Civil Liberties
Under the Constitution

Civil Liberties
Under the Constitution
THIRD EDITION

M. GLENN ABERNATHY
UNIVERSITY OF SOUTH CAROLINA

Harper & Row, Publishers
New York, Hagerstown, San Francisco, London

Sponsoring Editor: Dale Tharp
Project Editor: Karla B. Philip
Designer: Rita Naughton
Production Supervisor: Will C. Jomarrón
Compositor: Maryland Linotype Composition Co., Inc.
Printer and Binder: The Murray Printing Company

CIVIL LIBERTIES UNDER THE CONSTITUTION, Third Edition

Library of Congress Cataloging in Publication Data

Abernathy, Mabra Glenn, Date—
  Civil liberties under the Constitution.

  Bibliography: p.
  Includes index.
  1. Civil rights—United States.   I. United States.
Constitution. 1977.   II. Title.
KF4748.A2 1977   342'.73'08502643   76-18790
ISBN 0-06-040136-2

To David Fellman—
outstanding teacher, indefatigable scholar, and
warm friend

Contents

Preface

The proper study of civil liberties in America involves virtually the whole range of social science techniques and subject matter. It should include constitutional law, political theory, political action, sociology, economics, psychology, history, and the behavioral approaches to decision making, both public and private. Obviously one who attempts to treat civil liberties in a single modest volume is forced to omit most of these approaches and, to that extent, excludes substantial areas of highly relevant and important material necessary to a solid understanding of civil liberties in America. Choice must be made, however, and for reasons both of personal preference and pedagogical utility, this study concentrates primarily on the constitutional law aspect of civil liberties. Given the importance of the "rule of law" concept in Anglo-American history, it is felt that a firm grasp of the *law* with respect to civil liberties will provide a useful anchor, and a base will be established from which the student can more competently and fruitfully explore other modes of investigating the subject. In short, no limited approach to civil liberties can be more than an introduction to the broad subject, and the student should be warned of this fact at the outset. If this introductory analysis provides a framework for and stimulates interest in further study of so vital a subject, the venture will have been a success.

I should like to express my gratitude to Professors David Fellman, Robert J. Steamer, and Stephen L. Wasby for their critical review of the manuscript for the third edition, and for their valuable suggestions for improvement. In addition, I wish to thank Michael Briggs for his tireless attention to many of the tedious details of tracking down research notes and preparing the index.

Table of Cases

Boldface numbers indicate pages on which portions of opinions are quoted.

Civil Liberties
Under the Constitution

CHAPTER I
The Courts and Civil Rights

Until relatively recently, the focal point for official pronouncements concerning the nature and extent of American civil rights has been the judiciary. This is not an unreasonable approach in view of the impact of the institution of judicial review and the habituation of Anglo-Americans to judicial policy-making through centuries of development of the common law. These factors, despite the fact that constitutional conventions or legislative bodies initiated the statements of rights found in the state and federal constitutions, inexorably operate to place the stress on the judiciary as the locus for definitive elaboration of rights. Constitutional challenges to laws or official behavior are expected to reach final resolution only in a court decision, and the higher the court the more nearly final the decision. Despite its oversimplification, there is some element of truth in the statement by presidential candidate Charles Evans Hughes, "We are under the Constitution, but the Constitution is what the judges say it is."

More recently, legislative bodies and administrative agencies have been recognized as important participants in the creation and delineation of rights. Congress, for example, can both create new rights and destroy old ones. In the adoption of the National Labor Relations Act in 1935 a new right of defined categories of workers to organize and bargain collectively was created. And the old right of employers to discharge workers for union activity was demolished. Similarly, in the Civil Rights Act of 1964 a new right of access to places of public accommodation, irrespective of race or religion, was created, while the old right of choice in the operators (absent state laws to the contrary) was removed. In administering the nondiscrimination-in-education provisions of the Civil Rights Act of 1964, the Office of Education has essentially extended the meager phraseology of the Act to embrace additional rights. In great part, however, such participation in the process of rights-definition does not appear to displace the judiciary from its position of primacy in the public mind.

Unfortunately, this attitude sometimes engenders as a corollary the belief that the courts are the omnipresent *guardians* of civil rights. In other words, it is not uncommonly assumed that the courts of the nation stand ever ready to right all wrongs suffered to one's person or liberty or property. In a strictly limited sense this is true. If one has suffered an injury recognized by the law, and if he has the time, money, energy, witnesses, and evidence to prosecute his cause successfully in court, then a remedy is available to him. But this statement camouflages a multitude of barriers to the realization of effective judicial remedies for wronged individuals. Thus, while the bulk of this volume places heavy stress on judicial pronouncements defining and analyzing civil rights, it is well to enter a *caveat* initially concerning a number of important factors which serve to limit the effectiveness of courts as *guardians* of civil rights. The purpose of this chapter is to examine these factors, some of which are external to the judicial process while others stem from the courts' own evaluation of the limits to their appropriate role, and then to define the area in which courts *can* act to protect civil rights. [For an excellent discussion of the limitations on the impact of the United States Supreme Court on practices affecting criminal suspects, see Anthony G. Amsterdam, "The Rights of Suspects," in Norman Dorsen, ed., *The Rights of Americans* (New York: Random House, 1972), pp. 401–432.]

LIMITATIONS ON JUDICIAL POWER TO PROTECT RIGHTS

1. Failure to litigate. At the outset it is clear that the initiative in a civil suit must be taken by the injured party if the courts are to offer any assistance in righting the wrong. Even in criminal actions, a substantial burden rests on the injured party to push forward his cause if he expects satisfaction. If one suffers a criminal wrong, his complaint and testimony (if he is alive to give them) are usually a prerequisite to successful prosecution. And if, instead, he is the victim of an improper prosecution, it is up to him to carry the appeals necessary to try to get a reversal of the conviction. Thus our adversary system demands action, not childlike faith in some future retribution for one's enemies, if the judicial machinery is to be set in motion to safeguard rights. But every day sees abridgements of rights in some form take place with only a very small portion of these leading to actual litigation. Why is this so? Among the more obvious answers are cost, fear of reprisals, delay in reaching final settlement, and perhaps the bad character of the victim. Other factors as well contribute to this reluctance.

Most of us have from time to time suffered an actionable wrong from either private persons or public officials. But we recognize that a certain amount of friction is inevitable in the multitudinous contacts of modern living and prefer to ignore the minor encroachments on our rights. More to the point, one does not lightly undertake a lawsuit if he takes the time to calculate the potential costs in lawyer's fees, witnesses' fees, court costs, and his own time. Particularly is this true when the defendant in such proceedings is "judgment proof"—in other words, out of reach of any judgment against him for lack of money.

Delay in getting a decision more often than not works in favor of the defendant in civil actions. And the courts in many sections of the nation are falling further behind each year in disposing of cases on the dockets. In some of the larger cities, for example, the civil docket for jury trials is three to four years behind. Equity actions, such as a suit for an injunction to prevent impending injury, do not face this problem because they are disposed of without jury determinations. The magistrates' courts and other limited jurisdiction courts are much speedier in their handling of cases, but the quality of their decisions is frequently suspect, and these courts can normally handle only cases at law (no equity jurisdiction) involving relatively small amounts of money. Under such circumstances it is hard to criticize the injured party who throws up his hands in despair and either puts aside any thought of bringing suit or, after filing the action, settles out of court for considerably less than the alleged damages. [See Hans Zeisel, Harry Kalven, Jr., and Bernard Buchholz, *Delay in the Court* (Boston: Little, Brown, 1959).]

In the case of various unpopular minority groups or those dependent on the good will of the defendant, there is still additional cause for caution— the fear of reprisals. Economic pressures or even violence may be the reward for attempts to redress grievances through court action. In such event, suffering in silence may well seem to be the wiser course.

In the evolution of the administration of workmen's compensation laws in the various states it was the recognition of just these factors of cost, delay, and fear of reprisals which led legislatures to conclude that the determination of awards to injured employees bringing suit against their employers should be transferred from the courts to administrative agencies. [See Walter F. Dodd, *Administration of Workmen's Compensation* (New York: Oxford University Press, 1936), chap. 4.]

The heavy hand of officialdom may be visited much more frequently on those who have already had a history of criminal behavior. It is easier for officials to slip beyond the bounds of their authority when dealing with the habitual offender. But this is the class which would be fighting the greatest odds in bringing an action against the offending officials. Thus the questionable character of the would-be plaintiff might lead him to doubt seriously whether he could successfully prosecute a suit to vindicate his rights. Convicts and ex-convicts seldom sue sheriffs and police officers.

To move into slightly more technical aspects than the failure to litigate, there are several factors implicit either in our judicial procedure or statutes which restrict the availability of judicial remedies. Among the more important of these are: the requirement of "standing" to bring suit, the nonreviewability by courts of many administrative acts, the presumption of validity of official acts, the presumption of constitutionality of acts of the legislature, the difficulty of extending decisions beyond the specific facts and parties involved, and, finally, the limited remedies for private interference with free choice.

2. "Standing" to sue. The concept of "standing" to bring suit is a many-faceted problem. Basically, however, it is a requirement that the party bringing suit be able to show an injury recognized by the law, and one for which the law provides a remedy. Thus an individual cannot normally bring suit to redress a wrong suffered by another. (There are, of course, certain necessary exceptions, as in the case of parents, guardians, trustees, and others who may sue in behalf of those under their special care.) In addition, the injury must be real, not fancied, and must be one already suffered or immediately anticipated, not remote and speculative.

A standard illustration of the requirement that one must show injury to have "standing" to sue is the case of *Tileston* v. *Ullman,* 318 U.S. 44 (1943). Dr. Tileston, a Connecticut physician, challenged the constitutionality of a state law prohibiting "the use of drugs or instruments to prevent conception, and the giving of assistance or counsel in their use" on the ground that the law would prevent his giving professional advice to his patients whose lives would be endangered by childbearing. The United States Supreme Court dismissed the action, holding that no question was presented "which appellant has standing to assert." The allegations related to the potential dangers to his patients, not to him, and his patients were not parties to the proceeding. Thus, while the law might well present difficult questions of constitutionality, Dr. Tileston was not, in the context of this case, the appropriate person to raise them judicially.

The sequel to the case is *Griswold* v. *Connecticut,* 381 U.S. 479 (1965), in which the same law was again under attack in an appeal to the United States Supreme Court. This time, however, the appellants were appealing from a conviction in a Connecticut court for violation of the law. Since the injury was clear-cut and personal, they had the requisite "standing" to raise the constitutional issue, and the Court responded by rendering a decision on the merits. (A majority of five held the law to be an unconstitutional invasion of the right of privacy of married persons, while two other justices concurred on other grounds.)

The older rules relative to standing were somewhat restrictive, but beginning in 1968, several decisions of the Court have opened the way for broader access to the courts to attack governmental action. While the states have generally permitted suits by taxpayers attacking the validity of state appropriations, in *Frothingham* v. *Mellon,* 262 U.S. 447 (1923), the Court held that a *federal* taxpayer, merely as a taxpayer, did not have standing to challenge the constitutionality of a federal appropriation. But in *Flast* v. *Cohen,* 392 U.S. 83 (1968), the Court relaxed this rule to the extent of according standing when the plaintiff "alleges that congressional action under the taxing and spending clause is in derogation of those constitutional provisions which operate to restrict the exercise of the taxing and spending power." The case involved a challenge to the constitutionality of federal expenditures for textbooks and other instructional materials for religious schools, on the ground that such expenditures violated the establishment of religion clause of the First Amendment. In a more recent case, *Doe* v. *Bolton,* 410 U.S. 179 (1973), the Court held that both a married, pregnant woman and licensed physicians who had been consulted by pregnant women desiring abortions had standing to challenge Georgia's abortion laws. [For a discussion of standing cases, see Kenneth C. Davis, *Administrative Law: Cases—Text—Problems,* 5th ed. (St. Paul: West Pub. Co., 1973), chap. 5. For the special standing problems of environmentalists, see Christopher D. Stone, "Should Trees Have Standing? —Toward Legal Rights for Natural Objects," 45 *So. Cal. L. Rev.* 450 (1972).]

In general, economic injury sustained as a result of competition has not been held sufficient to accord standing to sue. Thus, in *Tennessee Power Co.* v. *T.V.A.,* 306 U.S. 118 (1939), where private power companies sought to enjoin T.V.A. from operating, claiming that the statute under which it was created was unconstitutional, the Court denied the competitors standing. But the Administrative Procedure Act, 5 U.S.C.A. §702, grants standing to a person "aggrieved by agency action within the meaning of a relevant statute." And in *Association of Data Processing Service Organizations* v. *Camp,* 397 U.S. 150 (1970), the Court held that private data processing companies had standing to challenge a ruling by the Comptroller of the Currency that national banks, as an incident to their banking services, could make data processing services available to other banks and to bank customers. The decision, however, turned on the interpretation of a statutory provision stating that "No bank service corporation may engage in any activity other than the performance of bank services for banks." Thus, if the competitive injury can be challenged under a relevant statute, the Court is willing to accord standing. In *Linda R.S.*

v. *Richard D.,* 410 U.S. 614 (1973), the Court pointed out that it is true that Congress may not confer jurisdiction on Article III federal courts to render advisory opinions, "but Congress may enact statutes creating legal rights, the invasion of which creates standing, even though no injury would exist without the statute."

In *Sierra Club* v. *Morton,* 405 U.S. 727 (1972), the Club sought a declaratory judgment and an injunction to restrain federal officials from approving the creation of an extensive ski-resort development in the scenic Mineral King Valley of the Sequoia National Forest. The Club claimed standing to maintain its "public interest" lawsuit because it had a special interest in the conservation and the sound maintenance of the national parks, game refuges, and forests of the country. The Court held those allegations insufficient since no specific injury to the members of the Club was alleged in the complaint. In a footnote to the opinion, however, it was suggested that the Club could easily rectify this error by amending the complaint to allege that the members actually used the area for hiking and camping and other recreational purposes, and that the development would cause direct, personal injury to the members.

Closely akin to this limitation of "standing" is the rule generally followed by judges (unless constitutional provisions require otherwise) that they will not render advisory opinions. One must present a proper case or controversy to a court, in an adversary proceeding, in order to test the validity of a statute or administrative order.

3. Presumption of validity of official acts. Another feature of judicial operation which limits the chances for successful attack on official restraints lies in the courts' presumption that the acts of public officials are valid. The courts do not automatically presume that all restraints on free choice are improper. The burden is thrown on the person attacking such acts to *prove* that they are improper. This is most readily seen in cases involving the claim that an act of the legislature is unconstitutional. As Mr. Justice Bushrod Washington wrote, over a century ago, "It is but a decent respect to the wisdom, integrity, and patriotism of the legislative body, by which any law is passed, to presume in favor of its validity, until its violation of the Constitution is proved beyond a reasonable doubt." [*Ogden* v. *Saunders,* 12 Wheat. 213 (1827).]

In the same general direction is the view of judges that acts of administrative officials should be accorded some presumption of validity. Thus a health officer who destroys food alleged by him to be unfit for consumption is presumed to have good reason for his action. The person whose property is so destroyed must bear the burden of proving bad faith on the part of the official, if an action is brought as a consequence.

The point to be made here is that the claimant who protests the operation of a law or the act of a public official must not only show that his view of the matter is a reasonable one, but he must also show that the approach involved in the law or administrative act is clearly an unreasonable one. Thus, in *Powell* v. *Pennsylvania,* 127 U.S. 678 (1888), a manufacturer of oleomargarine in Pennsylvania was unable to challenge successfully a state law prohibiting the manufacture of such products in that state. He offered to show by clear and convincing tests that his product was not unhealthful and was clearly safe for human consumption. But since he could not go further and prove that the law was clearly an unreasonable approach to protecting the citizens from unsafe products of other manufacturers, he lost his case.

Such a claimant, then, comes into court with the balances tilted against him. He must not merely equalize the weight in the opposite pan; he must add enough extra to tip the balance in his direction.

4. Difficulty in extending decisions beyond specific facts and parties involved in litigation. Technically, a decision rendered by a court binds only the parties to the suit then under consideration, and binds them only with respect to the controversy in which they are involved. If, however, the decision involves a constitutional question and is determined by the United States Supreme Court, then its effect may be considerably more far-reaching. Under our doctrine of precedent and the application of the national supremacy clause of Article VI of the United States Constitution, all state and federal judges are bound to apply the same constitutional rule if a case arises presenting a similar controversy. The point is, however, that a separate suit may be necessary to get a specific order directing that the Supreme Court's rule be followed. Two things then become apparent. First, a slight alteration of the facts presented may lead to a different decision by the Court in subsequent cases. Second, even if different parties present substantially the same fact situations, one Court decision does not by any means lead to a mass reaction on the part of legislators or administrators throughout the nation to bring their practices in line with the tenor of the Court's requirements.

The result is that inertia or opposition to a holding of a court, even the United States Supreme Court, could well mean that a prolonged period of litigation would be necessary to lead even to a partial acquiescence in the rule announced. This fact is nowhere better illustrated than in the long history of racial discrimination in according voting rights. The Fifteenth Amendment was proclaimed ratified in the year 1870. Yet until the implementation of the Voting Rights Act of 1965, almost a century later, many persons were still denied registration or voting rights solely on the grounds of race.

The words of the Fifteenth Amendment seem clear enough: "The right of citizens of the United States to vote shall not be denied or abridged by the United States or by any State on account of race, color, or previous condition of servitude." But a whole host of devices were employed to defeat the purposes of the Amendment. And in some parts of the South, as each device was held unconstitutional, a new one was substituted, which required a new course of litigation. A holding by the Court that denial of membership in the Democratic Party on account of race was unconstitutional did not preclude a state requirement that all applicants for registration give a "reasonable" interpretation of the United States Constitution. Thus a second case had to be brought and a second decision rendered on the new set of facts.

Even where the facts seem nearly identical, it still may be necessary to get a separate decree from a court in order to secure acquiescence. In 1948 the Supreme Court held unconstitiutional as an "establishment or religion" a "released time" program of an Illinois school board under which weekly religious instruction was given to public school students in the school buildings during regular school hours. [*McCollum* v. *Board of Education,* 333 U.S. 203 (1948).] It appears that similar programs are still in operation in various parts of the nation, but unless separate suits are brought to test the validity of such programs under the *McCollum* doctrine, they will continue indefinitely, in the absence of a legislative or administrative policy change. [See

Gordon Patric, "The Impact of a Court Decision: Aftermath of the McCollum Case," 6 *J. of Pub. L.* 455 (1957).] This lays open a key difference between the judicial process and the administrative process. The judicial process must await the sufficient irritation of the injured parties to energize its machinery. The administrative process has, by statutory grant, a built-in self-starting mechanism. The National Labor Relations Board, for example, may initiate its own action to halt unfair labor practices. It need not wait for some workman who has a greater than average allotment of courage to step forward and accuse his employer. And, in addition, the administrative tribunal has sufficient personnel to ensure, to a substantial degree at least, that its decisions are followed throughout all industries or areas where they may be applicable.

One way of broadening applications of decisions is to file a "class action" suit, the requirements for which are set out in Rule 23 of the Federal Rules of Civil Procedure. In general, the justification for bringing together a group of persons as a class to file as plaintiffs is that common questions of law may involve parties so numerous that joinder of all members is impractical and, further, that the risk of inconsistent disposition of separate cases or the refusal of the defendant to apply individual decisions to others similarly situated requires the issuance of a broader decree applicable to all members of the class. The courts have applied Rule 23 to permit a number of class action suits involving attacks on racial discrimination and have thus avoided the long delays occasioned by the requirement of separate suits by separate parties. In at least one area, however, the Court has applied the rule to restrict the opportunity for class actions. If the basis for federal jurisdiction is diversity of citizenship, the Congress has by statute provided that the amount in controversy must exceed $10,000 for the district courts to have jurisdiction. *Zahn* v. *International Paper Company,* 414 U.S. 291 (1973), involved a class action by petitioners, owners of property fronting on Lake Champlain in Vermont, on behalf of a class consisting of themselves and 200 lake-front property owners and lessees around the lake. They sought damages from International Paper Company, a New York corporation, for allegedly having permitted discharges from its pulp and paper-making plant to be carried into Lake Champlain, thereby polluting the waters of the lake and damaging the value and utility of the surrounding properties. The claim of each of the named plaintiffs was found to satisfy the $10,000 jurisdictional amount, but the District Court was convinced that not every individual owner in the class had suffered pollution damages in excess of $10,000. It then refused to permit the suit to proceed as a class action. The United States Supreme Court affirmed, with three justices dissenting. Thus each member of the class must claim the jurisdictional amount of damages, and if this cannot be shown, individual suits must be filed, with each plaintiff bearing the burden of expert testimony and with the additional drain on the resources of the judiciary.

5. Limited remedies for private interference with free choice. Another problem in the citizen's search for freedom from restriction lies in the fact that many types of interference stemming from private persons do not constitute actionable wrongs under the law. Private prejudice and private discrimination do not, in the absence of specific statutory provisions, offer grounds for judicial intervention in behalf of the sufferer. If one is denied admission to membership in a social club, for example, solely on the basis of his race or religion or political affiliation, he may understandably smart under the rejection, but the courts cannot help him (again assuming no statutory provision barring such distinctions). This statement is generally true as applied to other more important areas as well: for example, in employment outside the coverage of the Civil Rights Act of 1964, in admission to a purely private school, and in housing if the discrimination is not based on race or religion. To take the latter case, if a man chooses to sell his home to a member of his own economic group only, the courts at present offer no remedy to the would-be purchaser of another class. There are, then, many types of restraints on individual freedom of choice which are beyond the authority of courts to remove or ameliorate.

6. Political questions. Another self-imposed limitation on the courts' area of operation lies in the doctrine of political questions. In brief, this is the view that some problems are preeminently political in nature, and solutions should be sought in the political branches rather than in the courts. Even questions which turn on interpretations of the United States Constitution have occasionally been placed in this category, and the courts will refuse a remedy to those who claim injury. An illustration is found in the case of *Colegrove* v. *Green,* 328 U.S. 549 (1946), in which a citizen of Illinois sought a judicial remedy for the glaring inequalities of population in the arrangement of congressional districts in that state. He argued that he and others in the more populous districts were being denied equal protection of the laws because of their unequal voting power, in violation of the Fourteenth Amendment. The United States Supreme Court dismissed the case, although only three of the seven justices participating squarely viewed the question as a "political question." While *Baker* v. *Carr,* 369 U.S. 186 (1962), holds that such questions are now justiciable, Justice Frankfurter's statements on political questions in Colegrove are still instructive:

The Constitution has many commands that are not enforceable by courts because they clearly fall outside the conditions and purposes that circumscribe judicial action. Thus, "on demand of the executive authority," Article IV, Section 2, of a State it is the duty of a sister State to deliver up a fugitive from justice. But the fulfillment of this duty cannot be judicially enforced. *Kentucky* v. *Dennison, 24 How. 66.* The duty to see to it that the laws are faithfully executed cannot be brought under legal compulsion. *Mississippi* v. *Johnson, 4 Wall. 475.* Violation of the great guaranty of a republican form of government in States cannot be challenged in the courts. *Pacific Telephone Company* v. *Oregon, 223 U.S. 118.* The Constitution has left the performance of many duties in our governmental scheme to depend on the fidelity of the executive and legislative action and, ultimately, on the vigilance of the people in exercising their political rights.

While there are factors which limit courts in protecting civil liberties, there is, nevertheless, much that they can do in this area. Even in their restricted scope of operation, the courts exercise a vast influence over the activities of both officials and private persons who themselves may never be a party to litigation. Americans have traditionally shown great respect for judicial opinion, despite occasional periods during which the courts have been under heavy fire, and it has sometimes been important in the formation of the public opinion.

One of the key powers of the courts is that of judicial review—that is, the authority to review acts of the coordinate branches, in appropriate cases, and to refuse to give effect to such acts on the ground of their unconstitutionality. This power of judicial review is more typically an American judicial power than one belonging to judges in all countries. Many nations today, however, permit the courts at least a limited exercise of this authority. [The standard work on judicial review in America is Charles G. Haines, *The American Doctrine of Judicial Supremacy* (Berkeley: University of California Press, 1932). See also Charles L. Black, Jr., *The People and the Court* (New York: Macmillan, 1960); Edward McWhinney, *Judicial Review in the English-Speaking World* (Toronto: University of Toronto Press, 1956); David Deener, "Judicial Review in Modern Constitutional Systems," 46 *Amer. Pol. Sci. Rev.* 1079 (1952).] Without this vital power, the courts would be obliged to enforce any clear statement of policy by the legislative body, and no independent determination could be made of whether such policy constituted an undue abridgment of individual rights. The United States Supreme Court has increased its rate of declaring acts of Congress unconstitutional, and it still remains rather active in the area of checking excesses of state and local legislative zeal.

Constitutional challenges may be directed to specific administrative practices rather than to a statute, and this, too, is an important aspect of the broad doctrine of judicial review. For example, in *Escobedo* v. *Illinois,* 378 U.S. 478 (1964), the Court considered the constitutionality of a police refusal to allow the accused to consult counsel during interrogation, rather than the constitutionality of a statute. (Under the special circumstances of that case, the Court held the action unconstitutional.) While the bulk of challenged statutes or administrative actions are held valid, the threat of judicial review may serve as an important safeguard against unconstitutional action.

JUDICIAL REMEDIES FOR VIOLATIONS OF RIGHTS

Claims of denials of rights may be based on statutory or common-law grounds as well as on constitutional provisions. Whatever the basis for the alleged right, however, the more important specific *remedies* offered by the judicial process to wronged parties are encompassed in a relatively few procedures. And it is within the framework of these kinds of remedies that the courts serve to protect against injury or to assuage the wounds received.

1. Mandamus. Mandamus is an old common-law writ which may be usefully employed against public officials in specified circumstances. Briefly put, it is a writ commanding a public officer to perform some duty which the laws require him to do but which he refuses or neglects to perform. If he has any discretion in the matter, mandamus cannot be used. But if the law is clear in requiring the performance of some ministerial function, then mandamus may properly be sought to nudge the reluctant or negligent official along in the performance of his duties.

As an illustration, one who is clearly qualified under the law to be registered as a qualified elector may use the remedy of mandamus to force the registrar who arbitrarily denies registration to place his name in the register. Since the writ cannot be employed where the official has discretion, however, it could not issue against the legislature on complaint by teen-age citizens that the voting age should be reduced to sixteen. As the United States Supreme Court stated, in *Wilbur* v. *United States,* 281 U.S. 206, 218 (1930):

Where the duty in a particular situation is so plainly prescribed as to be free from doubt and equivalent to a positive command it is regarded as being so far ministerial that its performance may be compelled by mandamus, unless there be provision or implication to the contrary. But where the duty is not thus plainly prescribed but depends upon a statute the construction or application of which is not free from doubt, it is regarded as involving the character of a judgment or discretion which cannot be controlled by mandamus.

It is important to note as well that the writ does not issue to purely private persons, but can only be directed to public officials or persons performing some quasi-public function. Thus, while in its limited area it is useful, the restricted scope of application often makes it necessary for the citizen to seek other remedies.

2. Injunction. The injunction is primarily a preventive remedy and issues from a court of equity. It is considerably broader in its applications than mandamus and is far more frequently employed in civil rights questions. It can apply to either ministerial or discretionary functions and to either public officials or private persons. Equity picks up where the law ends and enables a judge to frame an order or decree to fit the necessities of the case under consideration. The injunction is one of the most useful tools of the equity judge. The broad operation of the injunctive remedy is well illustrated by the school segregation cases. The complainants sought injunctions directed to various local school officials ordering them to refrain from enforcing laws requiring racial segregation in the public schools. The 1955 decision of the United States Supreme Court left the lower district court judges free to frame such decrees as appeared advisable to accomplish the ends indicated in the 1954 decision. In some areas of the South, judges issued injunctions to restrain all further attempts to enforce the school segregation laws of the areas involved. In others, special longer range programs of gradual integration were specified in the decrees. In a few instances blanket injunctions were issued to restrain any and all attempts by either officials or private persons to interfere with the integration process.

Thus the injunction is particularly useful where there is a claim that some constitutional right is abridged by the operation of a law or administrative practice and the victim desires the intervention of a court to stop the abridgement. Violation of the terms of either a mandamus or an injunction subjects the violator to the possibility of citation for contempt, with broad leeway given to the judge in determining what punishment to impose.

3. Civil damage suit. Another important type of legal action to protect rights is the civil damage suit. If a citizen feels that he has been intentionally subjected to a deprivation of a right guaranteed by the law, he can intiate a suit for money damages against the offender. This is possible whether the defendant named is a private person or a public official. A person who without provocation assaults another leaves himself open to a damage suit in which the plaintiff may run up quite a list of items in the bill of damages: hospital or doctor's bills, mental and physical anguish, loss of time from work, and perhaps punitive damages as well. With the increasingly large jury verdicts in tort cases of various sorts, this type of action should pose a substantial deterrent against willful or malicious deprivation of rights. Exceptions are noted, of course, in those cases in which local sentiment runs against the plaintiff because of religion, race, past criminal activity, or some other factor which makes his cause unpopular.

While the civil suit for money damages might be useful in protecting private citizens against other private citizens, a more difficult problem is presented when the defendant is a public official, and the complaint arises from his official performance. If the official acts in good faith but makes an error of judgment, then the decision will normally run against the wronged citizen. The courts recognize that even competent, well-intentioned government personnel are sometimes known to err in the performance of their official duties. It would be a drastic rule indeed which would subject such persons to the expense of paying damages to all citizens who were inconvenienced by these mistakes. Judges and jurors might spend more time as defendants than in the pursuits of their vocations if this were allowed. Thus the plaintiff in such cases has an extra burden of proving willful or malicious deprivation of rights. This is much more difficult, and the difficulty is indicated in the relative rarity with which civil suits are successfully prosecuted against policemen, for example, for damages alleged to have been sustained by private persons in their contacts with these officials.

4. Criminal prosecution. Where the deprivation of one's rights is declared by the law to be a criminal offense, the offender may not only be forced to pay damages, but he also can be put to trial for committing a crime. Suppose one is injured by the unprovoked physical assault of another. Clearly this is a situation which involves the commission of both a private and a public wrong. The victim of such treatment can sue in a civil action for damages, while the government can bring a criminal prosecution. Except in those situations where the victim is locally unpopular for one reason or another, the increasing probability of criminal prosecution has served as one factor, among others, in lessening the frequency of police brutality in the past two or three decades. [See Caleb Foote, "Tort Remedies for Police Violations of Individual Rights," 39 *Minn. L. Rev.* 493 (1955), and Harry H. Shapiro, "Limitations in Prosecuting Civil Rights Violations," 46 *Cornell L.Q.* 532 (1961).]

5. Appellate court review. Deprivations of individual rights may take place or may be ignored in the course of judicial proceedings as well as elsewhere in life. Thus there must be some corrective which can operate on even the judicial process. The most important such device is to be found in the review of trial court proceedings by an appellate court. If errors of law are made in the trial court, or if a jury goes beyond its authority in rendering a verdict, then a case would be presented for the appropriate exercise of appellate court review and possible reversal. If a conviction is obtained under circumstances which render the possibility of a fair trial quite remote, such as mob domination or use of perjured testimony or "trial by newspaper," then an appellate court can reverse the conviction and demand a trial under more reasonable and proper conditions.

This power is a very important and highly valuable one. But it must be recognized that there are severe limitations on the effectiveness of this institution as a cure-all for mistakes in trial court proceedings. In the first place, less than five percent of the decisions of the trial courts in America are appealed. It is probably a fair assumption that in an appreciable number of the mass of unappealed cases reversible error occurred. But appellate review is not automatic, and if the losing party fails to perfect an appeal, the corrective powers of the higher courts cannot be brought to bear. In that event, the trial court decision, right or wrong, stands. In the second place, appellate courts as a general rule examine only the complaint that errors of *law* were made in the trial court, not errors in *fact-finding.* Since the disposition of large numbers of cases turns almost exclusively on the finding of facts, appeals would in most of these be completely futile.

Despite these limitations, the upper courts of both state and federal governments wield substantial powers to correct injustices in the trial courts. And it is argued by many that even where technically they might be powerless to act (e.g., under the rule of not disturbing a lower court finding of fact) there is always some point available on which a decision for reversal and an order for new trial can turn. At times the courts have even reversed on grounds which were not even raised by counsel seeking the review. These are very special cases, however, and the better view is to recognize that the power of review is useful but by no means a substitute for adequate staffing of the courts of first instance with competent personnel, and a high quality of advocacy on the part of counsel for both sides.

At this point the matter of how cases get to the United States Supreme Court deserves special treatment. Article III, Section 2, of the Constitution lists the kinds of cases and parties to which the federal judicial power extends. The Supreme Court has original jurisdiction in only two types of cases—those involving foreign ambassadors, ministers, or consuls and those in which a State is a party. In all the other cases listed in Section 2 the Court has appellate jurisdiction only, and even here the power to review is subject to "such exceptions" and "such regulations as the Congress shall make." Thus Congress has substantial authority to regulate the flow of appellate business to the Supreme Court. The previous provisions are included in Title 28, Chapter 81, of the United States Code. In general, Congress has divided the cases into two categories—those for which there is a "right" of review in the Supreme Court (called review by *appeal*) and those for which the Court has complete discretion as to whether it will grant or deny review (review by *writ of certiorari*). In applying these statutes, however, a third element comes into play. The Court reads the "right to review" sections very narrowly, and even where the case may seem to fit the statute, the Court has invented the device of dismissing most appeals from the state courts "for want of a substantial federal question." To understand fully the Court's appellate jurisdiction, then, one must look to three sources: (1) the Constitutional boundaries, which are set out in Article III, Section 2, (2) statutes of Congress which regulate appellate review, and (3) the Court's interpretations and applications of the Constitutional and statutory provisions.

The Supreme Court's appellate business issues from a number of different courts: the various federal courts, including the District Courts, the Courts of Appeals, the Court of Claims, and the Court of Customs and Patent Appeals, and also the state courts. While decisions of the District Courts normally reach the Supreme Court via the Courts of Appeals, Section 1253 of Title 28 provides for direct appeals from certain orders of District Courts in any civil action required by any act of Congress to be heard by a three-judge court. One illustration of such a case is the suit asking for an injunction to restrain the enforcement of a state law on the ground that the law violates the United States Constitution. In such a situation the case must be heard by a three-judge District Court, and the losing party has a right of appeal directly to the Supreme Court. Chief Justice Burger has argued that this provision for direct appeals places too great a burden on the Court and that Congress should at least make such direct review discretionary. The only cases where there is a right of appeal from the Courts of Appeals (Section 1254 of Title 28) are those where a party has relied on a state statute "held by a court of appeals to be invalid as repugnant to the Constitution, treaties or laws of the United States." All other cases coming to the Court from the Courts of Appeals and all cases coming up from the Court of Claims or the Court of Customs and Patent Appeals arrive by way of petitions for writs of certiorari, the granting of which is purely discretionary in the Court. (The matter of certified questions of law is omitted as relatively unimportant.) The writ of certiorari is an old common-law writ and historically was simply an order from a higher court to a lower court directing the latter to send up the record of a case for review. Thus, if a party has lost a decision in the United States Court of Appeals, and if his case does not fall in the category described as allowing appeal, he must petition the Supreme Court for a writ of certiorari directed to the Court of Appeal.

Aside from the various federal courts, the other source of appellate business for the Supreme Court is the state courts. But here the principle of federalism comes into play. As a broad generalization, the federal courts are established to deal with questions of federal law, and the state courts are established to handle questions of state law. There are obvious exceptions to this statement, since in diversity of jurisdiction cases the federal courts apply state law, and in many state cases questions of federal constitutional law are presented, but the generalization is still useful. The bulk of the cases decided in state courts do not involve questions of federal law, and therefore the decisions rendered in these courts will be final. Article VI of the Constitution states, however, that the United States Constitution, and the laws of the United States which shall be made in pursuance thereof, and all treaties made under the authority of the United States shall be the supreme law of the land, and the judges in every state shall be bound thereby. In the face of this doctrine of national supremacy, it would clearly be inappropriate to accord finality to State court decisions interpreting and applying federal laws, the United States Constitution, or treaties entered into by the United States. Thus provision is made for appellate review by the United States Supreme Court (*not* by any other federal court, however) of state court decisions which present "federal questions"—those involving federal laws, treaties, or the Constitution. Section 1257 of Title 28 provides that final judgments or decrees *rendered by the highest court of a state in which a decision could be had,* may be reviewed by *appeal* where the state court has held invalid a federal law or treaty, or where a state statute has been challenged as violative of a federal law, treaty, or the Constitution, and the state court has upheld the statute. All other federal question decisions rendered by state courts must be reviewed by writ of certiorari. It is important to note three prerequisites for getting Supreme Court review of state court decisions. First, a federal question must be presented. If the only issue for decision is, for example, the proper distribution of property under a will as determined by the relevant state laws, then there is no federal question presented and no basis for review. Second, the losing party must have carried his case to the highest state court in which he could get a decision. While this normally means that he must have gone to the State Supreme Court, the state laws frequently provide that decisions of lower courts shall be final. Where this is true, Section 1257 simply requires that he go as far as he can before petitioning the United States Supreme Court for review. Third, the state court decision on the federal questions must be crucial to the decision, for if it rests on an independent state law basis, review by the Supreme Court would be fruitless. Thus if a State law is held by the State court to be violative of both the United States Constitution and the state constitution, then review of the decision regarding the application of the United States Constitution only would be pointless, since the decision would stand on an independent state law ground.

Whether the cases arrive from state or federal courts, and whether they come up on appeal or certiorari, the members of the Court examine the questions presented to determine whether they merit action. In a great many petitions the justices consider the questions to be so frivolous that they do not consider them sufficiently "reviewworthy" even to discuss at conference, and review is denied or the appeal dismissed. Justice Brennan, in an interesting article discussing the workload of the Court ["The National Court of Appeals: Another Dissent," 40 *Univ. of Chi. L. Rev.* 473 (1973)], cited one illustration of such cases which presented the question, "Are Negroes in fact Indians and therefore entitled to Indians' exemptions from federal income taxes?"

Mention should be made of the effect of a denial of certiorari and the dismissal of an appeal "for want of a substantial federal question." The Court's own Rule 19, Section 1, gives the policy regarding certiorari:

1. A review on writ of certiorari is not a matter of right, but of sound judicial discretion, and will be granted only where there are special and important reasons therefor. The following, while neither controlling nor fully measuring the court's discretion, indicate the character of reasons which will be considered:

(a) Where a state court has decided a federal question of substance not theretofore determined by this court, or has decided it in a way probably not in accord with applicable decisions of this court.

(b) Where a court of appeals has rendered a decision in conflict with the decision of another court of appeals on the same matter; or has decided an important state or territorial question in a way in conflict with applicable state or territorial law; or has decided an important question of federal law which has not been, but should be, settled by this court; or has decided a federal question in a way in conflict with applicable decisions of this court; or has so far departed from the accepted and usual course of judicial proceedings, or so far sanctioned such a departure by a lower court, as to call for an exercise of this court's power of supervision.

Since the granting of the writ is purely discretionary, the accepted view is that a denial of the writ should not be construed in any way as a decision on the merits of the case. True, the result is that the decision of the court below stands, but denial of certiorari should not be interpreted as affirmance. The safe conclusion is that, for whatever reasons, there were not four members of the Court who wished to review the case, and nothing else should be read into the denial.

Dismissal of appeals "for want of a substantial federal question," however, is a different matter. In *Hicks* v. *Miranda*, 422 U.S. 332 (1975), the Court stated that such action constitutes a binding precedent as to the federal questions presented. The majority opinion indicated that summary disposition of an appeal, either by affirmance or by dismissal for want of a substantial federal question, is a disposition on the merits.

At various times during the Term of Court, conferences are held at which all cases which seem to merit attention are discussed, and the Justices then vote on whether they should grant or deny the requests. If four or more of the Justices vote to grant the petition, then the writ issues and the Court reviews the case. This "rule of four" is informal but has almost invariably been followed since the passage of the so-called Judges Act in 1925, which opened up the discretionary control by the Court of its appellate business. The necessity for such control is demonstrated by the fact that in the 1973 Term the Court had a total of 3,876 cases filed. It would have been impossible to dispose of any large percentage of these cases on the merits, and the only manageable approach is to allow the Court to select the cases it deems important to decide, and to dismiss appeals and deny certiorari in all others. In that 1973 Term the Court disposed of 188 cases by written opinion and 339 cases by Per Curiam decision. In the other 3,349 cases, the Court dismissed the appeals and denied petitions for review. The ratio of petitions for certiorari to appeals is about nine to one. More than 90 percent of the petitions for certiorari are denied, and more than 50 percent of the appeals are dismissed. Thus one who loses a case in a trial court and exclaims vehemently, "I'll carry this all the way to the Supreme Court," has a very heavy statistical probability running against him. The opportunity for appellate review is important, and both state and national law normally provide avenues for at least one such review of trial court decisions. But the enormous volume of judicial determinations of all courts in the United States militates against United States Supreme Court review except for a minute fraction of the total number.

6. Habeas Corpus. Another device available to vindicate one's legal rights is the writ of habeas corpus. Important though it is, it should be kept in mind that there are several limitations on its usefulness in the broad area of protecting personal liberties. Generally speaking, it is a device which can be used to test the legality of a physical restraint or detention. If a person is detained without any formal charge being placed against him, the writ may be used in effect to require that the man be released or a proper charge, supportable by some evidence or reliable information, be placed against him. If a prisoner has been tried and convicted, habeas corpus is still available as a potential remedy, since there is no time limit and no statute of limitations on its use. It cannot, however, be used as a substitute for ordinary appellate review, and the latter is a much broader device for raising issues concerning the interpretations of laws and the conduct of trials. Habeas corpus is referred to as a device for *collateral* attack on detention, since it opens up for investigation only such questions as are considered *jurisdictional* questions. Examples of such questions are whether the trial court which rendered judgment had authority over the person or the offense involved, or whether the prisoner was denied certain constitutional rights such as the right to counsel. On ordinary appellate review a great variety of additional points might be attacked which would be improper under habeas corpus, such as the judge's charge to the jury, the admissibility of evidence, or the competency of certain witnesses to testify. [For an excellent discussion of the history and uses of the writ of habeas corpus, see David Fellman, *The Defendant's Rights* (New York: Rinehart, 1958) chap. 5.] The writ is of special importance in dealing with detentions by the military, since there is no ordinary review of military court decisions by the civil courts. Thus the only method of bringing issues from the military tribunals to the civil courts is by petition for the writ of habeas corpus. Again it should be noted that in such cases the only ground for relief is that the sentencing court lacked jurisdiction.

While historically the writ had a relatively narrow application, the trend in the Court has been toward a definite liberalizing of the writ's uses. The "in custody" requirement for the availability of habeas corpus, for example, was held to have been met by one who was out of prison as a parolee, because of the stringent controls over the parolee exercised by the parole board. [*Jones* v. *Cunningham,* 371 U.S. 236 (1963).] And one formally charged with crime but released on bail would probably be held to meet the "in custody" test for habeas corpus purposes. In *Carafas* v. *LeVallee,* 391 U.S. 234 (1968), a prisoner filed an application for habeas corpus in federal court, alleging that illegally seized evidence had been used in securing his conviction in a state court. The application was dismissed by the District Court, and the Court of Appeals dismissed the appeal. Two weeks before filing a petition for certiorari in the United States Supreme Court, the petitioner was unconditionally released from the state prison. The Court held that the expiration of the sentence before the application for habeas corpus was finally adjudicated did not terminate federal jurisdiction, and because of the substantial disabilities which flowed from the conviction (ineligibility to engage in certain businesses, loss of voting rights, and others), the cause was not moot. Thus it was held that once federal jurisdiction attached in the District Court, it was not defeated by the release of the petitioner prior to completion of proceedings. (For a more detailed discussion of Habeas Corpus, see Chapter 4.)

SOURCES OF INTERFERENCE WITH PERSONAL FREEDOM

Since it is clear that the courts alone cannot adequately safeguard the liberties of the people, the question naturally arises of what additional forces may be deployed to achieve the necessary protection. In approaching the problem it is convenient to look at the various *sources* of interference with our personal freedom. Some may call for a different attack than others.

One important source is the legislative body, and this includes all such bodies from the national Congress down to the municipal council. A rather flagrant example of arbitrary legislative abridgment of rights is that of a municipal ordinance which required labor union organizers to get a permit from the mayor and city council before recruiting new members and to pay a license fee of $2,000, plus $500 for each member obtained! [Held unconstitutional on its face in *Staub* v. *City of Baxley,* 355 U.S. 313 (1958).] The preventive remedies for this source of interference are easily stated but obviously rather difficult to maintain. First, we must elect a high-caliber legislature, and second, we must see that those members of the citizenry who are interested in the protection of civil rights, whether they be a majority or a minority, maintain continual pressure on the legislative body to thwart attempts to adopt such policies as that illustrated above. The ideal may be impossible to attain, but any progress in that direction represents stronger protection of civil liberties.

A second source of abridgments of rights is the administrative process. Modern government by bureaucracy involves a great deal of delegation of decision-making power to what might well be called the fourth branch of the government. Such officials, even when they act in good faith, have the power to impose a tremendous variety of improper limitations on the citizen's exercise of free choices. One example of this sort of restriction was the action of the Postmaster General some years past in withdrawing second-class mail privileges from *Esquire* magazine on the ground that it did not meet the statutory test of being "published for the dissemination of information of a public character, or devoted to literature, the sciences, arts, or some special industry." Actually, he simply disapproved of the contents. Such a withdrawal does not completely bar the designated periodical from the mails, but the first-class rates for mailing are well-nigh prohibitive for commercial publishers in a competitive market. [The Court unanimously held the action to be an unauthorized censorship: *Hannegan* v. *Esquire*, 327 U.S. 146 (1946).]

The nonjudicial remedies against administrative interference are similar to those applicable to the legislature. The prestige of governmental administrative service must be sufficiently enhanced to attract and keep the ablest personnel among the citizenry. Second, the people, both as individuals and as members of organizations, must maintain a continual watch over the actions of administrative officials in those areas where improper interference with private rights is apt to occur. Such abridgments as do occur should be brought promptly to the attention of both administrative supervisors and policy officials who control the agency involved. Similarly, special recognition should be accorded administrative personnel who show particular concern for the rights of the individual. Third, the legislature must be held responsible for exercising care both in its grants of statutory authority to administrators and in its overseeing of their functions.

Making the bureaucracy responsible to the people is one of the most difficult problems in government today. A novel approach to the problem was development in Sweden in the office of the ombudsman. This official has discretion to investigate any administrative action or governmental agency omission impairing the rights of private persons, either on his own initiative or upon complaint filed with him. Denmark and Norway more recently adopted this institution, and considerable interest is now expressed in the United States. [See Donald C. Rowat, ed., *The Ombudsman: Citizen's Defender* (Toronto: University of Toronto Press, 1965); Walter Gellhorn, *Ombudsmen and Others: Citizens' Protectors in Nine Countries* (Cambridge: Harvard University Press, 1966); Walter Gellhorn, *When Americans Complain: Governmental Grievance Procedures* (Cambridge: Harvard University Press, 1966); and Stanley V. Anderson, ed., *Ombudsmen for American Government?* (Englewood Cliffs: Prentice-Hall, 1968).]

A third, and more widely publicized, source of violations of civil liberties lies in the personal malice or brutality of officials, particularly police officers. This is illustrated in peculiarly distasteful fashion by the case in which a city police chief and a sheriff's deputy forced a group of Jehovah's Witnesses to drink a half-pint of castor oil, in response to their request for police protection. [Held to come within the scope of acts punishable under the federal civil rights acts: *Catlette* v. *United States,* 132 F.2d 902 (4th C.A., 1943).] Many cases which are far more brutal come to light from time to time. In view of the vast number of daily contacts between police and citizen in the United States, the percentage of brutality cases must be extremely small. At least in this area, however, "small" must not be equated with "negligible." In discussing nonjudicial remedies, there is a strong tendency to propose that this type of evil will be adequately dispelled by the simple expedient of employing only well-educated young men who have passed rigid psychological tests for emotional stability. To some extent, more care in recruitment and training of policemen might well reduce the instances of police lawlessness. Assuredly this is an area in which progress can be made. But the habits and attitudes of the public toward police and law enforcement generally have a direct impact on the practices of the personnel involved. Low budgets and high pressures tend to push enforcement agencies into short-cut procedures. And community demands for unequal treatment of offenders, either on grounds of the character of the offender or of the offense, will usually find their response in the behavior of the enforcement agencies. Only if the community and the police maintain a genuine respect for following lawful procedures can such practices be minimized.

Unequal enforcement that is without brutality presents quite another problem. The average citizen is apt to hold that all criminal laws should be enforced against all offenders. A corollary would be the statement that selective enforcement constitutes a civil rights violation in that it denies equal protection of the laws. This same doctrinaire citizen would probably be enraged, however, if arrested for engaging in a penny-ante poker game on Saturday night with his close friends. As another illustration, laws against adultery are so rarely enforced in this country that one would surely hear indignant cries of "Discrimination!" if a prosecution were actually begun against one of the vast number (according to Professor Kinsey) of ordinary offenders. The suggestion is sometimes made that it would cleanse the consciences of both the police and the public if these rarely enforced criminal laws were repealed altogther. Then the laws remaining could be rewritten to make criminal *only* the specific acts which the community actively wants to see punished, and the police could push forward with full enforcement of *all* the laws.

There are several points at which these proposals are open to attack. First, the police, and (if closely questioned) in all probability the public, want to have available a full battery of weapons to use against persons in the community who are patently "undesirable." Then the prosecutor and the police who are forced by public pressures to act against a specific person can roam through the whole long list of criminal acts defined by the statutes or the common law to select the charges which can most easily be substantiated. A notorious but slippery racketeer might then be charged with adultery, when other offenders were overlooked. Admittedly, this is a sort of "The public will have its way" attitude on criminal law enforcement, but conversation with some students of the process would indicate that this conclusion is not too wide of the mark. A second difficulty with the suggested remedies lies in the extreme complexity of the task of statute writing. If the reader will but sit down and try to draft a bill which would punish only the forms of gambling which the average community thinks ought to be subjected to the criminal process, he will see the problem. The attempt to exclude the church bingo game, the matching for coffee, the friendly poker game (do the stakes determine the degree of friendliness?) and the annual bet on the homecoming football game—all of which the average community would probably consider as outside the proper confines of the criminal process—will either leave the statute so ponderous as to be unwieldy (perhaps even unconstitutionally vague) or else will leave loopholes through which the professional gambler can escape. Many enforcement officers much prefer to take a flat prohibition in the law and use the law with discretion. This is another way of saying that what is desired is unequal enforcement, and a serious question may be raised as to whether there is any acceptable realistic alternative. Still a third objection to the remedies proposed lies in the budget process, mentioned above. The law enforcement process is unalterably tied to the appropriation bill. Whatever the criminal code may proscribe, the police can investigate, patrol, and prevent only to the extent that money is appropriated for these purposes. Doubling the appropriation thus could very well have the effect of markedly increasing the statistical crime rate, in the sense that the resulting step-up in police activity would normally lead to the apprehension of more criminals. More financial support should mean a nearer approach to full enforcement of the laws. But in all probability no community gives the enforcement agencies anything approaching the annual sum necessary really to approximate full enforcement of all criminal laws. The police chief simply has to stretch his appropriation to cover as nearly as possible the types of crimes which arouse the greatest public indignation and those which are cheapest to enforce. The twilight zone of unenforced laws is reserved for use against those persons who cannot effectively be reached by the other laws but who have aroused the antagonism of either the public or the officialdom.

The final source of interference with the free choice of individuals is the action of private persons. There are standard judicial remedies for a great many types of private encroachment on private rights, e.g., in the use of the laws of trespass, assault, tort, and others. Nonjudicial remedies which would increase the protection against private interference would basically go in two directions: better enforcement of existing laws and the creation of new rights. Just as government created a new right in the labor field by the laws guaranteeing protection against discrimination for union membership, so governments of the states could create rights in other aspects of man's relations with man. Attempts to go beyond the usual application of standard remedies, however, and reduce further the area of private discrimination touch on the most difficult and sensitive area of all. It is perfectly reasonable to insist that governments act without undue discrimination or favoritism. In the arena of private action, however, the individual should be allowed more room for choice, even though the basic decisions might be considered irrational by others. Governments have stepped in to remove some areas of "free" choice because of inherent inequalities in the bargaining positions of the parties involved and the severe hardships to which large numbers of people might be subjected by others. This has been true, for example, in the matter of minimum wages, maximum hours, and workmen's compensation. In matters generally considered less necessitous than the right to make a living, governments have less frequently interfered with private choices. In the equal accommodations title of the Civil Rights Act of 1964, however, the Congress took action to remove from the area of free choice one of the most exacerbating instances of private discrimination—choice of customers on the basis of race or religion in places of public accommodation.

Freedom to choose associates in either social or vocational activities often leads to exclusivity, and the excluded groups may complain that something must be done by the government to afford them a wider range of choice. The policy which would lead to wider choices for the excluded group must to that extent reduce the freedom of selection of the former. The task of the policy-maker is to weigh the importance of the activity and the number of people involved, and to balance out the conflicting gains and losses in order to make a decision as to whether governmental action will be more or less beneficial than inaction.

In conclusion, one can say that while there is a tremendous area for exploration in the nonjudicial protections which may be offered to civil liberties, the judicial arena is still of vast importance in the field. The Court is, normally, the final judge of what most of the Constitution means; the state and federal courts interpret and apply the laws in appropriate cases; and some of the finest statements in the literature on human rights are to be found in the official opinions of judges on the state and federal bench. Since this is the case, and since this work is predominantly designed to describe the present law in the field of civil rights, the material and comment to follow will center heavily on the questions which have been presented for judicial decision.

CHAPTER 2
Civil Rights in the Federal System

For the beginning student in American civil rights, one of the most perplexing features is the complication presented by the federal pattern of government. To such persons it may come as a shock to find that the United States Constitution offers essentially a dual standard for national and state police or courts. The Constitution bars *federal* prosecution for serious crimes without grand jury indictment, but it permits a state to abolish the grand jury altogether. And until 1968 that same Constitution which guarantees the right of trial by jury to all persons charged with *federal* crimes allowed a state, if it chose to do so, to abolish the trial jury in all criminal cases, leaving the verdict to the judge. Further, until the fairly recent decision in *Gideon* v. *Wainwright,* 372 U.S. 335 (1963), the state could send persons to trial accused of even serious noncapital felonies without benefit of counsel, unless they could afford their own, while the Sixth Amendment demands court-appointed counsel for indigent *federal* defendants in all cases more serious than "petty offenses."

At the core of the matter is the fact that the Bill of Rights to the United States Constitution sets out various limitations on action by the *national* government, but it does not of its own terms in any way limit the *state* governments. Such protection as the Constitution provides against abridgment of civil rights by the state governments is to be found largely in the Civil War Amendments, and even these protections, with the exception of property rights, did not begin to take on substantial importance until the present century was well under way. Of course the most striking single development in the constitutional law of civil rights has been the "nationalization" of rights through the process of gradual "incorporation" of the various protections listed in the Bill of Rights into the due process clause of the Fourteenth Amendment. This process has been continuing for nearly half a century, and today most of the safeguards against national action described in the Bill of Rights are similarly operative against state action through the Fourteenth Amendment. Despite this fact, there remain some differences between the two sets of guarantees, and a sophisticated understanding of civil rights in America requires an analysis of the emergence of that law in the framework of the federal system.

To begin with the Philadelphia Convention, the national Constitution was designed to describe the powers and organization of the national government, without attempting to set up simultaneously a general pattern of state government. Certain limitations on state powers are to be found in that document, to be sure, but they are largely due to the desire to protect the integrity of national powers from state interference or to ensure that the states would not thwart the flow of interstate activities by means of burdensome discriminations. It must be recalled that the states existing in 1787 already had their own constitutions and framework of government, and the framers of the national Constitution did not take it upon themselves to tamper with those going concerns except as certain transfers of power from state to nation appeared necessary. In view of the purpose for which the Philadelphia Convention assembled, it would be surprising to find the framers drawing up a detailed list of safeguards to protect the citizen against the *state* government.

From an examination of the general purposes of the framers, it is a relatively easy second step to a realization that the Bill of Rights, added in 1791, protects the citizen only against the actions of the national government. A federal system had been established. Each governmental entity, nation and state, had its own constitution defining governmental organization, powers, and limitations. The state constitutions customarily had bills of rights describing guarantees operating against state officials. The national Bill of Rights operated against the national government. It would have seemed as curious in 1791 to argue that these amendments limited the state governments as it would to have claimed that federal courts were strictly bound by the requirements of state constitutions. The clamor from north to south for the addition of a bill of rights to the proposed Constitution of 1787 stemmed from distrust of national officials, not state officials. And Hamilton's response to such critics is further support for the view that the demands were restricted to protection against national abridgment of rights. In *The Federalist,* No. 84, he stated:

> I go further, and affirm that bills of rights, in the sense and to the extent in which they are contended for, are not only unnecessary in the proposed Constitution, but would even be dangerous. They would contain various exceptions to powers not granted; and, on this very account, would afford a colorable pretext to claim more than were granted. For why declare that things shall not be done which there is no power to do? Why, for instance, should it be said that the liberty of the press shall not be restrained, when no power is given by which restrictions may be imposed?

Hamilton was stressing the point that the government was one of delegated powers only, and in the absence of a delegation of authority to restrain the press there was no power to do so. Clearly he was speaking only of the national government, since the states have broad *reserved* powers and are not held to a specific list of enumerated powers as is the national government.

Finally, the group of amendments proposed by the first House of Representatives numbered seventeen, of which only one specifically limited the states. It provided that "no state should infringe the right of trial by jury in criminal cases, nor the rights of conscience, nor the freedom of speech or of the press." It is at least a reasonable conclusion to draw from this fact that the other provisions which omitted any reference to states were not intended to apply to the states. [For possible counter-arguments to this logic, see Herman Pritchett, *The American Constitution* (New York: McGraw-Hill, 1959), p. 371.] Despite these arguments, a judicial decision was required to dispose of the question finally. The case was *Barron* v. *Baltimore,* decided in 1833.

BARRON v. BALTIMORE
7 Peters 243 (1833)

[The case arose out of alleged damage to a wharf owned by Barron in the course of a paving program carried out by the City of Baltimore. In the completion of the program, certain streams were diverted from their usual course, and deposits of sand and gravel allegedly were built up at Barron's wharf to such an extent that access of vessels was prevented. A trial court verdict of $4,500 in Barron's favor was reversed by the Maryland Court of Appeals. Claiming that this action was a taking of his property for public use without just compensation, in violation of the Fifth Amendment to the United States Constitution, Barron took the question on writ of error to the United States Supreme Court. His contention was that the Fifth Amendment's broad language ought to be so construed as to restrain not only the power of the United States but also that of the State.]

Mr. Chief Justice Marshall delivered the opinion of the Court.

The judgment brought up by this writ of error having been rendered by the court of a State, this tribunal can exercise no jurisdiction over it, unless it be shown to come within the provisions of the twenty-fifth section of the Judicial Act.

The plaintiff in error contends that it comes within that clause in the Fifth Amendment to the Constitution, which inhibits the taking of private property for public use, without just compensation. He insists that this amendment, being in favor of the liberty of the citizen, ought to be so construed as to restrain the legislative power of a state, as well as that of the United States. If this proposition be untrue, the Court can take no jurisdiction of the cause.

The question thus presented is, we think, of great importance, but not of much difficulty.

The Constitution was ordained and established by the people of the United States for themselves, for their own government, and not for the government of the individual states. Each state established a constitution for itself, and, in that constitution, provided such limitations and restrictions on the powers of its particular government as its judgment dictated. The people of the United States framed such a government for the United States as they supposed best adapted to their situation, and best calculated to promote their interests. The powers they conferred on this government were to be exercised by itself; and the limitations on power, if expressed in general terms, are naturally, and, we think, necessarily applicable to the government created by the instrument. They are limitations of power granted in the instrument itself; not of distinct governments, framed by different persons and for different purposes.

If these propositions be correct, the Fifth Amendment must be understood as restraining the power of the general government, not as applicable to the states. In their several constitutions they have imposed such restrictions on their respective governments as their own wisdom suggested; such as they deemed most proper for themselves. It is a subject on which they judge exclusively, and with which others interfere no farther than they are supposed to have a common interest.

The counsel for the plaintiff in error insists that the Constitution was intended to secure the people of the several states against the undue exercise of power by their respective state governments; as well as against that which might be attempted by their general government. In support of this argument he relies on the inhibitions contained in the tenth section of the first article.

We think that section affords a strong if not a conclusive argument in support of the opinion already indicated by the Court.

[Here the Chief Justice compares some of the provisions of Article I, Section 9, with similar ones in Article I, Section 10. The former declares that "no bill of attainder or ex post facto law shall be passed." The latter declares that "no State shall pass any bill of attainder or ex post facto law." Marshall points out that despite the general wording of the prohibition in the former section it must be clear that it only applied to the Congress, because otherwise there would be no necessity for adding a separate phrase specifically forbidding the States to do these same things.]

If the original Constitution, in the ninth and tenth sections of the first article, draws this plain and marked line of discrimination between the limitations it imposes on the powers of the general government and on those of the states; if in every inhibition intended to act on state power, words are employed which directly express that intent, some strong reason must be assigned for departing from this safe and judicious course in framing the amendments, before that departure can be assumed.

We search in vain for that reason.

Had the people of the several states, or any of them, required changes in their constitutions; had they required additional safeguards to liberty from the apprehended encroachments of their particular governments, the remedy was in their own hands, and would have been applied by themselves. A convention would have been assembled by the discontented state, and the required improvements would have been made by itself. The unwieldy and cumbrous machinery of procuring a recommendation from two-thirds of Congress, and the assent of three-fourths of their sister states, could never have occurred to any human being as a mode of doing that which might be effected by the state itself. Had the framers of these amendments intended them to be limitations on the powers of the state governments, they would have imitated the framers of the original Constitution, and have expressed that intention. Had Congress engaged in the extraordinary occupation of improving the constitutions of the several states by affording the people additional protection from the exercise of power by their own governments in matters which concerned themselves alone, they would have declared this purpose in plain and intelligible language.

But it is universally understood, it is a part of the history of the day, that the great revolution which established the Constitution of the United States was not effected without immense opposition. Serious fears were extensively entertained that those powers which the patriot statesmen, who then watched over the interests of our country, deemed essential to union, and to the attainment of those invaluable objects for which union was sought, might be exercised in a manner dangerous to liberty. In almost every convention by which the Constitution was adopted, amendments to guard against the abuse of power were recommended. These amendments demanded security against the apprehended encroachments of the general government, not against those of the local governments.

In compliance with a sentiment thus generally expressed, to quiet fears thus extensively entertained, amendments were proposed by the required majority in Congress, and adopted by the states. These amendments contain no expression indicating an intention to apply them to the state governments. This Court cannot so apply them.

We are of opinion that the provision in the Fifth Amendment to the Constitution, declaring that private property shall not be taken for public use without just compensation, is intended solely as a limitation on the exercise of power by the government of the United States, and is not applicable to the legislation of the states. We are therefore of opinion, that there is no repugnancy between the several acts of the general assembly of Maryland, given in evidence by the defendants at the trial of this cause, in the court of that state, and the Constitution of the United States. This Court, therefore, has no jurisdiction of the cause; and it is dismissed.

Despite Marshall's logic and his historical analysis, one might argue that since the First Amendment specifically restricts Congress and the next seven are general in their language, all of these latter amendments were intended to apply fully to all governments within the United States. The answer to this contention is that in reality all of the provisions embodied in the first eight amendments were one lengthy addition to the Constitution, with no necessary logic or subtle, unexpressed intent behind the separation into eight articles. Thus the specific application of the opening sentence to Congress should be carried right on through as a limitation on the appropriate arm of the *national* government in each of the provisions of the Bill of Rights.

The citizen of Barron's day might have been impelled by that decision to sit down and browse through the whole Constitution to see just what sort of safeguards that document offered against the improper interference with his rights by the agents of state governments. At that time, 1833, he would have noted the protections in Article I, Section 10, regarding ex post facto laws and bills of attainder, to which Marshall referred in the above case, but virtually nothing else. A keen observer, however, might have spotted a potential weapon in Article IV, which states in Section 2, "The citizens of each State shall be entitled to all privileges and immunities of citizens in the several States." This sentence is not noteworthy for its clarity. The lay reader might readily conjure up an interpretation which would serve as a massive barrier to state deprivations of rights. The judicial interpretations of this clause, however, gave no great encouragement to such a view.

The clause is really a shorthand version of Article 4 of the Articles of Confederation, which in long and somewhat quaint fashion declared:

The better to secure and perpetuate mutual friendship and intercourse among the people of the different states in this Union, the free inhabitants of each of these states—paupers, vagabonds, and fugitives from justice, excepted—shall be entitled to all privileges and immunities of free citizens in the several states; and the people of each state shall have free ingress and regress to and from any other state, and shall enjoy therein all the privileges of trade and commerce, subject to the same duties, impositions, and restrictions, as the inhabitants thereof, respectively. . . .

If one examines the Constitutional provision in the light of its predecessor in the Articles of Confederation, then it immediately becomes apparent that the purpose of the clause was to protect out-of-state residents from burdensome discriminations in favor of local residents. The framers quite reasonably anticipated an ever-increasing flow of interstate travel and interstate commerce and presumably inserted the Article IV provision to safeguard against the erection of improper barriers to that development. [See Roger Howell, "The Privileges and Immunities of State Citizenship," *Johns Hopkins University Studies in History and Political Science,* Vol. 36, No. 3 (1918).] Under such an interpretation, however, it is clear that this clause would afford no solace to the individual who claims that his rights are abridged by his own state. At the outset, then, there is a serious limitation on the usefulness of the clause to protect one's rights broadly against state deprivation.

There is another question to be answered even where the allegation is made that a state has abridged the rights of an out-of-state resident. The question is, just what kinds of rights are protected by the clause? Not until 1825 was there anything approaching an official interpretation of what rights were covered. The controversy leading to this decision arose in New Jersey and concerned rights to gather oysters.

A New Jersey statute prohibited any person not a resident of New Jersey from gathering oysters in the state. One Corfield sailed his boat into the waters of New Jersey and took oysters. His boat was seized, and he was sued in trespass. Was New Jersey's reservation of its oysters inconsistent with Article IV, Section 2, of the Constitution? Justice Bushrod Washington, then on circuit, held the question under advisement from October term, 1824, until April term, 1825, and then gave his famous pronouncement on the meaning of the clause:

We feel no hesitation in confining these expressions to those privileges and immunities which are, in their nature fundamental; which belong, of right, to the citizens of all free governments; and which have, at all times, been enjoyed by the citizens of the several states which compose this Union, from the time of their becoming free, independent, and sovereign. What these fundamental principles are, it would perhaps be more tedious than difficult to enumerate. [The Justice then proceeds to risk tedium by recounting quite a list, including protection by the government; enjoyment of life and liberty; the right to acquire and possess property; the right of a citizen of one state to pass through, or reside in, other states for purposes of trade or profession; protection by the writ of habeas corpus; the right to institute and maintain court actions; exemption from higher taxes than are paid by other citizens of the state; and the elective franchise, as regulated by the laws of the particular state in which it is exercised.] These, and many others which might be mentioned, are, strictly speaking, privileges and immunities. [*Corfield* v. *Coryell,* 6 Fed. Cas. No. 3230, 546, 552 (1823).]

Considering the broad strokes with which Justice Washington outlined the "privileges and immunities" so protected, one might have expected him to have held oyster-taking in the protected category. He did not, however, and made a distinction between the private and personal rights covered and the common property of the people of a particular state, such as fish. He further held that the state was under no obligation to share property of this sort with citizens of other states. The precise holding of the case, with respect to fisheries, has been followed and even expanded to include game. But as to the list of general rights mentioned in the opinion, subsequent construction has in many ways permitted the state to differentiate between its citizens and nonresidents, or even new residents. Broadly speaking, these rights are subject to restrictions imposed under the police power of the state, and the Court has permitted reasonable discriminations by the state in protecting the health, safety, and welfare of its own citizens. The state may charge nonresidents a higher tuition for its schools or a higher fee for hunting and fishing licenses. It may require a specified period of residence within the state before allowing divorce actions to be maintained in its courts, and this rule was upheld against claims of abridgment of the right to travel and violation of the due process clause in *Sosna* v. *Iowa,* 419 U.S. 393 (1975). The state may not generally, however, deny nonresidents access to its courts.

[For an analysis of the clause and some of the major cases concerning it, see Lester S. Jayson, ed., *The Constitution of the United States of America, revised and annotated* (U.S. Government Printing Ofc., 1973), pp. 830–838.]

From both standpoints, then—the persons to whom the clause applies and the rights protected—the conclusion must be that this is a thin reed on which to rely for remedies against the state. To continue the search, what remained in the United States Constitution of the pre-Civil War period which would serve as a safeguard against abridgment of rights by the state? The answer is clear: nothing at all. The citizen of that period had to look to his own state laws and state constitution for redress of grievances against the officials of that government.

It should be apparent from this examination that not only did the pre-Civil War Constitution fail to restrain states in their general limitations on personal rights, but it also left the way open for the states to establish substantive and procedural standards in their respective bills of rights which were different from the protections afforded in the Bill of Rights to the United States Constitution. The net result was that the citizen had two separate packets of rights with two separate remedies for abuse, depending on which governmental entity committed the fault. The fact that many of the guarantees in the state and national constitutions were duplicated should not lead one to the conclusion that his rights against the two governments were identical. As pointed out earlier, even today the state can abolish indictment by grand jury, while the Fifth Amendment makes it mandatory in federal felony cases. This situation, then, is the first complication introduced into the area of civil rights by our federal system of government.

A second complication, and the reason for the chronological references above, was introduced by the addition of the Fourteenth Amendment to the Constitution. The relevant portions of that amendment are found in Section 1:

All persons born or naturalized in the United States, and subject to the jurisdiction thereof, are citizens of the United States and of the State wherein they reside. No State shall make or enforce any law which shall abridge the privileges or immunities of citizens of the United States; nor shall any State deprive any person of life, liberty, or property, without due process of law; nor deny to any person within its jurisdiction the equal protection of the laws.

With the addition of this amendment in 1868 we have the first major *national* restraint upon the governments of the states in the field of civil rights. It is important to note, however, that even this protection does not reach the sort of deprivation caused by private persons. The Fourteenth Amendment is clearly a bar to certain interference occasioned by states, but does not reach the great area of injury inflicted by private action. The problem of defining "state action" will be considered in more detail below.

The immediate question presented by the addition of the Fourteenth Amendment was what kinds of rights and immunities were covered and to what extent they were covered. To be more specific, did this new amendment incorporate the long list of guarantees in the Bill of Rights and require exactly these same standards to be met by all the states? If so, then the troublesome problem of two separate packets of rights would no longer plague us. If not, then at least two alternative interpretations could be made, one of which would make the amendment merely a general statement of principle, and the other build up yet a *third* category of rights and still further complicate the problem. Let us take up the various stages of development to follow the actual line of interpretation.

Over a period of years, class after class of beginning students has been asked to select the phrase from the Fourteenth Amendment which would appear to offer the most substantial protection against encroachment by the state government upon their rights. Almost without fail, the clause selected is, "No State shall make or enforce any law which shall abridge the privileges or immunities of citizens of the United States." And it would seem to be a reasonable choice. The words have the ring of freedom about them. Unfortunately, judicial interpretation has shown this answer to be altogether wrong. The leading decision on what the privileges and immunities clause means was rendered in 1873 in the *Slaughter-House Cases.* Professor Charles Fairman has certainly not overstated the point when he says that a full comprehension of this case yields the key to perhaps a good third of the entire constitutional law of the United States.

Despite the fact that the Fourteenth Amendment was primarily enacted to protect the newly freed Negro, it was a group of Southern whites who first invoked the amendment against the carpetbag laws of their own state.

SLAUGHTER-HOUSE CASES
16 Wallace 36 (1873)

[In 1869 the Republican legislature of Louisiana passed an act "to protect the health of the city of New Orleans," which incorporated a slaughter-house company and gave it a twenty-five-year monopoly on the slaughtering business in that city. The law required that all other butchers in New Orleans come to that company and pay for the use of its abattoir. The case went up through the state courts with the Republican courts, of course, sustaining the statute. It was argued before the United States Supreme Court that the statute violated four parts of the United States Constitution: the Thirteenth Amendment and the "privileges and immunities" clause, the "due process" clause, and the "equal protection" clause of the Fourteenth Amendment. Since the main thrust of the opinion was in response to the "privileges and immunities" argument, the other portions of the opinion will be reserved for later discussion.]

On Writ of Error to the Supreme Court of the State of Louisiana.

Mr. Justice Miller delivered the opinion of the Court.

The plaintiffs in error . . . allege that the Statute is a violation of the Constitution of the United States in these several particulars:

That it creates an involuntary servitude forbidden by the Thirteenth Article of Amendment;

That it abridges the privileges and immunities of citizens of the United States;

That it denies to the plaintiffs the equal protection of the laws; and,

That it deprives them of their property without due process of law; contrary to the provisions of the first section of the Fourteenth Article of Amendment.

This Court is thus called upon for the first time to give construction to these Articles.

We do not conceal from ourselves the great responsibility which this duty devolves upon us. No questions so far-reaching and pervading in their consequences, so profoundly interesting to the people of this country, and so important in their bearing upon the relations of the United States and of the several states to each other, and to the citizens of the states and of the United States have been before this Court during the official life of any of its present members. . . .

[Here the Justice discusses the background of the citizenship clause of Section 1, and the holding in the Dred Scott case, to the effect that a man of African descent, whether a slave or not, was not and could not be a citizen of a state or of the United States.]

To remove this difficulty primarily, and to establish a clear and comprehensive definition of citizenship which should declare what should constitute citizenship of the United States, and also citizenship of a state, the first clause of the first section was framed.

"All persons born or naturalized in the United States, and subject to the jurisdiction thereof, are citizens of the United States and of the State wherein they reside."

The first observation we have to make on this clause is that it puts at rest both the questions which we stated to have been the subject of differences of opinion. It declares that persons may be citizens of the United States without regard to their citizenship of a particular state, and it overturns the Dred Scott decision by making all persons born within the United States and subject to its jurisdiction citizens of the United States. That its main purpose was to establish the citizenship of the Negro can admit of no doubt. The phrase "subject to its jurisdiction" was intended to exclude from its operation children of ministers, consuls, and citizens or subjects of foreign states born within the United States.

The next observation is more important in view of the arguments of counsel in the present case. It is, that the distinction between citizenship of the United States and citizenship of a state is clearly recognized and established. Not only may a man be a citizen of the United States without being a citizen of a state, but an important element is necessary to convert the former into the latter. He must reside within the state to make him a citizen of it, but it is only necessary that he should be born or naturalized in the United States to be a citizen of the Union.

It is quite clear, then, that there is a citizenship of the United States, and a citizenship of a state, which are distinct from each other, and which depends upon different characteristics or circumstances in the individual.

We think this distinction and its explicit recognition in this Amendment of great weight in this argument, because the next paragraph of this same section, which is the one mainly relied on by the plaintiffs in error, speaks only of privileges and immunities of citizens of the United States, and does not speak of those of citizens of the several states. The argument, however, in favor of the plaintiffs rests wholly on the assumption that the citizenship is the same, and the privileges and immunities guaranteed by the clause are the same.

The language is: "No state shall make or enforce any law which shall abridge the privileges or immunities of citizens of the United States." It is a little remarkable, if this clause was intended as a protection to the citizen of a state against the legislative power of his own state, that the words "citizen of the state" should be left out when it is so carefully used, and used in contradistinction to "citizens of the United States" in the very sentence which precedes it. It is too clear for argument that the change in phraseology was adopted understandingly and with a purpose.

Of the privileges and immunities of the citizens of the United States, and of the privileges and immunities of the citizen of the state, and what they respectively are, we will presently consider; but we wish to state here that it is only the former which are placed by this clause under the protection of the Federal Constitution, and that the latter, whatever they may be, are not intended to have any additional protection by this paragraph of the Amendment.

If, then, there is a difference between the privileges and immunities belonging to a citizen of the United States as such, and those belonging to the citizen of the state as such, the latter must rest for their security and protection where they have heretofore rested; for they are not embraced by this paragraph of the Amendment.

The first occurrence of the words "privileges and immunities" in our constitutional history is to be found in the fourth of the Articles of the old Confederation.

[Here the Justice traces the development of the Article IV, Section 2, privileges and immunities clause in the Constitution, and cites Justice Washington's opinion in *Corfield* v. *Coryell,* discussed earlier in this chapter.]

In the case of *Paul* v. *Virginia,* the court, in expounding this clause of the Constitution, says that "the privileges and immunities secured to citizens of each state in the several states, by the provision in question, are those privileges and immunities which are common to the citizens in the latter states under their Constitution and laws by virtue of their being citizens."

The constitutional provision there alluded to did not create those rights, which it called privileges and immunities of citizens of the states. It threw around them in that clause no security for the citizen of the state in which they were claimed or exercised. Nor did it profess to control the power of the state governments over the rights of its own citizens.

Its sole purpose was to declare to the several states, that whatever those rights, as you grant or establish them to your own citizens, or as you limit or qualify, or impose restrictions on their exercise, the same, neither more nor less, shall be the measure of the rights of citizens of other states within your jurisdiction.

It would be the vainest show of learning to attempt to prove by citations of authority, that up to the adoption of the recent Amendments, no claim or pretense was set up that those rights depended on the Federal government for their existence or protection, beyond the very few express limitations which the Federal Constitution imposed upon the states—such, for instance, as the prohibition against ex post facto laws, bills of attainder, and laws impairing the obligation of contracts. But with the exception of these and a few other restrictions, the entire domain of the privileges and immunities of citizens of the states, as above defined, lay within the constitutional and legislative power of the states, and without that of the Federal government. Was it the purpose of the Fourteenth Amendment, by the simple declaration that no state should make or enforce any law which shall abridge the privileges and immunities of citizens of the United States, to transfer the security and protection of all the civil rights which we have mentioned, from the states to the Federal government? And where it is declared that Congress shall have the power to enforce that article, was it intended to bring within the power of Congress the entire domain of civil rights heretofore belonging exclusively to the states?

All this and more must follow, if the proposition of the plaintiffs in error be sound. For not only are these rights subject to the control of Congress whenever in its discretion any of them are supposed to be abridged by state legislation, but that body may also pass laws in advance, limiting and restricting the exercise of legislative power by the states, in their most ordinary and usual functions, as in its judgment it may think proper on all such subjects. And still further, such a construction followed by the reversal of the judgments of the supreme court of Louisiana in these cases would constitute this court a perpetual censor upon all legislation of the states, on the civil rights of their own citizens, with authority to nullify such as it did not approve as consistent with those rights, as they existed at the time of the adoption of this Amendment. The argument, we admit, is not always the most conclusive which is drawn from the consequences urged against the adoption of a particular construction of an instrument. But when, as in the case before us, these consequences are so serious, so far-reaching and pervading, so great a departure from the structure and spirit of our institutions; when the effect is to fetter and degrade the state governments by subjecting them to the control of Congress, in the exercise of powers heretofore universally conceded to them of the most ordinary and fundamental character; when in fact it radically changes the whole theory of the relations of the state and Federal governments to each other and of both these governments to the people; the argument has a force that is irresistible, in the absence of language which expresses such a purpose too clearly to admit of doubt.

We are convinced that no such results were intended by the Congress which proposed these amendments, nor by the legislatures of the states, which ratified them.

Having shown that the privileges and immunities relied on in the argument are those which belong to citizens of the states as such, and that they are left to the state governments for security and protection, and not by this article placed under the special care of the Federal government, we may hold ourselves excused from defining the privileges and immunities of citizens of the United States which no state can abridge, until some case involving those privileges may make it necessary to do so.

But lest it should be said that no such privileges and immunities are to be found if those we have been considering are excluded, we venture to suggest some which owe their existence to the Federal government, its national character, its Constitution, or its laws.

One of these is well described in the case of *Crandall* v. *Nevada*. It is said to be the right of the citizen of this great country, protected by implied guaranties of its Constitution, "to come to the seat of government to assert any claim he may have upon that government, to transact any business he may have with it, to seek its protection, to share its offices, to engage in administering its functions. He has the right of free access to its seaports, through which all operations of foreign commerce are conducted, to the sub-treasuries, land-offices, and courts of justice in the several states." And quoting from the language of Chief Justice Taney in another case, it is said "that, for all the great purposes for which the Federal government was established, we are one people with one common country; we are all citizens of the United States"; and it is as such citizens that their rights are supported in this court in *Crandall* v. *Nevada*.

Another privilege of a citizen of the United States is to demand the care and protection of the Federal government over his life, liberty, and property when on the high seas or within the jurisdiction of a foreign government. Of this there can be no doubt, nor that the right depends upon his character as a citizen of the United States. The right to peaceably assemble and petition for redress of grievances, the privilege of the writ of habeas corpus, are rights of the citizen guarantied by the Federal Constitution. The right to use the navigable waters of the United States, however they may penetrate the territory of the several states, and all rights secured to our citizens by treaties with foreign nations, are dependent upon citizenship of the United States, and not citizenship of a state. One of these privileges is conferred by the very article under consideration. It is that a citizen of the United States can, of his own volition, become a citizen of any state of the Union by a bona fide residence therein, with the same rights as other citizens of that state. To these may be added the rights secured by the thirteenth and fifteenth articles of amendment, and by the other clause of the fourteenth, next to be considered.

But it is useless to pursue this branch of the inquiry, since we are of opinion that the rights claimed by these plaintiffs in error, if they have any existence, are not privileges and immunities of citizens of the United States within the meaning of the clause of the fourteenth amendment under consideration. . . .

Judgment affirmed.

Justice Field, with Chief Justice Chase and Justices Swayne and Bradley concurring, rendered a dissenting opinion. He stated, in part:

The amendment does not attempt to confer any new privileges or immunities upon citizens, or to enumerate or define those already existing. It assumes that there are such privileges and immunities which belong of right to citizens as such, and ordains that they shall not be abridged by State legislation. If this inhibition has no reference to privileges and immunities of this character, but only refers, as held by the majority of the court in their opinion, to such privileges and immunities as were before its adoption specially designated in the Constitution or necessarily implied as belonging to citizens of the United States, it was a vain and idle enactment, which accomplished nothing, and most unnecessarily excited Congress and the people on its passage. With privileges and immunities thus designated or implied no State could ever have interfered by its laws, and no new constitutional provision was required to inhibit such interference. The supremacy of the Constitution and the laws of the United States always controlled any State legislation of that character.

Almost without exception, the interpretation given the privileges and immunities clause by the Court in the *Slaughter-House Cases* has remained the official view. The result has been that this clause affords no protection to the individual who claims that state officials have deprived him of rights which most of us consider the basic rights: freedom of speech, religious freedom, the right to engage in lawful occupations, freedom from improper police violence, and others of this nature. The initial reaction of many people to a reading of the opinion for the Court is frank surprise. One will frequently hear the remark that such a bad law *must* be unconstitutional, and the Court was derelict in its duty in refusing to hold it so. On the other hand, if Justice Miller's reasoning is carefully examined, it becomes clearer that the overall policy which he set out was beneficial in two important respects.

First, it recognized the existence of the two spheres of authority which the Constitution established in providing for the federal system of government. If we are to have a federal form, the agencies of the national government cannot be permitted to exercise a general supervisory power over every facet of state activity. This would make the states mere administrative subdivisions of the national government. A good case can be made for the unitary form of government, of course, but we have made no constitutional provision for such an arrangement. States are expected to operate more or less autonomously in many areas of policy-making, and it is improper for the arms of the national government to reach down to the purely local level to interfere with this discretionary power. State experiments in unemployment compensation or the use of the merit system of public employment which were dubbed "crackpot" in one period were in a later period adopted by all other states and the national government as well. And policies which are quite congenial to the residents of one state may find stubborn resistance in another. Thus Justice Miller's opinion shows a conscious refusal to stay the power of the state to experiment or to differ with its neighbors in the Union. It can quite properly be characterized as a strong "states-rights" decision.

A second beneficial aspect of the decision lies in the fact that the Court recognized the importance of judicial restraint in matters where the local citizenry should assume responsibility. The federal judges, with life tenure, are largely outside the control of the citizenry. The bench of even the states is not responsive to popular pressures to the degree to which the legislative and executive branches are. Thus errors committed by the judges may take longer to correct than would be the case with the other branches. The judge, then, must be constantly mindful of the ballot box as a remedy at least as important and perhaps more appropriate than judicial review for correcting the policy mistakes of governors and legislators.

An important consequence of the decision—whether beneficial or not depends upon the point of view—was its impact upon the possible enforcement legislation which Section 5 of the Fourteenth Amendment empowers Congress to enact. The fact of the matter seems to be that by the narrow coverage allowed to the privileges and immunities clause, the Court cut the heart out of one of the most potentially powerful weapons which Congress might have used to legislate in the civil rights area. The only remaining clauses of the amendment of importance for this purpose are the due process and the equal protection clauses. Looking at these three clauses from the legislator's viewpoint, which would afford the simplest framework for enforcement legislation? It would appear that the privileges and immunities clause is tailor-made for such a purpose. All one need do would be to set out a comprehensive list of the vast number of rights which the average person considers to flow from possession of United States citizenship, and then make it a crime for any agent of the state to abridge such rights. The restrictive decision in *Slaughter-House,* however, effectively blocked such an approach. The remaining two clauses are far more elusive as reference points for enforcement legislation. How does one frame a statute to protect a person from state deprivation of his liberty "without due process of law"? Except, perhaps, in the area of racial discrimination, how can a bill-drafter come to grips with the requirement of "equal protection of the laws," which allows so much flexibility in classifying the objects of legislation? Even leaving aside the important political barriers to passing civil rights laws, the technical difficulties in phrasing bills to accomplish the purposes without being unconstitutionally vague are formidable.

The decision in the *Slaughter-House Cases* is thus in the same vein as *Barron* v. *Baltimore.* Federal rights and state rights are two different things, and one must take care to make the proper distinction so that the correct remedy can be selected when abridgment is alleged. To this day, the rule of the *Slaughter-House Cases* with respect to the privileges and immunities clause is still good law. The only aberration was in 1935, when the Court held in *Colgate* v. *Harvey,* 296 U.S. 404 (1935), that the right of a citizen of the United States to do business in, or place a loan in, a state other than that of his residence was a privilege of national citizenship. Only five years later, however, the Court expressly overruled that decision in *Madden* v.

Kentucky, 309 U.S. 83 (1940), and returned to the old interpretation. *Madden* held that for a state to impose on its citizens a higher tax on out-of-state bank deposits than on those deposited within the state was not a violation of the privileges or immunities of national citizenship, since "the right to carry out an incident to a trade, business or calling such as the deposit of money in banks is not a privilege of national citizenship." And in *Snowden* v. *Hughes,* 321 U.S. 1 (1944), the Court held that the right to become a candidate for, and to be elected to, a state office was not among the privileges of United States citizenship but was an attribute of state citizenship. The complainant, then, had to look to his own state constitution and laws for redress of his injury, a least so far as this clause of the Constitution was concerned.

But what of the other two clauses in the Fourteenth Amendment—the due process and equal protection clauses? Are these no more useful as guarantees against state interference than the privileges and immunities clause proved to be? Again, the starting point is the *Slaughter-House* opinion of Justice Miller, but the subsequent developments have been vastly different. The appellants in the case argued most vigorously on the privileges and immunities ground, but the latter two clauses were tossed in for good measure. As to these claims, Justice Miller stated:

The argument has not been much pressed in these cases that the defendant's charter deprives the plaintiffs of their property without due process of law, or that it denies to them the equal protection of the law. The first of these paragraphs has been in the Constitution since the adoption of the Fifth Amendment, as a restraint upon the federal power. It is also to be found in some form of expression in the constitutions of nearly all the states, as a restraint upon the power of the states. This law, then, has practically been the same as it now is during the existence of the government, except so far as the present Amendment may place the restraining power over the states in this matter in the hands of the federal government.

We are not without judicial interpretation, therefore, both state and national, of the meaning of this clause. And it is sufficient to say that under no construction of that provision that we have ever seen, or any that we deem admissible, can the restraint imposed by the state of Louisiana upon the exercise of their trade by the butchers of New Orleans be held to be a deprivation of property within the meaning of that provision.

"Nor shall any State deny to any person within its jurisdiction the equal protection of the laws."

In the light of the history of these Amendments, and the pervading purpose of them, which we have already discussed, it is not difficult to give a meaning to this clause. The existence of laws in the states where the newly emancipated Negroes resided, which discriminated with gross injustice and hardship against them as a class, was the evil to be remedied by this clause, and by it such laws are forbidden.

If, however, the states did not conform their laws to its requirements, then by the fifth section of the Article of Amendment Congress was authorized to enforce it by suitable legislation. We doubt very much whether any action of a state not directed by way of discrimination against the Negroes as a class, or on account of their race, will ever be held to come within the purview of this provision. It is so clearly a provision for that race and that emergency, that a strong case would be necessary for its application to any other. But as it is a state that is to be dealt with, and not alone the validity of its laws, we may safely leave that matter until

Congress shall have exercised its power, or some case of state oppression, by denial of equal justice in its courts, shall have claimed a decision at our hands. We find no such case in the one before us, and do not deem it necessary to go over the argument again, as it may have relation to this particular clause of the Amendment. . . .

In almost perfunctory fashion, then, Justice Miller denied the contention that the due process clause barred the state from enforcing the butcher monopoly law. Except for his statements concerning the recognition of the federal form of government, it is not really clear just why such a law would not constitute a taking of property without due process of law. To fill the gap here, however, one may look to another opinion for the Court filed by Justice Miller a few years later. The case was *Davidson* v. *New Orleans*, 96 U.S. 97 (1878), and it dealt with the question of whether a special assessment on certain real estate, for the purpose of draining swamp lands, which allegedly would not benefit the assessed landowner, constituted a taking of property without due process of law. The Louisiana Supreme Court had held against the owner, and the United States Supreme Court reviewed the decision under the question stated. Justice Miller, speaking for the Court, gave a very narrow construction to the clause. In essence, his argument is summarized in the following statements:

It is not possible to hold that a party has, without due process of law, been deprived of his property, when, as regards the issues affecting it, he has, by the laws of the State, a fair trial in a court of justice, according to the modes of proceeding applicable to such a case. . . .

This proposition covers the present case. Before the assessment could be collected, or become effectual, the statute required that the tableau of assessments should be filed in the proper District Court of the State; that personal service of notice, with reasonable time to object, should be served on all owners who were known and within reach of process, and due advertisement made as to those who were unknown, or could not be found. This was compiled with; and the party complaining here appeared, and had a full and fair hearing in the court of the first instance, and afterwards in the Supreme Court. If this be not due process of law, then the words can have no definite meaning as used in the Constitution.

Judgment affirmed.

It is clear from this excerpt of Justice Miller's opinion that to him all that the term "due" process required of the state was "legal" process. If all the forms required by state constitution or statute were met, and if the injured party has his "day in court," then he could not successfully contend that the substance of the law should concern the federal courts under a claim of Fourteenth Amendment violation.

Unlike the privileges and immunities clause, however, the due process clause underwent a radical change from the interpretation which Justice Miller gave it. The concurring opinion of Justice Bradley in *Davidson* v. *New Orleans* foretold the direction in which later interpretations of the clause would move:

In the conclusion and general tenor of the opinion just read, I concur. But I think it narrows the scope of inquiry as to what is due process of law more than it should do.

It seems to me that private property may be taken by a State without due process of law in other ways than by mere direct enactment, or the want of a judicial proceeding. . . . I think, therefore, we are entitled, under the fourteenth amendment, not only to see that there is some process of law, but "due process of law," provided by the State law when a citizen is deprived of his property; and that, in judging what is "due process of law," respect must be had to the cause and object of the taking, whether under the taxing power, the power of eminent domain, or the power of assessment for local improvements, or none of these; and if found to be suitable or admissible in this special case, it will be adjudged to be "due process of law"; but if found to be arbitrary, oppressive, and unjust, it may be declared to be not "due process of law." Such an examination may be made without interfering with that large discretion which every legislative power has of making wide modifications in the forms of procedure in each case, according as the laws, habits, customs, and preferences of the people of the particular State may require.

The two cases just discussed indicate the strong reluctance of the majority on the United States Supreme Court in the 1870s to allow the Fourteenth Amendment to become a vehicle for wholesale judicial review by that Court of the laws and policies adopted by the states. However, the opinion of Justice Bradley, just quoted, contained the seeds of development of the due process clause into quite a different and stronger weapon of supervision. Beginning in the economic area, with close scrutiny of state laws interfering with the owner's use of property, the Court gradually toward the end of the nineteenth century assumed the power to determine whether such laws were so "arbitrary, oppressive, and unjust" as to amount to a deprivation of property without due process of law. For the purposes of examining non-economic civil rights, such as those generally specified in the national Bill of Rights, the Court was somewhat slower to draw on the due process clause as a basis for staying the power of the state. More and more frequently during the latter years of the nineteenth century the Court was criticized for placing the property protection of the Fourteenth Amendment ahead of protection to life and liberty. By the early part of the twentieth century at least some measure of success had been achieved by those who viewed the Fourteenth Amendment as a requirement of some kind of minimal standard in the area of criminal procedure. Efforts were made in arguing some of the cases to prove that in this area the Fourteenth Amendment really represented a shorthand adoption of the procedural guarantees listed in the Bill of Rights, and no state could provide less than this minimum group of safeguards.

One of the most important cases involving this approach was *Twining* v. *New Jersey*, decided in 1908. Counsel for Twining in effect tried to convince the Court that either the privileges and immunities clause or the due process clause, or both of them, included the whole list of rights which the Bill of Rights protects from national abridgment. The Court's analysis of the issues readily breaks into two parts to answer the contentions made under these two clauses of the Fourteenth Amendment.

TWINING *v.* NEW JERSEY

211 U.S. 78 (1908)

[Twining and Cornell, directors of a bank in New Jersey, were indicted for having knowingly exhibited a false paper to a state bank examiner with intent to deceive him as to the condition of the bank. At the trial the defendants called no witnesses and did not testify in their own behalf. In his charge to the jury the judge said: "Because a man does not go upon the stand you are not necessarily justified in drawing an inference of guilt. But you have a right to consider the fact that he does not go upon the stand where a direct accusation is made against him."

The defendants were convicted and sentenced to imprisonment for six and four years respectively. This was affirmed by the Court of Errors and Appeals, and the case was then carried to the United States Supreme Court on the claim that the charge to the jury constituted a form of self-incrimination which abridged their privileges and immunities as United States citizens and led to a deprivation of liberty without due process of law. The attempt was to show that the Fifth Amendment's protection against self-incrimination had been included in the Fourteenth Amendment as a protection against the states.]

Justice Moody delivered the opinion of the Court.

[On the "privileges and immunities" issue:]

The defendants contend, in the first place, that the exemption from self-incrimination is one of the privileges and immunities of citizens of the United States which the Fourteenth Amendment forbids the States to abridge. It is not argued that the defendants are protected by that part of the Fifth Amendment which provides that "no person . . . shall be compelled in any criminal case to be a witness against himself," for it is recognized by counsel that by a long line of decisions the first ten Amendments are not operative on the States. *Barron* v. *Baltimore,* 7 Pet. 243; . . . But it is argued that this privilege is one of the fundamental rights of National citizenship, placed under National protection by the Fourteenth Amendment, and it is specifically argued that the "privileges and immunities of citizens of the United States," protected against State action by that Amendment, include those fundamental personal rights which are protected against National action by the first eight Amendments; that this was the intention of the framers of the Fourteenth Amendment, and that this part of it would otherwise have little or no meaning and effect. These arguments are not new to this court and the answer to them is found in its decisions. The meaning of the phrase "privileges and immunities of citizens of the United States," as used in the Fourteenth Amendment, came under early consideration in the *Slaughter-House Cases,* 16 Wall. 36. . . .

. . . If, then, it be assumed, without deciding the point, that an exemption from compulsory self-incrimination is what is described as a fundamental right belonging to all who live under a free government, and incapable of impairment by legislation or judicial decision, it is, so far as the states are concerned, a fundamental right inherent in state citizenship, and is a privilege or immunity of that citizenship only. Privileges and immunities of citizens of the United States, on the other hand, are only such as arise out of the nature and essential character of the national government, or are specifically granted or secured to all citizens or persons by the Constitution of the United States. *Slaughter-House Cases* . . .

Thus, among the rights and privileges of national citizenship recognized by this court are the right to pass freely from state to state (*Crandall* v. *Nevada,* 6 Wall. 35); the right to petition Congress for a redress of grievances (*U.S.* v. *Cruikshank*); the right to vote for national officers (Ex parte *Yarbrough,* 115 U.S. 651); the right to enter the public lands (*U.S.* v. *Waddell,* 112 U.S. 76); the right to be protected against violence while in the lawful custody of a United States marshal (*Logan* v. *U.S.,* 144 U.S. 263); and the right to inform the United States authorities of violation of its laws (*Re Quarles,* 158 U.S. 532). . . . But assuming it to be true that the exemption from self-incrimination is not, as a fundamental right of national citizenship, included in the privileges and immunities of citizens of the United States, counsel insist that, as a right specifically granted or secured by the Federal Constitution, it is included in them. This view is based upon the contention which must now be examined, that the safeguards of personal rights which are enumerated in the first eight articles of amendment to the Federal Constitution, sometimes called the Federal Bill of Rights, though they were by those Amendments originally secured only against national action, are among the privileges and immunities of citizens of the United States, which this clause of the Fourteenth Amendment protects against state action. This view has been, at different times, expressed by justices of this court ... and was undoubtedly that entertained by some of those who framed the Amendment. It is, however, not profitable to examine the weighty arguments in its favor, for the question is no longer open in this court. The right of trial by jury in civil cases, guaranteed by the Seventh Amendment (*Walker* v. *Sauvinet*, 92 U.S. 90), and the right to bear arms, guaranteed by the Second Amendment (*Presser* v. *Illinois,* 116 U.S. 252), have been distinctly held not to be privileges and immunities of citizens of the United States, guaranteed by the Fourteenth Amendment against abridgment by the states, and in effect the same decision was made in respect of the guaranty against prosecution, except by indictment of a grand jury, contained in the Fifth Amendment (*Hurtado* v. *California,* 110 U.S. 516), and in respect of the right to be confronted with witnesses, contained in the Sixth Amendment (*West* v. *Louisiana,* 194 U.S. 258). In *Maxwell* v. *Dow* (176 U.S. 606), where the plaintiff in error had been convicted in a state court of a felony upon an information, and by a jury of eight persons, it was held that the indictment made indispensable by the Fifth Amendment, and the trial by jury, guaranteed by the Sixth Amendment, were not privileges and immunities of citizens of the United States, as those words were used in the Fourteenth Amendment. The discussion in that case ought not to be repeated. All the arguments for the other view were considered and answered, the authorities were examined and analyzed, and the decision rested upon the ground that this clause of the Fourteenth Amendment did not forbid the states to abridge the personal rights enumerated in the first eight Amendments, because those rights were not within the meaning of the clause "privileges and immunities of citizens of the United States.". . . We conclude, therefore, that the exemption from compulsory self-incrimination is not a privilege or immunity of national citizenship guaranteed by this clause of the Fourteenth Amendment against abridgment by the states.

[On the "due process" issue:]

The defendants, however, do not stop here. They appeal to another clause of the Fourteenth Amendment, and insist that the self-incrimination which they allege the instruction to the jury compelled was a denial of due process of law. This contention requires separate consideration, for it is possible that some of the personal rights safeguarded by the first eight Amendments against national action may also be safeguarded against state action, because a denial of them would be a denial of due process of law. . . . If this is so, it is not because those rights are enumerated in the first eight Amendments, but because they are of such a nature that they are included in the conception of due process of law. Few phrases of the law are so elusive of exact apprehension as this. Doubtless the difficulties of ascertaining its connotation have been increased in American jurisprudence, where it has been embodied in constitutions and put to new uses as a limit on legislative power. This court has always declined to give a comprehensive definition of it, and has preferred that its full meaning should be gradually ascertained by the process of inclusion and exclusion in the course of the decisions of cases as they arise. There are certain general principles, well settled, however, which narrow the field of discussion, and may serve as helps to correct conclusions. These principles grow out of the proposition universally accepted by American courts on the authority of Coke, that the words "due process of law" are equivalent in meaning to the words "law of the land," contained in that chapter of Magna Charta which provides that "no freeman shall be taken, or imprisoned, or disseised, or outlawed, or exiled, or any wise destroyed; nor shall we go upon him, nor send upon him, but by the lawful judgment of his peers or by the law of the land." . . . From the consideration of the meaning of the words in the light of their historical origin this court has drawn the following conclusions:

First. What is due process of law may be ascertained by an examination of those settled usages and modes of proceedings existing in the common and statute law of England before the emigration of our ancestors, and shown not to have been unsuited to their civil and political condition by having been acted on by them after the settlement of this country. . . . "A process of law," said Mr. Justice Matthews, . . . "which is not otherwise forbidden, must be taken to be due process of law, if it can show the sanction of settled usage both in England and in this country." *Hurtado* v. *California*, 110 U.S. 516, 528.

Second. It does not follow, however, that a procedure settled in English law at the time of the emigration, and brought to this country and practised by our ancestors, is an essential element of due process of law. If that were so, the procedure of the first half of the seventeenth century would be fastened upon the American jurisprudence like a straight-jacket, only to be unloosed by constitutional amendment. That, said Mr. Justice Matthews, in the same case, p. 529, "would be to deny every quality of the law but its age, and to render it incapable of progress or improvement." . . .

Third. But consistently with the requirements of due process, no change in ancient procedure can be made which disregards those fundamental principles, to be ascertained from time to time by judicial action, which have relation to process of law, and protect the citizen in his private right, and guard him against the arbitrary action of government. This idea has been many times expressed in differing words by this court, and it seems well to cite some expressions of it. . . . "This court has never attempted to define with precision the words 'due process of law.' . . . It is sufficient to say that there are certain immutable principles of justice which inhere in the very idea of free government which no member of the Union may disregard." *Holden* v. *Hardy*, 169 U.S. 366, 389. . . . "The limit of the full control which the state has in the proceedings of its courts, both in civil and criminal cases, is subject only to the qualification that such procedure must not work a denial of fundamental rights or conflict with specific and applicable provisions of the Federal Constitution." *West* v. *Louisiana*, 194 U.S. 258, 263.

The question under consideration may first be tested by the application of these settled doctrines of this court. If the statement of Mr. Justice Curtis, as elucidated in *Hurtado* v. *California*, is to be taken literally, that alone might almost be decisive. For nothing is more certain, in point of historical fact, than that the practice of compulsory self-incrimination in the courts and elsewhere existed for four hundred years after the granting of Magna Charta, continued throughout the reign of Charles I (though then beginning to be seriously questioned), gained at least some foothold among the early colonists of this country, and was not entirely omitted at trials in England until the eighteenth century. . . .

. . . We think it is manifest, from this review of the origin, growth, extent and limits of the exemption from compulsory self-incrimination in the English law, that it is not regarded as a part of the law of the land of Magna Charta or the due process of law, which has been deemed an equivalent expression, but, on the contrary, is regarded as separate from and independent of due process. It came into existence not as an essential part of due process, but as wise and beneficent rule of evidence developed in the course of judicial decision. This is a potent argument when it is remembered that the phrase was borrowed from English law and that to that law we must look at least for its primary meaning.

But . . . we prefer to rest our decision on broader grounds, and inquire whether the exemption from self-incrimination is of such a nature that it must be included in the conception of due process. Is it a fundamental principle of liberty and justice which inheres in the very idea of free government and is the inalienable right of a citizen of such a government? . . . One aid to the solution of the question is to inquire how the right was rated during the time when the meaning of due process was in a formative state, and before it was incorporated in American constitutional law. Did those who then were formulating and insisting upon the rights of the people entertain the view that the right was so fundamental that there could be no due process without it?

[The Court here reviews the historical background of state law on the subject and especially the attitude of the states at the time of the adoption of the Constitution and the Bill of Rights.] This survey does not tend to show that it was then in this country the universal or even general belief that the privilege ranked among the fundamental and inalienable rights of mankind; and what is more important here, it affirmatively shows that the privilege was not conceived to be inherent in due process of law, but, on the other hand, a right separate, independent, and outside of due process. Congress, in submitting the Amendments to the several states, treated the two rights as exclusive of each other. Such also has been the view of the states in framing their own Constitutions. . . . The inference is irresistible that it has been the opinion of constitution makers that the privilege, if fundamental in any sense, is not fundamental in due process of law, nor an essential part of it. . . .

. . . The essential elements of due process of law . . . are singularly few, though of wide application and deep significance. . . . Due process requires that the court which assumes to determine the rights of parties shall have jurisdiction . . . and that there shall be notice and opportunity for hearing given the parties. . . . Subject to these two fundamental conditions, which seem to be universally prescribed in all systems of law established by civilized countries, this court has, up to this time, sustained all state laws, statutory or judicially declared, regulating procedure, evidence, and methods of trial, and held them to be consistent with due process of law.

Even if the historical meaning of due process of law and the decisions of this court did not exclude the privilege from it, it would be going far to rate it as an immutable principle of justice which is the inalienable possession of every citizen of a free government. Salutary as the principle may seem to the great majority, it cannot be ranked with the right to hearing before condemnation, the immunity from arbitrary power not acting by general laws, and the inviolability of private property. The wisdom of the exemption has never been universally assented to since the days of Bentham; many doubt it today, and it is best defended not as an unchangeable principle of universal justice but as a law proved by experience to be expedient. . . .

Judgment affirmed.

Once again the Court refused to reconsider its narrow construction of the privileges and immunities clause laid down in *Slaughter-House Cases.*

Further, the opinion clearly states that the Court did not construe the due process clause as a total incorporation of all the Bill of Rights guarantees to be applied against the states. But the door was opened to some extent in the area of criminal procedure, and subsequent developments have widened the opening still further.

Justice Moody cautioned that the phrase "due process of law" was "elusive of exact apprehension." But he tried to give a few general guidelines. He pointed out that if a practice is of ancient origin and usage, and if it is not prohibited by law, then it is to be accepted as due process of law. He was unwilling to adopt as a corollary, however, the conclusion that *only* ancient practices could meet the test. Such a view would operate like a straitjacket to stop progress or improvement. Then what is the proper test to apply to newer criminal procedures? Justice Moody quoted two earlier opinions, and then gave his own summary statement: quoting from *Holden* v. *Hardy,* "There are certain immutable principles of justice which inhere in the very idea of free government which no member of the Union may disregard;" and, quoting from *West* v. *Louisiana,* "Such procedure must not work a denial of fundamental rights or conflict with specific and applicable provisions of the Federal Constitution." His own statement was, "Due process requires that the court which assumes to determine the rights of parties shall have jurisdiction . . . and that there shall be notice and opportunity for hearing given the parties."

Justice Cardozo expressed a similar view of the limited scope of the due process clause in *Palko* v. *Connecticut,* 302 U.S. 319 (1937), holding that the clause did not bar appeal by the state based on alleged errors of law in criminal cases and subsequent retrial if the state won the appeal. He stated that the only rights covered by the due process clause were those which "have been found to be implicit in the concept of ordered liberty, and thus, through the Fourteenth Amendment, become valid as against the States."

To say that the state can run its own affairs as long as it does not violate "immutable principles of justice" or "fundamental rights" is an invitation to every disappointed litigant to claim that in his case the state violated just such principles or rights. The pressures in this direction gradually increased, and in the period since *Twining* hundreds of cases have been reviewed by the Court in which every conceivable facet of the Bill of Rights guarantees has been described by eloquent counsel as an "immutable principle of justice" or a "fundamental right" or as a necessary feature of the requirement of "notice and opportunity for hearing," and therefore forever embedded in the Fourteenth Amendment concept of "due process of law."

Some of these pleas have been sufficiently convincing to lead a majority of the Court to agree with the contentions, and to this extent the procedural guarantees of the Bill of Rights have been incorporated into the Fourteenth Amendment. Thus the cases incorporating guarantees such as the right to counsel and freedom from self-incrimination are the doctrinal offspring of *Twining* v. *New Jersey.* In *Powell* v. *Alabama,* 287 U.S. 45 (1932), for example, holding that due process requires that counsel be afforded by the state to ignorant, illiterate, indigent defendants accused of a capital crime, Justice Sutherland paraphrased the *Twining* opinion in stating:

It never has been doubted by this court, or any other so far as we know, that notice and hearing are preliminary steps essential to the passing of an enforceable

judgment, and that they, together with a legally competent tribunal having jurisdiction of the case, constitute basic elements of the constitutional requirement of
due process of law. . . .

What, then, does a hearing include? Historically and in practice, in our own
country at least, it has always included the right to the aid of counsel when desired
and provided by the party asserting the right. The right to be heard would be, in
many cases, of little avail if it did not comprehend the right to be heard by
counsel. . . .

. . . All that it is necessary now to decide, as we do decide, is that in a capital
case, where the defendant is unable to employ counsel, and is incapable adequately
of making his own defense because of ignorance, feeble-mindedness, illiteracy, or
the like, it is the duty of the court, whether requested or not, to assign counsel
for him as a necessary requisite of due process of law. . . .

The first actual incorporation of one of the Bill of Rights guarantees took
place in *Chicago, Burlington & Quincy RR. Co.* v. *Chicago*, 166 U.S. 226 (1897),
holding that the compensation clause of the Fifth Amendment applied to the
states by way of the Fourteenth Amendment due process clause.

The *substantive* rights guaranteed by the Bill of Rights, such as speech,
press, and assembly, have also been incorporated into the Fourteenth Amendment, but the vehicle for the expansion here has been the word "liberty"
and not the phrase "due process of law." Thus in *Gitlow* v. *New York*, 268
U.S. 652 (1925), although the conviction for the crime of criminal anarchy
was affirmed, the majority opinion stated that, "For present purposes we
may and do assume that freedom of speech and of the press—which are
protected by the First Amendment from abridgment by Congress—are among
the fundamental personal rights and 'liberties' protected by the due process
clause of the Fourteenth Amendment from impairment by the States." For
our purposes here, however, it is immaterial which portion of the full due
process clause has been the vessel to contain the new right. The important
point is the extent to which the Fourteenth Amendment now includes Bill
of Rights guarantees against state abridgment.

In *Near* v. *Minnesota*, 283 U.S. 697 (1931), the majority opinion stated,
"It is no longer open to doubt that the liberty of the press and of speech
is within the liberty safeguarded by the due process clause of the Fourteenth Amendment from invasion by state action." By 1937 the Court was
willing to add freedom of assembly to the list. In *De Jonge* v. *Oregon*, 299
U.S. 353 (1937), Chief Justice Hughes, speaking for the Court, stated:

The right of peaceable assembly is a right cognate to those of free speech and
free press and is equally fundamental. . . . [T]he right is one that cannot be denied
without violating those fundamental principles of liberty and justice which lie at
the base of all civil and political institutions,—principles which the Fourteenth
Amendment embodies in the general terms of its due process clause.

Rounding out the incorporation of First Amendment rights into the Fourteenth, the Court in 1940 included religious freedom in the list. The case
was *Cantwell* v. *Connecticut*, 310 U.S. 296 (1940), and Justice Roberts, speaking for a unanimous Court, stated:

We hold that the statute, as construed and applied to the appellants, deprives
them of their liberty without due process of law in contravention of the Fourteenth
Amendment. The fundamental concept of liberty embodied in that Amendment

embraces the liberties guaranteed by the First Amendment. The First Amendment declares that Congress shall make no law respecting as establishment of religion or prohibiting the free exercise thereof. The Fourteenth Amendment has rendered the legislatures of the states as incompetent as Congress to enact such laws.

Although Justice Roberts included the prohibition against establishment of religion in his statement, *Cantwell* technically did not present that issue. The issue was squarely presented, however, in *Everson* v. *Board of Education,* 330 U.S. 1 (1947), and the Court held the establishment clause of the First Amendment to be applicable to the states through the Fourteenth Amendment.

The Fourth Amendment's protection against unreasonable searches and seizures was *partially* incorporated into the Fourteenth Amendment by the holding in *Wolf* v. *Colorado,* 338 U.S. 25 (1949), that the security of one's privacy against arbitrary intrusion by the police is "implicit in 'the concept of ordered liberty' and as such enforceable against the States through the Due Process Clause." Not until the decision in *Mapp* v. *Ohio,* 367 U.S. 643 (1961), however, did the Court presumably *fully* incorporate the Fourth Amendment by its holding that not only was an arbitrary search and seizure conducted by state officers unconstitutional, but it was also a violation of the Fourteenth Amendment for them to use evidence so obtained in a criminal prosecution.

In *Malloy* v. *Hogan,* 378 U.S. 1 (1964), the Court held that the Fifth Amendment's exemption from compulsory self-incrimination is also protected by the Fourteenth Amendment against abridgment by the states. And, lest any doubt remained that it was *full* incorporation which was intended, the Court in *Griffin* v. *California,* 380 U.S. 609 (1965), held that adverse comment by the judge on the failure of the accused to take the stand in his defense would violate the Fifth Amendment if occurring in a federal proceeding and, therefore, violated the Fourteenth Amendment in the case under review. The holding of the *Twining* case, then, is no longer ruling law.

In *Benton* v. *Maryland,* 395 U.S. 784 (1969), the Court specifically overruled *Palko* v. *Connecticut* and held that the double jeopardy clause of the Fifth Amendment is applicable to the states through the Fourteenth Amendment.

The Sixth Amendment's guarantee of a jury trial in criminal cases has long been considered inapplicable to state trials, but this right has now been incorporated as a result of the decision in *Duncan* v. *Louisiana,* 391 U.S. 145 (1968). The right to a "public trial" was employed as a Fourteenth Amendment right in *In re Oliver,* 333 U.S. 257 (1948), to reverse a contempt citation imposed during a secret proceeding. The Sixth Amendment also guarantees the accused the right "to be confronted with the witnesses against him," including the right of cross-examination. In *Pointer* v. *Texas,* 380 U.S. 400 (1965), the majority opinion stated:

We hold that petitioner was entitled to be tried in accordance with the protection of the confrontation guarantee of the Sixth Amendment, and that that guarantee, like the right against compelled self-incrimination, is "to be enforced against the States under the Fourteenth Amendment according to the same standards that protect those personal rights against federal encroachment." *Malloy* v. *Hogan.* . . .

A further protection of the Sixth Amendment for the criminal defendant is the right "to have compulsory process for obtaining witnesses in his favor." In *Washington* v. *Texas,* 388 U.S. 14 (1967), the Court incorporated this right into the Fourteenth Amendment. It further held that this right was denied by Texas statutes which provided that persons charged or convicted as coparticipants in the same crime could not testify for one another, although there was no bar to their testifying for the state. The final clause of the Sixth Amendment guarantees to defendants in federal prosecutions the right to have "the assistance of counsel" for their defense. As stated earlier, *Powell* v. *Alabama* partially incorporated this right into the Fourteenth Amendment by applying it to certain kinds of capital cases. Shortly thereafter it was extended to all capital cases, and full incorporation was accomplished in *Gideon* v. *Wainwright,* 372 U.S. 335 (1963).

In *Klopfer* v. *North Carolina,* 386 U.S. 213 (1967), the Court incorporated the "speedy trial" provision of the Sixth Amendment, stating: "We hold here that the right to a speedy trial is as fundamental as any of the rights secured by the Sixth Amendment."

Finally, in *Louisiana ex rel. Francis* v. *Resweber,* 329 U.S. 459 (1947), the majority "assumed" that the Eighth Amendment's prohibition against cruel and unusual punishments was binding on the state through the Fourteenth Amendment. This was accepted as a firm holding in *Robinson* v. *California,* 370 U.S. 660 (1962). While the Court has not yet ruled squarely that Fourteenth Amendment due process includes the Eighth Amendment prohibition of excessive bail, a number of lower federal courts have taken that prohibition for granted to such an extent that one can say that the bail provision probably does apply to the states.

The incorporation process has continued until at this juncture virtually all of the guarantees of the Bill of Rights have been drawn into the Fourteenth Amendment. There are a few of those guarantees, however, which still do not apply to the states through the absorption process. The Second Amendment right "to keep and bear arms" has not been incorporated, nor has the Third Amendment protection against the quartering of soldiers. And if the state wishes to abolish grand jury indictment and try criminals upon an information (a sworn written accusation by the prosecutor), the Fourteenth Amendment does not bar it, although the Fifth Amendment would prohibit such a substitution in a federal prosecution for a "capital or otherwise infamous crime." [*Hurtado* v. *California,* 110 U.S. 516 (1884).] While the right to jury trial in criminal cases has been incorporated, the Seventh Amendment guarantee of jury trial in civil suits at common law has not, so the state could abolish the civil jury altogether without, as yet, violating the Fourteenth Amendment.

It should also be noted that the phrase "due process of law" has been interpreted to include concepts not listed in the Bill of Rights at all. For example, in *Mooney* v. *Holohan,* 294 U.S. 103 (1935), the Court held that when a conviction is obtained by the presentation of testimony known to the prosecuting authorities to have been perjured, due process is violated. And while the Court will not weigh the sufficiency of evidence in reviewing state cases, convictions that are not supported by any evidence at all are void under the due process clause. *Thompson* v. *City of Louisville,* 362 U.S. 199 (1960), involved the conviction of Sam Thompson in police court on the charge of "loitering." The evidence and testimony showed only that he had gone into a small cafe while waiting for his bus, had eaten a dish of macaroni, and was "shuffling" about a small dance floor in time to juke-box music. The Court held that "there simply is no semblance of evidence" from which one could infer a violation of the city ordinance on loitering, and thus the conviction violated the Fourteenth Amendment.

There still remain, then, some differences between the standards set up by the Bill of Rights for federal proceedings and those which the Fourteenth Amendment has been construed as imposing upon states. The result of the line of decisions amplifying the due process clause of the Fourteenth Amendment is that the student of American civil rights must deal with *three separate* packets of rights: (1) the rights and safeguards which the Bill of Rights to the national Constitution guarantees against abridgment by the national government; (2) the rights which the state cannot abridge without violating the Fourteenth Amendment; and (3) the rights which the state constitution and laws guarantee against abridgment by the state government. [While these categories cover the bulk of the rights protected against governmental interference, there are, of course, a few rights specifically guaranteed in the main body of the Constitution in Article I, Sections 9 and 10 (safeguards against ex post facto laws, bills of attainder, and against suspension of the writ of habeas corpus), and in the Thirteenth (barring slavery), Fifteenth, Nineteenth, Twenty-fourth, and Twenty-sixth (barring various limitations on the right to vote) Amendments. Also, trial by jury in criminal cases is guaranteed in Article III, Section 2, of the Constitution.]

It should be kept in mind in comparing the due process requirements of the Fourteenth Amendment with state practices that the state provisions must be of general application. If the state guarantees certain procedures to one religious group, for example, and denies these protections to other sects, then there is a probable violation of the equal protection clause, even though the due process clause might permit the state to dispense with the procedure altogether. Thus the state can make available or abolish the civil jury. But it cannot make unreasonable classifications in determining that some persons may have a jury and others may not.

Recognition of the threefold pattern of civil rights in the American system is a prerequisite to a full understanding of the legal problems in the field. Federalism does, indeed, introduce a number of complications into the picture. This fact is particularly to be stressed when one turns to the area of national *protection* of civil rights.

CHAPTER 3
National Protection of Civil Rights

When one is faced with treatment which he considers a violation of some right, it is only natural to look about for a remedy. As pointed out in the first chapter, the remedies are many and varied, and they are not mutually exclusive. Whether the injured person singles out one approach to gaining satisfaction or combines several will depend on the nature of the injury and the degree of irritation which the offended person reaches. One point should be clear, however: The remedy for injuries to person or property or for interference with the ordinary lawful activities of the citizen is normally provided by *state* laws rather than *federal* laws. The usual tort action is brought under state law in state courts. Prosecution for criminal invasion of rights is usually brought under state law and in state courts. Under normal circumstances the laws and the administrative organization for their enforcement provide satisfactory results in the various state systems. The victim of trespass, assault, or improper denial of some license can certainly anticipate fair treatment in the disposition of his claims in the overwhelming bulk of the cases. Thus a careful observer could, with reason, conclude that the state remedies for abridgment of civil rights will normally work reasonably effectively to protect the individual.

There are two situations, however, which might lead this same observer to feel that state remedies alone are inadequate and that additional safeguards in the form of national laws should be added to the picture. The first turns on the character of the person injured and the second the character of the right abridged. If the person is a member of a class subjected to peculiar disabilities, in various communities, then an outside agency may be necessary to ensure equal treatment. This has frequently been pointed out with respect to minority racial or national groups or minority religious sects. The Negro, the Italian, the Puerto Rican, the Jehovah's Witness, or even the white Protestant may in certain areas and in certain periods be accorded heavy-handed treatment by local officials as compared with the treatment of the majority class. Many people have concluded that some sort of national legislation is necessary which can be employed, albeit sparingly and selectively, to push in the direction of equality of treatment.

As to the second situation, there are those who argue that the exercise of certain rights is so vital to the preservation of the democratic system that national safeguards must be provided to guarantee them against interference. Thus the rights of speech, press, assembly, and voting are placed in a preferred position in comparison with other rights. The theory here is that the system can tolerate (although not encourage) a noticeable margin of error in the disposition of ordinary criminal cases or ordinary civil suits to redress wrongs, but to permit abridgments of the rights of speech, press, assembly, and voting is to endanger the entire democratic fabric. Two of the most frequently criticized facets of state judicial systems are the incompetency of inferior court judges and the incompetency or bias of petit jurors. However exaggerated some of these allegations may be, there is no avoiding the conclusion that in both these institutions a great deal of improvement could be made. In practical terms this is the same as saying that the product turned out in many inferior state courts is sometimes pretty shoddy merchandise. Yet no serious drive is under way to adopt an amendment to the national Constitution which would either prescribe or give Congress the authority to prescribe the qualifications of state judges and jurors. Apparently the feeling is that the tolerance is fairly great for the disposition of cases involving what might be considered ordinary personal and property rights. By comparison, the subject of voting rights has received considerable attention at the national level for almost a hundred years. And the only national laws on civil rights to be adopted in this century, down to 1960, were laws to protect voting rights.

In addition to legislative action, the judicial and executive branches can also play a part in the protection of civil rights. Where the United States Constitution applies, the United States Supreme Court can, in appropriate cases, review the decisions of state courts and reverse aberrant interpretations of the Constitution. As pointed out earlier, obtaining such review requires a dogged litigant, a very careful handling of the issues from the trial court on up the ladder, and even an ample portion of luck in hitting the Court with a timely issue In terms of the Court's current emphasis. Nonetheless, a single, clear-cut decision of the Court on a point of constitutional interpretation will normally make itself felt in the state and federal courts throughout the country. The fact, therefore, that the Supreme Court cannot, as a practical matter, correct all the erroneous decisions of all the courts of the nation should not lead one to minimize the impact of the decisions which it does make.

The executive branch has powers which may also be employed very effectively to ensure equality of treatment in specialized areas and to afford protection for certain of the individual's rights. In personnel policies for federal employees, in awarding government contracts, in disbursing federal monies, in laying down enforcement policy for the Department of Justice, and even in general public statements of principle, the President can exercise considerable influence in the field of civil rights.

The major weapons available to the judicial branch have been discussed in earlier chapters. The area of civil rights authority of the federal legislative and executive branches will be taken up separately. Because of the complexities of defining the scope of Congress' powers, however, much the greater portion of the chapter will be devoted to that branch.

NATIONAL LEGISLATION TO PROTECT CIVIL RIGHTS

Laying aside the question of how far the Congress *should* go in the civil rights field, the first problem to consider is the question of how far Congress *can* constitutionally act in this area. And this question presents some of the most difficult and controversial issues in the whole field of constitutional law. Thus forewarned, the student should proceed carefully through the cases and analysis, making certain to grasp the fundamental principles involved.

With respect to domestic matters, the basic fact of Congress' legislative power is that every act passed by the Congress must be tied to some grant of authority in the Constitution. This tie may be somewhat indirect (thus the power may be spoken of as an "implied power"), but it still must be traceable to one or another of the delegated powers. It is not enough, then, that a proposed measure be a worthwhile or useful policy; it must be within that now rather broad list of powers which the Constitution, either directly or by implication, states that Congress can exercise. It is clear that one should not equate wisdom with constitutionality. Congress can constitutionally do a great many foolish things, such as declaring war on Canada, or adding one inch to the official measure of the yard, or abolishing paper money. Conversely, there are policies which might be considered useful to put into operation on the national level, but for which there is no constitutional authority. A national law on divorce or on disposition of property by will would fall into this category. Similarly, in the case of civil rights, there is much that Congress can do, but there are areas which thus far it cannot effectively reach for lack of constitutional authorization.

Delegations of power to Congress are scattered about through the Constitution, but the bulk of such powers are to be found in Article I. The first grant of power to be found which could be applied to civil rights deals with elections. And the matter of voting rights is a particularly good vehicle for examining the basic concepts in federal protection of civil rights. Article I, Section 4, provides:

The Times, Places and Manner of holding Elections for Senators and Representatives, shall be prescribed in each State by the Legislature thereof; but the Congress may at any time by Law make or alter such Regulations, except as to the Places of choosing Senators.

To reduce this clause to its most substantial grant of power, it says that Congress can regulate the *manner* of holding elections for candidates for Congress. If to this we join the stipulation in Article I, Section 2, that electors for the national house of representatives "shall have the qualifications requisite for Electors of the most numerous branch of the State Legislature," then it can be argued that the *qualified elector* has a constitutional right to vote for representatives to Congress, and that Congress has the constitutional power to protect that right by appropriate laws.

The Constitution does not specifically require popular election of presidential electors; instead, Article II, Section 1, leaves the matter to the legislature of each state. Since all states now provide for popular election of presidential electors, the question arises of whether a qualified elector has a federal right to participate in such elections. In *Burroughs* v. *United States,* 290 U.S. 534 (1934), the Court upheld the Federal Corrupt Practices Act of 1925 requiring the disclosure of facts as to contributions made to presidential campaigns. The opinion stated that the act sought to preserve the purity of presidential and vice-presidential elections, and "to say that Congress is without power to pass appropriate legislation to safeguard such an election from the improper use of money to influence the result is to deny to the nation in a vital particular the power of self protection." This decision would indicate, then, that the right of the elector to vote for presidential electors as well as members of Congress is a federal right. (A more detailed analysis of voting rights appears in Chapter 8.)

Elections for state and local officials stand on a different base, however, and the power of Congress is more restricted. Congressional authority is limited to those areas covered by the Fourteenth, Fifteenth, Nineteenth, Twenty-fourth, and Twenty-sixth Amendments, although it must be pointed out that such "limitation" still leaves Congress with rather broad authority. Thus, under the Fifteenth Amendment, Congress can prohibit the states from abridging the right to vote because of race even in a purely state election. But this power would not extend to the prohibition of purely private abridgments of the right to vote in a state election. This illustrates, then, the distinction between *federal* rights and *state* rights, as Justice Miller pointed out in the *Slaughter-House Cases* discussed earlier. The former are those protected by the Constitution and laws of the United States, and the latter are those protected only by the constitutions and laws of the states. The distinction between these two categories of rights is crucial to the task of defining congressional powers to protect civil rights.

The next step in the analysis is to understand clearly that neither state nor federal rights are static. New rights can be created, and, under many circumstances, old rights can be modified or destroyed. The United States Constitution does not of its own terms describe rights which are enforceable against abridgment by private persons. To put the matter another way, private action might violate laws, but it cannot violate the Constitution. The only exception to this statement is to be found in the Thirteenth Amendment which states flatly that neither slavery nor involuntary servitude shall exist within the United States. Presumably the victim of such treatment could obtain judicial relief even if Congress had never passed enforcement legislation. But the Constitution does describe rights, albeit vaguely, which are enforceable by appropriate judicial action against abridgment by state and federal officials. Even these, however, are not static. As already indicated, the Fourteenth Amendment has undergone tremendous expansion through judicial interpretation in the past half-century. As newer constructions have been given the due process and equal protection clauses of that Amendment, to that extent new federal rights have been created. Thus the United States Supreme Court can play an important role in creating new federal rights.

A second source of innovation is congressional enactments. Under its delegated powers Congress can not only provide protection for the rights set up by the Constitution, but it can also add new rights, and congressionally created rights normally run against private as well as official abridgment. For example, Article IV, Section 3, of the Constitution states that, "The Congress shall have Power to dispose of and make all needful Rules and Regulations respecting the Territory or other Property belonging to the United States." With this authority, Congress passed the Homestead Act of 1862, under which millions of acres of public lands were parceled out among pioneering home-seekers. By this act the Congress created a federal right in such homesteaders to use the land thus obtained free from improper interference by any person. While normally trespassers must be dealt with under state law (since the right to ordinary use of one's property is a state right), Congress can provide punishment for those who interfere with the exercise of a right which Congress creates. In *United States* v. *Waddell*, 112 U.S. 76 (1884), defendants were charged with using violence to drive a homesteader off his land which he had settled pursuant to the Federal Homestead Act. The Court held that the defendants' actions deprived the homesteader of rights secured to him by the laws of the United States and affirmed the application of congressional criminal provisions to the case. Similarly, the Court has held that when Congress enacts a criminal law, there is created a right in the individual to report violations of that law to a federal agent. Thus in *Motes* v. *United States*, 178 U.S. 458 (1900), the Court affirmed the conviction in a federal proceeding of defendants who had murdered a person who had informed federal revenue agents of the illegal operation of a still in Alabama. Thus when the claim of a privilege or immunity or right stems from some special relationship between the individual and the national government, there is a federal right. The cited cases demonstrate this relationship in the matters of voting in a federal election, lawful use of federal homestead property, and reporting a federal crime to a federal agent. Other illustrations will spring to mind where congressional action affords some special protection or bounty. In addition to this category, there is a federal right where the privilege or immunity is set up by the United States Constitution, even in the absence of any special relationship between the individual and the national government. The Fourteenth Amendment due process clause has been held to bar the use of coerced confessions in state criminal prosecutions. This means that there is a federal right against state use of such confessions. More broadly, there is a federal right not to be deprived of one's life by the state without due process of law. But since the Fourteenth Amendment limits only the actions of state officials and does not reach the acts of purely private persons, there is *no* federal right abridged when the private person takes the life of another. Just as was shown in the matter of voting, so it is with the other rights enjoyed by the individual in the United States: some federal rights run against abridgment by any person; other federal rights run only against abridgment by officials; and a great many rights are not federal at all, but must depend upon state law for their protection.

A third category of national rights would be those created by treaty action. The right to engage in ordinary lawful business is generally a state right only, but after a treaty was ratified between the United States and China there was created in Chinese aliens in this country a federal right to reside in the state of their choice and to engage in business there on equal terms with American citizens. Since Congress can pass appropriate laws to enforce the terms of treaty agreements, legislation could have been adopted to protect this right against encroachment even by private persons. In *Baldwin* v. *Franks*, 120 U.S. 678 (1887), the United States Supreme Court reviewed in habeas corpus proceedings the arrest of the petitioner for assaulting Chinese citizens and driving them out of a California town. The charge was made under Section 2 of the Act of April 20, 1871, which prohibited conspiracies to deprive another of equal protection of the laws or equal privileges or immunities under the laws. The Court directed petitioner's release, holding the section unconstitutional. The fact that the Chinese citizens were protected under a treaty might have afforded authority for congressional legislation, the Court held, but the provision of the 1871 law was so broadly worded that it covered action beyond the scope of congressional power.

The leading decision in the United States Supreme Court on the subject of congressional authority to protect civil rights came in the *Civil Rights Cases in 1883.*

CIVIL RIGHTS CASES
109 U.S. 3 (1883)

[The cases were brought under Sections 1 and 2 of the Civil Rights Act of March 1, 1875, which provided as follows:

"Sec. 1: That all persons within the jurisdiction of the United States shall be entitled to the full and equal enjoyment of the accommodations, advantages, facilities and privileges of inns, public conveyances on land or water, theaters and other places of public amusement; subject only to the conditions and limitations established by law and applicable alike to citizens of every race and color, regardless of any previous conditions of servitude.

"Sec. 2: That any person who shall violate the foregoing section by denying to any citizen, except for reasons by law applicable to citizens of every race and color, ... the full enjoyment of any of the accommodations ... or privileges in said section enumerated, ... shall for every such offense forfeit and pay the sum of $500 to the person aggrieved thereby, ... and shall also, for every such offense, be deemed guilty of a misdemeanor and, upon conviction thereof, shall be fined not less than $500 nor more than $1,000, or shall be imprisoned not less than thirty days nor more than one year."

Several cases arose in various courts, and these were handled together in the United States Supreme Court under the title *Civil Rights Cases.* They involved denial of accommodations because of race in a hotel, a theater, an opera house, and a railroad.]

Mr. Justice Bradley delivered the opinion of the Court....

... Has Congress constitutional power to make such a law? Of course, no one will contend that the power to pass it was contained in the Constitution before the adoption of the last three Amendments.... [But in the brief for the Negro litigants William Randolph stated (27 L. ed. 837): "Our case involves the rights of a citizen of one State traveling 'by a public conveyance by land' through another State, for the purpose of reaching a place in a third State. We maintain that so far as the Act of Congress applies to such a case, the power to pass it is beyond question. Independently of the 'power to enforce by appropriate legislation' the 14th Amendment, there are, as we conceive, at least two other clauses of the Constitution on either of which the Act may rest. The first is the power in Congress to regulate commerce with foreign Nations and among the several States ... and the other is the provision that 'The citizens of each State shall be entitled to all the privileges and immunities of citizens in the several States.'" And the Solicitor-General, S. F. Phillips, stated in his brief (27 L. ed. 837): "Inns are provided for the accommodation of travelers; for those passing from place to place. They are essential instrumentalities of commerce, which it was the province of the United States to regulate even prior to the recent Amendments to the Constitution."]

The first section of the Fourteenth Amendment, which is the one relied on, after declaring who shall be citizens of the United States, and of the several States, is prohibitory in its character, and prohibitory upon the States. It declares that: "No State shall make or enforce any law which shall abridge the privileges or immunities of citizens of the United States; nor shall any State deprive any person of life, liberty or property without due process of law; nor deny to any person within its jurisdiction the equal protection of the laws." It is State action of a particular character that is prohibited. Individual invasion of individual rights is not the subject-matter of the Amendment. It has a deeper and broader scope. It nullifies and makes void all State legislation, and State action of every kind, which impairs the privileges and immunities of citizens of the United States, or which injures them in life, liberty or property without due process of law, or which denies to any of them the equal protection of the laws. It not only does this, but, in order that the national will, thus declared, may not be a mere *brutum fulmen,* the last section of the Amendment invests Congress with power to enforce it by appropriate legislation. To enforce what? To enforce the prohibition. To adopt appropriate legislation for correcting the effects of such prohibited State laws and State Acts, and thus to render them effectually null, void and innocuous. This is the legislative power conferred upon Congress, and this is the whole of it. It does not invest Congress with power to legislate upon subjects which are within the domain of State legislation; but to provide modes of relief against State legislation, or State action, of the kind referred to. It does not authorize Congress to create a code of municipal law for the regulation of private rights; but to provide modes of redress against the operation of State laws, and the action of State officers executive or judicial, when these are subversive of the fundamental rights specified in the Amendment. Positive rights and privileges are undoubtedly secured by the Fourteenth Amendment; but they are secured by way of prohibition against State laws and State proceedings affecting those rights and privileges, and by power given to Congress to legislate for the purpose of carrying such prohibition into effect; and such legislation must, necessarily, be predicated upon such supposed State laws or State proceedings, and be directed to the correction of their operation and effect....

An apt illustration of this distinction may be found in some of the provisions of the original Constitution. Take the subject of contracts, for example; the Constitution prohibited the States from passing any law impairing the obligation of contracts. This did not give to Congress power to provide laws for the general enforcement of contracts; nor power to invest the courts of the United States with jurisdiction over contracts, so as to enable parties to sue upon them in those courts. It did, however, give the power to provide remedies by which the impairment of contracts by State legislation might be counteracted and corrected; and this power was exercised. The remedy which Congress actually provided was that contained in the 25th section of the Judiciary Act of 1789, 1 Stat. 85, giving to the Supreme Court of the United States jurisdiction by writ of error to review the final decisions of State courts whenever they should sustain the validity of a State statute or authority alleged to be repugnant to the Constitution or laws of the United States. By this means, if a State law was passed impairing the obligation of a contract, and the State tribunals sustained the validity of the law, the mischief could be corrected in this court. The legislation of Congress, and the proceedings provided for under it, were corrective in their character. No attempt was made to draw into the United States courts the litigation of contracts generally; and no such attempt would have been sustained....

And so in the present case, until some State law has been passed, or some State action through its officers or agents has been taken, adverse to the rights of citizens sought to be protected by the Fourteenth Amendment, no legislation of the United States under said Amendment, nor any proceedings under such legislation, can be called into activity; for the prohibitions of the Amendment are against State laws and acts done under State authority. Of course, legislation may and should be provided in advance to meet the exigency when it arises; but it should be adapted to the mischief and wrong which the Amendment was intended to provide against; and that is, State laws, or State action of some kind, adverse to the rights of the citizen secured by the Amendment. Such legislation cannot properly cover the whole domain of rights appertaining to life, liberty and property, defining them and providing for their vindication. That would be to establish a code of municipal law regulative of all private rights between man and man in society. It would be to make Congress take the place of the State Legislatures and to supersede them. It is absurd to affirm that, because the rights of life, liberty and property, which include all civil rights that men have, are, by the Amendment, sought to be protected against invasion on the part of the State without due process of law, Congress may, therefore, provide due process of law for their vindication in every case; and that, because the denial by a State to any persons, of the equal protection of the laws, is prohibited by the Amendment, therefore Congress may establish laws for their equal protection. . . .

An inspection of the law shows that it makes no reference whatever to any supposed or apprehended violation of the Fourteenth Amendment on the part of the States. It is not predicated on any such view. It proceeds *ex directo* to declare that certain acts committed by individuals shall be deemed offenses, and shall be prosecuted and punished by proceedings in the courts of the United States. It does not profess to be corrective of any constitutional wrong committed by the States; it does not make its operation to depend upon any such wrong committed. It applies equally to cases arising in States which have the justest laws respecting the personal rights of citizens, and whose authorities are ever ready to enforce such laws, as to those which arise in States that may have violated the prohibition of the Amendment. In other words, it steps into the domain of local jurisprudence, and lays down rules for the conduct of individuals in society towards each other, and imposes sanctions for the enforcement of those rules, without referring in any manner to any supposed action of the State or its authorities. . . .

In this connection it is proper to state that civil rights, such as are guaranteed by the Constitution against State aggression, cannot be impaired by the wrongful acts of individuals, unsupported by State authority in the shape of laws, customs or judicial or executive proceedings. The wrongful act of an individual, unsupported by any such authority, is simply a private wrong, or a crime of that individual; an invasion of the rights of the injured party, it is true, whether they affect his person, his property or his reputation; but if not sanctioned in some way by the State, or not done under State authority, his rights remain in full force, and may presumably be vindicated by resort to the laws of the State for redress. . . .

Of course, these remarks do not apply to those cases in which Congress is clothed with direct and plenary powers of legislation over the whole subject, accompanied with an express or implied denial of such power to the States, as in the regulation of commerce with foreign Nations, . . . the coining of money, the establishment of post offices and post-roads, the declaring of war, etc. In these cases, Congress has power to pass laws for regulating the subjects specified in every detail, and the conduct and transactions of individuals in respect thereof. But where a subject is not submitted to the general legislative power of Congress, but is only submitted thereto for the purpose of rendering effective some prohibition against particular State legislation or State action in reference to that subject, the power given is limited by its object, and any legislation by Congress in the matter must necessarily be corrective in its character, adapted to counteract and redress the operation of such prohibited State laws or proceedings of State officers. . . .

[The opinion then states that denials of accommodations do not constitute slavery or involuntary servitude, and therefore the Thirteenth Amendment, which does apply to private acts, would not cover the particular wrongs complained of. "It would be running the slavery argument into the ground, to make it apply to every act of discrimination which a person may see fit to make as to the guests he will entertain," or deal with in business.]

On the whole we are of opinion, that no countenance of authority for the passage of the law in question can be found in either the Thirteenth or Fourteenth Amendment of the Constitution; and no other ground of authority for its passage being suggested, it must necessarily be declared void, at least so far as its operation in the several States is concerned.

Justice Harlan dissenting. . . .

I am of the opinion that such discrimination practiced by corporations and individuals in the exercise of their public or *quasi*-public functions is a badge of servitude, the imposition of which Congress may prevent under its power, by appropriate legislation, to enforce the Thirteenth Amendment. . . .

[Justice Harlan then stated that if this is not sufficient, the Fourteenth Amendment adds even more to Congress' power: "All persons born or naturalized in the United States . . . are citizens of the United States and of the State wherein they reside." Congress may enforce this section. It may thus guarantee the interstate citizenship clause in Article IV, which would support the instant act.]

In every material sense applicable to the practical enforcement of the Fourteenth Amendment, railroad corporations, keepers of inns and managers of places of public amusements are agents or instrumentalities of the State, because they are charged with duties to the public, and are amenable, in respect of their duties and functions, to government regulation. It seems to me that, within the principle settled in *Ex parte Virginia,* a denial, by these instrumentalities of the State, to the citizen, because of his race, of that equality of civil rights secured to him by law, is a denial by the State, within the meaning of the Fourteenth Amendment. . . . [Justice Harlan then stated that, at least with respect to railroads, the act could be sustained as to interstate commerce under the power of Congress to regulate commerce. The fact that the act did not state that it was a regulation of commerce should not foreclose inspection under that power if it could thereby be upheld.]

The general principles enunciated by Justice Bradley in his opinion for the majority are still followed by the Court today. There have been substantial developments in the coverage of what he referred to as "State action," but the opinion is no less important for its fundamental distinction between the reach of congressional power under its "direct and plenary powers" and the lesser grant of authority in the Fourteenth Amendment. Since it is exactly this Fourteenth Amendment delegation of power which is so important in the rights field and which is so difficult to define, a substantial portion of the remainder of this chapter will be devoted to marking out the scope of legislative authority under the Fourteenth Amendment.

It was pointed out earlier that the restrictive interpretation which the Court, in the *Slaughter-House Cases,* gave to the Fourteenth Amendment privileges and immunities clause made the task of legislative enforcement of the amendment a difficult one. One of Congress' solutions to this problem was to adopt a provision which was rather general in its wording. It was declared unlawful for persons acting under color of law to deprive any person of rights "secured or protected by the Constitution *or* laws of the

United States." Now such a provision is clearly not limited to the bare coverage of the Fourteenth Amendment. For example, applied to voting in federal elections, this would be a perfectly proper exercise of congressional power even without the presence of the Fourteenth Amendment. It should be equally clear, however, that all Fourteenth Amendment violations could be construed as crimes under such a statute. Thus, in a sense, in applying the statute to a variety of deprivations one must engage in a bit of constitutional hopscotch: jumping from one section of the Constitution to another, depending on the particular right involved, to see what authority there might be for applying the law to the specific invasion alleged.

To confine ourselves to the coverage of the Fourteenth Amendment, however, there are two basic tests which must be met before there can be held to be a violation of the amendment. First, to use Justice Bradley's words in the *Civil Rights Cases,* "It is State action of a particular character that is prohibited. Individual invasion of individual rights is not the subject-matter of the Amendment." Second, the right claimed must be one which is protected by the Fourteenth Amendment. The absence of *either* of these facets in the case is fatal to a holding of Fourteenth Amendment violation. For example, the right to life is protected by the amendment, but only against improper deprivation by the *state.* A private lynching or murder would not fit the requirements. Similarly, there is no violation if the state bars persons from practicing medicine without a license, since even though the requisite state action is present, tho Fourteenth Amendment does not set up a right in every person to practice medicine on his own terms.

The enumeration of the rights protected by the Fourteenth Amendment is in large part the subject matter of the remainder of this book and cannot be encompassed in a single chapter. Thus the emphasis here will be on the elaboration of the concept of "state action," and the Fourteenth Amendment *rights* will be taken up category by category in the following chapters.

The Court rather early began the extension of the term "state action" to cover not only legislative action (indicated by the use of "law" in the privileges and immunities clause) but also action of the judicial and executive branches as well. And there was a vertical extension to include all governmental units subordinate to the state. The Court has found violations of the Amendment by the state courts [*Ex parte Virginia,* 100 U.S. 339 (1880)], legislatures [*Strauder* v. *West Virginia,* 100 U.S. 303 (1880)], executives [*Sterling* v. *Constantin,* 287 U.S. 378 (1932)], tax boards [*Raymond* v. *Chicago Union Traction Co.,* 207 U.S. 20 (1907)], boards of education [*West Virginia Board of Education* v. *Barnette,* 319 U.S. 624 (1943], counties [*Ward* v. *Love County,* 253 U.S. 17 (1920)], and cities [*Home Telephone & Telegraph Co.* v. *Los Angeles,* 227 U.S. 278 (1913)], among others. When any officer or employee of the state or any of its subordinate governmental units acts in pursuance of his official function as required by law, then there is state action within the meaning of the Fourteenth Amendment. The more complex questions concerning state action have arisen with respect to either operations not strictly classified as government operations, or acts of state agents which are not a part of their statutory duties. [See Glenn Abernathy, "Expansion of the State Action Concept Under the Fourteenth Amendment," 43 *Cornell L.Q.* 375 (1958); Thomas P. Lewis, "The Meaning of State Action," 60 *Colum. L. Rev.* 1083 (1960); and Jerre S. Williams, "The Twilight of State Action," 41 *Texas L. Rev.* 347 (1963).]

A question was raised very soon after the adoption of the Fourteenth Amendment, and even before the decision in the *Civil Rights Cases,* concerning the applicability of the Amendment to the act of a state judge in discriminating racially in the process of selecting jurors. Such discrimination was neither authorized nor prohibited by state law, but Judge Cole, of Virginia, on his own initiative excluded Negroes from jury service. The judge was indicted under Section 4 of the Act of Congress of March 1, 1875, which penalized officials for discriminating on grounds of race or color in the choosing of jurors. While in custody, he petitioned the United States Supreme Court for habeas corpus, alleging that the Act could not constitutionally be applied to him. The question, then, was whether the federal criminal law passed under authority of the equal protection clause of the Fourteenth Amendment could constitutionally be applied to official acts of a state judge who acted in his own discretion and not under statutory direction. In *Ex parte Virginia,* 100 U.S. 339 (1880), the Court held that such acts were within the prohibitions of the Fourteenth Amendment and the enforcement act passed under it. Justice Strong, speaking for the majority, stated:

... Whoever, by virtue of public position under a State government, deprives another of property, life, or liberty, without due process of law, or denies or takes away the equal protection of the laws, violates the constitutional inhibition; and as he acts in the name and for the State, and is clothed with the State's power, his act is that of the State. This must be so, or the constitutional prohibition has no meaning. Then the State has clothed one of its agents with power to annul or to evade it.

Suppose, however, that instead of merely acting where state law is silent, the official actually *violates* the law of his state while acting in his official capacity. Would such a situation come within the purview of the Fourteenth Amendment? In early cases dealing with attempts to obtain civil remedies against this type of official action, the Supreme Court vacillated, first saying "no," and then saying "sometimes." As Justice Roberts pointed out in *Screws v. United States,* 325 U.S. 91, 148 (1945), discussed below:

Although action taken under such circumstances has been deemed to be deprivation by a "State" of rights guaranteed by the Fourteenth Amendment for purposes of federal jurisdiction, the doctrine has had a fluctuating and dubious history. Compare *Barney* v. *City of New York,* 193 U.S. 430, with *Raymond* v. *Chicago Traction Co.,* 207 U.S. 20.

In *United States* v. *Classic,* 313 U.S. 299 (1941), state officers were convicted of willfully miscounting ballots in a federal election. And, of course, this sort of activity was a violation of Louisiana law as well. But the case does not squarely meet the issue as stated here, because Congress has broad powers to punish for federal election frauds even without the Fourteenth Amendment. Here the question is restricted to those rights for which the Fourteenth Amendment alone supports congressional legisaltion. It was not until 1945 that the United States Supreme Court squarely faced and answered the question with respect to federal criminal penalties. The case was *Screws v. United States,* a classic example of police brutality.

Screws, sheriff of Baker County, Georgia, aided by a local police officer and a deputy sheriff, arrested Hall, a Negro citizen of the United States, on a warrant charging theft of a tire. Hall was handcuffed and driven to the courthouse. There he was dragged from the car, and, while still handcuffed, beaten by all three men with their fists and with a two-pound solid-bar blackjack. The beating continued for fifteen to thirty minutes. Hall was then dragged, feet first, through the courthouse yard into the jail and thrown upon the floor, dying. An ambulance was called, but Hall died shortly afterward without regaining consciousness.

An indictment was returned against the three men charging, on one count, violation of Section 20 of the Criminal Code, 18 U.S.C. Section 242. This section provides:

> Whoever, under color of any law, statute, ordinance, regulation, or custom, willfully subjects, or causes to be subjected, any inhabitant of any State, Territory, or District to the deprivation of any rights, privileges, or immunities secured or protected by the Constitution and laws of the United States, or to different punishments, pains, or penalties, on account of such inhabitant being an alien, or by reason of his color, or race, than are prescribed for the punishment of citizens, shall be fined not more than $1,000 or imprisoned not more than one year, or both.

Convictions were obtained, and the United States Supreme Court reviewed the case on certiorari. Several constitutional issues were presented, but probably the most important dealt with the question of whether Congress, in enforcing the Fourteenth Amendment, could punish state acts which violated state laws. The answer to the question is complicated by the fact that when the Court applies a statute, it may not consider just the matter of constitutional power, but may have a second problem of determining the exact reach of the statute involved. Congress ordinarily does not exhaust the full scope of a constitutional grant of power when it gives effect to that grant by legislation. The key phrase in the section is "under color of any law." It might not have been designed by Congress to cover state acts in violation of state law, but certainly if it *were* so intended, the Fourteenth Amendment must justify such inclusion for it to be constitutional.

Another issue presented in the case was whether the section was a violation of the Fifth Amendment due process clause because it subjected persons to criminal penalties under vague and general phrases which did not adequately define just what sort of conduct was made criminal. The majority on the Court held against both claims, although the members were so badly split that there is no "opinion for the Court."

SCREWS *v.* UNITED STATES
325 U.S. 91 (1945)

Mr. Justice Douglas announced the judgment of the Court and delivered the following opinion, in which the Chief Justice, Mr. Justice Black and Mr. Justice Reed concur....

I

We are met at the outset with the claim that Section 20 is unconstitutional, insofar as it makes criminal acts in violation of the due process clause of the Fourteenth Amendment. The argument runs as follows: It is true that this Act as construed in *United States* v. *Classic* . . . was upheld in its application to certain ballot box frauds committed by state officials. But in that case the constitutional rights protected were the rights to vote specifically guaranteed by Art. I, Sections 2 and 4 of the Constitution. Here there is no ascertainable standard of guilt. There have been conflicting views in the Court as to the proper construction of the due process clause. The majority have quite consistently construed it in broad general terms. . . . In *Synder* v. *Massachusetts* . . . it was said that due process prevents state action which "offends some principle of justice so rooted in the traditions and conscience of our people as to be ranked as fundamental." The same standard was expressed in *Palko* v. *Connecticut* . . . in terms of a "scheme of ordered liberty.". . .

Is is said that the Act must be read as if it contained those broad and fluid definitions of due process and that if it is so read it provides no ascertainable standard of guilt. . . . In the instant case the decisions of the courts are, to be sure, a source of reference for ascertaining the specific content of the concept of due process. But even so the Act would incorporate by reference a large body of changing and uncertain law. That law is not always reducible to specific rules, is expressible only in general terms, and turns many times on the facts of a particular case. Accordingly, it is argued that such a body of legal principles lacks the basic specificity necessary for criminal statutes under our system of government. . . .

. . . Under that test a local law enforcement officer violates Section 20 and commits a federal offense for which he can be sent to the penitentiary if he does an act which some court later holds deprives a person of due process of law. And he is a criminal though his motive was pure and though his purpose was unrelated to the disregard of any constitutional guarantee. . . . Those who enforced local law today might not know for many months (and meanwhile could not find out) whether what they did deprived some one of due process of law. The enforcement of a criminal statute so construed would indeed cast law enforcement agencies loose at their own risk on a vast uncharted sea. . . .

We hesitate to say that when Congress sought to enforce the Fourteenth Amendment in this fashion it did a vain thing. We hesitate to conclude that for 80 years this effort of Congress, renewed several times, to protect the important rights of the individual guaranteed by the Fourteenth Amendment has been an idle gesture. . . . Only if no construction can save the Act from this claim of unconstitutionality are we willing to reach that result. We do not reach it, for we are of the view that if Section 20 is confined more narrowly than the lower courts confined it, it can be preserved as one of the sanctions to the great rights which the Fourteenth Amendment was designed to secure.

II

We recently pointed out that "willful" is a word "of many meanings, its construction often being influenced by its context.". . . But "when used in a criminal statute it generally means an act done with a bad purpose.". . . In that event something more is required than the doing of the act proscribed by the statute. . . . An evil motive to accomplish that which the statute condemns becomes a constituent element of the crime. . . . And that issue must be submitted to the jury under appropriate instructions. . . .

An analysis of the cases in which "willfully" has been held to connote more than an act which is voluntary or intentional would not prove helpful as each turns on its own peculiar facts. Those cases, however, make clear that if we construe "willfully" in Section 20 as connoting a purpose to deprive a person of a specific constitutional right, we would introduce no innovation. The Court, indeed, has recognized that the requirement of a specific intent to do a prohibited act may avoid those consequences to the accused which may otherwise render a vague or indefinite statute invalid. The constitutional vice in such a statute is the essential injustice to the accused of placing him on trial for an offense, the nature of which the statute does not define and hence of which it gives no warning. See *United States* v. *Cohen Grocery Co., supra.* But where the punishment imposed is only for an act knowingly done with the purpose of doing that which the statute prohibits, the accused cannot be said to suffer from lack of warning or knowledge that the act which he does is a violation of law. The requirement that the act must be willful or purposeful may not render certain, for all purposes, a statutory definition of the crime which is in some respects uncertain. But it does relieve the statute of the objection that it punishes without warning an offense of which the accused was unaware. . . .

Moreover, the history of Section 20 affords some support for that narrower construction. As we have seen, the word "willfully" was not added to the Act until 1909. Prior to that time it may be that Congress intended that he who deprived a person of any right protected by the Constitution should be liable without more. . . . But as we have seen, the word "willfully" was added to make the section "less severe." We think the inference is permissible that its severity was to be lessened by making it applicable only where the requisite bad purpose was present, thus requiring specific intent not only where discrimination is claimed but in other situations as well. We repeat that the presence of a bad purpose or evil intent alone may not be sufficient. We do say that a requirement of a specific intent to deprive a person of a federal right made definite by decision or other rule of law saves the Act from any charge of unconstitutionality on the grounds of vagueness. . . .

It is said, however, that this construction of the Act will not save it from the infirmity of vagueness since neither a law enforcement official nor a trial judge can know with sufficient definiteness the range of rights that are constitutional. But that criticism is wide of the mark. For the specific intent required by the Act is an intent to deprive a person of a right which has been made specific either by the express terms of the Constitution or laws of the United States or by decisions interpreting them. Take the case of a local officer who persists in enforcing a type of ordinance which the Court has held invalid as violative of the guarantees of free speech or freedom of worship. Or a local official continues to select juries in a manner which flies in the teeth of decisions of the Court. If those acts are done willfully, how can the officer possibly claim that he had no fair warning that his acts were prohibited by the statute? He violates the statute not merely because he has a bad purpose but because he acts in defiance of announced rules of law. He who defies a decision interpreting the Constitution knows precisely what he is doing. If sane, he hardly may be heard so say that he knew not what he did. Of course, willful conduct cannot make definite that which is undefined. But willful violators of constitutional requirements, which have been defined, certainly are in no position to say that they had no adequate advance notice that they would be visited with punishment. When they act willfully in the sense in which we use the word, they act in open defiance or in reckless disregard of a constitutional requirement which has been made specific and definite. When they are convicted for so acting, they are not punished for violating an unknowable something. . . .

. . . The fact that the defendants may not have been thinking in constitutional terms is not material where their aim was not to enforce local law but to deprive a citizen of a right and that right was protected by the Constitution. When they so act they at least act in reckless disregard of constitutional prohibitions or guarantees. Likewise, it is plain that basic to the concept of due process of law in a criminal case is a trial—a trial in a court of law, not a "trial by ordeal." *Brown* v. *Mississippi, 297 U.S. 278, 285.* It could hardly be doubted that they who "under color of any law, statute, ordinance, regulation, or custom" act with that evil motive violate Section 20. Those who decide to take the law into their own hands and act as prosecutor, jury, judge, and executioner plainly act to deprive a prisoner of the trial which due process of law guarantees him. And such a purpose need not be expressed; it may at times be reasonably inferred from all the circumstances attendant on the act. . . .

The difficulty here is that this question of intent was not submitted to the jury with the proper instructions. The court charged that petitioners acted illegally if they applied more force than was necessary to make the arrest effectual or to protect themselves from the prisoner's alleged assault. But in view of our construction of the word "willfully" the jury should have been further instructed that it was not sufficient that petitioners had a generally bad purpose. To convict it was necessary for them to find that petitioners had the purpose to deprive the prisoner of a constitutional right, e.g., the right to be tried by a court rather than by ordeal. And in determining whether that requisite bad purpose was present the jury would be entitled to consider all the attendant circustances—the malice of petitioners, the weapons used in the assault, its character and duration, the provocation, if any, and the like. . . .

III

It is said, however, that petitioners did not act "under color of any law" within the meaning of Section 20 of the Criminal Code. We disagree. We are of the view that petitioners acted under "color" of law in making the arrest of Robert Hall and in assaulting him. They were officers of the law who made the arrest. By their own admissions they assaulted Hall in order to protect themselves and to keep their prisoner from escaping. It was their duty under Georgia law to make the arrest effective. Hence, their conduct comes within the statute.

Some of the arguments which have been advanced in support of the contrary conclusion suggest that the question under Section 20 is whether Congress has made it a federal offense for a state officer to violate the law of his State. But there is no warrant for treating the question in state law terms. The problem is not whether state law has been violated but whether an inhabitant of a State has been deprived of a federal right by one who acts under "color of any law." He who acts under "color" of law may be a federal officer or a state officer. He may act under "color" of federal law or of state law. The statute does not come into play merely because the federal law or the state law under which the officer purports to act is violated. It is applicable when and only when someone is deprived of a federal right by that action. The fact that it is also a violation of state law does not make it any the less a federal offense punishable as such. Nor does its punishment by federal authority encroach on state authority or relieve the state from its responsibility for punishing state offenses.

We agree that when this statute is applied to the action of state officials, it should be construed so as to respect the proper balance between the States and the federal government in law enforcement. Violation of local law does not necessarily mean that federal rights have been invaded. The fact that a prisoner is assaulted, injured, or even murdered by state officials does not necessarily mean that he is deprived of any right protected or secured by the Constitution or laws of the United States. . . . The Fourteenth Amendment did not alter the basic relations between the States and the national government. . . . Our national government is one of delegated powers alone. Under our federal system the administration of criminal justice rests with the states except as Congress, acting within the scope of those delegated powers, has created offenses against the United States. . . . It is only state action of a "particular character" that is probihited by the Fourteenth Amendment and against which the Amendment authorizes Congress to afford relief. *Civil Rights Cases,* 109 U.S. 3, 11, 13. Thus Congress in Section 20 of the Criminal Code did not undertake to make all torts of state officials federal crimes. It brought within Section 20 only specified acts done "under color" of law and then only those acts which deprived a person of some right secured by the Constitution or laws of the United States. . . .

. . . We are not dealing here with a case where an officer not authorized to act nevertheless takes action. Here the state officers were authorized to make an arrest and to take such steps as were necessary to make the arrest effective. They acted without authority only in the sense that they used excessive force in making the arrest effective. It is clear that under "color" of law means under "pretense" of law. Thus acts of officers in the ambit of their personal pursuits are plainly excluded. Acts of officers who undertake to perform their official duties are included whether they hew to the line of their authority or overstep it. If, as suggested, the statute was designed to embrace only action which the State in fact authorized, the words "under color of any law" were hardly apt words to express the idea. . . .

Since there must be a new trial, the judgment below is

Reversed.

Mr. Justice Rutledge, concurring in the result.

For the compelling reason stated at the end of this opinion I concur in reversing the judgment and remanding the cause for further proceedings. But for that reason, my views would require that my vote be cast to affirm the judgment, for the reasons stated by Mr. Justice Murphy and others I feel forced, in the peculiar situation, to state.

The case comes here established in fact as a gross abuse of authority by state officers. . . . They do not come . . . as faithful state officers, innocent of crime. Justification has been foreclosed. Accordingly, their argument now admits the offense, but insists it was against the state alone, not the nation. So they have made their case in this Court.

In effect, the position urges it is murder they have done, not deprivation of constitutional right. Strange as the argument is the reason. It comes to this, that abuse of state power creates immunity to federal power. Because what they did violated the state's laws, the nation cannot reach their conduct. It may deprive the citizen of his liberty and his life. But whatever state officers may do in abuse of their official capacity can give this Government and its courts no concern. This, though the prime object of the Fourteenth Amendment and Section 20 was to secure these fundamental rights against wrongful denial by exercise of the power of the states. . . .

There could be no clearer violation of the Amendment or the statute. No act could be more final or complete, to denude the victim of rights secured by the Amendment's very terms. Those rights so destroyed cannot be restored. Nor could the part played by the state's power in causing their destruction be lessened, though other organs were not to repudiate what was done. The state's law might thus be vindicated. If so, the vindication could only sustain, it could not detract from the federal power. Nor could it restore what the federal power shielded. Neither acquittal nor conviction, though affirmed by the state's highest court, could resurrect what the wrongful use of state power has annihilated. There was in this case abuse of state power, which for the Amendment's great purposes was state action, final in the last degree, depriving the victim of his liberty and his life without due process of law. . . .

. . . Section 20 strikes only at abuse of official functions by the state officers. It does not reach out for crimes done by men in general. Not murder per se, but murder by state officers in the course of official conduct and done with the aid of state power is outlawed. These facts, inherent in the crime, give all the warning constitutionally required. For one, so situated, who goes so far in misconduct can have no excuse of innocence or ignorance.

Generally state officials know something of the individual's basic legal rights. If they do not, they should, for they assume that duty when they assume their office. Ignorance of the law is no excuse for men in general. It is less an excuse for men whose special duty is to apply it, and therefore to know and observe it. If their knowledge is not comprehensive, state officials know or should know when they pass the limits of their authority, so far at any rate that their action exceeds honest error of judgment and amounts to abuse of their office and its function. When they enter such a domain in dealing with the citizen's rights, they should do so at their peril, whether that be created by state or federal law. . . .

[Mr. Justice Rutledge then states that while his conviction is that the judgment should be affirmed, this would result in a lack of majority to dispose of the case. "Stalemate should not prevail for any reason, however compelling, in a criminal case, or, if avoidable, in any other." Accordingly, he concurs in voting to reverse the decision as required by the opinion of Mr. Justice Douglas.]

Mr. Justice Murphy dissenting.

I dissent. Robert Hall, a Negro citizen, has been deprived not only of the right to be tried by a court rather than by ordeal. He has been deprived of the right to life itself. That right belonged to him not because he was a Negro or a member of any particular race or creed. That right was his because he was an American citizen, because he was a human being. As such, he was entitled to all the respect and fair treatment that befits the dignity of man, a dignity that is recognized and guaranteed by the Constitution. Yet not even the semblance of due process has been accorded him. He has been cruelly and unjustifiably beaten to death by local police officers acting under color of authority derived from the state. It is difficult to believe that such an obvious and necessary right is indefinitely guaranteed by the Constitution or is foreign to the knowledge of local police officers so as to cast any reasonable doubt on the conviction under Section 20 of the Criminal Code of the perpetrators of this "shocking and revolting episode in law enforcement.". . .

It is axiomatic, of course, that a criminal statute must give a clear and unmistakable warning as to the acts which will subject one to criminal punishment. And courts are without power to supply that which Congress has left vague. But this salutary principle does not mean that if a statute is vague as to certain criminal acts but definite as to others the entire statute must fall. Nor does it mean that in the first case involving the statute to come before us we must delineate all the prohibited acts that are obscure and all those that are explicit. . . .

It is an illusion to say that the real issue in this case is the alleged failure of Section 20 fully to warn the state officials that their actions were illegal. The Constitution, Section 20 and their own consciences told them that. They knew that they lacked any mandate or authority to take human life unnecessarily or without due process of law in the course of their duties. They knew that their excessive and abusive use of authority would only subvert the ends of justice. The significant question, rather, is whether law enforcement officers and those entrusted with authority shall be allowed to violate with impunity the clear constitutional rights of the inarticulate and the friendless. Too often unpopular minorities, such as Negroes, are unable to find effective refuge from the cruelties of bigoted and ruthless authority. States are undoubtedly capable of punishing their officers who commit such outrages. But where, as here, the states are unwilling for some reason to prosecute such crimes the federal government must step in unless constitutional guarantees are to become atrophied. . . .

. . . We should therefore affirm the judgment.

Mr. Justice Roberts, Mr. Justice Frankfurter and Mr. Justice Jackson, dissenting . . .

Of course the petitioners are punishable. The only issue is whether Georgia alone has the power and duty to punish, or whether this patently local crime can be made the basis of a federal prosecution. The practical question is whether the States should be relieved from responsibility to bring their law officers to book for homicide, by allowing prosecutions in the federal courts for a relatively minor offense carrying a short sentence. The legal question is whether, for the purpose of accomplishing this relaxation of State responsibility, hitherto settled principles for the protection of civil liberties shall be bent and tortured. . . .

The Fourteenth Amendment prohibited a State from so acting as to deprive persons of new federal rights defined by it. Section 5 of the Amendment specifically authorized enabling legislation to enforce that prohibition. Since a State can act only through its officers, Congress provided for the prosecution of any officer who deprives others of their guaranteed rights and denied such an officer the right to defend by claiming the authority of the State for his action. In short, Congress said that no State can empower an officer to commit acts which the Constitution forbade the State from authorizing, whether such unauthorized command be given for the State by its legislative or judicial voice, or by a custom contradicting the written law. . . . The present prosecution is not based on an officer's claim that that for which the United States seeks his punishment was commanded or authorized by the law of his State. On the contrary, the present prosecution is based on the theory that Congress made it a federal offense for a State officer to violate the explicit law of his State. We are asked to construe legislation which was intended to effectuate prohibitions against States for defiance of the Constitution, to be equally applicable where a State duly obeys the Constitution, but an officer flouts State law and is unquestionably subject to punishment by the State for his disobedience. . . .

Such a distortion of federal power devised against recalcitrant State authority never entered the minds of the proponents of the legislation. [The opinion then discusses some of the legislative history of Section 20.]

Were it otherwise it would indeed be surprising. It was natural to give the shelter of the Constitution to those basic human rights for the vindication of which the successful conduct of the Civil War was the end of a long process. And the extension of federal authority so as to guard against evasion by any State of these newly created federal rights was an obvious corollary. But to attribute to Congress the making overnight of a revolutionary change in the balance of the political relations between the National Government and the States without reason, is a very different thing. And to have provided for the National Government to take over the administration of criminal justice from the States to the extent of making every lawless act of the policeman on the beat or in the station house, whether by way of third degree or the illegal ransacking for evidence in a man's house . . . , a federal offense, would have constituted a revolutionary break with the past overnight. The desire for such a dislocation in our federal system plainly was not contemplated by the Lyman Trumbulls and the John Shermans, and not even by the Thaddeus Stevenses. . . .

. . . It may well be that Congress could, within the bounds of the Fourteenth Amendment, treat action taken by a State official even though in defiance of State law and not condoned by ultimate State authority as the action of "a State." It has never been satisfactorily explained how a State can be said to deprive a person of liberty or property without due process of law when the foundation of the claim is that a minor official has disobeyed the authentic command of his State. . . . Although action taken under such circumstances has been deemed to be deprivation by a "State" of rights guaranteed by the Fourteenth Amendment for purposes of federal jurisdiction, the doctrine has had a fluctuating and dubious history. . . .

But assuming unreservedly that conduct such as that now before us, perpetrated by State officers in flagrant defiance of State law, may be attributed to the State under the Fourteenth Amendment, this does not make it action under "color of any law." Section 20 is much narrower than the power of Congress. Even though Congress might have swept within the federal criminal law any action that could be deemed within the vast reach of the Fourteenth Amendment, Congress did not do so. The presuppositions of our federal system, the pronouncements of the statesmen who shaped this legislation, and the normal meaning of language powerfully counsel against attributing to Congress intrusion into the sphere of criminal law traditionally and naturally reserved for the States alone. . . . In the absence of clear direction by Congress we should leave to the States the enforcement of their criminal law, and not relieve States of the responsibility for vindicating wrongdoing that is essentially local or weaken the habits of local law enforcement by tempting reliance on federal authority for an occasional unpleasant task of local enforcement. . . .

Since the majority of the Court do not share this conviction that the action of the Georgia peace officers was not perpetrated under color of law, we, too, must consider the constitutionality of Section 20. . . . [F]our members of the Court are of the opinion that this plain constitutional principle of definiteness in criminal statutes may be replaced by an elaborate scheme of constitutional exegesis whereby that which Congress has not defined the courts can define from time to time, with varying and conflicting definiteness in the decisions, and that, in any event, an undefined range of conduct may become sufficiently definite if only such undefined conduct is committed "willfully."

In subjecting to punishment "deprivation of any rights, privileges, or immunities secured or protected by the Constitution and laws of the United States," Section 20 on its face makes criminal deprivation of the whole range of undefined appeals to the Constitution. Such is the true scope of the forbidden conduct. Its domain is unbounded and therefore too indefinite. Criminal statutes must have more or less specific contours. This has none.

To suggest that the "right" deprivation of which is made criminal by Section 20 "has been made specific either by the express terms of the Constitution or by decisions interpreting it" hardly adds definiteness beyond that of the statute's own terms. . . . The illustrations given in the Court's opinion underline the inescapable vagueness due to the doubts and fluctuating character of decisions interpreting the Constitution.

This intrinsic vagueness of the terms of Section 20 surely cannot be removed by making the statute applicable only where the defendant has the "requisite bad purpose." Does that not amount to saying that the black heart of the defendant enables him to know what are the constitutional rights deprivation of which the statute forbids, although we as judges are not able to define their classes or their limits, or, at least, are not prepared to state what they are unless it be to say that Section 20 protects whatever rights the Constitution protects? . . .

. . . It is not denied that the Government's contention would make a potential offender against this act of any State official who as a judge admitted a confession of crime, or who as judge of a State court of last resort sustained admission of a confession, which we should later hold constitutionally inadmissible, or who as a public service commissioner issued a regulatory order which we should later hold denied due process or who as a municipal officer stopped any conduct we later should hold to be constitutionally protected. The Due Process Clause of the Fourteenth Amendment has a content the scope of which this Court determines only as cases come here from time to time and then not without close division and reversals of position. Such a dubious construction of a criminal statute should not be made unless language compels. . . .

We are told local authorities cannot be relied upon for courageous and prompt action, that often they have personal or political reasons for refusing to prosecute. If it be significantly true that crimes against local law cannot be locally prosecuted, it is an ominous sign indeed. In any event, the cure is a reinvigoration of State responsibility. It is not an undue incursion of remote federal authority into local duties with consequent debilitation of local responsibility. . . .

Admittedly, with four different opinions discussing two hard legal questions, the *Screws* case is not easy to decipher. Approaching it from the position of looking for similarities rather than differences, however, certain conclusions stand out. At least six of the justices agreed that the Fourteenth Amendment permitted Congress to punish state officials acting in defiance of state law in depriving one of rights protected by the Amendment. Although Justice Roberts did not specifically agree, he did say that "It may well be that Congress could, within the bounds of the Fourteenth Amendment," provide punishment for such action. Six of the justices held, further, that in adopting the "color of law" statute Congress in fact intended to cover illegal state acts such as that of Sheriff Screws. On the issue of vagueness, six justices held that the statute gave adequate notice, even though the exact scope of the due process and equal protection clauses is not clearly defined and even changes from time to time. This was the main thrust of Justice Douglas' stress on the word "willfully." He indicated that this saved the statute from indefiniteness simply because it put the burden on the prosecution to prove that the right involved in any given case was one of which state officials should be aware, and that the deprivation was to this extent a knowing deprivation of right. This was in answer to the very objection made by Justice Roberts, that a judge who admits a confession of crime, later held by the United States Supreme Court to be constitutionally inadmissible, would be a potential offender against the statute. If the claim of right has not yet been recognized in the laws of Congress or in the Supreme Court's interpretations of the Constitution, then the state official who denies the claim cannot have "willfully" deprived the claimant of any right. Thus there is a crucial difference between merely doing an act intentionally and doing the same act, *knowing* that it will deprive another of a constitutional right. The judge in the confession case would fall in the former category, and there would be no "willful" deprivation of right in the statutory sense. Once a clear-cut decision has been rendered by the Supreme Court on the admissibility of such confessions, however, subsequent judges who render decisions contrary to that holding might well be subject to prosecution on the ground that they could be charged with a *willful* act to deprive the claimant of a constitutional right.

Justice Douglas, in his opinion, stated that acts of officers "in the ambit of their personal pursuits are plainly excluded" from the coverage of the statute, or, presumably, the Fourteenth Amendment. And this would seem to be an eminently reasonable delineation of the extent of coverage. To hold differently and consider every act of a state officer or employee to be "state action" subject to the Fourteenth Amendment would appear to place an intolerable burden upon both the individual employee and the state. But this raises the question of where the line is drawn between the private and the official acts of state officials. Few cases are available to illustrate the judicial view of how the distinction is to be made. The extremes of the two categories are, of course, apparent. It is the part official, part private act which presents the difficulty.

Suppose that an officer takes an off-duty job as investigator or guard over private property. Would his acts in such related police capacity constitute "state action"? The answer seems to hinge on the specific facts in each case. The most notable case in this area to reach the United States Supreme Court is *Williams* v. *United States,* 341 U.S. 97 (1951). A Florida lumber company, having suffered numerous thefts, hired Williams, who operated a detective agency, to find the thieves. He held a special police officer's card issued by the City of Miami and had taken an oath and qualified as a special police officer. Williams and others over a period of three days took four men to a paint shack on the company's premises and used brutal methods to obtain a confession from each of them. One Ford, a policeman, was sent by his superior to lend authority to the proceedings. And Williams, who committed the assaults, went about flashing his badge.

The indictment charged a violation of Section 20 (now 18 U.S.C. 242) in that Williams, acting under color of law, used force to make each victim confess and that the victims were denied the right to be tried by due process of law. He was found guilty by a jury under instructions which conformed with the ruling of the Court in *Screws* v. *United States.* On certiorari, the Court affirmed the conviction. Justice Douglas, speaking for the majority, stated:

[T]his was an investigation conducted under the aegis of the state, as evidenced by the fact that a regular police officer was detailed to attend it. . . . There was, therefore, evidence that he acted under authority of Florida law; and the manner of his conduct of the interrogations makes clear that he was asserting the authority granted him and not acting in the role of a private person. In any event the charge to the jury drew the line between official and unofficial conduct which we explored in *Screws* v. *United States* . . . , and gave petitioner all of the protection which "color of law" as used in Section 20 offers.

The opinion then pointed out that while the right involved might be doubtful in other situations, no such difficulty was presented in the instant case. "It is as plain as a pikestaff that the present confessions would not be allowed in evidence whatever the school of thought concerning the scope and meaning of the Due Process Clause." On the issue of whether the deprivation was "willful," Justice Douglas quoted with approval the trial judge's charge to the jury:

The trial judge charged in part on this phase of the case: "The law denies to anyone acting under color of law ... the right to try a person by ordeal; that is, for the officer himself to inflict such punishment upon the person as he thinks the person should receive. Now in determining whether this requisite of willful intent was present in this case as to these counts, you gentlemen are entitled to consider all the attendant circumstances; the malice, if any, of the defendants toward these men; the weapon used in the assault, if any; and the character and duration of the investigation, if any, of the assault, and the time and manner in which it was carried out. All these facts and circumstances may be taken into consideration from the evidence that has been submitted for the purpose of determining whether the acts of the defendants were willful and for the deliberate and willful purpose of depriving these men of their Constitutional rights to be tried by a jury just like everyone else."

Another facet of the problem of delineating state action appears in the classification of the privately owned and managed operation which receives direct financial aid from the state. Is the act of such an agency an act of the state or is it a private act for purposes of the Fourteenth Amendment? Obviously, a categorical answer to the question is impossible. It would be a rather far-fetched doctrine which would consider as state agents all people on relief, unemployed persons benefiting under state compensation plans, persons on state retirement pensions, or all companies which profit from ordinary contract arrangements with the state. On the other hand, there are operations which might have begun as purely private, but which have become so enmeshed with the agencies of state government through grants or other special governmental treatment that they take on the character of state institutions. These, perhaps, should be considered as state agencies for the purposes of the Fourteenth Amendment.

In 1945 a question was raised concerning the status of the Enoch Pratt Free Library of Baltimore. Kerr, a Negro, sued for damages and an injunction on complaint that she was refused admission to a library training class conducted by the library to prepare persons for staff positions in the central library and its branches. She charged that the library was performing a governmental function, that she was rejected solely because of race, and that such rejection constituted state action prohibited by the Fourteenth Amendment. The library defended on the ground that it was a private corporation.

The library was established by Pratt in 1882. He erected a building and established a fund and gave them to the City of Baltimore on condition that the city would create a perpetual annuity of $50,000 for maintaining the library and branches. In giving legal effect to the terms of the gift, the Maryland legislature passed a statute and the city passed three ordinances. The real and personal property vested in the city by virtue of the act, as well as later acquisitions, were exempted from state and city taxes. In addition to the $50,000 annually appropriated, much greater sums were required to meet demands for increased services. In 1943 and 1944 more than half a million dollars was appropriated. In addition, the city paid large sums for bond interest, bond retirement, and the retirement funds for the library's employees. Salary checks were issued by the city's payroll officer and charged against the library's appropriation. The library budget was included in the regular city budget, and library employees were included within the municipal employees' retirement system.

In *Kerr* v. *Enoch Pratt Free Library,* 149 F.2d 212 (4th Cir. 1945) [*cert. denied,* 326 U.S. 721 (1945)], the Court of Appeals held that the library's action was state action within the meaning of the Fourteenth Amendment. The two criteria stressed by the court were control by the state over the library's activities and the volume or importance of governmental financial assistance afforded. The opinion indicated no line of demarcation to aid in determining how far along the spectrum from zero to complete control or complete financial support the state must go before the activity becomes that of the state. Nor is it easy to see where such a line can be drawn.

The state may aid a private operation in various ways other than by direct financial assistance. It may give the organization the power of eminent domain, it may grant tax exemptions, or it may give it a monopolistic status for certain purposes. Does the receipt of such assistance convert the organization into a state agency? According to Justice Harlan, in his dissent in the *Civil Rights Cases,* it would, especially if the state acquired special control powers in return.

One of the most thoroughly argued cases on the point to date is the case of *Dorsey* v. *Stuyvesant Town Corporation,* 299 N.Y. 512, 87 N.E.2d 541 (1949) [*cert. denied,* 339 U.S. 981 (1950)], decided by the New York Court of Appeals. Stuyvesant Town was built as an apartment housing development pursuant to a contract between the City of New York, Metropolitan Insurance Company, and its wholly owned subsidiary, Stuyvesant. Stuyvesant was organized under the state's Redevelopment Companies Law of 1942, as amended. The purpose of the law was to encourage private companies to enter the housing field. Under that law, the City of New York, by eminent domain, brought under one good title an area of eighteen blocks in the city, the area having been declared one of substandard housing. Stuyvesant acquired the property, including certain streets which the city had agreed to close, by paying to the city the cost of acquired land and buildings. The agreement provided that Stuyvesant would demolish the old buildings and construct new ones without expense to the city, and the city granted the corporation a twenty-five-year tax exemption to the extent of the enhanced value to be created by the project. Certain writers estimated the total tax exemption to reach approximaely $50,000,000. [See Walter J. Blum and Norman Bursler, "Tax Subsidies for Rental Housing," 15 *U. Chi. L. Rev.* 255, 269, n.22 (1948)]. The project represented an investment of about $90,000,000 of private funds by the Metropolitan Insurance Company. No state law barred the owner or operator of this project from discriminating, racially or otherwise, in his choice of tenants. While repeated attempts had been made in the state legislature to amend the redevelopment law to bar racial discrimination, all had failed as of that time. Although the matter was discussed in the city council, the agreement reached contained no bar to practice of racial discrimination by the landlord. When finally completed, the project housed approximately 25,000 persons. The contract gave the city the right to regulate rents and certain auditing privileges, and it prohibited the mortgage or sale of the property.

Dorsey, a Negro, was refused tenancy because of race and sued to enjoin Stuyvesant from denying accommodations because of race on the ground that to do so was in violation of the Fourteenth Amendment. The issue presented was whether the city's assistance in the form of eminent domain and tax exemptions and its reserved control over the housing operation made the Stuyvesant Corporation a state instrumentality within the meaning of the Fourteenth Amendment. By the close division of four-to-three the New York Court of Appeals held that Stuyvesant was not a state agency for purposes of the Fourteenth Amendment. The United States Supreme Court denied certiorari. The majority opinion stated that to argue that the housing development was barred from racial discrimination "on the ground that helpful co-operation between the State and the respondents transforms the activities of the latter into state action, comes perilously close to asserting that any State assistance to an organization which discriminates necessarily violates the Fourteenth Amendment." The dissenters argued that the degree of involvement by the city in the project was such that the requisite state action was present to invoke the prohibitions of the Fourteenth Amendment.

Burton v. *Wilmington Parking Authority*, 365 U.S. 715 (1961), dealt tangentially with the question of whether a lessee of state property who opens his business to the public comes within the Fourteenth Amendment's bar to racial discrimination. A parking building was owned and operated by the Parking Authority, an agency of the State of Delaware. It leased a portion of the building to a private corporation for the establishment of a restaurant. Plaintiff brought an action for declaratory and injunctive relief on the ground that the restaurant's racially discriminatory policy was state action barred by the Fourteenth Amendment. The Delaware Supreme Court held that the restaurant was operating in a purely private capacity and denied the relief. The United States Supreme Court reversed. Justice Clark, speaking for the majority, examined the lease arrangements and concluded:

Addition of all these activities, obligations and responsibilities of the Authority, the benefits mutually conferred, together with the obvious fact that the restaurant is operated as an integral part of a public building devoted to a public parking service, indicates that degree of state participation and involvement in discriminatory action which it was the design of the Fourteenth Amendment to condemn. It is irony amounting to grave injustice that in one part of a single building, erected and maintained with public funds by an agency of the State to serve a public purpose, all persons have equal rights, while in another portion, also serving the public, a Negro is a second-class citizen, offensive because of his race. . . . [N]o State may effectively abdicate its responsibilities by either ignoring them or by merely failing to discharge them whatever the motive may be. . . . By its inaction, the Authority, and through it the State, has not only made itself a party to the refusal of service, but has elected to place its power, property and prestige behind the admitted discrimination. . . .

The opinion went on to state, however, that the conclusions drawn from this case were by no means "universal truths on the basis of which every state leasing agreement is to be tested."

The status of a state licensee under the Fourteenth Amendment was discussed in *Moose Lodge No. 107* v. *Irvis* in 1972.

MOOSE LODGE NO. 107 *v.* IRVIS
407 U.S. 163 (1972)

[Irvis, a Negro guest of a white member of Moose Lodge (a private club), was refused service at the club's dining room and bar solely because of his race. The local lodge in Pennsylvania was bound by the constitution and bylaws of the national organization, whose bylaws contained a provision limiting membership in local lodges to white males. Irvis sought injunctive relief in the United States District Court under 42 U.S.C. Section 1983, on the theory that the refusal of service to him was "state action" for purposes of the equal protection clause of the Fourteenth Amendment, because the Pennsylvania Liquor Control Board, one of whose regulations required that "every club licensee shall adhere to the provisions of its constitution and bylaws," had issued the lodge a private club liquor license. The court entered a decree declaring the lodge's liquor license invalid "as long as it follows a policy of racial discrimination in its membership or operating policies or practices." Following the court's decision, the national organization altered its bylaws to make applicable to guests the same sort of racial restrictions as were applicable to members. Moose Lodge appealed directly to the Supreme Court.]

Mr. Justice Rehnquist delivered the opinion of the Court. . . .

Any injury to appellee from the conduct of Moose Lodge stemmed not from the Lodge's membership requirements, but from its policies with respect to the serving of guests of members. Appellee has standing to seek redress for injuries done to him, but may not seek redress for injuries done to others.

We believe that Moose Lodge is correct, therefore, in contending that the District Court in its decree went beyond the vindication of any claim that appellee had standing to litigate. Appellee did, however, have standing to litigate the constitutional validity of Moose Lodge's policies relating to the service of guests of members. . . .

Moose Lodge is a private club in the ordinary meaning of that term. It is a local chapter of a national fraternal organization having well defined requirements for membership. It conducts all of its activities in a building that is owned by it. It is not publicly funded. Only members and guests are permitted in any lodge of the order; one may become a guest only by invitation of a member or upon invitation of the house committee.

Appellee, while conceding the right of private clubs to choose members upon a discriminatory basis, asserts that the licensing of Moose Lodge to serve liquor by the Pennsylvania Liquor Control Board amounts to such State involvement with the club's activities as to make its discriminatory practices forbidden by the Equal Protection Clause of the Fourteenth Amendment. The relief sought and obtained by appellee in the District Court was an injunction forbidding the licensing by the liquor authority of Moose Lodge until it ceased its discriminatory practices. We conclude that Moose Lodge's refusal to serve food and beverages to a guest by reason of the fact that he was a Negro does not, under the circumstances here presented, violate the Fourteenth Amendment.

In 1883, this Court in *The Civil Rights Cases* . . . set forth the essential dichotomy between discriminatory action by the State, which is prohibited by the Equal Protection Clause, and private conduct, "however discriminatory or wrongful," against which that clause "erects no shield," *Shelley* v. *Kraemer*. . . . That dichotomy has been subsequently reaffirmed in *Shelley* v. *Kraemer, supra,* and in *Burton* v. *Wilmington Parking Authority* . . . (1961).

While the principle is easily stated, the question of whether particular discriminatory conduct is private, on the one hand, or amounts to "State action," on the other hand, frequently admits of no easy answer. "Only by sifting facts and weighing circumstances can the nonobvious involvement of the State in private conduct be attributed its true significance.". . .

The Court has never held, of course, that discrimination by an otherwise private entity would be violative of the Equal Protection Clause if the private entity receives any sort of benefit or service at all from the State, or if it is subject to state regulation in any degree whatever. Since state-furnished services include such necessities of life as electricity, water, and police and fire protection, such a holding would utterly emasculate the distinction between private as distinguished from State conduct set forth in *The Civil Rights Cases*... and adhered to in subsequent decisions. Our holdings indicate that where the impetus for the discrimination is private, the State must have "significantly involved itself with invidious discriminations"... in order for the discriminatory action to fall within the ambit of the constitutional prohibiton....

Here there is nothing approaching the symbiotic relationship between lessor and lessee that was present in *Burton,* where the private lessee obtained the benefit of locating in a building owned by the State created parking authority, and the parking authority was enabled to carry out its primary public purpose of furnishing parking space by advantageously leasing portions of the building constructed for that purpose to commercial lessees such as the owner of the Eagle Restaurant. Unlike *Burton,* the Moose Lodge building is located on land owned by it, not by any public authority. Far from apparently holding itself out as a place of public accommodation, Moose Lodge quite ostentatiously proclaims the fact that it is not open to the public at large. Nor is it located and operated in such surroundings that although private in name, it discharges a function or performs a service that would otherwise in all likelihood be performed by the State. In short, while Eagle was a public restaurant in a public building, Moose Lodge is a private social club in a private building....

The District Court was at pains to point out in its opinion what it considered to be the "pervasive" nature of the regulation of private clubs by the Pennsylvania Liquor Control Board. As that court noted, an applicant for a club license must make such physical alterations in its premises as the board may require, must file a list of the names and addresses of its members and employees, and must keep extensive financial records. The board is granted the right to inspect the licensed premises at any time when patrons, guests or members are present.

However detailed this type of regulation may be in some particulars, it cannot be said to in any way foster or encourage racial discrimination. Nor can it be said to make the State in any realistic sense a partner or even a joint venturer in the club's enterprise. The limited effect of the prohibition against obtaining additional club licenses when the maximum number of retail licenses allotted to a municipality has been issued, when considered together with the availability of liquor from hotel, restaurant, and retail licensees, falls far short of conferring upon club licensees a monopoly in the dispensing of liquor in any given municipality or in the State as a whole. We therefore hold that, with the exception hereafter noted, the operation of the regulatory scheme enforced by the Pennsylvania Liquor Control Board does not sufficiently implicate the State in the discriminatory guest policies of Moose Lodge so as to make the latter "State action" within the ambit of the Equal Protection Clause of the Fourteenth Amendment.

The District Court found that the regulations of the Liquor Control Board adopted pursuant to the statute affirmatively require that "every club licensee shall adhere to all the provisions of its constitution and bylaws." Appellant argues that the purpose of this provision "is purely and simply and plainly the prevention of subterfuge," pointing out that the bona fides of a private club, as opposed to a place of public accommodation masquerading as a private club, is a matter with which the State Liquor Control Board may legitimately concern itself. Appellee concedes this to be the case, and expresses disagreement with the District Court on this point. There can be no doubt that the label "private club" can and has been used to evade both regulations of State and local liquor authorities, and statutes requiring places of public accommodation to serve all persons without regard to race, color, religion, or national origin. . . .

The effect of this particular regulation on Moose Lodge under the provisions of the constitution placed in the record in the court below would be to place State sanctions behind its discriminatory membership rules, but not behind its guest practices, which were not embodied in the constitution of the lodge. Had there been no change in the relevant circumstances since the making of the record in the District Court, our holding in Part I of this opinion that appellee has standing to challenge only the guest practices of Moose Lodge would have a bearing on our disposition of this issue. Appellee stated upon oral argument, though, and Moose Lodge conceded in its Brief that the bylaws of the Supreme Lodge have been altered since the lower court decision to make applicable to guests the same sort of racial restrictions as are presently applicable to members.

Even though the Liquor control Board regulation in question is neutral in its terms, the result of its application in a case where the constitution and bylaws of a club required racial discrimination would be to invoke the sanctions of the State to enforce a concededly discriminatory private rule. State action, for purposes of the Equal Protection Clause, may emanate from rulings of administrative and regulatory agencies as well as from legislative or judicial action. . . . *Shelley* v. *Kraemer* makes it clear that the application of state sanctions to enforce such a rule would violate the Fourteenth Amendment. Although the record before us is not as clear as one would like, appellant has not persuaded us that the District Court should have denied any and all relief.

Appellee was entitled to a decree enjoining the enforcement of [the regulation] promulgated by the Pennsylvania Liquor Control Board insofar as that regulation requires compliance by Moose Lodge with provisions of its constitution and bylaws containing racially discriminatory provisions. He was entitled to no more. The judgment of the District Court is reversed, and the cause remanded with instructions to enter a decree in conformity with this opinion.

Reversed and remanded.

Mr. Justice Douglas, with whom Mr. Justice Marshall joins, dissenting.

My view of the First Amendment and the related guarantees of the Bill of Rights is that they create a zone of privacy which precludes government from interfering with private clubs or groups. The associational rights which our system honors permits all white, all black, all brown, and all yellow clubs to be formed. They also permit all Catholic, all Jewish, or all agnostic clubs to be established. Government may not tell a man or woman who his or her associates must be. The individual can be as selective as he desires. So the fact that the Moose Lodge allows only Caucasians to join or come as guests is constitutionally irrelevant, as is the decision of the Black Muslims to admit to their services only members of their race.

The problem is different, however, where the public domain is concerned. I have indicated in *Garner* v. *Louisiana* . . . and *Lombard* v. *Louisiana* . . . that where restaurants or other facilities serving the public are concerned and licenses are obtained from the State for operating the business, the "public" may not be defined by the proprietor to include only people of his choice; nor may a State or municipal service be granted only to some. . . .

Those cases are not precisely apposite, however, for a private club, by definition, is not in the public domain. And the fact that a private club gets some kind of permit from the State or municipality does not make it *ipso facto* a public enterprise or undertaking, any more than the grant to a householder of a permit to operate an incinerator puts the householder in the public domain. We must therefore examine whether there are special circumstances involved in the Pennsylvania scheme which differentiate the liquor license possessed by Moose Lodge from the incinerator permit.

Pennsylvania has a state store system of alcohol distribution. Resale is permitted by hotels, restaurants, and private clubs which all must obtain licenses from the Liquor Control Board. The scheme of regulation is complete and pervasive; and the state courts have sustained many restrictions on the licensees.... Once a license is issued the licensee must comply with many detailed requirements or risk suspension or revocation of the license. Among these requirements is Regulation No. 113.09 which says "Every club licensee shall adhere to all the provisions of its Constitution and Bylaws." This regulation means, as applied to Moose Lodge, that it must adhere to the racially discriminatory provision of the Constitution of its Supreme Lodge....

It is argued that this regulation only aims at the prevention of subterfuge and at enforcing Pennsylvania's differentiation between places of public accommodation and bona fide private clubs. It is also argued that the regulation only gives effect to the constitutionally protected rights of privacy and of association. But I cannot so read the regulation. While those other purposes are embraced in it, so is the restrictive membership clause. And we have held that "a State is responsible for the discriminatory act of a private party when the State, by its law, has compelled the act.".... The result, as I see it, is the same as though Pennslvania had put into its liquor licenses a provision that the license may not be used to dispense liquor to Blacks, Browns, Yellows—or atheists or agnostics. Regualtion No. 113.09 is thus an invidious form of state action.

Were this regulation the only infirmity in Pennsylvania's licensing scheme, I would perhaps agree with the majority that the appropriate relief would be a decree enjoining its enforcement. But there is another flaw in the scheme not so easily cured. Liquor licenses in Pennsylvania, unlike driver's licenses, or marriage licenses, are not freely available to those who meet racially neutral qualifications. There is a complex quota system.... What the majority neglects to say is that the Harrisburg quota, where Moose Lodge No. 107 is located, has been full for many years. No more club licenses may be issued in that city.

This state-enforced scarcity of licenses restricts the ability of blacks to obtain liquor, for liquor is commercially available *only* at private clubs for a significant portion of each week. Access by blacks to places that serve liquor is further limited by the fact that the state quota is filled. A group desiring to form a nondiscriminatory club which would serve blacks must purchase a license held by an existing club, which can exact a monopoly price for the transfer. The availability of such a license is speculative at best, however, for, as Moose Lodge itself concedes, without a liquor license a fraternal organization would be hard-pressed to survive.

Thus, the State of Pennsylvania is putting the weight of its liquor license, concededly a valued and important adjunct to a private club, behind racial discrimination....

I would affirm the judgment below.

Mr. Justice Brennan, with whom Mr. Justice Marshall joins, dissenting.

When Moose Lodge obtained its liquor license, the State of Pennsylvania became an active participant in the operation of the Lodge bar. Liquor licensing laws are only incidentally revenue measures; they are primarily pervasive regulatory schemes under which the State dictates and continually supervises virtually every detail of the operation of the licensee's business. Very few, if any, other licensed businesses experience such complete state involvement. Yet the Court holds that that involvement does not constitute "state action" making the Lodge's refusal to serve a guest liquor solely because of his race a violation of the Fourteenth Amendment. The vital flaw in the Court's reasoning is its complete disregard of the fundamental value underlying the "state action" concept. That value is discussed in my separate opinion in *Adickes* v. *Kress & Co.* . . . (1970):

"The state action doctrine reflects the profound judgment that denials of equal treatment, and particularly denials on account of race or color, are singularly grave when government has or shares responsibility for them. Government is the social organ to which all in our society look for the promotion of liberty, justice, fair and equal treatment, and the setting of worthy norms and goals for social conduct. Therefore something is uniquely amiss in a society where the government, the authoritative oracle of community values, involves itself in racial discrimination. Accordingly, . . . the cases that have come before us [in which] this Court has condemned significant state involvement in racial discrimination, however subtle and indirect it may have been and whatever form it may have taken, . . . represent vigilant fidelity to the constitutional principle that no State shall in any significant way lend its authority to the sordid business of racial discrimination."

Plainly, the State of Pennsylvania's liquor regulations intertwine the State with the operation of the Lodge bar in a "significant way [and] lend [the State's] authority to the sordid business of racial discrimination." . . . [Here the opinion quotes extensively from the District Court's opinion describing the pervasive types of regulations imposed by the Liquor Control Board on liquor licensees, including the right to require physical alterations, the supervision of financial arrangements and record-keeping, the right to inspect, and prohibitions against any "lewd, immoral or improper entertainment" or the allowing of "persons of ill repute" to frequent the premises.]

. . . The holder of a liquor license from the Commonwealth of Pennsylvania therefore is not like other licensees who conduct their enterprises at arm's-length from the state, even though they may have been required to comply with certain conditions, such as zoning or building requirements, in order to obtain or continue to enjoy the license which authorizes them to engage in their business. . . . Here by contrast beyond the act of licensing is the continuing and pervasive regulation of the licensees by the state to an unparalleled extent. The unique power which the state enjoys in this area, which has put it in the business of operating state liquor stores and in the role of licensing clubs, has been exercised in a manner which reaches intimately and deeply into the operation of the licensees. . . .

I therefore dissent and would affirm the final decree entered by the District Court.

Yet another question concerning the application of the Fourteenth Amendment is whether it can properly reach deprivations of rights which occur because of the *inaction* of a state official. An affirmative answer was indicated in the *Burton* opinion, above, as well as in some of the white primary cases, e.g., *Terry* v. *Adams*, 345 U.S. 461 (1953). But the Court has not squarely ruled on this specific point. Good illustrations are to be found in some of the cases reaching federal courts of appeals, however. In *Catlette* v. *United States*,

132 F.2d 902 (4th Cir. 1943), a group of Jehovah's Witnesses were refused the police protection they requested while engaged in religious activities. On the issue of whether the Fourteenth Amendment and 18 U.S.C. Section 52 (now Section 242) could apply to inaction of state officials the opinion stated:

> And since the failure of Catlette to protect the victims from group violence or to arrest the members of the mob who assaulted the victims constituted a violation of his common law duty, his dereliction in this respect comes squarely within the provisions of 18 U.S.C.A. Section 52.
>
> It is true that a denial of equal protection has hitherto been largely confined to affirmative acts of discrimination. The Supreme Court, however, has already taken the position that culpable official State inaction may also constitute a denial of equal protection.

In *Lynch* v. *United States*, 189 F.2d 476 (5th Cir. 1951), a federal court of appeals reviewed the conviction of a Georgia sheriff who had allowed Negro prisoners in his custody to be kidnapped and beaten by a Ku Klux Klan local. The sheriff claimed that he had been overpowered, but evidence was introduced which was sufficient to convince the jury that even if he didn't cooperate, he did nothing to apprehend or punish the offenders. The court of appeals upheld the conviction unanimously, the opinion stating, "There was a time when the denial of equal protection of the laws was confined to affirmative acts, but the law now is that culpable official inaction may also constitute a denial of equal protection."

It may be seen from the previous analysis that the concept of what constitutes state action is a broad one. And intentional denial by state action of the rights protected by the Fourteenth Amendment can be the subject of remedial legislation by Congress, as provided by the enforcement section of that amendment. Yet even today, despite the importance of recent civil rights acts, the century-old "color of law" statute, Section 242 of Title 18, remains one of the most important federal criminal provisions applicable to state deprivations of civil rights. Congress is not restricted to criminal provisions in protecting rights, of course, and may offer appropriate civil remedies as well. As a companion piece to Section 242 there are civil provisions applicable to "color of law" deprivations in Section 1983 of Title 42 of the United States Code.

Section 1983. Civil action for deprivation of rights.

> Every person who, under color of any statute, ordinance, regulation, custom, or usage, of any State or Territory, subjects or causes to be subjected, any citizen of the United States or other person within the jurisdiction thereof to the deprivation of any rights, privileges, or immunities secured by the Constitution and laws, shall be liable to the party injured in an action at law, suit in equity, or other proper proceeding for redress.

Since this section provides for suits for damages, injunctions, or special orders appropriate to the occasion, it is the key jurisdictional basis for litigation in federal courts seeking relief for state deprivations of federal rights. Most of the important segregation questions initiated in the federal courts, for example, have been partially or wholly Section 1983 actions. While normally the suit is for an injunction to halt the objectionable practice, the plaintiff may choose to sue for money damages under the section. In *Monroe* v. *Pape*, 365 U.S. 167 (1961), the Court examined the application of Section

1983 to an illegal search and seizure committed by municipal police. The complaint alleged that thirteen Chicago police officer broke into petitioners' home in the early morning, routed them from bed, made them stand naked in the living room, and ransacked every room, emptying drawers and ripping mattress covers. It further alleged that Mr. Monroe was then taken to the police station, detained for ten hours, interrogated about a recent murder, refused permission to call his family or his attorney, and finally released without charges preferred against him. A suit for damages was brought against the thirteen officers and the City of Chicago under Section 1983. The district court dismissed the complaint, and the court of appeals affirmed. The United States Supreme Court held that Congress did not intend in this act to make municipalities liable for injuries caused by their officers, but it further held that the section did provide remedies against the kind of state action alleged in the complaint, and thus the trial court should not have dismissed.

In addition, to the sections already discussed, in the period following the Civil War Congress passed a number of other statutes designed to protect civil rights. The Thirteenth Amendment was ratified in 1865, the Fourteenth in 1868, and the Fifteenth in 1870, all three containing enforcement clauses. During the years 1866–1875 Congress adopted seven broad civil rights statutes with a variety of sections outlining specific rights. These ranged from antipeonage provisions to prohibitions against denial of equal accommodations in inns—the section involved in the *Civil Rights Cases.* In less than thirty years after the passage of the last act, the program had ended in failure. [See Eugene Gressman, "The Unhappy History of Civil Rights Legislation," 50 *Mich. L. Rev.* 1323 (1952).] This failure was attributable to three causes: (1) Several key provisions were held unconstitutional by the United States Supreme Court. (2) Congress repealed a number of other provisions. (3) Administrative officers charged with enforcement were reluctant to use the authority remaining to them after the action of the Court and Congress.

The antipeonage provisions still remain, as 18 U.S.C. Sections 1581, 1583, and 1584. [See Sydney Brodie, "The Federally Secured Right to be Free from Bondage." 40 *Geo. L. J.* 367 (1952).] In addition to these, there are only three important criminal sections which survive. Section 242 has been discussed in some detail. Another, Section 243 of Title 18, makes it a criminal offense "for any officer or any person charged with any duty in the selection or summoning of jurors" to discriminate on grounds of race or color in the summoning of any citizen for service on federal or state juries. This is the section which was used in the prosecution of a Virginia judge in the case leading to *Ex parte Virginia.* The third remaining provision is Section 241 of Title 18, formerly Section 19 of the Criminal Code. In its present form it states:

Section 241. Conspiracy against rights of citizens.

If two or more persons conspire to injure, oppress, threaten, or intimidate any citizen in the free exercise or enjoyment of any right or privilege secured to him by the Constitution or laws of the United States, or because of his having so exercised the same; or

If two or more persons go in disguise on the highway, or on the premises of another, with intent to prevent or hinder his free exercise or enjoyment of any right or privilege so secured—

They shall be fined not more than $5,000 or imprisoned not more than ten years, or both.

It should be noted that Section 241 defines a felony with considerably stiffer penalties than are provided in Section 242, which defines a misdemeanor. Further, Section 241 does not require a finding of official action or action taken "under color of law." It is clear, then, that it was intended to reach certain kinds of acts of private persons. Two questions remain, however. First, what kinds of private acts are prohibited by the section? Second, can the section be employed against *officials* who engage in the proscribed conduct?

As to the first question, the previous analysis has already shown that the only kind of private action which can constitutionally be reached by the Congress is the interference with a federal right. As indicated, such rights are those created by Congress or arising out of the special relationship of national government to the individual. Thus private interference with an ordinary lawful speech or assembly could not be punishable under Section 241, but private interference with the attempt to vote in a federal election could properly be brought under its coverage.

The second question presents somewhat greater difficulties. There appear to be three possible approaches to the application of Section 241 to official action: (1) since Section 242 specifically covers acts "under color of law," to avoid duplication Section 241 logically should apply *only* to private acts; (2) Section 241 *can* be applied to officials, but since the primary purpose of the section was to reach private acts, it can reach only the kinds of interference for which Congress can punish private persons and does not extend to the full range of rights protected by the due process and equal protection clauses; or (3) Section 241 may be employed against official action as well as private action, and with respect to the former it extends to any deprivation for which Congress may constitutionally punish state officers. In effect, this last approach would mean that with respect to conspiracies including state officers, Section 241 would overlap Section 242 completely and offer substantially greater penalties in the bargain.

This question was discussed at length in *United States* v. *Williams,* 341 U.S. 70 (1951), but on this issue the Court split four-to-four and the question remained unresolved. This was a companion case to *Williams* v. *United States,* discussed earlier (arising out of a Section 242 prosecution), and was a prosecution for violation of Section 241. Justice Frankfurter, speaking for himself and three others, examined the legislative history of Section 241 and concluded that the rights which it protects "are those which Congress can beyond doubt constitutionally secure against interference by private individuals." He further examined the previous cases making the distinction between "rights that flow from the substantive powers of the Federal Government and may clearly be protected from private interference, and interests which the Constitution only guarantees from interference by States." He concluded that Section 241 does not extend "to rights which the Federal Constitution merely guarantees against abridgment by the States."

Four other members of the Court, taking the "plain words" approach to interpreting the statute, found no basis for making the differentiation stated by Justice Frankfurter. They felt that since the language was so similar the rights guarded by Sections 241 and 242 were identical when state officials were involved in the deprivation.

The definitive answer to the question was not given until 1966 when the Court handed down decisions in two important cases involving prosecutions under Sections 241 and 242. The first case was *United States* v. *Guest,* 383 U.S. 745 (1966), involving a Section 241 prosecution of six private persons. The second case was *United States* v. *Price,* 383 U.S. 787 (1966), involving prosecutions under both Section 241 and Section 242 of a group of eighteen persons, some of whom were private persons and some of whom were state officials.

UNITED STATES *v.* GUEST

383 U.S. 745 (1966)

[Six private persons were indicted in a United States District Court in Georgia for a conspiracy, in violation of 18 U.S.C. Section 241, to deprive Negro citizens of the free exercise and enjoyment of (1) the right to accommodations of motion picture theaters, restaurants, and other such places of public accommodation; (2) the right to equal utilization of public facilities operated by the state or any subdivision thereof; (3) the right to the use on the same terms as white citizens of the public streets and highways in the state; and (4) the right to travel freely to and from the state. Upon motion of the defendants the District Court dismissed the indictment, and the United States appealed directly to the Supreme Court. The Court dismissed the appeal as to the first allegation on the ground that since the dismissal below was rested on defective pleading, it had no jurisdiction to review on direct appeal.]

Mr. Justice Stewart delivered the opinion of the Court. . . .

The second numbered paragraph of the indictment alleged that the defendants conspired to injure, oppress, threaten, and intimidate Negro citizens of the United States in the free exercise and enjoyment of:

"The right to the equal utilization, without discrimination upon the basis of race, of public facilities in the vicinity of Athens, Georgia, owned, operated or managed by or on behalf of the State of Georgia or any subdivision thereof."

Correctly characterizing this paragraph as embracing rights protected by the Equal Protection Clause of the Fourteenth Amendment, the District Court held as a matter of statutory construction that 18 USC §241 does not encompass any Fourteenth Amendment rights, and further held as a matter of constitutional law that "any broader construction of §241 . . . would render it void for indefiniteness.". . . In so holding, the District Court was in error, as our opinion in *United States* v. *Price* . . . makes abundantly clear.

To be sure, *Price* involves rights under the Due Process Clause, whereas the present case involves rights under the Equal Protection Clause. But no possible reason suggests itself for concluding that §241—if it protects Fourteenth Amendment rights—protects rights secured by the one Clause but not those secured by the other. We have made clear in *Price* that when §241 speaks of "any right or privilege secured . . . by the Constitution or laws of the United States," it means precisely that.

Moreover, inclusion of Fourteenth Amendment rights within the compass of 18 USC §241 does not render the statute unconstitutionally vague. Since the gravamen of the offense is conspiracy, the requirement that the offender must act with a specific intent to interfere with the federal rights in question is satisfied. *Screws* v. *United States.* . . . And the rights under the Equal Protection Clause described by this paragraph of the indictment have been so firmly and precisely established by a consistent line of decisions in this Court, that the lack of specification of these rights in the language of §241 itself can raise no serious constitutional question on the ground of vagueness or indefiniteness.

Unlike the indictment in *Price,* however, the indictment in the present case names no person alleged to have acted in any way under the color of state law. The argument is therefore made that, since there exist no Equal Protection Clause rights against wholly private action, the judgment of the District Court on this branch of the case must be affirmed. On its face, the argument is unexceptionable. The Equal Protection Clause speaks to the State or to those acting under the color of its authority.

In this connection, we emphasize that §241 by its clear language incorporates no more than the Equal Protection Clause itself; the statute does not purport to give substantive, as opposed to remedial, implementation to any rights secured by that Clause. Since we therefore deal here only with the bare terms of the Equal Protection Clause itself, nothing said in this opinion goes to the question of what kinds of other and broader legislation Congress might constitutionally enact under §5 of the Fourteenth Amendment to implement that Clause or any other provision of the Amendment.

It is a commonplace that rights under the Equal Protection Clause itself arise only where there has been involvement of the State or of one acting under the color of its authority. The Equal Protection Clause "does not . . . add any thing to the rights which one citizen has under the Constitution against another." *United States* v. *Cruikshank.* . . . As Mr. Justice Douglas more recently put it, "The Fourteenth Amendment protects the individual against *state action,* not against wrongs done by *individuals." United States* v. *Williams.* . . . This has been the view of the Court from the beginning. . . . It remains the Court's view today. . . .

This case, however, requires no determination of the threshold level that state action must attain in order to create rights under the Equal Protection Clause. This is so because, contrary to the argument of the litigants, the indictment in fact contains an express allegation of state involvement sufficient at least to require the denial of a motion to dismiss. One of the means of accomplishing the object of the conspiracy, according to the indictment, was "By causing the arrest of Negroes by means of false reports that such Negroes had committed criminal acts.". . . [T]he allegation is broad enough to cover a charge of active connivance by agents of the State in the making of the "false reports," or other conduct amounting to official discrimination clearly sufficient to constitute denial of rights protected by the Equal Protection Clause. Although it is possible that a bill of particulars, or the proof if the case goes to trial, would disclose no cooperative action of that kind by officials of the State, the allegation is enough to prevent dismissal of this branch of the indictment.

III

The fourth numbered paragraph of the indictment alleged that the defendants conspired to injure, oppress, threaten, and intimidate Negro citizens of the United States in the free exercise and enjoyment of:

"The right to travel freely to and from the State of Georgia and to use highway facilities and other instrumentalities of interstate commerce within the State of Georgia."

The District Court was in error in dismissing the indictment as to this paragraph. The constitutional right to travel from one State to another, and necessarily to use the highways and other instrumentalities of interstate commerce in doing so, occupies a position fundamental to the concept of our Federal Union. It is a right that has been firmly established and repeatedly recognized. . . .

In *Edwards* v. *California*, . . . invalidating a California law which impeded the free interstate passage of the indigent, the Court based its reaffirmation of the federal right of interstate travel upon the Commerce Clause. . . .

Although there have been recurring differences in emphasis within the Court as to the source of the constitutional right of interstate travel, there is no need here to canvass those differences further. All have agreed that the right exists. Its explicit recognition as one of the federal rights protected by what is now 18 USC §241 goes back at least as far as 1904. . . . We reaffirm it now.

This does not mean, of course, that every criminal conspiracy affecting an individual's right of free interstate passage is within the sanction of 18 USC §241. A specific intent to interfere with the federal right must be proved, and at a trial the defendants are entitled to a jury instruction phrased in those terms. *Screws* v. *United States*. . . . Thus, for example, a conspiracy to rob an interstate traveler would not, of itself, violate §241. But if the predominant purpose of the conspiracy is to impede or prevent the exercise of the right of interstate travel, or to oppress a person because of his exercise of that right, then, whether or not motivated by racial discrimination, the conspiracy becomes a proper object of the federal law under which the indictment in this case was brought. Accordingly, it was error to grant the motion to dismiss on this branch of the indictment.

For these reasons, the judgment of the District Court is reversed and the case is remanded to that court for further proceedings consistent with this opinion.

It is so ordered.

Mr. Justice Clark, with whom Mr. Justice Black and Mr. Justice Fortas join, concurring.

I join the opinion of the Court in this case but believe it worthwhile to comment on its Part II in which the Court discusses [the second numbered paragraph of the indictment]. . . .

The Court carves out of its opinion the question of the power of Congress, under §5 of the Fourteenth Amendment, to enact legislation implementing the Equal Protection Clause or any other provision of the Fourteenth Amendment. The Court's interpretation of the indictment clearly avoids the question whether Congress, by appropriate legislation, has the power to punish private conspiracies that interfere with Fourteenth Amendment rights, such as the right to utilize public facilities. My Brother Brennan, however, says that the Court's disposition constitutes an acceptance of appellees' aforesaid contention as to §241 [that state action must be present]. Although the Court specifically rejects any such connotation, . . . it is, I believe, both appropriate and necessary under the circumstances here to say that there now can be no doubt that the specific language of §5 empowers the Congress to enact laws punishing all conspiracies—with or without state action—that interfere with Fourteenth Amendment rights.

Mr. Justice Harlan, concurring in part and dissenting in part.

I join Parts I and II of the Court's opinion, but I cannot subscribe to Part III in its full sweep. To the extent that it is there held that 18 USC §241 reaches conspiracies, embracing only the action of private persons, to obstruct or otherwise interfere with the right of citizens freely to engage in interstate travel, I am constrained to dissent. On the other hand, I agree that §241 does embrace state interference with such interstate travel, and I therefore consider that this aspect of the indictment is sustainable on the reasoning of Part II of the Court's opinion.

... While past cases do indeed establish that there is a constitutional "right to travel" between States free from unreasonable *governmental* interference, today's decision is the first to hold that such movement is also protected against *private* interference, and, depending on the constitutional source of the right, I think it either unwise or impermissible so to read the Constitution. . . .

Mr. Justice Brennan, with whom the Chief Justice and Mr. Justice Douglas join, concurring in part and dissenting in part.

I join Part I of the Court's opinion. I reach the same result as the Court on that branch of the indictment discussed in Part III of its opinion but for other reasons. . . . And I agree with so much of Part II as construes 18 USC §241 to encompass conspiracies to injure, oppress, threaten or intimidate citizens in the free exercise or enjoyment of Fourteenth Amendment rights and holds that, as so construed, §241 is not void for indefiniteness. I do not agree, however, with the remainder of Part II which holds, as I read the opinion, that a conspiracy to interfere with the exercise of the right to equal utilization of state facilities is not, within the meaning of §241, a conspiracy to interfere with the exercise of a "right . . . secured . . . by the Constitution" unless discriminatory conduct by state officers is involved in the alleged conspiracy. . . .

. . . I understand this to mean that, no matter how compelling the proof that private conspirators murdered, assaulted, or intimidated Negroes in order to prevent their use of state facilities, the prosecution under the second numbered paragraph must fail in the absence of proof of active connivance of law enforcement officers with the private conspirators in causing the false arrests. . . .

I cannot agree with that construction of §241. I am of the opinion that a conspiracy to interfere with the right to equal utilization of state facilities described in the second numbered paragraph of the indictment is a conspiracy to interfere with a "right . . . secured . . . by the Constitution" within the meaning of §241— without regard to whether state officers participated in the alleged conspiracy. I believe that §241 reaches such a private conspiracy, not because the Fourteenth Amendment of its own force prohibits such a conspiracy, but because §241, as an exercise of congressional power under §5 of that Amendment, prohibits *all* conspiracies to interfere with the exercise of a "right . . . secured . . . by the Constitution" and because the right to equal utilization of state facilities is a "right . . . secured . . . by the Constitution" within the meaning of that phrase as used in §241.

My difference with the Court stems from its construction of the term "secured" as used in §241. . . . The Court tacitly construes the term "secured" so as to restrict the coverage of §241 to those rights that are "fully protected" by the Constitution or another federal law. Unless private interferences with the exercise of the right in question are prohibited by the Constitution itself or another federal law, the right cannot, in the Court's view, be deemed "secured . . . by the Constitution or laws of the United States" so as to make §241 applicable to a private conspiracy to interfere with the exercise of that right. The Court then premises that neither the Fourteenth Amendment nor any other federal law prohibits private interferences with the exercise of the right to equal utilization of state facilities.

In my view, however, a right can be deemed "secured . . . by the Constitution or laws of the United States," within the meaning of §241, even though only governmental interferences with the exercise of the right are prohibited by the Constitution itself (or another federal law). The term "secured" means "created by, arising under or dependent upon,", . . rather than "fully protected." A right is "secured . . . by the Constitution" within the meaning of §241 if it emanates from the Constitution, if it finds its source in the Constitution. Section 241 must thus be viewed, in this context, as an exercise of congressional power to amplify prohibitions of the Constitution addressed, as is invariably the case, to government officers; contrary to the view of the Court, I think we are dealing here with a statute that seeks to implement the Constitution, not with the "bare terms" of the Constitution. Section 241 is not confined to protecting rights against private conspiracies that the Constitution or another federal law also protects against private interferences.... Many of the rights that have been held to be encompassed within §241 are not additionally the subject of protection of specific federal legislation or of any provision of the Constitution addressed to private individuals.... The reach of §241 should not vary with the particular constitutional provision that is the source of the right. For purposes of applying §241 to a private conspiracy, the standard used to determine whether, for example, the right to discuss public affairs or the right to vote in a federal election is a "right ... secured ... by the Constitution" is the very same standard to be used to determine whether the right to equal utilization of state facilities is a "right ... secured ... by the Constitution."

For me, the right to use state facilities without discrimination on the basis of race is, within the meaning of §241, a right created by, arising under and dependent upon the Fourteenth Amendment and hence is a right "secured" by that Amendment....

A majority of the members of the Court expresses the view today that §5 empowers Congress to enact laws punishing *all* conspiracies to interfere with the exercise of Fourteenth Amendment rights, whether or not state officers or others acting under the color of state law are implicated in the conspiracy....

I acknowledge that some of the decisions of this Court, most notably an aspect of the *Civil Rights Cases,* ... have declared that Congress' power under §5 is confined to the adoption of "appropriate legislation for correcting the effects of ... prohibited State laws and State acts, and thus to render them effectually null, void, and innocuous." I do not accept—and a majority of the Court today rejects— this interpretation of §5. It reduces the legislative power to enforce the provisions of the Amendment to that of the judiciary; and it attributes a far too limited objective to the Amendment's sponsors....

Viewed in its proper perspective, §5 of the Fourteenth Amendment appears as a positive grant of legislative power, authorizing Congress to exercise its discretion in fashioning remedies to achieve civil and political equality for all citizens.... I can find no principle of federalism nor word of the Constitution that denies Congress power to determine that in order adequately to protect the right to equal utilization of state facilities, it is also appropriate to punish other individuals— not state officers themselves and not acting in concert with state officers—who engage in the same brutal conduct for the same misguided purpose....

In the *Price* case, decided on the same day as the *Guest* case, the Court considered on direct appeal the dismissal of federal indictments arising out of the notorious murders of three civil rights workers in the state of Mississippi in 1964.

UNITED STATES *v.* PRICE
383 U.S. 787 (1966)

Mr. Justice Fortas delivered the opinion of the Court.

There are direct appeals from the dismissal in part of two indictments returned by the United States Grand Jury for the Southern District of Mississippi. The indictments allege assaults by the accused persons upon the rights of the asserted victims to due process of law under the Fourteenth Amendment. The indictment in No. 59 charges 18 persons with violations of 18 USC Section 241 (1964 ed.). In No. 60, the same 18 persons are charged with offenses based upon 18 USC Section 242 (1964 ed.). These are among the so-called civil rights statutes which have come to us from Reconstruction days. . . .

The sole question presented in these appeals is whether the specified statutes make criminal the conduct for which the individuals were indicted. It is an issue of construction, not of constitutional power. . . .

The events upon which the charges are based, as alleged in the indictments, are as follows: On June 21, 1964, Cecil Ray Price, the Deputy Sheriff of Neshoba County, Mississippi, detained Michael Henry Schwerner, James Earl Chaney and Andrew Goodman in the Neshoba County jail located in Philadelphia, Mississippi. He released them in the dark of that night. He then proceeded by automobile on Highway 19 to intercept his erstwhile wards. He removed the three men from their automobile, placed them in an official automobile of the Neshoba County Sheriff's office, and transported them to a place on an unpaved road.

[The indictment further alleged that these acts were a part of a conspiracy on the part of the 18 defendants to "punish" the three men, and that the three were unlawfully assaulted, shot and killed. The bodies were then transported to an earthen dam some five miles from Philadelphia, Mississippi.]

These are federal and not state indictments. They do not charge as crimes the alleged assaults or murders. The indictments are framed to fit the stated federal statutes, and the question before us is whether . . . the indictments charge offenses against the various defendants which may be prosecuted under the designated federal statutes. . . .

The indictment in No. 60 contains four counts, each of which names as defendants the three officials and 16 nonofficial persons. The First Count charges, on the basis of allegations substantially as set forth above, that all of the defendants conspired "to willfully subject" Schwerner, Chaney and Goodman "to the deprivation of their right, privilege and immunity secured and protected by the Fourteenth Amendment of the Constitution of the United States not to be summarily punished without due process of law by persons acting under color of the laws of the State of Mississippi." This is said to constitute a conspiracy to violate Section 242, and therefore an offense under 18 USC Section 371. The latter section, the general conspiracy statute, makes it a crime to conspire to commit any offense against the United States. The penalty for violation is the same as for direct violation of Section 242—that is, it would be a misdemeanor.

On a motion to dismiss, the District Court sustained this First Count as to all defendants. As to the sheriff, deputy sherif and patrolman, the court recognized that each was clearly alleged to have been acting "under color of law" as required by Section 242. As to the private persons, the District Court held that "[I]t is immaterial to the conspiracy that these private individuals were not acting under color of law" because the count charges that they were conspiring with persons who were so acting. . . .

No appeal was taken by the defendants from the decision of the trial court with respect to the First Count and it is not before us for adjudication.

The Second, Third and Fourth Counts of the indictment in No. 60 charge all of the defendants, not with conspiracy, but with substantive violations of Section 242. Each of these counts charges that the defendants, acting "under color of the laws of the State of Mississippi," "did wilfully assault, shoot and kill" Schwerner, Chaney and Goodman, respectively, "for the purpose and with the intent" of punishing each of the three and that the defendants "did thereby wilfully deprive" each "of rights, privileges and immunities secured and protected by the Constitution and the laws of the United States"—namely, due process of law.

The District Court held these counts of the indictment valid as to the sheriff, deputy sheriff and patrolman. But it dismissed them as against the nonofficial defendants because the counts do not charge that the latter were "officers in fact, or de facto in anything allegedly done by them 'under color of law.'"

We note that by sustaining these counts against the three officers, the court again necessarily concluded that an offense under Section 242 is properly stated by allegations of willful deprivation, under color of law, of life and liberty without due process of law. We agree. No other result would be permissible under the decisions of this Court. *Screws* v. *United States*. . . .

But we cannot agree that the Second, Third or Fourth Counts may be dismissed as against the nonofficial defendants. Section 242 applies only where a person indicted has acted "under color" of law. Private persons, jointly engaged with state officials in the prohibited action, are acting "under color" of law for purposes of the statute. To act "under color" of law does not require that the accused be an officer of the State. It is enough that he is a willful participant in joint activity with the State or its agents.

In the present case, according to the indictment, the brutal joint adventure was made possible by state detention and calculated release of the prisoners by a officer of the State. . . . Those who took advantage of participation by state officers in accomplishment of the foul purpose alleged must suffer the consequences of that participation. In effect, if the allegations are true, they were participants in official lawlessness, acting in willful concert with state officers and hence under color of law. . . .

Accordingly, we reverse the dismissal of the Second, Third and Fourth Counts of the indictment in No. 60 and remand for trial.

No. 59 charges each of the 18 defendants with a felony—violation of Section 241. This indictment is in one count. It charges that the defendants "conspired together . . . to injure, oppress, threaten and intimidate" Schwerner, Chaney and Goodman "in the free exercise and enjoyment of the right and privilege secured to them by the Fourteenth Amendment to the Constitution of the United States not to be deprived of life or liberty without due process of law by persons acting under color of the laws of Mississippi.". . . The penalty under Section 241 is a fine of not more than $5,000 or imprisonment for not more than 10 years, or both. . . .

The District Court dismissed the indictment as to all defendants. In effect, although Section 241 includes "rights or privileges secured by the Constitution or laws of the United States" without qualification or limitation, the Court held that it does not include rights protected by the Fourteenth Amendment. . . .

But the District Court purported to read the statutes with the gloss of *Williams I* [341 U.S. 70 (1951)]. In that case, the only case in which this Court has squarely confronted the point at issue, the Court did in fact sustain dismissal of an indictment under Section 241. But it did not, as the District Court incorrectly assumed, hold that Section 241 is inapplicable to Fourteenth Amendment rights. The Court divided equally on the issue. Four Justices, in an opinion by Mr. Justice Frankfurter, were of the view that Section 241 "only covers conduct which interferes with rights arising from the substantive powers of the Federal Government" —rights "which Congress can beyond doubt constitutionally secure against interference by private individuals."... Four other Justices, in an opinion by Mr. Justice Douglas, found no support for Mr. Justice Frankfurter's view in the language of the section, its legislative history, or its judicial interpretation up to that time. They read the statute as plainly covering conspiracies to injure others in the exercise of Fourteenth Amendment rights.... *Williams I* thus left the proper construction of Section 241, as regards its applicability to protect Fourteenth Amendment rights, an open question.

...On the basis of an extensive re-examination of the question, we conclude that the District Court erred; that Section 241 must be read as it is written—to reach conspiracies "to injure...any citizen in the free exercise or enjoyment of any right or privilege secured to him by the Constitution or laws of the United States..."; that this language includes rights or privileges protected by the Fourteenth Amendment; that whatever the ultimate coverage of the section may be, it extends to conspiracies otherwise within the scope of the section, participated in by officials alone or in collaboration with private persons; and that the indictment in No. 59 properly charges such a conspiracy in violation of Section 241....

[Here follows an examination of the language and the purposes of the statute.]

In this context, it is hardly conceivable that Congress intended Section 241 to apply only to a narrow and relatively unimportant category of rights. We cannot doubt that the purpose and effect of Section 241 was to reach assaults upon rights under the entire Constitution, including the Thirteenth, Fourteenth and Fifteenth Amendments, and not merely under part of it....

The present application of the statutes at issue does not raise fundamental questions of federal-state relationships. We are here concerned with allegations which squarely and indisputably involve state action in direct violation of the mandate of the Fourteenth Amendment—that no State shall deprive any person of life or liberty without due process of law.... In any event, the problem, being statutory and not constitutional, is ultimately, as it was in the beginning, susceptible of congressional disposition.

Reversed and remanded.

[Mr. Justice Black concurs in the judgment and opinion of the Court except insofar as the opinion relies upon the *Williams* cases.]

It has been seen that Section 242 of the Criminal Code has its civil counterpart in Section 1983 of Title 42 of the United States Code. Similarly, there is a civil provision, Section 1985(3) of Title 42, which is drawn in somewhat the same language as Section 241 of the Criminal Code. It is not really a twin section, however, since the types of deprivations covered are not identical. Both Section 241 and Section 1985(3) refer to conspiracies, but they are conspiracies to accomplish somewhat different purposes.

Section 1985(3). Conspiracies: to deprive citizens of rights or privileges.

If two or more persons in any State or Territory conspire or go in disguise on the highway or on the premises of another, for the purpose of depriving, either directly or indirectly, any person or class of persons of the equal protection of the laws, or of equal privileges and immunities under the laws; or for the purpose of preventing or hindering the constituted authorities of any State or Territory from giving or securing to all persons within such State or Territory the equal protection of the laws; or if two or more persons conspire to prevent by force, intimidation, or threat, any citizen who is lawfully entitled to vote, from giving his support or advocacy in a legal manner, toward or in favor of the election of any lawfully qualified person as an elector for President or Vice President, or as a Member of Congress of the United States; or to injure any citizen in person or property on account of such support or advocacy; in any case of conspiracy set forth in this section, if one or more persons engaged therein do, or cause to be done, any act in furtherance of the object of such conspiracy, whereby another is injured in his person or property, or deprived of having and exercising any right or privilege of a citizen of the United States, the party so injured or deprived may have an action for the recovery of damages occasioned by such injury or deprivation, against any one or more of the conspirators.

It should be noted that the section is narrower in scope than Section 241. Except for those clauses dealing with voting rights, Section 1985(3) is limited to deprivations of "equal protection of the laws" or "equal privileges and immunities under the law." It is harder to determine liability under such language than it is to find deprivation of "any right or privilege" secured by the Constitution or laws of the United States, as provided in Section 241. Further, Section 1985(3) provides only for an action to recover damages, and not equitable relief. In *Collins* v. *Hardyman,* 341 U.S. 641 (1951), the Court construed the statute as reaching only conspiracies under color of state law. In *Griffin* v. *Breckenridge,* 403 U.S. 88 (1971), the Court extended its application to purely private conspiracies aimed at invidiously discriminatory deprivation of the equal enjoyment of rights secured to all by law. Petitioners, Negro citizens of Mississippi, alleged that while travelling on the highway in an automobile driven by one Grady, a citizen of Tennessee, the white respondents, pursuant to a conspiracy, blocked the travellers' passage on the public highways, forced them from the car, held them at bay with firearms, and amidst threats of murder clubbed them, inflicting serious physical injury. They sued for damages under Section 1985(3). The District Court and the Court of Appeals, relying on *Collins* v. *Hardyman,* held that the complaint should be dismissed for failure to allege state action. The Supreme Court unanimously reversed. Justice Stewart, speaking for the Court, stated:

...On their face, the words of the statute fully encompass the conduct of private persons. The provision speaks simply of "two or more persons in any State or Territory" who "conspire or go in disguise on the highway or on the premises of another." Going in disguise, in particular, is in this context an activity so little associated with official action and so commonly connected with private marauders that this clause could almost never be applicable under the artificially restrictive construction of *Collins.* And since the "going in disguise" aspect must include private action, it is hard to see how the conspiracy aspect, joined by a disjunctive, could be read to require the involvement of state officers. . . . [The opinion then examines the section's companion statutory provisions, concluding that to read into 1985(3) a state action requirement would be unwarranted, since it would result in simply duplicating the coverage of one or more of the companion provisions. It further examined the legislative history of the section and concluded that Congress intended coverage of private action.]

It is thus evident that all indicators—text, companion provisions, and legislative history—point unwaveringly to §1985(3)'s coverage of private conspiracies. That the statute was meant to reach private action does not, however, mean that it was intended to apply to all tortious, conspiratorial interferences with the rights of others. . . . The language requiring intent to deprive of *equal* protection, or *equal* privileges and immunities, means that there must be some racial, or perhaps otherwise class-based, invidiously discriminatory animus behind the conspirators' action. The conspiracy, in other words, must aim at a deprivation of the equal enjoyment of rights secured by the law to all. . . .

As for the constitutional basis for the remedy against private conspiracies to deny Negroes their equal rights, the Court stated that the Thirteenth Amendment afforded ample power to Congress. Further, there was the allegation that one member was from another state, and the Court has "firmly established that the right of interstate travel is constitutionally protected, does not necessarily rest on the Fourteenth Amendment, and is assertable against private as well as governmental interference."

It would appear that the *Griffin* decision offers an important new weapon for identifiable minority groups to attempt to redress injuries inflicted by private action and motivated by "invidiously discriminatory animus."

A third civil provision derives from Section 1 of the Civil Rights Act of 1866. It was designed to protect the rights of blacks to acquire and convey real and personal property, but with rare exceptions, it lay unused for over a hundred years. It appears as Title 42 U.S.C. Section 1982 in the following form:

All citizens of the United States shall have the same right, in every State and Territory, as is enjoyed by white citizens thereof to inherit, purchase, lease, sell, hold, and convey real and personal property.

The constitutionality of Section 1982 as applied to private abridgments was upheld in *Jones* v. *Alfred Mayer Co.* in 1968.

JONES *v.* ALFRED MAYER CO.
392 U.S. 409 (1968)

Mr. Justice Stewart delivered the opinion to the Court.

In this case we are called upon to determine the scope and the constitutionality of an Act of Congress, 42 U.S.C. Sec. 1982, which provides that:

"All citizens of the United States have the same right, in every State and Territory, as is enjoyed by white citizens thereof to inherit, purchase, lease, sell, hold, and convey real and personal property."

[Petitioners filed a complaint in federal court alleging that the respondents had refused to sell them a home in the Paddock Woods community of St. Louis County for the sole reason that petitioner Jones is a Negro. Petitioners sought injunctive and other relief. The District Court dismissed and the Court of Appeals affirmed, concluding that Sec. 1982 applies only to state action and does not reach private refusals to sell.]

At the outset, it is important to make clear precisely what this case does *not* involve. Whatever else it may be, 42 U.S.C. Sec. 1982 is not a comprehensive open housing law. In sharp contrast to the Fair Housing Title (Title VIII) of the Civil Rights Act of 1968, . . . 82 Stat. 73, the statute in this case deals only with racial discrimination and does not address itself to discrimination on grounds of religion or national origin. It does not deal specifically with discrimination in the provision of services or facilities in connection with the sale or rental of a dwelling. . . . It does not empower a federal administrative agency to assist aggrieved parties. It makes no provision for intervention by the Attorney General. And, although it can be enforced by injunction, it contains no provision expressly authorizing a federal court to order the payment of damages. . . .

On its face . . . Sec. 1982 appears to prohibit *all* discrimination against Negroes in the sale or rental of property—discrimination by private owners as well as discrimination by public authorities. Indeed, even the respondents seem to concede that, if Sec. 1982 "means what it says"—to use the words of the respondents' brief—then it must encompass every racially motivated refusal to sell or rent and cannot be confined to officially sanctioned segregation in housing. Stressing what they consider to be the revolutionary implications of so literal a reading of Sec. 1982, the respondents argue that Congress cannot possibly have intended any such result. Our examination of the relevant history, however, persuades us that Congress meant exactly what it said. [The opinion here treats the history of the 1866 Act and concludes that private discrimination was within the reach of Congress' purpose in enacting the law.]

The remaining question is whether Congress has power under the Constitution to do what Sec. 1982 purports to do: to prohibit all racial discrimination, private and public in the sale and rental of property. Our starting point is the Thirteenth Amendment, for it was pursuant to that constitutional provision that Congress originally enacted what is now Sec. 1982. . . .

As its text reveals, the Thirteenth Amendment "is not a mere prohibition of State laws establishing or upholding slavery, but an absolute declaration that slavery or involuntary servitude shall not exist in any part of the United States." . . . It has never been doubted, therefore, "that the power vested in Congress to enforce the article by appropriate legislation," *ibid.,* includes the power to enact laws "direct and primary, operating upon the acts of individuals, whether sanctioned by State legislation or not.". . .

Thus, the fact that Sec. 1982 operates upon the unofficial acts of private individuals, whether or not sanctioned by state law, presents no constitutional problem. If Congress has power under the Thirteenth Amendment to eradicate conditions that prevent Negroes from buying and renting property because of their race or color, then no federal statute calculated to achieve that objective can be thought to exceed the constitutional power of Congress simply because it reaches beyond state action to regulate the conduct of private individuals. The constitutional question in this case, therefore, comes to this: Does the authority of Congress to enforce the Thirteenth Amendment "by appropriate legislation" include the power to eliminate all racial barriers to the acquisition of real and personal property? We think the answer to that question is plainly yes. . . .

Reversed.

Mr. Justice Douglas, concurring. . . .

Mr. Justice Harlan, whom Mr. Justice White joins, dissenting. . . .

For reasons which follow, I believe that the Court's construction of Sec. 1982 as applying to purely private action is almost surely wrong, and at the least is open to serious doubt. . . .

Another portion of the Civil Rights Act of 1866, now Title 42 U.S.C. Section 1981, provides in pertinent part that all persons within the jurisdiction of the United States "shall have the same right in every State and Territory to make and enforce contracts . . . as is enjoyed by white citizens." In *Runyon* v. *McCrary,* 44 L.W. 5034 (1976), the Court held that Section 1981 prohibits private, commercially operated, nonsectarian schools from denying admission to black applicants solely on the basis of race. Further, citing

Jones v. *Alfred Mayer*, the majority held that such application of the statute was a constitutional exercise of Congress' power to enforce the Thirteenth Amendment. Justice Stewart, for the majority, indicated that no opinion was being expressed on the application of Section 1981 to the question of the right of a private social organization to limit its membership on racial or any other grounds. Nor was any question presented of "the right of a private school to limit its student body to boys, to girls, or to adherents of a particular religious faith, since 42 U.S.C. Section 1981 is in no way addressed to such categories of selectivity."

On the same day that *Runyon* was decided, the Court held that Section 1981 prohibits racial discrimination in private employment against whites as well as nonwhites. The case was *McDonald* v. *Santa Fe Trail Company*, 44 L.W. 5067 (1976), and it arose out of the Company's discharge of certain white employees for allegedly misappropriating company property, at the same time that a similarly charged black employee was not dismissed. The Court held that an action could be maintained by the white employees under both Title VII of the Civil Rights Act of 1964 and 42 U.S.C. Section 1981.

On April 11, 1968, Congress adopted the Civil Rights Act of 1968, 82 Stat. 73, Title VIII of which is a "Fair Housing" provision. Section 804 is the substantive section of the Title, and it makes unlawful: (a) the refusal to sell or rent a dwelling to any person because of race, color, religion, or national origin; (b) discrimination in terms, conditions, or privileges of sale or rental of a dwelling because of race, color, religion, or national origin; (c) printing or publishing of any notice or advertisement with respect to the sale or rental of a dwelling that indicates any preference or limitation based on race, color, religion, or national origin; (d) representation to any person because of race, color, religion, or national origin that any dwelling is not available for inspection, sale, or rental when such dwelling is in fact so available; and (e) the inducement, for profit, of any person to sell or rent by representation regarding the entry into the neighborhood of a person of a particular race, color, religion, or national origin.

In general, enforcement of Title VIII is by negotiation or, if necessary, by civil suit filed by the Secretary of Housing and Urban Development in United States District Court. Where a pattern or practice of resistance to the provisions of Title VIII appears, the Attorney General may bring a civil action.

The two criminal and three civil sections discussed represent the most important statutory provisions in the federal code applicable to the general field of civil rights down to the year 1957. Many complaints were voiced that additional federal remedies were needed, particularly in the area of voting. It was pointed out that the federal government could initiate action only in the criminal sections. The civil provisions could be brought to bear only upon the initiative of private persons, many of whom could not bear the expense involved in long and complicated litigation. It was urged that at the very least a new law be adopted to permit the United States government to file an action to obtain appropriate remedies against voting abridgments. The first civil rights legislation to be passed since 1875 was enacted in 1957 in response to these demands. This was the Civil Rights Act of 1957 (71 Stat. 634). Further safeguards to voting rights were added in the Civil Rights Act of 1960, the Civil Rights Act of 1964, and culminating in the broad provisions of the Voting Rights Act of 1965. (The provisions of these acts dealing with voting are treated separately in Chapter 8, "Voting and Apportionment." The provisions of the Civil Rights Act of 1964 which apply to rights other than voting are discussed in Chapter 7, "Equal Protection of the Law.")

To summarize briefly the legislative powers of the national government to protect civil rights, the Congress can act to protect only those rights which derive in some fashion from the United States Constitution, or federal laws, or treaties adopted by the United States. The catalog of these federal rights is not static, and rights may be modified or expanded or new rights created by constitutional amendment, by legislation, or by entering into new treaty arrangements. And Congress may, by appropriate legislation, provide remedies for interference with any of these federal rights. The constitutional basis for congressional activity may vary with either the right involved or the source of the interference, however, and some care must be exercised in the remedies provided in order to deal precisely with a given deprivation. Potential sources of interference are state officers, private persons, and federal officers. The Fourteenth Amendment authorizes legislation protecting against deprivations of rights committed by the first group but not the others. Separate support must be found in the Constitution for remedies directed solely toward the latter sources. The broad delegated powers in Article I of the Constitution may be applied to any persons, official or private, and Congress has in these grants a rich source of authority to create new rights or provide stronger protections for older rights. Primarily grounded in the commerce power, the Civil Rights Act of 1964 for the first time set up a federal right not to be discriminated against on the basis of race or color in the enjoyment of various kinds of recreational and restaurant accommodations. Since the Fourteenth Amendment had already been construed to bar such discrimination on the part of state officials, the law is primarily directed toward private interference, but the "supremacy" clause dictates that state agencies as well as private persons are bound by the congressional enactments if the provisions of the laws apply to both. As to interference occasioned by federal administrators, Congress has ample power to provide remedies since it creates the positions and may clearly define the limits under which federal agencies may exercise their powers. As an illustration, the Post Office Department has on occasion, as one of several censorship devices, used a mail-block sanction (prohibiting the delivery of all mail to offending sources of allegedly obscene publications). Under a law passed by Congress in 1960, the mail-block sanction may not be used without an order from a federal court.

Finally, the treaty power may be employed to create new federal rights. The United States can constitutionally enter into a treaty agreement with Japan, for example, setting up reciprocal rights in the nationals of each country to enter lawful business pursuits while a legal resident of the other country. And this right of the resident Japanese alien in the United States could then be protected by Congress in giving effect to the terms of the treaty.

All nonfederal rights, however, stem from state laws and constitutions, and it is up to the states to provide remedies for interference with these rights. To repeat an earlier statement, the crucial problem in defining congressional powers to safeguard rights is the careful distinction between federal rights and state rights.

EXECUTIVE PROTECTION OF CIVIL RIGHTS

The general powers available to the federal judicial and legislative branches to protect civil rights have been discussed. It should not be overlooked, however, that the President of the United States has certain areas, albeit limited, in which he, too, can serve as a protector of rights.

In the first place, the President and Vice-President are the only elected federal officials who have as their constituency the whole of the nation. Senators and Representatives in Congress represent states or districts. In a real sense, then, the President is our only official national spokesman. In such position he can speak both for and to the American public. In periods of tension or crisis where there are potential dangers to the enjoyment of rights, the President can, by public statements and actions, serve as the conscience of the nation. As Franklin D. Roosevelt wrote shortly after his first election [quoted in Richard P. Longaker, *The Presidency and Individual Liberties* (Ithaca: Cornell University Press, 1961), p. 31]:

The Presidency is not merely an administrative office. That is the least of it. . . . It is preeminently a place of moral leadership. All of our great Presidents were leaders of thought at times when certain historic ideas in the life of the nation had to be clarified. . . . That is what the office is . . . a superb opportunity for re-applying, applying in new conditions, the simple rules of human conduct to which we always go back.

As chief legislator, the President has considerable influence from time to time on the programs which Congress will consider. Of course legislative suggestions, no matter from what source, must obtain approval of the Congress, but the President, by a variety of devices, can bring to bear appreciable pressures to gain support for his proposals. The Civil Rights Act of 1964 and the Voting Rights Act of 1965 are cases in point.

As chief administrator, the President has very substantial powers to protect the individual against federal abridgment of rights. In the areas of loyalty checks on federal employees, passport interference, instigation of deportation proceedings against aliens—in short, the entire range of federal administrative activity—the direction of activity and the energy with which it proceeds are largely under the control of the President. Of course the agencies and administrators must work within the statutory authority granted by Congress and within the congressional allocations of money. But despite these important boundaries, there is a vast area of discretion remaining to the President to determine how the congressional mandate will be carried out. Even taking into account the limitations of control over a giant bureaucracy, a President sensitive to the rights of the individual can exercise surveillance over the policies and procedures of the administrative agencies to ensure that at least in broad outline the executive branch will not become a source of unwarranted interference with individual liberty. His appointive and removal powers can be substantial weapons in guaranteeing performance in accordance with his policies. Thus in 1934 President Roosevelt appointed Huntington Cairns as special legal adviser to the Treasury Department. In administering the law barring importation of obscene literature, the Customs Bureau appeared to be following too restrictive an approach to decisions on exclusion of books and art from abroad. Mr. Cairns spent considerable time investigating the standards employed by customs inspectors, and his subsequent recommendations and influence were clearly in the direction of lessening censorship. [See Zechariah Chafee, *Government and Mass Communications* (Chicago: University of Chicago Press, 1947), pp. 254–275.]

In view of the limited corrective capacity of the judicial branch, such policies of restraint by the executive are of particular note in periods of pressure for conformity. During wartime, for example, overzealous United States attorneys might well be able to obain indictments and even convictions under the sedition laws against persons who merely express public discontent with the handling of military operations. Firm statements of presidential policy, normally through the Attorney General, exhorting restraint in the enforcement of such laws can have a beneficial effect in stemming the excesses of overenthusiastic prosecutors. On Attorney General Francis Biddle's insistence, for example, sedition cases during World War II were given very close scrutiny, in order to avoid the shotgun prosecutions which were all too common during World War I. In a directive to all United States Attorneys, he stated:[1]

This Department will oppose any curtailment of those rights beyond that absolutely necessary to the efficient conduct of the military and the war effort of the United States. Indeed, a further disregard for civil rights can only be viewed as distinctly injurious to national morale and subversive of the democratic ideals which the nation is seeking to defend.

Similarly, it appears that the Truman Administration followed a conscious policy of restraint in its treatment of conscientious objectors who refused to register, only rarely invoking the criminal process.

In yet a different direction the President has substantial control over such matters as personnel policies and other internal rules and regulations for the conduct of federal agencies. An illustration of the way this control can be employed to protect rights is the influence of the President in ending segregation in the armed forces. President Franklin Roosevelt initiated the moves in this direction, followed by increased pressures by Presidents Truman and Eisenhower. Desegregation was accomplished in the military in Korea and, by 1955, in the entire armed forces. Coupled with these moves was the decision to end segregation in schools on military posts and in federal facilities generally.

By executive order, Presidents Truman, Eisenhower, and Kennedy have pushed out even further to press for nondiscrimination in employment. In awarding government contracts the United States has the power to impose various conditions on the contracting parties. In 1941 President Roosevelt issued an executive order establishing a Committee on Fair Employment Practices and requiring that all federal defense contracts contain a stipulation obligating the contractor "not to discriminate against any worker because of race, creed, color, or national origin."[2] Under various titles and with varying effectiveness a committee for this purpose has been continued. Whatever the actual enforcement policy of these committees might be, it is clear that such a power of "government by contract" has enormous potential impact.

---

[1] Department of Justice Circular 3356, May 21, 1940, quoted in Richard P. Longaker, *The Presidency and Individual Liberties* (Ithaca: Cornell University Press, 1961), p. 134.
[2] See Richard P. Longaker, *op. cit.,* pp. 120–125, for an account of the handling of the nondiscrimination clause under the different administrations.

Since the President is also commander-in-chief of the national military arm, there is at least the possibility that under appropriate conditions he has ultimately at his disposal the armed might of the nation to guarantee the effectuation of national law and policy. Laying aside the question of presidential power to deploy troops outside the continental United States, there are important constitutional questions involved in the President's use of military force in the domestic United States.

One approach to the question of presidential power to use the military is to require that it be done within the limits of statutory authorization. Thus the President would be able to call out the military forces for domestic use only in situations spelled out by Congress. At least some adherence to this viewpoint is implicit in the fact that various authorizing statutes of this kind have been adopted by Congress almost from the beginning of the nation. As early as 1792, Congress authorized the President to call out the militia "whenever the laws of the United States shall be opposed or the execution thereof obstructed, in any state by combinations too powerful to be suppressed by the ordinary course of judicial proceedings or by the power vested in the marshals." The famous Whisky Rebellion was quenched under this provision in 1794.

The present version of this section is Section 332 of Title 10 of the United States Code:

Whenever the President considers that unlawful obstructions, combinations, or assemblages, or rebellion against the authority of the United States, make it impracticable to enforce the laws of the United States in any State or Territory by the ordinary course of judicial proceedings, he may call into Federal service such of the militia of any State, and use such of the armed forces, as he considers necessary to enforce those laws or to suppress the rebellion.

It was essentially in accordance with the authority given by this section that President Eisenhower in 1957 issued Executive Order No. 10730, ordering the Secretary of Defense to take appropriate steps to maintain order in the integration crisis in Little Rock, Arkansas. Within hours, Central High School in that city was under guard by the paratroopers of the 101st Airborne Division.

Probably the best answer to the question of presidential power to employ force inside the United States is given (although in a different context) by Professor Corwin, with his fine sense of the historical development of the office of the President. [See E. S. Corwin, *The President, Office and Powers,* 4th ed. (New York: New York University Press, 1957), p. 157.] He states that just as nature abhors a vacuum, so does a period of emergency. Something will be done in a crisis which demands action. If Congress has legislated, then probably the President will act within that authorization. If it has not, the President may act anyhow in preserving the "peace of the United States," to use the phrase of Justice Miller in *In re Neagle,* 135 U.S. 1 (1890). Casuistic arguments about presidential power to uphold the laws, the federal courts, and the Constitution of the United States will find little sympathy either in public opinion or, in all probability, in the federal courts.

Presidential powers to promote or protect civil rights are admittedly more elusive of understanding than are those of Congress. Further, the "visibility" with which the President or the executive agencies operate is much lower than is the case with Congress. When Congress passes, or fails to pass, important civil rights bills, a great deal of publicity and comment may be expected to follow. But executive decisions, particularly agency policy decisions, are less visible to the public, and it is considerably more difficult to arrive at a clear picture of just what the President and his subordinates in the executive branch are doing in the civil rights area at any given time. The mere fact that the picture relative to executive powers is cloudy, however, should not lead the observer to conclude that they are therefore minimal. It is hoped that the brief discussion and illustrations given will indicate sufficiently that there are tremendous weapons available to the President both for internal policing of federal practices and procedures and for external pressures on private and state action inimical to individual freedom.

JUDICIALLY CREATED RIGHTS

The general tools by which courts may protect rights created by statute or specifically described by constitutions have been discussed earlier. But the special role of the United States Supreme Court in the creation of new rights deserves separate attention. The phrases making up the various Articles of the Bill of Rights are not nearly so precise as is the statement in Article I, Section 3, which provides that the "Senate of the United States shall be composed of two Senators from each State." The construction given by the Court to such phrases as "freedom of speech," or "unreasonable searches and seizures," or "due process of law" may change markedly as the composition of the Court and the state of the society change. It is a "living Constitution" which we have, and, as every schoolboy knows, the opportunity is present for the Court to expand old rights and even to create new ones. The relatively clear statement in the Sixth Amendment that an accused shall have the right "to have the Assistance of Counsel for his defence" has undergone very great expansion since 1791. At the time of its ratification, this right probably was intended to extend no further than a guarantee that one accused of crime could employ an attorney of his choosing to aid in his defense. As of now, this right has been extended to guarantee that an indigent charged with any crime for which he might receive a jail sentence is entitled to a lawyer appointed by the government at government expense.

Broad phrases such as "due process of law" and "equal protection of the laws" offer the opportunity for the elevation to constitutional status of rights which are not even casually adverted to in the language of the Constitution. Among the list of "new rights" which the Court has fashioned in recent decades are: the right not to be discriminated against by governments on account of race; the right to equal apportionment of seats, based on population, in state legislatures; a relatively broad right against governmental discrimination based on sex; a right of prisoners to at least a limited form of legal assistance in preparing writs; a right to privacy; and others.

To illustrate the innovative potential which the Court has, and to point up the need for analytical flexibility in examining the topics to follow, the development of one of these rights—the Constitutional right to privacy—will be followed in some detail. When the Constitution and the Bill of Rights were ratified, neither statutes nor common-law rules established a right of privacy as such. And certainly there was no Constitutional provision which clearly provided a vehicle for its inclusion. The common law with regard to trespass, assault, slander and libel, and even nuisance (as applied to offensive noises and odors, for example) could be said to have tangential reference to privacy, but this would offer a piecemeal approach rather than an argument based on a full-fledged right of privacy.

The development of the law of privacy can be said to have originated with a law review article by Samuel D. Warren and Louis D. Brandeis, "The Right of Privacy," published in 1890 in the *Harvard Law Review* (4 *Harv. L. Rev.* 193). Out of a few fragments of the common law, the authors invented a brand new tort, the invasion of privacy. Dean Roscoe Pound reportedly said that the article did nothing less than add a chapter to the law. In the years following the publication of the article, a law of privacy gradually developed by statute and by common-law decisions in state courts. [For an excellent history of these developments, see Morris L. Ernst and Alan U. Schwartz, *Privacy: The Right to Be Let Alone* (New York: Macmillan, 1962).] But it was not until 1965 that the Supreme Court squarely held that the Constitution contained at least a limited right to privacy.

In *Griswold* v. *Connecticut,* 381 U.S. 479 (1965), a majority of the Court indicated that the Constitution creates "zones of privacy" which are beyond the scope of any legitimate search, and held invalid the Connecticut law barring the use of any drug or instrument for contraceptive purposes. Justice Douglas, for the majority, said: "Would we allow the police to search the sacred precincts of martial bedrooms for telltale signs of the use of contraceptives? The very idea is repulsive to the notions of privacy surrounding the marriage relationship." The constitutional basis for this right of privacy was seemingly found in the Fourth Amendment. The Justice stated: "We recently referred in *Mapp* v. *Ohio* . . . to the Fourth Amendment as creating a 'right to privacy, no less important than any other right carefully and particularly reserved to the people.' See Beaney, The Constitutional Right to Privacy, 1962 *Sup. Ct. Rev.* 212; Griswold, The Right to be Let Alone, 55 *Nw. U. L. Rev.* 216 (1960)."

Justice Goldberg, joined by the Chief Justice and Justice Brennan, concurred, but he referred to a different source for the "right of marital privacy." He stated that the Ninth Amendment was designed to protect additional fundamental rights not enumerated in the first eight amendments, and that a right of marital privacy was so "basic and fundamental and so deep-rooted in our society" that it could not be abridged without violating the Ninth Amendment. The ramifications of opening up broad construction of the Ninth Amendment to judicial review of state and federal legislation were pointedly criticized by dissenting Justices Black and Stewart.

A further extension of the "right to privacy" argument was successfully employed in the controversial abortion cases in 1973, in which the Court held unconstitutional the Texas and Georgia statutes which severely restricted the right of pregnant women to have legal abortions. The Texas case was *Roe* v. *Wade* and is illustrative of the reasoning in both cases.

ROE *v.* WADE
410 U.S. 113 (1973)

[A pregnant single woman (Roe) brought a class action challenging the constitutionality of the Texas criminal abortion laws, which prohibit procuring or attempting an abortion except on medical advice for the purpose of saving the mother's life. A licensed physician (Hallford), who had two state abortion prosecutions pending against him, was permitted to intervene in the class action. A separate action was filed by a married, childless couple, who alleged that if the wife became pregnant at some future date, they would wish to have an abortion. A three-judge District Court held that Roe and Hallford had standing to sue, but that the married, childless couple did not. As to the statutes, the court held them unconstitutionally vague and overbroad and issued a declaratory judgment so holding. In the Supreme Court the majority agreed that Roe had standing to sue. It was contended that Roe's claim was moot because her pregnancy had been terminated. The majority opinion stated: "If that termination makes a case moot, pregnancy litigation seldom will survive much beyond the trial state, and appellate review will be effectively denied. . . . Pregnancy provides a classic justification for a conclusion of nonmootness."]

Mr. Justice Blackmun delivered the opinion of the Court. . . .

The principal thrust of appellant's attack on the Texas statutes is that they improperly invade a right, said to be possessed by the pregnant woman, to choose to terminate her pregnancy. Appellant would discover this right in the concept of personal "liberty" embodied in the Fourteenth Amendment's Due Process Clause; or in personal, marital, familial, and sexual privacy said to be protected by the Bill of Rights or its penumbras, see *Griswold* v. *Connecticut*, . . . ; or among those rights reserved to the people by the Ninth Amendment. . . .

It is perhaps not generally appreciated that the restrictive criminal abortion laws in effect in a majority of States today are of relatively recent vintage. Those laws, generally proscribing abortion or its attempt at any time during pregnancy except when necessary to preserve the pregnant woman's life, are not of ancient or even of common law origin. Instead, they derive from statutory changes effected, for the most part, in the latter half of the 19th century. . . .

It is undisputed that at the common law, abortion performed *before* "quickening"—the first recognizable movement of the fetus in utero, appearing usually from the 16th to the 18th week of pregnancy—was not an indictable offense. . . .

Whether abortion of a *quick* fetus was a felony at common law, or even a lesser crime, is still disputed. Bracton, writing early in the 13th century, thought it homicide. But the later and predominant view, following the great common law scholars, has been that it was at most a lesser offense. . . .

England's first criminal abortion statute . . .came in 1803. It made abortion of a quick fetus, §1, a capital crime, but in §2 it provided lesser penalties for the felony of abortion before quickening, and thus preserved the quickening distinction. . . .

Three reasons have been advanced to explain historically the enactment of criminal abortion laws in the 19th century and to justify their continued existence.

It has been argued occasionally that these laws were the product of a Victorian social concern to discourage illicit sexual conduct. . . . The appellants and amici contend . . . that this is not a proper state purpose at all and suggest that, if it were, the Texas statutes are overbroad in protecting it since the law fails to distinguish between married and unwed mothers.

A second reason is concerned with abortion as a medical procedure. When most criminal abortion laws were first enacted, the procedure was a hazardous one for the woman. This was particularly true prior to the development of antisepsis. . . . Thus it has been argued that a State's real concern in enacting a criminal abortion law was to protect the pregnant woman, that is, to restrain her from submitting to a procedure that placed her life in serious jeopardy.

Modern medical techniques have altered this situation. Appellants and various amici refer to medical data indicating that abortion in early pregnancy, that is, prior to the end of first trimester, although not without its risk, is now relatively safe. . . .

The third reason is the State's interest—some phrase it in terms of duty—in protecting prenatal life. Some of the argument for this justification rests on the theory that a new human life is present from the moment of conception. The State's interest and general obligation to protect life then extends, it is argued, to prenatal life. Only when the life of the pregnant mother herself is at stake, balanced against the life she carries within her, should the interest of the embryo or fetus not prevail. . . .

Parties challenging state abortion laws have sharply disputed in some courts the contention that a purpose of these laws, when enacted, was to protect prenatal life. Pointing to the absence of legislative history to support the contention, they claim that most state laws were designed solely to protect the woman. . . . They claim that adoption of the "quickening" distinction through received common law and state statutes tacitly recognizes the greater health hazards inherent in late abortion and impliedly repudiates the theory that life begins at conception.

It is with these interests, and the weight to be attached to them, that this case is concerned.

The Constitution does not explicitly mention any right of privacy. In a line of decisions, however, going back perhaps as far as . . . [1891], the Court has recognized that a right of personal privacy, or a guarantee of certain areas or zones of privacy, does exist under the Constitution. In varying contexts the Court or individual Justices have indeed found at least the roots of that right in the First Amendment . . . ; in the Fourth and Fifth Amendments . . . ; in the penumbras of the Bill of Rights . . . ; in the Ninth Amendment . . . ; or in the concept of liberty guaranteed by the first section of the Fourteenth Amendment. . . . These decisions make it clear that only personal rights that can be deemed "fundamental" or "implicit in the concept of ordered liberty" . . . are included in this guarantee of personal privacy. They also make it clear that the right has some extension to activities relating to marriage . . . , procreation, . . . family relationships . . . , and child rearing and education. . . .

This right of privacy, whether it be founded in the Fourteenth Amendment's concept of personal liberty and restrictions upon state action, as we feel it is, or as the District Court determined, in the Ninth Amendment's reservation of rights to the people, is broad enough to encompass a woman's decision whether or not to terminate her pregnancy. The detriment that the State would impose upon the pregnant woman by denying this choice is apparent. Specific and direct harm medically diagnosable even in early pregnancy may be involved. Maternity, or additional offspring, may force upon the woman a distressful life and future. Psychological harm may be imminent. Mental and physical health may be taxed by child care. There is also the distress, for all concerned, associated with the unwanted child, and there is the problem of bringing a child into a family already unable, psychologically and otherwise, to care for it. In other cases, as in this one, the additional difficulties and continuing stigma of unwed motherhood may be involved. All these are factors the woman and her responsible physician necessarily will consider in consultation.

On the basis of elements such as these, appellants and some amici argue that the woman's right is absolute and that she is entitled to terminate her pregnancy at whatever time, in whatever way, and for whatever reason she alone chooses.

With this we do not agree.... The Court's decisions recognizing a right of privacy also acknowledge that some state regulation in areas protected by that right is appropriate. As noted above, a state may properly assert important interests in safeguarding health, in maintaining medical standards, and in protecting potential life.... The privacy right involved, therefore, cannot be said to be absolute....

We therefore conclude that the right of personal privacy includes the abortion decision, but that this right is not unqualified and must be considered against important state interests in regulation....

With respect to the State's important and legitimate interest in the health of the mother, the "compelling" point, in the light of present medical knowledge, is at approximately the end of the first trimester. This is so because of the now established medical fact ... that until the end of the first trimester mortality in abortion is less than mortality in normal childbirth. It follows that, from and after this point, a State may regulate the abortion procedure to the extent that the regulation reasonably relates to the preservation and protection of maternal health. Examples of permissible state regulation in this area are requirements as to the qualifications of the person who is to perform the abortion; as to the licensure of that person; as to the facility in which the procedure is to be performed, that is, whether it must be a hospital or may be a clinic or some other place of less-than-hospital status; as to the licensing of the facility; and the like....

With respect to the State's important and legitimate interest in potential life, the "compelling" point is at viability. This is so because the fetus then presumably has the capability of meaningful life outside the mother's womb. State regulation protective of fetal life after viability thus has both logical and biological justifications. If the State is interested in protecting fetal life after viability, it may go so far as to proscribe abortion during that period except when it is necessary to preserve the life or health of the mother....

To summarize and to repeat:

1. A state criminal abortion statute of the current Texas type, that excepts from criminality only a *life saving* procedure on behalf of the mother, without regard to pregnancy stage and without recognition of the other interests involved, is violative of the Due Process Clause of the Fourteenth Amendment.

(a) For the stage prior to approximately the end of the first trimester, the abortion decision and its effectuation must be left to the medical judgment of the pregnant woman's attending physician.

(b) For the stage subsequent to approximately the end of the first trimester, the State, in promoting its interest in the health of the mother, may, if it chooses, regulate the abortion procedure in ways that are reasonably related to maternal health.

(c) For the stage subsequent to viability the State, in promoting its interest in the potentiality of human life, may, if it chooses, regulate, and even proscribe, abortion except where it is necessary, in appropriate medical judgment, for the preservation of the life or health of the mother.

2. The State may define the term "physician," as it has been employed in ... this opinion, to mean only a physician currently licensed by the State, and may proscribe any abortion by a person who is not a physician as so defined....

Mr. Chief Justice Burger, concurring....

Mr. Justice Douglas, concurring....

Mr. Justice Stewart, concurring....

Mr. Justice White, with whom Mr. Justice Rehnquist joins, dissenting....

With all due respect, I dissent. I find nothing in the language or history of the Constitution to support the Court's judgment. The Court simply fashions and announces a new constitutional right for pregnant mothers and, with scarcely any reason or authority for its action, invests that right with sufficient substance to override most existing state abortion statutes. The upshot is that the people and the legislatures of the 50 States are constitutionally disentitled to weigh the relative importance of the continued existence and development of the fetus on the one hand against a spectrum of possible impacts on the mother on the other hand. As an exercise of raw judicial power, the Court perhaps has authority to do what it does today; but in my view its judgment is an improvident and extravagant exercise of the power of judicial review which the Constitution extends to this Court.

The Court apparently values the convenience of the pregnant mother more than the continued existence and development of the life or potential life which she carries. Whether or not I might agree with that marshalling of values, I can in no event join the Court's judgment because I find no constitutional warrant for imposing such an order of priorities on the people and legislatures of the States. . . .

Mr. Justice Rehnquist, dissenting. . . .

In *Planned Parenthood of Central Missouri* v. *Danforth*, 44 L.W. 5197 (1976), the Court held unconstitutional a section of Missouri's abortion law which required the husband's consent before permitting abortion and a section which required one parent's consent as a condition for an unmarried minor's abortion. As to the spouse's consent, the opinion stated that the requirement did not comport with the standards enunciated in *Roe* v. *Wade,* since the state cannot "delegate to a spouse a veto power which the state itself is absolutely and totally prohibited from exercising during the first trimester of pregnancy." On the requirement of parental consent, the opinion stated, "Just as with the requirement of consent from the spouse, so here, the State does not have the constitutional authority to give a third party an absolute, and possibly arbitrary, veto over the decision of the physician and his patient to terminate the patient's pregnancy, regardless of the reason for withholding the consent." The opinion stated further that any independent interest the parent may have in the termination of the minor daughter's pregnancy "is no more weighty than the right of privacy of the competent minor mature enough to have become pregnant."

The Court did uphold, however, the provision of the Missouri law which required that the woman submitting to abortion must consent in writing to the procedure and certify that "her consent is informed and freely given and is not the result of coercion."

It should not be assumed, of course, that the right of privacy is absolute. The claim may, at times, run into direct conflict with the First Amendment claim of newspapers of a right to inform the public. Whether one is a private citizen or a public figure or a public official, he or she may have said things or conducted himself in ways which he would not like to see upon the printed page. The legal issues raised by these situations largely arise in libel actions, which will be treated more fully later. (See the section "Libel" in Chapter 6.) One recent case involving the conflict between privacy and freedom of the press, however, is worthy of note at this point. *Cox Broadcasting Corporation* v. *Cohn,* 420 U.S. 469 (1975), involved the question of the liability of a television newsman who had broadcast the identity of a rape victim. A Georgia statute made it a misdemeanor to publish or broadcast the name of any rape victim. The reporter attended the trial of the persons charged with the rape and murder of a seventeen-year-old girl and learned the name of the girl from the indictments, which were public records. Later that day, he broadcast a news report of the proceedings, during which he named the victim of the crime. The father of the victim sued for money damages. The trial court held that the Georgia statute, by implication, gave a civil remedy for the invasion of privacy, and granted summary judgment over the defendant's claim of First Amendment privilege. The Georgia Supreme Court reversed and remanded for trial on common law grounds of "right of privacy or for the tort of public disclosure" which would bar summary judgment by the trial court. Upon motion for rehearing, the Court went further and held (1) that the statute represented an authoritative state policy that the name of a rape victim was not a matter of public concern, and (2) that the statute was a legitimate limitation on the First Amendment's right of expression. On appeal the United States Supreme Court reversed. Justice White, for the majority, stated that public records are of interest to those concerned with the administration of government, "and a public benefit is performed by the reporting of the true contents of the records by the media." He stated further that "the States may not impose sanctions for the publication of truthful information contained in official court records open to public inspection."

[For further treatment of the right to privacy, see: Francis X. Beytagh, "Privacy and a Free Press: A Contemporary Conflict in Values," 20 *N. Y. L. Forum* 453 (1975); Edward J. Blaustein, "The First Amendment and Privacy: The Supreme Court Justice and the Philosopher," 28 *Rutgers L. R.* 41 (1974); R. H. Clark, "Constitutional Sources of the Penumbral Right to Privacy," 19 *Villanova L. Rev.* 833 (1974).]

The right to privacy is but one of the emerging rights which the Court has elevated to constitutional status. In *Reed* v. *Reed,* 404 U.S. 71 (1971), the Court for the first time held void as a denial of equal protection a state law discriminating against women. A mandatory provision of the Idaho probate code gave preference to men over women when persons of the same entitlement class applied for appointment as administrator of a decedent's estate. The Court held that to give such preference, without a rational basis for the distinction, was to make "the very kind of arbitrary legislative choice forbidden by the Equal Protection Clause." Subsequent cases have invalidated a number of other laws, both federal and state, which classified on the basis of sex, and thus it may be said that at least a limited right not to be subjected to governmental discrimination based on sex has developed. (For a more extensive discussion, see the section "Sex Discrimination" in Chapter 7.)

In *O'Connor* v. *Donaldson,* 422 U.S. 563 (1975), the Court held that a state violates the due process clause when it confines, without treatment, a nondangerous mental patient who is capable of surviving safely in freedom by himself or with the help of willing and responsible family members or friends. Donaldson had been committed to a Florida State Hospital for nearly fifteen years, and his repeated requests for release had been rejected by the superintendent. The evidence showed that Donaldson was not dangerous, and, if mentally ill, had not received treatment. The Court affirmed the trial court's finding that upon these facts, O'Connor, the superintendent, had violated Donaldson's right to freedom. (The action arose as a suit for money damages, however, and the Court remanded for a consideration of O'Connor's liability under recent immunity decisions.) The holding of the Court can be restated, it would seem, to create a right to treatment for the nondangerous mental patient committed to a state mental hospital.

The few illustrations noted above show that the wide-ranging frontiers of civil rights law continue to move and that the Supreme Court has a major policy-making role in the redefinition of old rights and the creation of new ones. [For a collection of articles on some of the newer trends, see "New Developments in Traditional Civil Liberties," *Policy Studies Journal* (Winter, 1975), pp. 103–146.]

CHAPTER 4

The Rights of the Accused

One of the hardest tasks for the nonlawyer is the full appreciation of the value of procedural regularity. A commonly heard criticism of appellate courts is that they reverse criminal convictions "because of some technicality." Procedural requirements are sometimes viewed impatiently as mere obstructions to the efficient administration of criminal justice. What is being over-looked in these attacks on procedural "technicalities" is the realization that over the long pull of centuries these requirements have served as the grad-ually accumulating building blocks to form our most effective barrier against arbitrary governmental deprivation of life and liberty. As Justice Frankfurter succinctly stated it, "The history of liberty has largely been the history of observance of procedural safeguards." [*McNabb* v. *United States,* 318 U.S. 332, 347 (1943).]

The primary constitutionally guaranteed procedures in federal prosecu-tions are fairly explicitly stated in Article I, Section 9, and in the Bill of Rights. But the Fifth Amendment also contains the broad guarantee that no one can be deprived of life or liberty "without due process of law." The primary constitutionally guaranteed procedures in state prosecutions are contained in the due process and equal protection clauses of the Fourteenth Amendment. The Court has time and time again been faced with the task of giving content to the nebulous phrase "due process of law" in testing the validity of criminal procedures employed by the state or the federal government. In *Davidson* v. *New Orleans,* 96 U.S. 97, 104 (1877) Justice Miller said that if it were possible to define with precision the exact require-ments of due process, "no more useful construction could be furnished to any part of the fundamental law." Since the courts of the nation have uni-formly agreed that no such definition is possible, they have followed a course of defining the phrase, to quote Justice Miller again, "by the gradual process of judicial inclusion and exclusion, as the cases presented for decision shall require." In recognition of this practice, the approach here is to break up the criminal process into the more or less successive stages through which an accused may travel and examine the constitutional requirements at each stage. It will be seen that despite the absence of a precise definition of procedural due process, there is in the concept a general requirement that the procedures used at each stage must meet the test of "fundamental fairness."

In *Twining* v. *New Jersey,* 211 U.S. 78 (1908), the United States Supreme Court, through Justice Moody, made a tentative effort to point the way in approaching due process questions:

The essential elements of due process of law ... are singularly few, though of wide application and deep significance.... Due process requires that the court which assumes to determine the rights of parties shall have jurisdiction ... and that there shall be notice and opportunity for hearing given the parties. ... Subject to these two fundamental conditions, which seem to be universally prescribed in all systems of law established by civilized countries, this court has, up to this time, sustained all state laws, statutory or judicially declared, regulating procedure, evidence, and methods of trial, and held them to be consistent with due process of law.

We have in this statement what might be called the "hard core of due process"—jurisdiction, notice, and hearing. Taking these essential elements, along with the concept of fundamental fairness, the Court has over the years gradually elaborated the rules and principles which are followed today. At the same time, it must be noted that decisions expressing new requirements are often merely the bases for still further developments. Due process is by no means a static concept. Every term of Court sees refinements, modifications, and even reversals of former positions.

NOTICE OF WHAT CONDUCT IS MADE CRIMINAL

The "Void for Vagueness" Rule

To begin with the law which defines a crime, fairness demands that the law spell out with sufficient clarity just what it is that the legislature is trying to prohibit. Without this basic notice, the citizen surely should not be held accountable in a criminal prosecution which may result in a forfeiture of life, liberty, or property. Thus, in *United States* v. *Cohen Grocery Co.*, 255 U.S. 81 (1921), a World War I price-control statute which made it a crime to make "any unjust or unreasonable rate or charge" for "necessaries" was held unconstitutionally vague because it fixed no ascertainable standard of guilt. Similarly, in *Connally* v. *General Construction Company*, 269 U.S. 385 (1926), an Oklahoma statute was held invalid which made it a crime to pay "less than the current rate of per diem wages in the locality where the work is performed." The Court found that such vague directions as "current rate" and "locality where the work is performed" were not sufficiently clear to apprise an employer of just what rates of pay would be so low as to violate the law. Prosecutions under such a law, then, would be in violation of the due process clause because insufficient notice was given. [See Note, "The Void-for-Vagueness Doctrine in the Supreme Court," 109 *U. Pa. L. Rev.* 67 (1960).]

Of course a great many vague statutes have been upheld by the Court. Statute-making is hardly an exact science, and even areas of regulation which might appear to be relatively simple may turn out to present complexities in drafting which render absolute clarity impossible. And normally the Court takes into account the problem faced by the legislature. Thus a provision which proscribed the sale of goods at "unreasonably low prices for the purpose of destroying competition or eliminating a competitor" was upheld as applied because the statute required (and the indictment alleged) a "predatory intent" to sell below cost without a justifying business reason and therefore adequately notified the defendant of the nature of the offense. [*United States* v. *National Dairy Prod. Corp.*, 372 U.S. 29 (1963).] And in *Nash* v. *United States*, 229 U.S. 373 (1913), upholding the Sherman Act's prohibition against unreasonable restraints of trade, Justice Holmes pointed out that "the law is full of instances where a man's fate depends on his estimating rightly, that is, as the jury subsequently estimates it, some matter of degree." (It should be noted, however, that the Court is much more demanding of particularity when the statute may impinge on First Amendment freedoms.) The Court has also examined the statutes for the requirement of *scienter* in the definition of the crime, and words such as "willfully" or "knowingly" coupled with the proscribed conduct have been held to overcome the vice of vagueness, as in *Screws* v. *United States.*

A more recent application of the vagueness rule has been with respect to ordinances punishing "vagrancy" or "loitering." At least as such laws are generally written, the decision in *Papachristou* v. *City of Jacksonville,* 405 U.S. 156 (1972), would seem to render them invalid. The Jacksonville ordinance punished as vagrants

rogues and vagabonds, or dissolute persons who go about begging, . . . common night walkers, . . . lewd, wanton and lascivious persons, . . . persons wandering or strolling around from place to place without any lawful purpose or object, habitual loafers, . . . persons neglecting all lawful business and habitually spending their time by frequenting houses of ill fame, gaming houses, or places where alcoholic beverages are sold or served, persons able to work but habitually living upon the earnings of their wives or minor children. . . .

The case involved eight defendants who were convicted in municipal court of vagrancy, most of whom were either employed or were students. Four of the defendants were charged with "vagrancy—prowling by auto" for driving down the main street of Jacksonville early Sunday morning. The Court unanimously held the ordinance void for vagueness, both in the sense that "it 'fails to give a person of ordinary intelligence fair notice that his contemplated conduct is forbidden by the statute,'. . . and because it encourages arbitrary and erratic arrests and convictions." The opinion also stressed the unfettered discretion which the ordinance placed in the hands of the police. Justice Douglas, for the Court, gave an interesting essay on the value of "wandering or strolling about," and also pointed out that the punishment of persons neglecting all lawful business and frequenting places where alcoholic beverages are served might be applied to members of golf clubs or city clubs.

The Prohibition Against Ex Post Facto Laws

While ex post facto laws are normally considered separately from due process questions, the basic defect inherent in such laws is the failure to give adequate notice. To apply a criminal law retroactively, to the disadvantage of the accused, is to violate the most fundamental notions of fairness. Thus, even without the prohibitions against ex post facto laws in Article I, Sections 9 and 10 of the Constitution, the "due process" clauses of the Fifth and Fourteenth Amendments might be considered adequate to bar the application of such laws.

Whatever the framers of the Constitution might have intended, the Court has consistently held that only criminal laws can come within the meaning of ex post facto prohibitions. Retroactive civil laws, then, do not run afoul of this provision of the Constitution. The leading case on the subject is

Calder v. *Bull,* 3 Dall. 386, decided in 1798 and still ruling law. In holding that a Connecticut statute, which set aside a probate court ruling and granted a new hearing on the disposition of a will, was not ex post facto, Justice Chase stated the rule:

I will state what laws I consider ex post facto laws, within the words and the intent of the prohibition. 1st. Every law that makes an action done before the passing of the law, and which was innocent when done, criminal; and punishes such action. 2d. Every law that aggravates a crime, or makes it greater than it was, when committed. 3d. Every law that changes the punishment, and inflicts a greater punishment, than the law annexed to the crime, when committed. 4th. Every law that alters the legal rules of evidence, and receives less, or different, testimony, than the law required at the time of the commission of the offense, in order to convict the offender. All these, and similar laws, are manifestly unjust and oppressive. In my opinion, the true distinction is between ex post facto laws, and retrospective laws. Every ex post facto law must necessarily be retrospective; but every retrospective law is not an ex post facto law; the former, only, are prohibited.

In determining whether a particular retroactive criminal law is ex post facto, within the rule of *Calder* v. *Bull,* the Court requires a showing that the new law will disadvantage defendants generally, as a class, rather than merely a particular defendant. Thus to reduce the size of the criminal jury from twelve to eight, and apply the reduction retroactively, was held to come within the bar against ex post facto laws in *Thompson* v. *Utah,* 170 U.S. 343 (1898). This was on the theory that defendants generally could be convicted more easily with eight jurors than twelve under a requirement of unanimity. But in the same year, in *Thompson* v. *Missouri,* 171 U.S. 380 (1898), the Court held that a change in the rules of evidence, to permit admission of letters written by the accused to his wife, was not ex post facto, despite the fact that a comparison of the handwriting showed that Thompson wrote a prescription for strychnine used to commit murder. The conviction was sustained on the ground that under the new rule both the state and the defendant were allowed to avail themselves of this additional evidence, and it would not uniformly operate to the disadvantage of the accused. [See Oliver P. Field, "Ex Post Facto in the Constitution," 20 *Mich. L. Rev.* 315 (1922).]

Notice to the Accused of the Offense Charged Against Him

In addition to the general requirement that a statute be sufficiently clear to warn the citizenry of what the legislature is prohibiting, there is a more specific requirement of due process that the accused in a criminal proceeding be notified of the charge placed against him. Fairness demands that he know in advance just what the prosecution is for, in order that he may adequately attempt a defense. At an earlier stage in America this rule was carried to such extremes that indictments could be quashed unless the most minute details of the alleged crime were set forth—the manufacturer, the caliber, the color, and the model of the gun used to commit a murder, for example, and the physical location of the wound which was caused. The courts of today no longer require such lengthy descriptive essays in the indictments, but there must still appear a charge of sufficient clarity to apprise the accused of the nature of the offense charged. A good statement of the matter is found in *State* v. *Popolos,* 103 A.2d 511 (Maine, 1954), where the defendant questioned the adequacy of his indictment for perjury:

The essentials of an indictment for *perjury* in this State are set forth in a prescribed form by the legislature. But such a form is subject to constitutional restrictions and must be in compliance therewith. The statutes prescribing forms of indictment have removed many of the niceties of technical pleading and the indictment is made little more than a simple statement of the offense couched in ordinary language and with due regard for the rights of the accused. But they cannot change the requirements that the indictment must, as at common law, contain every averment that is necessary to inform the defendant of the particular circumstances of the charge against him. . . .

Under the Constitution of the United States and by provision of the Constitution of Maine the accused is entitled to be informed of the nature and cause of the accusation against him. These provisions are based on the presumption of innocence and require such certainty in indictments as will enable an innocent man to prepare for trial. But no greater particularity of allegation that may be of service to the accused in understanding the charge and preparing his defense is necessary. However, all the elements or facts necessary to the crime charged must be set out fully and clearly. . . .

The issue of adequate notice was brought to the United States Supreme Court in 1948 in a rather curious case. As the case appeared to that Court, the Supreme Court of Arkansas held that a conviction under one section of a law could not be sustained, but it was affirmed, nonetheless, since there appeared to be sufficient evidence to convict under another section, even though the defendant was never charged with the latter violation.

COLE *v.* ARKANSAS
333 U.S. 196 (1948)

[Arkansas adopted a law in 1943 making it a felony to interfere in specified ways with one's right to work. The two key sections provided, in part:

Section 1. It shall be unlawful for any person by the use of force or violence . . . to prevent or attempt to prevent any person from engaging in any lawful vocation within this State. . . .

Section 2. It shall be unlawful for any person acting in concert with one or more other persons, to assemble at or near any place where a "labor dispute" exists and by force or violence prevent . . . any person from engaging in any lawful vocation, or for any person acting . . . in concert with one or more other persons, to promote, encourage or aid any such unlawful assemblage.]

Mr. Justice Black delivered the opinion of the Court.

The petitioners were convicted of a felony in an Arkansas state court and sentenced to serve one year in the state penitentiary. . . . We granted certiorari because the record indicated that at least one of the questions presented was substantial. That question, in the present state of the record, is the only one we find it appropriate to consider. The question is: "Were the petitioners denied due process of law . . . in violation of the Fourteenth Amendment by the circumstance that their convictions were affirmed under a criminal statute for violation of which they had not been charged?"

The present convictions are under an information. The petitioners urge that the information charged them with a violation of Section 2 of Act 193 of the 1943

Arkansas Legislature and that they were tried and convicted of violating only Section 2. The State Supreme Court affirmed their convictions on the ground that the information had charged and the evidence had shown that the petitioners had violated Section 1 of the Arkansas Act which describes an offense separate and distinct from the offense described in Section 2. . . .

We therefore have this situation. The petitioners read the information as charging them with an offense under Section 2 of the Act, the language of which the information had used. The trial judge construed the information as charging an offense under Section 2. He instructed the jury to that effect. He charged the jury that petitioners were on trial for the offense of promoting an unlawful assemblage, not for the offense "of using force and violence." Without completely ignoring the judge's charge, the jury could not have convicted petitioner for having committed the separate, distinct, and substantially different offense defined in Section 1. Yet the State Supreme Court refused to consider the validity of the convictions under Section 2, for violation of which petitioners were tried and convicted. It affirmed their convictions as though they had been tried for violating Section 1, an offense for which they were neither tried nor convicted.

No principle of procedural due process is more clearly established than that notice of the specific charge, and a chance to be heard in a trial of the issues raised by that charge, if desired, are among the constitutional rights of every accused in a criminal proceeding in all courts, state or federal. . . . If, as the State Supreme Court held, petitioners were charged with a violation of Section 1, it is doubtful both that the information fairly informed them of that charge and that they sought to defend themselves against such a charge; it is certain that they were not tried for or found guilty of it. It is as much a violation of due process to send an accused to prison following conviction of a charge on which he was never tried as it would be to convict him upon a charge that was never made. . . .

We are constrained to hold that the petitioners have been denied safeguards guaranteed by due process of law—safeguards essential to liberty in a government dedicated to justice under law.

In the present state of the record we cannot pass upon those contentions which challenge the validity of Section 2 of the Arkansas Act. The judgment is reversed and remanded to the State Supreme Court for proceedings not inconsistent with this opinion.

Reversed and remanded.

UNREASONABLE SEARCHES AND SEIZURES

The Fourth Amendment to the United States Constitution begins with the phrase, "The right of the people to be secure in their persons, houses, papers, and effects, against unreasonable searches and seizures, shall not be violated . . ." The clear purport of the phrase is that not all seizures or searches are prohibited; it is only those which are *unreasonable* which are barred. The second part of the sentence states, "and no warrants shall issue, but upon probable cause, supported by oath or affirmation, and particularly describing the place to be searched, and the persons or things to be seized."

The phraseology of the Fourth Amendment raises two important questions of interpretation. First, what kinds of searches and seizures are "unreasonable"? Second, what sorts of information or observation are sufficient to constitute "probable cause" to believe that an offense was committed and that the things sought are in the place specified? The general bounds of the "probable cause" requirement become additionally important because of the fact that not all searches require a warrant, but even the exceptions demand that the officer meet this same test before proceeding, just as though he were attempting to obtain a warrant. [See Nelson B. Lasson, *The History and Development of the Fourth Amendment to the United States Constitution* (Baltimore: Johns Hopkins University Press, 1937) and Jacob W. Landynski, *Search and Seizure and the Supreme Court* (Baltimore: Johns Hopkins University Press, 1966).]

Search with a Valid Warrant

The two main procedural points involved in obtaining a warrant are: first, the warrant issues from a nonpolice officer in order to guarantee a somewhat more detached and neutral view of the matter, and second, the place to be searched, and the persons or things to be seized, must be specifically described. The first requirement has generally been thought to demand that a judicial officer issue the warrant. But in *Shadwick* v. *City of Tampa,* 407 U.S. 345 (1972), the Court made it clear that this was not necessarily the case and upheld the issuance of an arrest warrant (for the violation of a municipal ordinance) by a court clerk—a person who was not a judge or even a lawyer, but one who was attached to the court and was independent of the police. The second requirement, that of particularity, was a response to the despised "writs of assistance" under which the British made general searches during the colonial period.

Some of the basic aspects of Fourth Amendment application were treated in *Boyd* v. *United States,* 116 U.S. 616 (1886), and it is the leading case on one aspect of what may constitute an "unreasonable" search. While the case involved the validity of a production order issued by a court, rather than a search warrant as such, the primary issue was still the question of whether the Fourth Amendment was violated by an attempted seizure of private papers to be used in evidence against the owner. In the course of the majority opinion for the Court, it was pointed out that while it would be proper to authorize seizure of stolen goods or implements of crime or contraband, it would violate the Fourth and Fifth Amendments to seize "mere evidence" in the form of private papers in order to establish a criminal charge against the owner. This would be a seizure in order to compel self-incrimination.

Carried to its logical conclusion, the "mere evidence" rule as a protection against self-incrimination would appear to prohibit the taking of fingerprints or requiring one accused of drunken driving to take a breathalyzer test. The problem turns on a determination of just what kinds of inculpatory evidence taken from the person are contemplated in the term "self-incrimination." The Court reached this question in *Schmerber* v. *California,* 384 U.S. 757 (1966), and decided that the taking of a blood sample, under protest, of one accused of drunken driving, and the introduction of the results of the test in a prosecution, did not constitute a violation of the self-incrimination clause. The Court read the clause as a protection only against the use of matters of a "testimonial" or "communicative" nature, and thus did not extend to ordinary physical items of an evidentiary nature. This decision led to a reexamination of the "mere evidence" rule in *Warden* v. *Hayden* in 1967. While the case involved a search and seizure *without* a warrant, it has obvious relevance to the search with a warrant as well.

WARDEN *v.* HAYDEN
387 U.S. 294 (1967)

[Following the armed robbery of a cab company in Baltimore, Maryland, two cab drivers, attracted by shouts of "Holdup," followed a man who fled the company premises, and watched him enter a residence. One driver notified the company dispatcher by radio that the man was a Negro about 5'8" tall, wearing a light cap and dark jacket, and that he had entered the house on Cocoa Lane. The dispatcher relayed the information to police. Within minutes, police arrived at the house in a number of patrol cars. They searched the first and second floors and the cellar for the suspect. Hayden was found in an upstairs bedroom, and he was arrested when the officers on the first floor reported that no other man was in the house. One officer discovered a shotgun and a pistol in a flush tank in a bathroom adjoining the bedroom. Another officer, who was searching the cellar for "a man or the money" found, in a washing machine, a jacket and trousers of the type the fleeing man was said to have worn. A clip of ammunition for the pistol and a cap were found under the mattress of Hayden's bed. All these items of evidence were introduced against him at his trial.]

Mr. Justice Brennan delivered the opinion of the Court.

We review in this case the validity of the proposition that there is under the Fourth Amendment a "distinction between merely evidentiary materials, on the one hand, which may not be seized either under the authority of a search warrant or during the course of a search incident to arrest, and on the other hand, those objects which may validly be seized including the instrumentalities and means by which a crime is committed, the fruits of crime such as stolen property, weapons by which escape of the person arrested might be effected, and property the possession of which is a crime.". . .

We agree with the Court of Appeals that neither the entry without warrant to search for the robber, nor the search for him without warrant was invalid. . . . The police . . . acted reasonably when they entered the house and began to search for a man of the description they had been given and for weapons which he had used in the robbery or might use against them. The Fourth Amendment does not require police officers to delay in the course of an investigation if to do so would gravely endanger their lives or the lives of others. Speed here was essential, and only a thorough search of the house for persons and weapons could have insured that Hayden was the only man present and that the police had control of all weapons which could be used against them or to effect an escape. . . .

It is argued that, while the weapons, ammunition, and cap may have been seized in the course of a search for weapons, the officer who seized the clothing was searching neither for the suspect nor for weapons when he looked into the washing machine in which he found the clothing. . . .

We come, then, to the question whether, even though the search was lawful, the Court of Appeals was correct in holding that the seizure and introduction of the items of clothing violated the Fourth Amendment because they are "mere evidence.". . . We today reject the distinction as based on premises no longer accepted as rules governing the application of the Fourth Amendment. . . .

Nothing in the language of the Fourth Amendment supports the distinction between "mere evidence" and instrumentalities, fruits of crime, or contraband. On its face, the provision assures the "right of the people to be secure in their persons, houses, papers, and effects . . . ," without regard to the use to which any of these things are applied. This "right of the people" is certainly unrelated to the "mere evidence" limitation. Privacy is disturbed no more by .a search directed to a purely evidentiary object than it is by a search directed to an instrumentality, fruit, or contraband. . . . Indeed, the distinction is wholly irrational, since, depending on the circumstances, the same "papers and effects" may be "mere evidence" in one case and "instrumentality" in another. See Comment, 20 *U. Chi. L. Rev.* 319, 320–322 (1953).

In *Gouled* v. *United States* . . . the Court said that search warrants "may not be used as a means of gaining access to a man's house or office and papers solely for the purpose of making search to secure evidence to be used against him in a criminal or penal proceeding. . . ." The Court derived from *Boyd* v. *United States, supra,* the proposition that warrants "may be resorted to only when a primary right to such search and seizure may be found in the interest which the public or the complainant may have in the property to be seized, or in the right to the possession of it, or when a valid exercise of the police power renders possession of the property by the accused unlawful and provides that it may be taken.". . .

The items of clothing involved in this case are not "testimonial" or "communicative" in nature, and their introduction therefore did not compel respondent to become a witness against himself in violation of the Fifth Amendment. *Schmerber* v. *California,* 384 U.S. 757. This case thus does not require that we consider whether there are items of evidential value whose very nature precludes them from being the object of a reasonable search and seizure. . . .

The premise in *Gouled* that government may not seize evidence simply for the purpose of proving crime has . . . been discredited. The requirement that the Government assert in addition some property interest in material it seizes has long been a fiction, obscuring the reality that government has an interest in solving crime. *Schmerber* settled the proposition that it is reasonable, within the terms of the Fourth Amendment, to conduct otherwise permissible searches for the purpose of obtaining evidence which would aid in apprehending and convicting criminals. The requirements of the Fourth Amendment can secure the same protection of privacy whether the search is for "mere evidence" or for fruits, instrumentalities or contraband. There must, of course, be a nexus—automatically provided in the case of fruits, instrumentalities or contraband—between the item to be seized and criminal behavior. Thus in the case of "mere evidence," probable cause must be examined in terms of cause to believe that the evidence sought will aid in a particular apprehension or conviction. . . . The clothes found in the washing machine matched the description of those worn by the robber and the police therefore could reasonably believe that the items would aid in the identification of the culprit. . . .

The judgment of the Court of Appeals is

Reversed.

Mr. Justice Black concurs in the result.
Mr. Justice Fortas, with whom the Chief Justice joins, concurring. . . .
Mr. Justice Douglas, dissenting. . . .

Another question arising under searches with a warrant is: what things are subject to seizure? Since the warrant must describe the articles to be seized, it would seem reasonable to conclude that *only* such items described are subject to seizure. Generally speaking, this appears to be the rule that is followed, but officers may also seize other property if such property is related to the things described in the warrant, or if it is contraband. Thus in *Cofer* v. *United States,* 37 F.2d 677 (C.A. 5th, 1930), officers were held to have exceeded their power when they seized gun shells from a locked trunk while searching defendant's premises under a warrant directing a seizure of liquor. But in *Bennett* v. *United States,* 145 F.2d 270 (C.A. 4th, 1944), a seizure of counterfeit ration coupons was held reasonable under a warrant the affidavit for which mentioned only counterfeit apparatus. The ration coupons were considered to be "related objects" and therefore properly seized.

There is, in addition, the "plain view" doctrine, which in proper circumstances permits seizure of items without a warrant during a legitimate search. In *Coolidge* v. *New Hampshire,* 403 U.S. 443 (1971), Justice Stewart, for the majority, discussed the doctrine:

What the "plain view" cases have in common is that the police officer in each of them had a prior justification for an intrusion in the course of which he came inadvertently across a piece of evidence incriminating the accused. The doctrine serves to supplement the prior justification—whether it be a warrant for another object, hot pursuit, search incident to lawful arrest, or some other legitimate reason for being present unconnected with a search directed against the accused—and permits the warrantless seizure. Of course, the extension of the original justification is legitimate only where it is immediately apparent to the police that they have evidence before them; the "plain view" doctrine may not be used to extend a general exploratory search from one object to another until something incriminating at last emerges.

Although the law is not completely clear, it should be noted that the rule with respect to seizures under a search warrant is not necessarily identical to that concerning searches and seizures incident to a lawful arrest. The latter appears to give officers somewhat broader powers and is discussed separately below.

Search and Seizure Without a Warrant

The Fourth Amendment prohibits unreasonable searches and seizures and seems to suggest, as a generalization, that searches or seizures without a warrant are unreasonable. There are certain important exceptions to such a generalization, however. An arrest is, of course, a seizure, and an illegal arrest is an unconstitutional seizure under the Fourth Amendment, as indicated in *Henry* v. *United States,* 361 U.S. 98 (1959). But the Fourth Amendment does not demand a warrant in every case for the arrest to be lawful. Most arrests are made without warrants. At common law a warrant was required to arrest for any *misdemeanor* except a breach of the peace committed in the presence of the officer, and continuing at the time of the arrest. An arrest could be made for a *felony* without a warrant if the officer had reasonable ground to believe that a felony had been committed and the arrested person committed it. These rules have been modified by statute in most of the states. The general rule today is that an officer may arrest without warrant for *all* offenses committed in the presence of the officer, and may arrest a person for a *felony* without a warrant when he has reasonable cause to believe that a felony has been committed and reasonable cause to believe that such person has committed it. These are the exceptions, then, to a general requirement of a warrant prior to an *arrest.* [See Wayne R. LaFave, *Arrest* (Boston: Little, Brown, 1965).]

The argument that the Fourth Amendment permits warrantless arrests for felonies, based upon probable cause, only when exigent circumstances make obtaining a warrant impracticable was specifically rejected by the Court in *United States* v. *Watson*, 44 L.W. 4112 (1976). A postal inspector, having reliable information that respondent Watson possessed stolen credit cards, arrested him, without a warrant, in a public restaurant. A subsequent consent search of his nearby car revealed two such cards which were introduced in evidence against him. The trial court denied the motion to suppress, and he was convicted. The Court of Appeals held the warrantless arrest violative of the Fourth Amendment and ruled the evidence inadmissible as having been seized illegally. The Supreme Court reversed. The majority opinion pointed out that a statute specifically authorized postal inspectors to make warrantless felony arrests based upon probable cause, and the Fourth Amendment did not change the common-law rule to require that a warrant be obtained where practicable, at least when the arrest occurs in a police place.

In *United States* v. *Santana*, 44 L.W. 4970 (1976), the issue of the validity of a warrantless arrest turned on the question of whether the police action occurred in a public place and was thus governed by the *Watson* rule. On the basis of information that Santana had in her possession marked money used to make a heroin "buy" arranged by an undercover agent, police officers went to Santana's house. They saw her standing in the doorway of the house with a brown paper bag in her hand. As the officers approached, shouting "police," she retreated into the vestibule of her house, where they caught her. When she tried to escape, envelopes containing what was later determined to be heroin fell to the floor from the paper bag, and she was found to have been carrying some of the marked money on her person. After indictment, Santana moved to suppress the heroin and marked money. The District Court granted the motion on the ground that although the officers had probable cause to make the arrest, Santana's retreat into the vestibule did not justify a warrantless entry into the house on the ground of "hot pursuit." The Court of Appeals affirmed, but the Supreme Court reversed. The Court held, first, that while Santana was standing in the doorway of her house she was in a "public place" for purposes of the Fourth Amendment. Thus, the police intended to make a warrantless arrest in a public place upon probable cause, and the *Watson* rule was applicable. Second, by retreating into the privacy of the vestibule, Santana could not defeat an otherwise proper arrest that had been "set in motion in a public place, and is therefore proper under *Watson,* by the expedient of escaping to a private place." The conclusion was that this was a true case of "hot pursuit," and the decision was governed by *Warden* v. *Hayden,* since there was a need to act quickly to prevent destruction of evidence. Justice Marshall, joined by Justice Brennan, dissented on the ground that warrantless arrests must be justified by exigent circumstances, and none was asserted in this case.

As to *searches,* there are two important exceptions to the general requirement of a warrant. The first is a search conducted as an incident to a lawful arrest, and the second is a search of a movable vehicle based upon "probable cause" sufficient to have justified issuance of a warrant had it been requested. In these two situations a search without warrant is not *ipso facto* unreasonable, although the officers may by various improper procedures turn it into an unreasonable search. This would be the case, for example, if the extent of the search is too far-ranging or if the manner in which it is carried out is altogether improper.

The first of these exceptions is of ancient origin. For one reason, the officer should search the person of the accused and the immediate vicinity at least to be certain that there are no weapons by which the arrestee can effect an escape. In addition, the courts are agreed that an officer has the authority, following a lawful arrest, to make a search in order to prevent the destruction or loss of the fruits of the crime or the instruments by which it was committed. It is important to keep in mind, however, that for such a search to be justified without warrant, the arrest must be lawful on grounds independent of what the search turns up. The protection against unreasonable searches would be for the most part undermined if the arrest could be justified on the basis of evidence turned up by the search. Thus in *Johnson* v. *United States,* 333 U.S. 10 (1948), experienced narcotics officers, after a tip from an informer, went to a hotel room and immediately recognized the odor of burning opium emanating from the room. The officers knocked, and when a woman opened the door, one of the officers said, "I want you to consider yourself under arrest because we are going to search the room." On appeal after conviction, the United States Supreme Court held that at this point the officers had no ground for making the arrest, since they could not have known who was committing the crime. The Court held that the identification of the odor would have been "probable cause" sufficient to obtain a warrant, but that the arrest was invalid and the subsequent search, which indicated that no one else was present but the accused, could not validate the arrest. The government "is obliged to justify the arrest by the search and at the same time to justify the search by the arrest. This will not do. An officer gaining access to private living quarters under color of his office and of the law which he personifies must then have some valid basis in law for the intrusion. Any other rule ... would obliterate one of the most fundamental distinctions between our form of government, where officers are under the law, and the police-state where they are the law."

Two other questions concerning search incident to arrest were dealt with in *United States* v. *Rabinowitz,* 339 U.S. 56 (1950). These were the issues of the legitimate extent of such a search and also the legality of a search without a warrant which goes beyond the person of the accused to include his room, where the police have time to obtain a search warrant but fail to do so. The majority held that a thorough search of desk, safe, and file cabinets in a one-room office following arrest on a valid arrest warrant was not an unreasonable search within the bar of the Fourth Amendment. It further held that the fact that the police had ample time to procure a search warrant but failed to do so did not make the search unreasonable. Contradictions and vacillations in the line of decisions on these points led the Court to make yet another attempt at resolution in 1969.

CHIMEL v. CALIFORNIA
395 U.S. 752 (1969)

Mr. Justice Stewart delivered the opinion of the Court.

This case raises basic questions concerning the permissible scope under the Fourth Amendment of a search incident to a lawful arrest.

The relevant facts are essentially undisputed. Late in the afternoon of September 13, 1965, three police officers arrived at the Santa Ana, California, home of the petitioner with a warrant authorizing his arrest for the burglary of a coin shop.

The officers knocked on the door, identified themselves to the petitioner's wife, and asked if they might come inside. She ushered them into the house, where they waited 10 or 15 minutes until the petitioner returned home from work. When the petitioner entered the house, one of the officers handed him the arrest warrant and asked for permission to "look around." The petitioner objected, but was advised that "on the basis of the lawful arrest," the officers would nonetheless conduct a search. No search warrant had been issued.

Accompanied by the petitioner's wife, the officers then looked through the entire three-bedroom house, including the attic, the garage, and a small workshop. In some rooms the search was relatively cursory. In the master bedroom and sewing room, however, the officers directed the petitioner's wife to open drawers and "to physically move contents of the drawers from side to side so that [they] might view any items that would have come from [the] burglary." After completing the search, they seized numerous items—primarily coins, but also several medals, tokens, and a few other objects. The entire search took between 45 minutes and an hour.

At the petitioner's subsequent state trial on two charges of burglary, the items taken from his house were admitted into evidence against him, over his objection that they had been unconstitutionally seized. He was convicted, and the judgments of conviction were affirmed by both the California District Court of Appeal . . . and the California Supreme Court.

Without deciding the question, we proceed on the hypothesis that the California courts were correct in holding that the arrest of the petitioner was valid under the Constitution. This brings us directly to the question whether the warrantless search of the petitioner's entire house can be constitutionally justified as incident to that arrest. The decisions of this Court bearing upon that question have been far from consistent, as even the most cursory review makes evident.

Approval of a warrantless search incident to a lawful arrest seems first to have been articulated by the Court in 1914 as dictum in *Weeks* v. *United States*, 232 U.S. 383. . . .

[Here the opinion traces the decisions, and their inconsistencies, from *Weeks* v. *United States* to *Harris* v. *United States*].

In [*Harris* v. *United States*, 331 U.S. 145 (1947)] officers had obtained a warrant for Harris' arrest on the basis of his alleged involvement with the cashing and interstate transportation of a forged check. He was arrested in the living room of his four-room apartment, and in an attempt to recover two canceled checks thought to have been used in effecting the forgery, the officers undertook a thorough search of the entire apartment. . . . The Court rejected Harris' Fourth Amendment claim, sustaining the search as "incident to arrest." . . .

Only a year after Harris, however, the pendulum swung again. In *Trupiano* v. *United States*, 334 U.S. 699 (1948), agents raided the site of an illicit distillery, saw one of several conspirators operating the still, and arrested him, contemporaneously "seizing the illicit distillery." . . . The Court held that the arrest and others made subsequently had been valid, but that the unexplained failure of the agents to procure a search warrant—in spite of the fact that they had had more than enough time before the raid to do so—rendered the search unlawful. . . .

In 1950, two years after Trupiano, came *United States* v. *Rabinowitz*, 339 U.S. 56, the decision upon which California primarily relies in the case now before us. In Rabinowitz, federal authorities had been informed that the defendant was dealing in stamps bearing forged overprints. On the basis of that information they secured a warrant for his arrest, which they executed at his one-room business office. At the time of the arrest, the officers "searched the desk, safe, and file cabinets in the office for about an hour and a half," . . . and seized 573 stamps with forged overprints. The stamps were admitted into evidence at the defendant's trial, and this Court affirmed his conviction, rejecting the contention that the warrantless search had been unlawful. The Court held that the search in its entirety fell within the principle giving law enforcement authorities "[t]he right 'to search the place where the arrest is made in order to find and seize things connected with the crime. . . .' " Harris was regarded as "ample authority" for that conclusion. . . .

Rabinowitz has come to stand for the proposition, inter alia, that a warrantless search "incident to a lawful arrest" may generally extend to the area that is considered to be in the "possession" or under the "control" of the person arrested. And it was on the basis of that proposition that the California courts upheld the search of the petitioner's entire house in this case. That doctrine, however, at least in the broad sense in which it was applied by the California courts in this case, can withstand neither historical nor rational analysis.

Even limited to its own facts, the Rabinowitz decision was, as we have seen, hardly founded on an unimpeachable line of authority. As Mr. Justice Frankfurter commented in dissent in that case, the "hint" contained in Weeks was, without persuasive justification, "loosely turned into dictum and finally elevated to a decision.". . .

Only last Term in *Terry* v. *Ohio,* 392 U.S. 1, we emphasized that "the police must, whenever practicable, obtain advance judicial approval of searches and seizures through the warrant procedure,". . . and that "[t]he scope of [a] search must be 'strictly tied to and justified by' the circumstances which rendered its initiation permissible.". . . The search undertaken by the officer in that "stop and frisk" case was sustained under that test, because it was no more than a "protective . . . search for weapons.". . . But in a companion case, *Sibron* v. *New York,* 392 U.S. 40, we applied the same standard to another set of facts and reached a contrary result, holding that a policeman's action in thrusting his hand into a suspect's pocket had been neither motivated by nor limited to the objective of protection. Rather, the search had been made in order to find narcotics, which were in fact found.

A similar analysis underlies the "search incident to arrest" principle, and marks its proper extent. When an arrest is made, it is reasonable for the arresting officer to search the person arrested in order to remove any weapons that the latter might seek to use in order to resist arrest or effect his escape. Otherwise, the officer's safety might well be endangered, and the arrest itself frustrated. In addition, it is entirely reasonable for the arresting officer to search for and seize any evidence on the arrestee's person in order to prevent its concealment or destruction. And the area into which an arrestee might reach in order to grab a weapon or evidentiary items must, of course, be governed by a like rule. A gun on a table or in a drawer in front of one who is arrested can be as dangerous to the arresting officer as one concealed in the clothing of the person arrested. There is ample justification, therefore, for a search of the arrestee's person and the area "within his immediate control"—construing that phrase to mean the area from within which he might gain possession of a weapon or destructible evidence.

There is no comparable justification, however, for routinely searching rooms other than that in which an arrest occurs—or, for that matter, for searching through all the desk drawers or other closed or concealed areas in that room itself. Such searches, in the absence of well-recognized exceptions, may be made only under the authority of a search warrant. The "adherence to judicial processes" mandated by the Fourth Amendment requires no less. . . .

The petitioner correctly points out that one result of decisions such as Rabinowitz and Harris is to give law enforcement officials the opportunity to engage in searches not justified by probable cause, by the simple expedient of arranging to arrest suspects at home rather than elsewhere. We do not suggest that the petitioner is necessarily correct in his assertion that such a strategy was utilized here, but the fact remains that had he been arrested earlier in the day, at his place of employment rather than at home, no search of his house could have been made without a search warrant. In any event, even apart from the possibility of such police tactics, the general point so forcefully made by Judge Leonard Hand in *United States* v. *Kirchenblatt,* 16 F.2d 202, remains:

"After arresting a man in his house, to rummage at will among his papers in search of whatever will convict him, appears to us to be indistinguishable from what might be done under a general warrant; indeed, the warrant would give more protection, for presumably it must be issued by a magistrate. True, by hypothesis the power would not exist, if the supposed offender were not found on the premises; but it is small consolation to know that one's papers are safe only so long as one is not at home." Id., at 203.

Rabinowitz and Harris have been the subject of critical commentary for many years, and have been relied upon less and less in our own decisions. It is time, for the reasons we have stated, to hold that on their own facts, and insofar as the principles they stand for are inconsistent with those that we have endorsed today, they are no longer to be followed.

Application of sound Fourth Amendment principles to the facts of this case produces a clear result. The search here went far beyond the petitioner's person and the area from within which he might have obtained either a weapon or something that could have been used as evidence against him. There was no constitutional justification, in the absence of a search warrant, for extending the search beyond that area. The scope of the search was, therefore, "unreasonable" under the Fourth and Fourteenth Amendments, and the petitioner's conviction cannot stand.

Reversed.

Mr. Justice Harlan, concurring. . . .

Mr. Justice White, with whom Mr. Justice Black joins, dissenting. . . .

In *Terry* v. *Ohio,* 392 U.S. 1 (1968), and *Sibron* v. *New York,* 392 U.S. 40 (1968), the Court examined the validity of "stop and frisk" practices in two discrete situations. The first involved an experienced officer's observation of three men, his conclusion that they were contemplating a daylight robbery of a store, and his "patting down" procedure which revealed that two of the men carried guns. The second involved an officer's suspicion that Sibron possessed narcotics and the officer's subsequent search of Sibron's pocket, revealing heroin. Petitioners in each case claimed that the evidence was seized unconstitutionally and sought review of their convictions. The Court held that such warrantless searches had to meet the Fourth Amendment's requirements of probable cause and had to be based on reasonable grounds to believe the suspect to be armed and dangerous. It further distinguished between "patting down" the suspect and actually searching his pockets. Using these tests, the *Terry* evidence was held admissible, but the *Sibron* evidence was held to have been illegally seized. [See Paul G. Chevigny, "Police Abuses in Connection with the Law of Search and Seizure," 5 *Crim. L. Bull.* 3 (1969).]

In *Adams* v. *Williams,* 407 U.S. 143 (1972), the Court upheld a stop and frisk where the officer's suspicions rested on an informer's tip. The officer was alone in a patrol car in a high crime area when a person known to the officer approached his cruiser and informed him that an individual seated in a nearby vehicle was carrying narcotics and had a gun at his waist. The informant had apparently provided the officer with information in the past. The officer approached the vehicle, tapped on the car window, and asked the occupant to open the door. When he rolled down the window instead, the officer reached into the car and removed a fully loaded revolver from the occupant's waistband. The gun had not been visible from outside the car, but it was in precisely the place indicated by the informant. The officer then arrested him, and a search incident to the arrest uncovered substantial quantities of heroin on the defendant's person and in the car, and a machete and a second revolver were found hidden in the automobile. The defendant contended that absent a more reliable informant, or some corroboration of the tip, the policeman's actions were unreasonable under *Terry* standards. The Court disagreed, stating that "while the Court's decisions indicate that this informant's unverified tip may have been insufficient for a narcotics arrest or search warrant, . . . the information carried enough indicia of reliability to justify the officer's forcible stop of Williams." Three justices dissented, arguing, first, that the informant was not shown to have been reliable and, second, that the mere presence of the pistol was not sufficient to justify the arrest, since Williams might have been licensed to carry the gun legally.

The question of the extent of a search of the person, following arrest for a traffic violation, was considered in *United States* v. *Robinson* in 1973.

UNITED STATES *v.* ROBINSON
414 U.S. 218 (1973)

[A Washington D.C. police officer, having reason to believe that Robinson was operating a motor vehicle after the revocation of his operator's permit, signaled him to stop the automobile. Robinson stopped, and the three occupants got out of the car. At that point the officer informed the defendant that he was under arrest for "operating after revocation and obtaining a permit by misrepresentation." It was assumed by the lower courts, and conceded by the defendant, that the officer had probable cause to arrest and that he effected a full custody arrest. In accordance with police procedures, the officer then conducted a "patdown" of the defendant, during which the officer felt an object in the breast pocket of the heavy coat the defendant was wearing. He testified that he couldn't tell what the object was, nor actually the size of it. He reached into the pocket and pulled out a crumpled cigarette package. Upon looking in the package, he found fourteen gelatin capsules of white powder which he thought to be, and which later analysis proved to be, heroin. The heroin seized from the defendant was admitted into evidence at the trial which resulted in his conviction in the District Court. The Court of Appeals reversed, holding that the heroin had been obtained as a result of an unconstitutional search. The case came on certiorari to the Supreme Court.]

Mr. Justice Rehnquist delivered the opinion of the Court. . . .

It is well settled that a search incident to a lawful arrest is a traditional exception to the warrant requirement of the Fourth Amendment. This general exception has historically been formulated into two distinct propositions. The first is that a search may be made of the *person* of the arrestee by virtue of the lawful arrest. The second is that a search may be made of the area within the control of the arrestee.

Examination of this Court's decisions in the area show that these two propositions have been treated quite differently. The validity of the search of a person incident to a lawful arrest has been regarded as settled from its first enunciation, and has remained virtually unchallenged until the present case. The validity of the second proposition, while likewise conceded in principle, has been subject to differing interpretations as to the extent of the area which may be searched. . . .

[T]he broadly stated rule [regarding search of the person incident to lawful arrest], and the reasons for it, have been repeatedly affirmed in the decisions of this Court since *Weeks* v. *United States* nearly 60 years ago. Since the statements in the cases speak not simply in terms of an exception to the warrant requirement, but in terms of an affirmative authority to search, they clearly imply that such searches also meet the Fourth Amendment's requirement of reasonableness.

In its decision of this case, the majority of the Court of Appeals decided that even after a police officer lawfully places a suspect under arrest for the purpose of taking him into custody, he may not ordinarily proceed to fully search the prisoner. He must instead conduct a limited frisk of the outer clothing and remove such weapons that he may, as a result of that limited frisk, reasonably believe the suspect has in his possession. While recognizing that *Terry* v. *Ohio* . . . dealt with a permissible "frisk" incident to an investigative stop based on less than probable cause to arrest, the Court of Appeals felt that the principles of that case should be carried over to this probable cause arrest for driving while one's license is revoked. Since there would be no further evidence of such a crime to be obtained in a search of the arrestee, the Court held that only a search for weapons could be justified.

Terry v. *Ohio* did not involve an arrest for probable cause, and it made quite clear that the "protective frisk" for weapons which it approved might be conducted without probable cause. . . . The Court's opinion explicitly recognized that there is a "distinction in purpose, character, and extent between a search incident to an arrest and a limited search for weapons":

"The former, although justified in part by the acknowledged necessity to protect the arresting officer from assault with a concealed weapon, . . . is also justified on other grounds, and can therefore involve a relatively extensive exploration of the person. A search for weapons in the absence of probable cause to arrest, however, must, like any other search, be strictly circumscribed by the exigencies which justify its initiation. . . . Thus it must be limited to that which is necessary for the discovery of weapons wihch might be used to harm the officer or others nearby, and may realistically be characterized as something less than a 'full' search even though it remains a serious intrusion. . . ."

Terry, therefore, affords no basis to carry over to a probable cause arrest the limitations this Court placed on a stop-and-frisk search permissible without probable cause.

The Court of Appeals also relied on language in *Peters* v. *New York,* . . . a companion case to *Terry.* There the Court held that the police officer had authority to search Peters because he had probable cause to arrest him, and went on to say:

" . . . the incident search was obviously justified 'by the need to seize weapons and other things which might be used to assault an officer or effect an escape, as well as by the need to prevent the destruction of evidence of the crime.' . . . Moreover, it was reasonably limited in scope by these purposes. Officer Laskey did not engage in an unrestrained and thoroughgoing examination of Peters and his personal effects." . . .

We do not believe that the Court in *Peters* intended in one unexplained and unelaborated sentence to impose a novel and far reaching limitation on the authority to search the person of an arrestee incident to his lawful arrest. While the language from Peters was quoted with approval in *Chimel* v. *California*, . . . it is preceded by a full exposition of the traditional and unqualified authority of the arresting officer to search the arrestee's person. . . . We do not believe that either *Terry* or *Peters*, when considered in the light of the previously discussed statements of this Court, justified the sort of limitation upon that authority which the Court of Appeals fashioned in this case.

Virtually all of the statements of this Court affirming the existence of an unqualified authority to search incident to a lawful arrest are dicta. We would not therefore be foreclosed by principles of stare decisis from further examination into history and practice in order to see whether the sort of qualifications imposed by the Court of Appeals in this case were in fact intended by the Framers of the Fourth Amendment or recognized in cases decided prior to *Weeks*. [Here the opinion examines earlier authorities.]

While these earlier authorities are sketchy, they tend to support the broad statement of the authority to search incident to arrest found in the successive decisions of this Court, rather than the restrictive one which was applied by the Court of Appeals in this case. . . .

. . . [O]ur more fundamental disagreement with the Court of Appeals arises from its suggestion that there must be litigated in each case the issue of whether or not there was present one of the reasons supporting the authority for a search of the person incident to a lawful arrest. We do not think the long line of authorities of this Court dating back to *Weeks*, nor what we can glean from the history of practice in this country and in England, requires such a case by case adjudication. A police officer's determination as to how and where to search the person of a suspect whom he has arrested is necessarily a quick ad hoc judgment which the Fourth Amendment does not require to be broken down in each instance into an analysis of each step in the search. The authority to search the person incident to a lawful custodial arrest, while based upon the need to disarm and to discover evidence, does not depend on what a court may later decide was the probability in a particular arrest situation that weapons or evidence would in fact be found upon the person of the suspect. A custodial arrest of a suspect based on probable cause is a reasonable intrusion under the Fourth Amendment; that intrusion being lawful, a search incident to the arrest requires no additional justification. It is the fact of the lawful arrest which establishes the authority to search, and we hold that in the case of a lawful custodial arrest a full search of the person is not only an exception to the warrant requirement of the Fourth Amendment, but is also a "reasonable" search under that Amendment. . . .

Reversed.

Mr. Justice Powell, concurring. . . .

. . . [There] are areas of an individual's life about which he entertains legitimate expectations of privacy. I believe that an individual lawfully subjected to a custodial arrest retains no significant Fourth Amendment interest in the privacy of his person. . . . The search incident to arrest is reasonable under the Fourth Amendment because the privacy interest protected by that constitutional guarantee is legitimately abated by the fact of arrest.

Mr. Justice Marshall, with whom Mr. Justice Douglas and Mr. Justice Brennan join, dissenting.

Certain fundamental principles have characterized this Court's Fourth Amendment jurisprudence over the years. Perhaps the most basic of these was expressed by

Mr. Justice Butler, speaking for a unanimous Court in *Go-Bart Co.* v. *United States*, . . . : "There is no formula for the determination of reasonableness. Each case is to be decided on its own facts and circumstances." . . . The majority's approach represents a clear and marked departure from our long tradition of case-by-case adjudication of the reasonableness of searches and seizures under the Fourth Amendment. I continue to believe that "[t]he scheme of the Fourth Amendment becomes meaningful only when it is assured that at some point the conduct of those charged with enforcing the laws can be subjected to the more detached, neutral scrutiny of a judge who must evaluate the reasonableness of a particular search or seizure in light of the particular circumstances." *Terry* v. *Ohio*. . . . Because I find the majority's reasoning to be at odds with these fundamental principles, I must respectfully dissent. . . .

The majority also suggests that the Court of Appeals reached a novel and unprecedented result by imposing qualifications on the historically recognized authority to conduct a full search incident to a lawful arrest. Nothing could be further from the truth, as the Court of Appeals itself was so careful to point out. . . . The fact is that this question has been considered by several state and federal courts, the vast majority of which have held that absent special circumstances a police officer has no right to conduct a full search of the person incident to a lawful arrest for violation of a motor vehicle regulation. . . .

Accordingly, I think it disingenuous for the Court to now pronounce that what precedents exist on the question "tend to support the broad statement of the authority to search incident to arrest found in the successive decisions of this Court, rather than the restrictive one which was applied by the Court of Appeals in this case.". . . . It is disquieting, to say the least, to see the Court at once admit that "[v]irtually all of the statements of this Court affirming the existence of an unqualified authority to search incident to a lawful arrest are dicta" and concede that we are presented with an open question on which "further examination into history and practice" would be helpful, yet then conduct an examination into prior practice which is not only wholly superficial, but totally inaccurate and misleading.

The majority's attempt to avoid case-by-case adjudication of Fourth Amendment issues is not only misguided as a matter of principle, but is also doomed to fail as a matter of practical application. As the majority itself is well aware, . . . the powers granted the police in this case are strong ones, subject to potential abuse. . . . There is always the possibility that a police officer, lacking probable cause to obtain a search warrant, will use a traffic arrest as a pretext to conduct a search. . . . I suggest this possibility not to impugn the integrity of our police, but merely to point out that case-by-case adjudication will always be necessary to determine whether a full arrest was effected for purely legitimate reasons or, rather, as a pretext for searching the arrestee. . . .

The underlying rationale of a search incident to arrest of a traffic offender initially suggests as reasonable a search whose scope is similar to the protective weapons frisk permitted in *Terry*. . . .

The Government does not now contend that the search of respondent's pocket can be justified by any need to find and seize evidence in order to prevent its concealment or destruction, for as the Court of Appeals found, there are no evidence or fruits of the offense with which the respondent was charged. The only rationale for a search in this case, then, is the removal of weapons which the arrestee might use to harm the officer and attempt an escape. This rationale, of course, is identical to the rationale of the search permitted in *Terry*. . . .

The majority opinion fails to recognize that the search conducted by Officer

Jenks did not merely involve a search of respondent's person. It also included a separate search of effects found on his person. And even were we to assume, arguendo, that it was reasonable for Jenks to remove the object he felt in respondent's pocket, clearly there was no justification consistent with the Fourth Amendment which would authorize his opening the package and looking inside.

To begin with, after Jenks had the cigarette package in his hands, there is no indication that he had reason to believe or did in fact believe that the package contained a weapon. More importantly, even if the crumpled up cigarette package had in fact contained some sort of small weapon, it would have been impossible for respondent to have used it once the package was in the officer's hands. Opening the package therefore did not further the protective purpose of the search. . . .

The Government argues that it is difficult to see what constitutionally protected "expectation of privacy" a prisoner has in the interior of a cigarette pack. One wonders if the result in this case would have been the same were respondent a businessman who was lawfully taken into custody for driving without a license and whose wallet was taken from him by the police. Would it be reasonable for the police officer, because of the possibility that a razor blade was hidden somewhere in the wallet, to open it, remove all the contents, and examine each item carefully? Or suppose a lawyer lawfully arrested for a traffic offense is found to have a sealed envelope on his person. Would it be permissible for the arresting officer to tear open the envelope in order to make sure that it did not contain a clandestine weapon— perhaps a pin or a razor blade? . . . Would it not be more consonant with the purpose of the Fourth Amendment and the legitimate needs of the police to require the officer, if he has any question whatsoever about what the wallet or letter contains, to hold onto it until the arrestee is brought to the precinct station? . . .

The search conducted by Officer Jenks in this case went far beyond what was reasonably necessary to protect him from harm or to ensure that respondent would not effect an escape from custody. In my view, it therefore fell outside the scope of a properly drawn "search incident to arrest" exception to the Fourth Amendment's warrant requirement. I would affirm the judgment to the Court of Appeals holding that the fruits of the search should have been suppressed at respondent's trial.

It should be noted that some state courts have specifically refused to follow the rather harsh *Robinson* rule. [See, for example, *People* v. *Marsh,* 20 N.Y.2d. 98, 228 N.E.2d 783 (1967).]

The second general exception to the requirement of a warrant prior to search is in the situation of movable vehicles, such as automobiles, airplanes, or boats. The leading United States Supreme Court decision on the subject is *Carroll* v. *United States,* 267 U.S. 132 (1925), involving the admissibility of bottles of liquor seized from an automobile by federal prohibition agents without a warrant. Chief Justice Taft, after examining various federal statutes, stated for the Court:

We have made a somewhat extended reference to these statutes to show that the guaranty of freedom from unreasonable searches and seizures by the Fourth Amendment has been construed, practically since the beginning of the government, as recognizing a necessary difference between a search of a store, dwelling house, or other structure in respect of which a proper official warrant readily may be obtained, and a search of a ship, motor boat, wagon, or automobile for contraband goods, where it is not practicable to secure a warrant because the vehicle can be quickly moved out of the locality or jurisdiction in which the warrant must be sought.

It was brought out in that same opinion, however, that such an exception should not be construed by the police as carte blanche to search movable vehicles out of curiosity or mere suspicion: "In cases where seizure is impossible except without warrant, the seizing officer acts unlawfully and at his peril unless he can show the court probable cause."

In *Brinegar* v. *United States*, in 1949, the Court reaffirmed the principle announced in *Carroll* and also gave some attention to the matter of defining "probable cause."

BRINEGAR *v.* UNITED STATES
338 U.S. 160 (1949)

[Federal officers were patrolling a highway leading from known sources of liquor supply in Joplin, Missouri, to a probable illegal market in "dry" Oklahoma. They observed a car driven by a person whom one of the officers had arrested about five months previously for illegally transporting liquor and whom he knew to have a reputation for hauling liquor. On two prior occasions he had seen the same man loading liquor into his car in large quantities in Joplin, Missouri. The officers pursued the car at high speed and forced it off the road. The driver admitted he was transporting liquor. The liquor was seized and used as evidence at a trial in which the driver was convicted of violating federal liquor laws. At the trial the court denied a motion to suppress the evidence on the claim that there was no probable cause to believe that he was carrying liquor, and therefore the chase and detention were illegal, and the liquor was unlawfully seized.]

Mr. Justice Rutledge delivered the opinion of the Court. . . .

. . . The evidence here is undisputed, is admissible on the issue of probable cause, and clearly establishes that the agent had good ground for believing that Brinegar was engaged regularly throughout the period in illicit liquor running and dealing. . . .

Guilt in a criminal case must be proved beyond a reasonable doubt and by evidence confined to that which long experience in the common-law tradition, to some extent embodied in the Constitution, has crystallized into rules of evidence consistent with that standard. . . .

However, if those standards were to be made applicable in determining probable cause for an arrest or for search and seizure, more especially in cases such as this involving moving vehicles used in the commission of crime, few indeed would be the situations in which an officer, charged with protecting the public interest by enforcing the law, could take effective action toward that end. Those standards have seldom been so applied.

In dealing with probable cause, however, as the very name implies, we deal with probabilities. These are not technical; they are the factual and practical considerations of everyday life on which reasonable and prudent men, not legal technicians, act. The standard of proof is accordingly correlative to what must be proved.

"The substance of all the definitions" of probable cause "is a reasonable ground for belief of guilt.". . . And this "means less than evidence which would justify condemnation" or conviction, as Marshall, Ch. J., said for the Court more than a century ago. . . . Since Marshall's time, at any rate, it has come to mean more than bare suspicion: Probable cause exists where "the facts and circumstances within their [the officers'] knowledge, and of which they had reasonably trustworthy information, [are] sufficient in themselves to warrant a man of reasonable caution in the belief that" an offense has been or is being committed. *Carroll* v. *United States,* 267 U.S. 132, 162.

The rule of probable cause is a practical, non-technical conception affording the best compromise that has been found for accommodating . . . often opposing interests. Requiring more would unduly hamper law enforcement. To allow less would be to leave law-abiding citizens at the mercy of the officers' whim or caprice. . . .

Accordingly the judgment is

Affirmed.

Mr. Justice Jackson, joined by Justices Frankfurter and Murphy, dissenting.
. . . Undoubtedly the automobile presents peculiar problems for law enforcement agencies, is frequently a facility for the perpetration of crime and an aid in the escape of criminals. But if we are to make judicial exceptions to the Fourth Amendment for these reasons, it seems to me they should depend somewhat upon the gravity of the offense. If we assume, for example, that a child is kidnaped and the officers throw a roadblock about the neighborhood and search every outgoing car, it would be a drastic and undiscriminating use of the search. The officers might be unable to show probable cause for searching any particular car. However, I should candidly strive hard to sustain such an action, executed fairly and in good faith, because it might be reasonable to subject travelers to that indignity if it was the only way to save a life and detect a vicious crime. But I should not strain to sustain such a roadblock and universal search to salvage a few bottles of bourbon and catch a bootlegger. . . .

Searches for illegal aliens conducted by the United States Border Patrol have presented some special problems in the area of warrantless searches of automobiles. In *Almeida-Sanchez* v. *United States,* 413 U.S. 266 (1973), the defendant, while driving on a state highway in California, about twenty-five miles from the Mexican border, was stopped by a roving border patrol of the United States Immigration and Naturalization Service, and his automobile was searched for aliens. The patrol had no search warrant and had no probable cause to believe that the defendant had committed any offense. In the course of the search, marijuana was found in the automobile. In a Federal District Court the defendant was convicted of concealing and transporting illegally imported marijuana. The conviction was affirmed by the Court of Appeals, which held that under a federal statute and a regulation adopted by the Service under the statute, the patrol was authorized to look for aliens by stopping and searching automobiles within 100 miles of an international border, without either a warrant or probable cause. The United States Supreme Court reversed, holding that in the absence of probable cause or consent, the warrantless search of the automobile violated his Fourth Amendment rights, and that the search could not be justified either as the "functional equivalent" of a border search or under the Court's decisions allowing certain warrantless searches of automobiles and warrantless administrative inspections.

Justice Stewart, for the majority, stated that it is "undoubtedly within the power of the Federal Government to exclude aliens from the country," and that this power "can be effectuated by routine inspections and searches of individuals or conveyances seeking to cross our borders." Further, such searches may, in certain instances, take place not only at the border itself, but at its "functional equivalents" as well, as, for example, a search of the passengers and cargo of an airplane arriving at a St. Louis airport after a nonstop flight from Mexico City. But the search of petitioner's automobile on a road that lies at all points at least twenty miles from the Mexican border was of a wholly different sort and violated the Fourth Amendment right of petitioner to be free of unreasonable searches and seizures.

In *United States* v. *Ortiz,* 422 U.S. 891 (1975), the Court extended the rule of *Almeida-Sanchez* to bar searches of automobiles by the Border Patrol at an official checkpoint at San Clemente, California, some sixty-six road miles north of the Mexican border, where the choice of cars to be searched was purely discretionary in the Border Patrol officers, and probable cause was not shown to determine which cars were selected for search at the checkpoint. In a footnote to his opinion for the majority, however, Justice Powell pointed out that the Court was not deciding the issue of whether Border Patrol officers may lawfully stop motorists for *questioning* at an established checkpoint without reason to believe that a particular vehicle is carrying aliens, nor did the opinion suggest that probable cause would be required for all inspections of private motor vehicles. "It is quite possible, for example, that different considerations would apply to routine safety inspections required as a condition of road use."

In both *Almeida-Sanchez* and *Ortiz* the Government had argued vigorously that the public interest demands effective measures to control the illegal entry of aliens at the Mexican border. The immigration and Naturalization Service estimates that there may be as many as ten or twelve million aliens illegally in the country, and that some 85 percent of these are from Mexico. The Service argued that their special search measures were vital to achieve a reduction in such illegal entries. In *United States* v. *Brignoni-Ponce,* 422 U.S. 873 (1975), decided on the same day as *Ortiz,* the Court again reversed a conviction on Fourth Amendment grounds, but the majority stated that the full standard of "probable cause" would not be required of the Border Patrol when stopping cars without warrants in the border areas to check for illegal aliens. In *Brignoni-Ponce* the facts showed that the only ground for suspicion leading to the stopping of the car by the roving patrol was that the occupants appeared to be of Mexican ancestry. The Court held this to be insufficient. At the same time, Justice Powell, for the majority, stated that "Because of the limited nature of the intrusion, stops of this sort may be justified on facts that do not amount to the probable cause required for an arrest." *Terry* v. *Ohio* was mentioned as an analogy, where a limited search was approved when based on a reasonable suspicion. The rule was stated in this form: "Except at the border and its functional equivalents, officers on roving patrol may stop vehicles only if they are aware of specific articulate facts, together with rational inferences from those facts, that reasonably warrant suspicion that the vehicles contain aliens who may be illegally in the country."

[For discussion of the border search problem, see: Note, "Almeida-Sanchez and its Progeny," 17 *Arizona L. Rev.* 214 (1975), and Note, "Border Searches Revisited: The Constitutional Propriety of Fixed and Temporary Checkpoint Searches," 2 *Hastings Const. L. Q.* 251 (1975).]

The roving patrol cases seem to hold that to stop a car, based on "reasonable suspicion," to check for illegal aliens is not unreasonable, but such a stop initially justifies only a brief questioning and check of identification to determine whether the occupants are legal residents. A search would require probable cause. When the basis for stopping a car is probable cause to believe that it is transporting contraband, then a warrantless search of the vehicle, on the spot, is permissible. The *Robinson* case indicates that when a vehicle is stopped to cite the driver for a traffic violation, a search of the person as an incident to that arrest is not unreasonable. In addition, the "plain view" doctrine would extend the search to include those items inside the car which the officer could see, but a full search of the vehicle would seem to be unreasonable, absent probable cause to believe some crime other than the traffic violation is being committed which would involve the hidden portions of the car. If, however, the vehicle is stopped for the purpose of arresting the occupants where there is probable cause to believe them guilty of a crime other than a traffic violation, then these facts may support a probable cause determination sufficient to justify a full search of the vehicle for weapons used to commit the crime, or for the fruits of the crime, or for contraband. Thus the search can reasonably go beyond that permitted in a *Robinson* situation.

Problems have arisen, however, when warrantless searches of cars were made after the arrest and when the car was removed from the scene of the arrest. In *Preston* v. *United States,* 376 U.S. 364 (1964), the Court held void the search of a car in which the defendant had been riding, after it had been towed to the police garage. But in *Cooper* v. *California,* 386 U.S. 58 (1967), the Court held that such a warrantless search was valid if the purpose of seizing it and the later search were "closely related" to the reason for the defendant's arrest.

Chambers v. *Maroney,* 399 U.S. 42 (1970), involved the issue of probable cause in stopping a car and arresting the occupants, but it raised in addition the question of the legality of a warrantless search of the car after it had been driven from the scene of the arrest to the police station. A filling station in Pennsylvania was robbed by two men, each of whom displayed a gun. Currency was taken from the cash drawer, and the attendant was directed to place the coins in a glove, which was also taken. Two teen-agers, who had earlier noticed a blue compact station wagon circling the block near the station, saw the car speed away from a parking lot near the station. Upon learning that the station had been robbed, they called the police and reported that the car contained four men, and one was wearing a green sweater. The attendant told the police that one man was wearing a green sweater and the other wore a trench coat. A description of the car and the two robbers was broadcast over the police radio. Within an hour, a light blue compact station wagon answering the description and carrying four men was stopped by the police about two miles from the station. One of the occupants was wearing a green sweater and there was a trench coat in the car. The occupants were arrested and the car was driven to the police station. In the course of a thorough search of the car at the station, the police found concealed in a compartment under the dashboard two .38-caliber revolvers, a glove containing small change, and certain cards bearing the name of an attendant at another service station which had been robbed a week earlier. Chambers was indicted and convicted of both robberies. He attacked his conviction in a petition for habeas corpus, alleging that the arrest took place without probable cause and that the warrantless search of the car after its removal to the police station was unconstitutional, thus barring the use of the incriminating evidence obtained during the search. (Other claims of the petitioner are omitted from this discussion.)

The Court held, with little discussion, that "the police had ample cause to stop a light blue compact station wagon carrying four men and to arrest the occupants, one of whom was wearing a green sweater and one of whom had a trench coat with him in the car." On the question of the validity of the search, it was claimed that either the police had to search at the time of the arrest or they would be required to obtain a warrant. The Court disagreed. Justice White, for the majority, stated:

For constitutional purposes, we see no difference between on the one hand seizing and holding a car before presenting the probable cause issue to a magistrate and on the other hand carrying out an immediate search without a warrant. Given probable cause to search, either course is reasonable under the Fourth Amendment.

In *Cady* v. *Dombrowski,* 413 U.S. 433 (1973), the Court held valid the warrantless search of an automobile which had been involved in an accident, and which had been towed to a private garage. The driver of the car identified himself as a Chicago policeman. He was drunk and injured when found by the police in a Wisconsin rural area and was arrested, taken to a hospital, and placed under guard. One of the arresting officers, believing that Chicago police officers were required to carry their revolvers at all times, and observing that the injured man did not have a revolver when he was arrested, drove to the garage to search for the weapon. After a search of the interior failed to uncover the revolver, the officer searched the trunk and found bloodstained clothing. Later, a bloodstained body was located on the defendant's brother's farm in a nearby county. The defendant was charged with murder and was convicted in a trial at which the evidence taken from his car was introduced over his objections. The State argued that the search was reasonable in order to remove a weapon from a car which was vulnerable to intrusion by a vandal who might endanger the general public after stealing the revolver. In a five-to-four decision the Court held that the search was not "unreasonable" within the meaning of the Fourth Amendment.

In *Cardwell* v. *Lewis,* 417 U.S. 583 (1974), defendant was convicted of murder in a trial in which evidence was admitted that had been obtained from the seizure and examination of his automobile which, shortly after the defendant's arrest at a police office, had been towed to a police impoundment lot from a public parking lot. The examination, which was conducted on the day after the arrest, consisted of (1) the taking of paint samples from the exterior of the car, which samples were not different from foreign paint scrapings taken from the murder victim's automobile, and (2) the observation of the tread on a tire of the defendant's car which matched the cast of a tire impression made at the scene of the crime. In a habeas corpus proceeding, the United States District Court held that the seizure and examination of the car violated the Fourth and Fourteenth Amendments and ruled that the evidence should have been excluded. The Court of Appeals affirmed, but the Supreme Court reversed. Four members of the Court held that the seizure of the car from a public place, where access was not meaningfully restricted, was not unreasonable, and the "search" in this case, concededly made on the basis of probable cause, infringed no expectation of privacy, and thus the evidence was properly admissible. Justice Powell concurred, but solely on the ground that in a habeas corpus review of state convictions based on Fourth Amendment claims, the inquiry should be confined to the question whether the defendant had an opportunity to raise the issue in the state courts and to have it adjudicated fairly. The four dissenters argued vigorously that no exigent circumstances existed which would dispense with the requirement of a warrant prior to the seizure and search.

It should be clear that the search of persons of property without a warrant and without probable cause, but with proper consent voluntarily given, is valid under the Fourth Amendment. Questions may still arise, however, as to who may give consent for a particular search or whether consent was in fact voluntary. In *Schneckloth* v. *Bustamonte,* 412 U.S. 218 (1973), the issue presented was whether consent given to search an automobile should be considered "involuntary" if the accused was not aware that he had a right to refuse such consent. A police officer on routine patrol stopped a car for a minor traffic violation and found it to contain six men. When the driver could not produce a driver's license, the officer asked if any of the other five had any evidence of identification. One of the passengers produced a license and explained that the car was borrowed from his brother. The officer asked him if he could search the car, and the reply was, "Sure, go ahead." Prior to the search no one was threatened with arrest. The owner's brother opened the trunk and even assisted in the search. Under the rear seat were found three checks that had previously been stolen from a car wash. At subsequent trial upon a charge of possessing a check with intent to defraud, the defendant moved to suppress the evidence on the ground that the search and seizure were unconstitutional. The motion was denied, and accused was convicted. It was argued in the Supreme Court that consent could not be considered "voluntary" unless the accused was at the time aware of his right to refuse consent, and thus his permission would represent a "knowing and intelligent" waiver of such right. The majority of the Court rejected this argument, stating that "neither this Court's prior cases, nor the traditional definition of 'voluntariness' requires proof of knowledge of a right to refuse as the sine qua non of an effective consent to a search." It stated further that the State is required to demonstrate that the consent was in fact voluntarily given, and not the result of duress or coercion, express or implied, but "Voluntariness is a question of fact to be determined from all the circumstances, and while the subject's knowledge of a right to refuse is a factor to be taken into account, the prosecution is not required to demonstrate such knowledge as a prerequisite to establishing a voluntary consent." Three justices dissented, with Justice Brennan stating: "It wholly escapes me how our citizens can meaningfully be said to have waived something as precious as a constitutional guarantee without ever being aware of its existence." The dissenters were not impressed with the majority's view that a consent search is fundamentally different in nature from the waiver of a trial right.

It may be noted that some state courts, as a matter of state constitutional law, have ruled the other way on this issue. See, for example, *State* v. *Johnson,* 68 N.J. 349, 346 A.2d 66 (1975); *State* v. *Kaluna,* 520 P.2d 51 (Hawaii, 1974); and *People* v. *Brisendine,* 13 Cal.3rd 528, 531 P.2d 1099 (1975).

There is also the question of who is authorized to give consent. In *Chapman* v. *United States,* 365 U.S. 610 (1961), the Court held that a landlord could not validly consent to a search of a house he had rented to another, and in *Stoner* v. *California,* 376 U.S. 483 (1964), it was held that a night hotel clerk could not validly consent to a search of a customer's room. But in *United States* v. *Matlock,* 415 U.S. 164 (1974), the Court ruled that consent for the search of a home could be given by a woman who was living in the home and occupying the same bedroom with the defendant, even though they were not married. The majority made clear that the consent of one who possesses common authority over premises or effects is valid against the absent, nonconsenting person with whom that authority is shared.

Administrative Searches

In addition to the two well-recognized exceptions to the requirement of a search warrant (and the obvious one of consent), another situation was considered by the Court in 1959—the right of a health inspector to examine private premises without a warrant. The case was *Frank* v. *Maryland*, 359 U.S. 360 (1959), holding that conviction and fine for refusal to permit a health inspector to inspect the premises for rat infestation did not violate the Fourteenth Amendment. The majority opinion, through Justice Frankfurter, first stressed the point that the inspection was conducted solely to determine whether there were conditions existing which were forbidden by ordinance— not to gather evidence for a criminal prosecution. He further pointed to the long history of administrative inspections:

Inspection without a warrant, as an adjunct to a regulatory scheme for the general welfare of the community and not as a means of enforcing the criminal law, has antecedents deep in our history. For more than 200 years Maryland has empowered its officers to enter upon ships, carriages, shops, and homes in the service of the common welfare. . . .

Justice Douglas, joined by three others, filed a vigorous dissent. The close vote of five-to-four suggested a tenuous status for the Court's holding. Justice Frankfurter had indicated that as the complexities and problems of urban life increased, so would the need for freer governmental right to inspect. Others, however, argued that for the same reasons the government should be more severely limited in order to forestall mounting invasions of privacy without some probable cause requirement as included in the issuance of a search warrant. The controversy culminated in a reexamination of the question in 1967 and the overruling of *Frank* v. *Maryland*.

CAMARA *v.* MUNICIPAL COURT OF SAN FRANCISCO
387 U.S. 523 (1967)

[An inspector of the Division of Housing Inspection of the San Francisco Department of Public Health entered an apartment building to make a routine annual inspection for possible violations of the city's Housing Code. The building's manager informed the inspector that appellant, lessee of the ground floor, was using the rear of his leasehold as a personal residence. Claiming that the building's occupancy permit did not allow residential use of the ground floor, the inspector confronted appellant and demanded that he permit an inspection of the premises. Appellant refused to allow the inspection because the inspector lacked a search warrant. The inspector returned two days later, again without a warrant, and appellant again refused to allow an inspection. A citation was then mailed ordering appellant to appear at the district attorney's office. When appellant failed to appear, two inspectors returned to his apartment and informed him that he was required to permit an inspection under §503 of the Housing Code, which set up a right of entry for authorized city employees "at reasonable times" for the purpose of performing any duty imposed upon them by the Municipal Code. Appellant still refused to permit the search without a warrant. Thereafter he was arrested and charged with refusing to permit a lawful inspection. When his demurrer to the criminal complaint was denied, appellant filed this petition for a writ of prohibition.]

Mr. Justice White delivered the opinion of the Court. . . .

In *Frank* v. *Maryland*, this Court upheld the conviction of one who refused to permit a warrantless inspection of private premises for the purposes of locating and abating a suspected public nuisance. Although *Frank* can arguably be distinguished from these cases on its facts, the *Frank* opinion has generally been interpreted as carrying out an additional exception to the rule that warrantless searches are unreasonable under the Fourth Amendment. . . . The District Court of Appeal so interpreted *Frank* in this case, and that ruling is the core of appellant's challenge here. We proceed to a re-examination of the factors which persuaded the *Frank* majority to adopt this construction of the Fourth Amendment's prohibition against unreasonable searches.

To the *Frank* majority, municipal fire, health, and housing inspection programs "touch at most upon the periphery of the important interests safeguarded by the Fourteenth Amendment's protection against official intrusions,". . . because the inspections are merely to determine whether physical conditions exist which do not comply with minimum standards prescribed in local regulatory ordinances. Since the inspector does not ask that the property owner open his doors to a search for "evidence of criminal action" which may be used to secure the owner's criminal conviction, historic interests of "self-protection" jointly protected by the Fourth and Fifth Amendments are said not to be involved. . . .

We may agree that a routine inspection of the physical condition of private property is a less hostile intrusion that the typical policeman's search for the fruits and instrumentalities of crime. . . . But we cannot agree that the Fourth Amendment interests at stake in these inspection cases are merely "peripheral.". . . [E]ven the most law-abiding citizen has a very tangible interest in limiting the circumstances under which the sanctity of his home may be broken by official authority, for the possibility of criminal entry under the guise of official sanction is a serious threat to personal and family security. And even accepting *Frank's* rather remarkable premise, inspections of the kind we are here considering do in fact jeopardize "self-protection" interests of the property owner. Like most regulatory laws, fire, health, and housing codes are enforced by criminal processes. In some cities, discovery of a violation by the inspector leads to a criminal complaint. . . .

The final justification suggested for warrantless administrative searches is that the public interest demands such a rule: it is vigorously argued that the health and safety of entire urban populations is dependent upon enforcement of minimum fire, housing, and sanitation standards, and that the only effective means of enforcing such codes is by routine systematized inspections of all physical structures. . . . But we think this argument misses the mark. The question is not, at this stage at least, whether these inspections may be made, but whether they may be made without a warrant. . . . It has nowhere been urged that fire, health, and housing code inspection programs could not achieve their goals within the confines of a reasonable search warrant requirement. . . .

In summary, we hold that administrative searches of the kind at issue here are significant intrusions upon the interests protected by the Fourth Amendment, that such searches when authorized and conducted without a warrant procedure lack the traditional safeguards which the Fourth Amendment guarantees to the individual, and that the reasons put forth in *Frank* v. *Maryland* and in other cases for upholding these warrantless searches are insufficient to justify so substantial a weakening of the Fourth Amendment's protections. Because of the nature of the municipal programs under consideration, however, these conclusions must be the beginning, not the end of our inquiry. . . .

[The opinion then discusses the "probable cause" requirement of the Fourth Amendment, and the conclusion is reached that this requirement would not necessarily be the same for municipal code inspection programs as for criminal investigations. The standard of reasonableness is weighed in terms of the needs and goals of code enforcement. Thus "area inspections" would not be justified in a search for stolen goods, but in the enforcement of fire, sanitation, and housing codes, "such programs have a long history of judicial and public acceptance."]

Having concluded that the area inspection is a "reasonable" search of private property within the meaning of the Fourth Amendment, it is obvious that "probable cause" to issue a warrant to inspect must exist if reasonable legislative or administrative standards for conducting an area inspecton are satisfied with respect to a particular dwelling. Such standards, which will vary with the municipal program being enforced, may be based upon the passage of time, the nature of the building (*e.g.,* a multi-family apartment house), or the condition of the entire area, but they will not necessarily depend upon specific knowledge of the condition of the particular dwelling. It has been suggested that so to vary the probable cause test from the standard applied in criminal cases would be to authorize a "synthetic search warrant" and thereby to lessen the overall protections of the Fourth Amendment. *Frank* v. *Maryland.* . . . But we do not agree. The warrant procedure is designed to guarantee that a decision to search private property is justified by a reasonable governmental interest. But reasonableness is still the ultimate standard. If a valid public interest justifies the intrusion contemplated, then there is probable cause to issue a suitably restricted search warrant. . . .

Since our holding emphasizes the controlling standard of reasonableness, nothing we say today is intended to foreclose prompt inspections, even without a warrant, that the law has traditionally upheld in emergency situations. . . . (seizure of unwholesome food) . . . (compulsory small pox vaccination) . . . (health quarantine) . . . (summary destruction of tubercular cattle). On the other hand, in the case of most routine area inspections, there is no compelling urgency to inspect at a particular time or on a particular day. Moreover, most citizens allow inspections of their property without a warrant. Thus, as a practical matter and in light of the Fourth Amendment's requirement that a warrant specify the property to be searched, it seems likely that warrants should normally be sought only after entry is refused unless there has been a citizen complaint or there is other satisfactory reason for securing immediate entry. . . .

The judgment is vacated and the case is remanded for further proceedings not inconsistent with this opinion.

It is so ordered.

Mr. Justice Clark, with whom Mr. Justice Harlan and Mr. Justice Stewart join, dissenting. . . .

. . . As I read it, the Fourth Amendment guarantee of individual privacy is, by its language, specifically qualified. It prohibits only those searches that are "unreasonable." The majority seem to recognize this for they set up a new test for the long-recognized and enforced Fourth Amendment's "probable cause" requirement for the issuance of warrants. They would permit the issuance of paper warrants, in area inspection programs, with probable cause based on area inspection standards as set out in municipal codes, and with warrants issued by the rubber stamp of a willing magistrate. In my view, this degrades the Fourth Amendment.

Moreover, history supports the *Frank* disposition. Over 150 years of city *in rem* inspections for health and safety purposes have continuously been enforced. In only one case during all that period have the courts denied municipalities this right. . . .

. . . The majority seems to hold that warrants may be obtained after a refusal of initial entry; I can find no such constitutional distinction or command. This boxcar warrant will be identical as to every dwelling in the area, save the street number itself. I daresay they will be printed up in pads of a thousand or more—with space for the street number to be inserted—and issued by magistrates in broadcast fashion as a matter of course.

I ask: Why go through such an exercise, such a pretense? As the same essentials are being followed under present procedures, I ask: Why the ceremony, the delay, the expense, the abuse of the search warrant? In my view this will not only destroy its integrity but will degrade the magistrate issuing them and soon bring disrepute not only upon the practice but upon the judicial process. It will be very costly to the city in paperwork incident to the issuance of the paper warrants, in loss of time of inspectors and waste of the time of magistrates and will result in more annoyance to the public. It will also be more burdensome to the occupant of the premises to be inspected. Under a search warrant the inspector can enter any time he chooses. Under the existing procedures he can enter only at reasonable times and invariably the convenience of the occupant is considered. I submit that the identical grounds for action elaborated today give more support—both legal and practical— to the present practice as approved in *Frank* v. *Maryland, supra,* than it does to this legalistic facade that the Court creates. . . .

In the companion case of *See* v. *Seattle*, 387 U.S. 541 (1967), the Court held that the *Camara* rule applied to commercial structures as well as private residences.

A peculiar aspect of the administrative search is the unannounced late-night "bedcheck" by welfare agencies to ensure that deserted wives who are recipients of family support payments are not being visited by their husbands, thus forfeiting benefit rights. No warrant is used, but failure of the recipient to permit the search in itself is sufficient to withdraw support payments. In *Wyman* v. *James,* 400 U.S. 309 (1971), the Court held that such searches, with the coercive aspect of threatened termination of benefits, did not violate Fourth Amendment protections. [For criticism of the practice, see Albert M. Bendich, "Privacy, Poverty, and the Constitution," 54 *Calif. L. Rev.* 407 (1966), and Charles A. Reich, "Midnight Welfare Searches and the Social Security Act," 72 *Yale L. J.* 1347 (1963).]

WYMAN *v.* JAMES
400 U.S. 309 (1971)

Mr. Justice Blackmun delivered the opinion of the Court.

This appeal presents the issue whether a beneficiary of the program for Aid to Families with Dependent Children (AFDC) may refuse a home visit by the case worker without risking the termination of benefits.

The New York State and City social services commissioners appeal from a judgment and decree of a divided three-judge District Court holding invalid and unconstitutional in application §134 of the New York Social Services Law ... and granting injunctive relief ... The beneficiary's thesis, and that of the District Court majority, is that home visitation is a search and, when not consented to or when not supported by a warrant based on probable cause, violates the beneficiary's Fourth and Fourteenth Amendment rights. ...

When a case involves a home and some type of official intrusion into that home, as this case appears to do, an immediate and natural reaction is one of concern about Fourth Amendment rights and the protection which that Amendment is intended to afford. ...

This natural and quite proper protective attitude, however, is not a factor in this case, for the seemingly obvious and simple reason that we are not concerned here with any search by the New York social service agency in the Fourth Amendment meaning of that term. It is true that the governing statute and regulations appear to make mandatory the initial home visit and the subsequent periodic "contacts" (which may include home visits) for the inception and continuance of aid. It is also true that the caseworker's posture in the home visit is perhaps, in a sense, both rehabilitative and investigative. But this latter aspect, we think, is given too broad a character and far more emphasis than it deserves if it is equated with a search in the traditional criminal law context. We note, too, that the visitation in itself is not forced or compelled, and that the beneficiary's denial of permission is not a criminal act. If consent to the visitation is withheld, no visitation takes place. The aid then never begins or merely ceases, as the case may be. There is no entry of the home and there is no search. ...

There are a number of factors which compel us to conclude that the home visit proposed for Mrs. James is not unreasonable:

1. The public's interest in this particular segment of the area of assistance to the unfortunate is protection and aid for the dependent child whose family requires such aid for that child. The focus is on the *child* and, further, it is on the child who is *dependent*. There is no more worthy object of the public's concern. The dependent child's needs are paramount, and only with hesitancy would we relegate those needs, in the scale of comparative values, to a position secondary to what the mother claims as her rights.

2. The agency, with tax funds provided from federal as well as from state sources, is fulfilling a public trust. The State, working through its qualified welfare agency, has appropriate and paramount interest and concern in seeing and assuring that the intended and proper objects of that tax-produced assistance are the ones who benefit from the aid it dispenses. Surely it is not unreasonable, in the Fourth Amendment sense or in any other sense of that term, that the State have at its command a gentle means, of lmited extent and of practical and considerate application, of achieving that assurance.

3. One who dispenses purely private charity naturally has an interest in and expects to know how his charitable funds are utilized and put to work. The public, when it is the provider, rightly expects the same. It might well expect more, because of the trust aspect of public funds, and the recipient, as well as the caseworker, has not only an interest but an obligation. ...

7. Mrs. James, in fact, on this record presents no specific complaint of any unreasonable intrusion on her home and nothing which supports an inference that the desired home visit had as its purpose the obtaining of information as to criminal activity. She complains of no proposed visitation at an awkward or retirement hour. She suggests no forcible entry. She refers to no snooping. ... What Mrs. James appears to want from the agency which provides her and her infant son

with the necessities for life is the right to receive those necessities upon her own informational term, to utilize the Fourth Amendment as a wedge for imposing those terms, and to avoid questions of any kind. . . .

Mrs. Justice Douglas, dissenting. . . .

Mr. Justice Marshall, whom Mr. Justice Brennan joins, dissenting. . . .

Although the Court does not agree with my conclusion that the home visit is an unreasonable search, its opinion suggests that even if the visit were unreasonable, appellee has somehow waived her right to object. Surely the majority cannot believe that valid Fourth Amendment consent can be given under the threat of the loss of one's sole means of support. . . .

In deciding that the homes of AFDC recipients are not entitled to protection from warrantless searches by welfare caseworkers, the Court declines to follow prior case law and employs a rationale that, if applied to the claims of all citizens, would threaten the vitality of the Fourth Amendment. . . . I find no little irony in the fact that the burden of today's departure from principled adjudication is placed upon the lowly poor. Perhaps the majority has explained why a commercial warehouse deserves more protection than does this poor woman's home. I am not convinced; and therefore, I must respectfully dissent.

Admissibility of Evidence Obtained Illegally

The distinction between the question of unreasonable searches and the question of admissibility of illegally obtained evidence is important, because in *Weeks* v. *United States,* 232 U.S. 383 (1914), the Court held that the Fourth Amendment did not, according to the rule of *Weeks,* constitute a rule of evidence. The Court went on to state, however, that unless such evidence were excluded, the Fourth Amendment would present no effective bar to improper searches and seizures. Thus *Weeks* held that as a federal rule of evidence, which in its supervisory function the Supreme Court can lay down for all federal courts, evidence illegally obtained by federal officers could not be used in a federal prosecution. (A majority of the Court, however, has now construed the *Weeks* rule as a Fourth Amendment requirement.)

At this point the complications of the federal system again enter the picture. Fourth Amendment limitations do not necessarily spell out the coverage of Fourteenth Amendment due process limitations on the states. And federal exclusionary rules are not applicable to the states' criminal procedures unless they rise to the level of constitutional requirements. The Fourteenth Amendment test, in the words of Justice Cardozo in *Palko* v. *Connecticut,* is whether a particular procedure or safeguard is "of the very essence of a scheme of ordered liberty." In 1949, the United States Supreme Court in *Wolf* v. *Colorado,* 338 U.S. 25, held that for the states to permit the use of evidence obtained illegally in a criminal prosecution was not a violation of the Fourteenth Amendment. Justice Frankfurter's opinion for the majority adverted to the *Weeks* doctrine, pointing out that as of 1949, thirty states rejected the *Weeks* doctrine, while seventeen states were in agreement with it. In view of this survey, he stated:

The jurisdictions which have rejected the *Weeks* doctrine have not left the right of privacy without other means of protection. Indeed, the exclusion of evidence is a remedy which directly serves only to protect those upon whose person or premises something incriminating has been found. We cannot, therefore, regard it as a departure from basic standards to remand such persons, together with those who emerge scatheless from a search, to the remedies of private action and such protection as the internal discipline of the police, under the eyes of an alert public opinion, may afford. Granting that in practice the exclusion of evidence may be an effective way of deterring unreasonable searches, it is not for this Court to condemn as falling below the minimal standards assured by the Due Process Clause a State's reliance upon other methods which, if consistently enforced, would be equally effective. . . .

We hold, therefore, that in a prosecution in a State court for a State crime the Fourteenth Amendment does not forbid the admission of evidence obtained by an unreasonable search and seizure.

Despite the holding that illegally obtained evidence was not barred in a subsequent prosecution, Justice Frankfurter's opinion pointed out that "were a State affirmatively to sanction such police incursion into privacy it would run counter to the guaranty of the Fourteenth Amendment violation." Thus the majority held that arbitrary and illegal searches and seizures by the state constituted a Fourteenth Amendment violation, but this did not bar the introduction of the evidence so obtained in a prosecution. The apparent contradiction can be resolved in one way by making such conduct on the part of state officers actionable under the civil or criminal provisions of the Civil Rights Acts. This, of course, is exactly what the Court held in 1961 in the case of *Monroe* v. *Pape,* discussed earlier.

Justice Murphy, in one of the three dissenting opinions in the *Wolf* case, said:

The conclusion is inescapable that but one remedy exists to deter violations of the search and seizure clause. That is the rule which excludes illegally obtained evidence. Only by exclusion can we impress upon the zealous prosecutor that violation of the Constitution will do him no good. And only when that point is driven home can the prosecutor be expected to emphasize the importance of observing constitutional demands in his instructions to the police.

The frustrations experienced by some members of the Court, occasioned by adherence to the *Wolf* rule, were brought sharply to focus in the case of *Irvine* v. *California,* 374 U.S. 128 (1954). In *Irvine* the police, after having made a key to fit the door, made repeated illegal entries into the home of a suspected bookmaker. They installed a secret microphone in the home and moved it from room to room, including the Irvines' bedroom. For over a month the police eavesdropped on conversations in this way, and on the basis of information thus obtained Irvine was tried and convicted. The United States Supreme Court affirmed, on authority of the *Wolf* rule, but Justice Jackson, who announced the judgment of the Court and wrote the principal opinion, thoroughly excoriated the behavior of the police. He stated that what was done "would be almost incredible if it were not admitted. Few police measures have come to our attention that more flagrantly, deliberately, and persistently violated the fundamental principle declared by the Fourth Amendment as a restriction on the Federal Government." Justice Jackson made a novel suggestion in the case, indicating his strong feeling that the officers should not escape unscathed, even though the evidence was admissible:

If the officials have willfully deprived a citizen of the United States of a right or privilege secured to him by the Fourteenth Amendment, that being the right to be secure in his home against unreasonable searches, as defined in *Wolf* v. *Colorado,* their conduct may constitute a federal crime.... We believe the Clerk of this Court should be directed to forward a copy of the record in this case, together with a copy of this opinion, for attention of the Attorney General of the United States.

The dissatisfaction with *Wolf's* bifurcation of the Fourth Amendment culminated in 1961 in a landmark case in the area of searches and seizures. The case was *Mapp* v. *Ohio,* and a majority of the Court officially adopted the conclusion expressed by Justice Murphy in his dissent in the *Wolf* case.

MAPP *v.* OHIO
367 U.S. 643 (1961)

[Three Cleveland police officers had come to appellant's residence in 1957, demanding entry on information that "a person was hiding out in the home who was wanted for questioning in connection with a recent bombing" and that policy paraphernalia was hidden in the home. Appellant, after phoning her attorney, refused to admit them without a search warrant. They returned later with several additional officers and forcibly broke into the house. Mrs. Mapp demanded to see a warrant. A paper, claimed to be a warrant, was held up by one of the officers. She grabbed the "warrant" and placed it in her bosom. A struggle ensued in which the officers recovered the piece of paper and handcuffed appellant because she had been "belligerent" in resisting their official rescue of the "warrant" from her person. The entire first and second floors of the house were thoroughly searched, and the search spread to the basement. In a trunk in the basement officers found the obscene material, for possession of which she was ultimately convicted. At the trial no search warrant was produced by the prosecution, nor was the failure to produce one explained or accounted for. The Ohio Supreme Court stated that there was "considerable doubt as to whether there ever was any warrant for the search of defendant's home." That court, however, followed *Wolf* v. *Colorado* in holding that despite the illegal seizure, the evidence was admissible.]

Mr. Justice Clark delivered the opinion of the Court.

Appellant stands convicted of knowingly having had in her possession and under her control certain lewd and lascivious books, pictures, and photographs in violation of ... Ohio's Revised Code. As officially stated in the syllabus to its opinion, the Supreme Court of Ohio found that her conviction was valid though "based primarily upon the introduction in evidence of lewd and lascivious books and pictures unlawfully seized during an unlawful search of defendant's home...."

I

Seventy-five years ago, in *Boyd* v. *United States* ..., considering the Fourth and Fifth Amendments as running "almost into each other" on the facts before it, this Court held that the doctrines of those Amendments "apply to all invasions on the part of the government and its employees of the sanctity of a man's home and the privacies of life.".....

The Court noted that "constitutional provisions for the security of person and property should be liberally construed.... It is the duty of courts to be watchful for the constitutional rights of the citizen, and against any stealthy encroachments thereon.".....

Less than 30 years after *Boyd,* this Court, in *Weeks* v. *United States,* ... stated that "the Fourth Amendment ... put the courts of the United States and Federal officials, in the exercise of their power and authority, under limitations and restraints [and] ... forever secure[d] the people, their persons, houses, papers and effects against all unreasonable searches and seizures under the guise of law ... and the duty of giving to it force and effect is obligatory upon all entrusted under our Federal system with the enforcement of the laws.". ...

Finally, the Court in that case clearly stated that use of the seized evidence involved "a denial of the constitutional rights of the accused." At p. 398. Thus, in the year 1914, in the *Weeks* case, this Court "for the first time" held that "in a federal prosecution the Fourth Amendment barred the use of evidence secured through an illegal search and seizure." *Wolf* v. *Colorado* ... This Court has ever since required of federal law officers a strict adherence to that command which this Court has held to be a clear, specific, and constitutionally required—even if judicially implied—deterrent safeguard without insistence upon which the Fourth Amendment would have been reduced to "a form of words." *Holmes, J., Silverthorne Lumber Co.* v. *United States.* ...

II

In 1949, 35 years after *Weeks* was announced, this court, in *Wolf* v. *Colorado* ..., again for the first time, discussed the effect of the Fourth Amendment upon the States through the operation of the Due Process Clause of the Fourteenth Amendment. It said:

"We have no hesitation in saying that were a State affirmatively to sanction such police incursion into privacy it would run counter to the guaranty of the Fourteenth Amendment." At p. 28.

Nevertheless, after declaring that the "security of one's privacy against arbitrary intrusion by the police" is "implicit in the 'concept of ordered liberty' and as such enforceable against the States through the Due Process Clause,". . . and announcing that it "stoutly adhere[d]" to the *Weeks* decision, the Court decided that the *Weeks* exclusionary rule would not then be imposed upon the States as "an essential ingredient of the right.". . . The Court's reasons for not considering essential to the right to privacy, as a curb imposed upon the States by the Due Process Clause, that which decades before had been posited as part and parcel of the Fourth Amendment's limitation upon federal encroachment of individual privacy, were bottomed on factual considerations.

While they are not basically relevant to a decision that the exclusionary rule is an essential ingredient of the Fourth Amendment as the right it embodies is vouchsafed against the States by the Due Process Clause, we will consider the current validity of the factual grounds upon which *Wolf* was based. ...

... While in 1949, prior to the *Wolf* case, almost two-thirds of the States were opposed to the exclusionary rule, now, despite the *Wolf* case, more than half of those since passing upon it, by their own legislative or judicial decision, have wholly or partly adopted or adhered to the *Weeks* rule. ... Significantly, among those now following the rule is California which, according to its highest court, was "compelled to reach that conclusion because other remedies have completly failed to secure compliance with the constitutional provisions. . . ." In connection with this California case, we note that the second basis elaborated in *Wolf* in support of its failure to enforce the exclusionary doctrine against the States was that "other means of protection" have been afforded "the right to privacy.". . . The experience of California that such other remedies have been worthless and futile is buttressed by the experience of other States. The obvious futility of relegating the Fourth Amendment to the protection of other remedies has, moreover, been recognized by this Court since *Wolf*. See *Irvine* v. *California*. . . .

Likewise, time has set its face against what *Wolf* called the "weighty testimony" of *People* v. *Defore*. . . . There Justice (then Judge) Cardozo, rejecting adoption of the *Weeks* exclusionary rule in New York, had said that "[t]he Federal rule as it stands is either too strict or too lax.". . . However, the force of that reasoning has been largely vitiated by later decisions of this Court. These include the recent discarding of the "silver platter" doctrine which allowed federal judicial use of evidence seized in violation of the Constitution by state agents, *Elkins* v. *United States*, 364 U.S. 206, *supra;* the relaxation of the formerly strict requirements as to standing to challenge the use of evidence thus seized, so that now the procedure of exclusion, "ultimately referable to constitutional safeguards," is available to anyone even "legitimately on [the] premises" unlawfully searched, *Jones* v. *United States*, 362 U.S. 257 (1960); and, finally, the formulation of a method to prevent state use of evidence unconstitutionally seized by federal agents, *Rea* v. *United States*, 350 U.S. 214 (1956). . . .

It, therefore, plainly appears that the factual considerations supporting the failure of the *Wolf* Court to include the *Weeks* exclusionary rule when it recognized the enforceability of the right to privacy against the States in 1949, while not basically relevant to the constitutional consideration, could not, in any analysis, now be deemed controlling.

III

. . . And only last Term, after again carefully re-examining the *Wolf* doctrine in *Elkins* v. *United States* . . . the Court pointed out that "the controlling principles" as to search and seizure and the problem of admissibility "seemed clear" until the announcement in *Wolf* "that the Due Process Clause of the Fourteenth Amendment does not itself require state courts to adopt the exclusionary rule" of the *Weeks* case. . . . At the same time the Court pointed out, "the underlying constitutional doctrine which Wolf established . . . that the Federal Constitution . . . prohibits unreasonable searches and seizures by state officers" had undermined the "foundation upon which the admissibility of state-seized evidence in a federal trial originally rested. . . ." The Court concluded that it was therefore obliged to hold, although it chose the narrower ground on which to do so, that all evidence obtained by an unconstitutional search and seizure was inadmissible in a federal court regardless of its source. Today we once again examine *Wolf's* constitutional documentation of the right to privacy free from unreasonable state intrusion, and, after its dozen years on our books, are led by it to close the only courtroom door remaining open to evidence secured by official lawlessness in flagrant abuse of that basic right, reserved to all persons as a specific guarantee against that very same unlawful conduct. We hold that all evidence obtained by searches and seizures in violation of the Constitution is, by that same authority, inadmissible in a state court. . . .

V

. . . Moreover, our holding that the exclusionary rule is an essential part of both the Fourth and Fourteenth Amendments is not only the logical dictate of prior cases, but it also makes very good sense. There is no war between the Constitution and common sense. Presently, a federal prosecutor may make no use of evidence illegally seized, but a State's attorney across the street may, although he supposedly is operating under the enforceable prohibitions of the same Amendment. Thus, the State, by admitting evidence unlawfully seized, serves to encourage disobedience to the Federal Constitution which it is bound to uphold. Moreover, as was said in *Elkins,* "[t]he very essence of a healthy federalism depends upon the avoidance of needless conflict between state and federal courts.". . . Such a conflict, hereafter needless, arose this very Term, in *Wilson* v. *Schnettler,* 355 U.S. 381 (1961), in which, and in spite of the promise made by *Rea,* we gave full recognition to our practice in this regard by refusing to restrain a federal officer from testifying in a state court as to evidence unconstitutionally seized by him in the performance of his duties. Yet the double standard recognized until today hardly put such a thesis into practice. In nonexclusionary States, federal officers, being human, were by it invited to and did, as our cases indicated, step across the street to the State's attorney with their unconstitutionally seized evidence. Prosecution on the basis of that evidence was then had in a state court in utter disregard of the enforceable Fourth Amendment. If the fruits of an unconstitutional search had been inadmissible in both state and federal courts, this inducement to evasion would have been sooner eliminated. There would be no need to reconcile such cases as *Rea* and *Schnettler,* each pointing up the hazardous uncertainties of our heretofore ambivalent approach. . . .

There are those who say, as did Justice (then Judge) Cardozo that under our constitutional exclusionary doctrine "[t]he criminal is to go free because the constable has blundered.". . . In some cases this will undoubtedly be the result. But, as was said in *Elkins,* "there is another consideration—the imperative of judicial integrity.". . . The criminal goes free, if he must, but it is the law that sets him free. Nothing can destroy a govermnent more quickly than its failure to observe its own laws, or worse, its disregard of the charter of its own existence. . . .

The judgment of the Supreme Court of Ohio is reversed and the cause remanded for further proceedings not inconsistent with this opinion.

Reversed and Remanded.

Mr. Justice Black, concurring.

. . . I am still not persuaded that the Fourth Amendment, standing alone, would be enough to bar the introduction into evidence against an accused of papers and effects seized from him in violation of its commands. For the Fourth Amendment does not itself contain any provision expressly precluding the use of such evidence, and I am extremely doubtful that such a provision could properly be inferred from nothing more than the basic command against unreasonable searches and seizures. Reflection on the problem, however, in the light of cases coming before the Court since *Wolf,* has led me to conclude that when the Fourth Amendment's ban against unreasonable searches and seizures is considered together with the Fifth Amendment's ban against compelled self-incrimination, a constitutional basis emerges which not only justifies but actually requires the exclusionary rule. . . .

Mr. Justice Douglas, concurring. . . .

Mr. Justice Harlan, whom Mr. Justice Frankfurter and Mr. Justice Whittaker join, dissenting.

In overruling the *Wolf* case the Court, in my opinion, has forgotten the sense of judicial restraint which, with due regard for *stare decisis,* is one element that should enter into deciding whether a past decision of this Court should be overruled. Apart from that I also believe the *Wolf* rule represents sounder Constitutional doctrine than the new rule which now replaces it.

I

From the Court's statement of the case one would gather that the central, if not controlling, issue on this appeal is whether illegally state-seized evidence is Constitutionally admissible in a state prosecution, an issue which would of course face us with the need for re-examining *Wolf*. However, such is not the situation. For, although that question was indeed raised here and below among appellant's subordinate points, the new and pivotal issue brought to the Court by this appeal is whether Section 2905.34 of the Ohio Revised Code making criminal the *mere* knowing possession or control of obscene material, and under which appellant has been convicted, is consistent with the rights of free thought and expression assured against state action by the Fourteenth Amendment. That was the principal issue which was decided by the Ohio Supreme Court, which was tendered by appellant's Jurisdictional Statement, and which was briefed and argued in this Court.

In this posture of things, I think it fair to say that five members of this Court have simply "reached out" to overrule *Wolf*. With all respect for the views of the majority, and recognizing that *stare decisis* carries different weight in Constitutional adjudication than it does in nonconstitutional decision, I can perceive no justification for regarding this case as an appropriate occasion for re-examining *Wolf*....

The occasion which the Court has taken here is in the context of a case where the question was briefed not at all and argued only extremely tangentially.... I would think that our obligation to the States, on whom we impose this new rule, as well as the obligation of orderly adherence to our own processes would demand that we seek that aid which adequate briefing and argument lends to the determination of an important issue....

The preservation of a proper balance between state and federal responsibility in the administration of criminal justice demands patience on the part of those who might like to see things move faster among the States in this respect. Problems of criminal law enforcement vary widely from State to State.... For us the question remains, as it has always been, one of state power, not one of passing judgment on the wisdom of one state course or another. In my view this Court should continue to forbear from fettering the States with an adamant rule which may embarrass them in coping with their own peculiar problems in criminal law enforcement....

[Memorandum of Mr. Justice Stewart concurring in the reversal on the ground that the conviction was not consistent with "the rights of free thought and expression" guaranteed by the Fourteenth Amendment.]

Ker v. *California*, 374 U.S. 23 (1963), held that "the standard of reasonableness is the same under the Fourth and Fourteenth Amendments," thus clearly "incorporating" the Fourth Amendment.

The opinion in *Mapp*, however, left unanswered the question of whether the bar to admission of illegally obtained evidence should be applied retroactively and thus open the way for those in prison to attack their convictions where such evidence was used by the prosecution. The Court did not reach this issue until four years later, in *Linkletter* v. *Walker*, 381 U.S. 618 (1965), and by a seven-to-two vote held that the *Mapp* rule did not operate retrospectively upon cases finally decided prior to the *Mapp* case. Justice Clark, for the Court, pointed out that while the various federal courts of appeals had split on the issue, the "state courts which have considered the question have almost unanimously decided against application to cases finalized prior to *Mapp*." The petitioner contended that prior cases demonstrated that an absolute rule of retroaction prevails in the area of constitutional adjudication. Justice Clark gave a brief but instructive "outline of the history and theory of the problem presented" and concluded that "the Constitution neither prohibits nor requires retrospective effect." The doctrine of "void *ab initio*" was well stated in *Norton* v. *Shelby Co.,* 118 U.S. 425 (1886), in which the Court held that unconstitutional action "confers no rights; it imposes no duties; it affords no protection; it creates no office; it is, in legal contemplation, as inoperative as though it had never been passed." This Blackstonian view was opposed by the Austinian view that judges do more than merely discover law; they make law. And thus one cannot deny the existence of an overruled law as a juridical fact. Justice Clark stated, "We believe that the existence of the *Wolf* doctrine prior to *Mapp* is 'an operative fact and may have consequences which cannot justly be ignored. The past cannot always be erased by a new judicial declaration.' " He pointed out that the purpose in *Mapp* was to deter the lawless action of the police, and that purpose would not be served at this late date by the wholesale release of the guilty victims. He further suggested that retrospective application "would tax the administration of justice to the utmost." He concluded:

Finally, in each of the three areas in which we have applied our rule retrospectively the principle that we applied went to the fairness of the trial—the very integrity of the fact-finding process. Here, as we have pointed out, the fairness of the trial is not under attack. All that petitioner attacks is the admissibility of evidence, the reliability and relevancy of which is not questioned, and which may well have had no effect on the outcome.

[Justice Black, joined by Justice Douglas, dissented. He stated, "I am at a loss to understand why those who suffer from the use of evidence secured by a search and seizure in violation of the Fourth Amendment should be treated differently from those who have been denied other guarantees of the Bill of Rights."]

[See Oliver P. Field, *The Effect of an Unconstitutional Statute* (Minneapolis: University of Minnesota Press, 1935); Paul Freund, "New Vistas in Constitutional Law," 112 *U. Pa. L. Rev.* 631 (1964); Note, "Prospective Overruling and Retroactive Application in the Federal Courts," 71 *Yale L. J.* 907 (1962); Thomas S. Currier, "Time and Change in Judge-Made Law: Prospective Overruling," 51 *Va. L. Rev.* 201 (1965); and G. Gregory Fahlund, "Retroactivity and the Warren Court: The Strategy of a Revolution," 35 *Journal of Politics* 570 (1973).]

The exclusionary rule of *Weeks* and *Mapp* has been subjected to considerable criticism, and its future appears to be somewhat uncertain. It is argued that irrespective of the manner in which evidence is obtained, if it has probative value, it should be admissible. Other remedies than suppressing the evidence should be employed to stop illegal seizures. The classic statement of this position was made by Judge Cardozo while on the New York Court of Appeals: "Is the criminal to go free because the constable has blundered?" In a period of rising crime rates more and more police, judges, and scholars are echoing this sentiment. The need for modification of the exclusionary rule was strongly urged by Chief Justice Burger in a dissenting opinion in *Bivens* v. *Six Unknown Fed. Narcotics Agents,* 403 U.S. 388 (1971). The Court held that a violation of the Fourth Amendment's command against unreasonable searches and seizures, by a federal agent acting under color of federal authority, gave rise to a federal cause of action for damages. In dissent, the Chief Justice took the occasion to attack the exclusionary rule:

This evidentiary rule is unique to American jurisprudence. Although the English and Canadian legal systems are highly regarded, neither has adopted our rule. . . . Williams, *The Exclusionary Rule Under Foreign Law*—England, 52 *J. Crim L. C. & P. S.* 272 (1961).

I do not question the need for some remedy to give meaning and teeth to the constitutional guarantees against unlawful conduct by government officials. Without some effective sanction, these protections would constitute little more than rhetoric. . . . But the hope that this objective could be accomplished by the exclusion of reliable evidence from criminal trials was hardly more than a wistful dream. Although I would hesitate to abandon it until some meaningful substitute is developed, the history of the suppression doctrine demonstrates that it is both conceptually sterile and practically ineffective in accomplishing its stated objective. . . .

Some clear demonstration of the benefits and effectiveness of the exclusionary rule is required to justify it in view of the high price it extracts from society—the release of countless guilty criminals. . . . But there is no empirical evidence to support the claim that the rule actually deters illegal conduct of law enforcement officials. . . .

There are several reasons for this failure. The rule does not apply any direct sanction to the individual official whose illegal conduct results in the exclusion of evidence in a criminal trial. With rare exceptions law enforcement agencies do not impose direct sanctions on the individual officer responsible for a particular judicial application of the suppression doctrine. . . . Thus there is virtually nothing done to bring about a change in his practices. The immediate sanction triggered by the application of the rule is visited upon the prosecutor whose case against a criminal is either weakened or destroyed. The doctrine deprives the police in no real sense; except that apprehending wrongdoers is their business, police have no more stake in successful prosecutions than prosecutors or the public. . . .

Whatever educational effect the rule conceivably might have in theory is greatly diminished in fact by the realities of law enforcement work. Policemen do not have the time, inclination, or training to read and grasp the nuances of the appellate opinions that ultimately define the standards of conduct they are to follow. The issues that these decisions resolve often admit of neither easy nor obvious answers, as sharply divided courts on what is or is not "reasonable" amply demonstrate. Nor can judges, in all candor, forget that opinions sometimes lack helpful clarity. . . .

Although unfortunately ineffective, the exclusionary rule has increasingly been characterized by a single, monolithic, and drastic judicial response to all official violations of legal norms. Inadvertent errors of judgment that do not work any grave injustice will inevitably occur under the pressure of police work. These honest mistakes have been treated in the same way as deliberate and flagrant *Irvine*-type violations of the Fourth Amendment. For example, in *Miller* v. *United States* . . . reliable evidence was suppressed because of a police officer's failure to say a "few more words" during the arrest and search of a known narcotics peddler. . . .

I submit that society has at least as much right to expect rationally graded responses from judges in place of the universal "capital punishment" we inflict on all evidence when police error is shown in its acquisition. . . . Yet for over 55 years, and with increasing scope and intensity . . . , our legal system has treated vastly dissimilar cases as if they were the same. . . . [W]e can and should be faulted for clinging to an unworkable and irrational concept of law. My criticism is that we have taken so long to find better ways to accomplish these desired objectives. And there are better ways. . . .

Reasonable and effective substitutes can be formulated if Congress would take the lead, as it did for example in 1946 in the Federal Tort Claims Act. . . . The problems of both error and deliberate misconduct by law enforcement officials call for a workable remedy. Private damage actions against individual police officers concededly have not adequately met this requirement. . . .

I conclude, therefore, that an entirely different remedy is necessary, but it is one that in my view as as much beyond judicial power as the step the Court takes today. Congress should develop an administrative or quasi-judicial remedy against the government itself to afford compensation and restitution for persons whose Fourth Amendment rights have been violated. . . . Such a statutory scheme would have the added advantage of providing some remedy to the completely innocent persons who are sometimes the victim of illegal police conduct—something that the suppression doctrine, of course, can never accomplish. . . .

In a country that prides itself on innovation, inventive genius, and willingness to experiment, it is a paradox that we should cling for more than a half century to a legal mechanism that was poorly designed and never really worked. I can only hope now that the Congress will manifest a willingness to view realistically the hard evidence of the half-century history of the suppression doctrine revealing thousands of cases in which the criminal was set free because the constable blundered and virtually no evidence that innocent victims of police error—such as petitioner claims to be—have been afforded meaningful redress.

[For a thoughtful analysis of the exclusionary rule controversy and a plea for caution in making a change, see Bradley C. Canon, "Is the Exclusionary Rule in Failing Health? Some New Data and a Plea Against a Precipitous Conclusion," 62 *Ky. L. J.* 681 (1973–74).]

WIRETAPPING AND ELECTRONIC SURVEILLANCE

Following the logic of the decisions to date in the area of wiretapping and eavesdropping presents substantial difficulties. The constitutional issue was taken up in *Olmstead* v. *United States,* 277 U.S. 438 (1928). By a five-to-four vote the United States Supreme Court held that phone taps by federal officers did not violate the Fourth Amendment. Chief Justice Taft, speaking for the majority, stated:

The well known historical purpose of the Fourth Amendment, directed against general warrants and writs of assistance, was to prevent the use of governmental force to search a man's house, his person, his papers, and his effects, and to prevent their seizure against his will. . . .

The Amendment itself shows that the search is to be of material things—the person, the house, his papers or his effects. The description of the warrant necessary to make the proceeding lawful is that it must specify the place to be searched and the person or *things* to be seized. . . .

The United States takes no such care of telegraph or telephone messages as of mailed sealed letters. The Amendment does not forbid what was done here. There was no searching. There was no seizure. The evidence was secured by the use of the sense of hearing and that only. There was no entry of the houses or offices of the defendants. . . .

Congress may, of course, protect the secrecy of telephone messages by making them, when intercepted, inadmissible in evidence in Federal criminal trials, by direct legislation, and thus depart from the common law of evidence. But the courts may not adopt such a policy by attributing an enlarged and unusual meaning to the

Fourth Amendment. The reasonable view is that one who installs in his house a telephone instrument with connecting wires intends to project his voice to those quite outside, and that the wires beyond his house and messages while passing over them are not within the protection of the Fourth Amendment. Here those who intercepted the projected voices were not in the house of either party to the conversation. . . .

A standard which would forbid the reception of evidence if obtained by other than nice ethical conduct by government officials would make society suffer and give criminals greater immunity than has been known heretofore. In the absence of controlling legislation by Congress, those who realize the difficulties in bringing offenders to justice may well deem it wise that the exclusion of evidence should be confined to cases where rights under the Constitution would be violated by admitting it. . . .

[Justice Holmes gave a vigorous dissenting opinion, in the course of which he said:]

. . . It is desirable that criminals should be detected, and to that end that all available evidence should be used. It also is desirable that the government should not itself foster and pay for other crimes, when they are the means by which the evidence is to be obtained. If it pays its officers for having got evidence by crime I do not see why it may not as well pay them for getting it in the same way, and I can attach no importance to protestations of disapproval if it knowingly accepts and pays and announces that in the future it will pay for the fruits. We have to choose, and for my part I think it a less evil that some criminals should escape than that the government should play an ignoble part.

For those who agree with me, no distinction can be taken between the government as prosecutor and the government as judge. If the existing code does not permit district attorneys to have a hand in such dirty business, it does not permit the judge to allow such iniquities to succeed. . . . And if all that I have said so far be accepted, it makes no difference that in this case wire tapping is made a crime by the law of the state, not by the law of the United States. It is true that a state cannot make rules of evidence for courts of the United States, but the state has authority over the conduct in question, and I hardly think that the United States would appear to greater advantage when paying for an odious crime against state law than when inciting to the disregard of its own. . . .

[Justice Brandeis, also dissenting, made some prophetic statements about the "progress" of the various sciences in the art of prying into private lives:]

. . . The progress of science in furnishing the government with means of espionage is not likely to stop with wire-tapping. Ways may some day be developed by which the government, without removing papers from secret drawers, can reproduce them in court, and by which it will be enabled to expose to a jury the most intimate occurrences of the home. Advances in the psychic and related sciences may bring means of exploring unexpressed beliefs, thoughts and emotions. . . . Can it be that the Constitution affords no protection against such invasions of individual security? . . .

Decency, security, and liberty alike demand that government officials shall be subjected to the same rules of conduct that are commands to the citizen. In a government of laws, existence of the government will be imperiled if it fails to observe the law scrupulously. Our government is the potent, the omnipresent, teacher. For good or for ill, it teaches the whole people by its example. Crime is contagious. If the government becomes a law-breaker, it breeds contempt for law; it invites every man to become a law unto himself; it invites anarchy. To declare that in the administration of the criminal law the end justifies the means—to declare that the government may commit crimes in order to secure the conviction of a private criminal—would bring terrible retribution. Against that pernicious doctrine this Court should resolutely set its face.

[For an interesting treatment of the *Olmstead* case—"its genesis, its unfolding, and its impact"—see Walter F. Murphy, *Wiretapping on Trial: A Case Study in the Judicial Process* (New York: Random House, 1965).]

In his opinion for the majority, Chief Justice Taft suggested that if Congress so desired, it could bar the admission of intercepted telephone messages in federal criminal trials. Congress adopted the suggestions in passing the Federal Communications Act of 1934. The relevant portion of the Act is Section 605:

Unauthorized publication or use of communications. No person receiving or assisting in receiving, or transmitting, . . . any interstate or foreign communication by wire or radio shall divulge or publish the existence, contents, substance, purport, effect, or meaning thereof, . . . to any person other than the addressee . . . ; and no person not being authorized by the sender shall intercept any communication and divulge or publish the existence, contents, substance, purport, effect, or meaning of such intercepted communication to any person; . . . and no person having received such intercepted communication or having become acquainted with the contents, . . . or meaning of the same or any part thereof, knowing that such information was so obtained, shall divulge or publish the existence, contents, . . . or meaning of the same or any part thereof, or use the same . . . for his own benefit or for the benefit of another not entitled thereto. . . .

Section 501 of the Act made the willful and knowing violation of this section punishable by a fine of not more than $10,000 or by imprisonment for a term of not more than two years or both.

The Court faced the problem of interpreting the impact of Section 605 on admissibility of evidence in *Nardone* v. *United States,* 302 U.S. 379 (1937). The defendants, under indictment for smuggling alcohol, objected to the testimony of federal agents to the substance of telephone conversations by defendants which the agents had overheard by means of wiretaps. The trial judge rejected their contention, and they were convicted. On appeal, the Court reversed the conviction, holding that Section 605 comprehended federal agents in the phrase "no person" shall intercept and divulge communications by wire, and also holding that the prohibition against divulging the communication "to any person" barred the agents' testimony in court relative to the intercepted communication.

In a new trial following the first decision, Nardone and his codefendants were again convicted. On appeal, the defendants raised the issue of whether they could be barred from examining the prosecution to see whether it used the information obtained by the wiretap to acquire evidence. The Court of Appeals affirmed the trial judge's refusal to allow the examination. The Supreme Court, however, reversed in *Nardone* v. *United States,* 308 U.S. 338 (1939). It pointed out that merely to bar the testimony concerning conversations and at the same time to permit such illegally obtained information to be used to run down leads for evidence which *could* be admitted would be to "stultify the policy which compelled" the decision in the first *Nardone* case. It went on to say that the trial judge must allow to the accused an opportunity to prove, in wiretap situations, that "a substantial portion of the case against him was a fruit of the poisonous tree."

In *Berger* v. *New York*, 388 U.S. 41 (1967), the Court considered the validity of New York's permissive eavesdrop statute which permitted certain courts to issue "an ex parte order for eavesdropping," upon oath or affirmation of a district attorney or ranking police officers that there was reasonable ground to believe that evidence of crime might be thus obtained, and particularly describing the person whose communications, conversations, or discussions were to be overheard or recorded and the purpose thereof. The order would be effective for a period of no more than two months unless extended by the judge who signed the original order. In view of the rather widespread support for a "middle position" of outlawing eavesdrop testimony instigated by the government, except for that obtained under a special court order, the decision in *Berger* v. *New York* was awaited with more than usual interest. When it was announced, the square holding of the majority was that the New York statute was violative of the Fourth and Fourteenth Amendments. The vote was five-to-four on this point, although Justice Stewart joined the majority on other grounds.

BERGER *v.* NEW YORK

388 U.S. 41 (1967)

[Berger, the petitioner, was convicted on two counts of conspiracy to bribe the Chairman of the New York State Liquor Authority. The case arose out of a complaint by one Pansini, a bar owner, to the District Attorney that agents of the Authority had harassed him for his failure to pay a bribe for a liquor license. The District Attorney's office directed that Pansini, equipped with a recording device, interview an employee of the Authority. The employee advised Pansini that the price for a license was $10,000 and suggested that he contact one Neyer, an attorney. Neyer admitted having worked with the Authority employee, apparently concerning liquor licenses.

On the basis of this evidence an eavesdrop order was obtained permitting the installation of a recording device in Neyer's office. On the basis of leads obtained from this eavesdrop, a second order was obtained to plant a recorder in the office of one Steinman. After some two weeks of eavesdropping, a conspiracy was uncovered involving petitioner as "a go-between" for the principal conspirators and concerning the issuance of liquor licenses for the Playboy and Tenement Clubs of New York City. The parties stipulated that the State had no information on which to base its case except that obtained by the use of the eavesdrop evidence. Relevant portions of the recordings were received in evidence at the trial and were played to the jury, and petitioner was convicted.]

Mr. Justice Clark delivered the opinion of the Court.

This writ tests the validity of New York's permissive eavesdrop statute. . . . We have concluded that the language of New York's statute is too broad in its sweep resulting in a trespassory intrusion into a constitutionally protected area and is, therefore, violative of the Fourth and Fourteenth Amendments. . . .

Sophisticated electronic devices have now been developed (commonly known as "bugging") which are capable of eavesdropping on anyone in most any given situation. . . .

As science developed these detection techniques, lawmakers, sensing the resulting invasion of individual privacy, have provided some statutory protection for the public. Seven States, California, Illinois, Maryland, Massachusetts, Nevada, New York, and Oregon, prohibit surreptitious eavesdropping by mechanical or electronic device. However, all, save Illinois, permit official court-ordered eavesdropping. Some 36 States prohibit wiretapping. But of these, 27 permit "authorized" interception of some type. Federal law, as we have seen, prohibits interception and divulging or publishing of the content of wiretaps without exception. In sum, it is fair to say that wiretapping on the whole is outlawed, except for permissive use by law enforcement officials in some States; while electronic eavesdroping is—save for seven States—permitted both officially and privately. And, in six of the seven States electronic eavesdropping ("bugging") is permissible on court order. . . .

The Court was faced with its first wiretap case in 1928, *Olmstead* v. *United States*. . . . There the interception of Olmstead's telephone line was accomplished without entry upon his premises and was, therefore, found not to be proscribed by the Fourth Amendment. The basis of the decision was that the Constitution did not forbid the obtaining of evidence by wiretapping unless it involved actual unlawful entry into the house. . . .

The first "bugging" case reached the Court in 1942 in *Goldman* v. *United States*. . . . There the Court found that the use of a detectaphone placed against an office wall in order to hear private conversations in the office next door did not violate the Fourth Amendment because there was no physical trespass in connection with the relevant interception. And in *On Lee* v. *United States*. . . . (1952), we found that since "no trespass was committed" a conversation between Lee and a federal agent, occurring in the former's laundry and electronically recorded, was not condemned by the Fourth Amendment. Thereafter in *Silverman* v. *United States* . . . (1961), the Court found "that the eavesdropping was accomplished by means of an unauthorized physical penetration into the premises occupied by the petitioners.". . .

While New York's statute satisfies the Fourth Amendment's requirement that a neutral and detached authority be interposed between the police and the public, . . . the broad sweep of the statute is immediately observable. . . .

The Fourth Amendment commands that a warrant issue not only upon probable cause supported by oath or affirmation, but also "particularly describing the place to be searched, and the persons or things to be seized." New York's statute lacks this particularization. It merely says that a warrant may issue on reasonable ground to believe that evidence of crime may be obtained by the eavesdrop. It lays down no requirement for particularity in the warrant as to what specific crime has been or is being committed, nor "the place to be searched," or "the persons or things to be seized" as specifically required by the Fourth Amendment. The need for particularity and evidence of reliability in the showing required when judicial authorization of a search is sought is especially great in the case of eavesdropping. By its very nature eavesdropping involves an intrusion on privacy that is broad in scope. As was said in *Osborn* v. *United States,* 385 U.S. 323 (1966), the "indiscriminate use of such devices in law enforcement raises grave constitutional questions under the Fourth and Fifth Amendments," and imposes "a heavier responsibility on this Court in its supervision of the fairness of procedures. . . ." . . . There, two judges acting jointly authorized the installation of a device on the person of a prospective witness to record conversations between him and an attorney for a defendant then on trial in the United States District Court. The judicial authorization was based on an affidavit of the witness setting out in detail previous conversations between the witness and the attorney concerning the bribery of jurors in the case. The recording device was, as the Court said, authorized "under the most precise and discriminate circumstances, circumstances which fully met the 'requirement of particularity' " of the Fourth Amendment.... Among other safeguards, the order described the type of conversation sought with particularity, thus indicating the specific objective of the Government in entering the constitutionally protected area and the limitations placed upon the officer executing the warrant. Under it the officer could not search unauthorized areas; likewise, once the property sought, and for which the order was issued, was found the officer could not use the order as a passkey to further search. In addition, the order authorized one limited intrusion rather than a series or a continuous surveillance. And, we note that a new order was issued when the officer sought to resume the search and probable cause was shown for the succeeding one. Moreover, the order was executed by the officer with dispatch, not over a prolonged and extended period. In this manner no greater invasion of privacy was permitted than was necessary under the circumstances. Finally the officer was required to and did make a return on the order showing how it was executed and what was seized. Through these strict precautions the danger of an unlawful search and seizure was minimized.

On the contrary, New York's statute lays down no such "precise and discriminate" requirements.... New York's broadside authorization rather than being "carefully circumscribed" so as to prevent unauthorized invasions of privacy actually permits general searches by electronic devices, the truly offensive character of which was first condemned in *Entick* v. *Carrington, supra,* and which were then known as "general warrants.". . .

We believe the statute here is equally offensive. First . . . eavesdropping is authorized without requiring belief that any particular offense has been or is being committed; nor that the property sought, the conversations, be particularly described.... Secondly, authorization of eavesdroping for a two-month period is the equivalent of a series of intrusions, searches, and seizures pursuant to a single showing of probable cause.... During such . . . period the conversations of any and all persons coming into the area covered by the device will be seized indiscriminately and without regard to their connection to the crime under investigation . . . Third, the statute places no termination date on the eavesdrop once the conversation sought is seized. This is left entirely in the discretion of the officer. Finally, the statute's procedure, necessarily because its success depends on secrecy, has no requirement for notice as do conventional warrants, nor does it overcome this defect by requiring some showing of special facts.... In short, the statute's blanket grant of permission to eavesdrop is without adequate judicial supervision or protective procedures....

It is said with fervor that electronic eavesdropping is a most important technique of law enforcement and that outlawing it will severely cripple crime detection....

In any event we cannot forgive the requirements of the Fourth Amendment in the name of law enforcement. This is no formality that we require today but a fundamental rule that has long been recognized as basic to the privacy of every home in America.... Few threats to liberty exist which are greater than that posed by the use of eavesdropping devices....

It is said that neither a warrant nor a statute authorizing eavesdropping can be drawn so as to meet the Fourth Amendment's requirements. If that be true then the "fruits" of eavesdropping devices are barred under the Amendment. On the other hand this Court has in the past, under specific conditions and circumstances, sustained the use of eavesdropping devices. See *Goldman* v. *United States, supra; On Lee* v. *United States, supra; . . .* and *Osborn* v. *United States, supra.* . . . Our concern with the statute here is whether its language permits a trespassory invasion of the home, by general warrant, contrary to the command of the Fourth Amendment. As it is written, we believe that it does.

Reversed.

Mr. Justice Douglas, concurring.

I join the opinion of the Court because at long last it overrules *sub silentio Olmstead* v. *United States*... and its offspring and brings wiretapping and other electronic eavesdropping fully within the purview of the Fourth Amendment....

Mr. Justice Stewart, concurring in the result....

I think that "electronic eavesdropping, *as such,* or as it is permitted by this statute, is not an unreasonable search and seizure." The statute contains many provisions more stringent than the Fourth Amendment generally requires, as Mr. Justice Black has so forcefully pointed out....

I would hold that the affidavits on which the judicial order issued in this case did not constitute a showing of probable cause adequate to justify the authorizing order....

Accordingly, I would reverse the judgment.

Mr. Justice White, dissenting....

Mr. Justice Harlan, dissenting.

The Court in recent years has more and more taken to itself sole responsibility for setting the pattern of criminal law enforcement throughout the country....

Today's decision is in this mold. Despite the fact that the use of electronic eavesdropping devices as instruments of criminal law enforcement is currently being comprehensively addressed by the Congress and various other bodies in the country, the Court has chosen, quite unnecessarily, to decide this case in a manner which will seriously restrict, if not entirely thwart, such efforts, and will freeze further progress in this field, except as the Court may itself act or a Constitutional Amendment may set things right.

In my opinion what the Court is doing is very wrong, and I must respectfully dissent....

Mr. Justice Black, dissenting....

... [W]hile the Court faintly intimates to the contrary, it seems obvious to me that its holding, by creating obstacles that cannot be overcome, makes it completely impossible for the State or the Federal Government ever to have a valid eavesdropping statute. All of this is done, it seems to me, in part because of the Court's hostility to eavesdropping as "ignoble" and "dirty business" and in part because of fear that rapidly advancing science and technology is making eavesdropping more and more effective.... Neither of these, nor any other grounds that I can think of, are sufficient in my judgment to justify a holding that the use of evidence secured by eavesdropping is barred by the Constitution....

It was clear that the Court in *Berger* found the New York eavesdrop statute defective, but the more general impact of the decision was demonstrated later in the year in *Katz* v. *United States,* the "telephone booth" case.

KATZ *v.* UNITED STATES
389 U.S. 347 (1967)

Mr. Justice Stewart delivered the opinion of the Court.

The petitioner was convicted in the District Court for the Southern District of California under an eight-count indictment charging him with transmitting wagering information by telephone from Los Angeles to Miami and Boston, in violation of a federal statute. At trial the Government was permitted, over the petitioner's objection, to introduce evidence of the petitioner's end of telephone conversations, overheard by FBI agents who had attached an electronic listening and recording device to the outside of the public telephone booth from which he had placed his calls. In affirming his conviction, the Court of Appeals rejected the contention that the recordings had been obtained in violation of the Fourth Amendment, because "[t]here was no physical entrance into the area occupied by [the petitioner]." We granted certiorari in order to consider the constitutional questions thus presented. . . .

. . . [T]he Fourth Amendment cannot be translated into a general constitutional "right to privacy." That Amendment protects individual privacy against certain kinds of governmental intrusion, but its protections go further, and often have nothing to do with privacy at all. Other provisions of the Constitution protect personal privacy from other forms of governmental invasion. But the protection of a person's *general* right to privacy—his right to be let alone by other people—is, like the protection of his property and of his very life, left largely to the law of the individual States.

Because of the misleading way the issues have been formulated, the parties have attached great significance to the characterization of the telephone booth from which the petitioner placed his calls. The petitioner has strenuously argued that the booth was "a constitutionally protected area." The Government has maintained with equal vigor that it was not. But this effort to decide whether or not a given "area," viewed in the abstract, is "constitutionally protected" deflects attention from the problem presented by this case. For the Fourth Amendment protects people, not places. What a person knowingly exposes to the public, even in his own home or office, is not a subject of Fourth Amendment protection. . . . But what he seeks to preserve as private, even in an area accessible to the public, may be constitutionally protected. . . .

The Government stresses the fact that the telephone booth from which the petitioner made his calls was constructed partly of glass, so that he was as visible after he entered it as he would have been if he had remained outside. But what he sought to exclude when he entered the booth was not the intruding eye—it was the uninvited ear. He did not shed his right to do so simply because he made his calls from a place where he might be seen. No less than an individual in a business office, in a friend's apartment, or in a taxicab, a person in a telephone booth may rely upon the protection of the Fourth Amendment. One who occupies it, shuts the door behind him, and pays the toll that permits him to place a call is surely entitled to assume that the words he utters into the mouthpiece will not be broadcast to the world. To read the Constitution more narrowly is to ignore the vital role that the public telephone has come to play in private communication.

The Government contends, however, that the activities of its agents in this case should not be tested by Fourth Amendment requirements, for the surveillance technique they employed involved no physical penetration of the telephone booth from which the petitioner placed his calls. It is true that the absence of such penetration was at one time thought to foreclose further Fourth Amendment inquiry, *Olmstead* v. *United States*, . . . for that Amendment was thought to limit only searches and seizures of tangible property. But "[t]he premise that property interests control the right of the Government to search and seize has been discredited." *Warden* v. *Hayden*. . . .

We conclude that the underpinnings of Olmstead and Goldman have been so eroded by our subsequent decisions that the "trespass" doctrine there enunciated can no longer be regarded as controlling. The Government's activities in electronically listening to and recording the petitioner's words violated the privacy upon which he justifiably relied while using the telephone booth and thus constituted a "search and seizure" within the meaning of the Fourth Amendment. . . .

The question remaining for decision, then, is whether the search and seizure conducted in this case complied with constitutional standards. . . . [T]he surveillance was limited, both in scope and in duration, to the specific purpose of establishing the contents of the petitioner's unlawful telephonic communications. The agents confined their surveillance to the brief periods during which he used the telephone booth, and they took great care to overhear only the conversations of the petitioner himself.

Accepting this account of the Government's actions as accurate, it is clear that this surveillance was so narrowly circumscribed that a duly authorized magistrate, properly notified of the need for such investigation, specifically informed of the basis on which it was to proceed, and clearly apprised of the precise intrusion it would entail, could constitutionally have authorized, with appropriate safeguards, the very limited search and seizure that the Government asserts in fact took place. . . .

The Government . . . argues that surveillance of a telephone booth should be exempted from the usual requirement of advance authorization by a magistrate upon a showing of probable cause. We cannot agree. . . . The government agents here ignored "the procedure of antecedent justification . . . that is central to the Fourth Amendment," a procedure that we hold to be a constitutional precondition of the kind of electronic surveillance involved in this case. Because the surveillance here failed to meet that condition, and because it led to the petitioner's conviction, the judgment must be reversed.

It is so ordered.

Mr. Justice Marshall took no part in the consideration or decision of this case.

Mr. Justice Douglas, with whom Mr. Justice Brennan joins, concurring. . . .

Mr. Justice Harlan, concurring. . . .

Mr. Justice Black, dissenting.

If I could agree with the Court that eavesdropping carried on by electronic means . . . constitutes a "search" or "seizure," I would be happy to join the Court's opinion. . . .

My basic objection is twofold: (1) I do not believe that the words of the Amendment will bear the meaning given them by today's decision, and (2) I do not believe that it is the proper role of this Court to rewrite the Amendment in order "to bring it into harmony with the times" and thus reach a result that many people believe to be desirable. . . .

In 1968 Congress responded to increasing public pressures calling for action to reduce the high incidence of crime, by enacting the Omnibus Crime Control and Safe Streets Act of 1968, 82 Stat. 197. While a major thrust of the Act was the establishment of the Law Enforcement Assistance Administration to provide assistance to state and local law enforcement agencies, Title III of the Act was an attempt to regulate governmental wiretapping and electronic surveillance (and to prohibit private interception) in accord with the guidelines laid down by the Court in *Berger* and *Katz*. In general terms, the Act prohibits electronic surveillance by any federal agency unless first authorized by "the Attorney General, or any Assistant Attorney General specially designated by the Attorney General" and then submitted to a federal judge who is empowered to issue the order approving the interception of communications. Detailed provisions cover the documents and information necessary to accompany the application, as well as the regulations surrounding the issuance of the order itself. There are several exceptions to the requirement of judicial authorization prior to interception, but the two more important ones are (1) prior consent of one of the parties to the communication for the interception, and (2) any situation in which the President deems it necessary, to protect national security, to obtain foreign intelligence information or to protect national security information against foreign intelligence.

In the cases which have thus far reached the Supreme Court, the Court has demanded absolute adherence to the letter of the Act. In *United States* v. *Giordano*, 416 U.S. 505 (1974), the Court held that evidence of narcotics violations obtained by a court-ordered wiretap would have to be suppressed as unlawfully intercepted because the application had been approved by the Attorney General's Executive Assistant instead of by the Attorney General or an "Assistant Attorney General specially designated" by him as required by the Act.

The question of whether the President could, without a warrant, direct a wiretap to gather information on alleged attempts of *domestic* organizations to subvert the government was answered in *United States* v. *United States District Court* in 1972.

UNITED STATES *v.* UNITED STATES DISTRICT COURT
407 U.S. 297 (1972)

[The case arose out of a criminal proceeding in which the United States charged three defendants with conspiracy to destroy government property. One of the defendants, Plamondon, was charged with the dynamite bombing of an office of the Central Intelligence Agency in Ann Arbor, Michigan. The defendants moved to compel the United States to disclose whether wiretap evidence had been obtained for use as evidence and to conduct a hearing to determine whether it had been obtained illegally. The government conceded that it had intercepted communications without a warrant, but argued that the surveillance was lawful under the President's power to protect the national security. The District Court held that the evidence was illegally obtained, and the government filed for a writ of mandamus to set aside the court's order.]

Mr. Justice Powell delivered the opinion of the Court....

I

Title III of the Omnibus Crime Control and Safe Streets Act, 18 USC §§2510–2520, authorizes the use of electronic surveillance for classes of crimes carefully specified in 18 USC §2516. Such surveillance is subject to prior court order. Section 2518 sets forth the detailed and particularized application necessary to obtain such an order as well as carefully circumscribed conditions for its use. The Act represents a comprehensive attempt by Congress to promote more effective control of crime while protecting the privacy of individual thought and expression. Much of Title

III was drawn to meet the constitutional requirements for electronic surveillance enunciated by this court in *Berger* v. *New York* . . . and *Katz* v. *United States.* . . .

Together with the elaborate surveillance requirements in Title III, there is the following proviso, 18 USC §2511 (3):

"Nothing contained in this chapter or in section 605 of the Communications Act of 1934 shall limit the constitutional power of the President to take such measures as he deems necessary to protect the Nation against actual or potential attack or other hostile acts of a foreign power, to obtain foreign intelligence information deemed essential to the security of the United States, or to protect national security information against foreign intelligence activities. *Nor shall anything contained in this chapter be deemed to limit the constitutional power of the President to take such measures as he deems necessary to protect the United States against the overthrow of the Government by force or other unlawful means, or against any other clear and present danger to the structure or existence of the Government.* The contents of any wire or oral communication intercepted by authority of the President in the exercise of the foregoing powers may be received in evidence in any trial, hearing or other proceeding where such interception was reasonable, and shall not be otherwise used or disclosed except as is necessary to implement that power." (Emphasis supplied.)

The Government relies on §2511 (3). It argues that "in excepting national security surveillances from the Act's warrant requirement Congress recognized the President's authority to conduct such surveillances without prior judicial approval." . . . The section thus is viewed as a recognition or affirmance of a constitutional authority in the President to conduct warrantless domestic security surveillance such as that involved in this case.

We think the language of §2511 (3), as well as the legislative history of the statute, refutes this interpretation. The relevant language is that: "Nothing contained in this chapter . . . shall limit the constitutional power of the President to take such measures as he deems necessary to protect . . ." against the dangers specified. At most, this is an implicit recognition that the President does have certain powers in the specified areas. Few would doubt this . . . But so far as the use of the President's electronic surveillance power is concerned, the language is essentially neutral.

Section 2511 (3) certainly confers no power, as the language is wholly inappropriate for such purpose. It merely provides that the Act shall not be interpreted to limit or disturb such power as the President may have under the Constitution. In short, Congress simply left presidential powers where it found them. . . . The legislative history of §2511 (3) supports this interpretation. . . . The debate . . . explicitly indicates that nothing in §2511 (3) was intended to *expand* or to *contract* or to *define* whatever presidential surveillance powers existed in matters affecting the national security. . . . [W]e hold that the statute is not the measure of the executive authority asserted in this case. Rather, we must look to the constitutional powers of the President.

II

It is important at the outset to emphasize the limited nature of the question before the Court. This case raises no constitutional challenge to electronic surveillance as specifically authorized by Title III of the Omnibus Crime Control and Safe Streets Act of 1968. Nor is there any question or doubt as to the necessity of obtaining a warrant in the surveillance of crimes unrelated to the national security interest. . . . Further, the instant case requires no judgment on the scope of the President's surveillance power with respect to the activities of foreign powers, within or without his country. The Attorney General's affidavit in this case states that the surveillances were "deemed necessary to protect the nation from attempts of *domestic organizations* to attack and subvert the existing structure of Government" (emphasis supplied). There is no evidence of any involvement, directly or indirectly, of a foreign power.

Our present inquiry, though important, is therefore a narrow one. It addresses a question left open by *Katz*: "Whether safeguards other than prior authorization by a magistrate would satisfy the Fourth Amendment in a situation involving the national security...." The determination of this question requires the essential Fourth Amendment inquiry into the "reasonableness" of the search and seizure in question, and the way in which that "reasonableness" derives content and meaning through reference to the warrant clause....

We begin the inquiry by noting that the President of the United States has the fundamental duty, under Art. II, §1, of the Constitution, "to preserve, protect, and defend the Constitution of the United States." Implicit in that duty is the power to protect our Government against those who would subvert or overthrow it by unlawful means. In the discharge of this duty, the President—through the Attorney General—may find it necessary to employ electronic surveillance to obtain intelligence information on the plans of those who plot unlawful acts against the Government....

It has been said that "the most basic function of any government is to provide for the security of the individual and of his property."... And unless Government safeguards its own capacity to function and to preserve the security of its people, society itself could become so disordered that all rights and liberties would be endangered....

But a recognition of these elementary truths does not make the employment by Government of electronic surveillance a welcome development—even when employed with restraint and under judicial supervision. There is, understandably, a deep-seated uneasiness and apprehension that this capability will be used to intrude upon cherished privacy of law-abiding citizens. We look to the Bill of Rights to safeguard this privacy....

III

As the Fourth Amendment is not absolute in its terms, our task is to examine and balance the basic values at stake in this case: the duty of Government to protect the domestic security, and the potential danger posed by unreasonable surveillance to individual privacy and free expression. If the legitimate need of Government to safeguard domestic security requires the use of electronic surveillance, the question is whether the needs of citizens for privacy and free expression may not be better protected by requiring a warrant before such surveillance is undertaken. We must also ask whether a warrant requirement would unduly frustrate the efforts of Government to protect itself from acts of subversion and overthrow directed against it....

These Fourth Amendment freedoms cannot properly be guaranteed if domestic security surveillances may be conducted solely within the discretion of the executive branch. The Fourth Amendment does not contemplate the executive officers of Government as neutral and disinterested magistrates. Their duty and responsibility is to enforce the laws, to investigate and to prosecute.... But those charged with this investigative and prosecutorial duty should not be the sole judges of when to utilize constitutionally sensitive means in pursuing their tasks. The historical judgment, which the Fourth Amendment accepts, is that unreviewed executive discretion may yield too readily to pressures to obtain incriminating evidence and overlook potential invasions of privacy and protected speech.

It may well be that, in the instant case, the Government's surveillance of Plamondon's conversations was a reasonable one which readily would have gained prior judicial approval. But . . . the Fourth Amendment contemplates a prior judicial judgment, not the risk that executive discretion may be reasonably exercised. . . . The independent check upon executive discretion is not satisfied, as the Government argues, by "extremely limited" post-surveillance judicial review. Indeed, post-surveillance review would never reach the surveillances which failed to result in prosecutions. Prior review by a neutral and detached magistrate is the time tested means of effectuating Fourth Amendment rights. . . .

It is true that there have been some exceptions to the warrant requirement. . . . But those exceptions are few in number and carefully delineated; in general they serve the legitimate needs of law enforcement officers to protect their own well-being and preserve evidence from destruction. . . .

The Government argues that the special circumstances applicable to domestic security surveillances necessitate a further exception to the warrant requirement. It is urged that the requirement of prior judicial review would obstruct the President in the discharge of his constitutional duty to protect domestic security. We are told further that these surveillances are directed primarily to the collecting and maintaining of intelligence with respect to subversive forces, and are not an attempt to gather evidence for specific criminal prosecutions. It is said that this type of surveillance should not be subject to traditional warrant requirements which were established to govern investigation of criminal activity, not on-going intelligence gathering. . . .

The Government further insists that courts "as a practical matter would have neither the knowledge nor the techniques necessary to determine whether there was probable cause to believe that surveillance was necessary to protect national security." These security problems, the Government contends, involve "a large number of complex and subtle factors" beyond the competence of courts to evaluate. . . .

As a final reason for exemption from a warrant requirement, the Government believes that disclosure to a magistrate of all or even a significant portion of the information involved in domestic security surveillances "would create serious potential dangers to the national security and to the lives of informants and agents. . . . Secrecy is the essential ingredient in intelligence gathering; requiring prior judicial authorization would create a greater 'danger of leaks . . . , because in addition to the judge, you have the clerk, the stenographer and some other official like a law assistant or bailiff who may be apprised of the nature' of the surveillance.". . .

These contentions in behalf of a complete exemption from the warrant requirement, when urged on behalf of the President and the national security in its domestic implications, merit the most careful consideration. We certainly do not reject them lightly, especially at a time of worldwide ferment and when civil disorders in this country are more prevalent than in the less turbulent periods of our history. There is, no doubt, pragmatic force to the Government's position.

But we do not think a case has been made for the requested departure from Fourth Amendment standards. The circumstances described do not justify complete exemption of domestic security surveillance from prior judicial scrutiny. Official surveillance, whether its purpose be criminal investigation or on-going intelligence gathering, risks infringement of constitutionally protected privacy of speech. Security surveillances are especially sensitive because of the inherent vagueness of the domestic security concept, the necessarily broad and continuing nature of intelligence gathering, and the temptation to utilize such surveillances to oversee political dissent. We recognize, as we have before, the constitutional basis of the President's domestic security role, but we think it must be exercised in a manner compatible with the Fourth Amendment. In this case we hold that this requires an appropriate prior warrant procedure.

We cannot accept the Government's argument that internal security matters are too subtle and complex for judicial evaluation. Courts regularly deal with the most difficult issues of our society. There is no reason to believe that federal judges will be insensitive to or uncomprehending of the issues involved in domestic security cases. Certainly courts can recognize that domestic security surveillance involves different considerations from the surveillance of ordinary crime. If the threat is too subtle or complex for our senior law enforcement officers to convey its significance to a court, one may question whether there is probable cause for surveillance.

Nor do we believe prior judicial approval will fracture the secrecy essential to official intelligence gathering. The investigation of criminal activity has long involved imparting sensitive information to judical officers who have respected the confidentalities involved. Judges may be counted upon to be especially conscious of security requirements in national security cases. . . . Moreover, a warrant application involves no public or adversary proceedings: it is an ex parte request before a magistrate or judge. Whatever security dangers clerical and secretarial personnel may pose can be minimized by proper administrative measures, possibly to the point of allowing the Government itself to provide the necessary clerical assistance.

Thus, we conclude that the Government's concerns do not justify departure in this case from the customary Fourth Amendment requirement of judicial approval prior to initiation of a search or surveillance. Although some added burden will be imposed upon the Attorney General, this inconvenience is justified in a free society to protect constitutional values. Nor do we think the Government's domestic surveillance powers will be impaired to any significant degree. A prior warrant establishes presumptive validity of the surveillance and will minimize the burden of justification in post-surveillance judicial review. By no means of least importance will be the reassurance of the public generally that indiscriminate wiretapping and bugging of law-abiding citizens cannot occur.

IV

We emphasize, before concluding this opinion, the scope of our decision. As stated at the outset, this case involves only the domestic aspects of national security. We have not addressed, and express no opinion as, the issues which may be involved with respect to activities of foreign powers or their agents. Nor does our decision rest on the language of §2511 (3) or any other section of Title III of the Omnibus Crime Control and Safe Streets Act of 1968. That Act does not attempt to define or delineate the powers of the President to meet domestic threats to the national security. . . .

Moreover, we do not hold that the same type of standards and procedures prescribed by Title III are necessarily applicable to this case. We recognize that domestic security surveillance may involve different policy and practical considerations from the surveillance of "ordinary crime.". . . The exact targets of such surveillance may be more difficult to identify than in surveillance operations against many types of crime specified in Title III. . . . Thus, the focus of domestic surveillance may be less precise than that directed against more conventional types of crime. . . .

V

As the surveillance of Plamondon's conversations was unlawful, because conducted without prior judicial approval, the courts below correctly held that *Alder-*

man v. *United States* ... (1969) is controlling and that it requires disclosure to the accused of his own impermissibly intercepted conversations. As stated in Alderman, "the trial court can and should, where appropriate, place a defendant and his counsel under enforceable orders against unwarranted disclosure of the materials which they may be entitled to inspect."

The judgment of the Court of Appeals is hereby

Affirmed.

The Chief Justice concurs in the result.

Mr. Justice Rehnquist took no part in the consideration or decision of this case.

Mr. Justice Douglas, concurring. . . .

Mr. Justice White, concurring in the judgment. . . .

[On wiretapping and eavesdropping generally, see Alan F. Westin, *Privacy and Freedom* (New York: Atheneum, 1967) and Samuel Dash, Richard F. Schwartz, and Robert Knowlton, *The Eavesdroppers* (New Brunswick: Rutgers Univ. Press, 1959).]

SELF-INCRIMINATION

The privilege against self-incrimination is generally accepted as a landmark in the development of procedural guarantees. It became established in the common law as a revolt against procedures in which accused persons were questioned under oath by judges, both to get evidence and to obtain confessions. Immunity from such interrogation was written into the Fifth Amendment of the Constitution and provides that "no person . . . shall be compelled in any criminal case to be a witness against himself."

While it is sometimes suggested that the purpose of the privilege was simply to prevent torture, there is another reason as well. It lies in the general feeling that the concept of fair play demands that the individual not be required to accuse and convict himself out of his own mouth. The case against him must be built by the government without requiring of the accused that he make their case for them by his own testimony. This aspect of the privilege has important consequences. It is not confined, for example, merely to cases of criminal prosecution, but extends to all sorts of proceedings where testimony might be required and where the divulgences might lead to a later criminal prosecution of the witness. Thus the privilege can operate in civil cases and in legislative investigations, as well as in a criminal prosecution. The first case to rule squarely on the application of the privilege to testimony before congressional investigating committees was *Quinn* v. *United States*, 349 U.S. 155 (1955). In the opinion of the Court, upholding the application of the privilege, Chief Justice Warren said:

The privilege against self-incrimination is a right that was hard-earned by our forefathers. The reasons for its inclusion in the Constitution—and the necessities for its preservation—are to be found in the lessons of history. As early as 1650, remembrance of the horror of Star Chamber proceedings a decade before had firmly established the privilege in the common law of England. Transplanted to this country as part of our legal heritage, it soon made its way into various state constitutions and ultimately in 1791 into the federal Bill of Rights. The privilege, this Court has stated, "was generally regarded then, as now, as a privilege of great value, a protection to the innocent though a shelter to the guilty, and a safeguard against heedless, unfounded or tyrannical prosecutions." Coequally with our other constitutional guarantees, the Self-Incrimination Clause "must be accorded liberal construction in favor of the right it was intended to secure." Such liberal construction is particularly warranted in a prosecution of a witness for a refusal to answer, since the respect normally accorded the privilege is then buttressed by the presumption of innocence accorded a defendant in a criminal trial. To apply the privilege narrowly or begrudgingly—to treat it as an historical relic, at most merely to be tolerated—is to ignore its development and purpose.

The Invocation of the Privilege

In the case of a criminal defendant, invocation of the privilege is a very simple matter—he merely refuses to take the stand. By so doing, he precludes the prosecution from asking him any questions at all, incriminating or not. The defendant's counsel must weigh this advantage against the disadvantage that the jury may interpret such failure to defend himself as a sign of guilt, but the privilege is there if he chooses to use it. One problem which has arisen on this point is the constitutionality of permitting the trial judge to comment to the jury on the defendant's failure to take the stand. In *Twining* v. *New Jersey*, 211 U.S. 78 (1908), the Court held that it was not violative of the Fourteenth Amendment's privilege against self-incrimination for a state judge to charge the jury: "Because a man does not go upon the stand you are not necessarily justified in drawing an inference of guilt. But you have a right to consider the fact that he does not go upon the stand where a direct accusation is made against him." No case involving the Fifth Amendment's application directly to such a comment has been decided, since Congress by statute has required that federal judges specifically instruct juries that failure to take the stand should *not* be considered as evidence of guilt. But it was generally presumed that the Fifth Amendment would bar adverse comment in federal courts. In *Malloy* v. *Hogan,* 378 U.S. 1 (1964), the Court "incorporated" the Fifth Amendment privilege into the Fourteenth Amendment, thus imposing the federal standard upon the states. This inevitably led to the reexamination of the *Twining* rule, and in *Griffin* v. *California,* 380 U.S. 609 (1965), the Court held that "the Fifth Amendment, in its direct application to the federal government and its bearing on the States by reason of the Fourteenth Amendment, forbids either comment by the prosecution on the accused's silence or instructions by the court that such silence is evidence of guilt."

Suppose the person who is to be questioned is not a criminal defendant, but is instead a witness before a grand jury or a congressional committee. If he is under subpoena, he does not have the choice of refusing to "take the stand." How, then, does he invoke the privilege? The answer is that he must make a decision on each question as it is asked, as to whether he thinks his answer might incriminate him. If he concludes that it might do so, then he can refuse to answer, but he must in some way indicate that his refusal is based on the privilege.

As to whether the questioning body is absolutely bound by the witness' answer that his response might incriminate him, the answer is a qualified no. If the refusal is followed by a citation for contempt, and the question is before a court, the judge must make some sort of judgment as to whether there is any basis for fearing that an answer might incriminate the witness. The problem was discussed by Chief Justice Marshall while on circuit in the treason trial of Aaron Burr in 1807. During the course of the trial the attorney for the United States offered in evidence a paper in code. Burr's secretary was asked whether he understood the paper and declined to answer on the ground that he might incriminate himself. The court was asked to decide whether the excuse offered was sufficient to prevent his answering. In *United States* v. *Burr* [In re *Willie*], 25 Fed. Cas. 38, No. 14,692e (C.C.D. Va. 1807), the Chief Justice said:

When a question is propounded, it belongs to the court to consider and to decide whether any direct answer to it can implicate the witness. If this be decided in the negative, then he may answer it without violating the privilege which is secured to him by law. If a direct answer to it may criminate himself, then he must be the sole judge what his answer would be. The court cannot participate with him in this judgment, because they cannot decide on the effect of his answers without knowing what it would be; and a disclosure of that fact to the judges would strip him of the privilege which the law allows, and which he claims. It follows necessarily then, from this statement of things, that if the question be of such a description that an answer to it may or may not criminate the witness, according to the purport of that answer, it must rest with himself, who alone can tell what it would be, to answer the question or not. . . .

On examination of the question, the Chief Justice concluded that it could be answered without implicating the witness.

A similar approach was taken by Justice Clark, for the Court, in *Hoffman* v. *United States,* 341 U.S. 479 (1951), who stated: "The witness is not exonerated from answering merely because he declares that in so doing he would incriminate himself—his say-so does not of itself establish the hazard of incrimination. It is for the court to say whether his silence is justified . . . and to require him to answer if 'it clearly appears to the court that he is mistaken.' " He went on to say, however, just as did Chief Justice Marshall, that the witness cannot be required to make a complete revelation to prove his contention, or else the privilege is lost. By way of instruction, he stated: "[T]o sustain the privilege, it need only be evident from the implications of the question, in the setting in which it is asked, that a responsive answer to the question or an explanation of why it cannot be answered might be dangerous because injurious disclosure could result."

On occasion witnesses seem to plead the Fifth Amendment privilege when there would appear to be no basis whatever for a prosecution irrespective of the answer given. The general rule is that for the privilege to be invoked, there must be a real possibility of incrimination. However, this sometimes leaves the witness with the difficult problem of deciding when to stop answering questions after he has already answered several of them in a particular line of questioning. This was the problem presented in *Blau* v. *United States,* 340 U.S. 159 (1950). In response to questions by a grand jury about her employment by the Communist Party, the witness refused to answer and invoked the privilege. The government contended that it is not a crime merely to be an employee of the Party, and that she could not properly invoke the privilege. Petitioner was upheld in her refusal to answer:

At the time petitioner was called before the grand jury, the Smith Act was on the statute books making it a crime among other things to advocate knowingly the desirability of overthrow of the Government by force or violence.... These provisions made future prosecution of petitioner far more than "a mere imaginary possibility...." Whether such admissions by themselves would support a conviction under a criminal statute is immaterial. Answers to the questions asked by the grand jury would have furnished a link in the chain of evidence needed in a prosecution.

While in *Blau* the witness was charged with having invoked the privilege before it was necessary, in a subsequent case the question presented was whether the witness had waited too long to permit its invocation, thereby in effect waiving it by already answering incriminating questions. The case was *Rogers* v. *United States*, 340 U.S. 367 (1951), arising out of a federal grand jury investigation in Colorado. Petitioner testified that she had held the position of Treasurer of the Communist Party of Denver and had been in possession of the membership lists and dues records of the Party. At the time of the investigation she no longer held such position and denied having possession of the records. But she refused to identify the person to whom she had given the Party's books, stating to the court as her only reason: "I don't feel that I should subject a person or persons to the same thing that I'm going through." She later repeated her refusal, asserting this time the privilege against self-incrimination.

She was sentenced for contempt, the court of appeals affirmed, and the United States Supreme Court affirmed, three justices dissenting. Chief Justice Vinson, for the majority, first pointed out that the petitioner had no privilege with respect to the books of the Party. "Books and records kept 'in a representative rather than in a personal capacity cannot be the subject of the personal privilege against self-incrimination, even though production of the papers might tend to incriminate [their keeper] personally.'" He stated further that the *Blau* rule did not apply since she had already freely described her membership, activities, and office in the Party. "Since the privilege against self-incrimination presupposes a real danger of legal detriment arising from the disclosure, petitioner cannot invoke the privilege where response to the specific question in issue here would not further incriminate her. Disclosure of a fact waives the privilege as to details." Thus after admitting to office-holding in the Party, disclosure of acquaintance with her successor "presents no more than 'a mere imaginary possibility' of increasing the danger of prosecution."

The Scope of the Privilege

While the privilege "must be accorded liberal construction" and is "of great value," it does not extend to every divulgence which might have injurious consequences. In the first place, as the Court pointed out in *Rogers* v. *United States*, above, the privilege is purely personal and cannot be invoked to protect others. Similarly, the privilege can be claimed only by natural persons and not by corporations or other organizations. As was stated in *United States* v. *White*, 322 U.S. 694 (1944):

[T]he papers and effects which the privilege protects must be the private property of the person claiming the privilege, or at least in his possession in a purely personal capacity.... But individuals, when acting as representatives of a collective group, cannot be said to be exercising their personal rights and duties nor to be entitled to their purely personal privileges. . . . In their official capacity, therefore, they have no privilege against self-incrimination. And the official records and documents of the organization that are held by them in a representative rather than in a personal capacity cannot be the subject of the personal privilege against self-incrimination, even though production of the papers might tend to incriminate them personally.

Governments are, of course, empowered to grant immunity from prosecution to witnesses whom they wish to question. A Fifth Amendment problem may arise, however, if the extent of the immunity granted is too narrowly drawn and thus results in an abridgment of the privilege if the witness is compelled to testify. In 1954 Congress passed an immunity act which enabled Congress to compel testimony from witnesses in certain national security investigations. The immunity provision extended to a prohibition against prosecution for "any transaction, matter, or thing concerning which he is compelled to testify." In *Ullmann* v. *United States,* 350 U.S. 422 (1956), the Court upheld the act against claims of unconstitutionality on the grounds that: (1) the Fifth Amendment prohibits compulsion of what would otherwise be self-incriminating testimony irrespective of the grant of immunity, and (2) the grant of immunity was inadequate, since it did not extend to such injuries as loss of job or reputation. The majority held that the privilege is not a broad guarantee of a right to silence, and, further, the privilege only extends to a protection against criminal prosecution, not to other injurious consequences which might follow from divulgence of information.

In 1970 Congress passed another immunity act, but in so doing the "transactional immunity" provision found in the 1954 act was omitted. In *Kastigar* v. *United States* in 1972 the new act was tested.

KASTIGAR *v.* UNITED STATES
406 U.S. 441 (1972)

[A United States District Court ordered petitioners to appear before a grand jury and to answer its questions under a grant of immunity. The immunity was based upon a provision of the Organized Crime Control Act of 1970 stating that neither the compelled testimony nor any information directly or indirectly derived from such testimony could be used against the witness. Petitioners refused to answer the grand jury's questions and were found in contempt. The court rejected the contention that the Act abridged the privilege in that it still permitted prosecution for any crimes about which the petitioners might testify. The Court of Appeals affirmed, and the case came on certiorari to the Supreme Court.]

Mr. Justice Powell delivered the opinion of the Court. . . .

I

The power of government to compel persons to testify in court or before grand juries and other governmental agencies is firmly established in Anglo-American jurisprudence. . . . But the power to compel testimony is not absolute. There are a number of exemptions from the testimonial duty, the most important of which is the Fifth Amendment privilege against compulsory self-incrimination. . . .

Immunity statutes, which have historical roots deep in Anglo-American jurisprudence, are not incompatible with these values. Rather they seek a rational accommodation between the imperatives of the privilege and the legitimate demands of government to compel citizens to testify. The existence of these statutes reflects the importance of testimony, and the fact that many offenses are of such a character that the only persons capable of giving useful testimony are those implicated in the crime.... As Mr. Justice Frankfurter observed, speaking for the Court in *Ullmann* v. *United States*, ... such statutes have "become part of our constitutional fabric."....

II

Petitioners contend first that the Fifth Amendment's privilege against compulsory self-incrimination ... deprives Congress of power to enact laws which compel self-incrimination, even if complete immunity from prosecution is granted prior to the compulsion of the incriminatory testimony. In other words, petitioners assert that no immunity statute, however drawn, can afford a lawful basis for compelling incriminatory testimony. They ask us to reconsider and overrule *Brown* v. *Walker* ... and *Ullmann* v. *United States* ..., decisions which uphold the constitutionality of immunity statutes. We find no merit to this contention and reaffirm the decisions in *Brown* and *Ullmann*.

III

Petitioners' second contention is that the scope of immunity provided by the federal witness immunity statute ... is not co-extensive with the scope of the Fifth Amendment privilege against compulsory self-incrimination, and therefore is not sufficient to supplant the privilege and compel testimony over a claim of the privilege. The statute provides that when a witness is compelled by district court order to testify over a claim of the privilege: "the witness may not refuse to comply with the order on the basis of his privilege against self-incrimination; but no testimony or other information compelled under the order (or any information directly or indirectly derived from such testimony or other information) may be used against the witness in any criminal case, except a prosecution for perjury, giving a false statement, or otherwise failing to comply with the order."

The constitutional inquiry, rooted in logic and history, as well as in the decisions of this court, is whether the immunity granted under this statute is co-extensive with the scope of the privilege. If so, petitioners' refusals to answer based on the privilege were unjustified, and the judgments of contempt were proper.... If, on the other hand, the immunity granted is not as comprehensive as the protection afforded by the privilege, petitioners were justified in refusing to answer, and the judgments of contempt must be vacated....

Petitioners draw a distinction between statutes which provide transactional immunity and those which provide, as does the statute before us, immunity from use and derivative use. They contend that a statute must at a minimum grant full transactional immunity in order to be co-extensive with the scope of the privilege....

The statute's explicit proscription of the use in any criminal case of "testimony or other information compelled under the order (or any information directly or indirectly derived from such testimony or other information)" is consonant with Fifth Amendment standards. We hold that such immunity from use and derivative use is co-extensive with the scope of the privilege against self-incrimination, and therefore is sufficient to compel testimony over a claim of the privilege. While a grant of immunity must afford protection commensurate with that afforded by the privilege, it need not be broader. Transactional immunity, which accords full immunity from prosecution for the offense to which the compelled testimony relates, affords the witness considerably broader protection than does the Fifth Amendment privilege. The privilege has never been construed to mean that one who invokes it cannot subsequently be prosecuted. Its sole concern is to afford protection against being "forced to give testimony leading to the infliction of 'penalties affixed to . . . criminal acts.' " Immunity from the use of compelled testimony and evidence derived directly and indirectly therefrom affords this protection. It prohibits the prosecutorial authorities from using the compelled testimony in *any* respect, and it therefore insures that the testimony cannot lead to the infliction of criminal penalties on the witness. . . .

IV

. . . Petitioners argue that use and derivative use immunity will not adequately protect a witness from various possible incriminating uses of the compelled testimony: for example, the prosecutor or other law enforcement officials may obtain leads, names of witnesses, or other information not otherwise available which might result in a prosecution. It will be difficult and perhaps impossible, the argument goes, to identify, by testimony or cross-examination, the subtle ways in which the compelled testimony may disadvantage a witness, especially in the jurisdiction granting the immunity.

This argument presupposes that the statute's prohibition will prove impossible to enforce. The statute provides a sweeping proscription of any use, direct or indirect, of the compelled testimony and any information derived therefrom. . . . This total prohibition on use provides a comprehensive safeguard, barring the use of compelled testimony as an "investigatory lead," and also barring the use of any evidence obtained by focusing investigation on a witness as a result of his compelled disclosures.

A person accorded this immunity . . . and subsequently prosecuted, is not dependent for the preservation of his rights upon the integrity and good faith of the prosecuting authorities. As stated in *Murphy:* "Once a defendant demonstrates that he has testified, under a state grant of immunity, to matters related to the federal prosecution, the federal authorities have the burden of showing that their evidence is not tainted by establishing that they had an independent, legitimate source for the disputed evidence.". . . This burden of proof, which we reaffirm as appropriate, is not limited to a negation of taint; rather it imposes on the prosecution the affirmative duty to prove that the evidence it proposes to use is derived from a legitimate source wholly independent of the compelled testimony.

This is very substantial protection, commensurate with that resulting from invoking the privilege itself. . . . The statute, like the Fifth Amendment, grants neither pardon nor amnesty. Both the statute and the Fifth Amendment allow the government to prosecute using evidence from legitimate independent sources.

The statutory proscription is analogous to the Fifth Amendment requirement in cases of coerced confessions. A coerced confession, as revealing of leads as testimony given in exchange for immunity, is inadmissible in a criminal trial, but it does not bar prosecution. . . .

We conclude that the immunity provided by [the Act] leaves the witness and the prosecutorial authorities in substantially the same position as if the witness had claimed the Fifth Amendment privilege. . . . The judgment of the Court of Appeals . . . accordingly is

Affirmed.

Mr. Justice Brennan and Mr. Justice Rehnquist took no part in the consideration or decision of this case.

Mr. Justice Douglas, dissenting. . . .

When we allow the prosecution to offer only "use" immunity we allow it to grant far less than it has taken away. For while the precise testimony that is compelled may not be used, leads from that testimony may be pursued and used to convict the witness. My view is that the Framers put it beyond the power of Congress to *compel* anyone to confess his crimes. The Self-Incrimination Clause creates, as I said said before, "the federally protected right of silence," making it unconstitutional to use a law "to pry open one's lips and make him a witness against himself." *Ullmann* v. *United States* . . . That is indeed one of the chief procedural guarantees in our accusatorial system. Government acts in an ignoble way when it stoops to the end which we authorize today.

I would . . . hold that this attempt to dilute the Self-Incrimination Clause is unconstitutional.

Mr. Justice Marshall, dissenting. . . .

The Fifth Amendment gives a witness an absolute right to resist interrogation, if the testimony sought would tend to incriminate him. A grant of immunity may strip the witness of the right to refuse to testify, but only if it is broad enough to eliminate all possibility that the testimony will in fact operate to incriminate him. It must put him in precisely the same position, vis-a-vis the government that has compelled his testimony, as he would have been in had he remained silent in reliance on the privilege. . . .

I do not see how it can suffice merely to put the burden of proof on the Government. First, contrary to the Court's assertion, the Court's rule does leave the witness "dependent for the preservation of his rights upon the integrity and good faith of the prosecuting authorities." . . . Second, even their good faith is not a sufficient safeguard. For the paths of information through the investigative bureaucracy may well be long and winding, and even a prosecutor acting in the best of faith cannot be certain that somewhere in the depths of his investigative apparatus, often including hundreds of employees, there was not some prohibited use of the compelled testimony. . . . The Court today sets out a loose net to trap tainted evidence and prevent its use against the witness, but it accepts an intolerably great risk that tainted evidence will in fact slip through that net. . . .

The Problem of Immunity and Federalism

Both the states and the federal government have statutes trading immunity for information, and these date back more than a century. Some of the provisions apply to specific kinds of crimes, while others are more broadly drawn to cover any criminal offense. It is not uncommon to find a multiplicity of statutes in a single state dealing with the matter of immunity. New York, for example, has more than twoscore provisions under which witnesses may obtain immunity in return for giving testimony.

Since a single act can constitute both a federal and a state crime, the familiar complications of federalism arise in connection with immunity granted by one but not both jurisdictions. Does a grant of immunity by one jurisdiction carry with it insulation against prosecutions by the other based on the testimony? If not, is that fact sufficient to support a refusal to testify grounded on fear of incrimination?

As stated earlier, it was not until the decision in *Malloy* v. *Hogan*, 378

U.S. 1 (1964), that the Court fully incorporated the Fifth Amendment privilege into the Fourteenth Amendment. Justice Brennan, for the majority, stated: "The Fourteenth Amendment secures against state invasion the same privilege that the Fifth Amendment guarantees against federal infringement—the right of a person to remain silent unless he chooses to speak in the unfettered exercise of his own will, and to suffer no penalty, as held in *Twining*, for such silence." In so holding, the Court reversed a contempt conviction for petitioner's refusal to answer questions relating to gambling activities, and held that the *Twining* rule can no longer be accepted as the appropriate standard for the exercise of the privilege. Under the double standard of Fifth and Fourteenth Amendment self-incrimination protection, a form of legalized coerced confession had been supported by the Court where the federal government could force testimony by extending immunity and subsequently the state government could prosecute for state crimes revealed. Conversely, the federal prosecutor could use testimony exacted by state officials in return for the limited immunity from state prosecution. These cases were reconsidered, and overruled, in light of *Malloy* v. *Hogan*, in a decision rendered on the same day as that case, in *Murphy* v. *Waterfront Commission of New York Harbor*, 378 U.S. 52 (1964).

MURPHY *v.* WATERFRONT COMMISSION OF NEW YORK HARBOR
378 U.S. 52 (1964)

[Petitioners were subpoenaed to testify at a hearing conducted by the Waterfront Commission of New York Harbor concerning a work stoppage at the Hoboken piers. After refusing to respond to certain questions on the ground that the answers might tend to incriminate them, petitioners were granted immunity from prosecution under the laws of New Jersey and New York. Notwithstanding this grant of immunity, they still refused to respond to the questions on the ground that the answers might tend to incriminate them under *federal* law, to which the grant of immunity did not purport to extend. Petitioners were thereupon held in civil and criminal contempt of court. The New Jersey Supreme Court affirmed the civil contempt judgments, holding that a state may constitutionally compel a witness to give testimony which might be used in a federal prosecution against him.]

Mr. Justice Goldberg delivered the opinion of the Court.

We have held today that the Fifth Amendment privilege against self-incrimination must be deemed fully applicable to the States through the Fourteenth Amendment. *Malloy* v. *Hogan*. . . . This case presents a related issue: whether one jurisdiction within our federal structure may compel a witness, whom it has immunized from prosecution under its laws, to give testimony which might then be used to convict him of a crime against another such jurisdiction. . . .

I. The Policies of the Privilege

The privilege against self-incrimination "registers an important advance in the development of our liberty—'one of the great landmarks in man's struggle to make himself civilized.' ". . . It reflects many of our fundamental values and most noble aspirations: our unwillingness to subject those suspected of crime to the cruel trilemma of self-accusation, perjury or contempt; our preference for an accusatorial rather than an inquisitorial system of criminal justice; our fear that self-incriminating statements will be elicited by inhumane treatment and abuses; our sense of fair play which dictates "a fair state-individual balance by requiring the government to leave the individual alone until good cause is shown for disturbing him and by requiring the government in its contest with the individual to shoulder the entire load,"...; our respect for the inviolability of the human personality and of the right of each individual "to a private enclave where he may lead a private life,"...; our distrust of self-deprecatory statements; and our realization that the privilege, while sometimes "a shelter to the guilty," is often "a protection to the innocent."...

Most, if not all, of these policies and purposes are defeated when a witness "can be whipsawed into incriminating himself under both state and federal law even though" the constitutional privilege against self-incrimination is applicable to each.... This has become especially true in our age of "cooperative federalism," where the Federal and State Governments are waging a united front against many types of criminal activity.

Respondent contends... that we should adhere to the "established rule" that the constitutional privilege against self-incrimination does not protect a witness in one jurisdiction against being compelled to give testimony which could be used to convict him in another jurisdiction. This "rule" has three decisional facets: *United States* v. *Murdock,* 284 U.S. 141 [1931], held that the Federal Government could compel a witness to give testimony which might incriminate him under state law; *Knapp* v. *Schweitzer,* 357 U.S. 371 [1958], held that a State could compel a witness to give testimony which might incriminate him under federal law; and *Feldman* v. *United States,* 322 U.S. 487 [1944], held that testimony thus compelled by a State could be introduced into evidence in the federal courts.

Our decision today in *Malloy* v. *Hogan, supra,* necessitates a reconsideration of this rule. Our review of the pertinent cases in this Court and of their English antecedents reveals that *Murdock* did not adequately consider the relevant authorities and has been significantly weakened by subsequent decisions of this Court, and, further, that the legal premises underlying *Feldman* and *Knapp* have since been rejected....

[The opinion here gives a lengthy history of English and American cases on the self-incrimination issues through *Murdock, Knapp,* and *Feldman,* and then points out that in *Malloy* v. *Hogan* "the Court has today rejected" the rule which permits one government to use evidence obtained by another government under an immunity statute, "and with it, all the earlier cases resting on that rule."]

The foregoing makes it clear that there is no continuing legal vitality to, or historical justification for, the rule that one jurisdiction within our federal structure may compel a witness to give testimony which could be used to convict him of a crime in another jurisdiction.

IV. Conclusions

In light of the history, policies and purposes of the privilege against self-incrimination, we now accept as correct the construction given the privilege by the English courts and by Chief Justice Marshall and Justice Holmes.... We reject—as unsupported by history or policy—the deviation from that construction only recently adopted by this Court in *United States* v. *Murdock,* and *Feldman* v. *United States.* We hold that the constitutional privilege against self-incrimination protects a state witness against incrimination under federal as well as state law and a federal witness against incrimination under state as well as federal law.

We must now decide what effect this holding has on existing state immunity legislation. In *Counselman* v. *Hitchcock,* 142 U.S. 547 [1892], this Court considered a federal statute which provided that no "evidence obtained from a party or witness by means of a judicial proceeding ... shall be given in evidence, or in any manner used against him ... in any court of the United States ..." Nothwithstanding this statute, appellant, claiming his privilege against self-incrimination, refused to answer certain questions before a grand jury. The Court said "that legislation cannot abridge a constitutional privilege, and that it cannot replace or supply one, at least unless it is so broad as to have the same extent in scope and effect.". ... Applying this principle to the facts of that case, the Court upheld appellant's refusal to answer on the ground that the statute: "could not, and would not, prevent the use of his testimony to search out other testimony to be used in evidence against him or his property, in a criminal proceeding in such court ...", that it: "could not prevent the obtaining and the use of witnesses and evidence which should be attributable directly to the testimony he might give under compulsion, and on which he might be convicted, when otherwise, and if he had refused to answer, he could not possibly have been convicted ...", and that it: "affords no protection against that use of compelled testimony which consists in gaining therefrom a knowledge of the details of a crime, and of sources of information which may supply other means of convicting the witness or party.". ...

Applying the holding of that case to our holdings today that the privilege against self-incrimination protects a state witness against federal prosecution ... and that "the same standards must determine whether [a witness'] silence in either a federal or state proceeding is justified," *Malloy* v. *Hogan*, ... we hold the constitutional rule to be that a state witness may not be compelled to give testimony which may be incriminating under federal law unless the compelled testimony and its fruits cannot be used in any manner by federal officials in connection with a criminal prosecution against him. We conclude, moreover, that in order to implement this constitutional rule and accommodate the interests of the State and Federal Governments in investigating crime, the Federal Government must be prohibited from making any such use of compelled testimony and its fruits. This exclusionary rule, while permitting the States to secure information necessary for effective law enforcement, leaves the witness and the Federal Government in substantially the same position as if the witness had claimed his privilege in the absence of a state grant of immunity.

It follows that petitioners here may now be compelled to answer the questions propounded to them. At the time they refused to answer, however, petitioners had a reasonable fear, based on this Court's decision in *Feldman* v. *United States,* that the federal authorities might use the answers against them in connection with a federal prosecution. We have now overruled *Feldman* and hold that the Federal Government may make no such use of the answers. Fairness dictates that petitioners should now be afforded an opportunity, in light of this development, to answer the questions. ... Accordingly, the judgment of the New Jersey courts ordering petitioners to answer the questions may remain undisturbed. But the judgment of contempt is vacated and the cause remanded to the New Jersey Supreme Court for proceedings not inconsistent with this opinion.

It is so ordered.

Mr. Justice Black concurs in the judgment and opinion of the Court. ...

Mr. Justice Harlan, whom Mr. Justice Clark joins, concurring in the judgment.
Unless I wholly misapprehend the Court's opinion, its holding that testimony compelled in a state proceeding over a witness' claim that such testimony will

incriminate him may not be used against the witness in a federal criminal prosecution rests on *constitutional* grounds. On that basis, the contrary conclusion of *Feldman* v. *United States* ... is overruled.

I believe that the constitutional holding of *Feldman* was correct, and would not overrule it. To the extent, however, that the decision in that case may have rested also on a refusal to exercise this Court's "supervisory power" over the administration of justice in federal courts, I think that it can no longer be considered good law. ...

Part I of this opinion shows, I believe, that the Court's analysis of prior cases hardly furnishes an adequate basis for a new departure in constitutional law. Even if the Court's analysis were sound, however, it would not support reversal of the *Feldman* rule on *constitutional* grounds.

If the Court were correct in asserting that the "separate sovereignty" theory of self-incrimination should be discarded, that would, as the Court says, lead to the conclusion that "a state witness [is protected] against incrimation under federal as well as state law and a federal witness against incrimation under state as well as federal law.".... However, dealing strictly with the situation presented by this case, that conclusion does *not* in turn lead to a constitutional rule that the testimony of a state witness (or evidence to which his testimony leads) who is compelled to testify in state proceedings may not be used against him in a federal prosecution. Protection which the Due Process Clause affords against the *States* is quite obviously not any basis for a constitutional rule regulating the conduct of *federal* authorities in *federal* proceedings

The Court avoids this problem by mixing together the Fifth Amendment and the Fourteenth and talking about "the constitutional privilege against self-incrimination." Such an approach, which deals with "constitutional" rights at large, unrelated either to particular provisions of the Constitution or to relevant differences between the States and the Federal Government warns of the dangers for our federalism to which the "incorporation" theory of the Fourteenth Amendment leads. ...

The Court's reasons for overruling *Feldman* thus rest on an entirely new conception of the *Fifth Amendment,* namely that it applies to federal use of state-compelled incriminating testimony. The opinion, however, contains nothing at all to contradict the traditional, well-understood conception of the Fifth Amendment, to which, therefore, I continue to adhere. ...

Accordingly, I cannot accept the majority's conclusion that a rule prohibiting federal authorities from using in aid of a federal prosecution incriminating testimony compelled in state proceedings is constitutionally required.

I would, however, adopt such a rule in the exercise of our supervisory power over the administration of federal criminal justice. ... On this basis, I concur in the judgment of the Court.

Mr. Justice White, with whom Mr. Justice Stewart joins, concurring. ...

The Privilege, Registration Laws, and Compulsory Filing

Following the Kefauver Crime Committee investigation into crime and racketeering, Congress enacted the Gamblers' Occupational Tax Act in 1951. The Act levied a tax on persons engaged in the business of accepting wagers and required that they register with the Collector of Internal Revenue. In

United States v. *Kahriger*, 345 U.S. 22 (1953), the Court, by a six-to-three vote, upheld the registration requirement against the claim that it violated the protection against self-incrimination. The majority reasoned that the privilege "has relation only to past acts, not to future acts that may or may not be committed." In dissenting, Justice Black said he was sure that the Act "creates a squeezing device contrived to put a man in federal prison if he refuses to confess himself into a state prison as a violator of state gambling law."

In *Marchetti* v. *United States,* 390 U.S. 39 (1968), and *Grosso* v. *United States,* 390 U.S. 62 (1968), the Court overruled *Kahriger.* Justice Harlan, writing for the majority in both cases, stated:

Substantial hazards of incrimination as to past or present acts plainly may stem from the requirements to register and to pay the occupational tax. . . . In the first place, satisfaction of those requirements increases the likelihood that any past or present gambling offenses will be discovered and successfully prosecuted. It both centers attention upon the registrant as a gambler, and compels "injurious disclosures" which may provide or assist in the collection of evidence admissible in a prosecution for past or present offenses. . . .

In *Haynes* v. *United States*, 390 U.S. 85 (1968), the Court held void the registration requirements of the National Firearms Act of 1934. The defendant had been convicted for knowingly possessing a sawed-off shotgun which had not been registered with the Secretary of the Treasury. The Court held that a proper claim of the privilege against self-incrimination provides a full defense to prosecutions either for failure to register a firearm or for possession of an unregistered firearm under the Firearms Act.

In *Leary* v. *United States,* 395 U.S. 6 (1969), the Court held, without dissent, that the elaborate registration provisions of the Marihuana Tax Act violated the defendant's privilege against self-incrimination. There was a "real and appreciable" risk where the law required an order form which issued only upon identification as a transferee of marijuana, and further provided for notification of such status to state law officers.

In the context of Communist activities controls the Court has considered other federal registration requirements. The Subversive Activities Control Act of 1950 required Communist-action organizations, as defined by the statute, to register with the Attorney General, such registration to include a list of individual members. The Act further provided that if the officers of a Communist-action organization failed to register, then the individual members become criminally liable if they fail to register themselves within sixty days after the registration order issued. After lengthy litigation, the self-incrimination issues were substantially settled by the Court. (The cases are treated at some length in Chapter 6 and will only briefly be reviewed here.)

In *Communist Party of the United States* v. *Subversive Activities Control Board,* 367 U.S. 1 (1961), the Court held that as to the officers of the Communist Party, the issue of whether the registration order violated the privilege against self-incrimination was premature. Justice Frankfurter, for the Court, stated:

We cannot know now that the Party's officers will ever claim the privilege. . . . If a claim of privilege is made, it may or may not be honored by the Attorney

General. We cannot, on the basis of supposition that the privilege will be claimed and not honored, proceed now to adjudicate the constitutionality under the Fifth Amendment of the registration provisions.

In *Albertson* v. *Subversive Activities Control Board,* 382 U.S. 70 (1965), however, the Court faced the issue squarely and ruled that as to the individual member of a Communist-action organization required to register, the requirement violated the privilege against self-incrimination. Justice Brennan, for the Court, noted that the Act had an immunity provision applicable to registrants, but he found that the immunity offered was incomplete. "It does not preclude the use of the admission as an investigatory lead, a use which is barred by the privilege."

CONFESSIONS

While a confession is clearly a way in which one can incriminate himself, our present rules with respect to the use of confessions are not simply applications of the privilege to the subject of confessions. The privilege and the rule barring coerced confessions are different both in point of historical development and in the way they are applied. The privilege was firmly established by the late seventeenth century, but the rule barring forced confessions did not come until the late eighteenth century. In barring such confessions in federal proceedings, the Court did not rely on the Fifth Amendment privilege, but, instead, adopted a rule of evidence binding on the lower federal courts to accomplish the purpose. The phraseology of the privilege indicates strongly that it is to operate in official proceedings only—"in any criminal case." Such an interpretation would permit the use of a confession so long as it was obtained outside the formal proceedings of the court, grand jury, or legislative hearing. Thus a different basis than the privilege was considered necessary to afford the desired protection against coerced confessions. The federal bar to admission of coerced confessions originated, therefore, simply as a rule of evidence. Both this bar and the privilege against self-incrimination point in the same direction, of course, of guaranteeing to the accused fair play in the proceedings against him. As will be seen in the cases to follow, the prohibition against the use of coerced confessions has now been elevated to constitutional status as a requirement of due process of law.

Although the practice of barring coerced confessions in federal trials is an old one, it was not until 1936 that the Court held that the introduction of coerced confessions in state prosecutions violated the Fourteenth Amendment's due process clause. The case was *Brown* v. *Mississippi,* and the Court was faced with the problem of qualifying an earlier statement made in *Twining* v. *New Jersey* relative to self-incrimination and due process. In *Twining* the Court had held that in a state criminal case, judicial comment to the jury concerning defendant's refusal to take the stand in his defense was not a violation of due process of law. In the last sentence of his opinion for the Court, Justice Moody had stated "We think that the exemption from compulsory self-incrimination in the courts of the States is not secured by any part of the Federal Constitution." In *Brown* v. *Mississippi* the state used this statement to support their argument that coerced confessions were within the holding of the *Twining* case and thus their admission as evidence did not violate the due process clause.

BROWN *v.* MISSISSIPPI
297 U.S. 278 (1936)

[Three Negroes were arrested on March 30, 1934, for the murder of one Raymond Stewart. Testimony indicated that police officers administered sustained and brutal whippings to all three men until they confessed to the crime. They were then told that if they changed their story at any time, additional beatings would be given. They were indicted on April 4, 1934, and were then arraigned and pleaded not guilty. Counsel were appointed by the court to defend them, and trial was begun the next morning. Aside from the confessions, there was no evidence sufficient to warrant the submission of the case to the jury. Testimony as to the confessions was received over the objection of defendants' counsel. Defendants then testified that the confessions were false and had been procured by physical torture. The case went to the jury with instructions, upon the request of defendants' counsel, that if the jury had reasonable doubt as to the confessions having resulted from coercion, *and that they were not true,* they were not to be considered as evidence. The jury found the three defendants guilty, and they were sentenced to death. The Mississippi Supreme Court affirmed the judgment.]

Mr. Chief Justice Hughes delivered the opinion of the Court.

The question in this case is whether convictions, which rest solely upon confessions shown to have been extorted by officers of the state by brutality and violence, are consistent with the due process of law required by the Fourteenth Amendment of the Constitution of the United States. . . .

The grounds of the decision were (1) that immunity from self-incrimination is not essential to due process of law; and (2) that the failure of the trial court to exclude the confessions after the introduction of evidence showing their incompetency, in the absence of a request for such exclusion, did not deprive the defendants of life or liberty without due process of law; and that even if the trial court had erroneously overruled a motion to exclude the confessions, the ruling would have been mere error reversible on appeal, but not a violation of constitutional right. . . .

1. The state stresses the statement in *Twining* v. *New Jersey,* 211 US. 78, 114, that "exemption from compulsory self-incrimination in the courts of the states is not secured by any part of the Federal Constitution," and the statements in *Snyder* v. *Massachusetts,* 291 U.S. 97, 105, that "the privilege against self-incrimination may be withdrawn and the accused put upon the stand as a witness for the state." But the question of the right of the state to withdraw the privilege against self-incrimination is not here involved. The compulsion to which the quoted statements refer is that of the process of justice by which the accused may be called as a witness and required to testify. Compulsion by torture to extort a confession is a different matter.

The state is free to regulate the procedure of its courts in accordance with its own conceptions of policy, unless in so doing it "offends some principle of justice so rooted in the traditions and conscience of our people as to be ranked as fundamental." *Snyder* v. *Massachusetts, supra.* . . . The state may abolish trial by jury. It may dispense with indictment by a grand jury and substitute complaint or information. *Walker* v. *Sauvinet,* 92 U.S. 90; *Hurtado* v. *California,* 110 U.S. 516; *Snyder* v. *Massachusetts, supra.* But the freedom of the state in establishing its policy is the freedom of constitutional government and is limited by the requirement of due process of law. Because a state may dispense with a jury trial, it does not follow that it may substitute trial by ordeal. The rack and torture chamber may not be substituted for the witness stand. The state may not permit an accused to be hurried to conviction under mob domination—where the whole proceeding is but a mask—without supplying corrective process. *Moore* v. *Dempsey,* 261 U.S. 86. The state may not deny to the accused the aid of counsel. *Powell* v. *Alabama,* 287 U.S. 45. Nor may a state, through the action of its officers, contrive a conviction through the pretense of a trial which in truth is "but used as a means of depriving a defendant of liberty through a deliberate deception of court and jury by the presentation of testimony known to be perjured." *Mooney* v. *Holohan,* 294 U.S. 103. And the trial equally is a mere pretense where the state authorities have contrived a conviction resting solely upon confessions obtained by violence. The due process clause requires "that state action, whether through one agency or another, shall be consistent with the fundamental principles of liberty and justice which lie at the base of all our civil and political institutions." *Hebert* v. *Louisiana,* 272 U.S. 312. It would be difficult to conceive of methods more revolting to the sense of justice than those taken to procure the confessions of these petitioners, and the use of the confessions thus obtained as the basis for conviction and sentence was a clear denial of due process.

2. It is in this view that the further contention of the State must be considered. That contention rests upon the failure of counsel for the accused, who had objected to the admissibility of the confessions, to move for their exclusion after they had been introduced and the fact of coercion had been proved. It is a contention which proceeds upon a misconception of the nature of petitioners' complaint. That complaint is not of the commission of mere error, but of a wrong so fundamental that it made the whole proceeding a mere pretense of a trial and rendered the conviction and sentence wholly void. . . .

In the instance case, the trial court was fully advised by the undisputed evidence of the way in which the confessions had been procured. The trial court knew that there was no other evidence upon which conviction and sentence could be based. Yet it proceeded to permit conviction and to pronounce sentence. . . . The court thus denied a federal right fully established and specially set up and claimed, and the judgment must be reversed.

It is so ordered.

The Court has further made it clear that even though a coerced confession be considered truthful and reliable, its admission into evidence will void a conviction. Justice Frankfurter, speaking for the Court in *Rogers* v. *Richmond,* 365 U.S. 534 (1961), said:

Our decisions under [the Fourteenth] Amendment have made clear that convictions following the admission into evidence of confessions which are involuntary . . . cannot stand. This is so not because such confessions are unlikely to be true but because the methods used to extract them offend an underlying principle in the enforcement of our criminal law: that ours is an accusatorial and not an inquisitorial system—a system in which the State must establish guilt by evidence independently and freely secured and may not by coercion prove its charge against an accused out of his own mouth. . . .

From a fair reading of [expressions of the courts below], we cannot but conclude that the question whether Rogers' confessions were admissible into evidence was answered by reference to a legal standard which took into account the circumstance of probable truth or falsity. And this is not a permissible standard under the Due Process Clause of the Fourteenth Amendment.

In addition, in *Malinski* v. *New York,* 324 U.S. 401 (1945), the Court held that a conviction must be set aside where a coerced confession was admitted into evidence, even though other evidence was presented sufficient to sustain a conviction. As to the question of who determines whether a confession is voluntary, the New York rule, followed also in some other jurisdictions, required that the trial judge make a preliminary determination and exclude the confession if in no circumstances it could be deemed voluntary. But if the evidence presented a fair question as to its voluntariness, the judge was required to submit to the jury the determination of the voluntariness and truthfulness of the confession. In *Jackson* v. *Denno,* 378 U.S. 368 (1964), the Court, relying heavily on *Rogers* v. *Richmond* and *Malinski* v. *New York,* held that where a jury is returning a general verdict, it cannot be assumed that the jury could reliably distinguish the issue of voluntariness from the question of truthfulness, and the procedure thus violates Fourteenth Amendment due process. Justice White, for the majority, said, "The overall determination of the voluntariness of a confession has thus become an exceedingly sensitive task, one that requires facing the issue squarely, in illuminating isolation and unbeclouded by other issues and the effect of extraneous but prejudicial evidence." He also suggested the difficulty of ignoring a confession even after it has been found to be involuntary. "[T]he fact of a defendant's confession is solidly implanted in the jury's mind, for it has not only heard the confession, but it has been instructed to consider and judge its voluntariness and is in position to assess whether it is true or false." Thus the rule now imposed requires that a separate determination on voluntariness be made before the jury is brought into the picture.

As the Court settled the issue of the use of confessions obtained by physical torture, it moved on to take up the more difficult issue of the admissibility of confessions obtained after lengthy interrogation. [As will be seen, this aspect of the coerced confession problem moves ineluctably into conjunction with the question of the stage at which the right to counsel accrues, and is largely disposed of by the recent decision in *Miranda* v. *Arizona,* 384 U.S. 436 (1966), discussed below.] It has been a not uncommon practice for the police to take suspects to the police station "for investigation" in order to see whether interrogation will uncover additional information bearing on the commission of the crime. The wide variety of such situations which have come to the Court for appraisal has led to a group of decisions in which the members of the Court have been badly split on the rationale of the cases. *Ashcraft* v. *Tennessee,* 322 U.S. 143 (1944), involved a claim of coercion in the extraction of a confession after a 36-hour period of practically continuous questioning, under powerful electric lights, by relays of officers, experienced investigators, and highly trained lawyers. At the end of this period of interrogation, Ashcraft confessed to hiring another person to murder his wife. Justice Black, speaking for the majority, stated that the confession was "not voluntary but compelled." He stated further that the detention incommunicado and the 36-hour questioning were "so inherently coercive that its very existence is irreconcilable with the possession of mental freedom by a lone suspect against whom its full coercive force is brought to bear." Justice Jackson, with whom two other justices concurred, dissented vigorously. He stated:

A confession is wholly and incontestably voluntary only if a guilty person gives himself up to the law and becomes his own accuser. The Court bases its decision on the premise that custody and examination of a prisoner for 36 hours is "inherently coercive." Of course it is. And so is custody and examination for one hour. Arrest itself is inherently coercive, and so is detention.... Of course such acts put pressure upon the prisoner to answer questions, to answer them truthfully, and to confess if guilty.

But does the Constitution prohibit use of all confessions made after arrest because questioning, while one is deprived of freedom, is "inherently coercive"? The Court does not quite say so, but it is moving far and fast in that direction. The step it now takes is to hold this confession inadmissible because of the time taken in getting it.

... Always heretofore the ultimate question has been whether the confessor was in possession of his own will and self-control at the time of confession. For its bearing on this question the Court always has considered the confessor's strength or weakness, whether he was educated or illiterate, intelligent or moronic, well or ill, Negro or white....

The difficulty in maintaining consistency in the coerced confession decisions was well stated in *Culombe* v. *Connecticut*, 367 U.S. 568 (1961), reversing the conviction based on a confession of a mental defective who was subjected to psychological pressure during a four-day question period. The Court pointed out that it was impossible "precisely to delimit, or to surround with specific, all-inclusive restrictions, the power of interrogation allowed to state law enforcement officers in obtaining confessions. No single litmus-paper test for constitutionally impermissible interrogation has been evolved. ..." [For an analysis of the cases on coerced confessions, see *The Constitution of the United States of America*, 88th Cong., 1st Sess., Sen. Doc. No. 39 (U.S. Government Printing Ofc., 1964), pp. 1233–1251. An extensive bibliography and case analysis on police interrogation and coerced confessions is included in Justice Frankfurter's opinion in *Culombe*.] Justices Douglas and Black concurred, but they would have reversed the conviction solely on the ground of denial of counsel. Justice Douglas stated:

I find this case a simple one.... It is... controlled by the principle some of us have urged upon the Court in several prior cases.... That principle is that any accused—whether rich or poor—has the right to consult a lawyer before talking with the police....

It is said that if we enforced the guarantee of counsel by allowing a person, who is arrested, to obtain legal advice before talking with the police, we "would effectively preclude police questioning"... and "would constrict police activities in a manner that in many cases might impair their ability to solve crimes."... It is said that "any lawyer worth his salt will tell the suspect in no uncertain terms to make no statement to the police under any circumstances." *Watts* v. *Indiana* ... In other words an attorney is likely to inform his client, clearly and unequivocally, that "No person ... shall be compelled in any criminal case to be a witness against himself," as provided in the Fifth Amendment. This is the "evil" to be feared from contact between a police suspect and his lawyer.

Justice Douglas' remarks show clearly the conjunction of the privilege and the right to counsel at the interrogation stage. He and Justice Black waged a long campaign for acceptance of this view, culminating in success in *Miranda* v. *Arizona* in 1966.

Before proceeding further, a brief look should be taken at federal practice regarding admissibility of confessions. The Court has held coerced confessions inadmissible as a rule of evidence in federal prosecutions. In *McNabb* v. *United States*, 318 U.S. 332 (1943), the Court took another step and hold inadmissible a confession obtained by federal authorities who had not promptly taken the accused before a committing officer (as required by Rule 5 of the Federal Rules of Criminal Procedure). Thus the rule laid down was that a confession was inadmissible in a federal prosecution if secured during a period of unlawful detention. In *Upshaw* v. *United States,* 335 U.S. 410 (1948), the Court held that such confessions are inadmissible even though there is no proof of improper pressures brought to bear in obtaining the confessions. This was not construed as a requirement of the Constitution, but was in the exercise of the Court's supervisory power over the lower federal courts. The rule was followed in the highly controversial decision in *Mallory* v. *United States,* 354 U.S. 449 (1957), which reversed a conviction and death sentence for rape in a federal case. Washington, D.C., police had apprehended petitioner and others around two-thirty one afternoon. Petitioner was questioned for some forty-five minutes by four officers and strenuously denied his guilt. Around four o'clock the suspects were asked to submit to "lie detector" tests, and they agreed. Petitioner's questioning began at about eight o'clock, and after an hour and a half of interrogation he stated that he had committed the crime. At ten o'clock that evening the police attempted to reach a United States Commissioner for the purpose of arraignment. Failing in this, they had petitioner examined by a deputy coroner, who noted no indications of physical or psychological coercion, and around midnight he dictated his confession to a typist. Not until the following morning was he brought before a commissioner, although, as the Court stated, "arraignment could easily have been made in the same building in which the police headquarters were housed."

Justice Frankfurter, speaking for the Court, cited Rule 5 (a), requiring that officers take an arrested person "without unnecessary delay before the nearest available commissioner," and 5 (b) relative to the commissioner's function:

The commissioner shall inform the defendant of the complaint against him, of his right to retain counsel and of his right to have a preliminary examination. He shall also inform the defendant that he is not required to make a statement and that any statement made by him may be used against him. The commissioner shall allow the defendant reasonable time and opportunity to consult counsel and shall admit the defendant to bail as provided in these rules.

Again we see, this time in congressional legislation, the juxtaposition of the privilege and the right to counsel. In pointing out the purpose of Rule 5 (a) and (b), Justice Frankfurter said, "Not until he had confessed, when any judicial caution had lost its purpose, did the police arraign him." Thus the Court followed the *McNabb* rule in holding the confession inadmissible as a device to force the police to follow the congressional requirement of prompt arraignment and avoid the "tempting utilization of intensive interrogation, easily gliding into the evils of 'the third degree'."

A great deal of criticism from a variety of sources was leveled at the Court following both the *McNabb* and the *Mallory* decisions, and bills were introduced in Congress after each decision to protect the admissibility of voluntary confessions. Exhaustive hearings were conducted on the matter by a Senate subcommittee, and the published material contains a wealth of information on problems of confessions and police detention, proposed legislation, and journal articles. [See Hearings before the Subcommittee on Constitutional Rights of the Committee on the Judiciary, United States Senate, 85th Cong., 2nd Sess., *Confessions and Police Detention* (U.S. Government Printing Ofc., 1958).]

It has been pointed out by many writers that the *McNabb-Mallory* rule would not necessarily bar the use of damaging *admissions* (as opposed to confessions, or complete acknowledgment of guilt), such as the names of witnesses or a hidden weapon or the location of a buried body. [See, for example, M. C. Slough, "Confessions and Admissions," 28 *Fordham L. Rev.* 96 (1959).] Rather than abandon the rule because of each weakness, however, the Court has moved to strengthen it in an attempt to close the loophole. *Gideon* v. *Wainright,* 372 U.S. 335 (1963), had held that the Sixth Amendment's right to counsel was "incorporated" into the Fourteenth Amendment. But the key counsel decision in the context of the privilege against self-incrimination during police interrogation came in *Escobedo* v. *Illinois,* 378 U.S. 478 (1964).

Petitioner was arrested at 2:30 a.m. with a warrant and interrogated. He was released that afternoon pursuant to a writ of habeas corpus obtained by his lawyer. Several days later, he was again arrested and interrogated further. He asked to see his lawyer, who had arrived shortly thereafter at police headquarters, but the police refused. The lawyer asked permission to see Escobedo, and this request was refused. Notwithstanding repeated requests by each, the petitioner and his retained lawyer were afforded no opportunity to consult with each other during the course of the entire interrogation. During the course of the interrogation the petitioner made several damaging admissions implicating himself in the crime, and these statements were introduced into evidence. At no time was he advised of his constitutional right to remain silent. In reversing the conviction, Justice Goldberg stated for the majority of the Court:

> We hold ... that where, as here, the investigation is no longer a general inquiry into an unsolved crime but has begun to focus on a particular suspect, the suspect has been taken into police custody, the police carry out a process of interrogations that lends itself to eliciting incriminating statements, the suspect has requested and been denied an opportunity to consult with his lawyer, and the police have not effectively warned him of his absolute constitutional right to remain silent, the accused has been denied "the Assistance of Counsel" in violation of the Sixth Amendment to the Constitution as "made obligatory upon the States by the Fourteenth Amendment," *Gideon* v. *Wainright,* and that no statement elicited by the police during the interrogation may be used against him at a criminal trial.

The logical conclusion suggested by *Escobedo* came in *Miranda* v. *Arizona,* 384 U.S. 436 (1966). Four cases were brought together for decision, and without specific concentration on the facts of these cases, the Court sought to lay down the governing principles concerning interrogation and the Fifth Amendment privilege.

MIRANDA *v* ARIZONA

384 U.S. 436 (1966)

Mr. Chief Justice Warren delivered the opinion of the Court.

The cases before us raise questions which go to the roots of our concepts of American criminal jurisprudence: the restraints society must observe consistent with the Federal Constitution in prosecuting individuals for crime. More specifically, we deal with the admissibility of statements obtained from an individual who is subjected to custodial police interrogation and the necessity for procedures which assure that the individual is accorded his privilege under the Fifth Amendment to the Constitution not to be compelled to incriminate himself.

We dealt with certain phases of this problem recently in *Escobedo* v. *Illinois*. . . . There, as in the four cases before us, law enforcement officials took the defendant into custody and interrogated him in a police station for the purpose of obtaining a confession. The police did not effectively advise him of his right to remain silent or of his right to consult with his attorney. . . . We held that the statements thus made were constitutionally inadmissible.

This case has been the subject of judicial interpretation and spirited legal debate since it was decided two years ago. Both state and federal courts, in assessing its implications, have arrived at varying conclusions. . . . We granted certiorari in these cases . . . in order further to explore some facets of the problems, thus exposed, of applying the privilege against self-incrimination to in-custody interrogation, and to give concrete constitutional guidelines for law enforcement agencies and courts to follow.

We start here, as we did in *Escobedo*, with the premise that our holding is not an innovation in our jurisprudence, but is an application of principles long recognized and applied in other settings. We have undertaken a thorough reexamination of the *Escobedo* decision and the principles it announced, and we reaffirm it. . . . It was necessary in *Escobedo*, as here, to insure that what was proclaimed in the Constitution had not become but a "form of words," . . . in the hands of government officials. And it is in this spirit, consistent with our role as judges, that we adhere to the principles of *Escobedo* today.

Our holding will be spelled out with some specificity in the pages which follow, but briefly stated it is this: the prosecution may not use statements, whether exculpatory or inculpatory, stemming from custodial interrogation of the defendant unless it demonstrates the use of procedural safeguards effective to secure the privilege against self-incrimination. By custodial interrogation, we mean questioning initiated by law enforcement officers after a person has been taken into custody or otherwise deprived of his freedom of action in any significant way. As for the procedural safeguards to be employed, unless other fully effective means are devised to inform accused persons of their right of silence and to assure a continuous opportunity to exercise it, the following measures are required. Prior to any questioning, the person must be warned that he has a right to remain silent, that any statement he does make may be used as evidence against him, and that he has a right to the presence of an attorney, either retained or appointed. The defendant may waive effectuation of these rights, provided the waiver is made voluntarily, knowingly and intelligently. If, however, he indicates in any manner and at any stage of the process that he wishes to consult with an attorney before speaking, there can be no questioning. Likewise, if the individual is alone and indicates in any manner that he does not wish to be interrogated, the police may not question him. The mere fact that he may have answered some questions or volunteered some statements on his own does not deprive him of the right to refrain from answering any further inquiries until he has consulted with an attorney and thereafter consents to be questioned. . . .

An understanding of the nature and setting of this in-custody interrogation is essential to our decisions today. The difficulty in depicting what transpires at such interrogations stems from the fact that in this country they have largely taken place incommunicado. From extensive factual studies undertaken in the early 1930's including the famous Wickersham Report to Congress by a Presidential Commission, it is clear that police violence and the "third degree" flourished at that time. In a series of cases decided by this Court long after these studies, the police resorted to physical brutality—beatings, hanging, whipping—and to sustained and protracted questioning incommunicado in order to extort confessions. The Commission on Civil Rights in 1961 found much evidence to indicate that "some policemen still resort to physical force to obtain confessions.". . . The use of physical brutality and violence is not, unfortunately, relegated to the past or to any part of the country. Only recently in Kings County, New York, the police brutality beat, kicked and placed lighted cigarette butts on the back of a potential witness under interrogation for the purpose of securing a statement incriminating a third party. . . .

. . . [W]e stress that the modern practice of in-custody interrogation is psychologically rather than physically oriented. As we have stated before, "Since *Chambers* v. *Florida* . . . this Court has recognized that coercion can be mental as well as physical, and that the blood of the accused is not the only hallmark of an unconstitutional inquisition.". . . Interrogation still takes place in privacy. Privacy results in secrecy and this in turn results in a gap in our knowledge as to what in fact goes on in the interrogation rooms. A valuable source of information about present police practices, however, may be found in various police manuals and texts which document procedures employed with success in the past, and which recommend various other effective tactics. [The opinion here quotes at length from a number of manuals and texts on criminal investigation.]

Even without employing brutality, the "third degree" or the specific strategems described above, the very fact of custodial interrogation exacts a heavy toll on individual liberty and trades on the weakness of individuals. . . .

It is obvious that such an interrogation environment is created for no purpose other than to subjugate the individual to the will of his examiner. This atmosphere carries its own badge of intimidation. To be sure, this is not physical intimidation, but it is equally destructive of human dignity. The current practice of incommunicado interrogation is at odds with one of our Nation's most cherished principles—that the individual may not be compelled to incriminate himself. Unless adequate protective devices are employed to dispel the compulsion inherent in custodial surroundings, no statement obtained from the defendant can truly be the product of his free choice.

From the foregoing, we can readily perceive an intimate connection between the privilege against self-incrimination and police custodial questioning. . . .

. . . Our decision in no way creates a constitutional straightjacket which will handicap sound efforts at reform, nor is it intended to have this effect. We encourage Congress and the States to continue their laudable search for increasingly effective ways of protecting the rights of the individual while promoting efficient enforcement of our criminal laws. However, unless we are shown other procedures which are at least as effective in apprising accused persons of their right of silence and in assuring a continuous opportunity to exercise it, the following safeguards must be observed.

At the outset, if a person in custody is to be subjected to interrogation, he must first be informed in clear and unequivocal terms that he has a right to remain silent. For those unaware of the privilege, the warning is needed simply to make them aware of it—the threshold requirement for an intelligent decision as to its exercise. More important, such a warning is an absolute prerequisite in overcoming the inherent pressures of the interrogation atmosphere. It is not just the subnormal or woefully ignorant who succumb to an interrogator's imprecations, whether implied or expressly stated, that the interrogation will continue until a confession is obtained or that silence in the face of accusation is itself damning and will bode ill when presented to a jury. Further, the warning will show the individual that his interrogators are prepared to recognize his privilege should he choose to exercise it. . . .

The warning of the right to remain silent must be accompanied by the explanation that anything said can and will be used against the individual in court. This warning is needed in order to make him aware not only of the privilege, but also of the consequences of foregoing it. . . .

The circumstances surrounding in-custody interrogation can operate very quickly to overbear the will of one merely made aware of his privilege by his interrogators. Therefore, the right to have counsel present at the interrogation is indispensable to the protection of the Fifth Amendment privilege under the system we delineate today. Our aim is to assure that the individual's right to choose between silence and speech remains unfettered throughout the interrogation process. . . .

An individual need not make a pre-interrogation request for a lawyer. While such request affirmatively secures his right to have one, his failure to ask for a lawyer does not constitute a waiver. No effective waiver of the right to counsel during interrogation can be recognized unless specifically made after the warnings we here delineate have been given. The accused who does not know his rights and therefore does not make a request may be the person who most needs counsel. . . .

Accordingly we hold that an individual held for interrogation must be clearly informed that he has the right to consult with a lawyer and to have the lawyer with him during interrogation. . . . As with the warnings of the right to remain silent and that anything stated can be used in evidence against him, this warning is an absolute prerequisite to interrogation. No amount of circumstantial evidence that the person may have been aware of this right will suffice to stand in its stead. Only through such a warning is there ascertainable assurance that the accused was aware of this right.

If an individual indicates that he wishes the assistance of counsel before any interrogation occurs, the authorities cannot rationally ignore or deny his request on the basis that the individual does not have or cannot afford a retained attorney. The financial ability of the individual has no relationship to the scope of the rights involved here. The privilege against self-incrimination secured by the Constitution applies to all individuals. The need for counsel in order to protect the privilege exists for the indigent as well as the affluent. . . .

In order fully to apprise a person interrogated of the extent of his rights under this system then, it is necessary to warn him not only that he has the right to consult with an attorney, but also that if he is indigent a lawyer will be appointed to represent him. Without this additional warning, the admonition of the right to consult with counsel would often be understood as meaning only that he can consult with a lawyer if he has one or has the funds to obtain one. . . .

This does not mean, as some have suggested, that each police station must have a "station house lawyer" present at all times to advise prisoners. It does mean, however, that if police propose to interrogate a person they must make known to him that he is entitled to a lawyer and that if he cannot afford one, a lawyer will be provided for him prior to any interrogation. If authorities conclude that they will not provide counsel during a reasonable period of time in which investigation in the field is carried out, they may refrain from doing so without violating the person's Fifth Amendment privilege so long as they do not question him during that time.

If the interrogation continues without the presence of an attorney and a statement is taken, a heavy burden rests on the government to demonstrate that the defendant knowingly and intelligently waived his privilege against self-incrimination and his right to retained or appointed counsel. . . .

The warnings required and the waiver necessary in accordance with our opinion today are, in the absence of a fully effective equivalent, prerequisites to the admissibility of any statement made by a defendant. No distinction can be drawn between statements which are direct confessions and statements which amount to "admissions" of part or all of an offense. The privilege against self-incrimination protects the individual from being compelled to incriminate himself in any manner; it does not distinguish degrees of incrimination. . . .

Our decision is not intended to hamper the traditional function of police officers in investigating crime. . . . When an individual is in custody on probable cause, the police may, of course, seek out evidence in the field to be used at trial against him. Such investigation may include inquiry of persons not under restraint. General on-the-scene questioning as to facts surrounding a crime or other general questioning of citizens in the fact-finding process is not affected by our holding. It is an act of responsible citizenship for individuals to give whatever information they may have to aid in law enforcement. In such situations the compelling atmosphere inherent in the process of in-custody interrogation is not necessarily present.

In dealing with statements obtained through interrogation, we do not purport to find all confessions inadmissable. Confessions remain a proper element in law enforcement. Any statement given freely and voluntarily without any compelling influences is, of course, admissible in evidence. The fundamental import of the privilege while an individual is in custody is not whether he is allowed to talk to the police without the benefit of warnings and counsel, but whether he can be interrogated. There is no requirement that police stop a person who enters a police station and states that he wishes to confess to a crime, or a person who calls the police to offer a confession or any other statement he desires to make. Volunteered statements of any kind are not barred by the Fifth Amendment and their admissibility is not affected by our holding today.

To summarize, we hold that when an individual is taken into custody or otherwise deprived of his freedom by the authorities in any significant way and is subjected to questioning, the privilege against self-incrimination is jeopardized. Procedural safeguards must be employed to protect the privilege, and unless other fully effective means are adopted to notify the person of his right of silence and to assure that the exercise of the right will be scrupulously honored, the following measures are required. He must be warned prior to any questioning that he has the right to remain silent, that anything he says can be used against him in a court of law, that he has the right to the presence of an attorney, and that if he cannot afford an attorney one will be appointed for him prior to any questioning if he so desires. Opportunity to exercise the rights must be afforded to him throughout the interrogation. After such warnings have been given, and such opportunity afforded him, the individual may knowingly and intelligently waive these rights and agree to answer questions or make a statment. But unless and until such warnings and waiver are demonstrated by the prosecution at trial, no evidence obtained as a result of interrogation can be used against him. . . .

[The Court finds that in each of the four cases under review confessions were obtained without appropriate warnings of constitutional rights.]

Mr. Justice Clark, dissenting [in part]. . . .

Such a strict constitutional specific inserted at the nerve center of crime detection may well kill the patient. Since there is at this time a paucity of information and an almost total lack of empirical knowledge on the practical operation of requirements truly comparable to those announced by the majority, I would be more restrained lest we go too far too fast. . . .

Mr. Justice Harlan, whom Mr. Justice Stewart and Mr. Justice White join, dissenting.

I believe the decision of the Court represents poor constitutional law and entails harmful consequences for the country at large. How serious these consequences may prove to be only time can tell. . . .

What the Court largely ignores is that its rules impair, if they will not eventually serve wholly to frustrate, an instrument of law enforcement that has long and quite reasonably been thought worth the price paid for it. There can be little doubt that the Court's new code would markedly decrease the number of confessions. To warn the suspect that he may remain silent and remind him that his confession may be used in court are minor obstructions. To require also an express waiver by the suspect and an end to questioning whenever he demurs must heavily handicap questioning. And to suggest or provide counsel for the suspect simply invites the end of the interrogation. . . .

How much harm this decision will inflict on law enforcement cannot fairly be predicted with accuracy. Evidence on the role of confessions is notoriously incomplete . . . . , and little is added by the Court's reference to the FBI experience and the resources believed wasted in interrogation. . . . We do know that some crimes cannot be solved without confessions, that ample expert testimony attests to their importance in crime control, and that the Court is taking a real risk with society's welfare in imposing its new regime on the country. The social costs of crime are too great to call the new rules anything but a hazardous experimentation. . . .

Mr. Justice White, with whom Mr. Justice Harlan and Mr. Justice Stewart join, dissenting. . . .

It may be noted that after Miranda's conviction was reversed, the State of Arizona retried him. His confession was not introduced in evidence, but the prosecution found a new witness—Miranda's common-law wife—who gave testimony sufficiently damaging to result in a second conviction and a resulting sentence of from twenty to thirty years on each count of kidnapping and rape. [For an excellent description of the entire Miranda case, from commission of the crime to final disposition, see Richard C. Cortner and Clifford M. Lytle, *Modern Constitutional Law* (New York: Free Press, 1971), pp. 158–198.]

In *Johnson* v. *New Jersey*, 384 U.S. 719 (1966), the Court held that *Miranda* and *Escobedo* would not be applied retroactively, and thus the rules of those cases would apply prospectively from the dates the decisions were handed down.

HARRIS *v.* NEW YORK
401 U.S. 222 (1971)

Mr. Chief Justice Berger delivered the opinion of the Court.

We granted the writ in this case to consider petitioner's claim that a statement made by him to police under circumstances rendering it inadmissible to establish the prosecution's case in chief under *Miranda* v. *Arizona* ... may not be used to impeach his credibility.

The State of New York charged petitioner in a two-count indictment with twice selling heroin to an undercover police officer. ...

Petitioner took the stand in his own defense. He admitted knowing the undercover police officer but denied a sale on January 4. He admitted making a sale of contents of a glassine bag to the officer on Jaunary 6 but claimed it was baking soda and part of a scheme to defraud the purchaser.

On cross-examination petitioner was asked seriatim whether he had made specified statements to the police immediately following his arrest on January 7—statements that partially contradicted petitioner's direct testimony at trial. In response to the cross-examination, petitioner testified that he could not remember virtually any of the questions or answers recited by the prosecutor. ...

The trial judge instructed the jury that the statements attributed to petitioner by the prosecution could be considered only in passing on petitioner's credibility and not as evidence of guilt. In closing summations both counsel argued the substance of the impeaching statements. The jury then found petitioner guilty of the second count of the indictment. ...

At trial the prosecution made no effort in its case in chief to use the statements allegedly made by petitioner, conceding that they were inadmissible under *Miranda* v. *Arizona*. ...

Some comments in the *Miranda* opinion can indeed be read as indicating a bar to use of an uncounseled statement for any purpose, but discussion of that issue was not at all necessary to the Court's holding and cannot be regarded as controlling. *Miranda* barred the prosecution from making its case with statements of an accused made while in custody prior to having or effectively waiving counsel. It does not follow from *Miranda* that evidence inadmissible against an accused in the prosecution's case in chief is barred for all purposes, provided of course that the trustworthiness of the evidence satisfies legal standards. ...

... The impeachment process here undoubtedly provided valuable aid to the jury in assessing petitioner's credibility, and the benefits of this process should not be lost, in our view, because of the speculative possibility that impermissible police conduct will be encouraged thereby. Assuming that the exclusionary rule has a deterrent effect on proscribed police conduct, sufficient deterrence flows when the evidence in question is made unavailable to the prosecution in its case in chief.

Every criminal defendant is privileged to testify in his own defense, or to refuse to do so. ... The shield provided by *Miranda* cannot be perverted into a license to use perjury by way of a defense, free from the risk of confrontation with prior inconsistent utterances. We hold, therefore, that petitioner's credibility was appropriately impeached by use of his earlier conflicting statements.

Affirmed.

Mr. Justice Black dissents.

Mr. Justice Brennan, with whom Mr. Justice Douglas and Mr. Justice Marshall join, dissenting. ...

The objective of deterring improper police conduct is only part of the larger objective of safeguarding the integrity of our adversary system. The "essential mainstay" of that system ... is the privilege against self-incrimination, which for that reason has occupied a central place in our jurisprudence since before the Nation's birth. ... These values are plainly jeopardized if an exception against admission of tainted statements is made for those used for impeachment purposes.

Moreover, it is monstrous that courts should aid or abet the law-breaking police officer.... The Court today tells the police that they may freely interrogate an accused incommunicado and without counsel and know that although any statement they obtain in violation of *Miranda* can't be used on the State's direct case, it may be introduced if the defendant has the temerity to testify in his own defense. This goes far toward undoing much of the progress made in conforming police methods to the Constitution. I dissent.

Another problem which is sometimes treated in the context of coerced confessions, although not involving testimonial utterances in any way, is the question of the legality of obtaining evidence from the actual person of the accused. Use of the person for identification purposes has long been sanctioned. The point was discussed by Justice Holmes in *Holt* v. *United States,* 218 U.S. 245, 252–253, in 1910:

Another objection is based upon an extravagant extension of the Fifth Amendment. A question arose as to whether a blouse belonged to the prisoner. A witness testified that the prisoner put it on and it fitted him. It is objected that he did this under the same duress that made his statements inadmissible, and that it should be excluded for the same reasons. But the prohibition of compelling a man in a criminal court to be witness against himself is a prohibition of the use of physical or moral compulsion *to extort communications from him,* not an exclusion of his body as evidence when it may be material. The objection in principle would forbid a jury to look at a prisoner and compare his features with a photograph in proof. (Italics added.)

As Justice Holmes stated, the person may even be used in supplying evidentiary proof over and above mere identification—as in trying on a blouse found at the scene of the crime. The problem is really one of coerced *evidence* rather than coerced confessions, although it is frequently put in the latter category. The question of how far the police can go in obtaining evidence from the person of the accused is thus better viewed as simply a due process question rather than in the context of self-incrimination. In this framework it is easier to distinguish the holdings in the two cases to follow: *Rochin* v. *California* and *Breithaupt* v. *Abram.*

ROCHIN *v.* CALIFORNIA
342 U.S. 165 (1952)

Mr. Justice Frankfurter delivered the opinion of the Court.

Having "some information that [the petitioner] was selling narcotics," three deputy sheriffs of the County of Los Angeles, on the morning of July 1, 1949, made for the two-story dwelling house in which Rochin lived with his mother, his common-law wife, brothers and sisters. Finding the outside door open, they entered and then forced open the door to Rochin's room on the second floor. Inside they found petitioner sitting partly dressed on the side of the bed, upon which his wife was lying. On a "night stand" beside the bed the deputies spied two capsules. When asked "Whose stuff is this?" Rochin seized the capsules and put them in his mouth. A struggle ensued, in the course of which the three officers "jumped upon him" and attempted to extract the capsules. The force they applied proved unavailing against Rochin's resistance. He was handcuffed and taken to a hospital. At the direction of one of the officers a doctor forced an emetic solution through a tube into Rochin's stomach against his will. This "stomach pumping" produced vomiting. In the vomited matter were found two capsules which proved to contain morphine.

Rochin was brought to trial before a California Superior Court, sitting without a jury, on the charge of possessing "a preparation of morphine".... Rochin was convicted and sentenced to sixty days' imprisonment. The chief evidence against him was the two capsules. They were admitted over petitioner's objection, although the means of obtaining them was frankly set forth in the testimony by one of the deputies, substantially as here narrated.

On appeal, the District Court of Appeal affirmed the conviction, despite the finding that the officers "were guilty of unlawfully breaking into and entering defendant's room and were guilty of unlawfully assaulting and battering, torturing and falsely imprisoning the defendant at the alleged hospital.".... The Supreme Court of California denied without opinion Rochin's petition for a hearing. Two justices dissented from this denial. . . .

This Court granted certiorari ... because a serious question is raised as to the limitations which the Due Process Clause of the Fourteenth Amendment imposes on the conduct of criminal proceedings by the States. . . .

. . . Regard for the requirements of the Due Process Clause "inescapably imposes upon this Court an exercise of judgment upon the whole course of the proceedings [resulting in a conviction] in order to ascertain whether they offend those canons of decency and fairness which express the notions of justice of English-speaking peoples even toward those charged with the most heinous offenses." *Malinski* v. *New York*. . . . These standards of justice are not authoritatively formulated anywhere as though they were specifics. Due process of law is a summarized constitutional guarantee of respect for those personal immunities which, as Mr. Justice Cardozo twice wrote for the Court, are "so rooted in the traditions and conscience of our people as to be ranked as fundamental," *Snyder* v. *Massachusetts*, 291 U.S. 97, 105, or are "implicit in the concept of ordered liberty." *Palko* v. *Connecticut*, 302 U.S. 319, 325. . . .

Applying these general considerations to the circumstances of the present case, we are compelled to conclude that the proceedings by which this conviction was obtained do more than offend some fastidious squeamishness or private sentimentalism about combatting crime too energetically. It is conduct that shocks the conscience. Illegally breaking into the privacy of the petitioner, the struggle to open his mouth and remove what was there, the forcible extraction of his stomach's contents—this course of proceeding by agents of government to obtain evidence is bound to offend even hardened sensibilities. They are methods too close to the rack and the screw to permit of constitutional differentiation.

It has long since ceased to be true that due process of law is heedless of the means by which otherwise relevant and credible evidence is obtained. Even before the series of recent cases enforced the constitutional principle the States could not base convictions upon confessions, however much verified, but obtained by coercion. These decisions are not arbitrary exceptions to the comprehensive right of States to fashion their own rules of evidence for criminal trials. They are not sports in our constitutional law but applications of a general principle. They are only instances of the general requirement that States in their prosecutions respect certain decencies of civilized conduct. Due process of law, as a historic and generative principle, precludes defining, and thereby confining, these standards of conduct more precisely than to say that convictions cannot be brought about by methods that offend "a sense of justice." See Mr. Chief Justice Hughes, speaking for a unanimous Court in *Brown* v. *Mississippi*, 297 U.S. 278, 285, 286. It would be a stultification of the responsibility which the course of constitutional history has cast upon this Court to hold that in order to convict a man the police cannot extract by force what is in his mind but can extract what is in his stomach.

To attempt in this case to distinguish what lawyers call "real evidence" from verbal evidence is to ignore the reasons for excluding coerced confessions. Use of involuntary verbal confessions in State criminal trials is constitutionally obnoxious not only because of their unreliability. They are inadmissible under the Due Process Clause even though statements contained in them may be independently established as true. Coerced confessions offend the community's sense of fair play and decency. So here, to sanction the brutal conduct which naturally enough was condemned by the court whose judgment is before us, would be to afford brutality the cloak of law. Nothing would be more calculated to discredit law and thereby to brutalize the temper of a society. . . .

We are not unmindful that hypothetical situations can be conjured by shading imperceptibly from the circumstances of this case and by gradations producing practical differences despite seemingly logical extensions. But the Constitution is "intended to preserve practical and substantial rights, not to maintain theories." *Davis* v. *Mills*, 194 U.S. 451, 457.

On the facts of this case the conviction of the petitioner has been obtained by methods that offend the Due Process Clause. The judgment below must be

Reversed.

Mr. Justice Minton took no part in the consideration or decision of this case.

Mr. Justice Black, concurring.

Adamson v. *California*, 332 U.S. 46, 68–123, sets out reasons for my belief that state as well as federal courts and law enforcement officers must obey the Fifth Amendment's command that "No person . . . shall be compelled in any criminal case to be a witness against himself." I think a person is compelled to be a witness against himself not only when he is compelled to testify, but also when, as here, incriminating evidence is forcibly taken from him by a contrivance of modern science. Cf. *Boyd* v. *United States*, 116 U.S. 616; . . . California convicted this petitioner by using against him evidence obtained in this manner, and I agree with Mr. Justice Douglas that the case should be reversed on this ground. . . .

Mr. Justice Douglas, concurring. . . .

As an original matter it might be debatable whether the provision in the Fifth Amendment that no person "shall be compelled in any criminal case to be a witness against himself" serves the ends of justice. Not all civilized legal procedures recognize it. But the choice was made by the Framers, a choice which sets a standard for legal trials in this country. The Framers made it a standard of due process for prosecutions by the Federal Government. If it is a requirement of due process for a trial in the federal court house, it is impossible for me to say it is not a requirement of due process for a trial in the state court house. . . . Of course an accused can be compelled to be present at the trial, to stand, to sit, to turn this way or that, and to try on a cap or a coat. See *Holt* v. *United States*, 218 U.S. 245, 252, 253. But I think that words taken from his lips, capsules taken from his stomach, blood taken from his veins are all inadmissible provided they are taken from him without his consent. They are inadmissible because of the command of the Fifth Amendment. . . .

In his concurring opinion, Justice Douglas put "blood taken from his veins" in the same area of constitutional protection as capsules taken from the stomach. He stated that in either case they are inadmissible if taken from the accused without his consent. Five years later the Court was faced with this exact question In *Breithaupt* v. *Abram*. Differences in approach among the justices which were indicated In *Rochin* resulted in a sharp split in the vote in *Breithaupt*.

BREITHAUPT *v.* ABRAM

352 U.S. 432 (1957)

Mr. Justice Clark delivered the opinion of the Court.

Petitioner, while driving a pickup truck on the highways of New Mexico, was involved in a collision with a passenger car. Three occupants of the car were killed and petitioner was seriously injured. A pint whiskey bottle, almost empty, was found in the glove compartment of the pickup truck. Petitioner was taken to a hospital and while lying unconscious in the emergency room the smell of liquor was detected on his breath. A state patrolman requested that a sample of petitioner's blood be taken. An attending physician, while petitioner was unconscious, withdrew a sample of about 20 cubic centimeters of blood by use of a hypodermic needle. This sample was delivered to the patrolman and subsequent laboratory analysis showed this blood to contain about .17 per cent alcohol.

Petitioner was thereafter charged with involuntary manslaughter. Testimony regarding the blood test and its result was admitted into evidence at trial over petitioner's objection. This included testimony of an expert that a person with .17 per cent alcohol in his blood was under the influence of intoxicating liquor. Petitioner was convicted and sentenced for involuntary manslaughter. He did not appeal the conviction. Subsequently, however, he sought release from his imprisonment by a petition for a writ of habeas corpus to the Supreme Court of New Mexico. That court, after argument, denied the writ.... Petitioner contends that his conviction, based on the result of the involuntary blood test, deprived him of his liberty without that due process of law guaranteed him by the Fourteenth Amendment to the Constitution. We granted certiorari....

It has been clear since *Weeks* v. *United States*, 232 U.S. 383, that evidence obtained in violation of rights protected by the Fourth Amendment to the Federal Constitution must be excluded in federal criminal prosecutions. There is argument on behalf of petitioner that the evidence used here, the result of the blood test, was obtained in violation of the Due Process Clause of the Fourteenth Amendment in that the taking was the result of an unreasonable search and seizure violative of the Fourth Amendment. Likewise, he argues that by way of the Fourteenth Amendment there has been a violation of the Fifth Amendment in that introduction of the test result compelled him to be a witness against himself. Petitioner relies on the proposition that "the generative principles" of the Bill of Rights should extend the protections of the Fourth and Fifth Amendments to his case through the Due Process Clause of the Fourteenth Amendment. But *Wolf* v. *Colorado* ... answers this contention in the negative.... New Mexico has rejected, as it may, the exclusionary rule set forth in *Weeks*.... Therefore, the rights petitioner claims afford no aid to him here for the fruits of the violations, if, any, are admissible in the State's prosecution.

Petitioner's remaining and primary assault on his conviction is not so easily unhorsed. He urges that the conduct of the state officers here offends that "sense of justice" of which we spoke in *Rochin* v. *California*. . . . But we see nothing comparable here to the facts in *Rochin*.

Basically the distinction rests on the fact that there is nothing "brutal" or "offensive" in the taking of a sample of blood when done, as in this case, under the protective eye of a physician. To be sure, the driver here was unconscious when the blood was taken, but the absense of conscious consent, without more, does not necessarily render the taking a violation of a constitutional right; and certainly the test as administered here would not be considered offensive by even the most delicate. Furthermore, due process is not measured by the yardstick of personal reaction or the sphygmogram of the most sensitive person, but by that whole community sense of "decency and fairness" that has been woven by common experience into the fabric of acceptable conduct. It is on this bedrock that this Court has established the concept of due process. The blood test procedure has become routine in our everyday life. It is a ritual for those going into the military service as well as those applying for marriage licenses. Many colleges require such tests before permitting entrance and literally millions of us have voluntarily gone through the same, through a longer routine, in becoming blood donors. Likewise, we note that a majority of our States have either enacted statutes in some form authorizing tests of this nature or permit findings so obtained to be admitted in evidence. We therefore conclude that a blood test taken by a skilled technician is not such "conduct that shocks the conscience," *Rochin, supra,* . . . nor such a method of obtaining evidence that it offends a "sense of justice," *Brown* v. *Mississippi*. . . . This is not to say that the indiscriminate taking of blood under different conditions, or by those not competent to do so may not amount to such "brutality" as would come under the *Rochin* rule. The chief law-enforcement officer of New Mexico, while at the Bar of this Court, assured us that every proper medical precaution is afforded an accused from whom the blood is taken.

The test upheld here is not attacked on the ground of any basic deficiency or of injudicious application, but admittedly is a scientifically accurate method of detecting alcoholic content in the blood, thus furnishing an exact measure upon which to base a decision as to intoxication. Modern community living requires modern scientific methods of crime detection lest the public go unprotected. The increasing slaughter on our highways, most of which should be avoidable, now reaches the astounding figures only heard of on the battlefield. The States, through safety measures, modern scientific methods, and strict enforcement of traffic laws, are using all reasonable means to make automobile driving less dangerous.

As against the right of an individual that his person be held inviolable, even against so slight an intrusion as is involved in applying a blood test of the kind to which millions of Americans submit as a matter of course nearly every day, must be set the interests of society in the scientific determination of intoxication, one of the great causes of the mortal hazards of the road. And the more so since the test likewise may establish innocence, thus affording protection against the treachery of judgment based on one or more of the senses. Furthermore, since our criminal law is to no small extent justified by the assumption of deterrence, the individual's right to immunity from such invasion of the body as is involved in a properly safeguarded blood test is far outweighed by the value of its deterrent effect due to public realization that the issue of driving while under the influence of alcohol can often by this method be taken out of the confusion of conflicting contentions.

For these reasons the judgment is

Affirmed.

Mr. Chief Justice Warren, with whom Mr. Justice Black and Mr. Justice Douglas join, dissenting:

The judgment in this case should be reversed if *Rochin* v. *California* ... is to retain its vitality and stand as more than an instance of personal revulsion against particular police methods. I cannot agree with the Court when it says, "We see nothing comparable here to the facts in *Rochin*." It seems to me the essential elements of the cases are the same and the same result should follow.

There is much in the Court's opinion concerning the hazards on our nation's highways, the efforts of the States to enforce the traffic laws and the necessity for the use of modern scientific methods in the detection of crime. Everybody can agree with these sentiments, and yet they do not help us particularly in determining whether this case can be distinguished from *Rochin*. That case grew out of police efforts to curb the narcotics traffic, in which there is surely a state interest of at least as great magnitude as the interest in highway law enforcement. . . .

. . . Of course, one may consent to having his blood extracted or his stomach pumped and thereby waive any due process objection. . . . But where there is no affirmative consent, I cannot see that it should make any difference whether one states unequivocally that he objects or resorts to physical violence in protest or is in such condition that he is unable to protest. The Court, however, states that "the absence of conscious consent, without more, does not necessarily render the taking a violation of a constitutional right." This implies that a different result might follow if petitioner had been conscious and had voiced his objection. I reject the distinction. . . . I cannot accept an analysis that would make physical resistance by a prisoner a prerequisite to the existence of his constitutional rights. . . .

Only personal reaction to the stomach pump and the blood test distinguish them. To base the restriction which the Due Process Clause imposes on state criminal procedures upon such reactions is to build on shifting sands. We should, in my opinion, hold that due process means at least that law enforcement officers in their efforts to obtain evidence from persons suspected of crime must stop short of bruising the body, breaking skin, puncturing tissue or extracting body fluids, whether they contemplate doing it by force or by stealth.

Viewed according to this standard the judgment should be reversed.

Mr. Justice Douglas, with whom Mr. Justice Black joins, dissenting. . . .

As I understood today's decision there would be a violation of due process if the blood had been withdrawn from the accused after a struggle with the police. But the sanctity of the person is equally violated and his body assaulted where the prisoner is incapable of offering resistance as it would be if force were used to overcome his resistance. In both cases evidence is used to convict a man which had been obtained from him on an involuntary basis. I would not draw a line between the use of force on the one hand and trickery, subterfuge, or any police technique which takes advantage of the inability of the prisoner to resist on the other. Nor would I draw a line between involuntary extraction of words from his lips, the involuntary extraction of the contents of his stomach, and the involuntary extraction of fluids of his body when the evidence obtained is used to convict him. Under our system of government, police cannot compel people to furnish the evidence necessary to send them to prison. Yet there is compulsion here, following the violation by the police of the sanctity of the body of an unconscious man. . . .

In *Schmerber* v. *California*, 384 U.S. 757 (1966), the Court ruled on the admissibility of a blood test report on intoxication where the blood sample was taken from the injured petitioner despite his refusal, on the advice of counsel, to consent to the test. He contended that the admission of such evidence violated due process under the Fourteenth Amendment, his privilege against self-incrimination under the Fifth Amendment, his right to counsel under the Sixth Amendment, and the prohibitions against unreasonable searches and seizures under the Fourth Amendment, as these have been incorporated into the Fourteenth Amendment. The Court stated that in view of the important decisions rendered since *Breithaupt* v. *Abram* (*viz., Escobedo* v. *Illinois, Malloy* v. *Hogan,* and *Mapp* v. *Ohio*), certiorari was granted to reconsider the questions. Justice Brennan, speaking for a majority of five, stated: "We hold that the privilege protects an accused only from being compelled to testify against himself, or otherwise provide the State with evidence of a testimonial or communicative nature, and that the withdrawal of blood and use of the analysis in question in this case did not involve compulsion to these ends." The due process contention was rejected squarely on the basis of *Breithaupt,* and the majority concluded that no substantial right to counsel issue was presented. On the Fourth Amendment claim, the Court stated that there was probable cause to believe petitioner to be intoxicated, that the officer therefore made a lawful arrest, and that the ordering of the blood test without a warrant was "an appropriate incident to petitioner's arrest" in order to prevent the "destruction of evidence" by normal physiological elimination of blood alcohol. Justices Harlan and Stewart concurred, with the only additional comment that "While agreeing with the Court that the taking of this blood test involved no testimonial compulsion, I would go further and hold that apart from this consideration the case in no way implicates the Fifth Amendment." Chief Justice Warren and Justices Black and Douglas dissented, following their views expressed in *Breithaupt.*

While taking fingerprints may not implicate the Fifth Amendment, the procedures employed may still run afoul of the protection of the Fourth Amendment. *Davis* v. *Mississippi,* 394 U.S. 721 (1969), involved the admissibility of fingerprints taken at a police station in a trial and conviction for rape. The victim could give no better description of her assailant than that he was a Negro youth. Fingerprints were found on a window sill, and over a period of ten days the police, without warrants, took at least twenty-four Negro youths to police headquarters where they were questioned briefly, fingerprinted, and released. The petitioner's prints matched those taken from the window sill, and he was tried and convicted. The Court reversed the conviction, holding that the unauthorized detention and fingerprinting of large numbers of persons, without probable cause to arrest, violated the Fourth Amendment.

In *United States* v. *Dionisio,* 410 U.S. 1 (1973), however, the Court held that a grand jury witness could be compelled to furnish a voice exemplar, and the fact that some twenty persons were subpoenaed for this purpose, without probable cause, did not require a holding of violation of either the Fourth or the Fifth Amendments. Dionisio had been held in contempt for refusing to comply with the instruction, but the Court of Appeals reversed on authority of *Davis,* reasoning that the dragnet effect had the same invidious effect on Fourth Amendment rights as had occurred in that case. The Supreme Court held, through Justice Stewart, that "Since neither the summons to appear before the grand jury, nor its directive to make a voice recording infringed upon any interest protected by the Fourth Amendment, there was no justification for requiring the grand jury to satisfy even the minimal requirement of 'reasonableness' imposed by the Court of Appeals." A person's voice, like his facial characteristics or handwriting, "is repeatedly produced for others to hear." And there is no intrusion which would present a Fourth Amendment violation. In *United States* v. *Mara*, 410 U.S. 19 (1973), the Court upheld the right of a grand jury to require the production of handwriting exemplars even though no preliminary showing of reasonableness was made.

The Court has also held admissible fingernail scrapings taken in a police station from one who was not under arrest but where probable cause to arrest existed. The case was *Cupp* v. *Murphy*, 412 U.S. 291 (1973). Murphy's wife was killed by strangulation in her home, and abrasions and lacerations were found on her throat. There was no sign of a break-in or robbery. Murphy, who was not living with his wife, was notified, and he voluntarily went to the station house for questioning. There the police noticed a dark spot on Murphy's finger and suspected that it might be dried blood. They asked if they might take a sample of scrapings and were refused. They took a sample anyhow, over his protest, and found it to contain traces of skin and blood cells and also fabric from the victim's nightgown. This evidence was admitted at the trial and Murphy was convicted of second-degree murder. In reversing the District Court's denial of habeas corpus, the Court of Appeals concluded that, absent arrest or other exigent circumstances, the search was unconstitutional. The Supreme Court reversed, holding that "on the facts of the case, considering the existence of probable cause, the very limited intrusion undertaken incident to the station-house detention, and the ready destructibility of the evidence," there was no violation of the Fourth Amendment.

THE RIGHT TO COUNSEL

One of the most important rights of one accused of crime is the right to be represented by counsel. At common law a defendant had the right to employ counsel when charged with a misdemeanor, but not in cases of treason or felony. The theory apparently was that the Crown might err in petty offenses, but in the graver charges no case would be brought unless the evidence was so clear that guilt was evident. Therefore no lawyer was necessary, and the judge would see that procedures were fair. Full right of counsel was not extended by Parliament until 1836, much later than in the United States. Congress provided for the assistance of counsel in the original Judiciary Act of 1789, and in most of the original states the right was granted to accused persons whether in misdemeanor or felony cases.

It should be noted, however, that the original meaning of the right to counsel extended only to permission for the accused to employ and bring in to the trial a lawyer of his choosing. No general provision was made for the indigent defendant who might want and even badly need counsel, but who was too poor to employ a lawyer. Thus the Sixth Amendment provision for "assistance of counsel for his defense" in "all criminal prosecutions" was permissive only. It imposed no duty on the government to provide free counsel. The Federal Crimes Act of 1790, however, provided that counsel must be appointed in all capital cases at the request of the defendant. And Delaware, Pennsylvania, and South Carolina by 1789 had similar provisions. Connecticut apparently went further and the judges appointed counsel upon request if they felt that the accused needed it. With these exceptions, the "right to counsel" only gave the accused the right to hire a lawyer. In construing the federal requirement under the Sixth Amendment and under the Act of 1790, the Court held that neither the Constitution nor the statutes made court-appointed counsel mandatory in noncapital cases. Referring to the 1790 statute, which required counsel in all capital cases, the Court said, "There would appear to be a negative pregnant here." *United States* v. *Van Duzee,* 140 U.S. 169, 173 (1891). Thus it concluded that no appointment need be made in any other type of case. It did leave the trial court with discretion to appoint counsel in noncapital cases if the judge saw fit, but it held that there was neither constitutional nor statutory duty to do so. As recently as 1931 this interpretation received official recognition. The Wickersham Commission, appointed by President Hoover to investigate law enforcement, stated in its report in that year: "[T]he right guaranteed is one of employing counsel, not one of having counsel provided by the Government." [U.S. National Commission on Law Observance and Enforcement, *Report on Prosecution* 30 (U.S. Government Printing Ofc., 1931). See William M. Beaney, *The Right of Counsel in American Courts* (Ann Arbor University of Michigan Press, 1955); J. A. C. Grant, "Our Common Law Constitution," 40 *B. U. L. Rev.* 1, 5–10 (1960); David Fellman, *The Defendant's Rights* (New York: Rinehart, 1958), chap. 7.]

While the exact scope of the Sixth Amendment's right to counsel was as yet undefined, the Court had occasion in 1932 to examine the question of the application of the Fourteenth Amendment's due process clause to the matter of counsel in state criminal proceedings. This was in the famous Scottsboro case of *Powell* v. *Alabama.*

POWELL *v.* ALABAMA
287 U.S. 45 (1932)

Mr. Justice Sutherland delivered the opinion of the Court.

These cases were argued together and submitted for decision as one case.

The petitioners, hereafter referred to as defendants, are negroes charged with the crime of rape, committed upon the persons of two white girls. The crime is said to have been committed on March 25, 1931. The indictment was returned in a state court of first instance on March 31, and the record recites that on the same day the defendants were arraigned and entered pleas of not guilty. There is a further recital to the effect that upon the arraignment they were represented by counsel. But no counsel had been employed, and aside from a statement made by the trial judge several days later during a colloquy immediately preceding the trial, the record does not disclose when, or under what circumstances, an appointment of counsel was made, or who was appointed. During the colloquy referred to, the trial judge, in response to a question, said that he had appointed all the members of the bar for the purpose of arraigning the defendants and then of course anticipated that the members of the bar would continue to help the defendants if no counsel appeared. Upon the argument here both sides accepted that as a correct statement of the facts concerning the matter.

There was a severance upon the request of the state, and the defendants were tried in three several groups. as indicated above. As each of the three cases was called for trial, each defendant was arraigned, and, having the indictment read to him, entered a plea of not guilty. Whether the original arraignment and pleas were regarded as ineffective is not shown. Each of the three trials was completed within a single day. Under the Alabama statute the punishment for rape is to be fixed by the jury, and in its discretion may be from ten years' imprisonment to death. The juries found defendants guilty and imposed the death penalty upon all. The trial court overruled motions for new trials and sentenced the defendants in accordance with the verdicts. The judgments were affirmed by the state supreme court. . . .

. . . It is perfectly apparent that the proceedings, from beginning to end, took place in an atmosphere of tense, hostile and excited public sentiment. During the entire time, the defendants were closely confined or were under military guard. The record does not disclose their ages, except that one of them was nineteen; but the record clearly indicates that most, if not all, of them were youthful, and they are constantly referred to as "the boys." They were ignorant and illiterate. All of them were residents of other states, where alone members of their families or friends resided.

However guilty defendants, upon due inquiry, might prove to have been, they were, until convicted, presumed to be innocent. It was the duty of the court having their cases in charge to see that they were denied no necessary incident of a fair trial. . . . The sole inquiry which we are permitted to make is whether the federal Constitution was contravened . . . whether the defendants were in substance denied the right of counsel, and if so, whether such denial infringes the due process clause of the Fourteenth Amendment. . . .

It is hardly necessary to say that, the right to counsel being conceded, a defendant should be afforded a fair opportunity to secure counsel of his own choice. Not only was that not done here, but such designation of counsel as was attempted was either so indefinite or so close upon the trial as to amount to a denial of effective and substantial aid in that regard. This will be amply demonstrated by a brief review of the record.

[The opinion then quotes from the record, indicating clearly that no specific designation of counsel was made until the time of trial, and even then on the basis of a volunteer who stated, "I will go ahead and help do anything I can do."]

And in this casual fashion the matter of counsel in a capital case was disposed of. . . .

. . . In any event, the circumstance lends emphasis to the conclusion that during perhaps the most critical period of the proceedings against these defendants, that is to say, from the time of their arraignment until the beginning of their trial, when consultation, thorough-going investigation and preparation were vitally important, the defendants did not have the aid of counsel in any real sense, although they were as much entitled to such aid during that period as at the trial itself. . . .

. . . The defendants, young, ignorant, illiterate, surrounded by hostile sentiment, haled back and forth under guard of soldiers, charged with an atrocious crime regarded with especial horror in the community where they were to be tried, were thus put in peril of their lives within a few moments after counsel for the first time charged with any degree of responsibility began to represent them. . . .

It never has been doubted by this court, or any other so far as we know, that notice and hearing are preliminary steps essential to the passing of an enforceable judgment, and that they, together with a legally competent tribunal having jurisdiction of the case, constitute basic elements of the constitutional requirement of due process of law. . . .

What, then, does a hearing include? Historically and in practice, in our own country at least, it has always included the right to the aid of counsel when desired and provided by the party asserting the right. The right to be heard would be, in many cases, of little avail if it did not comprehend the right to be heard by counsel. Even the intelligent and educated layman has small and sometimes no skill in the science of law. If charged with crime, he is incapable, generally, of determining for himself whether the indictment is good or bad. He is unfamiliar with the rules of evidence. Left without the aid of counsel he may be put on trial without a proper charge, and convicted upon incompetent evidence, or evidence irrelevant to the issue or otherwise inadmissible. He lacks both the skill and knowledge adequately to prepare his defense, even though he have a perfect one. He requires the guiding hand of counsel at every step in the proceedings against him. Without it, though he be not guilty, he faces the danger of conviction because he does not know how to establish his innocence. If that be true of men of intelligence, how much more true is it of the ignorant and illiterate, or those of feeble intellect. If in any case, civil or criminal, a state or federal court were arbitrarily to refuse to hear a party by counsel, employed by and appearing for him, it reasonably may not be doubted that such a refusal would be a denial of a hearing, and, therefore, of due process in the constitutional sense. . . .

In the light of the facts outlined in the forepart of this opinion—the ignorance and illiteracy of the defendants, their youth, the circumstances of public hostility, the imprisonment and the close surveillance of the defendants by the military forces, the fact that their friends and families were all in other states and communication with them necessarily difficult, and above all that they stood in deadly peril of their lives—we think the failure of the trial court to give them reasonable time and opportunity to secure counsel was a clear denial of due process.

But passing that, and assuming their inability, even if opportunity had been given to employ counsel, as the trial court evidently did assume, we are of opinion that, under the circumstances just stated, the necessity of counsel was so vital and imperative that the failure of the trial court to make an effective appointment of counsel was likewise a denial of due process within the meaning of the Fourteenth Amendment. Whether this would be so in other criminal prosecutions, or under other circumstances, we need not determine. All that it is necessary now to decide, as we do decide, is that in a capital case, where the defendant is unable to employ counsel, and is incapable adequately of making his own defense because of ignorance, feeble-mindedness, illiteracy, or the like, it is the duty of the court, whether requested or not, to assign counsel for him as a necessary requisite of due process of law; and that duty is not discharged by an assignment at such a time or under such circumstances as to preclude the giving of effective aid in the preparation and trial of the case. . . . In a case such as this, whatever may be the rule in other cases, the right to have counsel appointed, when necessary, is a logical corollary from the constitutional right to be heard by counsel. . . .

The judgments must be reversed and the causes remanded for further proceedings not inconsistent with this opinion.

Judgments reversed.

7-2

[Justice Butler, joined by Justice McReynolds, dissented.]

Justice Sutherland was careful in stating the decision to confine the ruling to the peculiar facts of the case. At the same time, there was dictum which could give encouragement to those who wished to see the Fourteenth Amendment right to counsel for the indigent defendant broadened. Further encouragement was offered by the decision in *Johnson* v. *Zerbst*, 304 U.S. 458 (1938), which clarified the Sixth Amendment right to counsel. Johnson was charged with passing counterfeit notes and tried in federal court. At trial, he stated that he had no lawyer, and—in response to an inquiry of the court—stated that he was ready for trial. The judge neither advised him of his right to counsel nor offered a court-appointed attorney. Johnson was convicted of the felony and sentenced to four and one-half years in prison. While in prison, he filed a petition for habeas corpus, alleging that his trial without counsel violated the Sixth Amendment. The Supreme Court held that the Sixth Amendment right to counsel extends to the *appointment* of counsel for indigent defendants in federal criminal proceedings unless the accused waives the right. The holding also involved two important subsidiary points. First, the defendant may waive counsel, but such waiver must be "intelligent and competent." The duty placed on the trial judge is clear; he must make certain that under the circumstances of the charge, the possible penalties, and the capabilities of the accused, that a request to proceed without counsel would not result in serious disability to the accused. Second, failure to meet the Sixth Amendment requirement with respect to counsel is a jurisdictional defect, and therefore the collateral remedy of habeas corpus may properly be employed.

In 1942, however, the majority made it clear that they did not intend to equate the Fourteenth Amendment requirement with that of the Sixth Amendment. The case was *Betts* v. *Brady,* 316 U.S. 455 (1942), which dealt with a trial for robbery in the state court of Maryland. Petitioner was too poor to employ counsel, so informed the judge at his arraignment, and requested that counsel be appointed for him. The judge refused, pointing out that counsel was appointed for indigent defendants only in prosecutions for murder and rape. The trial proceeded, without a jury, and the judge found him guilty. The sentence imposed was eight years. A majority of the United States Supreme Court held that under the circumstances of the case, no denial of a fair trial could be inferred. Thus counsel was not a constitutional necessity. Justice Black, joined by Justices Douglas and Murphy, dissented, and thus began a sustained campaign by a minority of the justices to equate the Fourteenth Amendment rule with that of the Sixth Amendment as announced in *Johnson* v. *Zerbst.* The campaign culminated in victory in 1963, when *Betts* v. *Brady* was squarely overruled in the case of *Gideon* v. *Wainwright.*

One additional case out of the host of cases between *Powell* and *Gideon* is worthy of note because of the peculiar twist it gave to the rule announced by Justice Sutherland in *Powell* v. *Alabama.* The case was *Bute* v. *Illinois,* 333 U.S. 640 (1948). Roy Bute, a fifty-seven-year-old man, pleaded guilty and was convicted of "taking indecent liberties with children." He was sentenced to one to twenty years in jail. After he had served eight years in jail, in 1946, he filed a writ of error in the Supreme Court of Illinois, claiming that he had been denied representation by counsel. His writ was denied, and the United States Supreme Court granted certiorari. In a five-to-four decision the denial was affirmed. The majority could find no fundamental unfairness in the trial and nothing unusual in the status of the defendant which would have demanded counsel. Justice Sutherland had stated in *Powell* that the accused must have appointed counsel if it is a capital case *and* if the accused is ignorant, feeble-minded, illiterate, "or the like." Justice Burton, for the majority in the *Bute* case, changed this "and" to "or." The result was two rules: counsel must be furnished in every capital case and also in every noncapital felony case where special facts seem to make it mandatory for a fair trial. His statement was:

In a noncapital state felony case, this Court has recognized the constitutional right of the accused to the assistance of counsel for his defense when there are special circumstances showing that, otherwise, the defendant would not enjoy that fair notice and adequate hearing which constitute the foundation of due process of law in the trial of any criminal charge.

As more and more "special circumstances" requiring counsel impressed themselves upon the majority of the Court (such as youth, inability to speak English, complexity of the issues involved in the case, "loaded" suggestions by officers of the state to plead guilty), the pressures both of argument and case-load pushed almost inexorably in the direction of a more clear-cut rule. The decision was unanimous when it finally came in 1963 in *Gideon* v. *Wainwright*.

GIDEON *v.* WAINWRIGHT
372 U.S. 335 (1963)

Mr. Justice Black delivered the opinion of the Court.

Petitioner was charged in a Florida state court with having broken and entered a poolroom with intent to commit a misdemeanor. This offense is a felony under Florida law. Appearing in court without funds and without a lawyer, petitioner asked the court to appoint counsel for him, [a request denied by the court on the ground that the law of Florida required appointment only in capital cases].

Put to trial before a jury, Gideon conducted his defense about as well as could be expected from a layman. He made an opening statement to the jury, cross-examined the State's witnesses, presented witnesses in his own defense, declined to testify himself, and made a short argument "emphasizing his innocence to the charge contained in the Information filed in this case." The jury returned a verdict of guilty, and petitioner was sentenced to serve five years in the state prison. Later, petitioner filed in the Florida Supreme Court this habeas corpus petition attacking his conviction and sentence on the ground that the trial court's refusal to appoint counsel for him denied him rights "guaranteed by the Constitution and the Bill of Rights by the United States Government." Treating the petition for habeas corpus as properly before it, the State Supreme Court, "upon consideration thereof" but without an opinion, denied all relief. Since 1942, when *Betts* v. *Brady*, 316 U.S. 455, was decided by a divided Court, the problem of a defendant's federal constitutional right to counsel in a state court has been a continuing source of controversy and litigation in both state and federal courts. To give this problem another review here, we granted certiorari. . . . Since Gideon was proceeding *in forma pauperis*, we appointed counsel to represent him and requested both sides to discuss in their briefs and oral arguments the following: "Should this Court's holding in *Betts* vs. *Brady* . . . be reconsidered?"

I

The facts upon which Betts claimed that he had been unconstitutionally denied the right to have counsel appointed to assist him are strikingly like the facts upon which Gideon here bases his federal constitutional claim. . . . Since the facts and circumstances of the two cases are so nearly indistinguishable, we think the *Betts* v. *Brady* holding if left standing would require us to reject Gideon's claim that the

Constitution guarantees him the assistance of counsel. Upon full reconsideration we conclude that *Betts* v. *Brady* should be overruled.

II

... We accept *Betts* v. *Brady's* assumption, based as it was on our prior cases, that a provision of the Bill of Rights which is "fundamental and essential to a fair trial" is made obligatory upon the States by the Fourteenth Amendment. We think the Court in *Betts* was wrong, however, in concluding that the Sixth Amendment's guarantee of counsel is not one of these fundamental rights. Ten years before *Betts* v. *Brady*, this Court, after full consideration of all the historical data examined in *Betts*, had unequivocally declared that "the right to the aid of counsel is of this fundamental character." *Powell* v. *Alabama*, 287 U.S. 45, 68, (1932). While the Court at the close of its *Powell* opinion did by its language, as this Court frequently does, limit its holding to the particular facts and circumstances of that case, its conclusions about the fundamental nature of the right to counsel are unmistakable. Several years later, in 1936, the Court reemphasized what it had said about the fundamental nature of the right to counsel in this language:

"We concluded that certain fundamental rights, safeguarded by the first eight amendments against federal action, were also safeguarded against state action by the due process clause of the Fourteenth Amendment, and among them the fundamental right of the accused to the aid of counsel in a criminal prosecution." *Grosjean* v. *American Press Co.,* 297 U.S. 233, 243, 244 (1936).

And again in 1938 this Court said:

"[The assistance of counsel] is one of the safeguards of the Sixth Amendment deemed necessary to insure fundamental human rights of life and liberty.... The Sixth Amendment stands as a constant admonition that if the constitutional safeguards it provides be lost, justice will not 'still be done.'" *Johnson* v. *Zerbst*, 304 U.S. 458, 462 (1938)....

In light of these and many other prior decisions of this Court, it is not surprising that the *Betts* Court, when faced with the contention that "one charged with crime, who is unable to obtain counsel, must be furnished counsel by the State," conceded that "expressions in the opinions of this court lend color to the argument...." 316 U.S., at 462, 463. The fact is that in deciding as it did—that "appointment of counsel is not a fundamental right, essential to a fair trial"—the Court in *Betts* v. *Brady* made an abrupt break with its own well-considered precedents. In returning to these old precedents, sounder we believe than the new, we but restore constitutional principles established to achieve a fair system of justice. Not only these precedents but also reason and reflection require us to recognize that in our adversary system of criminal justice, any person haled into court, who is too poor to hire a lawyer, cannot be assured a fair trial unless counsel is provided for him. This seems to us to be an obvious truth. Governments, both state and federal, quite properly spend vast sums of money to establish machinery to try defendants accused of crime. Lawyers to prosecute are everywhere deemed essential to protect the public's interest in an orderly society. Similarly, there are few defendants charged with crime, few indeed, who fail to hire the best lawyers they can get to prepare and present their defenses. That government hires lawyers to prosecute and defendants who have the money hire lawyers to defend are the strongest indications of the widespread belief that lawyers in criminal courts are necessities, not luxuries. The right of one charged with crime to counsel may not be deemed fundamental and essential to fair trials in some countries, but it is in ours. From the very beginning, our state and national constitutions and laws have laid great emphasis on procedural and substantive safeguards designed to assure fair trials before impartial tribunals in which every defendant stands equal before the law. This noble idea cannot be realized if the poor man charged with crime has to face his accusers without a lawyer to assist him. A defendant's need for a lawyer is nowhere better stated than in the moving words of Mr. Justice Sutherland in *Powell* v. *Alabama*. . . .

The Court in *Betts* v. *Brady* departed from the sound wisdom upon which the Court's holding in *Powell* v. *Alabama* rested. Florida, supported by two other States, has asked that *Betts* v. *Brady* be left intact. Twenty-two States, as friends of the Court, argue that *Betts* was "an anachronism when handed down" and that it should now be overruled. We agree.

The judgment is reversed and the cause is remanded to the Supreme Court of Florida for further action not inconsistent with this opinion.

Reversed.

[Justices Douglas, Clark, and Harlan each filed separate concurring opinions.]

Another aspect of the right to counsel to be considered is the minimal offense to which it applies. Since the Sixth Amendment extends the right to "all criminal prosecutions," it is arguably a right enforceable even in cases involving petty offenses. The Court did not rule squarely on the question until 1972 in *Argersinger* v. *Hamlin*.

ARGERSINGER *v.* HAMLIN
407 U.S. 25 (1972)

Mr. Justice Douglas delivered the opinion of the Court.

Petitioner, an indigent, was charged in Florida with carrying a concealed weapon, an offense punishable by imprisonment up to six months and a $1,000 fine. The trial was to a judge and petitioner was unrepresented by counsel. He was sentenced to serve 90 days in jail and brought this habeas corpus action in the Florida Supreme Court, alleging that, being deprived of his right to counsel, he was unable as an indigent layman properly to raise and present to the trial court good and sufficient defenses to the charges for which he stands convicted. The Florida Supreme Court . . . , in ruling on the right to counsel, followed the line we marked out in *Duncan* v. *Louisiana* . . . as respects the right to trial by jury and held that the right to court-appointed counsel extends to trials "for nonpetty offenses punishable by more than six months imprisonment.". . .

The case is here on a petition for certiorari which we granted. We reverse.

The Sixth Amendment, which in enumerated situations has been made applicable to the States by reason of the Fourteenth Amendment, . . . provides specified standards for "all criminal prosecutions."

One is the requirement of a "public trial." *In re Oliver, supra,* held that the right to a "public trial" was applicable to a state proceeding even though only a 60-day sentence was involved. . . .

Another guarantee is the right to be informed of the nature and cause of the accusation. Still another, the right of confrontation. . . . And another, compulsory process for obtaining witnesses in one's favor. . . . We have never limited these rights to felonies nor to lesser but serious offenses. . . .

The right to trial by jury, also guaranteed by the Sixth Amendment by reason of the Fourteenth, was limited by *Duncan* v. *Louisiana, supra,* to trials where the potential punishment was imprisonment of six months or more. But as the various opinions in *Baldwin* v. *New York* . . . make plain, the right to trial by jury has a different genealogy and is brigaded with a system of trial to a judge alone. . . .

While there is historical support for limiting the "deep commitment" to trial by jury to "serious criminal cases," there is no such support for a similar limitation on the right to assistance of counsel:

"Originally, in England, a person charged with treason or felony was denied the aid of counsel, except in respect of legal questions which the accused himself might suggest. At the same time parties in civil cases and persons accused of misdemeanors were entitled to the full assistance of counsel. . . . [It] appears that in at least twelve of the thirteen colonies the rule of the English common law, in the respect now under consideration, had been definitively rejected and the right to counsel fully recognized in all criminal prosecutions, save that in one or two instances the right was limited to capital offenses or to the more serious crimes. . . ." *Powell* v. *Alabama.*

The Sixth Amendment thus extended the right to counsel beyond its common-law dimensions. But there is nothing in the language of the Amendment, its history, or in the decisions of this Court, to indicate that it was intended to embody a retraction of the right in petty offenses wherein the common law previously did require that counsel be provided. . . .

We reject, therefore, the premise that since prosecutions for crimes punishable by imprisonment for less than six months may be tried without a jury, they may always be tried without a lawyer. The assistance of counsel is often a requisite to the very existence of a fair trial. . . . even in a petty offense prosecution. We are by no means convinced that legal and constitutional questions involved in a case that actually leads to imprisonment even for a brief period are any less complex than when a person can be sent off for six months or more. . . .

The trial of vagrancy cases is illustrative. While only brief sentences of imprisonment may be imposed, the cases often bristle with thorny constitutional questions. See *Papachristou* v. *Jacksonville.* . . .

Beyond the problem of trials and appeals is that of the guilty plea, a problem which looms large in misdemeanor as well as in felony cases. Counsel is needed so that the accused may know precisely what he is doing, so that he is fully aware of the prospect of going to jail or prison, and so that he is treated fairly by the prosecution.

In addition, the volume of misdemeanor cases, far greater in number than felony prosecutions, may create an obsession for speedy dispositions, regardless of the fairness of the result. The Report by the President's Commission on Law Enforcement and Administration of Justice, *The Challenge of Crime in a Free Society*, p. 128 (1967), states: "For example, until legislation last year increased the number of judges, the District of Columbia Court of General Sessions had four judges to process the preliminary stages of more than 1,500 felony cases, 7,500 serious misdemeanor cases, and 38,000 petty offenses and an equal number of traffic offenses per year. An inevitable consequence of volume that large is the almost total preoccupation in such a court with the movement of cases. The calendar is long, speed often is substituted for care, and casually arranged out-of-court compromise too often is substituted for adjudication. . . ."

That picture is seen in almost every report. "The misdemeanor trial is characterized by insufficient and frequently irresponsible preparation on the part of the defense, the prosecution, and the court. Everything is rush, rush.". . .

There is evidence of the prejudice which results to misdemeanor defendants from this "assembly-line justice." One study concluded that "Misdemeanants represented by attorneys are five times as likely to emerge from police court with all charges dismissed as are defendants who face similar charges without counsel." ACLU, Legal Counsel for Misdemeanants, Preliminary Report, 1 (1970). . . .

We hold, therefore, that absent a knowing and intelligent waiver, no person may be imprisoned for any offense, whether classified as petty, misdemeanor, or felony, unless he was represented by counsel at his trial. . . .

We do not sit as an ombudsman to direct state courts how to manage their affairs but only to make clear the federal constitutional requirement. How crimes should be classified is largely a state matter. The fact that traffic charges technically fall within the category of "criminal prosecutions" does not necessarily mean that many of them will be brought into the class where imprisonment actually occurs. . . .

Under the rule we announce today, every judge will know when the trial of a misdemeanor starts that no imprisonment may be imposed, even though local law permits it, unless the accused is represented by counsel. He will have a measure of the seriousness and gravity of the offense and therefore know when to name a lawyer to represent the accused before the trial starts.

The run of misdemeanors will not be affected by today's ruling. But in those that end up in the actual deprivation of a person's liberty, the accused will receive the benefit of "the guiding hand of counsel" so necessary when one's liberty is in jeopardy.

Reversed.

Mr. Justice Brennan, with whom Mr. Justice Douglas and Mr. Justice Stewart join, concurring.

I join the opinion of the Court and add only an observation upon its discussion of legal resources. . . . Law students as well as practicing attorneys may provide an important source of legal representation for the indigent. The Council on Legal Education for Professional Responsibility (CLEPR) informs us that more than 125 of the country's 147 accredited law schools have established clinical programs in which faculty-supervised students aid clients in a variety of civil and criminal matters. . . . These programs supplement practice rules enacted in 38 States authorizing students to practice law under prescribed conditions. . . . Given the huge increase in law school enrollments over the past few years, . . . I think it plain that law students can be looked to to make a significant contribution, quantitatively and qualitatively, to the representation of the poor in many areas, including cases reached by today's decision.

Mr. Chief Justice Burger, concurring in the result. . . .

Trial judges sitting in petty and misdemeanor cases—and prosecutors—should recognize exactly what will be required by today's decision. Because no individual can be imprisoned unless he is represented by counsel, the trial judge and the prosecutor will have to engage in a predictive evaluation of each case to determine whether there is a significant likelihood that, if the defendant is convicted, the trial judge will sentence him to a jail term. The judge can preserve the option of a jail sentence by offering counsel to any defendant unable to retain counsel on his own. This need to predict will place a new load on courts already overburdened and already compelled to deal with far more cases in one day than is reasonable and proper. Yet the prediction is not one beyond the capacity of an experienced judge, aided as he should be by the prosecuting officer. . . .

Mr. Justice Powell, with whom Mr. Justice Rehnquist joins, concurring in the result. . . .

There is a middle course, between the extremes of Florida's six-month rule and the Court's rule, which comports with the requirement of the Fourteenth Amendment. I would adhere to the principle of due process that requires fundamental fairness in criminal trials, a principle which I believe encompasses the right to counsel in petty cases whenever the assistance of counsel is necessary to assure a fair trial. . . .

Serious consequences also may result from convictions not punishable by imprisonment. Stigma may attack to a drunken driving conviction or a hit-and-run escapade. Losing one's driver's license is more serious for some individuals than a brief stay in jail. . . .

When the deprivation of property rights and interests is of sufficient consequence, denying the assistance of counsel to indigents who are incapable of defending themselves is a denial of due process. . . .

A landmark decision was rendered in 1967 which extended the right to counsel to juvenile court proceedings where delinquency is charged. The case was *In re Gault,* 387 U.S. 1 (1967), and the decision will presumably have a marked impact on the organization and procedures of juvenile courts in the nation. (The majority opinion is excerpted in the section "The Right to a Fair Hearing" below.)

Stage at Which the Right to Counsel Accrues

The Sixth Amendment refers to "prosecutions" but makes no mention of detention, interrogation, preliminary hearings, or the other pretrial stages which an accused must face. Then when does the right to counsel accrue? In 1932, in *Powell* v. *Alabama,* Justice Sutherland stated that the defendant "requires the guiding hand of counsel at every step in the proceedings against him." It was not until the decision in *Miranda* v. *Arizona* in 1966, however, that the Court officially adopted the view that the right extends to the interrogation stage.

Prior to the decision in *Gideon,* the primary thrust of litigation in the counsel cases was to broaden the categories of cases in which appointed counsel was guaranteed at the *trial stage.* Even so, the issue of when the right first obtained in the chronology of criminal procedure began to appear in some of the pre-*Gideon* cases. In *Hamilton* v. *Alabama,* 368 U.S. 52 (1961), for example, the Court held that appointment of counsel for indigent defendants must be made as early as the arraignment stage if this is "a critical stage in a criminal proceeding." Petitioner was convicted of the capital crime of breaking and entering a dwelling at night with intent to ravish, and was not afforded counsel until the trial stage. In reversing, the Court pointed out that under Alabama law the arraignment was the only stage at which the defense of insanity could be pleaded, that pleas in abatement could be made, or that motions to quash based on the ground that the grand jury was improperly drawn could be made.

In *United States* v. *Wade,* 388 U.S. 218 (1967), the Court held that a post-indictment police lineup was a "critical state of the prosecution" at which the defendant was as much entitled to the aid of counsel as at the trial itself, and the police conduct of such a lineup without notice to and in the absence of his counsel denied the accused his Sixth Amendment right to counsel. In 1956 the Court held in *Griffin* v. *Illinois,* 351 U.S. 12, that indigent defendants have a constitutional right to a free transcript on appeal:

"destitute defendants must be afforded as adequate appellate review as defendants who have money enough to buy transcripts." This holding suggested that indigents might also have a right to counsel on appeal, and the Court so held in *Douglas* v. *California,* 372 U.S. 353 (1963). Quoting the opinion of Justice Traynor of the California Supreme Court, Justice Douglas stated: "denial of counsel on appeal to an indigent would seem to be a discrimination at least as invidious as that condemned in *Griffin* v. *Illinois.*" But in *Ross* v. *Moffitt,* 417 U.S. 600 (1974), the Court distinguished *Douglas* and held that neither the due process clause nor the equal protection clause of the Fourteenth Amendment required that a State, after appointing counsel for an indigent's first appeal of right from his conviction to an intermediate state court, must also appoint counsel for the indigent's subsequent discretionary appeal to the highest state court.

Gagnon v. *Scarpelli,* 411 U.S. 778 (1973), presented the questions whether a previously sentenced probationer is entitled to a hearing when his probation is revoked and, if so, whether he is entitled to be represented by appointed counsel at such a hearing. The Court held that the probationer was entitled to a hearing, but refused to lay out a firm requirement of counsel. The opinion stated that the decision as to the need for counsel "must be made on a case-by-case basis in the exercise of a sound discretion by the state authority charged with responsibility for administering the probation and parole system." It was stated further that, "Although the presence and participation of counsel will probably be both undesirable and constitutionally unnecessary in most revocation hearings, there will remain certain cases in which fundamental fairness . . . will require that the State provide at its expense counsel for indigent probationers or parolees."

Effective Representation by Counsel

In the majority opinion in *Powell* it was pointed out that "the failure of the trial court to make an effective appointment of counsel" was a denial of due process. Appointment must be made in time to be of some assistance to the accused. "That duty is not discharged by an assignment at such time or under such circumstances as to preclude the giving of effective aid in the preparation and trial of the case." *Miranda* held that assignment must be made at the interrogation stage if the right is not waived. And in the case where the police feel that evidence is sufficient that no interrogation is necessary, *Hamilton* v. *Alabama* indicates that assignment must be made early enough to protect the interests of the defendant fully. A second interpretation of the requirement of "effective" representation raises the question of the competence of counsel handling the case. A losing defendant may protest that, through inefficiency or neglect, counsel appointed by the court was so incompetent that the conviction was obtained without due process of law. Obviously, appellate courts will be reluctant to overturn convictions under such a claim, both out of consideration for the orderly disposition of cases and also out of concern for the lawyer's standing as a professional man, heavily dependent upon his reputation. In retrospect, most trials could probably have been conducted more effectively had certain changes in strategy been made. But such a conclusion standing alone is insufficient to support a claim of denial of due process. The deficiencies must be so glaring and gross that the appellate court can see that on its face the trial was patently unfair. Thus, in *Sanchez* v. *Indiana,* 199 Ind. 235, 157 N.W. 1 (1927), reversal was obtained where counsel, hired by friends of an eighteen-year-old illiterate Mexican, was unaware of forcible process for obtaining witnesses, failed to object to obviously incompetent evidence, failed to submit instructions, and failed to produce character witnesses for the defendant, who had no previous criminal record.

It has been held that proper representation is not satisfied by the appointment of nonlawyers, even though they are law students, in *Jones* v. *Georgia,* 57 Ga. App. 344, 195 S.E. 316 (1938). And if the court appoints a single lawyer to represent two or more defendants being tried jointly, there must not be a conflict of interest as to the defendants which would result in a deprivation of fair representation. On the whole, however, the burden on the claimant of proving gross incompetence of counsel has only rarely been successfully met.

A number of cases have been decided which dealt with the question of whether guilty pleas can appropriately be challenged on the ground of ineffective counsel in habeas corpus actions where the petitioner attempted to show that constitutional deprivations antedating the plea were known to counsel and that he failed to file all appropriate motions concerning such deprivations. The claims have involved improper grand jury constitution, coerced confessions, and others. In *McMann* v. *Richardson,* 397 U.S. 759 (1970), the Court laid down the general rule by which federal collateral attacks on convictions based on guilty pleas rendered with the advice of counsel were to be governed:

> Whether a plea of guilty is unintelligent and therefore vulnerable when motivated by a confession erroneously thought admissible in evidence depends as an initial matter, not on whether a court would retrospectively consider counsel's advice to be right or wrong, but on whether that advice was within the range of competence demanded of attorneys in criminal cases.

Thus, to prevail, the petitioner must establish that his attorney's advice to plead guilty without having made inquiry into the composition of the grand jury [as in *Tollett* v. *Henderson,* 411 U.S. 258 (1973)] rendered that advice outside "the range of competence demanded of attorneys in criminal cases." And the mere finding that the grand jury was unconstitutionally selected would not automatically result in a finding that the advice to plead guilty was indicative of incompetence.

THE RIGHT TO A FAIR HEARING

In addition to the guarantees already discussed, there are other requirements of the Sixth Amendment, and of due process generally, which are held to be requirements of a fair hearing. The Sixth Amendment guarantees the accused in a federal prosecution the right to a "public trial." The due process clause of the Fourteenth Amendment also assures this right in state proceedings. The Court so ruled in *In re Oliver,* 333 U.S. 257 (1948), holding invalid the criminal contempt conviction of a witness before a Michigan judge, sitting as a "one-man grand jury," and conducting the proceeding in secret. The Court stated:

> The traditional Anglo-American distrust for secret trials has been variously ascribed to the notorious use of this practice by the Spanish Inquisition, to the

excesses of the English Court of Star Chamber, and to the French monarchy's abuse of the *lettre de cachet*. All of these institutions obviously symbolized a menace to liberty.

Further, since publicity may be given to the proceedings, both witnesses and officials may tend to operate in more honest and trustworthy fashion. [See Max Radin, "The Right to a Public Trial," 6 *Temp. L. Q.* 381 (1932) and Charles W. Quick, "A Public Criminal Trial," 60 *Dick. L. Rev.* 21 (1955).]

Due process also includes the right of the accused to be present at his trial in order to face his accusers and advise with his lawyer. Thus trials *in absentia* would seem normally to be unconstitutional in the United States. But in *Illinois* v. *Allen*, 397 U.S. 337 (1970), the Court held that the removal of a disruptive defendant from the courtroom during a criminal trial was not violative of his constitutional right to be present at trial.

ILLINOIS *v.* ALLEN
397 U.S. 337 (1970)

Mr. Justice Black delivered the opinion of the Court. . . .

One of the most basic of the rights guaranteed by the Confrontation Clause is the accused's right to be present in the courtroom at every stage of his trial. . . . The question presented in this case is whether an accused can claim the benefit of this constitutional right to remain in the courtroom while at the same time he engages in speech and conduct which is so noisy, disorderly, and disruptive that it is exceedingly difficult or wholly impossible to carry on the trial. . . . [The opinion here describes in detail the obstreperous conduct, the interruptions, and abusive language on the part of the defendant, resulting in the judge's order of removal from the courtroom for substantial portions of the trial.]

. . . Although mindful that courts must indulge every reasonable presumption against the loss of constitutional rights, . . . we explicitly hold today that a defendant can lose his right to be present at trial if, after he has been warned by the judge that he will be removed if he continues his disruptive behavior, he nevertheless insists on conducting himself in a manner so disorderly, disruptive, and disrespectful of the court that his trial cannot be carried on with him in the courtroom. Once lost, the right to be present can, of course, be reclaimed as soon as the defendant is willing to conduct himself consistently with the decorum and respect inherent in the concept of courts and judicial proceedings.

It is essential to the proper administration of criminal justice that dignity, order, and decorum be the hallmarks of all court proceedings in our country. The flagrant disregard in the courtroom of elementary standards of proper conduct should not and cannot be tolerated. We believe trial judges confronted with disruptive, contumacious, stubbornly defiant defendants must be given sufficient discretion to meet the circumstances of each case. No one formula for maintaining the appropriate courtroom atmosphere will be best in all situations. We think there are at least three constitutionally permissible ways for a trial judge to handle an obstreperous defendant like Allen: (1) bind and gag him, thereby keeping him present; (2) cite him for contempt; (3) take him out of the courtroom until he promises to conduct himself properly.

Trying a defendant for a crime while he sits bound and gagged before the judge and jury would to an extent comply with that part of the Sixth Amendment's purposes that accords the defendant an opportunity to confront the witnesses at the trial. But even to contemplate such a technique, much less see it, arouses a feeling that no person should be tried while shackled and gagged except as a last resort....

It is not pleasant to hold that the respondent Allen was properly banished from the court for a part of his own trial. But our courts, palladiums of liberty as they are, cannot be treated disrespectfully with impunity. Nor can the accused be permitted by his disruptive conduct indefinitely to avoid being tried on the charges brought against him. It would degrade our country and our judicial system to permit our courts to be bullied, insulted, and humiliated and their orderly progress thwarted and obstructed by defendants brought before them charged with crimes.... Being manned by humans, the courts are not perfect and are bound to make some errors. But, if our courts are to remain what the Founders intended, the citadels of justice, their proceedings cannot and must not be infected with the sort of scurrilous, abusive language and conduct paraded before the Illinois trial judge in this case. The record shows that the Illinois judge at all times conducted himself with that dignity, decorum, and patience that befits a judge. Even in holding that the trial judge had erred, the Court of Appeals praised his "commendable patience under severe provocation."

We do not hold that removing this defendant from his own trial was the only way the Illinois judge could have constitutionally solved the problem he had. We do hold, however, that there is nothing whatever in this record to show that the judge did not act completely within his discretion....

The judgment of the Court of Appeals is

Reversed.

Mr. Justice Brennan, concurring....

Mr. Justice Douglas....

We should not reach the merits but should reverse the case for staleness of the record and affirm the denial of relief by the District Court. After all, behind the issuance of a writ of habeas corpus is the exercise of an informed discretion. The question, how to proceed in a criminal case against a defendant who is a mental case, should be resolved only on a full and adequate record....

The mere fact that the superficial formalities of a trial are adhered to is not sufficient to meet the test of due process, if the result is dictated by external pressures. In *Moore* v. *Dempsey*, 261 U.S. 86 (1923), the Court reviewed the conviction of five Negroes in an Arkansas court for the murder of a white man. The trial court and the neighborhood were "thronged with an adverse crowd that threatened the most dangerous consequences to anyone interfering with the desired result." The trial lasted about forty-five minutes, and in less than five minutes the jury brought in a verdict of guilty of murder. According to the allegations and affidavits "no juryman could have voted for an acquittal and continued to live in Phillips County and if any prisoner by any chance had been acquitted by a jury he could not have escaped the mob." In reversing the denial of habeas corpus, Justice Holmes, for the Court, quoted from an earlier case, stating that "if the State, supplying no corrective process, carries into execution a judgment of death or imprisonment based upon a verdict thus produced by mob domination, the State deprives the accused of his life or liberty without due process of law."

Due process also demands that the trial be conducted by an unbiased judge. The best-known case on the point is *Tumey* v. *Ohio*, 273 U.S. 510

(1927), involving a conviction for violation of the liquor laws of the state. The mayor was authorized to try such offenses without a jury, and he received, in addition to his salary, the costs imposed on the defendant in case of conviction. Further, also in the event of conviction, the municipality received half the fine levied. In reversing, Chief Justice Taft stated for the Court:

All questions of judicial qualification may not involve constitutional validity. Thus matters of kinship, personal bias, state policy, remoteness of interest would seem generally to be matters merely of legislative discretion.... But it certainly violates the Fourteenth Amendment and deprives a defendant in a criminal case of due process of law to subject his liberty or property to the judgment of a court, the judge of which has a direct, personal, substantial pecuniary interest in reaching a conclusion against him in his case....

... Every procedure which would offer a possible temptation to the average man as a judge to forget the burden of proof required to convict the defendant, or which might lead him not to hold the balance nice, clear, and true between the state and the accused denies the latter due process of law.

In *Dugan* v. *Ohio,* 277 U.S. 61 (1928), however, the Court, in refusing to reverse a conviction, emphasized that the judge's pecuniary interest had to be "direct, personal, and substantial" in order to disqualify him under the *Tumey* rule. It held that the interest was too remote in this case, which involved a mayor-judge on a fixed salary, who was a member of the city commission and was paid from the city's general fund, into which one-half of the fines of convicted persons was paid. [See John P. Frank, "Disqualification of Judges," 56 *Yale L. J.* 605 (1947).]

Ward v. *Monroeville,* 409 U.S. 57 (1972), presented a situation where the mayor was given broad executive powers and was also the chief conservator of the peace. In addition, a major part of the village income was derived from the fines, forfeitures, costs, and fees imposed by him in his mayor's court. The Court found that the "possible temptation" to forget the burden of proof required to convict defendants was too great in this case to be constitutionally acceptable.

The Sixth Amendment guarantees the accused a right "to be confronted with the witnesses against him," and, as a corollary thereto, the right to cross-examine them. In fact, the right of "confrontation" is intended primarily to afford to the accused an opportunity to cross-examine. The policy behind this requirement is well stated in Wigmore's *Textbook on the Law of Evidence* (Brooklyn: Foundation Press, 1935), Sec. 242:

[It is insisted upon because] the experience of the last three centuries of judicial trials has demonstrated convincingly that in disputed issues one cannot depend on the mere assertion of anybody, however plausible, without scrutiny into its bases. All the weaknesses that may affect a witness' trustworthiness—observation, memory, bias, interest, and the like—may otherwise lurk unrevealed; modifying circumstances omitted in his tale may give his facts an entirely different effect, if disclosed; and cross-examination is the best way to get at these.

In *Jencks* v. *United States,* 353 U.S. 657 (1957), the Court held that when the government calls its informers to the stand as witnesses in a criminal prosecution, it cannot refuse to produce the statements and reports of such informers in the possession of the government, if requested by the defendant as necessary aids to adequate cross-examination. The decision was criticized on the ground that it would open up the confidential and secret files of the government to general inspection by criminals, but the Court stated that the government must make the choice of either granting defendants full rights of cross-examination or proceeding without the desired testimony. [See Robert B. McKay, "The Right of Confrontation," 1959 *Wash. U. L. Q.* 122 (1959) and Barrie M. Karen, "The Right to Production for Inspection of Documents in Possession of the Government: Guaranteed by the Due Process Clause?" 31 *So. Calif. L. Rev.* 78 (1957).]

In *Pointer* v. *Texas,* 380 U.S. 400 (1965), the Court "incorporated" the Sixth Amendment right of confrontation into the Fourteenth Amendment due process clause. At the defendant's trial in a state court on a charge of robbery, the state, over defendant's objections, introduced the transcript of a witness' testimony given at the preliminary hearing, at which defendant was not represented by counsel and had no opportunity to cross-examine the witness. The state showed that the witness had moved out of Texas with no intention of returning. Defendant was convicted, and his conviction affirmed by the appellate court. On certiorari, the United States Supreme Court reversed. Justice Black, for the Court, stated:

It cannot seriously be doubted at this late date that the right of cross-examination is included in the right of an accused in a criminal case to confront the witnesses against him. And probably no one, certainly no one experienced in the trial of lawsuits, would deny the value of cross-examination in exposing falsehood and bringing out the truth in the trial of a criminal case. . . .

There are few subjects, perhaps, upon which this Court and other courts have been more nearly unanimous than in their expressions of belief that the right of confrontation and cross-examination is an essential and fundamental requirement for the kind of fair trial which is this country's constitutional goal. . . .

. . . We hold that petitioner was entitled to be tried in accordance with the protection of the confrontation guarantee of the Sixth Amendment, and that that guarantee, like the right against compelled self-incrimination, is "to be enforced against the States under the Fourteenth Amendment according to the same standards that protect those personal rights against federal encroachment." *Malloy* v. *Hogan.* . . .

The Court followed *Pointer* in *Douglas* v. *Alabama,* 380 U.S. 415 (1965). Defendant was charged with assault with intent to murder. An accomplice, who had been tried separately and found guilty, was called as a witness by the state but invoked his privilege against self-incrimination because he planned to appeal his conviction. The solicitor then produced a confession purportedly signed by the witness and, under the guise of cross-examination to refresh the witness' recollection, read from the document, pausing after every few sentences to ask him, before the jury, "Did you make that statement?" Each time, the witness invoked the privilege. Defendant's counsel objected to the reading, but defendant was convicted and the state supreme court affirmed. The Court unanimously reversed, holding that in the circumstances, petitioner's inability to cross-examine the witness as to the alleged confession "plainly denied him the right of cross-examination secured by the Confrontation Clause."

In *Washington* v. *Texas,* 388 U.S. 14 (1967), the Court "incorporated" the Sixth Amendment right to have compulsory process for obtaining witnesses in his favor into the Fourteenth Amendment. It further held that this right was denied by Texas statutes which provided that persons charged or convicted as coparticipants in the same crime could not testify for one another, although there was no bar to their testifying for the state. The witness Washington wished to call had previously been convicted of the same crime, sentenced to fifty years in prison, and was confined in the Dallas County jail. On the basis of the statutes, the trial judge refused to allow the witness to testify. The United States Supreme Court unanimously reversed. Chief Justice Warren, for eight of the members, stated:

The right to offer the testimony of witnesses, and to compel their attendance, if necessary, is in plain terms the right to present a defense, the right to present the defendant's version of the facts as well as the prosecution's to the jury so it may decide where the truth lies. Just as an accused has the right to confront the prosecution's witnesses for the purpose of challenging their testimony, he has the right to present his own witnesses to establish a defense. The right is a fundamental element of due process of law.

It was argued that such witnesses should be disqualified on the ground that they are particularly likely to commit perjury. The Chief Justice pointed out that "the absurdity of the rule" is demonstrated by the fact that the accused accomplice could testify for the prosecution. It was further suggested that such witnesses would be more apt to lie for their coparticipants. The response by the Chief Justice was: "To think that criminals will lie to save their fellows but not to obtain favors from the prosecution for themselves is indeed to clothe the criminal class with more nobility than one might expect to find in the public at large."

One of the most important decisions of recent years involving criminal procedure came in 1967 in *In re Gault,* 387 U.S. 1 (1967). In that case the Court held that juvenile delinquency proceedings which may lead to commitment in state institutions must measure up to the essentials of due process and fair treatment. An Arizona juvenile court had committed a fifteen-year-old boy to the state industrial school for the period of his minority, unless officially discharged sooner. The boy was taken into custody by the county sheriff, without notice to his parents, on a complaint charging the defendant with making on obscene telephone call. The juvenile judge held a hearing at which the boy, his mother, his older brother, and two probation officers appeared. No transcript or recording was made, the complainant was not present, and no one was sworn. Later testimony by the juvenile judge was to the effect that the judge questioned the defendant at this hearing and that he admitted making lewd statements over the telephone. Neither the boy nor his parents was advised of his right to counsel or to remain silent. At a second hearing the following week, still without transcript or recording, the defendant and another boy, charged with participating in the same telephone call, were questioned further. Witnesses differed in their recollections of the defendant's testimony at this hearing. His parents recalled that he admitted only to having dialed the number, and that the other boy had made the remarks. The mother asked that the complainant be present to testify as to which boy had done the talking. The judge stated that she did not have to be present. At the conclusion of the hearing the defendant was committed to the state industrial school. Since no appeal was permitted by statute, the commitment was attacked by habeas corpus. The trial court dismissed, and the Arizona Supreme Court affirmed. The United States Supreme Court considered the case on appeal and reversed.

IN RE GAULT
387 U.S. 1 (1967)

Mr. Justice Fortas delivered the opinion of the Court. . . .

[Appellants] urge that we hold the Juvenile Code of Arizona invalid on its face or as applied in this case because, contrary to the Due Process Clause of the Fourteenth Amendment, the juvenile is taken from the custody of his parents and committed to a state institution pursuant to proceedings in which the Juvenile Court has virtually unlimited discretion, and in which the following basic rights are denied:

1. Notice of the charges;
2. Right to counsel;
3. Right to confrontation and cross-examination;
4. Privilege against self-incrimination;
5. Right to a transcript of the proceedings; and
6. Right to appellate review. . . .

We do not in this opinion consider the impact of these constitutional provisions upon the totality of the relationship of the juvenile and the state. . . . We consider only the problems presented to us by this case. These relate to the proceedings by which a determination is made as to whether a juvenile is a "delinquent" as a result of alleged misconduct on his part, with the consequence that he may be committed to a state institution. . . .

From the inception of the juvenile court system, wide differences have been tolerated—indeed insisted upon—between the procedural rights accorded to adults and those of juveniles. . . .

The early reformers were appalled by adult procedures and penalties, and by the fact children could be given long prison sentences and mixed in jails with hardened criminals. . . . The apparent rigidities, technicalities, and harshness which they observed in both substantive and procedural criminal law were therefore to be discarded. The idea of crime and punishment was to be abandoned. The child was to be "treated" and "rehabilitated" and the procedures, from apprehension through institutionalization, were to be "clinical" rather than punitive.

These results were to be achieved, without coming to conceptual and constitutional grief, by insisting that the proceedings were not adversary, but that the State was proceeding as *parens patriae*. The Latin phrase proved to be a great help to those who sought to rationalize the exclusion of juveniles from the constitutional scheme; but its meaning is murky and its historic credentials are of dubious relevance. . . .

Accordingly, the highest motives and most enlightened impulses led to a peculiar system for juveniles, unknown to our law in any comparable context. The constitutional and theoretical basis for this peculiar system is—to say the least—debatable. And in practice . . . the results have not been entirely satisfactory. Juvenile court history has again demonstrated that unbridled discretion, however benevolently motivated, is frequently a poor substitute for principle and procedure. In 1937, Dean Pound wrote: "The powers of the Star Chamber were a trifle in comparison with those of our juvenile courts. . . ." The absence of substantive standards has not necessarily meant that children receive careful, compassionate, individualized treatment. The absence of procedural rules based upon constitutional principle has not always produced fair, efficient, and effective procedures. Departures from established principles of due process have frequently resulted not in enlightened procedure, but in arbitrariness. . . .

It is claimed that juveniles obtain benefits from the special procedures applicable to them which more than offset the disadvantages of denial of the substance of normal due process. As we shall discuss, the observance of due process standards, intelligently and not ruthlessly administered, will not compel the States to abandon or displace any of the substantive benefits of the juvenile process. . . .

. . . For example, the commendable principles relating to the processing and treatment of juveniles separately from adults are in no way involved or affected by the procedural issues under discussion. Further, we are told that one of the important benefits of the special juvenile court procedures is that they avoid classifying the juvenile as a "criminal." The juvenile offender is now classed as a "delinquent." There is, of course, no reason why this should not continue. It is disconcerting, however, that this term has come to involve only slightly less stigma than the term "criminal" applied to adults. . . .

Beyond this, it is frequently said that juveniles are protected by the process from disclosure of their deviational behavior. . . . This claim of secrecy, however, is more rhetoric than reality. Disclosure of court records is discretionary with the judge in most jurisdictions. . . .

In any event, there is no reason why, consistently with due process, a State cannot continue, if it deems it appropriate, to provide and to improve provision for the confidentiality of records of police contacts and court action relating to juveniles. . . .

Further, it is urged that the juvenile benefits from informal proceedings in the court. The early conception of the juvenile court proceeding was one in which a fatherly judge touched the heart and conscience of the erring youth by talking over his problems, by paternal advice and admonition, and in which, in extreme situations, benevolent and wise institutions of the State provided guidance and help "to save him from a downward career.". . . But recent studies have, with surprising unanimity, entered sharp dissent as to the validity of this gentle conception. They suggest that the appearance as well as the actuality of fairness, impartiality and orderliness—in short, the essentials of due process—may be a more impressive and more therapeutic attitude so far as the juvenile is concerned. . . .

Ultimately, however, we confront the reality of that portion of the juvenile court process with which we deal in this case. A boy is charged with misconduct. The boy is committed to an institution where he may be restrained of liberty for years. . . .

In view of this, it would be extraordinary if our Constitution did not require the procedural regularity and the exercise of care implied in the phrase "due process." Under our Constitution, the condition of being a boy does not justify a kangaroo court. . . .

If Gerald had been over 18, he would not have been subject to Juvenile Court proceedings. For the particular offense immediatly involvd, the maximum punishment would have been a fine of $5 to $50, or imprisonment in jail for not more than two months. Instead, he was committed to custody for a maximum of six years. If he had been over 18 and had committed an offense to which such a sentence might apply, he would have been entitled to substantial rights under the Constitution of the United States as well as under Arizona's laws and constiuttion. . . . So wide a gulf between the State's treatment of the adult and of the child requires a bridge sturdier than mere verbiage, and reasons more persuasive than cliche can provide. . . .

Notice of Charges

. . . The applicable Arizona statute provides for a petition to be filed in Juvenile Court, alleging in general terms that the child is "neglected, dependent, or delinquent." The statute explicitly states that such a general allegation is sufficient, "without alleging the facts.". . .

We cannot agree with the court's conclusion that adequate notice was given in this case. . . . Due process of law requires notice of the sort we have described—that is, notice which would be deemed constitutionally adequate in a civil or criminal proceeding. . .

Right to Counsel

Appellants charge that the Juvenile Court proceedings were fatally defective because the court did not advise Gerald or his parents of their right to counsel, and proceeded with the hearing, the adjudication of delinquency and the order of commitment in the absence of counsel for the child and his parents or an express waiver of the right thereto. . . . The court argued that "The parent and the probation officer may be relied upon to protect the infant's interests." Accordingly it rejected the proposition that "due process requires that an infant have a right to counsel." . . . We do not agree. . . . The child "requires the guiding hand of counsel at every step in the proceedings against him.". . .

Confrontation, Self-Incrimination, Cross-Examination

Appellants urge that the writ of habeas corpus should have been granted because of the denial of the rights of confrontation and cross-examination in the Juvenile Court hearings, and because the privilege against self-incrimination was not observed. The Juvenile Court Judge testified at the habeas corpus hearing that he had proceeded on the basis of Gerald's admissions at the two hearings. . . .

It would indeed be surprising if the privilege against self-incrimination were available to hardened criminals but not to children. The language of the Fifth Amendment, applicable to the States by operation of the Fourteenth Amendment, is unequivocal and without exception. And the scope of the privilege is comprehensive. . . .

Against the application to juveniles of the right to silence, it is argued that juvenile proceedings are "civil" and not "criminal," and therefore the privilege should not apply. . . .

. . . For this purpose, at least, commitment is a deprivation of liberty. It is incarceration against one's will, whether it is called "criminal" or "civil.". . .

We conclude that the constitutional privilege against self-incrimination is applicable in the case of juveniles as it is with respect to adults. . . .

. . . Apart from the "admission," there was nothing upon which a judgment or finding might be based. There was no sworn testimony. Mrs. Cook, the complainant, was not present. . . .

. . . We now hold that, absent a valid confession, a determination of delinquency and an order of commitment to a state institution cannot be sustained in the absence of sworn testimony subjected to the opportunity for cross-examination in accordance with our law and constitutional requirements. . . .

[Justices Black and White concurred. Justice Harlan concurred in part and dissented in part. Justice Stewart dissented.]

In *In re Winship*, 397 U.S. 358 (1970), the Court examined the New York rule permitting conviction in juvenile delinquency proceedings based on a "preponderance of evidence." The Court reversed, holding that the due process clause protected an accused juvenile in a criminal prosecution against conviction except upon proof beyond a reasonable doubt. But in *McKeiver* v.

Pennsylvania, 403 U.S. 528 (1971), in a badly fragmented set of opinions, the Court held that the Fourteenth Amendment does not require a jury trial in criminal proceedings in juvenile courts.

In 1975 the Court examined the issue of whether public school students could be suspended from school without a hearing within the due process clause of the Fourteenth Amendment. The case was *Goss* v. *Lopez.*

GOSS *v.* LOPEZ
419 U.S. 565 (1975)

Mr. Justice White delivered the opinion of the Court. . . .

Ohio law . . . empowers the principal of an Ohio public school to suspend a pupil for misconduct for up to 10 days or to expel him. In either case, he must notify the student's parents within 24 hours and state the reasons for his actions. A pupil who is expelled, or his parents, may appeal the decision to the Board of Education and in connection therewith shall be permitted to be heard at the board meeting. The board may reinstate the pupil following the hearing. No similar procedure is provided . . . for a suspended student. . . .

The nine named appellees, each of whom alleged that he or she had been suspended from public high school in Columbus for up to 10 days without a hearing . . . filed an action against the Columbus Board of Education and various administrators . . . under 42 USC §1983. The complaint sought a declaration that [the Ohio law] was unconstitutional in that it permitted public school administrators to deprive plaintiffs of their rights to an education without a hearing of any kind, in violation of the procedural due process component of the Fourteenth Amendment. It also sought to enjoin the public school officials from issuing future suspensions pursuant to [the law] and to require them to remove references to the past suspensions from the records of the students in question.

The proof below established that the suspensions in question arose out of a period of widespread student unrest . . . during February and March of 1971. Six of the named plaintiffs . . . were students at the Marion-Franklin High School and were each suspended for 10 days on account of disruptive or disobedient conduct committed in the presence of the school administrator who ordered the suspension. One of these, Tyrone Washington, was among a group of students demonstrating in the school auditorium while a class was being conducted there. He was ordered by the school principal to leave, refused to do so and was suspended. Rudolph Sutton, in the presence of the principal, physically attacked a police officer who was attempting to remove Tyrone Washington from the auditorium. He was immediately suspended. The other four Marion-Franklin students were suspended for similar conduct. None was given a hearing to determine the operative facts underlying the suspension, but each, together with his or her parents, was offered the opportunity to attend a conference, subsequent to the effective date of the suspension, to discuss the student's future. . . .

[A three-judge District Court granted the relief sought by plaintiffs.]

At the outset, appellants contend that because there is no constitutional right to an education at public expense, the Due Process Clause does not protect against expulsions from the public school system. This position misconceives the nature of the issue and is refuted by prior decisions. . . .

Here, on the basis of state law, appellees plainly had legitimate claims of entitlement to a public education. [The Ohio Code] directs local authorities to provide a free education to all residents between six and 21 years of age, and a compulsory attendance law requires attendance for a school year of not less than 32 weeks. . . .

Although Ohio may not be constitutionally obligated to establish and maintain a public school system, it has nevertheless done so and has required its children to attend. Those young people do not "shed their constitutional rights" at the schoolhouse door. *Tinker* v. *Des Moines School District.* . . . The authority possessed by the State to prescribe and enforce standards of conduct in its schools, although concededly very broad, must be exercised consistently with constitutional safeguards. Among other things, the State is constrained to recognize a student's legitimate entitlement to a public education as a property interest which is protected by the Due Process Clause and which may not be taken away for misconduct without adherence to the minimum procedures required by that clause. . . .

Appellants proceed to argue that even if there is a right to a public education protected by the Due Process Clause generally, the clause comes into play only when the State subjects a student to a "severe detriment or grievous loss." The loss of 10 days, it is said, is neither severe nor grievous and the Due Process Clause is therefore of no relevance. . . .

A short suspension is of course a far milder deprivation than expulsion. But, "education is perhaps the most important function of state and local governments." *Brown* v. *Board of Education* . . . , and the total exclusion from the educational process for more than a trivial period, and certainly if the suspension is for 10 days, is a serious event in the life of the suspended child. Neither the property interest in educational benefits temporarily denied nor the liberty interest in reputation, which is also implicated, is so insubstantial that suspensions may constitutionally be imposed by any procedure the school chooses, no matter how arbitrary. . . .

We do not believe that school authorities must be totally free from notice and hearing requirements if their schools are to operate with acceptable efficiency. Students facing temporary suspension have interests qualifying for protection of the Due Process Clause, and due process requires, in connection with a suspension of 10 days or less, that the student be given oral or written notice of the charges against him and, if he denies them, an explanation of the evidence the authorities have and an opportunity to present his side of the story. The clause requires at least these rudimentary precautions against unfair or mistaken findings of misconduct and arbitrary exclusion from school.

There need be no delay between the time "notice" is given and the time of the hearing. In the great majority of cases the disciplinarian may informally discuss the alleged misconduct with the student minutes after it has occurred. We hold only that, in being given an opportunity to explain his version of the facts at this discussion, the student first be told what he is accused of doing and what the basis of the accusation is. Lower courts which have addressed the question of the *nature of the procedures required in short suspension cases* have reached the same conclusion. . . .

Since the hearing may occur almost immediately following the misconduct, it follows that as a general rule notice and hearing should precede removal of the student from school. We agree with the District Court, however, that there are recurring situations in which prior notice and hearing cannot be insisted upon. Students whose presence pose a continuing danger to persons or property or an ongoing threat of disrupting the academic process may be immediately removed from school. In such cases, the necessary notice and rudimentary hearing should follow as soon as practicable, as the District Court indicated. . . .

We stop short of construing the Due Process Clause to require, countrywide, that hearings in connection with short suspensions must afford the student the opportunity to secure counsel, to confront and cross-examine witnesses supporting the charge or to call his own witnesses to verify his version of the incident. Brief disciplinary suspensions are almost countless. To impose in each such case even truncated trial type procedures might well overwhelm administrative facilities in many places and, by diverting resources, cost more than it would save in educational effectiveness. Moreover, further formalizing the suspension process and escalating its formality and adversary nature may not only make it too costly as a regular disciplinary tool but also destroy its effectiveness as part of the teaching process.

On the other hand, requiring effective notice and informal hearing permitted the student to give his version of the events will provide a meaningful hedge against erroneous action. At least the disciplinarian will be alerted to the existence of disputes about facts and arguments about cause and effect. He may then determine himself to summon the accuser, permit cross-examination and allow the student to present his own witnesses. In more difficult cases, he may permit counsel. In any event, his discretion will be more informed and we think the risk of error substantially reduced. . . .

We should also make it clear that we have addressed ourselves solely to the short suspension, not exceeding 10 days. Longer suspensions or expulsions for the remainder of the school term, or permanently, may require more formal procedures. Nor do we put aside the possibility that in unusual situations, although involving only a short suspension, something more than the rudimentary procedures will be required. . . .

Affirmed.

Mr. Justice Powell, with whom the Chief Justice, Mr. Justice Blackmun, and Mr. Justice Rehnquist join, dissenting. . . .

No one can foresee the ultimate frontiers of the new "thicket" the Court now enters. Today's ruling appears to sweep within the protected interest in education a multitude of discretionary decisions in the educational process. Teachers and other school authorities are required to make many decisions that may have serious consequences for the pupil. . . . [I]n many of these situations, the pupil can advance the same types of speculative and subjective injury given critical weight in this case. The District Court, relying upon generalized opinion evidence, concluded that a suspended student may suffer psychological injury in one or more of the ways set forth in the margin below. The Court appears to adopt this rationale. . . .

It hardly need be said that if a student, as a result of a day's suspension, suffers "a blow" to his "self-esteem," "feels powerless," views "teachers with resentment," or feels "stigmatized by his teachers," identical psychological harms will flow from many other routine and necessary school decisions. The student who is given a failing grade, who is not promoted, who is excluded from certain extracurricular activities, who is assigned to a school reserved for children of less than average ability, or who is placed in the "vocational" rather than the "college preparatory" track, is unlikely to suffer any less psychological injury than if he were suspended for a day for a relatively minor infraction.

If, as seems apparent, the Court will now require due process procedures whenever such routine school decisions are challenged, the impact upon public education will be serious indeed. The discretion and judgment of federal courts across the land will be substituted for that of the 50 state legislatures, the 14,000 school boards and the 2,000,000 teachers who heretofore have been responsible for the administration of the American public school system. If the Court perceives a rational and analytically sound distinction between the discretionary decision by school authorities to suspend a pupil for a brief period, and the types of discretionary school decisions described above, it would be prudent to articulate it in today's opinion. Otherwise, the federal courts should prepare themselves for a vast new role in society. . . .

DOUBLE JEOPARDY

Protection against double jeopardy was firmly grounded in the common law well before the addition of the Fifth Amendment provision that no person shall be "subject for the same offense to be twice put in jeopardy of life or limb." In fact the English rule today, embodying the common law principle, is tighter than our own, since the law does not even permit English appellate courts to send criminal cases back for new trials. The choice is between correction of errors below, if possible, or simply vacating the judgment of conviction, so rigidly is the rule against double jeopardy construed.

Since jeopardy means the danger of conviction, *indictment* for crime does not put a person in jeopardy, and therefore repeated indictments do not constitute double jeopardy. Jeopardy does not attach until the trial actually begins. If trial is without a jury, jeopardy commonly attaches when the first witness is sworn or when the court has begun to hear evidence. If the case is tried to a jury, jeopardy begins when the jury is impaneled and sworn. The general rule is that only under exceptional circumstances can the trial be halted after this stage and the accused subjected later to a second trial. Such would be the case where a juror is disqualified or the jury fails to reach a verdict. The latter situation was involved in *United States* v. *Perez*, 9 Wheat. 579 (1824), in which the Court stated:

The prisoner has not been convicted or acquitted, and may again be put upon his defense. We think, that in all cases of this nature, the law has invested courts of justice with the authority to discharge a jury from giving any verdict, whenever, in their opinion, taking all the circumstances into consideration, there is a manifest necessity for the act, or the ends of public justice would otherwise be defeated.

The double jeopardy clause would bar having the government secure a mistrial solely to afford the prosecution a chance to improve its preparation of the case. In *Brock* v. *North Carolina*, 344 U.S. 424 (1953), however, the Court held that the Fourteenth Amendment did not preclude the state's second trial of the defendant after the first trial was declared a mistrial on motion of the prosecution when two of the state's key witnesses, apparently without warning, refused to answer incriminating questions. The witnesses had already been convicted, but were awaiting word on an appeal and refused to talk in the interim. They lost their appeals and were then willing to testify in the later trial.

Double Jeopardy and Criminal Appeals

The federal law is clear that the government has no right to appeal after a verdict of acquittal, since the protection against double jeopardy encompasses such an action. Such was the holding in *Kepner* v. *United States*, 195 U.S. 100 (1904). This reaffirmed a similar holding based on common law considerations in *United States* v. *Sanges*, 144 U.S. 310, 323 (1892). Since jeopardy does not attach merely upon indictment, however, a judgment to quash an indictment is appealable by the Government. The old Fourteenth Amendment rule (no longer valid) was laid down in *Palko* v. *Connecticut*, 302 U.S. 319 (1937). The Court held there that where errors of law, to the prejudice of the State, were committed in the trial court, the State could appeal for a new trial. In *Benton* v. *Maryland*, 395 U.S. 784 (1969), however, the Court incorporated the Fifth Amendment's protection against double jeopardy into the Fourteenth Amendment and overruled *Palko*.

At the common law, and still in England, the appellate court was barred from ordering a retrial following conviction, even if material error was found in the trial proceedings. American courts have followed a practice of ordering a wholly new trial if the convicted defendant appealed and "reversible errors" were found to have occurred in the first trial. In *United States* v. *Keen*, 6 Fed. Cas. 686 (1839), Justice McLean, on circuit, vigorously rejected the view that the constitutional provision prohibited a new trial on the defendant's motion after a conviction, or that it "guarantees to him the right of being hung, to protect him from the danger of a second trial." The theory followed here seems to be that since the request is made by the defendant, the claim of double jeopardy is implicitly waived. There is no particular difficulty with this approach if the defendant obtains a new trial on the same charge for which conviction resulted in the first trial. A problem arises, however, if the conviction is for a lesser included offense of the original charge and on subsequent retrial the defendant again faces the more serious original charge. In *Palko*, for example, the defendant was tried for first degree murder. He was convicted of second degree murder. At the new trial he was again tried, and convicted, of *first* degree murder. The Court held in 1957, in *Green* v. *United States*, that such a procedure in the federal courts would violate the Fifth Amendment's protection against double jeopardy.

GREEN *v.* UNITED STATES
335 U.S. 184 (1957)

Opinion of the Court by Mr. Justice Black, announced by Mr. Justice Douglas,

This case presents a serious question concerning the meaning and application of that provision of the Fifth Amendment to the Constitution which declares that no person shall

". . . be subject for the same offence to be twice put in jeopardy of life or limb. . . ."

The petitioner, Everett Green, was indicted by a District of Columbia grand jury on two counts. The first charged that he had committed arson by maliciously setting fire to a house. The second accused him of causing the death of a woman by this alleged arson which if true amounted to murder in the first degree punishable by death. Green entered a plea of not guilty to both counts and the case was tried by a jury. After each side had presented its evidence the trial judge instructed the jury that it could find Green guilty of arson under the first count and of either (1) first degree murder or (2) second degree murder under the second count. The trial judge treated second degree murder, which is defined by the District Code as the killing of another with malice aforethought, and is punishable by imprisonment for a term of years or for life, as an offense included within the language charging first degree murder in the second count of the indictment.

The jury found Green guilty of arson and of second degree murder but did not find him guilty on the charge of murder in the first degree. Its verdict was silent on that charge. The trial judge accepted the verdict, entered the proper judgments and dismissed the jury. Green was sentenced to one to three years' imprisonment for arson and five to twenty years' imprisonment for murder in the second degree. He appealed the conviction of second degree murder. The Court of Appeals reversed that conviction because it was not supported by evidence and remanded the case for a new trial. . . .

On remand Green was tried again for first degree murder under the original indictment. At the outset of this second trial he raised the defense of former jeopardy but the court overruled his plea. This time a new jury found him guilty of first degree murder and he was given the mandatory death sentence. Aagin he appealed. Sitting *en banc,* the Court of Appeals rejected his defense of former jeopardy . . . and affirmed the conviction. . . .

The constitutional prohibition against "doubly jeopardy" was designed to protect an individual from being subjected to the hazards of trial and possible conviction more than once for an alleged offense. . . .

The underlying idea, one that is deeply ingrained in at least the Anglo-American system of jurisprudence, is that the State with all its resources and power should not be allowed to make repeated attempts to convict an individual for an alleged offense, thereby subjecting him to embarrassment, expense and ordeal and compelling him to live in a continuing state of anxiety and insecurity, as well as enhancing the possibility that even though innocent he may be found guilty.

In accordance with this philosophy it has long been settled under the Fifth Amendment that a verdict of acquittal is final, ending a defendant's jeopardy, and even when "not followed by any judgment, is a bar to a subsequent prosecution for the same offence." *United States* v. *Ball,* . . . Thus it is one of the elemental principles of our criminal law that the Government cannot secure a new trial by means of an appeal even though an acquittal may appear to be erroneous. . . .

At common law a convicted person could not obtain a new trial by appeal except in certain narrow instances. As this harsh rule was discarded courts and legislatures provided that if a defendant obtained the reversal of a conviction by his own appeal he could be tried again for the same offense. Most courts regarded the new trial as a second jeopardy but justified this on the ground that the appellant had "waived" his plea of former jeopardy by asking that the conviction be set aside. Other courts viewed the second trial as continuing the same jeopardy which had attached at the first trial by reasoning that jeopardy did not come to an end until the accused was acquitted or his conviction became final. But whatever the rationalization, this Court has also held that a defendant can be tried a second time for an offense when his prior conviction for that same offense had been set aside on appeal. *United States* v. *Ball,* 163 U.S. 662.

In this case, however, we have a much different question. . . . For the reasons stated hereafter, we conclude that this second trial for first degree murder placed Green in jeopardy twice for the same offense in violation of the Constitution.

Green was in direct peril of being convicted and punished for first degree murder at his first trial. He was forced to run the gantlet once on that charge and the jury refused to convict him. When given the choice between finding him guilty of either first or second degree murder it chose the latter. In this situation the great majority of cases in this country have regarded the jury's verdict as an implicit acquittal on the charge of first degree murder. . . . In brief, we believe this case can be treated no differently, for purposes of former jeopardy, than if the jury had returned a verdict which expressly read: "We find the defendant not guilty of murder in the first degree but guilty of murder in the second degree."

After the original trial, but prior to his appeal, it is indisputable that Green could not have been tried again for first degree murder for the death resulting from the fire. A plea of former jeopardy would have absolutely barred a new prosecution even though it might have been convincingly demonstrated that the jury erred in failing to convict him of that offense. And even after appealing the conviction of second degree murder he still could not have been tried a second time for first degree murder had his appeal been unsuccessful.

Nevertheless the Government contends that Green "waived" his constitutional defense of former jeopardy to a second prosecution on the first degree murder charge by making a *successful appeal* of his improper conviction of second degree murder. We cannot accept this paradoxical contention. . . .

Reduced to plain terms, the Government contends that in order to secure the reversal of an erroneous conviction of one offense, a defendant must surrender his valid defense of former jeopardy not only on that offense but also on a different offense for which he was not convicted and which was not involved in his appeal. . . . The law should not, and in our judgment does not, place the defendant in such an incredible dilemma. Conditioning an appeal of one offense on a coerced surrender of a valid plea of former jeopardy on another offense exacts a forfeiture in plain conflict with the constitutional bar against double jeopardy. . . .

Reversed.

Mr. Justice Frankfurter, whom Mr. Justice Burton, Mr. Justice Clark and Mr. Justice Harlan join, dissenting. . . .

In 1969, in *Benton* v. *Maryland,* the Court incorporated the Fifth Amendment's protection against double jeopardy into the Fourteenth Amendment. Following the federal rule announced in *Green* v. *United States,* the Court held that due process barred the State from subjecting a defendant to charges on retrial other than those for which he was convicted at the initial trial. *Palko* and, by implication, *Brock* v. *North Carolina* were overruled.

BENTON *v.* MARYLAND
395 U.S. 784 (1969)

[In a Maryland state court trial on charges of burglary and larceny, the jury found the defendant not guilty of larceny, but convicted him on the burglary count, for which he was sentenced to ten years in prison. Because both the grand and petit juries in the case had been unconstitutionally selected, the Maryland Court of Appeals remanded the case to the trial court, where the defendant was given the option of demanding reindictment and retrial, which he did. At the second trial, again for both larceny and burglary, the defendant's motion to dismiss the larceny charge as subjecting him to double jeopardy was denied, he was found guilty of both offenses, and he was given concurrent sentences of fifteen years on the burglary count and five years for larceny. The newly created Maryland Court of Special Appeals rejected the defendant's double jeopardy claim on the merits, and the Maryland Court of Appeals denied discretionary review.]

Mr. Justice Marshall delivered the opinion of the Court.

In 1937, this Court decided the landmark case of *Palko* v. *Connecticut.* . . . Palko, although indicted for first-degree murder, had been convicted of murder in the second degree after a jury trial in a Connecticut state court. The State appealed and won a new trial. Palko argued that the Fourteenth Amendment incorporated, as against the States, the Fifth Amendment requirement that no person "be twice put in jeopardy of life or limb." The Court disagreed. Federal double jeopardy standards were not applicable against the States. Only when a kind of jeopardy subjected a defendant to "a hardship so acute and shocking that our polity will not endure it,"... did the Fourteenth Amendment apply. The order for a new trial was affirmed. In subsequent appeals from state courts, the Court continued to apply this lesser *Palko* standard. See, e.g., *Broch* v. *North Carolina*. ...

Recently, however, this Court has "increasingly looked to the specific guarantees of the [Bill of Rights] to determine whether a state criminal trial was conducted with due process of law." *Washington* v. *Texas* ... (1967). In an increasing number of cases, the Court "has rejected the notion that the Fourteenth Amendment applies to the States only a 'watered-down, subjective version of the individual guarantees of the Bill of Rights. ...'"... Only last Term we found that the right to trial by jury in criminal cases was "fundamental to the American scheme of justice," *Duncan* v. *Louisiana* ... (1968), and held that the Sixth Amendment right to a jury trial was applicable to the States through the Fourteenth Amendment. For the same reasons, we today find that the double jeopardy prohibition of the Fifth Amendment represents a fundamental ideal in our constitutional heritage, and that it should apply to the States through the Fourteenth Amendment. Insofar as it is inconsistent with this holding, *Palko* v. *Connecticut* is overruled.

Palko represented an approach to basic constitutional rights which this Court's recent decisions have rejected. It was cut of the same cloth as *Betts* v. *Brady* ... , the case which held that a criminal defendant's right to counsel was to be determined by deciding in each case whether the denial of that right was "shocking to the universal sense of justice." ... Our recent cases have thoroughly rejected the Palko notion that basic constitutional right can be denied by the States as long as the totality of the circumstances does not disclose a denial of "fundamental fairness." Once it is decided that a particular Bill of Rights guarantee is "fundamental to the American scheme of justice," ... the same constitutional standards apply against both the State and Federal Governments. Palko's roots had thus been cut away years ago. We today only recognize the inevitable.

The fundamental nature of the guarantees against double jeopardy can hardly be doubted. Its origins can be traced to Greek and Roman Times, and it became established in the common law of England long before this Nation's independence.... Today, every State incorporates some form of the prohibition in its constitution or common law.... This underlying notion has from the very beginning been part of our constitutional tradition. Like the right to trial by jury, it is clearly "fundamental to the American scheme of justice." The validity of petitioner's larceny conviction must be judged, not by the watered-down standard enunciated in *Palko,* but under this Court's interpretations of the Fifth Amendment double jeopardy provision.

It is clear that petitioner's larceny conviction cannot stand once federal double jeopardy standards are applied. Petitioner was acquitted of larceny in his first trial. Because he decided to appeal his burglary conviction, he is forced to suffer retrial on the larceny count as well. As this Court held in *Green* v. *United States*, ... "conditioning an appeal of one offense on a coerced surrender of a valid plea of former jeopardy on another offense exacts a forfeiture in plain conflict with the constitutional bar against double jeopardy."

Maryland argues that *Green* does not apply to this case because petitioner's original indictment was absolutely void. One cannot be placed in "jeopardy" by a void indictment, the State argues. This argument sounds a bit strange, however, since petitioner could quietly have served out his sentence under this "void" indictment had he not appealed his burglary conviction. . . . Petitioner was acquitted of larceny. He has, under *Green,* a valid double jeopardy plea which he cannot be forced to waive. Yet Maryland wants the earlier acquittal set aside, over petitioner's objections, because of a defect in the indictment. This it cannot do. Petitioner's larceny conviction cannot stand.

Petitioner argues that his burglary conviction should be set aside as well. He contends that some evidence, inadmissible under state law in a trial for burglary alone, was introduced in the joint trial for both burglary and larceny, and that the jury was prejudiced by this evidence. This question was not decided by the Maryland Court. . . . Accordingly, we think it "just under the circumstances,". . . to vacate the judgment below and remand for consideration of this question. The judgment is vacated and the case is remanded for further proceedings not inconsistent with this opinion.

It is so ordered.

Mr. Justice White, concurring. . . .

Mr. Justice Harlan, whom Mr. Justice Stewart joins, dissenting. . . .

I would hold, in accordance with *Palko* v. *Connecticut* . . . that the due Process Clause of the Fourteenth Amendment does not take over the Double Jeopardy Clause of the Fifth, as such. Today *Palko* becomes another casualty in the so far unchecked march toward "incorporating" much, if not all, of the Federal Bill of Rights into the Due Process Clause. This march began, with a Court majority, in 1961 when *Mapp* v. *Ohio* . . . was decided and, before the present decision, found its last stopping point in *Duncan* v. *Louisiana* . . . ., decided at the end of last Term. I have at each step in the march expressed my opposition . . .; more particularly in the *Duncan* case I undertook to show that the "selective incorporation" doctrine finds no support either in history or in reason. Under the pressures of the closing days of the Term, I am content to rest on what I have written in prior opinions, save to raise my voice again in protest against a doctrine which so subtly, yet profoundly, is eroding many of the basics of our federal system. . . .

In *North Carolina* v. *Pearce,* 395 U.S. 711 (1969), the Court examined another double jeopardy issue—the problem of the successful appellant who is given more severe sentence upon retrial than at the first trial. The Court held that while such sentences were not *ipso facto* unconstitutional, any punishment already exacted must be "fully credited," and where more severe punishment is given, the judge's reasons for doing so must affirmatively appear, and the factual data upon which the increased sentence is based must be made a part of the record for the purpose of reviewing the constitutionality of such sentence.

Chaffin v. *Stynchcombe,* 412 U.S. 17 (1973), involved the imposition of a more severe sentence upon retrial, but in this case the sentence was set by the jury. The defendant was convicted of a felony in a Georgia criminal court, and the jury, pursuant to Georgia procedure, sentenced him to fifteen years in prison. A United States District Court, granting habeas corpus relief, ordered a new trial. After retrial, before a different judge and jury, he was again convicted, and the second jury sentenced him to life imprisonment. He again pursued habeas corpus relief, but the District Court denied his claim of due process violation. The Court of Appeals affirmed and, on certiorari, the Supreme Court also affirmed. The majority held that the higher sentence did not violate the due process clause so long as the jury was not informed of the prior sentence and the second sentence was not otherwise shown to be a product of vindictiveness. Further, there was no need for extending to jury resentencing the restrictions, applicable to judge resentencing, that the record must show the reasons for the higher sentence, based on the defendant's conduct after the original sentencing.

In *Michigan* v. *Payne*, 412 U.S. 47 (1973), the Court held that the *Pearce* rule was not retroactive. Justice Powell, for the majority, stated that the test repeatedly utilized to ascertain whether "new" constitutional protections in the area of criminal procedure are to be applied retroactively calls for the consideration of three criteria: (a) the purpose to be served by the new standards, (b) the extent of the reliance by law enforcement authorities on the old standards, and (c) the effect on the administration of justice of a retroactive application of the new standards. Applying these criteria, he found that *Pearce* should not be applied retroactively.

Blackledge v. *Perry*, 417 U.S. 21 (1974), dealt with the matter of prosecutor vindictiveness after one convicted of a misdemeanor filed an appeal. While serving a prison term in North Carolina, Perry became involved in an altercation with another inmate. Perry was charged with the misdemeanor of assault with a deadly weapon and was convicted in the State District Court. While his appeal was pending in the Superior Court, where he had the right to a trial *de novo*, the prosecutor obtained an indictment covering the same conduct for the felony offense of assault with a deadly weapon with intent to kill inflicting serious bodily injury. Perry entered a plea of guilty and was sentenced to a term of five to seven years in the penitentiary, instead of the six-month sentence he had received in the District Court. Later, in a habeas corpus action in the United States District Court, Perry claimed that the felony indictment violated the double jeopardy clause and also violated the due process clause as expressed in the *Pearce* rule. When the case came on to the Supreme Court, only the latter claim was discussed. The opinion for the majority, through Justice Stewart, stated that the lesson that emerges from *Pearce* and *Chaffin* is that "the Due Process Clause is not offended by all possibilities of increased punishment upon retrial after appeal, but only by those that pose a realistic likelihood of 'vindictiveness.' " The majority concluded that the facts justified such a finding in this case. It was pointed out that if the prosecutor may "up the ante" through a felony indictment whenever a convicted misdemeanant pursues his statutory appellate remedy, the State can insure that only the most hardy defendants will brave the hazards of a *de novo* trial. An additional issue in the case was whether, because of his guilty plea, Perry was barred from raising his constitutional claims in a federal habeas corpus proceeding by the decisions in *McMann* v. *Richardson* and *Tollott* v. *Henderson* (discussed earlier). The Court distinguished those cases, stating that while the claims presented were of constitutional dimension, "none went to the very power of the State to bring the defendant into court to answer the charge brought against him."

Trial for Multiple Related Offenses

Double jeopardy issues of a special sort may be presented when an accused is tried on multiple counts—entirely in a single trial or in successive trials—arising out of the execution of a single criminal plot. Three facets of this situation occur, each presenting separate problems. (1) The criminal law has developed in a fashion which results in a great deal of overlapping, and consequently a single criminal *act* may in fact be chargeable as two or more *offenses*. In defining criminal offenses the law has operated like the pathologist's knife in splitting the total transaction into several discrete parts, each of which constitutes a separate crime. Thus a burglary might actually be broken down into the separate charges of conspiracy to commit burglary, possession of burglar's tools with intent to commit burglary, and burglary. (2) A criminal may commit several crimes on a single occasion, as, for example, by robbing five different customers in a tavern. In so doing, he has committed five separate crimes and may be so charged. The problem arises when he is tried *seriatim* on these charges, rather than in one trial. (3) A third double jeopardy issue stems from the fact that we live under a federal system, and a single act may constitute both a state crime and a federal crime.

The constitutionality of trying a defendant on closely related charges is usually determined by whether additional facts must be proved in the additional charges. If so, then there is no double jeopardy. If the same facts would support a conviction on the additional charges, then double jeopardy occurs. Thus it is permissible to try an accused both for conspiracy to commit a crime and for the substantive crime. It is also permissible to try for breaking and entertaining with intent to commit larceny and, additionally, for committing the larceny. But if the additional charge is an *included* offense the situation is different. Bank robbery and conspiracy to commit bank robbery are capable of separate treatment and may even be tried as different trials, since either crime may take place without the other. But murder includes the lesser crime of manslaughter, and if trial is had on either charge, a later trial on the other is precluded.

When a criminal robs several persons on a single occasion, he has committed multiple crimes of an identical nature. The question then arises of whether he can be tried in a series of trials under these circumstances or whether the prohibition against double jeopardy limits the government to a single trial. Two cases involving this issue under the Fourteenth Amendment were decided in 1958. They were *Hoag* v. *New Jersey,* 356 U.S. 464 (1958), and *Ciucci* v. *Illinois,* 356 U.S. 571 (1958).

The *Hoag* case involved the robbery of five persons one evening in a New Jersey tavern. Hoag was indicted separately for robbery of three of the victims, and the indictments were joined for trial. At this trial acquittal resulted. All five victims were called as witnesses in the trial. Subsequently, Hoag was indicted, tried, and convicted for robbing a fourth person at the tavern. The same issues of identification of Hoag as a participant in the robbery and the credibility of Hoag's alibi were presented at the second trial. Hoag argued that in these circumstances his second trial was in violation of the due process protection against double jeopardy. The Supreme Court of New Jersey sustained the conviction, and on certiorari the United States Supreme Court affirmed by a five-to-three vote. The majority took into account the fact that several of the witnesses, to the surprise of the State, failed to identify Hoag as one of the robbers after having done so during the police investigation, and concluded that this was not an attempt on the part of the State to wear the accused out by a multitude of cases with accumulated trials. The dissenters argued that "Hoag is made to run the gantlet twice," since the only contested issue was whether he was one of the robbers. This they felt clearly violated the constitutional protection against double jeopardy.

In the same term of Court, a similar holding followed in *Ciucci* v. *Illinois,* 356 U.S. 571 (1958). In this case the vote was five-to-four, with Mr. Justice Brennan participating and voting with the dissenters. Ciucci's wife and three children were found dead with bullet wounds in their heads in a burning building. Ciucci was charged on four separate murder indictments and tried three successive times, first for the murder of his wife, and then for the murder of two of the three children. At each of the trials the prosecution introduced into evidence details of all four deaths. Under Illinois law, the jury fixed the penalty for first degree murder. Ciucci was convicted in each of the three trials. The sentences by the three different juries increased successively from 20 years for the wife, to 45 years for the first child, to death for the second child. The same majority as in *Hoag,* in a per curiam opinion, affirmed the judgment on authority of *Hoag* and *Palko.* In 1970, in the wake of *Benton* v. *Maryland,* the Court overruled this position in *Ashe* v. *Swenson.*

ASHE *v.* SWENSON
397 U.S. 436 (1970)

[Six men engaged in a poker game were robbed by three or four masked gunmen. Six weeks after being acquitted in a state trial for the robbery of one of the players, the defendant was tried for the robbery of another of the players and was convicted. The witnesses in the two trials were for the most part the same, and the State's evidence establishing the facts of the robbery was uncontradicted, but the testimony identifying the defendant as one of the robbers was substantially stronger at the second trial. The Supreme Court of Missouri affirmed the conviction, holding that the "plea of former jeopardy must be denied." A collateral attack upon the conviction in the state courts five years later was also unsuccessful. The defendant then brought a habeas corpus proceedings in the United States District Court, claiming that the second prosecution had violated his right not to be twice put in jeopardy. The District Court denied the writ, the Court of Appeals affirmed, and the Supreme Court granted certiorari.]

Mr. Justice Stewart delivered the opinion of the Court.

As the District Court and the Court of Appeals correctly noted, the operative facts here are virtually identical to those of *Hoag* v. *New Jersey.* . . . Viewing the question presented solely in terms of Fourteenth Amendment due process—whether the course that New Jersey had pursued had "led to fundamental unfairness,". . . —this Court declined to reverse the judgment of conviction, because "in the circumstances shown by this record, we cannot say that petitioner's later prosecution and conviction violated due process.". . . The Court found it unnecessary to decide whether "collateral estoppel"—the principle that bars relitigation between the same parties of issues actually determined at a previous trial—is a due process requirement in a state criminal trial. . . . And in the view the Court took of the issues presented, it did not, of course, even approach consideration of whether collateral estoppel is an ingredient of the Fifth Amendment guarantee against double jeopardy.

The doctrine of *Benton* v. *Maryland* . . . puts the issues in the present case in a perspective quite different from that in which the issues were perceived in *Hoag* v. *New Jersey.* The question is no longer whether collateral estoppel is a requirement of due process, but whether it is a part of the Fifth Amendment's guarantee against double jeopardy. . . .

"Collateral estoppel" is an awkward phrase, but it stands for an extremely important principle in our adversary system of justice. It means simply that when an issue of ultimate fact has once been determined by a valid and final judgment, that issue cannot again be litigated between the same parties any any future lawsuit.... The federal decisions have made clear that the rule of collateral estoppel in criminal cases is not to be applied with the hypertechnical and archaic approach of a 19th century pleading book, but with realism and rationality. Where a previous judgment of acquittal was based upon a general verdict, as is usually the case, this approach requires a court to "examine the record of a prior proceeding, taking into account the pleadings, evidence, charge, and other relevant matter, and conclude whether a rational jury could have grounded its verdict upon an issue other than that which the defendant seeks to foreclose from consideration."...

Straightforward application of the federal rule to the present case can lead to but one conclusion.... The single rationally conceivable issue in dispute before the jury was whether the petitioner had been one of the robbers. And the jury by its verdict found that he had not....

The ultimate question to be determined, then, in the light of *Benton* v. *Maryland, supra,* is whether this established rule of federal law is embodied in the Fifth Amendment guarantee against double jeopardy. We do not hesitate to hold that it is. For whatever else that constitutional guarantee may embrace,... it surely protects a man who has been acquitted from having to "run the gantlet" a second time....

The question is not whether Missouri could validly charge the petitioner with six separate offenses for the robbery of the six poker players. It is not whether he could have received a total of six punishments if he had been convicted in a single trial of robbing the six victims. It is simply whether, after a jury determined by its verdict that the petitioner was not one of the robbers, the State could constitutionally hale him before a new jury to litigate that issue again....

The judgment is reversed, and the case is remanded to the Court of Appeals for the Eighth Circuit for further proceedings consistent with this opinion.

[Separate concurring opinions were written by Justice Black, Justice Harlan, and Justice Brennan, who was joined by Justices Douglas and Marshall. Chief Justice Burger dissented.]

Another multiple offense problem arises when a single act constitutes a crime under state law and also under municipal ordinance. The question of whether dual prosecution in such situations constitutes double jeopardy was considered in *Waller* v. *Florida*, decided on the same day as *Ashe*.

WALLER *v.* FLORIDA
397 U.S. 387 (1970)

Mr. Chief Justice Burger delivered the opinion of the Court....

Petitioner was one of a number of persons who removed a canvas mural which was affixed to a wall inside the City Hall of St. Petersburg, Florida. After the mural was removed, the petitioner and others carried it through the streets of St. Petersburg until they were confronted by police officers. After a scuffle, the officers recovered the mural, but in a damaged condition.

The petitioner was charged by the City of St. Petersburg with the violation of two ordinances: first, destruction of city property; and second, disorderly breach of the peace. He was found guilty in the municipal court on both counts, and a sentence of 180 days in the county jail was imposed.

Thereafter an information was filed against the petitioner by the State of Florida charging him with grand larceny. It is conceded that this information was based on the same acts of the petitioner as were involved in the violation of the two city ordinances. . . . Thereafter petitioner was tried in the Circuit Court of Florida by a jury and was found guilty of the felony of grand larceny. . . .

On appeal, the District Court of Appeal of Florida considered and rejected petitioner's claim that he had twice been put in jeopardy because prior to his conviction of grand larceny, he had been convicted by the municipal court of an included offense of the crime of grand larceny. . . . [The District Court of Appeal quoted the Florida Supreme Court saying:]

" 'This double jeopardy argument has long been settled contrary to the claims of the petitioner. We see no reason to recede from our established precedent on the subject. Long ago it was decided that an act committed within municipal limits may be punished by city ordinance even though the same act is also proscribed as a crime by a state statute. An offender may be tried for the municipal offense in the city court and for the crime in the proper state court. Conviction or acquittal in either does not bar prosecution in the other.' ". . .

. . . Whether in fact and law petitioner committed separate offenses which could support separate charges was not decided by the Florida courts, nor do we reach that question. What is before us is the asserted power of the two courts within one State to place petitioner on trial for the same alleged crime.

In *Benton* v. *Maryland* . . . this Court declared the double jeopardy provisions of the Fifth Amendment applicable to the States. . . . Here, as in *North Carolina* v. *Pearce* . . . *Benton* should be applied to test petitioner's conviction. . . .

Florida does not stand alone in treating municipalities and the State as separate sovereign entities, each capable of imposing punishment for the same alleged crime. Here, respondent State of Florida seeks to justify this separate sovereignty theory by asserting that the relationship between a municipality and the state is analogous to the relationship between a State and the Federal Government. Florida's chief reliance is placed upon this Court's holdings in *Bartkus* v. *Illinois* . . . and *Abbate* v. *United States* . . . which permitted successive prosecutions by the Federal and State Governments as separate sovereigns. . . .

[The] provisions of the Florida Constitution demonstrate that the judicial power to try petitioner on the first charges in municipal court springs from the same organic law that created the state court of general jurisdiction in which petitioner was tried and convicted for a felony. Accordingly, the apt analogy to the relationship between municipal and state governments is to be found in the relationship between the government of a Territory and the Government of the United States. The legal consequence of that relationship was settled in *Grafton* v. *United States*, 206 U.S. 333 (1907), where this Court held that a prosecution in a court of the United States is a bar to a subsequent prosecution in a territorial court, since both are arms of the same sovereign. . . .

Thus *Grafton*, not *Fox* v. *Ohio*, *supra*, or its progeny, *Bartkus* v. *Illinois* . . . or *Abbate* v. *United States* . . . controls, and we hold that on the basis of the facts upon which the Florida District Court of Appeal relied petitioner could not lawfully be tried both by the municipal government and by the State of Florida. In this context a "dual sovereignty" theory is an anachronism, and the second trial constituted double jeopardy violative of the Fifth and Fourteenth Amendments to the United States Constitution. . . . [Judgment in the second trial vacated, and the cause remanded for further proceedings in accord with this opinion.]

[Justices Black and Brennan wrote concurring opinions.]

The final aspect of the multiple offense problems to be considered is that of trial by both federal and state authority where a single act constitutes a crime against both jurisdictions. Beginning in 1852 in *Moore* v. *Illinois,* 14 How. 13, the Court has indicated in a number of cases that trials by both jurisdictions in such instances would not violate the prohibitions against double jeopardy. While the most recent decision to date on the point, *Bartkus* v. *Illinois,* follows this rule, the opinions in *Benton, Ashe,* and *Waller* suggest that it is now on very tenuous ground.

BARTKUS *v.* ILLINOIS

359 U.S. 121 (1959)

Mr. Justice Frankfurter delivered the opinion of the Court.

Petitioner was tried in the Federal District Court for the Northern District of Illinois on December 18, 1953, for robbery of a federally insured savings and loan association . . . in violation of 18 U.S.C. Sec. 2113. The case was tried to a jury and resulted in an acquittal. On January 8, 1954, an Illinois grand jury indicted Bartkus. The facts recited in the Illinois indictment were substantially identical to those contained in the prior federal indictment. The Illinois indictment charged that these facts constituted a violation of Illinois Revised Statutes, 1951 c. 38, Sec. 501, a robbery statute. Bartkus was tried and convicted in the Criminal Court of Cook County and was sentenced to life imprisonment under the Illinois Habitual Criminal Statute. . . .

The Illinois trial considered and rejected petitioner's plea of *autrefois acquit.* That ruling and other alleged errors were challenged before the Illinois Supreme Court which affirmed the conviction. . . .

The state and federal prosecutions were separately conducted. It is true that the agent of the Federal Bureau of Investigation who had conducted the investigation on behalf of the Federal Government turned over to the Illinois prosecuting officials all the evidence he had gathered against the petitioner. Concededly, some of that evidence had been gathered after acquittal in the federal court. The only other connection between the two trials is to be found in a suggestion that the federal sentencing of the accomplices who testified against petitioner in both trials was purposely continued by the federal court until after they testified in the state trial. The record establishes that the prosecution was undertaken by state prosecuting officials within their discretionary responsibility and on the basis of evidence that conduct contrary to the penal code of Illinois had occurred within their jurisdiction. It establishes also that federal officials acted in cooperation with state authorities, as is the conventional practice between the two sets of prosecutors throughout the country. It does not support the claim that the State of Illinois in bringing its prosecution was merely a tool of the federal authorities, who thereby avoided the prohibition of the Fifth Amendment against a retrial of a federal prosecution after an acquittal. It does not sustain a conclusion that the state prosecution was a sham and a cover for a federal prosecution, and thereby in essential fact another federal prosecution. . . .

Constitutional challenge to successive state and federal prosecutions based upon the same transaction or conduct is not a new question before the Court though it has now been presented with conspicuous ability. The Fifth Amendment's proscription of double jeopardy has been invoked and rejected in over twenty cases of real or hypothetical successive state and federal prosecution cases before this Court. While *United States* v. *Lanza,* 260 U.S. 377 [1922], was the first case in which we squarely held valid a federal prosecution arising out of the same facts which had been the basis of a state conviction, the validity of such a prosecution by the Federal Government has not been questioned by this Court since the opinion in *Fox* v. *State of Ohio,* 5 How. 410, more than one hundred years ago....

In a dozen cases decided by this Court [before *United States* v. *Lanza*] this Court had occasion to reaffirm the principle first enunciated in *Fox* v. *State of Ohio.* Since *Lanza* the Court has five times repeated the rule that successive state prosecutions are not in violation of the Fifth Amendment. Indeed Mr. Justice Holmes once wrote of this rule that it "is too plain to need more than statement."...

The experience of state courts in dealing with successive prosecutions by different governments is obviously also relevant in considering whether or not the Illinois prosecution of Bartkus violated due process of law. Of the twenty-eight States which have considered the validity of successive state and federal prosecutions as against a challenge of violation of either a state constitutional double-jeopardy provision or a common-law evidentiary rule of *autrefois acquit* and *autrefois convict,* twenty-seven have refused to rule that the second prosecution was or would be barred. These States were not bound to follow this Court and its interpretation of the Fifth Amendment. The rules, constitutional, statutory, or common law which bound them drew upon the same experience as did the Fifth Amendment, but were and are of separate and independent authority....

With this body of precedent as irrefutable evidence that state and federal courts have for years refused to bar a second trial even though there had been a prior trial by another government for a similar offense, it would be disregard of a long, unbroken, unquestioned course of impressive adjudication for the Court now to rule that due process compels such a bar. A practical justification for rejecting such a reading of due process also commends itself in aid of this interpretation of the Fourteenth Amendment. In *Screws* v. *United States,* 325 U.S. 91, defendants were tried and convicted in a federal court under federal statutes with maximum sentences of a year and two years respectively. But the state crime there involved was a capital offense. Were the federal prosecution of a comparatively minor offense to prevent state prosecution of so grave an infraction of state law, the result would be a shocking and untoward deprivation of the historic right and obligation of the States to maintain peace and order within their confines. It would be in derogation of our federal system to displace the reserved power of States over state offenses by reason of prosecution of minor federal offenses by federal authorities beyond the control of the States....

Precedent, experience, and reason all support the conclusion that Alphonse Bartkus has not been deprived of due process of law by the State of Illinois.

Affirmed.

Mr. Justice Black, with whom the Chief Justice and Mr. Justice Douglas concur, dissenting....

The Court's holding further limits our already weakened constitutional guarantees against double prosecutions. *United States* v. *Lanza* ... allowed federal conviction and punishment of a man who had been previously convicted and punished for the identical acts by one of our States. Today, for the first time in its history, this Court upholds the state conviction of a defendant who had been *acquitted* of the same offense in the federal courts. I would hold that a federal trial following either state acquittal or conviction is barred by the Double Jeopardy Clause of the Fifth Amendment. *Abbate* v. *United States,* 359 U.S. 187 (dissenting opinion). And, quite apart from whether that clause is as fully binding on the States as it is on the Federal Government, . . . I would hold that Bartkus' conviction cannot stand. For I think double prosecutions for the same offense are so contrary to the spirit of our free country that they violate even the prevailing view of the Fourteenth Amendment, expressed in *Palko* v. *Connecticut*. . . .

The Court apparently takes the position that a second trial for the same act is somehow less offensive if one of the trials is conducted by the Federal Government and the other by a State. Looked at from the standpoint of the individual who is being prosecuted, this notion is too subtle for me to grasp. If double punishment is what is feared, it hurts no less for two "Sovereigns" to inflict it than for one. If danger to the innocent is emphasized, that danger is surely no less when the power of State and Federal Governments is brought to bear on one man in two trials, than when one of these "Sovereigns" proceeds alone. In each case, inescapably, a man is forced to face danger twice for the same conduct.

The Court, without denying the almost universal abhorrence of such double prosecutions, nevertheless justifies the practice here in the name of "federalism." This, it seems to me, is a misuse and desecration of the concept. Our Federal Union was conceived and created "to establish Justice" and to "secure the Blessings of Liberty," not to destroy any of the bulwarks on which both freedom and justice depend. We should, therefore, be suspicious of any supposed "requirements" of "federalism" which result in obliterating ancient safeguards. I have been shown nothing in the history of our Union, in the writings of its Founders, or elsewhere, to indicate that individual rights deemed essential by both State and Nation were to be lost through the combined operations of the two governments. Nor has the Court given any sound reason for thinking that the successful operation of our dual system of government depends in the slightest on the power to try people twice for the same act.

Implicit in the Court's reliance on "federalism" is the premise that failure to allow double prosecutions would seriously impair law enforcement in both State and Nation. For one jurisdiction might provide minor penalties for acts severely punished by the other and by accepting pleas of guilty shield wrongdoers from justice. I believe this argument fails on several grounds. In the first place it relies on the unwarranted assumption that State and Nation will seek to subvert each other's laws. It has elsewhere been persuasively argued that most civilized nations do not and have not needed the power to try people a second time to protect themselves even when dealing with foreign lands. . . .

Ultimately, the Court's reliance on federalism amounts to no more than the notion that, somehow, one act becomes two because two jurisdictions are involved. Hawkins, in his Pleas of the Crown, long ago disposed of a similar contention made to justify two trials for the same offense by different counties as "a mere Fiction or Construction of Law, which shall hardly take Place against a Maxim made in Favour of Life." It was discarded as a dangerous fiction then, it should be discarded as a dangerous fiction now. . . .

I would reverse.

[Mr. Justice Brennan, joined by Chief Justice Warren and Mr. Justice Douglas, dissented on the ground that the unusual extent of federal assistance and participation in the state trial made it "actually a second federal prosecution" barred by the double jeopardy provisions of the Fifth Amendment.]

Immediately following the decisions in *Bartkus* and *Abbate,* in 1959, the then Attorney General, William P. Rogers, announced for the Department of Justice a policy that no federal prosecution would be initiated following a state prosecution on a charge arising out of the same act unless unusual circumstances appeared. Even here, it was stated, the Attorney General himself would have to approve the decision to prosecute.

The majority and dissenting opinions in *Bartkus,* taken together with the action of Attorney General Rogers, raise the interesting question of the degree to which official discretion can be permitted, in order to retain flexibility, in the face of our traditional repugnance to double punishment. They are also illustrative of the point that care must be exercised in erecting any rule to the level of a constitutional requirement, since this tends to remove any "play at the joints" in the application of the rule.

[See J. A. C. Grant, "Successive Prosecutions by State and Nation," 4 *U.C.L.A. L. Rev.* 1 (1956) and Walter T. Fisher, "Double Jeopardy, Two Sovereignties and the Intruding Constitution," 28 *U. Chi. L. Rev.* 591 (1961).]

TRIAL BY JURY

Trial by jury in criminal cases has been probably the most venerated and often praised of any of the procedural guarantees of the Constitution. It has undergone a slow erosion, however, and is only used in the more important cases in England. In the United States a similar trend is evident, and increasingly the jury trial is being waived. In addition, several states have reduced the number of jurors required or changed the unanimity requirement or both. But in federal trials the right to a jury is specifically guaranteed. The guarantee of jury trial in criminal cases is found both in Article III and in the Sixth Amendment of the Constitution. Article III, Section 2, Clause 3, states:

The trial of all crimes, except in cases of impeachment, shall be by jury; and such trial shall be held in the State where the said crimes shall have been committed; but when not committed within any State, the trial shall be at such place or places as the Congress may by law have directed.

The Sixth Amendment states:

In all criminal prosecutions the accused shall enjoy the right to a speedy and public trial, by an impartial jury of the State and district wherein the crime shall have been committed. . . .

While the Sixth Amendment guarantees the right of jury trial "in all criminal prosecutions," and Article III states that the trial "of all Crimes" shall be by jury, the Court has uniformly held that the Constitution does not require that petty offenses be tried to a jury. This, too, is a common-law feature of jury trial. The rule was stated in *District of Columbia* v. *Colts,* 282 U.S. 63 (1930). Colts was charged with having operated a motor vehicle in the district at a greater rate of speed than twenty-two miles an hour (the legal limit) recklessly, "in such manner and condition so as to endanger property and individuals." He demanded trial by jury but was refused. In reviewing his conviction the court of appeals reversed the judgment, holding that the offense went beyond the character of a petty offense, and therefore the accused was constitutionally entitled to trial by jury. The United States Supreme Court affirmed this decision. Justice Sutherland, for a unanimous Court, stated:

It will be seen that the respondent is not charged merely with the comparatively slight offense of exceeding the twenty-two mile limit of speed . . . or merely with driving recklessly . . . ; but with the grave offense of having driven at the forbidden rate of speed and recklessly, "so as to endanger property and individuals."

By section 165 of title 18 of the D.C. Code, . . . the Constitution is made the test—as, of course, it must be—to determine whether the accused be entitled to a jury trial. Article 3, Section 2, Cl. 3, of the Constitution provides that, "The Trial of all Crimes, except in Cases of Impeachment, shall be by Jury." This provision is to be interpreted in the light of common law, according to which petty offenses might be proceeded against summarily before a magistrate sitting without a jury. See *Callan* v. *Wilson,* 127 U.S. 540, 557. That there may be many offenses called "petty offenses" which do not rise to the degree of crimes within the meaning of Article 3, and in respect of which Congress may dispense with a jury trial, is settled. . . .

Whether a given offense is to be classed as a crime, so as to require a jury trial, or as a petty offense, triable summarily without a jury, depends primarily upon the nature of the offense. The offense here charged is not merely *malum prohibitum,* but in its very nature is *malum in se.* It was an indictable offense at common law . . . when horses, instead of gasoline, constituted the motive power. The New Jersey Court of Errors and Appeals, in *State* v. *Rodgers, supra,* has discussed the distinction between traffic offenses of a petty character, subject to summary proceedings without indictment and trial by jury, and those of a serious character, amounting to public nuisances indictable at common law; and its examination of the subject makes clear that the offense now under review is of the latter character.

An interesting aspect of the right to a jury trial involves the question of whether the defendant has a right to waive jury trial and allow the judge to render the verdict. Rule 23 (a) of the Federal Rules of Criminal Procedure provides:

Cases required to be tried by jury shall be so tried unless defendant waives a jury trial in writing with the approval of the court and the consent of the government.

The validity of the requirement of the consent of the government to the waiver was challenged, and upheld, in *Singer* v. *United States,* 380 U.S. 24 (1965). Singer was charged with violations of the mail fraud statute and offered to waive a trial by jury. The trial court approved, but the government refused to give its consent. Petitioner was subsequently convicted by a jury, and the Court granted certiorari to consider his claim that the Sixth Amendment affords an unconditional right in a federal criminal case for the defendant to have his case decided by a judge alone if he considers it to be to his advantage. The Court unanimously denied this interpretation and held Rule 23 (a) to be valid. "The ability to waive a constitutional right does not ordinarily carry with it the right to insist upon the opposite of that right. . . . [A]lthough he can waive his right to be confronted by the witnesses against him, it has never been seriously suggested that he can thereby compel the Government to try the case by stipulation." The Chief Justice pointed out that if the consent of the judge or prosecutor to waiver is withheld, "the result is simply that the defendant is subject to an impartial trial by jury—the very thing that the Constitution guarantees him."

Incorporation

Until 1968 the Court followed the *Palko* rule of "fundamental fairness" with respect to the use of jury trials in state prosecutions and even indicated in several cases that the State could abolish the criminal jury altogether without violating the Fourteenth Amendment. In *Duncan* v. *Louisiana*, 391 U.S. 145 (1968), however, the Court incorporated the Sixth Amendment jury trial guarantee into the Fourteenth Amendment.

DUNCAN *v.* LOUISIANA
391 U.S. 145 (1968)

Mr. Justice White delivered the opinion of the Court.

Appellant, Gary Duncan, was convicted of simple battery in the . . . District Court of Louisiana. Under Louisiana law simple battery is a misdemeanor, punishable by a maximum of two years' imprisonment and a $300 fine. Appellant sought trial by jury, but because the Louisiana Constitution grants jury trials only in cases in which capital punishment or imprisonment at hard labor may be imposed, the trial judge denied the request. Appellant was convicted and sentenced to serve 60 days in the parish prison and pay a fine of $150. Appellant sought review in the Supreme Court of Louisiana, asserting that the denial of jury trial violated rights guaranteed to him by the United States Constitution. The Supreme Court . . . denied appellant a writ of certiorari. . . .

The test for determining whether a right extended by the Fifth and Sixth Amendments with respect to federal criminal proceedings is also protected against state action by the Fourteenth Amendment has been phrased in a variety of ways in the opinions of this Court. The question has been asked whether a right is among those " 'fundamental principles of liberty and justice which lie at the base of all our civil and political institutions,' ". . . ; whether it is "basic in our system of jurisprudence,". . . ; and whether it is "a fundamental right, essential to a fair trial,". . . . . Because we believe that trial by jury in criminal cases is fundamental to the American scheme of justice, we hold that the Fourteenth Amendment guarantees a right of jury trial in all criminal cases which—were they to be tried in a federal court—would come within the Sixth Amendment's guarantee. Since we consider the appeal before us to be such a case, we hold that the Constitution was violated when appellant's demand for jury trial was refused. . . .

We are aware of prior cases in this Court in which the prevailing opinion contains statements contrary to our holding today that the right to jury trial in serious criminal cases is a fundamental right and hence must be recognized by the States as part of their obligation to extend due process of all to all persons within their jurisdiction. . . . None of these cases, however, dealt with a State which had purported to dispense entirely with a jury trial in serious criminal cases. . . .

The guarantees of jury in the Federal and State Constitutions reflect a profound judgment about the way in which law should be enforced and justice administered. A right to jury trial is granted to criminal defendants in order to prevent oppression by the Government. Those who wrote our constitutions knew from history and experience that it was necessary to protect against unfounded criminal charges brought to eliminate enemies and against judges too responsive to the voice of higher authority. . . . The deep commitment of the Nation to the right of jury trial in serious criminal cases as a defense against arbitrary law enforcement qualifies for protection under the Due Process Clause of the Fourteenth Amendment, and must therefore be respected by the States. . . .

. . . It is doubtless true that there is a category of petty crimes or offenses which is not subject to the Sixth Amendment jury trial provision and should not be subject to the Fourteenth Amendment jury trial requirement here applied to the States. Crimes carrying possible penalties up to six months do not require a jury trial if they otherwise qualify as petty offenses. *Cheff* v. *Schnackenberg,* 384 U.S. 373 (1966). But the penalty authorized for a particular crime is of major relevance in determining whether it is serious or not and may in itself, if severe enough, subject the trial to the mandates of the Sixth Amendment. . . .

We need not, however, settle in this case the exact location of the line between petty offenses and serious crimes. It is sufficient for our purposes to hold that a crime punishable by two years in prison is, based on past and contemporary standards in this country, a serious crime and not a petty offense. Consequently, appellant was entitled to a jury trial and it was error to deny it.

The judgment below is reversed and the case is remanded for proceedings not inconsistent with this opinion.

Mr. Justice Fortas, concurring. . . .
Mr. Justice Black, with whom Mr. Justice Douglas joins, concurring. . . .
Mr. Justice Harlan, whom Mr. Justice Stewart joins, dissenting. . . .

Number of Jurors

At common law the jury numbered twelve, and it has long been assumed that the Sixth Amendment jury contemplated twelve as a constitutional requirement. If so, then the decision in *Duncan* v. *Louisiana* would demand that state criminal juries also number twelve. The Court examined this question in 1970, in *Williams* v. *Florida,* and held that the Constitution did not require juries of twelve.

WILLIAMS *v.* FLORIDA
399 U.S. 78 (1970)

[Prior to his trial for robbery in the State of Florida, petitioner filed a pretrial motion to impanel a twelve-man jury instead of the six-man jury provided by Florida law in all but capital cases. That motion was denied, and in the subsequent trial petitioner was convicted as charged and was sentenced to life imprisonment. The District Court of Appeals affirmed, rejecting petitioner's claim that his Sixth Amendment rights had been violated.]

Mr. Justice White delivered the opinion of the Court.

In *Duncan* v. *Louisiana* . . . we held that the Fourteenth Amendment guarantees a right to trial by jury in all criminal cases which—were they to be tried in a federal court—would come within the Sixth Amendment's guarantee. Petitioner's trial for robbery . . . clearly falls within the scope of that holding. . . . The question in this case then is whether the constitutional guarantee of a trial by "jury" necessarily requires trial by exactly 12 persons, rather than some lesser number— in this case six. We hold that the 12-man panel is not a necessary ingredient of "trial by jury," and that respondent's refusal to impanel more than the six members provided for by Florida law did not violate petitioner's Sixth Amendment rights as applied to the States through the Fourteenth.

We had occasion in *Duncan* v. *Louisiana,* . . . to review briefly the oft-told history of the development of trial by jury in criminal cases. That history revealed a long tradition attaching great importance to the concept of relying on a body of one's peers to determine guilt or innocence as a safeguard against arbitrary law enforcement. That same history, however, affords little insight into the considerations which gradually led the size of that body to be generally fixed at 12. Some have suggested that the number 12 was fixed upon simply because that was the number of the presentment jury from the hundred, from which the petty jury developed. Other, less circular but more fanciful reasons for the number 12 have been given, "but they were all brought forward after the number was fixed," and rest on little more than mystical or superstitious insights into the significance of "12." Lord Coke's explanation that the "number of twelve is much respected in holy writ, as 12 apostles, 12 stones, 12 tribes, etc." is typical. In short, while sometime in the 14th century the size of the jury at common law came to be fixed generally at 12, that particular feature of the jury system appears to have been an historical accident, unrelated to the great purposes which gave rise to the jury in the first place. The question before us is whether this accidental feature of the jury has been immutably codified into our Constitution.

This Court's earlier decisions have assumed an affirmative answer to this question. The leading case so construing the Sixth Amendment is *Thompson* v. *Utah,* 170 U.S. 343 (1898).... In reaching its conclusion, the Court announced that the Sixth Amendment was applicable to the defendant's trial when Utah was a territory, and that the jury referred to in the Amendment was a jury "constituted, as it was at common law, of twelve persons, neither more nor less.".....

While "the intent of the Framers" is often an elusive quarry, the relevant constitutional history casts considerable doubt on the easy assumption in our past decisions that if a given feature existed in a jury at common law in 1789, then it was necessarily preserved in the Constitution....

We do not pretend to be able to divine precisely what the word "jury" imported to the Framers, the First Congress, or the States in 1789. It may well be that the usual expectation was that the jury would consist of 12, and that hence, the most likely conclusion to be drawn is simply that little thought was actually given to the specific question we face today. But there is absolutely no indication in "the intent of the Framers" of an explicit decision to equate the constitutional and common law characteristics of the jury.... The relevant inquiry, as we see it, must be the function which the particular feature performs and its relation to the purposes of the jury trial. Measured by this standard, the 12-man requirement cannot be regarded as an indispensable component of the Sixth Amendment.

[The opinion here examines the functions of group deliberation, cross-section representation of the community, and protection against governmental oppression, and concludes that these functions are equally well served with juries of six.]

We conclude, in short, as we began: the fact that the jury at common law was composed of precisely 12 is an historical accident, unnecessary to effect the purposes of the jury system and wholly without significance "except to mystics."....

Affirmed.

Mr. Justice Blackmun took no part in the consideration or decision of this case.
Mr. Chief Justice Burger, concurring....
Mr. Justice Harlan, concurring in part and dissenting in part....
Mr. Justice Stewart, concurring....
Mr. Justice Black, with whom Mr. Justice Douglas joins, concurring....
Mr. Justice Marshall, dissenting in part....

In *Colgrove* v. *Battin,* 413 U.S. 149 (1973), the Court followed the *Williams* rationale in holding that the Seventh Amendment's guarantee of jury trial in civil suits at common law was not violated by a local United States District Court rule providing for juries of six in such cases. The petitioner contended that the local rule (1) violated the Seventh Amendment; (2) violated the statutory provision, 28 U.S.C. §2072, that rules "shall preserve the right of trial by jury as at common law and as declared by the Seventh Amendment"; and (3) was rendered invalid by Federal Rules of Civil Procedure 83 because "inconsistent with" Federal Rules of Civil Procedure 48 that provides for juries of less than twelve when stipulated by the parties. The majority of five held that the Seventh Amendment did not bind the federal courts to the exact procedural incidents or details of jury trial according to the common law. As in *Williams,* the majority then concluded that the results of studies of juries of six and of twelve indicated that there was no discernible difference between the results reached by the two different-sized juries, and that a jury of six satisfies the Seventh Amendment's guarantee of trial by jury in civil cases. As to the contention that the local rule was inconsistent with Rule 48, the Court held that Rule 48 deals only with stipulation *by the parties* and does not purport to prevent court rules which provide for civil juries of reduced size. Only two of the four dissenters reached the constitutional issue, while the other two argued that Congress had not intended to permit federal courts to use a jury of six unless the parties so stipulated.

Requirement of Unanimity

APODACA *v.* OREGON

406 U.S. 404 (1972)

[Pursuant to Oregon constitutional provisions authorizing a verdict by ten of twelve jurors in criminal cases, except for first degree murder verdicts, three defendants were convicted of criminal offenses other than first degree murder in separate state prosecutions. Two were convicted by eleven-to-one verdicts and one by a ten-to-two verdict. The Court of Appeals of Oregon affirmed the convictions, rejecting the defendants' contention that conviction by less than a unanimous jury violated the right to trial by jury specified by the Sixth Amendment and made applicable to the states by the Fourteenth Amendment. The Oregon Supreme Court denied review.]

Mr. Justice White announced the judgment of the Court and an opinion in which the Chief Justice, Mr. Justice Blackmun, and Mr. Justice Rehnquist joined....

In *Williams* v. *Florida* ... (1970), we had occasion to consider a related issue: whether the Sixth Amendment's right to trial by jury requires that all juries consist of 12 men. After considering the history of the 12-man requirement and the functions it performs in contemporary society, we concluded that it was not of constitutional stature. We reach the same conclusion today with regard to the requirement of unanimity.

I

Like the requirement that juries consist of 12 men, the requirement of unanimity arose during the Middle Ages and had become an accepted feature of the common-law jury by the 18th century. But, as we observed in *Williams,* "the relevant constitutional history casts considerable doubt on the easy assumption ... that if a given feature existed in a jury at common law in 1789, then it was necessarily preserved in the Constitution.". . .

As we observed in *Williams,* one can draw conflicting inferences from [the] legislative history. One possible inference is that Congress eliminated references to unanimity and to the other "accustomed requisites" of the jury because those requisites were thought already to be implicit in the very concept of jury. A contrary explanation, which we found in *Williams* to be the more plausible, is that the deletion was intended to have some substantive effect. . . . Surely one fact that is absolutely clear from this history is that, after a proposal had been made to specify precisely which of the common-law requisites of the jury were to be preserved by the Constitution, the Framers explicitly rejected the proposal and instead left such specification to the future. . . .

II

Our inquiry must focus upon the function served by the jury in contemporary society. . . . As we said in *Duncan*, the purpose of trial by jury is to prevent oppression by the Government by providing a "safeguard against the corrupt or overzealous prosecutor and against the compliant, biased, or eccentric judge.". . . "Given this purpose, the essential feature of a jury obviously lies in the interposition between the accused and his accuser of the commonsense judgment of a group of laymen.". . . A requirement of unanimity, however, does not materially contribute to the exercise of this commonsense judgment. As we said in *Williams,* a jury will come to such a judgment as long as it consists of a group of laymen representative of a cross section of the community who have the duty and the opportunity to deliberate, free from outside attempts at intimidation, on the question of a defendant's guilt. In terms of this function we perceive no difference between juries required to act unanimously and those permitted to convict or acquit by votes of 10 to two or 11 to one. Requiring unanimity would obviously produce hung juries in some situations where nonunanimous juries will convict or acquit. But in either case, the interest of the defendant in having the judgment of his peers interposed between himself and the officers of the State who prosecute and judge him is equally well served.

III

Petitioners nevertheless argue that unanimity serves other purposes constitutionally essential to the continued operation of the jury system. Their principal contention is that a Sixth Amendment "jury trial". . . should be held to require a unanimous jury verdict in order to give substance to the reasonable doubt standard otherwise mandated by the Due Process Clause. . . .

We are quite sure, however, that the Sixth Amendment itself has never been held to require proof beyond a reasonable doubt in criminal cases. The reasonable doubt standard developed separately from both the jury trial and the unanimous verdict. . . . The reasonable doubt argument is rooted, in effect, in due process and has been rejected in *Johnson* v. *Louisiana, ante.*

IV

Petitioners also cite quite accurately a long line of decisions of this Court upholding the principle that the Fourteenth Amendment requires jury panels to reflect a cross section of the community. . . . They then contend that unanimity is a necessary precondition for effective application of the cross section requirement, because a rule permitting less than unanimous verdicts will make it possible for convictions to occur without the acquiescence of minority elements within the community. . . .

We . . . cannot accept petitioners' . . . assumption—that minority groups, even when they are represented on a jury, will not adequately represent the viewpoint of those groups simply because they may be outvoted in the final result. They will be present during all deliberations, and their views will be heard. We cannot assume that the majority of the jury will refuse to weigh the evidence and reach a decision upon rational grounds, just as it must now do in order to obtain unanimous verdicts, or that a majority will deprive a man of his liberty on the basis of prejudice when a minority is presenting a reasonable argument in favor of acquittal. We simply find no proof for the notion that a majority will disregard its instructions and cast its votes for guilt or innocence based on prejudice rather than the evidence.

We accordingly affirm the judgment of the Court of Appeals of Oregon.

It is so ordered.

Mr. Justice Blackmun, concurring.

I join the Court's opinion and judgment in each of these cases. I add only the comment . . . that in so doing I do not imply that I regard a State's split verdict system as a wise one. My vote means only that I cannot conclude that the system is constitutionally offensive. Were I a legislator, I would disfavor it as a matter of policy. Our task here, however, is not to pursue and strike down what happens to impress us as undesirable legislative policy.

I do not hesitate to say, either, that a system employing a 7–5 standard, rather than a 9–3 or 75% minimum, would afford me great difficulty. . . .

Mr. Justice Powell, concurring. . . .

. . . I concur in the plurality opinion in this case insofar as it concludes that a defendant in a state court may constitutionally be convicted by less than a unanimous verdict, but I am not in accord with a major premise upon which that judgment is based. Its premise is that the concept of a jury trial, as applicable to the States under the Fourteenth Amendment, must be identical in every detail to the concept required in federal courts by the Sixth Amendment. I do not think that all of the elements of jury trial within the meaning of the Sixth Amendment are necessarily embodied in or incorporated into the Due Process Clause of the Fourteenth Amendment. . . .

In an unbroken line of cases reaching back into the late 1800's, the Justices of this Court have recognized, virtually without dissent, that unanimity is one of the indispensable features of *federal* jury trial. . . . It therefore seems to me, in accord both with history and precedent, that the Sixth Amendment requires a unanimous jury verdict to convict in a federal criminal trial. . . .

The question, therefore, which should be addressed in this case is whether unanimity is in fact so fundamental to the essentials of jury trial that this particular requirement of the Sixth Amendment is necessarily binding on the States under the Due Process Clause of the Fourteenth Amendment. . . . Since I do not view Oregon's less than unanimous jury verdict requirement as violative of the due process guarantee of the Fourteenth Amendment, I concur in the Court's affirmance of these convictions.

Mr. Justice Douglas, with whom Mr. Justice Brennan and Mr. Justice Mrashall concur, dissenting. . . .

The plurality approves a procedure which diminishes the reliability of a jury. First, it eliminates the circumstances in which a minority or jurors (a) could have rationally persuaded the entire jury to acquit, or (b) while unable to persuade the majority to acquit, nonetheless could have convinced them to convict only on a lesser-included offense. Second, it permits prosecutors in Oregon ... to enjoy a conviction-acquittal ratio substantially greater than that ordinarily returned by unanimous juries.

The diminution of verdict reliability flows from the fact that nonunanimous juries need not debate and deliberate as fully as must unanimous juries. As soon as the requisite majority is attained, further consideration is not required ... even though the dissident jurors might, if given the chance, be able to convince the majority. Such persuasion does in fact occasionally occur in States where the unanimous requirement applies. . . .

The rationale of *Williams* can have no application here. *Williams* requires that the change be neither more nor less advantageous to either the State or the defendant. It is said that such a showing is satisfied here since a ... 2:10 verdict will result in acquittal. Yet experience shows that the less than unanimous jury overwhelmingly favors the States. . . .

The requirements of a unanimous jury verdict in criminal cases and proof beyond a reasonable doubt are so embedded in our constitutional law and touch so directly all the citizens and are such important barricades of liberty that if they are to be changed they should be introduced by constitutional amendment. . . .

Mr. Justice Brennan, with whom Mr. Justice Marshall joins, dissenting. . . .

Mr. Justice Stewart, with whom Mr. Justice Brennan and Mr. Justice Marshall join, dissenting. . . .

In *Duncan* v. *Louisiana* . . . the Court squarely held that the Sixth Amendment right to trial by jury in a federal criminal case is made wholly applicable to state criminal trials by the Fourteenth Amendment. Unless *Duncan* is to be overruled, therefore, the only relevant question here is whether the Sixth Amendment's guarantee of trial by jury embraces a guarantee that the verdict of the jury must be unanimous. The answer to that question is clearly "yes," as my Brother Powell has cogently demonstrated in that part of his concurring opinion that reviews almost a century of Sixth Amendment adjudication.

Until today, it has been universally understood that a unanimous verdict is an essential element of a Sixth Amendment jury trial. . . .

I would follow these settled Sixth Amendment precedents and reverse the judgment before us.

Mr. Justice Marshall, with whom Mr. Justice Brennan joins, dissenting. . . .

. . . The Court asserts that when a jury votes nine to three for conviction, the doubts of the three do not impeach the verdict of the nine. The argument seems to be that since, under *Williams,* nine jurors are enough to convict, the three dissenters are mere surplusage. But there is all the difference in the world between three jurors who aren't there, and three jurors who entertain doubts after hearing all the evidence. In the first case we can never know, and it is senseless to ask, whether the prosecutor might have persuaded additional jurors had they been present. But in the second case we know what has happened: the prosecutor has tried and failed to persuade those jurors of the defendant's guilt. In such circumstances, it does violence to language and to logic to say that the government has proved the defendant's guilt beyond a reasonable doubt. . . .

It should be noted that while five of the Justices in *Apodaca* held that the Fourteenth Amendment did not impose a unanimity requirement on state

criminal juries, there were also five Justices who stated that they construed the Sixth Amendment to demand unanimity in *federal* criminal trials.

Selection of Jurors

The Court has long held that the systematic and intentional exclusion of any class of persons, otherwise eligible to serve, from the jury lists is constitutionally invalid. Thus it was held as early as 1880 in *Strauder* v. *West Virginia,* 100 U.S. 303, that trial of a Negro defendant by a jury from which all Negroes were excluded by law was a denial of equal protection guaranteed by the Fourteenth Amendment. A long series of subsequent cases have uniformly followed this rule. *Avery* v. *Georgia,* 345 U.S. 559 (1953), presented a novel process for exclusion of Negroes. Prospective jurors had their names printed on tickets, with white persons on white tickets and Negroes on yellow tickets. The tickets were placed in a box, and a judge drew out the required number. These were given to the sheriff, who in turn handed them to the clerk, who typed up the final list for the panel. In the *Avery* case not a single Negro was selected to serve on a panel of sixty. The Court concluded that such a procedure established a prima facie case of discrimination, which the State failed to overcome. In *Hernandez* v. *Texas,* 347 U.S. 475 (1954), the Court reversed the conviction of Hernandez upon a finding that no person with a Mexican or Latin-American name had served on a jury in that county for twenty-five years. As the Court has often pointed out, however, there is no constitutional requirement of proportional representation or even that a particular jury have members of the race or economic class of the defendant. Carried to such an extreme, a bank robber would be able to claim one or more of his trade on the jury trying him. For the state to exclude any category, however, it must show reasons relevant to the function which the jury is required to perform, and not exclude merely on grounds of race or sex or whether one is salaried or an hourly wage earner. The issue of exclusion or exemption of women from jury service was considered in *Taylor* v. *Louisiana* in 1975.

TAYLOR *v.* LOUISIANA

419 U.S. 522 (1975)

[Prior to trial in a state court in Louisiana on a kidnapping charge, the defendant, a male, sought to quash the petit jury venire from which his jury would be selected, contending that women had been systematically excluded from the venire, thus depriving him of his federal constitutional right to a fair trial by a properly selected jury. The Louisiana Constitution excluded women from jury service selection unless they had previously filed a written declaration of their desire to be subject to jury service. Of the persons eligible for jury service in the judicial district in which Taylor was tried, 53 percent were women, but no more than 10 percent of the persons on the jury wheel were women, and none was selected for service on the defendant's venire. The motion to quash was denied, and at a trial before an all-male jury the defendant was convicted. The Supreme Court of Louisiana affirmed, holding the constitutional provision valid.]

Mr. Justice White delivered the opinion of the Court. . . .

The Louisiana jury selection system does not disqualify women from jury service, but in operation its conceded systematic impact is that only a very few women, grossly disproportionate to the number of eligible women in the community, are called for jury service. In this case, no women were on the venire from which the petit jury was drawn. The issue we have, therefore, is whether a jury selection system which operates to exclude from jury service an identifiable class of citizens constituting 53% of eligible jurors in the community comports with the Sixth and Fourteenth Amendments.

The State first insists that Taylor, a male, has no standing to object to the exclusion of women from his jury. But Taylor's claim is that he was constitutionally entitled to a jury drawn from a venire constituting a fair cross section of the community and that the jury that tried him was not such a jury by reason of the exclusion of women. Taylor was not a member of the excluded class; but there is no rule that claims such as Taylor presents may be made only by those defendants who are members of the group excluded from jury service. In *Peters* v. *Kiff* . . . (1972), the defendant, a white man, challenged his conviction on the ground that Negroes had been systematically excluded from jury service. Six members of the Court agreed that petitioner was entitled to present the issue and concluded that he had been deprived of his federal rights. Taylor, in the case before us, was similarly entitled to tender and have adjudicated the claim that the exclusion of women from jury service deprived him of the kind of fact finder to which he was constitutionally entitled.

The background against which this case must be decided includes our holding in *Duncan* v. *Louisiana* . . . (1968), that the Sixth Amendment's provision for jury trial is made binding on the States by virtue of the Fourteenth Amendment. Our inquiry is whether the presence of a fair cross section of the community on venires, panels or lists from which petit juries are drawn is essential to the fulfillment of the Sixth Amendment's guarantee of an impartial jury trial in criminal prosecutions.

The Court's prior cases are instructive. Both in the course of exercising its supervisory powers over trials in federal courts and in the constitutional context, the Court has unambiguously declared that the American concept of the jury trial contemplates a jury drawn from a fair cross section of the community. A unanimous Court stated in *Smith* v. *Texas* . . . (1940), that "it is part of the established tradition in the use of juries as instruments of public justice that the jury be a body truly representative of the community.". . .

The unmistakable import of this Court's opinions, at least since 1941, *Smith* v. *Texas, supra,* and not repudiated by intervening decisions, is that the selection of a petit jury from a representative cross section of the community is an essential component of the Sixth Amendment right to a jury trial. . . .

We accept the fair cross-section requirement as fundamental to the jury trial guaranteed by the Sixth Amendment and are convinced that the requirement has solid foundation. The purpose of a jury is to guard against the exercise of arbitrary power—to make available the commonsense judgment of the community as a hedge against the overzealous or mistaken prosecutor and in preference to the professional or perhaps overconditioned or biased response of a judge. . . . This prophylactic vehicle is not provided if the jury pool is made up of only special segments of the populace or if large, distinctive groups are excluded from the pool. Community participation in the administration of the criminal law, moreover, is not only consistent with our democratic heritage but is also critical to public confidence in the fairness of the criminal justice system. Restricting jury service to only special groups or excluding identifiable segments playing major roles in the community cannot be squared with the constitutional concept of jury trial. . . .

We are also persuaded that the fair cross section requirement is violated by the systematic exclusion of women, who in the judicial district involved here amounted to 53% of the citizens eligible for jury service. This conclusion necessarily entails the judgment that women are sufficiently numerous and distinct from men that if they are systematically eliminated from jury panels, the Sixth Amendment's fair cross section requirement cannot be satisfied. . . .

There remains the argument that women as a class serve a distinctive role in society and that jury service would so substantially interfere with that function that the State has ample justification for excluding women from service unless they volunteer, even though the result is that almost all jurors are men. . . .

The States are free to grant exemptions from jury service to individuals in case of special hardship or incapacity and to those engaged in particular occupations the uninterrupted performance of which is critical of the community's welfare. . . . It would not appear that such exemptions would pose substantial threats that the remaining pool of jurors would not be representative of the community. A system excluding all women, however, is a wholly different matter. It is untenable to suggest these days that it would be a special hardship for each and every woman to perform jury service or that society cannot spare *any* women from their present duties. This may be the case with many, and it may be burdensome to sort out those who should not be exempted from those who should serve. But that task is performed in the case of men, and the administrative convenience in dealing with women as a class is insufficient justification for diluting the quality of community judgment represented by the jury in criminal trials. . . .

It should also be emphasized that in holding that petit juries must be drawn from a source fairly representative of the community we impose no requirement that petit juries actually chosen must mirror the community and reflect the various distinctive groups in the population. Defendants are not entitled to a jury of any particular composition . . . , but the jury wheels, pools of names, panels or venires from which juries are drawn must not systematically exclude distinctive groups in the community and thereby fail to be reasonably representative thereof.

The judgment of the Louisiana Supreme Court is reversed and the case remanded to that court for further proceedings not inconsistent with this opinion.

So ordered.

Mr. Chief Justice Burger concurred in the result.

Mr. Justice Rehnquist, dissenting.

The Court's opinion reverses a conviction without a suggestion, much less a showing, that the appellant has been unfairly treated or prejudiced in any way by the manner in which his jury was selected. In so doing, the Court invalidates a jury selection system which it approved by a substantial majority only 13 years ago. I disagree with the Court and would affirm the judgment of the Supreme Court of Louisiana.

The majority opinion canvasses various of our jury trial cases, beginning with *Smith* v. *Texas*. . . . Relying on carefully chosen quotations, it concludes that the "unmistakable import" of our cases is that the fair cross section requirement "is an essential component of the Sixth Amendment right to a jury trial." I disagree. Fairly read, the only "unmistakable import" of those cases is that due process and equal protection prohibit jury selection systems which are likely to result in biased or partial juries. . . .

Absent any suggestion that appellant's trial was unfairly conducted, or that its result was unreliable, I would not require Louisiana to retry him (assuming the

State can once again produce its evidence and witnesses) in order to impose on him the sanctions which its laws provide.

In *Daniel* v. *Louisiana,* 420 U.S. 31 (1975), decided one week after *Taylor,* the Court held that the rule of *Taylor* v. *Louisiana* would not be applied retroactively.

Impartial Juries

The Sixth Amendment requires that the federal jury, in addition to some of the common-law aspects, must be "impartial." The Court apparently incorporated this requirement into the Fourteenth Amendment in *Parker* v. *Gladden,* 385 U.S. 363 (1966). In so doing it reversed a conviction following a trial during which a bailiff, assigned to shepherd the sequestered jury, had stated to one of the jurors, in the presence of others, that the defendant was guilty. As in *Turner* v. *Louisiana,* 379 U.S. 466 (1965), where a similar situation occurred, the Court held this to be a denial of the right of confrontation also.

There are three stages at which issues of partiality may occur in connection with jury trial: (1) when the general jury panel is drawn for a term of court; (2) when the jurors are drawn from the general panel for a specific case; and (3) during the course of the trial. Problems at the first stage result from improper exclusions in either the law or the administration of the juror qualification law. The problem at the second stage is basically that of eliminating jurors who have an improper bias in the specific case on which they might serve. At the third stage the issue is presented if jurors are improperly influenced, as by bribery or other illegal persuasion, during the course of the trial.

The first of these stages presents the most difficult constitutional problem, and is the one to be treated here. The second stage can normally be handled by the method of examining prospective jurors under oath and removing ("for cause") those found to be unduly prejudiced or to have an interest in the case. (In addition, each side is allowed a specified number of "peremptory" challenges for which no reason need by assigned.) On occasion, because of unusual notoriety, it may be impossible to impanel an impartial jury in the locality in which the crime occurred. In such instances the guarantee of impartiality can only be met by granting a continuance or a change of venue to allow the trial to take place in another location. (The problem of "trial by newspaper" is treated at some length in Chapter 6, in the section "Free Press v. Fair Administration of Justice.")

The third problem is partially avoided by careful admonition of jurors in advance by the judge and, frequently, by close guard during the course of the trial. Violators are dealt with severely, and tampering with the jury is ground for declaring a mistrial (if the trial is still in progress) or vacating the judgment (if the trial has been concluded).

One problem concerning the "impartial jury" was presented by the fact that government employees served on juries in criminal cases brought by the United States In the District of Columbia. In *Crawford* v. *United States,* 212 U.S. 183 (1909), the Court decided, on common-law grounds, that such employees were disqualified in federal criminal proceedings. As the number of government employees in the district increased and jury panels became more difficult to fill, Congress in 1935 removed the disqualification by statute. The act was held valid in *United States* v. *Wood,* 299 U.S. 123 (1936). By a narrow majority the Court in *Frazier* v. *United States,* 335 U.S. 497 (1948), held that government employees as a class are not disqualified by an implied bias against defendants. Of course, individual employees may be disqualified if shown to have actual bias.

Even though the general panel and the specific jury are chosen in accordance with statutory and constitutional requirements, subjection of the jury to improper pressures during the course of a trial may be sufficient to violate the accused's right to an impartial jury. This was the claim made in *Turner* v. *Louisiana,* 379 U.S. 466 (1965), in challenging a conviction for murder. During the three-day trial, two deputy sheriffs, who were the two principal prosecution witnesses, were charged with the supervision of the jurors. Thus they were in continuous company with the jurors. They drove the jurors to a restaurant for each meal, and to their lodgings each night. The deputies ate with them, conversed with them, and did errands for them.

Defendant's counsel moved for a mistrial when the deputies testified, but the court denied the motions on the ground that there was no showing that either deputy had talked with any member of the jury about the case itself. Defendant was convicted and sentenced to death, and the Louisiana Supreme Court affirmed.

On certiorari, the United States Supreme Court reversed, with Justice Clark filing the only dissenting vote. Justice Stewart, for the majority, discussed the due process problem:

> In the constitutional sense, trial by jury in a criminal case necessarily implies at the very least that the "evidence developed" against a defendant shall come from the witness stand in a public courtroom where there is full judicial protection of the defendant's right of confrontation, of cross-examination, and of counsel. What happened in this case operated to subvert these basic guarantees of trial by jury. . . . [T]he credibility which the jury attached to the testimony of these two key witnesses must inevitably have determined whether Wayne Turner was to be sent to his death. To be sure, their credibility was assailed by Turner's counsel through cross-examination in open court. But the potentialities of what went on outside the courtroom during the three days of the trial may well have made these courtroom proceedings little more than a hollow formality. . . .
> . . . We deal here not with a brief encounter, but with a continuous and intimate association throughout a three-day trial—an association which gave these witnesses an opportunity, as [one deputy] put it, to renew old friendships and make new acquaintances among the members of the jury. . . . [T]he relationship was one which could not but foster the jurors' confidence in those who were their official guardians during the entire period of the trial. And Turner's fate depended upon how much confidence the jury placed in these two witnesses.

Justice Clark "with regret" dissented. In view of the fact that "no prejudice whatever is shown," and in view of the widespread acceptance of the practice of permitting an officer who testifies in a case also to be in charge of the jury, he felt that it could not be considered violative of the Fourteenth Amendment's due process clause.

[See James Bradley Thayer, *A Preliminary Treatise on Evidence at the Common Law* (Boston: Little, Brown, 1898); Sir Patrick Devlin, *Trial by Jury* (London: Stevens, 1956); Felix Frankfurter and Thomas G. Gorcoran, "Petty Federal Offenses and the Constitutional Guaranty of Trial by Jury," 39 *Harv.*

L. Rev. 917 (1926); and Harry Kalven, Jr., and Hans Zeisel, *The American Jury* (Boston: Little, Brown, 1966).]

GUILTY PLEAS

The previous sections treating various aspects of trial procedures should not, of course, lead to the conclusion that the usual course of a criminal prosecution involves a full court trial. The far more common practice is for the defendant to plead guilty and for the judge to pass sentence, thus by-passing the trial aspects completely. The Task Force Report *The Courts,* prepared by the President's Commission on Law Enforcement and Adminis-tration of Justice in 1967, suggests that guilty pleas account for 90 percent of all convictions, and perhaps as high as 95 percent of misdemeanor convic-tions. A substantial percentage of guilty pleas are a result of negotiations between the prosecutor and the defendant (or his attorney)—a process commonly termed "plea bargaining." The three customary bargaining points are: (1) the recommendation of a lesser sentence than might normally be given; (2) the reduction of the charge to a lesser offense; and (3) the dis-missal of some charges where multiple offenses or charges are listed in the indictment.

There is considerable unease and suspicion surrounding the process of plea bargaining, and in 1973 the United States National Advisory Commission on Criminal Justice Standards and Goals went so far as to recommend its abolition by 1978. This does not appear to be the view of most court special-ists, however, who prefer to retain the process but provide certain reforms. (See the *Report on Courts* of the Advisory Commission, p. 49.) Certainly our system of criminal justice has come to rely upon a steady flow of guilty pleas. There are not enough personnel—judges, prosecutors, or defense coun-sel—or even enough courtrooms to operate a system in which most de-fendants go to trial. Despite this fact, it is clear that the process of plea bargaining carries with it certain problems. Some of these are: (1) suspicion that the process may be employed for purely political gain by the prosecutor; (2) the question of the propriety of offering a defendant an inducement to surrender his right to trial; (3) the gamble on the defendant's part that the judge will, in fact, assign a lesser sentence; or (4) the potential for deliberate overcharging by the prosecutor to exert pressure for a guilty plea.

The most important Supreme Court decision to date on the guilty plea and subsequent sentencing is *Santobello* v. *New York* in 1971.

SANTOBELLO *v.* NEW YORK
404 U.S. 257 (1971)

[After being indicted on two felony gambling counts under New York statutes, and after negotiating with the prosecuting attorney, the defendant withdrew his not guilty plea and entered a guilty plea to a lesser included offense, the prosecutor agreeing to make no recommendation as to the sentence to be imposed. The New York trial court accepted the guilty plea and set a date for a sentencing hearing, which was subsequently postponed. Some six months later, after several days, the hearing was held, at which a new prosecuting attorney appeared. Apparently un-aware of the previous prosecutor's commitment, he recommended that the maximum one-year sentence be imposed. Although the defendant objected and sought adjournment of the sentencing hearing, the judge stated that he was not influenced by the prosecutor's recommendation and imposed the maximum sentence on the basis of a presentence report. The Appellate Division of the New York Supreme Court affirmed, and the Court of Appeals denied leave to appeal.]

Mr. Chief Justice Burger delivered the opinion of the Court.

We granted certiorari in this case to determine whether the State's failure to keep a commitment concerning the sentence recommendation on a guilty plea required a new trial. . . .

This record represents another example of an unfortunate lapse in orderly prosecutorial procedures, in part, no doubt, because of the enormous increase in the workload of the often understaffed prosecutor's offices. The heavy workload may well explain these episodes, but it does not excuse them. The disposition of criminal charges by agreement between the prosecutor and the accused, sometimes loosely called "plea bargaining," is an essential component of the administration of justice. Properly administered, it is to be encouraged. If every criminal charge were subjected to a full-scale trial, the States and the Federal Government would need to multiply by many times the number of judges and court facilities.

Disposition of charges after plea discussions is not only an essential part of the process but a highly desirable part for many reasons. It leads to prompt and largely final disposition of most criminal cases; it avoids much of the corrosive impact of enforced idleness during pretrial confinement for those who are denied release pending trial; it protects the public from those accused persons who are prone to continue criminal conduct even while on pretrial release; and, by shortening the time between charge and disposition, it enhances whatever may be the rehabilitative prospects of the guilty when they are ultimately imprisoned. . . .

However, all of these considerations presuppose fairness in securing agreement between an accused and a prosecutor. It is now clear, for example, that the accused pleading guilty must be counseled, absent a waiver. *Moore* v. *Michigan*, 355 U.S. 155 (1957). Fed. Rule Crim. Proc. 11, governing pleas in federal courts, now makes clear that the sentencing judge must develop, *on the record,* the factual basis for the plea, as, for example, by having the accused describe the conduct that gave rise to the charge. The plea must, of course, be voluntary and knowing and if it was induced by promises, the essence of those promises must in some way be made known. There is, of course, no absolute right to have a guilty plea accepted. . . . A court may reject a plea in exercise of sound judicial discretion. . . .

On this record, petitioner "bargained" and negotiated for a particular plea in order to secure dismissal of more serious charges, but also on condition that no sentence recommendation would be made by the prosecutor. It is now conceded that the promise to abstain from a recommendation was made, and at this stage the prosecution is not in a good position to argue that its inadvertent breach of agreement is immaterial. The staff lawyers in a prosecutor's office have the burden of "letting the left hand know what the right hand is doing" or has done. That the breach of agreement was inadvertent does not lessen its impact.

We need not reach the question whether the sentencing judge would or would not have been influenced had he known all the details of the negotiations for the plea. He stated that the prosecutor's recommendation did not influence him and we have no reason to doubt that. Nevertheless, we conclude that the interests of justice and appropriate recognition of the duties of the prosecution in relation to promises made in the negotiation of pleas of guilty will be best served by remanding the case to the state courts for further consideration. The ultimate relief to which petitioner is entitled we leave to the discretion of the state court, which is in a better position to decide whether the circumstances of this case require only that there be specific performance of the agreement on the plea, in which case petitioner should be resentenced by a different judge, or whether, in the view of the state court, the circumstances require granting the relief sought by petitioner, i.e., the opportunity to withdraw his plea of guilty. We emphasize that this is in no sense to question the fairness of the sentencing judge; the fault here rests on the prosecutor, not on the sentencing judge.

The judgment is vacated and the case is remanded for reconsideration not inconsistent with this opinion.

Mr. Justice Douglas, concurring. . . .

I join the opinion of the Court and favor a constitutional rule for this as well as for other pending or on-coming cases. Where the "plea bargain" is not kept by the prosecutor, the sentence must be vacated and the state court will decide in light of the circumstances of each case whether due process requires (a) that there be specific performance of the plea bargain or (b) that the defendant be given the option to go on trial on the original charges. One alternative may do justice on one case, and the other in a different case. In choosing a remedy, however, a court ought to accord a defendant's preference considerable, if not controlling, weight inasmuch as the fundamental rights flouted by a prosecutor's breach of a plea bargain are those of the defendant, not of the State.

Mr. Justice Marshall, with whom Mr. Justice Brennan and Mr. Justice Stewart join, concurring in part and dissenting in part.

I agree with much of the majority's opinion, but conclude that petitioner must be permitted to withdraw his guilty plea. . . .

Here, petitioner never claimed any automatic right to withdraw a guilty plea before sentencing. Rather, he tendered a specific reason why, in his case, the plea should be vacated. His reason was that the prosecutor had broken a promise made in return for the agreement to plead guilty. When a prosecutor breaks the bargain, he undercuts the basis for the waiver of constitutional rights implicit in the plea. This, it seems to me, provides the defendant ample justification for rescinding the plea. . . .

CRUEL AND UNUSUAL PUNISHMENTS

The Eighth Amendment provides that "cruel and unusual punishments" shall not be inflicted. The phraseology derives from the English Bill of Rights of 1689, and similar provisions were found in colonial records in this country. Presumably the guarantee bars such ancient practices as branding, drawing and quartering, burning alive, or crucifixion. But the death penalty as such has not been held to violate the provision as long as it is carried out without unnecessary cruelty. In upholding execution by a firing squad, in *Wilkerson* v. *Utah*, 99 U.S. 130 (1879), the Court stated, "Difficulty would attend the effort to define with exactness the extent of the constitutional provision which provides that cruel and unusual punishments shall not be inflicted, but it is safe to affirm that punishments of torture, . . . and all others in the same line of unnecessary cruelty, are forbidden by that Amendment to the Constitution."

Not only the *manner* of punishment but also the severity of the penalty in relation to the crime has been considered an appropriate issue within the scope of the guarantee. In *Weems* v. *United States,* 217 U.S. 349 (1910), the Court held invalid a Philippine statute prescribing fine and imprisonment in irons from twelve to twenty years for entry of a known false statement in a public record, on the ground that the gross disparity between this punishment and that imposed for other more serious crimes violated the prohibition against cruel and unusual punishments.

In *Louisiana ex rel. Francis* v. *Resweber,* 329 U.S. 459 (1947), four members of the Court assumed, "but without so deciding," that the Eighth Amendment's prohibition was binding on the states through the Fourteenth Amendment. The case involved a claim of cruel and unusual punishment where petitioner had been placed in the electric chair and the switch thrown, without consequent death, and the subsequent setting of a second date for execution. The state contended that the failure was due to a mechanical defect, that it was unintended, and that a subsequent execution would not be a denial of due process. The petitioner contended that to force him to undergo the strain of preparing for execution, actually to place him in the electric chair and throw the switch, and then to send him back to prison to be subjected to the whole process again, was a cruel and unusual punishment even if unintentional. By a five-to-four vote the Court upheld the state's position, stressing that it was an unforeseeable accident with "no purpose to inflict unnecessary pain." Four justices dissented, pointing out that the intent of the executioner was immaterial to the issue of cruel and unusual punishment, and protesting "death by installments."

In *Trop* v. *Dulles,* 356 U.S. 86 (1958), the Court held invalid the denationalization of a native-born citizen convicted by a court-martial of desertion from the military or naval forces in time of war and dismissed or dishonorably discharged. One of the grounds for invalidation was that divestiture of citizenship in such case was a cruel and unusual punishment. Chief Justice Warren, speaking for four members of the Court, said, "This Court has had little occasion to give precise content to the Eighth Amendment," but the scope of the Amendment "is not static. The Amendment must draw its meaning from the evolving standards of decency that mark the progress of a maturing society."

On the merits, the Chief Justice stated that denationalization in this case was a violation of the Eighth Amendment:

> There may be involved no physical mistreatment, no primitive torture. There is instead the total destruction of the individual's status in organized society. It is a form of punishment more primitive than torture, for it destroys for the individual the political existence that was centuries in the development. . . . His very existence is at the sufferance of the country in which he happens to find himself. . . . In short, the expatriate has lost the right to have rights.

Concurring separately, Justice Brennan agreed that such punishment was unduly severe in relationship to the power Congress was exercising, but he stopped short of holding it violative of the Eighth Amendment.

More recently, in *Robinson* v. *California,* 370 U.S. 660 (1962), the Court held invalid a California statute making it a misdemeanor for a person to "be addicted to the use of narcotics," subject to a mandatory jail term of not less than ninety days. Justice Stewart, speaking for five members of the Court, pointed out that the statute was not the usual one which punished for the use, purchase, sale, or possession of narcotics, but it was rather a statute "which makes the 'status' of narcotic addiction a criminal offense, for which the offender may be prosecuted 'at any time before he reforms.'" He concluded:

We hold that a state law which imprisons a person thus afflicted as a criminal, even though he has never touched any narcotic drug within the State or been guilty of any irregular behavior there, inflicts a cruel and unusual punishment in violation of the Fourteenth Amendment. To be sure, imprisonment for ninety days is not, in the abstract, a punishment which is either cruel or unusual. But the question cannot be considered in the abstract. Even one day in prison would be a cruel and unusual punishment for the "crime" of having a common cold.

For many years campaigns have been waged to try to abolish capital punishment. It is argued that neither on grounds of morality nor utility can such a severe penalty be justified. While some measure of success has been achieved in the fact that over the past two decades a number of states have abolished the death penalty, the proponents of abolition have long sought a decision from the Supreme Court that capital punishment was a violation of the Eighth Amendment's bar to cruel and unusual punishments. The Court managed to avoid the issue for many years, however, by denial of certiorari, as in *Rudolph* v. *Alabama,* 375 U.S. 889 (1963), with three Justices registering a strong dissent. The decision finally came, although limited in scope, in 1972 in *Furman* v. *Georgia,* 408 U.S. 238. By a vote of five-to-four the Court held that the death penalty, *as then imposed,* constituted cruel and unusual punishment in violation of the Eighth Amendment. The four Nixon appointees dissented. Nine separate opinions were filed, and the majority was split on the rationale for the decision. Justices Brennan and Marshall were the only members to state that the death penalty was *per se* a violation of the Eighth Amendment. Others of the majority stressed the discriminatory aspects of the sentence, citing studies which showed that the poor, the disadvantaged, and the minorities were the primary recipients of such sentences, and the broad discretion in juries to mete out either the death penalty or a term in prison. Justice Stewart emphasized the point that the Eighth Amendment "cannot tolerate the infliction of a sentence of death under legal systems that permit this unique penalty to be so wantonly and so freakishly imposed." Following the decision, states with capital punishment laws began revision of their statutes to try to meet the objections outlined in *Furman.* Some read *Furman* as ordering a complete removal of sentencing discretion and adopted new laws making the death penalty mandatory for specified crimes. Others provided for various degrees of discretion in the sentencing body but specified guidelines to be used in the decision to order the death penalty.

On July 2, 1976, the Court rendered decisions on the constitutionality of the new death penalty statutes of five states—Georgia, Florida, Texas, Louisiana, and North Carolina. Some 600 prisoners on death row in various states had been anxiously awaiting the verdict. The statutes of North Carolina and Louisiana were held invalid on the ground that the mandatory death sentence did not allow for appropriate differentiation between persons convicted of the same crime, and thus violated the Eighth Amendment's requirement of "civilized standards" for punishment. The statutes of the other three states were upheld as providing for properly controlled sentencing discretion. A majority of seven held clearly that capital punishment *per se* was not unconstitutional. The Georgia case contains fuller analyses and is selected for illustration. (The other cases are *Profitt* v. *Florida*, 44 L.W. 5256, *Jurek* v. *Texas*, 44 L.W. 5262, *Woodson* v. *North Carolina*, 44 L.W. 5267, and *Roberts* v. *Louisiana*, 44 L.W. 5281.)

GREGG *v.* GEORGIA
44 L.W. 5230 (1976)

[The petitioner, Troy Gregg, was charged with committing armed robbery and murder on the basis of evidence that he had killed and robbed two men.]

Mr. Justice Stewart, Mr. Justice Powell, and Mr. Justice Stevens announced the judgment of the Court and filed an opinion delivered by Mr. Justice Stewart.

The issue in this case is whether the imposition of the sentence of death for the crime of murder under the law of Georgia violates the Eighth and Fourteenth Amendments.

I

The trial judge submitted the murder charges to the jury on both felony-murder and nonfelony-murder theories. He also instructed on the issue of self-defense but declined to instruct on manslaughter. He submitted the robbery case to the jury on both an armed-robbery theory and on the lesser included offense of robbery by intimidation. The jury found the petitioner guilty of two counts of armed robbery and two counts of murder.

At the penalty stage, which took place before the same jury, neither the prosecutor nor the petitioner's lawyer offered any additional evidence. Both counsel, however, made lengthy arguments dealing generally with the propriety of capital punishment under the circumstances and with the weight of the evidence of guilt. The trial judge instructed the jury that it could recommend either a death sentence or a life prison sentence on each count. The judge further charged the jury that in determining what sentence was appropriate the jury was free to consider the facts and circumstances presented by the parties, if any, in mitigation or aggravation.

Finally, the judge instructed the jury that it "would not be authorized to consider [imposing] the sentence of death" unless it first found beyond a reasonable doubt one of these aggravating circumstances:

"One—That the offense of murder was committed while the offender was engaged in the commission o[f] two other capit[a]l felonies, towit the armed ro[b]bery of [Simons and Moore].

"Two—That the offender committed the offense of murder for the purpose of receiving money and the automobile described in the indictment.

"Three—The offense of murder was outrageously and wantonly vile, horrible and inhuman, in that they [*sic*] involved the depravity of the mind of the defendant."

Finding the first and second of these circumstances, the jury returned verdicts of death on each count.

The Supreme Court of Georgia affirmed the convictions and the imposition of the death sentences for murder.... After reviewing the trial transcript and the record, including the evidence, and comparing the evidence and sentence in similar cases in accordance with the requirements of Georgia law, the court concluded that, considering the nature of the crime and the defendant, the sentences of death had not resulted from prejudice or any other arbitrary factor and were not excessive or disproportionate to the penalty applied in similar cases. The death sentences imposed for armed robbery, however, were vacated on the grounds that the death penalty had rarely been imposed in Georgia for that offense and that the jury improperly considered the murders as aggravating circumstances for the robberies after having considered the armed robberies as aggravating circumstances for the murders. . . .

II

Before considering the issues presented it is necessary to understand the Georgia statutory scheme for the imposition of the death penalty. The Georgia statute, as amended after our decision in *Furman* v. *Georgia*, . . . retains the death penalty for six categories of crime: murder, kidnapping for ransom or where the victim is harmed, armed robbery, rape, treason, and aircraft hijacking. . . . The capital defendant's guilt or innocence is determined in the traditional manner, either by a trial judge or a jury, in the first stage of a bifurcated trial.

If a trial is by jury, the trial judge is required to charge lesser included offenses when they are supported by any view of the evidence. . . . After a verdict, finding, or plea of guilty to a capital crime, a presentence hearing is conducted before whomever made the determination of guilt. The sentencing procedures are essentially the same in both bench and jury trials. . . .

. . . Before a convicted defendant may be sentenced to death, however, the jury, or the trial judge in cases tried without a jury, must find beyond a reasonable doubt one of the 10 aggravating circumstances specified in the statute.* The sentence of death may be imposed only if the jury (or judge) finds one of the statutory aggravating circumstances and then elects to impose that sentence. . . . If the verdict is death the jury or judge must specify the aggravating circumstance(s) found. . . . In jury cases, the trial judge is bound by the jury's recommended sentence. . . .

In addition to the conventional appellate process available in all criminal cases, provision is made for special expedited direct review by the Supreme Court of Georgia of the appropriateness of imposing the sentence of death in the particular case. The court is directed to consider "the punishment as well as any errors enumerated by way of appeal," and to determine:

"(1) Whether the sentence of death was imposed under the influence of passion, prejudice, or any other arbitrary factor, and

---

* The statute provides in part: . . .

"(1) The offense of murder, rape, armed robbery, or kidnapping was committed by a person with a prior record of conviction for a capital felony, or the offense of murder was committed by a person who has a substantial history of serious assaultive criminal convictions.

"(2) The offense of murder, rape, armed robbery, or kidnapping was committed while the offender was engaged in the commission of another capital felony, or aggravated battery, or the offense of murder was committed while the offender was engaged in the commission of burglary or arson in the first degree.

"(3) The offender by his act of murder, armed robbery, or kidnapping knowingly created a great risk of death to more than one person in a public place by means of a weapon or device which would normally be hazardous to the lives of more than one person.

"(4) The offender committed the offense of murder for himself or another, for the purpose of receiving money or any other thing of monetary value.

"(5) The murder of a judicial officer, former judicial officer, district attorney or solicitor or former district attorney or solicitor during or because of the exercise of his official duty.

"(6) The offender caused or directed another to commit murder or committed murder as an agent or employee of another person.

"(7) The offense of murder, rape, armed robbery, or kidnapping was outrageously or wantonly vile, horrible or inhuman in that it involved torture, depravity of mind, or an aggravated battery to the victim.

"(8) The offense of murder was committed against any peace officer, corrections employee or fireman while engaged in the performance of his official duties.

"(9) The offense of murder was committed by a person in, or who has escaped from, the lawful custody of a peace officer or place of lawful confinement.

"(10) The murder was committed for the purpose of avoiding, interfering with, or preventing a lawful arrest or custody in a place of lawful confinement, of himself or another.

"(2) Whether, in cases other than treason or aircraft hijacking, the evidence supports the jury's or judge's finding of a statutory aggravating circumstance as enumerated [in the law], and

"(3) Whether the sentence of death is excessive or disproportionate to the penalty imposed in similar cases, considering both the crime and the defendant.". . . If the court affirms a death sentence, it is required to include in its decision reference to similar cases that it has taken into consideration. . . .

. . . Under its special review authority, the court may either affirm the death sentence or remand the case for resentencing. In cases in which the death sentence is affirmed there remains the possibility of executive clemency.

III

We address initially the basic contention that the punishment of death for the crime of murder is, under all circumstances, "cruel and unusual" in violation of the Eighth and Fourteenth Amendments of the Constitution. . . . [Here the opinion reviews the history of the "cruel and unusual" provision of the Eighth Amendment and concludes with the statement that history and precedent strongly support a negative answer to the question of whether capital punishment is violative of that provision. "The imposition of the death penalty for the crime of murder has a long history of acceptance both in the United States and in England."]

Four years ago, the petitioners in Furman and its companion cases predicated their argument primarily upon the asserted proposition that standards of decency had evolved to the point where capital punishment no longer could be tolerated. The petitioners in those cases said, in effect, that the evolutionary process had come to an end, and that standards of decency required that the Eighth Amendment be construed finally as prohibiting capital punishment for any crime regardless of its depravity and impact on society. This view was accepted by two Justices. Three other Justices were unwilling to go so far; focusing on the procedures by which convicted defendants were selected for the death penalty rather than on the actual punishment inflicted, they joined in the conclusion that the statutes before the Court were constitutionally invalid.

The petitioners in the capital cases before the Court today renew the "standards of decency" argument, but developments during the four years since Furman have undercut substantially the assumptions upon which their argument rested. Despite the continuing debate, dating back to the 19th century, over the morality and utility of capital punishment, it is now evident that a large proportion of American society continues to regard it as an appropriate and necessary criminal sanction.

The most marked indication of society's endorsement of the death penalty for murder is the legislative response to Furman. The legislatures of at least 35 States have enacted new statutes that provide for the death penalty for at least some crimes that result in the death of another person. And the Congress of the United States, in 1974, enacted a statute providing the death penalty for aircraft piracy that results in death. . . .

The jury also is a significant and reliable objective index of contemporary values because it is so directly involved. . . . Indeed, the actions of juries in many States since Furman is fully compatible with the legislative judgments, reflected in the new statutes, as to the continued utility and necessity of capital punishment in appropriate cases. At the close of 1974 at least 254 persons had been sentenced to death since Furman, and by the end of March 1976, more than 460 persons were subject to death sentences.

As we have seen, however, the Eighth Amendment demands more than that a challenged punishment be acceptable to contemporary society. The Court also must ask whether it comports with the basic concept of human dignity at the core of the Amendment. . . .

The death penalty is said to serve two principal social purposes: retribution and deterrence of capital crimes by prospective offenders.

In part, capital punishment is an expression of society's moral outrage at particularly offensive conduct. This function may be unappealing to many, but it is essential in an ordered society that asks its citizens to rely on legal processes rather than self-help to vindicate their wrongs. . . . "Retribution is no longer the dominant objective of the criminal law," . . . but neither is it a forbidden objective nor one inconsistent with our respect for the dignity of men. . . . Indeed, the decision that capital punishment may be the appropriate sanction in extreme cases is an expression of the community's belief that certain crimes are themselves so grievous an affront to humanity that the only adequate response may be the penalty of death.

Statistical attempts to evaluate the worth of the death penalty as a deterrent to crimes by potential offenders have occasioned a great deal of debate. The results simply have been inconclusive. . . .

Although some of the studies suggest that the death penalty may not function as a significantly greater deterrent than lesser penalties, there is no convincing empirical evidence either supporting or refuting this view. We may nevertheless assume safely that there are murderers, such as those who act in passion, for whom the threat of death has little or no deterrent effect. But for many others, the death penalty undoubtedly is a significant deterrent. There are carefully contemplated murders, such as murder for hire, where the possible penalty of death may well enter into the cold calculus that precedes the decision to act. And there are some categories of murder, such as murder by a life prisoner, where other sanctions may not be adequate.

The value of capital punishment as a deterrent of crime is a complex factual issue the resolution of which properly rests with the legislatures, which can evaluate the results of statistical studies in terms of their own local conditions and with a flexibility of approach that is not available to the courts. . . . Indeed, many of the post-*Furman* statutes reflect just such a responsible effort to define those crimes and those criminals for which capital punishment is most probably an effective deterrent.

In sum, we cannot say that the judgment of the Georgia legislature that capital punishment may be necessary in some cases is clearly wrong. Considerations of federalism, as well as respect for the ability of a legislature to evaluate, in terms of its particular state the moral consensus concerning the death penalty and its social utility as a sanction, require us to conclude, in the absence of more convincing evidence, that the infliction of death as a punishment for murder is not without justification and thus is not unconstitutionally severe. . . .

We hold that the death penalty is not a form of punishment that may never be imposed, regardless of the circumstances of the offense, regardless of the character of the offender, and regardless of the procedure followed in reaching the decision to impose it.

IV

We now consider whether Georgia may impose the death penalty on the petitioner in this case.

A

While *Furman* did not hold that the infliction of the death penalty *per se* violates the Constitution's ban on cruel and unusual punishments, it did recognize that the penalty of death is different in kind from any other punishment imposed under our system of criminal justice. Because of the uniqueness of the death penalty, *Furman* held that it could not be imposed under sentencing procedures that created a substantial risk that it would be inflicted in an arbitrary and capricious manner. . . .

Furman mandates that where discretion is afforded a sentencing body on a matter so grave as the determination of whether a human life should be taken or spared, that discretion must be suitably directed and limited so as to minimize the risk of wholly arbitrary and capricious action. . . .

While some have suggested that standards to guide a capital jury's sentencing deliberations are impossible to formulate, the fact is that such standards have been developed. When the drafters of the Model Penal Code faced this problem, they concluded "that it is within the realm of possibility to point to the main circumstances of aggravation and of mitigation that should be weighed, *and weighed against each other,* when they are presented in a concrete case.". . . While such standards are by necessity somewhat general, they do provide guidance to the sentencing authority and thereby reduce the likelihood that it will impose a sentence that fairly can be called capricious and arbitrary. Where the sentencing authority is required to specify the factors it relied upon in reaching its decision, the further safeguard of meaningful appellate review is available to ensure that death sentences are not imposed capriciously or in a freakish manner.

In summary, the concerns expressed in *Furman* that the penalty of death not be imposed in an arbitrary or capricious manner can be met by a carefully drafted statute that ensures that the sentencing authority is given adequate information and guidance. As a general proposition these concerns are best met by a system that provides for a bifurcated proceeding at which the sentencing authority is apprised of the information relevant to the imposition of sentence and provided with standards to guide its use of the information.

We do not intend to suggest that only the above-described procedures would be permissible under *Furman* or that any sentencing system constructed along these general lines would inevitably satisfy the concerns of *Furman,* for each distinct system must be examined on an individual basis. Rather, we have embarked upon this general exposition to make clear that it is possible to construct capital-sentencing systems capable of meeting *Furman's* constitutional concerns.

B

We now turn to consideration of the constitutionality of Georgia's capital-sentencing procedures. . . .

These procedures require the jury to consider the circumstances of the crime and the criminal before it recommends sentence. No longer can a Georgia jury do as Furman's jury did: reach a finding of the defendant's guilt and then, without guidance or direction, decide whether he should live or die. Instead, the jury's attention is directed to the specific circumstances of the crime: Was it committed in the course of another capital felony? Was it committed for money? Was it committed upon a peace officer or judicial officer? Was it committed in a particularly heinous way or in a manner that endangered the lives of many persons? In addition, the jury's attention is focused on the characteristics of the person who committed the crime: Does he have a record of prior convictions for capital offenses? Are there any special facts about this defendant that mitigate against imposing capital punishment (e.g., his youth, the extent of his cooperation with the police, his emotional state at the time of the crime). As a result, while some jury discretion still exists, "the discretion to be exercised is controlled by clear and objective standards so as to produce non-discriminatory application.". . .

As an important additional safeguard against arbitrariness and caprice, the Georgia statutory scheme provides for automatic appeal of all death sentences to the State's supreme court. That court is required by statute to review each sentence of death and determine whether it was imposed under the influence of passion or prejudice, whether the evidence supports the jury's finding of a statutory aggravating circumstance, and whether the sentence is disproportionate compared to those sentences imposed in similar cases. . . .

The petitioner contends, however, that the changes in the Georgia sentencing procedures are only cosmetic, that the arbitrariness and capriciousness condemned by *Furman* continue to exist in Georgia—both in traditional practices that still remain and in the new sentencing procedures adopted in response to *Furman*.

I

First, the petitioner focuses on the opportunities for discretionary action that are inherent in the processing of any murder case under Georgia law. He notes that the state prosecutor has unfettered authority to select those persons whom he wishes to prosecute for a capital offense and to plea bargain with them. Further, at the trial the jury may choose to convict a defendant of a lesser included offense rather than find him guilty of a crime punishable by death, even if the evidence would support a capital verdict. And finally, a defendant who is convicted and sentenced to die may have his sentence commuted by the Governor of the State and the Georgia Board of Pardons and Paroles.

The existence of these discretionary stages is not determinative of the issues before us. At each of these stages an actor in the criminal justice system makes a decision which may remove a defendant from consideration as a candidate for the death penalty. *Furman*, in contrast, dealt with the decision to impose the death sentence on a specific individual who had been convicted of a capital offense. Nothing in any of our cases suggests that the decision to afford an individual defendant mercy violates the Constitution. *Furman* held only that, in order to minimize the risk that the death penalty would be imposed on a capriciously selected group of offenders, the decision to impose it had to be guided by standards so that the sentencing authority would focus on the particularized circumstances of the crime and the defendant. . . .

V

The basic concern of *Furman* centered on those defendants who were being condemned to death capriciously and arbitrarily. Under the procedures before the Court in that case, sentencing authorities were not directed to give attention to the nature or circumstances of the crime committed or to the character or record of the defendant. Left unguided, juries imposed the death sentence in a way that could only be called freakish. The new Georgia sentencing procedures, by contrast, focus the jury's attention on the particularized nature of the crime and the particularized characteristics of the individual defendant. While the jury is permitted to consider any aggravating or mitigating circumstances, it must find and identify at least one statutory aggravating factor before it may impose a penalty of death. In this way the jury's discretion is channeled. No longer can a jury wantonly and freakishly impose the death sentence; it is always circumscribed by the legislative guidelines. In addition, the review function of the Supreme Court of Georgia affords additional assurance that the concerns that prompted our decision in *Furman* are not present to any significant degree in the Georgia procedure applied here.

For the reasons expressed in this opinion, we hold that the statutory system under which Gregg was sentenced to death does not violate the Constitution. Accordingly, the judgment of the Georgia Supreme Court is affirmed.

It is so ordered.

Mr. Justice White, with whom the Chief Justice and Mr. Justice Rehnquist join, concurring in the judgment. . . .

III

The threshold question in this case is whether the death penalty may be carried out for murder under the Georgia legislative scheme consistent with the decision in *Furman* v. *Georgia.* . . . Petitioner argues that, as in *Furman,* the jury is still the sentencer; that the statutory criteria to be considered by the jury on the issue of sentence under Georgia's new statutory scheme are vague and do not purport to be all inclusive; and that, in any event, there are *no* circumstances under which the jury is required to impose the death penalty. Consequently, the petitioner argues that the death penalty will inexorably be imposed in as discriminatory, standardless, and rare a manner as it was imposed under the scheme declared invalid in *Furman.*

The argument is considerably overstated. The Georgia Legislature has made an effort to identify those aggravating factors which it considers necessary and relevant to the question whether a defendant convicted of capital murder should be sentenced to death. The jury which imposes sentence is instructed on all statutory aggravating factors which are supported by the evidence, and is told that it may not impose the death penalty unless it unanimously finds at least one of those factors to have been established beyond a reasonable doubt. The Georgia Legislature has plainly made an effort to guide the jury in the exercise of its discretion, while at the same time permitting the jury to dispense mercy on the basis of factors too intangible to write into a statute and I cannot accept the naked assertion that the effort is bound to fail. . . .

Petitioner also argues that decisions made by the prosecutor—either in negotiating a plea to some offense lesser than capital murder or in simply declining to charge capital murder—are standardless and will inexorably result in the wanton and freakish imposition of the penalty condemned by the judgment in *Furman.* I address this point separately because the cases in which no capital offense is charged escape the view of the Georgia Supreme Court and are not considered by it in determining whether a particular sentence is excessive or disproportionate.

Petitioner's argument that prosecutors behave in a standardless fashion in deciding which cases to try as capital felonies is unsupported by any facts. Petitioner simply asserts that since prosecutors have the power not to charge capital felonies they will exercise that power in a standardless fashion. This is untenable. Absent facts to the contrary, it cannot be assumed that prosecutors will be motivated in their charging decision by factors other than the strength of their case and the likelihood that a jury would impose the death penalty if it convicts. Unless prosecutors are incompetent in their judgments, the standards by which they decide whether to charge a capital felony will be the same as those by which the jury will decide the questions of guilt and sentence. Thus defendants will escape the death penalty through prosecutorial charging decisions only because the offense is not sufficiently serious; or because the proof is insufficiently strong. This does not cause the system to be standardless any more than the jury's decision to impose life imprisonment on a defendant whose crime is deemed insufficiently serious or its decision to acquit someone who is probably guilty but whose guilt is not established beyond a reasonable doubt. Thus the prosecutor's charging decisions are unlikely to have removed from the sample of cases considered by the Georgia Supreme Court any which are truly "similar." If the cases really were "similar" in relevant respects, it is unlikely that prosecutors would fail to prosecute them as capital cases; and I am unwilling to assume the contrary. . . .

I therefore concur in the judgment of affirmance.

Statement of The Chief Justice and Mr. Justice Rehnquist:

We join the opinion of Mr. Justice White, agreeing with its analysis that Georgia's system of capital punishment comports with the Court's holding in *Furman* v. *Georgia*. . . .

Mr. Justice Blackmun, concurring in the judgment. . . .

Mr. Justice Brennan, dissenting.

The Cruel and Unusual Punishments Clause "must draw its meaning from the evolving standards of decency that mark the progress of a maturing society." The opinions of Mr. Justice Stewart, Mr. Justice Powell, and Mr. Justice Stevens today hold that "evolving standards of decency" require focus not on the essence of the death penalty itself but primarily upon the procedures employed by the State to single out persons to suffer the penalty of death. . . .

In *Furman* v. *Georgia* . . . I read "evolving standards of decency" as requiring focus upon the essence of the death penalty itself and not primarily or solely upon the procedures under which the determination to inflict the penalty upon a particular person was made. . . .

This Court inescapably has the duty, as the ultimate arbiter of the meaning of our Constitution, to say whether, when individuals condemned to death stand before our Bar, "moral concepts" require us to hold that the law has progressed to the point where we should declare that the punishment of death, like punishments on the rack, the screw and the wheel, is no longer morally tolerable in our civilized society. My opinion in *Furman* v. *Georgia* concluded that our civilization and the law had progressed to this point and that therefore the punishment of death, for whatever crime and under all circumstances, is "cruel and unusual" in violation of the Eighth and Fourteenth Amendment of the Constitution. I shall not again canvass the reason that led to that conclusion. I emphasize only that foremost among the "moral concepts" recognized in our cases and inherent in the Clause is the primary moral principle that the State, even as it punishes, must treat its citizens in a manner consistent with their intrinsic worth as human beings—a punishment must not be so severe as to be degrading to human dignity. A judicial determination whether the punishment of death comports with human dignity is therefore not only permitted but compelled by the Clause. . . .

I do not understand that the Court disagrees that "[i]n comparison to all other punishments today . . . the deliberate extinguishment of human life by the State is uniquely degrading to human dignity." . . . For three of my Brethren hold today that mandatory infliction of the death penalty constitutes the penalty cruel and unusual punishment. I perceive no principled basis for this limitation. Death for whatever crime and under all circumstances "is truly an awesome punishment. The calculated killing of a human being by the State involves, by its very nature, a denial of the executed person's humanity. . . . An executed person has indeed 'lost the right to have rights.' ". . . Death is not only an unusually severe punishment, unusual in its pain, in its finality, and in its enormity, but it serves no penal purpose more effectively than a less severe punishment; therefore the principle inherent in the Clause that prohibits pointless infliction of excessive punishment when less severe punishment can adequately achieve the same purposes invalidates the punishment. . . .

The fatal constitutional infirmity in the punishment of death is that it treats "members of the human race as nonhumans, as objects to be toyed with and discarded. [It is] thus inconsistent with the fundamental premise of the Clause that even the vilest criminal remains a human being possessed of common human dignity.". . . . As such it is a penalty that "subjects the individual to a fate forbidden by the principle of civilized treatment guaranteed by the [Clause]." I therefore would hold, on that ground alone, that death is today a cruel and unusual punishment prohibited by the Clause. "Justice of this kind is obviously no less shocking than the crime itself, and the new 'official' murder, far from offering redress for the offense committed against society, adds instead a second defilement to the first.". . .

Mr. Justice Marshall, dissenting.

In *Furman* v. *Georgia* . . . I set forth at some length my views on the basic issue presented to the Court in these cases. The death penalty, I concluded, is a cruel and unusual punishment prohibited by the Eighth and Fourteenth Amendments. That continues to be my view. . . .

In *Furman* I concluded that the death penalty is constitutionally invalid for two reasons. First, the death penalty is excessive. . . . And second, the American people, fully informed as to the purposes of the death penalty and its liabilities, would in my view reject it as morally unacceptable. . . .

Since the decision in *Furman*, the legislatures of 35 States have enacted new statutes authorizing the imposition of the death sentence for certain crimes, and Congress has enacted a law providing the death penalty for air piracy resulting in death. . . . I would be less than candid if I did not acknowledge that these developments have a significant bearing on a realistic assessment of the moral acceptability of the death penalty to the American people. But if the constitutionality of the death penalty turns, as I have urged, on the opinion of an *informed* citizenry, then even the enactment of new death statutes cannot be viewed as conclusive. In *Furman*, I observed that the American people are largely unaware of the information critical to a judgment on the morality of the death penalty, and concluded that if they were better informed they would consider it shocking, unjust, and unacceptable. . . . A recent study, conducted after the enactment of the post-*Furman* statutes, has confirmed that the American people know little about the death penalty, and that the opinions of an informed public would differ significantly from those of a public unaware of the consequences and effects of the death penalty.

Even assuming, however, that the post-*Furman* enactment of statutes authorizing the death penalty renders the prediction of the views of an informed citizenry an uncertain basis for a constitutional decision, the enactment of those statutes has no bearing whatsoever on the conclusion that the death penalty is unconstitutional because it is excessive. An excessive penalty is invalid under the Cruel and Unusual Punishments Clause "even though popular sentiment may favor" it. . . . The inquiry here, then, is simply whether the death penalty is necessary to accomplish the legitimate legislative purposes in punishment, or whether a less severe penalty— life imprisonment—would do as well. . . .

The two purposes that sustain the death penalty as nonexcessive in the Court's view are general deterrence and retribution. In *Furman*, I canvassed the relevant data on the deterrent effect of capital punishment. . . . The state of knowledge at that point, after literally centuries of debate, was summarized as follows by a United Nations Committee:

"It is generally agreed between the retentionists and abolitionists, whatever their opinions about the validity of comparative studies of deterrence, that the data

which now exist show no correlation between the existence of capital punishment and lower rates of capital crime.". . .
The available evidence, I concluded in *Furman*, was convincing that "capital punishment is not necessary as a deterrent to crime in our society.". . .

The other principal purpose said to be served by the death penalty is retribution. The notion that retribution can serve as a moral justification for the sanction of death finds credence in the opinion of my Brothers Stewart, Powell, and Stevens, and that of my Brother White in *Roberts* v. *Louisiana, post.* . . . It is this notion that I find to be the most disturbing aspect of today's unfortunate decision. . . .

My Brothers Stewart, Powell, and Stevens offer the following explanation of the retributive justification for capital punishment:

"The instinct for retribution is part of the nature of man, and channeling that instinct in the administration of criminal justice serves an important purpose in promoting the stability of a society governed by law. When people begin to believe that organized society is unwilling or unable to impose upon criminal offenders the punishment they 'deserve,' then there are sown the seeds of anarchy—of self-help, vigilante justice, and lynch law.". . .
This statement is wholly inadequate to justify the death penalty. . . . It simply defies belief to suggest that the death penalty is necessary to prevent the American people from taking the law into their own hands.

In a related vein, it may be suggested that the expression of moral outrage through the imposition of the death penalty serves to reinforce basic moral values— that it marks some crimes as particularly offensive and therefore to be avoided. . . .
This contention, like the previous one, provides no support for the death penalty. It is inconceivable that any individual concerned about conforming his conduct to what society says is "right" would fail to realize that murder is "wrong" if the penalty were simply life imprisonment. . . .

There remains for consideration, however, what might be termed the purely retributive justification for the death penalty—that the death penalty is appropriate, not because of its beneficial effect on society, but because the taking of the murderer's life is itself morally good. Some of the language of the plurality's opinion appears positively to embrace this notion of retribution for its own sake as a justification for capital punishment. . . . The mere fact that the community demands the murderer's life in return for the evil he has done cannot sustain the death penalty, for as the plurality reminds us, "the Eighth Amendment demands more than that a challenged punishment be acceptable to contemporary society.". . . . To be sustained under the Eighth Amendment, the death penalty must "[comport] with the basic concept of human dignity at the core of the Amendment,". . . ; the objective in imposing it must be "[consistent] with our respect for the dignity of other men.". . . Under these standards, the taking of life "because the wrong-doer deserves it" surely must fall, for such a punishment has as its very basis the total denial of the wrong-doer's dignity and worth.

The death penalty, unnecessary to promote the goal of deterrence or to further any legitimate notion of retribution, is an excessive penalty forbidden by the Eighth and Fourteenth Amendments. I respectfully dissent from the Court's judgment upholding the sentences of death imposed upon the petitioners in these cases.

In separate decisions the Court upheld the death penalty statutes of Texas and Florida. Although different from the Georgia statute, the majority of the Court found that in each case the sentencing body was guided by standards and was required to consider both aggravating and mitigating factors in reaching its decision on whether to impose the death penalty or life imprisonment. The North Carolina and Louisiana statutes were held unconstitutional because conviction for specified crimes mandated the death penalty with no latitude for discretion in the sentencing body to consider either aggravating or mitigating circumstances.

[On cruel and unusual punishments generally, see David Fellman, *The Defendant's Rights* (New York: Rinehart, 1958) chap. 11; James S. Campbell, "Revival of the Eighth Amendment: Development of Cruel Punishment Doctrine by the Supreme Court," 16 *Stan. L. Rev.* 996 (1964); Michael Meltsner, *Cruel and Unusual: The Supreme Court and Capital Punishment* (New York: Morrow, 1974); and Larry C. Berkson, *The Concept of Cruel and Unusual* Punishment (Lexington, Mass.: Heath, 1975).]

HABEAS CORPUS

There are several varieties of writs of habeas corpus. The one which is commonly referred to, however, as "the" writ, when the shorthand title is employed, is *habeas corpus ad subjiciendum et recipiendum.* It stems from the common law, with certain important extensions made by the famous Habeas Corpus Act adopted by Parliament in 1679. The writ is purely procedural in character. Its primary function is to provide a procedure whereby a speedy inquiry may be made by a judge into the legality of a detention on a criminal charge. More broadly, however, it can be used to test the legality of any restraint of person.

Since the writ is available to test the legality of detentions, it may be brought into play either before trial or after conviction and sentence. In the latter situation, however, it should be noted that habeas corpus is not a substitute for appeal. Allegations of error may be properly considered on appeal which are outside the scope of attack by habeas corpus. As a generalization, habeas corpus represents only a collateral attack on the detention, and concerns contentions which mainly reach questions of the jurisdiction of the committing court or agency. The Court has, however, tended to broaden the category of issues which it will accept as "jurisdictional questions." Under older approaches, a showing in a return to a writ that the prisoner was held under final process based upon a judgment of a court of competent jurisdiction closed the inquiry. This same rule was carried over into the Judiciary Act of 1789. But in 1867 Congress made a major change in the law. It extended the availability of the writ to state as well as federal prisoners, and made it applicable to restraints of liberty "in violation of the constitution, or of any treaty or law of the United States."

It should be clear that a court could have jurisdiction over a specific party and cause of action, but that procedure might be employed in the course of the trial "in violation of the constitution." Thus the act of 1867 opened the way for a much broader scope of "review" than was formerly the case. It still, however, does not permit the use of habeas corpus to reach ordinary assignments of error, such as an erroneous charge to the jury or the admission of improper evidence, where such claims do not rise to the status of constitutional rights. Thus appellate review should not be neglected under the mistaken belief that habeas corpus can serve the same purposes. While there is no time limit on the availability of the writ, unlike the situation with respect to appeals, the writ is narrower in its application. At the same time, there are procedural aspects of the use of the writ which afford more flexibility than is the case with appeal. Appeals are normally carried to a specified court, while any coordinate trial court may entertain a petition for habeas corpus.

That the scope of the writ is not confined to common-law rules or even, for that matter, to earlier American judicial interpretation, was made clear in *Johnson* v. *Zerbst,* 304 U.S. 458 (1938), discussed earlier in this chapter. In holding that habeas corpus was an appropriate remedy for attacking a federal conviction denying the Sixth Amendment right to counsel, the majority, through Justice Black, stated:

> The scope of inquiry in habeas corpus proceedings has been broadened—not narrowed—since the adoption of the Sixth Amendment. . . . A court's jurisdiction at the beginning of trial may be lost "in the course of the proceedings" due to failure to complete the court—as the Sixth Amendment requires—by providing Counsel for an accused who is unable to obtain Counsel, who has not intelligently waived this constitutional guaranty, and whose life or liberty is at stake. If this requirement of the Sixth Amendment is not complied with, the court no longer has jurisdiction to proceed. The judgment of conviction pronounced by a court without jurisdiction is void, and one imprisoned thereunder may obtain release by habeas corpus.

More recently, a majority of the Court asserted the right to expand the writ by judicial interpretation and to permit its use for a purpose unknown to the common law, to bring a prisoner into court to argue his own appeal. Justice Murphy, for the majority, in *Price* v. *Johnston,* 334 U.S. 266, 282 (1948), stated:

> [W]e do not conceive that a circuit court of appeals, in issuing a writ of habeas corpus under Section 262 of the Judicial Code, is necessarily confined to the precise forms of that writ in vogue at the common law or in the English judicial system. Section 262 says that the writ must be agreeable to the usages and principles of "law," a term which is unlimited by the common law or the English law. And since "law" is not a static concept, but expands and develops as new problems arise, we do not believe that the forms of the *habeas corpus* writ authorized by Section 262 are only those recognized in this country in 1789, when the original Judiciary Act containing the substance of this section came into existence.

A dramatic use for habeas corpus is illustrated by cases in which the evidence or testimony indicates that the whole trial proceedings are infected with basic unfairness. Such a case was *Moore* v. *Dempsey,* 261 U.S. 86 (1923), discussed earlier, where evidence showed the entire trial to have been under mob domination. Justice Holmes, for the majority, stated:

> We assume . . . that the corrective process supplied by the state may be so adequate that interference by habeas corpus ought not to be allowed. It certainly is true that mere mistakes of law in the course of a trial are not to be corrected in that way. But if the case is that the whole proceeding is a mask,—that counsel, jury, and judge were swept to the fatal end by an irresistible wave of public passion, and that the state courts failed to correct the wrong,—neither perfection in the machinery for correction nor the possibility that the trial court and counsel saw no other way of avoiding an immediate outbreak of the mob can prevent this court from securing to the petitioners their constitutional rights.

The general rule is that the writ of habeas corpus is unavailable unless the petitioner is under detention or in custody in some fashion. Over the years, however, the Court has substantially liberalized the application of the "in custody" requirement for purposes of utilizing habeas corpus.

In *Jones* v. *Cunningham,* 371 U.S. 236 (1963), the Court faced the question of whether the "in custody" requirement of 28 U.S.C. 2241 was sufficiently met in the supervisory control exercised over a parolee by the state parole board. Petitioner had ben sentenced as a recidivist in state court and filed a petition for habeas corpus in federal district court alleging the invalidity of his conviction on the ground of denial of right to counsel. The superintendent of the prison was named as respondent. The petition was dismissed and appeal was taken. Before the appeal was argued, the prisoner was paroled, and he moved to add the parole board as respondents. The court of appeals refused on the ground that the board did not have physical custody of the prisoner and dismissed the petition on the ground that the case was moot because the petitioner was out of prison. On certiorari, the United States Supreme Court unanimously reversed. The Court agreed that the case was moot as to the prison superintendent, but it held that the stringent controls over the parolee exercised by the parole board met the "in custody" requirement of the statute necessary to the issuance of habeas corpus. The lower courts were thus ordered to proceed to a decision on the merits of petitioner's case.

In *Carafas* v. *LaVallee,* 391 U.S. 234 (1968), a prisoner filed an application for habeas corpus in federal court, alleging that illegally seized evidence had been used in securing his conviction in a state court. The application was dismissed by the District Court, and the Court of Appeals dismissed the appeal. Two weeks before filing a petition for certiorari in the United States Supreme Court, the petitioner was unconditionally released from the state prison. The Court held that the expiration of the sentence before the application for habeas corpus was finally adjudicated did not terminate federal jurisdiction, and because of the substantial disabilities which flowed from the conviction (ineligibility to engage in certain businesses, loss of voting rights, and others), the cause was not moot. Thus it was held that once federal jurisdiction attached in the District Court, it was not defeated by the release of the petitioner prior to completion of proceedings.

For federal courts to intervene in state criminal process through the device of habeas corpus is, of course, to raise delicate questions of federal-state relations. For this reason, the federal code requires that state prisoners exhaust their state remedies, including habeas corpus, prior to petitioning federal courts for the writ. The normal appellate route for state prisoners is to proceed through the state courts as far as allowable, and then, if a federal question is presented, to petition the United States Supreme Court for certiorari.

FAY *v.* NOIA

372 U.S. 391 (1963)

[Noia was convicted with two others in 1942 of a felony murder. The sole evidence against each defendant was his signed confession. The other defendants, but not Noia, appealed their convictions. These appeals were unsuccessful, but subsequent legal proceedings resulted in their release upon findings that the confessions had been coerced. Noia petitioned for habeas corpus in the United States District Court, where it was stipulated that his confession was also corced. The District Court denied relief on the ground that since Noia had failed to appeal, he did not satisfy the requirements of 28 U.S.C. §2254 whereby "An applicant for a writ of habeas corpus in behalf of a person in custody pursuant to the judgment of a State court shall not be granted unless it appears that the applicant has exhausted the remedies available in the courts of the State. . . ." The Court of Appeals reversed.]

Mr. Justice Brennan delivered the opinion of the Court.

This case presents important questions touching the federal habeas corpus jurisdiction . . . in its relation to state criminal justice. The narrow question is whether the respondent Noia may be granted federal habeas corpus relief from imprisonment under a New York conviction now admitted by the State to rest upon a confession obtained from him in violation of the Fourteenth Amendment, after he was denied state post-conviction relief because the coerced confession claim had been decided against him at the trial and Noia had allowed the time for a direct appeal to lapse without seeking review by a state appellate court.

We affirm the judgment of the Court of Appeals but reach that court's result by a different course of reasoning. We hold: (1) Federal courts have *power* under the federal habeas statute to grant relief despite the applicant's failure to have pursued a state remedy not available to him at the time he applies; the doctrine under which state procedural defaults are held to constitute an adequate and independent state law ground barring direct Supreme Court review is not to be extended to limit the power granted the federal courts under the federal habeas statute. (2) Noia's failure to appeal was not a failure to exhaust "the remedies available in the courts of the State" as required by §2254; that requirement refers only to a failure to exhaust state remedies still open to the applicant at the time he files his application for habeas corpus in the federal court. (3) Noia's failure to appeal cannot under the circumstances be deemed an intelligent and understanding waiver of his right to appeal such as to justify the withholding of federal habeas corpus relief.

The question has been much mooted under what circumstances, if any, the failure of a state prisoner to comply with a state procedural requirement, as a result of which the state courts decline to pass on the merits of his federal defense, bars subsequent resort to the federal courts for relief on habeas corpus. Plainly it is a question that has important implications for federal-state relations in the area of the administration of criminal justice. It cannot be answered without a preliminary inquiry into the historical development of the writ of habeas corpus.

We do well to bear in mind the extraordinary prestige of the Great Writ, *habeas corpus ad subjiciendum,* in Anglo-American jurisprudence: "the most celebrated writ in the English law." 3 *Blackstone Commentaries* 129. . . . It is perhaps the most important writ known to the constitutional law of England, affording as it does a swift and imperative remedy in all cases of illegal restraint or confinement. . . .

. . . The principle that judicial as well as executive restraints may be intolerable received dramatic expression in *Bushell's Case* . . . (1670). Bushell was one of the jurors in the trial, held before the Court of Oyer and Terminer at the Old Bailey, of William Penn and William Mead on charges of tumultuous assembly and other crimes. When the jury brought in a verdict of not guilty, the court ordered the jurors committed for contempt. Bushell sought habeas corpus, and the Court of Common Pleas, in a memorable opinion by Chief Justice Vaughn, ordered him discharged from custody. . . . [The opinion here gives a lengthy treatment of the history of the application of the writ.]

And so, although almost 300 years have elapsed since Bushell's Case, changed conceptions of the kind of criminal proceedings so fundamentally defective as to make imprisonment pursuant to them constitutionally intolerable should not be allowed to obscure the basic continuity in the conception of the writ as the remedy for such imprisonments. . . .

The breadth of the federal courts' power of independent adjudication on habeas corpus stems from the very nature of the writ, and conforms with the classic English practice. As put by Mr. Justice Holmes . . . : "If the petition discloses facts that amount to a loss of jurisdiction in the trial court, jurisdiction could not be restored by any decision above." It is of the historical essence of habeas corpus that it lies to test proceedings so fundamentally lawless that imprisonment pursuant to them is not merely erroneous but void. Hence, the familiar principle that *res judicata* is inapplicable in habeas proceedings. . . .

We have reviewed the development of habeas corpus at some length because the question of the instant case has obvious importance to the proper accommodation of a great constitutional privilege and the requirements of the federal system. Our survey discloses nothing to suggest that the Federal District Court lacked the *power* to order Noia discharged because of a procedural forfeiture he may have incurred under state law. On the contrary, the nature of the writ at common law, the language and purpose of the Act of February 5, 1867, and the course of decisions in this Court extending over nearly a century are wholly irreconcilable with such a limitation. . . . Obedient to this purpose, we have consistently held that federal court jurisdiction is conferred by the allegation of an unconstitutional restraint and is not defeated by anything that may occur in the state court proceedings. State procedural rules plainly must yield to this overriding federal policy. . . .

Although we hold that the jurisdiction of the federal courts on habeas corpus is not affected by procedural defaults incurred by the applicant during the state court proceedings, we recognize a limited discretion in the federal judge to deny relief to an applicant under certain circumstances. Discretion is implicit in the statutory command that the judge, after granting the writ and holding a hearing of appropriate scope, "dispose of the matter as law and justice require," . . . ; and discretion was the flexible concept employed by the federal courts in developing the exhaustion rule. . . . We therefore hold that the federal habeas judge may in his discretion deny relief to an applicant who has deliberately by-passed the orderly procedure of the state courts and in so doing has forfeited his state court remedies.

But we wish to make very clear that this grant of discretion is not to be interpreted as a permission to introduce legal fictions into federal habeas corpus. The classic definition of waiver enunciated in *Johnson* v. *Zerbst* . . . —"an intentional relinquishment or abandonment of a known right or privilege"—furnishes the controlling standard. . . .

The application of the standard we have adumbrated to the facts of the instant case is not difficult. Under no reasonable view can the State's version of Noia's reason for not appealing support an inference of deliberate by-passing of the state court system. For Noia to have appealed in 1942 would have been to run a substantial risk of electrocution. His was the grisly choice whether to sit content with life imprisonment or to travel the uncertain avenue of appeal which, if successful, might well have led to a retrial and death sentence. . . .

...Our decision today swings open no prison gates. Today as always few indeed is the number of state prisoners who eventually win their freedom by means of federal habeas corpus. Those few who are ultimately successful are persons whom society has grievously wronged and for whom belated liberation is little enough compensation....

Affirmed.

Mr. Justice Clark, dissenting.

I agree fully with and join the opinion of my Brother Harlan. Beyond question the federal courts until today have had no power to release a prisoner in respondent Noia's predicament, there being no basis for such power in either the Constitution or the statute. But the Court today in releasing Noia makes an "abrupt break" not only with the Constitution and the statute but also with its past decisions, disrupting the delicate balance of federalism so foremost in the minds of the Founding Fathers and so uniquely important in the field of law enforcement. The short of it is that Noia's incarceration rests entirely on an adequate and independent state ground—namely, that he knowingly failed to perfect any appeal from his conviction of murder. While it may be that the Court's "decision today swings open no prison gates," the Court must admit in all candor that it effectively swings closed the doors of justice in the face of the State, since it certainly cannot prove its case 20 years after the fact....

Mr. Justice Harlan, whom Mr. Justice Clark and Mr. Justice Stewart join, dissenting.

This decision, both in its abrupt break with the past and in its consequences for the future, is one of the most disquieting that the Court has rendered in a long time....

I dissent from the Court's opinion and judgment for the reason that the federal courts have no *power,* statutory or constitutional, to release the respondent Noia from state detention. This is because his custody by New York does not violate any federal right, since it is pursuant to a conviction whose validity rests upon an adequate and independent state ground which the federal courts are required to respect....

The history of federal habeas corpus jurisdiction, I believe, leaves no doubt that today's decision constitutes a square rejection of long-accepted principles governing the nature and scope of the Great Writ....

It is the adequacy, or fairness, of the state ground that should be the controlling question in this case. This controlling question the Court does not discuss.

New York asserts that a claim of the kind involved here must be raised on timely appeal if it is to be preserved, and contends that in permitting an appeal it has provided a reasonable opportunity for the claim to be made....In other words, the State claims that it may constitutionally detain a man pursuant to a judgment of conviction, regardless of any error that may have led to that conviction, if the relevant facts were reasonably available and an appeal was not taken....

...Certainly the State has a vital interest in requiring that appeals be taken on the basis of facts known at the time, since the first assertion of a claim many years later might otherwise require release long after it was feasible to hold a trial....Many federal decisions have held that a federal prisoner held pursuant to a federal conviction may not assert such a claim in collateral proceedings when it was not, but could have been, asserted on appeal....

I recognize that Noia's predicament may well be thought one that strongly calls for correction. But the proper course to that end lies with the New York Governor's powers of executive clemency, not with the federal courts. Since Noia is detained pursuant to a state judgment whose validity rests on an adequate and independent state ground, the judgment below should be reversed.

Fay v. *Noia* appeared to remove the final barriers to broad collateral reexamination of state criminal convictions in federal habeas corpus proceedings. But in 1976 the Court made a major policy shift away from *Fay* and, at the same time, gave strong indications that the exclusionary rule of *Mapp* v. *Ohio* might be applied selectively "in the light of competing policies." In *Stone* v. *Powell,* 44 L.W. 5313 (1976), a majority of six members held that "where the State has provided an opportunity for full and fair litigation of a Fourth Amendment claim, the Constitution does not require that a state prisoner be granted federal habeas corpus relief on the ground that evidence obtained in an unconstitutional search or seizure was introduced at his trial." Justice Powell, for the majority, stated that the rule was not absolute which barred illegally seized evidence, since it is admissible in grand jury proceedings and may be admitted to impeach the credibility of a defendant in the trial itself. He further pointed out some of the defects and costs in the application of the rule which "deflects the truthfinding process and often frees the guilty." Nonetheless, he concluded that the exclusionary rule should be implemented at trial and on direct appeal of state court convictions. "But the additional contribution, if any, of the consideration of search-and-seizure claims of state prisoners on collateral review is small in relation to the costs." Chief Justice Burger, in a concurring opinion, would have gone even further in the shift away from *Mapp,* stating that "it seems clear to me that the exclusionary rule has been operative long enough to demonstrate its flaws. The time has come to modify its reach, even if is retained for a small and limited category of cases."

[See Zechariah Chafee, "The Most Important Human Right in the Constitution," 32 *B. U. L. Rev.* 144 (1952); David Fellman, *The Defendant's Rights* (New York: Rinehart, 1958), chap. 5; William J. Brennan, Jr., "Federal Habeas Corpus and State Prisoners: An Exercise in Federalism," 7 *Utah L. Rev.* 423 (1961); Curtis R. Reitz, "Federal Habeas Corpus: Impact of an Abortive State Proceeding," 74 *Harv. L. Rev.* 1315 (1961); and Paul M. Bator, "Finality in Criminal Law and Federal Habeas Corpus for State Prisoners," 76 *Harv. L. Rev.* 441 (1963).]

A specialized use of habeas corpus is its function as a narrow form of civil court review of military detention. Many of the procedural requirements of the Bill of Rights are made inapplicable to military trials. Article I of the Constitution authorizes Congress "to make rules for the government and regulation of the land and naval forces," and the Fifth Amendment, either specifically or by implication, exempts courts-martial from the requirements of grand jury indictment and jury trial. Under the Uniform Code of Military Justice, adopted by Congress in 1950, substantial guarantees in favor of the accused were added to the old provisions, and careful appellate review procedures are set out *within* the military establishment. The long-established rule, however, is that there is no ordinary appellate review by the civil courts over the judgments of courts-martial. [See Earl Warren, "The Bill of Rights and the Military," 37 *N.Y.U. L. Rev.* 181 (1962) and James Snedeker, "Habeas Corpus and Court-Martial Prisoners," 6 *Vand. L. Rev.* 288 (1953).] For this reason, the writ of habeas corpus occupies an exceptional place in the relationship of the two systems. It is the single judicial remedy by which any civil collateral attack can be made on a military detention. And its application is severely limited to the single question of whether the sentencing court had jurisdiction.

As the Court said in *Hiatt* v. *Brown*, 339 U.S. 103 (1950), "It is well settled that 'by habeas corpus the civil courts exercise no supervisory or correcting power over the proceedings of a court-martial. . . . The single inquiry, the test, is jurisdiction.' *Re Grimley*, 137 U.S. 147 (1890)." A case illustrative of the utility of habeas corpus to test military court jurisdiction is that of *Toth* v. *Quarles*, decided in 1955.

UNITED STATES *ex. rel.* TOTH *v.* QUARLES
350 U.S. 11 (1955)

Mr. Justice Black delivered the opinion of the Court.

After serving with the United States Air Force in Korea, Robert W. Toth was honorably discharged. He returned to his home in Pittsburgh and went to work in a steel plant. Five months later he was arrested by military authorities on charges of murder and conspiracy to commit murder while an airman in Korea. At the time of arrest he had no relationship of any kind with the military. He was taken to Korea to stand trial before a court-martial under authority of a 1950 Act of Congress. The Court of Appeals sustained the Act, rejecting the contention that civilian ex-servicemen like Toth could not constitutionally be subjected to trial by court-martial. . . . We granted certiorari to pass upon this important constitutional question. . . .

The Court has held that the Article I clause just quoted authorizes Congress to subject persons actually in the armed service to trial by court-martial for military and naval offenses. Later it was held that court-martial jurisdiction could be exerted over a dishonorably discharged soldier then a military prisoner serving a sentence imposed by a prior court-martial. It has never been intimated by this Court, however, that Article I military jurisdiction could be extended to civilian ex-soldiers who had severed all relationship with the military and its institutions. To allow this extension of military authority would require an extremely broad construction of the language used in the constitutional provision relied on. For given its natural meaning, the power granted Congress "To make Rules" or regulate "the land and naval Forces" would seem to restrict court-martial jurisdiction to persons who are actually members or part of the armed forces. There is a compelling reason for construing the clause this way: any expansion of court-martial jurisdiction like that in the 1950 Act necessarily encroaches on the jurisdiction of federal courts set up under Article III of the Constitution where persons on trial are surrounded with more constitutional safeguards than in military tribunals.

Article III provides for the establishment of a court system as one of the separate but coordinate branches of the National Government. It is the primary, indeed the sole business of these courts to try cases and controversies between individuals and between individuals and the Government. This includes trial of criminal cases. These courts are presided over by judges appointed for life, subject only to removal by impeachment. Their compensation cannot be diminished during their continuance in office. The provisions of Article III were designed to give judges maximum freedom from possible coercion or influence by the executive or legislative branches of the Government. But the Constitution and the Amendments in the

Bill of Rights show that the Founders were not satisfied with leaving determination of guilt or innocence to judges, even though wholly independent. They further provided that no person should be held to answer in those courts for capital or other infamous crimes unless on the presentment or indictment of a grand jury drawn from the body of the people. Other safeguards designed to protect defendants against oppressive governmental practices were included. . . .

We find nothing in the history or constitutional treatment of military tribunals which entitles them to rank along with Article III courts as adjudicators of the guilt or innocence of people charged with offenses for which they can be deprived of their life, liberty or property. Unlike courts, it is the primary business of armies and navies to fight or be ready to fight wars should the occasion arise. But trial of soldiers to maintain discipline is merely incidental to an army's primary fighting function. To the extent that those responsible for performance of this primary function are diverted from it by the necessity of trying cases, the basic fighting purpose of armies is not served. And conceding to military personnel that high degree of honesty and sense of justice which nearly all of them undoubtedly have, it still remains true that military tribunals have not been and probably never can be constituted in such way that they can have the same kind of qualifications that the Constitution has deemed essential to fair trials of civilians in federal courts. For instance, the Constitution does not provide life tenure for those performing judicial functions in military trials. They are appointed by military commanders and may be removed at will. Nor does the Constitution protect their salaries as it does judicial salaries. Strides have been made toward making courts-martial less subject to the will of the executive department which appoints, supervises and ultimately controls them. But from the very nature of things, courts have more independence in passing on the life and liberty of people than do military tribunals. . . .

Fear has been expressed that if this law is not sustained discharged soldiers may escape punishment altogether for crimes they commit while in the service. But that fear is not warranted and was not shared by the Judge Advocate General of the Army who made a strong statement against passage of the law. He asked Congress to "confer jurisdiction upon Federal courts to try any person for an offense denounced by the [military] code if he is no longer subject thereto. This would be consistent with the fifth amendment of the Constitution.". . . It is conceded that it was wholly within the constitutional power of Congress to follow this suggestion and provide for federal district court trials of discharged soldiers accused of offenses committed while in the armed services. This concession is justified. U.S. Const., Art. III, Section 2. . . . There can be no valid argument, therefore, that civilian ex-servicemen must be tried by court-martial or not tried at all. If that is so it is only because Congress has not seen fit to subject them to trial in federal district courts.

None of the other reasons suggested by the Government are sufficient to justify a broad construction of the constitutional grant of power to Congress to regulate the armed forces. That provision itself does not empower Congress to deprive people of trials under Bill of Rights safeguards, and we are not willing to hold that power to circumvent those safeguards should be inferred through the Necessary and Proper Clause. It is impossible to think that the discipline of the Army is going to be disrupted, its morale impaired, or its orderly processes disturbed, by giving ex-servicemen the benefit of a civilian court trial when they are actually civilians. And we are not impressed by the fact that some other countries which do not have our Bill of Rights indulge in the practice of subjecting civilians who were once soldiers to trials by courts-martial instead of trials by civilian courts.

Determining the scope of the constitutional power of Congress to authorize trial by court-martial presents another instance calling for limitation to *"the least possible power adequate to the end proposed."* We hold that Congress cannot subject civilians like Toth to trial by court-martial. They, like other civilians, are entitled to have the benefit of safeguards afforded those tried in the regular courts authorized by Article III of the Contsitution.

[Justice Reed, joined by Justices Burton and Minton, dissented. Justice Minton, joined by Justice Burton, dissented.]

O'CALLAHAN *v.* PARKER
395 U.S. 258 (1969)

[Petitioner, a sergeant in the United States Army stationed in Hawaii, while on an evening pass and dressed in civilian clothes, broke into a girl's hotel room in Honolulu and assaulted and attempted to rape her. He was apprehended by a hotel security officer who delivered him to the Honolulu city police for questioning, and after determining that he was a soldier, the city police delivered him to the military police. He was charged with attempted rape, housebreaking, and assault with intent to rape, in violation of the Uniform Code of Military Justice, and was tried and convicted by court-martial on all counts. While under confinement at a federal prison, he filed a petition for habeas corpus in a federal District Court alleging that the court-martial was without jurisdiction to try him for non-military offenses committed off-post while on an evening pass. The District Court dismissed, and the Court of Appeals affirmed.]

Mr. Justice Douglas delivered the opinion of the Court.

A court-martial is not yet an independent instrument of justice but remains to a significant degree a specialized part of the overall mechanism by which military discipline is preserved.

That a system of specialized military courts, proceeding by practices different from those obtaining in the regular courts and in general less favorable to defendants, is necessary to an effective national defense establishment, few would deny. But the justification for such a system rests on the special needs of the military, and history teaches that expansion of military discipline beyond its proper domain carries with it a threat to liberty. . . .

While the Court of Military Appeals takes cognizance of some constitutional rights of the accused who are court-martialed, courts-martial as an institution are singularly inept in dealing with the nice subtleties of constitutional law. . . .

The mere fact that petitioner was at the time of his offense and of his court-martial on active duty in the Armed Forces does not automatically dispose of this case under our prior decisions.

We have held in a series of decisions that court-martial jurisdictions cannot be extended to reach any person not a member of the Armed Forces at the times of both the offense and the trial. Thus, discharged soldiers cannot be court-martialed for offenses committed while in service. *Toth* v. *Quarles.* . . . Similarly, neither civilian employees of the Armed Forces overseas . . . nor civilian dependents of military personnel accompanying them overseas . . . may be tried by court-martial. . . .

The fact that courts-martial have no jurisdiction over nonsoldiers, whatever their offense, does not necessarily imply that they have unlimited jurisdiction over soldiers, regardless of the nature of the offenses charged. Nor do the cases of this Court suggest any such interpretation. . . .

We have concluded that the crime to be under military jurisdiction must be service connected, lest "cases arising in the land or naval forces, or in the Militia, when in actual service in time of War or public danger," as used in the Fifth Amendment, be expanded to deprive every member of the armed services of the benefits of an indictment by a grand jury and a trial by a jury of his peers. . . .

In the present case petitioner was properly absent from his military base when he committed the crimes with which he is charged. There was no connection—not even the remotest one—between his military duties and the crimes in question. The crimes were not committed on a military post or enclave; nor was the person whom he attacked performing any duties relating to the military. Moreover, Hawaii, the situs of the crime, is not an armed camp under military control, as are some of our far-flung outposts.

Finally, we deal with peacetime offenses, not with authority stemming from the war power. Civil courts were open. . . . The offenses did not involve any question of the flouting of military authority, the security of a military post, or the integrity of military property.

We have accordingly decided that since petitioner's crimes were not service connected, he could not be tried by court-martial but rather was entitled to trial by the civilian courts.

Reversed.

Mr. Justice Harlan, whom Mr. Justice Stewart and Mr. Justice White join, dissenting. . . .

The Court does not explain the scope of the "service-connected" crimes as to which court-martial jurisdiction is appropriate, but it appears that jurisdiction may extend to "nonmilitary" offenses in appropriate circumstances. . . .

Whatever role an *ad hoc* judicial approach may have in some areas of the law, the Congress and the military are at least entitled to know with some certainty the allowable scope of court-martial jurisdiction. Otherwise, the infinite permutations of possibly relevant factors are bound to create confusion and proliferate litigation over the jurisdictional issue in each instance. Absolutely nothing in the language, history, or logic of the Constitution justifies this uneasy state of affairs which the Court has today created.

I would affirm the judgment of the Court of Appeals.

A final aspect of the writ of habeas corpus concerns the form and the procedure accompanying its use. The prisoner or his lawyer or a friend petitions an appropriate judge to issue the writ. While there is no rigid requirement of a particular form, there are certain essential allegations and statements of fact which must be presented in order for consideration to be given the petition. Illustrative of the general pattern is the following type of petition to a federal District Court Judge:

To the Honorable _____ Judge, of the United States District Court, for the District of _____, _____ Division.

Your petitioner [name] alleges that he is unlawfully imprisoned and detained by _____ in the [institution] in the city of _____, county of _____ under and by virtue of a pretended writ or warrant issued by [identity of judge or officer issuing warrant or commitment, if known]. His imprisonment and detention are unlawful in that [statement of facts showing illegality]. The petitioner has exhausted all other remedies before filing this petition. [Statement of facts showing what federal, state or administrative remedies, as the case may be, have been sought and the disposition of such requests.]

Wherefore _____, your petitioner, prays that a Writ of Habeas Corpus issue out of this court to _____, commanding him forthwith to have the body of this petitioner before the court together with the cause of his detention and to abide the further order of the court herein.

_____,
Petitioner

Dated _____, 19___

Upon receipt of such a petition alleging facts which would support a charge of illegal detention, the judge issues the writ, directed to the warden or other person detaining the petitioner, ordering him to bring the prisoner before the judge for hearing. While the judge may doubt the authenticity of the claims of petitioner, if a proper statement is made, the writ issues. However, as Justice Jackson pointed out in *Brown* v. *Allen,* 344 U.S. 443, 547 (1953), "Unless it state facts which, if proved, would warrant relief, the applicant is not entitled as of right to a hearing." This factor normally presents no problem to the prisoner, however, since most penitentiaries have among the inmates at least one expert on drawing petitions for habeas corpus. Judges have often complained, however, that since the issuance of the writ is very nearly automatic and since there is no limit on the number of petitions a prisoner may file, that the writ is all too often used merely as a device to get a few days vacation from the prison. Justice Jackson, again in *Brown* v. *Allen,* stated:

[T]his Court has sanctioned progressive trivialization of the writ until floods of stale, frivolous and repetitious petitions inundate the docket of the lower courts and swell our own. Judged by our own disposition of habeas corpus matters, they have, as a class, become peculiarly undeserving. It must prejudice the occasional meritorious application to be buried in a flood of worthless ones. He who must search a haystack for a needle is likely to end up with the attitude that the needle is not worth the search. Nor is it any answer to say that few of these petitions in any court really result in the discharge of the petitioner. That is condemnation of the procedure which has encouraged frivolous cases.

The "needle" referred to by Justice Jackson turns out to represent between 1 percent and 2 percent of the total petitions handled in federal courts. Many people, especially the prisoners concerned, feel that even this small return on the time invested is worth the effort.

RIGHTS OF PRISONERS

Increasingly in recent years persons confined in prisons have been filing suits requesting injunctive relief against a variety of restrictions imposed upon them during incarceration. The suits include complaints against censorship of mail, refusal to allow receipt of obscene publications, imposition of punishment while in prison without the due process safeguards of notice, hearing, access to witnesses, or counsel, and the failure to furnish library facilities and legal assistance to aid in the preparation of habeas corpus applications or civil rights actions. *Wolff* v. *McDonnell,* decided in 1974, indicates the Court's view on some of these claims. [See also *Procunier* v. *Martinez,* 416 U.S. 396 (1974).]

WOLFF v. MCDONNELL
418 U.S. 539 (1974)

Mr. Justice White delivered the opinion of the Court.

We granted the petition for writ of certiorari in this case ... because it raises important questions concerning the administration of a state prison.

Respondent, on behalf of himself and other inmates of the Nebraska Penal and Correctional Complex ... filed a complaint under 42 USC §1983 challenging several of the practices, rules, and regulations of the Complex. For present purposes, the pertinent allegations were that disciplinary proceedings did not comply with the Due Process Clause of the Fourteenth Amendment to the Federal Constitution; that the inmate legal assistance program did not meet constitutional standards, and that the regulations governing the inspection of mail to and from attorneys for inmates were unconstitutionally restrictive. Respondent requested damages and injunctive relief.

After an evidentiary hearing, the District Court granted partial relief. ... [The Court of Appeals reversed in part and affirmed in part.]

We begin with the due process claim. An understanding of the issues involved requires a detailing of the prison disciplinary regime set down by Nebraska statutes and prison regulations.

Section 16 of the Nebraska Treatment and Corrections Act ... provides that the chief executive officer of each penal facility is responsible for the discipline of inmates in a particular institution. The statute provides for a range of possible disciplinary action. "Except in flagrant or serious cases, punishment for misconduct shall consist of deprivation of privileges. In cases of flagrant or serious misconduct, the chief executive officer may order that a person's reduction of term ... [good-time credit] be forfeited or withheld and also that the person be confined in a disciplinary cell." Each breach of discipline is to be entered in the person's file together with the disposition or punishment therefor. ...

[Major misconduct must be reported to an Adjustment Committee, composed of the Associate Warden Custody, the Correctional Industries Superintendent, and the Reception Center Director. This Committee is directed to review and evaluate all misconduct reports, conduct investigations, make findings, and impose disciplinary actions. Based on the testimony, the District Court found that the following procedures were in effect when an inmate is written up or charged with a prison violation: (a) the chief correction supervisor reviews the "write-ups" on the inmates by the officers of the Complex daily; (b) the convict is called to a conference with the chief correction supervisor and the charging party; (c) following the conference, a conduct report is sent to the Adjustment Committee: (d) there follows a hearing before the Adjustment Committee and the report is read to the inmate and discussed; (e) if the inmate denies the charge he may ask questions of the party writing him up; (f) the Adjustment Committee can conduct additional investigations if it desires; and (g) punishment is imposed.]

Petitioners assert that the procedure for disciplining prison inmates for serious misconduct is a matter of policy raising no constitutional issue. If the position implies that prisoners in state institutions are wholly without the protections of the Constitution and the Due Process Clause, it is plainly untenable. Lawful imprisonment necessarily makes unavailable many rights and privileges of the ordinary citizen, a "retraction justified by the considerations underlying our penal system.". . . But though his rights may be diminished by the needs and exigencies of the institutional environment, a prisoner is not wholly stripped of constitutional protections when he is imprisoned for crime. . . .

Of course, as we have indicated, the fact that prisoners retain rights under the Due Process Clause in no way implies that these rights are not subject to restrictions imposed by the nature of the regime to which they have been lawfully committed. . . . Prison disciplinary proceedings are not part of a criminal prosecution, and the full panoply of rights due a defendant in such proceedings does not apply. . . . In sum, there must be mutual accommodation between institutional needs and objectives and the provisions of the Constitution that are of general application. . . .

. . . But the State having created the right to good time and itself recognizing that its deprivation is a sanction authorized for major misconduct, the prisoner's interest has real substance and is sufficiently embraced within Fourteenth Amendment "liberty" to entitle him to those minimum procedures appropriate under the circumstances and required by the Due Process Clause to insure that the state-created right is not arbitrarily abrogated. . . .

. . . We hold that written notice of the charges must be given to the disciplinary-action defendant in order to inform him of the charges and to enable him to marshall the facts and prepare a defense. At least a brief period of time after the notice, no less than 24 hours, should be allowed to the inmate to prepare for the appearance before the Adjustment Committee.

We also hold that there must be a "'written statement by the fact-finders as to the evidence relied on and reasons" for the disciplinary action. . . .

We are also of the opinion that the inmate facing disciplinary proceedings should be allowed to call witnesses and present documentary evidence in his defense when permitting him to do so will not be unduly hazardous to institutional safety or correctional goals. Ordinarily, the right to present evidence is basic to a fair hearing; but the unrestricted right to call witnesses from the prison population carries obvious potential for disruption and for interference with the swift punishment that in individual cases may be essential to carrying out the correctional program of the institution. . . .

Confrontation and cross-examination present greater hazards to institutional interests. If confrontation and cross-examination of those furnishing evidence against the inmate were to be allowed as a matter of course, as in criminal trials, there would be considerable potential for havoc inside the prison walls. Proceedings would inevitably be longer and tend to unmanageability. . . . Although some States do seem to allow cross-examination in disciplinary hearings, we are not apprised of the conditions under which the procedure may be curtailed; and it does not appear that confrontation and cross-examination are generally required in this context. We think that the Constitution should not be read to impose the procedure at the present time and that adequate bases for decision in prison disciplinary cases can be arrived at without cross-examination. . . .

The insertion of counsel into the disciplinary process would inevitably give the proceedings a more adversary cast and tend to reduce their utility as a means to further correctional goals. There would also be delay and very practical problems in providing counsel in sufficient numbers at the time and place where hearings are to be held. At this stage of the development of these procedures we are not prepared to hold that inmates have a right to either retained or appointed counsel in disciplinary proceedings.

Where an illiterate inmate is involved, however, or where the complexity of the issue makes it unlikely that the inmate will be able to collect and present the evidence necessary for an adequate comprehension of the case, he should be free to seek the aid of a fellow inmate, or if that is forbidden, to have adequate substitute aid in the form of help from the staff or from a sufficiently competent inmate designated by the staff. . . .

The issue of the extent to which prison authorities can open and inspect incoming mail from attorneys to inmates, has been considerably narrowed in the course of this litigation. . . . Petitioners now concede that they cannot open and *read* mail from attorneys to inmates, but contend that they may open all letters from attorneys as long as it is done in the presence of the prisoners. . . .

. . . We think it entirely appropriate that the State require any such communications to be specially marked as originating from an attorney, with his name and address being given, if they are to receive special treatment. It would also certainly be permissible that prison authorities require that a lawyer desiring to correspond with a prisoner, first identify himself and his client to the prison officials, to assure that the letters marked privileged are actually from members of the bar. At to the ability to open the mail in the presence of inmates, this could in no way constitute censorship, since the mail would not be read. Neither could it chill such communications, since the inmate's presence insures that prison officials will not read the mail. The possibility that contraband will be enclosed in letters, even those from apparent attorneys, surely warrants prison officials' opening the letters. . . .

The last issue presented is whether the Complex must make available, and if so has made available, adequate legal assistance, under *Johnson* v. *Avery, supra,* for the preparation of habeas corpus petitions and civil rights actions by inmates. The issue arises in the context of a challenge to a regulation providing, in pertinent part:

"Legal Work

"A legal advisor has been appointed by the Warden for the benefit of those offenders who are in need of legal assistance. This individual is an offender who has general knowledge of the law procedure. He is not an attorney and can not represent you as such.

"No other offender than the legal advisor is permitted to assist you in the preparation of legal documents unless with the specific written permission of the Warden.". . .

In *Johnson* v. *Avery,* an inmate was disciplined for violating a prison regulation which prohibited inmates from assisting other prisoners in preparing habeas corpus petitions. The Court held that "unless and until the State provides some reasonable alternative to assist inmates in the preparation of petitions for postconviction relief," inmates could not be barred from furnishing assistance to each other. . . .

Petitioners contend that *Avery* is limited to assistance in the preparation of habeas corpus petitions and disputes the direction of the Court of Appeals to the District Court that the capacity of the inmate adviser be assessed in light of the demand for assistance in civil rights actions as well as in the preparation of habeas writs. Petitioners take too narrow a view of that decision. . . .

. . . [W]hile it is true that only in habeas actions may relief be granted which will shorten the term of confinement . . . it is more pertinent that both actions serve to protect basic constitutional rights. The right of access to the courts, upon which *Avery* was premised, is founded in the Due Process Clause and assures that no person will be denied the opportunity to present to the judiciary allegations concerning violations of fundamental constitutional rights. It is futile to contend that the Civil Rights Act of 1871 has less importance in our constitutional scheme than does the Great Writ. The recognition by this Court that prisoners have certain constitutional rights which can be protected by civil rights actions would be diluted if inmates, often "totally or functionally illiterate," were unable to articulate their complaints to the courts. Although there may be additional burdens on the Complex, if inmates may seek help from other inmates, or from the inmate adviser if he proves adequate, in both habeas and civil rights actions, this should not prove overwhelming. At present only one inmate serves as legal adviser and it may be expected that other qualified inmates could be found for assistance if the Complex insists on naming the inmates from whom help may be sought. . . .

Affirmed in part, reversed in part, and remanded.

Mr. Justice Marshall, with whom Mr. Justice Brennan joins, dissenting in part. . . .

Mr. Justice Douglas, dissenting. . . .

CHAPTER 5
Religious Freedom

The part played by religious enthusiasts in the settlement and development of America is an oft-told story. What is sometimes overlooked, however, is the fact that religious liberty did not reach fruition with the landing of the Pilgrims. On the contrary, the attainment of the present broad measure of religious freedom in America is a story of long, and sometimes bitter, struggle extending over more than three centuries. Even today, there are controverted areas of policy and practice in which various minority sects are claiming abridgment of their constitutional guarantees of religious liberty.

The Puritans brought with them to New England the conviction that men have a right and a duty to associate voluntarily for religious purposes. For this group, however, religious freedom meant only freedom to practice the true faith—Puritanism. They not only did not accept the principle of religious toleration; they went further and used the arm of government both to prosecute dissenters and to enforce observance of certain of the church laws. Thus we have depicted in the history of the Massachusetts Bay Colony two of the primary enemies of religious freedom—active support of religion by the government and governmental suppression of certain religious exercises.

In Massachusetts Bay, Puritanism was the official faith. In the Virginia charter of 1609 the doctrine and rites of the Church of England were established by law. While most other faiths were apparently to be tolerated, the charter particularly excluded "persons who affected the 'superstitions of the Church of Rome.'" In New Netherlands the Dutch Reformed Church had the exclusive right of public worship. And in the Spanish colonies the Inquisition was imported to guarantee the repression of non-Catholic heresies.

At the mid-seventeenth century only two of the English colonies, Rhode Island and Maryland, offered substantial religious freedom. Not until almost the outbreak of the Revolutionary War did the attitude on religious liberty begin to soften and governmental policy toward minority sects show signs of easing. Changes in the law followed, with Virginia leading the way by its adoption of religious toleration in the Declaration of Rights accompanying its 1776 constitution. Pennsylvania in the same year and Massachusetts in 1780 guaranteed to all faiths the freedom to worship publicly. These were measures directed to *one* of the problems of religious freedom—that of *free exercise* of religion. And while they were important gains, they represented actually only a strong start along a long road. Some of the most important developments, in fact, have come in the period since 1940.

Another major hurdle to overcome in the advance toward religious freedom was disestablishment and the abolition of taxation for religious purposes.

These problems arise from the presence of *active government support* of religion, especially where the support is for a specific religion. Modifications were made in the latter years of the Revolution, and in 1785 Jefferson's famous Act for Establishing Religious Freedom passed the Virginia legislature. Other states followed, although New England was much slower to succumb to the trend. The Connecticut constitution of 1818 provided for separation of church and state, but this chapter of the struggle was not closed until the last state, Massachusetts, adopted a constitutional amendment in 1833 to remove the state from active promotion of a particular religion.

Since 1833, and particularly since the end of World War II, the problem of governmental support of religion has broadened, and the controversies have presented issues more difficult of logical resolution. There is probably fairly general agreement in the United States that government should not actively show a preference for one religious sect. But suppose government promotes all religious sects equally. Does this present a threat to religious freedom? Does the fact that the overwhelming majority of people in the United States profess a preference for Christianity justify Sunday Closing Laws? Is religious liberty endangered by either promoting or permitting religious exercises in the public schools? Does government act improperly if it includes religious schools among the beneficiaries of aid-to-education appropriation bills? These questions are less easily disposed of than those involving the clear-cut issue of preferential treatment.

The theory behind the argument for virtually complete separation of church and state is fairly easy to state. It rests on a view that religious liberty is best protected when government remains absolutely neutral on matters of religion. The problem, however, is that one man's neutrality is another man's hostility. To some, government is neutral toward religion if it does not support or even permit religious exercises in public schools during the school day. It is neither promoting sectarian religion nor is it prohibiting the child from engaging in religious observance, so long as it takes place outside the ambit of public school activities. To others, the denial of permission to use a portion of the school day for religious exercises is to *interfere* with religious freedom and therefore is outright governmental hostility. The newer cases raising the separation issue have presented questions which are more and more difficult of logical resolution. The result has frequently been more readily defensible as simply a convenient place to draw the line, rather than the logical necessities of applying the broad principle of "separation of church and state."

The two aspects of religious liberty—freedom from governmental establishment of religion and the free exercise of religion—will be taken up separately in this chapter. In the First Amendment both aspects are covered in the phrase "Congress shall make no law respecting an establishment of religion, or prohibiting the free exercise thereof."

SEPARATION OF CHURCH AND STATE

The establishment clause of the First Amendment has long since been rephrased in the general literature and in the popular mind to become simply a guarantee of "separation of church and state." The controversy over separation in America has its roots in the debate between John Cotton and Roger Williams in Massachusetts Bay Colony in the first half of the seventeenth century. It has continued at intervals ever since. But the first case to reach the United States Supreme Court in which the Court really came to grips with the question of applying the First Amendment's establishment clause (albeit through the Fourteenth Amendment) did not arrive until 1947. State courts for some years have been faced with establishment issues, although most of these are of twentieth century vintage. Thus we have the somewhat strange situation of a burgeoning body of relatively new case law on a controversy which in America is as old as the colonial settlements themselves.

Aid to Religious Schools

EVERSON v. BOARD OF EDUCATION
330 U.S. 1 (1947)

Mr. Justice Black delivered the opinion of the Court.

A New Jersey statute authorizes its local school districts to make rules and contracts for the transportation of children to and from schools.* The appellee, a township board of education, acting pursuant to this statute, authorized reimbursement to parents of money expended by them for the bus transportation of their children on regular buses operated by the public transportation system. Part of this money was for the payment of transportation of some children in the community to Catholic parochial schools. These church schools give their students, in addition to secular education, regular religious instruction conforming to the religious tenets and modes of worship of the Catholic Faith. The superintendent of these schools is a Catholic priest.

The appellant, in his capacity as a district taxpayer, filed suit in a State court challenging the right of the Board to reimburse parents of parochial school students. He contended that the statute and the resolution passed pursuant to it violated both the State and the Federal Constitutions. That court held that the legislature was without power to authorize such payment under the State constitution. 132 N.J.L. 98. The New Jersey Court of Errors and Appeals reversed, holding that neither the statute nor the resolution passed pursuant to it was in conflict with the State constitution or the provisions of the Federal Constitution in issue. 133 N.J.L. 350. The case is here on appeal under 28 U.S.C. Section 344(a).

Since there has been no attack on the statute on the ground that a part of its language excludes children attending private schools operated for profit from enjoying State payment for their transportation, we need not consider this exclusionary language; it has no relevancy to any constitutional question here presented. Futhermore, if the exclusion clause had been properly challenged, we do not know whether New Jersey's highest court would construe its statutes as precluding payment of the school transportation of any group of pupils, even those of a private school run for profit. Consequently, we put to one side the question as to the validity of the statute against the claim that it does not authorize payment for the transportation generally of school children in New Jersey.

The only contention here is that the State statute and the resolution, insofar as they authorized reimbursement to parents of children attending parochial schools,

---

* Whenever in any district there are children living remote from any schoolhouse, the board of education of the district may make rules and contracts for the transportation of such children to and from school, including the transportation of school children to and from school other than a public school, except such school as is operated for profit in whole or in part. . . ."

violate the Federal Constitution in these two respects, which to some extent overlap. First. They authorize the State to take by taxation the private property of some and bestow it upon others, to be used for their own private purposes. This, it is alleged, violates the due process clause of the Fourteenth Amendment. Second. The statute and the resolution forced inhabitants to pay taxes to help support and maintain schools which are dedicated to, and which regularly teach, the Catholic Faith. This is alleged to be a use of State power to support church schools contrary to the prohibition of the First Amendment which the Fourteenth Amendment made applicable to the states. . . .

It is much too late to argue that legislation intended to facilitate the opportunity of children to get a secular education serves no public purposes. . . . The same thing is no less true of legislation to reimburse needy parents, or all parents, for payment of the fares of their children so that they can ride in public busses to and from schools rather than run the risk of traffic and other hazards incident to walking or "hitch-hiking.'. . . Nor does it follow that a law has a private rather than a public purpose because it provided that tax-raised funds will be paid to reimburse individuals on account of money spent by them in a way which furthers a public program. . . . Subsidies and loans to individuals such as farmers and home owners, and to privately owned transportation systems, as well as many other kinds of businesses, have been common-place practice in our state and national history. . . .

Second. The New Jersey statute is challenged as a "law respecting the establishment of religion." The First Amendment, as made applicable to the states by the Fourteenth, *Murdock* v. *Pennsylvania,* 319 U.S. 105, commands that a state "shall make no law respecting an establishment of religion, or prohibiting the free exercise thereof.". . . These words of the First Amendment reflected in the minds of early Americans a vivid mental picture of conditions and practices which they fervently wished to stamp out in order to preserve liberty for themselves and for their posterity. Doubtless their goal has not been entirely reached; but so far has the Nation moved toward it that the expression "law respecting the establishment of religion," probably does not so vividly remind present-day Americans of the evils, fears, and political problems that caused that expression to be written into our Bill of Rights. Whether this New Jersey law is one respecting the "establishment of religion" requires an understanding of the meaning of that language, particularly with respect to the imposition of taxes. Once again, therefore, it is not inappropriate briefly to review the background and environment of the period in which that constitutional language was fashioned and adopted. . . . [Here the opinion reviews the historical events and concludes with the interpretation that the First Amendment was intended to bar the government from adopting measures to "tax, to support, or otherwise to assist any or all religions. . . ."]

The "establishment of religion" clause of the First Amendment means at least this. Neither a state nor the Federal Government can set up a church. Neither can pass laws which aid one religion, aid all religions, or prefer one religion over another. Neither can force nor influence a person to go to or to remain away from church against his will or force him to profess a belief or disbelief in any religion. No person can be punished for entertaining or professing religious beliefs or disbeliefs, for church attendance or non-attendance. No tax in any amount, large or small, can be levied to support any religious activities or institutions, whatever they may be called, or whatever form they may adopt to teach or practice religion. Neither a state nor the Federal Government can, openly or secretly, participate in the affairs of any religious organizations or groups and vice versa.

In the words of Jefferson, the clause against establishment of religion by law was intended to erect "a wall of separation between Church and State." *Reynolds* v. *United States,* 98 U.S. 145, 164.

We must consider the New Jersey statute in accordance with the foregoing limitations imposed by the First Amendment. But we must not strike that state statute down if it is within the State's constitutional power even though it approaches the verge of that power. . . . New Jersey cannot consistently with the "establishment of religion" clause of the First Amendment contribute tax-raised funds to the support of an institution which teaches the tenets and faith of any church. On the other hand, other language of the amendment commands that New Jersey cannot hamper its citizens in the free exercise of their own religion. Consequently, it cannot exclude individual Catholics, Lutherans, Mohammedans, Baptists, Jews, Methodists, Non-believers, Presbyterians, or the members of any other faith, *because of their faith, or lack of it,* from receiving the benefits of public welfare legislation. While we do not mean to intimate that a state could not provide transportation only to children attending public schools, we must be careful, in protecting the citizens of New Jersey against state-established churches, to be sure that we do not inadvertently prohibit New Jersey from extending its general state law benefits to all its citizens without regard to their religious belief.

Measured by these standards, we cannot say that the First Amendment prohibits New Jersey from spending tax-raised funds to pay the bus fares of parochial school pupils as a part of a general program under which it pays the fares of pupils attending public and other schools. It is undoubtedly true that children are helped to get to church schools. There is even a possibility that some of the children might not be sent to the church schools if the parents were compelled to pay their children's bus fares out of their own pockets when transportation to a public school would have been paid for by the state. The same possibility exists where the state requires a local transit company to provide reduced fares to school children including those attending parochial schools, or where a municipally owned transportation system undertakes to carry all school children free of charge. Moreover, state-paid policemen, detailed to protect children going to and from church schools from the very real hazards of traffic, would serve much the same purpose and accomplish much the same result as state provisions intended to guarantee free transportation of a kind which the state deems to be best for the school children's welfare. And parents might refuse to risk their children to the serious danger of traffic accidents going to and from parochial schools, the approaches to which were not protected by policemen. Similarly, parents might be reluctant to permit their children to attend schools which the state had cut off from such general government services as ordinary police and fire protection, connections for sewage disposal, public highways and sidewalks. Of course, cutting off church schools from these services, so separate and so indisputably marked off from the religious function, would make it far more difficult for the schools to operate. But such is obviously not the purpose of the First Amendment. That Amendment requires the state to be neutral in its relations with groups of religious believers and non-believers; it does not require the state to be their adversary. State power is no more to be used so as to handicap religions than it is to favor them.

This Court has said that parents may, in the discharge of their duty under state compulsory education laws, send their children to a religious rather than a public school if the school meets the secular educational requirements which the state has power to impose. See *Pierce* v. *Society of Sisters,* 268 U.S. 510. It appears that these parochial schools meet New Jersey's requirements. The state contributes no money to the schools. It does not support them. Its legislation, as applied, does no more than provide a general program to help parents get their children, regardless of their religion, safely and expeditiously to and from accredited schools.

The First Amendment has erected a wall between church and state. That wall must be kept high and impregnable. We could not approve the slightest breach. New Jersey has not breached it here.

Affirmed.

Mr. Justice Jackson, dissenting. . . .

Whether the taxpayer constitutionally can be made to contribute aid to parents of students because of their attendance at parochial schools depends upon the nature of those schools and their relation to the Church. . . .

It is no exaggeration to say that the whole historic conflict in temporal policy between the Catholic Church and non-Catholics comes to a focus in their respective school policies. The Roman Catholic Church, counseled by experience in many ages and many lands and with all sorts and conditions of men, takes what, from the viewpoint of its own progress and the success of its mission, is a wise estimate of the importance of education to religion. It does not leave the individual to pick up religion by chance. It relies on early and indelible indoctrination in the faith and order of the Church by the word and example of persons consecrated to the task. . . .

I should be surprised if any Catholic would deny that the parochial school is a vital, if not the most vital, part of the Roman Catholic Church. If put to the choice, that venerable institution, I should expect, would forego its whole service for mature persons before it would give up education of the young, and it would be a wise choice. Its growth and cohesion, discipline and loyalty, spring from its schools. Catholic education is the rock on which the whole structure rests, and to render tax aid to its Church school is indistinguishable to me from rendering the same aid to the Church itself.

It is of no importance in this situation whether the beneficiary of this expenditure of tax-raised funds is primarily the parochial school and incidentally the pupil, or whether the aid is directly bestowed on the pupil with indirect benefits to the school. The state cannot maintain a Church and it can no more tax its citizens to furnish free carriage to those who attend a Church. The prohibition against establishment of religion cannot be circumvented by a subsidy, bonus or reimbursement of expense to individuals for receiving religious instruction and indoctrination. . . .

Mr. Justice Frankfurter joins in this opinion.

Mr. Justice Rutledge, with whom Mr. Justice Frankfurter, Mr. Justice Jackson and Mr. Justice Burton agree, dissenting. . . .

This case forces us to determine squarely for the first time what was "an establishment of religion" in the First Amendment's conception; and by that measure to decide whether New Jersey's action violates its command.

[Here the opinion contains a survey of the "generating history" of the religious clause of the First Amendment.]

In view of this history no further proof is needed that the Amendment forbids any appropriation, large or small, from public funds to aid or support any and all religious exercises. But if more were called for, the debates in the First Congress and this Court's consistent expressions, whenever it has touched on the matter directly, supply it. . . .

Compulsory attendance upon religious exercises went out early in the process of separating church and state, together with forced observance of religious forms and ceremonies. Test oaths and religions qualification for office followed later. These things none devoted to our great tradition of religious liberty would think of bringing back. Hence today, apart from efforts to inject religious training or exercises and sectarian issues into the public schools, the only serious surviving threat to maintaining that complete and permanent separation of religion and civil power which the First Amendment commands is through use of the taxing power to support religion, religious establishments, or establishments having a religious foundation whatever their form or special religious function.

Does New Jersey's action furnish support for religion by use of the taxing power? Certainly it does, if the test remains undiluted as Jefferson and Madison made it, that money taken by taxation from one is not to be used or given to support another's religious training or belief, or indeed one's own. Today as then the furnishing of "contributions of money for the propagation of opinions which he disbelieves" is the forbidden exaction; and the prohibition is absolute for whatever measure brings that consequence and whatever amount may be sought or given to that end.

The funds used here were raised by taxation. The Court does not dispute, nor could it, that their use does in fact give aid and encouragement to religious instruction. It only concludes that this aid is not "support" in law. But Madison and Jefferson were concerned with aid and support in fact, not as a legal conclusion "entangled in precedents.". . . Here parents pay money to send their children to parochial school and funds raised by taxation are used to reimburse them. This not only helps the children to get to school and the parents to send them. It aids them in a substantial way to get the very thing which they are sent to the particular school to secure, namely, religious training and teaching. . . .

Despite the close vote in the case and the controversy aroused by the decision, *Everson* remains as ruling law on the bus transportation issue. However, the earlier cautions concerning the impact of federalism on civil rights must be called to mind here. All the Court held in *Everson* was that the New Jersey bus transportation scheme did not violate the United States Constitution. Obviously the case did not hold that the state was *required* to furnish such transportation. Less obviously, perhaps, it in no way foreclosed a decision by the state courts that such a scheme would violate *state* constitutional provisions relative to separation of church and state. In our federal system the state supreme court is the final judge of the construction of the state constitution. And a practice may be held violative of state constitutional provisions even though it does not offend against the United States Constitution, and even though the constitutional phraseology is identical. In fact, the bus transportation issue was litigated under state constitutional provisions in several states both before and after the *Everson* decision, and the weight of authority among the state courts is against such transportation. [The cases are canvassed in David Fellman, *Religion in American Public Law* (Boston: Boston University Press, 1965), pp. 81–83.]

The issue of aid to religion at the federal level arose in 1961 with President Kennedy's proposals to provide federal grants to assist *public* elementary and secondary schools. Pressure developed to extend the assistance to private schools as well, including sectarian schools. The positions of those who opposed and those who supported federal aid to church-related schools were compromised in the passage of the Elementary and Secondary School Improvement Act of 1965. About one-fourth of the more than $1,000,000,000 to be provided was to be earmarked for the purchase of textbooks and for the establishment of supplementary education centers, both of which would be under the control of the public schools, but the benefits to be shared by pupils in the parochial schools.

BOARD OF EDUCATION *v.* ALLEN
392 U.S. 236 (1968)

Mr. Justice White delivered the opinion of the Court.

A law of the State of New York requires local public school authorities to lend textbooks free of charge to all students in grades seven through 12; students attending private schools are included. This case presents the question whether this statute is a "law respecting an establishment of religion, or prohibiting the free exercise thereof," and so in conflict with the First and Fourteenth Amendments to the Constitution, because it authorizes the loan of textbooks to students attending parochial schools. We hold that the law is not in violation of the Constitution. . . .

Everson v. *Board of Education* . . . is the case decided by this Court that is most nearly in point for today's problem. . . .

Everson and later cases have shown that the line between state neutrality to religion and state support of religion is not easy to locate. . . . Based on *Everson, Zorach, McGowan,* and other cases, *Abington School District* v. *Schempp* . . . fashioned a test subscribed to by eight Justices for distinguishing between forbidden involvements of the State with religion and those contacts which the Establishment clause permits:

"The test may be stated as follows: what are the purpose and the primary effect of the enactment? If either is the advancement or inhibition of religion then the enactment exceeds the scope of legislative power as circumscribed by the Constitution. That is to say that to withstand the strictures of the Establishment Clause there must be a secular legislative purpose and a primary effect that neither advances nor inhibits religion. *Everson* v. *Board of Education.* . . ."

The test is not easy to apply, but the citation of *Everson* by the *Schempp* Court to support its general standard made clear how the *Schempp* rule would be applied to the facts of *Everson*. The statute upheld in *Everson* would be considered a law having "a secular legislative purpose and a primary effect that neither advances nor inhibits religion." We reach the same result with respect to the New York law. . . .

Of course books are different from buses. Most bus rides have no inherent religious significance, while religious books are common. However, the language of Sec. 701 does not authorize the loan of religious books, and the State claims no right to distribute religious literature. Although the books loaned are those required by the parochial school for use in specific courses, each book loaned must be approved by the public school authorities; only secular books may receive approval. . . . In judging the validity of the statute on this record we must proceed on the assumption that books loaned to students are books that are not unsuitable for use in the public schools because of religious content. . . .

The judgment is affirmed.

Mr. Justice Harlan, concurring. . . .

Mr. Justice Black, dissenting. . . .

I still subscribe to the belief that tax-raised funds cannot constitutionally be used to support religious schools, buy their school books, erect their buildings, pay their teachers, or pay any other of their maintenance expenses, even to the extent of one penny. . . . And I still believe that the only way to protect minority religious groups from majority groups in this country is to keep the wall of separation between church and state high and impregnable as the First and Fourteenth Amendments provide. The Court's affirmance here bodes nothing but evil to religious peace in this country.

Mr. Justice Douglas, dissenting. . . .

Whatever may be said of *Everson,* there is nothing ideological about a bus. There is nothing ideological about a school lunch, or a public nurse, or a scholarship. . . . The textbook goes to the very heart of education in a parochial school. It is the chief, although not solitary, instrumentality for propagating a particular religious creed or faith. How can we possibly approve such state aid to a religion? . . .

The initiative to select and requisition "the books desired" is with the parochial school. Powerful religious-political pressures will therefore be on the state agencies to provide the books that are desired.

These then are the battlegrounds where control of textbook distribution will be won or lost. Now that "secular" textbooks will pour into religious schools, we can rest assured that a contest will be on to provide those books for religious schools which the dominant religious group concludes best reflect the theocentric or other philosophy of the particular church. . . .

It has long been the policy of governmental units to accord special treatment to religious and other charitable organizations in the form of exemptions from property taxes. While such exemptions do not constitute an appropriation of tax money for religious purposes, they obviously represent a valuable monetary benefit, and money not spent for taxes may be used to expand religious operations. The Court considered the First Amendment implications of such exemptions in *Walz* v. *Tax Commission of the City of New York* in 1970.

WALZ *v.* TAX COMMISSION OF THE CITY OF NEW YORK
397 U.S. 664 (1970)

[The plaintiff, an owner of real property, brought suit in the New York courts to enjoin the New York City Tax Commission from granting property tax exemptions to religious organizations for religious properties used solely for religious worship. Such exemptions were authorized by state constitutional and statutory provisions, but the plaintiff contended that the exemptions indirectly required the plaintiff to make a contribution to religious bodies, thereby violating the religion clauses of the First Amendment. The court dismissed the complaint, and the New York Court of Appeals affirmed.]

Mr. Chief Justice Burger delivered the opinion of the Court.

The course of constitutional neutrality in this area cannot be an absolutely straight line; rigidity could well defeat the basic purpose of these provisions, which is to insure that no religion be sponsored or favored, none commanded, and none inhibited. . . .

The legislative purpose of a property tax exemption is neither the adavncement nor the inhibition of religion; it is neither sponsorship nor hostility. New York, in common with the other States, has determined that certain entities that exist in a harmonious relationship to the community at large, and that foster its "moral or mental improvement," should not be inhibited in their activities by property taxation or the hazard of loss of those properties for nonpayment of taxes. It has not singled out one particular church or religious group or even churches as such; rather, it has granted exemption to all houses of religious worship within a broad class of property owned by nonprofit, quasi-public corporations which include hospitals, libraries, playgrounds, scientific, professional, historical and patriotic groups. The State has an affirmative policy that considers these groups as beneficial and stabilizing influences in community life and finds this classification useful, desirable, and in the public interest. . . .

Determining that the legislative purpose of tax exemption is not aimed at establishing, sponsoring, or supporting religion does not end the inquiry, however. We must also be sure that the end result—the effect—is not an excessive government entanglement with religion. The test is inescapably one of degree. Either course, taxation of churches or exemption, occasions some degree of involvement with religion. Elimination of exemption would tend to expand the involvement of government by giving rise to tax valuation of church property, tax liens, tax foreclosures, and the direct confrontations and conflicts that follow in the train of those legal processes. . . . The exemption creates only a minimal and remote involvement between church and state and far less than taxation of churches. It restricts the fiscal relationship between church and state, and tends to complement and reinforce the desired separation insulating each from the other. . . .

All of the 50 States provide for tax exemption of places of worship, most of them doing so by constitutional guarantees. For so long as federal income taxes have had any potential impact on churches—over 75 years—religous organizations have been expressly exempt from the tax. . . .

Nothing in this national attitude toward religious tolerance and two centuries of uninterrupted freedom from taxation has given the remotest sign of leading to an established church or religion and on the contrary it has operated affirmatively to help guarantee the free exercise of all forms of religious beliefs. . . . If taxation can be seen as this first step toward "establishment" of religion, as Mr. Justice Douglas fears, the second step has been long in coming. Any move which realistically "establishes" a church or tends to do so can be dealt with "while this Court sits.". . .

Affirmed.

Mr. Justice Brennan, concurring. . . .

The existence from the beginning of the Nation's life of a practice, such as tax exemptions for religious organizations, is not conclusive of its constitutionality. But such practice is a fact of considerable import in the interpretation of abstract constitutional language. On its face, the Establishment Clause is reasonably susceptible of different interpretations regarding the exemptions. This Court's interpretation of the clause, accordingly, is appropriately influenced by the reading it has received in the practices of the Nation. As Mr. Justice Holmes observed in an analogous context, in resolving such questions of interpretation, "a page of history is worth a volume of logic.". . . The more longstanding and widely accepted a practice, the greater its impact upon constitutional interpretation. History is particularly compelling in the present case because of the undeviating acceptance given religious tax exemptions from our earliest days as a Nation. Rarely if ever has this Court considered the constitutionality of a practice for which the historical support is so overwhelming. . . .

The exemptions have continued uninterrupted to the present day. They are in force in all 50 States. No judicial decision, state or federal, has ever held that they violate the Establishment Clause. . . .

Tax exemptions and general subsidies . . . are qualitatively different. Though both provide economic assistance, they do so in fundamentally different ways. A subsidy involves the direct transfer of public monies to the subsidized enterprise and uses resources exacted from taxpayers as a whole. An exemption, on the other hand, involves no such transfer. It assists the exempted enterprise only passively, by relieving a privately funded venture of the burden of paying taxes. In other words, "in the case of direct subsidy, the state forcibly diverts the income of both believers and nonbelievers to churches," while "in the case of an exemption, the state merely refrains from diverting to its own uses income independently generated by the churches through voluntary contributions.". . .

. . . Moreover, the termination of exemptions would give rise, as the Court says, to the necessity for "tax valuation of church property, tax liens, tax foreclosures, and the direct confrontation and conflicts that follow in the train of those legal processes.". . . Whether Government grants or withholds the exemptions, it is going to be involved with religion. . . .

Mr. Justice Harlan, concurring. . . .

Mr. Justice Douglas, dissenting. . . .

There are many states in which private school (largely sectarian) enrollment at the elementary and secondary level represents a substantial percentage of the total school population. As costs have increased over the past several years, private schools have faced severe budgetary difficulties, and their supporters have mounted strong pressures for at least minimal financial aid from public funds. Two arguments have been forcefully presented: (1) as a matter of public policy, the government should promote a strong private school sector in order to encourage diversity of training and educational choice, and (2) from the standpoint of equity, those who support both private and public schools, but who do not use or burden the public school system, should receive governmental assistance to insure the continued viability of the private schools.

A number of proposals for aid to private schools have been adopted in response to these pleas, and almost immediately they have been challenged by persons or organizations who contend that such aid represents an unconstitutional establishment of religion insofar as it assists sectarian schools. The following cases represent the more important decisions with respect to these various school-aid devices.

LEMON *v.* KURTZMAN
403 U.S. 602 (1971)

Mr. Chief Justice Burger delivered the opinion of the Court.

These two appeals raise questions as to Pennsylvania and Rhode Island statutes providing state aid to church-related elementary and secondary schools. Both statutes are challenged as violative of the Establishment and Free Exercise Clauses of the First Amendment and the Due Process Clause of the Fourteenth Amendment.

Pennsylvania has adopted a statutory program that provides financial support to nonpublic elementary and secondary schools by way of reimbursement for the cost of teachers' salaries, textbooks, and instructional materials in specified secular subjects. Rhode Island has adopted a statute under which the State pays directly to teachers in nonpublic elementary schools a supplement of 15% of their annual salary. Under each statute state aid has been given to church-related educational institutions as well as other private schools. We hold that both statutes are unconstitutional. . . .

(a) Rhode Island Program

The District Court made extensive findings on the grave potential for excessive entanglement that inheres in the religious character and purpose of the Roman Catholic elementary schools of Rhode Island, to date the sole beneficiaries of the Rhode Island Salary Supplement Act. . . .

In *Allen* the Court refused to make assumptions, on a meager record, about the religious content of the textbooks that the State would be asked to provide. We cannot, however, refuse there to recognize that teachers have a substantially different ideological character than books. In terms of potential for involving some aspect of faith or morals in secular subjects, a textbook's content is ascertainable, but a teacher's handling of a subject is not. We cannot ignore the dangers that a teacher under religious control and discipline poses to the separation of the religious from the purely secular aspects of pre-college education.

In our view the record shows these dangers are present to a substantial degree. . . . The teacher is employed by a religious organization, subject to the direction and discipline of religious authorities, and works in a system dedicated to rearing children in a particular faith. These are not lessened by the fact that most of the lay teachers are of the Catholic faith. Inevitably some of a teacher's responsibilities hover on the border between secular and religious orientation.

We need not and do not assume that teachers in parochial schools will be guilty of bad faith or any conscious design to evade the limitations imposed by the statute and the First Amendment. We simply recognize that a dedicated religious person, teaching in a school affiliated with his or her faith and operated to inculate its tenets, will inevitably experience great difficulty in remaining religiously neutral. . . .

(b) Pennsylvania Program

The Pennsylvania statute also provides state aid to church-related schools for teachers' salaries. . . .

As we noted earlier, the very restrictions and surveillance necessary to ensure that teachers pay a strictly nonideological role give rise to entanglements between church and state. The Pennsylvania statute, like that of Rhode Island, fosters this kind of relationship. Reimbursement is not only limited to courses offered in the public schools and materials approved by state officials, but the statute excludes "any subject matter expressing religious teaching, or the morals or forms of worship of an sect." In addition schools seeking reimbursement must maintain accounting procedures that require the State to establish the cost of the secular as distinguished from the religious instruction.

The Pennsylvania statute, moreover, has the further defect of providing state financial aid directly to the church-related school. This factor distinguishes both *Everson* and *Allen,* for in both those cases the Court was careful to point out that state aid was provided to the student and his parents—not to the church-related school. . . . The history of government grants of a continuing cash subsidy indicates that such programs have almost always been accompanied by varying measures of control and surveillance. . . .

A broader base of entanglement of yet a different character is presented by the divisive political potential of these state programs. In a community where such a large number of pupils are served by church-related schools, it can be assumed that state assistance will entail considerable political activity. . . . Candidates will be forced to declare and voters to choose. It would be unrealistic to ignore the fact that many people confronted with issues of this kind will find their votes aligned with their faith.

Ordinarily political debate and division, however vigorous or even partisan, are normal and healthy manifestations of our democratic system of government, but political division along religious lines was one of the principal evils against which the First Amendment was intended to protect. . . .

Mr. Justice Harlan, concurring. . . .

Mr. Justice Douglas, whom Mr. Justice Black joins, concurring. . . .

In *Tilton* v. *Richardson,* 403 U.S. 672 (1971), the Court upheld that portion of the Higher Education Facilities Act of 1963 which provided federal construction grants for college and university facilities (excluding facilities used for sectarian instruction or as places of worship, or those used as part of a program of a school or department of divinity), but held unconstitutional that portion of the Act providing for a 20-year limitation on the religious use of the facilities constructed with federal funds. The Court pointed out that it "cannot be assumed that a substantial structure has no value after that period and hence the unrestricted use of a valuable property is in effect a contribution of some value to a religious body."

In *Hunt* v. *McNair,* 413 U.S. 734 (1973), a South Carolina taxpayer sued state officials for declaratory and injunctive relief against the operation of the South Carolina Educational Facilities Act insofar as it authorized the state-created Educational Facilities Authority to issue revenue bonds for the benefit of the Baptist College at Charleston. Under the arrangement, the Authority was permitted to issue bonds (at the lower interest rates for tax-exempt state bonds than the private Baptist College could obtain), the proceeds of which would be used to finance the construction of buildings and facilities for the college. The plan provided that the college would convey title to such projects to the Authority, and the Authority would lease back to the college, with reconveyance to the college upon full repayment of the bonds.

The Court held that the scheme did not violate the establishment clause because (1) the statute had a secular purpose in seeking to aid institutions of higher education, whether or not they had religious affiliations; (2) the Baptist College's operations were not oriented significantly toward sectarian rather than secular education, since there were no religious qualifications for faculty membership or student admission, and its percentage of Baptist students was roughly equal to the percentage of Baptists in that area of the state; (3) the bond issuance would not have the primary effect of advancing or inhibiting religion, because the project would not include any buildings or facilities used for religious purposes; and (4) the transaction would not foster an excessive entanglement with religion merely because the college had a formalistic relationship with the state or because the Authority might foreclose if the college should fail to make the prescribed rental payments or otherwise default in its obligations.

At the same time, the Court added a refinement to the "primary effect" test, the second of the three tests applied in *Lemon* v. *Kurtzman:*

Aid normally may be thought to have a primary effect of advancing religion when it flows to an institution in which religion is so pervasive that a substantial portion of its functions are subsumed in the religious mission or when it funds a specifically religious activity in an otherwise substantially secular setting.

A measure of at least one state's concern and interest in helping the private schools is indicated by the rapidity with which the legislature of Pennsylvania reacted to the decision in *Lemon* v. *Kurtzman.* That decision came on June 28, 1971, and on August 27, 1971, the legislature promulgated a new aid law, entitled the "Parent Reimbursement Act for Nonpublic Education," providing funds to reimburse parents for a portion of tuition expenses incurred in sending their children to nonpublic schools. In *Sloan* v. *Lemon,* 413 U.S. 825 (1973), the Court held this act also unconstitutional because "at bottom its intended consequence is to preserve and support religion-oriented institutions." On the same day, in *Committee for Public Education* v. *Nyquist,* a more elaborate aid statute of New York was held invalid.

COMMITTEE FOR PUBLIC EDUCATION *v.* NYQUIST
413 U.S. 756 (1973)

[Amendments to New York's education and tax laws established three financial aid programs for nonpublic elementary and secondary schools. The first section provides for direct money grants to "qualifying" schools to be used for maintenance and repair of facilities and equipment. A "qualifying" school is a nonpublic, nonprofit elementary or secondary school serving a high concentration of pupils from low-income families. The annual grant is $30 per pupil, or $40 if the facilities are more than twenty-five years old, but not to exceed 50 percent of the average per-pupil cost for such services in the public schools. Section 2 establishes a tuition reimbursement plan for parents of children attending nonpublic elementary or secondary schools. Reimbursement is provided in amounts up to $50 per grade school child and $100 per high school student to parents with an annual taxable income of less than $5,000. Sections 3, 4, and 5 provide tax relief to parents failing to qualify for tuition reimbursement. Each taxpayer-parent is entitled to deduct a specified sum from his gross income for each child attending a nonpublic school. The amount of the deduction is unrelated to the amount of tuition actually paid and decreases as the amount of taxable income increases. Parents with adjusted gross incomes of more than $25,000 receive no deduction.

The Committee for Public Education filed for an injunction in the United States District Court for the Southern District of New York, alleging that each of the three aid provisions constituted an invalid aid to religion. A three-judge court found that the maintenance and tuition reimbursement provisions were unconstitutional, but that the income tax relief provided in the law was valid. Appeal to the Supreme Court.]

Mr. Justice Powell delivered the opinion of the Court. . . .

Most of the cases coming to this Court raising Establishment Clause questions have involved the relationship between religion and education. Among these religion-education precedents, two general categories of cases may be identified:

those dealing with religious activities within the public schools, and those involving public aid in varying forms to sectarian institutions.... Taken together, these decisions dictate that to pass muster under the Establishment Clause the law in question, first must reflect a clearly secular legislative purpose..., second, must have a primary effect that neither advances nor inhibits religion,... and, third, must avoid excessive government entanglement with religion....

In applying these criteria to the three distinct forms of aid involved in this case, we need touch only briefly on the requirement of a "secular legislative purpose." As the recitation of legislative purposes appended to New York's law indicates, each measure is adequately supported by legitimate, nonsectarian state interests. We do not question the propriety, and fully secular content, of New York's interest in preserving a healthy and safe educational environment for all of its school children. And we do not doubt—indeed, we fully recognize—the validity of the State's interests in promoting pluralism and diversity among its public and nonpublic schools. Nor do we hesitate to acknowledge the reality of its concern for an already overburdened public school system that might suffer in the event that a significant percentage of children presently attending nonpublic schools should abandon those schools in favor of the public schools.

But the propriety of a legislature's purposes may not immunize from further scrutiny a law which either has a primary effect that advances religion, or which fosters excessive entanglements between Church and State. Accordingly, we must weigh each of the three aid provisions challenged here against these criteria of effect and entanglement.

The "maintenance and repair" provisions of §1 authorize direct payments to nonpublic schools, virtually all of which are Roman Catholic schools in low-income areas.... So long as expenditures do not exceed 50% of comparable expenses in the public school system, it is possible for a sectarian elementary or secondary school to finance its entire "maintenance and repair" budget from state tax-raised funds. No attempt is made to restrict payments to those expenditures related to the upkeep of facilities used exclusively for secular purposes, nor do we think it possible within the context of these religion-oriented institutions to impose such restrictions. Nothing in the statute, for instance, bars a qualifying school from paying out of state funds the salaries of employees who maintain the school chapel, or the cost of renovating classrooms in which religion is taught, or the cost of heating and lighting those same facilities. Absent appropriate restrictions on expenditures for these and similar purposes, it simply cannot be denied that this section has a primary effect that advances religion in that it subsidizes directly the religious activities of sectarian elementary and secondary schools.

The state officials nevertheless argue that these expenditures for "maintenance and repair" are similar to other financial expenditures approved by this Court. Primarily they rely on *Everson* v. *Board of Education; Board of Education* v. *Allen* ...; and *Tilton* v. *Richardson*. In each of those cases it is true that the Court approved a form of financial assistance which conferred undeniable benefits upon private, sectarian schools. But a close examination of those cases illuminates their distinguishing characteristics....

These cases simply recognize that sectarian schools perform secular, educational functions as well as religious functions, and that some forms of aid may be channeled to the secular without providing direct aid to the sectarian. But the channel is a narrow one, as the above cases illustrate. Of course, it is true in each case that the provision of such neutral, nonideological aid, assisting only the secular functions of sectarian schools, served indirectly and incidentally to promote the religious function by rendering it more likely that children would attend sectarian schools and by freeing the budgets of those schools for use in other non-secular areas. But an indirect and incidental effect beneficial to religious institutions has never been thought a sufficient defect to warrant the invalidation of a state law....

What we have said demonstrates that New York's maintenance and repair provisions violate the Establishment Clause because their effect, inevitably, is to subsidize and advance the religious mission of sectarian schools....

New York's tuition reimbursement program also fails the "effect" test, for much the same reasons that govern its maintenance and repair grants.... There can be no question that these grants could not, consistently with the Establishment Clause, be given directly to sectarian schools, since they would suffer from the same deficiency that renders invalid the grants for maintenance and repair. In the absence of an effective means of guaranteeing that the state aid derived from public funds will be used exclusively for secular, neutral, and nonideological purposes, it is clear from our cases that direct aid in whatever form is invalid.... The controlling question here, then, is whether the fact that the grants are delivered to parents rather than schools is of such significance as to compel a contrary result. The State and intervenor-appellees rely on *Everson* and *Allen* for their claim that grants to parents, unlike grants to institutions, respect the "wall of separation" required by the Constitution....

In *Everson,* the Court found the bus fare program analogous to the provision of services such as police and fire protection, sewage disposal, highways, and sidewalks for parochial schools.... Such services, provided in common to all citizens, are "so separate and so indisputably marked off from the religious function,"... that they may fairly be viewed as reflections of a neutral posture toward religious institutions. *Allen* is founded upon a similar principle. The Court there repeatedly emphasized that upon the record in that case there was no indication that textbooks would be provided for anything other than purely secular courses....

The tuition grants here are subject to no such restrictions. There has been no endeavor "to guarantee the separation between secular and religious educational functions and to ensure that State financial aid supports only the former." *Lemon v. Kurtzman....* Indeed, it is precisely the function of New York's law to provide assistance to private schools, the great majority of which are sectarian. By reimbursing parents for a portion of their tuition bill, the State seeks to relieve their financial burdens sufficiently to assure that they continue to have the option to send their children to religion-oriented schools. And while the other purposes for that aid—to perpetuate a pluralistic educational environment and to protect the fiscal integrity of overburdened public schools—are certainly unexceptionable, the effect of the aid is unmistakably to provide desired financial support for nonpublic, sectarian institutions....

Sections 3, 4, and 5 establish a system for providing income tax benefits to parents of children attending New York's nonpublic schools....

In practical terms there would appear to be little difference, for purposes of determining whether such aid has the effect of advancing religion, between the tax benefit allowed here and the tuition grant allowed under §2. The qualifying parent under either program receives the same form of encouragement and reward for sending his children to nonpublic schools. The only difference is that one parent receives an actual cash payment while the other is allowed to reduce by an arbitrary amount the sum he would otherwise be obliged to pay over to the State. We see no answer to Judge Hays' dissenting statement below that "in both instances the money involved represents a charge made upon the state for the purpose of religious education.". . .

. . . [A]ppellees place their strongest reliance on *Walz* v. *Tax Comm'n* in which New York's property tax exemption for religious organizations was upheld. We think that *Walz* provides no support for appellees' position. Indeed, its rationale plainly compels the conclusion that New York's tax package violates the Establishment Clause.

Tax exemptions for church property enjoyed an apparently universal approval in this country both before and after the adoption of the First Amendment. . . . We know of no historical precedent for New York's recently promulgated tax relief program. Indeed, it seems clear that tax benefits for parents whose children attend parochial schools are a recent innovation, occasioned by the growing financial plight of such nonpublic institutions and designed, albeit unsuccessfully, to tailor state aid in a manner not incompatible with the recent decisions of this Court. . . . A proper respect for both the Free Exercise and the Establishment Clauses compels the State to pursue a course of "neutrality" toward religion. . . . Special tax benefits, however, cannot be squared with the principle of neutrality established by the decisions of this Court. To the contrary, insofar as such benefits render assistance to parents who send their children to sectarian schools, their purpose and inevitable effect are to aid and advance those religious institutions. . . .

One further difference between tax exemptions for church property and tax benefits for parents should be noted. The exemption challenged in *Walz* was not restricted to a class composed exclusively or even predominantly of religious institutions. Instead, the exemption covered all property devoted to religious, educational, or charitable purposes. As the parties here must concede, tax reductions authorized by this law flow primarily to the parents of children attending sectarian, nonpublic schools. . . .

In conclusion, we find the *Walz* analogy unpersuasive, and in light of the practical similarity between New York's tax and tuition reimbursement programs, we hold that neither form of aid is sufficiently restricted to assure that it will not have the impermissible effect of advancing the sectarian activities of religious schools. . . .

Mr. Chief Justice Burger, joined in part by Mr. Justice White, and joined by Mr. Justice Rehnquist, concurring in part and dissenting in part.

I join in that part of the Court's opinion . . . which holds the New York "maintenance and repair" provision unconstitutional under the Establishment Clause because it is a direct aid to religion. I disagree, however, with the Court's decisions in *Nyquist* and in *Sloan* v. *Lemon* . . . to strike down the New York and Pennsylvania tuition grant programs and the New York tax relief provisions. I believe the Court's decisions on those statutory provisions ignore the teachings of *Everson* v. *Board of Education* . . . and *Board of Education* v. *Allen*, . . . and fail to observe what I thought the Court had held in *Walz* v. *Tax Comm'n*. . . . I therefore dissent as to those aspects of the two holdings. . . .

The tuition grant and tax relief programs now before us are, in my view, indistinguishable in principle, purpose, and effect from the statutes in *Everson* and *Allen*. In the instant cases, as in *Everson* and *Allen,* the States have merely attempted to equalize the costs incurred by parents in obtaining an education for their children. The only discernible difference between the programs in *Everson* and *Allen* and these cases is in the method of the distribution of benefits: here the particular benefits of the Pennsylvania and New York statutes are given only to

parents of private schoolchildren, while in *Everson* and *Allen* the statutory benefits were made available to parents of both public and private schoolchildren. But
to regard that difference as constitutionally meaningful is to exalt form over substance. It is beyond dispute that the parents of public schoolchildren in New
York and Pennsylvania presently receive the "benefit" of having their children
educated totally at state expense; the statutes enacted in those States and at issue
here merely attempt to equalize that "benefit" by giving to parents of private
schoolchildren, in the form of dollars or tax deductions, what the parents of
public schoolchildren receive in kind. It is no more than simple equity to grant
partial relief to parents who support the public schools they do not use....

Mr. Justice White, joined in part by the Chief Justice and Mr. Justice Rehnquist, dissenting....

I am quite unreconciled to the Court's decision in *Lemon* v. *Kurtzman* ...
(1971). I thought then, and I think now, that the Court's conclusion there was not
required by the First Amendment and is contrary to the long-range interests of the
country. I therefore have little difficulty in accepting the New York maintenance
grant, which does not and could not, by its terms, approach the actual repair and
maintenance cost incurred in connection with the secular education services performed for the State in parochial schools. But, accepting *Lemon* and the invalidation of the New York maintenance grant, I would, with The Chief Justice and
Mr. Justice Rehnquist, sustain the New York and Pennsylvania tuition grant
statutes and the New York tax credit provisions....

The reimbursement and tax benefit plans today struck down, no less than the
plans in *Everson* and *Allen,* are consistent with the principle of neutrality. New
York has recognized that parents who are sending their children to nonpublic
schools are rendering the State a service by decreasing the costs of public education
and by physically relieving an already overburdened public school system. Such
parents are nonetheless compelled to support public school services unused by
them and to pay for their own children's education. Rather than offering "an
incentive to parents to send their children to sectarian schools,"... as the majority
suggests, New York is effectuating the secular purpose of the equalization of the
costs of educating New York children that are borne by parents who send their
children to nonpublic schools....

The increasing difficulties faced by private schools in our country are no
reason at all for this Court to readjust the admittedly rough-hewn limits on
governmental involvement with religion which are found in the First and Fourteenth Amendments. But, quite understandably, these difficulties can be expected
to lead to efforts on the part of those who wish to keep alive pluralism in education to obtain through legislative channels forms of permissible public assistance
which were not thought necessary a generation ago. Within the limits permitted
by the Constitution, these decisions are quite rightly hammered out on the legislative anvil. If the Constitution does indeed allow for play in the legislative joints,
Walz, supra, ... the Court must distinguish between a new exercise of power within
constitutional limits and an exercise of legislative power which transgresses those
limits. I believe the Court has failed to make that distinction here, and I therefore dissent.

In *Meek* v. *Pittenger,* 421 U.S. 349 (1975), the Court upheld that portion
of a Pennsylvania law which provided for loan of textbooks "acceptable for
use in" the public schools to children enrolled in nonpublic elementary and

secondary schools. But the remainder of the act which provided various "auxiliary services" was held to be violative of the establishment clause. The services included counseling, testing, psychological services, speech and hearing therapy, and related services for exceptional, remedial, or educationally disadvantaged students, "and such other secular, neutral, nonideological services as are of benefit to nonpublic school-children" and are provided to those in the public schools. Further provision was made for instructional equipment (projectors, recorders, and laboratory paraphernalia) and instructional materials (periodicals, photographs, maps, charts, recordings, and films). The majority found that although such aid was ostensibly limited to secular materials, the massive aid provided was neither indirect nor incidental and amounted to a direct and substantial advancement of religious activity. It also found the auxiliary services unconstitutional since excessive entanglement would be required for Pennsylvania to be assured that the public school professional staff members providing the services did not advance the religious mission of the church-related schools in which they were to serve.

In 1971 a Maryland statute was enacted that authorized the payment of state funds to any private institution of higher education within the state that met certain minimum criteria and did not award "only seminarian or theological degrees." The aid was in the form of an annual fiscal year subsidy to qualifying colleges and universities. The amounts were based upon the number of students, excluding those in seminarian or theological academic programs. The grants were noncategorical, but could not be utilized by the institutions for sectarian purposes. The assistance program was primarily administered by the Maryland Council for Higher Education, which, in order to insure compliance with statutory restrictions, (1) determined the eligibility of applicant institutions, and (2) examined applications to insure that only nonsectarian uses for the money were planned. At the end of the fiscal year the recipient institution was required to file a financial statement showing the specific purposes for which the money was used.

Suit was brought by four Maryland citizens and taxpayers challenging the statutory scheme as violative of the establishment clause. In addition to the responsible state officials, plaintiffs joined as defendants four Roman Catholic colleges, claiming that they were constitutionally ineligible for this form of aid. The Federal District Court, applying the three-part requirement of *Lemon* v. *Kurtzman,* upheld the statute and denied relief. On direct appeal, the Supreme Court affirmed in *Roemer* v. *Board of Public Works of Maryland,* 44 L.W. 4939 (1976). The vote was five to four, and there was no majority opinion. Appellants did not challenge the District Court's finding respecting the first part of *Lemon*'s three-part test—that the purpose of Maryland's aid program was the secular one of supporting private higher education generally, as an economic alternative to a wholly public system. The focus of the argument was on the second and third parts, those concerning the primary effect of advancing religion and excessive church-state entanglement.

In the plurality opinion by Justice Blackmum, joined by the Chief Justice and Justice Powell, it was concluded that the picture painted of the four Maryland colleges was "similar in almost all respects to that of the church-affiliated colleges considered in *Tilton* and *Hunt,*" and that the institutions were not "so permeated by religion that the secular side cannot be separated from the sectarian." Further, it was concluded that the aid was extended only to the secular side and could not be used to support a "specially religious activity." Thus, the aid did not violate the "primary effect of advancing religion" test.

As to the "excessive entanglement" test, the plurality found no greater problem here than in *Tilton* and the statute was upheld against this claim.

As the District Court pointed out, ongoing, annual supervision of college facilities was explicitly foreseen in *Tilton* . . . and even more so in *Hunt*. . . . *Tilton* and *Hunt* would be totally indistinguishable, at least in terms of annual supervision, if funds were used under the present statute to build or maintain physical facilities devoted to secular use. The present statute contemplates annual decisions by the Council as to what is a "sectarian purpose," but, as we have noted, the secular and sectarian activities of the colleges are easily separated. Occasional audits are possible here, but we must accept the District Court's finding that they would be "quick and non-judgmental.". . . They and the other contacts between the Council and the colleges are not likely to be any more entangling than the inspections and audits incident to the normal process of the colleges' accreditations by the State.

Justice White, joined by Justice Rehnquist, concurred in the result but objected to the use of the "excessive entanglement" test. He stated that, "I have never understood the constitutional foundation for this added element; it is at once both insolubly paradoxical . . . and . . . a 'blurred, indistinct and variable barrier.' " He argued that if the purpose of the legislation is secular and if the primary effect of the aid program is not advancement of religion, that is enough to sustain the program against constitutional challenge, "and I would say no more."

Justice Brennan, joined by Justice Marshall, dissented on the ground that the statute provided a general subsidy to religious schools from public funds, and that such a provision exposes state money for use in advancing religion, no matter the vigilance to avoid it. In a separate dissent, Justice Stewart stressed the point that theology courses were a compulsory part of the curriculum at each of the appellee institutions, and that they were not taught merely as part of the academic discipline. Thus, the aid provided did in fact advance religion. Justice Stevens added an interesting reversal to the usual no-aid-to-religion argument in stating:

I would add emphasis to the pernicious tendency of a state subsidy to tempt religious schools to compromise their religious mission without wholly abandoning it. The disease of entanglement may infect a law discouraging wholesome religious activity as well as a law encouraging the propagation of a given faith.

"Released Time" Programs

It has been a long-established practice in many public school districts of the United States to include various kinds of religious exercises as a part of the school program. In some of these districts specific times are set aside during the school week when pupils are "released" from regular classes in order to attend some sort of religious program in the school building. An establishment issue is clearly presented by such practices, but the first case on that issue to reach the United States Supreme Court did not arrive until 1948. It dealt with the "released time" program followed in Champaign, Illinois.

ILLINOIS *ex. rel.* McCOLLUM *v.* BOARD OF EDUCATION
333 U.S. 203 (1948)

Mr. Justice Black delivered the opinion of the Court.

This case relates to the power of a state to utilize its tax-supported public school system in aid of religious instruction insofar as that power may be restricted by the First and Fourteenth Amendments to the Federal Constitution.

The appellant, Vashti McCollum, began this action for mandamus against the Champaign Board of Education in the Circuit Court of Champaign County, Illinois. Her asserted interest was that of a resident and taxpayer of Champaign and of a parent whose child was then enrolled in the Champaign public schools. . . .

Appellant's petition for mandamus alleged that religious teachers, employed by private religious groups, were permitted to come weekly into the school buildings during the regular hours set apart for secular teaching, and then and there for a period of thirty minutes substitute their religious teaching for the secular education provided under the compulsory education law. The petitioner charged that this joint public-school religious-group program violated the First and Fourteenth Amendments to the United States Constitution. The prayer of her petition was that the Board of Education be ordered to "adopt and enforce rules and regulations prohibiting all instruction in and teaching of religious education in all public schools in Champaign School District Number 71, . . . and in all public school houses and buildings in said district when occupied by public schools.". . .

Although there are disputes between the parties as to various inferences that may or may not properly be drawn from the evidence concerning the religious program, the following facts are shown by the record without dispute. In 1940 interested members of the Jewish, Roman Catholic, and a few of the Protestant faiths formed a voluntary association called the Champaign Council on Religious Education. They obtained permission from the Board of Education to offer classes in religious instruction to public school pupils in grades four to nine inclusive. Classes were made up of pupils whose parents signed printed cards requesting that their children be permitted to attend; they were held weekly, thirty minutes for the lower grades, forty-five minutes for the higher. The council employed the religious teachers at no expense to the school authorities, but the instructors were subject to the approval and supervision of the superintendent of schools. The classes were taught in three separate religious groups by Protestant teachers, Catholic priests, and a Jewish rabbi, although for the past several years there have apparently been no classes instructed in the Jewish religion. Classes were conducted in the regular classrooms of the school building. Students who did not choose to take the religious instruction were not released from public school duties; they were required to leave their classrooms and go to some other place in the school building for pursuit of their secular studies. On the other hand, students who were released from secular study for the religious instructions were required to be present at the religious classes. Reports of their presence or absence were to be made to their secular teachers.

The foregoing facts, without reference to others that appear in the record, show the use of tax-supported property for religious instruction and the close cooperation between the school authorities and the religious council in promoting religious education. The operation of the state's compulsory education system thus assists and is integrated with the program of religious instruction carried on by separate religious sects. Pupils compelled by law to go to school for secular education are released in part from their legal duty upon the condition that they attend the religious classes. This is beyond all question a utilization of the tax-established and tax-supported public school system to aid religious groups to spread their faith. And it falls squarely under the ban of the First Amendment (made applicable to the States by the Fourteenth) as we interpreted it in *Everson* v. *Board of Education,* 330 U.S. 1. . . . The majority in the *Everson* case, and the minority . . . , agreed that the First Amendment's language, properly interpreted, had erected a wall of separation between Church and State. They disagreed as to the facts shown by the record and as to the proper application of the First Amendment's language to those facts.

Recognizing that the Illinois program is barred by the First and Fourteenth Amendments if we adhere to the views expressed both by the majority and the minority in the *Everson* case, counsel for the respondents challenge those views as dicta and urge that we reconsider and repudiate them. They argue that historically the First Amendment was intended to forbid only government preference of one religion over another, not an impartial governmental assistance of all religions. In addition they ask that we distinguish or overrule our holding in the *Everson* case that the Fourteenth Amendment made the "establishment of religion" clause of the First Amendment applicable as a prohibition against the States. After giving full consideration to the arguments presented we are unable to accept either of these contentions.

To hold that a State cannot consistently with the First and Fourteenth Amendments utilize its public school system to aid any or all religious faiths or sects in the dissemination of their doctrines and ideals does not, as counsel urge, manifest a governmental hostility to religion or religious teachings. A manifestation of such hostility would be at war with our national tradition as embodied in the First Amendment's guaranty of the free exercise of religion. For the First Amendment rests upon the premise that both religion and government can best work to achieve their lofty aims if each is left free from the other within its respective sphere. Or, as we said in the *Everson* case, the First Amendment has erected a wall between Church and State which must be kept high and impregnable.

Here not only are the state's tax-supported public school buildings used for the dissemination of religious doctrines. The State also affords sectarian groups an invaluable aid in that it helps to provide pupils for their religious classses through use of the state's compulsory public school machinery. This is not separation of Church and State.

The cause is reversed and remanded to the State Supreme Court for proceedings not inconsistent with this opinion.

Reversed and remanded.

Mr. Justice Frankfurter delivered the following opinion, in which Mr. Justice Jackson, Mr. Justice Rutledge and Mr. Justice Burton join. [Mr. Justice Rutledge and Mr. Justice Burton concurred also in the Court's opinion.] . . .

Religious education so conducted on school time and property is patently woven into the working scheme of the school. The Champaign arrangement thus presents powerful elements of inherent pressure by the school system in the interest of religious sects. The fact that this power has not been used to discriminate is beside the point. Separation is a requirement to abstain from fusing functions of Government and of religious sects, not merely to treat them all equally. That a child is offered an alternative may reduce the constraint; it does not eliminate the operation of influence by the school in matters sacred to conscience and outside the school's domain. The law of imitation operates, and non-conformity is not an outstanding characteristic of children. The result is an obvious pressure upon children to attend.

Again, while the Champaign school population represents only a fraction of the more than two hundred and fifty sects of the nation, not even all the practicing sects in Champaign are willing or able to provide religious instruction. The children belonging to these non-participating sects will thus have inculcated in them a feeling of separatism when the school should be the training ground for habits of community, or they will have religious instruction in a faith which is not that of their parents. As a result, the public school system of Champaign actively furthers inculcation in the religious tenets of some faiths, and in the process sharpens the consciousness of religious differences at least among some of the children committed to its care. These are consequences not amenable to statistics. But they are precisely the consequences against which the Constitution was directed when it prohibited the Government common to all from becoming embroiled, however innocently, in the destructive conflicts of which the history of even this country records some dark pages. . . .

We renew our conviction that "we have staked the very existence of our country on the faith that complete separation between the state and religion is best for the state and best for religion." *Everson* v. *Board of Education.* If nowhere else, in the relation between Church and State, "good fences make good neighbors."

Mr. Justice Jackson, concurring. . . .

Mr. Justice Reed, dissenting. . . .

Mr. Jefferson, as one of the founders of the University of Virginia, a school which from its establishment in 1819 has been wholly governed, managed and controlled by the State of Virginia, was faced with the same problem that is before this Court today: the question of the constitutional limitation upon religious education in public schools. In his annual report as Rector, to the President and Directors of the Literary Fund . . . Mr. Jefferson set forth his views at some length. These suggestions of Mr. Jefferson were adopted and c. II, Section 1, of the Regulations of the University of October 4, 1824, provided that:

"Should the religious sects of this State, or any of them, according to the invitation held out to them, establish within, or adjacent to, the precincts of the University, schools for instruction in the religion of their sect, the students of the University will be free, and expected to attend religious worship at the establishment of their respective sects, in the morning, and in time to meet their school in the University at its stated hour."

Thus, the "wall of separation between church and State" that Mr. Jefferson built at the University which he founded did not exclude religious education from that school. The difference between the generality of his statements on the separation of church and state and the specificity of his conclusions on education are considerable. A rule of law should not be drawn from a figure of speech. . . .

Well-recognized and long-established practices support the validity of the Illinois statute here in question. That statute, as construed in this case, is comparable to those in many states. . . .

The practices of the federal government offer many examples of this kind of "aid" by the state to religion. The Congress of the United States has a chaplain for each House who daily invokes divine blessings and guidance for the proceedings. The armed forces have commissioned chaplains from early days. They conduct the public services in accordance with the liturgical requirements of their respective faiths, ashore and afloat, employing for the purpose property belonging to the United States and dedicated to the services of religion. Under the Servicemen's

Readjustment Act of 1944, eligible veterans may receive training at government expense for the ministry in denominational schools. The schools of the District of Columbia have opening exercises which "include a reading from the Bible without note or comment, and the Lord's prayer."

In the United States Naval Academy and the United States Military Academy, schools wholly supported and completely controlled by the federal government, there are a number of religious activities. Chaplains are attached to both schools. Attendance at church services on Sunday is compulsory at both the Military and Naval Academies. . . .

. . . Devotion to the great principle of religious liberty should not lead us into a rigid interpretation of the constitutional guarantee that conflicts with accepted habits of our people. This is an instance where, for me, the history of past practices is determinative of the meaning of a constitutional clause not a decorous introduction to the study of its text. The judgment should be affirmed.

The decision in the *McCollum* case was greeted with a storm of protest. One of America's most eminent scholars in constitutional law, Professor E. S. Corwin, argued that the establishment clause only barred the government from setting up an official church or showing preference for one religion over another. [See E. S. Corwin, "The Supreme Court as National School Board," 14 *Law & Contempt. Prob.* 3 (1949).] But groups supporting the viewpoint of the majority took encouragement from the decision and plans were soon under way to initiate suits testing the "released time" programs in other parts of the nation. The New York City program was brought before the Court for examination only four years after *McCollum*. In *Zorach* v. *Clauson* the Court beat a strategic retreat and upheld this "dismissed time" program in which the pupils were permitted to leave the school grounds during the school day for their religious instruction.

ZORACH *v.* CLAUSON
343 U.S. 306 (1952)

Mr. Justice Douglas delivered the opinion of the Court.

New York City has a program which permits its public schools to release students during the school day so that they may leave the school buildings and school grounds and go to religious centers for religious instruction or devotional exercises. A student is released on written request of his parents. Those not released stay in the classrooms. The churches make weekly reports to the schools, sending a list of children who have been released from public school but who have not reported for religious instruction.

This "released time" program involves neither religious instruction in public school classrooms nor the expenditure of public funds. All costs, including the application blanks, are paid by the religious organizations. The case is therefore unlike *McCollum* v. *Board of Education*, 333 U.S. 203, which involved a "released time" program from Illinois. In that case the classrooms were turned over to religious instructors. We accordingly held that the program violated the First Amendment which (by reason of the Fourteenth Amendment) prohibits the states from establishing religion or prohibiting its free exercise.

Appellants, who are taxpayers and residents of New York City and whose children attend its public schools, challenge the present law, contending it is in essence not different from the one involved in the *McCollum* case. Their argument, stated elaborately in various ways, reduces itself to this: the weight and influence of the school is put behind a program for religious instruction; public school teachers police it, keeping tab on students who are released; the classroom activities come to a halt while the students who are released for religious instruction are on leave; the school is a crutch on which the churches are leaning for support in their religious training; without the cooperation of the schools this "released time" program, like the one in the *McCollum* case, would be futile and ineffective. The New York Court of Appeals sustained the law against this claim of unconstitutionality. . . .

There is a suggestion that the system involves the use of coercion to get public school students into religious classrooms. There is no evidence in the record before us that supports that conclusion. The present record indeed tells us that the school authorities are neutral in this regard and do no more than release students whose parents so request. If in fact coercion were used, if it were established that any one or more teachers were using their office to persuade or force students to take the religious instruction, a wholly different case would be presented. Hence we put aside the claim of coercion both as respects the "free exercise" of religion and "an establishment of religion" within the meaning of the First Amendment. . . .

. . . There cannot be the slightest doubt that the First Amendment reflects the philosophy that Church and State should be separated. And so far as interference with the "free exercise" of religion and an "establishment" of religion are concerned, the separation must be complete and unequivocal. The First Amendment within the scope of its coverage permits no exception; the prohibition is absolute. The first Amendment, however, does not say that in every and all respects there shall be a separation of Church and State. Rather, it studiously defines the manner, the specific ways, in which there shall be no concert or union or dependency one on the other. That is the common sense of the matter. Otherwise the state and religion would be aliens to each other—hostile, suspicious, and even unfriendly. Churches could not be required to pay even property taxes. Municipalities would not be permitted to render police or fire protection to religious groups. Policemen who helped parishioners into their places of worship would violate the Constitution. Prayers in our legislative halls; the appeals to the Almighty in the messages of the Chief Executive; the proclamations making Thanksgiving Day a holiday; "so help me God" in our courtroom oaths—these and all other references to the Almighty that run through our laws, our public rituals, our ceremonies would be flouting the First Amendment. A fastidious atheist or agnostic could even object to the supplication with which the Court opens each session: "God save the United States and this Honorable Court."

We would have to press the concept of separation of Church and State to these extremes to condemn the present law on constitutional grounds. The nullification of this law would have wide and profound effects. A Catholic student applies to his teacher for permission to leave the school during hours on a Holy Day of Obligation to attend a mass. A Jewish student asks his teacher for permission to be excused for Yom Kippur. A Protestant wants the afternoon off for a family baptismal ceremony. In each case the teacher requires parental consent in writing. In each case the teacher, in order to make sure the student is not a truant, goes further and requires a report from the priest, the rabbi, or the minister. The teacher in other words cooperates in a religious program to the extent of making it possible for her students to participate in it. Whether she does it occasionally for a few students, regularly for one, or pursuant to a systematized program designed to further the religious needs of all the students does not alter the character of the act.

We are a religious people whose institutions presuppose a Supreme Being. We guarantee the freedom to worship as one chooses. We make room for as wide a variety of beliefs and creeds as the spiritual needs of man deem necessary. We sponsor an attitude on the part of government that shows no partiality to any one group and that lets each flourish according to the zeal of its adherents and the appeal of its dogma. When the state encourages religious instruction or cooperates with religious authorities by adjusting the schedule of public events to sectarian needs, it follows the best of our traditions. For it then respects the religious nature of our people and accommodates the public service to their spiritual needs. To hold that it may not would be to find in the Constitution a requirement that the government show a callous indifference to religious groups. That would be preferring those who believe in no religion over those who do believe. Government may not finance religious groups nor undertake religious instruction nor blend secular and sectarian education nor use secular institutions to force one or some religion on any person. But we find no constitutional requirement which makes it necessary for government to be hostile to religion and to throw its weight against efforts to widen the effective scope of religious influence. The government must be neutral when it comes to competition between sects. It may not thrust any sect on any person. It may not make a religious observance compulsory. It may not coerce anyone to attend church, to observe a religious holiday, or to take religious instruction. But it can close its doors or suspend its operations as to those who want to repair to their religious sanctuary for worship or instruction. No more than that is undertaken here.

This program may be unwise and improvident from an educational or a community viewpoint. That appeal is made to us on a theory, previously advanced, that each case must be decided on the basis of "our own prepossessions.". . . Our individual preferences, however, are not the constitutional standard. The constitutional standard is the separation of Church and State. The problem, like many problems in constitutional law, is one of degree. . . .

In the *McCollum* case the classrooms were used for religious instruction and the force of the public school was used to promote that instruction. Here, as we have said, the public schools do no more than accommodate their schedules to a program of outside religious instruction. We follow the *McCollum* case. But we cannot expand it to cover the present released time program unless separation of Church and State means that public institutions can make no adjustments of their schedules to accommodate the religious needs of the people. We cannot read into the Bill of Rights such a philosophy of hostility to religion.

Affirmed.

Mr. Justice Black, dissenting. . . .

I see no significant difference between the invalid Illinois system and that of New York here sustained. Except for the use of the school buildings in Illinois, there is no difference between the systems which I consider even worthy of mention. In the New York program, as in that of Illinois, the school authorities release some of the children on the condition that they attend the religious classes, get reports on whether they attend, and hold the other children in the school building until the religious hour is over. . . . *McCollum* . . . held that Illinois could not constitutionally manipulate the compelled classroom hours of its compulsory school machinery so as to channel children into sectarian classes. Yet that is exactly what the Court holds New York can do. . . .

Difficulty of decision in the hypothetical situations mentioned by the Court, but not now before us, should not confuse the issues in this case. Here the sole question is whether New York can use its compulsory education laws to help religious sects get attendants presumably too unenthusiastic to go unless moved to do so by the pressure of this state machinery. That this is the plan, purpose, design and consequence of the New York program cannot be denied. The state thus makes religious sects beneficiaries of its power to compel children to attend secular schools. Any use of such coercive power by the state to help or hinder some religious sects or to prefer all religious sects over nonbelievers or vice versa is just what I think the First Amendment forbids. In considering whether a state has entered this forbidden field the question is not whether it has entered too far but whether it has entered at all. New York is manipulating its compulsory education laws to help religious sects get pupils. This is not separation but combination of Church and State. . . .

Mr. Justice Frankfurter, dissenting. . . .

Mr. Justice Jackson, dissenting.

This released time program is founded upon a use of the State's power of coercion, which, for me, determines its unconstitutionality. Stripped to its essentials, the plan has two stages: first, that the State compel each student to yield a large part of his time for public secular education; and, second, that some of it be "released" to him on condition that he devote it to sectarian religious purposes.

No one suggests that the Constitution would permit the State directly to require this "released" time to be spent "under the control of a duly constituted religious body." This program accomplishes that forbidden result by indirection. If public education were taking so much of the pupils' time as to injure the public or the students' welfare by encroaching upon their religious opportunity, simply shortening everyone's school day would facilitate voluntary and optional attendance at Church classes. But that suggestion is rejected upon the ground that if they are made free many students will not go to the Church, Hence, they must be deprived of freedom for this period, with Church attendance put to them as one of the two permissible ways of using it.

The greater effectiveness of this system over voluntary attendance after school hours is due to the truant officer who, if the youngster fails to go to the Church school, dogs him back to the public schoolroom. Here schooling is more or less suspended during the "released time" so the nonreligious attendants will not forge ahead of the churchgoing absentees. But it serves as a temporary jail for a pupil who will not go to Church. It takes more subtlety of mind than I possess to deny that this is governmental constraint in support of religion. It is as unconstitutional, in my view, when exerted by indirection as when exercised forthrightly.

As one whose children, as a matter of free choice, have been sent to privately supported Church schools, I may challenge the Court's suggestion that opposition to this plan can only be antireligious, atheistic, or agnostic. My evangelistic brethren confuse an objection to compulsion with an objection to religion. It is possible to hold a faith with enough confidence to believe that what should be rendered to God does not need to be decided and collected by Caesar.

The day that this country ceases to be free for irreligion it will cease to be free for religion—except for the sect that can win political power. The same epithetical jurisprudence used by the Court today to beat down those who oppose pressuring children into some religion can devise as good epithets tomorrow against those who object to pressuring them into a favored religion. And, after all, if we concede to the State power and wisdom to single out "duly constituted religious" bodies as exclusive alternatives for compulsory secular instruction, it would be logical to also uphold the power and wisdom to choose the true faith among those "duly constituted." We start down a rough road when we begin to mix compulsory public education with compulsory godliness.

A number of Justices just short of a majority of the majority that promulgates today's passionate dialectics joined in answering them in *Illinois ex rel. McCollum* v. *Board of Education,* 333 U.S. 203. The distinction attempted between that case and this is trivial, almost to the point of cynicism, magnifying its nonessential details and disparaging compulsion which was the underlying reason for invalidity. A reading of the Court's opinion in that case along with its opinion in this case will show such difference of overtones and undertones as to make clear that the *McCollum* case has passed like a storm in a teacup. The wall which the Court was professing to erect between Church and State has become even more warped and twisted than I expected. Today's judgment will be more interesting to students of psychology and of the judicial processes than to students of constitutional law.

As pointed out in the majority opinion, the New York courts refused to consider plaintiff's offers of proof of coercion. [A description of some of the practices under the released time program in New York City, with quotations from affidavits filed in the Supreme Court, Kings County, is given in Note, "Released Time Reconsidered: The New York Plan Is Tested," 61 *Yale L. J.* 405 (1952).] In one of the affidavits, for example, it was alleged that in one sixth grade classroom the students who did not attend the religious programs were given very difficult long division arithmetic problems during every released time hour, while those who went to their religious exercises were excused from this work. [On the released time issue generally, see George E. Reed, "Church-State and the Zorach Case," 27 *Notre Dame Law.* 529 (1952); Paul G. Kauper, "Church, State and Freedom: A Review," 52 *Mich. L. Rev.* 829 (1954); and Leo Pfeffer, "Released Time and Religious Liberty: A Reply," 53 *Mich. L. Rev.* 91 (1954).]

Some indication of the importance of the retention in school of nonparticipants is shown in the finding of one investigator that several such programs of religious instruction collapsed from nonattendance when they were shifted to the time immediately after school hours and the nonparticipating student was free to go home or play as the alternative to a religious program. [See Gordon Patric, "The Impact of a Court Decision: Aftermath of the McCollum Case," 6 *Journal of Public Law* 455 (1957).]

The Bible and Prayer in Public Schools

The decisions by the United States Supreme Court on the use of Bible-reading and prayer in the public schools have stirred protest and controversy to an extent rarely equaled in the history of the Court. It should not be forgotten, however, that litigation on these issues is by no means new. While these decisions were the first in which the Court ruled on the validity of such practices under the United States Constitution, the issues have been litigated in various forms under *state* constitutional provisions for over a hundred years, and in the appellate courts of nearly half the states. The earliest reported case is a Maine case, *Donahoe* v. *Richards,* 38 Me. 376 (1854), in which the court held that a regulation adopting the King James version of the Bible as a textbook, binding upon all pupils, was not a violation of the rights of conscience or religion guaranteed by the state constitution. Of the twenty-three state appellate courts which have considered the issue of Bible-reading in the public schools, seventeen held that the practices challenged did not violate state or federal constitutional provisions, but the courts of six states held the practices invalid under state constitutional provisions. A Wisconsin decision, *State ex rel. Weiss* v. *District Board of Edgerton,* 76 Wis. 177, 44 N.W. 967 (1890), was the earliest of these decisions ruling against Bible-reading. [The cases are canvassed in David Fellman, *Religion in American Public Law* (Boston: Boston University Press, 1965), pp. 98–99. See also Robert E. Cushman, "The Holy Bible and the Public Schools," 40 *Cornell L. Q.* 475 (1955).] Thus the issue was already a very old one even in the judicial arena by the time it reached the United States Supreme Court, and, further, twenty-five percent of the twenty-three states ruling on the question had ruled *against* the validity of Bible-reading in the public schools. The first decision to come from the Supreme Court did not come until 1962, however, and it involved the so-called Regents' prayer in the state of New York.

The State Board of Regents of New York has broad supervisory powers over the public school system. The Board adopted the following prayer and recommended that the various school districts use it in daily exercises: "Almighty God we acknowledge our dependence upon Thee and we beg Thy blessings upon us, our parents, our teachers and our country." In *Engel* v. *Vitale,* 370 U.S. 421 (1962), the Court held that such a state-sponsored prayer program was an establishment of official religion in violation of the Constitution. In response to the claim that such a construction indicated hostility toward religion or toward prayer, Justice Black, for the Court, stated:

> Nothing, of course, could be more wrong. . . . It is neither sacrilegious nor anti-religious to say that each separate government in this country should stay out of the business of writing or sanctioning official prayers and leave that purely religious function to the people themselves and to those the people choose to look to for religious guidance. . . .

The criticism which the Court received after the *McCollum* decision was mild by comparison with the tempest which blew up following *Engel* v. *Vitale.* Fresh charges were leveled that the members of the majority were atheistic or even Communist-inspired. And another round of proposals was aired calling for mass impeachments. Much of the initial anger was dispelled, however, as more people actually read the opinions, and officials of a number of different religious organizations issued public statements pointing out that the decision gave constitutional status to what they had long argued—that the church and the home, rather than the public schools, should be the primary centers of religious instruction. On legal grounds, however, Professor Sutherland of the Harvard Law School criticized the decision on the ground that the *de minimis* rule should have been employed by the Court to avoid ruling on such a small religious exercise. [Arthur E. Sutherland, Jr., "Establishment According to Engel," 76 *Harv. L. Rev.* 25 (1962).] And Dean Erwin Griswold of the Harvard Law School criticized Justice Black for what he considered to be an extreme absolutist position in barring all religion from public activity. [Erwin Griswold, "Absolute Is in the Dark," 8 *Utah L. Rev.* 167 (1963).]

Despite the fact that the opinion was carefully written to apply only to governmentally written prayers, it was not difficult to make the necessary extension to predict the treatment to be accorded Bible-reading and the recitation of the Lord's Prayer as officially sponsored exercises in the public schools. One year later, almost to the day, the Court decided companion cases from Pennsylvania and Maryland and held such exercises unconstitutional.

SCHOOL DISTRICT OF ABINGTON TOWNSHIP v. SCHEMPP (NO. 142) MURRAY v. CURLETT (NO. 119)
374 U.S. 203 (1963)

Mr. Justice Clark delivered the opinion of the Court.

Once again we are called upon to consider the scope of the provision of the First Amendment to the United States Constitution which declares that "Congress shall make no law respecting an establishment of religion or prohibiting the free exercise thereof...." These companion cases present the issues in the context of state actions requiring that schools begin each day with readings from the Bible. While raising the basic questions under slightly different factual situations, the cases permit of joint treatment. In light of the history of the First Amendment and of our cases interpreting and applying its requirements, we hold that the practices at issue and the laws requiring them are unconstitutional under the Establishment Clause, as applied to the states through the Fourteenth Amendment....

I

The Facts in Each Case: No. 142. The Commonwealth of Pennsylvania by law ... requires that "At least ten verses from the Holy Bible shall be read, without comment, at the opening of each public school on each school day. Any child shall be excused from such Bible reading, or attending such Bible reading, upon the written request of his parent or guardian."...

On each school day at the Abington High School between 8:15 and 8:30 A.M., while the pupils are attending their home rooms or advisory sections, opening exercises are conducted pursuant to the statute. The exercises are broadcast into each room in the school building through an intercommunications system and are conducted under the supervision of a teacher by students attending the school's radio and television workshop. Selected students from this course gather each morning in the school's workshop studio for the exercises, which include readings by one of the students of 10 verses of the Holy Bible, broadcast to each room in the building. This is followed by the recitation of the Lord's Prayer, likewise over the intercommunications system, but also by the students in the various classrooms, who are asked to stand and join in repeating the prayer in unison. The exercises are closed with the flag salute and such pertinent announcements as are of interest to the students. Participation in the opening exercises, as directed by the statute, is voluntary. The student reading the verses from the Bible may select the passages and read from any version he chooses, although the only copies furnished by the school are the King James version, copies of which were circulated to each teacher by the school district. During the period in which the exercises have been conducted the King James, the Douay and the Revised Standard versions of the Bible have been used, as well as the Jewish Holy Scriptures. There are no prefatory statements, no questions asked or solicited, no comments or explanations made and no interpretations given at or during the exercises. The students and parents are advised that the student may absent himself from the classroom or, should he elect to remain, not participate in the exercises.

It appears from the record that in schools not having an intercommunications system the Bible reading and the recitation of the Lord's Prayer were conducted by the homeroom teacher, who chose the text of the verses and read them herself or had students read them in rotation or by volunteers. This was followed by a standing recitation of the Lord's Prayer, together with the Pledge of Allegiance to the flag by the class in unison and a closing announcement of routine school items of interest.

At the first trial Edward Schempp and the children testified as to specific religious doctrines purveyed by a literal reading of the Bible "which were contrary to the religious beliefs which they held and to their familial teaching.". . . The children testified that all of the doctrines to which they referred were read to them at various times as part of the exercises. Edward Schempp testified at the second trial that he had considered having Roger and Donna excused from attendance at the exercises but decided against it for several reasons, including his belief that the children's relationships with their teachers and classmates would be adversely affected.

Expert testimony was introduced by both appellants and appellees at the first trial, which testimony was summarized by the trial court as follows:

"Dr. Solomon Grayzel testified that there were marked differences between the Jewish Holy Scriptures and the Christian Holy Bible, the most obvious of which was the absence of the New Testament in the Jewish Holy Scriptures. Dr. Grayzel testified that portions of the New Testament were offensive to Jewish tradition and that, from the standpoint of Jewish faith, the concept of Jesus Christ as the Son of God was 'practically blasphemous.' He cited instances in the New Testament which, assertedly, were not only sectarian in nature but tended to bring the Jews into ridicule or scorn. . . .

"Dr. Luther A. Weigle, an expert witness for the defense, testified in some detail as to the reasons for and the methods employed in developing the King James and the Revised Standard Versions of the Bible. On direct examination, Dr. Weigle stated that the Bible was nonsectarian within the Christian faiths.". . .

No. 119. In 1905 the Board of School Commissioners of Baltimore City adopted a rule. . . . The rule provided for the holding of opening exercises in the schools of the city consisting primarily of the "reading, without comment, of a chapter of the Holy Bible and/or the use of the Lord's Prayer." The petitioners, Mrs. Madalyn Murray and her son, William J. Murray, III, are both professed atheists. Following unsuccessful attempts to have the respondent school board rescind the rule this suit was filed for mandamus to compel its rescission or cancellation. It was alleged that William was a student in a public school of the city and Mrs. Murray, his mother, was a taxpayer therein; that it was the practice under the rule to have a reading on each school morning from the King James version of the Bible; that at petitioners' insistence the rule was amended to permit children to be excused from the exercise on request of the parent and that William had been excused pursuant thereto; that nevertheless the rule as amended was in violation of the petitioners' rights "to freedom of religion under the First and Fourteenth Amendments" and in violation of "the principle of separation between church and state, contained therein. . . ." The petition particularized the petitioners' atheistic beliefs and stated that the rule, as practiced, violated their rights "in that it threatens their religious liberty by placing a premium on belief as against non-belief and subjects their freedom of conscience to the rule of the majority; it pronounces belief in God as the source of all moral and spiritual values, equating these values with religious values, and thereby renders sinister, alien and suspect the beliefs and ideas of. . . . Petitioners, promoting doubt and question of their morality, good citizenship and good faith."

The respondents demurred and the trial court, recognizing that the demurrer admitted all facts well pleaded, sustained it without leave to amend. The Maryland Court of Appeals affirmed, the majority of four justices holding the exercise not in violation of the First and Fourteenth Amendments, with three justices dissenting. . . .

"The government is neutral, and, while protecting all, it prefers none, and it disparages none."

Before examining this "neutral" position in which the Establishment and Free Exercise Clauses of the First Amendment place our government it is well that we discuss the reach of the Amendment under the cases of this Court.

[The opinion here contains numerous quotations from the various previous cases on religious freedom.]

The wholesome "neutrality" of which this Court's cases speak thus stems from a recognition of the teachings of history that powerful sects or groups might bring about a fusion of governmental and religious functions or a concert or dependency of one upon the other to the end that official support of the State or Federal Government would be placed behind the tenets of one or of all orthodoxies. This the Establishment Clause prohibits. And a further reason for neutrality is found in the Free Exercise Clause, which recognizes the value of religious training, teaching and observance and, more particularly, the right of every person to freely choose his own course with reference thereto, free of any compulsion from the state. This the Free Exercise Clause guarantees. Thus, as we have seen, the two clauses may overlap. As we have indicated, the Establishment Clause has been directly considered by this Court eight times in the past score of years and, with only one Justice dissenting on the point, it has consistently held that the clause withdrew all legislative power respecting religious belief or the expression thereof. The test may be stated as follows: what are the purpose and the primary effect of the enactment? If either is the advancement or inhibition of religion then the enactment exceeds the scope of legislative power as circumscribed by the Constitution. That is to say that to withstand the strictures of the Establishment Clause there must be a secular legislative purpose and a primary effect that neither advances nor inhibits religion. . . . The Free Exercise Clause, likewise considered many times here, withdraws from legislative power, state and federal, the exertion of any restraint on the free exercise of religion. Its purpose is to secure religious liberty in the individual by prohibiting any invasions thereof by civil authority. Hence it is necessary in a free exercise case for one to show the coercive effect of the enactment as it operates against him in the practice of his religion. The distinction between the two clauses is apparent—a violation of the Free Exercise Clause is predicated on coercion while the Establishment Clause violation need not be so attended.

Applying the Establishment Clause principles to the cases at bar, we find that the States are requiring the selection and reading at the opening of the school day of verses from the Holy Bible and the recitation of the Lord's Prayer by the students in unison. These exercises are prescribed as part of the curricular activities of students who are required by law to attend school. They are held in the school buildings under the supervision and with the participation of teachers employed in those schools. None of these factors, other than compulsory school attendance, was present in the program upheld in *Zorach* v. *Clauson*. The trial court in No. 142 has found that such an opening exercise is a religious ceremony and was intended by the State to be so. We agree with the trial court's finding as to the religious character of the exercises. Given that finding the exercises and the law requiring them are in violation of the Establishment Clause.

There is no such specific finding as to the religious character of the exercises in No. 119, and the State contends (as does the State in No. 142) that the program is an effort to extend its benefits to all public school children without regard to their religious belief. Included within its secular purposes, it says, are the promotion of moral values, the contradictions to the materialistic trends of our times, the perpetuation of our institutions and the teaching of literature. The case came up on demurrer, of course, to a petition which alleged that the uniform practice under the rule had been to read from the King James version of the Bible and that the exercise was sectarian. The short answer, therefore, is that the religious character of the exercise was admitted by the State. But even if its purpose is not strictly religious, it is sought to be accomplished through readings, without comment, from the Bible. Surely the place of the Bible as an instrument of religion cannot be gainsaid, and the State's recognition of the pervading religious character of the ceremony is evident from the rule's specific permission of the alternative use of the Catholic Douay version as well as the recent amendment permitting nonattendance at the exercises. None of these factors is consistent with the contention that the Bible is here used either as an instrument for nonreligious moral inspiration or as a reference for the teaching of secular subjects.

The conclusion follows that in both cases the laws require religious exercises and such exercises are being conducted in direct violation of the rights of the appellees and petitioners. Nor are these required exercises mitigated by the fact that individual students may absent themselves upon parental request, for that fact furnishes no defense to a claim of unconstitutionality under the Establishment Clause. See *Engel* v. *Vitale, supra* (370 U.S. at 430). Further, it is no defense to urge that the religious practices here may be relatively minor encroachments on the First Amendment. The breach of neutrality that is today a trickling stream may all too soon become a raging torrent and, in the words of Madison, "it is proper to take alarm at the first experiment on our liberties." Memorial and Remonstrance Against Religious Assessments, quoted in *Everson, supra,* 330 U.S. at 65.

It is insisted that unless these religious exercises are permitted a "religion of secularism" is established in the schools. . . . We do not agree, however, that this decision in any sense has that effect. In addition, it might well be said that one's education is not complete without a study of comparative religion or the history of religion and its relationship to the advancement of civilization. It certainly may be said that the Bible is worthy of study for its literary and historic qualities. Nothing we have said here indicates that such study of the Bible or of religion, when presented objectively as part of a secular program of education, may not be effected consistent with the First Amendment. But the exercises here do not fall into those categories. They are religious exercises, required by the States in violation of the command of the First Amendment that the Government maintain strict neutrality, neither aiding nor opposing religion.

Finally, we cannot accept that the concept of neutrality, which does not permit a State to require a religious exercise even with the consent of the majority of those affected, collides with the majority's right to free exercise of religion. While the Free Exercise Clause clearly prohibits the use of state action to deny the rights of free exercise to *anyone*, it has never meant that a majority could use the machinery of the State to practice its beliefs. Such a contention was effectively answered by Mr. Justice Jackson for the Court in *West Virginia State Board of Education* v. *Barnette,* 319 U.S. 624, 638 (1943):

"The very purpose of a Bill of Rights was to withdraw certain subjects from the vicissitudes of political controversy, to place them beyond the reach of majorities and officials and to establish them as legal principles to be applied by the courts. One's right to . . . freedom of worship . . . and other fundamental rights may not be submitted to vote; they depend on the outcome of no elections.". . .

[Judgment in No. 142 affirmed. Judgment in No. 119 reversed and the cause remanded.]

Mr. Justice Douglas, concurring. . . .

Mr. Justice Brennan, concurring. . . .

Attendance at the public schools has never been compulsory; parents remain morally and constitutionally free to choose the academic environment in which they wish their children to be educated. The relationship of the Establishment Clause of the First Amendment to the public school system is preeminently that of reserving such a choice to the individual parent, rather than vesting it in the majority of voters of each State or school district. The choice which is thus preserved is between a public secular education with its uniquely democratic values, and some form of private, or sectarian education, which offers values of its own. In my judgment the First Amendment forbids the State to inhibit that freedom of choice by diminishing the attractiveness of either alternative—either by restricting the liberty of the private schools to inculcate whatever values they wish, or by jeopardizing the freedom of the public school from private or sectarian pressures. . . .

The line between permissible and impermissible forms of involvement between government and religion has already been considered by the lower federal and state courts. I think a brief survey of certain of these forms of accommodation will reveal that the First Amendment commands not official hostility toward religion, but only a strict neutrality in matters of religion. Moreover, it may serve to suggest that the scope of our holding today is to be measured by the special circumstances under which these cases have arisen, and by the particular dangers to church and state which religious exercises in the public schools present. It may be helpful for purposes of analysis to group these other practices and forms of accommodation into several rough categories.

A. *The Conflict Between Establishment and Free Exercise.*—There are certain practices, conceivably violative of the Establishment Clause, the striking down of which might seriously interfere with certain religious liberties also protected by the First Amendment. Provisions for churches and chaplains to military establishments for those in the armed services may afford one such example. The like provision by state and federal governments for chaplains in penal institutions may afford another example. It is argued that such provisions may be assumed to contravene the Establishment Clause, yet be sustained on constitutional grounds as necessary to secure to the members of the Armed Forces and prisoners those rights of worship guaranteed under the Free Exercise Clause. Since government has deprived such persons of the opportunity to practice their faith at places of their choice, the argument runs, government may, in order to avoid infringing the free exercise guarantees, provide substitutes where it requires such persons to be. . . .

The State must be steadfastly neutral in all matters of faith, and neither favor nor inhibit religion. In my view, government cannot sponsor religious exercises in the public schools without jeopardizing that neutrality. On the other hand, hostility, not neutrality, would characterize the refusal to provide chaplains and places of worship for prisoners and soldiers cut off by the State from all civilian opportunities for public communion, the withholding of draft exemptions for ministers and conscientious objectors, or the denial of the temporary use of an empty public building to a congregation whose place of worship has been destroyed by fire or flood. I do not say that government *must* provide chaplains or draft exemptions, or that the courts should intercede if it fails to do so.

B. *Establishment and Exercises in Legislative Bodies.*—The saying of invocational prayers in legislative chambers, state or federal, and the appointment of legislative chaplains, might well represent no involvement of the kind prohibited by the Establishment Clause. Legislators, federal and state, are mature adults who may presumably absent themselves from such public and ceremonial exercises without incurring any penalty, direct or indirect....

C. *Non-Devotional Use of the Bible in the Public Schools.*—The holding of the Court today plainly does not foreclose teaching *about* the Holy Scriptures or about the differences between religious sects in classes in literature or history. Indeed, whether or not the Bible is involved, it would be impossible to teach meaningfully many subjects in the social sciences or the humanities without some mention of religion. To what extent, and at what points in the curriculum religious materials should be cited, are matters which the courts ought to entrust very largely to the experienced officials who superintend our Nation's public schools. They are experts in such matters, and we are not....

D. *Uniform Tax Exemptions Incidentally Available to Religious Institutions.*— Nothing we hold today questions the propriety of certain tax deductions or exemptions which incidentally benefit churches and religious institutions, along with many secular charities and nonprofit organizations. If religious institutions benefit, it is in spite of rather than because of their religious character. For religious institutions simply share benefits which government makes generally available to educational, charitable, and eleemosynary groups. There is no indication that taxing authorities have used such benefits in any way to subsidize worship or foster belief in God. And as among religious beneficiaries, the tax exemption or deduction can be truly nondiscriminatory, available on equal terms to small as well as large religious bodies, to popular and unpopular sects, and to those organizations which reject as well as those which accept a belief in God....

F. *Activities Which, Though Religious in Origin, Have Ceased to Have Religious Meaning.*—As we noted in our Sunday Law decision, nearly every criminal law on the books can be traced to some religious principle or inspiration. But that does not make the present enforcement of the criminal law in any sense an establishment of religion, simply because it accords with widely held religious principles. As we said in *McGowan* v. *Maryland*, 366 U.S. 420, 442, "the 'Establishment' clause does not ban federal or state regulation of conduct whose reason or effect merely happens to coincide or harmonize with the tenets of some or all religions." This rationale suggests that the use of the motto "In God We Trust" on currency, on documents and public buildings and the like may not offend the clause. It is not that the use of those four words can be dismissed as *"de minimis"*—for I suspect there would be intense opposition to the abandonment of that motto. The truth is that we have simply interwoven the motto so deeply into the fabric of our civil polity that its present use may well not present that type of involvement which the First Amendment prohibits.

This general principle might also serve to insulate the various patriotic exercises and activities used in the Public schools and elsewhere which, whatever may have been their origins, no longer have a religious purpose or meaning. The reference to divinity in the revised pledge of allegiance, for example, may merely recognize the historical fact that our Nation was believed to have been founded "under God." Thus reciting the pledge may be no more of a religious exercise than the reading aloud of Lincoln's Gettysburg Address, which contains an allusion to the same historical fact. . . .

Mr. Justice Goldberg, with whom Mr. Justice Harlan joins, concurring. . . .

Mr. Justice Stewart, dissenting. . . .

It might . . . be argued that parents who want their children exposed to religious influences can adequately fulfill that wish off school property and outside school time. With all its surface persuasiveness, however, this argument seriously misconceives the basic constitutional justification for permitting the exercises at issue in these cases. For a compulsory state educational system so structures a child's life that if religious exercises are held to be an impermissible activity in schools, religion is placed at an artificial and state-created disadvantage. Viewed in this light, permission of such exercises for those who want them is necessary if the schools are truly to be neutral in the matter of religion. And a refusal to permit religious exercises thus is seen, not as the realization of state neutrality, but rather as the establishment of a religion of secularism, or at the least, as government support of the beliefs of those who think that religious exercises should be conducted only in private. . . .

Our decisions made clear that there is no constitutional bar to the use of government property for religious purposes. On the contrary, this Court has consistently held that the discriminatory barring of religious groups from public property is itself a violation of First and Fourteenth Amendment guarantees. *Fowler* v. *Rhode Island*, 345 U.S. 67; *Niemotko* v. *Maryland*, 340 U.S. 268. . . .

It is clear that the dangers of coercion involved in the holding of religious exercises in a schoolroom differ qualitatively from those presented by the use of similar exercises or affirmations in ceremonies attended by adults. Even as to children, however, the duty laid upon government in connection with religious exercises in the public schools is that of refraining from so structuring the school environment as to put any kind of pressure on a child to participate in those exercises; it is not that of providing an atmosphere in which children are kept scrupulously insulated from any awareness that some of their fellows may want to open the school day with prayer, or of the fact that there exist in our pluralistic society differences of religious belief. . . .

. . . [R]eligious exercises are not constitutionally invalid if they simply reflect differences which exist in the society from which the school draws its pupils. They become constitutionally invalid only if their administration places the sanction of secular authority behind one or more particular religious or irreligious beliefs. . . .

Viewed in this light, it seems to me clear that the records in both of the cases before us are wholly inadequate to support an informed or responsible decision. Both cases involve provisions which explicitly permit any student who wishes, to be excused from participation in the exercises. There is no evidence in either case as to whether there would exist any coercion of any kind upon a student who did not want to participate. . . .

What our Constitution indispensably protects is the freedom of each of us, be he Jew or Agnostic, Christian or Atheist, Buddhist or Free-thinker, to believe or disbelieve, to worship or not worship, to pray or keep silent, according to his own conscience, uncoerced and unrestrained by government. It is conceivable that these school boards, or even all school boards, might eventually find it impossible to administer a system of religious exercises during school hours in such a way as to meet this constitutional standard—in such a way as completely to free from any kind of official coercion those who do not affirmatively want to participate. But I think we must not assume that school boards so lack the qualities of inventiveness and good will as to make impossible the achievement of that goal.

I would remand both cases for further hearings.

Opposition to the prayer decisions led to an enormous mail campaign demanding that members of Congress introduce constitutional amendments to permit prayer and Bible-reading in the public schools. During the 88th Congress, through the third week of March 1964, 146 proposals for such constitutional amendments were introduced in the House and sent to the House Judiciary. A group of House members supporting amendment met to join forces behind a single proposal. The result was the "Becker Amendment," named for representative Frank Becker of New York who had sponsored the first prayer amendment bill in the 88th Congress. The text was as follows (H. J. Res. 693):

Sec. 1. Nothing in this Constitution shall be deemed to prohibit the offering, reading from, or listening to prayers or Biblical Scriptures, if participation therein is on a voluntary basis, in any governmental or public school, institution or place.

Sec. 2. Nothing in this Constitution shall be deemed to prohibit making reference to belief in, reliance upon, or invoking the aid of God or a Supreme Being in any governmental or public document, proceeding, activity, ceremony, school, institution, or place, or upon any coinage, currency, or obligation of the United States.

Sec. 3. Nothing in this Article shall constitute an establishment of religion

Although the House Judiciary Committee held hearings on the proposals, action was delayed sufficiently long until supporters of the Court's decisions mounted strong counter pressures, and no amendment proposal has passed the Congress to date. [For an account of the legislative history of the proposals, the stands taken by various church groups, and testimony before the Judiciary Committee, see *Congressional Quarterly Weekly Report,* No. 18 (May 1, 1964), pp. 881–885.]

An interesting aspect of the Bible in the public schools was presented in New Jersey in litigation involving the free distribution of Gideon Bibles at a group of public schools. One of the primary methods of operation of the Gideons International is the placing of Bibles in hotels, hospitals, and schools. A local chapter of the organization asked the Board of Education of the Borough of Rutherford for permission to distribute copies to public school children in the municipality. The volume contained the Book of Psalms, Proverbs, and the New Testament, all in the King James version. At a meeting of the Board of Education to consider the request, objections were voiced by a Catholic priest and a Jewish rabbi, on the grounds that the Gideons' New Testament was sectarian and forbidden to Catholic and Jewish children under the laws of their respective religions. The proposal passed, however, with only one dissenting vote.

Arrangements were made for forms to be sent to school by parents who wished their children to receive the free copies of the Bible. It was ordered that the distribution was to take place after school, and no other pupils were to be in the room when the Bibles were distributed.

Two plaintiffs, one Jewish and one Catholic, sought an injunction in a

New Jersey Court to restrain the Board of Education from carrying out its plan for Bible distribution. Each contended that the Gideon Bible is "a sectarian work of peculiar religious value and significance to members of the Protestant faith," and that its distribution to children of their faiths violated the teachings, tenets and principles of their respective religions. Prior to the case, however, the Catholic child transferred schools and his issue became moot. In *Tudor* v. *Board of Education of Rutherford,* 14 N.J. 31 (1953), the New Jersey Supreme Court held the proposal unconstitutional. Chief Justice Vanderbilt, for the court, said in part:

This brings us to the heart of our problem here—namely, whether the resolution of the Board of Education displays that favoritism that is repugnant to our constitution. By permitting the distribution of the Gideon Bible, has the Board of Education established one religious sect in preference to another? Although as to the Catholic plaintiff this action has become moot due to the withdrawal of his child from the public schools of Rutherford, some testimony was presented at the trial as to his claim of sectarianism so we will at times refer to such testimony in our opinion. Our decision, however, is based upon the claim of the Jewish plaintiff that the resolution of the Rutherford Board of Education constitutes a preference of one religion over the Hebrew faith.

A review of the testimony at the trial convinces us that the King James version or Gideon Bible is unacceptable to those of the Jewish faith. In this regard Rabbi Joachim Prinz testified:

"The New Testament is in profound conflict with the basic principles of Judaism. It is not accepted by the Jewish people as a sacred book. The Bible of the Jewish people is the Old Testament. The New Testament is not recognized as part of the Bible. The teachings of the New Testament are in complete and profound conflict with what Judaism teaches. It presupposes the concept of Jesus of Nazareth as a divinity, a concept which we do not accept.". . .

. . . Nor is there any doubt that the King James version of the Bible is as unacceptable to Catholics as the Douay version is to Protestants. According to the testimony in this case the canon law of the Catholic Church provides that "Editions of the original text of the sacred scriptures published by non-Catholics are forbidden *ipso jure.*". . .

We find from the evidence presented in this case that the Gideon Bible is a sectarian book, and that the resolution of the defendant Board of Education to permit its distribution through the public school system . . . was in violation of the First Amendment of the United States Constitution, as incorporated into the Fourteenth Amendment, and of Article 1, paragraph 4, of the New Jersey Constitution. It therefore must be set aside. . . .

[The Chief Justice then quoted from certain of the expert testimony elicited from a psychologist and a professor of education to the effect that the student is not really free to make a choice but will feel that "he will be something of an outcast and a pariah if he does not go along with this procedure," and also that the distribution would create tensions among the religious groups and divide the children in terms of receiving or not receiving Bibles.]

We cannot accept the argument that here, as in the *Zorach* case, the State is merely "accommodating" religion. It matters little whether the teachers themselves will distribute the Bibles or whether that will be done by members of the Gideons International. The same vice exists, that of preference of one religion over another. This is all the more obvious when we realize the motive of the Gideons. . . . The society is engaged in missionary work, accomplished in part by placing the King James version of the Bible in the hands of public school children throughout the United States. To achieve this end it employs the public school system as the medium of distribution. It is at the school that the pupil receives the request slip to take to his parents for signature. It is at the school that the pupil actually receives his Gideon Bible. In other words, the public school machinery is used to bring about the distribution of these Bibles to the children of Rutherford. In the eyes of the pupils and their parents the Board of Education has placed its stamp of approval upon this distribution, and in fact, upon the Gideon Bible itself. . . . Dr. William Heard Kilpatrick stated:

"The Protestants would feel that the school is getting behind this thing; the Catholics would feel that the school is getting behind a Protestant affair; the Jews would feel that the school is getting behind the Protestant religion as opposed to their religion; and the people who don't accept any religion would feel that the school is actually trying to teach the religion through this means."

This is more than mere "accommodation" of religion permitted in the *Zorach* case. The school's part in this distribution is an active one and cannot be sustained on the basis of a mere assistance to religion.

. . . To permit the distribution of the King James version of the Bible in the public schools of this state would be to cast aside all the programs made in the United States and throughout New Jersey in the field of religious toleration and freedom. We would be renewing the ancient struggles among the various religious faiths to the detriment of all. This we must decline to do. . . .

More recently some groups, particularly some of the Jewish organizations, have raised questions concerning the propriety of so-called Christological observances in the public schools—Easter programs, Christmas programs, nativity scenes, and other programs or activities specifically associated with Christian beliefs. As of this date the attempts to resolve such issues have taken place primarily in the lower level political arenas—representations before school boards, principals, or city councils—rather than in the courts. One such attack was carried forward in the courts of Florida, however. Suit was brought against the Dade County Board of Instruction challenging Bible-reading, prayer, baccalaureate exercises, religious census for students, and alleged religious tests for the employment and promotion of teachers in the public schools. The Florida Supreme Court upheld the Board on all counts, *Chamberlin* v. *Dade County Board of Public Instruction,* 143 So.2d 21 (1963). On appeal, the United States Supreme Court vacated the judgment and re-manded the case for reconsideration in the light of the *Murray* and *Schempp* cases. [374 U.S. 487 (1963).] The Florida Supreme Court then reaffirmed its judgment, 160 So.2d 97 (1964), and the case went back to the United States Supreme Court on appeal. In *Chamberlin* v. *Dade County Board of Public Instruction,* 377 U.S. 402 (1964), the Court rendered the following *per curiam* opinion reversing the Florida Supreme Court:

. . . The judgment of the Florida Supreme Court is reversed with respect to the issues of the constitutionality of prayer, and of devotional Bible reading . . . in the public schools of Dade County. . . . As to the other questions raised, the appeal is dismissed for want of properly presented federal questions. . . .

Mr. Justice Douglas, with whom Mr. Justice Black agrees, concurring in part.
I join in reversing the Supreme Court of Florida on the main issue in the case.

The "other questions raised" which the Court refuses to consider . . . involve the constitutionality under the First and Fourteenth Amendments of baccalaureate services in the schools, a religious census among pupils, and a religious test for teachers. The Florida Supreme Court disposed of those issues on the authority of *Doremus* v. *Board of Education* . . . which held that a taxpayer lacks standing to challenge religious exercises in the public schools. . . . I think it is arguable that appellant-taxpayers do have standing to challenge these practices.

I think, however, that two of those "other questions"—the baccalaureate services and the religious census—do not present substantial federal questions, and so I concur in the dismissal of the appeal as to them. As to the religious test for teachers, I think a substantial question is presented. . . .

Mr. Justice Stewart would note probable jurisdiction of this appeal and set it down for argument on the merits.

Sunday Closing Laws and the Establishment Clause

One of the clearest legacies bequeathed to us by the American Puritans is the Sunday Blue Law. Whatever the errors perpetuated concerning the Puritan's capacity for sin and pleasure—and the adjective "puritanical" is illustrative of such error—the accounts of his rigid and sober Sabbath observance are grounded in solid fact. Now, more than three hundred years later, we still retain laws which bar many kinds of mercantile and manufacturing operations on Sunday. For those persons whose Sabbath observance is on Sunday this is a congenial arrangement. For others, it may introduce a certain conflict in accommodating their religious and business interests to the Sunday Closing Law. At the very least, they may feel that the state is adopting punitive legislation which favors certain religious sects and penalizes others. Despite the clear indication that Sunday Laws were originally adopted as a means of promoting Christian observance, the earlier court decisions have uniformly upheld such laws, as in the case of *Petit* v. *Minnesota,* 177 U.S. 164 (1900), where a state law forbidding Sunday labor except works of necessity or charity was upheld. The first detailed examination of Sunday Laws by the United States Supreme Court under the claims of establishment of religion and abridgment of free exercise of religion did not occur, however, until 1961. In that year four cases involving the Sunday Laws of Massachusetts, Pennsylvania, and Maryland were decided, and in each case the laws were upheld against the claims of violation of religious liberty. The Maryland case, *McGowan* v. *Maryland*, covers the establishment arguments most thoroughly and will be presented as illustrative of the Court's view on that issue. (Since the Sunday laws contain a myriad of exceptions and exemptions from the closing requirement, the question of improper classification under the equal protection clause naturally arises, but this issue has been omitted from the cutting below since it does not relate directly to the matter of religious liberty.)

McGOWAN v. MARYLAND

366 U.S. 420 (1961)

Mr. Chief Justice Warren delivered the opinion of the Court.

The issues in this case concern the constitutional validity of Maryland criminal statutes, commonly known as Sunday Closing Laws or Sunday Blue Laws. . . .

Appellants are seven employees of a large discount department store located on a highway in Anne Arundel County, Maryland. They were indicted for the Sunday sale of a three-ring loose-leaf binder, a can of floor wax, a stapler and staples, and a toy submarine in violation of Md. Ann. Code, Art. 27 §521. Generally, this section prohibited, throughout the State, the Sunday sale of all merchandise except the retail sale of tobacco products, confectioneries, milk, drugs and medicines, and newspapers and periodicals. Recently amended, this section also now excepts from the general prohibition the retail sale in Anne Arundel County of all foodstuffs, automobile and boating accessories, flowers, toilet goods, hospital supplies and souvenirs. It now further provides that any retail establishment in Anne Arundel County which does not employ more than one person other than the owner may operate on Sunday.

Although appellants were indicted only under §521, in order properly to consider several of the broad constitutional contentions, we must examine the whole body of Maryland Sunday laws. Several sections of the Maryland statutes are particularly relevant to evaluation of the issues presented. . . .

The remaining statutory sections concern a myriad of exceptions for various counties, districts of counties, cities, and towns throughout the State. Among the activities allowed in certain areas on Sunday are such sports as football, baseball, golf, tennis, bowling, croquet, basketball, lacrosse, soccer, hockey, swimming, softball, boating, fishing, skating, horseback riding, stock car racing and pool or billiards. Other immunized activities permitted in some regions of the State include group singing or playing of musical instruments; the exhibition of motion pictures; dancing; the operation of recreation centers, picnic grounds, swimming pools, skating rinks and miniature golf courses. . . .

. . . Appellants were convicted and each was fined five dollars and costs. . . .

III

The final questions for decision are whether the Maryland Sunday Closing laws conflict with the Federal Constitution's provisions for religious liberty. . . . But appellants allege only economic injury to themselves; they do not allege any infringement of their own religious freedoms due to Sunday closing. In fact, the record is silent as to what appellants' religious beliefs are. Since the general rule is that "a litigant may only assert his own constitutional rights or immunities," *United States* v. *Raines,* 362 U.S. 17, 22, we hold that appellants have no standing to raise this contention. . . .

Secondly, appellants contend that the statutes violate the guarantee of separation of church and state in that the statutes are laws respecting an establishment of religion contrary to the First Amendment, made applicable to the states by the Fourteenth Amendment. . . . Appellants here concededly have suffered direct economic injury, allegedly due to the imposition on them of the tenets of the Christian religion. We find that, in these circumstances, these appellants have standing to complain that the statutes are laws respecting an establishment of religion.

The essence of appellant's "establishment" argument is that Sunday is the Sabbath day of the predominant Christian sects; that the purpose of the enforced stoppage of labor on that day is to facilitate and encourage church attendance; that the purpose of setting Sunday as a day of universal rest is to induce people with no religion or people with marginal religious beliefs to join the predominant Christian sects; that the purpose of the atmosphere of tranquility created by Sunday closing is to aid the conduct of church services and religious observance of the sacred day. In substantiating their "establishment" argument, appellants rely on the wording of the present Maryland statutes, on earlier versions of the current Sunday laws and on prior judicial characterizations of these laws by the Maryland Court of Appeals. Although only the constitutionality of §521, of the section under which appellants have been convicted, is immediately before us in this litigation, inquiry into the history of Sunday Closing Laws in our country, in addition to an examination of the Maryland Sunday closing statutes in their entirety and of their history, is relevant to the decision of whether the Maryland Sunday Law in question is one respecting an establishment of religion. There is no dispute that the original laws which dealt with Sunday labor were motivated by religious forces. But what we must decide is whether present Sunday legislation having undergone extensive changes from the earliest forms, still retains its religious character.

Sunday Closing Laws go far back into American history, having been brought to the colonies with a background of English legislation dating to the thirteenth century. . . . The law of the colonies to the time of the Revolution and the basis of the Sunday laws in the States was 29 Charles II, c. 7 (1677). It provided, in part:

"For the better observation and keeping holy the Lord's day, commonly called Sunday: be it enacted . . . that all the laws enacted and in force concerning the observation of the Lord's day, *and repairing to the church thereon,* be carefully put in execution; and that all and every person and persons whatsoever shall upon every Lord's day apply themselves to the observation of the same, by exercising themselves thereon in the duties of piety and true religion, publicly and privately; and that no tradesman, artificer, workman, laborer, or other person whatsoever, *shall do or exercise any worldly labor or business or work* of their ordinary callings upon the Lord's day, . . ." (Emphasis added.)

Observation of the above language, and of that of the prior mandates, reveals clearly that the English Sunday legislation was in aid of the established church.

The American colonial Sunday restrictions arose soon after settlement. Starting in 1650, the Plymouth Colony proscribed servile work, unnecessary travelling, sports, and the sale of alcoholic beverages on the Lord's day and enacted laws concerning church attendance. . . .

But, despite the strongly religious origin of these laws, beginning before the eighteenth century, nonreligious arguments for Sunday closing began to be heard more distinctly and the statutes began to lose some of their totally religious flavor. In the middle 1700's, Blackstone wrote, "[T]he keeping one day in the seven holy, as a time of relaxation and refreshment as well as for public worship, is of admirable service to a state considered merely as civil institution. It humanizes, by the help of conversation and society, the manners of the lower classes; which would otherwise degenerate into a sordid ferocity and savage selfishness of spirit; it enables the industrious workman to pursue his occupation in the ensuing week with health and cheerfulness." 4 Bl. Comm. 63. . . . With the advent of the First Amendment, the colonial provisions requiring church attendance were soon repealed. . . .

More recently, further secular justifications have been advanced for making Sunday a day of rest, a day when people may recover from the labors of the week just passed and may physically and mentally prepare for the week's work to come. In England, during the First World War, a committee investigating the health conditions of munitions workers reported that "if the maximum output is to be secured and maintained for any length of time, a weekly period of rest must be allowed. . . . On economic and social grounds alike this weekly period of rest is best provided on Sunday."

The proponents of Sunday closing legislation are no longer exclusively representatives of religious interests. Recent New Jersey Sunday legislation was supported by labor groups and trade associations. . . .

. . . Some of our States now enforce their Sunday legislation through Departments of Labor, e.g., SC Code Ann (1952), §64–5. Thus have Sunday laws evolved from the wholly religious sanctions that originally were enacted.

Moreover, litigation over Sunday closing laws is not novel. Scores of cases may be found in the state appellate courts relating to sundry phases of Sunday enactments. Religious objections have been raised there on numerous occasions but sustained only once, in *Ex parte Newman,* 9 Cal 502 (1858); and that decision was overruled three years later, in *Ex parte Andrews,* 18 Cal. 678. . . .

However, it is equally true that the "Establishment" Clause does not ban federal or state regulation of conduct whose reason or effect merely happens to coincide or harmonize with the tenets of some or all religions. In many instances, the Congress or state legislatures conclude that the general welfare of society, wholly apart from any religious considerations, demands such regulation. Thus, for temporal purposes, murder is illegal. And the fact that this agrees with the dictates of the Judaeo-Christian religions while it may disagree with others does not invalidate the regulation. So too with the questions of adultery and polygamy. . . .

In light of the evolution of our Sunday Closing Laws through the centuries, and of their more or less recent emphasis upon secular considerations, it is not difficult to discern that as present written and administered, most of them, at least, are of a secular rather than of a religious character, and that presently they bear no relationship to establishment of religion as those words are used in the Constitution of the United States.

Throughout this century and longer, both the federal and state governments have oriented their activities very largely toward improvements of the health, safety, recreation and general well-being of our citizens. Numerous laws affecting public health, safety factors in industry, laws affecting hours and conditions of labor of women and children, week-end diversion at parks and beaches, and cultural activities of various kinds, now point the way toward the good life for all. Sunday Closing Laws, like those before us, have become part and parcel of this great governmental concern wholly apart from their original purposes or connotations. The present purpose and effect of most of them is to provide a uniform day of rest for all citizens; the fact that this day is Sunday, a day of particular significance for the dominant Christian sects, does not bar the State from achieving its secular goals. To say that the States cannot prescribe Sunday as a day of rest for these purposes solely because centuries ago such laws had their genesis in religion would give a constitutional interpretation of hostility to the public welfare rather than one of mere separation of church and state.

We now reach the Maryland statutes under review. . . .

Considering the language and operative effect of the current statutes, we no longer find the blanket prohibition against Sunday work or bodily labor. To the contrary, we find . . . the Sunday sale of tobaccos and sweets and a long list of sundry articles which we have enumerated above. . . . the Sunday operation of bathing beaches, amusement parks and similar facilities; . . . the Sunday sale of alcoholic beverages, . . . Sunday bingo and the Sunday playing of pin-ball machines and slot machines, activities generally condemned by prior Maryland Sunday legislation. Certainly, these are not works of charity or necessity. . . . These provisions, along with those which permit various sports and entertainments on Sunday, seem clearly to be fashioned for the purpose of providing a Sunday atmosphere of recreation, cheerfulness, repose and enjoyment. Coupled with the general proscription against other types of work, we believe that the air of the day is one of relaxation rather than one of religion. . . .

But, this does not answer all of appellants' contentions. We are told that the State has other means at its disposal to accomplish its secular purpose, other courses that would not even remotely or incidentally give state aid to religion. . . . It is true that if the State's interest were simply to provide for its citizens a periodic respite from work, a regulation demanding that everyone rest one day in seven, leaving the choice of the day to the individual, would suffice.

However, the State's purpose is not merely to provide a one-day-in-seven work stoppage. In addition to this, the State seeks to set one day apart from all others as a day of rest, repose, recreation and tranquility—a day which all members of the family and community have the opportunity to spend and enjoy together, a day in which there exists relative quiet and disassociation from the everday intensity of commercial activities, a day in which people may visit friends and relatives who are not available during working days.

Obviously, a State is empowered to determine that a rest-one-day-in-seven statute would not accomplish this purpose; that it would not provide for a general cessation of activity, a special atmosphere of tranquility, a day which all members of the family or friends and relatives might spend together. Furthermore, it seems plain that the problems involved in enforcing such a provision would be exceedingly more difficult than those in enforcing a common-day-of-rest provision.

Moreover, it is common knowledge that the first day of the week has come to have special significance as a rest day in this country. . . . Sunday is a day apart from all others. The cause is irrelevant; the fact exists. It would seem unrealistic for enforcement purposes and perhaps detrimental to the general welfare to require a State to choose a common-day-of-rest other than that which most persons would select of their own accord. For these reasons, we hold that the Maryland statutes are not laws respecting an establishment of religion. . . .

Accordingly, the decision is

Affirmed.

Separate opinion of Mr. Justice Frankfurter, whom Mr. Justice Harlan joins. . . .

Mr. Justice Douglas, dissenting.

The question is not whether one day out of seven can be imposed by a State as a day of rest. The question is not whether Sunday can by force of custom and habit be retained as a day of rest. The question is whether a State can impose criminal sanctions on those who, unlike the Christian majority that make up our society, worship on a different day or do not share the religious scruples of the majority. . . .

With that as my starting point I do not see how a State can make protesting citizens refrain from doing innocent acts on Sunday because the doing of those acts offends sentiments of their Christian neighbors. . . .

. . . The "establishment" clause protects citizens also against any law which selects any religious custom, practice, or ritual, puts the force of government behind it, and fines, imprisons, or otherwise penalizes a person for not observing it. The Government plainly could not join forces with one religious group and decree a universal and symbolic circumcision. Nor could it require all children to be baptized or give tax exemptions only to those whose children were baptized.

Could it require a fast from sunrise to sunset throughout the Moslem month of Ramadan? I should think not. Yet why then can it make criminal the doing of other acts, as innocent as eating, during the day that Christians revere? . . .

The issue of these cases would therefore be in better focus if we imagined that a state legislature controlled by orthodox Jews and Seventh Day Adventists, passed a law making it a crime to keep a shop open on Saturdays. Would a Baptist, Catholic, Methodist, or Presbyterian be compelled to obey that law or go to jail or pay a fine? Or suppose Moslems grew in political strength here and got a law through a state legislature making it a crime to keep a shop open on Fridays? Would the rest of us have to submit under the fear of criminal sanctions? . . .

It seems to me plain that by these laws the States compel one, under sanction of law, to refrain from work or recreation on Sunday because of the majority's religious views about that day. The State by law makes Sunday a symbol of respect or adherence. Refraining from work or recreation in deference to the majority's religious feelings about Sunday is within every person's choice. By what authority can government compel it?

Cases are put where acts that are immoral by our standards but not by the standards of other religious groups are made criminal. That category of cases, until today, has been a very restricted one confined to polygamy . . . and other extreme situations. . . . None of the actions made constitutionally criminal today involves the doing of any act that any society has deemed to be immoral. . . .

The State can of course require one day of rest a week: one day when every shop or factory is closed. Quite a few States make that requirement. Then the "day of rest" becomes purely and simply a health measure. But the Sunday laws operate differently. They force minorities to obey the majority's religious feelings of what is due and proper for a Christian community; they provide a coercive spur to the "weaker brethren," to those who are indifferent to the claims of a Sabbath through apathy or scruple. Can there be any doubt that Christians, now aligned vigorously in favor of these laws, would be as strongly opposed, if they were prosecuted under a Moslem law that forbade them from engaging in secular activities on days that violated Moslem scruples?

There is an "establishment" of religion in the constitutional sense if any practice of any religious group has the sanction of law behind it. There is an interference with the "free exercise" of religion if what in conscience one can do or omit doing is required because of the religious scruples of the community. Hence I would declare each of those laws unconstitutional as applied to the complaining parties, whether or not they are members of a sect which observes as their Sabbath a day other than Sunday.

When these laws are applied to Orthodox Jews . . . or to Sabbatarians their vice is accentuated. If the Sunday laws are constitutional, Kosher markets are on a five-day week. Thus those laws put an economic penalty on those who observe Saturday rather than Sunday as the Sabbath. For the economic pressures on these minorities, created by the fact that our communities are predominantly Sunday-minded, there is no recourse. When, however, the State uses its coercive powers—here the criminal law—to compel minorities to observe a second Sabbath, not their own, the State undertakes to aid and "prefer one religion over another" contrary to the commands of the Constitution. . . .

THE "FREE EXERCISE" OF RELIGION

As previously pointed out, the First Amendment contains two clauses designed to safeguard religious liberty—the establishment clause and the free exercise clause. These are, of course, but complementary facets of the overall protection for religious freedom. While the one shades off into the other, it is still useful to separate the two facets for analysis. As Justice Frankfurter stated in his concurring opinion in *McGowan* v. *Maryland*:

Within the discriminating phraseology of the First Amendment, distinction has been drawn between cases raising "establishment" and "free exercise" questions. Any attempt to formulate a bright-line distinction is bound to founder. In view of the competition among religious creeds, whatever "establishes" one sect disadvantages another, and vice versa. But it is possible historically, and therefore helpful analytically—no less for problems arising under the Fourteenth Amendment, illuminated as that Amendment is by our national experience, than for problems arising under the First—to isolate in general terms the two largely overlapping areas of concern reflected in the two constitutional phrases, "establishment" and "free exercise." . . .

Religious minorities were too busy struggling for their existence during the earlier period of American development to feel that they could turn to the courts for protection against majority rules which merely pinched but did not destroy. As the major battles were won in the political arena—freedom to engage in public worship, freedom from taxes to support religion, and freedom from the onus of an established religion—the climate was prepared for settling the secondary sources of friction by the calmer method of litigation. Thus it was not until the latter quarter of the nineteenth century that the first major case on religious liberty reached the United States Supreme Court. The case was *Reynolds* v. *United States,* decided in 1879, and it dealt with the constitutionality of a law prohibiting polygamous marriages as applied to a Mormon whose religion encouraged such a practice.

Permissible Areas of Restraint—Protection of Morals, Health, and Safety

Reynolds was convicted in a district court of the Territory of Utah of the crime of bigamy, in violation of federal statutes which prohibited bigamy in any place under exclusive jurisdiction of the United States. He admitted to having entered into a second marriage, but as a Mormon, he alleged that "it was the duty of male members of said Church, circumstances permitting, to practice polygamy," and for the United States to punish him for enjoying this prescription of his Church was to abridge his First Amendment right to free exercise of religion. In *Reynolds* v. *United States,* 98 U.S. 145 (1879), the Court unanimously denied his claim. Chief Justice Waite, for the Court, examined the statutory history relating to the practice and concluded: "Polygamy has always been odious among the Northern and Western Nations of Europe and, until the establishment of the Mormon Church, was almost exclusively a feature of the life of Asiatic and African people." He stated that since before, during, and after the adoption of the First Amendment the law had punished bigamous marriages, "it is impossible to believe that the constitutional guaranty of religious freedom was intended to prohibit legislation in respect to this most important feature of social life."

As the *Reynolds* opinion makes clear, the First Amendment was not intended, and has not been so construed, to set up an absolute right to engage in a course of action just because one's religion happens to dictate it. Reasonable restrictions adopted by governments in furtherance of the health, safety, and convenience of the community may be enforced even against claims of violation of religious freedom.

The state has a well-recognized interest in the proper care and maintenance of children, and every state has laws charging parents with due attention to the health needs of their minor children. Issues have arisen, however, as a result of parental decisions to rely on prayer or special religious ceremony rather than normal medical assistance for the cure of sick children. There is no question but that a competent adult may freely choose whether to submit to medical treatment or not. The question arises, however, whether the parent is constitutionally free to make the same choices on religious grounds for his or her minor children. Typical of the general view of state courts is that expressed in *Craig* v. *State of Maryland*, decided by the Maryland Supreme Court.

CRAIG *v.* STATE OF MARYLAND
220 Md. 590, 155 A.2d 684 (1959)

[Defendants, father and mother, refused, on religious grounds, to call for medical care for their child, afflicted with pneumonia. As members of the Church of God they based their belief in divine healing on the Epistle of James 5:14, 15—"If there be any sick among you, let him call in the Elders of the Church." The child died and the parents were tried and convicted of involuntary manslaughter, on the theory that they were grossly negligent in failing to provide medical care. Appellants claim that such statutes as Maryland's requiring medical care for children violate their free exercise of religion protected by the Constitution of the United States.]

[The opinion by Justice Prescott first points out that the holding in *Regina* v. *Wagstaffe*, to the effect that parents of a sick child who omit to call in medical assistance because of their religious belief are not guilty of manslaughter, is irrelevant because it is a common law decision, and Maryland has by statute charged parents with medical care for their children.]

Appellants claim that such statutes violate their free exercise of religion protected by the Constitution of the United States.

The authorities are practically unanimous in holding to the contrary of the appellants' contention here. . . .

In prosecutions for the breach of a duty imposed by statute to furnish necessary medical aid to a minor child, the particular religious belief of the person charged with the offense constitutes no defense. . . . *People* v. *Pierson,* 176 N.Y. 201, 68 N.E. 243, 63 L.R.A. 187, seems to be a leading case upon the subject. After a most interesting and enlightening discourse upon the origin of medical science, the growth of legends of miracles and the intertwining of religion into the treating of sickness, the court held that a statute making the failure to furnish medical attention to a child a misdemeanor as applied to a person believing that prayer was the proper cure for illness was not violative of a New York constitutional provision guaranteeing the freedom of religious worship, since the religious belief secured by the Constitution did not extend to practices inconsistent with the peace or safety of the State, which involved the protection of the lives and health of its children and in the obedience of its citizens to its laws. The appellants were, and are, at perfect liberty to believe in the religion of their selection; they may pray, anoint and call in the Elders of their church in case of sickness of their minor children; but they, like all parents, must also obey the mandate of Article 72A, Section 1, by providing medical aid when the circumstances properly call for the same. . . .

The appellants' contention that they were denied "equal protection of the laws". . . is likewise without merit. It is based upon . . . Article 43, Section 140, which provides that "[N]othing in this subtitle . . . shall prevent any Christian Science practitioner duly registered in the Christian Science Journal . . . from treating human ills in accordance with the tenets of Christian Science or from making an adequate charge for services performed." They complain that they were prosecuted for treating human ills by prayer, when the above section permits Christian Scientists to render such treatment legally. They were, however, not prosecuted because they prayed, but for their alleged negligent failure to provide medical care. While Section 140 *permits* the treating of human ills in accordance with the tenets of Christian Science, it does not, in any manner, render such treatment the legal equivalent of medical care; hence Christian Science parents find themselves under the same duty to provide medical care for their minor children under the provisions of Article 72A, Section 1, when the circumstances require such care, as do all other parents. There is no discrimination here that violates the equal protection clause.

[The judgments were reversed, however, and the cases remanded for new trials. No testimony was entered to show that the parents were aware of the seriousness of the disease until two or three days prior to death. Testimony of doctors was that at that stage antibiotics probably would not have helped. Thus the evidence was insufficient to sustain a finding that gross negligence was the proximate cause of death.]

The only case thus far to reach the United States Supreme Court involving a conflict between child care laws and the claim of free exercise of religion is *Prince* v. *Massachusetts,* 321 U.S. 158 (1944). It concerned the validity of the application of the state's child labor law to the guardian of a nine-year-old girl, who was permitted by the guardian to engage in "preaching work" and the sale and distribution of religious literature on the public streets after school hours. The defendant objected on the ground of interference with her religious freedom. By a five-to-four vote the Court held the application of such a criminal law valid as a reasonable police regulation designed to protect the welfare of children, even against the competing claim of religious exercise. The Court noted that the authority of the State as *parens patriae* "is not nullified merely because the parent grounds his claim to control the child's course of conduct on religion or conscience." The Court stated further:

The state's authority over children's activities is broader than over like actions of adults. This is peculiarly true of public activities and in matters of employment. A democratic society rests, for its continuance, upon the healthy, well-rounded growth of young people into full maturity as citizens, with all that implies. It may secure this against impeding restraints and dangers within a broad range of selection. Among evils most appropriate for such action are the crippling effects of child employment, more especially in public places, and the possible harms arising from other activities subject to all the diverse influences of the street. It is too late now to doubt that legislation appropriately designed to reach such evils is within the state's police power, whether against the parent's claim to control of the child or one that religious scruples dictate contrary action.

Justice Murphy dissented on the ground that the particular prohibition of religious activities by children in this case was unreasonable, suggesting that "the reasonableness that justifies the prohibition of the ordinary distribution of literature in the public streets by children is not necessarily the reasonableness that justifies such a drastic restriction when the distribution is part of their religious faith."

Where religious practices endanger the health or safety of others in the community, the courts have had no difficulty applying the normal police power regulations to such practices. As one illustration, a number of state supreme courts have dealt with claims of violation of religious freedom in the convictions of persons who engage in handling poisonous snakes as a part of their religious ritual. Such convictions have uniformly been upheld against claims of violation of the free exercise clauses of state constitutions. Illustrative of the cases is *Harden* v. *State of Tennessee,* 188 Tenn. 17, 216 S.W.2d 708 (1949).

Harden and others were convicted of violating a statute making it unlawful for any person to handle or display any poisonous or dangerous snake in such manner as to endanger the life or health of any person. They were members of a religious denomination believing that the handling of poisonous snakes was a test of the sincerity of their faith and, further, that non-believers would be converted to their faith upon witnessing this miracle of safely handling such snakes. The Tennessee Supreme Court, in upholding the conviction, pointed out:

Aside from the fact that such handling of a rattlesnake is commonly known to be fraught with danger, there is in this record affirmative evidence that at this particular church at least one worshipper was bitten by a poisonous snake and died from the effects thereof within a few hours.

Reasonable minds must agree that the aforementioned practice of so handling poisonous snakes as a part of the religious services of this Church is dangerous to the life and health of people.

The court stated further that the statute did not interfere with the conscience of the defendants, or their beliefs concerning snakes, but that society had a right to protection of life and health which was equally as precious as defendants' right to free exercise of religion.

The courts of the states have also upheld state laws which require affirmative action to prevent disease, as well as the requirements of caring for ill minor children. The compulsory vaccination laws have been upheld in general in *Jacobson* v. *Massachusetts,* 197 U.S. 11 (1905), and convictions for failure to vaccinate children as a condition for admission to public school have been upheld against religious challenge, as in *Anderson* v. *State,* 84 Ga. App. 259, 65 S.E. 2d 848 (1951). Fluoridation has been upheld against the challenge from members of religious sects opposed to medication that such a program violates their religious liberty, as in *Baer* v. *City of Bend,* 206 Ore. 221, 292 P. 2d 134 (1956). It is interesting to note that such groups do not normally oppose *chlorination* of water although they do oppose *fluoridation.* The distinction apparently is drawn on the basis that chlorination merely kills certain bacteria, while flouridation specifically is designed to serve as a caries preventive and is therefore a form of medication.

Another area in which the police power has been deemed to take precedence over claims of religious liberty is protection against fraud. Spiritual healing and faith healing have probably been with us since the earliest case of illness. Since normal physiological processes will rectify three-fourths of all illness, and psychosomatic disorders may respond to readjustment of mental state, the reportable "cures" of healers may reach impressive percentage figures. Claimants of special supernatural powers to heal the sick have often been sincerely convinced that they possessed such talents. Others have formed religious sects which included as an article of faith the belief that participation in certain kinds of religious ritual would result in curing illness. Where there is a clear nexus between religious belief or practice and the attempts to heal the sick, government denies religious freedom if it attempts actively to intervene. On the other hand, there are those who, without any prompting of religious conviction, set up healing enterprises with all the panoply and trappings of religion and play upon the credulity of the ignorant and the desperation of the incurably ill solely for financial gain. The general view is that the latter category of healers can properly be made the object of prosecutions for fraud, although there are strong dissents from this view.

The United States Supreme Court in 1944 considered the issue of the constitutionality under the First Amendment of prosecution of faith healers for mail fraud. The "I Am" cult was established in California by one Guy Ballard. The founders and leaders of the movement were subjected to a mail fraud prosecution. Guy Ballard claimed that he and his wife Edna and their child had been selected by St. Germain (dead since A.D. 488) as earthly representatives of the true religion. As a consequence of such divine designation Guy Ballard could heal incurable diseases and take spots off clothing, or at least so their doctrine taught. Funds were received from believers to carry on the work of the cult, and the mails were used for this purpose, as well as for the sale of various types of printed matter describing the doctrines of the cult. Very substantial profits were made on the printed material.

The federal government charged that the mails had been used to defraud. The major question throughout was just what the jury was supposed to decide: whether the Ballards could cure the incurable, or whether the Ballards *believed* that they could cure the incurable. The trial judge decided that the jury could only examine the latter, that is, the question of whether the Ballards honestly believed what they taught.

Before the case was concluded Guy Ballard died, following an operation, but his wife and child were convicted, fined, and given suspended prison sentences. The Court of Appeals reversed on the ground that the trial judge improperly charged the jury as to the defendants' sincerity. This decision was appealed, and the United States Supreme Court, agreeing with the view of the trial judge, reversed the decision of the Court of Appeals. Justice Douglas, speaking for the Court in *United States* v. *Ballard,* 322 U.S. 78 (1944), stated that this approach was in line with the First Amendment protection of religious freedom. Clearly, he said, the Constitution did not countenance an examination into the truth or falsity of beliefs, for then any religious group could be brought into court to prove the validity of its teachings, and religious freedom would be at an end. The majority, however, voted to remand the case for the disposition of other issues, with three justices dissenting. Justice Jackson was the lone dissenter on the question of the government's right to try the Ballards. He was by no means impressed with what he called "humbug, untainted by any trace of truth," but he felt that a jury simply would not be able to distinguish the beliefs of the Ballards from the credibility of such beliefs in reaching their verdict. In view of this difficulty he felt that the only safe course from the standpoint of religious freedom was to rule out such trials altogether. Even the more orthodox ministers or clergymen might be hard pressed on occasion if they were subjected to a sincerity test for everything said in the pulpit before the collection plate was passed. [For an interesting treatment of *Ballard,* see David Fellman, *The Limits of Freedom* (New Brunswick: Rutgers University Press, 1959), pp. 6–19.]

Compulsory Patriotic Exercises and Religious Freedom

In the public schools of many states there are compulsory exercises which include the salute to the flag and the recitation of the pledge of allegiance. The Jehovah's Witnesses sect believes that such a gesture of respect for the flag as saluting is forbidden by the commands of Scripture. Reliance is especially placed on the third, fourth, and fifth verses of Chapter 20 of Exodus prohibiting false gods, graven images, and bowing down to such images. In 1940 the United States Supreme Court faced the issue of whether children in the public schools could be expelled for refusal on religious grounds to participate in the flag salute exercises. In *Minersville School District* v. *Gobitis,* 310 U.S. 586 (1940), the Court held that such provisions did not unconstitutionally abridge religious liberty. Justice Frankfurter, for the majority, stated:

We are dealing with an interest inferior to none in the hierarchy of legal values. National unity is the basis of national security.... To stigmatize legislative judgment in providing for this universal gesture of respect for the symbol of our national life in the setting of the common school as a lawless inroad on that freedom of conscience which the Constitution protects, would amount to no less than the pronouncement of pedagogical and psychological dogma in a field where courts possess no marked and certainly no controlling competence. The influences which help toward a common feeling for the common country are manifold. Some may seem harsh and others no doubt are foolish. Surely, however, the end is legitimate. And the effective means for its attainment are still so uncertain and so unauthenticated by science as to preclude us from putting the widely prevalent belief in flag-saluting beyond the pale of legislative power. It mocks reason and denies our whole history to find in the allowance of a requirement to salute our flag on fitting occasions the seeds of sanction for obeisance to a leader.... Where all the effective means of inducing political changes are left free from interference, education in the abandonment of foolish legislation is itself a training in liberty. To fight out the wise use of legislative authority in the forum of public opinion and before legislative assemblies rather than to transfer such a contest to the judicial arena, serves to vindicate the self-confidence of a free people.

Justice Stone was the only dissenter in the case. In a vigorous dissent he stated:

... [B]y this law the state seeks to coerce these children to express a sentiment which, as they interpret it, they do not entertain, and which violates their deepest religious convictions.... History teaches us that there have been but few infringements of personal liberty by the state which have not been justified, as they are here, in the name of righteousness and the public good, and few which have not been directed, as they are now, at politically helpless minorities.... I cannot conceive that in prescribing, as limitations upon the powers of government, the freedom of the mind and spirit secured by the explicit guarantees of freedom of speech and religion, [the framers] intended or rightly could have left any latitude for a legislative judgment that the compulsory expression of belief which violates religious convictions would better serve the public interest than their protection.

The *Minersville* decision was subjected to wide criticism. In an unusual step, three justices took the occasion of a dissenting opinion in a case arising in 1942 to announce that they felt the *Minersville* case was "wrongly decided." With Justice Stone, this made four members opposing that decision. Justice Byrnes, a member of the *Minersville* majority, resigned and was replaced by Justice Rutledge in 1943. In that same year the issue was relitigated in the case of *West Virginia State Board of Education* v. *Barnette.*

WEST VIRGINIA STATE BOARD OF EDUCATION *v.* BARNETTE
319 U.S. 624 (1943)

Mr. Justice Jackson delivered the opinion of the Court....

The Board of Education on January 9, 1942, adopted a resolution containing recitals taken largely from the Court's *Gobitis* opinion and ordering that the salute to the flag become "a regular part of the program of activities in the public schools," that all teachers and pupils "shall be required to paritcipate in the salute honoring the Nation represented by the Flag; provided, however, that refusal to salute the Flag be regarded as an Act of insubordination, and shall be dealt with accordingly."...

Failure to conform is "insubordination" dealt with by expulsion. Readmission is denied by statute until compliance. Meanwhile the expelled child is "unlawfully absent" and may be proceeded against as a delinquent. His parents or guardians are liable to prosecution, and if convicted are subject to fine not exceeding $50 and jail term not exceeding thirty days.

Appellees, citizens of the United States and of West Virginia, brought suit in the United States District Court for themselves and others similarly situated asking its injunction to restrain enforcement of these laws and regulations against Jehovah's Witnesses. The Witnesses are an unincorporated body teaching that the obligation imposed by law of God is superior to that of laws enacted by temporal government. Their religious beliefs include a literal version of Exodus, Chapter 20, verses 4 and 5, which says: "Thou shalt not make unto thee any graven image, or any likeness of anything that is in heaven above, or that is in the earth beneath, or that is in the water under the earth; thou shalt not bow down thyself to them, nor serve them." They consider that the flag is an "image within this command." For this reason they refuse to salute it.

Children of this faith have been expelled from school and are threatened with exclusion for no other cause. Officials threaten to send them to reformatories maintained for criminally inclined juveniles. Parents of such children have been prosecuted and are threatened with prosecutions for causing delinquency.

... The cause was submitted on the pleadings to a District Court of three judges. It restrained enforcement as to the plaintiffs and those of that class. The Board of Education brought the case here by direct appeal.

This case calls upon us to reconsider a precedent decision, as the Court throughout its history often has been required to do. Before turning to the *Gobitis* case, however, it is desirable to notice certain characteristics by which this controversy is distinguished.

The freedom asserted by these appellees does not bring them into collision with rights asserted by any other individual. It is such conflicts which most frequently require intervention of the State to determine where the rights of one end and those of another begin.... The sole conflict is between authority and rights of the individual. The State asserts power to condition access to public education on making a prescribed sign and profession and at the same time to coerce attendance by punishing both parent and child. The latter stand on a right of self-determination in matters that touch individual opinion and personal attitude. . . .

There is no doubt that, in connection with the pledges, the flag salute is a form of utterance. . . .

. . . To sustain the compulsory flag salute we are required to say that a Bill of Rights which guards the individual's right to speak his own mind, left it open to public authorities to compel him to utter what is not in his mind. . . .

Nor does the issue as we see it turn on one's possession of particular religious views or the sincerity with which they are held. While religion supplies appellees' motive for enduring the discomforts of making the issue in this case, many citizens who do not share their religious views hold such a compulsory rite to infringe constitutional liberty of the individual. It is not necessary to inquire whether nonconformist beliefs will exempt from the duty to salute unless we first find power to make the salute a legal duty.

The *Gobitis* decision, however, *assumed*, as did the argument in that case and in this, that power exists in the State of impose the flag salute discipline upon school children in general. The Court only examined and rejected a claim based on religious beliefs of immunity from an unquestioned general rule. The question which underlies the flag salute controversy is whether such a ceremony so touching matters of opinion and political attitude may be imposed upon the individual by official authority under powers committed to any political organization under our Constitution. We examine rather than assume existence of this power and, against this broader definition of issues in this case, re-examine specific grounds assigned for the *Gobitis* decision. . . .

3. The *Gobitis* opinion reasoned that this is a field "where courts possess no marked and certainly no controlling competence," that it is committed to the legislatures as well as the courts to guard cherished liberties and that it is constitutionally appropriate to "fight out the wise use of legislative authority in the forum of public opinion and before legislative assemblies rather than to transfer such a contest to the judicial arena," since all the "effective means of inducing political changes are left free."

The very purpose of a Bill of Rights was to withdraw certain subjects from the vicissitudes of political controversy, to place them beyond the reach of majorities and officials and to establish them as legal principles to be applied by the courts. One's rights to life, liberty, and property, to free speech, a free press, freedom of worship and assembly, and other fundamental rights may not be submitted to vote; they depend on the outcome of no elections. . . .

4. Lastly, and this is the very heart of the *Gobitis* opinion, it reasons that "national unity is the basis of national security," that the authorities have "the right to select appropriate means for its attainment," and hence reaches the conclusion that such compulsory measures toward "national unity" are constitutional. Upon the verity of this assumption depends our answer in this case.

National unity as an end which officials may foster by persuasion and example is not in question. The problem is whether under our Constitution compulsion as here employed is a permissible means for its achievement.

Struggles to coerce uniformity of sentiment in support of some end thought essential to their time and country have been waged by many good as well as by evil men. Nationalism is a relatively recent phenomenon but at other times and places the ends have been racial or territorial security, support of a dynasty or regime, and particular plans for saving souls. As first and moderate methods to attain unity have failed, those bent on its accomplishment must resort to an ever increasing severity. As governmental pressure toward unity becomes greater, so strife becomes more bitter as to whose unity it shall be. Probably no deeper division of our people could proceed from any provocation than from finding it necessary to choose what doctrine and whose program public educational officials shall compel youth to unite in embracing. Ultimate futility of such attempts to compel coherence is the lesson of every such effort from the Roman drive to stamp out Christianity as a disturber of its pagan unity, the Inquisition, as a means to religious and dynastic unity, the Siberian exiles as a means to Russian unity, down to the fast failing efforts of our present totalitarian enemies. Those who begin coercive elimination of dissent soon find themselves exterminating dissenters. Compulsory unification of opinion achieves only the unanimity of the graveyard.

It seems trite but necessary to say that the First Amendment to our Constitution was designed to avoid those ends by avoiding these beginnings. There is no mysticism in the American concept of the State or of the nature or origin of its authority. We set up government by consent of the governed, and the Bill of Rights denies those in power any legal opportunity to coerce that consent. Authority here is to be controlled by public opinion, not public opinion by authority.

The case is made difficult not because the principles of its decision are obscure but because the flag involved is our own. Nevertheless, we apply the limitations of the Constitution with no fear that freedom to be intellectually and spiritually diverse or even contrary will disintegrate the social organization. To believe that patriotism will not flourish if patriotic ceremonies are voluntary and spontaneous instead of a compulsory routine is to make an unflattering estimate of the appeal of our institutions to free minds. We can have intellectual individualism and the rich cultural diversities that we owe to exceptional minds only at the price of occasional eccentricity and abnormal attitudes. When they are so harmless to others or to the State as those we deal with here, the price is not too great. But freedom to differ is not limited to things that do not matter much. That would be a mere shadow of freedom. The test of its substance is the right to differ as to things that touch the heart of the existing order.

If there is any fixed star in our constitutional constellation, it is that no official, high or petty, can prescribe what shall be orthodox in politics, nationalism, religion, or other matters of opinion or force citizens to confess by word or act their faith therein. If there are any circumstances which permit an exception, they do not now occur to us.

We think the action of the local authorities in compelling the flag salute and pledge transcends constitutional limitations on their power and invades the sphere of intellect and spirit which it is the purpose of the First Amendment to our Constitution to reserve from all official control.

The decision of this Court in *Minersville School District* v. *Gobitis* and the holdings of those few *per curiam* decisions which preceded and foreshadowed it are overruled, and the judgment enjoining enforcement of the West Virginia Regulation is

Affirmed.

Mr. Justice Roberts and Mr. Justice Reed adhere to the views expressed by the Court in *Minersville School District* v. *Gobitis* ... and are of the opinion that the judgment below should be reversed.

Mr. Justice Black and Mr. Justice Douglas concurring. . . .

Mr. Justice Murphy concurring. . . .

Mr. Justice Frankfurter, dissenting.

One who belongs to the most vilified and persecuted minority in history is not likely to be insensible to the freedoms guaranteed by our Constitution. Were my purely personal attitude relevant I should wholeheartedly associate myself with the general libertarian views in the Court's opinion, representing as they do the thought and action of a lifetime. But as judges we are neither Jew nor Gentile, neither Catholic nor agnostic. We owe equal attachment to the Constitution and are equally bound by our judicial obligations whether we derive our citizenship from the earliest or the latest immigrants to these shores. As a member of this Court I am not justified in writing my private notions of policy into the Constitution, no matter how deeply I may cherish them or how mischievous I may deem their disregard. The duty of a judge who must decide which of two claims before the Court shall prevail, that of a State to enact and enforce laws within its general competence or that of an individual to refuse obedience because of the demands of his conscience, is not that of the ordinary person. It can never be emphasized too much that one's own opinion about the wisdom or evil of a law should be excluded altogether when one is doing one's duty on the bench. The only opinion of our own even looking in that direction that is material is our opinion of whether legislators could in reason have enacted such a law. In the light of all the circumstances, including the history of this question in this Court, it would require more daring than I possess to deny that reasonable legislators could have taken the action which is before us for review. Most unwillingly, therefore, I must differ from my brethren with regard to legislation like this. I cannot bring my mind to believe that the "liberty" secured by the Due Process Clause gives this Court authority to deny to the State of West Virginia the attainment of that which we all recognize as a legitimate legislative end, namely, the promotion of good citizenship, by employment of the means here chosen. . . .

The reason why from the beginning even the narrow judicial authority to nullify legislation has been viewed with a jealous eye is that it serves to prevent the full play of the democratic process. The fact that it may be an undemocratic aspect of our scheme of government does not call for its rejection or its disuse. But it is the best of reasons, as this Court has frequently recognized, for the greatest caution in its use. . . .

Under our constitutional system the legislature is charged solely with civil concerns of society. If the avowed or intrinsic legislative purpose is either to promote or to discourage some religious community or creed, it is clearly within the constitutional restrictions imposed on legislatures and cannot stand. But it by no means follows that legislative power is wanting whenever a general non-discriminatory civil regulation in fact touches conscientious scruples or religious beliefs of an individual or a group. Regard for such scruples or beliefs undoubtedly presents one of the most reasonable claims for the exertion of legislative accommodation. It is, of course, beyond our power to rewrite the State's requirement, by providing exemptions for those who do not wish to participate in the flag salute or by making some other accommodations to meet their scruples. That wisdom might suggest the making of such accommodations and that school administration would not find it too difficult to make them and yet maintain the ceremony for those not refusing to conform, is outside our province to suggest. Tact, respect, and generosity toward variant views will always commend themselves to those charged with the duties of legislation so as to achieve a maximum of good will and to require a minimum of unwilling submission to a general law. But the real question is, who is to make such accommodations, the courts or the legislature? . . .

Conscientious scruples, all would admit, cannot stand against every legislative compulsion to do positive acts in conflict with such scruples. We have been told that such compulsions override religious scruples only as to major concerns of the state. But the determination of what is major and what is minor itself raises questions of policy. For the way in which men equally guided by reason appraise importance goes to the very heart of policy. Judges should be very diffident in setting their judgment against that of a state in determining what is and what is not a major concern, what means are appropriate to proper ends, and what is the total social cost in striking the balance of imponderables. . . .

. . . I think I appreciate fully the objections to the law before us. But to deny that it presents a question upon which men might reasonably differ appears to me to be intolerance. And since men may so reasonably differ, I deem it beyond my constitutional power to assert my view of the wisdom of this law against the view of the state of West Virginia. . . .

Of course patriotism cannot be enforced by the flag salute. But neither can the liberal spirit be enforced by judicial invalidation of illiberal legislation. Our constant preoccupation with the constitutionality of legislation rather than with its wisdom tends to preoccupation of the American mind with a false value. The tendency of focussing attention on constitutionality is to make constitutionality synonymous with wisdom, to regard a law as all right if it is constitutional. Such an attitude is a great enemy of liberalism. Particularly in legislation affecting freedom of thought and fredom of speech much which should offend a free-spirited society is constitutional. Reliance for the most precious interests of civilization, therefore, must be found outside of their vindication in courts of law. Only a persistent positive translation of the faith of a free society into the convictions and habits and actions of a community is the ultimate reliance against unabated temptations to fetter the human spirit.

[For a thorough treatment of the flag salute cases, see David Manwaring, *Render Unto Caesar: The Flag Salute Controversy* (Chicago: University of Chicago Press, 1962).]

Free Exercise of Religion and the Problems of Sabbatarians

In *McGowan* v. *Maryland*, discussed earlier, Maryland's Sunday Laws were challenged on the ground that they represented an establishment of religion. In companion cases decided on the same day as *McGowan* (*Gallagher* v. *Crown Kosher Super Market of Massachusetts* and *Braunfeld* v. *Brown*) Sunday Closing Laws were challenged by members of the Orthodox Jewish faith on the ground that they were an interference with the free exercise of their religion. The essence of the claim was that their religion required them to remain closed on Saturday, and that if they were compelled to remain closed on Sunday as well, the effect of the law would be to compel them to make a choice between going out of business or violating their religious beliefs and remaining open on Saturday. In *Gallagher*, for example, it was testified that the market had been conducting about one-third of its weekly business on Sunday, and that to close on that day would be ruinous.

BRAUNFELD v. BROWN
366 U.S. 599 (1961)

Mr. Chief Justice Warren announced the judgment of the Court and an opinion in which Mr. Justice Black, Mr. Justice Clark, and Mr. Justice Whittaker concur.

This case concerns the constitutional validity of the application to appellants of the Pennsylvania criminal statute, enacted in 1959, which proscribes the Sunday retail sale of certain enumerated commodities. Among the questions presented are whether the statute is a law respecting an establishment of religion and whether the statute violates equal protection. Since both of these questions, in reference to this very statute, have already been answered in the negative, ... and since appellants present nothing new regarding them, they need not be considered here. Thus, the only question for consideration is whether the statute interferes with the free exercise of appellants' religion.

Appellants are merchants in Philadelphia who engage in the retail sale of clothing and home furnishings within the proscription of the statute in issue. Each of the appellants is a member of the Orthodox Jewish faith, which requires the closing of their places of business and a total abstention from all manner of work from nightfall each Friday until nightfall each Saturday. They instituted a suit in the court below seeking a permanent injunction against the enforcement of the 1959 statute. ...

A three-judge court was properly convened and it dismissed the complaint. ... On appeal brought under 28 USC Section 1253, we noted probable jurisdiction. ...

Appellants contend that the enforcement against them of the Pennsylvania statute will prohibit the free exercise of their religion because, due to the statute's compulsion to close on Sunday, appellants will suffer substantial economic loss, to the benefit of their non-Sabbatarian competitors, if appellants also continue their Sabbath observance by closing their businesses on Saturday; that this result will either compel appellants to give up their Sabbath observance, a basic tenet of the Orthodox Jewish faith, or will put appellants at a serious economic disadvantage if they continue to adhere to the Sabbath. Appellants also assert that the statute will operate so as to hinder the Orthodox Jewish faith in gaining new adherents. And the corollary to these arguments is that if the free exercise of appellants' religion is impeded, that religion is being subjected to discriminatory treatment by the State. ...

Concededly, appellants and all other persons who wish to work on Sunday will be burdened economically by the State's day of rest mandate; and appellants point out that their religion requires them to refrain from work on Saturday as well. Our inquiry then is whether, in these circumstances, the First and Fourteenth Amendments forbid application of the Sunday Closing Law to appellants.

Certain aspects of religious exercise cannot, in any way, be restricted or burdened by either federal or state legislation. Compulsion by law of the acceptance of any creed or the practice of any form of worship is strictly forbidden. The freedom to hold religious beliefs and opinions is absolute. ...

However, the freedom to act, even when the action is in accord with one's religious convictions, is not totally free from legislative restrictions. ... As pointed out in *Reynolds* v. *United States* ... legislative power over mere opinion is forbidden but it may reach people's actions when they are found to be in violation of important social duties or subversive of good order, even when the actions are demanded by one's religion. ...

But ... the statute at bar does not make unlawful any religious practices of appellants; the Sunday law simply regulates a secular activity and, as applied to appellants, operates so as to make the practice of their religious beliefs more expensive. Furthermore, the law's effect does not inconvenience all members of the Orthodox Jewish faith but only those who believe it necessary to work on Sunday. And even these are not faced with as serious a choice as forsaking their religious practices or subjecting themselves to criminal prosecution. Fully recognizing that the alternatives open to appellants and others similarly situated—retaining their present occupations and incurring economic disadvantage or engaging in some other commercial activity which does not call for either Saturday or Sunday labor—may well result in some financial sacrifice in order to observe their religious beliefs, still the option is wholly different than when the legislation attempts to make a religious practice itself unlawful.

To strike down, without the most critical scrutiny, legislation which imposes only an indirect burden on the exercise of religion, i.e., legislation which does not make unlawful the religious practice itself, would radically restrict the operating latitude of the legislature. Statutes which tax income and limit the amount which may be deducted for religious contributions impose an indirect economic burden on the observance of the religion of the citizen whose religion requires him to donate a greater amount to his church; statutes which require the courts to be closed on Saturday and Sunday impose a similar indirect burden on the observance of the religion of the trial lawyer whose religion requires him to rest on a weekday. The list of legislation of this nature is nearly limitless. . . .

Of course, to hold unassailable all legislation regulating conduct which imposes solely an indirect burden on the observance of religion would be a gross oversimplification. If the purpose or effect of a law is to impede the observance of one or all religions or is to discriminate invidiously between religions, that law is constitutionally invalid even though the burden may be characterized as being only indirect. But if the State regulates conduct by enacting a general law within its power, the purpose and effect of which is to advance the State's secular goals, the statute is valid despite its indirect burden on religious observance unless the State may accomplish its purpose by means which do not impose such a budren. . . .

As we pointed out in *McGowan* v. *Maryland* . . . we cannot find a State without power to provide a weekly respite from all labor and, at the same time, to set one day of the week apart from the others as a day of rest, repose, recreation and tranquillity. . . .

However, appellants . . . contend that the State should cut an exception from the Sunday labor proscription for those people who, because of religious conviction, observe a day of rest other than Sunday. By such regulation, appellants contend, the economic disadvantages imposed by the present system would be removed and the State's interest in having all people rest one day would be satisfied.

A number of States provide such an exemption, and this may well be the wiser solution to the problem. But our concern is not with the wisdom of legislation but with its constitutional limitation. Thus, reason and experience teach that to permit the exemption might well undermine the State's goal of providing a day that, as best possible, eliminates the atmosphere of commercial noise and activity. Although not dispositive of the issue, enforcement problems would be more difficult since there would be two or more days to police rather than one and it would be more difficult to observe whether violations were occurring.

Additional problems might also be presented by a regulation of this sort. To allow only people who rest on a day other than Sunday to keep their businesses open on that day might well provide the people with an economic advantage over their competitors who must remain closed on that day; this might cause the Sunday-observers to complain that their religions are being discriminated against. With this competitive advantage existing, there could well be the temptation for some, in order to keep their businesses open on Sunday, to assert that they have religious convictions which compel them to close their businesses on what had formerly been their least profitable day. This might make necessary a state-conducted inquiry into the sincerity of the individual's religious beliefs, a practice which a State might believe would itself run afoul of the spirit of constitutionally protected religious guarantees. Finally, in order to keep the disruption of the day at a minimum, exempted employers would probably have to hire employees who themselves qualified for the exemption because of their own religious beliefs, a practice which a State might feel to be opposed to its general policy prohibiting religious discrimination in hiring. For all of these reasons, we cannot say that the Pennsylvania statute before us is invalid, either on its face or as applied.

Mr. Justice Harlan concurs in the judgment. Mr. Justice Brennan and Mr. Justice Stewart concur in our disposition of appellants' claims under the Establishment Clause and the Equal Protection Clause. Mr. Justice Frankfurter and Mr. Justice Harlan have rejected appellants' claim under the Free Exercise Clause in a separate opinion.

Accordingly, the decision is

Affirmed.

Separate opinion of Mr. Justice Frankfurter, whom Mr. Justice Harlan joins [relating to all four of the Sunday law cases]. . . .

Mr. Justice Brennan, concurring and dissenting.

I agree with the Chief Justice that there is no merit in appellants' establishment and equal-protection claims. I dissent, however, as to the claim that Pennsylvania has prohibited the free exercise of appellants' religion. . . .

[The complaint alleges that] "Plaintiff, Abraham Braunfeld, will be unable to continue in his business if he may not stay open on Sunday and he will thereby lose his capital investment." In other words, the issue in this case—and we do not understand either appellees or the Court to contend otherwise—is whether a State may put an individual to a choice between his business and his religion. The Court today holds that it may. But I dissent, believing that such a law prohibits the free exercise of religion. . . .

What, then, is the compelling state interest which impels the Commonwealth of Pennsylvania to impede appellants' freedom of worship? . . . It is the mere convenience of having everyone rest on the same day. It is to defend this interest that the Court holds that a State need not follow the alternative route of granting an exemption for those who in good faith observe a day of rest other than Sunday.

It is true, I suppose, that the granting of such an exemption would make Sundays a little noisier, and the task of police and prosecutor a little more difficult. It is also true that a majority—21—of the 34 States which have general Sunday regulations have exemptions of this kind. We are not told that those States are significantly noisier, or that their police are significantly more burdened, than Pennsylvania's. Even England, not under the compulsion of a written constitution, but simply influenced by considerations of fairness, has such an exemption for some activities. The Court conjures up several difficulties with such a system which seem to me more fanciful than real. . . .

In fine, the Court, in my view, has exalted administrative convenience to a constitutional level high enough to justify making one religion economically disadvantageous. . . .

I would reverse this judgment and remand for a trial of appellants' allegations, limited to the free-exercise-of-religion issue.

Mr. Justice Stewart, dissenting.

I agree with substantially all that Mr. Justice Brennan has written. Pennsylvania has passed a law which compels an Orthodox Jew to choose between his religious faith and his economic survival. That is a cruel choice. It is a choice which I think no State can constitutionally demand. For me this is not something that can be swept under the rug and forgotten in the interest of enforced Sunday togetherness. I think the impact of this law upon these appellants grossly violates their constitutional right to the exercise of their religion.

Mr. Justice Douglas, dissenting. [This dissent to the holding in *McGowan* v. *Maryland applies* to all four Sunday Law cases.]

The question is not whether one day out of seven can be imposed by a State as a day of rest. The question is not whether Sunday can by force of custom and habit be retained as a day of rest. The question is whether a State can impose criminal sanctions on those who, unlike the Christian majority that makes up our society, worship on a different day or do not share the religious scruples of the majority. . . .

[The Justice here takes up the "establishment" issue, included in the excerpts quoted earlier in *McGowan* v. *Maryland.*]

When these laws are applied to Orthodox Jews, as they are in [*Gallagher* and *Braunfeld*], or to Sabbatarians their vice is accentuated. If the Sunday laws are constitutional, Kosher markets are on a five-day week. Thus those laws put an economic penalty on those who observe Saturday rather than Sunday as the Sabbath. For the economic pressures on these minorities, created by the fact that our communities are predominantly Sunday-minded, there is no recourse. When, however, the State uses its coercive powers—here the criminal law—to compel minorities to observe a second Sabbath, not their own, the State undertakes to aid and "prefer one religion over another"—contrary to the command of the Constitution. . . .

The reverse side of an "establishment" is a burden on the "free exercise" of religion. Receipt of funds from the state benefits the established church directly; laying an extra tax on nonmembers benefits the established church indirectly. Certainly the present Sunday laws place Orthodox Jews and Sabbatarians under extra burdens because of their religious opinions or beliefs. Requiring them to abstain from their trade or business on Sunday reduces their work-week to five days, unless they violate their religious scruples. This places them at a competitive disadvantage and penalizes them for adhering to their religious beliefs.

. . . The special protection which Sunday laws give the dominant religious groups and the penalty they place on minorities whose holy day is Saturday constitute in my view state interference with the "free exercise" of religion.

An unusual aspect of the problem faced by a Sabbatarian in a Sunday-observing society is the question of eligibility for unemployment compensation in the face of a refusal to accept any job requiring Saturday work. Does denial by the state agency of such compensation constitute abridgment of religious freedom for the Saturday worshiper? The Court decided the issue in a case arriving from South Carolina in 1963, *Sherbert* v. *Verner*, 374 U.S. 398 (1963).

The appellant in the case became a member of the Seventh-day Adventist Church in 1957 at a time when her employer permitted her to work a five-day week. In 1959 the work week was changed to six days, including Saturday, for all shifts in the mill. Appellant was discharged by her employer because she refused to work on Saturday, the Sabbath Day of her faith. She was unable to obtain other employment for which she was qualified because of her refusal to take Saturday work and filed for unemployment compensation benefits under the state law. The appellee Employment Security Commission found her disqualified for benefits by their interpretation of the provision disqualifying persons who fail to accept "suitable work when offered" by the employment office. The South Carolina Supreme Court sustained this finding.

With two dissenting votes, the United States Supreme Court reversed, holding the decision of the Commission to be an abridgment of the free exercise of religion. Justice Brennan, for the majority, stated:

> Here not only is it apparent that appellant's declared ineligibility for benefits derives solely from the practice of her religion, but the pressure upon her to forego that practice is unmistakable. The ruling forces her to choose between following the precepts of her religion and forfeiting benefits, on the one hand, and abandoning one of the precepts of her religion in order to accept work, on the other hand. Governmental imposition of such a choice puts the same kind of burden upon the free exercise of religion as would a fine imposed against appellant for her Saturday worship.

The Court noted further that South Carolina law expressly saves the Sunday worshipper from penalties or from discrimination because of refusal, based on his religion, to work on Sunday. "The unconstitutionality of the disqualification of the Sabbatarian is thus compounded by the religious discrimination which South Carolina's general statutory scheme necessarily effects." The Court could find no strong state interest in enforcing the eligibility provisions against the claim of free exercise of religion. To this extent it found the state interest asserted "is wholly dissimilar to the interests which were found to justify the less direct burden upon religious practices in *Braunfeld* v. *Brown*," namely, the provision of one uniform day of rest for all workers.

Justice Stewart concurred, but he stated that he did not see how the decision could be reconciled with that in *Braunfeld* v. *Brown*, since in both cases the state forced the citizen to make a choice between his religion and his economic welfare. Justice Harlan dissented, joined by Justice White, on the ground that Mrs. Sherbert's denial of benefits was no different from that of "any other claimant ... denied benefits who was not 'available for work' for personal reasons." Justice Harlan also stated that the decision was inconsistent with that in *Braunfeld* v. *Brown*.

A comparison of the *Braunfeld* and *Sherbert* cases would seem to point to a conclusion that governmental "neutrality" in the religion cases cannot but be a relativistic characterization. Attempts to treat the establishment clause purely in terms of governmental neutrality will on occasion lead to situations where, as Justice Stewart pointed out in his opinion in the *Sherbert* case, the establishment clause and the free exercise clause "will run into head-on collision." South Carolina's "neutrality" in applying its nondiscrimInatory unemployment compensation law without regard for its impact upon particular religious minorities was construed by the Court as a kind of *hostility* violative of the free exercise clause. Yet for the state to make a specific exception in the application of its law on grounds of religious belief (as the *Sherbert* majority required in order to meet "the governmental obligation of neutrality in the face of religious differences") can also be construed as a kind of governmental *preference* based on religion and thus violative of the establishment clause. If to ignore religious aspects is hostility and to take religious customs or practices into account is aid or preference, then indeed neutrality may be merely chimerical.

To stamp "In God We Trust" on our coins and to insert "under God" in the pledge of allegiance is, in a measure at least, to give governmental support to religion. For the government to strike out these phrases would surely be construed by many Americans as hostility to religion. By such a definition, neutrality is simply the absence of a conscious policy. Once the issue is raised, however, a policy decision is in fact made, whether the proposal is adopted or rejected, and the position of neutrality is then erased. Only a *de minimis* rule circumvents the issue.

Some of the opinions in the religion cases seem to suggest that the establishment clause approaches an absolute prohibition—a real wall of separation—while the free exercise clause involves weighing of interests. Other opinions lay stress on the direct versus indirect effect test. Neither approach solves both the logical and the practical problems presented, nor perhaps would any other. The balancing test can, however, be employed usefully in the mixed free exercise and establishment cases. The *Sunday Law Cases* presented such mixed issues, and the majority and concurring opinions devoted considerable space to such matters as enforcement problems, the interest of the state in a designated day of rest, and the interference with the individual's religion which such laws occasioned. And Justice Brennan stated for the Court in *Sherbert* v. *Verner,* "We must . . . consider whether some compelling state interest . . . justifies the substantial infringement of appellant's First Amendment right." [See Paul Kauper, "Schempp and Sherbert: Studies in Neutrality and Accommodation," 1963 *Religion and the Public Order* 3; Comment, "A Braunfeld v. Brown Test for Indirect Burdens on the Free Exercise of Religion," 48 *Minn. L. Rev.* 1165 (1964); and P. B. Kurland, *Religion and the Law: of Church and State and the Supreme Court* (Chicago: University of Chicago Press, 1962).]

Religious Oaths

Whatever may be the constitutional status of formal governmental religious declarations or practices (as in the mottoes on coins or the religious exercises in governmental ceremonies), it is clear that when government requires an affirmation of religious belief, it oversteps the bounds of the First Amendment. The governmental requirement of a religious test oath is thus unconstitutional. The Court dealt with the issue in 1961 in considering the validity of a Maryland constitutional provision held to require a belief in God as a qualification for holding public office.

TORCASO v. WATKINS
367 U.S. 488 (1961)

Mr. Justice Black delivered the opinion of the Court.

Article 37 of the Declaration of Rights of the Maryland Constitution provides:

"[N]o religious test ought ever to be required as a qualification for any office of profit or trust in this State, other than a declaration of belief in the existence of God. . . ."

The appellant Torcaso was appointed to the office of Notary Public by the Governor of Maryland but was refused a commission to serve because he would not declare his belief in God. He then brought this action in a Maryland Circuit Court to compel issuance of his commission, charging that the State's requirement that he declare this belief violated "the First and Fourteenth Amendments to the Constitution of the United States. . . ." The Circuit Court rejected these federal constitutional contentions, and the highest court of the State, the Court of Appeals, affirmed, holding that the state constitutional provision is self-executing and requires declaration of belief in God as a qualification for office without need for implementing legislation. The case is therefore properly here on appeal under 28 USC Sec. 1257(2).

There is, and can be, no dispute about the purpose or effect of the Maryland Declaration of Rights requirement before us—it sets up a religious test which was designed to and, if valid, does bar every person who refuses to declare a belief in God from holding a public "office of profit or trust" in Maryland. The power and authority of the State of Maryland thus is put on the side of one particular sort of believers—those who are willing to say they believe in "the existence of God." It is true that there is much historical precedent for such laws. Indeed, it was largely to escape religious test oaths and declarations that a great many of the early colonists left Europe and came here hoping to worship in their own way. It soon developed, however, that many of those who had fled to escape religious test oaths turned out to be perfectly willing, when they had the power to do so, to force dissenters from their faith to take test oaths in conformity with that faith. This brought on a host of laws in the new Colonies imposing burdens and disabilities of various kinds upon varied beliefs depending largely upon what group happened to be politically strong enough to legislate in favor of its own beliefs. The effect of all this was the formal or practical "establishment" of particular religious faiths in most of the Colonies, with consequent burdens imposed on the free exercise of the faiths of nonfavored believers. . . .

When our Constitution was adopted, the desire to put the people "securely beyond the reach" of religious test oaths brought about the inclusion in Article 6 of that document of a provision that "no religious Test shall ever be required as a Qualification to any Office or public Trust under the United States.". . . Not satisfied, however, with Article 6 and other guarantees in the original Constitution, the First Congress proposed and the states very shortly thereafter adopted our Bill of Rights, including the First Amendment. That Amendment broke new constitutional ground in the protection it sought to afford to freedom of religion, speech, press, petition and assembly. Since prior cases in this Court have thoroughly explored and documented the history behind the First Amendment, the reasons for it, and the scope of the religious freedom it protects, we need not cover that ground again. What was said in our prior cases we think controls our decision here. . . .

The Maryland Court of Appeals thought, and it is argued here, that this Court's later holding and opinion in *Zorach* v. *Clauson* . . . had in part repudiated the statement in the *Everson* opinion . . . previously reaffirmed in *McCollum*. But the Court's opinion in *Zorach* specifically stated: "We follow the *McCollum* case.". . . Nothing decided or written in *Zorach* lends support to the idea that the Court there intended to open up the way for government, state or federal, to restore the historically and constitutionally discredited policy of probing religious beliefs by test oaths or limiting public offices to persons who have, or perhaps more properly profess to have, a belief in some particular kind of religious concept.

We repeat and again reaffirm that neither a State nor the Federal Government can constitutionally force a person "to profess a belief or disbelief in any religion." Neither can constitutionally pass laws nor impose requirements which aid all religions as against nonbelievers, and neither can aid those religions based on a belief in the existence of God as against those religious founded on different beliefs.*

In upholding the State's religious test for public office the highest court of Maryland said:

"The petitioner is not compelled to believe or disbelieve, under threat of punishment or other compulsion. True, unless he makes the declaration of belief he cannot hold public office in Maryland, but he is not compelled to hold office."

The fact, however, that a person is not compelled to hold public office cannot possibly be an excuse for barring him from office by state-imposed criteria forbidden by the Constitution. This was settled by our holding in *Wieman* v. *Updegraff*, 344 U.S. 183. We there pointed out that whether or not "an abstract right to public employment exists," Congress could not pass a law providing " '. . . that no federal employee shall attend Mass or take any active part in missionary work.' "

This Maryland religious test for public office unconstitutionally invades the appellant's freedom of belief and religion and therefore cannot be enforced against him.

The judgment of the Supreme Court of Maryland is accordingly reversed and the cause is remanded for further proceedings not inconsistent with this opinion.

Reversed and Remanded.

Mr. Justice Frankfurter and Mr. Justice Harlan concur in the result.

Several of the justices in *United States* v. *Ballard* and the *Sunday Law Cases* and *Sherbert* v. *Verner* referred to the delicate ground of governmental inquiry into religious beliefs. *Torcaso v. Watkins* held that government may not condition office holding on the affirmation of a belief in the existence of God. A related problem is presented in the draft law exemption granted by statute to conscientious objectors. The constitutional issue of forcing one to perform military service against his religious convictions has not squarely arisen because of the exemption provided in all national conscription laws since the first one in 1917. But draft boards have been faced with the problems of applying the exemptions to claimant conscientious objectors. In so doing, they inquired into the beliefs of the claimant for exemption and the evidence indicating the tenacity with which he held to the principle of nonviolence—for example, whether he acquired his convictions before or after the outbreak of hostilities. Obviously the claimant cannot be given exemption merely for the asking, and the Court has held, in *Dickinson* v. *United States*, 346 U.S. 389 (1953), that the claim of ministerial exemption is subject to judicial review. A number of cases have reached the Supreme Court since World War II dealing with both the exemption from

---

* Among religions in this country which do not teach what would generally be considered a belief in the existence of God are Buddhism, Taoism, Ethical Culture, Secular Humanism and others. . . .

combatant service for conscientious objectors and the exemption for ordained ministers. In general the cases have dealt with either statutory construction or with the fairness of administrative procedures or findings. [For a collection of the cases dealing with conscientious objectors, see Annotation, "Who Is Entitled to Exemption as a Conscientious Objector Within the Universal Military Training and Service Act," 13 L ed 2d 1186.]

An interesting aspect of the problem was presented in *United States* v. *Seeger,* 380 U.S. 163 (1965), a consolidated group of cases which treats comprehensively the background of legislation as to conscientious objectors. The cases raised the question of the constitutionality, under the First Amendment, of the section of the Universal Military Training and Service Act which defines the term "religious training and belief" (for purposes of the exemption) as "an individual's belief in a relation to a Supreme Being involving duties superior to those arising from any human relation, but [not including] essentially political, sociological, or a merely personal moral code." Seeger stated that he was conscientiously opposed to war in any form by reason of his "religious" belief, but preferred to leave open the question as to his belief in a Supreme Being. He stated further that his was a "belief in and devotion to goodness and virtue for their own sakes, and a religious faith in a purely ethical creed," without belief in God, "except in the remotest sense." His belief was found to be sincere and made in good faith. He was classified 1-A and ordered to report for induction into the armed forces. Upon refusal he was tried and convicted for refusal to submit to induction. The court of appeals reversed, and the government sought review on writ of certiorari. In another of the cases Forest Peter was convicted in a federal district court in California on a charge of refusing to submit to induction. He had stated that he was not a member of a religious sect or organization, but that he conscientiously objected to war, and felt it a violation of his moral code to take human life. As to whether his conviction was religious, he quoted with approval the Reverend John Holmes' definition of a religion as "the consciousness of some power manifest in nature which helps man in the ordering of his life in harmony with its demands . . . ; it is man thinking his highest, feeling his deepest, and living his best." As to his belief in a Supreme Being, Peter stated that he supposed "you could call that a belief in the Supreme Being or God. These just do not happen to be the words I use." He was classified 1-A, convicted for failure to report for induction, and the court of appeals affirmed.

The United States Supreme Court unanimously affirmed the reversal of Seeger's conviction and reversed the conviction of Peter, without, however, reaching the constitutional issues raised. The Court concluded that the statutory purpose, in using the expression "Supreme Being" rather than the designation "God," "was merely clarifying the meaning of religious training and belief so as to embrace all religions and to exclude essentially political, sociological, or philosophical views." Justice Clark, for the Court, then formulated the appropriate test: "We believe that under this construction, the test of belief 'in a relation to a Supreme Being' is whether a given belief that is sincere and meaningful occupies a place in the life of its possessor parallel to that filled by the orthodox belief in God of one who clearly qualifies for the exemption." He said further, "This construction avoids imputing to Congress an intent to classify different religious beliefs, exempting some and excluding others, and is in accord with the well-established congressional policy of equal treatment for those whose opposition to service is grounded in their religious tenets." In support of the construction given the Act, various theological authorities and even the Schema of the recent Ecumenical Council were cited to indicate the "ever-broadening understanding of the modern religious community." [See Francis Heisler, "The Law versus the Conscientious Objector," 20 *U. Chi. L. Rev.* 441 (1953); Selective Service System, *Conscientious Objection* (Special Monograph No. 11, 1950); and J. D. Tietz, "Jehovah's Witnesses: Conscientious Objectors," 28 *So. Calif. L. Rev.* 123 (1955).]

Several conscientious objector cases of note were decided in 1970 and 1971. *Welsh* v. *United States,* 398 U.S. 333 (1970) involved a draft registrant's application for exemption based on his conscientious scruples against participating in any war and on his belief that killing was morally wrong, but he stated that his views were not "religious" in the traditional sense. The application was denied, and he was convicted of refusing to submit to induction. The Supreme Court reversed the conviction, with five members agreeing that the proper test was whether the opposition to war stemmed from moral, ethical, or religious beliefs about what was right and wrong, and whether such beliefs were held with the strength of traditional convictions.

In *Gillette* v. *United States,* 401 U.S. 437 (1971), however, the Court held that the statutory conscientious objector status did not have to be accorded one who objects to the Vietnam War, but not to participation in a war of national defense or a war sponsored by the United Nations as a peace-keeping measure.

In *Clay (Ali)* v. *United States,* 403 U.S. 698 (1971), the Court reversed the conviction of Muhammad Ali for willful refusal to submit to induction. The *per curiam* opinion stated: "In order to qualify for classification as a conscientious objector, a registrant must satisfy three basic tests. He must show that he is conscientiously opposed to war in any form. *Gillette* v. *United States....* He must show that this opposition is based upon religious training and belief, as the term has been construed in our decisions. *United States* v. *Seeger, ... Welsh* v. *United States....* And he must show that this objection is sincere." The Court found that Ali's case satisfied all three tests and that the conviction must be reversed.

In *Mulloy* v. *United States,* 398 U.S. 410 (1970), the Court held unanimously that when a local draft board is presented with a nonfrivolous, prima facie claim for a change in classification based on new factual allegations which were not conclusively refuted by other information in the registrant's file, the board's refusal to reopen the classification, thereby depriving the registrant of his right to an administrative appeal, constituted an abuse of discretion, rendering invalid a subsequent order to report for induction, and requiring reversal of a conviction for refusal to submit to induction.

Compulsory Public Education Laws and Religious Freedom

Aside from the Bible and prayer cases, which presented establishment issues primarily, there have been two important areas of conflict between educational policy and religious freedom. The first issue discussed was the flag salute controversy, treated earlier. The second was the attempt by the state of Oregon to require all children to attend *public* schools through the eighth grade in the face of parental choice of private sectarian elementary school education. Although the case, *Pierce* v. *Society of Sisters,* was decided on a purely secular application of the Fourteenth Amendment's protection to the "liberty" of parents and teachers, the religious freedom application is clear.

PIERCE *v.* SOCIETY OF SISTERS
268 U.S. 510 (1925)

Mr. Justice McReynolds delivered the opinion of the Court.

These appeals are from decrees, based upon undenied allegations, which granted preliminary orders restraining appellants from threatening or attempting to enforce the Compulsory Education Act adopted November 7, 1922, under the initiative provision of her Constitution by the voters of Oregon. They present the same points of law; there are no controverted questions of fact. Rights said to be guaranteed by the Federal Constitution were specially set up, and appropriate prayers asked for their protection.

The challenged act, effective September 1, 1926, requires every parent, guardian, or other person having control or charge or custody of a child between eight and sixteen years to send him "to a public school for the period of time a public school shall be held during the current year" in the district where the child resides; and failure so to do is declared a misdemeanor. There are exemptions—not specially important here—for children who are not normal, or who have completed the eighth grade, or whose parents or private teachers reside at considerable distances from any public school, or who hold special permits from the county superintendent. The manifest purpose is to compel general attendance at public schools by normal children, between eight and sixteen, who have not completed the eighth grade. And without doubt enforcement of the statute would seriously impair, perhaps destroy, the profitable features of appellees' business, and greatly diminish the value of their property.

Appellee the Society of Sisters is an Oregon corporation, organized in 1880, with power to care for orphans, educate and instruct the youth, establish and maintain academies or schools, and acquire necessary real and personal property. It has long devoted its property and effort to the secular and religious education and care of children, and has acquired the valuable good will of many parents and guardians.... The Compulsory Education Act of 1922 has already caused the withdrawal from its schools of children who would otherwise continue, and their income has steadily declined. The appellants, public officers, have proclaimed their purpose strictly to enforce the statute....

[Appellee Hill Military Academy is a private corporation engaged in operating for profit an elementary, college preparatory, and military training school for boys. The average attendance is one hundred, and the annual fees received for each student amount to some $800.]

No question is raised concerning the power of the state reasonably to regulate all schools, to inspect, supervise, and examine them, their teachers and pupils; to require that all children of proper age attend some school, that teachers shall be of good moral character and patriotic disposition, that certain studies plainly essential to good citizenship must be taught, and that nothing be taught which is manifestly inimical to the public welfare.

The inevitable practical result of enforcing the act under consideration would be destruction of appellees' primary schools, and perhaps all other private primary schools for normal children within the state of Oregon. Appellees are engaged in a kind of undertaking not inherently harmful, but long regarded as useful and meritorious. Certainly there is nothing in the present records to indicate that they have failed to discharge their obligations to patrons, students, or the state. And there are no peculiar circumstances or present emergencies which demand extraordinary measures relative to primary education.

Under the doctrine of *Meyer* v. *Nebraska,* 262 U.S. 390, we think it entirely plain that the Act of 1922 unreasonably interferes with the liberty of parents and guardians to direct the upbringing and education of children under their control. As often heretofore pointed out, rights guaranteed by the Constitution may not be abridged by legislation which has no reasonable relation to some purpose within the competency of the state. The fundamental theory of liberty upon which all governments in this Union repose excludes any general power of the State to standardize its children by forcing them to accept instruction from public teachers only. The child is not the mere creature of the State; those who nurture him and direct his destiny have the right, coupled with the high duty, to recognize and prepare him for additional obligations.

Appellees are corporations and therefore, it is said, they cannot claim for themselves the liberty which the Fourteenth Amendment guarantees. Accepted in the proper sense, this is true. . . . But they have business and property for which they claim protection. These are threatened with destruction through the unwarranted compulsion which appellants are exercising over present and prospective patrons of their schools. And this court has gone very far to protect against loss threatened by such action. . . .

The decrees are

Affirmed.

It should be noted that *Pierce* v. *Society of Sisters* held only that the state could not constitutionally prohibit parents from sending their children to a nonpublic school. It can normally require all children to attend *some* school through a specified grade or until reaching a specified age. And although *Pierce* offers substantial protections to the continued operation of the private school, the state clearly has the power to demand minimum standards in such schools, such as curriculum and teacher accreditation, if the private schools are to be allowed as alternatives to the public schools. [See Fred F. Beach and Robert F. Will, "The State and Non-public Schools" (U.S. Office of Ed., Misc. No. 28, 1958).]

In 1972 the Court decided a free-exercise case brought by members of the Old Order Amish religion challenging Wisconsin's compulsory school laws. The Amish were willing to send their children to school through the eighth grade, but they contended that formal education at the high school level or beyond would inculcate values at marked variance with Amish religious values. They viewed secondary school education as an impermissible exposure of their children to a "worldly" influence in conflict with their beliefs, specifically objecting to the schools' emphasis on competition, intellectual accomplishment, and worldly success rather than stressing Amish values of "goodness," wisdom, and community welfare. In *Wisconsin* v. *Yoder,* 406 U.S. 205 (1972), the Court held that in view of the substantial interference with the religious development of the Amish children occasioned by the requirement of secondary school education and the absence of a showing of impairment of the physical or mental health of the children or their ability to be self-supporting, the state's interest in the compulsory educational system was not so compelling as to warrant interference with the Amish' free exercise of religion. [For a detailed treatment of the case, see Richard C. Cortner, *The Supreme Court and Civil Liberties Policy* (Palo Alto: Mayfield, 1975), pp. 153–182.]

Prior Restraints on the Free Exercise of Religion

In many of the previous free exercise cases the judicial approach has been to make a determination of the interest the state may have in maintaining a specific policy and the kind and degree of restraint on the individual's exercise of religion. To say, therefore, that the individual may practice his religion freely so long as he does not violate the criminal laws of the state is too facile a generalization. If the statement were true as given, then no interference which took the form of a penal statute would violate the guarantee of religious freedom. The crux of the problem is the determination of whether the application of a criminal provision in a particular exercise of religion situation is an improper infringement of that exercise. And the weighing of interests involved in each separate fact situation can result in a decision either in favor of the claimed immunity or against it, depending on how a majority of the Court may view the weight of the state's and the individual's interests. Thus in *Reynolds* and *Prince* the Court upheld the application of criminal statutes barring polygamy and certain forms of child labor, respectively, against the claims of religious freedom. But in *West Virginia Board of Education* v. *Barnette* the Court held that to punish the parent and to expel the child who refused on religious grounds to salute the flag in public school exercises was violative of the constitutional protection to free exercise of religion. Whether a particular criminal law can constitutionally be applied to restrict religious exercise will turn on the kind and degree of interference and the value to the state of imposing the restraint.

There is one category of First Amendment restrictions, however, concerning which the Court has taken a virtually absolutist position—those laws or official practices which impose "prior restraints" on First Amendment freedoms. The theory here is that if a course of action is not *malum in se* or *malum prohibita* (is not, for example, in the category of human sacrifice or polygamy or forced child labor of certain kinds) then it is a violation of First Amendment guarantees to require permits or licenses as conditions of engaging in the religious activity. This is in essence the doctrine of "no previous restraints." It does not, of course, halt the application of the ordinary criminal provisions to the conduct of the participants. Delivering a religious sermon is not *per se* unlawful, but the time, the place, and the kind of language used may still be such as to justify criminal penalties. The point of the "no previous restraint" doctrine, however, is that one cannot be barred at the outset the right to participate in an ordinarily lawful religious exercise or have that right conditioned on permission given by some governmental official.

In the setting in which the cases have frequently come to the Court, the crucial question is often whether the *general* course of action engaged in by the religious claimant can properly be declared unlawful by the state. If the decision is that such activity in general cannot be declared unlawful, then no prior permit or license, unless nondiscretionary in nature, can be required for the First Amendment exercise. Specific crimes committed in the course of the normally lawful activity may be punished, but the presence of such illegal aspects in past or similar activity may not be used to justify the attempt to impose prior restraints in the first place. Punishment for these must come under the application of the appropriate criminal laws and represent separate issues.

The cases on religious freedom and prior restraint generally show a clear overlap with free speech issues. Indeed, the prior restraint issues in their most familiar setting involve matters of communication and oral persuasion. But since not all prior restraints of speech are clearly unconstitutional (see, for example, *Prince* v. *Massachusetts,* discussed earlier), the attempt has been made to establish a more generalized rationale for the doctrine. (See Chapter 6 for a more detailed discussion of prior restraints.) The first case to come to the United States Supreme Court involving the prior restraint doctrine as applied to religious freedom was *Cantwell* v. *Connecticut,* decided in 1940.

CANTWELL *v.* CONNECTICUT
310 U.S. 296 (1940)

Mr. Justice Roberts delivered the opinion of the Court.

Newton Cantwell and his two sons, Jessee and Russell, members of a group known as Jehovah's Witnesses, and claiming to be ordained ministers, were arrested in New Haven, Connecticut, and each was charged by information in five counts, with statutory and common-law offenses. After trial in the Court of Common Pleas of New Haven County each of them was convicted on the third count, which charged a violation of Section 6294 of the General Statutes of Connecticut, and on the fifth count, which charged commission of the common-law offenses of inciting a breach of the peace. . . .

The facts adduced to sustain the convictions on the third count follow. On the day of their arrest the appellants were engaged in going singly from house to house on Cassius Street in New Haven. They were individually equipped with a bag containing books and pamphlets on religious subjects, a portable phonograph and a set of records, each of which, when played, introduced, and was a description of, one of the books. Each appellant asked the person who responded to his call for permission to play one of the records. If permission was granted he asked the person to buy the book described and, upon refusal, he solicited such contribution towards the publication of the pamphlets as the listener was willing to make. If a contribution was received, a pamphlet was delivered upon condition that it would be read.

Cassius Street is in a thickly populated neighborhood, where about ninety per cent of the residents are Roman Catholics. A phonograph record, describing a book entitled "Enemies," included an attack on the Catholic religion. None of the persons interviewed were members of Jehovah's Witnesses.

The statute under which the appellants were charged provides:

"No person shall solicit money, services, subscriptions or any valuable thing for any alleged religious, charitable or philanthropic cause, from other than a member of the organization for whose benefit such person is soliciting or within the county in which such person or organization is located unless such cause shall have been approved by the secretary of the public welfare council. Upon application of any person in behalf of such cause, the secretary shall determine whether such cause is a religious one or is a bona fide object of charity or philanthropy and conforms to reasonable standards of efficiency and integrity, and, if he shall so find, shall approve the same and issue to the authority in charge a certificate to that effect. Such certificate may be revoked at any time. Any person violating any provision of this section shall be fined not more than one hundred dollars or imprisoned not more than thirty days or both."

The appellants claimed that their activities were not within the statute but consisted only of distribution of books, pamphlets, and periodicals. The State Supreme Court construed the finding of the trial court to be that "in addition to the sale of the books and the distribution of the pamphlets the defendants were also soliciting contributions or donations of money for an alleged religious cause, and thereby came within the purview of the statute." It overruled the contention that the Act, as applied to the appellants, offends the due process clause of the Fourteenth Amendment, because it abridges or denies religious freedom and liberty of speech and press. The court stated that it was the solicitation that brought the appellants within the sweep of the Act and not their other activities in the dissemination of literature. It declared the legislation constitutional as an effort by the State to protect the public against fraud and imposition in the solicitation of funds for what purported to be religious, charitable, or philanthropic causes.

The facts which were held to support the conviction of Jesse Cantwell on the fifth count were that he stopped two men in the street, asked, and received, permission to play a phonograph record, and played the record "Enemies," which attacked the religion and church of the two men, who were Catholics. Both were incensed by the contents of the record and were tempted to strike Cantwell unless he went away. On being told to be on his way he left their presence. There was no evidence that he was personally offensive or entered into any argument with those he interviewed.

The court held that the charge was not assault or breach of the peace or threats on Cantwell's part, but invoking or inciting others to beach of the peace, and that the facts supported the conviction of that offense.

First. We hold that the statute, as construed and applied to the appellants, deprives them of their liberty without due process of law in contravention of the Fourteenth Amendment. The fundamental concept of liberty embodied in that Amendment embraces the liberties guaranteed by the First Amendment. . . . No one would contest the proposition that a State may not, by statute, wholly deny the right to preach or to disseminate religious views. Plainly such a previous and absolute restraint would violate the terms of the guarantee. It is equally clear that a State may by general and non-discriminatory legislation regulate the times, the places, and the manner of soliciting upon its streets, and of holding meeting thereon; and may in other respects safeguard the peace, good order and comfort of the community, without unconstitutionally invading the liberties protected by the Fourteenth Amendment. The appellants are right in their insistence that the Act in question is not such a regulation. If a certificate is procured, solicitation is permitted without restraint but, in the absence of a certificate, solicitation is altogether prohibited.

The appellants urge that to require them to obtain a certificate as a condition of soliciting support for their views amounts to a prior restraint on the exercise of their religion within the meaning of the Constitution. The State insists that the Act, as construed by the Supreme Court of Connecticut, imposes no previous restraint upon the dissemination of religious views or teaching but merely safeguards against the perpetration of frauds under the cloak of religion. Conceding that this is so, the question remains whether the method adopted by Connecticut to that end transgresses the liberty safeguarded by the Constitution.

The general regulation, in the public interest, of solicitation, which does not involve any religious test and does not unreasonably obstruct or delay the collection of funds, is not open to any constitutional objection, even though the collection be for a religious purpose. Such regulation would not constitute a prohibited previous restraint on the free exercise of religion or interpose an inadmissible obstacle to its exercise.

It will be noted, however, that the Act requires an application to the secretary of the public welfare council of the State; that he is empowered to determine whether the cause is a religious one, and that the issue of a certificate depends upon his affirmative action. If he finds that the cause is not that of religion, to solicit for it becomes a crime. He is not to issue a certificate as a matter of course. His decision to issue or refuse it involves appraisal of facts, the exercise of judgment, and the formation of an opinion. He is authorized to withhold his approval if he determines that the cause is not a religious one. Such a censorship of religion as the means of determining its right to survive is a denial of liberty protected by the First Amendment and included in the liberty which is within the protection of the Fourteenth.

Nothing we have said is intended even remotely to imply that, under the cloak of religion, persons may, with impunity, commit frauds upon the public. Certainly penal laws are available to punish such conduct. Even the exercise of religion may be at some slight inconvenience in order that the state may protect its citizens from injury. Without doubt a State may protect its citizens from fraudulent solicitation by requiring a stranger in the community, before permitting him publicly to solicit funds for any purpose, to establish his identity and his authority to act for the cause which he purports to represent. The State is likewise free to regulate the time and manner of solicitation generally, in the interest of public safety, peace, comfort or convenience. But to condition the solicitation of aid for the perpetuation of religious views or systems upon a license, the grant of which rests in the exercise of a determination by state authority as to what is a religious cause, is to lay a forbidden burden upon the exercise of liberty protected by the Constitution.

Second. We hold that, in the circumstances disclosed, the conviction of Jesse Cantwell on the fifth count must be set aside. Decision as to the lawfulness of the conviction demands the weighing of two conflicting interests. The fundamental law declares the interest of the United States that the free exercise of religion be not prohibited and that freedom to communicate information and opinion be not abridged. The State of Connecticut has an obvious interest in the preservation and protection of peace and good order within her borders. We must determine whether the alleged protection of the State's interest, means to which end would, in the absence of limitation by the Federal Constitution, lie wholly within the State's discretion, has been pressed, in this instance, to a point where it has come into fatal collision with the overriding interest protected by the federal compact. . . .

Having these considerations in mind, we note that Jesse Cantwell, on April 25, 1938, was upon a public street, where he had a right to be, and where he had a right peacefully to impart his views to others. There is no showing that his deportment was noisy, truculent, overbearing or offensive. He requested of two pedestrians permission to play them a phonograph record. The permission was granted. It is not claimed that he intended to insult or affront the hearers by playing the record. It is plain that he wished only to interest them in his propaganda. The sound of the phonograph is not shown to have disturbed residents of the street, to have drawn a crowd, or to have impeded traffic. Thus far he had invaded no right or interest of the public or of the men accosted.

The record played by Cantwell embodies a general attack on all organized religious systems as instruments of Satan and injurious to man; it then singles out the Roman Catholic Church for strictures couched in terms which naturally would offend not only persons of that persuasion, but all others who respect the honestly held religious faith of their fellows. The hearers were in fact highly offended. One of them said he felt like hitting Cantwell and the other that he was tempted to throw Cantwell off the street. . . .

Cantwell's conduct, in the view of the court below, considered apart from the effect of his communication upon his hearers, did not amount to a breach of the peace. One may, however, be guilty of the offense if he commit acts or make statements likely to provoke violence and disturbance of good order, even though no such eventuality be intended. Decisions to this effect are many, but examination discloses that, in practically all, the provocative language which was held to amount to a breach of the peace consisted of profane, indecent, or abusive remarks directed to the person of the hearer. Resort to epithets or personal abuse is not in any proper sense communication of information or opinion safeguarded by the Constitution, and its punishment as a criminal act would raise no question under that instrument. . . .

Although the contents of the record not unnaturally aroused animosity, we think that, in the absence of a statute narrowly drawn to define and punish specific conduct as constituting a clear and present danger to a substantial interest of the State, the petitioner's communication, considered in the light of the constitutional guarantees, raised no such clear and present menace to public peace and order as to render him liable to conviction of the common law offense in question.

The judgment affirming the convictions on the third and fifth counts is reversed and the cause is remanded for further proceedings not inconsistent with this opinion.

Reversed.

It should be noted that the holding of *Cantwell* v. *Connecticut* reaches only those discretionary practices on the part of officials which would allow them to make distinctions between what is and what is not a religious cause. The Court did not hold that every requirement of obtaining a permit prior to embarking on religious solicitation would be unconstitutional. It did, however, point out that such requirements would have to be rather severely limited to such purposes as identification and notification in order to protect against fraud to escape the strictures of the First Amendment's protections to speech and religion.

In *Cox* v. *State of New Hampshire,* 312 U.S. 569 (1941), the Court reviewed a conviction of five Jehovah's Witnesses for violation of a statute prohibiting parades upon a public street without a special license. As construed by the state courts, the statute required prior application for a license and payment of a fee which was scaled according to a reasonable estimate of the expense of policing the particular parade. The statute was further construed as allowing no discretion in the licensing board except as necessity might dictate changes in time or route for such parades. The Court held the statute valid and found that it was administered in a fair and nondiscriminatory manner consistent with the requirements of the Constitution.

The issue of the validity of the fee requirement prior to parading was discussed separately in the *Cox* case and the requirement was upheld. The decision cannot be read, however, as supporting all license taxes on the exercise of First Amendment rights. The Court's discussion was confined to the problems of administering the municipal function of policing traffic in the public ways. Other types of religious exercise requiring no such special attention could be treated quite differently by the Court in dealing with license tax requirements. However, in the next year after *Cox*, the Court was faced with a challenge to a municipal ordinance which imposed a license tax on all persons who sold or canvassed for the sale of printed matter. There was no discrimination against sellers of religious literature; the license fee applied to all alike. Jehovah's Witnesses in Opelika, Alabama, raised the issue of abridgment of religious freedom in the application of such a fee requirement to their missionary efforts. In a five-to-four decision in *Jones* v. *Opelika,* 316 U.S. 584 (1942), the Court upheld the ordinance as applied to the Jehovah's Witnesses. The opinion for the majority stated that "The First Amendment does not require a subsidy in the form of fiscal exemption." This judgment was vacated in the following year, however, when in *Murdock* v. *Pennsylvania,* 319 U.S. 105 (1943), the Court reversed its position and held such fees unconstitutional as applied to the sale of religious literature. In this case Jehovah's Witnesses attacked the license requirement of the City of Jeanette, Pennsylvania. Justice Douglas, speaking for a majority of five, stated:

The hand distribution of religious tracts is an age-old form of missionary evangelism—as old as the history of printing presses. It has been a potent force in various religious movements down through the years. This form of evangelism is utilized today on a large scale by various religious sects whose colporteurs carry the Gospel to thousands upon thousands of homes and seek through personal visitations to win adherents to their faith. It is more than preaching; it is more than distribution of religious literature. It is a combination of both. Its purpose is as evangelical as the revival meeting. This form of religious activity occupies the same high estate under the First Amendment as do worship in the churches and preaching from the pulpits. It has the same claim to protection as the more orthodox and conventional exercises of religion. It also has the same claim as the others to the guarantees of freedom of speech and freedom of the press.

It was alleged in justification for the license fee that the religious literature was distributed with a solicitation of funds, and thus utilized ordinary commercial methods. Justice Douglas responded that the mere fact that the religious literature is "sold" by itinerant preachers rather than "donated" does not transform evangelism into a commercial enterprise. "If it did, then the passing of the collection plate in church would make the church service a commercial project. The constitutional rights of those spreading their religious beliefs through the spoken and printed word are not to be gauged by standards governing retailers or wholesalers of books." He stated further that an itinerant evangelist does not become "a mere book agent by selling the Bible or religious tracts to help defray his expenses or to sustain him."

The Justice was careful to say, however, that he did not mean that religious groups and the press are free from all financial burdens of government. Normal income taxes or property taxes levied on one who engages in religious activities are a different matter. But in this case, it was "a flat tax imposed on the exercise of a privilege granted by the Bill of Rights," and therefore a prior restraint on the free exercise of religion.

The *Murdock* decision was followed in *Follett* v. *Town of McCormick,* 321 U.S. 573 (1944), invalidating a similar municipal tax imposed on a Jehovah's Witness who maintained his home in the municipality and who earned his living by means of the sale of religious literature. [For discussions of some of the earlier Jehovah's Witnesses cases, see Hollis W. Barber, "Religious Liberty v. Police Power—Jehovah's Witnesses," 41 *Am. Pol. Sci.*

Rev. 226 (1947); and Edward F. Waite, "The Debt of Constitutional Law to Jehovah's Witnesses," 28 *Minn. L. Rev.* 209 (1944).]

The Free Exercise Clause and Judicial Settlement of Church Disputes

Church organizations are no less subject to rifts and dissensions than are other groups, despite their presumably nobler aims. When these differences involve matters of religious beliefs and doctrines, then the warring factions are left to their own devices, if peaceable, to settle the disputes. But when, as is sometimes the case, the differences shift over to issues of property rights, then questions are raised which have traditionally been within the purview of the civil courts. To say this, however, is not to throw the door open to judicial interference in the property relationships of church groups. For it is clear that courts, as well as legislative bodies, have potentialities for interfering with religion through the simple device of awarding title to the properties to the specific faction which the court chooses to promote. This is the danger area in the judicial settlement of church disputes. When arguments arise between factions over who gets the pulpit, how can the courts select one of the groups as the official, legally constituted congregation without being guilty of abridging religious freedom? The courts cannot evade the responsibility of settling property disputes peaceably, but they cannot invade the sphere of religion by interjecting their own views on matters of doctrine. How can they reconcile these requirements? The United States Supreme Court faced this question for the first time in 1872 in the case of *Watson* v. *Jones.*

WATSON *v.* JONES
13 Wallace 679 (1872)

[A number of Southern churches withdrew from the General Assembly of the Presbyterian Church and formed the Presbyterian Church of The Confederate States following a division of opinion over the question of slavery. The congregation of the Walnut Street Church of Louisville, Kentucky, split irreconcilably over the question of adherence to the northern or southern branch and came to court to settle the property issues. The Trial Court held for the anti-slavery group, and the appellate court affirmed.]

Mr. Justice Miller delivered the opinion of the Court.

This case belongs to a class, happily rare in our courts, in which one of the parties to a controversy, essentially ecclesiastical, resorts to the judicial tribunals of the State for the maintenance of rights which the Church has refused to acknowledge, or found itself unable to protect. Much as such dissensions among the members of a religious society should be regretted, a regret which is increased when passing from the control of the judicial and legislative bodies of the entire organization to which the society belongs, an appeal is made to the secular authority; the courts when so called on must perform their functions as in other cases. . . .

The questions which have come before the civil courts concerning the rights to property held by ecclesiastical bodies, may, so far as we have been able to examine them, be profitably classified under three general heads, which of course do not include cases governed by considerations applicable to a church established and supported by law as the religion of the State.

1. The first of these is when the property which is the subject of controversy has been, by the deed or will of the donor, or other instrument by which the property is held, by the express terms of the instrument devoted to the teaching, support or spread of some specific form of religious doctrine or belief.

2. The second is when the property is held by a religious congregation which, by the nature of its organization, is strictly independent of other ecclesiastical associations, and so far as church government is concerned, owes no fealty or obligation to any higher authority.

3. The third is where the religious congregation or ecclesiastical body holding the property is but a subordinate member of some general church organization in which there are superior ecclesiastical tribunals with a general and ultimate power of control more or less complete in some supreme judicatory over the whole membership of that general organization.

In regard to the first of these classes it seems hardly to admit a rational doubt that an individual or an association of individuals may dedicate property by way of trust to the purpose of sustaining, supporting and propagating definite religious doctrines or principles, providing that in doing so they violate no law of morality, and give to the instrument by which their purpose is evidenced, the formalities which the laws require. And it would seem also to be the obvious duty of the court, in a case properly made, to see that the property so dedicated is not diverted from the trust which is thus attached to its use. So long as there are persons qualified within the meaning of the original dedication, and who are willing to teach the doctrines or principles prescribed in the act of dedication, and so long as there is any one so interested in the execution of the trust as to have a standing in court, it must be that they can prevent the diversion of the property or fund to other and different uses. This is the general doctrine of courts of equity as to charities, and it seems equally applicable to ecclesiastical matters.

In such case, if the trust is confided to a religious congregation of the independent or congregational form of church government, it is not in the power of the majority of that congregation, however preponderant, by reason of a change of views on religious subjects, to carry the property so confided to them to the support of new and conflicting doctrine. A pious man building and dedicating a house of worship to the sole and exclusive use of those who believe in the doctrine of the Holy Trinity, and placing it under the control of a congregation which at the time holds the same belief, has a right to expect that the law will prevent that property from being used as a means of support and dissemination of the Unitarian doctrine, and as a place of Unitarian worship. Nor is the principle varied when the organization to which the trust is confided is of the second or associated form of church government. The protection which the law throws around the trust is the same. And though the task may be a delicate one and a difficult one, it will be the duty of the court in such cases, when the doctrine to be taught or the form of worship to be used is definitely and clearly laid down, to inquire whether the party accused of violating the trust is holding or teaching a different doctrine, or using a form of worship which is so far variant as to defeat the declared objects of the trust. ...

The second class of cases which we have described has reference to the case of a church of a strictly congregational or independent organization, governed solely within itself, either by a majority of its members or by such other local organism as it may have instituted for the purpose of ecclesiastical government; and to property held by such a church, either by way of purchase or donation, with no other specific trust attached to it in the hands of the church than that it is for the use of that congregation as a religious society.

In such cases, where there is a schism which leads to a separation into distinct and conflicting bodies, the rights of such bodies to the use of the property must be determined by the ordinary principles which govern voluntary associations. If the principle of government in such cases is that the majority rules, then the numerical majority of members must control the right to the use of the property. If there be within the congregation officers in whom are vested the powers of such control, then those who adhere to the acknowledged organism by which the body is governed are entitled to the use of the property. The minority in choosing to separate themselves into a distinct body, and refusing to recognize the authority of the governing body, can claim no rights in the property from the fact that they had once been members of the church or congregation. This ruling admits of no inquiry into the existing religious opinions of those who comprise the legal or regular organization; for, if such was permitted, a very small minority, without any officers of the church among them, might be found to be the only faithful supporters of the religious dogmas of the founders of the Church. There being no such trust imposed upon the property when purchased or given, the court will not imply one for the purpose of expelling from its use those who by regular succession and order constitute the Church, because they may have changed in some respect their views of religious truth. . . .

But the third of these classes of cases is the one which is oftenest found in the courts, and which, with reference to the number and difficulty of the questions involved, and to other considerations, is every way the most important.

It is the case of property acquired in any of the usual modes for the general use of a religious congregation which is itself part of a large and general organization of some religious denomination, with which it is more or less intimately connected by religious views and ecclesiastical government.

The case before us is one of this class, growing out of a schism which has divided the congregation and its officers and the presbytery and synod, and which appeals to the courts to determine the right to the use of the property so acquired. Here is no case of property devoted forever by the instrument which conveyed it, or by an specific declaration to its owner, to the support of any special religious dogmas, or any pecular form of worship, but of property purchased for the use of a religious congregation, and so long as any existing religious congregation can be ascertained to be that congregation, or its regular and legitimate successor, it is entitled to the use of the property. In the case of an independent congregation we have pointed out how this identity, or succession, is to be ascertained, but in cases of this character we are bound to look at the fact that the local congregation is itself but a member of a much larger and more important religious organization, and is under its government and control, and is bound by its orders and judgments. There are in the Presbyterian system of ecclesiastical government, in regular succession, the Presbytery over the session or local church, the Synod over the Presbytery, and the General Assembly over all. These are called in the language of the church organs "judicatories," and they entertain appeals from the decisions of those below, and prescribe corrective measures in other cases.

In this class of cases we think the rule of action which should govern the civil courts, founded in a broad and sound view of the relations of church and state under our system of laws, and supported by a preponderating weight of judicial authority is, that, whenever, the questions of discipline or of faith, or ecclesiastical rule, custom or law have been decided by the highest of these church judicatories to which the matter has been carried, the legal tribunals must accept such decisions as final, and as binding on them, in their application to the case before them. . . .

In this country the full and free right to entertain any religious belief, to practice any religious principle, and to teach any religious doctrine which does not violate the laws of morality and property, and which does not infringe personal rights, is conceded to all. The law knows no heresy, and is committed to the support of no dogma, the establishment of no sect. The right to organize voluntary religious associations to assist in the expression and dissemination of any religious doctrine, and to create tribunals for the decision of controverted questions of faith within the association, and for the ecclesiastical government of all the individual members, congregations and officers within the general association, is unquestioned. All who unite themselves to such a body do so with an implied consent to this government, and are bound to submit to it. But it would be a vain consent and would lead to the total subversion of such religious bodies, if any one aggrieved by one of their decisions could appeal to the secular courts and have them reversed. It is of the essence of these religious unions, and of their right to establish tribunals for the decision of questions arising among themselves, that those decisions should be binding in all cases of ecclesiastical cognizance, subject only to such appeals as the organism itself provides for. . . .

[Here Justice Miller reviews other cases decided in state courts on similar questions of disposition of religious disputes.]

We cannot better close this review of the authorities than in the language of the Supreme Court of Pennsylvania, in the case of *The German Ref. Ch.* v. *Seibert:* "The decisions of ecclesiastical courts, like every other judicial tribunal, are final, as they are the best judges of what constitutes an offense against the word of God and the discipline of the Church. Any other than those courts must be incompetent judges of matters of faith, discipline and doctrine; and civil courts, if they should be so unwise as to attempt to supervise their judgments on matters which come within their jurisdiction, would only involve themselves in a sea of uncertainty and doubt which would do anything but improve either religion or good morals." . . .

But we need pursue this subject no further. Whatever may have been the case before the Kentucky court, the appellants in the case presented to us have separated themselves wholly from the church organization to which they belonged when this controversy commenced. They now deny its authority, denounce its action and refuse to abide by its judgments. They have first erected themselves into a new organization, and have since joined themselves to another totally different, if not hostile, to the one to which they belonged when the difficulty first began. Under any of the decisions which we have examined, the appellants, in their present position, have no right to the property, or to the use of it, which is the subject of this suit. . . .

Affirmed.

Justice Miller's clear and careful categorization of property questions in ecclesiastical disputes coming before the civil courts is still followed today. He described three types of cases and stated the governing principle for each. First, if the property has been set up in trust for the propagation of a specific doctrine, then the civil courts will enforce such purpose irrespective of the desires of the governing body of the church or the majority of its members. If no such arrangement is present, however, then the applicable rule for disposition of the property turns on whether the body is a self-governing congregational church or a hierarchical (centrally-organized) church. In the former case, the court applies a majority-rule principle and seeks to determine which faction in the dispute constitutes the majority. In the latter case, however, it is immaterial whether the protesting faction constitutes a majority or not. The court will follow the decision of the proper hierarchical or institutional authority, and its inquiry is limited to determining what that authority's decision is.

Watson v. *Jones* was used in 1952 as authority for holding unconstitutional a New York statute which undertook to determine proprietary use of the St. Nicholas Cathedral in New York. Two separate factions claimed the cathedral, each contending that it was the duly authorized proprietor or agent of the Russian Orthodox Church. By statute the legislature of New York in 1945 attempted to free the Russian Orthodox churches in that state from control of the Moscow church authorities—the Patriarch of Moscow and the Holy Synod—and leave them under the control of the Russian Church in America—a North American organization exclusively. Thus one faction claimed occupancy by virtue of an appointment by the Patriarch of Moscow, while the opposing group claimed under the statute. The New York Court of Appeals, following the statute, held for the latter group. In *Kedroff* v. *St. Nicholas Cathedral,* 344 U.S. 94 (1952), the United States Supreme Court reversed. After examining the complicated factual setting of the case, Justice Reed, speaking for the majority, stated:

We conclude that [the statute] undertook by its terms to transfer the control of the New York churches of the Russian Orthodox religion from the central governing hierarchy of the Russian Orthodox Church, the Patriarch of Moscow and the Holy Synod, to the governing authorities of the Russian Church in America, a church organization limited to the diocese of North America and the Aleutian Islands. This transfer takes place by virtue of the statute. Such a law violates the Fourteenth Amendment. It prohibits in this country the free exercise of religion. Legislation that regulates church administration, the operation of the churches, the appointment of clergy, by requiring conformity to church statutes "adopted at a general convention (sobor) held in the City of New York . . ." prohibits the free exercise of religion. Although this statute requires the New York churches to "in all other respects conform to, maintain and follow the faith, doctrine, ritual, communion, discipline, canon law, traditions and usages of the Eastern Confession (Eastern Orthodox or Greek Catholic Church)," their conformity is by legislative fiat and subject to legislative will. . . .

This legislation . . . in the view of the Court of Appeals, gave the use of the churches to the Russian Church in America on the theory that this church would most faithfully carry out the purposes of the religious trust. Thus dangers of political use of church pulpits would be minimized. Legislative power to punish subversive action cannot be doubted. If such action should be actually attempted by a cleric, neither his robe nor his pulpit would be a defense. . . . Here there is a transfer by statute of control over churches. This violates our rule of separation between church and state. That conclusion results from the purpose, meaning and effect of the New York legislation stated above, considered in the light of the history and decisions considered below. . . .

[Here Justice Reed discusses hierarchical churches and gives a detailed treatment of *Watson* v. *Jones.*]

. . . The opinion radiates . . . a spirit of freedom for religious organizations, an independence from secular control or manipulation—in short, power to decide for themselves, free from state interference, matters of church government as well as those of faith and doctrine. Freedom to select the clergy, where no improper methods of choice are proven, we think, must now be said to have a federal constitutional protection as part of the free exercise of religion against state interference. . . .

The Supreme Court reversed and remanded the *Kedroff* case to the New York Court of Appeals. That court then reached the same decision as it had earlier, but this time on common-law grounds. In *Kreshik* v. *St. Nicholas Cathedral*, 363 U.S. 190 (1960), the Supreme Court reversed again. In a *per curiam* opinion the Court stated:

[T]he decision now under review rests on the same premises which were found to have underlain the enactment of the statute struck down in *Kedroff*. . . . But it is established doctrine that "[i]t is not of moment that the State has here acted solely through its judicial branch, for whether legislative or judicial, it is still the application of state power which we are asked to scrutinize.". . . Accordingly, our ruling in *Kedroff* is controlling here, and requires dismissal of the complaint.

While the Court in *Watson* reached its decision on nonconstitutional grounds, it is clear that the rule was accorded constitutional status in *Kedroff*. The Court followed the line of *Watson-Kedroff* in disposing of the church dispute issue in *Presbyterian Church* v. *Hull Memorial Church*, 393 U.S. 440 (1969). Two local Presbyterian churches in Georgia had voted to withdraw from the Presbyterian Church in the United States (the hierarchical general church organization), because of the latter's alleged departure from its original doctrines and tenets. In a suit to enjoin the general church from trespassing on the local churches' property, the Georgia trial court submitted the case to a jury on the theory that Georgia law implies a trust of local church property for the benefit of the general church on the sole condition that the general church adhere to its tenets of faith and practice existing at the time of affiliation by the local churches. Thus, the jury was instructed to determine whether the actions of the general church amounted to a "fundamental or substantial abandonment of the original tenets and doctrines" of the general church. The jury returned a verdict for the local churches, and the injunction was issued. The Court unanimously reversed. Justice Brennan, for the Court, said:

Civil courts do not inhibit free exercise of religion merely by opening their doors to disputes involving church property. And there are neutral principles of law, developed for use in all property disputes, which can be applied without "establishing" churches to which property is awarded. But First Amendment values are plainly jeopardized when church property litigation is made to turn on the resolution by civil courts of controversies over religious doctrine and practice. If civil courts undertake to resolve such controversies in order to adjudicate the property dispute, the hazards are ever present of inhibiting the free development of religious doctrine and of implicating secular interests in matters of purely ecclesiastical concern. . . .

CHAPTER 6

Freedom of Speech, Press, and Assembly

The freedoms of speech, press, and assembly occupy a peculiar position relative to the democratic process, and one shared only by the various aspects of the right to participate in elections. Trial by jury, freedom from self-incrimination, and the right to counsel are assuredly important procedural guarantees against arbitrary deprivation of life and liberty. But the democratic process could be maintained even if these guarantees were changed. The First Amendment guarantees freedom from establishment of religion, and there is apparently widespread approval of this policy in the United States. But a change to some specific established church in this nation would have no necessary impact on the characterization of the United States as a democratic nation. England has an established church and yet is clearly democratic by the usual procedural standards. To restrict substantially the rights of speech, press, assembly, and voting, however, is to cut the arteries that feed the heart of the democratic model. However one may choose to define democracy, the list of characteristics must include at least certain minimal procedural features: widespread adult suffrage, reasonably frequent elections, reasonable access to the ballot on the part of candidates, popular selection of major policy-making officials, and decision by majority rule. Those rights which are necessary to ensure free interchange of ideas and to guarantee that a continuing and shifting majority may be arrived at freely would certainly seem to be in a special category in terms of constitutional immunity. The most important institutions for the preservation of the democratic process are those which safeguard the opportunity for the reversal of the public policy if a sufficient majority demands it. The important rights in this category would be access to the ballot, both as a voter and as a candidate, and the freedoms of speech, press, and assembly. Serious inroads on the exercise of any of these rights may result in a corresponding curtailment of the ease with which public policy can be changed, even though a majority may desire the change. Thus while encroachments on other types of personal rights might be inconvenient or even obnoxious, the dangers to democratic form must be considerably less as long as the channels for formulating public opinion and focusing majority demands remain open. It is this general proposition which accounts for the apparently paradoxical position in which many champions of personal liberties find themselves with respect to treatment of Communists in the United States. Free speech and association are vital in a democracy, but some restraints even on these must be permitted if there is a real danger that the group using them to gain political power will close off the channels and institutions by which reversal of policy can be accomplished by majority demand.

The conclusion that certain rights guaranteed in the Constitution are in a special position in a democracy is not drawn from any specific phraseology of the Constitution. It is derived logically from the assumption that the democratic system is the appropriate organizational scheme for a reasonably educated society but one in which knowledge will always be incomplete. The channels of communication, of receiving new information, and of persuasion, and the institutions for legally influencing the determination of public policy deserve special care if the democratic model is to function according to blueprint. Such a view is somewhat akin to the "preferred position" doctrine which for a time enjoyed considerable publicity in the opinions of the Court. That doctrine, however, was squarely tied to the First Amendment in its entirety and was never extended to cover voting rights as well, as does the statement here.

THE SCOPE OF THE RIGHTS

The words "speech, press, and assembly" have certain obvious connotations which have required no special analysis to fit them under the First Amendment coverage of these words. A candidate's speech requesting votes, the publication of books and newspapers, and a meeting to discuss public questions are clearly within the scope of application of the First Amendment. Certain other aspects of these words have, however, been less clearly subsumed under the proper interpretation of the bare phraseology of the First Amendment, and their addition has been slower and somewhat more controversial. Probably the best illustration of this slow expansion of the scope of the rights is in the position of motion pictures under the First Amendment. The question of whether commercial movies were entitled to constitutional protection as speech and press first reached the Supreme Court in 1915, in *Mutual Film Corporation* v. *Industrial Commission,* 236 U.S. 230. The Court in that case held that the exhibition of motion pictures was a "business pure and simple, originated and conducted for profit like other spectacles, not to be regarded, nor intended to be regarded by the Ohio Constitution . . . as part of the press of the country or as organs of public opinion." This view held until 1952, when the Court overruled that portion of the *Mutual Film Corporation* decision in *Burstyn* v. *Wilson,* 343 U.S. 495. The Court stated squarely in the latter case that the "liberty of expression by means of motion pictures is guaranteed by the First and Fourteenth Amendments."

In 1940 the Court held that picketing of a plant in the course of a labor dispute came within the meaning of "speech" in the First Amendment. The case was *Thornhill* v. *Alabama,* 310 U.S. 88, and the opinion for a nearly unanimous Court stated:

In the circumstances of our times the dissemination of information concerning the facts of a labor dispute must be regarded as within that area of free discussion that is guaranteed by the Constitution. . . . The range of activities proscribed by Section 3448, whether characterized as picketing or loitering or otherwise, embraces nearly every practicable, effective means whereby those interested—including the employees directly affected—may enlighten the public on the nature and causes of a labor dispute. The safeguarding of these means is essential to the securing of an informed and educated public opinion with respect to a matter which is of public concern.

In *Cox* v. *State of New Hampshire,* 312 U.S. 569 (1941), the Court made the logical extension from *Thornhill* and accepted the view that parades could be properly brought under the rubric of speech and assembly protected by the Constitution.

The "press" protected by the First Amendment extends to handbills and circulars, as well as the standard forms of books and magazines and newspapers. As the Court stated in *Lovell* v. *Griffin,* 303 U.S. 444 (1938):

The liberty of the press is not confined to newspapers and periodicals. It necessarily embraces pamphlets and leaflets. These indeed have been historic weapons in the defense of liberty, as the pamphlets of Thomas Paine and others in our own history abundantly attest. The press in its historic connotation comprehends every sort of publication which affords a vehicle of information and opinion.

Nor has the Court ignored the impact of technological developments on the traditional forms of speech and press. As indicated earlier, in 1952 it held that movies were a form of expression guaranteed by the First and Fourteenth Amendments. And in 1948, in *Saia* v. *New York,* 334 U.S. 558, the Court held that the use of amplifying systems in delivering speeches did not take them out of the area of protection of the First Amendment. Justice Douglas stated for the Court, "Loud-speakers are today indispensable instruments of effective public speech. The sound truck has become an accepted method of political campaigning. It is the way people are reached."

Finally, the right of assembly has been expanded beyond the simple concept of a physical assemblage to include the even more significant right of association. In *NAACP* v. *Alabama,* 357 U.S. 449 (1958), Justice Harlan, speaking for a unanimous Court, stated:

Effective advocacy of both public and private points of view, particularly controversial ones, is undeniably enhanced by group association, as this Court has more than once recognized by remarking upon the close nexus between the freedoms of speech and assembly. . . . It is beyond debate that freedom to engage in association for the advancement of beliefs and ideas is an inseparable aspect of the "liberty" assured by the Due Process Clause of the Fourteenth Amendment, which embraces freedom of speech.

Even these few cases illustrate the breadth which the Court is willing to accord to the words of the First Amendment. The words "speech," "press," and "assembly" are not applied in coldly formalistic fashion. Instead, it is the substance of the rights which is examined and their importance in a free democratic system. Thus, as Justice Harlan put it in the NAACP case, what the First Amendment protects is "effective advocacy of both public and private points of view." To introduce novel vehicles of expression, then, is merely to change the angle from which resulting problems of reconciliation might be viewed; it is not to step outside the First Amendment's scope of application.

As has already been discussed, the rights guaranteed by the First Amendment are explicitly guaranteed against abridgment by Congress. It has also been noted that over the past several decades the Court has, through a succession of decisions, gradually "incorporated" these same rights into the liberties which the due process clause of the Fourteenth Amendment protects against invasion by the state. In the area of First Amendment rights, then, it is usually safe to use First Amendment cases and Fourteenth Amendment cases interchangeably in discussing the validity of restrictions placed by government—whether state or federal—on the exercise of those rights. The process of "incorporation" began with *Gitlow* v. *New York*, 268 U.S. 652 (1925). Benjamin Gitlow was indicted in the supreme court of New York for the crime of criminal anarchy, as defined by statute. His conviction was affirmed by the New York appellate courts. The case was taken on writ of error to the United States Supreme Court under the contention that the statute was repugnant to the due process clause of the Fourteenth Amendment. The Court affirmed the judgment of the New York Court of Appeals, but on the issue of whether a state law unduly restrictive of freedom of speech and press could be held to violate the Fourteenth Amendment the Court gave, almost casually, one of its most momentous decisions. Justice Sanford, for the Court, said, "For present purposes we may and do assume that freedom of speech and of the press—which are protected by the First Amendment from abridgment by Congress—are among the fundamental personal rights and liberties protected by the due process clause of the Fourteenth Amendment from impairment by the States." With such a modest statement did the Court begin the vastly important process of "incorporation" of the First Amendment rights into the Fourteenth Amendment's "liberty" safeguarded by the concept of due process of law.

Freedom of assembly, the third of the rights covered in this chapter, was brought under the protection of the Fourteenth Amendment's due process clause in 1937 in *De Jonge* v. *Oregon*, 229 U.S. 353. The appellant in that case was indicted for violation of the Criminal Syndicalism Law of Oregon, was found guilty as charged, and was sentenced to imprisonment for seven years. The law defined "criminal syndicalism" as "the doctrine which advocates crime, physical violence, sabotage or any unlawful acts or methods as a means of accomplishing or effecting industrial or political change or revolution." The charge was that De Jonge assisted in the conduct of a meeting called under the auspices of the Communist Party. The defense contended that the meeting was lawful, orderly, and public, and that no unlawful conduct was taught or advocated at the meeting. In holding the Fourteenth Amendment applicable to assemblies, as well as to speech and press, the Court, through Chief Justice Hughes, first cited *Gitlow* v. *New York*. The opinion then stated:

Freedom of speech and of the press are fundamental rights which are safeguarded by the due process clause of the Fourteenth Amendment of the Federal Constitution. . . . The right of peaceable assembly is a right cognate to those of free speech and free press and is equally fundamental. . . . The First Amendment of the Federal Constitution expressly guarantees that right against abridgment by Congress. But explicit mention there does not argue exclusion elsewhere. For the right is one that cannot be denied without violating those fundamental principles of liberty and justice which lie at the base of all civil and political institutions,— principles which the Fourteenth Amendment embodies in the general terms of its due process clause.

Two important points should be noted, then, concerning the Constitution's protection of speech, press, and assembly. First, the rights have been broadly construed to include picketing, parading, carrying placards, distributing handbills or circulars, using amplifying equipment, movies, and organizational associations as well as mere congregations of people. Second, the rights guaranteed in the First Amendment against abridgment by the national government have been incorporated totally into the "liberty" guaranteed in the Fourteenth Amendment against state encroachment.

PREVIOUS RESTRAINTS

It should be obvious that the First Amendment was not intended and has not been construed to protect every utterance, publication, or assembly. The traditional approach is to consider that certain well-recognized exceptions to the exercise of First Amendment rights were tacitly included in defining the scope of the Amendment's protections. As Justice Thomas M. Cooley stated, with respect to the Bill of Rights, "They are conservatory instruments rather than reformatory." [*Weimer* v. *Bunbury,* 30 Mich. 201, 214 (1874).] Despite the broad language, then, existing limitations on the exercise of those rights were not necessarily abolished.

Since the First Amendment rights are not absolute, the essential problem to be faced is the delineation of the kinds of restraints on speech, press, and assembly which are constitutionally permissible from those which are not. There are widely differing views on the appropriate answer to this problem, and the present chapter depicts the application of some of these views to the central areas of controversy surrounding First Amendment rights. There is one area, however, on which there seems to be fairly general agreement. This is in the theory that the First Amendment forbids the imposition of most *prior* restraints on the exercise of First Amendment rights. The standard citation is Blackstone's *Commentaries* (IV, 151), in which he states that "the liberty of the press . . . consists in laying no *previous* restraints upon publications and not in freedom from censure for criminal matter when published." Broadening the statement to include other rights, it would indicate that government cannot hinder speech or press or assembly *before* the speaking or printing or assembling takes place, but can punish or obstruct as it may choose *afterward.* As Thomas Jefferson often urged, Blackstone was no model for those interested in human liberty to follow. Probably the most trenchant statements on this aspect of Blackstone are those of Professor Zechariah Chafee, Jr., in his book *Free Speech in the United States:*[1]

This Blackstonian theory dies hard, but it ought to be knocked on the head once for all. In the first place, Blackstone was not interpreting a constitution, but trying to state the English law of his time, which had no censorship and did have extensive libel prosecutions. Whether or not he stated that law correctly, an entirely different view of the liberty of the press was soon afterwards enacted in Fox's Libel Act, . . . so that Blackstone's view does not even correspond to the English law of the last hundred and twenty-five years. Furthermore, Blackstone is notoriously unfitted to be an authority on the liberties of American colonists, since he upheld the right of Parliament to tax them, and was pronounced by one of his own colleagues to have been "we all know, an anti-republican lawyer."

[1] Zechariah Chafee, Jr., *Free Speech in the United States* (Cambridge: Harvard University Press, 1948), pp. 9–11. Reprinted by permission of the publishers.

Not only is the Blackstonian interpretation of our free speech clauses inconsistent with eighteenth-century history, . . . but it is contrary to modern decisions, thoroughly artificial, and wholly out of accord with a common sense view of the relations of state and citizen. In some respects this theory goes altogether too far in restricting state action. The total prohibition of previous restraint would not allow the government to prevent a newspaper from publishing the sailing dates of transports or the number of troops in a sector. It would forbid the removal of an indecent poster from a billboard. . . .

On the other hand, it is hardly necessary to argue that the Blackstonian definition gives very inadequate protection to the freedom of expression. A death penalty for writing about socialism would be as effective suppression as a censorship. The government which holds twenty years in prison before a speaker and calls him free to talk resembles the peasant described by Galsworthy:

"The other day in Russia an Englishman came on a street-meeting shortly after the first revolution had begun. An extremist was addressing the gathering and telling them that they were fools to go on fighting, that they ought to refuse and go home, and so forth. The crowd grew angry, and some soldiers were for making a rush at him; but the chairman, a big burly peasant, stopped them with these words: 'Brothers, you know that our country is now a country of free speech. We must listen to this man, we must let him say anything he will. But, brothers, when he's finished, we'll bash his head in!' "

Professor Chafee has thus pointed out that the Blackstonian statement is at the same time too extreme a restriction on governmental powers of censorship and too liberal in its grant of governmental power to punish after the fact. The Court has not treated the former issue definitively, but it has clearly refused to apply the First Amendment so as to permit the kinds of punishment which would have the same stifling effect as prior restraints. It is the impact of the restriction on the exercise of First Amendment rights which is the important consideration, rather than the mere formal determination of whether the restraining hand of government is laid on before or after the exercise of the right. Nevertheless, the Court has taken a near absolutist position on the invalidity of prior restraints. It is apt to use a balancing test on the issue of liability for punishment after the speech, publication, or assembly, but the rule generally is a firm one relative to prior restraints. A case illustrative of the Court's approach is *Near* v. *Minnesota*, dealing with limitations on the press.

NEAR *v.* MINNESOTA
283 U.S. 697 (1931)

Mr. Chief Justice Hughes delivered the opinion of the Court.

Chapter 285 of the Session Laws of Minnesota for the year 1925 . . . provides for the abatement, as a public nuisance, of a "malicious, scandalous defamatory newspaper, magazine or other periodical." Section 1 of the act is as follows:

"Section 1: Any person who, as an individual, or as a member or employee of a firm, or association or organization, or as an officer, director, member or employee of a corporation, shall be engaged in the business of regularly or customarily producing, publishing or circulating, having in possession, selling or giving away,

(a) an obscene, lewd and lascivious newspaper, magazine, or other periodical, or

(b) a malicious, scandalous and defamatory newspaper, magazine or other periodical, is guilty of a nuisance, and all persons guilty of such nuisance may be enjoined, as hereinafter provided. . . .

"In actions brought under (b) above, there shall be available the defense that the truth was published with good motives and for justifiable ends and in such actions the plaintiff shall not have the right to report [sic] to issues or editions of periodicals taking place more than three months before the commencement of the action.". . .

Under this statute, [section one, clause (b)], the county attorney of Hennepin county brought this action to enjoin the publication of what was described as a "malicious, scandalous and defamatory newspaper, magazine and periodical," known as "The Saturday Press," published by the defendants in the city of Minneapolis. . . .

Without attempting to summarize the contents of the voluminous exhibits attached to the complaint, we deem it sufficient to say that the articles charged in substance that a Jewish gangster was in control of gambling, bootlegging and racketeering in Minneapolis, and that law enforcing officers and agencies were not energetically performing their duties. Most of the charges were directed against the chief of police; he was charged with gross neglect of duty, illicit relations with gangsters, and with participation in graft. The county attorney was charged with knowing the existing conditions and with failure to take adequate measures to remedy them. The mayor was accused of inefficiency and dereliction. One member of the grand jury was stated to be in sympathy with the gangsters. A special grand jury and a special prosecutor were demanded to deal with the situation in general, and, in particular, to investigate an attempt to assassinate one Guilford, one of the original defendants, who, it appears from the articles, was shot by gangsters after the first issue of the periodical had been published. There is no question but that the articles made serious accusations against the public officers named and others in connection with the prevalence of crimes and the failure to expose and punish them.

[Initially an order was made by the district court of the State directing the defendants to show cause why a temporary injunction should not issue and meanwhile forbidding the defendants to circulate certain editions of the periodical and from publishing or circulating future editions "containing malicious, scandalous and defamatory matter of the kind alleged in plaintiff's complaint herein or otherwise."

The defendants demurred to the complaint, challenging the constitutionality of the statute. The district court overruled the demurrer, certified the question of constitutionality to the state supreme court, and the supreme court held the statute to be valid. Thereupon, Near answered the complaint and denied that the articles were malicious, scandalous or defamatory as alleged. He expressly invoked the protection of the "due process" clause of the Fourteenth Amendment.]

The district court made findings of fact, which followed the allegations of the complaint and found in general terms that the editions in question were "chiefly devoted to malicious, scandalous and defamatory articles," concerning the individuals named. The court further found that the defendants through these publications "did engage in the business of regularly and customarily producing, publishing and circulating a malicious, scandalous and defamatory newspaper," and that "the said publication under said name of The Saturday Press, or any other name, constitutes a public nuissance under the laws of the state." Judgment was thereupon entered adjudging that "the newspaper, magazine and periodical known as The Saturday Press," as a public nuisance, "be and is hereby abated." The judgment perpetually enjoined the defendants "from producing, editing, publishing, circulating, having in their possession, selling or giving away any publication whatsoever which is a malicious, scandalous or defamatory newspaper, as defined by law," and also "from further conducting said nuisance under the name and title of said The Saturday Press or any other name or title."

The defendant Near appealed from this judgment to the supreme court of the state, again asserting his right under the Federal Constitution, and the judgment was affirmed upon the authority of the former decision. 179 Minn. 40. With respect to the contention that the judgment went too far, and prevented the defendants from publishing any kind of a newspaper, the court observed that the assignments of error did not go to the form of the judgment and that the lower court had not been asked to modify it. The court added that it saw no reason "for defendants to construe the judgment as restraining them from operating a newspaper in harmony with the public welfare, to which all must yield," that the allegations of the complaint had been found to be true, and though this was an equitable action defendants had not indicated a desire "to conduct their business in the usual and legitimate manner."

From the judgment as thus affirmed, the defendant Near appeals to this court.

This statute, for the suppression as a public nuisance of a newspaper or periodical, is unusual, if not unique, and raises questions of grave importance transcending the local interests involved in the particular action. It is no longer open to doubt that the liberty of the press and of speech is within the liberty safeguarded by the due process clause of the Fourteenth Amendment from invasion by state action. It was found impossible to conclude that this essential personal liberty of the citizen was left unprotected by the general guaranty of fundamental rights of person and property. . . .

The appellee insists that the questions of the application of the statute to appellant's periodical, and of the construction of the judgment of the trial court, are not presented for review; that appellant's sole attack was upon the constitutionality of the statute, however it might be applied. The appellee contends that no question either of motive in the publication, or whether the decree goes beyond the direction of the statute, is before us. . . .

With respect to these contentions it is enough to say that in passing upon constitutional questions the court has regard to substance and not to mere matters of form, and that, in accordance with familiar principles, the statute must be tested by its operation and effect. . . . That operation and effect we think are clearly shown by the record in this case. We are not concerned with mere errors of the trial court, if there be such, in going beyond the direction of the statute as construed by the supreme court of the state. It is thus important to note precisely the purpose and effect of the statute as the state court has construed it.

First. The statute is not aimed at the redress of individual or private wrongs. Remedies for libel remain available and unaffected. The statute, said the state court, "is not directed at threatened libel but at an existing business which, generally speaking, involves more than libel." It is aimed at the distribution of scandalous matter as "detrimental to public morals and to the general welfare," tending "to disturb the peace of the community" and "to provoke assaults and the commission of crime." In order to obtain an injunction to suppress the future publication of the newspaper or periodical, it is not necessary to prove the falsity of the charges that have been made in the publication condemned. In the present action there was no allegation that the matter published was not true. It is alleged, and the statute requires the allegation, that the publication was "malicious." But, as in prosecutions for libel, there is no requirement of proof by the state of malice in fact as distinguished from malice inferred from the mere publication of the defamatory matter. The judgment in this case proceeded upon the mere proof of publication. The statute permits the defense, not of the truth alone, but only that the truth was published with good motives and for justifiable ends. It is apparent that under the statute the publication is to be regarded as defamatory if it injures reputation, and that it is scandalous if it circulates charges of reprehensible conduct, whether criminal or otherwise, and the publication is thus deemed to invite public reprobation and to constitute a public scandal. . . .

Second. The statute is directed not simply at the circulation of scandalous and defamatory statements with regard to private citizens, but at the continued publication by newspapers and periodicals of charges against public officers of corruption, malfeasance in office, or serious neglect of duty. Such charges by their very nature create a public scandal. They are scandalous and defamatory within the meaning of the statute, which has its normal operation in relation of publications dealing prominently and chiefly with the alleged derelictions of public officers.

Third. The object of the statute is not punishment, in the ordinary sense, but suppression of the offending newspaper or periodical. The reason for the enactment, as the state court has said, is that prosecutions to enforce penal statutes for libel do not result in "efficient repression or suppression of the evils of scandal.". . . Under this statute, a publisher of a newspaper or periodical, undertaking to conduct a campaign to expose and to censure official derelictions, and devoting his publication principally to that purpose, must face not simply the possibility of a verdict against him in a suit or prosecution for libel, but a determination that his newspaper or periodical is a public nuisance to be abated, and that this abatement and suppression will follow unless he is prepared with legal evidence to prove the truth of the charges and also to satisfy the court that, in addition to being true, the matter was published with good motives and for justifiable ends.

This suppression is accomplished by enjoining publication and that restraint is the object and effect of the statute.

Fourth. The statute not only operates to suppress the offending newspaper or periodical but to put the publisher under an effective censorship. . . .

If we cut through mere details of procedure, the operation and effect of the statute in substance is that public authorities may bring the owner or publisher of a newspaper or periodical before a judge upon a charge of conducting a business of publishing scandalous and defamatory matter—in particular that the matter consists of charges against public officers of official dereliction—and unless the owner or publisher is able and disposed to bring competent evidence to satisfy the judge that the charges are true and are published with good motives and for justifiable ends, his newspaper or periodical is suppressed and further publication is made punishable as a contempt. This is the essence of censorship.

The question is whether a statute authorizing such proceedings in restraint of publication is consistent with the conception of the liberty of the press as historically conceived and guaranteed. In determining the extent of the constitutional protection, it has been generally, if not universally, considered that it is the chief purpose of the guaranty to prevent previous restraints upon publication. The struggle in England, directed against the legislative power of the licenser, resulted in renunciation of the censorship of the press. . . . Here, as Madison said, "The great and essential rights of the people are secured against legislative as well as against executive ambition. They are secured, not by laws paramount to prerogative, but by constitutions paramount to laws. This security of the freedom of the press requires that it should be exempt not only from previous restraint by the executive, as in Great Britain, but from legislative restraint also." Report on the Virginia Resolutions, Madison's Works, vol. 4, p. 543. This court said, in *Patterson* v. *Colorado,* 205 U.S. 454, 462: "In the first place, the main purpose of such constitutional provisions is 'to prevent all such *previous restraints* upon publications as had been practised by other governments,' and they do not prevent the subsequent punishment of such as may be deemed contrary to the public welfare."...

...In the present case, we have no occasion to inquire as to the permissible scope of subsequent punishment. For whatever wrong the appellant has committed or may commit, by his publications, the state appropriately affords both public and private redress by its libel laws. As has been noted, the statute in question does not deal with punishments; it provides for no punishment, except in case of contempt for violation of the court's order, but for suppression and injunction, that is, for restraint upon publication.

The objection has also been made that the principle as to immunity from previous restraint is not absolutely unlimited. But the limitation has been recognized only in exceptional cases. "When a nation is at war many things that might be said in time of peace are such a hindrance to its effort that their utterance will not be endured so long as men fight and that no court could regard them as protected by any constitutional right." *Schenck* v. *United States,* 249 U.S. 47, 52. No one would question but that a government might prevent actual obstruction to its recruiting service or the publication of the sailing dates of transports or the number and location of troops. On similar grounds, the primary requirements of decency may be enforced against obscene publications. The security of the community life may be protected against incitements to acts of violence and the overthrow by force of orderly government. The constitutional guaranty of free speech does not "protect a man from an injunction against uttering words that may have all the effect of force. *Gompers* v. *Bucks Stove & Range Co.,* 221 U.S. 418, 439." *Schenck* v. *United States, supra.* These limitations are not applicable here. Nor are we now concerned with questions as to the extent of authority to prevent publications in order to protect private rights according to the principles governing the exercise of the jurisdiction of courts of equity. (See 29 *Harvard Law Rev.* 640.)

The exceptional nature of its limitations places in a strong light the general conception that liberty of the press, historically considered and taken up by the Federal Constitution, has meant, principally, although not exclusively, immunity from previous restraints or censorship....

The importance of this immunity has not lessened. While reckless assaults upon public men, and efforts to bring obloquy upon those who are endeavoring faithfully to discharge official duties, exert a baleful influence and deserve the severest condemnation in public opinion, it cannot be said that this abuse is greater, and it is believed to be less, than that which characterized the period in which our institutions took shape. Meanwhile, the administration of government has become more complex, the opportunities for malfeasance and corruption have multiplied, crime has grown to most serious proportions, and the danger of its protection by unfaithful officials and of the impairment of the fundamental security of life and property by criminal alliances and official neglect, emphasizes the primary need of a vigilant and courageous press, especially in great cities. The fact that the liberty of the press may be abused by miscreant purveyors of scandal does not make any the less necessary the immunity of the press from previous restraint in dealing with official misconduct. Subsequent punishment for such abuses as may exist is the appropriate remedy, consistent with constitutional privilege....

Equally unavailing is the insistence that the statute is designed to prevent the circulation of scandal which tends to disturb the public peace and to provoke assaults and the commission of crime. Charges of reprehensible conduct, and in particular of official malfeasance, unquestionably create a public scandal, but the theory of the constitutional guaranty is that even a more serious public evil would be caused by authority to prevent publication. . . .

Judgment reversed.

[Mr. Justice Butler wrote a dissenting opinion, concurred in by Justices Van Devanter, McReynolds, and Sutherland.]

The majority opinion in the case did not reach the issue of whether the publisher was constitutionally free of any liability for the specific charges made in his newspaper. The point stressed was that in view of the post-publication remedy of a libel action, the injunction against future publication of similar charges was in the nature of a previous restraint. While the decision might be construed as a bar to the use of the injunctive remedy as a limitation on the press, a later case shows that the injunction is constitutionally permissible in special circumstances if the procedural safeguards are adequate. The case is *Kingsley Books, Inc.* v. *Brown,* decided in 1957.

KINGSLEY BOOKS, INC. *v.* BROWN
354 U.S. 436 (1957)

Mr. Justice Frankfurter delivered the opinion of the Court.

This is a proceeding under Sec. 22-a of the New York Code of Criminal Procedure. . . . This section supplements the existing conventional criminal provision dealing with pornography by authorizing the chief executive, or legal officer, of a municipality to invoke a "limited injunctive remedy," under closely defined procedural safeguards, against the sale and distribution of written and printed matter found after due trial to be obscene, and to obtain an order for the seizure, in default of surrender, of the condemned publications.

A complaint dated September 10, 1954, charged appellants with displaying for sale paper-covered obscene booklets, fourteen of which were annexed, under the general title of "Nights of Horror." The complaint prayed that appelants be enjoined from further distribution of the booklets, that they be required to surrender to the sheriff for destruction all copies in their possession, and, upon failure to do so, that the sheriff be commanded to seize and destroy those copies. The same day the appellants were ordered to show cause within four days why they should not be enjoined *pendente lite* from distributing the booklets. Appellants consented to the granting of an injunction *pendente lite* and did not bring the matter to issue promptly, as was their right under subdivision 2 of the challenged section, which provides that the persons sought to be enjoined "shall be entitled to a trial of the issues within two days of the conclusion of the trial." After the case came to trial, the judge, sitting in equity, found that the booklets annexed to the complaint and introduced in evidence were clearly obscene—were "dirt for dirt's sake"; he enjoined their further distribution and ordered their destruction. He refused to enjoin "the sale and distribution of later issues" on the ground that "to rule against a volume not offered in evidence would . . . impose an unreasonable prior restraint upon freedom of the press.". . .

Neither in the New York Court of Appeals, nor here, did appellants assail the legislation insofar as it outlaws obscenity. The claim they make lies within a very narrow compass. Their attack is upon the power of New York to employ the remedial scheme of Section 22-a.... Resort to this injunctive remedy, it is claimed, is beyond the constitutional power of New York in that it amounts to a prior censorship of literary product and as such is violative of that "freedom of thought, and speech" which has been "withdrawn by the Fourteenth Amendment from encroachment by the states.".... Reliance is particularly placed upon *Near* v. *Minnesota*....

We need not linger over the suggestion that something can be drawn out of the Due Process Clause of the Fourteenth Amendment that restricts New York to the criminal process in seeking to protect its people against the dissemination of pornography. It is not for this Court thus to limit the State in resorting to various weapons in the armory of the law. Whether proscribed conduct is to be visited by a criminal prosecution or by a *qui tam* action or by an injunction or by some or all of these remedies in combination, is a matter within the legislature's range of choice.... If New York chooses to subject persons who disseminate obscene "literature" to criminal prosecution and also to deal with such books as deodands of old, or both, with due regard, of course, to appropriate opportunities for the trial of the underlying issue, it is not for us to gainsay its selection of remedies....

... The phrase "prior restraint" is not a self-wielding sword. Nor can it serve as a talismanic test. The duty of closer analysis and critical judgment in applying the thought behind the phrase has thus been authoritatively put by one who brings weighty learning to his support of constitutionally protected liberties: "What is needed," writes Professor Paul A. Freund, "is a pragmatic assessment of its operation in the particular circumstances. The generalization that prior restraint is particularly obnoxious in civil liberties cases must yield to more particularistic analysis." The Supreme Court and Civil Liberties, 4 *Vand. L. Rev.* 533, 539.

Wherein does Section 22-a differ in its effective operation from the type of statute upheld in *Alberts?* Section 311 of California's Penal Code provides that "Every person who willfully and lewdly . . . keeps for sale . . . any obscene . . . book ... is guilty of a misdemeanor...." Section 1141 of New York's Penal Law is similar. One would be bold to assert that the *in terrorem* effect of such statutes less restrains booksellers in the period before the law strikes than does Section 22-a. Instead of requiring the bookseller to dread that the offer for sale of a book may, without prior warning, subject him to a criminal prosecution with the hazard of imprisonment, the civil procedure assures him that such consequences cannot follow unless he ignores a court order specifically directed to him for a prompt and carefully circumscribed determination of the issue of obscenity. Until then, he may keep the book for sale and sell it on his own judgment rather than steer "nervously among the treacherous shoals.". . .

Criminal enforcement and the proceeding under Section 22-a interfere with a book's solicitation of the public precisely at the same stage. In each situation the law moves after publication; the book need not in either case have yet passed into the hands of the public. . . .

Nor are the consequences of a judicial condemnation for obscenity under Section 22-a more restrictive of freedom of expression than the result of conviction for a misdemeanor. In *Alberts,* the defendant was fined $500, sentenced to sixty days in prison, and put on probation for two years on condition that he not violate the obscenity statute. Not only was he completely separated from society for two months but he was also seriously restrained from trafficking in all obscene publications for a considerable time. Appellants, on the other hand, were enjoined from displaying for sale or distributing only the particular booklets theretofore published and adjudged to be obscene. Thus, the restraint upon appellants as merchants in obscenity was narrower than that imposed on Alberts.

Section 22-a's provision for the seizure and destruction of the instruments of ascertained wrongdoing expresses resort to a legal remedy sanctioned by the long history of Anglo-American law. See Holmes, The Common Law, 24–26. . . .

It only remains to say that the difference between *Near* v. *Minnesota, supra,* and this case is glaring in fact. The two cases are no less glaringly different when judged by the appropriate criteria of constitutional law. Minnesota empowered its courts to enjoin the dissemination of future issues of a publication because its past issues had been found offensive. In the language of Mr. Chief Justice Hughes, "This is of the essence of censorship.". . . As such, it was found unconstitutional. This was enough to condemn the statute wholly apart from the fact that the proceeding in *Near* involved not obscenity but matters deemed to be derogatory to a public officer. Unlike *Near,* Section 22-a is concerned solely with obscenity and, as authoritatively construed, it studiously withholds restraint upon matters not already published and not yet found to be offensive.

The judgment is

Affirmed.

Mr. Chief Justice Warren, dissenting. . . .

Mr. Justice Douglas, joined by Mr. Justice Black, dissenting. . . .

Mr. Justice Brennan, dissenting. . . .

The jury represents a cross-section of the community and has a special aptitude for reflecting the view of the average person. Jury trial of obscenity therefore provides a peculiarly competent application of the standard for judging obscenity which, by its definition, calls for an appraisal of material according to the average person's application of contemporary community standards. A statute which does not afford the defendant, of right, a jury determination of obscenity falls short, in my view, of giving proper effect to the standard fashioned as the necessary safeguard demanded by the freedoms of speech and press for material which is not obscene. Of course, as with jury questions generally, the trial judge must initially determine that there is a jury question, *i.e.,* that reasonable men may differ whether the material is obscene. . . .

[On prior restraint generally, see Zechariah Chafee, Jr., *Free Speech in the United States* (Cambridge: Harvard University Press, 1948), pp. 9–30, 400–435; Paul A. Freund, "The Supreme Court and Civil Liberties," 4 *Vand. L. Rev.* 533, 537–545 (1951); and Thomas I. Emerson, "The Doctrine of Prior Restraint," 20 *Law and Contemp. Prob.* 648 (1955).]

In 1971 the Court faced the issue of freedom of the press versus the national security in *New York Times Co.* v. *United States,* the "Pentagon Papers Case."

NEW YORK TIMES CO. *v.* UNITED STATES
403 U.S. 713 (1971)

[In June 1971 Professor Daniel Ellsberg released to the press a large portion of a 47-volume Pentagon study entitled *History of the United States Decision-Making Process on Vietnam Policy*—some 7,000 pages of material still classified "Top Secret-Sensitive" by the Defense Department. On June 13 the *New York*

Times published the first installment of a scheduled five-part series on how the United States got involved in Vietnam. On June 18 the *Washington Post* published the first in its series of articles based on the "Pentagon Papers." The Department of Justice in two separate District Courts requested temporary restraining orders to halt further publication of the papers by the *Times* and the *Post*. Both District Courts denied the requests. On June 19 the Court of Appeals, District of Columbia, temporarily restrained the *Post* from continuing its series, and the District Judge scheduled a hearing for June 21 on the Justice Department's request for an injunction. The Court of Appeals for the Second Circuit issued a restraining order against the *Times* to allow the Government to appeal the District Court decision in New York. After secret hearings in both District Courts, the Court of Appeals for the Second Circuit continued its restraining order and the *Times* filed an appeal to the Supreme Court, while the Court of Appeals in Washington upheld the District Court decision there that the government had failed to prove that the *Post* articles would endanger the national security, but extended the restraining order to give the government time for an appeal to the Supreme Court. Both cases were handled on writs of certiorari and decided on June 30, 1971.]

PER CURIAM.

We granted certiorari in these cases in which the United States seeks to enjoin the *New York Times* and the *Washington Post* from publishing the contents of a classified study entitled "History of U.S. Decision-Making Process on Viet Nam Policy."

"Any system of prior restraints of expression comes to this Court bearing a heavy presumption against its constitutional validity." *Bantam Books, Inc.* v. *Sullivan* . . . ; see also *Near* v. *Minnesota*. . . . The Government "thus carries a heavy burden of showing justification for the enforcement of such a restraint." *Organization for a Better Austin* v. *Keefe*. . . . The District Court for the Southern District of New York in the *New York Times* case and the District Court for the District of Columbia and the Court of Appeals for the District of Columbia Circuit in the *Washington Post* case held that the Government had not met that burden. We agree.

The judgment of the Court of Appeals for the District of Columbia Circuit is therefore affirmed. The order of the Court of Appeals for the Second Circuit is reversed and the case is remanded with directions to enter a judgment affirming the judgment of the District Court for the Southern District of New York. The stays entered June 25, 1971, by the Court are vacated. The mandates shall issue forthwith.

So ordered.

Mr. Justice Black, with whom Mr. Justice Douglas joins, concurring.

I adhere to the view that the Government's case against the *Washington Post* should have been dismissed and that the injunction against the *New York Times* should have been vacated without oral orgument when the cases were first presented to this Court. I believe that every moment's continuance of the injunctions against these newspapers amounts to a flagrant, indefensible, and continuing violation of the First Amendment. . . . In my view it is unfortunate that some of my Brethren are apparently willing to hold that the publication of news may sometimes be enjoined. Such a holding would make a shambles of the First Amendment. . . .

In the First Amendment the Founding Fathers gave the free press the protection it must have to fulfill its essential role in our democracy. The press was to serve the governed, not the governors. . . . Only a free and unrestrained press can effectively expose deception in government. And paramount among the responsibilities of a free press is the duty to prevent any part of the government from deceiving the people and sending them off to distant lands to die of foreign fevers and foreign shot and shell. In my view, far from deserving condemnation for their courageous reporting, the *New York Times,* the *Washington Post,* and other newspapers should be commended for serving the purpose that the Founding Fathers saw so clearly. . . .

Mr. Justice Douglas, with whom Mr. Justice Black joins, concurring. . . .

The dominant purpose of the First Amendment was to prohibit the widespread practice of governmental suppression of embarrassing information. It is common knowledge that the First Amendment was adopted against the widespread use of the common law of seditious libel to punish the dissemination of material that is embarrassing to the powers-that-be. . . . The present cases will, I think, go down in history as the most dramatic illustration of that principle. A debate of large proportions goes on in the Nation over our posture in Vietnam. That debate antedated the disclosure of the contents of the present documents. The latter are highly relevant to the debate in progress.

Secrecy in government is fundamentally anti-democratic, perpetuating bureaucratic errors. Open debate and discussion of public issues are vital to our national health. On public questions there should be "open and robust debate.". . .

Mr. Justice Brennan, concurring.

I write separately in these cases only to emphasize what should be apparent: that our judgment in the present cases may not be taken to indicate the propriety, in the future, of issuing temporary stays and restraining orders to block the publication of material sought to be suppressed by the Government. . . .

The error which has pervaded these cases from the outset was the granting of any injunctive relief whatsoever, interim or otherwise. The entire thrust of the Government's claim throughout these cases has been that publication of the material sought to be enjoined "could," or "might," or "may" prejudice the national interest in various ways. But the First Amendment tolerates absolutely no prior judicial restraints of the press predicated upon surmise or conjecture that untoward consequences may result. . . . Thus, only governmental allegation and proof that publication must inevitably, directly and immediately cause the occurrence of an event kindred to imperiling the safety of a transport already at sea can support even the issuance of an interim restraining order. In no event may mere conclusions be sufficient: for if the Executive Branch seeks judicial aid in preventing publication, it must inevitably submit the basis upon which that aid is sought to scrutiny by the judiciary. And therefore, every restraint issued in this case, whatever its form, has violated the First Amendment—and none the less so because that restraint was justified as necessary to afford the court an opportunity to examine the claim more thoroughly. Unless and until the Government has clearly made out its case, the First Amendment commands that no injunction may issue.

Mr. Justice Stewart, with whom Mr. Justice White joins, concurring. . . .

In the absence of the governmental checks and balances present in other areas of our national life, the only effective restraint upon executive policy and power in the areas of national defense and international affairs may lie in an enlightened citizenry—in an informed and critical public opinion which alone can here protect the values of democratic government. . . .

Yet it is elementary that the successful conduct of international diplomacy and the maintenance of an effective national defense require both confidentiality and secrecy. . . .

I think there can be but one answer to this dilemma, if dilemma it be. The responsibility must be where the power is. If the Constitution gives the Executive a large degree of unshared power in the conduct of foreign affairs and the maintenance of our national defense, then under the Constitution the Executive must have the largely unshared duty to determine and preserve the degree of internal security necessary to exercise that power successfully. . . . [I]t is clear to me that it is the constitutional duty of the Executive—as a matter of sovereign prerogative and not as a matter of law as the courts know law—. . . to protect the confidentiality necessary to carry out its responsibilities in the fields of international relations and national defense. . . .

. . . [I]n the cases before us we are asked neither to construe specific regulations nor to apply specific laws. We are asked, instead, to perform a function that the Constitution gave to the Executive, not the Judiciary. . . . I join the judgments of the Court.

Mr. Justice White, with whom Mr. Justice Stewart joins, concurring.

I concur in today's judgments, but only because of the concededly extraordinary protection against prior restraints enjoyed by the press under our constitutional system. I do not say that in no circumstances would the First Amendment permit an injunction against publishing information about government plans or operations. Nor, after examining the materials the Government characterizes as the most sensitive and destructive, can I deny that revelation of these documents will do substantial damage to public interests. Indeed, I am confident that their disclosure will have that result. But I nevertheless agree that the United States has not satisfied the very heavy burden which it must meet to warrant an injunction against publication in these cases, at least in the absence of express and appropriately limited congressional authorization for prior restraints in circumstances such as these. . . .

Mr. Justice Marshall, concurring. . . .

The problem here is whether in this particular case the Executive Branch has authority to invoke the equity jurisdiction of the courts to protect what it believes to be the national interest. . . .

It would . . . be utterly inconsistent with the concept of separation of power for this Court to use its power of contempt to prevent behavior that Congress has specifically declined to prohibit. . . .

Either the Government has the power under statutory grant to use traditional criminal law to protect the country or, if there is no basis for arguing that Congress has made the activity a crime, it is plain that Congress has specifically refused to grant the authority the Government seeks from this Court. In either case this Court does not have authority to grant the requested relief. It is not for this Court to fling itself into every breach perceived by some Government official nor is it for this Court to take on itself the burden of enacting law, especially law that Congress has refused to pass. . . .

Mr. Chief Justice Burger, dissenting. . . .

Only those who view the First Amendment as an absolute in all circumstances —a view I respect, but reject—can find such a case as this to be simple or easy.

This case is not simple for another and more immediate reason. We do not know the facts of the case. No District Judge knew all the facts. No Court of Appeals judge knew all the facts. No member of this Court knows all the facts. . . .

I suggest we are in this posture because these cases have been conducted in unseemly haste. Mr. Justice Harlan covers the chronology of events demonstrating the hectic pressures under which these cases have been processed and I need not restate them. . . .

The consequence of all this melancholy series of events is that we literally do not know what we are acting on. As I see it we have been forced to deal with litigation concerning rights of great magnitude without an adequate record, and surely without time for adequate treatment either in the prior proceedings or in this Court. . . . I agree with Mr. Justice Harlan and Mr. Justice Blackmun but I am not prepared to reach the merits.

I would affirm the Court of Appeals for the Second Circuit and allow the District Court to complete the trial aborted by our grant of certiorari meanwhile preserving the *status quo* in the *Post* case. I would direct that the District Court on remand give priority to the *Times* case to the exclusion of all other business on that court but I would not set arbitrary deadlines. . . .

Mr. Justice Harlan, with whom the Chief Justice and Mr. Justice Blackmun join, dissenting. . . .

With all respect, I consider that the Court has been almost irresponsibly feverish in dealing with these cases. . . .

Forced as I am to reach the merits of these cases, I dissent from the opinion and judgments of the Court. . . .

It is plain to me that the scope of the judicial function in passing upon the activities of the Executive Branch of the Government in the field of foreign affairs is very narrowly restricted. This view is, I think, dictated by the concept of separation of powers upon which our constitutional system rests. . . .

I agree that, in performance of its duty to protect the values of the First Amendment against political pressures, the judiciary must review the initial Executive determination to the point of satisfying itself that the subject matter of the dispute does lie within the proper compass of the President's foreign relations power. . . . Moreover, the judiciary may properly insist that the determination that disclosure of the subject matter would irreparably impair the national security be made by the head of the Executive Department concerned—here the Secretary of State or the Secretary of Defense—after actual personal consideration by that officer. . . .

But in my judgment the judiciary may not properly go beyond these two inquiries and redetermine for itself the probable impact of disclosure on the national security. . . .

I can see no indication in the opinions of either the District Court or the Court of Appeals in the *Post* litigation that the conclusions of the Executive were given even the deference owing to an administrative agency, much less that owing to a co-equal branch of the Government operating within the field of its constitutional prerogative. . . .

Mr. Justice Blackmun, dissenting. . . .

With such respect as may be due to the contrary view, this, in my opinion, is not the way to try a law suit of this magnitude and asserted importance. It is not the way for federal courts to adjudicate, and to be required to adjudicate, issues that allegedly concern the Nation's vital welfare. . . .

The First Amendment, after all, is only part of an entire Constitution. Article II of the great document vests in the Executive Branch primary power over the conduct of foreign affairs and places in that branch the responsibility for the Nation's safety. Each provision of the Constitution is important, and I cannot subscribe to a doctrine of unlimited absolutism for the First Amendment at the cost of downgrading other provisions. First Amendment absolutism has never commanded a majority of this Court. . . . What is needed here is a weighing, upon properly developed standards, of the broad right of the press to print and of the very narrow right of the Government to prevent. Such standards are not yet developed. The parties here are in disagreement as to what those standards should be. But even the newspapers concede that there are situations where restraint is in order and is constitutional. . . .

I therefore would remand these cases. . . .

Concern over previous restraints is, of course, both understandable and supportable. Censorship denies the proscribed book the light of day altogether, with no chance for an impact on the reading public. If the book is in fact one which it is illegal to sell or display for sale, then one might raise the question of whether it is not indeed more desirable to keep it off the shelf altogether. This is to overlook the crucial stage of the problem, however, which is the actual determination of whether the book falls within the statutory ban. Three aspects of this fact-finding stage deserve careful scrutiny before a decision can be reached on the issue of denial of First Amendment rights. These are (1) the test to be employed to determine whether or not the publication is proscribed by law (whether under obscenity, national security provisions, or others), (2) the procedures to be followed in arriving at a decision, and (3) the special competence required of the person or persons who actually make the finding. To the majority in *Kingsley Books* it appeared that examination of such factors as these was a more appropriate approach (the "pragmatic assessment" suggested by Professor Freund) than the use of the phrase "prior restraint" as a talismanic test.

The real difficulty in attempting to apply a "prior restraint" test to limitations on the press (and its included forms, such as movies) lies in the face that a multi-stage process is involved. A manuscript is prepared, then it is published, then it is distributed in volume to various distributors and retailers, and finally it is actually placed in the hands of the reading public. To complicate the process further, advance copies of some books are specially printed and sent out for review or other purposes prior to the general publication date. Must the government wait to proceed under its criminal laws until members of the public have actually purchased copies at retail outlets to avoid the claim of "prior restraint"? If only one copy need be sold at retail to avoid such a charge, then it might be argued, as did Justice Frankfurter in *Kingsley Books,* that the practical distinction is nonexistent. As what stage do restraints clearly become "prior" restraints?

In applying the doctrine to freedom of speech, without the several stages involved in press cases, there are fewer difficulties. Either the speech is permitted to be given or it is not. If not, there may be an issue of prior restraint. But if penalties are imposed afterward, no such issue is presented. Thus in

Thomas v. *Collins,* 323 U.S. 516 (1945), the question presented was the constitutionality of an injunction issued under a Texas statute which forbade solicitation of members for labor unions without an organizer's card having first been obtained from the Secretary of State. Five members of the United States Supreme Court held the requirement to be unconstitutional. Justice Rutledge, for the majority, stated:

> If the exercise of the rights of free speech and free assembly cannot be made a crime, we do not think this can be accomplished by the device of requiring previous registration as a condition for exercising them and making such a condition the foundation for restraining in advance their exercise and for imposing a penalty for violating such a restraining order.

A special aspect of the prior restraint problem was presented in *Kunz* v. *New York* in 1951, when a permit granted to a street-speaker was later revoked because of the content of some of the speeches.

KUNZ *v.* NEW YORK
340 U.S. 290 (1951)

Mr. Chief Justice Vinson delivered the opinion of the Court.

New York City has adopted an ordinance which makes it unlawful to hold public worship meetings on the streets without first obtaining a permit from the city police commissioner. Appellant, Carl Jacob Kunz, was convicted and fined $10 for violating this ordinance by holding a religious meeting without a permit. The conviction was affirmed by the . . . New York Court of Appeals, three judges dissenting. . . . The case is here on appeal, it having been urged that the ordinance is invalid under the Fourteenth Amendment.

Appellant is an ordained Baptist minister who speaks under the auspices of the "Outdoor Gospel Work," of which he is the director. He has been preaching for about six years, and states that it is his conviction and duty to "go out on the highways and byways and preach the word of God." In 1946, he applied for and received a permit under the ordinance in question, there being no question that appellant comes within the classes of persons entitled to receive permits under the ordinance.* This permit, like all others, was good only for the calendar year in which issued. In November, 1946, his permit was revoked after a hearing by the police commissioner. The revocation was based on evidence that he had ridiculed and denounced other religious beliefs in his meetings.

Although the penalties of the ordinance apply to anyone who "ridicules and denounces other religious beliefs," the ordinance does not specify this as a ground for permit revocation. Indeed, there is no mention in the ordinance of any power of revocation. However, appellant did not seek judicial or administrative review of the revocation proceedings, and any question as to the propriety of the revocation is not before us in this case. In any event, the revocation affected appellant's rights to speak in 1946 only. Appellant applied for another permit in 1947, and again in 1948, but was notified each time that this application was "disapproved," with no reason for the disapproval being given. On September 11, 1948, appellant was arrested for speaking at Columbus Circle in New York City without a permit. It is from the conviction which resulted that this appeal has been taken.

---

* The New York Court of Appeals has construed the ordinance to require that all initial requests for permits by eligible applicants must be granted. 300 N.Y. at 276.

Appellant's conviction was thus based upon his failure to possess a permit for 1948. We are here concerned only with the proprietary of the action of the police commissioner in refusing to issue that permit. Disapproval of the 1948 permit application by the police commissioner was justified by the New York courts on the ground that a permit had previously been revoked "for good reasons." It is noteworthy that there is no mention in the ordinance of reasons for which such a permit application can be refused. This interpretation allows the police commissioner, an administrative official, to exercise discretion in denying subsequent permit applications on the basis of his interpretation, at that time, of what is deemed to be conduct condemned by the ordinance. We have here, then, an ordinance which gives an administrative official discretionary power to control in advance the right of citizens to speak on religious matters on the streets of New York. As such, the ordinance is clearly invalid as a prior restraint on the exercise of First Amendment rights.

In considering the right of a municipality to control the use of public streets for the expression of religious views, we start with the words of Mr. Justice Roberts that "Wherever the title of streets and parks may rest, they have immemorially been held in trust for the use of the public and, time out of mind, have been used for purposes of assembly, communicating thoughts between citizens, and discussing public questions." *Hague* v. *C.I.O.*, 307 U.S. 496, 515. Although this Court has recognized that a statute may be enacted which prevents serious interference with normal usage of streets and parks, *Cox* v. *New Hampshire*, 312 U.S. 569, we have consistently condemned licensing systems which vest in an administrative official discretion to grant or withhold a permit upon broad criteria unrelated to proper regulation of public places. In *Cantwell* v. *Connecticut*, 310 U.S. 296 (1940), this Court held invalid an ordinance which required a license for soliciting money for religious causes. Speaking for a unanimous Court, Mr. Justice Roberts said: "But to condition the solicitation of aid for the perpetuation of religious views or systems upon a license, the grant of which rests in the exercise of a determination by state authority as to what is a religious cause, is to lay a forbidden burden upon the exercise of liberty protected by the Constitution." 310 U.S. at 307. . . .

The court below has mistakenly derived support for its conclusion from the evidence produced at the trial that appellant's religious meetings had, in the past, caused some disorder. There are appropriate public remedies to protect the peace and order of the community if appellant's speeches should result in disorder or violence. "In the present case, we have no occasion to inquire as to the permissible scope of subsequent punishment." *Near* v. *Minnesota*, 283 U.S. 697, 715. We do not express any opinion on the propriety of punitive remedies which the New York authorities may utilize. We are here concerned with suppression—not punishment. It is sufficient to say that New York cannot vest restraining control over the right to speak on religious subjects in an administrative official where there are no appropriate standards to guide his action.

Reversed.

Mr. Justice Black concurs in the result.

Mr. Justice Frankfurter, concurring in the result. . . .

Mr. Justice Jackson, dissenting. . . .

At these meetings, Kunz preached, among many other things of like tenor, that "The Catholic Church makes merchandise out of souls," that Catholicism is "a religion of the devil," and that the Pope is "the anti-Christ." The Jews he denounced as "Christ-killers," and he said of them, "All the garbage that didn't believe in Christ should have been burnt in the incinerators. It's a shame they all weren't.". . .

This Court today initiates the doctrine that language such as this, in the environment of the street meeting, is immune from prior municipal control. We would have a very different question if New York had presumed to say that Kunz could not speak his piece in his own pulpit or hall. But it has undertaken to restrain him only if he chooses to speak at street meetings. There is a world of difference. The street preacher takes advantage of people's presence on the streets to impose his message upon what, in a sense, is a captive audience. A meeting on private property is made up of an audience that has volunteered to listen. The question, therefore, is not whether New York could, if it tried, silence Kunz, but whether it must place its streets at his service to hurl insults at the passerby. . . .

Of course, as to the press, there are the best of reasons against any licensing or prior restraint. Decisions such as *Near* v. *Minnesota, supra,* hold any licensing or prior restraint of the press unconstitutional, and I heartily agree. But precedents from that field cannot reasonably be transposed to the street-meeting field. The impact of publishing on public order has no similarity with that of a street meeting. Publishing does not make private use of public property. It reaches only those who choose to read, and, in that way, is analogous to a meeting held in a hall where those who come do so by choice. Written words are less apt to incite or provoke to mass action than spoken words, speech being the primitive and direct communication with the emotions. Few are the riots caused by publication alone, few are the mobs that have not had their immediate origin in harangue. The vulnerability of various forms of communication to community control must be proportioned to their impact upon other community interests.

It is suggested that a permit for a street meeting could be required if the ordinance would prescribe precise standards for its grant or denial. . . .

Of course, standards for administrative action are always desirable, and the more exact the better. But I do not see how this Court can condemn municipal ordinances for not setting forth comprehensive First Amendment standards. This Court never has announced what those standards must be, it does not now say what they are, and it is not clear that any majority could agree on them. In no field are there more numerous individual opinions among the Justices. . . . It seems hypercritical to strike down local laws on their faces for want of standards when we have no standards. And I do not find it required by existing authority. I think that where speech is outside of constitutional immunity the local community or the State is left a large measure of discretion as to the means for dealing with it. . . .

Turning then to the permit system as applied by the Court of Appeals, whose construction binds us, we find that issuance the first time is required. Denial is warranted only in such unusual cases as where an applicant has had a permit which has been revoked for cause and he asserts the right to continue the conduct which was the cause for revocation. If anything less than a reasonable certainty of disorder was shown, denial of a permit would be improper. The procedure by which that decision is reached commends itself to the orderly mind—complaints are filed, witnesses are heard, opportunity to cross-examine is given, and decision is reached by what we must assume to be an impartial and reasonable administrative officer, and, if he denies the permit, the applicant may carry his cause to the courts. He may thus have a civil test of his rights without the personal humiliation of being arrested as presenting a menace to public order. It seems to me that this procedure better protects freedom of speech than to let everyone speak without leave, but subject to surveillance and to being ordered to stop in the discretion of the police. . . .

If any two subjects are intrinsically incendiary and divisive, they are race and religion. Racial fears and hatreds have been at the root of the most terrible riots that have disgraced American civilization. They are ugly possibilities that overhang every great American city. The "consecrated hatreds of sect" account for more than a few of the world's bloody disorders. These are the explosives which the Court says Kunz may play with in the public streets, and the community must not only tolerate but aid him. I find no such doctrine in the Constitution.

In this case there is no evidence of a purpose to suppress speech, except to keep it in bounds that will not upset good order. If there are abuses of censorship or discrimination in administering the ordinance, as well there may be, they are not proved in this case. This Court should be particularly sure of its ground before it strikes down, in a time like this, the going practical system by which New York has sought to control its street-meeting problem. . . .

It should be noted that the Court did not flatly proscribe the requirement of a permit in the *Kunz* decision. But where such requirements pertain, they cannot admit of official discretion which would allow arbitrary or capricious distinctions among applicants. In *Niemotko* v. *Maryland,* 340 U.S. 268 (1951), involving the operation of an "amorphous practice" (as the Chief Justice called it) of requiring a permit from the city council before holding a meeting in a public park, there is an indication that a permit requirement which is completely nondiscretionary and is used merely for the purpose of notification and for scheduling use in orderly fashion would not be considered an unconstitutional restraint. Chief Justice Vinson, speaking for the majority in *Niemotko,* stated:

This Court has many times examined the licensing systems by which local bodies regulate the use of their parks and public places. . . . In those cases this Court condemned statutes and ordinances which required that permits be obtained from local officials as a prerequisite to the use of public places, on the grounds that a license requirement constituted a prior restraint on freedom of speech, press and religion, and, *in the absence of narrowly drawn, reasonable and definite standards for the officials to follow,* must be invalid. [Emphasis added.]

It would seem that a little prior restraint may be tolerated if there is some substantial community interest to be served in imposing the limitation. Thus, again, Justice Frankfurter's conclusion may be recalled, to the effect that the phrase "prior restraint" is not a self-wielding sword.

In another area of speech and press the Court has shown even more flexibility in its applications of the rule of no previous restraint. This is the matter of licensing of motion pictures. A very few states and less than a score of cities have provisions requiring that an exhibitor obtain a permit prior to the showing of any motion picture publicly. These laws or ordinances generally allow the licensing agency to refuse a permit if the film is obscene or would tend to corrupt morals or incite to crime. In *Burstyn, Inc.* v. *Wilson,* 343 U.S. 495 (1952), the Court first held that "expression by means of motion pictures is included within the free speech and free press guaranty of the First and Fourteenth Amendments." The controversy arose over the decision of the New York Board of Regents to rescind a license granted earlier for the showing of the film *The Miracle* on the ground that it fell under the statutory ban against exhibiting "sacrilegious" movies. The Court refused to rule squarely on the issue of the constitutionality of licensing movies. Instead the decision to reverse was based on the narrower ground of adequacy of standards in the use of the word "sacrilegious." Justice Clark, for the Court, stated:

New York's highest court says there is "nothing mysterious" about the statutory provision applied in this case: "It is simply this: that no religion, as that word is understood by the ordinary, reasonable person, shall be treated with contempt, mockery, scorn and ridicule. . . ." This is far from the kind of narrow exception to freedom of expression which a state may carve out to satisfy the adverse demands of other interests of society. In seeking to apply the broad and all-inclusive definition of "sacrilegious" given by the New York courts, the censor is set adrift upon a boundless sea amid a myriad of conflicting currents of religious views, with no charts but those provided by the most vocal and powerful orthodoxies. New York cannot vest such unlimited restraining control over motion pictures in a censor.

The Court followed a similar approach in reversing several subsequent state court decisions on the apparent ground of inadequacy of standards. Without explanation and citing only the *Burstyn* case in *Per Curiam* decisions, the Court reversed: New York's denial of a license for the showing of *La Ronde* (under the statutory standard of "immoral" and "tending to corrupt morals") in *Commercial Pictures* v. *Regents,* 346 U.S. 587 (1954); Ohio's ban on the film *M* (which had been found to "undermine confidence in the enforcement of law and government" and which could lead "unstable persons to increased immorality and crime") in *Superior Films* v. *Department of Education of Ohio,* 346 U.S. 587 (1954); and a Kansas ban on *The Moon is Blue* (under a statutory standard barring films that were "obscene, indecent, or immoral, or such as tend to debase or corrupt morals") in *Holmby Productions* v. *Vaughn,* 350 U.S. 870 (1955).

Not until 1961 did the Court squarely come to grips with the issue of whether the licensing requirement for the exhibiting of motion pictures was *per se* an unconstitutional prior restraint. The case was *Times Film Corporation* v. *City of Chicago,* 365 U.S. 43 (1961). The Municipal Code of the City of Chicago required submission of all motion pictures for examination prior to their public exhibition. An exhibitor applied for a permit, as required by the ordinance, and tendered the license fee but refused to submit the film for examination. The City refused to issue the permit, and the corporation sued for injunctive relief, arguing that the requirement of submission of the film constituted, on its face, a prior restraint within the prohibition of the First and Fourteenth Amendments. By a five-to-four vote the Court upheld the ordinance requirement of prior submission. Justice Clark, for the majority, stated:

Petitioner would have us hold that the public exhibition of motion pictures must be allowed under any circumstances. The State's sole remedy, it says, is the invocation of criminal process under the Illinois pornography statute, . . . and then only after a transgression. But this position, as we have seen, is founded upon the claim of absolute privilege against prior restraint under the First Amendment—a claim without sanction in our cases. . . . Chicago emphasizes here its duty to protect its people against the dangers of obscenity in the public exhibition of motion pictures. To this argument petitioner's only answer is that regardless of the capacity for, or extent of such an evil, previous restraint cannot be justified. With this we cannot agree. We recognized in *Burstyn,* that "capacity for evil ... may be relevant in determining the permissible scope of control,". . . and that motion pictures were not "necessarily subject to the precise rules governing any other particular method of expression. Each method," we said, "tends to present its own peculiar problems." . . . It is not for this Court to limit the State in its selection of the remedy it deems most effective to cope with such a problem, absent, of course, a showing of unreasonable strictures on individual liberty resulting from its application in particular circumstances. *Kingsley Books, Inc.,* v. *Brown.* . . . We, of course, are not holding that city officials may be granted the power to prevent the showing of any motion picture they deem unworthy of a license. . . .

FREEDMAN *v.* MARYLAND
380 U.S. 51 (1965)

Mr. Justice Brennan delivered the opinion of the Court.

Appellant sought to challenge the constitutionality of the Maryland motion picture censorship statute ... and exhibited the film "Revenge at Daybreak" at his Baltimore theatre without first submitting the picture to the State Board of Censors as required by §2 thereof. The State concedes that the picture does not violate the statutory standards and would have received a license if properly submitted, but the appellant was convicted of a §2 violation despite his contention that the statute in its entirety unconstitutionally impaired freedom of expression. The Court of Appeals of Maryland affirmed. . . . We reverse.

In *Times Film Corp.* v. *City of Chicago* ... we considered and upheld a requirement of submission of motion pictures in advance of exhibition. The Court of Appeals held, on the authority of that decision, that "the Maryland censorship law must be held to be not void on its face as violative of the freedoms protected against State action by the First and Fourteenth Amendments.". . . This reliance on Times Film was misplaced. The only question tendered for decision in that case was "whether a prior restraint was necessarily unconstitutional *under all circumstances.*" . . . In rejecting the proffered proposition in *Times Film* the Court emphasized, however, that "it is that question alone which we decide,". . . and it would therefore be inaccurate to say that *Times Film* upheld the specific features of the Chicago censorship ordinance.

Unlike the petitioner in *Times Film,* appellant does not argue that §2 is unconstitutional simply because it may prevent even the first showing of a film whose exhibition may legitimately be the subject of an obscenity prosecution. He presents a question quite distinct from that passed on in *Times Film;* accepting the rule in *Times Film,* he argues that §2 constitutes an invalid prior restraint because, in the context of the remainder of the statute, it presents a danger of unduly suppressing protected expression. He focuses particularly on the procedure for an initial decision by the censorship board, which, without any judicial participation, effectively bars exhibition of any disapproved film, unless and until the exhibitor undertakes a time-consuming appeal to the Maryland courts and succeeds in having the Board's decision reversed. [The procedure outlined by the statute provided that the Board's disapproval could be appealed, in which case the film would be reexamined by two or more members of the Board and a decision promptly rendered. Appeal from this decision was to the Baltimore City Court, with further right of appeal from their decision to the Court of Appeals of Maryland.]

Thus there is no statutory provision for judical participation in the procedure which bars a film, nor even assurance of prompt judicial review. Risk of delay is built into the Maryland procedure, as is borne out by experience; in the only reported case indicating the length of time required to complete an appeal, the initial judicial determination has taken four months and final vindication of the film on appellate review, six months. . . .

Although the Court has said that motion pictures are not "necessarily subject to the precise rules governing any other particular method of expression,". . . it is as true here as of other forms of expression that "any system of prior restraints of expression comes to this Court bearing a heavy presumption against its constitutional validity.". . . Because the censor's business is to censor, there inheres the danger that he may well be less responsive than a court—part of an independent branch of government—to the constitutionally protected interests in free expression. And if it is made unduly onerous, by reason of delay or otherwise, to seek judicial review, the censor's determination may in practice be final.

Applying the settled rule of our cases, we hold that a noncriminal process which requires the prior submission of a film to a censor avoids constitutional infirmity only if it takes place under procedural safeguards designed to obviate the dangers of a censorship system. First, the burden of proving that the film is unprotected expression must rest on the censor. . . . Second, while the State may require advance submission of all films, in order to proceed effectively to bar all showings of unprotected films, the requirement cannot be administered in a manner which would lend an effect of finality to the censor's determination whether a film constitutes protected expression. The teaching of our cases is that, because only a judicial determination in an adversary proceeding ensures the necessary sensitivity to freedom of expression, only a procedure requiring a judical determination suffices to impose a valid final restraint. . . . To this end, the exhibitor must be assured, by statute or authoritative judicial construction, that the censor will, within a specified brief period, either issue a license or go to court to restrain showing the film. Any restraint imposed in advance of a final judicial determination on the merits must similarly be limited to preservation of the status quo for the shortest fixed period compatible with sound judicial resolution. . . .

Without these safeguards, it may prove too burdensome to seek review of the censor's determination. Particularly in the case of motion pictures, it may take very little to deter exhibition in a given locality. The exhibitor's stake in any one picture may be insufficient to warrant a protracted and onerous course of litigation. The distributor, on the other hand, may be equally unwilling to accept the burdens and delays of litigation in a particular area when, without such difficulties, he can freely exhibit his film in most of the rest of the country; for we are told that only four States and a handful of municipalities have active censorship laws. . . .

. . . We hold, therefore, that appellant's conviction must be reversed. The Maryland scheme fails to provide adequate safeguards against undue inhibition of protected expression, and this renders the §2 requirement of prior submission of films to the Board an invalid previous restraint.

How or whether Maryland is to incorporate the required procedural safeguards in the statutory scheme is, of course, for the State to decide. But a model is not lacking: In *Kingsley Books, Inc.* v. *Brown* . . . we upheld a New York injunctive procedure designed to prevent the sale of obscene books. That procedure postpones any restraint against sale until a judicial determination of obscenity following notice and an adversary hearing. The statute provides for a hearing one day after joinder of issue; the judge must hand down his decision within two days after termination of the hearing. The New York procedure operates without prior submission to a censor, but the chilling effect of a censorship order, even one which requires judicial action for its enforcement, suggests all the more reason for expeditious determination of the question whether a particular film is constitutionally protected. . . .

Reversed.

Mr. Justice Douglas, whom Mr. Justice Black joins, concurring.

On several occasions I have indicated my view that movies are entitled to the same degree and kind of protection under the First Amendment as other forms of expression. . . . I do not believe any form of censorship—no matter how speedy or prolonged it may be—is permissible. As I see it, a pictorial presentation occupies as preferred a position as any other form of expression. If censors are banned from the publishing business, from the pulpit, from the public platform—as they are— they should be banned from the theatre. I would not admit the censor even for the limited role accorded him in *Kingsley Books, Inc.* v. *Brown*. . . .

[See John R. Verani, "Motion Picture Censorship and the Doctrine of Prior Restraint," 3 *Houston L. Rev.* 11 (1965); and Ernest Giglio, "Prior Restraint of Motion Pictures," 69 *Dick. L. Rev.* 379 (1965).]

It may be seen from the various opinions expressed in the cases presented thus far that discussion of the specific doctrine of previous restraint tends to slide over into the more generalized concept of censorship. The latter word is quite commonly employed in the literature to denote any form of restraint, before or after publication, aside from criminal prosecutions, which effectively impairs consumption of the various forms of speech or press. Thus a decision of the Postmaster General to classify a magazine as not entitled to the second-class mailing privilege is certainly not a previous restraint, in the traditional usage, but it will clearly reduce (or possibly rule out altogether) the circulation of the magazine. Since the terms are sometimes used interchangeably in discussions of previous restraint, it is appropriate to consider here some of the postpublication administrative practices which limit freedom of speech and press.

Periodicals which are granted the second-class mail privilege have by this fact gained a valuable asset. Without such a privilege the standard postage rates would be so high for many such publications that costs would be prohibitive. Even if this were not the result, the periodical would suffer a serious competitive disadvantage. The Court has held that Congress need not open the privilege to publications of all types, and Congress has set conditions which must be met in order to qualify. The relevant requirement (one of four) is:

Except as otherwise provided by law, the conditions upon which a publication shall be admitted to the second class are as follows . . . *Fourth*. It must be originated and published for the dissemination of information of a public character, or devoted to literature, the sciences, arts, or some special industry, and having a legitimate list of subscribers. Nothing herein contained shall be so construed as to admit to the second-class rate regular publications designed primarily for advertising purposes, or for free circulation, or for circulation at nominal rates.

Esquire Magazine was granted a second-cass permit in 1933. In 1943, pursuant to 39 U.S.C.A. Sec. 232, the Postmaster General held a hearing and revoked the permit. The publisher then brought suit to enjoin the Postmaster General from revoking the permit. The Supreme Court considered the issue in *Hannegan* v. *Esquire, Inc.*, 327 U.S. 146 (1946). Justice Douglas, for a unanimous Court, stated that the Postmaster General acted improperly. The opinion cites the Postmaster General's statements in support of the conclusion to revoke. It should be noted that the decision to revoke was not based on a finding of obscenity, for in that case the magazine would be altogether nonmailable. It rested, intead, on a conclusion that the fourth condition set down by Congress was not met:

The plain language of this statute does not assume that a publication must in fact be "obscene" within the intendment of the postal obscenity statutes before it can be found not to be "originated and published for the disemination of information of a public character, or devoted to literature, the sciences, arts, or some special industry."

Writings and pictures may be indecent, vulgar, and risque and still not be obscene in a technical sense. Such writings and pictures may be in that obscure and treacherous borderland zone where the average person hesitates to find them technically obscene, but still may see ample proof that they are morally improper and not for the public welfare and the public good. When such writings or pictures occur in isolated instances their dangerous tendencies and malignant qualities may be considered of lesser importance.

When, however, they become a dominant and systematic feature they most certainly cannot be said to be for the public good, and a publication which uses them in that manner is not making the "special contribution to the public welfare" which Congress intended by the Fourth condition.

A publication to enjoy these unique mail privileges and special preferences is bound to do more than refrain from disseminating material which is obscene or bordering on the obscene. It is under a positive duty to contribute to the public good and the public welfare. . . .

Justice Douglas pointed out that most of the magazine issues offered in evidence and under attack were predominantly made up of material which was not challenged. He continued:

But petitioner's predecessor found that the objectionable items, though a small percentage of the total bulk, were regular recurrent features which gave the magazine its dominant tone or characteristic. These include jokes, cartoons, pictures, articles, and poems. They were said to reflect the smoking-room type of humor, featuring, in the main, sex. Some witnesses found the challenged items highly objectionable, calling them salacious and indecent. Others thought they were only racy and risque. Some condemned them as being merely in poor taste. Other witnesses could find no objection to them.

An examination of the items makes plain, we think, that the controversy is not whether the magazine publishes "information of a public character" or is devoted to "literature" or to the "arts." It is whether the contents are "good" or "bad." To uphold the order of revocation would, therefore, grant the Postmaster-General a power of censorship. Such a power is so abhorrent to our traditions that a purpose to grant it should not be easily inferred. . . .

We may assume that Congress has a broad power of classification and need not open second-class mail to publications of all types. The categories or publications entitled to that classification have indeed varied through the years. And the Court held in *Ex parte Jackson*, 96 U.S. 727, that Congress could constitutionally make it a crime to send fraudulent or obscene material through the mails. But grave constitutional questions are immediately raised once it is said that the use of mails is a privilege which may be extended or withheld on any grounds whatsoever.... Under that view the second-class rate could be granted on condition that certain economic or political ideas not be disseminated. The provisions of the Fourth condition would have to be far more explicit for us to assume that Congress made such a radical departure from our traditions and undertook to clothe the Postmaster General with the power to supervise the tastes of the reading public of the country.

It is plain, as we have said, that the favorable second class rates were granted periodicals meeting the requirements of the Fourth condition, so as that the public good might be served through a dissemination of the class of periodicals described. But that is a far cry from assuming that Congress had any idea that each applicant for the second class rate must convince the Postmaster-General that his publication positively contributes to the public good or public welfare....

It should be noted that the Court's decision in the *Esquire* case came off as an issue of statutory intent rather than First Amendment application. It thus left undetermined the constitutional area of restrictions which Congress might impose as limitations on the second-class mail privilege. In *Donaldson* v. *Read Magazine*, 333 U.S. 178 (1948), however, the Court sustained a Court order forbidding the delivery of mail and money orders to a magazine conducting a puzzle contest which the Postmaster General had found to be fraudulent. The Court stated that freedom of the press does not include the right to raise money by deception of the public. The mail-block sanction (prohibiting the delivery of *all* mail to offending sources of "obscene" publications and other articles) is a formidable weapon in the hands of the Post Office Department. Under a 1960 act of Congress, the mail-block sanction may not be used without an order from a federal court. At one time the Department declared nondeliverable such works as James Jones' *From Here to Eternity,* as well as some of the works of John O'Hara, John Steinbeck, and Ernest Hemingway. [See Edward De Grazia, "Obscenity and the Mail: A Study of Administrative Restraint," 20 *Law and Contemporary Problems* 608–620 (Autumn, 1955).] Under its interpretation of the Foreign Agents Registration Act of 1938, the Post Office Department has held that it can seize and destroy foreign propaganda coming into this country via the mails. Under this interpretation it delayed a shipment of seventy-five copies of Lenin's *State and Revolution* to be used in a history course at Brown University until the university authorities satisfied the Department as to the usefulness of the book to the University and the restrictions placed on its accessibility. [See Jay A. Sigler, "Freedom of the Mails: A Developing Right," 54 *Geo. L. J.* 30 (1965).]

Another form of administrative proceeding involving censorship from time to time has been the enforcement of customs controls on the importation of books or paintings. Until the law was changed by Congress in 1930, customs officials prevented the entry of such classics as Voltaire's *Candide, The Arabian Nights,* and Boccaccio's *Decameron,* as well as a number of modern works. The fact that many of the books were published in the United States did not seem to affect the application of the section barring "obscene" works. In 1930 the Congress amended the Tariff Act to authorize importation of classics and books of recognized scientific and literary merit when imported for noncommercial purposes. The act also provided that upon seizure of a book, the collector was required to notify the federal district attorney, who was to institute proceedings in the federal district court for the forfeiture of the book. Any party in interest could demand a trial by jury. In 1933 a copy of *Ulysses* was seized by the customs officials, but in an important decision by Judge Woolsey, the book was held not to come within the statutory ban on "obscene" works and therefore was not subject to seizure and confiscation. The case was *United States* v. *One Book Called "Ulysses,"* 5 F. Supp. 182 (1933). The decision was affirmed by the Court of Appeals, 72 F. 2d 705 (1934), and resulted in relative freedom from customs censorship. Nonetheless, the Tariff Act provision, Title 19 United States Code, Section 1305, remains and may be applied in appropriate cases if supported by judicial order. [See Jay A. Sigler, "Customs Censorship," 15 *Clev.-Mar. L. Rev.* 58 (1966).]

It can be said that the Court has taken a strong stand against previous restraints on First Amendment rights, although the opinions do indicate a few exceptional situations where such restraints might be allowable. Censorship devices which operate after publication but still effectively bar public consumption of a film, book, or painting, have been treated less stringently, but the Court examines the standards employed by the censors with great care. Thus it is not unconstitutional to require that movie films be licensed for showing, but the statutory guidelines for denial of license must be carefully drawn. Book publishers may print their books, but they may not send obscene books through the mail. Further, the Post Office Department might request and receive a court order setting up a mail-block sanction against offending publishers. The publishers might get the books as far as the retailers, only to face an injunction barring the sale of their books at that juncture. And, finally, the customs bureau is directed to stop the importation of obscene books into the United States.

What is the Court's attitude on restraints imposed after the speech is made or after the book has been made available to the public? As Chafee pointed out so clearly, the Blackstone approach would leave the speaker or the writer at the mercy of the law once he had exercised his right to put his ideas before the public. Such an attitude would make a mockery of the constitutional guarantees. Recognizing this, the Court and thoughtful writers on the subject have explored several approaches in their attempts to set out workable doctrines as decisional rules for determining the permissible areas of restraint on First Amendment rights. The development of these approaches is taken up in the following section.

DOCTRINES ADVANCED AS TESTS OF CONSTITUTIONALITY OF FIRST AMENDMENT RESTRAINTS

Probably the best known judicial test in the First Amendment area is the "clear and present danger" test formulated by Justice Holmes in *Schenck* v. *United States* in 1919. The case presented the delicate issue of the area of criticism and dissent allowable during time of war. The decision holds that the rights of speech and press are not and were not intended to be absolute rights, but must be subject to certain reasonable restraints. At the same time, Justice Holmes, for a unanimous Court, set out his controversial proposition regarding the requirements necessary to support such restraints.

SCHENCK *v.* UNITED STATES
249 U.S. 47 (1919)

Mr. Justice Holmes delivered the opinion of the Court.

This is an indictment in three counts. The first charges a conspiracy to violate the Espionage Act of June 15, 1917, ... by causing and attempting to cause insubordination, etc., in the military and naval forces of the United States, and to obstruct the recruiting and enlistment service of the United States, when the United States was at war with the German Empire, to-wit, that the defendants willfully conspired to have printed and circulated to men who had been called and accepted for military service under the Act of May 18, 1917, a document set forth and alleged to be calculated to cause such insubordination and obstruction.... The second count alleges a conspiracy to commit an offense against the United States, to-wit, to use the mails for the transmission of matter declared to be nonmailable by ... the Act of June 15, 1917, to-wit, the above mentioned document, ... The third count charges an unlawful use of the mails for the transmission of the same matter and otherwise as above. The defendants were found guilty on all the counts. They set up the First Amendment to the Constitution forbidding Congress to make any law abridging the freedom of speech, or of the press, and bringing the case here on that ground have argued some other points also of which we must dispose....

The document in question upon its first printed side recited the first section of the Thirteenth Amendment, said that the idea embodied in it was violated by the Conscription Act and that a conscript is little better than a convict. In impassioned language it intimated that conscription was despotism in its worst form and a monstrous wrong against humanity in the interest of Wall Street's chosen few. It said, "Do not submit to intimidation," but in form at least confined itself to peaceful measures such as a petition for the repeal of the act. The other and later printed side of the sheet was headed "Assert Your Rights." It stated reasons for alleging that any one violated the Constitution when he refused to recognize "your right to assert your opposition to the draft," and went on, "If you do not assert and support your rights, you are helping to deny or disparage rights which it is the solemn duty of all citizens and residents of the United States to retain." It described the arguments on the other side as coming from cunning politicians and a mercenary capitalist press, and even silent consent to the conscription law as helping to support an infamous conspiracy. It denied the power to send our citizens away to foreign shores to shoot up the people of other lands, and added that words could not express the condemnation such cold-blooded ruthlessness deserves, &c., &c., winding up, "You must do your share to maintain, support and uphold the rights of the people of this country." Of course the document would not have been sent unless it had been intended to have some effect, and we do not see what effect it could be expected to have upon persons subject to the draft except to influence them to obstruct the carrying of it out. The defendants do not deny that the jury might find against them on this point.

But it is said, suppose that that was the tendency of the circular, it is protected by the First Amendment to the Constitution. Two of the strongest expressions are said to be quoted respectively from well-known public men. It well may be that the prohibition of laws abridging the freedom of speech is not confined to previous restraints, although to prevent them may have been the main purpose, as intimated in *Patterson* v. *Colorado,* 205 U.S. 454, 462. We admit that in many places and in ordinary times the defendants saying all that was said in the circular would have been within their constitutional rights. But the character of every act depends upon the circumstances in which it is done. *Aikens* v. *Wisconsin,* 195 U.S. 194,

205, 206. The most stringent protection of free speech would not protect a man in falsely shouting fire in a theatre and causing a panic. It does not even protect a man from an injunction against uttering words that may have all the effect of force. *Gompers v. Bucks Stove & Range Co.,* 221 U.S. 418, 439. The question in every case is whether the words used are used in such circumstances and are of such a nature as to create a clear and present danger that they will bring about the substantive evils that Congress has a right to prevent. It is a question of proximity and degree. When a nation is at war many things that might be said in time of peace are such a hindrance to its effort that their utterance will not be endured so long as men fight and that no Court could regard them as protected by any constitutional right. It seems to be admitted that if an actual obstruction of the recruiting service were proved, liability for words that produced that effect might be enforced. The Statute of 1917, in Section 4, punishes conspiracies to obstruct as well as actual obstruction. If the act (speaking, or circulating a paper), its tendency and the intent with which it is done, are the same, we perceive no ground for saying that success alone warrants making the act a crime. . . .

Judgments affirmed.

Nine months after the *Schenck* case the Court decided *Abrams* v. *United States,* 250 U.S. 616 (1919). (For an excellent treatment of this case see Chafee, *Free Speech in the United States,* pp. 108–140.) In August 1918, while the United States was still at war with Germany, American troops were ordered to Vladivostok as a move to hinder the success of the Russian Revolution. Abrams and others began meeting in their "third-floor back" in New York's East Side and decided to protest against the attack on the Russian Revolution, with which they strongly sympathized. They printed several thousand leaflets and distributed them. There were general exhortations to munitions workers to strike in order to prevent American interference in the Revolution. There was no evidence that any of the leaflets reached any munitions workers or that anyone was led to stop war work. The five defendants were convicted and sentenced to twenty years imprisonment. The United States Supreme Court affirmed the convictions. The majority found that the defendants had intended to "urge, incite, and advocate" curtailment of production necessary to the war with Germany and were thus guilty of violation of the Sedition Act of 1918. Justice Holmes, with Justice Brandeis concurring, dissented. His opinion stated in part:

I never have seen any reason to doubt that the questions of law that alone were before this Court in the cases of *Schenck, Frohwerk* and *Debs,* . . . were rightly decided. I do not doubt for a moment that by the same reasoning that would justify punishing persuasion to murder, the United States constitutionally may punish speech that produces or is intended to produce a clear and imminent danger that it will bring about forthwith certain substantive evils that the United States constitutionally may seek to prevent. The power undoubtedly is greater in time of war than in time of peace because war opens dangers that do not exist at other times.

But as against dangers peculiar to war, as against others, the principle of the right to free speech is always the same. It is only the present danger of immediate evil or an intent to bring it about that warrants Congress in setting a limit to the expression of opinion where private rights are not concerned. Congress certainly cannot forbid all effort to change the mind of the country. Now nobody can suppose that the surreptitious publishing of a silly leaflet by an unkown man, without more, would present any immediate danger that its opinions would hinder the success of the government arms or have any appreciable tendency to do so. Publishing those opinions for the very purpose of obstructing, however, might indicate a greater danger and at any rate would have the quality of an attempt. So I assume that the second leaflet if published for the purposes alleged in the fourth count might be punishable. But it seems pretty clear to me that nothing less than that would bring these papers within the scope of this law. . . .

I do not see how anyone can find the intent required by the statute in any of the defendants' words. The second leaflet is the only one that affords even a foundation for the charge, and there, without invoking the hatred of German militarism expressed in the former one, it is evident from the beginning to the end that the only object of the paper is to help Russia and stop American intervention there against the popular government—not to impede the United States in the war that it was carrying on. To say that two phrases taken literally might import a suggestion of conduct that would have interference with the war as an indirect and probably undesired effect seems to me by no means enough to show an attempt to produce that effect. . . .

Persecution for the expression of opinions seems to me perfectly logical. If you have no doubt of your premises or your power and want a certain result with all your heart you naturally express your wishes in law and sweep away all opposition. To allow opposition by speech seems to indicate that you think the speech impotent, as when a man says that he has squared the circle, or that you do not care wholeheartedly for the result, or that you doubt either your power or your premises. But when men have realized that time has upset many fighting faiths, they may come to believe even more than they believe the very foundation of their own conduct that the ultimate good desired is better reached by free trade in ideas—that the best test of truth is the power of the thought to get itself accepted in the competition of the market, and that truth is the only ground upon which their wishes safely can be carried out. That at any rate is the theory of our Constitution. It is an experiment, as all life is an experiment. Every year if not every day we have to wager our salvation upon some prophecy based upon imperfect knowledge. While that experiment is part of our system I think that we should be eternally vigilant against attempts to check the expression of opinions that we loathe and believe to be fraught with death, unless they so imminently threaten immediate interference with the lawful and pressing purposes of the law that an immediate check is required to save the country. I wholly disagree with the argument of the Government that the First Amendment left the common law as to seditious libel in force. I had conceived that the United States through many years had shown its repentance for the Sedition Act of 1798, by repaying fines that it imposed. Only the emergency that makes it immediately dangerous to leave the correction of evil counsels to time warrants making any exception to the sweeping command, "Congress shall make no law . . . abridging the freedom of speech." Of course I am speaking only of expressions of opinion and exhortations, which were all that were uttered here, but I regret that I cannot put into more impressive words my belief that in their conviction upon this indictment the defendants were deprived of their rights under the Constitution of the United States.

It seems to be a reasonable inference from Justice Holmes' pronouncements in the two preceding cases that the Court itself would have the final word on whether a given speech or publication presented the requisite "clear and present danger"—at least where the issue was appropriately raised. In

Gitlow v. *New York,* 268 U.S. 652 (1925), however, the majority gave the doctrine a different cast.

GITLOW *v.* NEW YORK
268 U.S. 652 (1925)

[Benjamin Gitlow was convicted in the Supreme Court of New York of the statutory crime of criminal anarchy, in that he and others published and distributed various papers advocating the revolutionary overthrow of the government. He was a member of the Left Wing section of the Socialist Party and participated in the publication and circulation of a Left Wing Manifesto in the official organ entitled "The Revolutionary Age." Several thousand copies of the paper were distributed by mail and by direct sale. The manifesto called for a "Communist revolution" and mobilizing the "power of the proletariat in action," through mass industrial revolts developing into mass political strikes and "revolutionary mass action" for the purpose of conquering and destroying the parliamentary state and establishing in its place the "system of Communist Socialism."]

Justice Sanford delivered the opinion of the Court....

By enacting the present statute the state has determined, through its legislative body, that utterances advocating the overthrow of organized government by force, violence, and unlawful means, are so inimical to the general welfare, and involve such danger of substantive evil, that they may be penalized in the exercise of its police power. That determination must be given great weight.... That utterances inciting to the overthrow of organized government by unlawful means present a sufficient danger of substantive evil to bring their punishment within the range of legislative discretion is clear. Such utterances, by their very nature, involve danger to the public peace and to the security of the state. They threaten breaches of the peace and ultimate revolution. And the immediate danger is none the less real and substantial because the effect of a given utterance cannot be accurately foreseen....

We cannot hold that the present statute is an arbitrary or unreasonable exercise of the police power of the state, unwarrantably infringing the freedom of speech or press; and we must and do sustain its constitutionality.

This being so it may be applied to every utterance—not too trivial to be beneath the notice of the law—which is of such a character and used with such intent and purpose as to bring it within the prohibition of the statute.... In other words, when the legislative body has determined generally, in the constitutional exercise of its discretion, that utterances of a certain kind involve such danger of substantive evil that they may be punished, the question whether any specific utterance coming within the prohibited class is likely, in and of itself, to bring about the substantive evil, is not open to consideration. It is sufficient that the statute itself be constitutional, and that the use of the language comes within its prohibition.

It is clear that the question in such cases is entirely different from that involved in those cases where the statute merely prohibits certain acts involving the danger of substantive evil, without any reference to language itself, and it is sought to apply its provisions to language used by the defendant for the purpose of bringing about the prohibited results.... And the general statement in the *Schenck* case that the "question in every case is whether the words are used in such circumstances and are of such a nature as to create a clear and present danger that they will bring about the substantive evils,"—upon which great reliance is placed in the defendant's argument,—was manifestly intended, as shown by the context, to apply only in cases of this class, and has no application to those like the present, where the legislative body itself has previously determined the danger of substantive evil arising from utterances of a specified character. . . .

Justice Holmes, joined by Justice Brandeis, dissenting. . . .

If I am right, then I think that the criterion sanctioned by the full court in *Schenck* v. *United States* . . . applies: "The question in every case is whether the words used are used in such circumstances and are of such a nature as to create a clear and present danger that they will bring about the substantive evils that [the state] has a right to prevent." It is true that in my opinion this criterion was departed from in *Abrams* v. *United States*, . . . but the convictions that I expressed in that case are too deep for it to be possible for me as yet to believe that it and *Schaefer* v. *United States* . . . have settled the law. If what I think the correct test is applied, it is manifest that there was no present danger of an attempt to over-throw the government by force on the part of the admittedly small minority who shared the defendant's views. It is said that this Manifesto was more than a theory, that it was an incitement. Every idea is an incitement. It offers itself for belief, and, if believed, it is acted on unless some other belief outweighs it, or some failure of energy stifles the movement at its birth. The only difference between the expression of an opinion and an incitement in the narrower sense is the speaker's enthusiasm for the result. Eloquence may set fire to reason. But whatever may be thought of the redundant discourse before us, it had no chance of starting a present conflagration. If, in the long run, the beliefs expressed in proletarian dictatorship are destined to be accepted by the dominant forces of the community, the only meaning of free speech is that they should be given their chance and have their way.

If the publication of this document had been laid as an attempt to induce an uprising against government at once, and not at some indefinite time in the future, it would have presented a different question. The object would have been one with which the law might deal, subject to the doubt whether there was any danger that the publication could produce any result; or, in other words, whether it was not futile and too remote from possible consequences. But the indictment alleges the publication and nothing more.

Since Justice Holmes had formulated the "clear and present danger" statement and had written the opinion for a unanimous Court when it first appeared in the official reports, and since Justice Sanford was not even on the Court when the *Schenck* case was decided, Justice Sanford's attempt to explain the appropriate application of the doctrine might seem to indicate considerable temerity, if not outright effrontery. The majority in *Abrams* had disagreed with Justice Holmes, but no mention was made by them of the clear and present danger test.

It appears that the majority in *Gitlow* employed the normal test of reason-ableness coupled with the presumption of validity accorded legislative deter-minations. Speech was to be accorded no different treatment than any other area subject to legislative restraint, and the statutory finding of clear and present danger was to be conclusive upon the courts. It seems equally clear that the Holmes test was either purposely designed or, at the very least, used as a judicial tool for according special protection to the rights of ex-pression against overzealous application of restraints. It did not purport to set up an absolute freedom to speak and publish, but as Justice Holmes applied the phrase it was a useful mechanism for broadening the permissible area of speech and press and for allowing the courts to examine more critically than before the restraints on those rights. Justice Black's gloss on the doctrine affords the maximum scope. In his opinion for the Court in *Bridges* v. *California,* 314 U.S. 252 (1941), he stated, "What finally emerges from the 'clear and present danger' cases is a working principle that the substantive evil must be extremely serious and the degree of imminence extremely high before utterances can be punished." On the other hand, Justice Frankfurter minimized the utility of the phrase. In his concurring opinion in *Pennekamp* v. *Florida,* 328 U.S. 331 (1946), he stated:

"Clear and present danger" was never used by Mr. Justice Holmes to express a technical legal doctrine or to convey a formula for adjudicating cases. It was a literary phrase not to be distorted by being taken from its context. In its setting it served to indicate the importance of freedom of speech to a free society but also to emphasize that its exercise must be compatible with the preservation of other freedoms essential to a democracy and guaranteed by our Constitution. When those other attributes of a democracy are threatened by speech, the Constitution does not deny power to the states to curb it.

The years since *Schenck* and *Gitlow* have seen a variety of different, even tortured, applications of the clear and present danger doctrine. [See, for example, the opinions in *Dennis* v. *United States,* 341 U.S. 494 (1951).] It has been subjected to criticism as well as praise, and to avoid this collateral controversy the Court today seems to feel that it can handle First Amendment cases more easily by simply omitting reference to the doctrine altogether. The one exception in recent years is *Wood* v. *Georgia,* 370 U.S. 375 (1962), in which the test was applied to invalidate a conviction for contempt of court based upon a sheriff's criticism of certain judges which allegedly interfered with a grand jury proceeding. Two justices dissented, but all justices accepted the application of the test in the case.

While the customary view has been that the clear and present danger doctrine had as its primary function the *broadening* of the permissible area of First Amendment freedoms, there have been some who have argued that to use such a test is to *restrict* First Amendment rights and therefore to violate the Constitution. The foremost exponent of this view has been Alexander Meiklejohn.

In his book *Free Speech and Its Relation to Self-Government,* Professor Meiklejohn argued that the protection accorded freedom of speech by the First Amendment was absolute, unqualified, and admits of no exceptions. But he made an interesting distinction between "public" speech (on matters concerning government, public policy, and the welfare of the nation) and "private" speech (on all other nonpublic matters). Public speech comes under the absolute protection of the First Amendment, while private speech is protected by the Fifth Amendment's protection accorded the "liberty" of the people, and thus such speech can be restricted if the restrictions meet the test of due process of law. He argued that the "clear and present danger" test, while better than the *Gitlow* approach, would still be an improper restraint on freedom of speech if employed in a case involving *public* discussion rather than speech concerning *private* matters. In 1962, in a public interview with Professor Edmond Cahn, Justice Black indicated an even stronger position in favor of freedom of speech than did Professor Meiklejohn. Some questions and Justice Black's answers follow:[2]

Suppose we start with one of the key sentences in your James Madison Lecture where you said, "It is my belief that there *are* 'absolutes' in our Bill of Rights, and that they were put there on purpose by men who knew what words meant and meant their prohibitions to be 'absolutes.' " Will you please explain your reasons for this.

JUSTICE BLACK: My first reason is that I believe the words do mean what they say. I have no reason to challenge the intelligence, integrity or honesty of the men who wrote the First Amendment. . . .

I learned a long time ago that there are affirmative and negative words. The beginning of the First Amendment is that "Congress shall make no law." I understand that it is rather old-fashioned and shows a slight naivete to say that "no law" means no law. It is one of the most amazing things about the ingeniousness of the times that strong arguments are made, which *almost* convince me, that it is very foolish of me to think "no law" means no law. But what it *says* is "Congress shall make no law respecting an establishment of religion," and so on.

I have to be honest about it. I confess not only that I think the Amendment means what it says but also that I may be slightly influenced by the fact that I do not think Congress *should* make any law with respect to these subjects. . . .

CAHN: Some of your colleagues would say that it is better to interpret the Bill of Rights so as to permit Congress to take what it considers reasonable steps to preserve the security of the nation even at some sacrifice of freedom of speech and association. Otherwise what will happen to the nation and the Bill of Rights as well? What is your view of this?

JUSTICE BLACK: . . . Of course, I want this country to do what will preserve it. I want it to be preserved as the kind of Government it was intended to be. I would not desire to live at any place where my thoughts were under the suspicion of government and where my words could be censored by government, and where worship, whatever it was or wasn't, had to be determined by an officer of the government. That is not the kind of government I want preserved.

I agree with those who wrote our Constitution, that too much power in the hands of officials is a dangerous thing. What was government created for except to serve the people? Why was a Constitution written for the first time in this country except to limit the power of government and those who were selected to exercise it at the moment?

My answer to the statement that this Government should preserve itself is yes. The method I would adopt is different, however, from that of some other people. I think it can be preserved only by leaving people with the utmost freedom to think and to hope and to talk and to dream if they want to dream. I do not think this Government must look to force, stifling the minds and aspirations of the people. Yes, I believe in self-preservation, but I would preserve it as the founders said, by leaving people free. I think here, as in another time, it cannot live half slave and half free. . . .

CAHN: Do you make an exception in freedom of speech and press for the law of defamation? That is, are you willing to allow people to sue for damages when they are subjected to libel or slander?

[2] "Justice Black and First Amendment 'Absolutes': A Public Interview," 37 *N.Y.U. L. Rev.* 549 (1962). Reprinted by permission of the *New York University Law Review* and Justice Black.

JUSTICE BLACK: My view of the First Amendment, as originally ratified, is that it said Congress should pass none of these kinds of laws. As written at that time, the Amendment applied only to Congress. I have no doubt myself that the provision, as written and adopted, intended that there should be no libel or defamation law in the United States under the United States Government, just absolutely none so far as I am concerned. . . .

My belief is that the First Amendment was made applicable to the states by the Fourteenth. I do not hesitate, so far as my own view is concerned, as to what should be and what I hope will sometime be the constitutional doctrine that just as it was not intended to authorize damage suits for mere words as distinguished from conduct as far as the Federal Government is concerned, the same rule should apply to the states. . . .

I believe with Jefferson that it is time enough for government to step in to regulate people when they *do* something, not when they *say* something, and I do not believe myself that there is *any* halfway ground if they enforce the protections of the First Amendment. . . .

CAHN: Is there any kind of obscene material, whether defined as hardcore pornography or otherwise, the distribution and sale of which can be constitutionally restricted in any manner whatever, in your opinion?

JUSTICE BLACK: I will say it can in this country, because the courts have held that it can.

CAHN: Yes, but you won't get off so easily. I want to know what you think.

JUSTICE BLACK: My view is, without deviation, without exception, without any ifs, buts, or whereases, that freedom of speech means that you shall not do something to people either for the views they have or the views they express or the words they speak or write.

There is strong argument for the position taken by a man whom I admire very greatly, Dr. Meiklejohn, that the First Amendment really was intended to protect *political* speech, and I do think that was the basic purpose; that plus the fact that they wanted to protect *religious* speech. Those were the two main things they had in mind.

It is the law that there can be an arrest made for obscenity. It was the law in Rome that they could arrest people for obscenity after Augustus became Caesar. Tacitus says that then it became obscene to criticize the Emperor. It is not any trouble to establish a classification so that whatever it is that you do not want said is within that classification. So far as I am concerned, I do not believe there is any halfway ground for protecting freedom of speech and press. If you say it is half free, you can rest assured that it will not remain as much as half free. Madison explained that in his great Remonstrance when he said in effect, "If you make laws to force people to speak the words of Christianity, it won't be long until the same power will narrow the sole religion to the most powerful sect in it." I realize that there are dangers in freedom of speech, but I do not believe there are any halfway marks.

CAHN: Do you subscribe to the idea involved in the clear and present danger rule?

JUSTICE BLACK: I do not.

The "abolutist" position on First Amendment rights has never gained the acceptance of a majority on the Court, but it is a recurring theme in many of the dissenting opinions of Justice Black, who was frequently joined by Chief Justice Warren and Justice Douglas.

Another approach to the judicial handling of restrictions on freedom of expression is the "preferred position" doctrine. In *Thomas* v. *Collins*, 323 U.S. 516 (1945), the doctrine finds its first official expression supported by a majority of the Court. The case dealt with the validity of a labor organizer's conviction for contempt of court for violating an order that he refrain from addressing a meeting until he first registered and obtained an organizer's card as required by Texas law. In holding the requirement invalid, and thus the conviction as well, Justice Rutledge, speaking for the majority, stated:

The case confronts us again with the duty our system places on this Court to say where the individual's freedom ends and the State's power begins. Choice on that border, now as always delicate, is perhaps more so where the usual presumption supporting legislation is balanced by the preferred place given in our scheme to the great, the indispensable democratic freedoms secured by the First Amendment. That priority gives these liberties a sanctity and a sanction not permitting dubious intrusions. And it is the character of the right, not of the limitation, which determines what standard governs the choice.

The "preferred position" doctrine was by no means first stated in *Thomas* v. *Collins*, since variations on this theme were presented at least as early as 1788 in letters of Thomas Paine and Thomas Jefferson. [Edmond Cahn gives an interesting historical analysis in "The Firstness of the First Amendment," 65 *Yale L. J.* 464 (1956).] But this case is the first in which a majority of the Court acquiesced in its use. It seems to have made its first appearance in the judicial opinions in Justice Stone's now famous "footnote 4" in his opinion for the Court in *United States* v. *Carolene Products Company*, 304 U.S. 144, 152, n. 4 (1938). In it he stated:

There may be narrower scope for operation of the presumption of constitutionality when legislation appears on its face to be within a specific prohibition of the Constitution, such as those of the first ten Amendments, which are deemed equally specific when held to be embraced within the Fourteenth. . . .

It is unnecessary to consider now whether legislation which restricts those political processes which can ordinarily be expected to bring about repeal of undesirable legislation, is to be subjected to more exacting judicial scrutiny under the general prohibitions of the Fourteenth Amendment than are most other types of legislation.

In effect, the theory of this doctrine is that the presumption of validity of legislation under attack is reversed when the questioned legislation affects adversely First Amendment freedom of expression. Thus, while formerly the Court took the view that state or federal laws were constitutional until proved otherwise, the "preferred position" concept would shift the burden of proof to the government to show that the attempted restriction was not unconstitutional. By the late 1940s, however, the Court was wavering on the use of this concept, and in 1949 Justice Frankfurter frankly expressed his distrust of its use. The occasion was the Court's consideration of a Trenton, New Jersey, sound truck ordinance in *Kovacs* v. *Cooper*, 336 U.S. 77 (1949). In the course of his opinion concurring with the majority in holding the ordinance constitutional, Justice Frankfurter took issue with Justice Reed's acceptance of the "preferred position" concept. He stated:

My brother Reed speaks of "The preferred position of freedom of speech," though, to be sure, he finds that the Trenton ordinance does not disregard it. This is a phrase that has uncritically crept into some recent opinions of this Court. I deem it a mischievous phrase, if it carries the thought, which it may subtly imply, that any law touching communication is infected with presumptive invalidity. It is not the first time in the history of constitutional adjudication that such a doctrinaire attitude has disregarded the admonition most to be observed in exercising the Court's reviewing power over legislation, "that it is a *constitution* we are expounding," *McCulloch* v. *Maryland*. . . . I say the phrase is mischievous because it radiates a constitutional doctrine without avowing it. . . .

Behind the notion sought to be expressed by the formula as to "the preferred position of freedom of speech" lies a relevant consideration in determining whether an enactment relating to the liberties protected by the Due Process Clause of the Fourteenth Amendment is violative of it. In law also, doctrine is illuminated by history. The ideas now governing the constitutional protection of freedom of speech derive essentially from the opinions of Mr. Justice Holmes.

The philosophy of his opinions on that subject arose from a deep awareness of the extent to which sociological conclusions are conditioned by time and circumstance. Because of this awareness Mr. Justice Holmes seldom felt justified in opposing his own opinion to economic views which the legislature embodied in law. But since he also realized that the progress of civilization is to a considerable extent the displacement of error which once held sway as official truth by beliefs which in turn have yielded to other beliefs, for him the right to search for truth was of a different order than some transient economic dogma. And without freedom of expression, thought becomes checked and atrophied. Therefore, in considering what interests are so fundamental as to be enshrined in the Due Process Clause, those liberties of the individual which history has attested as the indispensable conditions of an open as against a closed society come to this Court with a momentum for respect lacking when appeal is made to liberties which derive merely from shifting economic arrangements. Accordingly, Mr. Justice Holmes was far more ready to find legislative invasion where free inquiry was involved than in the debatable area of economics. See my Mr. Justice Holmes and the Supreme Court, 58 et seq.

The objection of summarizing this line of thought by the phrase "the preferred position of freedom of speech" is that it expresses a complicated process of constitutional adjudication by a deceptive formula. And it was Mr. Justice Holmes who admonished us that "To rest upon a formula is a slumber that, prolonged, means death." Collected Legal Papers, 306. Such a formula makes for mechanical jurisprudence . . .

A careful reading of Justice Frankfurter's opinion might lead to the conclusion that he accepts the idea of a gradation of rights, with freedom of expression on public matters as foremost, but he disapproves of a shorthand "doctrine" to express the differentiation. [For further reading of the "preferred position" concept, as well as a detailed analysis of Justice Frankfurter's position, see Robert B. McKay, "The Preference for Freedom," 34 *N.Y.U. L. Rev.* 1182 (1959).]

More recently the Court has tended to stress a "balancing" test, although some members strongly object to its use, preferring instead something closer to the absolute position. It seems that the first use of the "balancing" test by the Court is to be found in Chief Justice Vinson's opinion for the majority in *American Communications Ass'n, CIO* v. *Douds*, 339 U.S. 382 (1950), in which the Court upheld the non-Communist affidavit provision of the Labor Management Relations Act of 1947. In the course of his opinion he stated:

So far as the *Schenck* case itself is concerned, imminent danger of any substantive evil that Congress may prevent justifies the restriction of speech. . . . But in suggesting that the substantive evil must be serious and substantial, it was never the intention of this Court to lay down an absolutist test measured in terms of danger to the Nation. When the effect of a statute or ordinance upon the exercise of First Amendment freedoms is relatively small and the public interest to be protected is substantial, it is obvious that a rigid test requiring a showing of imminent danger to the security of the Nation is an absurdity. . . .

When particular conduct is regulated in the interest of public order, and the regulation results in an indirect, conditional, partial abridgment of speech, the duty of the courts is to determine which of these two conflicting interests demands the greater protection under the particular circumstances presented. The high place in which the right to speak, think, and assemble as you will was held by the Framers of the Bill of Rights and is held today by those who value liberty both as a means and an end indicates the solicitude with which we must view any assertion of personal freedoms. . . .

On the other hand, legitimate attempts to protect the public, not from the remote possible effects of noxious ideologies, but from present excesses of direct, active conduct are not presumptively bad because they interfere with and, in some of its manifestations, restrain the exercise of First Amendment rights. . . . In essence, the problem is one of weighing the probable effects of the statute upon the free exercise of the right of speech and assembly against the congressional determination that political strikes are evils of conduct which cause substantial harm to interstate commerce and that Communists and others identified by Section 9(h) pose continuing threats to the public interest when in positions of union leadership. We must, therefore, undertake the "delicate and difficult task . . . to weigh the circumstances and to appraise the substantiality of the reason advanced in support of the regulation of the free enjoyment of the rights." *Schneider* v. *Irvington,* 308 U.S. 147, 161.

Justices Frankfurter, Harlan, and Clark were leading supporters of the "balancing" test in the period beginning in 1950. In *Dennis* v. *United States,* 341 U.S. 494 (1951), upholding sections of the Smith Act of 1940, Justice Frankfurter made the following statements in his concurring opinion:

The demands of free speech in a democratic society as well as the interest in national security are better served by candid and informed weighing of the competing interests, within the confines of the judicial process, than by announcing dogmas too inflexible for the non-Euclidian problems to be solved.

But how are competing interests to be assessed? Since they are not subject to quantitative ascertainment, the issue necessarily resolves itself into asking, who is to make the adjustment?—who is to balance the relevant factors and ascertain which interest is in the circumstances to prevail? Full responsibility for the choice cannot be given to the courts. Courts are not representative bodies. They are not designed to be a good reflex of a democratic society. Their judgment is best informed, and therefore most dependable, within narrow limits. Their essential quality is detachment, founded on independence. History teaches that the independence of the judiciary is jeopardized when courts become embroiled in the passions of the day and assume primary responsibility in choosing between competing political, economic and social pressures.

Primary responsibility for adjusting the interests which compete in the situation before us of necessity belongs to the Congress. The nature of the power to be exercised by this Court has been delineated in decisions not charged with the emotional appeal of situations such as that now before us. We are to set aside the judgment of those whose duty it is to legislate only if there is no reasonable basis for it. . . .

... Free-speech cases are not an exception to the principle that we are not legislators, that direct policy-making is not our province. How best to reconcile competing interests is the business of legislatures, and the balance they strike is a judgment not to be displaced by ours, but to be respected unless outside the pale of fair judgment. . . .

. . . A survey of the relevant decisions indicates that the results which we have reached are on the whole those that would ensue from careful weighing of conflicting interests. The complex issues presented by regulation of speech in public places by picketing, and by legislation prohibiting advocacy of crime have been resolved by scrutiny of many factors besides the imminence and gravity of the evil threatened. The matter has been well summarized by a reflective student of the Court's work. "The truth is that the clear-and-present-danger test is an oversimplified judgment unless it takes account also of a number of other factors: the relative seriousness of the danger in comparison with the value of the occasion for speech or political activity; the availability of more moderate controls than those which the state has imposed; and perhaps the specific intent with which the speech or activity is launched. No matter how rapidly we utter the phrase 'clear and present danger,' or how closely we hyphenate the words, they are not a substitute for the weighing of values. They tend to convey a delusion of certitude when what is most certain is the complexity of the strands in the web of freedoms which the judge must disentangle." Freund, *On Understanding the Supreme Court*, 27–28.

Justice Harlan made use of the "balancing" test in his opinion for a unanimous Court in *NAACP* v. *Alabama,* 357 U.S. 449 (1958), in which the Court held invalid the order of an Alabama court requiring the disclosure of membership rolls of the Alabama affiliates of the National Association for the Advancement of Colored People. Justice Harlan's opinion pointed out that "the production order, in the respects here drawn in question, must be regarded as entailing the likelihood of a substantial restraint upon the exercise by petitioner's members of their right to freedom of association." He then stated: "We turn to the final question whether Alabama has demonstrated an interest in obtaining the disclosures it seeks from petitioner which is sufficient to justify the deterrent effect which we have concluded these disclosures may well have on the free exercise by petitioner's members of their constitutionally protected right of association." The phraseology is thus clearly indicative of the employment of a "balancing" test of constitutionality. And Justice Clark, in his dissenting opinion in *Talley* v. *California,* 362 U.S. 60 (1960), dealing with the constitutionality of a Los Angeles ordinance requiring the name and address of sponsors on any handbills distributed, said: "[B]efore passing upon the validity of the ordinance, I would weigh the interests of the public in its enforcement against the claimed right of Talley."

Justices Black and Douglas were vigorous opponents of the use of the "balancing" test in the First Amendment area. In *Barenblatt* v. *United States,* 360 U.S. 109 (1959), in which the Court upheld the conviction for contempt of Congress for refusal to answer committee questions concerning Communist Party membership, and in which Barenblatt grounded his refusal on First Amendment protection to belief and associated activity, Justice Black dissented, saying:

The First Amendment says in no equivocal language that Congress shall pass no law abridging freedom of speech, press, assembly or petition. The activities of this Committee, authorized by Congress, do precisely that, through exposure, obloquy and public scorn. . . .

(A) I do not agree that laws directly abridging First Amendment freedoms can be justified by a congressional or judicial balancing process. There arc, of course, cases suggesting that a law which primarily regulates conduct but which might also indirectly affect speech can be upheld if the effect on speech is minor in relation to the need for control of the conduct. With these cases I agree. Typical of them are *Cantwell* v. *State of Connecticut,* 310 U.S. 296, and *Schneider* v. *Irvington,* 308 U.S. 147. Both of these involved the right of a city to control its streets. . . . In so holding, we, of course, found it necessary to "weigh the circumstances." But we did not in *Schneider,* any more than in *Cantwell,* even remotely suggest that a law directly aimed at curtailing speech and political persuasion could be saved through a balancing process. . . .

To apply the Court's balancing test under such circumstances is to read the First Amendment to say "Congress shall pass no law abridging freedom of speech, press, assembly and petition, unless Congress and the Supreme Court reach the joint conclusion that on balance the interests of the Government in stifling these freedoms is greater than the interest of the people in having them exercised." This is closely akin to the notion that neither the First Amendment nor any other provision of the Bill of Rights should be enforced unless the Court believes it is *reasonable* to do so. Not only does this violate the genius of our *written* Constitution, but it runs expressly counter to the injunction to Court and Congress made by Madison when he introduced the Bill of Rights.

It can be seen that there are a variety of "doctrines," "principles," or "tests" which have been employed or suggested for determining the validity of restraints on First Amendment freedom of expression. But there is substantial disagreement among the members of the Court and among leading scholars as to the appropriate test to employ. The problem is further complicated by the fact that some of the members of the Court have stated that First Amendment cases must be categorized and different tests employed for the different categories. Justice Black indicated as much in the portion of his dissent in *Barenblatt* quoted above. Thus a street regulation which indirectly affects speech may be handled under a "balancing" test, but a straight restriction on First Amendment freedom of expression may not be. Justice Jackson, in his concurring opinion in the *Dennis* case, suggested a different division. Discussing the "clear and present danger" test, he stated:

I would save it, unmodified, for application as a "rule of reason" in the kind of case for which it was devised. When the issue is criminality of a hot-headed speech on a street corner, or circulation of a few incendiary pamphlets, or parading by some zealots behind a red flag, or refusal of a handful of school childen to salute our flag, it is not beyond the capacity of the judicial process to gather, comprehend, and weigh the necessary materials for decision whether it is a clear and present danger of substantive evil or a harmless letting off of steam. It is not a prophecy, for the danger in such cases has matured by the time of trial or it was never present. The test applies and has meaning where a conviction is sought to be based on a speech or writing which does not directly or explicitly advocate a crime but to which such tendency is sought to be attributed by construction or by implication from external circumstances. The formula in such cases favors freedoms that are vital to our society, and, even if sometimes applied too generously, the consequences cannot be grave. But its recent expansion has extended, in particular to Communists, unprecedented immunities. Unless we are to hold our Government captive in a judge-made trap, we must approach the problem of a well-organized, nationwide conspiracy, such as I have described, as realistically as our predecessors faced the trivialities that were being prosecuted until they were checked with a rule of reason. . . .

The authors of the clear and present danger test never applied it to a case like this, nor would I. If applied as it is proposed here, it means that the Communist plotting is protected during its period of incubation; its preliminary stages of organization and preparation are immune from the law; the Government can move only after imminent action is manifest, when it would, of course, be too late.

[For further treatment of the various doctrines applied to freedom of expression, see Zechariah Chafee, Jr., *Free Speech in the United States, passim;* Thomas I. Emerson, "Toward a General Theory of the First Amendment," 72 *Yale L. J.* 877 (1963); and Charles B. Nutting, "Is the First Amendment Obsolete?" 30 *Geo. Wash. L. Rev.* 167 (1961). On the "clear and present danger" test, see Chester J. Antieau, "The Rule of Clear and Present Danger —Its Origin and Application," 13 *U. Det. L. J.* 198 (1950); Chester J. Antieau, "The Rule of Clear and Present Danger: Scope of Its Applicability," 48 *Mich. L. Rev.* 811 (1950); and Robert B. McKay, "The Preference for Freedom," 34 *N.Y.U. L. Rev.* 1182 (1959). On the "absolutist" approach, see Alexander Meiklejohn, "The Balancing of Self-Preservation Against Political Freedom," 49 *Calif. L. Rev.* 4 (1961), and "The First Amendment Is an Absolute," 1961 *Sup. Ct. Rev.* 245. On the "balancing" test, see Wallace Mendelson, "On the Meaning of the First Amendment: Absolutes in the Balance," 50 *Calif. L. Rev.* 821 (1962); and Laurent B. Frantz, "The First Amendment in the Balance," 71 *Yale L. J.* 1424 (1962).]

The contrapuntal application of these doctrines in the major areas of First Amendment controversy can be most easily seen in the categorized examination of the cases. The remaining portion of this chapter will be devoted to delineating the scope of protection offered in the more important areas of governmental restraint on freedom of expression.

INTERNAL SECURITY

One of the most notorious instances of governmental repression of freedom of expression in American history was the enactment of the Sedition Act of 1798. There were a number of interesting aspects of the operation of the law. Although the verdict of history has been that it was unconstitutional, the act was never challenged in the United States Supreme Court. The act expired by its own terms in 1801, after two years of operation. And despite the furor the act aroused, only ten persons were convicted under it, although many more were indicted but never tried. One Jared Peck was indicted under the act for circulating a petition to Congress asking that the act be repealed. [For the best account of the Alien and Sedition Acts, see James Morton Smith, *Freedom's Fetters* (Ithaca: Cornell University Press, 1956).] The important portions of the act prohibited the writing, printing, or uttering "any false, scandalous and malicious writings against the government of the United States, or either house of the Congress of the United States, or the President" with intent to defame them, or to bring them into contempt or disrepute, or "to excite any unlawful combinations therein, for opposing or resisting any law of the United States. . . ." The punishment was a fine not exceeding $2,000 and imprisonment not exceeding two years.

The next important pieces of federal legislation restricting speech and press did not come until World War I, with the enactment of the Espionage Act of 1917 and the Sedition Act of 1918. As indicated earlier, these acts were upheld in *Schneck* v. *United States* and *Abrams* v. *United States,* along with four other cases decided in the period 1919–1920. The Espionage Act penalized the circulation of false statements made with intent to interfere with military success, or attempts to cause insubordination in the military and naval forces of the United States or to obstruct the recruiting and enlistment service of the United States. The Sedition Act further prohibited speeches or acts obstructing the sale of government bonds, or speaking or writing anything intended to cause contempt for the American form of government, the Constitution, the flag, or the military uniforms, or urging any curtailment of production of things necessary to the prosecution of the war with intent to hinder its prosecution, or supporting the cause of any country at war with us, or opposing the cause of the United States therein. The penalty was $10,000 fine or twenty years imprisonment or both. Nearly a thousand persons were convicted under these two acts, out of about two thousand cases prosecuted. In his *Free Speech in the United States* Professor Chafee devoted a chapter to these prosecutions. He stated:

... Almost all the convictions were for expressions of opinion about the merits and conduct of the war.

It became criminal to advocate heavier taxation instead of bond issues, to state that conscription was unconstitutional though the Supreme Court had not yet held it valid, to say that the sinking of merchant vessels was legal, to urge that a referendum should have preceded our declarations of war, to say that war was contrary to the teachings of Christ. Men have been punished for criticising the Red Cross and the Y.M.C.A., while under the Minnesota Espionage Act it has been held a crime to discourage women from knitting by the remark, "No soldier ever sees these socks." [p. 51.]

More recently the Congress enacted the Alien Registration Act of 1940, better known simply as the Smith Act. The Act contains provisions similar to those of New York's Criminal Anarchy Act of 1902, which was upheld in *Gitlow* v. *New York.* It was not until 1951, however, that the United States Supreme Court decided the issue of the constitutionality of the Smith Act. Prior to that case, *Dennis* v. *United States,* the Act had been invoked only twice. In 1941, eighteen Trotskyites were convicted under the Act, and their convictions were affirmed by the Court of Appeals. [*Dunne* v. *United States,* 138 F.2d 137 (C.A. 8th, 1943).] The Supreme Court denied certiorari. A second trial, involving alleged pro-Nazis, was dropped before completion in 1944. [*United States* v. *McWilliams,* 163 F.2d 695 (C.A. D.C., 1947).]

In 1948, eleven top members of the American Community Party were indicted for conspiracies prohibited by Section 3 of the Smith Act. The trial in the District Court in New York was a marathon proceeding, running for nine months and resulting in conviction. The convictions were affirmed by the court of appeals with an opinion by Judge Learned Hand. [*United States* v. *Dennis,* 183 F.2d 201 (C.A. 2d, 1950).] The Supreme Court granted certiorari, limiting review to the constitutional issues raised without examining such issues as the sufficiency of the evidence.

DENNIS v. UNITED STATES
341 U.S. 494 (1951)

Mr. Chief Justice Vinson announced the judgment of the Court and an opinion in which Mr. Justice Reed, Mr. Justice Burton and Mr. Justice Minton join.

Petitioners were indicted in July, 1948, for violation of the conspiracy provisions of the Smith Act, 54 Stat. 671, 18 U.S.C. (1946 ed.) Section 11.... A verdict of guilty as to all the petitioners was returned by the jury.... The Court of Appeals affirmed the convictions. 183 F. 2d 201. We granted certiorari ... limited to the following two questions: (1) Whether either Section 2 or Section 3 of the Smith Act, inherently or as construed and applied in the instant case, violates the First Amendment and other provisions of the Bill of Rights; (2) whether either Section 2 or Section 3 of the Act, inherently or as construed and applied in the instant case, violates the First and Fifth Amendments because of indefiniteness.

Sections 2 and 3 of the Smith Act ... provide as follows:

"Sec. 2.

"(a) It shall be unlawful for any person—

"(1) to knowingly or wilfully advocate, abet, advise, or teach the duty, necessity, desirability, or propriety of overthrowing or destroying any government in the United States by force or violence, or by the assassination of any officer of such government;

"(2) with intent to cause the overthrow or destruction of any government in the United States, to print, publish, edit, issue, circulate, sell, distribute, or publicly display any written or printed matter advocating, advising, or teaching the duty, necessity, desirability, or propriety of overthrowing or destroying any government in the United States by force or violence;

"(3) to organize or help to organize any society, group, or assembly of persons who teach, advocate, or encourage the overthrow or destruction of any government in the United States by force or violence; or to be or become a member of, or affiliate with, any such society, group, or assembly of persons, knowing the purpose thereof....

"Sec. 3. It shall be unlawful for any person to attempt to commit, or to conspire to commit, any of the acts prohibited by the provisions of ... this title."

The indictment charged the petitioners with wilfully and knowingly conspiring (1) to organize as the Communist Party of the United States of America a society, group and assembly of persons who teach and advocate the overthrow and destruction of the Government of the United States by force and violence, and (2) knowingly and wilfully to advocate and teach the duty and necessity of overthrowing and destroying the Government of the United States by force and violence. The indictment further alleged that Section 2 of the Smith Act proscribes these acts and that any conspiracy to take such action is a violation of Section 3 of the Act....

I

It will be helpful in clarifying the issues to treat next the contention that the trial judge improperly interpreted the statute by charging that the statute required an unlawful intent before the jury could convict. More specifically, he charged that the jury could not find the petitioners guilty under the indictment unless they found that petitioners had the intent "to overthrow ... the Government of the United States by force and violence as speedily as circumstances would permit.".

... We hold that the statute requires as an essential element of the crime proof of the intention of those who are charged with its violation to overthrow the Government by force and violence....

II

The obvious purpose of the statute is to protect existing Government, not from change by peaceable, lawful and constitutional means, but from change by violence, revolution and terrorism. That it is within the *power* of the Congress to protect the Government of the United States from armed rebellion is a proposition which requires little discussion. Whatever theoretical merit there may be to the argument that there is a "right" to rebellion against dictatorial governments is without force where the existing structure of the government provides for peaceful and orderly change. We reject any principle of government helplessness in the face of preparation for revolution, which principle, carried to its logical conclusion, must lead to anarchy. No one could conceive that it is not within the power of Congress to prohibit acts intended to overthrow the Government by force and violence. The question with which we are concerned here is not whether Congress has such *power*, but whether the *means* which it has employed conflict with the First and Fifth Amendments to the Constitution.

One of the bases for the contention that the means which Congress has employed are invalid takes the form of an attack on the face of the statute on the grounds that by its terms it prohibits academic discussion of the merits of Marxism-Leninism, that it stifles ideas and is contrary to all concepts of a free speech and a free press. Although we do not agree that the language itself has that significance, we must bear in mind that it is the duty of the federal courts to interpret federal legislation in a manner not inconsistent with the demands of the Constitution. . . .

The very language of the Smith Act negates the intepretation which petitioners would have us impose on that act. It is directed at advocacy, not discussion. Thus, the trial judge properly charged the jury that they could not convict if they found that petitioners did "no more than pursue peaceful studies and discussions or teachings and advocacy in the realm of ideas." He further charged that it was not unlawful "to conduct in an American college and university a course explaining the philosophical theories set forth in the books which have been placed in evidence." Such a charge is in strict accord with the statutory language, and illustrates the meaning to be placed on those words. Congress did not intend to eradicate the free discussion of political theories, to destroy the traditional rights of Americans to discuss and evaluate ideas without fear of governmental sanctions. Rather Congress was concerned with the very kind of activity in which the evidence showed these petitioners engaged.

III

. . . No important case involving free speech was decided by this Court prior to *Schenck* v. *United States*, 249 U.S. 47 (1919). . . . Writing for a unanimous Court, Justice Holmes stated that the "question in every case is whether the words used are used in such circumstances and are of such a nature as to create a clear and present danger that they will bring about the substantive evils that Congress has a right to prevent." . . .

. . . But . . . neither Justice Holmes nor Justice Brandeis ever envisioned that a shorthand phrase should be crystallized into a rigid rule to be applied inflexibly without regard to the circumstances of each case. Speech is not absolute, above and beyond control by the legislature when its judgment, subject to review here, is that certain kinds of speech are so undesirable as to warrant criminal sanction. Nothing is more certain in modern society than the principle that there are no absolutes, that a name, a phrase, a standard has meaning only when associated with the considerations which gave birth to the nomenclature. . . . To those who would paralyze our Government in the face of impending threat by encasing it in a semantic straitjacket we must reply that all concepts are relative.

In this case we are squarely presented with the application of the "clear and present danger" test, and must decide what that phrase imports. We first note that many of the cases in which this Court has reversed convictions by use of this or similar tests have been based on the fact that the interest which the States was attempting to protect was itself too insubstantial to warrant restriction of speech.... Overthrow of the Government by force and violence is certainly a substantial enough interest for the Government to limit speech. Indeed, this is the ultimate value of any society, for if a society cannot protect its very structure from armed internal attack, it must follow that no subordinate value can be protected. If, then, this interest may be protected, the literal problem which is presented is what has been meant by the use of the phrase "clear and present danger" of the utterances bringing about the evil within the power of Congress to punish.

Obviously, the words cannot mean that before the Government may act, it must wait until the *putsch* is about to be executed, the plans have been laid and the signal is awaited. If Government is aware that a group aiming at its overthrow is attempting to indoctrinate its members and to commit them to a course whereby they will strike when the leaders feel the circumstances permit, action by the Government is required. The argument that there is no need for Government to concern itself, for Government is strong, it possesses ample powers to put down a rebellion, it may defeat the revolution with ease needs no answer. For that is not the question. Certainly an attempt to overthrow the Government by force, even though doomed from the outset because of inadequate numbers or power of the revolutionists, is a sufficient evil for Congress to prevent. The damage which such attempts create both physically and politically to a nation makes it impossible to measure the validity in terms of the probability of success, or the immediacy of a successful attempt. In the instant case the trial judge charged the jury that they could not convict unless they found that petitioners intended to overthrow the Government "as speedily as circumstances would permit." This does not mean, and could not properly mean, that they would not strike until there was certainty of success. What was meant was that the revolutionists would strike when they thought the time was ripe. We must therefore reject the contention that success or probability of success is the criterion.

The situation with which Justices Holmes and Brandeis were concerned in *Gitlow* was a comparatively isolated event bearing little relation in their minds to any substantial threat to the safety of the community.... They were not confronted with any situation comparable to the instant one—the development of an apparatus designed and dedicated to the overthrow of the Government, in the context of world crisis after crisis.

Chief Judge Learned Hand, writing for the majority below, interpreted the phrase as follows: "In each case [courts] must ask whether the gravity of the 'evil,' discounted by its improbability, justifies such invasion of free speech as is necessary to avoid the danger." We adopt this statement of the rule. As articulated by Chief Judge Hand, it is as succinct and inclusive as any other we might devise at this time. It takes into consideration those factors which we deem relevant, and relates their significances. More we cannot expect from words.

Likewise, we are in accord with the court below, which affirmed the trial court's finding that the requisite danger existed. The mere fact that from the period 1945 to 1948 petitioner's activities did not result in an attempt to overthrow the Government by force and violence is of course no answer to the fact that there was a group that was ready to make the attempt. The formation by petitioners of such a highly organized conspiracy, with rigidly disciplined members subject to call when the leaders, these petitioners, felt that the time had come for action, coupled with the inflammable nature of world conditions, similar uprisings in other countries, and the touch-and-go nature of our relations with countries with whom petitioners were in the very least ideologically attuned, convince us that their convictions were justified on this score. And this analysis disposes of the contention that a conspiracy to advocate, as distinguished from the advocacy itself, cannot be constitutionally restrained, because it comprises only the preparation. It is the existence of the conspiracy which creates the danger. . . .

IV

[The Chief Justice then considers the contention that the trial judge should have submitted for jury determination the question of whether sufficient danger existed to apply the law rather than making this decision himself as a matter of law.]

When facts are found that establish the violation of a statute the protection against conviction afforded by the First Amendment is a matter of law. The doctrine that there must be a clear and present danger of a substantive evil that Congress has a right to prevent is a judicial rule to be applied as a matter of law by the courts. The guilt is established by proof of facts. Whether the First Amendment protects the activity which constitutes the violation of the statute must depend upon a judicial determination of the scope of the First Amendment applied to the circumstances of the case. . . .

V

There remains to be discussed the question of vagueness—whether the statute as we have interpreted it is too vague, not sufficiently advising those who would speak of the limitations upon their activity. . . .

We hold that Sections 2(a)(1), 2(a)(3) and 3 of the Smith Act, do not inherently, or as construed or applied in the instant case, violate the First Amendment and other provisions of the Bill of Rights, or the First and Fifth Amendments because of indefiniteness. Petitioners intended to overthrow the Government of the United States as speedily as the circumstances would permit. Their conspiracy to organize the Communist Party and to teach and advocate the overthrow of the Government of the United States by force and violence created a "clear and present danger" of an attempt to overthrow the Government by force and violence. They were properly and constitutionally convicted for violation of the Smith Act. The judgments of conviction are

Affirmed.

Mr. Justice Clark took no part in the consideration or decision of this case.

Mr. Justice Frankfurter, concurring in affirmance of the judgment. . . .

The language of the First Amendment is to be read not as barren words found in a dictionary but as symbols of historic experience illumined by the presuppositions of those who employed them. Not what words did Madison and Hamilton use, but what was it in their minds which they conveyed? Free speech is subject to prohibition of those abuses of expression which a civilized society may forbid. . . . Absolute rules would inevitably lead to absolute exceptions, and such exceptions would eventually corrode the rules. The demands of free speech in a democratic society as well as the interest in national security are better served by candid and informed weighing of the competing interests, within the confines of the judicial process, then by announcing dogmas too inflexible for the non-Euclidian problems to be solved. . . .

II

We have recognized and resolved conflicts between speech and competing interests in six different types of cases. . . .

I must leave to others the ungrateful task of trying to reconcile all these decisions. In some instances we have too readily permitted juries to infer deception from error, or intention from argumentative or critical statements. . . .In other instances we weighed the interest in free speech so heavily that we permitted essential conflicting values to be destroyed. . . . Viewed as a whole, however, the decisions express an attitude toward the judicial function and a standard of values which for me are decisive of the case before us.

First.—Free-speech cases are not an exception to the principle that we are not legislators, that direct policy-making is not our province. How best to reconcile competing interests is the business of legislatures, and the balance they strike is a judgment not to be displaced by ours, but to be respected unless outside the pale of fair judgment. . . .

Second.—A survey of the relevant decisions indicates that the results which we have reached are on the whole those that would ensue from careful weighing of conflicting interests. The complex issues presented by regulation of speech . . . have been resolved by scrutiny of many factors besides the imminence and gravity of the evil threatened. . . .

Third.—Not every type of speech occupies the same position on the scale of values. There is no substantial public interest in permitting certain kinds of utterances: "the lewd and obscene, the profane, the libelous, and the insulting or 'fighting' words—those which by their very utterance inflict injury or tend to incite an immediate breach of the peace." *Chaplinsky* v. *New Hampshire,* 315 U.S. 568, 572. We have frequently indicated that the interest in protecting speech depends on the circumstances of the occasion. . . .

The defendants have been convicted of conspiring to organize a party of persons who advocate the overthrow of the Government by force and violence. . . .

On any scale of values which we have hitherto recognized, speech of this sort ranks low. . . .

III

These general considerations underlie decision of the case before us.

On the one hand is the interest in security. The Communist Party was not designed by these defendants as an ordinary political party. . . . The jury found that the Party rejects the basic premise of our political system—that change is to be brought about by nonviolent constitutional process. The jury found that the Party advocates the theory that there is a duty and necessity to overthrow the Government by force and violence. . . .

. . . We may take judicial notice that the Communist doctrines which these defendants have conspired to advocate are in the ascendancy in powerful nations who cannot be acquitted of unfriendliness to the institutions of this country. We may take account of evidence brought forward at this trial and elsewhere, much of which has long been common knowledge. In sum, it would amply justify a legislature in concluding that recruitment of additional members for the Party would create a substantial danger to national security. . . .

On the other hand is the interest in free speech. The right to exert all governmental powers in aid of maintaining our institutions and resisting their physical overthrow does not include intolerance of opinions and speech that cannot do harm although opposed and perhaps alien to dominant, traditional opinion. . . .

. . . A public interest is not wanting in granting freedom to speak their minds even to those who advocate the overthrow of the Government by force. For, as the evidence in this case abundantly illustrates, coupled with such advocacy is criticism of defects in our society. Criticism is the spur to reform. . . . Suppressing advocates of overthrow inevitably will also silence critics who do not advocate overthrow but fear that their criticism may be so construed. No matter how clear we may be that the defendants now before us are preparing to overthrow our Government at the propitious moment, it is self-delusion to think that we can punish them for their advocacy without adding to the risks run by loyal citizens who honestly believe in some of the reforms these defendants advance. It is a sobering fact that in sustaining the conviction before us we can hardly escape restriction on the interchange of ideas. . . .

It is not for us to decide how we would adjust the clash of interests which this case presents were the primary responsibility for reconciling it ours. Congress has determined that the danger created by advocacy of overthrow justifies the ensuing restriction on freedom of speech. . . .

. . . [I]t is relevant to remind that in sustaining the power of Congress in a case like this nothing irrevocable is done. The democratic process at all events is not impaired or restricted. Power and responsibility remain with the people and immediately with their representation. All the Court says is that Congress was not forbidden by the Constitution to pass this enactment and a prosecution under it may be brought against a conspiracy such as the one before us. . . .

Mr. Justice Jackson, concurring.

This prosecution is the latest of never-ending, because never successful, quests for some legal formula that will secure an existing order against revolutionary radicalism. It requires us to reappraise, in the light of our own times and conditions, constitutional doctrines devised under other circumstances to strike a balance between authority and liberty. . . .

If we must decide that this Act and its application are constitutional only if we are convinced that petitioner's conduct creates a "clear and present danger" of violent overthrow, we must appraise imponderables, including international and national phenomena which baffle the best informed foreign offices and our most experienced politicians. We would have to foresee and predict the effectiveness of Communist propaganda, opportunities for infiltration, whether, and when, a time will come that they consider propitious for action, and whether and how fast our existing government will deteriorate. And we would have to speculate as to whether an approaching Communist *coup* would not be anticipated by a nationalistic fascist movement. No doctrine can be sound whose application requires us to make a prophecy of that sort in the guise of a legal decision. The judicial process simply is not adequate to a trial of such far-flung issues. The answers given would reflect our own political predilections and nothing more.

The authors of the clear and present danger test never applied it to a case like this, nor would I. If applied as it is proposed here, it means that Communist plotting is protected during its period of incubation; its preliminary stages of organization and preparation are immune from the law; the Government can move only after imminent action is manifest, when it would, of course, be too late. . . .

There is lamentation in the dissents about the injustice of conviction in the absence of some overt act. Of course, there has been no general uprising against the Government, but the record is replete with acts to carry out the conspiracy alleged, acts such as always are held sufficient to consummate the crime where the statute requires an overt act. . . .

I do not suggest that Congress could punish conspiracy to advocate something, the doing of which it may not punish. Advocacy or exposition of the doctrine of communal property ownership, or any political philosophy unassociated with advocacy of its imposition by force or seizure of government by unlawful means could not be reached through conspiracy prosecution. But it is not forbidden to put down force or violence, it is not forbidden to punish its teaching or advocacy, and the end being punishable, there is no doubt of the power to punish conspiracy for the purpose. . . .

The law of conspiracy has been the chief means at the Government's disposal to deal with the growing problems created by such organizations. I happen to think it is an awkward and inept remedy, but I find no constitutional authority for taking this weapon from the Government. There is no constitutional right to "gang up" on the Government.

While I think there was power in Congress to enact this statute and that, as applied in this case, it cannot be held unconstitutional, I add that I have little faith in the long-range effectiveness of this conviction to stop the rise of the Communist movement. . . . No decision by this Court can forestall revolution whenever the existing government fails to command the respect and loyalty of the people and sufficient distress and discontent is allowed to grow up among the masses. . . .

Mr. Justice Black, dissenting. . . .

At the outset I want to emphasize what the crime involved in this case is, and what it is not. These petitioners were not charged with an attempt to overthrow the Government. They were not charged with overt acts of any kind designed to overthrow the Government. They were not even charged with saying anything or writing anything designed to overthrow the Government. The charge was that they agreed to assemble and to talk and publish certain ideas at a later date: The indictment is that they conspired to organize the Communist Party and to use speech or newspapers and other publications in the future to teach and advocate the forcible overthrow of the Government. No matter how it is worded, this is a virulent form of prior censorship of speech and press, which I believe the First Amendment forbids. I would hold Section 3 of the Smith Act authorizing this prior restraint unconstitutional on its face and as applied.

. . . The opinions for affirmance indicate that the chief reason for jettisoning the [clear and present danger] rule is the expressed fear that advocacy of Communist doctrine endangers the safety of the Republic. Undoubtedly, a governmental policy of unfettered communication of ideas does entail dangers. To the Founders of this Nation, however, the benefits derived from free expression were worth the risk. . . . I have always believed that the First Amendment is the keystone of our Government, that the freedoms it guarantees provide the best insurance against destruction of all freedom. At least as to speech in the realm of public matters, I believe that the "clear and present danger" test does not "mark the furthermost constitutional boundaries of protected expression" but does "no more than recognize a minimum compulsion of the Bill of Rights." *Bridges* v. *California*, 314 U.S. 252, 263.

So long as this Court exercises the power of judicial review of legislation, I cannot agree that the First Amendment permits us to sustain laws suppressing freedom of speech and press on the basis of Congress' or our own notions of mere "reasonableness." Such a doctrine waters down the First Amendment so that it amounts to little more than an admonition to Congress. The Amendment as so construed is not likely to protect any but those "safe" or orthodox views which rarely need its protection. . . .

Public opinion being what it now is, few will protest the conviction of these Communist petitioners. There is hope, however, that in calmer times, when present pressures, passions and fears subside, this or some later Court will restore the First Amendment liberties to the high preferred place where they belong in a free society.

Mr. Justice Douglas, dissenting. . . .

The next important case to come before the Court involving the Smith Act was *Yates* v. *United States,* 354 U.S. 298 (1957). Other prosecutions of lesser Communists had taken place in the interval since *Dennis,* but the Court had not reviewed any of the convictions. In *Yates* the Court imposed no limitations upon its grant of certiorari to review the convictions of fourteen Communists under the same Smith Act sections involved in the *Dennis* case. Thus it was free to examine the whole record and consider the sufficiency of the evidence supporting the convictions. Three primary issues were presented in the case. First, the petitioners contended that the conviction for "organizing" the Community Party was barred by the three-year statute of limitations, since the Party was "organized," within the meaning of the statute, by 1945 at the latest, and the indictment was returned in 1951. Justice Harlan, for the majority, agreed with this contention. He pointed out that the statute did not define what was meant by "organize," and that, "In these circumstances we should follow the familiar rule that criminal statutes are to be strictly construed and give to 'organize' its narrow meaning, that is, that the word refers only to acts entering into the creation of a new organization, and not to acts thereafter performed in carrying on its activities, even though such acts may loosely be termed 'organizational.' "

A second issue presented by petitioners was that the instructions to the jury were fatally defective in that the trial court refused to charge that, in order to convict, the jury must find that the advocacy which the defendants conspired to promote was directed at promoting unlawful action and not mere persuasion to accept forcible overthrow as abstract doctrine. The majority agreed with this second contention also. Justice Harlan stated:

In failing to distinguish between advocacy of forcible overthrow as an abstract doctrine and advocacy of action to that end, the District Court appears to have been led astray by the holding in *Dennis* that advocacy of violent action to be taken at some future time was enough. . . . [W]e are unable to regard the District Court's charge upon this aspect of the case as adequate. The jury was never told that the Smith Act does not denounce advocacy in the sense of preaching abstractly the forcible overthrow of the Government. We think that the trial court's statement that the proscribed advocacy must include the "urging," "necessity," and "duty" of forcible overthrow, and not merely its "desirability" and "propriety," may not be regarded as a sufficient substitute for charging that the Smith Act reaches only advocacy of action for the overthrow of government by force and violence. The essential distinction is that those to whom the advocacy is addressed must be urged to *do* something, now or in the future, rather than merely to *believe* in something.

Although the holding on the first two issues already required reversal of the convictions, the Court went one step further to consider the sufficiency of the evidence against the fourteen petitioners, "to see whether there are individuals as to whom acquittal is unequivocally demanded." After putting aside all evidence relating to the "organizing" charge alone as well as that not directly connected to a charge of advocacy in the sense of a call to forcible action, Justice Harlan found the record "strikingly deficient." As to five of the defendants he found no overt acts to support the conviction other than mere membership in the Party or as officers or functionaries, and their acquittal was ordered. As to the other nine defendants, the majority found evidence indicating "action" in their holding of classes teaching illegal action as well as other participation in "underground apparatus"—which might support a finding of guilty under a proper charge to the jury. The cases of these nine, then, were remanded for new trials.

The *Yates* decision represents somewhat of a withdrawal from the broad language of Chief Justice Vinson in the *Dennis* case and, in fact, draws in question the very validity of the convictions in the earlier case. Since the decision came off on statutory construction rather than constitutional issues, the Congress might have revised the Smith Act to reach *any* advocacy of overthrow of the government by violence, thus presenting the constitutional issue squarely, but such revision has not been made. Congress did disagree with the Court's construction of the "organizing" section, however, and in 1962 amended the Act to include within the meaning of that section the continued recruitment or expansion of organizational activity.

Neither *Dennis* nor *Yates,* however, reached the question of the validity of the "membership" section of the Smith Act. The section appeared to raise even more serious questions of constitutionality than the two preceding sections, and the Government was somewhat slow to proceed under the "membership" charge alone. In *Scales* v. *United States,* 367 U.S. 203 (1961), the Court ruled on the issue for the first time.

SCALES *v.* UNITED STATES
367 U.S. 203 (1961)

Mr. Justice Harlan delivered the opinion of the Court.

Our writ issued in this case . . . to review . . . petitioner's conviction under the so-called membership clause of the Smith Act. 18 USC Section 2385. The Act, among other things, makes a felony the acquisition or holding of knowing membership in any organization which advocates the overthrow of the Government of the United States by force or violence.

The validity of this conviction is challenged on statutory, constitutional, and evidentiary grounds, and further on the basis of certain alleged trial and procedural errors. . . . For reasons given in this opinion we affirm the Court of Appeals.

I

Statutory Challenge

Petitioner contends that the indictment fails to state an offense against the United States. The claim is that Section 4(f) of the Internal Security Act of 1950, 64 Stat 987, . . . constitutes a *pro tanto* repeal of the membership clause of the Smith Act by excluding from the reach of that clause membership in any Communist organization. . . .

We turn first to the provision itself, and find that, as to petitioner's construction of it, the language is at best ambiguous if not suggestive of a contrary conclusion. Section 4(f) provides that membership or office-holding in a Communist organization shall not constitute *"per se* a violation of subsection (a) or subsection

(c) of this section or of any other criminal statute." Petitioner would most plainly be correct if the statute under which he was indicted purported to proscribe membership in Communist organizations, as such, and to punish membership *per se* in an organization engaging in proscribed advocacy....

... The natural tendency of the first sentence of subsection (f) as to the criminal provisions specifically mentioned is to provide clarification of the meaning of those provisions, that is, that an offense is not made out on proof of *mere* membership in a Communist organization....

... Although we think that the membership clause on its face goes beyond making mere Party membership a violation, in that it requires a showing both of illegal Party purposes and of a member's knowledge of such purposes, we regard the first sentence of Section 4(f) as a clear warrant for construing the clause as requiring not only knowing membership, but active and purposive membership, purposive that is as to the organization's criminal ends.... By its terms, then, subsection (f) does not effect a *pro tanto* repeal of the membership clause; at most it modifies it....

[The opinion then takes up an examination of the legislative history of the Internal Security Act of 1950, and Justice Harlan concludes that it does not bar this prosecution.]

II

Constitutional Challenge to the Membership Clause on its Face

Petitioner's constitutional attack goes both to the statute on its face and as applied ...

It will bring the constitutional issues into clearer focus to notice first the premises on which the case was submitted to the jury. The jury was instructed that in order to convict it must find that within the three-year limitations period (1) the Communist Party advocated the violent overthrow of the Government, in the sense of present "advocacy of action" to accomplish that end as soon as circumstances were propitious; and (2) petitioner was an "active" member of the Party, and not merely "a nominal, passive, inactive or purely technical" member, with knowledge of the Party's illegal advocacy and a specific intent to bring about violent overthrow "as speedily as circumstances would permit."

The constitutional attack upon the membership clause, as thus construed, is that the statute offends (1) the Fifth Amendment, in that it impermissibly imputes guilt to an individual merely on the basis of his associations and sympathies, rather than because of some concrete personal involvement in criminal conduct; and (2) the First Amendment, in that it infringes free political expression and association....

Fifth Amendment

Any thought that due process puts beyond the reach of the criminal law all individual associational relationships, unless accompanied by the commission of specific acts of criminality, is dispelled by familiar concepts of the law of conspiracy and complicity....

What must be met, then, is the argument that membership, even when accompanied by the elements of knowledge and specific intent, affords an insufficient quantum of participation in the organization's alleged criminal activity, that is, an insufficiently significant form of aid and encouragement to permit the imposition of criminal sanctions on that basis....

In an area of the criminal law which this Court has indicated more than once demands its watchful scrutiny . . . , these factors have weight and must be found to be overborne in a total constitutional assessment of the statute. We think, however, they are duly met when the statute is found to reach only "active" members having also a guilty knowledge and intent, and which therefore prevents a conviction on what otherwise might be regarded as merely an expression of sympathy with the alleged criminal enterprise, unaccompanied by any significant action in its support or any commitment to undertake such action. . . .

First Amendment

Little remains to be said concerning the claim that the statute infringes First Amendment freedoms. It was settled in *Dennis* that the advocacy with which we are here concerned is not constitutionally protected speech, and it was further established that a combination to promote such advocacy, albeit under the aegis of what purports to be a political party, is not such association as is protected by the First Amendment. We can discern no reason why membership, when it constitutes a purposeful form of complicity in a group engaging in this same forbidden advocacy, should receive any greater degree of protection from the guarantees of that Amendment.

If it is said that the mere existence of such an enactment tends to inhibit the exercise of constitutionally protected rights, in that it engenders an unhealthy fear that one may find himself unwittingly embroiled in criminal liability, the answer surely is that the statute provides that a defendant must be proven to have knowledge of the proscribed advocacy before he may be convicted. . . . The clause does not make criminal all association with an organization, which has been shown to engage in illegal advocacy. There must be clear proof that a defendant "specifically intend[s] to accomplish [the aims of the organization] by resort to violence." *Noto* v. *United States*. . . . Thus the member for whom the organization is a vehicle for the advancement of legitimate aims and policies does not fall within the ban of the statute: he lacks the requisite specific intent "to bring about the overthrow of the government as speedily as circumstances would permit." Such a person may be foolish, deluded, or perhaps merely optimistic, but he is not by this statute made a criminal.

We conclude that petitioner's constitutional challenge must be overruled.

III

Evidentiary Challenge

Only in rare instances will this Court review the general sufficiency of the evidence to support a criminal conviction, for ordinarily that is a function which properly belongs to and ends with the Court of Appeals. We do so in this case and in . . . *Noto* v. *United States* . . . , our first review of convictions under the membership clause of the Smith Act—not only to make sure that substantive constitutional standards have not been thwarted, but also to provide guidance for the future to the lower courts in an area which borders so closely upon constitutionally protected rights. . . .

[Justice Harlan here examines the testimony introduced to prove the illegal purposes and general "character of the organization of which he is charged with being a member." As to the specific acts of the defendant, Justice Harlan cited testimony and evidence showing that Scales had recruited members, sent out Communist literature, instructed and guided new members, arranged for scholarships to study at official Communist Party schools, and advised one member to "infiltrate the Civilian Defense setup" in New York.]

We conclude that this evidence sufficed to make a case for the jury on the issue of illegal Party advocacy. *Dennis* and *Yates* have definitely laid at rest any doubt but that present advocacy of *future* action for violent overthrow satisfies statutory and constitutional requirements equally with advocacy of *immediate* action to that end....Hence this record cannot be considered deficient because it contains no evidence of advocacy for immediate overthrow....

The sufficiency of the evidence as to other elements of the crime requires no exposition. Scales' "active" membership in the Party is indisputable, and that issue was properly submitted to the jury under instructions that were entirely adequate. The elements of petitioner's "knowledge" and "specific intent" ... require no further discussion of the evidence beyond that already given as to Scales' utterances and activities. Compare *Noto* v. *United States*.... They bear little resemblance to the fragmentary and equivocal utterances and conduct which were found insufficient in *Nowak* v. *United States*, 356 U.S. 660....

We hold that this prosecution does not fail for insufficiency of the proof....

The judgment of the Court of Appeals must be

Affirmed.

Mr. Justice Black, dissenting.

... My reasons for dissenting from this decision are primarily those set out by Mr. Justice Brennan—that Section 4(f) of the Subversive Activities Control Act bars prosecutions under the membership clause of the Smith Act—and Mr. Justice Douglas—that the Amendment absolutely forbids Congress to outlaw membership in a political party or similar association merely because one of the philosophical tenets of that group is that the existing government should be overthrown by force at some distant time in the future when circumstances may permit....

... I think it is important to point out the manner in which this case re-emphasizes the freedom-destroying nature of the "balancing test" presently in use by the Court to justify its refusal to apply specific constitutional protections of the Bill of Rights. In some of the recent cases in which it has "balanced" away the protections of the First Amendment, the Court has suggested that it was justified in the application of this "test" because no direct abridgment of First Amendment freedoms was involved, the abridgment in each of these cases being, in the Court's opinion, nothing more than "an incident of the informed exercise of a valid governmental function." A possible implication of that suggestion was that if the Court were confronted with what it would call a direct abridgment of speech, it would not apply the "balancing test" but would enforce the protections of the First Amendment according to its own terms. This case causes me to doubt that such an implication is justified. Petitioner is being sent to jail for the express reason that he has associated with people who have entertained unlawful ideas and said unlawful things, and that of course is a *direct* abridgment of his freedoms of speech and assembly—under any definition that has ever been used for that term. Nevertheless, even as to this admittedly direct abridgment, the Court relies upon its prior decisions to the effect that the Government has power to abridge speech and assembly if its interest in doing so is sufficient to outweigh the interest in protecting these First Amendment freedoms.

This, I think, demonstrates the unlimited breadth and danger of the "balancing test" as it is currently being applied by a majority of this Court. Under that "test," the question in every case in which a First Amendment right is asserted is not whether there has been an abridgment of that right, not whether the abridgment of that right was intentional on the part of the Government, and not whether there is any other way in which the Government could accomplish a lawful aim without an invasion of the constitutionally guaranteed rights of the people. It is, rather, simply whether the Government has an interest in abridging the right involved and, if so, whether that interest is of sufficient importance, in the opinion of a majority of this Court, to justify the Government's action in doing so. This doctrine, to say the very least, is capable of being used to justify almost any action Government may wish to take to suppress First Amendment freedoms.

Mr. Justice Douglas, dissenting.

When we allow petitioner to be sentenced to prison for six years for being a "member" of the Communist Party, we make a sharp break with traditional concepts of First Amendment rights and make serious Mark Twain's lighthearted comment that, "It is by the goodness of God that in our country we have those three unspeakably precious things: freedom of speech, freedom of conscience, and the prudence never to practice either of them." . . .

We legalize today guilt by association, sending a man to prison when he committed no unlawful act. Today's break with tradition is a serious one. It borrows from the totalitarian philosophy. . . .

The case is not saved by showing that petitioner was an active member. None of the activity constitutes a crime. . . .

Belief in the principle of revolution is deep in our traditions. The Declaration of Independence proclaims it. . . .

This right of revolution has been and is a part of the fabric of our institutions. . . .

Mr. Justice Brennan, with whom the Chief Justice and Mr. Justice Douglas, join, dissenting. . . .

States, of course, have long had various kinds of sedition statutes of their own. No particular problems were presented by such laws, other than those taken up in the cases above, until the enactment of the Smith Act. The issue then presented was one of national supremacy: did the federal law supersede the state laws on sedition and thereby render them unenforceable? In *Pennsylvania* v. *Nelson,* 350 U.S. 497 (1956), the Court held that in passing the Smith Act Congress intended to occupy the field, and affirmed the Pennsylvania Supreme Court's reversal of a conviction under the state statute. The Court pointed out as additional support for its decision the strong possibility of interference by the state enforcement authorities with the overall program of the federal government.

Although the cases thus far discussed point up some rather sharp differences of opinion among the justices regarding the validity of some of the major antisubversion sections of the Smith Act, the Court is unanimous in its view that *overt acts* in aid of revolution may appropriately be punished. Justices Black and Douglas stressed, however, that restrictions imposed prior to engagement in overt action unconstitutionally inhibit freedom of thought and association. At the core of the differences of opinion on these questions appears to be the divergence of attitude on whether making speeches, organizing groups, and associating for common purposes can appropriately be considered as "overt action." A minority of the Court did not think such stages could be so held, and this conclusion led them to dissent in a number of cases involving a variety of restrictions primarily directed at subversive organizations. The important right of association was the central issue in many of these cases, particularly those involving the various kinds of non-Communist oaths. [On the validity of state criminal syndicalism laws, see *Brandenburg* v. *Ohio*, 395 U.S. 444 (1969), later in this chapter.]

In the Taft-Hartley Act of 1947 Congress provided that the services of the NLRB and the protections of the Act would be denied to labor organizations whose officers failed to file affidavits with the Board that they were not Communist Party members and did not believe in overthrow of the governmnt by force. This requirement was upheld in *American Communications Ass'n., CIO* v. *Douds*, 339 U.S. 382 (1950). Chief Justice Vinson in his opinion for the Court stated:

> Government's interest here is not in preventing the dissemination of Communist doctrine or the holding of particular beliefs because it is feared that unlawful action will result therefrom if free speech is practiced. Its interest is in protecting the free flow of commerce from what Congress considers to be substantial evils of conduct that are not the products of speech at all. Section 9(h), in other words, . . . regulates harmful conduct which Congress has determined is carried on by persons who may be identified by their political affiliations and beliefs.

Justices Jackson and Frankfurter concurred in the result as to the non-membership portion but dissented as to the "belief" portion of the affidavit. Justice Black dissented on the ground that both provisions were unconstitutional. He stated that "Never before has this Court held that the Government could for any reason attaint persons for their political beliefs or affiliations. It does so today."

Many states and cities have adopted policies demanding non-Communist oaths from governmental employees. In 1948 Los Angeles adopted an ordinance requiring all employees to file an oath stating that they had neither advocated overthrow of the government by violence nor been a member of an organization which advocated such action and also to file an affidavit stating whether they were or ever had been a member of the Communist Party. The validity of the ordinance was tested in *Garner* v. *Board of Public Works*, 341 U.S. 716 (1951). Five members of the Court held that both the oath and the affidavit were valid, although Justice Clark, for the majority, said, "We assume that *scienter* is implicit in each clause of the oath." Thus innocent membership was not to be punished. Two members of the Court felt that the affidavit was valid but not the oath, since the ordinance did not by its terms clearly specify "knowing" membership as the basis for denial of employment. Justices Douglas and Black considered both requirements to be bills of attainder and ex post facto.

The following year, in *Wieman* v. *Updegraff*, 344 U.S. 183 (1952), the Court unanimously invalidated an oath requirement of Oklahoma which barred from governmental employment persons who were or had been members of proscribed organizations, irrespective of their knowledge of the purposes of such organizations. Justice Clark, for the Court, stated:

> Under the Oklahoma Act, the fact of association alone determines disloyalty and disqualification; it matters not whether association existed innocently or knowingly. To thus inhibit individual freedom of movement is to stifle the flow of democratic expression and controversy at one of its chief sources. We hold that the distinction observed between the case at bar and *Garner* . . . is decisive. Indis-

criminate classification of innocent with knowing activity must fall as an assertion of arbitrary power. The oath offends due process.

Employees have also been removed from public positions when found to belong to subversive organizations. New York's Feinberg Law, passed in 1949, provided that after an inquiry and notice and hearing the Board of Regents should prepare a list of subversive organizations. Thereafter membership in any of these organizations should constitute prima facie evidence of disqualification for employment in the public schools. The law was upheld by the Supreme Court in *Adler* v. *Board of Education of the City of New York,* 342 U.S. 485 (1952). Justice Minton, speaking for the majority, stated that persons have no right to work for the state in the school system on their own terms. If they do not choose to work for the school system upon the reasonable terms laid down by the proper authorities of New York, "they are at liberty to retain their beliefs and associations and go elsewhere."

Public employees have also been dismissed for refusal to answer questions about membership in subversive organizations, even when the alleged association took place many years earlier. A Brooklyn College professor was discharged on the ground that claiming the Fifth Amendment privilege before a Senate committee, which had questioned him concerning his political affiliations prior to 1941, was "equivalent to a resignation" under the Charter of the City of New York. In *Slochower* v. *Board of Higher Education,* 350 U.S. 551 (1956), the Court reversed the judgment, but at the same time it suggested that the city could use whatever facts it chose to make an inquiry to see whether Slochower's continued employment was "inconsistent with a real interest of the State."

New York City accepted the suggestion, and two employees who refused to answer questions concerning Communist membership were discharged. Lerner, a subway conductor, was removed as a person of "doubtful trust and reliability" for his "lack of candor," and Beilan, a public school teacher, was dismissed for "incompetency." The judgments were affirmed by the Court in *Lerner* v. *Casey,* 357 U.S. 468 (1958), and *Beilan* v. *Board of Public Education,* 357 U.S. 399 (1958), respectively. A similar result obtained in a Los Angeles County employee's dismissal for refusal to testify concerning his subversive activity before a subcommittee of the House Un-American Activities Committee in the face of a state statute requiring all public employees to give such testimony "on pain of discharge." *Nelson* v. *County of Los Angeles,* 362 U.S. 1 (1960).

The application of associational or belief tests to examinations for admission to the bar presents a specialized aspect of the same problem. In 1945, in the case of *In Re Summers,* 325 U.S. 561, the Court sustained Illinois' denial of admission to the bar of an applicant on the sole ground that as a conscientious objector to military service, he could not in good faith take the required oath to support the constitution of the state. Justice Reed, speaking for the majority of five, stressed that "the responsibility for choice as to the personnel of its bar rests with Illinois." He stated further, however, that men could not be excluded from the practice of law "or indeed from following any other calling, simply because they belong to any of our religious groups." But he did not find any such discrimination in the action of the Illinois Supreme Court. Justice Black, for the four dissenting members, objected that by its requirement Illinois had set up a test oath "designed to impose civil disabilities upon men for their beliefs rather than for unlawful conduct."

In 1957 the Court had occasion to examine, at least partially, the issue of whether Communist membership could constitutionally be made a basis for denial of admission to the bar. The case was *Schware* v. *Board of Bar Examiners*, 353 U.S. 232 (1957). Three aspects of Schware's past conduct led the New Mexico Board to conclude that "he failed to satisfy the Board of the requisite moral character." (1) From 1934 to 1937 he had used several aliases, apparently to avoid anti-Semitism; (2) he had been arrested several times, including twice for "suspicion of criminal syndicalism," although not convicted; and (3) from 1932 to 1940 he had been a member of the Communist Party, having joined at the age of 18 in his last year of high school. At the hearing he made a strong case for exemplary conduct since 1940, with three years of honorable service as a paratrooper, the operation of a business to support his family and his law school study, and the testimony of teachers and associates in support of his character. The State Supreme Court affirmed the denial of admission and stressed the previous Communist membership. The United States Supreme Court unanimously reversed, although the members split six-to-three on their reasons. Justice Black, for the majority, said: "We conclude that his past membership in the Communist Party does not justify an inference that he presently has bad moral character." Justice Frankfurter, in the concurring opinion, took a somewhat narrow view in saying: "to hold, as the [state] court did, that Communist affiliation for six to seven years up to 1940, fifteen years prior to the court's assessment of it, in and of itself made the petitioner 'a person of questionable character' is so dogmatic an inference as to be wholly unwarranted."

It does not appear that the holding in *Schware* bars the state from taking past Communist membership into account in making decisions regarding admissions to the bar, but it clearly cannot be considered as conclusively establishing bad moral character or as alone a ground for denial of admission.

As in the public employment cases, the problem of refusal to answer questions concerning Communist membership as affecting acceptability has been presented. In the first Konigsberg case, *Konigsberg* v. *State Bar of California,* 353 U.S. 252 (1957), the relevant requirement used as a basis for denial of admission to the bar was that applicants must be of good moral character and not advocate the overthrow of the government. The Court held that the denial of a license, based largely upon the applicant's refusal to answer questions concerning Communist Party membership, violated due process, since the record did not warrant finding that he failed to prove that he was of good moral character and did not advocate overthrow. At subsequent hearings before the bar committee Konigsberg again refused to answer questions relating to membership in the Communist Party, and again the committee declined to certify him. In the second Konigsberg case, *Konigsberg* v. *State Bar of California,* 366 U.S. 36 (1961), the Court held, in a five-to-four decision, that the state could properly deny the application on the ground that by refusing to answer the questions, the applicant had obstructed the committee in the performance of its required investigation into his qualifications. According to the majority, this was permissible despite the fact that the applicant's evidence of good moral character was unrebutted and he unequivocally asserted his disbelief in violent overthrow and stated that he had never knowingly been a member of an organization advocating such action. The applicant had refused, however, to answer questions dealing with Communist Party membership on the ground that they unconstitutionally impinged upon rights of free speech and association. Justice Harlan, for the Court, cited *Beilan* v. *Board of Public Education* in stating: "As regards the questioning of public employees relative to Communist Party membership it has already been held that the interest in not subjecting speech and association to the deterrence of subsequent disclosure is outweighed by the State's interest in ascertaining the fitness of the employee for the post he holds, and hence that such questioning does not infringe constitutional protections." He went on to conclude that the "State's interest in having lawyers who are devoted to the law in its broadest sense, including not only its substantive provisions, but also its procedures for orderly change, is clearly sufficient to outweigh the minimal effect upon free association occasioned by compulsory disclosure in the circumstances here presented."

A vigorous dissenting opinion was filed by Justice Black, with two justices concurring, and another by Justice Brennan. They argued that both on constitutional grounds and as a matter of a finding based on the record, the denial of license should have been reversed.

A similar result was reached in *In Re Anastaplo,* 366 U.S. 82 (1961), dealing with an Illinois decision to deny admission to the bar to an applicant who refused to answer questions about membership in the Communist Party.

The cases above indicate a somewhat ambivalent attitude on the part of the Court toward the extent to which membership in the Communist Party may be considered relevant in denying or terminating various kinds of public or quasi-public employment. One explanation for the ambivalence during the period spanned by the cases (1952–1961) is that not until 1958, in the decision in *NAACP* v. *Alabama* (discussed below), did the Court squarely recognize a constitutional right of association. Once having accorded this right First Amendment status, however, subsequent decisions demonstrate greater reluctance to uphold governmental restrictions which directly impinge on the right of association. *Scales* v. *United States,* decided in 1961, pointed to a new rule: mere membership in the Communist Party, without active furtherance of unlawful purposes, could not constitutionally be punished. The *Scales* decision came on statutory rather than constitutional grounds, but the constitutional implications were clear nonetheless.

In *Elfbrandt* v. *Russell,* 384 U.S. 11 (1966), the Court held unconstitutional an Arizona loyalty oath for state employees which subjected to discharge and prosecution for perjury any person who took the oath and "knowingly and willfully becomes or remains a member of the communist party" or any other organization having as one of its purposes the overthrow of the government of Arizona. A majority of five held the statute invalid since it did not require a showing that an employee was an active member with the specific intent of assisting in achieving the unlawful ends of a proscribed organization. Justice Douglas, for the majority, said, "This Act threatens the cherished freedom of association protected by the First Amendment." He said further:

Those who join an organization but do not share its unlawful purposes and who do not participate in its unlawful activities surely pose no threat, either as citizens or as public employees. Laws such as this which are not restricted in scope to those who join with the "specific intent" to further illegal action impose, in effect, a conclusive presumption that the member shares the unlawful aims of the organization.

The decision in *Elfbrandt* invited a new attack on New York's Feinberg Law. Several faculty members of the State University of New York brought suit in a federal district court for declaratory and injunctive relief against the New York plan, formulated partly in statutes and partly in administrative regulations. A three-judge court upheld the plan, but on direct appeal, in *Keyishian* v. *Board of Regents of New York*, 385 U.S. 589 (1967), the Supreme Court reversed, overruling *Adler* and holding the Feinberg Law to be unconstitutional.

Three sections of the New York law were challenged as being unconstitutionally vague: (1) a section requiring removal for "treasonable or seditious" utterances or acts; (2) a section barring employment of any person who "by word of mouth or writing willfully and deliberately advocates, advises or teaches the doctrine" of forceful overthrow of government; and (3) a section requiring the disqualification of an employee involved with the distribution of written material "containing or advocating, advising or teaching the doctrine" of forceful overthrow, and who himself "advocates, advises, teaches, or embraces the duty, necessity or propriety of adopting the doctrine contained therein."

A majority of five held these sections to be unconstitutionally vague, on the ground that they were "plainly susceptible to sweeping and improper application" and might "reasonably be construed to cover mere expression of belief." As to the provisions of the Feinberg Law making Communist Party membership, as such, prima facie evidence of disqualification, the majority followed *Elfbrandt* in holding that "legislation which sanctions membership unaccompanied by specific intent to further the unlawful goals of the organization or which is not active membership violates constitutional limitations."

In the course of his opinion for the majority, Justice Brennan gave an impressive statement in support of academic freedom:

> Our Nation is deeply committed to safeguarding academic freedom, which is of transcendent value to all of us and not merely to the teachers concerned. That freedom is therefore a special concern of the First Amendment, which does not tolerate laws that cast a pall of orthodoxy over the classroom. "The vigilant protection of constitutional freedoms is nowhere more vital than in the community of American schools."... The classroom is peculiarly the "marketplace of ideas." The Nation's future depends upon leaders trained through wide exposure to that robust exchange of ideas which discovers the truth "out of a multitude of tongues, [rather] than through any kind of authoritative selection."

In *United States* v. *Robel*, 389 U.S. 258 (1967), the Court held unconstitutional a section of the Subversive Activities Control Act of 1950 which makes it a crime, when a Communist-action organization is under a final order to register, "for any member of that organization to engage in any employment in any defense facility." Robel was a member of the Communist Party and a machinist in a West Coast shipyard at the time the Communist Party was ordered to register and the yard was declared a "defense facility." In affirming the dismissal of Robel's indictment, Chief Justice Warren, for the majority, stated that the statute cast too broad a net "indiscriminately trapping membership which can be constitutionally punished and membership which cannot be so proscribed. It is made irrelevant to the statute's operation that an individual may be a passive or inactive member of a designated organization, that he may be unaware of the organization's unlawful aims, or that he may disagree with those unlawful aims." Thus the section contained the "fatal defect of overbreadth."

A special problem involving the right of association concerns governmental power, by statute or order, to compel individuals to disclose their membership in various organizations or to compel organizations to disclose their membership lists. The major recent cases on these questions have held that the Constitution protects against such compulsory disclosure.

NAACP v. *Alabama,* 357 U.S. 449 (1958) involved the validity of an Alabama court order directing the disclosure of membership lists in the Alabama affiliate of the NAACP. The organization offered to produce all requested papers and information except those showing names and addresses of officers and members. The Alabama court held the NAACP in contempt and a fine of $100,000 was adjudged. The United States Supreme Court unanimously held the registration requirement invalid. Speaking for the Court, Justice Harlan stated:

> Effective advocacy of both public and private points of view, particularly controversial ones, is undeniably enhanced by group association, as this Court has more than once recognized by remarking upon the close nexus between the freedoms of speech and assembly. . . . It is beyond debate that freedom to engage in association for the advancement of beliefs and ideas is an inseparable aspect of the "liberty" assured by the Due Process Clause of the Fourteenth Amendment, which embraces freedom of speech. . . . Of course, it is immaterial whether the beliefs sought to be advanced by association pertain to political, economic, religious or cultural matters, and state action which may have the effect of curtailing the freedom to associate is subject to the closest scrutiny.

The main problem presented in the case was to distinguish the Alabama requirement from the Klan registration law of New York which the Court had held constitutional in *New York ex rel. Bryant* v. *Zimmerman,* 278 U.S. 63 (1928). On this point Justice Harland stated:

> That case involved markedly different considerations in terms of the interest of the State in obtaining disclosure. . . . In its opinion, the Court took care to emphasize the nature of the organization which New York sought to regulate. The decision was based on the particular character of the Klan's activities, involving acts of unlawful intimidation and violence, which the Court assumed was before the state legislature when it enacted the statute, and of which the Court itself took judicial notice. . . . And we conclude that Alabama has fallen short of showing a controlling justification for the deterrent effect on the free enjoyment of the right to associate which disclosure of membership lists is likely to have.

[See Joseph B. Robison, "Protection of Associations from Compulsory Disclosure of Membership," 58 *Col. L. Rev.* 614 (1958).]

Despite the distinction which the opinion indicated between the Klan registration law and the NAACP registration, the holding in the NAACP case raises doubts as to the continued vitality of the *Zimmerman* decision.

In *Shelton* v. *Tucker,* 364 U.S. 479 (1960), the Court dealt with an Arkansas statute which compelled every teacher in a state-supported school to file annually an affidavit listing every organization to which he had belonged or regularly contributed within the preceding five years. Plaintiffs challenged the validity of the statute under the Fourteenth Amendment due process clause. By the narrow margin of five-to-four the Court held the requirement unconstitutional. All members of the Court agreed that the state has a right to investigate the competence and fitness of those whom it hires to teach in its schools. They further appeared to agree that some check into the associational ties would be relevant to the matter of competence. But the majority felt that to inquire into *every* such organizational relationship—church affiliation, political party, social club and others—was to permit unlimited scope to such an inquiry and therefore to violate the freedom of association. As Justice Stewart stated for the majority, "Many such relationships could have no possible bearing upon the teacher's occupational competence or fitness."

Justice Frankfurter, dissenting, felt that the state was entitled to know whether a teacher might "have so many divers associations, so many divers commitments, that they consume his time and energy and interest at the expense of his work or even of his professional dedication." He also stated that, on the record, he could not attribute to the state a purpose to inhibit constitutional rights. But he added, "Of course, if the information gathered by the required affidavits is used to further a scheme of terminating the employment of teachers solely because of their membership in unpopular organizations, that use will run afoul of the Fourteenth Amendment."

The more recent issue of compulsory disclosure of membership involves the application of the Subversive Activities Control Act of 1950 (which is Title I of the Internal Security Act of 1950), which requires the registration with the Attorney General of all Communist-action organizations, as well as all Communist-front organizations. In the case of an organization which is ordered to register by the Subversive Activities Control Board, registration must take place within thirty days of the date upon which the Board's order becomes final. Registration is to be accompanied by a statement containing, among other information, the names and addresses of each person who has been an officer and each person who has been a member during the past twelve months. Once an organization has registered, it must file an annual report containing the same information required in the registration statement. The procedures and requirements of registration for Communist fronts are identical with those for Communist-action organizations, except that fronts need not list their nonofficer members.

Under Section 7(h) of the Act, if the officers of a Communist-action organization fail to register as ordered by the Board, then the individual members are required to register themselves within sixty days after the registration order becomes final. Section 8 provides criminal penalties to be imposed upon organizations, officers, and individuals who fail to register or to file statements as required: a fine of not more than $10,000 for each offense by an organization; a fine of not more than $10,000 or imprisonment for not more than five years or both for each offense by an officer or individual; and each day of failure to register constituting a separate offense.

After more than a year of hearings, the Subversive Activities Control Board in 1953 issued an order requiring that the Communist Party of the United States register in the manner prescribed by the Act. After protracted litigation, the Court of Appeals for the District of Columbia Circuit affirmed the registration order. The Party petitioned the Supreme Court for review, basing its objections to the order on three broad grounds: alleged procedural errors in the Board's taking of testimony, improper construction of the Act, and the unconstitutionality of the Act as constituting a bill of attainder, as violative of freedom of expression and association, and as violative of the privilege against self-incrimination. By a five-to-four vote the Court upheld the judgment of the court of appeals in *Communist Party of the United States* v. *Subversive Activities Control Board,* 367 U.S. 1 (1961).

The majority, through Justice Frankfurter, held that many of the alleged consequences of the Act were prematurely presented and the prejudicial effects only speculative, without support in the record. They refused, therefore, to reach several of the claims of appellants. The majority specifically held, however, that the Act was not a bill of attainder, since the Act applies to a class of activity, not to the Communist Party as such. On the claim of violation of freedom of expression and association, Justice Frankfurter stated, "The present case differs from *Thomas* v. *Collins* and from *National Association for Advancement of Colored People, Bates,* and *Shelton* in the magnitude of the public interests which the registration and disclosure provisions are designed to protect and in the pertinence which registration and disclosure bear to the protection of those interests." He reviewed the legislative findings of the threat to national security from the Communist-action organizations and the purpose of the Act as preventing "the world-wide Communist conspiracy from accomplishing its purpose in this country." He stated further:

Congress, when it enacted the Subversive Activities Control Act, did attempt to cope with precisely such a danger. In light of its legislative findings, based on voluminous evidence collected during years of investigation, we cannot say that that danger is chimerical, or that the registration requirement of Section 7 is an ill-adjusted means of dealing with it. In saying this, we are not insensitive to the fact that the public opprobrium and obloquy which may attach to an individual listed with the Attorney General as a member of a Communist-action organization is no less considerable than that with which members of the National Association for the Advancement of Colored People were threatened in *National Association for Advancement of Colored People* and *Bates.* But while an angry public opinion, and the evils which it may spawn, are relevant considerations in adjudging . . . the validity of legislation that, in effecting disclosure, may thereby entail some restraints on speech and association, the existence of an ugly public temper does not, as such and without more, incapacitate government to require publicity demanded by rational interests high in the scale of national concern. Where the mask of anonymity which an organization's members wear serves the double purpose of protecting them from popular prejudice and of enabling them to cover over a foreign-directed conspiracy, infiltrate into other groups, and enlist the support of persons who would not, if the truth were revealed, lend their support, . . . it would be a distortion of the First Amendment to hold that it prohibits Congress from removing the mask.

An additional claim of the Party was that the registration requirements of the Act could not be imposed and exacted consistently with the Fifth Amendment's self-incrimination clause. It was argued that the officers of the Party are compelled, in the very act of filing a signed registration statement, to admit that they *are* Party officers—an admission which the Court has held incriminating. Justice Frankfurter's response was that the claim was premature:

Manifestly, insofar as this contention is directed against the provisions . . . requiring that designated officers file registration statements in default of registration by an organization, it is prematurely raised in the present proceeding. The duties imposed by those provisions will not arise until and unless the Party fails to register. At this time their application is wholly contingent and conjectural. . . .

The sequel to the case came in 1965 in the case of *Albertson* v. *Subversive Activities Control Board,* 382 U.S. 70 (1965). After the Communist Party had failed to comply with an order requiring it to furnish the Attorney General a list of the Party's members, the Attorney General, acting pursuant to provisions of the Subversive Activities Control Act, requested that the Subversive Activities Control Board grant orders requiring petitioners to register as individual members of the Party. The Board granted the orders, and the Court of Appeals for the District of Columbia affirmed, expressing the view that the constitutional issues raised by the petitioners were not ripe for adjudication and would be ripe only in a prosecution for failure to register if the petitioners did not register. The United States Supreme Court voted unanimously to reverse, holding that the orders violated the Fifth Amendment privilege against self-incrimination. Justice Brennan, for the Court, stated that admission of membership may be used to prosecute the registrant under the membership clause of the Smith Act. He stated further:

Section 4(f) of the Act, the purported immunity provision, does not save the registration orders from petitioners' Fifth Amendment challenge. . . . [T]he immunity granted by §4(f) is not complete. . . . With regard to the act of registering . . . §4(f) provides only that the admission of Party membership thus required shall not per se constitute a violation of §§4(a) and (c) or any other criminal statute, or "be received in evidence" against a registrant in any criminal prosecution; it does not preclude the use of the admission as an investigatory lead, a use which is barred by the privilege.

It is not an easy matter to sum up the Court's delineation of the constitutional rights to free expression when applied to matters touching on internal security, especially as related to restrictions on Communists. But a few signposts have been erected, indicating at least general directions. At the outset, it is apparent that in the hard cases involving the issue of freedom of expression versus internal security the Court takes a long, close look at the procedures used in applying the given restrictions. While procedural matters have generally been dealt with in a previous chapter, the point here is that where freedom of expression is being abridged, the statutory and constitutional procedural requirements are apt to be applied somewhat more rigorously than in some other areas. Once these requirements are met, however, the Court has permitted both the national and the state governments to impose a variety of restrictions on Communists. [For a compilation of such restrictions and court decisions relative to them, see the Fund for the Republic publication, *Digest of the Public Record of Communism in the United States* (New York: Fund for the Republic, 1955).] Both governments may bar *active* Communists from employment. In addition, a refusal to answer official inquiries concerning such participation can be taken into account in determining "competence" or "good moral character" in connection with retention of governmental employment or admission to the bar. But where associational tests range too widely and reach ordinarily lawful organizational ties, then the Court tends to hold that First Amendment rights of belief and association have been abridged. Thus it may be true that there is no "right" to government employment, but this is not to say that governments can set requirements which are unrelated to the proper performance of the employment position or which classify applicants in an unreasonable fashion.

The Court has upheld a congressional requirement that before becoming eligible for the services of the National Labor Relations Board, and thus the statutory benefits of the Wagner Act, a labor organization must file with the Board an affidavit executed by each officer of such organization that he is not a member of the Communist Party or affiliated with it. In 1959, however, this requirement of the Taft-Hartley Act was replaced by a provision making it a crime for a member of the Communist Party to serve as an officer or employee of a labor union (except in clerical or custodial positions). In *United States* v. *Brown,* 381 U.S. 437 (1965), the Court by a five-to-four vote held this section unconstitutional as a bill of attainder. The Chief Justice, for the majority, stated that the statute did not "set forth a generally applicable rule decreeing that any person who commits certain acts or possesses certain characteristics . . . . shall not hold union office, and leave to courts and juries the job of deciding what persons have committed the specified acts or possessed the specified characteristics." Instead it simply designated the persons—members of the Communist Party—and such designation "is not the substitution of a semantically equivalent phrase" and is therefore a bill of attainder.

In *Schneiderman* v. *United States,* 320 U.S. 118 (1943), the Court indicated that Congress might exclude all Communist aliens from entering the United States. And in *Harisiades* v. *Shaughnessy,* 342 U.S. 580 (1952), it was held that Congress could constitutionally deport all aliens who had been members of the Communist Party, including even those whose membership had ceased prior to the passage of the statute requiring such deportation. Thus aliens and immigrants are in a particularly vulnerable position. [See Milton R. Konvitz, *Civil Rights in Immigration* (Ithaca: Cornell University Press, 1953); Lena L. Orlow, "The Immigration and Nationality Act in Operation," 29 *Temple L. Q.* 153 (1956); Blanch L. Freedman, "The Loyalty-Security Program—Its Effect in Immigration and Deportation," 15 *Law. Guild Rev.* 135 (1955); and Comment, "The Alien and the Constitution," 20 *U. of Chi. L. Rev.* 547 (1953).]

The advocacy of revolution can constitutionally be punished unless it is limited to the advocacy of *belief in the doctrine* of overthrow of the government by violence. And organizing a group or becoming an active member of a group dedicated to teaching the overthrow of the government by violence may constitutionally be punished. Restrictions on Communists unsupported by a showing of potential danger to the nation or to maintenance of order appear to be subjected to close scrutiny, however. Thus in *Aptheker* v. *Secretary of State,* 378 U.S. 500 (1964), the Court held that Section 6 of the Subversive Activities Control Act, which bars the application for or use of a passport by a member of an organization ordered to register by the Board as a Communist-action organization, was an undue restriction on the right to travel abroad and therefore an unconstitutional abridgment of the liberty guaranteed by the Fifth Amendment. [See Leonard B. Boudin, "The Constitutional Right to Travel," 56 *Column. L. Rev.* 47 (1956).] More recently, in *Lamont* v. *Postmaster General,* 381 U.S. 301 (1965), the Court held unconstitutional a federal statute requiring a request in writing as a prerequisite to the delivery of nonsealed mail from abroad which was classified as containing Communist propaganda material. This case is particularly noteworthy in that for the first time in our history the United States Supreme Court held a *federal* statute unconstitutional as an abridgment of First Amendment rights. [See Jay A. Sigler, "Freedom of the Mails: a Developing Right," 54 *Geo. L. J.* 30 (1965).]

At least in the treatment of citizens, it appears that the Court is more willing to take up cases dealing with anti-Communist restrictions than it was in the decade following World War II and is requiring a relatively close relationship between the restriction and the protection of the nation's security before upholding the peripheral attacks on Communists.

[The literature on loyalty-security problems is enormous. See Thomas I. Emerson, David Haber, and Norman Dorsen, *Political and Civil Rights in the United States,* 3rd ed., 2 vols. (Boston: Little, Brown, 1967), chap. 3, especially the bibliographic references. See also John L. O'Brian, *National Security and Individual Freedom* (Cambridge: Harvard University Press, 1955); Harold W. Chase, *Security and Liberty: The Problem of Native Communists, 1947–1955* (Garden City: Doubleday, 1955); and Walter Gellhorn, ed., *The States and Subversion* (Ithaca: Cornell University Press, 1952).]

REGULATION OF TRAFFIC AND MAINTENANCE OF PUBLIC PEACE AND ORDER

The state may place the exercise of speech and assembly under reasonable police regulations for a variety of purposes, and some of the most oft-cited illustrations of this power are in the areas of traffic control and the preservation of public order. Of course the previously treated decisions dealing with prior restraints are applicable in this area, just as in other types of expression, but if the state avoids this error, it is permitted a reasonable range of control.

A good illustration of the Court's view of an improper and a proper statutory handling of a permissible area of regulation is to be seen in two cases dealing with the regulation of sound amplification equipment in urban streets and parks. In *Saia* v. *New York,* 334 U.S. 558 (1948), the Court found a prior restraint in a city ordinance forbidding the use of sound amplification devices except for "public dissemination . . . of items of news and matters of public concern . . . provided that the same be done under permission obtained from the Chief of Police." Refused a second permit on the ground that complaints had been reported concerning his prior speeches and sermons using a loud-speaker, appellant, a minister of the Jehovah's Witnesses, delivered a speech, without a permit and again using a loud-speaker, in a park normally used for recreation purposes. By a five-to-four majority the Court held the ordinance unconstitutional on its face as a prior restraint on the right of free speech. It should be noted, however, that the opinion for the Court pointed out that reasonable regulation of the use of loud-speaker was within the range of state power. Justice Douglas, for the majority, stated:

Noise can be regulated by regulating decibels. The hours and place of public discussion can be controlled. But to allow the police to bar the use of loud-speakers because their use can be abused is like barring radio receivers because they too make a noise. The police need not be given the power to deny a man the use of his radio in order to protect a neighbor against sleepless nights. The same is true here.

Any abuses which loud-speakers create can be controlled by narrowly drawn statutes. When a city allows an official to ban them in his uncontrolled discretion, it sanctions a device for suppression of free communication of ideas. In this case a permit is denied because some persons were said to have found the sound annoying. In the next one a permit may be denied because some people find the ideas annoying. Annoyance at ideas can be cloaked in annoyance at sound. The power of censorship inherent in this type of ordinance reveals its vice.

Justice Frankfurter, joined in dissent by Justices Reed and Burton, pointed out that there is an important difference in ordinary human speech and the use of modern amplifying devices which "afford easy, too easy, opportunities for aural aggression." Considering this and the fact that people had complained, it did not seem to him unreasonable or unconstitutional to refuse a license to the appellant for the time and place requested. Justice Jackson dissented separately, stating that this was not even a free speech issue.

[C]an it be that society has no control of apparatus which, when put to un-regulated proselyting, propaganda and commercial uses, can render life unbearable? It is intimated that the city can control the decibels; if so, why may it not prescribe zero decibels as appropriate to some places? It seems to me that society has the right to control, as to place, time and volume, the use of loud-speaking devices for any purpose, provided its regulations are not unduly arbitrary, capricous or discriminatory.

The second loud-speaker case also came on a five-to-four vote, but this time upholding a regulation. The case was *Kovacs* v. *Cooper*, 336 U.S. 77 (1949), involving the validity of a Trenton, New Jersey, ordinance which provided:

That it shall be unlawful for any person, firm or corporation . . . to play, use or operate for advertising purposes, or for any other purpose whatsoever, on or upon the public streets, alleys or thoroughfares in the City of Trenton, any device known as a sound truck, loud speaker or sound-amplifier, or radio or phonograph with a loud speaker or sound amplifier, or any other instrument known as a calliope or any instrument of any kind or character which emits therefrom loud and raucous noises and is attached to and upon any vehicle operated or standing upon said streets or public places aforementioned.

Although five justices held the regulation valid, there was no opinion for the Court. Justice Reed, speaking for three members, seemingly accepted the construction placed on the ordinance by the New Jersey Supreme Court, namely that the ordinance applied only to vehicles with sound amplifiers "emitting loud and raucous noises" and did not prohibit sound trucks altogether. On this basis he stated, "We think that the need for reasonable protection in the homes or business houses from the distracting noises of vehicles equipped with such sound amplifying devices justifies the ordinance."

Justice Frankfurter concurred, repeating the views expressed in his *Saia* dissent. Justice Jackson also concurred separately, saying:

I join the judgment sustaining the Trenton ordinance because I believe that operation of mechanical sound-amplifying devices conflicts with quiet enjoyment of home and park and with safe and legitimate use of street and market place, and that it is constitutionally subject to regulation or prohibition by the state or municipal authority. . . .

But I agree with Mr. Justice Black that this decision is a repudiation of that in *Saia* v. *New York*. . . . Like him, I am unable to find anything in this record to warrant a distinction because of "loud and raucous" tones of this machine . . . Trenton, as the ordinance reads to me, unconditionally bans all sound trucks from the city streets. Lockport relaxed its prohibition with a proviso to allow their use, even in areas set aside for public recreation, when and where the Chief of Police saw no objection. Comparison of this our 1949 decision with our 1948 decision, I think, will pretty hopelessly confuse municipal authorities as to what they may or may not do.

Justice Black, joined by Justices Douglas and Rutledge, dissented on the ground that the "ordinance is on its face, and as construed and applied in this case by that state's courts, an absolute and unqualified prohibition of amplifying devices on any of Trenton's streets at any time, at any place, for any purpose, and without regard to how noisy they may be." He indicated clearly, however, that reasonable regulation would meet the test of constitutionality. The opinion stated:

I would agree without reservation to the sentiment that "unrestrained use throughout a municipality of all sound amplifying devices would be intolerable." And of course cities may restrict or absolutely ban the use of amplifiers on busy streets in the business area. A city ordinance that reasonably restricts the volume of sound, or the hours during which an amplifier may be used, does not in my mind infringe the constitutionally protected area of free speech. It is because this ordinance does none of these things, but is instead an absolute prohibition of all uses of an amplifier on any of the streets of Trenton at any time that I must dissent.

Justice Murphy dissented separately.

While reconciliation of the two cases may not be easy, a head-count of the voting in the cases shows that Chief Justice Vinson was the only member to change his vote from *Saia* to *Kovacs* relative to the power to enforce the respective ordinances. Since he did not write an opinion in either case, it is not possible to state precisely the basis for his shift. Once again, however, it is clear from a reading of the opinions that an ordinance limiting the volume, time, and place of the use of sound trucks or public sound amplification equipment in some reasonable manner would pass constitutional muster.

The problem of regulating street processions while at the same time avoiding the pitfall of prior restraint and affording broad protection to First Amendment rights was well illustrated in the case of *Cox* v. *New Hampshire*, 312 U.S. 569 (1941), discussed earlier. The Court upheld a reasonable and nondiscriminatory permit requirement for the holding of parades as a proper municipal regulation of the use of the streets.

Feiner v. *New York*, 340 U.S. 315 (1951) illustrates the application of a municipal ordinance prohibiting disorderly conduct to the attempted exercise of free speech. Feiner addressed a group of listeners on a street corner in Syracuse, New York. A racially mixed crowd of some seventy-five or eighty people gathered on the sidewalks and spilled into the street. He urged the audience to attend a speech later that night on the subject of racial discrimination, and during the appeal referred to President Truman as a "bum," to the American Legion as "a Nazi Gestapo," and to the Mayor of Syracuse as a "champagne-sipping bum." He also said that "colored people don't have equal rights and they should rise up in arms and fight for them."

Two officers were sent to the meeting and stated that the crowd was restless and there was some pushing, shoving, and milling around. One man said to the police officers, "If you don't get that S.O.B. off, I will go over and get him off there myself." The police officers told Feiner to stop speaking, and when he refused, arrested him for disorderly conduct. In finding Feiner guilty the trial judge concluded that the police officers were justified in taking action to prevent a breach of the peace, and the New York Court of Appeals affirmed.

A majority of six in the United States Supreme Court considered that the facts clearly indicated sufficient evidence of a possible breach of the peace to warrant Feiner's arrest for disorderly conduct. The Chief Justice, speaking for the majority, stated that "Petitioner was neither arrested nor convicted for the making or the content of his speech. Rather it was the reaction which it actually engendered." He stated further:

> We are well aware that the ordinary murmurings and objections of a hostile audience cannot be allowed to silence a speaker, and are also mindful of the possible danger of giving overzealous police officials complete discretion to break up otherwise lawful public meetings. . . . But we are not faced here with such a situation. It is one thing to say that the police cannot be used as an instrument for the oppression of unpopular views, and another to say that, when as here the speaker passes the bounds of argument or persuasion and undertakes incitement to riot, they are powerless to prevent a breach of the peace.

Justices Black and Douglas gave vigorous dissenting opinions, Justice Minton concurring with the latter. Justice Black stated:

> As to the existence of a dangerous situation on the street corner, it seems far-fetched to suggest that the "facts" show any imminent threat of riot or uncontrollable disorder. It is neither unusual nor unexpected that some people at public street meetings mutter, mill about, push, shove, or disagree, even violently, with the speaker. Indeed, it is rare where controversial topics are discussed that an outdoor crowd does not do some or all of these things. Nor does one isolated threat to assault the speaker forbode disorder. . . .
>
> Moreover, assuming that the "facts" did indicate a critical situation, I reject the implication of the Court's opinion that the police had no obligation to protect petitioner's constitutional right to talk. But if, in the name of preserving order, they ever can interfere with a lawful public speaker, they first must make all reasonable efforts to protect him. Here the policemen did not even pretend to try to protect petitioner. . . . Their duty was to protect petitioner's right to talk, even to the extent of arresting the man who threatened to interfere. Instead, they shirked that duty and acted only to suppress the right to speak.

The decision in the *Feiner* case indicates the importance of the fact-finding aspect of the cases. The members of the Court sometimes disagree on the law and sometimes on the way that the facts should be read. While the appellate courts do not as a rule upset lower court findings of fact, the United States Supreme Court has often pointed out that in First Amendment cases it will feel free to make its own determination of the facts. The majority in *Feiner* found the facts to support a conviction for disorderly conduct, while the minority read them differently and concluded that the problem was one of a hostile audience interfering with a lawful speech. As to the law, however, it is clear that a reasonably administered municipal prohibition against disorderly conduct may be upheld even though it regulates speech or assembly.

Profane and Abusive Language: The "Fighting Words" Doctrine

Chaplinsky v. *New Hampshire,* 315 U.S. 568 (1942), involved a state law providing that:

No person shall address any offensive, derisive or annoying word to any other person who is lawfully in any street or other public place, nor call him by any offensive or derisive name, nor make any noise or exclamation in his presence and hearing with intent to deride, offend or annoy him or to prevent him from pursuing his lawful business or occupation.

The state court construed the statute as prohibiting "words likely to cause an average addressee to fight," or "face-to-face words plainly likely to cause a breach of the peace by the addressee." Appellant was a Jehovah's Witness who, after getting into an argument on a public sidewalk, called a city marshal a "damned Fascist" and a "Goddamned racketeer." His conviction under the statute was unanimously upheld by the United States Supreme Court against a claim of invasion of First Amendment freedom of expression. Justice Murphy, for the Court, stated:

There are certain well-defined and narrowly limited classes of speech, the prevention and punishment of which have never been thought to raise any Constitutional problem. These include the lewd and obscene, the profane, the libelous, and the insulting or "fighting" words—those which by their very utterance inflict injury or tend to incite an immediate breach of the peace. It has been well observed that such utterances are no essential part of any exposition of ideas and are of such slight social value as a step to truth that any benefit that may be derived from them is clearly outweighed by the social interest in order and morality.

A case frequently cited in the context of "fighting words" is *Terminiello* v. *Chicago,* 337 U.S. 1 (1949), although the decision in the United States Supreme Court did not come off on that issue. Terminiello spoke in an auditorium in Chicago to a crowd of about 800 persons. He criticized Democrats, Jews, and Communists in a speech full of racial and political hatred. A crowd of over a thousand gathered outside in protest, yelling "Fascists, Hitlers!" A cordon of police assigned to the meeting was unable to stop the smashing of doors, the breaking of windows, and other acts of violence. Terminiello was arrested and convicted of violating a breach of the peace ordinance. In charging the jury, however, the judge defined breach of the peace to include speech which "stirs the public to anger, invites dispute, brings about a condition of unrest or creates a disturbance." By a five-to-four vote the Court reversed the conviction on the ground that the charge to the jury interpreting the statute permitted the punishment of speech that was protected by the Constitution. Justice Douglas, for the majority, stated:

A function of free speech under our system of government is to invite dispute. It may indeed best serve its high purpose when it induces a condition of unrest, creates dissatisfaction with conditions as they are, or even stirs people to anger. Speech is often provocative and challenging. It may strike at prejudices and preconceptions and have profound unsettling effects as it presses for acceptance of an idea.... The ordinance as construed by the trial court seriously invaded this province. It permitted conviction of petitioner if his speech stirred people to anger, invited public dispute, or brought about a condition of unrest. A conviction resting on any of these grounds may not stand.

There were dissents on the ground that no one had raised any issue regarding the charge to the jury at any stage of the proceedings, and thus the question was not open to them. Justices Jackson and Burton further dissented on the ground that the jury was justified in finding a breach of the peace in the facts of the case, and the conviction should have been affirmed.

In view of the basis for the majority decision, the *Terminiello* case must be confined to the issue of whether speech which invites dispute and stirs the public to anger can for those reasons only be restricted. Thus it stands as no authority for what a municipality can or cannot do to punish a man who says the things which Terminiello did under the circumstances of his speech. The Court simply did not reach that question in deciding the case.

COHEN *v.* CALIFORNIA
403 U.S. 15 (1971)

[On April 26, 1968, Cohen was observed in the Los Angeles County Courthouse in the corridor outside the Municipal Court wearing a jacket bearing the words "Fuck the Draft" which were plainly visible. There were women and children present in the corridor. Cohen was arrested and convicted of violating a state law which prohibits "maliciously and willfully disturbing the peace or quiet of any neighborhood or person,... by ... offensive conduct..." and sentenced to thirty days imprisonment. The California Court of Appeals affirmed.]

Mr. Justice Harlan delivered the opinion of the Court.

This case may seem at first blush too inconsequential to find its way into our books, but the issue it presents is of no small constitutional significance....

The conviction quite clearly rests upon the asserted offensiveness of the *words* Cohen used to convey his message to the public. The only "conduct" which the State sought to punish is the fact of communication. Thus, we deal here with a conviction resting solely upon "speech,"... not upon any separated identifiable conduct.... Further, the State certainly lacks power to punish Cohen for the underlying content of the message the inscription conveyed. At least so long as there is no showing of an intent to incite disobedience to or disruption of the draft, Cohen could not, consistently with the First and Fourteenth Amendments, be punished for asserting the evident position on the inutility or immorality of the draft his jacket reflected....

Appellant's conviction, then, rests squarely upon his exercise of the "freedom of speech" protected from arbitrary governmental interference by the Constitution and can be justified, if at all, only as a valid regulation of the manner in which he exercised that freedom, not as a permissible prohibition on the substantive message it conveys....

In the first place, Cohen was tried under a statute applicable throughout the entire State. Any attempt to support this conviction on the ground that the statute seeks to preserve an appropriately decorous atmosphere in the courthouse where

Cohen was arrested must fail in the absence of any language in the statute that would have put appellant on notice that certain kinds of otherwise permissible speech or conduct would nevertheless, under California law, not be tolerated in certain places. . . .

In the second place, as it comes to us, this case . . . is not an obscenity case. Whatever else may be necessary to give rise to the States' broader power to prohibit obscene expression, such expression must be, in some significant way, erotic. . . . It cannot plausibly be maintained that this vulgar allusion to the Selective Service System would conjure up such psychic stimulation in anyone likely to be confronted with Cohen's crudely defaced jacket.

This Court has also held that the States are free to ban the simple use, without a demonstration of additional justifying circumstances, of so-called "fighting words," those personally abusive epithets which, when addressed to the ordinary citizen, are, as a matter of common knowledge, inherently likely to provoke violent reaction. *Chaplinsky* v. *New Hampshire.* . . . While the four-letter word displayed by Cohen in relation to the draft is not uncommonly employed in a personally provocative fashion, in this instance it was clearly not "directed to the person of the hearer." . . . There is, as noted above, no showing that anyone who saw Cohen was in fact violently aroused or that appellant intended such a result.

Finally, in arguments before this Court much has been made of the claim that Cohen's distasteful mode of expression was thrust upon unwilling or unsuspecting viewers, and that the State might therefore legitimately act as it did in order to protect the sensitive from otherwise unavoidable exposure to appellant's crude form of protest. Of course, the mere presumed presence of unwitting listeners or viewers does not serve automatically to justify curtailing all speech capable of giving offense. . . . The ability of government, consonant with the Constitution, to shut off discourse solely to protect others from hearing it is . . . dependent upon a showing that substantial privacy interests are being invaded in an essentially intolerable manner. Any broader view of this authority would effectively empower a majority to silence dissidents simply as a matter of personal predilections. . . .

. . . [T]he principle contended for by the State seems inherently boundless. How is one to distinguish this from any other offensive word? Surely the State has no right to cleanse public debate to the point where it is grammatically palatable to the most squeamish among us. Yet no readily ascertainable general principle exists for stopping short of that result were we to affirm the judgment below. For, while the particular four-letter word being litigated here is perhaps more distasteful than most others of its genre, it is nevertheless often true that one man's vulgarity is another's lyric. Indeed, we think it is largely because government officials cannot make principled distinctions in this area that the Constitution leaves matters of taste and style so largely to the individual.

Additionally, we cannot overlook the fact, because it is well illustrated by the episode involved here, that much linguistic expression serves a dual communicative function: it conveys not only ideas capable of relatively precise, detached explication, but otherwise inexpressible emotions as well. In fact, words are often chosen as much for their emotive as their cognitive force. We cannot sanction the view that the Constitution, while solicitous of the cognitive content of individual speech, has little or no regard for that emotive function which, practically speaking, may often be the more important element of the overall message sought to be communicated. . . .

Mr. Justice Blackmun, with whom The Chief Justice and Mr. Justice Black join, dissenting. [Mr. Justice White concurred in part.]

GOODING v. WILSON
405 U.S. 518 (1972)

[Appellee Wilson was one of a group of persons who picketed a building housing the 12th Army Corps Headquarters, carrying signs opposing the war in Vietnam. When the police tried to remove the pickets from the door, a scuffle ensued. Testimony showed that Wilson addressed the police as follows: "White son of a bitch, I'll kill you." "You son of a bitch, I'll choke you to death." "You son of a bitch, if you ever put your hands on me again, I'll cut you all to pieces." Wilson was charged and convicted of using opprobrious words and abusive language in violation of a Georgia law which provides: "Any person who shall, without provocation, use to or of another, and in his presence . . . opprobrious words or abusive language, tending to cause a breach of the peace . . . shall be guilty of a misdemeanor." The Georgia Supreme Court affirmed the conviction. Wilson then sought habeas corpus relief in a federal District Court, which held that the Georgia statute was unconstitutionally vague and broad and set aside the conviction.]

Mr. Justice Brennan delivered the opinion of the Court. . . .

[The statute] punishes only spoken words. It can therefore withstand appellee's attack upon its facial constitutionality only if, as authoritatively construed by the Georgia courts, it is not susceptible of application to speech, although vulgar or offensive, that is protected by the First and Fourteenth Amendments, *Cohen* v. *California.* . . .

"Although a statute may be neither vague, overbroad, nor otherwise invalid as applied to the conduct charged against a particular defendant, he is permitted to raise its vagueness or unconstitutional overbreadth as applied to others. And if the law is found deficient in one of these respects, it may not be applied to him either, until and unless a satisfactory limiting construction is placed on the statute. The statute, in effect, is stricken down on its face. This result is deemed justified since the otherwise continued existence of the statute in unnarrowed form would tend to suppress constitutionally protected rights." *Coates* v. *City of Cincinnati,* . . . In other words, the statute must be carefully drawn or be authoritatively construed to punish only unprotected speech and not be susceptible of application to protected expression. . . .

Appellant does not challenge these principles but contends that the Georgia statute is narrowly drawn to apply only to a constitutionally unprotected class of words—"fighting" words—"those which by their very utterance inflict injury or tend to incite an immediate breach of the peace." . . . Our decisions since *Chaplinsky* have continued to recognize state power constitutionally to punish "fighting" words under carefully drawn statutes not also susceptible of application to protected expression. . . . We have, however, made our own examination of the Georgia cases, both those cited and others discovered in research. That examination brings us to the conclusion, in argeement with the courts below, that the Georgia appellate decisions have not construed [the statute] to be limited in application, as in *Chaplinsky,* to words that "have a direct tendency to cause acts of violence by the person to whom, individually, the remark is addressed." . . .

Mr. Justice Powell and Mr. Justice Rehnquist took no part in the consideration or decision of this case.

Mr. Chief Justice Burger, dissenting.

I fully join in Mr. Justice Blackmun's dissent against the bizarre result reached by the Court. It is not merely odd, it is nothing less than remarkable that the Court can find a state statute void on its face, not because of its language—which is the traditional test—but because of the way courts of that State have applied the statute in a few isolated cases, decided as long ago as 1905 and generally long before this Court's decision in *Chaplinsky* v. *New Hampshire.* . . . Even if all of those cases had been decided yesterday, they do nothing to demonstrate that the narrow language of the Georgia statute has any significant potential for sweeping application to suppress or deter important protected speech. . . .

. . . And if the early Georgia cases cited by the majority establish any proposition, it is that the statute, as its language so clearly indicates, is aimed at preventing precisely that type of personal, face-to-face, abusive and insulting language likely to provoke a violent retaliation—self-help, as we euphemistically call it—that the *Chaplinsky* case recognized could be validly prohibited. The facts of the case now before the Court demonstrate that the Georgia statute is serving that valid and entirely proper purpose. There is no persuasive reason to wipe the statute from the books, unless we want to encourage victims of such verbal assaults to seek their own private redress. . . .

Mr. Justice Blackmun, with whom The Chief Justice joins, dissenting.

It seems strange indeed, that in this day a man may say to a police officer, who is attempting to restore access to a public building, "White son of a bitch, I'll kill you" and "You son of a bitch, I'll choke you to death,". . . and yet constitutionally cannot be prosecuted and convicted under a state statute that makes it a misdemeanor to "use to or of another, and in his presence . . . opprobrious words or abusive language, tending to cause a breach of the peace. . . ." This, however, is precisely what the Court pronounces as the law today.

The Supreme Court of Georgia, when the conviction was appealed, unanimously held the other way. . . . Surely any adult who can read—and I do not exclude this appellee-defendant from that category—should reasonably expect no other conclusion. The words . . . are clear. They are also concise. They are not in my view, overbroad or incapable of being understood. Except perhaps for the "big" word "opprobrious"—and no point is made of its bigness—any Georgia schoolboy would expect that this defendant's fighting and provocative words to the officers were covered. . . . Common sense permits no other conclusion. This is demonstrated by the fact that the appellee, and this Court, attack the statute, not as it applies to the appellee, but as it conceivably might apply to others who might utter other words. . . .

In *Eaton* v. *City of Tulsa*, 415 U.S. 697 (1974), the Court reversed a contempt citation which had been imposed on petitioner because of his use of an expletive during the course of a trial for an alleged violation of a Tulsa ordinance. During cross-examination, in response to a question asked him by the assistant city prosecutor, the following exchange occurred:

Q. What did you do?

A. I sensed something from behind me and I turned maybe enough to look over my shoulder. At the time I turned and looked over my shoulder I could see this guy's face and shoulders coming at me; almost simultaneously he hit me and he knocked me over on my back a bench down. Luckily, somebody grabbed him and pulled him back, and I got up off of my back after being knocked down on my back, wrenched my elbow, got up to a vertical posture where I would have some kind of defensibility and moved up to where I had some square footing.

Q. What's defensibility?

A. I think that would be a place where you were able to get your feet to stand square so you would be half ready for some chicken shit that had jumped you from behind.

THE COURT: Mr. Eaton, you will have until tomorrow morning to show me why you should not be held in direct contempt of this Court. I'm not going to put up with that kind of language in this Court.

THE WITNESS: That's fine. I don't feel as though I need to put up with why I received this.

THE COURT: Mr. Eaton, did you hear what I just said?

THE WITNESS: Yes, sir.

Petitioner was found guilty of contempt and fined $50 plus costs. The Oklahoma Court of Criminal Appeals affirmed. The Supreme Court reversed, and the Per Curiam opinion stated:

This single isolated usage of street vernacular, not directed at the judge or any officer of the court, cannot constitutionally support the conviction of criminal contempt. . . . In using the expletive in answering the question on cross-examination "it is not charged that [petitioner] here disobeyed any valid court order, talked loudly, acted boisterously, or attempted to prevent the judge or any other officer of the court from carrying on his court duties.". . . In the circumstances, the use of the expletive thus cannot be held to "constitute an imminent . . . threat to the administration of justice."

Justice Powell, concurring, stated that "the controlling fact, in my view, and one that should be emphasized, is that petitioner received no prior warning or caution from the trial judge with respect to court etiquette."

Demonstrations and Protest Speech

EDWARDS v. SOUTH CAROLINA
372 U.S. 229 (1963)

Mr. Justice Stewart delivered the opinion of the Court.

The petitioners, 187 in number, were convicted in a magistrate's court in Columbia, South Carolina, of the common-law crime of breach of the peace. Their convictions were ultimately affirmed by the South Carolina Supreme Court. . . . We granted certiorari . . . to consider the claim that these convictions cannot be squared with the Fourteenth Amendment of the United States Constitution.

There was no substantial conflict in the trial evidence. Late in the morning of March 2, 1961, the petitioners, high school and college students of the Negro race, met at the Zion Baptist Church in Columbia. From there, at about noon, they walked in separate groups of about 15 to the South Carolina State House grounds, an area of two city blocks open to the general public. Their purpose was "to submit a protest to the citizens of South Carolina, along with the Legislative Bodies of South Carolina, our feelings and our dissatisfaction with the present condition of discriminatory actions against Negroes, in general, and to let them know that we were dissatisfied and that we would like for the laws which prohibited Negro privileges in this State to be removed."

Already on the State House grounds when the petitioners arrived were 30 or more law enforcement officers, who had advance knowledge that the petitioners were coming. Each group of petitioners entered the grounds through a driveway and parking area known in the record as the "horseshoe." As they entered, they were told by the law enforcement officials that "they had a right, as a citizen, to go through the State House grounds, as any other citizen has, as long as they were peaceful." During the next half hour or 45 minutes, the petitioners, in the same small groups, walked single file or two abreast in an orderly way through the grounds, each group carrying placards bearing such messages as "I am proud to be a Negro," and "Down with segregation."

During this time a crowd of some 200 to 300 onlookers had collected in the horseshoe area and on the adjacent sidewalks. There was no evidence to suggest that these onlookers were anything but curious, and no evidence at all of any threatening remarks, hostile gestures, or offensive language on the part of any member of the crowd. The City Manager testified that he recognized some of the onlookers, whom he did not identify, as "possible trouble makers," but his subsequent testimony made clear that nobody among the crowd actually caused or threatened any trouble. There was no obstruction of pedestrian or vehicular traffic within the State House grounds. . . . Although vehicular traffic at a nearby street intersection was slowed down somewhat, an officer was dispatched to keep traffic moving. There were a number of bystanders on the public sidewalk adjacent to the State House grounds, but they all moved on when asked to do so, and there was no impediment of pedestrian traffic. Police protection at the scene was at all times sufficient to meet any foreseeable possibility of disorder.

In the situation and under the circumstances thus described, the police authorities [actually the order issued from the City Manager, as the footnote excerpts from the trial record show] advised the petitioners that they would be arrested if they did not disperse within 15 minutes. Instead of dispersing, the petitioners engaged in what the City Manager described as "boisterous," "loud," and "flamboyant" conduct, which, as his later testimony made clear, consisted of listening to a "religious harangue" by one of their leaders, and loudly singing "The Star Spangled Banner" and other patriotic and religious songs, while stamping their feet and clapping their hands. After 15 minutes had passed, the police arrested the petitioners and marched them off to jail.

Upon this evidence the state trial court convicted the petitioners of breach of the peace, and imposed sentences ranging from a $10 fine or five days in jail, to a $100 fine or 30 days in jail. In affirming the judgments, the Supreme Court of South Carolina said that under the law of that State the offense of breach of the peace "is not susceptible of exact definition," but that the "general definition of the offense" is as follows:

"In general terms, a breach of the peace is a violation of public order, a disturbance of the public tranquility, by any act or conduct inciting to violence . . . , it includes any violation of any law enacted to preserve peace and good order. It may consist of an act of violence or an act likely to produce violence. It is not necessary that the peace be actually broken to lay the foundation for a prosecution for this offense. If what is done is unjustifiable and unlawful, tending with sufficient directness to break the peace, no more is required. Nor is actual personal violence an essential element in the offense. . . ."

The petitioners contend that there was a complete absence of any evidence of the commission of this offense, and that they were thus denied one of the most basic elements of due process of law. . . . Whatever the merits of this contention, we need not pass upon it in the present case. The state courts have held that the petitioners' conduct constituted breach of the peace under state law, and we may accept their decision as binding upon us to that extent. *But it nevertheless remains our duty in a case such as this to make an independent examination of the whole record.* [Emphasis supplied.] ... And it is clear to us that in arresting, convicting, and punishing the petitioners under the circumstances disclosed by this record, South Carolina infringed the petitioners' constitutionally protected rights of speech, free assembly, and freedom to petition for redress of their grievances.

... The circumstances in this case reflect an exercise of these basic constitutional rights in their most pristine and classic form. The petitioners felt aggrieved by laws of South Carolina which allegedly "prohibited Negro privileges in this State." They peaceably assembled at the site of the State Government and there peaceably expressed their grievances "to the citizens of South Carolina, along with the Legislative Bodies of South Carolina." Not until they were told by police officials that they must disperse on pain of arrest did they do more. Even then, they but sang patriotic and religious songs after one of their leaders had delivered a "religious harangue." There was no evidence or threat of violence on their part, or on the part of any member of the crowd watching them. Police protection was "ample."

This, therefore, was a far cry from the situation in *Feiner* v. *New York*, ... where two policemen were faced with a crowd which was "pushing, shoving, and milling around,". . . where at least one member of the crowd "threatened violence if the police did not act,". . . where "the crowd was pressing closer around petitioner and the officer,". . . and where "the speaker passes the bounds of argument or persuasion and undertakes incitement to riot.". . . And the record is barren of any evidence of "fighting words." See *Chaplinsky* v. *New Hampshire*. . . .

We do not review in this case criminal convictions resulting from the even-handed application of a precise and narrowly drawn regulatory statute evincing a legislative judgment that certain specific conduct be limited or proscribed. If, for example, the petitioners had been convicted upon evidence that they had violated a law regulating traffic, or had disobeyed a law reasonably limiting the periods during which the State House grounds were open to the public, this would be a different case. . . . These petitioners . . . were convicted upon evidence which showed no more than that the opinions which they were peaceably expressing were sufficiently opposed to the views of the majority of the community to attract a crowd and necessitate police protection. . . .

For these reasons we conclude that these criminal convictions cannot stand.

Reversed.

Mr. Justice Clark, dissenting. . . .

. . . Petitioners, of course, had a right to peaceable assembly, to espouse their cause and to petition, but in my view the manner in which they exercised those rights was by no means the passive demonstration which this Court relates; rather, as the City Manager of Columbia testified, "a dangerous situation was building up" which South Carolina's courts expressly found had created "an actual interference with traffic and an imminently threatened disturbance of the peace of the community." Since the Court does not attack the state courts' findings and accepts the convictions as "binding" to the extent that the petitioners' conduct constituted a breach of the peace, it is difficult for me to understand its understatement of the facts and reversal of the convictions. . . .

. . . Here the petitioners were permitted without hindrance to exercise their rights of free speech and assembly. Their arrests occurred only after a situation arose in which the law-enforcement officials on the scene considered that a dangerous disturbance was imminent. The County Court found that "the evidence is clear that the officers were motivated solely by a proper concern for the preservation

of order and the protection of the general welfare in the face of an actual interference with traffic and an imminently threatened disturbance of the peace of the
community." In affirming, the South Carolina Supreme Court said the action of
the police was "reasonable and motivated solely by a proper concern for the preservation of order and prevention of further interference with traffic upon the public
streets and sidewalks.". . .

. . . [I]n *Feiner* v. *New York* . . . we upheld a conviction for breach of the peace
in a situation no more dangerous than that found here. There the demonstration
was conducted by only one person and the crowd was limited to approximately
80. . . . Here 200 youthful Negro demonstrators were being aroused to a "fever
pitch" before a crowd of some 300 people who undoubtedly were hostile. . . . It is
my belief that anyone conversant with the almost spontaneous combustion in some
Southern communities in such a situation will agree that the City Manager's action
may well have averted a major catastrophe.

The gravity of the danger here surely needs no further explication. The imminence of that danger has been emphasized at every stage of this proceeding, from
the complaints charging that the demonstrations "tended directly to immediate
violence" to the State Supreme Court's affirmance on the authority of Feiner (US)
supra. This record, then, shows no steps backward from a standard of "clear and
present danger." But to say that the police may not intervene until the riot has
occurred is like keeping out the doctor until the patient dies. I cannot subscribe to
such a doctrine. . . .

I would affirm the convictions.

The "demonstration" has developed into a widely used weapon in the
arsenal of peaceful protest. In many of its forms it is simply a variation of
the old tool of the picket line. Since it has normally been used to protest
a practice or custom much more widespread than the boundaries of a single
company, however, and involves an attempt to change entire communities'
practices, it carries with it more of the traditional aspects and justifications
for considering it as an exercise of freedom of speech than do some of the
more narrowly drawn picketing issues. Certainly the majority opinion in
Edwards illustrates this interpretation. Justice Stewart said, "The circumstances in this case reflect an exercise of these basic constitutional rights in
their most pristine and classic form." This is not to say that there is an
absolute right to "demonstrate" in large crowds in any and every circumstance, but it is a clear warning that so long as the participants are not
engaged in clearly unlawful conduct, the state must show a strong justification for any interference and the justification must be supported by the
facts, subject to independent examination by the United States Supreme
Court. The position was reiterated in *Henry* v. *Rock Hill,* 376 U.S. 776 (1964),
reversing convictions for breach of the peace where there had been a peaceful assemblage at a city hall, with the participants carrying signs and singing
songs to protest segregation and where no violence had occurred.

A touchier question was presented in the review of a conviction for
picketing in front of a courthouse in Baton Rouge, Louisiana. The appellant
Cox was convicted on three charges: (1) breach of the peace, (2) obstructing
public passages, and (3) picketing before a courthouse. The charges were
based on his conduct during a demonstration of some 2,000 Negro college
students protesting racial discrimination. The convictions were separated
into two appeals, the first, No. 24, dealing with the first two charges and the

second, No. 49, dealing with the charge of picketing before the courthouse. The Court voted unanimously to reverse the convictions on the first charge of breach of the peace. While there was disagreement on the bases for reversal, most of the justices used reasoning similar to that in the *Edwards* case. Justice Black concurred on the ground that the breach of the peace statute on its face and as construed by the state courts was so broad as to be unconstitutionally vague. On the second charge the Court voted seven-to-two for reversal. *Cox* v. *Louisiana,* 379 U.S. 536 (1965). Justice Goldberg, for five members of the Court, held that the conviction for unlawfully obstructing public passages was an unwarranted abridgment of the leader's freedom of speech and assembly because the city authorities permitted or prohibited parades or street meetings in their completely uncontrolled discretion. He stated that, "Although the statute here involved on its face precludes all street assemblies and parades, it has not been so applied and enforced by the Baton Rouge authorities. City officials who testified for the state clearly indicated that certain meetings and parades are permitted in Baton Rouge, even though they have the effect of obstructing traffic, provided prior approval is obtained." Justices Black and Clark concurred on the separate ground that since the statute expressly permitted picketing for the publication of labor union views, to deny picketing for other free speech uses was forbidden by the "equal protection" clause of the Fourteenth Amendment. Justice White and Harlan dissented from the reversal of the conviction of obstructing public passages, stating that the statute had not been applied as an "open-ended licensing statute."

The appeal on the third charge of picketing before a courthouse is reported separately as *Cox* v. *Louisiana,* 379 U.S. 559 (1965), and the Court reversed by a vote of five-to-four. The conviction was for violations of a Louisiana statute which prohibited picketing or parading in or near a state court "with the intent of interfering with, obstructing or impeding the administration of justice, or with the intent of influencing any judge, juror, witness, or court officer, in the discharge of his duty." Justice Goldberg, speaking for the majority, denied appellant's contention that the statute was invalid on its face. He pointed out that the statute was modeled after an identical statute pertaining to the federal judiciary, passed by Congress in 1949 (64 Stat. 1018) and "unlike the two previously considered, is a precise, narrowly drawn regulatory statute which proscribes certain specific behavior."

The majority went on to find, further, that in applying the statute the state could properly arrest and convict for the kind of demonstration held in this instance—a protest gathering objecting to the arrest of a number of the students and held in the vicinity of the courthouse where the students' trials would take place and where the judges were located who would be trying the students' cases. Justice Goldberg made a distinction between regulations of "speech in its pristine form," such as newspaper comment or a telegram by a citizen to a public official, and "expression mixed with particular conduct." Noting that the case involved the latter form of expression, he concluded that appellant's argument that no clear and present danger was presented should be rejected on the ground that the legislature could properly have made a determination "based on experience that such conduct inherently threatens the judicial process."

Despite these statements in support of a general power to forbid what was done by the demonstrators in this case, however, the majority voted to reverse the convictions on the ground that prior permission was granted by the police and that the meeting did not acquire any illegal aspects afterward which would make refusal to obey a dispersal order a legitimate basis for arrest and conviction on the charge of picketing before a courthouse. The opinion pointed out that the demonstration took place on the far side of the street from the couthouse steps, and that the record showed that the officials present gave permission for Cox to conduct the demonstration at this point. This testimony "was corroborated by the State's witnesses themselves." Justice Goldberg said that "under all the circumstances of this case, after the public officials acted as they did, to sustain appellant's later conviction for demonstrating where they told him he could 'would be to sanction an indefensible sort of entrapment by the State—convicting a citizen for exercising a privilege which the State had clearly told him was available to him.'"

ADDERLEY v. FLORIDA
385 U.S. 39 (1966)

Mr. Justice Black delivered the opinion of the Court.

Petitioners, Harriett Louise Adderley and 31 other persons, were convicted by a jury . . . on a charge of "trespass with a malicious and mischievous intent" upon the premises of the county jail contrary to . . . Florida statutes. . . . Petitioners, apparently all students of the Florida A. & M. University in Tallahassee, had gone from the school to the jail about a mile away, along with many other students, to "demonstrate" at the jail their protests of arrests of other protesting students the day before, and perhaps to protest more generally against state and local policies and practices of racial segregation, including segregation of the jail. The county sheriff, legal custodian of the jail and jail grounds, tried to persuade the students to leave the jail grounds. When this did not work, he notified them that they must leave, that if they did not leave he would arrest them for trespassing, and that if they resisted he would charge them with that as well. Some of the students left but others, including petitioners, remained and they were arrested. On appeal the convictions were affirmed. . . . [P]etitioners applied to us for certiorari contending that, in view of petitioners' purpose to protest against jail and other segregation policies, their conviction denied them "rights of free speech, assembly, petition, due process of law and equal protection of the laws as guaranteed by the Fourteenth Amendment. . . ."

Petitioners have insisted from the beginning of this case that it is controlled by and must be reversed because of our prior cases of *Edwards* v. *South Carolina* . . . and *Cox* v. *Louisiana*. . . . We cannot agree. . . .

. . . The South Carolina breach-of-the-peace statute was . . . struck down as being so broad and all embracing as to jeopardize speech, press, assembly and petition, under the constitutional doctrine enunciated in *Cantwell* v. *Connecticut* . . . and followed in many subsequent cases. And it was on this same ground of vagueness that in *Cox* v. *Louisiana* . . . the Louisiana breach-of-the-peace law used to prosecute Cox was invalidated.

The Florida trespass statute under which these petitioners were charged cannot be challenged on this ground. It is aimed at conduct of one limited kind, that is, for one person or persons to trespass upon the property of another with a malicious and mischievous intent. There is no lack of notice in this law, nothing to entrap or fool the unwary. . . .

Petitioners next argue that "petty criminal statutes may not be used to violate minorities' constitutional rights." This of course is true, but this abstract proposition gets us nowhere in deciding this case.

Petitioners here contend that "Petitioners' convictions are based on a total lack of relevant evidence." If true, this would be a denial of due process. . . . Both in the petition for certiorari and in the brief on the merits petitioners state that their summary of the evidence "does not conflict with the facts contained in the Circuit Court's opinion" which was in effect affirmed by the District Court of Appeal . . . That statement is correct and petitioners' summary of facts, as well as that of the Circuit Court, shows an abundance of facts to support the jury's verdict of guilty in this case. . . .

Under the foregoing testimony the jury was authorized to find that the State had proven every essential element of the crime, as it was defined by the state court. That interpretation is, of course, binding on us, leaving only the question of whether conviction of the state offense, thus defined, unconstitutionally deprives petitioners of their rights to freedom of speech, press, assembly or petition. We hold it does not. The sheriff, as jail custodian, had power, as the state courts have here held, to direct that this large crowd of people get off the grounds. There is not a shred of evidence in this record that this power was exercised, or that its exercise was sanctioned by the lower courts, because the sheriff objected to what was being sung or said by the demonstrators or because he disagreed with the objectives of their protest. The record reveals that he objected only to their presence on that part of the jail grounds reserved for jail uses. There is no evidence at all that on any other occasion had similarly large groups of the public been permitted to gather on this portion of the jail grounds for any purpose. Nothing in the Constitution of the United States prevents Florida from even-handed enforcement of its general trespass statute against those refusing to obey the sheriff's order to remove themselves from what amounted to the curtilage of the jailhouse. The State, no less than a private owner of property, has power to preserve the property under its control for the use to which it is lawfully dedicated. For this reason there is no merit to the petitioners' argument that they had a constitutional right to stay on the property, over the jail custodian's objections, because this "area chosen for the peaceful civil rights demonstration was not only 'reasonable' but also particularly appropriate. . . ." Such an argument has as its major unarticulated premise the assumption that people who want to propagandize protests or views have a constitutional right to do so whenever and however and wherever they please. That concept of constitutional law was vigorously and forthrightly rejected in two of the cases petitioners rely on. . . . We reject it again. The United States Constitution does not forbid a State to control the use of its own property for its own lawful nondiscriminatory purpose.

Affirmed.

Mr. Justice Douglas, with whom The Chief Justice, Mr. Justice Brennan, and Mr. Justice Fortas concur, dissenting. . . .

. . . When we allow Florida to construe her "malicious trespass" statute to bar a person from going on property knowing it is not his own and to apply that prohibition to public property, we discard *Cox* and *Edwards*. Would the case be any different if, as is common, the demonstration took place outside a building which housed both the jail and the legislative body? I think not.

There may be some public places which are so clearly committed to other purposes that their use for the airing of grievances is anomalous. There may be some instances in which assemblies and petitions for redress of grievances are not consistent with other necessary purposes of public property. A noisy meeting may be out of keeping with the serenity of the statehouse or the quiet of the courthouse. No one, for example, would suggest that the Senate gallery is the proper place for a vociferous protest rally. And in other cases it may be necessary to adjust the right to petition for redress of grievances to the other interests inhering in the uses to which the public property is normally put. . . . But this is quite different from saying that all public places are off limits to people with grievances. . . . And it is farther yet from saying that the "custodian" of the public property in his discretion can decide when public places shall be used for the communication of ideas, especially the constitutional right to assemble and petition for redress of grievances. . . . For to place such discretion in any public official, be he the "custodian" of the public property or the local police commissioner . . . is to place those who assert their First Amendment rights at his mercy. It gives him the awesome power to decide whose ideas may be expressed and who shall be denied a place to air their claims and petition their government. Such power is out of step with all our decisions prior to today. . . .

GREGORY *v.* CHICAGO
394 U.S. 111 (1969)

Mr. Chief Justice Warren delivered the opinion of the Court.

This is a simple case. Petitioners, accompanied by Chicago police and an assistant city attorney, marched in a peaceful and orderly procession from city hall to the mayor's residence to press their claims for desegregation of the public schools. Having promised to cease singing at 8:30 P.M., the marchers did so. Although petitioners and the other demonstrators continued to march in a completely lawful fashion, the onlookers became unruly as the number of bystanders increased. Chicago police, to prevent what they regarded as an impending civil disorder, demanded that the demonstrators, upon pain of arrest, disperse. When this command was not obeyed, petitioners were arrested for disorderly conduct.

Petitioners' march, if peaceful and orderly, falls well within the sphere of conduct protected by the First Amendment. . . . There is no evidence in this record that petitioners' conduct was disorderly. Therefore, under the principle first established in *Thompson* v. *City of Louisville,* . . . convictions so totally devoid of evidentiary support violate due process.

The opinion of the Supreme Court of Illinois suggests that petitioners were convicted not for the manner in which they conducted their march but rather for their refusal to disperse when requested to do so by Chicago police. . . . However reasonable the police request may have been and however laudable the police motives, petitioners were charged and convicted for holding a demonstration not for a refusal to obey a police officer. . . .

The judgments are

Reversed.

Mr. Justice Douglas, while joining the separate opinion of Mr. Justice Black, also joins this opinion.

Mr. Justice Stewart and Mr. Justice White concurring. . . .

Mr. Justice Black, with whom Mr. Justice Douglas joins, concurring.

This we think is a highly important case which requires more detailed consideration than the Court's opinion gives it. . . .

. . . [B]oth police and demonstrators made their best efforts faithfully to discharge their responsibilities as officers and citizens, but they were nevertheless unable to restrain these hostile hecklers within decent and orderly bounds. These facts disclosed by the record point unerringly to one conclusion, namely, that when groups with diametrically opposed, deep-seated views are permitted to air their emotional grievances, side by side, on city streets, tranquility and order cannot be maintained even by the joint efforts of the finest and best officers and of those who desire to be the most law-abiding protestors of their grievances.

It is because of this truth, and a desire both to promote order and to safeguard First Amendment freedoms, that this Court has repeatedly warned States and governmental units that they cannot regulate conduct connected with these freedoms through use of sweeping, dragnet statutes that may, because of vagueness, jeopardize these freedoms. In those cases, however, we have been careful to point out the Constitution does not bar enactment of laws regulating conduct, even though connected with speech, press, assembly, and petition, if such laws specifically bar only the conduct deemed obnoxious and are carefully and narrowly aimed at that forbidden conduct. The dilemma revealed by this record is a crying example of a need for some such narrowly drawn law. . . .

The disorderly conduct ordinance under which these petitioners were charged and convicted is not, however, a narrowly drawn law. . . . To the contrary, it might better be described as a meat ax ordinance, gathering in one comprehensive definition of an offense a number of words which have a multiplicity of meanings, some of which would cover activity specifically protected by the First Amendment. . . .

The so-called "diversion tending to a breach of the peace" here was limited entirely and exclusively to the fact that when the policeman in charge of the special police detail concluded that the hecklers observing the march were dangerously close to rioting and that the demonstrators and others were likely to be engulfed in that riot, he ordered Gregory and his demonstrators to leave, and Gregory—standing on what he deemed to be his constitutional rights—refused to do so. . . . To let a policeman's command become equivalent to a criminal statute comes dangerously near making our government one of men rather than of law. . . . There are ample ways to protect the domestic tranquility without subjecting First Amendment freedoms to such a clumsy and unwieldy weapon.

The city of Chicago, recognizing the serious First Amendment problems raised by the disorderly conduct ordinance as it is written, argues that these convictions should nevertheless be affirmed in light of the narrowing construction placed on the ordinance by the Illinois Supreme Court in this case. . . . Whatever the validity of the Illinois Supreme Court's construction, this was simply not the theory on which these petitioners were convicted. In explaining the elements of the offense to the jury, the trial judge merely read the language of the ordinance. The jury was not asked to find whether, as the Illinois Supreme Court's construction apparently requires, there was "an imminent threat of violence," or whether the police had "made all reasonable efforts to protect the demonstrators." Rather, it was sufficient for the jury to decide that petitioners had made "an improper noise" or a "diversion tending to a breach of the peace," or had "collect[ed] in bodies or crowds for unlawful purposes, or for any purpose, to the annoyance or disturbance of other persons.". . .

In agreeing to the reversal of these convictions, however, we wish once more to say that we think our Federal Constitution does not render the States powerless to regulate the conduct of demonstrators and picketers, conduct which is more than "speech," more than "press," more than "assembly," and more than "petition" as those terms are used in the First Amendment. Narrowly drawn statutes regulating the conduct of demonstrators and picketers are not impossible to draft.... Speech and press are, of course, to be free, so that public matters can be discussed with impunity. But picketing and demonstrating can be regulated like other conduct of men. We believe that the homes of men, sometimes the last citadel of the tired, the weary and the sick, can be protected by government from noisy, marching, tramping, threatening picketers and demonstrators bent on filling the minds of men, women, and children with fears of the unknown.

For these reasons we concur in the reversal....

Mr. Justice Harlan, concurring in the result....

BRANDENBURG *v.* OHIO
395 U.S. 444 (1969)

[The defendant, a leader of a Ku Klux Klan group, spoke at a Klan rally at which a large wooden cross was burned and some of the other persons present were carrying firearms. His remarks included such statements as: "Bury the niggers," "the niggers should be returned to Africa," and "send the Jews back to Israel." He was convicted under the Ohio Criminal Syndicalism statute of "advocat[ing] ... the duty, necessity, or propriety of crime, sabotage, violence, or unlawful methods of terrorism as a means of accomplishing industrial or political reform" and of "voluntarily assembl[ing] with any society, group or assemblage of persons formed to teach or advocate the doctrines of criminal syndicalism." On appeal, he challenged the constitutionality of the statute under the First and Fourteenth Amendments, but the intermediate appellate court of Ohio affirmed, without opinion, and the Supreme Court of Ohio dismissed his appeal.]

PER CURIAM....

In 1927, this Court sustained the constitutionality of California's Criminal Syndicalism Act, ... the text of which is quite similar to that of the laws of Ohio. *Whitney* v. *California*.... The Court upheld the statute on the ground that, without more, "advocating" violent means to effect political and economic change involves such danger to the security of the State that the State may outlaw it. ... But *Whitney* has been thoroughly discredited by later decisions. See *Dennis* v. *United States*.... These later decisions have fashioned the principle that the constitutional guarantees of free speech and free press do not permit a State to forbid or proscribe advocacy of the use of force or of law violation except where such advocacy is directed to inciting or producing imminent lawless action and is likely to incite or produce such action. As we said in *Noto* v. *United States*, ... "the mere abstract teaching ... of the moral propriety or even moral necessity for a resort to force and violence, is not the same as preparing a group for violent action and steeling it to such action."... A statute which fails to draw this distinction impermissibly intrudes upon the freedoms guaranteed by the First and Fourteenth Amendments....

... [W]e are here confronted with a statute which, by its own words and as applied, purports to punish mere advocacy and to forbid, on pain of criminal punishment, assembly with others merely to advocate the described type of action. Such a statute falls within the condemnation of the First and Fourteenth Amendments. The contrary teaching of *Whitney* v. *California, supra,* cannot be supported, and that decision is therefore overruled.

Reversed.

Mr. Justice Black, concurring. . . .
Mr. Justice Douglas, concurring. . . .

In *United States* v. *O'Brien,* 391 U.S. 367 (1968), the defendant was convicted for violating federal law by burning his draft card. The Court of Appeals reversed on the ground that the statute was unconstitutional as a law abridging freedom of speech. The Supreme Court reinstated the judgment and sentence of the District Court. Chief Justice Warren, for the majority, said, "We cannot accept the view that an apparently limitless variety of conduct can be labelled 'speech' whenever the person engaging in the conduct intends thereby to express an idea." He stated further that the power to classify and conscript manpower for military service is "beyond question," and that the issuance of draft cards was a legitimate and substantial administrative aid in the functioning of the system.

Street v. *New York,* 394 U.S. 576 (1969), involved a conviction for burning an American flag on a street corner. After learning that civil rights leader James Meredith had been shot by a sniper in Mississippi, the accused set fire to his flag. After a policeman approached and learned that Street had burned the flag, the accused stated: "If they did that to Meredith, we don't need an American flag." Following a nonjury trial in the New York City Criminal Court, the accused was convicted and given a suspended sentence for malicious mischief consisting of a violation of a New York statute making it a misdemeanor publicly to mutilate, defile, or cast contempt upon an American flag either by words or act. The conviction was affirmed by the New York Court of Appeals. On appeal, the United States Supreme Court reversed and remanded. A majority of five held that the accused had a constitutional right to express his opinion about the flag, even if his opinion was defiant or contemptuous, and that since he might have been convicted for the words used rather than merely the deed, the case would have to be remanded. Four judges dissented, arguing that the conviction was based on the deed rather than the words and was therefore constitutional.

In *Spence* v. *Washington,* 418 U.S. 405 (1974), the Court reversed a conviction under a Washington statute which prohibited the placing of any "word, figure, mark, picture, design, . . . of any nature upon any flag" of the United States. Spence had affixed to both surfaces of a flag a large peace symbol of removable tape and had then displayed the flag from his apartment window. The Per Curiam opinion for five members of the Court stated that the defendant was not charged under a flag desecration statute, nor did he permanently disfigure the flag or destroy it. "His message was direct, likely to be understood, and within the contours of the First Amendment. Given the protected character of his expression and in light of the fact that no interest the State may have in preserving the physical integrity of a privately-owned flag was significantly impaired on these facts, the conviction must be invalidated."

TINKER *v.* DES MOINES SCHOOL DISTRICT
393 U.S. 503 (1969)

Mr. Justice Fortas delivered the opinion of the Court.

Petitioner John F. Tinker, 15 years old, and petitioner Christopher Eckhardt, 16 years old, attended high schools in Des Moines. Petitioner Mary Beth Tinker, John's sister, was a 13-year-old student in junior high school. [As part of a plan formulated by a group of adults and students in the city, the petitioners wore black armbands to their schools to publicize their objections to the hostilities in Vietnam and their support for a truce, despite the fact that they were aware that the school authorities a few days previously had adopted a policy that any student wearing an armband to school would be asked to remove it, on penalty of suspension until he returned without the armband. After refusal to remove the armbands, the students were suspended. Petitioners filed a suit for injunction in federal court. The District Court dismissed the complaint, holding the order a reasonable measure to prevent disturbance of school discipline. The Court of Appeals affirmed.]

The problem presented by the present case does not relate to regulation of the length of skirts or the type of clothing, to hair style or deportment. . . . It does not concern aggressive, disruptive action or even group demonstrations. Our problem involves direct, primary First Amendment rights akin to "pure speech."

The school officials banned and sought to punish petitioners for a silent, passive, expression of opinion, unaccompanied by any disorder or disturbance on the part of petitioners. There is here no evidence whatever of petitioners' interference, actual or nascent, with the school's work or of collision with the rights of other students to be secure and to be let alone. Accordingly, this case does not concern speech or action that intrudes upon the work of the school or the rights of other students. . . .

In order for the State in the person of school officials to justify prohibition of a particular expression of opinion, it must be able to show that its action was caused by something more than a mere desire to avoid the discomfort and unpleasantness that always accompany an unpopular viewpoint. Certainly where there is no finding and no showing that the exercise of the forbidden right would "materially and substantially interfere with the requirements of appropriate discipline in the operation of the school," the prohibition cannot be sustained. . . .

It is also relevant that the school authorities did not purport to prohibit the wearing of all symbols of political or controversial significance. The record shows that students in some of the schools wore buttons relating to national political campaigns, and some even wore the Iron Cross, traditionally a symbol of nazism. The order prohibiting the wearing of armbands did not extend to these. Instead, a particular symbol—black armbands worn to exhibit opposition to this Nation's involvement in Vietnam—was singled out for prohibition. Clearly, the prohibition of expression of one particular opinion, at least without evidence that it is necessary to avoid material and substantial interference with school work or discipline, is not constitutionally permissible.

In our system, state-operated schools may not be enclaves of totalitarianism. School officials do not possess absolute authority over their students. Students in school as well as out of school are "persons" under our Constitution. They are possessed of fundamental rights which the State must respect, just as they themselves must respect their obligations to the State. In our system, students may not be regarded as closed-circuit recipients of only that which the State chooses to communicate. They may not be confined to the expression of those sentiments that are officially approved. In the absence of a specific showing of constitutionally valid reasons to regulate their speech, students are entitled to freedom of expression of their views. . . .

Reversed and remanded.

Mr. Justice Stewart, concurring. . . .

Mr. Justice White, concurring. . . .

Mr. Justice Black, dissenting.

The Court's holding in this case ushers in what I deem to be an entirely new era in which the power to control pupils by the elected "officials of state supported public schools ..." in the United States is in ultimate effect transferred to the Supreme Court. ...

Assuming that the Court is correct in holding that the conduct of wearing armbands for the purpose of conveying political ideas is protected by the First Amendment ... the crucial remaining questions are whether students and teachers may use the school at their whim as a platform for the exercise of free speech—"symbolic" or "pure"—and whether the Courts will allocate to themselves the function of deciding how the pupils' school day will be spent. While I have always believed that under the First and Fourteenth Amendments neither the State nor Federal Government has any authority to regulate or censor the content of speech, I have never believed that any person has a right to give speeches or engage in demonstrations where he pleases and when he pleases. This Court has already rejected such a notion. ...

While the record does not show that any of these armband students shouted, used profane language or were violent in any manner, a detailed report by some of them shows their armbands caused comments, warnings by other students, the poking of fun at them, and a warning by an older football player that other, nonprotesting students had better let them alone. There is also evidence that the professor of mathematics had his lesson period practically "wrecked" chiefly by disputes with Beth Tinker, who wore her armband for her "demonstration." Even a casual reading of the record shows that this armband did divert students' minds from their regular lessons, and that talk, comments, etc., made John Tinker "self-conscious" in attending school with his armband. While the absence of obscene or boisterous and loud disorder perhaps justifies the Court's statement that the few armband students did not actually "disrupt" the classwork, I think the record overwhelmingly shows that the armbands did exactly what the elected school officials and principals foresaw it would, that is, took the students' minds off their classwork and diverted them to thoughts about the highly emotional subject of the Vietnam war. And I repeat that if the time has come when pupils of state-supported schools, kindergarten, grammar school or high school, can defy and flaunt orders of school officials to keep their minds on their own school work, it is the beginning of a new revolutionary era of permissiveness in this country fostered by the judiciary. The next logical step, it appears to me, would be to hold unconstitutional laws that bar pupils under 21 or 18 from voting, or from being elected members of the Boards of Education. ...

... The truth is that a teacher of kindergarten, grammar school, or high school pupils no more carries into a school with him a complete right to freedom of speech and expression than an anti-Catholic or anti-Semitic carries with him a complete freedom of speech and religion into a Catholic church or Jewish synagogue. Nor does a person carry with him into the United States Senate or House, or to the Supreme Court, or any other court, a complete constitutional right to go into those places contrary to their rules and speak his mind on any subject he pleases. ...

In my view, teachers in state-controlled public schools are hired to teach there. Although Mr. Justice McReynolds may have intimated to the contrary in *Myers v. Nebraska, supra,* certainly a teacher is not paid to go into school and teach subjects the State does not hire him to teach as a part of its selected curriculum. Nor are public school students sent to the schools at public expense to broadcast political or any other views to educate and inform the public. The original idea of schools, which I do not believe is yet abandoned as worthless or out of date, was that children had not yet reached the point of experience and wisdom which enabled them to teach all of their elders. It may be that the Nation has outworn the old-fashioned slogan that "children are to be seen not heard," but one may, I hope, be permitted to harbor the thought that taxpayers send children to school on the premise that at their age they need to learn, not teach. . . .

Change has been said to be truly the law of life but sometimes the old and the tried and true are worth holding. The schools of this Nation have undoubtedly contributed to giving us tranquility and to making us a more law-abiding people. Uncontrolled and uncontrollable liberty is an enemy to domestic peace. We cannot close our eyes to the fact that some of the country's greatest problems are crimes committed by the youth, too many of school age. . . . One does not need to be a prophet to know that after the Court's holding today that some students in Iowa schools and indeed in all schools will be ready, able, and willing to defy their teachers on practically all orders. This is the more unfortunate for the schools since groups of students all over the land are already running loose, conducting break-ins, sit-ins, lie-ins, and smash-ins. . . . Students engaged in such activities are apparently confident that they know far more about how to operate public school systems than do their parents, teachers, and elected school officials. It is no answer to say that the particular students here have not yet reached such high points in their demands to attend classes in order to exercise their political pressures. Turned loose with lawsuits for damages and injunctions against their teachers like they are here, it is nothing but wishful thinking to imagine that young, immature students will not soon believe it is their right to control the schools rather than the right of the States that collect the taxes to hire the teachers for the benefit of the pupils. This case, therefore, wholly without constitutional reasons in my judgment, subjects all the public schools in the country to the whims and caprices of their loudest-mouthed, but maybe not their brightest, students. I, for one, am not fully persuaded that school pupils are wise enough, even with this Court's expert help from Washington, to run the 23,390 public school systems in our 50 States. I wish, therefore, wholly to disclaim any purpose on my part, to hold that the Federal Constitution compels the teachers, parents, and elected school officials to surrender control of the American public school system to public school students. I dissent.

Mr. Justice Harlan, dissenting. . . .

SPECIAL ASPECTS OF FREEDOM OF THE PRESS

While the broader aspects of the topics previously discussed apply to all forms of expression—speech, press, and assembly—and thus have not been dealt with in their applications to isolated First Amendment rights, there are certain special problems which have arisen in connection with the press and other news media which require separate treatment. Among the foremost is that of reconciling the demands of a free press with the need for fair administration of justice. Another is the definition and proper treatment of obscene publications within the demands of the First Amendment. In addition there are problems of delineating the appropriate area of regulation of the press in its character as a normal commercial enterprise, and the application of state laws in such areas as libel and the regulation of distribution of handbills. Insofar as regulations may run afoul of the general interdiction against prior restraints, the earlier discussion of that rule in this chapter applies, as in the important free press case *Near* v. *Minnesota.* In general, this section will deal with the constitutional issues presented by some of the postpublication regulations or burdens on the various facets of the press.

Free Press v. Fair Administration of Justice

While a democratic society must accord a high place to the freedom of news media to inform the public, the right to a fair trial, both in civil and criminal cases, is entitled to no less regard. A conflict between these two values arises when newspaper or radio or television communications prior to a trial or during a trial are of such a nature as to threaten the impartiality of verdicts or sentences. The issue with respect to criminal cases has been dealt with to some extent in the earlier chapter on the rights of the accused.

Under his common-law powers the judge in Anglo-American courts has long had the power to punish for contempt persons who interfere with or obstruct the administration of justice. The application of this power to a newspaper, of course, raises First Amendment questions. In the companion cases of *Bridges* v. *California* and *Times-Mirror Company* v. *Superior Court of California*, 314 U.S. 252 (1941), the Court for the first time had occasion to review a state's exercise of the contempt power in punishing a publisher for statements appearing during the course of a trial. Justice Black, in his opinion for the Court, recited the facts:

The Los Angeles Times Editorials. The Times-Mirror Company, publisher of the Los Angeles Times, and L. D. Hotchkiss, its managing editor, were cited for contempt for the publication of three editorials. Both found by the trial court to be responsible for one of the editorials, the company and Hotchkiss were each fined $100. The company alone was held responsible for the other two, and was fined $100 more on account of one, and $300 more on account of the other.

The $300 fine presumably marks the most serious offense. The editorial thus distinguished was entitled "Probation for Gorillas?" After vigorously denouncing two members of a labor union who had previously been found guilty of assaulting nonunion truck drivers, it closes with the observation: "Judge A. A. Scott will make a serious mistake if he grants probation to Matthew Shannon and Kennan Holmes. This community needs the example of their assignment to the jute mill." Judge Scott had previously set a day (about a month after the publication) for passing upon the application of Shannon and Holmes for probation and for pronouncing sentence. . . .

The Bridges Telegram. While a motion for a new trial was pending in a case involving a dispute between an A.F. of L. union and a C.I.O. union of which Bridges was an officer, he either caused to be published or acquiesced in the publication of a telegram which he had sent to the Secretary of Labor. The telegram referred to the judge's decision as "outrageous"; said that attempted enforcement of it would tie up the port of Los Angeles and involve the entire Pacific Coast; and concluded with the announcement that the C.I.O. union, representing some twelve thousand members, did "not intend to allow state courts to override the majority vote of members in choosing its officers and representatives and to override the National Labor Relations Board."

Apparently Bridges' conviction is not rested at all upon his use of the word "outrageous." The remainder of the telegram fairly construed appears to be a statement that if the court's decree should be enforced there would be a strike. It is not claimed that such a strike would have been in violation of the terms of the decree, nor that in any other way it would have run afoul of the law of California. On no construction, therefore, can the telegram be taken as a threat either by Bridges or the union to follow an illegal course of action.

By a five-to-four vote the Court reversed the contempt citations in both cases. Justice Black, for the majority, examined and refuted the argument that "the power of judges to punish by contempt out-of-court publications tending to obstruct the orderly and fair administration of justice in a pending case was deeply rooted in English common law at the time the Constitution was adopted," and therefore the usual constitutional immunity guaranteed to other types of utterances could not be applied in this case. The opinion stated further:

... [W]e are convinced that the judgments below result in a curtailment of expression that cannot be dismissed as insignificant. If they can be justified at all, it must be in terms of some serious substantive evil which they are designed to avert. The substantive evil here sought to be averted has been variously described below. It appears to be double: disrespect for the judiciary; and disorderly and unfair administration of justice. The assumption that respect for the judiciary can be won by shielding judges from published criticism wrongly appraises the character of American public opinion. For it is a prized American privilege to speak one's mind, although not always with perfect good taste, on all public institutions. And an enforced silence, however limited, solely in the name of preserving the dignity of the bench, would probably engender resentment, suspicion, and contempt much more than it would enhance respect.

The other evil feared, disorderly and unfair administration of justice, is more plausibly associated with restricting publications which touch upon pending litigation. The very word "trial" connotes decisions on the evidence and arguments properly advanced in open court. Legal trials are not like elections, to be won through the use of the meeting-hall, the radio, and the newspaper. But we cannot start with the assumption that publications of the kind here involved actually do threaten to change the nature of legal trials, and that to preserve judicial impartiality, it is necessary for judges to have a contempt power by which they can close all channels of public expression to all matters which touch upon pending cases. We must therefore turn to the particular utterances here in question and the circumstances of their publication to determine to what extent the substantive evil of unfair administration of justice was a likely consequence, and whether the degree of likelihood was sufficient to justify summary punishment.

[As to the *Times-Mirror* editorials, the opinion pointed out that from the past position of the paper on labor controversies there could have been little doubt of its attitude toward the probation of the two union members.]

In view of the paper's long-continued militancy in this field, it is inconceivable that any judge in Los Angeles would expect anything but adverse criticism from it in the event probation were granted. Yet such criticism after final disposition of the proceedings would clearly have been privileged. Hence, this editorial, given the most intimidating construction it will bear, did no more than threaten future adverse criticism which was reasonably to be expected anyway in the event of a lenient disposition of the pending case. To regard it, therefore, as in itself of substantial influence upon the course of justice would be to impute to judges a lack of firmness, wisdom, or honor, which we cannot accept as a major premise.

The majority felt that there was no more danger of intimidation or interference with justice in the Bridges telegram than in the editorials and reversed the judgment in this case also. Justice Frankfurter filed a long dissenting opinion, concurred in by Chief Justice Stone and Justices Roberts and Byrnes. He said, "A trial is not a 'free trade in ideas,' nor is the best test of truth in a courtroom 'the power of the thought to get itself accepted in the competition of the market.'" He continued:

A court is a forum with strictly defined limits for discussion. It is circumscribed in the range of its inquiry and in its methods by the Constitution, by laws, and by age-old traditions. Its judges are restrained in their freedom of expression by historic compulsions resting on no other officials of government. They are so circumscribed precisely because judges have in their keeping the enforcement of rights and the protection of liberties which, according to the wisdom of the ages, can only be enforced and protected by observing such methods and traditions. . . .

It is suggested that threats, by discussion, to untrammeled decisions by courts are the most natural expressions when public feeling runs highest. But it does not follow that states are left powerless to prevent their courts from being subverted by outside pressure when the need for impartiality and fair proceeding is greatest. To say that the framers of the Constitution sanctified veiled violence through coercive speech directed against those charged with adjudications is not merely to make violence an ingredient of justice; it mocks the very ideal of justice by respecting its forms while stultifying its uncontaminated exercise.

The case illustrates the milder strictures employed in the United States against newspaper comment while a case is *sub judice*. In England the rule is much tighter, and the fines are apt to be far more severe. In 1949 the Lord Chief Justice fined the London *Daily Mirror* £10,000 and sentenced the editor to three months in jail for comments published concerning a murder trial then under way. [See Donald M. Gillmor, "Free Press and Fair Trial in English Law," 22 *Wash. & Lee L. Rev.* 17 (1965).] In the United States Supreme Court the cases indicate that the evidence supporting a contempt finding must point to a strong threat of subversion of justice before such a judgment will be upheld. In *Pennekamp* v. *Florida,* 328 U.S. 331 (1946), the publisher of the *Miami Herald* was fined for contempt for having published various editorials and a cartoon criticizing a local judge for interfering with the prosecutor's attempts to combat crime in the Miami area. The Supreme Court reversed. Even though some of the cases were still pending, the Court unanimously held that the criticism did not create a danger to fair judicial administration of the "clearness and immediacy necessary to close the doors of permissible public comment." And in *Craig* v. *Harney,* 331 U.S. 367 (1947), a divided Court held that publication, while a motion for a new trial was pending, of an unfair report of the facts of a civil case, accompanied by criticism of the judge for taking the case from the jury, was protected by the Constitution. The press called the action of the trial judge "arbitrary action" and a "travesty on justice." It deplored the fact that the elected judge was a "layman" and not a "competent attorney." The case dealt with an attempt by a property owner to evict a serviceman from business property for nonpayment of rent, and public opinion seemingly was strongly in favor of the serviceman. The jury had twice returned a verdict in his favor despite an instructed verdict for the plaintiff. The motion for new trial followed the jury's third verdict in compliance with the judge's instruction. Subsequently the newspaper personnel involved in the editorials and reports were adjudged guilty of contempt. Justice Douglas, speaking for the majority voting to reverse, stated:

A judge who is part of such a dramatic episode can hardly help but know that his decision is apt to be unpopular. But the law of contempt is not made for the protection of judges who may be sensitive to the winds of public opinion. Judges are supposed to be men of fortitude, able to thrive in a hardy climate. Conceivably a campaign could be so managed and so aimed at the sensibilities of a particular judge and the matter pending before him as to cross the forbidden line. But the episodes we have here do not fall in that category. Nor can we assume that the trial judge was not a man of fortitude.

[Justice Fanrkfurter, joined by Chief Justice Vinson, dissented, pointing out that the newspapers involved were under common control and were the only papers of general circulation in the area. He stated:]

It can hardly be a compelling presumption that such papers so controlled had no influence, at a time when patriotic fervor was running high, in stirring up sentiment of powerful groups in a small community in favor of a veteran to whom, it was charged, a great wrong had been done. It would seem a natural inference, as the court below in effect found, that these newspapers whipped up public opinion against the judge to secure reversal of his action and then professed merely to report public opinion. We cannot say that the Texas Court could not properly find that these newspapers asked of the judge, and instigated powerful sections of the community to ask of the judge, that which no one has any business to ask of a judge, except the parties and their counsel in open court, namely, that he should decide one way rather than another.

[Justice Jackson dissented separately, saying:]

From our sheltered position, fortified by life tenure and other defenses to judicial independence, it is easy to say that this local judge ought to have shown more fortitude in the face of criticism. But he had no such protection. He was an elective judge, who held for a short term. I do not take it that an ambition of a judge to remain a judge is either unusual or dishonorable. Moreover, he was not a lawyer, and I regard this as a matter of some consequence. A lawyer may gain courage to render a decision that temporarily is unpopular because he has confidence that his profession over the years will approve it, despite its unpopular reception, as has been the case with many great decisions. But this judge had no anchor in professional opinion. Of course, the blasts of these little papers in this small community do not jolt us, but I am not so confident that we would be indifferent if a news monopoly in our entire jurisdiction should perpetrate this kind of an attack on us.

The previous decisions have presented the problem of unusual pressures on judges by newspapers to have them dispose of cases in particular ways. A problem is also presented when pretrial publicity in criminal cases is of such a nature as to threaten impartial decisions by jurors. The usual procedure for developing this issue is to appeal a conviction on the ground that a fair trial was denied because of the prejudicial effect of the publicity. In *Shepherd* v. *Florida*, 341 U.S. 50 (1951), this was one of the grounds suggested in requesting a reversal of the conviction of four Negroes. The majority reversed, although the decision came on the ground that discrimination had been practiced in the selection of the grand jury. Justices Frankfurter and Jackson, however, argued further that inflammatory newspaper comment made a fair trial in the community impossible.

Contempt proceedings have also been initiated against persons publishing prejudicial comment upon pending criminal cases. A Maryland trial court, in 1949, punished for contempt a broadcasting company which prior to a murder trial had announced that the person arrested had confessed to the crime, that he had a long criminal record, and that he went to the scene of the crime with officers, re-enacted the crime, and dug up the knife which he had used to commit the murder. The Maryland court of appeals reversed the contempt conviction on the basis of *Bridges, Pennekamp,* and *Craig.* The United States Supreme Court denied certiorari, *Maryland* v. *Baltimore Radio Show,* 338 U.S. 912 (1950), but Justice Frankfurter filed an opinion stressing the point that such denial should not be construed as approving the decision below. He set out in an appendix the course of English decisions dealing with situations in which publications were claimed to have injuriously affected the prosecutions for crime awaiting jury determination, and as to freedom of press in England cited the Report of the Royal Commission on the Press, Cmd. No. 7700, and the debate thereon in the House of Commons, July 28, 1949 (467 H.C. Deb., 5th Ser., 2683–2794).

In *Irvin* v. *Dowd,* 366 U.S. 717 (1961), the petitioner was indicted for murder in Indiana and was granted a change of venue to an adjoining county. His request for a second change of venue and a continuance, sought on the ground of local prejudice, was denied. He was convicted and sentenced to death. After lengthy litigation, the issue came to the United States Supreme Court on certiorari to review a denial of habeas corpus. By unanimous vote the Court vacated the judgment, holding that pretrial publicity had prejudiced the chances for a fair trial in the second county. Justice Clark's opinion for the Court states:

Finally, and with remarkable understatement, the headlines reported that "impartial jurors are hard to find." The panel consisted of 430 persons. The court itself excused 268 of those on challenges for cause as having fixed opinions as to the guilt of petitioner.... An examination of the 2,783-page *voir dire* record shows that 370 prospective jurors or almost 90 percent of those examined on the point (10 members of the panel were never asked whether or not they had any opinion) entertained some opinion as to guilt—ranging in intensity from mere suspicion to absolute certainty.... With his life at stake, it is not requiring too much that petitioner be tried in an atmosphere undisturbed by so huge a wave of public passion and by a jury other than one in which two-thirds of the members admit, before hearing any testimony, to possessing a belief in his guilt.

A flagrant example of pretrial publicity is presented in *Rideau* v. *Louisiana,* 373 U.S. 73 (1963). Following a confession televised from a jail cell, Rideau moved for a change of venue. The motion was denied, and the defendant was tried, convicted, and sentenced to death for murder. On certiorari, the United States Supreme Court reversed, with the majority holding that due process required a trial before a jury drawn from a community of people who had not seen and heard the televised interview. The facts are recited in Justice Stewart's opinion for the Court:

[A] man robbed a bank in Lake Charles, Louisiana, kidnapped three of the bank's employees, and killed one of them. A few hours later the petitioner... was apprehended by the police and lodged in ... jail in Lake Charles. The next morning a moving picture film with a sound track was made of an "interview" in the jail between Rideau and the Sheriff of Calcasieu Parish. This "interview" lasted approximately 20 minutes. It consisted of interrogation by the sheriff and admissions by Rideau that he had perpetrated the bank robbery, kidnapping, and murder. Later the same day the filmed "interview" was broadcast over a television station in Lake Charles, and some 24,000 people in the community saw and heard it on television. The sound film was again shown on television the next day to an estimated audience of 53,000 people. The following day the film was again broadcast by the same television station, and this time approximately 29,000 people saw and heard the "interview" on their television sets. Calcasieu Parish has a population of approximately 150,000 people. . . .

Three members of the jury which convicted him had stated on *voir dire* that they had seen and heard Rideau's televised "interview" with the sheriff on at least one occasion. . . . Rideau's counsel had requested that three jurors be excused for cause, having exhausted all of their peremptory challenges, but these challenges for cause had been denied by the trial judge.

[In holding the denial of the motion for change of venue and the subsequent trial unconstitutional, Justice Stewart stated:]

For anyone who has ever watched television the conclusion cannot be avoided that this spectacle, to the tens of thousands of people who saw and heard it, in a very real sense *was* Rideau's trial—at which he pleaded guilty to murder. Any subsequent court proceedings in a community so pervasively exposed to such a spectacle could be but a hollow formality.

Justices Clark and Harlan dissented on the ground that the record did not show that the adverse publicity "fatally infected the trial." On this basis they distinguished the case from *Irvin* v. *Dowd*.

The most vivid recent situation involving the clash between the freedom of the news media and the right of an accused to an impartial determination of his guilt took place following the assassination of President Kennedy in November, 1963. A crime of such magnitude was bound to lead to enormous pressures on the police and prosecutor for even the most trivial piece of information concerning the assassin which could be transmitted by radio, television, and newspaper to people all over the world. And much that would be considered of an evidentiary nature was released to these media prior to and after the arrest of Lee Harvey Oswald. Had he not been murdered prior to the trial, a serious question would have been presented of whether the three days of saturation coverage precluded an impartial jury determination. The President's Commission on the Assassination took cognizance of this aspect of the events and in the official report, issued in 1964, stated as the last of twelve recommendations:

The commission recommends that the representatives of the bar, law enforcement associations, and the news media work together to establish ethical standards concerning the collection and presentation of information to the public so that there will be no interference with pending criminal investigations, court proceedings, or the right to a fair trial.

In 1965 the Court faced the issue of whether televising and broadcasting a criminal trial of considerable notoriety denied the accused due process of law. The case involved a state prosecution for swindling against Billie Sol Estes in Texas. At a pretrial hearing the defense moved to prevent telecasting, broadcasting by radio and news photography and also moved for a continuance. In a two-day hearing arguments were heard on these motions. These hearings were carried live by both radio and television, and news photography was permitted throughout. At least twelve cameramen were present, "cables and wires were snaked across the courtroom floor, three microphones were on the judge's bench and others were beamed at the jury box and the counsel table," as Justice Clark described the scene. A venire of jurymen had been summoned and was present in the courtroom during the entire hearing. The motion for continuance was granted. At the trial itself, a booth was constructed at the back of the courtroom with an aperture to permit cameramen an unrestricted view of the courtroom. All television cameras and newsreel photographers were restricted to the area of the booth when shooting film or telecasting. Live telecasting was permitted only for the opening and closing arguments of the state, the return of the jury's verdict, and its receipt by the trial judge. Videotapes of the entire proceeding without sound were permitted, however, although the cameras operated only intermittently. Estes was convicted, and the Texas Court of Criminal Appeals affirmed, over the claim of denial of due process under the Fourteenth Amendment because of the televising and broadcasting of proceedings.

By the close decision of five-to-four the Court reversed in *Estes* v. *Texas,* 381 U.S. 532 (1965), although the majority was divided on the applicable rule governing the televising and broadcasting of criminal trials. Thus the holding of the case is limited to the use of these media in trials of considerable notoriety. Justice Harlan, in a concurring opinion, indicated that he would not necessarily vote the same way in a trial less highly publicized and involving a "run-of-the-mill case."

The state argued that no prejudice had been shown by petitioner as a result of the televising and that the public has a right to know what goes on in the courts. Justice Clark, for the majority, responded that our system of law must prevent even the probability of unfairness, and even though "one cannot put his finger on its specific mischief and prove with particularity wherein he was prejudiced," it *may* cause prejudice to an accused. Add to this the fact that forty-eight of the states and the Federal Rules bar the use of television in the courtroom and the conclusion was that "its use would be inconsistent with our concepts of due process in this field."

As to the dangers, Justice Clark enumerated four potential threats to the fair administration of justice: (1) the distraction of jurors because of their self-consciousness and unease when being televised, (2) the impairment of the quality of testimony because of the witnesses' knowledge that they are being viewed by a vast audience, (3) the additional burden and responsibility placed on the trial judge because of the necessity for supervision of the telecasting, leading perhaps to the diversion of attention from the proper conduct of the trial, and (4) the impact of television on the defendant as a form of mental harassment. He stated further, "A defendant on trial for a specific crime is entitled to his day in court, not in a stadium, or a city or nationwide arena. The heightened public clamor resulting from radio and television coverage will inevitably result in prejudice."

Chief Justice Warren, joined by Justices Douglas and Goldberg, stated flatly that he believed "that it violates the Sixth Amendment for federal courts and the Fourteenth Amendment for state courts to allow criminal trials to be televised to the public at large." On the issue of guaranteeing a public trial, he stated that this requirement was met when "a courtroom has facilities for a reasonable number of the public to observe the proceedings, which facilities are not so small as to render the openness negligible and not so large as to distract the trial participants from their proper function, when the public is free to use these facilities, and when all those who attend the trial are free to report what they observed at the proceedings."

The dissenters in the case were unwilling to lay down a flat constitutional bar to televised criminal trials and stressed the point that no actual prejudice was proved in the case. They indicated that a lack of information on the effect of cameras in the courtroom should make the Court wary of a decision which would preclude intelligent assessment of the probable hazards involved in their use.

In an important decision in 1966, *Sheppard* v. *Maxwell*, the Court undertook to suggest some appropriate steps which trial judges should employ to safeguard against prejudicial reporting in criminal trials. The occasion was the review of proceedings at a notorious murder trial.

SHEPPARD *v.* MAXWELL
384 U.S. 333 (1966)

[Petitioner, accused of murdering his wife, was tried before a jury in the Court of Common Pleas of Cuyahoga County, Ohio. Both before and during the trial, which began two weeks before an election in which the trial judge and the chief prosecutor were candidates for judgeships, the petitioner was the subject of extensive newspaper, radio, and television publicity. The publicity included many matters unfavorable to the defendant which were never presented in court. The trial judge denied various requests by defense counsel for a continuance, change of venue, mistrial, and interrogation of the jurors as to their exposure to the publicity. During the trial, which lasted nine weeks, reporters were seated at a press table inside the bar, a few feet from the jury box, and most of the seats in the courtroom were filled with representatives of the news media. Radio broadcasting was done from a room next to the room where the jury recessed and deliberated. Courtroom proceedings which were supposed to be private were overheard and reported by the press, and the noise of newsmen moving in and out of the courtroom made it difficult for counsel and witnesses to be heard. The trial judge made no effort to control the release of leads, information, and gossip to the press by the prosecuting attorneys, the coroner, police officers, or witnesses. Petitioner was convicted of second degree murder. The Ohio Supreme Court affirmed, and the United States Supreme Court denied certiorari. Several years later, petitioner instituted habeas corpus proceedings in a federal district court, which held that he had been denied a fair trial and was entitled to be released. The Court of Appeals reversed. The Supreme Court granted certiorari.]

Mr. Justice Clark delivered the opinion of the Court. . . .

The principle that justice cannot survive behind walls of silence has long been reflected in the "Anglo-American distrust for secret trials.". . . A responsible press has always been regarded as the handmaiden of effective judicial administration, especially in the criminal field. Its function in this regard is documented by an impressive record of service over several centuries. The press does not simply publish information about trials but guards against the miscarriage of justice by subjecting the police, prosecutors, and judicial processes to extensive public scrutiny and criticism. This Court has, therefore, been unwilling to place any direct limitations on the freedom traditionally exercised by the news media for "[w]hat transpires in the court room is public property.". . .

But the Court has also pointed out that "[l]egal trials are not like elections, to be won through the use of the meeting-hall, the radio, and the newspaper.". . .

While we cannot say that Sheppard was denied due process by the judge's refusal to take precautions against the influence of pretrial publicity alone, the court's later rulings must be considered against the setting in which the trial was held. In light of this background, we believe that the arrangements made by the judge with the news media caused Sheppard to be deprived of that "judicial serenity and calm to which [he] was entitled.". . . The fact is that bedlam reigned at the courthouse during the trial and newsmen took over practically the entire courtroom, hounding most of the participants in the trial, especially Sheppard. . . .

The carnival atmosphere at trial could easily have been avoided since the courtroom and courthouse premises are subject to the control of the court. As we stressed in *Estes,* the presence of the press at judicial proceedings must be limited when it is apparent that the accused might otherwise be prejudiced or disadvantaged. Bearing in mind the massive pretrial publicity, the judge should have adopted stricter rules governing the use of the courtroom by newsmen, as Sheppard's counsel requested. The number of reporters in the courtroom itself could have been limited at the first sign that their presence would disrupt the trial. They certainly should not have been placed inside the bar. Furthermore, the judge should have more closely regulated the conduct of newsmen in the courtroom. For instance, the judge belatedly asked them not to handle and photograph trial exhibits lying on the counsel table during recesses.

Secondly, the court should have insulated the witnesses. All of the newspapers and radio stations apparently interviewed prospective witnesses at will, and in many instances disclosed their testimony. . . .

Thirdly, the court should have made some effort to control the release of leads, information, and gossip to the press by police officers, witnesses, and the counsel for both sides. Much of the information thus disclosed was inaccurate, leading to groundless rumors and confusion. . . . Under such circumstances, the judge should have at least warned the newspapers to check the accuracy of their accounts. And it is obvious that the judge should have further sought to alleviate this problem by imposing control over the statements made to the news media by counsel, witnesses, and especially the Coroner and police officers. The prosecution repeatedly made evidence available to the news media which was never offered in the trial. Much of the "evidence" disseminated in this fashion was clearly inadmissible. The exclusion of such evidence in court is rendered meaningless when a news media makes it available to the public. . . .

More specifically, the trial court might well have proscribed extrajudicial statements by any lawyer, party, witness, or court official which divulged prejudicial matters, such as the refusal of Sheppard to submit to interrogation or take any lie detector tests; any statement by Sheppard to officials; the identity of prospective witnesses or their probable testimony; any belief in guilt or innocence; or like statements concerning the merits of the case. . . . In addition, reporters who wrote or broadcasted prejudicial stories, could have been warned as to the impropriety of publishing material not introduced in the proceedings. . . .

From the cases coming here we note that unfair and prejudicial news comment on pending trials has become increasingly prevalent. Due process requires that the accused receive a trial by an impartial jury free from outside influences. Given the pervasiveness of modern communications and the difficulty of effacing prejudicial publicity from the minds of the jurors, the trial courts must take strong measures to ensure that the balance is never weighed against the accused.... Neither prosecutors, counsel for defense, the accused, witnesses, court staff nor enforcement officers coming under the jurisdiction of the court should be permitted to frustrate its function. Collaboration between counsel and the press as to information affecting the fairness of a criminal trial is not only subject to regulation, but is highly censurable and worthy of disciplinary measures.

...The case is remanded to the District Court with instructions to issue the writ and order that Sheppard be released from custody unless the State puts him to its charges again within a reasonable time.

It is so ordered.

Mr. Justice Black dissents.

While the *Sheppard* case presented the situation of undue laxity on the part of a trial judge in dealing with the media, the Court in 1976 faced a problem at the other extreme—an absolute "gag rule" imposed by a Nebraska judge on the media and applicable until the trial jury was actually impanelled. The order was occasioned by a sensational murder case. Police had found the six members of a family murdered in their home in Sutherland, Nebraska, a town of about 850 people. On the following day a suspect was arrested. Three days later, upon request by the prosecuting and defense attorneys, the County Court entered an order prohibiting anyone in attendance at pretrial proceedings from releasing or authorizing for public dissemination any testimony given or evidence given. A preliminary hearing was held on the same day, open to the public but subject to the order. The defendant was bound over for trial in the District Court on charges that he had committed the murders in the course of a sexual assault. Several members of the media then petitioned the District Court for leave to intervene, asking that the restrictive order be vacated. District Judge Stuart entered his own restrictive order which, as modified by the Nebraska Supreme Court, prohibited reporting of three matters: (1) the existence and nature of any confessions or admissions made by the defendant to law enforcement officers, (2) any confessions or admissions made to any third parties, except members of the press, and (3) other facts "strongly implicative" of the accused. The Nebraska Supreme Court held that the order was necessary, in view of the publicity surrounding the crime, in order to assure trial by an impartial jury.

The United States Supreme Court reviewed the case on certiorari and in *Nebraska Press Association* v. *Stuart,* 44 L.W. 5149 (1976), unanimously reversed. While the defendant had already been tried, convicted, and sentenced to death, the case was on appeal to the Nebraska Supreme Court, and the United States Supreme Court held that the "gag rule" issue was not moot, stating that "jurisdiction is not necessarily defeated simply because the order attacked has expired, if the underlying dispute between the parties is one 'capable of repetition, yet evading review.'" On the merits, the Court held that there was no finding that alternative measures short of prior restraint on the press would not have protected the accused's right to a fair trial. Such alternatives were "discussed with obvious approval in *Sheppard* v. *Maxwell.*" To the extent that the order prohibited the reporting of evidence at the open preliminary hearing, it violated the settled principle stated in *Sheppard* that "there is nothing that proscribes the press from reporting events that transpire in the courtroom." In some circumstances the hearing might have been closed to the public, but once it was open, "what transpired there could not be subject to prior restraint." Finally, the portion of the order restraining publication of other facts "strongly implicative" of the accused was held to be too vague and too broad to survive the scrutiny given to restraints on First Amendment rights.

[On the subject of fair trial and free press, see George D. Haimbaugh, Jr., "Free Press v. Fair Trial: The Contribution of Mr. Justice Frankfurter," 26 *U. Pitt. L. Rev.* 491 (1965); Carolyn Jaffee, "The Press and the Oppressed— A Study of Prejudicial News Reporting in Criminal Cases," 56 *J. Crim. L.* 1 (1965); Vermont Royster, "Free Press and a Fair Trial," 43 *N.C. L. Rev.* 364 (1965); Symposium, "Free Press vs. Fair Trial," 41 *N. Dak. L. Rev.* 7, 156 (1964–65); Edward G. Hudon, "Freedom of the Press versus Fair Trial: the Remedy Lies with the Courts," 1 *Valparaiso U. L. Rev.* 8 (1966); A.B.A. Advisory Comm. on Fair Trial and Free Press, *Standards Relating to Fair Trial and Free Press, Tentative Draft* (New York: Institute of Judicial Administration, 1966); Hearings on S.290 before the Subcommittee on Constitutional Rights and the Subcommittee on Improvements in Judicial Machinery of the Senate Committee on the Judiciary, *Free Press and Fair Trial*, 89th Cong., 1st Sess. (1965); and Association of the Bar of the City of New York, Special Committee on Radio, Television, and the Administration of Justice, *Freedom of the Press and Fair Trial: Final Report with Recommendations* (New York: Columbia University Press, 1967).]

Newsman's Privilege

BRANZBURG *v.* HAYES
408 U.S. 665 (1972)

[The Supreme Court granted certiorari in three cases to consider newsmen's constitutional privilege from giving grand jury testimony. Branzburg, a reporter for the *Louisville Courier-Journal,* published a story in 1969 describing in detail his observations of two young persons synthesizing hashish from marihuana, an activity which, they asserted, earned them about $5,000 in three weeks. The article stated that Branzburg had promised not to reveal the identity of the two hashish makers. He was subpoenaed by the county grand jury but refused to identify the individuals he had seen possessing marihuana or the persons he had seen making hashish. A state trial court judge ordered petitioner to answer these questions and rejected his contention that the Kentucky reporters' privilege statute, the First Amendment, or the Kentucky Constitution authorized his refusal to answer. Petitioner then sought prohibition and mandamus in the Kentucky Court of Appeals, but the Court denied the petition.

A second case involving Branzburg arose from a later story which described in detail the use of drugs in Frankfort, Kentucky. A number of conversations with several unnamed drug users were recounted. Subpoenaed to appear before another county grand jury, petitioner moved to quash the summons. The Court of Appeals once again denied the requested writs.

The two other cases involved newsmen from Massachusetts and California, respectively, who carried out in-depth interviews with local Black Panther Party members and other black militant groups. In each case they were ordered to appear before grand juries and answer questions concerning possible violations of a number of criminal statutes. In the Massachusetts case, the courts refused the motion to quash. In the California case, involving a federal grand jury, the Court of Appeals held that absent compelling reasons for requiring his testimony, he was privileged to withold it. The United States petitioned for certiorari.]

Opinion of the Court by Mr. Justice White, announced by The Chief Justice.

The issue in these cases is whether requiring newsmen to appear and testify before State or federal grand juries abridges the freedom of speech and press guaranteed by the First Amendment. We hold that it does not. . . .

Petitioners Branzburg and Pappas and respondent Caldwell press First Amendment claims that may be simply put: that to gather news it is often necessary to agree either not to identify the source of information published or to publish only part of the facts revealed, or both; that if the reporter is nevertheless forced to reveal these confidences to a grand jury, the source so identified and other confidential sources of other reporters will be measurably deterred from furnishing publishable information, all to the detriment of the free flow of information protected by the First Amendment. Although petitioners do not claim an absolute privilege against official interrogation in all circumstances, they assert that the reporter should not be forced either to appear or to testify before a grand jury or at a trial until and unless sufficient grounds are shown for believing that the reporter possesses information relevant to a crime the grand jury is investigating, that the information the reporter has is unavailable from other sources, and that the need for the information is sufficiently compelling to override the claimed invasion of First Amendment interests occasioned by the disclosure. . . . The heart of the claim is that the burden on news gathering resulting from compelling reporters to disclose confidential information outweighs any public interest in obtaining the information.

We do not question the significance of free speech, press or assembly to the country's welfare. Nor is it suggested that news gathering does not qualify for First Amendment protection; without some protection for seeking out the news, freedom of the press could be eviscerated. But this case involves no intrusions upon speech or assembly, no prior restraint or restriction on what the press may publish, and no express or implied command that the press publish what it prefers to withhold. . . .

The sole issue before us is the obligation of reporters to respond to grand jury subpoenas as other citizens do and to answer questions relevant to an investigation into the commission of crime. Citizens generally are not constitutionally immune from grand jury subpoenas; and neither the First Amendment nor other constitutional provision protects the average citizen from disclosing to a grand jury information that he has received in confidence. The claim is, however, that reporters are exempt from these obligations because if forced to respond to subpoenas and identify their sources or disclose other confidences, their informants will refuse or be reluctant to furnish newsworthy information in the future. This asserted burden on news gathering is said to make compelled testimony from newsmen constitutionally suspect and to require a privileged position for them.

It is clear that the First Amendment does not invalidate every incidental burdening of the press that may result from the enforcement of civil or criminal statutes of general applicability. Under prior cases, otherwise valid laws serving substantial public interests may be enforced against the press as against others, despite the possible burden that may be imposed. . . .

The prevailing view is that the press is not free with impunity to publish everything and anything it desires to publish. Although it may deter or regulate what is said or published, the press may not circulate knowing or reckless falsehoods damaging to private reputation without subjecting itself to liability for damages, including punitive damages, or even criminal prosecution. . . . A newspaper or a journalist may also be punished for contempt of court, in appropriate circumstances. . . .

It has generally been held that the First Amendment does not guarantee the press a constitutional right of special access to information not available to the public generally. . . . Despite the fact that news gathering may be hampered, the press is regularly excluded from grand jury proceedings, our own conferences, the meetings of other official bodies gathered in executive session, and the meetings of private organizations. . . .

It is thus not surprising that the great weight of authority is that newsmen are not exempt from the normal duty of appearing before a grand jury and answering questions relevant to a criminal investigation. At common law, courts consistently refused to recognize the existence of any privilege authorizing a newsman to refuse to reveal confidential information to a grand jury. . . . In 1958, a news gatherer asserted for the first time that the First Amendment exempted confidential information from public disclosure pursuant to a subpoena issued in a civil suit, . . . but the claim was denied, and this argument has been almost uniformly rejected since then, although there are occasional dicta that, in circumstances not presented, a newsman might be excused. . . .

A number of States have provided newsmen a statutory privilege of varying breadth, but the majority have not done so, and none has been provided by federal statute. Until now the only testimonial privilege for unofficial witnesses that is rooted in the Federal Constitution is the Fifth Amendment privilege against compelled self-incrimination. We are asked to create another by interpreting the First Amendment to grant newsmen a testimonial privilege that other citizens do not enjoy. This we decline to do. Fair and effective law enforcement aimed at providing security for the person and property of the individual is a fundamental function of government, and the grand jury plays an important, constitutionally mandated role in this process. On the records now before us, we perceive no basis for holding that the public interest in law enforcement and in ensuring effective grand jury proceedings is insufficient to override the consequential, but uncertain, burden on news gathering which is said to result from insisting that reporters, like other citizens, respond to relevant questions put to them in the course of a valid grand jury investigation or criminal trial. . . .

Accepting the fact, however, that an undetermined number of informants not themselves implicated in crime will nevertheless, for whatever reason, refuse to talk to newsmen if they fear identification by a reporter in an official investigation we cannot accept the argument that the public interest in possible future news about crime from undisclosed, unverified sources must take precedence over the public interest in pursuing and prosecuting those crimes reported to the press by informants and in thus deterring the commission of such crimes in the future.

[I]t is obvious that agreements to conceal information relevant to commission of crime have very little to recommend them from the standpoint of public policy. Historically, the common law recognized a duty to raise the "hue and cry" and report felonies to the authorities. Misprision of a felony—that is, the concealment of a felony . . .—was often said to be a common law crime. The first Congress passed a statute . . . which is still in effect, defining a federal crime of misprision. . . . It is apparent from this statute, as well as from our history and that of England, that concealment of crime and agreements to do so are not looked upon with favor. Such conduct deserves no encomium, and we decline now to afford it First Amendment protection by denigrating the duty of a citizen, whether reporter or informer, to respond to grand jury subpoena and answer relevant questions put to him. . . .

At the federal level, Congress has freedom to determine whether a statutory newsman's privilege is necessary and desirable and to fashion standards and rules as narrow or broad as deemed necessary to address the evil discerned and, equally important, to re-fashion those rules as experience from time to time may dictate. There is also merit in leaving state legislatures free, within First Amendment limits, to fashion their own standards in light of the conditions and problems with respect to the relations between law enforcement officials and press in their own areas. . . .

Finally, as we have earlier indicated, news gathering is not without its First Amendment protections, and grand jury investigations if instituted or conducted other than in good faith, would pose wholly different issues for resolution under the First Amendment. Official harassment of the press undertaken not for purposes of law enforcement but to disrupt a reporter's relationship with his news sources would have no justification. Grand juries are subject to judicial control and subpoenas to motions to quash. We do not expect courts will forget that grand juries must operate within the limits of the First Amendment as well as the Fifth. . . .

Mr. Justice Powell, concurring in the opinion of the Court. . . .

Mr. Justice Douglas, dissenting. . . .

It is my view that there is no "compelling need" that can be shown which qualifies the reporter's immunity from appearing or testifying before a grand jury, unless the reporter himself is implicated in a crime. His immunity in my view is therefore quite complete, for absent his involvement in a crime, the First Amendment protects him against an appearance before a grand jury, and if he is involved in a crime, the Fifth Amendment stands as a barrier. Since in my view there is no area of inquiry not protected by a privilege, the reporter need not appear for the futile purpose of invoking one to each question. And, since in my view a newsman has an absolute right not to appear before a grand jury it follows for me that a journalist who voluntarily appears before that body may invoke his First Amendment privilege to specific questions. . . .

The press has a preferred position in our constitutional scheme not to enable it to make money, not to set newsmen apart as a favored class, but to bring fulfillment to the public's right to know. The right to know is crucial to the governing powers of the people, to paraphrase Alexander Meiklejohn. Knowledge is essential to informed decisions. . . .

The record in this case is replete with weighty affidavits from responsible newsmen, telling how important are the sanctity of their sources of information. When we deny newsmen that protection, we deprive the people of the information needed to run the affairs of the Nation in an intelligent way. . . .

Mr. Justice Stewart, with whom Mr. Justice Brennan and Mr. Justice Marshall join, dissenting.

The Court's crabbed view of the First Amendment reflects a disturbing insensitivity to the critical role of an independent press in our society. . . . The Court thus invites state and federal authorities to undermine the historic independence of the press by attempting to annex the journalistic profession as an investigative arm of government. Not only will this decision impair performance of the press' constitutionally protected functions, but it will, I am convinced, in the long run, harm rather than help the administration of justice. . . .

The right to gather news implies . . . a right to a confidential relationship between a reporter and his source. This proposition follows as a matter of simple logic once three factual predicates are recognized: (1) newsmen require informants to gather news; (2) confidentiality—the promise or understanding that names or certain aspects of communications will be kept off-the-record—is essential to the creation and maintenance of a news-gathering relationship with informants; and (3) the existence of an unbridled subpoena power—the absense of a constitutional right protecting, in *any* way, a confidential relationship from compulsory process—will either deter sources from divulging information or deter reporters from gathering and publishing information. . . .

The reporter must speculate about whether contact with a controversial source or publication of controversial material will lead to a subpoena. In the event of a subpoena, under today's decision, the newsman will know that he must choose between being punished for contempt if he refuses to testify, or violating his profession's ethics and impairing his resourcefulness as a reporter if he discloses confidential information. . . .

Accordingly, when a reporter is asked to appear before a grand jury and reveal confidences, I would hold that the government must (1) show that there is probable cause to believe that the newsman has information which is clearly relevant to a specific probable violation of law; (2) demonstrate that the information sought cannot be obtained by alternative means less destructive of First Amendment rights; and (3) demonstrate a compelling and overriding interest in the information.

This is not to say that a grand jury could not issue a suboena until such a showing were made, and it is not to say that a newsman would be in any way privileged to ignore any subpoena that was issued. Obviously, before the government's burden to make such a showing were triggered, the reporter would have to move to quash the subpoena, asserting the basis on which he considered the particular relationship a confidential one. . . .

Libel

In the past it has been commonplace to cite libelous and obscene publications as exceptions to the general rule of constitutional protection afforded the press. In more recent years, however, questions have been raised as to whether even these kinds of publications should necessarily be placed outside the pale of First Amendment protection. Justice Black, in a public interview quoted earlier [37 *N.Y.U. L. Rev.* 549 (1962)], stated that he had no doubt that the First Amendment intended that there should be no libel or defamation law in the United States, and that the Constitution was not intended "to authorize damage suits for mere words as distinguished from conduct."

The Court has not yet adopted the absolute protection argued for by Justice Black, but when the allegedly libelous statements are directed toward official conduct, the Court indicated in *New York Times Co.* v. *Sullivan,* 376 U.S. 254 (1964), that actual malice must be shown to support a judgment against the press.

NEW YORK TIMES CO. *v.* SULLIVAN
376 U.S. 254 (1964)

[A civil libel action was filed in Montgomery, Alabama, by Montgomery's Commissioner of Public Affairs, whose duties included the supervision of the police department. The action was brought against the *New York Times* for publication of a paid advertisement describing the mistreatment of Negro students protesting segregation in Montgomery, and also against four individuals whose names, among others, appeared in the advertisement. The advertisement stated in part:

"In Montgomery, Alabama, after students sang 'My County, 'Tis of Thee' on the State Capitol steps, their leaders were expelled from school, and truckloads of police armed with shotguns and tear-gas ringed the Alabama State College Campus. When the entire student body protested to state authorities by refusing to re-register, their dining hall was padlocked in an attempt to starve them into submission." . . .

"Again and again the Southern violators have answered Dr. King's peaceful protests with intimidation and violence. They have bombed his home almost killing his wife and child. They have assaulted his person. They have arrested him seven times—for 'speeding,' 'loitering' and similar 'offenses.' And now they have charged him with 'perjury'—a *felony* under which they could imprison him for *ten years*. . . ."

Sullivan contended that both paragraphs accused the Montgomery police, and hence him, as the commissioner who supervised the police, of answering Dr. King's protests with intimidation and violence. It was uncontroverted that some of the statements contained in the two paragraphs were not accurate descriptions of events which occurred. For example, the campus dining hall was not padlocked, the police did not "ring" the campus, although there were large numbers deployed near it, and Dr. King had been arrested only four times rather than seven.

The jury awarded plaintiff damages of $500,000 against all defendants, and the judgment on the verdict was affirmed by the Supreme Court of Alabama on the grounds that the statements in the advertisement were libelous *per se,* false, and not privileged, and that the evidence showed malice on the part of the newspaper.]

Mr. Justice Brennan delivered the opinion of the Court.

We are required for the first time in this case to determine the extent to which the constitutional protections for speech and press limit a State's power to award damages in a libel action brought by a public official against critics of his official conduct. . . .

The cost of the advertisement was approximately $4800, and it was published by the Times upon an order from a New York advertising agency acting for the signatory Committee. The agency submitted the advertisement with a letter from A. Philip Randolph, Chairman of the Committee, certifying that the persons whose names appeared on the advertisement had given their permission. Mr. Randolph was known to the Times' Advertising Acceptability Department as a responsible person, and in accepting the letter as sufficient proof of authorization it followed its established practice. . . . The manager of the Advertising Acceptability Department testified that he had approved the advertisement for publication because he knew nothing to cause him to believe that anything in it was false, and because it bore the endorsement of "a number of people who are well known and whose reputation" he "had no reason to question." Neither he nor anyone else at the Times made an effort to confirm the accuracy of the advertisement, either by checking it against recent Times news stories relating to some of the described events or by some other means.

Alabama law denies a public officer recovery of punitive damages in a libel action brought on account of a publication concerning his official conduct unless he first makes a written demand for a public retraction and the defendant fails or refuses to comply. . . . Respondent served such a demand upon each of the petitioners. None of the individual petitioners responded to the demand, primarily because each took the position that he had not authorized the use of his name on the advertisement and therefore had not published the statements that respondent alleged to have libeled him. The Times did not publish a retraction in response to the demand, but wrote respondent a letter stating among other things, that "we . . . are somewhat puzzled as to how you think the statements in any way reflect on you," and "you might, if you desire, let us know in what respect you claim that the statements in the advertisement reflect on you." Respondent filed this suit a few days later without answering the letter. [The Times did later print a retraction of the advertisement for its possible application to the Governor of Alabama, but not for the respondent.] . . .

The trial judge submitted the case to the jury under instructions that the statements in the advertisement were "libelous per se" and were not privileged, so that petitioners might be held liable if the jury found that they had published the advertisement and that the statements were made "of and concerning" respondent. The jury was instructed that, because the statements were libelous *per se,* "the law . . . implies legal injury from the bare fact of publication itself," "falsity and malice are presumed," and "punitive damages may be awarded by the jury even though the amount of actual damages is neither found nor shown." . . .

In affirming the judgment, the Supreme Court of Alabama sustained the trial judge's rulings and instructions in all respects. . . . In sustaining the trial court's determination that the verdict was not excessive, the court said that malice could be inferred from the Times' "irresponsibility" in printing the advertisement while "the Times in its own files had articles already published which would have demonstrated the falsity of the allegations in the advertisement" . . . .

. . . We reverse the judgment. We hold that the rule of law applied by the Alabama courts is constitutionally deficient for failure to provide the safeguards for freedom of speech and of the press that are required by the First and Fourteenth Amendments in a libel action brought by a public official against critics of his official conduct. We further hold that under the proper safeguards the evidence presented in this case is constitutionally insufficient to support the judgment for the respondent. . . .

Respondent relies heavily, as did the Alabama courts, on statements of this Court to the effect that the Constitution does not protect libelous publications. Those statements do not foreclose our inquiry here. None of the cases sustained the use of libel laws to impose sanctions upon expression critical of the official conduct of public officials. . . .

Thus we consider this case against the background of a profound national commitment to the principle that debate on public issues should be uninhibited, robust, and wide-open, and that it may well include vehement, caustic, and sometimes unpleasantly sharp attacks on government and public officials. . . . The present advertisement, as an expression of grievance and protest on one of the major issues of our time, would seem clearly to qualify for the constitutional protection. The question is whether it forfeits that protection by the falsity of some of its factual statements and by its alleged defamation of respondent.

Authoritative interpretations of the First Amendment guarantees have consistently refused to recognize an exception for any test of truth—whether administered by judges, juries, or administrative officials—and especially one that puts the burden of proving truth on the speaker. . . . The constitutional protection does not turn upon "the truth, popularity, or social utility of the ideas and beliefs which are offered." . . .

Injury to official reputation affords no more warrant for repressing speech that would otherwise be free than does factual error. Where judicial officers are involved, this Court has held that concern for the dignity and reputation of the courts does not justify the punishment as criminal contempt of criticism of the judge or his decision. . . . This is true even though the utterance contains "half-truths" and "misinformation." . . . If judges are to be treated as "men of fortitude, able to thrive in a hardy climate," . . . surely the same must be true of other government officials, such as elected city commissioners. Criticism of their official conduct does not lose its constitutional protection merely because it is effective criticism and hence diminishes their official reputations.

If neither factual error nor defamatory content suffices to remove the constitutional shield from criticism of official conduct, the combination of the two elements is no less inadequate. . . .

A rule compelling the critic of official conduct to guarantee the truth of all his factual assertions—and to do so on pain of libel judgments virtually unlimited in amount—leads to a . . . "self-censorship." Allowance of the defense of truth, with the burden of proving it on the defendant, does not mean that only false speech will be deterred. Even courts accepting this defense as an adequate safeguard have recognized the difficulties of adducing legal proofs that the alleged libel was true in all its factual particulars. . . . Under such a rule, would-be critics of official conduct may be deterred from voicing their criticism, even though it is believed to be true and even though it is in fact true, because of doubt whether it can be proved in court or fear of the expense of having to do so. They tend to make only statements which "steer far wider of the unlawful zone." . . . The rule thus dampens the vigor and limits the variety of public debate. It is inconsistent with the First and Fourteenth Amendments.

The constitutional guarantees require, we think, a federal rule that prohibits a public official from recovering damages for a defamatory falsehood relating to his official conduct unless he proves that the statement was made with "actual malice"— that is, with knowledge that it was false or with reckless disregard of whether it was false or not. . . .

We conclude that such a privilege is required by the First and Fourteenth Amendments. . . . [T]he judgment must be reversed and remanded. . . .

Since respondent may seek a new trial, we deem that considerations of effective judicial administration require us to review the evidence in the present record to determine whether it could constitutionally support a judgment for respondent. . . .

Applying these standards, we consider that the proof presented to show actual malice lacks the convincing clarity which the constitutional standard demands, and hence that it would not constitutionally sustain the judgment for respondent under the proper rule of law. . . . The statement by the Times' Secretary that, apart from the padlocking allegation, he thought the advertisement was "substantially correct," affords no constitutional warrant for the Alabama Supreme Court's conclusion that it was a "cavalier ignoring of the falsity of the advertisement [from which] the jury could not have but been impressed with the bad faith of the Times, and its maliciousness inferable therefrom." . . . We think the evidence against the Times supports at most a finding of negligence in failing to discover the misstatements, and is constitutionally insufficient to show the recklessness that is required for a finding of actual malice. . . .

We also think the evidence was constitutionally defective in another respect: it was incapable of supporting the jury's finding that the allegedly libelous statements were made "of and concerning" respondent. . . . Although the statements may be taken as referring to the police, they did not on their face make even an oblique reference to respondent as an individual. Support for the asserted reference must, therefore, be sought in the testimony of respondent's witnesses. But none of them suggested any basis for the belief that respondent himself was attacked in the advertisement beyond the bare fact that he was in overall charge of the Police Department and thus bore official responsibility for police conduct. . . .

This proposition has disquieting implications for criticism of governmental conduct. . . . [It would transmute] criticisms of government, however impersonal it may seem on its face, into personal criticism, and hence potential libel, of the officials of whom the government is composed. . . . Raising as it does the possibility that a good-faith critic of government will be penalized for his criticism, the proposition relied on by the Alabama courts strikes at the very center of the constitutionally protected area of free expression. We hold that such a proposition may not constitutionally be utilized to establish that an otherwise impersonal attack on governmental operations was a libel of an official responsible for those operations. Since it it was relied on exclusively here, and there was no other evidence to connect the statements with respondent, the evidence was constitutionally insufficient to support a finding that the statements referred to respondent. . . .

Reversed and remanded.

Mr. Justice Black with whom Mr. Justice Douglas joins, concurring. . . .

. . . I base my vote to reverse on the belief that the First and Fourteenth Amendments not merely "delimit" a State's power to award damages to "a public official against critics of his official conduct" but completely prohibit a State from exercising such a power. The Court goes on to hold that a State can subject such critics to damages if "actual malice" can be proved against them. "Malice," even as defined by the Court, is an elusive, abstract concept, hard to prove and hard to disprove. The requirement that malice be proved provides at best an evanescent protection for the right critically to discuss public affairs and certainly does not measure up to the sturdy safeguard embodied in the First Amendment. Unlike the Court, therefore, I vote to reverse exclusively on the ground that the Times and the individual defendants had an absolute, unconditional constitutional right to publish in the Times advertisement their criticisms of the Montgomery agencies and officials. . . . An unconditional right to say what one pleases about public affairs is what I consider to be the minimum guarantee of the First Amendment. . . .

Mr. Justice Goldberg, with whom Mr. Justice Douglas joins, concurring in the result. . . .

In my view, the First and Fourteenth Amendments to the Constitution afford to the citizen and to the press an absolute, unconditional privilege to criticize official conduct despite the harm which may flow from excesses and abuses. . . . In a democratic society, one who assumes to act for the citizens in an executive, legislative, or judicial capacity must expect that his official acts will be commented upon and criticized. Such criticism cannot, in my opinion, be muzzled or deterred by the courts at the instance of public officials under the label of libel. . . .

This is not to say that the Constitution protects defamatory statements directed against the private conduct of a public official or private citizen. Freedom of press and of speech insures that government will respond to the will of the people and that changes may be obtained by peaceful means. Purely private defamation has little to do with the political ends of a self-governing society. The imposition of liability for private defamation does not abridge the freedom of public speech or any other freedom protected by the First Amendment. . . .

The rule of the *New York Times* case was followed in *Garrison* v. *Louisiana,* 379 U.S. 64 (1964), in reversing a conviction for criminal defamation.

During a dispute with the judges of a criminal court of New Orleans, the district attorney for the parish held a press conference at which he attributed a large backlog of pending criminal cases to the inefficiency, laziness, and excessive vacations of the judges, and accused them of hampering his enforcement of the vice laws by refusing to authorize the expenses for the necessary investigations. The Court held that the *New York Times* rule limiting the awarding of civil damages in cases of alleged false criticism of public officials to instances of actual malice was also applicable to criminal sanctions for such criticism.

Subsequent decisions of the Court have applied the *New York Times* standard to the reporting of incidents of "public interest," to "public figures," even though such persons are not public officials, and to the activities of public officials which they engaged in prior to assuming public position. *Time, Inc.* v. *Hill,* 385 U.S. 374 (1967), arose from the publication in *Life Magazine* of an article reporting that a new play portrayed an experience suffered by Hill and his family. The article was entitled "True Crime Inspires Tense Play," with the subtitle, "The ordeal of a family trapped by convicts gives Broadway a new thriller, 'The Desperate Hours.' " Hill alleged that the article falsely reported that the play was based on his family's experience and sued for libel. The Court reversed the award of damages below on the ground that an improper standard was employed by the trial court. The majority opinion stated, "We hold that the constitutional protections for speech and press preclude the application of the New York statute to redress false reports of matters of public interest in the absence of proof that the defendant published the report with knowledge of its falsity or in reckless disregard of the truth."

The *Hill* standard was applied, but with a different result, in *Cantrell* v. *Forest City Publishing Co.,* 419 U.S. 245 (1974). The Company published a news story concerning the collapse of a bridge across the Ohio River in which forty-three persons were killed, including the plaintiff's husband. Some months later, reporter and photographer were sent to the Cantrell home to do a follow-up story. They talked with the Cantrell children while Mrs. Cantrell was away. The story contained several misstatements of fact, particularly regarding nonexistent conversations with Mrs. Cantrell concerning the family's poverty. She sued, alleging mental distress and humiliation by the false statements in the article, which had made them objects of pity and ridicule. The jury awarded compensation based on a "false light" invasion of privacy theory, finding that the story had been published while known to be false. The Sixth Circuit reversed, but the Supreme Court reversed that holding, stating that a publisher is vicariously liable for damages caused by its reporters' knowing falsehoods.

In *Curtis Publishing Co.* v. *Butts,* 388 U.S. 130 (1967), the Court extended the *Times* rule to cover "public figures." The *Saturday Evening Post* had published an article entitled "The Story of a College Football Fix," in which it was stated that "Wally" Butts, University of Georgia football coach, had revealed to "Bear" Bryant, University of Alabama football coach, Georgia's plays, defensive patterns, and all the significant secrets Georgia's football team possessed. This reportedly occurred shortly before the two teams were to play a conference game. Butts sued for libel in a diversity action in federal court and won a jury verdict of more than $3,000,000. The trial court reduced the award to $460,000, and the Court of Appeals affirmed. The Supreme Court affirmed, but there was no majority opinion. A majority of the justices did, however, hold that the rule of *New York Times* was constitutionally demanded in the case of "public figures" as well as public officials. It was further held that the evidence supported the jury verdict in view of the failure of the *Post* to check the accuracy of the very serious allegations made against a well-known football coach, although the majority on the merits was a different group of justices and included some who would require a lesser standard for "public figures" than for public officials.

Greenbelt Cooperative Publishing Ass'n. v. *Bresler,* 398 U.S. 6 (1970), involved a libel action against a newspaper brought by a private real-estate developer. New articles had reported that at city council meetings certain citizens had characterized as "blackmail" the plaintiff's negotiating position with the city council in seeking to obtain zoning variances for certain property owned by the plaintiff at the same time that the city was attempting to buy other property from the plaintiff for school building purposes. The plaintiff contended that the defendants should be held liable for the knowing use of falsehood, since the word "blackmail" was intended to charge the plaintiff with the crime of blackmail, and since the defendants knew that the plaintiff had committed no such crime. The trial court's charge to the jury stated that the plaintiff could recover if the publications had been made with malice *or* with a reckless disregard of whether they were true or false. Judgment was entered for the plaintiff, the Maryland Court of Appeals affirmed, and on certiorari the United States Supreme Court reversed and remanded. The majority held that the plaintiff's status in the course of the negotiations with school officials and the city council brought him clearly within the "public figure" category as defined in *Curtis Publishing Co.* v. *Butts.* Thus the constitutional standard permitted recovery only if it was established that the defamatory publication was false *and* that it was made with knowledge of its falsity or in reckless disregard of whether it was false or true. Further, the majority thought it "simply impossible to believe" that a reader who reached the word "blackmail" would have considered it to be more than "rhetorical hyperbole."

In 1971 the Court reworked the rule of *New York Times* v. *Sullivan* to extend even further the media's protection against libel action. *Rosenbloom* v. *Metromedia,* 403 U.S. 29 (1971), involved a libel action against a radio station as a result of news stories of petitioner's arrest for possession of obscene literature, and stories concerning petitioner's lawsuit against certain officials alleging that the magazines he distributed were not obscene and seeking injunctive relief from police interference with his business. The latter stories did not mention petitioner's name, but used the terms "smut literature racket" and "girlie-book peddlers." Following his acquittal of criminal obscenity charges, petitioner sued in a diversity suit in federal court seeking damages under Pennsylvania's libel law. The jury found for petitioner and awarded $25,000 in general damages and $725,000 in punitive damages, which was reduced by the court on remittitur to $25,000. The Court of Appeals reversed, and the Supreme Court affirmed by a five-to-three vote, with Justice Douglas not participating. There was no majority opinion. Justice Brennan wrote an opinion which was joined by the Chief Justice and Justice Blackmun, however, in which the "public official" or "public figure" test was revised to focus on whether the matter publicized was "an event of public or general concern." It was argued that this would protect the media under the *Sullivan* test if the subject matter was of public concern, whether the person involved was public or private. And it would protect the purely *private* activity of even public officials or public figures against careless defamation. Justice Black concurred, reiterating his position that the First Amendment bars all libel actions against the news media "even when statements are broadcast with knowledge they are false." Justice White concurred in the result.

In *Monitor Patriot Co.* v. *Roy,* 401 U.S. 265 (1971), the Court held that the *Sullivan* test applied to a newspaper's characterization of a candidate for the United States Senate as a "former small-time bootlegger." The trial court had charged the jury that if the libel was in the "public sector" and concerned the plaintiff's fitness for office, then the *Sullivan* rule applied, but that if the libel was in the "private sector," the plaintiff need only show that the article was false and had not been published in good faith for a justifiable purpose with a belief founded on reasonable grounds of the truth of the matter published. The jury found against the newspaper, and the New Hampshire Supreme Court affirmed. The United States Supreme Court reversed and remanded, holding that the *Sullivan* test was the proper rule since, as a matter of constitutional law, a charge of criminal conduct, no matter how remote in time or place, could never be irrelevant to a candidate's fitness for office.

GERTZ *v.* WELCH
418 U.S. 323 (1974)

[A Chicago policeman named Nuccio was convicted of murder. The victim's family retained Gertz, a reputable attorney, to represent them in a civil suit against the officer. An article appearing in Welch's magazine alleged that the murder trial was part of a Communist conspiracy to discredit the local police, and it falsely stated that Gertz had arranged Nuccio's "frame-up," implied that Gertz had a criminal record, and labeled him a "Communist-fronter." Petitioner brought this diversity libel action against respondent. After the jury returned a verdict for petitioner for $50,000, the District Court decided that the standard announced in *New York Times* should have been applied to the suit. Concluding that this standard protects media discussion of a public issue without regard to whether the person defamed is a public official or a public figure, the court made its own finding that petitioner had failed to prove malice or reckless disregard for the truth and therefore entered judgment n.o.v. for respondent. The Court of Appeals affirmed.]

Mr. Justice Powell delivered the opinion of the Court. . . .

[The opinion begins with a lengthy analysis of the Court's libel decisions from *New York Times* v. *Sullivan* through *Rosenbloom* v. *Metromedia.*]

The *New York Times* standard defines the level of constitutional protection appropriate to the context of defamation of a public person. Those who, by reason of the notoriety of their achievements or the vigor and success with which they seek the public's attention, are properly classed as public figures and those who hold governmental office may recover for injury to reputation only on clear and convincing proof that the defamatory falsehood was made with knowledge of its falsity or with reckless disregard for the truth. This standard administers an extremely powerful antidote to the inducement to media self-censorship of the common-law rule of strict liability for libel and slander. And it exacts a correspondingly high price from the victims of defamatory falsehood. Plainly many deserving plantiffs, including some intentionally subjected to injury, will be unable to surmount the barrier of the *New York Times* test. Despite this substantial abridgment of the state law right to compensation for wrongful hurt to one's reputation, the Court has concluded that the protection of the *New York Times* privilege should be available to publishers and broadcasters of defamatory falsehood concerning public officials and public figures. . . . We think that these decisions are correct, but we do not find their holdings justified solely by reference to the interest of the press and broadcast media in immunity from liability. Rather, we believe that the *New York Times* rule states an accommodation between this concern and the limited state interest present in the context of libel actions brought by public persons. For the reasons stated below, we conclude that the state interest in compensating injury to the reputation of private individuals requires that a different rule should obtain with respect to them. . . .

. . . [W]e have no difficulty in distinguishing among defamation plaintiffs. The first remedy of any victim of defamation is self-help—using available opportunities to contradict the lie or correct the error and thereby to minimize its adverse impact on reputation. Public officials and public figures usually enjoy significantly greater access to the channels of effective communication and hence have a more realistic opportunity to counteract false statements than private individuals normally enjoy. Private individuals are therefore more vulnerable to injury, and the state interest in protecting them is correspondingly greater.

More important than the likelihood that private individuals will lack effective opportunities for rebuttal, there is a compelling normative consideration underlying the distinction between public and private defamation plaintiffs. An individual who decides to seek governmental office must accept certain necessary consequences of that involvement in public affairs. He runs the risk of closer public scrutiny than might otherwise be the case. And society's interest in the officers of government is not strictly limited to the formal discharge of official duties. . . .

Those classed as public figures stand in a similar position. Hypothetically, it may be possible for someone to become a public figure through no purposeful action of his own, but the instances of truly involuntary public figures must be exceedingly rare. . . .

We hold that, so long as they do not impose liability without fault, the States may define for themselves the appropriate standard of liability for a publisher or broadcaster of defamatory falsehood injurious to a private individual. . . .

Our accommodation of the competing values at stake in defamation suits by private individuals allows the States to impose liability on the publisher or broadcaster of defamatory falsehood on a less demanding showing than that required by *New York Times*. . . . But this Countervailing state interest extends no further than compensation for actual injury. . . . [W]e hold that the States may not permit recovery of presumed or punitive damages, at least when liability is not based on a showing of knowledge of falsity or reckless disregard for the truth. . . .

We therefore conclude that the *New York Times* standard is inapplicable to this case and that the trial court erred in entering judgment for respondent. Because the jury was allowed to impose liability without fault and was permitted to presume damages without proof of injury, a new trial is necessary. We reverse and remand for further proceedings in accord with this opinion.

It is so ordered.

Mr. Justice Blackmun, concurring. . . .
Mr. Chief Justice Burger, dissenting. . . .
Mr. Justice Douglas, dissenting. . . .

Mr. Justice Brennan, dissenting. . . .
Mr. Justice White, dissenting. . . .

The *Gertz* rule was applied in *Time, Inc.* v. *Firestone,* 44 L.W. 4262 (1976), although the case was remanded for reconsideration. Mary Alice Firestone sued her husband, "the scion of one of America's wealthier families," for separate maintenance. Her husband filed a counterclaim for divorce on grounds of extreme cruelty and adultery. A Florida Circuit Court granted the divorce. Although there was discussion of the allegations of adultery in the court's final judgment, there was some ambiguity concerning the actual finding on this point. *Time* magazine published a report stating that the divorce was granted "on grounds of extreme cruelty and adultery." The former wife demanded a retraction, but *Time* declined. She sued for libel and won a judgment for $100,000, and the Florida Supreme Court affirmed. The United States Supreme Court reversed and remanded. The majority held that Mary Alice Firestone was not a "public figure" because she did not meet the *Gertz* tests of occupying a role "of especial prominence in the affairs of society," nor had she "thrust [herself] to the forefront of particular public controversies in order to influence the resolution of the issues involved." Thus, the *New York Times* standard did not apply. The *Gertz* decision does state, however, that liability cannot be imposed without fault, and the Court did not discover in the opinions of the various Florida courts a specific finding of fault on the part of *Time* magazine. The judgment was reversed and the case remanded for reconsideration in light of this deficiency.

Cox Broadcasting Corporation v. *Cohn,* 420 U.S. 469 (1975), involved the question of the liability of a television newsman who had broadcast the identity of a rape victim. A Georgia statute made it a misdemeanor to publish or broadcast the name of any rape victim. The reporter attended the trial of the persons charged with the rape and murder of a seventeen-year-old girl and learned the name of the girl from the indictments, which were public records. Later that day, he broadcast a news report of the proceedings, during which he named the victim of the crime. The father of the victim sued for money damages. The Georgia Supreme Court held that the name of a rape victim was not a matter of public concern and that the statute was a legitimate limitation on the First Amendment's right of expression. On appeal, the United States Supreme Court reversed. Justice White, for the majority, stated that public records are of interest to those concerned with the administration of government, "and a public benefit is performed by the reporting of the true contents of the records by the media." He stated further that the "States may not impose sanctions for the publication of truthful information contained in official court records open to public inspection."

Handbill Regulation and "Green River" Ordinances

The earlier cases involving restraints on the distribution of handbills were largely decided on the basis that such limitations constituted prior restraints on free speech and press. Justice Frankfurter gives a brief résumé of the cases in his concurring opinion in *Kunz* v. *New York,* 340 U.S. 290 (1951):

The easiest cases have been those in which the only interest opposing free communication was that of keeping the streets of the community clean. This could scarcely justify prohibiting the dissemination of information by handbills or censoring their contents. In *Lovell* v. *City of Griffin,* 303 U.S. 444 (1937), an ordinance requiring a permit to distribute pamphlets was held invalid where the licensing standard was "not limited to ways which might be regarded as inconsistent with the maintenance of public order or as involving disorderly conduct, the molestation of the inhabitants, or the misuse or littering of the streets." . . . In *Hague* v. *C.I.O.,* 307 U.S. 496 (1939), a portion of the ordinance declared invalid prohibited the distribution of pamphlets. In *Schneider* v. *New Jersey, Town of Irvington,* 308 U.S. 147 (1939), three of the four ordinances declared invalid by the Court prohibited the distribution of pamphlets. In *Jamison* v. *Texas,* 318 U.S. 413 (1943), the Court again declared invalid a municipal ordinance prohibiting the distribution of all handbills.

Other cases have dealt with regulations of commercial handbills and with an ordinance requiring that handbills disclose the name of the distributor. *Valentine* v. *Chrestensen,* 316 U.S. 52 (1942), is an illustration of the former. The respondent had printed a handbill advertising tours of a former navy submarine, which he owned, at a stated admission fee. He was told by the police commissioner that distribution of such a handbill would violate the city sanitary code which prohibited distribution of commercial and advertising matter in the streets. He was told that an exception was made for literature devoted to "information" or public matters. He then printed on the reverse side of his handbills a protest against the city dock department for refusing him wharfage facilities for the exhibition of his submarine. He was advised that this form still violated the ordinance and was restrained from distributing the handbills. The Court unanimously upheld the ordinance as applied to such handbills, clearly differentiating between the state's power to proscribe the dissemination of information and opinion and its power to regulate commercial advertising.

In more recent decisions *Chrestensen*'s continued vitality has been questioned, and the Court has indicated that the holding merely upheld a reasonable regulation of the manner in which commercial advertising could be distributed. *Virginia State Board of Pharmacy* v. *Virginia Citizens Consumer Council, Inc.,* 44 L.W. 4686 (1976), held unconstitutional a Virginia statute which prohibited pharmacists from advertising prices of prescription drugs. The suit was brought by consumers rather than by pharmacists, but the Court held that there was a First Amendment right of pharmacists to engage in truthful, nondeceptive advertising, and "If there is a right to advertise, there is a reciprocal right to receive the advertising, and it may be asserted by these appellees." Thus, commercial speech, while subject to reasonable regulation, is not wholly outside the protection of the First and Fourteenth Amendments. In a footnote to the majority opinion, however, it was stated that no opinion was being expressed as to regulations of commercial advertising by other professions, such as physicians and lawyers, which "render professional *services* of almost infinite variety and nature, with the consequent enhanced possibility for confusion and deception if they were to undertake certain kinds of advertising."

In *Talley* v. *California,* 362 U.S. 60 (1960), the Court reviewed the conviction of appellant who was convicted in a Los Angeles Municipal Court for violating a municipal ordinance making it a criminal offense to distribute "any handbill in any place under any circumstances," unless it had printed on it the names and addresses of the persons who prepared, distributed, or sponsored it. The Court divided six-to-three in reversing the conviction. Justice Black, speaking for the Court, found the ordinance void on its face, citing *Lovell* v. *Griffin.* Counsel for the state urged that the ordinance was aimed at providing a way to identify those responsible for fraud, false advertising, and libel. Justice Black stated, however, that "the ordinance is in no manner so limited, nor have we been referred to any legislative history indicating such a purpose." He stated further:

There can be no doubt that such an identification requirement would tend to restrict freedom to distribute information and thereby freedom of expression....

Anonymous pamphlets, leaflets, brochures and even books have played an important role in the progress of mankind. Persecuted groups and sects from time to time throughout history have been able to criticize oppressive practices and laws either anonymously or not at all....

We have recently had occasion to hold in two cases that there are times and circumstances when States may not compel members of groups engaged in the dissemination of ideas to be publicly identified. *Bates* v. *Little Rock* ... ; *National Association for Advancement of Colored People* v. *Alabama,* ... The reason for those holdings was that identification and fear of reprisal might deter perfectly peaceful discussions of public matters of importance. This broad Los Angeles ordinance is subject to the same infirmity. We hold that it, like the Griffin, Georgia, ordinance, is void on its face.

Justice Clark, joined by Justices Frankfurter and Whittaker, dissented. He pointed out that Talley had made no showing that a restraint upon his freedom of speech would result from the enforcement of the ordinance and concluded that "the substantiality of Los Angeles' interest in the enforcement of the ordinance sustains its validity." He also stated that the case was controlled by prior decisions in which "this Court has approved laws requiring no less than Los Angeles' ordinance:" one upholding an Act of Congress requiring newspapers using the second-class mails to publish the names of their editors, publishers, and owners; a second upholding the Federal Regulation of Lobbying Act requiring registration; and, third, the stated policy of a majority of states prohibiting the anonymous distribution of materials relating to candidates and elections.

Special problems have arisen with respect to speech and handbill activities in privately owned "company towns" and in privately owned shopping centers, both of which are generally open to the public. In *Marsh* v. *Alabama,* 326 U.S. 501 (1946), the Court reversed a trespass conviction of a Jehovah's Witness who undertook to distribute religious literature on a sidewalk near a post office on property owned by the Gulf Shipbuilding Corporation. The majority opinion pointed out that there was nothing to distinguish the town and its shopping district from any other town and shopping center except the fact that the title to the property belonged to a private corporation. To apply trespass law to one distributing religious literature in such an area was held to violate his First and Fourteenth Amendment rights.

In *Amalgamated Food Employees Union* v. *Logan Valley Plaza,* 391 U.S. 308 (1968), the Court extended the rationale of *Marsh* to peaceful picketing of a store, located in a large shopping center, by nonemployees who were protesting the fact that the store was employing a wholly nonunion staff. The opinion, however, noted that the scope of the holding was limited and added, "We are, therefore, not called upon to consider whether respondents' property rights could, consistently with the First Amendment, justify a bar on picketing which was not thus directly related in its purpose to the use to which the shopping center property was being put."

The question of the right to deliver handbills in a privately owned shopping center came to the court in *Lloyd Corporation* v. *Tanner,* 407 U.S. 551 (1972). The respondents attempted to distribute handbills, which invited the public to a meeting to protest the draft and the Vietnam War, in the interior mall area of a large privately owned shopping center. The owner had a strict no-handbilling rule, and his security guards requested the respondents, under threat of arrest, to stop the distribution. They then secured an injunction from a United States District Court in Oregon against interference with their continued distribution of noncommercial handbills in a peaceful and orderly manner in areas open to general public access. The Court of Appeals affirmed, but the Supreme Court reversed and remanded with directions to vacate the injunction. In an opinion by Justice Powell for five members of the Court, it was held that while generally open to the public, the shopping center was not so dedicated to public use as to require the shopping center owner to permit handbilling in the center which was unrelated to the shopping center's operations. *Marsh* was distinguished on the ground that it involved a company town which had all the attributes of a municipality. *Logan Valley* was distinguished on the ground that the picketing there was designed to convey a message to patrons of a particular store, so located as to preclude other reasonable access to patrons of the store. The dissenters argued that the mall was the functional equivalent of a public business district, and that the First Amendment protected the right to distribute handbills. Justice Marshall, for the dissenters, stated, "As I read the opinion of the Court, it is an attack not only on the rationale of *Logan Valley,* but also on this Court's longstanding decision in *Marsh* v. *Alabama.*"

Any doubt as to the continued vitality of *Logan Valley* was removed in 1976 when the Court overruled that decision in *Hudgens* v. *N. L. R. B.,* 44 L.W. 4281. Striking warehouse employees, who were members of a union, started to picket their employer's retail store located in a privately owned shopping center. They departed, however, when an agent of the owner of the shopping center threatened that they would be arrested for trespassing. The union then filed an unfair labor charge with the N.L.R.B., alleging interference with the employees' rights under the N.L.R.B. Relying on *Logan Valley* in addition to the Act, the Board held that union members could not be enjoined from exercising their First Amendment right to picket in a shopping center which was the equivalent of a municipality's business district. The Court of Appeals enforced the Board's cease-and-desist order, holding that the Board had met the requirement of *Lloyd Corp.* v. *Tanner* of proving that less intrusive locations for picketing were either unavailable or ineffective.

On certiorari, the Supreme Court reversed and remanded. The majority opinion indicated that a large self-contained shopping center was not the functional equivalent of a municipality, and therefore the First and Fourteenth Amendments had no application to this case. It stated further that the *Lloyd* case amounted to a total rejection of *Logan Valley,* and the striking employees in the case at bar "did not have a First Amendment right to enter this shopping center for the purpose of advertising their strike." It followed that the rights and liabilities of the parties were dependent exclusively upon the Labor Relations Act, and the case was remanded to the Board for a determination of those issues.

"Green River" ordinances (so called because of earlier adoption by the City of Green River, Wyoming) are those which prohibit various kinds of door-to-door solicitation without the prior permission of the householder. In *Martin v. Struthers*, 319 U.S. 141 (1943), a divided Court held that a munici- pality could not constitutionally prohibit a person from going from door to door knocking on doors and ringing doorbells for the purpose of distributing to the householder a handbill announcing a religious meeting. The com- munity's interest in preventing crime and in assuring privacy in an industrial community where many residents worked night shifts and had to sleep during the day was held insufficient to justify the ordinance in the case of persons involved in religious communication by handbill. Justice Frankfurter filed a strong dissent stressing the need to recognize the householder's privacy.

In *Breard* v. *City of Alexandria*, 341 U.S. 622 (1951), however, the Court sustained a similar ordinance applying to various kinds of commercial solicitation.

BREARD *v.* CITY OF ALEXANDRIA
341 U.S. 622 (1951)

[Appellant was a representative of Keystone Readers Service, Inc., and was arrested while going from door to door soliciting subscriptions for nationally known magazines. He argued that the ordinance was an abridgment of his freedom of speech and press. Justice Reed, speaking for the majority, stated:]

. . . We agree that the fact that periodicals are sold does not put them beyond the protection of the First Amendment. The selling, however, brings into the transaction a commercial feature. . . .

The case that comes nearest to supporting appellant's contention is *Martin* v. *Struthers.* . . . There a municipal ordinance forbidding anyone summoning the occupants of a residence to the door to receive advertisements was held invalid as applied to the free distribution of dodgers "advertising a religious meeting." Atten- tion was directed in note 1 of that case to the fact that the ordinance was not aimed "solely at commercial advertising." It was said: "The ordinance does not control anything but the distribution of literature, and in that respect it substitutes the judgment of the community for the judgment of the individual householder."

The decision to release the distributor was because: "Freedom to distribute information to every citizen wherever he desires to receive it is so clearly vital to the preservation of a free society that, putting aside reasonable police and health regulations of time and manner of distribution, it must be fully preserved."

There was dissent even to this carefully phrased application of the principles of the First Amendment. As no element of the commercial entered into this free solicitation and the opinion was narrowly limited to the precise fact of the free distribution of an invitation to religious services, we feel that it is not necessarily inconsistent with the conclusion reached in this case. . . .

This makes the constitutionality of Alexandria's ordinance turn upon a balanc- ing of the conveniences between some householder's desire for privacy and the pub- lisher's right to distribute publications in the precise way that those soliciting for him think brings the best results. The issue brings into collision the rights of the hospitable housewife, peering on Monday morning around her chained door, with those of Mr. Breard's courteous, well-trained but possibly persistent solicitor, offering a bargain on culture and information through a joint subscription to *Satevepost, Pic* and *Today's Woman....*

... We think those communities that have found these methods of sale obnoxious may control them by ordinance.... We see no abridgment of the principles of the First Amendment in this ordinance.

[Justice Black, joined by Justice Douglas, dissented. He stated:]

Today's decision marks a revitalization of the judicial views which prevailed before this Court embraced the philosophy that the First Amendment gives a preferred status to the liberties it protects. I adhere to that preferred position philosophy. It is my belief that the freedom of the people of this Nation cannot survive even a little governmental hobbling of religious or political ideas, whether they be communicated orally or through the press.

The constitutional sanctuary for the press must necessarily include liberty to publish and circulate. In view of our economic system, it must also include freedom to solicit paying subscribers. Of course homeowners can if they wish forbid newsboys, reporters or magazine solicitors to ring their doorbells. But when the homeowner himself has not done this, I believe that the First Amendment ... bars laws like the present ordinance which punish persons who peacefully go from door to door as agents of the press.

Miscellaneous Regulations Applicable to the Press

While the press is accorded special protection under the First and Fourteenth Amendments, newspapers are not for this reason exempt from all ordinary regulatory measures fairly applied by state or national governments. Newspapers are, after all, commercial enterprises and may be subjected to normal governmental restraints generally applicable to other business operations. The crucial test in any given case is whether the regulation was adopted as a device to limit the freedom of the press.

Newspapers are liable for ordinary taxes, but may a tax be exacted as punishment of newspapers for political opposition? This was the issue in *Grosjean* v. *American Press Co.*, 297 U.S. 233 (1936). In 1934 the Louisiana legislature, dominated by Huey Long, imposed a tax of 2 percent of gross receipts on all newspapers in the state with a circulation of more than 20,000 copies a week. Thirteen newspapers, all hostile to Long, were affected by the tax, while there were four other daily papers and some 120 weekly newspapers, favorable to Long, which were not subject to the tax. Justice Sutherland, speaking for a unanimous Court, examined the pattern of British taxation of newspapers in the eighteenth and nineteenth centuries, remarking, "These duties were quite commonly characterized as 'taxes on knowledge,' a phrase used for the purpose of describing the effect of the exactions and at the same time condemning them." He concluded that the First and Fourteenth Amendments were meant to bar taxes imposed to restrict the free flow of information.

It is not intended by anything we have said to suggest that the owners of newspapers are immune from any of the ordinary forms of taxation for support of the government. But this is not an ordinary form of tax, but one single in kind, with a long history of hostile misuse against the freedom of the press.

The predominant purpose of the grant of immunity here invoked was to preserve an untrammeled press as a vital source of public information. ... The tax here involved is bad not because it takes money from the pockets of the appellees. If that were all, a wholly different question would be presented. It is bad because, in the light of its history and of its present setting, it is seen to be a deliberate and calculated device in the guise of a tax to limit the circulation of information to which the public is entitled in virtue of the constitutional guaranties. A free press stands as one of the great interpreters between the government and the people. To allow it to be fettered is to fetter ourselves.

In view of the persistent search for new subjects of taxation, it is not without significance that, with the single exception of the Louisiana statute, so far as we can discover, no state during the one hundred fifty years of our national existence has undertaken to impose a tax like that now in question.

The form in which the tax is imposed is in itself suspicious. It is not measured or limited by the volume of advertisements. It is measured alone by the extent of the circulation of the publication in which the advertisements are carried, with the plain purpose of penalizing the publishers and curtailing the circulation of a selected group of newspapers.

Having reached the conclusion that the act imposing the tax in question is unconstitutional under the due process of law clause because it abridges the freedom of the press, we deem it unnecessary to consider the further grounds assigned that it also constitutes a denial of the equal protection of the laws.

Several national regulations adopted under the commerce power have been successfully applied to the press against claims of First Amendment violation. In *The Associated Press* v. *National Labor Relations Board,* 301 U.S. 103 (1937), the Court held that the National Labor Relations Act could be applied to the newspaper business just as it could to other business enterprises in interstate commerce. The case arose after the Board had ordered the reinstatement of a copy editor for the Associated Press who had been fired for attempting to organize a union. The Court said, "The publisher of a newspaper has no special immunity from the application of general laws. ... The regulation here in question has no relation whatever to the impartial distribution of news."

A similar holding obtained in *Oklahoma Press Publishing Co.* v. *Walling,* 327 U.S. 186 (1946), in which a newspaper publisher was held subject to the provisions of the Fair Labor Standards Act. And in *Associated Press* v. *United States,* 326 U.S. 1 (1945), it was held that the Sherman Antitrust Act could constitutionally be applied to newspapers, and for the Associated Press to enforce its bylaws severely restricting competition was an unreasonable restraint of trade in violation of the Act. Justice Black, for the majority, said, "The First Amendment affords not the slightest support for the contention that a combination to restrain trade in news and views has any constitutional immunity."

In 1973 the State of Florida adopted a "right of reply" statute which provided that if a candidate for nomination or election was assailed regarding his personal character or official record by any newspaper, the candidate had the right to demand that the newspaper print, free of cost to the candidate, any reply the candidate might make to the newspaper's charges. The reply had to appear in as conspicuous a place and in the same kind of type as the charges which prompted the reply, provided it did not take up more space than the charges. Failure to comply with the statute constituted a first-degree misdemeanor. In *Miami Herald Publishing Company* v. *Tornillo,* 418 U.S. 241 (1974), the Court held unanimously that the statute violated the First Amendment guarantee of a free press.

The *Tornillo* case is one feature of a whole new civil liberties policy issue, that of the right of access to the media. [See Jerome A. Barron, *Freedom of the Press for Whom?* (Bloomington, Ind.: Indiana University Press, 1973), and Francisco J. Lewels, "Restoring the Free Marketplace: Minority Access to the Media," 4 *Policy Studies Journal* 103 (1975).] An aspect of the issue involving access to radio and television time was presented in a group of four cases, with the decision coming under *Columbia Broadcasting System* v. *Democratic National Committee,* 412 U.S. 94 (1973). The Federal Communications Commission had rejected contentions that the general policy of certain radio and television broadcast licensees of not selling any editorial advertising time to individuals or groups wishing to speak out on public issues violated the Federal Communications Act of 1934 and the First Amendment. The contentions were asserted in actions instituted by a national organization of businessmen opposed to United States involvement in Vietnam and by the Democratic National Committee. The complainants had argued that responsible individuals and groups had a right to purchase advertising time to comment on public issues without regard to whether the broadcaster had complied with the Commission's "fairness doctrine" requiring that a broadcaster provide adequate coverage of public issues, fairly reflecting differing viewpoints. The Court of Appeals reversed the Commission and remanded to the Commission to develop regulations governing the airing of editorial advertisements. The opinion stated that "a flat ban on paid public issue announcements is in violation of the First Amendment, at least when other sorts of paid announcements are accepted." The Supreme Court reversed, holding that neither the Communications Act nor the First Amendment requires broadcasters to accept paid editorial advertisements. Chief Justice Burger, speaking for six members of the Court, stated that great weight must be afforded to the decisions of Congress and the experience of the F.C.C. He noted that Congress has consistently rejected efforts to impose on broadcasters a "common carrier" right of access for all persons wishing to speak out on public issues. Instead, it reposed in the F.C.C. regulatory authority by which the fairness doctrine was evolved to require that the broadcaster's coverage of important public issues must be adequate and must fairly reflect differing viewpoints. No private individual or group, therefore, has a right to command the use of broadcast facilities. Further, the F.C.C. was justified in concluding that the public interest in having access to the marketplace of "ideas and experience" would not be served by ordering a right of access to advertising time. There is a substantial risk that such a system would be monopolized by those who were wealthy, and the public accountability which now rests with the broadcaster would be diluted.

Justice Brennan, joined by Justice Marshall, dissented. He stated that the First Amendment must be construed to safeguard "not only the right of the public to *hear* debate, but also the right of individuals to *participate* in that debate and to attempt to persuade others to their points of view. He pointed out that as the system now operates, any person wishing to market beer, soap, toothpaste, or deodorant has direct, personal, and instantaneous access to the electronic media. But a similar individual "seeking to discuss war, peace, pollution, or the suffering of the poor is denied this right to speak." He felt that the differential treatment accorded "commercial" and "controversial" speech clearly violated the First Amendment. [See Louis L. Jaffe, "The Editorial Responsibility of the Broadcaster: Reflections on Fairness and Access," 85 *Harv. L. Rev.* 768 (1972).]

OBSCENITY AND PORNOGRAPHY

Earlier forms of censorship were primarily concerned with stamping out heresy or sedition. More recently, while considerations of security are important, the principal impetus for control of publications and movies is a concern for morality and the prohibition of obscenity. The common-law crime of "obscene libel" developed in England in the early part of the eighteenth century. The established rule of the old common law received its formulation in the opinion of Chief Justice Cockburn in the case of *Regina* v. *Hicklin* (1968), L.R. 3 Q. B. 360. The case dealt with a pamphlet purporting to describe the morals—or lack of morals—of Catholic priests in connection with the confessional. The long title was *The Confessional Unmasked: showing the depravity of the Roman Priesthood, the iniquity of the Confessional and the questions put to females in confession.* It was printed and circulated at cost by an anti-Catholic group which had as its main purpose the election of Protestants to Parliament. The case involved a request for a destruction order, rather than a prosecution, and in allowing the order the Chief Justice laid down the test for obscenity:

I think the test of obscenity is this, whether the tendency of the matter charged as obscenity is to deprave and corrupt those whose minds are open to such immoral influences, and into whose hands a publication of this sort may fall.

This rule has apparently been followed by the English courts down to the enactment of the Obscene Publications Act of 1959, which changed "tendency" to "effect" and omitted the application to "those whose minds are open to such immoral influences." [On the English law generally, see Norman St. John-Stevas, *Obscenity and the Law* (New York: Macmillan, 1956), and John Chandos, ed., *To Deprave and Corrupt* (New York: Association Press, 1962).]

The objection to the Hicklin test, of course, is that it fixes a standard for the community's reading matter geared to the feeblest mentality or most suggestible individual in the community. While the test may have been followed to some extent by American judges, it was explicitly rejected in 1933 by federal judge John Woolsey in *United States* v. *One Book Called Ulysses,* 5 F. Supp. 182 (1933), a case involving a customs official's denial of entry of James Joyce's *Ulysses.* [*Aff'd.* 72 F. 2d 705 (1934) by Judges Augustus N. and Learned Hand.] Since then American judges have preferred to use as a standard of judgment the effect of the book upon normal, average, healthy persons.

The United States Supreme Court made a historic decision in 1957 when it ruled squarely for the first time on the subject of the censorship of books. The case was *Butler* v. *Michigan,* 352 U.S. 380 (1957). The state statute made it a misdemeanor to sell to the *general reading public* any obscene book, "tending to incite minors to violent or depraved or immoral acts," or "tending to the corruption of the morals of youth." The appellant was convicted of violating the statute by selling a copy of a paper-bound reprint of John Griffin's *The Devil Rides Outside.*

The Court unanimously voted to set aside the conviction. Justice Frankfurter, for the Court, stated:

> The State insists that, by thus quarantining the general reading public against books not too rugged for grown men and women in order to shield juvenile innocence, it is exercising its power to promote the general welfare. Surely, this is to burn the house to roast the pig. . . . We have before us legislation not reasonably restricted to the evil with which it is said to deal. The incidence of this enactment is to reduce the adult population of Michigan to reading only what is fit for children.

At the same term of Court, and also for the first time, the problem of legislative control of publications alleged to be obscene was considered. The opinion was written jointly for the companion cases of *Roth* v. *United States* and *Alberts* v. *California,* 354 U.S. 476 (1957). Roth was convicted in a federal court of violating the federal statute which forbids the mailing of obscene literature, by sending a publication called *American Aphrodite.* Alberts was convicted for advertising such books as *Sword of Desire, She Made It Pay,* and *The Business Side of the Oldest Business,* in violation of a California law which forbids the writing, publishing, or selling of obscene books.

ROTH *v.* UNITED STATES
ALBERTS *v.* CALIFORNIA
354 U.S. 476 (1957)

Mr. Justice Brennan delivered the opinion of the Court. . . .

The dispositive question is whether obscenity is utterance within the area of protected speech and press.* Although this is the first time the question has been squarely presented to this Court, either under the First Amendment or under the Fourteenth Amendment, expressions found in numerous opinions indicate that this Court has always assumed that obscenity is not protected by the freedoms of speech and press. . . .

The guaranties of freedom of expression in effect in 10 of the 14 States which by 1792 had ratified the Constitution, gave no absolute protection for every utterance. Thirteen of the 14 States provided for the prosecution of libel, and all of those States made either blasphemy or profanity, or both, statutory crimes. As early as 1712, Massachusetts made it criminal to publish "any filthy, obscene, or profane song, pamphlet, libel or mock sermon" in imitation or mimicking of religious services. . . . Thus, profanity and obscenity were related offenses.

In light of this history, it is apparent that the unconditional phrasing of the First Amendment was not intended to protect every utterance. . . . At the time of the adoption of the First Amendment, obscenity law was not as fully developed as libel law, but there is sufficiently contemporaneous evidence to show that obscenity, too, was outside the protection intended for speech and press. . . .

All ideas having even the slightest redeeming social importance—unorthodox ideas, controversial ideas, even ideas hateful to the prevailing climate of opinion— have the full protection of the guaranties, unless excludable because they encroach upon the limited area of more important interests. But implicit in the history of

---

* No issue is presented in either case concerning the obscenity of the material involved.

the First Amendment is the rejection of obscenity as utterly without redeeming social importance. This rejection for that reason is mirrored in the universal judgment that obscenity should be restrained, reflected in the international agreement of over 50 nations,** in the obscenity laws of all of the 48 States, and in the 20 obscenity laws enacted by the Congress from 1842 to 1956. . . . We hold that obscenity is not within the area of constitutionally protected speech or press.

It is strenuously urged that these obscenity statutes offend the constitutional guaranties because they punish incitation to impure sexual *thoughts,* not shown to be related to any overt antisocial conduct which is or may be incited in the persons stimulated to such *thoughts.* . . .

However, sex and obscenity are not synonymous. Obscene material is material which deals with sex in a manner appealing to prurient interest.*** The portrayal of sex, *e.g.,* in art, literature and scientific works, is not itself sufficient reason to deny material the constitutional protection of freedom of speech and press. Sex, a great and mysterious motive force in human life, has indisputably been a subject of absorbing interest to mankind through the ages; it is one of the vital problems of human interest and public concern. . . .

The early leading standard of obscenity allowed material to be judged merely by the effect of an isolated excerpt upon particularly susceptible persons. *Regina* v. *Hicklin* [1868] L.R. 3 Q.B. 360. Some American courts adopted this standard but later decisions have rejected it and substituted this test: whether to the average person, applying contemporary community standards, the dominant theme of the material taken as a whole appeals to prurient interest. The *Hicklin* test, judging obscenity by the effect of isolated passages upon the most susceptible persons, might well encompass material legitimately treating with sex, and so it must be rejected as unconstitutionally restrictive of the freedoms of speech and press. On the other hand, the substituted standard provides safeguards adequate to withstand the charge of constitutional infirmity. . . .

It is argued that the statutes do not provide reasonably ascertainable standards of guilt and therefore violate the constitutional requirements of due process. . . .

Many decisions have recognized that these terms of obscenity statutes are not precise. This Court, however, has consistently held that lack of precision is not itself offensive to the requirements of due process. . . . These words [obscene, lewd, lascivious, or filthy or indecent], applied according to the proper standard for judging obscenity, already discussed, give adequate warning of the conduct proscribed and mark " . . . boundaries sufficiently distinct for judges and juries fairly to administer the law." . . .

[Chief Justice Warren concurred in the result.]

[Justice Harlan concurred in *Alberts* and dissented in *Roth.* He stated that "Congress has no substantive power over sexual morality," and such powers as the federal government has in this field are insufficient to support a statute so broadly phrased as to reach the transmission of books which, under the judge's

---

** Agreement for the Suppression of the Circulation of Obscene Publications, 37 stat. 1511; Treaties in Force 209 (U.S. Department of State, October 31, 1956).
*** *I.e.,* material having a tendency to excite lustful thoughts. . . .
   We perceive no significant difference between the meaning of obscenity developed in the case law and the definition of the A.L.I., Model Penal Code, Section 207.10 (2) (Tent. Draft No. 6, 1957), *viz.:*
   " . . . A thing is obscene if, considered as a whole, its predominant appeal is to prurient interest, i.e., a shameful or morbid interest in nudity, sex, or excretion, and if it goes substantially beyond customary limits of candor in description or representation of such matters. . . ." . . .

charge "tend to stir sexual impulses and lead to sexually impure thoughts." He stated further that he did not think the federal statute could be constitutionally construed to reach other than "what the Government has termed as 'hard-core' pornography."]

Mr. Justice Douglas, with whom Mr. Justice Black concurs, dissenting.

When we sustain these convictions, we make the legality of a publication turn on the purity of thought which a book or tract instills in the mind of the reader. I do not think we can approve that standard and be faithful to the command of the First Amendment, which by its terms is a restraint on Congress and which by the Fourteenth is a restraint on the States. . . .

By these standards punishment is inflicted for thoughts provoked, not for overt acts nor antisocial conduct. This test cannot be squared with our decisions under the First Amendment. . . . This issue cannot be avoided by saying that obscenity is not protected by the First Amendment. The question remains what is the constitutional test of obscenity?

The tests by which these convictions were obtained require only the arousing of sexual thoughts. Yet the arousing of sexual thoughts and desires happens every day in normal life in dozens of ways. Nearly 30 years ago a questionnaire sent to college and normal school women graduates asked what things were most stimulating sexually. Of 409 replies, 9 said "music"; 18 said "pictures"; 29 said "dancing"; 40 said "drama"; 95 said "books"; and 218 said "man." Alpert, Judicial Censorship of Obscene Literature, 52 Harv. L. Rev. 40, 73. . . .

If we were certain that impurity of sexual thoughts impelled to action, we would be on less dangerous ground in punishing the distributors of this sex literature. But it is by no means clear that obscene literature, as so defined, is a significant factor in influencing substantial deviations from the community standards. . . .

The absence of dependable information on the effect of obscene literature on human conduct should make us wary. It should put us on the side of protecting society's interest in literature, except and unless it can be said that the particular publication has an impact on action that the government can control.

As noted, the trial judge in the *Roth* case charged the jury in the alternative that the federal obscenity statute outlaws literature dealing with sex which affends "the common conscience of the community." That standard is, in my view, more inimical still to freedom of expression.

. . . Certainly that standard would not be an acceptable one if religion, economics, politics or philosophy were involved. How does it become a constitutional standard when literature treating with sex is concerned?

Any test that turns on what is offensive to the community's standards is too loose, too capricious, too destructive of freedom of expression to be squared with the First Amendment. Under that test, juries can censor, suppress what they don't like, provided the matter relates to "sexual impurity" or has a tendency "to excite lustful thoughts." This is community censorship in one of its worst forms. It creates a regime where in the battle between the literati and the Philistines, the Philistines are certain to win. If experience in this field teaches anything, it is that "censorship of obscenity has almost always been both irrational and indiscriminate." . . .

I would give the broad sweep of the First Amendment full support. I have the same confidence in the ability of our people to reject noxious literature as I have in their capacity to sort out the true from the false in theology, economics, politics, or any other field.

A new gloss was added to the law of obscenity in three decisions in 1966. In *Ginzburg* v. *United States,* 383 U.S. 463 (1966), defendants challenged their convictions for having violated the federal obscenity statute by using the mail for distributing allegedly obscene literature—namely, the magazine *Eros,* containing articles and photo essays on love and sex; a biweekly newsletter, dedicated to "keeping sex an art and preventing it from becoming a science"; and "The Housewife's Handbook on Promiscuity." On certiorari, the Supreme Court by a five-to-four vote affirmed the convictions. In so holding, the majority stated that even through the publications, standing alone, might not be obscene, the question of obscenity "may include consideration of the setting in which the publications were presented as an aid to determining the question of obscenity, and assume without deciding that the prosecution could not have succeeded otherwise." "We view the publications against a background of commercial exploitation of erotica solely for the sake of their prurient appeal." The Court found ample evidence to support a finding that the publisher pointedly directed his advertising and distribution campaign to prurient appeal. Justice Brennan stated:

Besides testimony as to the merit of the material, there was abundant evidence to show that each of the accused publications was originated or sold as stock in trade of the sordid business of pandering—"the business of purveying textual or graphic matter openly advertised to appeal to the erotic interest of their customers."

With respect to the "Handbook," the government drew a distinction between the author's solicitation and that of petitioners. The author had printed the work privately and canvassed persons whose names appeared on membership lists of medical and psychiatric associations, asserting its value as an adjunct in therapy. According to the United States Attorney, the author "never had widespread indiscriminate distribution of the Handbook and, consequently, the Post Office Department did not interfere." The majority of the Court accepted this distinction in applying the definition of obscenity, stating:

Petitioners, however, did not sell the book to such a limited audience, or focus their claims for it on its supposed therapeutic or educational value; rather, they deliberately emphasized the sexually provocative aspects of the work, in order to catch the salaciously disposed.

Thus the majority added to the *Roth* test of obscenity another consideration, whether in the context of the production, sale, and publicity for the publication there is substantial evidence of "exploitation by those who would make a business of pandering to 'the widespread weakness for titillation by pornography.' " And the finding of the latter fact "in close cases . . . may be probative with respect to the nature of the material in question and thus satisfy the *Roth* test."

There were four separate dissenting opinions. Justice Stewart expressed the views that (1) the defendants were denied due process because they were never charged with "commercial exploitation," or "pandering," or "titillation"; (2) no federal statute made conduct of this kind a criminal offense; (3) any such criminal statute would be unconstitutionally vague; and (4) the Court had no power to deny a defendant the First Amendment protections because it disapproves of his sordid business.

A second obscenity case, decided on the same day, was *Mishkin* v. *New York,* 383 U.S. 502 (1966). Mishkin was convicted of violating New York law by preparing obscene books, publishing obscene books, and possessing obscene books with intent to sell them. Fifty books were involved in the case. As stated by Justice Brennan, "They portray sexuality in many guises. Some depict relatively normal heterosexual relations, but more depict such deviations as sado-masochism, fetishism, and homosexuality." By a six-to-three vote the Court affirmed the conviction. Appellant attacked his conviction on three grounds: (1) the statutory proscriptions against "sadistic" or "masochistic" or "obscene" materials are impermissibly vague and thus the statute is invalid on its face; (2) the books were not in fact obscene; and (3) the proof of *scienter* was inadequate.

The Court stated that the New York courts have interpreted "obscenity" to cover only so-called hard-core pornography, and since this is a more rigorous test than the *Roth* definition, the constitutional criteria are satisfied. The second challenge rested in part on the *Roth* requirement that the material be judged on the basis of its appeal to the "average" or "normal" person. It was argued that material concerning deviant sexual practices, such as flagellation, fetishisms, and lesbianism, do not satisfy the prurient-appeal requirement because the "average" person would be disgusted rather than erotically stimulated. In response Justice Brennan, for the majority, stated:

> We adjust the prurient-appeal requirement to social realities by permitting the appeal of this type of material to be assessed in terms of the sexual interests of its intended and probable recipient group; and since our holding requires that the recipient group be defined with more specificity than in terms of sexually immature persons, it also avoids the inadequacy of the most-susceptible-person facet of the *Hicklin* test.

On the issue of *scienter*, the Court quoted the New York Court of Appeals statement that "It is not innocent but *calculated purveyance* of filth which is exorcised," and stated that there was adequate proof that appellant was aware of the character of the material which he purposely had prepared and sold.

In a third case decided on the same day, *A Book Named "John Cleland's Memoirs of a Woman of Pleasure"* v. *Attorney General of Massachusetts,* 383 U.S. 413 (1966), the Court reviewed the judgment of a Massachusetts court of equity that the book *Memoirs of a Woman of Pleasure* (commonly known as *Fanny Hill*), written by John Cleland in about 1750, was obscene. By a six-to-three vote the Court reversed, but the majority was so badly split that there was no "opinion for the Court." Three justices, through Justice Brennan, held that the *Roth* test required a finding that the book be *"utterly without redeeming social value"* to be classified as obscene; that each of the three facets of the *Roth* test is to be applied independently; and that "the social value of the book can neither be weighed against nor canceled by its prurient appeal or patent offensiveness." Thus the Massachusetts court erred in holding that a book need not be "unqualified worthless before it can be deemed obscene." The opinion brought this holding in line with *Ginzburg* by stating that there was no evidence presented that the book was "commercially exploited for the sake of prurient appeal, to the exclusion of all other values," but that such a finding might justify the conclusion that the book was utterly without redeeming social importance.

Another aspect of the enforcement of obscenity laws was the basis for reversal in *Smith* v. *California,* 361 U.S. 147 (1959). Smith was the proprietor of a bookstore and was convicted of violating a Los Angeles ordinance which made it unlawful to possess any obscene or indecent book in any place where books were sold or kept for sale. The ordinance was construed as imposing a strict criminal liability, without requiring any element of *scienter*, i.e., knowledge by the defendant of the contents of the book upon which the criminal charge was based. The Court unanimously reversed the conviction, although there were five separate opinions. Justice Brennan, speaking for five members, held that the requirement of strict liability on the bookseller unconstitutionally hindered freedom of speech and press. He stated:

[I]f the bookseller is criminally liable without knowledge of the contents, and the ordinance fulfills its purposes, he will tend to restrict the books the sells to those he has inspected; and thus the State will have imposed a restriction upon the distribution of constitutionally protected as well as obscene literature.... If the contents of bookshops and periodical stands were restricted to material of which their proprietors had made an inspection, they might be depleted indeed.... The bookseller's self-censorship, compelled by the State, would be a censorship affecting the whole public, hardly less virulent for being privately administered.

In *Bantam Books, Inc.* v. *Sullivan*, 372 U.S. 58 (1963), the Court dealt with the constitutionality of certain forms of informal suppression of distribution of books by a state commission. The Rhode Island legislature created the "Rhode Island Commission to Encourage Morality in Youth" which, among other duties, was charged with educating the public concerning any obscene publications and with investigating and recommending the prosecution of all violations of relevant statutes. The Commission evolved the practice of sending notices to distributors that certain designated books or magazines had been found to be objectionable for sale, distribution, or display to persons under 18 years of age, asking for their cooperation, and reminding them of the Commission's duty to recommend prosecution of sellers of obscenity. Copies of the lists of objectionable publications were also circulated to local police departments, and the distributors were so advised. The normal result of such notification was for the distributor to halt further circulation of the listed publications, to withdraw from retailers all unsold copies, and to return all unsold copies to the publishers.

Appellants, four New York publishers of paperback books, brought the action in the Superior Court of Rhode Island (1) to declare the law creating the Commission unconstitutional and (2) to declare unconstitutional and enjoin the acts and practices of the Commission under the law. With only one dissent, the Court held that the law creating the Commission was valid, but the practice of informal suppression constituted a system of prior administrative restraints. The opinion for the majority noted that "although the Commission's supposed concern is limited to youthful readers, the 'cooperation' it seeks from distributors invariably entails the complete suppression of the listed publications; adult readers are equally deprived of the opportunity to purchase the publications in the State." The fact that such a result could be accomplished without any judicial determination of the issue of obscenity was a fatal defect in its failure to furnish the procedural safeguards required for restricting the freedom of the press.

In *Ginsberg* v. *New York*, 390 U.S. 629 (1968), the Court examined the question of the constitutionality on its face of a New York criminal obscenity statute which prohibited the sale to minors under 17 years of age of material defined to be obscene on the basis of its appeal to them, whether or not it would be obscene to adults. Appellant was convicted under the statute for selling two "girlie" magazines to a sixteen-year-old boy. The Court upheld the statute against the claim that the *Roth-Memoirs* test was the appropriate standard, and held that the State could properly bar the sale of materials to minors which it could not constitutionally exclude from distribution to adults.

STANLEY v. GEORGIA
394 U.S. 557 (1969)

Mr. Justice Marshall delivered the opinion of the Court.

An investigation of appellant's alleged bookmaking activities led to the issuance of a search warrant for appellant's home. Under authority of this warrant, federal and state agents secured entrance ... [W]hile looking through a desk drawer in an upstairs bedroom, one of the federal agents, accompanied by a state officer, found three reels of eight-millimeter film. Using a projector and screen found in an upstairs living room, they viewed the films. The state officer concluded that they were obscene and seized them. Since a further examination of the bedroom indicated that appellant occupied it, he was charged with possession of obscene matter and placed under arrest. He was later indicted for "knowingly hav[ing] possession of obscene matter" in violation of Georgia law. Appellant was tried before a jury and convicted. The Supreme Court of Georgia affirmed. . . .

It is now well established that the Constitution protects the right to receive information and ideas. . . . The right to receive information and ideas, regardless of their social worth . . . is fundamental to our free society. Moreover, in the context of this case—a prosecution for mere possession of printed or filmed matter in the privacy of a person's own home—that right takes on an added dimension. For also fundamental is the right to be free, except in very limited circumstances, from unwanted governmental intrusions into one's privacy. . . .

These are the rights that appellant is asserting in the case before us. He is asserting the right to read or observe what he pleases—the right to satisfy his intellectual and emotional needs in the privacy of his own home. He is asserting the right to be free from state inquiry into the contents of his library. Georgia contends that appellant does not have these rights, that there are certain types of materials that the individual may not read or even possess. Georgia justifies this assertion by arguing that the films in the present case are obscene. But we think that mere categorization of these films as "obscene" is insufficient justification for such a drastic invasion of personal liberties guaranteed by the First and Fourteenth Amendments. Whatever may be the justifications for other statutes regulating obscenity, we do not think they reach into the privacy of one's own home. If the First Amendment means anything, it means that a State has no business telling a man, sitting alone in his own house, what books he may read or what films he may watch. Our whole constitutional heritage rebels at the thought of giving government the power to control men's minds.

And yet, in the face of these traditional notions of individual liberty, Georgia asserts the right to protect the individual's mind from the effects of obscenity. We are not certain that this argument amounts to anything more than the assertion that the State has the right to control the moral content of a person's thoughts. To some, this may be a noble purpose, but it is wholly inconsistent with the philosophy of the First Amendment. . . . Whatever the power of the state to control public dissemination of ideas inimical to the public morality, it cannot constitutionally premise legislation on the desirability of controlling a person's private thoughts. . . .

Reversed and remanded.

Mr. Justice Black, concurring. . . .

Mr. Justice Stewart, with whom Mr. Justice Brennan and Mr. Justice White join, concurring in the result. . . .

Even in the much criticized case of *United States* v. *Rabinowitz* . . . the Court emphasized that "exploratory searches . . . cannot be undertaken by officers, with or without a warrant." . . . This record presents a bald violation of that basic constitutional rule. To condone what happened here is to invite a government official to use a seemingly precise and legal warrant only as a ticket to get into a man's home, and, once inside, to launch forth upon unconfined searches and indiscriminate seizures as if armed with all the unbridled and illegal power of a general warrant. . . .

UNITED STATES *v.* REIDEL
402 U.S. 351 (1971)

Mr. Justice White delivered the opinion of the Court.

Section 1461 of Title 18, USC, prohibits the knowing use of the mails for the delivery of obscene matter. The issue presented by the jurisdictional statement in this case is whether Sec. 1461 is constitutional as applied to the distribution of obscene material to willing recipients who state that they are adults. The District Court held that it was not. We disagree and reverse the judgment. . . .

In *Roth* v. *United States* . . . Roth was convicted under Sec. 1461 for mailing obscene circulars and advertising. The Court affirmed the conviction. . . . *Roth* has not been overruled. It remains the law on this Court and governs this case. . . .

Stanley v. *Georgia* . . . compels no different result. . . . [I]t neither overruled nor disturbed the holding in *Roth*. . . . The Court made its point expressly: "*Roth* and the cases following that decision are not impaired by today's holding. . . ."

The District Court ignored both *Roth* and the express limitations on the reach of the *Stanley* decision. Relying on the statement in *Stanley* that "the Constitution protects the right to receive information and ideas . . . regardless of their social worth," . . . the trial judge reasoned that "if a person has the right to receive and possess this material, then someone must have the right to deliver it to him." He concluded that Sec. 1461 could not be validly applied "where obscene material is not directed at children, or it is not directed at an unwilling public, where the material such as in this case is solicited by adults. . . ."

The District Court gave *Stanley* too wide a sweep. To extrapolate from Stanley's right to have and peruse obscene material in the privacy of his own home a First Amendment right in Reidel to sell it to him would effectively scuttle *Roth*, the precise result that the Stanley opinion abjured. . . .

Reidel is in a wholly different position. He has no complaints about governmental violations of his private thoughts or fantasies, but stands squarely on a claimed First Amendment right to do business in obscenity and use the mails in the process. But *Roth* has squarely placed obscenity and its distribution outside the reach of the First Amendment and they remain there today. *Stanley* did not overrule *Roth* and we decline to do so now. . . .

The judgment of the District Court is

Reversed.

Mr. Justice Harlan, concurring. . . .
Mr. Justice Marshall, concurring. . . .
Mr. Justice Black, with whom Mr. Justice Douglas joins, dissenting. . . .

Roth v. *United States* was decided in 1957, and it represented the Court's first effort to provide a definition of that unprotected area of speech and publication denoted as "obscenity." While that effort was subscribed to by a majority of the Court, it was not until 1973, in *Miller* v. *California*, that the Court could again marshal a clear majority behind a revised definition of obscenity. The *Memoirs* gloss, for example, which altered the *Roth* test to require that the prosecution must prove that a work was "*utterly* without redeeming social value," had only plurality support. The problem, of course, arose from the fact that the membership of the Court split into at least three different ideological camps for purposes of dealing with obscenity cases. One group argued from an absolutist position and contended that all such restraints were in violation of the First Amendment. At the other end of the constitutional spectrum, a second group took a more traditional due process approach and contended that unless state regulations of obscenity were irrational or unreasonable, they should be upheld. The middle group attempted to establish a definitional standard for obscenity and apply this to the specific publication or movie on a case-by-case approach. The result of this fragmentation was that cases could be *disposed* of by a majority vote, but it was nearly impossible to muster a majority behind a single rationale for the disposition. A shift in the personnel of the Court between 1957 and 1973, however, opened the way for a different alignment on the obscenity issue, and the redefinition which came in *Miller* v. *California* had the support of five of the Justices.

MILLER *v.* CALIFORNIA
413 U.S. 15 (1973)

Mr. Chief Justice Burger delivered the opinion of the Court.

This is one of a group of "obscenity-pornography" cases being reviewed by the Court in a re-examination of standards enunciated in earlier cases involving what Mr. Justice Harlan called "the intractable obscenity problem.". . .

Appellant conducted a mass mailing campaign to advertise the sale of illustrated books, euphemistically called "adult" material. After a jury trial, he was convicted of . . . a misdemeanor, by knowingly distributing obscene matter. . . . Appellant's conviction was specifically based on his conduct in causing five unsolicited advertising brochures to be sent through the mail in an envelope addressed to a restaurant in Newport Beach, California. The envelope was opened by the manager of the restaurant and his mother. They had not requested the brochures; they complained to the police.

The brochures advertise four books entitled "Intercourse," "Man-Woman," "Sex Orgies Illustrated," and "An Illustrated History of Pornography," and a film entitled "Marital Intercourse." While the brochures contain some descriptive printed material, primarily they consist of pictures and drawings very explicitly depicting men and women in groups of two or more engaging in a variety of sexual activities, with genitals often prominently displayed.

This case involves the application of a State's criminal obscenity statute to a situation in which sexually explicit materials have been thrust by aggressive sales action upon unwilling recipients who had in no way indicated any desire to reccive such materials. This Court has recognized that the States have a legitimate interest in prohibiting dissemination or exhibition of obscene material when the mode of dissemination carries with it a significant danger of offending the sensibilities of unwilling recipients or of exposure to juveniles. *Stanley* v. *Georgia* ... *Ginsberg* v. *New York.* . . . It is in this context that we are called on to define the standards which must be used to identify obscene material that a State may regulate without infringing the First Amendment as applicable to the States through the Fourteenth Amendment.

[The opinion here discusses the standards announced in *Roth* v. *United States* and *Memoirs* v. *Massachusetts*.]

While *Roth* presumed "obscenity" to be "utterly without redeeming social value," *Memoirs* required that to prove obscenity it must be affirmatively established that the material is *"utterly* without redeeming social value." Thus, even as they repeated the words of *Roth*, the *Memoirs* plurality produced a drastically altered test that called on the prosecution to prove a negative, i.e., that the material was *"utterly* without redeeming social value"—a burden virtually impossible to discharge under our criminal standards of proof. . . .

Apart from the initial formulation in the *Roth case,* no majority of the Court has at any given time been able to agree on a standard to determine what constitutes obscene, pornographic material subject to regulation under the States' police power. . . . This is not remarkable, for in the area of freedom of speech and press the courts must always remain sensitive to any infringement on genuinely serious literary, artistic, political, or scientific expression. This is an area in which there are few eternal verities.

The case we now review was tried on the theory that the California Penal Code . . . approximately incorporates the three-stage *Memoirs* test, . . . But now the *Memoirs* test has been abandoned as unworkable by its author and no member of the Court today supports the *Memoirs* formulation.

This much has been categorically settled by the Court, that obscene material is unprotected by the First Amendment. . . . We acknowledge, however, the inherent dangers of undertaking to regulate any form of expression. State statutes designed to regulate obscene materials must be carefully limited. . . . As a result, we now confine the permissible scope of such regulation to works which depict or describe sexual conduct. That conduct must be specifically defined by the applicable state law, as written or authoritatively construed. A state offense must also be limited to works which, taken as a whole, appeal to the prurient interest in sex, which portray sexual conduct in a patently offensive way, and which, taken as a whole, do not have serious literary, artistic, political, or scientific value.

The basic guidelines for the trier of fact must be: (a) whether "the average person, applying contemporary community standards" would find that the work, taken as a whole, appeals to the prurient interest . . . , (b) whether the work depicts or describes, in a patently offensive way, sexual conduct specifically defined by the applicable state law, and (c) whether the work, taken as a whole, lacks serious literary, artistic, political, or scientific value. We do not adopt as a constitutional standard the *"utterly* without redeeming social value" test of *Memoirs* v. *Massachusetts* . . . ; that concept has never commanded the adherence of more than three Justices at one time. . . . If a state law that regulates obscene material is thus limited, as written or construed, the First Amendment values applicable to the States through the Fourteenth Amendment are adequately protected by the ultimate power of appellate courts to conduct an independent review of constitutional claims when necessary. . . .

We emphasize that it is not our function to propose regulatory schemes for the States. That must await their concrete legislative efforts. It is possible, however, to give a few plain examples of what a state statute could define for regulation under the second part (b) of the standard announced in this opinion, *supra:*

(a) Patently offensive representations or descriptions of ultimate sexual acts, normal or perverted; actual or simulated.

(b) Patently offensive representations or descriptions of masturbation, excretory functions, and lewd exhibition of the genitals.

Sex and nudity may not be exploited without limit by films or pictures exhibited or sold in places of public accommodation any more than live sex and nudity can be exhibited or sold without limit in such public places. At a minimum, prurient, patently offensive depiction or description of sexual conduct must have serious literary, artistic, political, or scientific value to merit First Amendment protection. . . .

It is certainly true that the absence, since *Roth,* of a single majority view of this Court as to proper standards for testing obscenity has placed a strain on both state and federal courts. But today, for the first time since *Roth* was decided in 1957, a majority of this Court has agreed on concrete guidelines to isolate "hard core" pornography from expression protected by the First Amendment. Now we may abandon the casual practice of *Redrup* v. *New York* . . . and attempt to provide positive guidance to the federal and state courts alike.

This may not be an easy road, free from difficulty. But no amount of "fatigue" should lead us to adopt a convenient "institutional" rationale—an absolutist, "anything goes" view of the First Amendment—because it will lighten our burdens. . . . Nor should we remedy "tension between state and federal courts" by arbitrarily depriving the States of a power reserved to them under the Constitution, a power which they have enjoyed and exercised continuously from before the adoption of the First Amendment to this day. . . .

Under a national Constitution, fundamental First Amendment limitations on the powers of the States do not vary from community to community, but this does not mean that there are, or should or can be, fixed, uniform national standards of precisely what appeals to the "prurient interest" or is "patently offensive." These are essentially questions of fact, and our nation is simply too big and too diverse for this Court to reasonably expect that such standards could be articulated for all 50 States in a single formulation, even assuming the prerequisite consensus exists. . . . The adversary system, with lay jurors as the usual ultimate factfinders in criminal prosecutions, has historically permitted triers-of-fact to draw on the standards of their community, guided always by limiting instructions on the law. To require a State to structure obscenity proceedings around evidence of a *national* "community standard" would be an exercise in futility. . . .

We conclude that neither the State's alleged failure to offer evidence of "national standards," nor the trial court's charge that the jury consider state community standards, were constitutional errors. Nothing in the First Amendment requires that a jury must consider hypothetical and unascertainable "national standards" when attempting to determine whether certain materials are obscene as a matter of fact. . . .

It is neither realistic nor constitutionally sound to read the First Amendment as requiring that the people of Maine or Mississippi accept public depiction of conduct found tolerable in Las Vegas, or New York City. . . . People in different States vary in their tastes and attitudes, and this diversity is not to be strangled by the absolutism of imposed uniformity.... We hold the requirement that the jury evaluate the materials with reference to "contemporary standards of the State of California" serves this protective purpose and is constitutionally adequate.

The dissenting Justices sound the alarm of repression. But, in our view, to equate the free and robust exchange of ideas and political debate with commercial exploitation of obscene material demeans the grand conception of the First Amendment and its high purposes in the historic struggle for freedom.... The First Amendment protects works which, taken as a whole, have serious literary, artistic, political or scientific value, regardless of whether the government or a majority of the people approve of the ideas these works represent.... But the public portrayal of hard core sexual conduct for its own sake, and for the ensuing commercial gain, is a different matter....

In sum we (a) reaffirm the *Roth* holding that obscene material is not protected by the First Amendment, (b) hold that such material can be regulated by the States, subject to the specific safeguards enunciated above, without a showing that the material is "*utterly* without redeeming social value," and (c) hold that obscenity is to be determined by applying "contemporary community standards,".... not "national standards."....

Vacated and remanded for further proceedings.

Mr. Justice Douglas, dissenting.

Today we leave open the way for California to send a man to prison for distributing brochures that advertise books and a movie under freshly written standards defining obscenity which until today's decision were never the part of any law....

Today the Court retreats from the earlier formulations of the constitutional test and undertakes to make new definitions. This effort, like the earlier ones, is earnest and well-intentioned. The difficulty is that we do not deal with constitutional terms, since "obscenity" is not mentioned in the Constitution or Bill of Rights. And the First Amendment makes no such exception from "the press" which it undertakes to protect nor, as I have said on other occasions, is an exception necessarily implied, for there was no recognized exception to the free press at the time the Bill of Rights was adopted which treated "obscene" publications differently from other types of papers, magazines, and books. So there are no constitutional guidelines for deciding what is and what is not "obscene." The Court is at large because we deal with tastes and standards of literature. What shocks me may be sustenance for my neighbor. What causes one person to boil up in rage over one pamphlet or movie may reflect only his neurosis, not shared by others. We deal here with problems of censorship which, if adopted, should be done by constitutional amendment after full debate by the people.

Obscenity cases usually generate tremendous emotional outbursts. They have no business being in the courts. If a constitutional amendment authorized censorship, the censor would probably be an administrative agency. Then criminal prosecutions could follow as, if and when publishers defied the censor and sold their literature. Under that regime a publisher would know when he was on dangerous ground. Under the present regime—whether the old standards or the new ones are used—the criminal law becomes a trap. A brand new test would put a publisher behind bars under a new law improvised by the courts after the publication. That was done in *Ginzburg* and has all the evils of an ex post facto law.

My contention is that until a civil proceeding has placed a tract beyond the pale, no criminal prosecution should be sustained. For no more vivid illustration of vague and uncertain laws could be designed than those we have fashioned. . . .

No such protective procedure has been designed by California in this case. Obscenity—which even we cannot define with precision—is a hodge-podge. To send men to jail for violating standards they cannot understand, construe, and apply is a monstrous thing to do in a Nation dedicated to fair trials and due process. . . .

The idea that the First Amendment permits government to ban publications that are "offensive" to some people puts an ominous gloss on freedom of the press. That test would make it possible to ban any paper or any journal or magazine in some benighted place. The First Amendment was designed "to invite dispute," to induce "a condition of unrest," to create dissatisfaction with conditions as they are," and even to stir "people to anger.". . . The idea that the First Amendment permits punishment for ideas that are "offensive" to the particular judge or jury sitting in judgment is astounding. . . .

Mr. Justice Brennan, with whom Mr. Justice Stewart and Mr. Justice Marshall join, dissenting. . . .

On the same date that the *Miller* decision was made, the Court decided *Paris Adult Theatre I* v. *Slaton,* 413 U.S. 49 (1973). The case involved a civil action for an injunction to restrain the Theatre from continued exhibition of an obscene film. The Theatre had displayed a sign on the door stating: "Adult Theatre—You must be 21 and able to prove it. If viewing the nude body offends you, Please Do Not Enter." Its contention was that the showing of obscene films was constitutionally protected since they were exhibited only to consenting adults. The Court refused to accept this application of the First Amendment and held the exhibitor bound by the state law as long as the law met the standards announced in *Miller* v. *California*. Chief Justice Burger, for the majority, stated:

We categorically disapprove the theory . . . that obscene, pornographic films acquire constitutional immunity from state regulation simply because they are exhibited for consenting adults only. This holding was properly rejected by the Georgia Supreme Court. Although we have often pointedly recognized the high importance of the state interest in regulating the exposure of obscene materials to juveniles and unconsenting adults, . . . this Court has never declared these to be the only legitimate state interests permitting regulation of obscene material. The States have a long-recognized legitimate interest in regulating the use of obscene material in local commerce and in all places of public accommodation, as long as these regulations do not run afoul of specific constitutional prohibitions. . . .

In particular, we hold that there are legitimate state interests at stake in stemming the tide of commercialized obscenity, even assuming it is feasible to enforce effective safeguards against exposure to juveniles and to the passerby. Rights and interests "other than those of the advocates are involved.". . . These include the interest of the public in the quality of life and the total community environment, the tone of commerce in the great city centers, and, possibly, the public safety itself. . . .

[See Walter Berns, "Pornography v. Democracy: The Case for Censorship," 22 *The Public Interest* 3 (1971).]

While the Court in *Miller* held that in defining the "community standard" the trial court was not required to employ a "national standard," it held in *Hamling* v. *United States,* 418 U.S. 87 (1974), that it was not reversible error for the trial judge to charge the jury to employ national community standards in determining obscenity, since there was nothing to indicate that the use of statewide community standards would have materially affected the deliberations of the jury in California.

Jenkins v. *Georgia,* 418 U.S. 153 (1974), involved the conviction of a Georgia theater manager for showing the motion picture *Carnal Knowledge* in violation of a state obscenity statute. The trial occurred before the *Miller* decision was rendered by the Court, and the trial court gave instructions directing the jury, which viewed the film, to apply "community standards" in determining obscenity, without specifying what "community." Since the case was on appeal at the time the *Miller* decision was made, the Court held that the defendant was entitled to receive any benefit available to him under that ruling. The majority further held that in state obscenity prosecutions, juries could properly be instructed to apply "community standards" without specifying what "community" since "the Constitution does not require that juries be instructed in state obscenity cases to apply the standards of a hypothetical statewide community." *Miller* approved the use of such instructions; it did not mandate their use. What *Miller* makes clear is that state juries need not be instructed to apply "national standards." But after the Court viewed the film (as is its custom), the majority concluded that, the jury verdict to the contrary notwithstanding, the film "could not be found under the *Miller* standards to depict sexual conduct in a patently offensive way," and thus reversed the conviction. The dissenting opinion of Justice Brennan pointed to the obvious problem resulting from the new *Miller-Jenkins* approach to obscenity: any time a film is found to be obscene and comes to the Court on review, the Court will have to look at the film and decide whether to substitute judgment for the trial court. "One cannot say with certainty that material is obscene until at least five members of this Court, applying inevitably obscure standards, have pronounced it so."

A final note should be added with respect to the seizure of materials alleged to be obscene. The general rule appears to be that if the seizure takes place under a proper warrant, an adversary hearing and judicial determination of obscenity does not have to precede the seizure. But in *Heller* v. *New York,* 413 U.S. 483 (1973), it was stated in the majority opinion that the hearing and judicial determination must be prompt:

In addition, on a showing to the trial court that other copies of the film are not available to the exhibitor, the court should permit the seized film to be copied so that showing can be continued pending a judicial determination of the obscenity issue in an adversary proceeding. Otherwise, the film must be returned.

[On obscenity questions generally, see: Martin Shapiro, "Obscenity Law: a Public Policy Analysis," 20 *J. Pub. L.* 503 (1971); Walter Gellhorn, "Dirty Books, Disgusting Pictures, and Dreadful Laws," 8 *Ga. L. Rev.* 291 (1974); Note, "Morality and the Broadcast Media: a Constitutional Analysis of FCC Regulatory Standards," 84 *Harv. L. Rev.* 664 (1971); Note, "Obscenity and the Right to Be Let Alone: the Balancing of Constitutional Rights," 6 *Ind. L. Rev.* 490 (1973); and *The Report of the Commission on Obscenity and Pornography* (Washington, D.C.: U.S. Gov't Printing Office, 1970).]

CHAPTER 7
Equal Protection of the Law

Much of the developing law in the area of civil rights can in essence be characterized as a drive for equality under the law. The concept of equality has played an important part in American legal and political development since its overt statement by Thomas Jefferson in the Declaration's famous words, "We hold these truths to be self-evident, that all men are created equal. . . ." The movement has been sporadic and has taken differing directions and emphases, sometimes stressing the economic, at other times the legal or the social. In the Revolutionary and post-Revolutionary periods substantial gains were made in the area of religious equality, with the gradual elimination of taxes for religious support, disestablishment, and the removal of restrictions on public worship for some of the minority sects. During the Jacksonian period religious tests for office-holding began to disappear and political equality was further extended by the removal of property qualifications for both voters and candidates for public office. In economic thought it was one of the firm tenets of Jacksonian democracy that progress could be assured for all if the legislative policy of granting exclusive grants of privilege could be stopped and everyone afforded equal opportunity to engage in business enterprise. The Civil War era saw the adoption of a minimal program of racial equality in the abolition of slavery. Even in the period of Manchester Liberalism in the latter third of the nineteenth century, when the doctrines of Herbert Spencer held sway, it was a somewhat twisted concept of equality which was interwoven into the fabric of social Darwinism. All men had an equal opportunity to compete for economic survival and leadership. By fencing off government from entering the struggle to lay down ground rules for the economic "game," equality was supposedly secured and the victors were entitled to the spoils because they were the fittest. The theory, of course, took no account of the fact that the competition could never be equal between persons who entered the struggle with substantially unequal financial assets. A great deal of legislation since the adoption of the Sherman Antitrust Act in 1890 has been prompted by the desire to equalize the competitive battle in the economic arena, including labor's bargaining position as against management.

Except in the area of voting rights and in certain aspects of economic rights, there was little governmental activity, either legislative or judicial, to extend the guarantees of equality prior to World War II. The Fourteenth Amendment, with its equal protection clause, was ratified in 1868, but cases were rarely won by litigants who based their attacks on the invalidity of legislative classifications. Distinctions based on race were upheld unless they were found to abridge political or property rights. And virtually all distinctions based on sex, except for those impairing voting rights, could be validly imposed. With few exceptions, it was not until the post-World War II period that Congress and the federal courts began a concerted drive to eliminate some of the major inequalities based on race, sex, religion, and economic level.

It was not until the 1950s, during the Warren Court period, that the potential of the equal protection clause began to be realized. Beginning with *Brown* v. *Board of Education* in 1954, the Court has rendered key decisions under this clause resulting in prohibitions against governmental race discrimination, the requirement of fair apportionment of population in establishing election districts, substantial equality of rights for indigents in the criminal process, and the gradual elimination of a number of disabilities imposed by law on women.

While under the traditional view of the equal protection clause the State was allowed broad leeway to classify for purposes of legislation, a new and more rigid standard was developed during the period of the Warren Court to test the validity of state laws which affected special classes or special rights. Thus the discussion to follow will first take up cases illustrating the traditional approach and then will move to the "new" equal protection tests developed by the Warren Court.

THE TRADITIONAL VIEW

In the traditional approach to the judicial treatment of equal protection cases, the issues raised could usually be resolved into two questions: (1) Was the specific law involved administered impartially? and (2) Did the legislature, in adopting a law providing for differential treatment of segments of the public, set up a reasonable classification of the objects or persons treated, in view of the overall purposes of the law? Stated differently, the second question might be: Did the legislature make "invidious distinctions" in the law?

An early case on the first issue was *Yick Wo* v. *Hopkins,* 118 U.S. 356 (1886). The board of supervisors of San Francisco enacted an ordinance providing that no one should carry on a laundry within the county "without having first obtained the consent of the board of supervisors, except the same be located in a building constructed either of brick or stone." Yick Wo, a Chinese subject resident in San Francisco, petitioned for a license to carry on a laundry in the same building in which he had been doing so for twenty-two years. His application was refused, and he was arrested and fined $10 for continuing in business without the license. After failure to pay the fine he was committed to jail, where he petitioned for a writ of habeas corpus. He had received certificates from the fire wardens and the health officer showing that his premises were safe and in sanitary condition. At the time the ordinance was passed, there were about 320 laundries in San Francisco of which about 240 were owned and operated by Chinese. It was admitted that all applications for a license made by Chinese persons were refused, while the petitions of all others, with one exception, were granted. About 150 Chinese were arrested for noncompliance, while, as stated in Yick Wo's petition, "those who are not subjects of China and who are conducting eighty-odd laundries under similar conditions, are left unmolested." The Supreme Court of California discharged the writ, but the United States

Supreme Court reversed, holding the application of the law violative of the equal protection clause.

Justice Matthews, for the Court, stated:

In the present cases we are not obliged to reason from the probable to the actual, and pass upon the validity of the ordinances complained of, as tried merely by the opportunities which their terms afford, of unequal and unjust discrimination in their administration. For the cases present the ordinances in actual operation, and the facts shown establish an administration directed so exclusively against a particular class of persons as to warrant and require the conclusion that ... they are applied by the public authorities charged with their administration ... with a mind so unequal and oppressive as to amount to a practical denial by the State of that equal protection of the laws which is secured ... by the broad and benign provisions of the Fourteenth Amendment.... Though the law itself be fair on its face and impartial in appearance, yet, if it is applied and administered by public authority with an evil eye and an unequal hand, so as practically to make unjust and illegal discriminations between persons in similar circumstances, material to their rights, the denial of equal justice is still within the prohibition of the Constitution. ...

A similar issue, although in quite another context, was presented in *Niemotko* v. *Maryland,* 340 U.S. 268 (1951). Niemotko and others, who were Jehovah's Witnesses, scheduled Bible talks in the public park of Havre de Grace, Maryland. Although there was no ordinance prohibiting or regulating the use of this park, it had been the custom for organizations and individuals desiring to use it for meetings and celebrations of various kinds to obtain a permit from the park commissioner. In conformity with this practice, the group requested permission to use the park on four consecutive Sundays. The park commissioner refused.

The group appealed this refusal to the city council, and a hearing was held by the council. The evidence indicated that the only questions asked of the Witnesses at the hearing pertained to their alleged refusal to salute the flag, their views on the Bible, and other issues irrelevant to unencumbered use of the public parks. After the hearing, the council denied the request, although permits had been customarily granted for similar purposes, including meetings of religious and fraternal organizations. Niemotko was later arrested for attempting to hold the meeting without a permit and convicted of disorderly conduct. The Maryland appellate court denied certiorari, and on appeal the United States Supreme Court unanimously held the convictions violative of equal protection of the laws. Chief Justice Vinson, for the Court, stated:

The conclusion is inescapable that the use of the park was denied because of the City Council's dislike for or disagreement with the Witnesses on their views. The right to equal protection of the laws, in the exercise of those freedoms of speech and religion protected by the First and Fourteenth Amendments, has a firmer foundation than the whims or personal opinions of a local governing body.

Because of limited resources, enforcement agencies often follow policies of selective enforcement of various laws. Presumably if such selectivity is based on race or religion, it would run afoul of the equal protection clause, as in the two cases discussed above. But suppose the only basis for the policy is the judicious allocation of scarce policing resources. This situation presents a more difficult question, and one which the Court has not fully explored. In one case, however, the Court expressly recognized the dilemma of the enforcing agency and approved a selective enforcement order of the FTC. The Commission obtained a cease and desist order against one firm engaged in illegal price arrangements. The firm complained that several other business competitors were following the same practices, and that it was unfair to subject one to serious financial loss without at the same time punishing the others. In *Moog Industries* v. *FTC,* 335 U.S. 411 (1958), the Court rejected the argument, and, after stressing the "specialized experienced judgment" of the Commission, concluded that "the Commission alone is empowered to develop that enforcement policy best calculated to achieve the ends contemplated by Congress and to allocate its available funds and personnel in such a way as to execute its policy efficiently and economically." [See Wayne R. LaFave, "The Police and Nonenforcement of the Law" (Two Pts.), 1962 *Wis. L. Rev.* 104, 179.]

The second aspect of the problem of equal protection concerns actual classification by the legislature in the application of a statute. It is almost impossible to conceive of a law which does not in some way employ classification. And it would place an intolerable burden on the legislature to have to deal with all evils in the community at once, or even to deal with all aspects of a single evil, in order to meet the test of equal protection. Thus the legislature can, if it chooses, attack community ills more or less piecemeal. It can try to solve problems one at a time, and it can even deal with some aspects of a given problem while ignoring others. In short, the equal protection clause does not fasten upon the legislature an iron rule of uniform treatment.

The legislature is thus free to "classify" the objects of its attention, treating some in one fashion and others differently. It is then free to discriminate. But if it *does* discriminate, the equal protection requirement demands that the legislative classification not be arbitrary and unreasonable and that the distinctions employed bear some rational relationship to the lawful purposes to be accomplished. Even here, however, there is a strong presumption in the courts that discriminations in legislation are based on adequate grounds. As indicated in *Crescent Oil Company* v. *Mississippi,* 257 U.S. 129, 137 (1921), every set of facts sufficient to sustain a classification which can reasonably be conceived of as having existed when the law was adopted will be assumed. Further, since the legislature is free to try to correct one evil without reaching others, it is no defense to show that a challenged law could easily have been broadened to correct other very similar evils. As Justice Holmes stated in *Keokee Consolidated Coke Company* v. *Taylor* 234 U.S. 224 (1914), "it is established by repeated decisions that a statute aimed at what is deemed an evil, and hitting it presumably where experience shows it to be most felt, is not to be upset by thinking up and enumerating other instances to which it might have been applied equally well, so far as the Court can see."

A famous case which involved in part the equal protection issue was *Buck* v. *Bell,* 274 U.S. 200 (1927), in which a state law providing for the sterilization of mental defectives was challenged. A Virginia law of 1924 provided that after complying with very careful procedural requirements to protect patients from possible abuse, *institutionalized* mental defectives could be ordered sterilized. No provision was made for sterilization of such persons who were not living in various institutions specified in the law. The main thrust of argument in the case was that it deprived the affected persons of their liberty without due process of law, and in upholding the provisions the opinion was primarily directed to that issue. The law was also challenged, however, on the ground that the differential treatment accorded institutional inmates and those outside institutions violated the equal protection clause. In upholding the statute against this claim, Justice Holmes, for the Court, stated:

But, it is said, however it might be if this reasoning were applied generally, it fails when it is confined to the small number who are in the institutions named and is not applied to the multitudes outside. It is the usual last resort of constitutional arguments to point out shortcomings of this sort. But the answer is that the law does all that is needed when it does all that it can, indicates a policy, applies it to all within the lines, and seeks to bring within the lines all similarly situated so far and so fast as its means allow. Of course so far as the operations enable those who otherwise must be kept confined to be returned to the world, and thus open the asylum to others, the equality aimed at will be more nearly reached.

In 1942 the Court held that an Oklahoma law providing for the sterilization of certain kinds of criminals and not others went beyond the bounds of reasonable classification. The case was *Skinner* v. *Oklahoma,* 316 U.S. 535 (1942). The law provided for the sterilization of habitual criminals and defined such persons as those convicted three or more times for crimes "amounting to felonies involving moral turpitude." The act provided for exceptions, however, for "offenses arising out of the violation of the prohibitory laws, revenue acts, embezzlement, or political offenses." One of Skinner's felonies was that of stealing chickens. Upon conviction for his third felony, the State began sterilization proceedings under the act, and Skinner appealed. In holding the law invalid, the Court pointed out that while one who was convicted three times for stealing chicken could be sterilized, the law exempted the embezzler from such treatment even though he might have stolen large amounts of money. Justice Douglas, for the Court, said: "When the law lays an unequal hand on those who have committed intrinsically the same quality of offense and sterilizes one and not the other, it has made as invidious a discrimination as if it had selected a particular race or nationality for oppresive treatment." He stated further, "The equal protection clause would indeed be a formula of empty words if such conspicuously artificial lines could be drawn."

In matters of economic regulation, an area in which the Court has almost gone out of the business of invalidating legislation on due process grounds, the state has exceedingly large powers of classification. In *Williamson* v. *Lee Optical Company,* 348 U.S. 483 (1955), for example, the Court examined an Oklahoma law which made it unlawful for any person not a licensed optometrist or ophthalmologist to fit lenses to the face or to duplicate or replace lenses except upon written prescriptive authority of a licensed ophthalmologist or optometrist. Sellers of ready-to-wear glasses were exempt, however, from the regulations, and the claim was made that the exemption rendered the law invalid under the equal protection clause. The Court unanimously disallowed the claim. Justice Douglas, for the Court, stated:

The problem of legislative classification is a perennial one, admitting of no doctrinaire definition. Evils in the same field may be of different dimensions and proportions, requiring different remedies. Or so the legislature may think.... Or the reform may take one step at a time, addressing itself to the phase of the problem which seems most acute to the legislative mind.... The legislature may select one phase of one field and apply a remedy there, neglecting the others.... The prohibition of the Equal Protection Clause goes no further than the invidious discrimination. We cannot say that that point has been reached here. For all this record shows, the ready-to-wear branch of this business may not loom large in Oklahoma or may present problems of regulation distinct from the other branch.

The "hands-off" attitude implicit in Justice Douglas' statement is fairly typical of the judicial restraint exhibited by the Court when faced with classifications affecting the economic or related areas. Thus states may classify cities by population and provide different powers or obligations for each class. The Social Security Act may be applied to large firms and exempt small firms. And license-tax or property-tax laws may differentiate by size or function. The constitutional requirement in each case is that the classification not be arbitrary, capricious, or irrational. Thus the traditional view of the equal protection clause was fairly aptly described by Justice Holmes as "the usual last resort of constitutional arguments." And so long as the Court finds no "invidious discrimination," this pattern of judicial restraint still applies in many areas of governmental regulatory policy.

THE NEW EQUAL PROTECTION

Brown v. *Board of Education* and its progeny held that governmental discrimination based on race was invalid under the equal protection clause. While the language of the opinion did not specifically suggest a new formula for considering equal protection claims generally, it at least opened the way for such a development. By the late 1960s, the Court began to apply its new, stricter standard. The rule is fairly easily stated although the application is more difficult. When government legislates or acts either on the basis of a "suspect" category or with respect to a "fundamental right," the traditional standard is ignored, and the Court subjects the action to a "strict scrutiny." If it is a state law which is being examined, the Court will demand that there be shown a "compelling state interest" justifying the law's classification. If the regulation does not set up a suspect category or restrict a fundamental right, then the lesser invidious-discrimination test is still the standard. Race is, of course, the most suspect of categories, but the Court has now included "alienage" in this group as well. In *Graham* v. *Richardson,* 403 U.S. 365 (1971), the Court struck down statutes of Arizona and Pennsylvania which substantially limited welfare benefits to United States citizens. In holding the laws violative of the equal protection clause, Justice Blackmun, for the Court, stated:

Under traditional equal protection principles, a State retains broad discretion to classify as long as its classification has a reasonable basis.... But the Court's decisions have established that classifications based on alienage, like those based on nationality or race, are inherently suspect and subject to close judicial scrutiny. Aliens as a class are a prime example of a "discrete and insular" minority... for whom such heightened judicial solicitude is appropriate.

In 1973 the Court applied the *Graham* rule to invalidate a Connecticut provision which denied aliens admission to the bar.

IN RE GRIFFITHS
413 U.S. 717 (1973)

[Appellant Fre Le Poole Griffiths, a citizen of the Netherlands, came to the United States in 1965 as a visitor. In 1967 she married a citizen of the United States and became a resident of Connecticut. After graduation from law school, she applied in 1970 for permission to take the Connecticut bar examination. The County Bar Association found her qualified in all respects except that she was not a citizen of the United States as required by the Connecticut Practice Book, and on that account refused to allow her to take the examination. The Superior Court denied her petition for a decree that she be permitted to take the examination and be declared eligible for admission, and the Supreme Court of Connecticut affirmed.]

Mr. Justice Powell delivered the opinion of the Court. . . .

The Court has consistently emphasized that a State which adopts a suspect classification "bears a heavy burden of justification," . . . a burden which, though variously formulated, requires the State to meet certain standards of proof. In order to justify the use of a suspect classification, a State must show that its purpose or interest is both constitutionally permissible and substantial, and that its use of the classification is "necessary . . . to the accomplishment" of its purpose or the safeguarding of its interest.

Resident aliens, like citizens, pay taxes, support the economy, serve in the armed forces, and contribute in myriad other ways to our society. It is appropriate that a State bear a heavy burden when it deprives them of employment opportunities.

We hold that the Committee, acting on behalf of the State, has not carried its burden. The State's ultimate interest here implicated is to assure the requisite qualifications of persons licensed to practice law. It is undisputed that a State has a constitutionally permissible and substantial interest in determining whether an applicant possesses " 'the character and general fitness requisite for an attorney and counselor-at-law.' " . . . But no question is raised in this case as to appellant's character or general fitness. Rather, the sole basis for disqualification is her status as a resident alien.

The Committee defends [the rule] that applicants for admission to the bar be citizens of the United States on the ground that the special role of the lawyer justifies excluding aliens from the practice of law. . . . In order to establish a link between citizenship and the powers and responsibilities of the lawyer in Connecticut, the Committee contrasts a citizen's undivided allegiance to this country with a resident alien's possible conflict of loyalties. From this, the Committee concludes that a resident alien lawyer might in the exercise of his functions ignore his responsibilities to the courts or even his clients in favor of the interest of a foreign power.

We find these arguments unconvincing. It in no way denigrates a lawyer's high responsibilities to observe that the powers "to sign writs and subpoenas, take recognizances, [and] administer oaths" hardly involve matters of state policy or acts or such unique responsibility as to entrust them only to citizens. Nor do we think that the practice of law offers meaningful opportunities adversely to affect the interest of the United States. Certainly the Committee has failed to show the relevance of citizenship to any likelihood that a lawyer will fail to protect faithfully the interest of his clients.

Nor would the possibility that some resident aliens are unsuited to the practice of law be a justification for a wholesale ban. . . .

... Although, as we have acknowledged, a State does have a substantial interest in the qualifications of those admitted to the practice of law, the arguments advanced by the Committee fall short of showing that the classification established ... is necessary to the promoting or safeguarding of this interest. ...

Mr. Chief Justice Burger, with whom Mr. Justice Rehnquist joins, dissenting. ...

In recent years the Court, in a rather casual way, has articulated the code phrase "suspect classification" as though it embraced a reasoned constitutional concept. Admittedly, it simplifies judicial work as do "per se" rules, but it tends to stop analysis while appearing to suggest an analytical process. ...

Mr. Justice Rehnquist, dissenting. ...

In *Hampton* v. *Mow Sun Wong,* 44 L.W. 4737 (1976), the Court held that a federal regulation, adopted not by the president or Congress but by the Civil Service Commission, generally barring noncitizens from employment in the federal civil service, deprives lawfully admitted resident aliens of liberty without due process in violation of the Fifth Amendment. In the opinion for the Court by Justice Stevens (his first on the Court), however, it was pointed out that the concept of equal justice under law, included in the Fifth Amendment's guarantee of due process, and the equal protection clause of the Fourteenth Amendment were not always coextensive. "There may be overriding national interests which justify selective federal legislation that would be unacceptable for an individual State." Justice Stevens stated further:

We do not agree, however, with the petitioners' primary submission that the federal power over aliens is so plenary that any agent of the National Government may arbitrarily subject all resident aliens to different substantive rules than those applied to citizens. ... We may assume with the petitioners that if the Congress or the President had expressly imposed the citizenship requirement, it would be justified by the national interest in providing an incentive for aliens to become naturalized, or possibly even as providing the President with an expendable token for treaty negotiating purposes; but we are not willing to presume that the Chairman of the Civil Service Commission, or any of the other original defendants, was deliberately fostering an interest so far removed from his normal responsibilities.

In *Mathews* v. *Diaz,* 44 L.W. 4748 (1976), the Court held that a federal statute which conditions permanent resident aliens' eligibility for Medicare supplemental insurance on five years continuous residence in the United States does not constitute invidious discrimination within a class of aliens or deprive ineligible aliens of liberty or property in violation of the Fifth Amendment's due process clause.

At this writing only race (or national origin) and alienage have been declared to be "inherently suspect" categories, although one would certainly assume that religion would be included. While some members of the Court would include classifications based on sex as suspect, a majority of the Justices have not so held as yet. (See the treatment of the cases under "Sex Discrimination," below.)

In a number of cases the Court has declared that there is a constitutional right to travel across state lines. An application of the equal protection clause to a state law allegedly impairing this "fundamental right" is found in *Shapiro*

v. *Thompson*, which dealt with residence requirements for the receipt of welfare assistance.

SHAPIRO *v.* THOMPSON
394 U.S. 618 (1969)

Mr. Justice Brennan delivered the opinion of the Court.

These three appeals were restored to the calendar for reargument . . . Each is an appeal from a decision of a three-judge District Court holding unconstitutional a State or District of Columbia statutory provision which denies welfare assistance to residents of the State or District who have not resided within their jurisdictions for at least one year immediately preceding their applications for such assistance. We affirm the judgments of the District Courts in the three cases. . . .

There is no dispute that the effect of the waiting-period requirement in each case is to create two classes of needy resident families indistinguishable from each other except that one is composed of residents who have resided a year or more, and the second of residents who have resided less than a year, in the jurisdiction. On the basis of this sole difference the first class is granted and the second class is denied welfare aid upon which may depend the ability of the families to obtain the very means to subsist—food, shelter, and other necessities of life. In each case, the District Court found that appellees met the test for residence in their jurisdictions, as well as all other eligibility requirements except the requirement of residence for a full year prior to their applications. On reargument, appellees' central contention is that the statutory prohibition of benefits to residents of less than a year creates a classification which constitutes an invidious discrimination denying them equal protection of the laws. We agree. The interests which appellants assert are promoted by the classification either may not constitutionally be promoted by government or are not compelling governmental interests.

Primarily, appellants justify the waiting-period requirement as a protective device to preserve the fiscal integrity of state public assistance programs. It is asserted that people who require welfare assistance during their first year of residence in a State are likely to become continuing burdens on state welfare programs. Therefore, the argument runs, if such people can be deterred from entering the jurisdiction by denying them welfare benefits during the first year, state programs to assist long-time residents will not be impaired by a substantial influx of indigent newcomers.

There is weighty evidence that exclusion from the jurisdiction of the poor who need or may need relief was the specific objective of these provisions. In the Congress, sponsors of federal legislation to eliminate all residence requirements have been consistently opposed by representatives of state and local welfare agencies who have stressed the fears of the States that elimination of the requirements would result in a heavy influx of individuals into States providing the most generous benefits. . . .

We do not doubt that the one-year waiting-period device is well suited to discourage the influx of poor families in need of assistance. . . . But the purpose of inhibiting migration by needy persons into the State is constitutionally impermissible.

This Court long ago recognized that the nature of our Federal Union and our constitutional concepts of personal liberty unite to require that all citizens be free to travel throughout the length and breadth of our land uninhibited by statutes, rules, or regulations which unreasonably burden or restrict this movement. . . .

We have no occasion to ascribe the source of this right to travel interstate to a particular constitutional provision. It suffices that, as Mr. Justice Stewart said for the Court in *United States* v. *Guest,* . . . : "The constitutional right to travel from one State to another . . . occupies a position fundamental to the concept of our Federal Union. It is a right that has been firmly established and repeatedly recognized. . . ."

Thus, the purpose of deterring the in-migration of indigents cannot serve as justification for the classification created by the one-year waiting period, since that purpose is constitutionally impermissible. . . .

Alternatively, appellants argue that even if it is impermissible for a State to attempt to deter the entry of all indigents, the challenged classification may be justified as a permissible state attempt to discourage those indigents who would enter the State solely to obtain larger benefits. We observe first that none of the statutes before us is tailored to serve that objective. . . .

More fundamentally, a State may no more try to fence out those indigents who seek higher welfare benefits than it may try to fence out indigents generally. Implicit in any such distinction is the notion that indigents who enter a State with the hope of securing higher welfare benefits are somehow less deserving than indigents who do not take this consideration into account. But we do not perceive why a mother who is seeking to make a new life for herself and her children should be regarded as less deserving because she considers, among other factors, the level of a State's public assistance. Surely such a mother is no less deserving than a mother who moves into a particular State in order to take advantage of its better educational facilities. . . .

Appellants next advance as justification certain administrative and related governmental objectives allegedly served by the waiting-period requirement. They argue that the requirement (1) facilitates the planning of the welfare budget; (2) provides an objective test of residency; (3) minimizes the opportunity for recipients fraudulently to receive payments from more than one jurisdiction; and (4) encourages early entry of new residents into the labor force.

At the outset, we reject appellants' argument that a mere showing of a rational relationship between the waiting period and these four admittedly permissible state objectives will suffice to justify the classification. . . . The waiting-period provision denies welfare benefits to otherwise eligible applicants solely because they have recently moved into the jurisdiction. But in moving from State to State or to the District of Columbia appellees were exercising a constitutional right, and any classification which serves to penalize the exercise of that right, unless shown to be necessary to promote a *compelling* government interest, is unconstitutional. . . . [Here the opinion takes up each of the four justifications claimed, and the conclusion is that they either are not achieved by the residence period or can be better achieved by other reasonable methods.]

We conclude therefore that appellants in these cases do not use and have no need to use the one-year requirement for the governmental purposes suggested. Thus, even under traditional equal protection tests a classification of welfare applicants according to whether they have lived in the State for one year would seem irrational and unconstitutional. But, of course, the traditional criteria do not apply in these cases. Since the classification here touches on the fundamental right of interstate movement, its constitutionality must be judged by the stricter standard of whether it promotes a *compelling* state interest. Under this standard, the waiting-period requirement clearly violates the Equal Protection Clause. . . .

Affirmed.

Mr. Justice Stewart, concurring. . . .

Mr. Chief Justice Warren, with whom Mr. Justice Black joins, dissenting. . . .

Mr. Justice Harlan, dissenting. . . .

In upholding the equal protection argument, the Court has applied an equal protection doctrine of relatively recent vintage: the rule that statutory classifications which either are based upon certain "suspect" criteria or affect "fundamental rights" will be held to deny equal protection unless justified by a "compelling" governmental interest. . . .

The "compelling interest" doctrine, which today is articulated more explicitly than ever before, constitutes an increasingly significant exception to the long-established rule that a statute does not deny equal protection if it is rationally related to a legitimate governmental objective. The "compelling interest" doctrine has two branches. The branch which requires that classifications based upon "suspect" criteria be supported by a compelling interest apparently had its genesis in cases involving racial classifications, which have, at least since *Korematsu* v. *United States* . . . , have been regarded as inherently "suspect.". . .

I think that this branch of the "compelling interest" doctrine is sound when applied to racial classifications, for historically the Equal Protection Clause was largely a product of the desire to eradicate legal distinctions founded upon race. However, I believe that the more recent extensions have been unwise. . . .

The second branch of the "compelling interest" principle is even more troublesome. For it has been held that a statutory classification is subject to the "compelling interest" test if the result of the classification may be to affect a "fundamental right," regardless of the basis of the classification. . . .

I think this branch of the "compelling interest" doctrine particularly unfortunate and unnecessary. It is unfortunate because it creates an exception which threatens to swallow the standard equal protection rule. Virtually every state statute affects important rights. This Court has repeatedly held, for example, that the traditional equal protection standard is applicable to statutory classifications affecting such fundamental matters as the right to pursue a particular occupation, the right to receive greater or smaller wages or to work more or less hours, and the right to inherit property. Rights such as these are in principle indistinguishable from those involved here, and to extend the "compelling interest" rule to all cases in which such rights are affected would go far toward making this Court a "superlegislature." This branch of the doctrine is also unnecessary. When the right affected is one assured by the Federal Constitution, any infringement can be dealt with under the Due Process Clause. But when a statute affects only matters not mentioned in the Federal Constitution and is not arbitrary or irrational, I must reiterate that I know of nothing which entitles this Court to pick out particular human activities, characterize them as "fundamental," and give them added protection under an unusually stringent equal protection test. . . .

In addition to the right to travel interstate, the Court has clearly indicated that voting rights are among the "fundamental rights" of citizens. In *Dunn* v. *Blumstein,* 405 U.S. 330 (1972), the Court held that there was no compelling state interest in enforcing a one-year durational residence requirement for voting. The State of Tennessee contended that the requirement would contribute to the goal of a more knowledgeable and intelligent voter. Justice Marshall, for the Court, said: "Knowledge or competence has never been a criterion for participation in Tennessee's electoral process for longtime residents. . . . If the State seeks to assure intelligent use of the ballot, it may not try to serve this interest only with respect to new arrivals."

In a variety of cases claimants have attempted to achieve the advantage of the "strict scrutiny" rule by contentions that challenged laws either set up "suspect" categories or impaired "fundamental rights." Laws discriminating on the basis of legitimacy of birth or on the basis of wealth have been so challenged, for example, but thus far the Court has not held these to be suspect classifications. It should not be assumed, however, that such a denial automatically results in a holding that the law meets the equal protection test. Laws which classify must still overcome the "invidious discrimination" claim even if they do not involve the strict scrutiny standard. In *Weber* v. *Aetna Casualty & Surety Co.,* 406 U.S. 164 (1972), for example, a Louisiana workman's compensation law was challenged which allowed illegitimate children to recover benefits only if there were not enough legitimate children to exhaust the maximum benefits under the statute. In holding the classification invalid, Justice Powell, for the Court, stated:

Obviously, no child is responsible for his birth and penalizing the illegitimate child is an ineffectual—as well as an unjust—way of deterring the parent. Courts are powerless to prevent the social opprobrium suffered by these hapless children, but the Equal Protection Clause does enable us to strike down discriminatory laws relating to status of birth where—as in this case—the classification is justified by no legitimate state interest, compelling or otherwise.

The problem of the indigent who is disadvantaged in his contacts with governmental action or policy may raise serious equal protection questions. The long history of the development of the right of the indigent to appointed counsel when charged with a jailable criminal offense took place largely within the context of the due process clause. But there were clearly equal protection overtones in much of the language employed by the Court in the various decisions. The issue was more clearly raised in a case involving a convicted indigent who was fined, but who was sentenced to a term in jail because of his inability to pay the fine. In *Tate* v. *Short,* 401 U.S. 395 (1971), the Court reversed the conviction, holding that the sentence of imprisonment "worked an invidious discrimination solely because the defendant was too poor to pay the fine, and therefore violated the Equal Protection Clause." The Court suggested alternatives for imprisonment, including the payment of fines in installments.

A case which combined the contentions that poverty (or wealth) is a suspect classification and that education is a fundamental right was *San Antonio* v. *Rodriguez,* 411 U.S. 1 (1973). At issue was the question of whether interdistrict disparities in school expenditures—with larger budgets in the richer districts and smaller budgets in the poorer districts—constituted a violation of the equal protection clause.

SAN ANTONIO *v.* RODRIGUEZ
411 U.S. 1 (1973)

[The financing of public schools in Texas is a combination of state aid and local contribution based on property taxes. Appellees brought this class action contending that the state's reliance on local property taxation favors the more affluent districts and violates the equal protection clause because of substantial interdistrict disparities in per-pupil expenditures in the school system. Appellees are residents of the Edgewood Independent School District, a predominantly Mexican American area. The average assessed property value per pupil is $5,900—the lowest in the metropolitan area. At a tax rate of $1.05 per $100—the highest in the metropolitan area—the district contributed $26 per child for the 1967–1968 school year above the legal minimum required. The combined state-local total was $248 per pupil, and federal funds brought the total to $356 per pupil.

In Alamo Heights district the assessed property value per pupil was over $49,000. The local tax rate of $.85 per $100 yielded an excess of $333 per pupil over its required minimum. The combined state-local total was $558 per pupil, and federal funds brought the total to $594 per student.]

Mr. Justice Powell delivered the opinion of the Court. . . .

Despite . . . recent increases, substantial interdistrict disparities in school expenditures found by the District Court to prevail in San Antonio and in varying degrees throughout the State still exist. And it was these disparities, largely attributable to differences in the amounts of money collected through local property taxation, that led the District Court to conclude that Texas' dual system of public school finance violated the Equal Protection Clause. The District Court held that the Texas system discriminates on the basis of wealth in the manner in which education is provided for its people. Finding that wealth is a "suspect" classification and that education is a "fundamental" interest, the District Court held that the Texas system could be sustained only if the State could show that it was premised upon some compelling state interest. On this issue the court concluded that "not only are defendants unable to demonstrate compelling state interests . . . they fail even to establish a reasonable basis for these classifications.". . .

We are unable to agree that this case, which in significant aspects is *sui generis,* may be so neatly fitted into the conventional mosaic of constitutional analysis under the Equal Protection Clause. Indeed, for the several reasons that follow, we find neither the suspect classification nor the fundamental interest analysis persuasive.

The precedents of this Court provide the proper starting point. The individuals or groups of individuals who constituted the class discriminated against in our prior cases shared two distinguishing characteristics: because of their impecunity they were completely unable to pay for some desired benefit, and as a consequence, they sustained an absolute deprivation of a meaningful opportunity to enjoy that benefit. . . .

Only appellees' first possible basis for describing the class disadvantaged by the Texas school finance system—discrimination against a class of definably "poor" persons——might arguably meet the criteria established in these prior cases. Even a cursory examination, however, demonstrates that neither of the two distinguishing characteristics of wealth classifications can be found there. First, in support of their charge that the system discriminates against the "poor," appellees have made no effort to demonstrate that it operates to the peculiar disadvantages of any class fairly definable as indigent, or as composed of persons whose incomes are beneath any designated poverty level. Indeed, there is reason to believe that the poorest families are not necessarily clustered in the poorest property districts. . . .

Second, neither appellees nor the District Court addressed the fact that, unlike each of the foregoing cases, lack of personal resources has not occasioned an absolute deprivation of the desired benefit. The argument here is not that the children in districts having relatively low assessable property values are receiving no public education; rather, it is that they are receiving a poorer quality education than that available to children in districts having more assessable wealth. Apart from the unsettled and disputed question whether the quality of education may be determined by the amount of money expended for it, a sufficient answer to appellees' argument is that at least where wealth is involved the Equal Protection Clause does not require absolute equality or precisely equal advantages. Nor, indeed, in view of the infinite variables affecting the educational process, can any system assure equal quality of education except in the most relative sense. . . .

[The opinion here rejects the argument that the system discriminates on the basis of family income.]

This brings us, then, to the third way in which the classification scheme might be defined—*district* wealth discrimination. Since the only correlation indicated by the evidence is between district propety wealth and expenditures, it may be argued that discrimination might be found without regard to the individual income characteristics of district residents. . . .

However described, it is clear that appellees' suit asks this Court to extend its most exacting scrutiny to review a system that allegedly discriminates against a large, diverse, and amorphous class, unified only by the common factor of residence in districts that happen to have less taxable wealth than other districts. The system of alleged discrimination and the class it defines have none of the traditional indicia of suspectness: the class is not saddled with such disabilities, or subjected to such a history of purposeful unequal treatment, or relegated to such a position of political powerlessness as to command extraordinary protection from the majoritarian political process.

We thus conclude that the Texas system does not operate to the preculiar disadvantage of any suspect class. But in recognition of the fact that this Court has never heretofore held that wealth discrimination alone provides an adequate basis for invoking strict scrutiny, appellees have not relied solely on this contention. They also assert that the State's system impermissibly interferes with the exercise of a "fundamental" right and that accordingly the prior decisions of this Court require the application of the strict standard of judicial review. . . .

In *Brown* v. *Board of Education,* . . . a unanimous Court recognized that "education is perhaps the most important function of state and local governments.". . . What was said there in the context of racial discrimination has lost none of its vitality with the passage of time. . . .

Nothing this Court holds today in any way detracts from our historic dedication to public education. We are in complete agreement with the conclusion of the three-judge panel below that "the grave significance of education both to the individual and to our society" cannot be doubted. But the importance of a service performed by the State does not determine whether it must be regarded as fundamental for purposes of examination under the Equal Protection Clause. . . .

. . . It is not the province of this Court to create substantive constitutional rights in the name of guaranteeing equal protection of the laws. Thus the key to discovering whether education is "fundamental" is not to be found in comparisons of the relative societal significance of education as opposed to subsistence or housing. Nor is it to be found by weighing whether education is as important as the right to travel. Rather, the answer lies in assessing whether there is a right to education explicitly or implicitly guaranteed by the Constitution. . . .

Education, of course, is not among the rights afforded explicit protection under our Federal Constitution. Nor do we find any basis for saying it is implicitly so protected. As we have said, the undisputed importance of education will not alone cause this Court to depart from the usual standard for reviewing a State's social and economic legislation. . . .

We need not rest our decision, however, solely on the inappropriateness of the strict scrutiny test. A century of Supreme Court adjudication under the Equal Protection Clause affirmatively supports the application of the traditional standard of review, which requires only that the State's system be shown to bear some rational relationship to legitimate state purposes. This case represents far more than a challenge to the manner in which Texas provides for the education of its children. We have here nothing less than a direct attack on the way in which Texas has chosen to raise and disburse state and local tax revenues. We are asked to condemn the State's judgment in conferring on political subdivisions the power to tax local property to supply revenues for local interests. In so doing, appellees would have the Court intrude in an area in which it has traditionally deferred to state legislatures. This Court has often admonished against such interference with the State's fiscal policies under the Equal Protection Clause. . . .

. . . The very complexity of the problems of financing and managing a state-wide public school system suggest that "there will be more than one constitutionally permissible method of solving them," and that, within the limits of rationality, "the legislature's efforts to tackle the problems" should be entitled to respect. . . . On even the most basic questions in this area the scholars and educational experts are divided. Indeed, one of the hottest sources of controversy concerns the extent to which there is a demonstrable correlation between educational expenditures and the quality of education—an assumed correlation underlying virtually every legal conclusion drawn by the District Court in this case. . . .

. . . The Texas plan is not the result of hurried, ill-conceived legislation. It certainly is not the product of purposeful discrimination against any group or class. . . . In its essential characteristics the Texas plan for financing public education reflects what many educators for a half century have thought was an enlightened approach to a problem for which there is no perfect solution. We are unwilling to assume for ourselves a level of wisdom superior to that of legislators, scholars, and educational authorities in 49 States, especially where the alternatives proposed are only recently conceived and nowhere yet tested. The constitutional standard under the Equal Protection Clause is whether the challenged state action rationally furthers a legitimate state purpose or interest. . . . We hold that the Texas plan abundantly satisfies this standard. . . .

Mr. Justice Stewart, concurring. . . .

Mr. Justice Brennan, dissenting.
Although I agree with my Brother White that the Texas statutory scheme is devoid of any rational basis, and for that reason is violative of the Equal Protection Clause, I also record my disagreement with the Court's rather distressing assertion that a right may be deemed "fundamental" for the purposes of equal protection analysis only if it is "explicitly or implicitly guaranteed by the Constitution.". . .

Here, there can be no doubt that education is inextricably linked to the right to participate in the electoral process and to the rights of free speech and association guaranteed by the First Amendment. . . . This being so, any classification affecting education must be subjected to strict judicial scrutiny, and since even the State concedes that the statutory scheme now before us cannot pass constitutional muster under this stricter standard of review, I can only conclude that the Texas school financing scheme is constitutionally invalid.

Mr. Justice White, with whom Mr. Justice Douglas and Mr. Justice Brennan join, dissenting. . . .

Perhaps the majority believes that the major disparity in revenues provided and permitted by the Texas system is inconsequential. I cannot agree, however, that the difference of the magnitude appearing in this case can sensibly be ignored, particularly since the State itself considers it so important to provide opportunities to exceed the minimum state educational expenditures. . . .

. . . [I]n the present case we would blink reality to ignore the fact that school districts, and students in the end, are differentially affected by the Texas school financing scheme with respect to their capability to supplement the Minimum Foundation School Pogram. At the very least, the law discriminates against those children and their parents who live in districts where the per-pupil tax base is sufficiently low to make impossible the provision of comparable school revenues by resort to the real property tax which is the only device the State extends for this purpose.

Mr. Justice Marshall, with whom Mr. Justice Douglas concurs, dissenting.

The Court today decides, in effect, that a State may constitutionally vary the quality of education which it offers its children in accordance with the amount of taxable wealth located in the school districts within which they reside. The majority's decision represents an abrupt departure from the mainstream of recent state and federal court decisions concerning the unconstitutionality of state educational financing schemes dependent upon taxable local wealth. More unfortunately, though, the majority's holding can only be seen as a retreat from our historic commitment to equality of educational opportunity and as unsupportable acquiescence in a system which deprives children in their earliest years of the chance to reach their full potential as citizens. The Court does this despite the absence of any substantial justification for a scheme which arbitrarily channels educational resources in accordance with the fortuity of the amount of taxable wealth within each district.

In my judgment, the right of every American to an equal start in life, so far as the provision of a state service as important as education is concerned, is far too vital to permit state discrimination on grounds as tenuous as those presented by this record. Nor can I accept the notion that it is sufficient to remit these appellees to the vagaries of the political process which, contrary to the majority's suggestion, has proven singularly unsuited to the task of providing a remedy for this discrimination. I, for one, am unsatisfied with the hope of an ultimate "political" solution sometime in the indefinite future while, in the meantime, countless children unjustifiably receive inferior educations that "may affect their hearts and minds in a way unlikely ever to be undone.". . .

The appellants do not deny the disparities in educational funding caused by variations in taxable district property wealth. They do contend, however, that whatever the differences in per pupil spending among Texas districts, there are no discriminatory consequences for the children of the disadvantaged districts. . . .

In my view, though, even an unadorned restatement of this contention is sufficient to reveal its absurdity. Authorities concerned with educational quality no doubt disagree as to the significance of variations in per pupil spending. . . . That a child forced to attend an underfunded school with poorer physical facilities, less experienced teachers, larger classes, and a narrower range of courses than a school with substantially more funds—and thus with greater choice in educational planning—may nevertheless excel is to the credit of the child, not the State. . . .

Even if the Equal Protection Clause encompassed some theory of constitutional adequacy, discrimination in the provision of educational opportunity would certainly seem to be a poor candidate for its application. Neither the majority nor appellants informs us how judicially manageable standards are to be derived for determining how much education is "enough" to excuse constitutional discrimination. . . .

[On the "new" equal protection approach, see Wallace Mendelson, "From Warren to Burger: The Rise and Decline of Substantive Equal Protection," 66 *Am. Pol. Sci. Rev.* 1226 (1972); and Arthur B. Winter, "The Changing Parameters of Substantive Equal Protection: From the Warren to the Burger Era," 23 *Emory L. J.* 657 (1974).]

RACE DISCRIMINATION

The single most dramatic change in the broad movement toward equal rights since the abolition of slavery has been the reversal in constitutional interpretation which now bars governmental discrimination based on race. For most of the period since 1865 the law looked in two directions with regard to racial discrimination. It was held unconstitutional for the state explicitly to deny to persons because of their race a right enjoyed by members of other races, but, under the decision in *Plessy* v. *Ferguson* in 1896, it was not unconstitutional for the state to dispense governmental benefits and employ its police powers along lines separated on the basis of race. The Louisiana statute upheld in that case required "equal but separate accommodations for the white and colored races" in railway coaches. The phrase has been reversed and since that time has been referred to as the "separate but equal" doctrine. The landmark decision in the area of race discrimination, *Brown* v. *Board of Education of Topeka,* 347 U.S. 483 (1954), although technically confined to education, has been subsequently broadened to a holding that separate facilities are *inherently unequal,* and therefore governmental discrimination on the basis of race cannot meet the test of equal protection of the laws. [The literature on the subject of racial discrimination is enormous, but for an excellent treatment of the development of the law through the *Brown* case, see A. P. Blaustein and C. C. Ferguson, Jr., *Desegregation and the Law* (New Brunswick: Rutgers University Press, 1957). See, also, Jack Greenberg, *Race Relations and American Law* (New York: Columbia University Press, 1959). An invaluable reference source is the *Race Relations Law Reporter* (Nashville: Vanderbilt University School of Law, published quarterly, 1956–1974).]

Following the bitterly criticized decision in *Dred Scott* v. *Sandford,* 19 Howard 393 (1857), holding that the Constitution did not contemplate acquisition of United States citizenship by Negroes, the Thirteenth, Fourteenth, and Fifteenth Amendments were adopted. As a package, these amendments were clearly intended to elevate the Negro to at least equal *legal* status with other United States citizens. The extent to which they limit private and quasi-public discrimination based on race is actually still a matter of argument, although the question is largely moot since the adoption of the Civil Rights Act of 1964. (The issue of what is considered "state action" under the Fourteenth and Fifteenth Amendments has been discussed in Chapter 3.) But it required nearly a century of litigation to reach a clear holding that all governmental distinctions based on race were unconstitutional. One of the earliest post-Civil War cases on the application of the Fourteenth Amendment to racial discrimination was decided in 1880 and dealt with the constitutionality of a statutory bar to jury service for Negroes. The case was *Strauder* v. *West Virginia* and was decided by a Court whose members had lived through the Civil War and observed the activity of the subsequent Congresses in adopting constitutional amendments and legislation designed to protect the Negro.

STRAUDER *v.* WEST VIRGINIA
100 U.S. 303 (1880)

[Strauder, a Negro, was convicted of murder in a West Virginia court by an all-white jury. Under state law only white male citizens were liable for jury service. A petition for removal of the cause to the federal circuit court on the ground of racial discrimination in the selection of jurors was denied, and the trial proceeded in state court. The state supreme court affirmed the conviction and the United States Supreme Court reviewed the conviction on writ of error.]

Mr. Justice Strong delivered the opinion of the Court.

[The Fourteenth Amendment] is one of a series of constitutional provisions having a common purpose; namely, securing to a race recently emancipated, a race that through many generations had been held in slavery, all the civil rights that the superior race enjoy.... At the time when they were incorporated into the Constitution, it required little knowledge of human nature to anticipate that those who had long been regarded as an inferior and subject race would, when suddenly raised to the rank of citizenship, be looked upon with jealousy and positive dislike, and that state laws might be enacted or enforced to perpetuate the distinctions that had before existed. Discriminations against them had been habitual.... They especially needed protection against unfriendly action in the States where they were resident. It was in view of these considerations the Fourteenth Amendment was framed and adopted.

It was designed to assure to the colored race the enjoyment of all the civil rights that under the law are enjoyed by white persons, and to give to that race the protection of the general government, in that enjoyment, whenever it should be denied by the States....

If this is the spirit and meaning of the amendment, whether it means more or not, it is to be construed liberally, to carry out the purposes of its framers.... It ordains that no State shall deprive any person of life, liberty, or property, without due process of law, or deny to any person within its jurisdiction the equal protection of the laws. What is this but declaring that the law in the States shall be the same for the black as for the white; that all persons, whether colored or white, shall stand equal before the laws of the States, and, in regard to the colored race, for whose protection the amendment was primarily designed, that no discrimination shall be made against them by law because of their color? The words of the amendment, it is true, are prohibitory, but they contain a necessary implication of a positive immunity, or right, most valuable to the colored race,—the right to exemption from unfriendly legislation against them distinctively as colored,—exemption from legal discriminations, inplying inferiority in civil society, lessening the security of their enjoyment of the rights which others enjoy, and discriminations which are steps towards reducing them to the condition of a subject race....

In view of these considerations, it is hard to see why the statute of West Virginia should not be regarded as discriminating against a colored man when he is put upon trial for an alleged criminal offense against the State. It is not easy to comprehend how it can be said that while every white man is entitled to a trial by a jury selected from persons of his own race or color, or rather, selected without discrimination against his color, and a negro is not, the latter is equally protected by the law with the former. Is not protection of life, and liberty against race or color prejudice a right, a legal right, under the constitutional amendment? And how can it be maintained that compelling a colored man to submit to a trial for his life by a jury drawn from a panel from which the State has expressly excluded every man of his race, because of color alone, however well qualified in other respects, is not a denial to him of equal legal protection? . . .

The Fourteenth Amendment makes no attempt to enumerate the rights it is designed to protect. It speaks in general terms, and those are as comprehensive as possible. Its language is prohibitory; but every prohibition implies the existence of rights and immunities, prominent among which is an immunity from inequality of legal protection, either for life, liberty, or property. Any state action that denies this immunity to a colored man is in conflict with the Constitution. . . .

Reversed.

[Justice Field, joined by Justice Clifford, dissented.]

The bar against state discrimination on race in jury service has been applied uniformly by the Court since *Strauder,* although it extends only to a requirement that racial discrimination not be employed in the selection process and does not command that a given racial distribution be found on a particular jury. Thus in *Hernandez* v. *Texas,* 347 U.S. 475 (1954), the Court reversed the conviction of a Mexican-American where the record showed a systematic exclusion of Mexican-Americans from juries. (See the discussion of jury trial in Chapter 4.)

Despite the sweeping statements in Justice Strong's opinion concerning the scope of protection offered by the Fourteenth Amendment against racial discrimination, the Court, less than twenty years later, in 1896, was prepared to uphold, with only one dissent, the power of the state to require racial segregation. The case was *Plessy* v. *Ferguson,* and the dissenter, Justice Harlan, was the only remaining member who had voted with the majority in the *Strauder* case. (Justice Field also remained, but he had dissented in the earlier case.)

PLESSY *v.* FERGUSON
163 U.S. 537 (1896)

[A Louisiana statute, passed in 1890, required all railway companies carrying passengers in the state to provide "equal but separate accommodations for the white and colored races," and also that no person should be permitted to occupy seats in coaches other than the ones assigned to his race. Plessy alleged that he was seven-eights Caucasian and one-eighth African blood, that he took a seat in a white coach, and upon his refusal to leave the coach was forcibly ejected, imprisoned, and charged with violation of the act. He petitioned for a writ of prohibition directed against the trial court on the ground that the statute was unconstitutional under the Thirteenth and Fourteenth Amendments. The Louisiana Supreme Court held the statute constitutional and denied the relief sought.]

Mr. Justice Brown . . . delivered the opinion of the court.

That it does not conflict with the Thirteenth Amendment, which abolished slavery and involuntary servitude, . . . is too clear for argument. Slavery implies involuntary servitude,—a state of bondage; the ownership of mankind as a chattel, or, at least, the control of the labor and services of one man for the benefit of another. . . .

By the Fourteenth Amendment . . . the states are forbidden from making or enforcing any law which shall . . . deny to any person within their jurisdiction the equal protection of the laws. . . .

The object of the amendment was undoubtedly to enforce the absolute equality of the two races before the law, but in the nature of things it could not have been intended to abolish distinctions based upon color, or to enforce social, as distinguished from political, equality, or a commingling of the two races upon terms unsatisfactory to either. Laws permitting, and even requiring, their separation in places where they are liable to be brought into contact do not necessarily imply the inferiority of either race to the other, and have been generally, if not universally, recognized as within the competency of the state legislatures in the exercise of their police power. The most common instance of this is connected with the establishment of separate schools for white and colored children, which has been held to be a valid exercise of the legislative power even by courts of states where the political rights of the colored race have been longest and most earnestly enforced.

One of the earliest of these cases is that of *Roberts* v. *City of Boston,* 5 Cush. 198 (1849), in which the Supreme Judicial Court of Massachusetts held that the general school committee of Boston had power to make provision for the instruction of colored children in separate schools established exclusively for them, and to prohibit their attendance upon the other schools. . . . Similar laws have been enacted by Congress under its general power of legislation over the District of Columbia . . . as well as by the legislatures of many of the states, and have been generally, if not uniformly, sustained by the courts. . . .

The distinction between laws interfering with the political equality of the Negro and those requiring the separation of the two races in schools, theatres, and railway carriages has been frequently drawn by this court. . . .

We consider the underlying fallacy of the plaintiff's argument to consist in the assumption that the enforced separation of the two races stamps the colored race with a badge of inferiority. If this be so, it is not by reason of anything found in the act, but solely because the colored race chooses to put that construction upon it. The argument necessarily assumes that if . . . the colored race should become the dominant power in the state legislature, and should enact a law in precisely similar terms, it would thereby relegate the white race to an inferior position. We imagine that the white race, at least, would not acquiesce in this assumption. The argument also assumes that social prejudices may be overcome by legislation and that equal rights cannot be secured to the Negro except by an enforced commingling of the two races. We cannot accept this proposition. If the two races are to meet upon terms of social equality, it must be the result of natural affinities, a mutual appreciation of each other's merits, and a voluntary consent of individuals. . . .

Legislation is powerless to eradicate racial instincts or to abolish distinctions based upon physical differences, and the attempt to do so can only result in accentuating the difficulties of the present situation. If the civil and political rights of both races be equal, one cannot be inferior to the other civilly or politically. If one race be inferior to the other socially, the Constitution of the United States cannot put them upon the same plane. . . .

The judgment of the court below is, therefore,

Affirmed.

Mr. Justice Brewer did not hear the argument or participate in the decision of this case.

Mr. Justice Harlan, dissenting: . . .

In respect of civil rights, common to all citizens, the Constitution of the United States does not, I think, permit any public authority to know the race of those entitled to be protected in the enjoyment of such rights. . . .

It was said in argument that the statute of Louisiana does not discriminate against either race but prescribes a rule applicable alike to white and colored citizens. But this argument does not meet the difficulty. Everyone knows that the statute in question had its origin in the purpose, not so much to exclude white persons from railroad cars occupied by blacks, as to exclude colored people from coaches occupied or assigned to white persons. . . . The thing to accomplish was, under the guise of giving equal accommodations for whites and blacks, to compel the latter to keep to themselves while travelling in railroad passenger coaches. No one would be so wanting in candor as to assert the contrary. The fundamental objection, therefore, to the statute is that it interferes with the personal freedom of citizens. . . .

The white race deems itself to be the dominant race in this country. And so it is, in prestige, in achievements, in education, in wealth, and in power. So, I doubt not, it will continue to be for all time, if it remains true to its great heritage and holds fast to the principles of constitutional liberty. But in the views of the Constitution, in the eye of the law, there is in this country no superior, dominant, ruling class of citizens. There is no caste here. Our Constitution is color-blind and neither knows nor tolerates classes among citizens. In respect of civil rights, all citizens are equal before the law. The humblest is the peer of the most powerful. The law regards man as man and takes no account of his surroundings or of his color when his civil rights as guaranteed by the supreme law of the land are involved. . . .

The arbitrary separation of citizens, on the basis of race, while they are on a public highway, is a badge of servitude wholly inconsistent with the civil freedom and the equality before the law established by the Constitution. It cannot be justified upon any legal grounds.

If evils will result from the commingling of the two races upon public highways established for the benefit of all, they be infinitely less than those that will surely come from state legislation regulating the enjoyment of civil rights upon the basis of race. We boast of the freedom enjoyed by our people above all other peoples. But it is difficult to reconcile that boast with a state of the law which, practically, puts the brand of servitude and degradation upon a large class of our fellow citizens, our equals before the law. The thin disguise of "equal" accommodations for passengers in railroad coaches will not mislead anyone, nor atone for the wrong this day done. . . .

It is difficult to reconcile the holding in *Plessy* with the language of Justice Strong in *Strauder* v. *West Virginia*. As Justice Harlan pointed out in his dissent in *Plessy*, it was clear to everyone that the equal but separate provisions in transportation and other laws were designed to perpetuate a caste system, even though the facilities for the two races might be equal.

As a matter of fact, segregated facilities were rarely equal, but it was not until almost fifty years later that the Court came to grips with this issue.

If it was not unconstitutional for the state to segregate by race in transportation, then it was felt that it would be equally permissible to segregate in other areas such as education, parks, and swimming pools. The so-called Jim Crow laws became a pattern in the South and racial segregation in "social" activities was maintained, while under the *Strauder* rule and the Fifteenth Amendment at least most of the "political" arena was presumed to be constitutionally bound to a policy of freedom from racial differentiation. [See C. Vann Woodward, *The Strange Career of Jim Crow,* 2d ed. (New York: Oxford, 1966).]

Even this kind of rough distinction between "social" and "political" did not always obtain, however, as became evident when the issue of racial zoning in residential property came to the Court in 1917.

BUCHANAN *v.* WARLEY

245 U.S. 60 (1971)

[In 1914 the City of Louisville, Kentucky, in order "to prevent conflict and ill-feeling between the white and colored races in the City of Louisville," enacted an ordinance which prohibited any Negro from moving into and occupying a residence in a block in which more than half the houses were occupied by whites and, conversely, prohibited whites from moving into a block in which the houses were predominantly Negro-occupied. Warley, a Negro, contracted with Buchanan for the purchase of a home in a block largely occupied by white residents. Buchanan then refused to complete the sale on the ground that the ordinance forbade it. Warley brought an action for specific performance on the contention that the ordinance violated the Fourteenth Amendment and thus was no defense to an action for specific performance. The Kentucky courts upheld the ordinance, and the case was carried to the Supreme Court for review on a writ of error.]

Mr. Justice Day delivered the opinion of the Court. . . .

That there exists a serious and difficult problem arising from a feeling of race hostility which the law is powerless to control, and to which it must give a measure of consideration, may be freely admitted. But its solution cannot be promoted by depriving citizens of their constitutional rights and privileges.

As we have seen, this court has held laws valid which separated the races on the basis of equal accommodations in public conveyances, and courts of high authority have held enactments lawful which provide for separation in the public schools of white and colored pupils where equal privileges are given. But in view of the rights secured by the Fourteenth Amendment to the federal Constitution such legislation must have its limitations, and cannot be sustained where the exercise of authority exceeds the restraints of the Constitution. We think these limitations are exceeded in laws and ordinances of the character now before us.

It is the purpose of such enactments, and, it is frankly avowed it will be their ultimate effect, to require by law, at least in residential districts, the compulsory separation of the races on account of color. Such action is said to be essential to the maintenance of the purity of the races, although it is to be noted in the ordinance under consideration that the employment of colored servants in white families is permitted, and near-by residences of colored persons not coming within the blocks, as defined in the ordinance, are not prohibited.

The case presented does not deal with an attempt to prohibit the amalgamation of the races. The right which the ordinance annulled was the civil rights of a white man to dispose of his property if he saw fit to do so to a person of color and of a colored person to make such disposition to a white person.

It is urged that this proposed segregation will promote the public peace by preventing race conflicts. Desirable as this is, and important as is the preservation of the public peace, this aim cannot be accomplished by laws or ordinances which deny rights created or protected by the federal Constitution.

It is said that such acquisitions by colored persons depreciate property owned in the neighborhood by white persons. But property may be acquired by undesirable white neighbors or put to disagreeable though lawful uses with like results.

We think this attempt to prevent the alienation of the property in question to a person of color was not a legitimate exercise of the police power of the State, and is in direct violation of the fundamental law enacted in the Fourteenth Amendment of the Constitution preventing state interference with property rights except by due process of law. That being the case, the ordinance cannot stand.

It should be noted that the decision came off on the ground that for the state so to restrict the property owner was a deprivation of property without due process of law. Technically, then, the holding did not interfere with the earlier interpretation of the equal protection clause that racial segregation imposed by law in nonpolitical areas was not barred. It did, however, point up the anomaly in such an interpretation, and the Court was sharply criticized for giving greater protection to the property rights of Negroes than to their personal rights. In rebuttal it was contended that the Congress following the Civil War had enacted legislation specifically to protect the right of all citizens "to inherit, purchase, lease, sell, hold, and convey real and personal property" (14 Stat. 27, 1866), while it also established schools for the District of Columbia on a racially segregated basis. Thus it was argued that the Congress intended to protect property rights through the Fourteenth Amendment but did not intend for that Amendment to restrict racial segregation imposed by law. As a consequence of the decision in *Buchanan* v. *Warley,* the practice developed of incorporating racially restrictive covenants in deeds conveying property. (The cases involving the validity of the enforcement of such covenants by the state are taken up below.)

Taking the decisions in *Strauder, Plessy,* and *Buchanan* together, it would appear that by the end of World War I a rough rule had been developed that the state could not make racial distinctions in the area of political or property rights, but racial segregation in "social" areas could be imposed by law on a "separate but equal" basis. Added to this is the holding in the *Civil Rights Cases,* 109 U.S. 3 (1883), (discussed in Chapter 3) that the Fourteenth Amendment barred only *state* action of certain types and not racial barriers set up by *private* action. This decision was double-edged in that it not only limited judicial remedies in actions brought under the Fourteenth Amendment, but it also, and to the same extent, limited the scope of legislation adopted by Congress to enforce the provisions of the Fourteenth Amendment. The rule of *Strauder-Plessy-Buchanan,* and the rule of the *Civil Rights Cases,* however, suggested three broad avenues of attack on racial discrimination. Within the framework of these decisions it was still possible to enter the judicial arena and argue (1) that a given right was political in nature and that the state should be barred from making any kind of racial distinctions in its exercise, or (2) that a given facility, required by state law to be segregated, was operated in such fashion that Negroes were not in fact being treated equally with whites, or (3) that a particular form of racial discrimination, though nominally imposed by private action, was in some manner being furthered by the active assistance or participation of the state in such fashion as to bring the imposition within the category of "state action" prohibited by the Fourteenth or Fifteenth Amendments.

The first approach has been used repeatedly in such areas as racial discrimination in jury selection and in voting rights. Despite the clear holding in *Strauder,* the Court has repeatedly found it necessary to review, and reverse, convictions of Negroes where a long-continued pattern of discrimination in the selection of jurors was followed. And in *Pierre* v. *Louisiana,* 306 U.S. 354 (1939), the Court held unanimously that even in the grand jury the Negro defendant was constitutionally entitled to a panel free from selection methods which discriminated against Negroes because of their race. (The discussion of racial discrimination in voting will be reserved for Chapter 8.)

The second approach is the one which was ultimately successful in barring racial segregation in public schools in the landmark case of *Brown* v. *Board of Education* in 1954. It is not suggested that the earlier cases brought on this ground were part of an organized, frontal assault on the whole concept of segregation by race. They were, in fact, sporadic, isolated cases, and not until after the end of World War II was there a conscious strategy employed to press the case for exact equality of facilities to the point that separate facilities were by this very fact unequal.

The earlier cases arguing inequality of facilities were brought in situations where the Negro was offered no facilities whatever in an area where they were available to whites. The Court had little difficulty finding a violation of the Fourteenth Amendment in such instances where there was no pretense of affording separate but equal treatment. In *McCabe* v. *Atchison, T. & S.F. Ry.,* 235 U.S. 151 (1914), the Court held void a separate coach law of Oklahoma which permitted carriers to provide sleeping and dining cars only for white persons, notwithstanding the state's contention that there was little demand for them by colored persons. Nearly twenty-five years later a similar issue was presented, this time in the field of education, and again the Court held the state provision to be a violation of the equal protection of the laws. The state of Missouri maintained a law school at its university for white students but had none at the state university for Negroes. It provided by statute for the payment of tuition fees for any of its Negro citizens to study law "at the university of any adjacent state," but refused to admit them to the white law school. In *Missouri ex rel. Gaines* v. *Canada,* 305 U.S. 337 (1938), the Court unanimously held that petitioner had been denied equal protection of the laws. Chief Justice Hughes, speaking for the Court, stated:

The admissibility of laws separating the races in the enjoyment of privileges afforded by the State rests wholly upon the equality of the privileges which the laws give to the separated groups within the State. The question here is not of a duty of the State to supply legal training, or of the quality of the training which it does supply, but of its duty when it provides such training to furnish it to the residents of the State upon the basis of an equality of right. By the operation of the laws of Missouri a privilege has been created for white law students which is denied to negroes by reason of their race. The white resident is afforded legal education within the State; the negro resident having the same qualifications is refused it there and must go outside the State to obtain it. That is a denial of the equality of legal right to the enjoyment of the privilege which the State has set up, and the provision for the payment of tuition fees in another State does not remove the discrimination. . . . That resort may mitigate the inconvenience of the discrimination but cannot serve to validate it.

Nor can we regard the fact that there is but a limited demand in Missouri for the legal education of negroes as excusing the discrimination in favor of whites. We had occasion to consider a cognate question in the case of *McCabe* v. *Atchison, T. & S.F. Ry. Co.* . . . We found that argument to be without merit. It made, we said, the constitutional right "depend upon the number of persons who may be discriminated against, whereas the essence of the constitutional right is that it is a personal one. Whether or not particular facilities shall be provided may doubtless be conditioned upon there being a reasonable demand therefor; but, if facilities are provided, substantial equality of treatment of persons traveling under like conditions cannot be refused. It is the individual who is entitled to the equal protection of the laws, and if he is denied by a common carrier, acting in the matter under the authority of a state law, a facility or convenience in the course of his journey which, under substantially the same circumstances, is furnished to another traveler, he may properly complain that his constitutional privilege has been invaded." *Id.*, 235 U.S. 161, 162. . . .

The *McCabe* and *Gaines* cases can, of course, be confined to the narrow holding that privileges created by law for white persons cannot be denied to Negroes, although they can be constitutionally provided on a segregated basis. There are phrases in the two opinions, however, which suggest that the segregated facilities should in fact be equal. The opinion in *McCabe* states that "substantial equality of treatment . . . cannot be refused." And in *Gaines* the Court refers to "the equality of legal right to the enjoyment of the privilege which the State has set up." Not yet, however, did the Court squarely hold that separate facilities had to be truly equal to meet the requirements of equal protection.

Meanwhile a sort of collateral attack on segregation by race was undertaken in the field of interstate transportation. In *Mitchell* v. *United States,* 313 U.S. 80 (1941), the Court held that for a railroad to deny Pullman car accommodations to a Negro solely because of his race was in violation of the provision of the Interstate Commerce Act forbidding "any undue or unreasonable prejudice or disadvantage in any respect whatsoever." The decision stands with *McCabe* and *Gaines*, however, as a case involving absolute denial of a facility rather than the equality of separately provided facilities. The next approach was to argue that separate facilities required by state law on interstate carriers was an undue burden on interstate commerce. This argument was successful in *Morgan* v. *Virginia,* 328 U.S. 373 (1946), in which the Court held that the mandatory reseating of passengers when a state line was crossed was a burden on interstate commerce not supportable under the police power of the state. In the absence of state laws, however, private regulations of carriers requiring segregation of passengers remained unaffected by this ruling. This gap was closed by the ruling in *Henderson* v. *United States,* 339 U.S. 816 (1950), in which the Court held that the nondiscrimination requirement of the Interstate Commerce Act barred a railroad from enforcing its rule providing for segregated dining facilities on its cars. And *Boynton* v. *Virginia,* 364 U.S. 454 (1960), extended the holding to the terminal and restaurant facilities of interstate bus carriers.

Discrimination in Public Schools

In the same year that the *Henderson* case was decided, the Court decided two other cases in the field of higher education which squarely opened the way for an attack on segregated facilities on the ground that accommodations for Negroes were not in actuality equal to those for white persons. *McLaurin* v. *Oklahoma State Regents,* 339 U.S. 637 (1950), involved a Negro in the graduate school of the University of Oklahoma. Under the requirements of the *Gaines* holding, the state had provided that qualified Negroes could be admitted to white state schools where the Negro school did not offer the requested course of study. Once McLaurin was admitted, however, rigid segregation practices prevailed within the University. He was assigned a special "colored" seat in each classroom, a special table was provided for him in the library, and he was required to eat in a segregated portion of the cafeteria. The Court declared these conditions unconstitutional on the ground that they would "impair and inhibit his ability to study, to engage in discussions and exchange views with other students."

On the same day as *McLaurin,* the Court rendered its decision in *Sweatt* v. *Painter,* involving the petition of a Negro for admission to the University of Texas Law School.

SWEATT *v.* PAINTER
339 U.S. 629 (1950)

[Petitioner applied for admission to the University of Texas Law School, but his application was rejected solely because he was a Negro. He applied for mandamus to compel his admission on the ground that there was no Negro law school in Texas. The court did not issue mandamus, but continued the case for six months to allow the State to supply substantially equal facilities. A Negro law school was opened by the State, and the court denied the writ, but petitioner refused to register in the new school. A new hearing was held on the issue of the equality of the educational facilities at the newly established school as compared with the University of Texas Law School. Finding that the new school offered petitioner "privileges, advantages, and opportunties for the study of law substantially equivalent to those offered by the State to white students at the University of Texas," the trial court denied mandamus, and the Court of Civil Appeals affirmed.]

Mr. Chief Justice Warren delivered the opinion of the Court. . . .

The University of Texas Law School, from which petitioner was excluded, was staffed by a faculty of sixteen full-time and three part-time professors, some of whom are nationally recognized authorities in their field. Its student body numbered 850. The library contained over 65,000 volumes. Among the other facilities available to the students were a law review, moot court facilities, scholarship funds, and Order of the Coif affiliation. The school's alumni occupy the most distinguished positions in the private practice of the law and in the public life of the State. It may properly be considered one of the nation's ranking law schools.

The law school for Negroes which was to have opened in February, 1947, would have no independent faculty or library. The teaching was to be carried on by four members of the University of Texas Law School faculty, who were to maintain their offices at the University of Texas while teaching at both institutions. Few of the 10,000 volumes ordered for the library had arrived; nor was there any full-time librarian. The school lacked accreditation.

Since the trial of this case, respondents report the opening of a law school at the Texas State University for Negroes. It is apparently on the road to full accreditation. It has a faculty of five full-time professors; a student body of 23; a library of some 16,500 volumes serviced by a full-time staff; a practice court and legal aid association; and one alumnus who has become a member of the Texas Bar.

Whether the University of Texas Law School is compared with the original or the new law school for Negroes, we cannot find substantial equality in the educational opportunities offered white and Negro law students by the State. In terms of number of the faculty, variety of courses and opportunity for specialization, size of the student body, scope of the library, availability of law review and similar activities, the University of Texas Law School is superior. What is more important, the University of Texas Law School possesses to a far greater degree those qualities which are incapable of objective measurement but which make for greatness in a law school. Such qualities, to name but a few, include reputation of the faculty, experience of the administration, position and influence of the alumni, standing in the community, traditions and prestige. It is difficult to believe that one who had a free choice between these law schools would consider the question close.

. . . The law school to which Texas is willing to admit petitioner excludes from its student body members of the racial groups which number 85 per cent of the population of the State and include most of the lawyers, witnesses, jurors, judges and other officials with whom petitioner will inevitably be dealing with when he becomes a member of the Texas Bar. With such a substantial and significant segment of society excluded, we cannot conclude that the education offered petitioner is substantially equal to that which he would receive if admitted to the University of Texas Law School. . . .

In holding that the Texas practice violated the equal protection clause, the Court refused, however, to reexamine the separate but equal doctrine. Nonetheless, the decision and the general tenor of the Court's opinion suggested strongly that the time might be ripe for such a reexamination. To make a point of the opportunities of students for "intellectual commingling" in the *McLaurin* case and to examine and recognize "those qualities which are incapable of objective measurement" such as reputation of the faculty, the school's standing in the community, and the "position and influence of the alumni," as the Court did in *Sweatt,* is certainly to give strong intimations that separate facilities in education are inherently unequal and therefore unconstitutional. Actions were brought in several states and in the District of Columbia with the hope that this issue could ultimately be squarely raised in the United States Supreme Court. In December, 1952, the Court heard argument in its appellate review of four cases involving segregated school laws in the states of Kansas, Virginia, South Carolina, and Delaware, and one case involving the validity of maintaining segregated public schools in the District of Columbia. In December of the following year, 1953, the cases were reargued on certain questions propounded by the Court. Finally, on May 17, 1954, the Court handed down its momentous decision that governmentally enforced racial segregation in public schools was unconstitutional. The state cases, decided together and reported officially under the name of the Kansas case, *Brown* v. *Board of Education of Topeka, Kansas,* were based on the equal protection clause of the Fourteenth Amendment. The District of Columbia case, *Bolling* v. *Sharpe,* was based on an equal protection requirement as implied in the due process clause of the Fifth Amendment.

BROWN *v.* BOARD OF EDUCATION OF TOPEKA
347 U.S. 483 (1954)

Mr. Chief Justice Warren delivered the opinion of the Court.

These cases come to us from the States of Kansas, South Carolina, Virginia, and Delaware. They are premised on different facts and different local conditions, but a common legal question justifies their consideration together in this consolidated opinion.

In each of the cases, minors of the Negro race, through their legal representatives, seek the aid of the courts in obtaining admission to the public schools of their community on a nonsegregated basis. In each instance, they had been denied admission to schools attended by white children under laws requiring or permitting segregation according to race. This segregation was alleged to deprive the plantiffs of the equal protection of the laws under the Fourteenth Amendment. In each of the cases other than the Delaware case, a three-judge federal district court denied relief to the plantiffs on the so-called "separate but equal" doctrine announced by this Court in *Plessy* v. *Ferguson,* 163 U.S. 537. Under that doctrine, equality of treatment is accorded when the races are provided substantially equal facilities, even though these facilities be separate. In the Delaware case, the Supreme Court of Delaware adhered to that doctrine, but ordered that the plantiffs be admitted to the white schools because of their superiority to the Negro schools.

The plaintiffs contend that segregated public schools are not "equal" and cannot be made "equal," and that hence they are deprived of the equal protection of the laws. Because of the obvious importance of the question presented, the Court took jurisdiction. Argument was heard in the 1952 Term, and reargument was heard this Term on certain questions propounded by the Court.

[The order was issued on June 8, 1953, 345 U.S. 972, and requested counsel "to discuss particularly" five questions. The first three questions are answered in the instant case, but questions 4 and 5 are set out for still further argument in the following Term. The five questions were:

"1. What evidence is there that the Congress which submitted and the State legislatures and conventions which ratified the Fourteenth Amendment contemplated or did not contemplate, understood or did not understand, that it would abolish segregation in public schools?

"2. If neither the Congress in submitting nor the States in ratifying the Fourteenth Amendment understood that compliance with it would require the immediate abolition of segregation in public schools, was it nevertheless the understanding of the framers of the Amendment

(a) that future Congresses might, in the exercise of their power under section 5 of the Amendment, abolish such segregation, or

(b) that it would be within the judicial power, in light of future conditions, to construe the Amendment as abolishing such segregation of its own force?

"3. On the assumption that the answers to questions 2(a) and (b) do not dispose of the issue, is it within the judicial power, in construing the Amendment, to abolish segregation in public schools,

"4. Assuming it is decided that segregation in public schools violated the Fourteenth Amendment

(a) would a decree necessarily follow providing that, within the limits set by normal geographic school districting, Negro children should forthwith be admitted to schools of their choice, or

(b) may this Court, in the exercise of its equity powers, permit an effective gradual adjustment to be brought about from existing segregated systems to a system not based on color distinctions?

"5. On the assumption on which questions 4(a) and (b) are based, and assuming further that this Court will exercise its equity powers to the end described in question 4(b),

(a) should this Court formulate decrees in these cases;

(b) if so, what specific issues should the decrees reach;

(c) should this Court appoint a special master to hear evidence with a view to recommending specific terms for such decrees;

(d) should this Court remand to the courts of first instance with directions to frame decrees in these cases, and if so what general directions should the decrees of this Court include and what procedures should the courts of first instance follow in arriving at the specific terms of more detailed decrees?" 345 U.S. 972.

The Attorney General of the United States participated both Terms as *amicus curiae.*]

Reargument was largely devoted to the circumstances surrounding the adoption of the Fourteenth Amendment in 1868. It covered exhaustively consideration of the Amendment in Congress, ratification by the states, then existing practices in racial segregation, and the views of proponents and opponents of the Amendment. This discussion and our own investigation convince us that, although these sources cast some light, it is not enough to resolve the problem with which we are faced. At best, they are inconclusive. The most avid proponents of the post-War Amendments undoubtedly intended them to remove all legal distinctions among "all persons born or naturalized in the United States." Their opponents, just as certainly, were antagonistic to both the letter and the spirit of the Amendments and wished them to have the most limited effect. What others in Congress and the state legislatures had in mind cannot be determined with any degree of certainty.

An additional reason for the inconclusive nature of the Amendment's history, with respect to segregated schools, is the status of public education at that time. In the South, the movement toward free common schools, supported by general taxation, had not yet taken hold. Education of white children was largely in the hands of private groups. Education of Negroes was almost nonexistent, and practically all of the race were illiterate. In fact, any education of Negroes was forbidden by law in some states. Today, in contrast, many Negroes have achieved outstanding success in the arts and sciences as well as in the business and professional world. It is true that public school education at the time of the Amendment had advanced further in the North, but the effect of the Amendment on Northern States was generally ignored in the congressional debates. Even in the North, the conditions of public education did not approximate those existing today. The curriculum was usually rudimentary; ungraded schools were common in rural areas; the school term was but three months a year in many states; and compulsory school attendance was virtually unknown. As a consequence, it is not surprising that there should be so little in the history of the Fourteenth Amendment relating to its intended effect on public education.

In the first cases in this Court construing the Fourteenth Amendment, decided shortly after its adoption, the Court interpreted it as proscribing all state-imposed discriminations against the Negro race.* The doctrine of "separate but equal" did

---

* *Slaughter-House Cases,* 16 Wall. 36, 67–72 (1873); *Strauder* v. *West Virginia,* 100 U.S. 303, 307–308 (1880).... See also *Virginia* v. *Rives,* 100 U.S. 313 (1880); *Ex parte Virginia,* 100 U.S. 339, 344–345 (1880).

not make its appearance in this Court until 1896 in the case of *Plessy* v. *Ferguson, supra,* involving not education but transportation.** American courts have since labored with the doctrine for over half a century. In this Court, there have been six cases involving the "separate but equal" doctrine in the field of public education. In *Cumming* v. *County Board of Education,* 175 U.S. 528, and *Gong Lum* v. *Rice,* 275 U.S. 78, the validity of the doctrine itself was not challenged. In more recent cases, all on the graduate school level, inequality was found in that specific benefits enjoyed by white students were denied to Negro students of the same educational qualifications. *Missouri ex rel. Gaines* v. *Canada,* 305 U.S. 337; *Sipuel* v. *Oklahoma,* 332 U.S. 631; *Sweatt* v. *Painter,* 339 U.S. 629; *McLaurin* v. *Oklahoma State Regents,* 339 U.S. 637. In none of these cases was it necessary to re-examine the doctrine to grant relief to the Negro plaintiff. And in *Sweatt* v. *Painter, supra,* the Court expressly reserved decision on the question whether *Plessy* v. *Ferguson* should be held inapplicable to public education.

In the instant cases, that question is directly presented. Here, unlike *Sweatt* v. *Painter,* there are findings below that the Negro and white schools involved have been equalized, or are being equalized, with respect to buildings, curricula, qualifications and salaries of teachers, and other "tangible" factors. Our decision, therefore, cannot turn on merely a comparison of these tangible factors in the Negro and white schools involved in each of the cases. We must look instead to the effect of segregation itself on public education.

In approaching this problem we cannot turn the clock back to 1868 when the Amendment was adopted, or even to 1896 when *Plessy* v. *Ferguson* was written. We must consider public education in the light of its full development and its present place in American life throughout the Nation. Only in this way can it be determined if segregation in public schools deprives these plaintiffs of the equal protection of the laws.

Today, education is perhaps the most important function of state and local governments. Compulsory school attendance laws and the great expenditures for education both demonstrate our recognition of the importance of education to our democratic society. It is required in the performance of our most basic public responsibilities, even service in the armed forces. It is the very foundation of good citizenship. Today it is a principal instrument in awakening the child to cultural values, in preparing him for later professional training, and in helping him to adjust normally to his environment. In these days, it is doubtful that any child may reasonably be expected to succeed in life if he is denied the opportunity of an education. Such an opportunity, where the state has undertaken to provide it, is a right which must be made available to all on equal terms.

We come then to the question presented: Does segregation of children in public schools solely on the basis of race, even though the physical facilities and other "tangible" factors may be equal, deprive the children of the minority group of equal education opportunities? We believe that it does.

In *Sweatt* v. *Painter, supra,* in finding that a segregated law school for Negroes could not provide them equal educational opportunities, this Court relied in large part on "those qualities which are incapable of objective measurement but which make for greatness in a law school," In *McLaurin* v. *Oklahoma State Regents, supra,* the Court, in requiring that a Negro admitted to a white graduate school be treated

** The doctrine apparently originated in *Roberts* v. *City of Boston,* 59 Mass. 198, 206 (1850), upholding school segregation against attack as being violative of a state constitutional guarantee of equality....

like all other students, again resorted to intangible considerations: "... his ability to study, to engage in discussions and exchange views with other students, and, in general, to learn his profession." Such considerations apply with added force to children in grade and high schools. To separate them from others of similar age and qualifications solely because of their race generates a feeling of inferiority as to their status in the community that may affect their hearts and minds in a way unlikely ever to be undone. The effect of this separation on their educational opportunities was well stated by a finding in the Kansas case by a court which nevertheless felt compelled to rule against the Negro plaintiffs:

"Segregation of white and colored children in public schools has a detrimental effect upon the colored children. The impact is greater when it has the sanction of the law; for the policy of separating the races is usually interpreted as denoting the inferiority of the negro group. A sense of inferiority affects the motivation of a child to learn. Segregation with the sanction of law, therefore, has a tendency to [retard] the educational and mental development of negro children and to deprive them of some of the benefits they would receive in a racial[ly] integrated school system."

Whatever may have been the extent of psychological knowledge at the time of *Plessy* v. *Ferguson,* this finding is amply supported by modern authority.*** Any language in *Plessy* v. *Ferguson* contrary to this finding is rejected.

We conclude that in the field of public education the doctrine of "separate but equal" has no place. Separate educational facilities are inherently unequal. Therefore, we hold that the plaintiffs and others similarly situated for whom the actions have been brought are, by reason of the segregation complained of, deprived of the equal protection of the laws guaranteed by the Fourteenth Amendment. This disposition makes unnecessary any discussion whether such segregation also violates the Due Process Clause of the Fourteenth Amendment.

Because these are class actions, because of the wide applicability of this decision, and because of the great variety of local conditions, the formulation of decrees in these cases presents problems of considerable complexity. On reargument, the consideration of appropriate relief was necessarily subordinated to the primary question—the constitutionality of segregation in public education. We have now announced that such segregation is a denial of the equal protection of the laws. In order that we may have the full assistance of the parties in formulating decrees, the cases will be restored to the docket, and the parties are requested to present further argument on Questions 4 and 5 previously propounded by the Court for the reargument this term. . . .

It is so ordered.

In *Bolling* v. *Sharpe,* 347 U.S. 497 (1954), decided the same day, the Court held that racial segregation enforced by the federal government in the public schools of the District of Columbia was violative of the Fifth Amendment. The case was treated separately because there is no equal protection clause applicable to the federal government. The Court, however, had no difficulty

*** K. B. Clark, *Effect of Prejudice and Discrimination on Personality Development* (Midcentury White House Conference on Children and Youth, 1950); Witmer and Kotinsky, *Personality in the Making* (1952), c. VI; Deutscher and Chein, "The Psychological Effects of Enforced Segregation: a Survey of Social Science Opinion," 26 *J. Psychol.* 259 (1948); Chein, "What Are the Psychological Effects of Segregation Under Conditions of Equal Facilities?" 3 *Int. J. Opinion and Attitude Res.* 229 (1949); Brameld, *Educational Costs in Discrimination and National Welfare* (MacIver, ed., 1949), 44–48; Frazier, *The Negro in the United States* (1949), 674–681. And see generally Gunnar Myrdal, *An American Dilemma* (1944).

in reading the requirement into the due process clause of the Fifth Amendment. It was pointed out that classifications may be so arbitrary and unjust as to be violative of due process, and racial discrimination by the federal government fell into this category. Chief Justice Warren, for the Court, stated:

In view of our decision that the Constitution prohibits the states from maintaining racially segregated public schools, it would be unthinkable that the same Constitution would impose a lesser duty on the Federal Government. We hold that racial segregation in the public schools of the District of Columbia is a denial of the due process of law guaranteed by the Fifth Amendment to the Constitution.

In two landmark decisions, then, coming near the end of the term in 1954, the Court held that governmentally enforced racial segregation in the public schools was forbidden by the Constitution. Two points should be noted. First, the Court did not in these decisions state that the Constitution commanded governmental *integration* of the schools. It stated only that the policy of forcible segregation by the governments of the nation was invalid. Second, although *Plessy* v. *Ferguson* was not squarely overruled, and the decisions were technically limited to segregation in public education, the Court did say that any language in *Plessy* "contrary to this finding is rejected," and the clear import of the decision was a renunciation of *Plessy*. The final step in overruling *Plessy* was taken in *Gayle* v. *Browder,* 352 U.S. 903 (1956), which held invalid, under the equal protection clause, a city ordinance requiring segregation on motor buses operated within the city of Montgomery, Alabama.

Having held that racial segregation enforced by government in the public schools was unconstitutional, the Court was then faced with the question of how best to implement the decision. As stated in the *Brown* opinion, the Court decided to hear further argument on this question before issuing any enforcement decree. Argument was heard in April 1955, and the opinion and judgments were announced in May 1955.

BROWN *v.* BOARD OF EDUCATION OF TOPEKA
349 U.S. 294 (1955)

Mr. Chief Justice Warren delivered the opinion of the Court.

These cases were decided on May 17, 1954. The opinions of that date, declaring the fundamental principle that racial discrimination in public education is unconstitutional, are incorporated herein by reference. All provisions of federal, state, or local law requiring or permitting such discrimination must yield to this principle. There remains for consideration the manner in which relief is to be accorded.

Because these cases arose under different local conditions and their disposition will involve a variety of local problems, we requested further argument on the question of relief. In view of the nationwide importance of the decision, we invited the Attorney General of the United States and the Attorneys General of all states requiring or permitting racial discrimination in public education to present their views on that question. . . .

These presentations were informative and helpful to the Court in its consideration of the complexities arising from the transition to a system of public education freed of racial discrimination. . . .

Full implementation of these constitutional principles may require solution of varied local school problems. School authorities have the primary responsibility for elucidating, assessing, and solving these problems; courts will have to consider whether the action of school authorities constitutes good faith implementation of the governing constitutional principles. Because of their proximity to local conditions and the possible need for further hearings, the courts which originally heard these cases can best perform this judicial appraisal. Accordingly, we believe it appropriate to remand the cases to those courts.

In fashioning and effectuating the decrees, the courts will be guided by equitable principles. Traditionally, equity has been characterized by a practical flexibility in shaping its remedies and by a facility for adjusting and reconciling public and private needs. These cases call for the exercise of these traditional attributes of equity power. At stake is the personal interest of the plaintiffs in admission to public schools as soon as practicable on a nondiscriminatory basis. To effectuate this interest may call for elimination of a variety of obstacles in making the transition to school systems operated in accordance with the constitutional principles set forth in our May 17, 1954, decision. Courts of equity may properly take into account the public interest in the elimination of such obstacles in a systematic and effective manner. But it should go without saying that the vitality of these constitutional principles cannot be allowed to yield simply because of disagreement with them.

While giving weight to these public and private considerations, the courts will require that the defendants make a prompt and reasonable start toward full compliance with our May 17, 1954 ruling. Once such a start has been made, the courts may find that additional time is necessary to carry out the ruling in an effective manner. The burden rests upon the defendants to establish that such time is necessary in the public interest and is consistent with good faith compliance at the earliest practicable date. To that end, the courts may consider problems related to administration, arising from the physical condition of the school plant, the school transportation system, personnel, revision of school districts and attendance areas into compact units to achieve a system of determining admission to the public schools on a nonracial basis, and revision of local laws and regulations which may be necessary in solving the foregoing problems. They will also consider the adequacy of any plans the defendants may propose to meet these problems and to effectuate a transition to a racially nondiscriminatory school system. During this period of transition, the courts will retain jurisdiction of these cases.

The judgments below, except that in the Delaware case, are accordingly reversed and the cases are remanded to the District Courts to take such proceedings and enter such orders and decrees consistent with this opinion as are necessary and proper to admit to public schools on a racially nondiscriminatory basis with all deliberate speed the parties to these cases. . . .

Despite the fact that *Brown* v. *Board of Education* had been decided ten years earlier, little progress toward desegregation in public schools had been made in the deep South by the time of the passage of the Civil Rights Act of 1964. Title IV of the Act provided for various assistance in the preparation and implementation of plans for the desegregation of public schools and, in addition, provided that the Attorney General could initiate suits to obtain relief for persons denied equal protection in the utilization of public schools or colleges. The primary weapon for ending racial segregation in schools and other federally aided state programs, however, was the Title VI provision for cutting off federal funds as penalty for failure to desegregate. The substantive and main procedural provisions are covered in Sections 601 and 602:

Sec. 601. No person in the United States shall, on the ground of race, color, or national origin, be excluded from participation in, be denied the benefits of, or be subjected to discrimination under any program or activity receiving Federal financial assistance.

Sec. 602. Each Federal department and agency which is empowered to extend Federal financial assistance to any program or activity, by way of grant, loan, or contract other than a contract of insurance or guaranty, is authorized and directed to effectuate the provisions of section 601 with respect to such program or activity by issuing rules, regulations, or orders of general applicability which shall be consistent with achievement of the objectives of the statute authorizing the financial assistance in connection with which the action is taken. No such rule, regulation, or order shall become effective unless and until approved by the President. Compliance with any requirement adopted pursuant to this section may be effected (1) by the termination of or refusal to grant or to continue assistance under such program or activity to any recipient as to whom there has been an express finding on the record, after opportunity for hearing, of a failure to comply with such requirement, but such termination or refusal shall be limited to the particular political entity, or part thereof, or other recipient as to whom such a finding has been made and, shall be limited in its effect to the particular program, or part thereof, in which such noncompliance has been so found, or (2) by any other means authorized by law: *Provided, however,* That no such action shall be taken until the department or agency concerned has advised the appropriate person or persons of the failure to comply with the requirement and has determined that compliance cannot be secured by voluntary means. In the case of any action terminating, or refusing to grant or continue, assistance because of failure to comply with a requirement imposed pursuant to this section, the head of the Federal department or agency shall file with the committees of the House and Senate having legislative jurisdiction over the program or activity involved a full written report of the circumstances and the grounds for such action. No such action shall become effective until thirty days have elapsed after the filing of such report.

On April 29, 1965, the Office of Education of the Department of Health, Education and Welfare issued a statement of policy for the implementation of the Title VI provisions. A key aspect of the policy statement lies in the fact that instead of approaching the problem with a view of *cutting off* funds during the year for school systems which failed to desegrate, the Office of Education demanded that school systems *prove their eligibility* for the funds by filing appropriate plans or court orders for desegregation and assurances of implementation with the Commissioner of Education. The basic requirements of the General Statement of Policies are covered in the following sections:

II. *Methods of Compliance—General.*

Elementary and secondary schools or school systems may qualify for Federal financial assistance by:

A. Executing an Assurance of Compliance (HEW Form 441), if the requirements specified in III below are satisfied; or

B. Submitting a final order of a court of the United States for the desegregation of the school or school system which satisfies the requirements . . . below, together with an Initial Compliance Report . . . ; or

C. Submitting a plan for the desegregation of the school system which the Commissioner of Education determines is adequate to accomplish the purposes of the Civil Rights Act . . . ; together with an Initial Compliance Report . . . ; and

D. Implementing the Assurance, final court order or desegregation plan in good faith so as to effectuate the basic objective set forth in section 601 of Title VI. . . .

III. *Methods of Compliance—Assurance of Compliance (HEW Form 441).*

An Assurance of Compliance . . . that will qualify a school system for Federal financial assistance may not be executed by a school system in which:

A. The race, color, or national origin of pupils is a factor in their initial assignment, reassignment, or transfer to a particular school or class within a school; or

B. Teachers or other staff who serve pupils remain segregated on the basis of the race, color, or national origin of the pupils in a school; or

C. Any activity, facility or other service, including transportation, provided or sponsored by a school system is segregated on the basis of race, color, or national origin; or

D. There remain any other practices characteristic of dual or segregated school systems.

IV. *Methods of Compliance—Court Orders.*

A. A school system subject to a final order of a court of the United States will be eligible for Federal financial assistance only if the order directs desegregation of the school system; it does not suffice if the order merely directs school authorities to admit certain named persons or otherwise fails to require the elimination of a dual or segregated system of schools based on race, color, or national origin. . . .

V. *Methods of Compliance—Plans for the Desegregation of School Systems.*

[Eligibility may be obtained by submitting a desegregation plan which provides for assignment of pupils on the basis of appropriate geographic attendance areas or freedom of choice exercised by the pupil and his parents or a combination of geographic attendance areas and freedom of choice and which also provides for desegregation of all facets of the school system described in Part III, above.]

One of the many responses to the *Brown* decisions was the adoption by some states of some form of "freedom of choice" plan, under which parents could formally designate a choice of schools which their children would attend. Since approval or rejection of such choices was presumably based on strictly nonracial factors, it was argued that the plan was not in violation of the *Brown* decisions barring forced segregation. In the case to follow, however, the Court made a major policy shift and held that states with formerly segregated schools would be required by Constitution to take affirmative steps to *integrate* the public school system rather than merely remaining neutral.

GREEN v. SCHOOL BOARD OF NEW KENT COUNTY
391 U.S. 430 (1968)

Mr. Justice Brennan delivered the opinion of the Court.

The question for decision is whether, under all the circumstances here, respondent School Board's adoption of a "freedom-of-choice" plan which allows a pupil to choose his own public school constitutes adequate compliance with the Board's responsibility "to achieve a system of determining admission to the public schools on a nonracial basis. . .". . . .

Petitioners brought this action in March, 1965, seeking injunctive relief against respondent's continued maintenance of an alleged racially segregated school system. New Kent County is a rural county in Eastern Virginia. About one-half of its population of some 4,500 are Negroes. There is no residential segregation in the county; persons of both races reside throughout. The school system has only two schools, the New Kent school on the east side of the county and the George W. Watkins school on the west side. . . . The School Board operates one white combined elementary and high school (New Kent), and one Negro combined elementary and high school (George W. Watkins). There are no attendance zones. Each school serves the entire county. . . . Under [the State's Pupil Placement Act] children were each year automatically reassigned to the school previously attended unless upon their application the State Board assigned them to another school. . . . To September, 1964, no Negro pupil had applied for admission to the New Kent school under this statute and no white pupil had applied for admission to the Watkins school. . . .

It was such dual systems that 14 years ago *Brown I* held unconstitutional and a year *Brown II* held must be abolished; school boards operating such school systems were *required* by *Brown II* "to effectuate a transition to a racially non-discriminatory school system.". . . It is of course true that for the time immediately after *Brown II* the concern was with making an initial break in a long-established pattern of excluding Negro children from schools attended by white children. The principal focus was on obtaining for those Negro children courageous enough to break with tradition a place in the "white" schools. . . . Under *Brown II* that immediate goal was only the first step, however. The transition to a unitary, nonracial system of public education was and is the ultimate end to be brought about; it was because of the "complexities arising from the transition to a system of public education freed of racial discrimination" that we provided for "all deliberate speed" in the implementation of the principles of *Brown I.* . . .

The School Board contends that it has fully discharged its obligation by adopting a plan by which every student, regardless of race, may "freely" choose the school he will attend. The Board attempts to cast the issue in its broadest form by arguing that its "freedom-of-choice" plan may be faulted only by reading the Fourteenth Amendment as universally requiring "compulsory integration," a reading it insists the wording of the Amendment will not support. But that argument ignores the thrust of *Brown II.* . . . *Brown II* was a call for the dismantling of well-entrenched dual systems tempered by an awareness that complex and multi-faceted problems would arise which would require time and flexibility for a successful resolution. School boards such as the respondent then operating state-compelled dual systems were nevertheless clearly charged with the affirmative duty to take whatever steps might be necessary to convert to a unitary system in which racial discrimination would be eliminated root and branch. . . . The constitutional rights of Negro school children articulated in *Brown I* permit no less than this; and it was to this end that *Brown II* commanded school boards to bend their efforts. . . . The burden on a school board today is to come forward with a plan that promises realistically to work, and promises realistically to work *now.* . . .

We do not hold that "freedom of choice" can have no place in such a plan. We do not hold that a "freedom-of-choice" plan might of itself be unconstitutional, although that argument has been urged upon us. Rather, all we decide today is that in desegregating a dual system a plan utilizing "freedom of choice" is not an end in itself. . . .

The New Kent School Board's "freedom-of-choice" plan cannot be accepted as a sufficient step to "effectuate a transition" to a unitary system. In three years of operation not a single white child has chosen to attend Watkins school and although 115 Negro children enrolled in New Kent school in 1967 . . . 85% of the Negro children in the system still attend the all-Negro Watkins school. In other words, the school system remains a dual system. Rather than further the dismantling of the dual system, the plan has operated simply to burden children and their parents with a responsibility which *Brown II* placed squarely on the School Board. The Board must be required to formulate a new plan and, in light of other courses which appear open to the Board, such as zoning, fashion steps which promise realistically to convert promptly to a system without a "white" school and a "Negro" school, but just schools. . . . [Reversed and remanded.]

It is so ordered.

In response to the *Green* decision, a number of district courts began to include in their desegregation orders a directive that white and black students in different schools be interchanged in order to achieve an integrated, unitary system. The protest over "busing" orders was enormous and led to the examination of that issue in *Swann* in 1971.

SWANN *v.* CHARLOTTE-MECKLENBURG BOARD OF EDUCATION
402 U.S. 1 (1971)

[The Charlotte-Mecklenburg school system, which includes the city of Charlotte, North Carolina, had more than 84,000 students in 107 schools in the 1968–1969 school year. Approximately 29 percent of the pupils were Negro, about two-thirds of whom (some 14,000 students) attended 21 schools which were at least 99 percent Negro. This resulted from a desegregation plan approved by the District Court in 1965, at the start of this litigation. In 1968 petitioner Swann moved for further relief based on *Green* v. *School Board of New Kent County*. The District Court ordered the school board in 1969 to provide a plan for faculty and student desegregation. Finding the board's submission unsatisfactory, the Court appointed an expert (Finger) to submit a desegregation plan. The Court in 1970 adopted the board's plan, as modified, for the junior and senior high schools, and the Finger plan for the elementary schools. The latter plan desegregated all the elementary schools by the technique of grouping two or three outlying schools with one black inner city school, by transporting black students from grades one through four to the outlying white schools, and by transporting white students from the fifth and sixth grades from the outlying white schools to the inner city black school. The Court of Appeals affirmed portions of the order but vacated the order respecting elementary schools, fearing that the plan would unreasonably burden the pupils and the Board.]

Mr. Chief Justice Burger delivered the opinion of the Court.

We granted certiorari in this case to review important issues as to the duties of school authorities and the scope of powers of federal courts under this Court's mandates to eliminate racially separate public schools established and maintained by state action. . . .

This case and those argued with it arose in states having a long history of maintaining two sets of schools in a single school system deliberately operated to carry out a governmental policy to separate pupils in schools solely on the basis of race. That was what *Brown* v. *Board of Education* was all about. These cases present us with the problem of defining in more precise terms than heretofore the scope of the duty of school authorities and district courts in implementing *Brown I* and the mandate to eliminate dual systems and establish unitary systems at once. . . .

The problems encountered by the district courts and courts of appeal make plain that we should now try to amplify guidelines, however incomplete and imperfect, for the assistance of school authorities and courts. . . .

If school authorities fail in their affirmative obligations under these holdings, judicial authority may be invoked. Once a right and a violation have been shown, the scope of a district court's equitable powers to remedy past wrongs is broad, for breadth and flexibility are inherent in equitable remedies. . . .

The school authorities argue that the equity powers of federal district courts have been limited by Title IV of the Civil Rights Act of 1964, 42 U.S.C. Sec. 2000c. The language and the history of Title IV shows that it was not enacted to limit but to define the role of the Federal Government in the implementation of the *Brown I* decision. . . . [Section 2000c-6 provides that "nothing herein shall empower any official or court of the United States to issue any order seeking to achieve a racial balance in any school by requiring the transportation of pupils or students from one school to another . . . to achieve such racial balance. . . ."]

The proviso in Sec. 2000c-6 is in terms designed to foreclose any interpretation of the Act as expanding the *existing* powers of federal courts to enforce the Equal Protection Clause. There is no suggestion of an intention to restrict those powers or withdraw from courts their historic equitable remedial powers. The legislative history of Title IV indicates that Congress was concerned that the Act might be read as creating a right of action under the Fourteenth Amendment in the situation of so-called "de facto segregation," where racial imbalance exists in the schools but with no showing that this was brought about by discriminatory action of state authorities. In short, there is nothing in the Act which provides us material assistance in answering the question of remedy for state-imposed segregation in violation of *Brown I*. The basis of our decision must be the prohibition of the Fourteenth Amendment that no State shall "deny to any person within its jurisdiction the equal protection of the laws.". . .

In *Green,* we pointed out that existing policy and practice with regard to faculty, staff, transportation, extra-curricular activities, and facilities were among the most important indicia of a segregated system. . . . Independent of student assignment, where it is possible to identify a "white school" or a "Negro school" simply by reference to the racial composition of teachers and staff, the quality of school buildings and equipment, or the organization of sports activities, a *prima facie* case of violation of substantive constitutional rights under the Equal Protection Clause is shown. . . .

The construction of new schools and the closing of old ones is one of the most important functions of local school authorities and also one of the most complex. . . . The result of this will be a decision which, when combined with one technique or another of student assignment, will determine the racial composition of the student body in each school in the system. Over the long run, the consequences of the choices will be far reaching. People gravitate toward school facilities, just as schools are located in response to the needs of people. . . . It may well promote segregated residential patterns which, when combined with "neighborhood zoning," further lock the school system into the mold of separation of the races. Upon a proper showing a district court may consider this in fashioning a remedy. . . .

(1) *Racial Balances or Racial Quotas.* . . .

We do not reach in this case the question whether a showing that school segregation is a consequence of other types of state action, without any discriminatory action by the school authorities, is a constitutional violation requiring remedial action by a school desegregation decree. This case does not present that question and we therefore do not decide it. . . .

In this case it is urged that the District Court has imposed a racial balance requirement of 71%–29% on individual schools. The fact that no such objective was actually achieved—and would appear to be impossible—tends to blunt that claim, yet in the opinion and order of the District Court . . . we find that court directing:

"that efforts should be made to reach 71–29 ratio in the various schools so that there will be no basis for contending that one school is racially different from the others. . . ."

The District Judge went on to acknowledge that variation "from that norm may be unavoidable." This contains intimations that the "norm" is a fixed mathematical racial balance reflecting the pupil constituency of the system. If we were to read the holding of the District Court to require, as a matter of substantive constitutional right, any particular degree of racial balance or mixing, that approach would be disapproved and we would be obliged to reverse. The constitutional command to desegregate schools does not mean that every school in every community must always reflect the racial composition of the school system as a whole. . . .

Awareness of the racial composition of the whole school system is likely to be a useful starting point in shaping a remedy to correct past constitutional violations. In sum, the very limited use made of mathematical ratios was within the equitable remedial discretion of the District Court.

(2) *One-Race Schools.*

The record in this case reveals that familiar phenomenon that in metropolitan areas minority groups are often found concentrated in one part of the city. . . . Schools all or predominately of one race in a district of mixed population will require close scrutiny to determine that school assignments are not part of state-enforced segregation.

In light of the above, it should be clear that the existence of some small number of one-race, or virtually one-race, schools within a district is not in and of itself the mark of a system which still practices segregation by law. . . .

The court should scrutinize such schools, and the burden upon the school authorities will be to satisfy the court that their racial composition is not the result of present or past discriminatory action on their part. . . .

(3) *Remedial Altering of Attendance Zones.*

The maps submitted in these cases graphically demonstrate that one of the principal tools employed by school planners and by courts to break up the dual school system has been a frank—and sometimes drastic—gerrymandering of school districts and attendance zones. An additional step was pairing, "clustering," or "grouping" of schools with attendance assignments made deliberately to accomplish the transfer of Negro students out of formerly segregated Negro schools and transfer of white students to formerly all-Negro schools. More often than not, these zones are neither compact nor contiguous; indeed they may be on opposite ends of the city. As an interim corrective measure, this cannot be said to be beyond the broad remedial powers of a court.

Absent a constitutional violation there would be no basis for judicially ordering assignment of students on a racial basis. All things being equal, with no history of discrimination, it might well be desirable to assign pupils to schools nearest their homes. But all things are not equal in a system that has been deliberately constructed and maintained to enforce racial segregation. The remedy for such segregation may be administratively awkward, inconvenient, and even bizarre in some situations and may impose burdens on some; but all awkwardness and inconvenience cannot be avoided in the interim period when remedial adjustments are being made to eliminate the dual school systems. . . .

We hold that the pairing and grouping of noncontiguous school zones is a permissible tool and such action is to be considered in light of the objectives sought. . . .

(4) *Transportation of Students.*

The scope of permissible transportation of students as an implement of a remedial decree has never been defined by this Court and by the very nature of the problem it cannot be defined with precision. No rigid guidelines as to student transportation can be given for application to the infinite variety of problems presented in thousands of situations. . . . The District Court's conclusion that assignment of children to the school nearest their home serving their grade would not produce an effective dismantling of the dual system is supported by the record.

Thus the remedial techniques used in the District Court's order were within that court's power to provide equitable relief; implementation of the decree is well within the capacity of the school authority.

The decree provided that the buses used to implement the plan would operate on direct routes. . . . The trips for elementary school pupils average about seven miles and the District Court found that they would take "not over 35 minutes at the most." This system compares favorably with the transportation plan previously operated in Charlotte under which each day 23,600 students on all grade levels were transported an average of 15 miles one way for an average trip requiring over an hour. In these circumstances, we find no basis for holding that the local school authorities may not be required to employ bus transportation as one tool of school desegregation. Desegregation plans cannot be limited to the walk-in school.

An objection to transportation of students may have validity when the time or distance of travel is so great as to risk either the health of the children or significantly impinge on the educational process. District courts must weigh the soundness of any transportation plan in light of what is said in subdivisions (1), (2), and (3) above. . . .

On the facts of this case, we are unable to conclude that the order of the District Court is not reasonable, feasible and workable. . . .

It does not follow that the communities served by such systems will remain demographically stable, for in a growing, mobile society, few will do so. Neither school authorities nor district courts are constitutionally required to make year-by-year adjustments of the racial composition of student bodies once the affirmative duty to desegregate has been accomplished and racial discrimination through official action is eliminated from the system. This does not mean that federal courts are without power to deal with future problems; but in the absence of a showing that either the school authorities or some other agency of the State has deliberately attempted to fix or alter demographic patterns to affect the racial composition of the schools, further intervention by a district court should not be necessary. . . .

The order of the District Court . . . is . . . affirmed.

It is so ordered.

In 1976 the Court cited with approval the statement in *Swann* that annual adjustments would not be constitutionally required of school districts in order to maintain a given racial composition. The Pasadena, California, Board of Education was ordered by a federal District Court in 1970 to implement a desegregation plan which would provide that there would be no school "with a majority of any minority students." In 1974 the District Court stated that such requirement was an inflexible one to be applied anew each school year even though changes in the racial mix were occasioned by the operation of normal demographic factors beyond the control of the Board. In *Pasadena City Board of Education* v. *Spanger,* 44 L.W. 5114 (1976), the Court reversed, holding that where shifts in the racial composition of schools resulted from changes in the residential patterns of the city and were not attributable to any segregative action on the part of school officials, neither the school officials nor the District Court "were constitutionally required to make year-by-year adjustments of racial composition of student bodies once the affirmative duty to desegregate has been accomplished and racial discrimination through official action is eliminated from the system."

As the Southern public schools began to achieve substantial integration, attention was directed to systems outside the South, many of which, especially in the North, were far more segregated than the reordered systems in the South. *Swann* suggested that where segregation was *de facto* only, as a result of residential housing patterns of one-race neighborhoods rather than as a result of governmental policy, the Court would not necessarily require the "elimination root and branch" of the segregated school system. More and more Negroes, and many Southern whites, began to point out that if segregation was wrong in the public schools, and if a unitary system was in fact required by the Constitution, then the rule should apply throughout the country, irrespective of whether segregation had developed *de jure, de facto,* or in any other manner. In his impassioned statement regarding segregated school systems in *Brown I,* Chief Justice Warren said, "To separate them from others of similar age and qualifications solely because of their race generates a feeling of inferiority as to their status in the community that may affect their hearts and minds in a way unlikely ever to be undone." And if racially segregated neighborhoods lead to racially segregated schools, it was argued, then the same damage is done and it is immaterial whether the result was produced by purposeful governmental policy or not. In fact, evidence began to accumulate that in some areas outside the South governmental units had encouraged the development of segregated schools by such devices as the location of new schools and the drawing of attendance lines. One such case involved Denver, Colorado, and came to the Court as *Keyes* v. *School District No. 1* in 1973.

KEYES *v.* SCHOOL DISTRICT NO. 1
413 U.S. 921 (1973)

[Petitioners filed suit in District Court for an order directing the desegregation of the schools in the Park Hill area of Denver, Colorado, and also "for the School

District as a whole." The court found that for a period of almost a decade, the School Board had engaged in an unconstitutional policy of deliberate racial segregation with respect to the Park Hill schools. The court issued the order to desegregate those schools, but as to the remaining areas, the court fractionated the district and held that petitioners had to make a fresh showing of de jure segregation in each area of the city for which they sought relief. The court found that petitioners did not prove that the Board had followed a like policy with respect to the core city or other areas within the district. Nevertheless, the court went on to hold that the proofs established that the segregated core city schools were educationally inferior to the predominantly white schools in other parts of the district. Therefore, although all-out desegregation would not be decreed, the decree did demand some desegregation and certain educational improvements for those schools. The Court of Appeals affirmed the Park Hill order but reversed the order respecting the core city schools.]

Mr. Justice Brennan delivered the opinion of the Court. . . .

. . . We have never suggested that plaintiffs in school desegregation cases must bear the burden of proving the elements of de jure segregation as to each and every school or each and every student within the school system. Rather, we have held that where plaintiffs prove that a current condition of segregated schooling exists within a school district where a dual system was compelled or authorized by statute at the time of our decision in *Brown* v. *Board of Education,* . . . the State automatically assumes an affirmative duty "to effectuate a transition to a racially nondiscriminatory school system," . . . that is, to eliminate from the public schools within their school system "all vestiges of state-imposed segregation." . . .

This is not a case, however, where a statutory dual system has ever existed. Nevertheless, where plaintiffs prove that the school authorities have carried out a systematic program of segregation affecting a substantial portion of the students, schools, teachers, and facilities within the school system, it is only common sense to conclude that there exists a predicate for a finding of the existence of a dual school system. Several considerations support this conclusion. First, it is obvious that a practice of concentrating Negroes in certain schools by structuring attendance zones or designating "feeder" schools on the basis of race has the reciprocal effect of keeping other nearby schools predominantly white. Similarly, the practice of building a school . . . to a certain size and in a certain location, "with conscious knowledge that it would be a segregated school," . . . has a substantial reciprocal effect on the racial composition of other schools. So also, the use of mobile classrooms, the drafting of student transfer policies, the transportation of students, and the assignment of faculty and staff, on racially identifiable bases, have the clear effect of earmarking schools according to their racial composition, and this, in turn, together with the elements of student assignment and school construction, may have a profound reciprocal effect on the racial composition of residential neighborhoods within a metropolitan area, thereby causing further racial concentration within the schools. . . .

In short, common sense dictates the conclusion that racially inspired school board actions have an impact beyond the particular schools that are the subjects of those actions. . . . [P]roof of state-imposed segregation in a substantial portion of the district will suffice to support a finding by the trial court of the existence of a dual system. Of course, where that finding is made, as in cases involving statutory dual systems, the school authorities have an affirmative duty "to effectuate a transition to a racially nondiscriminatory school system." . . .

On remand, therefore, the District Court should decide in the first instance whether respondent School Board's deliberate racial segregation policy with respect to the Park Hill schools constitutes the entire Denver school system a dual school system. . . .

The District Court proceeded on the premise that the finding as to the Park Hill schools was irrelevant to the consideration of the rest of the district, and began its examination of the core city schools by requiring that petitioners prove all of the essential elements of de jure segregation—that is, stated simply, a current condition of segregation resulting from intentional state action directed specifically to the core city schools. . . .

Although petitioners had already proved the existence of intentional school segregation in the Park Hill schools, this crucial finding was totally ignored when attention turned to the core city schools. Plainly, a finding of intentional segregation as to a portion of a school system is not devoid of probative value in assessing the school authorities' intent with respect to other parts of the same school system. On the contrary, where, as here, the case involves one school board, a finding of intentional segregation on its part in one portion of a school system is highly relevant to the issue of the board's intent with respect to other segregated schools in the system. . . .

Applying these principles in the special context of school desegregation cases, we hold that a finding of intentionally segregative school board actions in a meaningful portion of a school system, as in this case, creates a presumption that other segregated schooling within the system is not adventitious. It establishes, in other words, a prima facie case of unlawful segregative design on the part of school authorities, and shifts to those authorities the burden of proving that other segregated schools within the system are not also the result of intentionally segregative actions. This is true even if it is determined that different areas of the school district should be viewed independently of each other because, even in that situation, there is high probability that where school authorities have effectuated an intentionally segregative policy in a meaningful portion of the school system, similar impermissible considerations have motivated their actions in other areas of the system. We emphasize that the differentiating factor between de jure segregation and so-called de facto segregation to which we referred in *Swann* is *purpose* or *intent* to segregate. . . .

In discharging that burden, it is not enough, of course, that the school authorities rely upon some allegedly logical, racially neutral explanation for their actions. Their burden is to adduce proof sufficient to support a finding that segregative intent was not among the factors that motivated their actions. The courts below attributed much significance to the fact that many of the Board's actions in the core city area antedated our decision in *Brown*. We reject any suggestion that remoteness in time has any relevance to the issue of intent. If the actions of school authorities were to any degree motivated by segregative intent and the segregation resulting from those actions continues to exist, the fact of remoteness in time certainly does not make those actions any less "intentional.". . .

. . . If the District Court determines that the Denver school system is a dual school system, respondent School Board has the affirmative duty to desegregate the entire system "root and branch.". . . If the District determines, however, that the Denver school system is not a dual school system by reason of the Board's actions in Park Hill, the court . . . will afford respondent School Board the opportunity to rebut petitioners' prima facie case of intentional segregation in the core city schools raised by the finding of intentional segregation in the Park Hill schools. . . . If respondent Board fails to rebut petitioners' prima facie case, the District Court must, as in the case of Park Hill, decree all-out desegregation of the core city schools. . . .

Mr. Chief Justice Burger concurs in the result.

Mr. Justice White took no part in the decision of this case.

Mr. Justice Douglas.
While I join the opinion of the Court, I agree with my Brother Powell that there is, for the purpose of the Equal Protection Clause of the Fourteenth Amendment as applied to the school cases, no difference between de facto and de jure segregation. The school board is a state agency and the lines that it draws, the locations it selects for school sites, the allocation it makes of students, the budgets it prepares are state action for Fourteenth Amendment purposes. . . .

Mr. Justice Powell concurring in part and dissenting in part.
I concur in the remand of this case for further proceedings in the District Court, but on grounds that differ from those relied upon by the Court.
This is the first school desegregation case to reach this Court which involves a major city outside the South. It comes from Denver, Colorado, a city and a State which have not operated public schools under constitutional or statutory provisions which mandated or permitted racial segregation. . . . The Court has inquired only to what extent the Denver public school authorities may have contributed to the school segregation which is acknowledged to exist in Denver. . . .
The situation in Denver is generally comparable to that in other large cities across the country in which there is a substantial minority population and where desegregation has not been ordered by the federal courts. There is segregation in the schools of many of these cities fully as pervasive as that in southern cities prior to the desegregation decrees of the past decade and a half. The focus of the school desegregation problem has now shifted from the South to the country as a whole. Unwilling and footdragging as the process was in most places, substantial progress toward achieving integration has been made in southern States.* No comparable progress has been made in many nonsouthern cities with large minority populations primarily because of the de facto/de jure distinction nurtured by the courts and accepted complacently by many of the same voices which denounced the evils of segregated schools in the South. But if our national concern is for those who attend such schools, rather than for perpetuating a legalism rooted in history rather than present reality, we must recognize that the evil of operating separate schools is no less in Denver than in Atlanta.
In my view we should abandon a distinction which long since has outlived its time, and formulate constitutional principles of national rather than merely regional application. . . . In a series of decisions extending from 1954 to 1971 the concept of state neutrality was transformed into the present constitutional doctrine requiring affirmative state action to desegregate school systems. The keystone case was *Green* v. *County School Board,* . . . where school boards were declared to have "the affirmative duty to take whatever steps might be necessary to convert to a unitary system in which racial discrimination would be eliminated root and branch.". . .
[T]he doubt as to whether the affirmative-duty concept would flower into a new constitutional principle of general application was laid to rest by *Swann* v. *Charlotte-Mecklenburg Board of Education,* . . . in which the duty articulated in

---

* According to the 1971 [HEW] estimate, 43.9% of Negro pupils attended majority white schools in the South as opposed to only 27.8% who attended such schools in the North and West. Fifty-seven percent of all Negro pupils in the North and West attend schools with over 80% minority population as opposed to 32.2% who do so in the South. . . .

Green was applied to the urban school system of metropolitan Charlotte, North Carolina. . . .

In *Swann,* the Court further noted it was concerned only with States having "a long history" of officially imposed segregation and the duty of school authorities in those States to implement *Brown I.* . . . In so doing, the Court refrained from even considering whether the evolution of constitutional doctrine from *Brown I* to *Green/Swann* undercut whatever logic once supported the de facto/de jure distinction. In imposing on metropolitan southern school districts an affirmative duty, entailing large-scale transportation of pupils, to eliminate segregation in the schools, the Court required these districts to alleviate conditions which in large part did *not* result from historic, state-imposed de jure segregation. Rather, the familiar root cause of segregated schools in *all* the biracial metropolitan areas of our country is essentially the same: one of segregated residential and migratory patterns the impact of which on the racial composition of the schools was often perpetuated and rarely ameliorated by action of public school authorities. This is a national, not a southern, phenomenon. And it is largely unrelated to whether a particular State had or did not have segregative schools laws.

Whereas *Brown I* rightly decreed the elimination of state-imposed segregation in that particular section of the country where it did exist, *Swann* imposed obligations on southern school districts to eliminate conditions which are not regionally unique but are similar both in origin and effect to conditions in the rest of the country. As the remedial obligations of *Swann* extend far beyond the elimination of the outgrowths of the state-imposed segregation outlawed in *Brown,* the rationale of Swann points inevitably toward a uniform, constitutional approach to our national problem of school segregation.

The Court's decision today, while adhering to the de jure/de facto distinction, will require the application of the *Green/Swann* doctrine of "affirmative duty" to the Denver School Board despite the absence of any history of state-mandated school segregation. . . . I concur in the Court's position that the public school authorities are the responsible agency of the State, and that if the affirmative-duty doctrine is sound constitutional law for Charlotte, it is equally so for Denver. I would not, however, perpetuate the de jure/de facto distinction nor would I leave to petitioners the initial tortuous effort of identifying "segregative acts" and deducing "segregative intent." I would hold, quite simply, that where segregated public schools exist within a school district to a substantial degree, there is a prima facie case that the duly constituted public authorities . . . are sufficiently responsible to warrant imposing upon them a nationally applicable burden to demonstrate they nevertheless are operating a genuinely integrated school system.

The principal reason for abandonment of the de jure/de facto distinction is that, in view of the evolution of the holding in *Brown I* into the affirmative-duty doctrine, the distinction no longer can be justified on a principled basis. In decreeing remedial requirements for the Charlotte-Mecklenburg school district, *Swann* dealt with a metropolitan, urbanized area in which the basic causes of segregation were generally similar to those in all sections of the country, and also largely irrelevant to the existence of historic, state-imposed segregation at the time of the *Brown* decision. Further, the extension of the affirmative-duty concept to include compulsory student transportation went well beyond the mere remedying of that portion of school segregation for which former state segregation laws were ever responsible. Moreover, as the Court's opinion today abundantly demonstrates, the facts deemed necessary to establish de jure discrimination present problems of subjective intent which the courts cannot fairly resolve. . . .

Public schools are creatures of the State, and whether the segregation is state-created or state-assisted or merely state-perpetuated should be irrelevant to constitutional principle. . . .

It makes little sense to find prima facie violations and the consequent affirmative duty to desegregate solely in those States with state-imposed segregation at the time of the *Brown* decision. The history of state-imposed segregation is more widespread in our country than the de jure/de facto distinction has traditionally cared to recognize. . . .

As the Court's opinion virtually compels the finding on remand that Denver has a "dual school system," that city will then be under an "affirmative duty" to desegregate its entire system "root and branch.". . . Again, the critical question is what ought this constitutional duty to entail. . . .

To the extent that *Swann* may be thought to require large-scale or long-distance transportation of students in our metropolitan school districts, I record my profound misgivings. Nothing in our Constitution commands or encourages any such court-compelled disruption of public education. . . . In the balancing of interests so appropriate to a fair and just equitable decree, transportation orders should be applied with special caution to any proposal as disruptive of family life and interests—and ultimately of education itself—as extensive transportation of elementary-age children solely for desegregation purposes. . . .

The existing state of law has failed to shed light and provide guidance on the two issues addressed in this opinion: (i) whether a constitutional rule of uniform, national application should be adopted with respect to our national problem of school desegregation and (ii), if so, whether the ambiguities of *Swann*, construed to date almost uniformly in favor of extensive transportation, should be redefined to restore a more viable balance among the various interests which are involved. With all deference, it seems to me that the Court today has addressed neither of these issues in a way that will afford adequate guidance to the courts below in this case or lead to a rational, coherent national policy. . . .

Mr. Justice Rehnquist, dissenting. . . .

Milliken v. *Bradley*, 418 U.S. 717 (1974), dealt with an attempt to desegregate the public schools in the city of Detroit. The District Court ultimately concluded that the defendant school system had engaged in unconstitutional activities which had resulted in de jure segregation in the city school district. The court ordered the submission of desegregation plans for the city alone, and also for the three-county metropolitan area, even though the suburban school districts were not parties to the action and there was no claim that they had committed any constitutional violations. The court concluded that to effectively desegregate the Detroit schools it would be necessary to include neighboring districts as well, and ordered the preparation of a plan with a desegregation area including 53 suburban school districts plus Detroit and with the acquisition of a number of school buses to transport students between and among the various districts to achieve integration. The Supreme Court reversed by a five-to-four vote, holding that a federal court could not properly impose a multi-district, areawide remedy to a single district de jure segregation problem unless it was first established that unconstitutional racially discriminatory acts of the other districts had caused inter-district segregation, or that district lines—which could not be considered as mere arbitrary lines drawn for political convenience—had been deliberately drawn on the basis of race. The dissenters pointed out that the majority decision left the District Court with no effective remedy for correcting widespread and pervasive segregation in the metropolitan area, since a remedy limited to the city of Detroit would probably result in the Detroit school system becoming a substantially all-Negro system by increasing flight of whites from the city to the suburbs.

Private Discrimination

Hard on the heels of the second *Brown* decision the Court in 1956, in *Gayle* v. *Browder,* extended the *Brown* rule to the field of transportation, and thus to all areas under governmental regulation. By 1956, then, the Court had officially ruled that any governmentally imposed policy of segregation by race in any area of activity was in violation of the equal protection of the laws. In addition, the transportation cases involving interstate commerce, discussed earlier in this chapter, had laid down a firm rule that racial discrimination in interstate carriers or in restaurant and terminal facilities operated in conjunction with an interstate carrier violated the nondiscrimination clause of the Interstate Commerce Act. Thus the second broad avenue of attack on racial segregation—that separated facilities required by law were not equal—resulted in a firm holding that the separate but equal doctrine was unconstitutional.

Such decisions, however, only affected practices in the public sector or those properly brought by Congress within the application of its commerce power. There still remained an enormous area of private or quasi-public operations in which race discrimination was practiced and which could not readily be fitted into the framework of decisions relating to enforcement of racially discriminatory legislation or governmental regulations. For these areas a third attack was developed in the courts. The basic approach was fairly simple, although the development of the legal doctrines to support it required a great deal of expert legal scholarship and sustained pressure-group strategy of a kind peculiar to the process of "judicial lobbying." [For an account of this aspect of litigation, see Clement Vose, *Caucasians Only: The Supreme Court, the N.A.A.C.P., and the Restrictive Covenant Cases* (Berkeley: University of California Press, 1959).] The approach was simply to bring as much activity as possible within the concept of "state action" rather than private action. The Fourteenth Amendment bars racial discrimination imposed by "state action," so the more agencies and activities which could be classified within that category, the fewer sectors would remain in which discrimination could validly be carried on under the Constitution.

The first area of attack under this approach was racial discrimination in the Democratic primaries in the South, with a long series of cases beginning in the 1920s and culminating in a square holding in 1953 that a Democratic primary was a governmental institution and that no person could be barred from participation because of his race. (The voting cases will be discussed in the following chapter.) Since a political right was involved, and since the Fifteenth Amendment clearly prohibited governmental discrimination based on race in voting, it did not require the abrogation of the "separate but equal" doctrine to support the Negro claimant's argument. Thus in the category of political and property rights the "state action" approach could be, and was, utilized even before the demise of "separate but equal." Once the claimed right was clearly brought into the magic circle of political and property rights, it was then only necessary to make a proper showing that the denial of the right was in some fair manner carried out under the aegis of governmental authority and a decision could be obtained that racially discriminatory enforcement would violate the Fourteenth and Fifteenth Amendments.

It was pointed out earlier that following the decision in *Buchanan* v. *Warley,* holding that racial zoning by ordinance violated the Fourteenth Amendment, the practice developed of incorporating racially restrictive covenants in deeds conveying property. By the terms of the contract, a buyer of such property would agree never to sell the property to persons of African descent, or Oriental descent, or whatever other nationality the covenant excluded. Presumably, if the buyer violated the agreement and attempted to convey the property to a person in the excluded category, the original seller could file an action in a court of equity and have the later conveyance set aside. But this raised an interesting constitutional issue. Does the participation of the state, in a judicial proceeding setting aside a contract as contrary to a racially restrictive covenant, inject sufficient governmental activity into the transaction to bring it within the category of "state action" within the meaning of the Fourteenth Amendment? If so, then the rule of *Buchanan* v. *Warley* should govern and such participation should be unconstitutional. If not, then the Fourteenth Amendment would not apply, and private discrimination is not barred by the Constitution. After a number of abortive attempts to present the issue before the United States Supreme Court, various organizations interested in the problem of discrimination in residential property were successful in bringing two cases to the Court for decision in 1948. The cases were *Shelley* v. *Kraemer* and *McGhee* v. *Sipes,* and they illustrate clearly the attack on discrimination through broadening the scope of coverage of "state action."

SHELLEY *v.* KRAEMER
334 U.S. 1 (1948)

Mr. Chief Justice Vinson delivered the opinion of the Court.

These cases present for our consideration questions relating to the validity of court enforcement of private agreements, generally described as restrictive covenants, which have as their purpose the exclusion of persons of designated race or color from the ownership or occupancy of real property. Basic constitutional issues of obvious importance have been raised. . . .

I

Whether the equal protection clause of the Fourteenth Amendment inhibits judicial enforcement by state courts of restrictive covenants based on race or color is a question which this Court has not heretofore been called upon to consider. . . .

It cannot be doubted that among the civil rights intended to be protected from discriminatory state action by the Fourteenth Amendment are the rights to acquire, enjoy, own, and dispose of property. Equality in the enjoyment of property rights was regarded by the framers of that Amendment as an essential pre-condition to the realization of other basic civil rights and liberties which the Amendment was intended to guarantee. . . .

This Court has given specific recognition to the same principle. *Buchanan* v. *Warley,* 245 U.S. 60 (1917).

It is likewise clear that restrictions on the right of occupancy of the sort sought to be created by the private agreements in these cases could not be squared with the requirements of the Fourteenth Amendment if imposd by state statute or local ordinance. . . .

But the present cases, unlike those just discussed, do not involve action by state legislatures or city councils. Here the particular patterns of discrimination and the areas in which the restrictions are to operate, are determined, in the first instance, by the terms of agreements among private individuals. Participation of the State consists in the enforcement of the restrictions so defined. The crucial issue with which we are here confronted is whether this distinction removes these cases from the operation of the prohibitory provisions of the Fourteenth Amendment.

Since the decision of this Court in the *Civil Rights Cases,* 109 U.S. 3 (1883), the principle has become firmly embedded in our constitutional law that the action inhibited by the first section of the Fourteenth Amendment is only such action as may fairly be said to be that of the States. That Amendment erects no shield against merely private conduct, however discriminatory or wrongful. We conclude, therefore, that the restrictive agreements standing alone cannot be regarded as violative of any rights guaranteed to petitioners by the Fourteenth Amendment. So long as the purposes of those agreements are effectuated by voluntary adherence to their terms, it would appear clear that there has been no action by the State and the provisions of the Amendment have not been violated. . . .

But here there was more. These are cases in which the purposes of the agreements were secured only by judicial enforcement by the state courts of the restrictive terms of the agreements. The respondents urge that judicial enforcement of private agreements does not amount to state action; or, in any event, the participation of the State is so attenuated in character as not to amount to state action within the meaning of the Fourteenth Amendment. Finally, it is suggested, even if the States in these cases may be deemed to have acted in the constitutional sense, their action did not deprive petitioners of rights guaranteed by the Fourteenth Amendment. We move to a consideration of these matters.

II

That the action of state courts and judicial officers in their official capacities is to be regarded as action of the State within the meaning of the Fourteenth Amendment, is a proposition which has long been established by decisions of this Court. That principle was given expression in the earlier cases involving the construction of the terms of the Fourteenth Amendment.. . .

III

Against this background of judicial construction, extending over a period of some three-quarters of a century, we are called upon to consider whether enforcement by state courts of the restrictive agreements in these cases may be deemed to be the acts of those States; and if so, whether that action has denied these petitioners the equal protection of the laws which the Amendment was intended to secure.

We have no doubt that there has been state action in these cases in the full and complete sense of the phrase. The undisputed facts disclose that petitioners were willing purchasers of properties upon which they desired to establish homes. The owners of the properties were willing sellers; and contracts of sale were accordingly consummated. It is clear that but for the active intervention of the state courts, supported by the full panoply of state power, petitioners would have been free to occupy the properties in question without restraint.

These are not cases, as has been suggested, in which the States have merely abstained from action, leaving private individuals free to impose such discriminations as they see fit. Rather, these are cases in which the States have made available to such individuals the full coercive power of government to deny to petitioners, on the grounds of race or color, the enjoyment of property rights in premises which petitioners are willing and financially able to acquire and which the grantors are willing to sell. . . .

The enforcement of the restrictive agreements by the state courts in these cases was directed pursuant to the common-law policy of the States as formulated by those courts in earlier decisions. . . . We have noted that previous decisions of this Court have established the proposition that judicial action is not immunized from the operation of the Fourteenth Amendment simply because it is taken pursuant to the state's common-law policy. Nor is the Amendment ineffective simply because the particular pattern of discrimination, which the State has enforced, was defined initially by the terms of a private agreement. State action, as that phrase is understood for the purposes of the Fourteenth Amendment, refers to exertions of state power in all forms. And when the effect of that action is to deny rights subject to the protection of the Fourteenth Amendment, it is the obligation of this Court to enforce the constitutional commands.

We hold that in granting judicial enforcement of the restrictive agreements in these cases, the States have denied petitioners the equal protection of the laws and that, therefore, the action of the state courts cannot stand. . . .

Reversed.

Mr. Justice Reed, Mr. Justice Jackson, and Mr. Justice Rutledge took no part in the consideration or decision of these cases.

Since the Court stated that the covenants were not violative of the Constitution but that state enforcement of such clauses was, the *Shelley* decision resulted in a revised method of attempting to maintain racially restrictive covenants. *Barrows* v. *Jackson,* 346 U.S. 249 (1953), raised the question of whether the state violated the Fourteenth Amendment by permitting an action for damages for breach of contract to be maintained in its courts against a property owner who conveyed the property in violation of a racial covenant. A California property owner sold a home to a Negro, contrary to the deed restrictions. She was sued by three neighbors on the ground that the value of their property had dropped sharply since Negroes moved in. The Court held that since California could not incorporate in a statute or enforce in equity such discriminatory policies, it could not furnish its coercive power to force payment of damages and thereby accomplish the same result.

The *Shelley* decision also had its impact on federal policies which affected housing. The national government has provided both for supervision of mortgage lenders and for assistance in financing homes. The Fourteenth Amendment does not reach private discrimination, but national power to support and regulate lending practices extends to the individual pieces of property covered by such loans or financial support. A year and a half after *Shelley,* the FHA ruled that it would not provide mortgage insurance for property on which racially restrictive covenants were recorded after February 15, 1950

[FHA *Underwriting Manual,* sec. 303 (December 1949).] This represented a substantial change in policy, since the earlier *Manual* even contained a model restrictive covenant. The VA has followed similar policies designed to promote open occupancy without respect to race. These kinds of pressures are relatively slight to date, but they illustrate the fact that the executive branch can pick up where the courts leave off and can employ additional tools to further a policy of equal opportunity irrespective of race. [For additional material on government and housing, see the 1961 United States Commission on Civil Rights Report No. 4, *Housing* (Washington: United States Government Printing Office, 1961).]

The decisions in *Shelley* and *Barrows* stimulated further litigation in the program to attack racial discrimination via the "state action" route. *Burton* v. *Wilmington Park Authority,* 365 U.S. 715 (1961), raised the question of whether the policy of racial discrimination followed by a private leaseholder of state property in operating a restaurant was "state action" barred by the Fourteenth Amendment. Eagle Coffee Shoppe, Inc., was a restaurant located in a state-owned automobile parking building in Wilmington, Delaware. The Wilmington Parking Authority, a state agency, leased a portion of the building to Eagle for twenty years, renewable for another ten. The lease contained no requirement that the restaurant services be made available to the general public on a nondiscriminatory basis, and Eagle refused to serve Negroes. In an action for injunctive relief, petitioner claimed that in the circumstances of the lease of state property to serve the public, the action of Eagle was state action violative of the equal protection clause of the Fourteenth Amendment. The Delaware Supreme Court held that Eagle was acting in "a purely private capacity" under its lease, that its action was not that of the Authority, and therefore the discriminatory policies were not furthered by state action within the contemplation of the Fourteenth Amendment. The United States Supreme Court reversed. Pointing out some of the interrelationships between the Parking Authority and Eagle, Justice Clark, speaking for the majority, stated, "The State has so far insinuated itself into a position of interdependence with Eagle that it must be recognized as a joint participant in the challenged activity, which, on that account, cannot be considered to have been so 'purely private' as to fall without the scope of the Fourteenth Amendment."

[The "state action" problem has been discussed in the context of federal legislative power in Chapter 3.]

The California experience with the controversial area of open-housing policy presented a novel aspect of the combination of state action and private discrimination. The problem came to the Court in 1967 in *Reitman* v. *Mulkey.*

REITMAN *v.* MULKEY
387 U.S. 369 (1967)

[In 1959 California passed the Unruh Act guaranteeing equal accommodations, without regard to race, color, or religion, "in all business establishments of every kind whatsoever," and providing for actions for damages for violation of the law. In 1963 the California legislature adopted the Rumford Fair Housing Act, which prohibited racial discrimination in the sale or rental of any private dwelling containing more than four units. In 1964, however, by initiative, the voters of California adopted a constitutional amendment, Art. I, §26, providing in part as follows: "Neither the State nor any subdivision or agency thereof shall deny, limit or abridge, directly or indirectly, the right of any person, who is willing or desires to sell, lease or rent any part or all of his real property, to decline to sell, lease or rent such property to such person or persons as he, in his absolute discretion, chooses."

The real property covered by the amendment was limited to residential property and contained an exception for state-owned real estate. Petitioners sued under the equal accommodations guarantees of the Unruh Act, alleging that they had been refused apartment accommodations solely on account of their race. An injunction and damages were demanded. Defendants moved for summary judgment on the ground that the equal accommodations sections had been made inapplicable to the renting of apartments by the adoption of §26 of Art. I of the constitution. The trial court granted the motion, and the California Supreme Court reversed, holding the amendment invalid under the Fourteenth Amendment equal protection clause.]

Mr. Justice White delivered the opinion of the Court. . . .

We affirm the judgments of the California Supreme Court. . . .

To reach this result, the state court examined certain prior decisions in this Court in which discriminatory state action was identified. Based on these cases, . . . it concluded that a prohibited state involvement could be found "even where the state can be charged with only encouraging," rather than commanding discrimination. . . . The judgment of the California court was that §26 unconstitutionally involves the State in racial discriminations and is therefore invalid under the Fourteenth Amendment. . . .

The California court could very reasonably conclude that §26 would and did have wider impact than a mere repeal of existing statutes. . . . The right to discriminate, including the right to discriminate on racial grounds, was now embodied in the State's basic charter, immune from legislative, executive, or judicial regulation at any level of the state government. Those practicing racial discriminations need no longer rely soley on their personal choice. They could now invoke express constitutional authority, free from censure or interference of any kind from official sources. . . .

. . . Here the California court, armed as it was with the knowledge of the facts and circumstances concerning the passage and potential impact of §26, and familiar with the milieu in which that provision would operate, has determined that the provision would involve the State in private racial discriminations to an unconstitutional degree. We accept this holding of the California court. . . .

. . . Here we are dealing with a provision which does not just repeal an existing law forbidding private racial discriminations. Section 26 was intended to authorize, and does authorize, racial discrimination in the housng market. The right to discriminate is now one of the basic policies of the State. The California Supreme Court believes that the section will significantly encourage and involve the State in private discriminations. We have been presented with no persuasive considerations indicating that this judgment should be overturned.

Mr. Justice Harlan, whom Mr. Justice Black, Mr. Justice Clark, and Mr. Justice Stewart join, dissenting. . . .

This type of alleged state involvement, simply evincing a refusal to involve itself at all, is of course very different from that illustrated in such cases as *Lombard, Peterson, Evans,* and *Burton, supra,* where the Court found active involvement of state agencies and officials in specific acts of discrimination. It is also quite different from cases in which a state enactment could be said to have the obvious purpose of fostering discrimination. . . . I believe the state action required to bring the Fourteenth Amendment into operation must be affirmative and purposeful, actively fostering discrimination. Only in such a case is ostensibly "private" action more properly labeled "official." I do not believe that the mere enactment of §26, on the showing made here, falls within this class of cases. . . .

More recently, in *Jones* v. *Alfred' Mayer Co.,* 392 U.S. 409 (1968), the Court upheld the validity of an 1866 Act of Congress (now 42 U.S.C. §1982) which guaranteed to all citizens the same right enjoyed by white citizens to inherit, purchase, lease, sell, hold, and convey real and personal property. (See Chapter 3 for a cutting of the case.)

Another portion of the Civil Rights Act of 1866 (now Title 42 U.S.C. Section 1981) provides in pertinent part that all persons within the jurisdiction of the United States "shall have the same right in every State and Territory to make and enforce contracts . . . as is enjoyed by white citizens." In *Runyon* v. *McCrary,* 44 L.W. 5034 (1976), the Court held that Section 1981 prohibits private, commercially operated, nonsectarian schools from denying admission to black applicants solely on the basis of race. And in *McDonald* v. *Santa Fe Trail Company,* 44 L.W. 5067 (1976), it was held that whites as well as nonwhites could maintain an action to challenge racial discrimination in private employment under Section 1981.

On April 11, 1968, Congress adopted the Civil Rights Act of 1968, 82 Stat. 73, Title VIII of which is a "Fair Housing" provision. Section 804 is the substantive section of the Title, and it makes unlawful: (a) the refusal to sell or rent a dwelling to any person because of race, color, religion, or national origin; (b) discrimination in terms, conditions, or privileges of sale or rental of a dwelling because of race, color, religion, or national origin; (c) printing or publishing of any notice or advertisement with respect to the sale or rental of a dwelling that indicates any preference or limitation based on race, color, religion, or national origin; (d) representation to any person because of race, color, religion, or national origin that any dwelling is not available for inspection, sale, or rental when such dwelling is in fact so available; and (e) the inducement, for profit, of any person to sell or rent by representation regarding the entry into the neighborhood of a person of a particular race, color, religion, or national origin.

In general, enforcement of Title VIII is by negotiation or, if necessary, by civil suit filed by the Secretary of Housing and Urban Development in a United States District Court. Where a pattern or practice of resistance to the provisions of Title VIII appears, the Attorney General may bring a civil action.

Since 1960 several cases growing out of convictions for restaurant "sit-in" demonstrations have been carried to the United States Supreme Court. Various arguments were presented by the Negro appellants in these cases, including (1) that the restaurants had, by virtue of state licensing and special state regulation, become state instrumentalities, (2) that for the state police and courts to enforce trespass laws in support of restaurant-keepers' racially discriminatory policies was to inject unconstitutional state action under the *Shelley* rule, and (3) where segregated facilities exist in response to general and widespread community custom, state enforcement of such rules is tantamount to state legislation adopting the rule as law and thus violates the Fourteenth Amendment to the same extent as the segregation ordinance did in *Gayle* v. *Browder.* One such case was *Lombard* v. *Louisiana,* 373 U.S. 267 (1963). In *Peterson* v. *Greenville,* 373 U.S. 244 (1963), decided the same day, the Court reversed trespass convictions in a municipal court, following lunch counter "sit-ins," on the ground that a city ordinance required segregated eating facilities, and the convictions had the effect of enforcing the ordinance in violation of the Fourteenth Amendment. In *Lombard,* however, no such ordinance was involved. After having been refused service at the refreshment counter of a Five-and-Ten-Cent store in New Orleans, three Negroes and one white person refused to leave when requested to do so by the restaurant manager. They were convicted in a Louisiana state court of criminal mischief under a statute including within that designation the taking of temporary possession of, or the remaining in, a place of business after being ordered to leave by the person in charge of such business. On appeal the Supreme Court of Louisiana affirmed. On certiorari, the Supreme Court of the United States reversed. In an opinion by Chief Justice Warren, for eight members of the Court, it was held that despite the absence of an ordinance requiring segregation of restaurant facilities, "we conclude that this case is governed by the principles announced in *Peterson* v. *Greenville.*" This conclusion was reached on the ground that public statements of various city officials in effect reached the level of an official command that segregation be continued and such command "has at least as much coercive effect as an ordinance."

Justice Douglas concurred, but on much more expansive grounds. He stated:

> ... If this were an intrusion of a man's home or yard or farm or garden, the property owner could seek and obtain the aid of the State against the intruder. For the Bill of Rights, as applied to the States through the Due Process Clause of the Fourteenth Amendment, casts its weight on the side of the privacy of homes. ...
>
> But a restaurant, like the other departments of this retail store where Negroes were served, though private property within the protection of the Fifth Amendment, has no aura of constitutionally protected privacy about it. Access by the public is the very reason for its existence. ...
>
> State licensing and surveillance of a business serving the public ... brings its service into the public domain. This restaurant needs a permit from Louisiana to operate; and during the existence of the license the State has broad powers of visitation and control. This restaurant is thus an instrumentality of the State since the State charges it with duties to the public and supervises its performance. The State's interest in and activity with regard to its restaurants extends far beyond any mere income-producing licensing requirement.
>
> There is no constitutional way, as I see it, in which a State can license and supervise a business serving the public and endow it with the authority to manage that business on the basis of *apartheid,* which is foreign to our Constitution.

The majority of the Court has not accepted Justice Douglas' suggestion that a private business becomes a state instrumentality by virtue of state licensing and special state regulation. In *Lombard,* however, the Court did look beyond the requirements of statutes or ordinances and found coercive state action in the public statements of officials sufficient to invalidate trespass convictions.

In the 1963 Term, the Court was faced with more than a dozen cases attacking racial segregation in private establishments along "state action" lines. The case in which the state action argument was most fully discussed, although it was not the ground on which the case was disposed of, was *Bell v. Maryland* in 1964.

BELL *v.* MARYLAND
378 U.S. 226 (1964)

Mr. Justice Brennan delivered the opinion of the Court.

Petitioners, 12 Negro students, were convicted in a Maryland state court as a result of their participation in a "sit-in" demonstration at Hooper's restaurant in the City of Baltimore in 1960.... [Petitioners] went to Hooper's restaurant to engage in what their counsel describes as a "sit-in protest" because the restaurant would not serve Negroes.... Petitioners did not leave when requested to by the hostess and the manager; instead they went to tables, took seats, and refused to leave, insisting that they be served.... Mr. Hooper then went to the police station and swore out warrants, and petitioners were accordingly arrested.

The statute under which the convictions were obtained was the Maryland criminal trespass law.... The convictions were affirmed by the Maryland Court of Appeals....

We do not reach the questions that have been argued under the Equal Protection and Due Process Clauses of the Fourteenth Amendment. It appears that a significant change has taken place in the applicable law of Maryland since these convictions were affirmed by the Court of Appeals. [Since that date, Maryland enacted laws that abolish the crime of which petitioners were convicted. These laws accord petitioners a right to be served in the restaurant and make unlawful the refusal of service because of race.] Under this Court's settled practice in such circumstances, the judgments must consequently be vacated and reversed and the case remanded so that the state court may consider the effect of the supervening change in state law....

Mr. Justice Goldberg, with whom The Chief Justice joins, and with whom Mr. Justice Douglas joins . . . concurring.

I join in the opinion and the judgment of the Court and would therefore have no occasion under ordinary circumstances to express my views on the underlying constitutional issue. Since, however, the dissent at length discusses this constitutional issue and reaches a conclusion with which I profoundly disagree, I am impelled to state the reasons for my conviction that the Constitution guarantees to all Americans the right to be treated as equal members of the community with respect to public accommodations....

The Thirteenth, Fourteenth and Fifteenth Amendments do not permit Negroes to be considered as second-class citizens in any respect of our public life.... We make no racial distinctions between citizens in exacting from them the discharge of public responsibilities. The heaviest duties of citizenship—military service, taxation, obedience to laws—are imposed evenhandedly upon black and white.... Our fundamental law which insures such an equality of public burdens, in my view, similarly insures an equality of public benefits....

[Here follows an analysis of the congressional intent behind the Civil Rights Act of 1866 and the Fourteenth Amendment with the conclusion that the purpose was "to ensure that the constitutional concept of citizenship with all attendant rights and privileges would henceforth embrace Negroes. It follows that Negroes as citizens necessarily became entitled to share the right, customarily possessed by other citizens, of access to public accommodations."]

A State applying its statutory or common law to deny rather than protect the right of access to public accommodations has . . . denied the constitutionally intended equal protection. Indeed, in light of the assumption so explicitly stated in the *Civil Rights Cases,* it is significant that Mr. Justice Bradley, who spoke for the Court, had earlier in correspondence with Circuit Judge Woods. . . . concluded that: "Denying includes inaction as well as action. And denying the equal protection of the laws includes the omission to protect, as well as the omission to pass laws for protection." These views are fully consonant with this Court's recognition that state conduct which might be described as "inaction" can nevertheless constitute responsible "state action" within the meaning of the Fourteenth Amendment. See, e.g., *Marsh* v. *Alabama,* . . . *Shelley* v. *Kraemer,* . . . *Terry* v. *Adams,* . . . *Burrows* v. *Jackson.* . . .

In the present case the responsibility of the judiciary in applying the principles of the Fourteenth Amendment is clear. The State of Maryland has failed to protect petitioners' constitutional right to public accommodations and is now prosecuting them for attempting to exercise that right. The decision of Maryland's highest court in sustaining these trespass convictions cannot be described as "neutral," for the decision is as affirmative in effect as if the State had enacted an unconstitutional law explicitly authorizing racial discrimination in places of public accommodation. A State, obligated under the Fourteenth Amendment to maintain a system of law in which Negroes are not denied protection in their claim to be treated as equal members of the community, may not use its criminal trespass laws to frustrate the constitutionally granted right. Nor, it should be added, may a State frustrate this right by legitimating a proprietor's attempt at self-help. . . .

My brother Douglas convincingly demonstrates that the dissent has constructed a straw man by suggesting that this case involves "a property owner's right to choose his social or business associates." . . . The restaurant involved in this case is concededly open to a large segment of the public. Restaurants such as this daily open their doors to millions of Americans. These establishments provide a public service as necessary today as the inns and carriers of Blackstone's time. It should be recognized that the claim asserted by the Negro petitioners concerns such public establishments and does not infringe upon the rights of property owners or personal associational interests.

Petitioners frankly state that the "extension of constitutional guarantees to the authentically private choices of man is wholly unacceptable, and any constitutional theory leading to that result would have reduced itself to absurdity." Indeed, the constitutional protection extended to privacy and private association assures against the imposition of social equality. As noted before, the Congress that enacted the Fourteenth Amendment was particularly conscious that the "civil" rights of man should be distinguished from his "social" rights. Prejudice and bigotry in any form are regrettable, but it is the constitutional right of every person to close his home or club to any person or to choose his social intimates and business partners solely on the basis of personal prejudices including race. These and other rights pertaining to privacy and private association are themselves constitutionally protected liberties.

We deal here, however, with a claim of equal access to public accommodations. This is not a claim which significantly impinges upon personal associational interests; nor is it a claim infringing upon the control of private property not dedicated to public use. A judicial ruling on this claim inevitably involves the liberties and freedoms both of the restaurant proprietor and of the Negro citizen. The dissent would hold in effect that the restaurant proprietor's interest in choosing customers on the basis of race is to be preferred to the Negro's right to equal treatment by a business serving the public. The history and purposes of the Fourteenth Amendment indicate, however, that the Amendment resolves this apparent conflict of liberties in favor of the Negro's right to equal public accommodations. . . . As the history of the common law and, indeed, of our own times graphically illustrates, the interests of proprietors of places of public accommodation have always been adapted to the citizen's felt need for public accommodations, a need which is basic and deep-rooted. This history and the purposes of the Fourteenth Amendment compel the conclusion that the right to be served in places of public accommodation regardless of color cannot constitutionally be subordinated to the proprietor's interest in discriminatorily refusing service. . . .

Mr. Justice Black, with whom Mr. Justice Harlan and Mr. Justice White join, dissenting.

This case does not involve the constitutionality of any existing or proposed state or federal legislation requiring restaurant owners to serve people without regard to color. The crucial issue which the case does present but which the Court does not decide is whether the Fourteenth Amendment, of itself, forbids a State to enforce its trespass laws to convict a person who comes into a privately owned restaurant, is told that because of his color he will not be served, and over the owner's protest refuses to leave. We dissent from the Court's refusal to decide that question. For reasons stated, we think that the question should be decided and that the Fourteenth Amendment does not forbid this application of a State's trespass laws. . . .

. . . [O]ur affirmance of the state court's holding that the Maryland trespass statute is constitutional as applied would in no way hamper or bar decision of further state questions which the Maryland court might deem relevant to protect the rights of the petitioners in accord with Maryland law. Recognition of this power of state courts after we affirm their holdings on federal questions is a commonplace occurrence. . . .

Petitioners, but not the Solicitor General, contend that their conviction for trespass under the state statute was by itself the kind of discriminatory state action forbidden by the Fourteenth Amendment. This contention, on its face, has plausibility when considered along with general statements to the effect that under the Amendment forbidden "state action" may be that of the Judicial as well as of the Legislative or Executive Branch of Government. But a mechanical application of the Fourteenth Amendment to this case cannot survive analysis. The Amendment does not forbid a State to prosecute for crimes committed against a person or his property, however prejudiced or narrow the victim's views may be. Nor can whatever prejudice and bigotry the victim of a crime may have be automatically attributed to the State that prosecutes. Such a doctrine would not only be based on a fiction; it would also severely handicap a State's efforts to maintain a peaceful and orderly society. Our society has put its trust in a system of criminal laws to punish lawless conduct. To avert personal feuds and violent brawls it has led its people to believe and expect that wrongs against them will be vindicated in the courts. Instead of attempting to take the law into their own hands, people have been taught to call for police protection to protect their rights wherever possible. . . . None of our past cases justifies reading the Fourteenth Amendment in a way that might well penalize citizens who are law-abiding enough to call upon the law and its officers for protection instead of using their own physical strength or dangerous weapons to preserve their rights.

In contending that the State's prosecution of petitioners for trespass is state action forbidden by the Fourteenth Amendment, petitioners rely chiefly on *Shelley* v. *Kraemer, supra.* That reliance is misplaced....

It seems pretty clear that the reason judicial enforcement of the restrictive covenants in *Shelley* was deemed state action was not merely the fact that a state court had acted, but rather that it had acted "to deny to petitioners, on the grounds of race or color, the enjoyment of property rights in premises which petitioners are willing and financially able to acquire and which the grantors are willing to sell."... In other words, this Court held that state enforcement of the convenants had the effect of denying to the parties their federally guaranteed right to own, occupy, enjoy, and use their property without regard to race or color. Thus, the line of cases from *Buchanan* through *Shelley* establishes these propositions: (1) When an owner of property is willing to sell and a would-be purchaser is willing to buy, then the Civil Rights Act of 1866 ... prohibits a State, whether through its legislature, executive, or judiciary, from preventing the sale on the grounds of the race or color of one of the parties.... (2) Once a person has become a property owner, then he acquires all the rights that go with ownership.... This means that the property owner may, in the absence of a valid statute forbidding it, sell his property to whom he pleases and admit to that property whom he will; so long as both parties are willing parties, then the principles stated in Buchanan and Shelley protect this right. But equally, when one party is unwilling, as when the property owner chooses *not* to sell to a particular person or *not* to admit that person, then, as this Court emphasized in *Buchanan,* he is entitled to rely on the guarantee of due process of law, that is, "law of the land," to protect his free use and enjoyment of property and to know that only by valid legislation, passed pursuant to some constitutional grant of power, can anyone disturb this free use. . . . [P]etitioners would have us say that Hooper's federal right must be cut down and he must be compelled— though no statute said he must—to allow people to force their way into his restaurant and remain there over his protest. We cannot subscribe to such a mutilating, one-sided interpretation of federal guarantees the very heart of which is equal treatment under law to all. We must never forget that the Fourteenth Amendment protects "life, liberty, or property" of all people generally, not just some people's "life," some people's "liberty," and some kind of "property."...

We, like the Solicitor General, reject the argument that the State's protection of Hooper's desire to choose customers on the basis of race by prosecuting trespassers is enough, standing alone, to deprive Hooper of his right to operate the property in his own way. But we disagree with the contention that there are other circumstances which, added to the State's prosecution for trespass, justify a finding of state action. There is no Maryland law, no municipal ordinance, and no official proclamation or action of any kind that shows the slightest state coercion of, or encouragement to, Hooper to bar Negroes from his restaurant. Neither the State, the city, nor any of their agencies has leased publicly owned property to Hooper. It is true that the State and city regulate the restaurants—but not by compelling restaurants to deny service to customers because of their race. License fees are collected, but this licensing has no relationship to race. Under such circumstances, to hold that a State must be held to have participated in prejudicial conduct of its licensees is too big a jump for us to take. Businesses owned by private persons do not become agencies of the State because they are licensed; to hold that they do would be completely to negate all our private ownership concepts and practices....

Our Brother Goldberg in his opinion argues that he Fourteenth Amendment, of its own force and without the need of congressional legislation, prohibits privately owned restaurants from discriminating on account of color or race....

... [T]here is nothing whatever in the material cited to support the proposition that the Fourteenth Amendment, without congressional legislation, prohibits owners of restaurants and other places to refuse service to Negroes. [Here follows an examination of some of the debates in Congress between 1864 and 1874.]

We have confined ourselves entirely to those debates cited in Brother Goldberg's opinion the better to show how, even on its own evidence, the opinion's argument that the Fourteenth Amendment without more prohibits discrimination by restaurants and other such places rests on a wholly inadequate historical foundation. When read and analyzed, the argument is shown to rest entirely on what speakers are said to have believed bills and statutes of the time were meant to do. Such proof fails entirely when the question is, not what statutes did, but rather what the Constitution does. ...

... We express no views as to the power of Congress, acting under one or another provision of the Constitution, to prevent racial discrimination in the operation of privately owned businesses, nor upon any particular form of legislation to that end. Our sole conclusion is that Section 1 of the Fourteenth Amendment, standing alone, does not prohibit privately owned restaurants from choosing their own customers. ...

The issue of the validity of state enforcement of trespass laws in support of a restaurant owner's policy of racial discrimination has largely become moot as a consequence of the enactment of the Civil Rights Act of 1964 (78 Stat. 241). [For an account of the legislative history of the Act, see Congressional Quarterly Service, *Revolution in Civil Rights* (Washington, D.C.: Congressional Quarterly, Inc., 1965), pp. 41–70.] The Act reaches discrimination in places of public accommodation if the operations affect interstate commerce or if supported by state action. The issue of what constitutes state action is still viable, however, in areas not covered by the definition of "public accommodations" in the Act, such as barber shops or local dance halls or private schools. [See Richard A. Lang, Jr., "State Action Under the Equal Protection Clause and the Remaining Scope of Private Choice," 50 *Cornell L. Q.* 473–505 (1965).]

The public accommodations title of the Civil Rights Act of 1964 is similar in coverage to the first two sections of the old Civil Rights Act of 1875 which were held unconstitutional in the *Civil Rights Cases* in 1883. The former is primarily grounded in Congress' power to regulate commerce, however, while the latter was largely based on the Civil War Amendments. The relevant provisions of the new Act are found in Title II.

Title II—Injunctive Relief Against Discrimination
in Places of Public Accommodation

Sec. 201. (a) All persons shall be entitled to the full and equal enjoyment of the goods, services, facilities, privileges, advantages, and accommodations of any place of public accommodation, as defined in this section, without discrimination or segregation on the ground of race, color, religion, or national origin.

(b) Each of the following establishments which serves the public is a place of public accommodation within the meaning of this title if its operations affect commerce, or if discrimination or segregation by it is supported by State action:

(1) any inn, hotel, motel, or other establishment which provides lodging to transient guests, other than an establishment located within a building which contains not more than five rooms for rent or hire and which is actually occupied by the proprietor of such establishment as his residence;

(2) any restaurant, cafeteria, lunchroom, lunch counter, soda fountain, or other facility principally engaged in selling food for consumption on the premises including, but not limited to, any such facility located on the premises of any retail establishment; or any gasoline station;

(3) any motion picture house, theater, concert hall, sports arena, stadium or other place of exhibition or entertainment; and

(4) any establishment (A)(i) which is physically located within the premises of any establishment otherwise covered by this subsection, or (ii) within the premises of which is physically located any such covered establishment, and (B) which holds itself out as serving patrons of such covered establishment.

(c) The operations of an establishment affect commerce within the meaning of this title if (1) it is one of the establishments described in paragraph (1) of subsection (b); (2) in the case of an establishment described in paragraph (2) of subsection (b), it serves or offers to serve interstate travelers or a substantial portion of the food which it serves, or gasoline or other products which it sells, has moved in commerce; (3) in the case of an establishment described in paragraph (3) of subsection (b), it customarily presents films, performances, athletic teams, exhibitions, or other sources of entertainment which move in commerce; and (4) in the case of an establishment described in paragraph (4) of subsection (b), it is physically located within the premises of, or there is physically located within its premises, an establishment the operations of which affect commerce within the meaning of this subsection. For purposes of this section, "commerce" means travel, trade, traffic, commerce, transportation, or communication among the several States or between the District of Columbia and any State, or between any foreign country or any territory or possession and any State or the District of Columbia, or between points in the same State but through any other State or the District of Columbia or a foreign country.

(d) Discrimination or segregation by an establishment is supported by State action within the meaning of this title if such discrimination or segregation (1) is carried on under color of any law, statute, ordinance, or regulation; or (2) is carried on under color of any custom or usage required or enforced by officials of the State or political subdivision thereof; or (3) is required by action of the State or political subdivision thereof.

(e) The provisions of this title shall not apply to a private club or other establishment not in fact open to the public, except to the extent that the facilities of such establishment are made available to the customers or patrons of an establishment within the scope of subsection (b).

Sec. 202. All persons shall be entitled to be free, at any establishment or place, from discrimination or segregation of any kind on the ground of race, color, religion, or national origin, if such discrimination or segregation is or purports to be required by any law, statute, ordinance, regulation, rule, or order of a State or any agency or political subdivision thereof.

[Sec. 203 prohibits the intimidation or coercion of any person with the purpose of interfering with any right or privilege secured by Sections 201 and 202. Sec. 204 provides for the issuance of restraining orders in the event of such attempted intimidation or coercion, upon application of the aggrieved person, and permits the Attorney General to intervene if he certifies that the case is of general public importance. The court is also permitted, in justifiable cases, to appoint an attorney for the complainant and to authorize the commencement of the civil action without the payment of fees, costs, or security. The court may also allow the prevailing party a reasonable attorney's fee as part of the costs.]

Sec. 206. (a) Whenever the Attorney General has reasonable cause to believe that any person or group of persons is engaged in a pattern or practice of resistance to the full enjoyment of any of the rights secured by this title, and that the pattern or practice is of such a nature and is intended to deny the full exercise of the rights herein described, the Attorney General may bring a civil action in the appropriate district court of the United States by filing with it a complaint... requesting such preventive relief... as he deems necessary to insure the full enjoyment of the rights herein described. . . .

Sec. 207. (a) The district courts of the United States shall have jurisdiction of proceedings instituted pursuant to this title and shall exercise the same without regard to whether the aggrieved party shall have exhausted any administrative or other remedies that may be provided by law.

(b) The remedies provided in this title shall be the exclusive means of enforcing the rights based on this title, but nothing in this title shall preclude any individual or any State or local agency from asserting any right based on any other Federal or State law not inconsistent with this title, including any statute or ordinance requiring nondiscrimination in public establishments or accommodations, or from pursuing any remedy, civil or criminal, which may be available for the vindication or enforcement of such right.

As expected, cases were initiated very quickly questioning the constitutionality of Title II of the Civil Rights Act of 1964. Two such cases were argued on the opening day of the 1964 Term of the Court, only three months after the passage of the Act. *Heart of Atlanta Motel* v. *United States*, 379 U.S. 241 (1964), came on direct appeal from a three-judge district court in Georgia which had sustained the constitutionality of the Title II provisions and had enjoined the motel owner-operator from discriminating against Negroes on account of race or color. *Katzenbach* v. *McClung*, 379 U.S. 294 (1964), came on direct appeal from a three-judge district court in Alabama which had held the Act unconstitutional as applied to "Ollie's Barbecue" in Birmingham and enjoined enforcement against the restaurant. Decisions were handed down in these two companion cases in December 1964, only two months after argument and five months after enactment of the law.

HEART OF ATLANTA MOTEL *v.* UNITED STATES
379 U.S. 241 (1964)

[The owner of a motel which solicited and received patronage from interstate travelers brought suit in a District Court for declaratory and injunctive relief against the enforcement of the public accommodations sections of the Civil Rights Act of 1964, contending that the sections exceeded the commerce power of Congress, deprived him of liberty and property without due process of law, took his property without just compensation, and subjected him to involuntary servitude. The three-judge court held the provisions constitutional and enjoined the owner from discriminating against Negroes on account of race or color. The Court reviewed the decision on direct appeal.]

Mr. Justice Clark delivered the opinion of the Court. . . . .

[The opinion takes up the Civil Rights Act of 1875, with somewhat similar language to that in the 1964 Act, and the decision in the *Civil Rights Cases* holding the earlier act unconstitutional.]

We think that decision inapposite, and without precedential value in determining the constitutionality of the present Act. Unlike Title II of the present legislation, the 1875 Act broadly proscribed discrimination in "inns, public conveyances on land or water, theaters, and other public places of amusement," without limiting the categories of affected businesses to those impinging upon interstate commerce. In contrast, the applicability of Title II is carefully limited to enterprises having a direct and substantial relation to the interstate flow of goods and people, except where state action is involved. Further, the fact that certain kinds of businesses may not in 1875 have been sufficiently involved in interstate commerce to warrant bringing them within the ambit of the commerce power is not necessarily dispositive of the same question today. . . . The sheer increase in volume of interstate traffic alone would give discriminatory practices which inhibit travel a far larger impact upon the nation's commerce than such practices had in the economy of another day. Finally, there is language in the *Civil Rights Cases* which indicates that the Court did not fully consider whether the 1875 Act could be sustained as an exercise of the commerce power. . . .

[The opinion then takes up the evidence and testimony reported in various congressional committee hearings to the effect that racial discrimination had "a qualitative as well as quantitative effect on interstate travel by Negroes." The evidence indicated that the uncertainty of finding facilities for food and lodging, stemming from racial discrimination, "had the effect of discouraging travel on the part of a substantial portion of the Negro community."]

The power of Congress to deal with these obstructions depends on the meaning of the Commerce Clause. Its meaning was first enunciated 140 years ago by the great Chief Justice John Marshall in *Gibbons* v. *Ogden*, 9 Wheat. 1 (1824). . . .

In short, the determinative test of the exercise of power by the Congress under the Commerce Clause is simply whether the activity sought to be regulated is "commerce which concerns more than one state" and has a real and substantial relation to the national interest. . . .

It is said that the operation of the motel here is of a purely local character. But, assuming this to be true, "if it is interstate commerce that feels the pinch, it does not matter how local the operation that applies the squeeze." *United States* v. *Women's Sportswear Mfrs. Ass'n.*, 336 U.S. 460, 464 (1949). . . . As Chief Justice Stone put it in *United States* v. *Darby, supra:*

"The power of Congress over interstate commerce is not confined to the regulation of commerce among the states. It extends to those activities intrastate which so affect interstate commerce or the exercise of the power of Congress over it as to make regulation of them appropriate means to the attainment of a legitimate end, the exercise of the granted power of Congress to regulate interstate commerce. . . . "

Thus the power of Congress to promote interstate commerce also includes the power to regulate the local incidents thereof, including local activities in both the States of origin and destination, which might have a substantial and harmful effect upon that commerce. One need only examine the evidence which we have discussed above to see that Congress may—as it has—prohibit racial discrimination by motels serving travelers, however "local" their operations may appear.

Nor does the Act deprive appellant of liberty or property under the Fifth Amendment. The commerce power invoked here by the Congress is a specific and plenary one authorized by the Constitution itself. The only questions are: (1) whether Congress had a rational basis for finding that racial discrimination by motels affected commerce, and (2) if it had such a bias, whether the means it selected to eliminate that evil are reasonable and appropriate. If they are, appellant has no "right" to select its guests as it sees fit free from governmental regulation.

There is nothing novel about such legislation. Thirty-two States now have it on their books either by statute or executive order and many cities provide such regulations. Some of these Acts go back fourscore years. It has been repeatedly held by this Court that such laws do not violate the Due Process Clause of the Fourteenth Amendment....

... As a result the constitutionality of such state statutes stands unquestioned. "The authority of the Federal Government over interstate commerce does not differ," it was held in *United States* v. *Rock Royal Co-op, Inc.,* 307 U.S. 533 (1939), "in extent or character from that retained by the states over intrastate commerce." ...

... Neither do we find any merit in the claim that the Act is a taking of property without just compensation. The cases are to the contrary....

We find no merit in the remainder of appellant's contentions, including that of "involuntary servitude.".... We could not say that the requirements of the Act in this regard are in any way "akin to African slavery." *Butler* v. *Perry,* 240 U.S. 328, 332 (1916).

Katzenbach v. *McClung,* 379 U.S. 294 (1964), raised many of the same questions which were disposed of in the companion motel case. The appellees did raise one additional issue, however, which the Court took care of separately. The restaurant was located some distance from interstate highways and railroad and bus stations, and it catered to local family and white-collar trade. In the preceding year the restaurant had purchased locally approximately $150,000 worth of food, of which about $70,000 was for meat that it bought from a local supplier who had procured it from outside the state. In his opinion for the Court upholding the application of the Act to Ollie's Barbecue, Justice Clark stated the question and gave the response:

... There is no claim that interstate travelers frequented the restaurant. The sole question, therefore, narrows down to whether Title II, as applied to a restaurant receiving about $70,000 worth of food which has moved in commerce, is a valid exercise of the power of Congress. The Government has contended that Congress had ample basis upon which to find that racial discrimination at restaurants which receive from out of state a substantial portion of the food served does, in fact, impose commercial burdens of national magnitude upon interstate commerce. The appellees' major argument is directed to this premise. They urge that no such basis existed. It is to that question that we now turn....

[The opinion then refers to testimony at hearings before the Senate Committee on Commerce, including testimony that in areas where discrimination is widely practiced there was less spending per capita by Negroes, after discounting income differences, in restaurants and like establishments. "The diminutive spending springing from a refusal to serve Negroes and their total loss as customers, has, regardless of the absence of direct evidence, a close connection to interstate commerce. The fewer customers a restaurant enjoys the less food it sells and consequently the less it buys."]

We believe that this testimoney afforded ample basis for the conclusion that established restaurants in such areas sold less interstate goods because of the discrimination, that interstate travel was obstructed directly by it, that business in general suffered and that many new businesses refrained from establishing there as a result of it....

It goes without saying that, viewed in isolation, the volume of food purchased by Ollie's Barbecue from sources supplied from out of state was insignificant when compared with the total foodstuffs moving in commerce. But, as our late Brother Jackson said for the Court in *Wickard* v. *Filburn,* 317 U.S. 111, 127–128 (1942):

"That appellee's own contribution to the demand for wheat may be trivial by itself is not enough to remove him from the scope of federal regulation where, as here, his contribution, taken together with that of many others similarly situated, is far from trivial." . . .

. . . The activities that are beyond the reach of Congress are "those which are completely within a particular State, which do not affect other States, and with which it is not necessary to interfere, for the purpose of executing some of the general powers of the government." *Gibbons* v. *Ogden,* 9 Wheat 1, 195 (1824). This rule is as good today as it was when Chief Justice Marshall laid it down almost a century and a half ago.

[On the issue of racial discrimination in state-licensed private clubs, see *Moose Lodge No. 107* v. *Irvis,* 407 U.S. 163 (1972). The case cutting appears in Chapter 3.]

A third important provision of the Civil Rights Act of 1964 is the Title VII provision setting up a right of equal employment opportunity irrespective of race, color, religion, sex, or national origin. Though the impact of this Title has not been so immediate or dramatic as that of the equal accommodations sections, the long-term effect of this provision, if implemented, will probably be of more importance in assuring real equality of opportunity for all persons than any of the other provisions of the Act. Equal educational opportunity alone does not instill motivation to learn or to remain in school through advanced grades. And equal access to public accommodations is no great personal triumph for the man whose menial occupation does not pay enough to permit him to stay in motels or eat in restaurants. Assurance of equal chances to compete and to advance in the economic arena, however, at least offers the potential for encouraging the fuller utilization of educational opportunities and the realization of some of the benefits of the equal accommodations provisions.

The first section of Title VII defines the persons and organizations to which the terms of the Title extend. It covers labor unions, employers engaged in an industry affecting commerce, employment agencies, and others. In general the provisions apply to employers and labor unions with twenty-five or more employees or members, but operating on a sliding scale with exemption the first year for those with less than one hundred, the second year for those with less than seventy-five, the third year for those with less than fifty, and those with less than twenty-five thereafter. Since the effective date for this Title was July 2, 1965, the maximum coverage was reached on July 2, 1968. Section 701 (b) further states that the term "employer" does not include:

(1) the United States, a corporation wholly owned by the Government of the United States, an Indian tribe, or a State or political subdivision thereof, (2) a bona fide private membership club (other than a labor organization) which is exempt from taxation under section 501 (c) of the Internal Revenue Code of 1954: . . . *Provided further,* That it shall be the policy of the United States to insure equal employment opportunities for Federal employees without discrimination because of race, color, religion, sex or national origin and the President shall utilize his existing authority to effectuate this policy.

The substantive provisions of the Title are found in the following section:

Sec. 703. (a) It shall be an unlawful employment practice for an employer—

(1) to fail or refuse to hire or to discharge any individuals, or otherwise to discriminate against any individual with respect to his compensation, terms, conditions, or privileges of employment, because of such individual's race, color, religion, sex, or national origin; or

(2) to limit, segregate, or classify his employees in any way which would deprive or tend to deprive any individual of employment opportunities or otherwise a lversely affect his status as an employee, because of such individual's race, color, religion, sex, or national origin. . . .

Subsections (b), (c), and (d) impose similar limitations on the referral policies of employment agencies, membership policies of labor unions, and training program policies of either employers or labor organizations.

There are two primary exceptions to the nondiscrimination provisions. First, classification on the basis of religion, sex, or national origin may be made if such classification is "a bona fide occupational qualification reasonably necessary to the normal operation of that particular business or enterprise." (Note that the provision does not permit an exception based on race.) Second, schools may hire employees of a particular religion if they are "in whole or in substantial part, owned, supported, controlled, or managed by a particular religion," or if the curriculum of any such school "is directed toward the propagation of a particular religion."

The final subsection, (j), states that nothing in the title shall be interpreted to require *preferential* treatment based on race, religion, sex, or national origin "on account of an imbalance which may exist" in the number of persons in any category employed by any employer (or admitted to membership in any labor union, etc.) in comparison with the total number of persons in such category in the community. Thus a "quota" system of hiring is not demanded by the title.

Section 705 of Title VII provides for the creation of a five-member Equal Employment Opportunity Commission. It is given the power to furnish various kinds of technical assistance to further compliance with the title, to make such technical studies "as are appropriate to effectuate the purposes and policies of this title," and to perform other advising and consulting functions. It is charged with reporting annually to the Congress and to the President concerning the action it has taken, "and shall make such further reports on the cause of and means of eliminating discrimination and such recommendations for further legislation as may appear desirable." The Commission also has authority to examine witnesses under oath and to require the production of documentary evidence relevant or material to the investigation. The Commission has further authority to issue suitable procedural regulations to carry out the provisions of Title VII.

GRIGGS *v.* DUKE POWER CO.
401 U.S. 424 (1971)

Mr. Chief Justice Burger delivered the opinion of the Court.

We granted the writ in this case to resolve the question whether an employer is prohibited by the Civil Rights Act of 1964, Title VII, from requiring a high school education or passing of a standardized general intelligence test as a condition of employment in or transfer to jobs when (a) neither standard is shown to be significantly related to successful job performance, (b) both requirements operate to disqualify Negroes at a substantially higher rate than white applicants, and (c) the jobs in question formerly had been filled only by white employees as part of a long-standing practice of giving preference to whites. . . .

The District Court found that prior to . . . the effective date of the Civil Rights Act of 1964, the Company openly discriminated on the basis of race in the hiring and assigning of employees at its Dan River plant. . . .

The objective of Congress in the enactment of Title VII is plain from the language of the statute. It was to achieve equality of employment opportunities and remove barriers that have operated in the past to favor an identifiable group of white employees over other employees. Under the Act, practices, procedures, or tests neutral on their face, and even neutral of intent, cannot be maintained if they operate to "freeze" the status quo of prior discriminatory employment practices. . . .

. . . Congress did not intend by Ttitle VII, however, to guarantee a job to every person regardless of qualifications. In short, the Act does not command that any person be hired simply because he was formerly the subject of discrimination, or because he is a member of a minority group. Discriminatory preference for any group, minority or majority, is precisely and only what Congress has proscribed. What is required by Congress is the removal of artificial, arbitrary, and unnecessary barriers to employment when the barriers operate invidiously to discriminate on the basis of racial or other impermissible classification. . . . The touchstone is business necessity. If an employment practice which operates to exclude Negroes cannot be shown to be related to job performance, the practice is prohibited.

On the record before us, neither the high school completion requirement nor the general intelligence test is shown to bear a demonstrable relationship to successful performance of the jobs for which it was used. Both were adopted, as the Court of Appeals noted, without meaningful study of their relationship to job-performance ability. Rather, a vice president of the Company testified, the requirements were instituted on the Company's judgment that they generally would improve the overall quality of the work force.

The evidence, however, shows that employees who have not completed high school or taken the tests have continued to perform satisfactorily and make progress in departments for which the high school and test criteria are now used. . . .

The facts of this case demonstrate the inadequacy of broad and general testing devices as well as the infirmity of using diplomas or degrees as fixed measures of capability. History is filled with examples of men and women who rendered highly effective performance without the conventional badges of accomplishment in terms of certificates, diplomas, or degrees. Diplomas and tests are useful servants, but Congress has mandated the common-sense proposition that they are not to become masters of reality.

The Company contents that its general intelligence tests are specifically permitted by §703(h) of the Act. That section authorizes the use of "any professionally developed ability test" that is not "designed, intended *or used* to discriminate because of race. . . ." (Emphasis added.) . . .

Nothing in the Act precludes the use of testing or measuring procedures; obviously they are useful. What Congress has forbidden is giving these devices and mechanisms controlling force unless they are demonstrably a reasonable measure of job performance. Congress has not commanded that the less qualified be preferred over the better qualified simply because of minority origins. Far from disparaging job qualifications as such, Congress has made such qualifications the controlling factor, so that race, religion, nationality, and sex become irrelevant. What Congress has commanded is that any tests used must measure the person for the job and not the person in the abstract. . . .

Mr. Justice Brennan took no part in the consideration or decision of this case.

In *Washington* v. *Davis,* 44 L.W. 4789 (1976), various unsuccessful black candidates for positions as police officers in the District of Columbia challenged the constitutionality of certain of the written tests, claiming discriminatory racial impact. It should be noted that while there was considerable discussion of Title VII standards in the opinion of the Court, the case was brought on due process grounds rather than under Title VII because, at the time the action was brought, Title VII did not apply to governmental units. (Amendments to the Act in 1972 did extend the provisions to such units.) The Court held that the mere fact that a governmental test had a racially disproportionate impact (four times as many blacks as whites failed the test) was insufficient, standing alone, to require a decision that the test violated the Fifth Amendment's prohibition against invidious discrimination. The claimants were required to make a further showing that the test was adopted with a racially discriminatory purpose. Justice White, for the majority, indicated that Title VII imposed a more rigorous standard than did the Fifth and Fourteenth Amendments. He stated:

Under Title VII, Congress provided that when hiring and promotion practices disqualifying substantially disproportionate numbers of blacks are challenged, discriminatory purpose need not be proved, and that it is an insufficient response to demonstrate some rational basis for the challenged practices. It is necessary, in addition, that they be "validated" in terms of job performance in any one of several ways, perhaps by ascertaining the minimum skill, ability or potential necessary for the positon at issue and determining whether the qualifying tests are appropriate for the selection of qualified applicants for the job in question. However this process proceeds, it involves a more probing judicial review of, and less deference to, the seemingly reasonable acts of administrators and executives than is appropriate under the Constitution where special racial impact, without discriminatory purpose, is claimed. We are not disposed to adopt this more rigorous standard for the purposes of applying the Fifth and the Fourteenth Amendments in cases such as this.

The Court accepted the District Court's finding that the challenged test, measuring verbal skills, was directly related to the requirements of the police training program and that a positive relationship between the test and that program was sufficient to validate the test.

Despite the statements in *Griggs* to the effect that Congress, in the 1964 Act, intended to make distinctions based on race irrelevant—"the Act does not command that any person be hired simply because he was formerly the subject of discrimination, or because he is a member of a minority group" —some courts have issued decrees which set up minority quotas for purposes of hiring or promotion. Two divergent approaches to such decrees may be noted in decisions coming from the United States Courts of Appeals for the Second and Third Circuits in 1975. *Oburn* v. *Shapp* (3rd Cir., 44 L.W. 2088, 1975) dealt with a quota system imposed on the Pennsylvania state police. Plaintiffs were white applicants for the position of state trooper who asserted that they were discriminated against because the state police were following a racial quota system of hiring dictated by a District Court consent decree. The decree established a temporary hiring goal requiring that at least one-third of those selected as police cadets should be minorities. A District Court denied the request for injunctive relief, and the Third Circuit Court of Appeals affirmed, pointing out that courts of appeals have held it be reversible error for a district court to withhold quota relief where other forms of remedy fail to eliminate racially discriminatory practices or effects. The court accepted the position of the state police that their interest in off-setting prior discrimination constituted a remedial purpose sufficient to warrant the use of racial quotas.

The Second Circuit did not look favorably, however, on the "reverse discrimination" policy inherent in the quota system. A District Court had concluded that a particular New York civil service examination was unconstitutionally discriminatory in its effect and had imposed a minority employment quota for such positions in the State of New York. The Court of Appeals reversed, *Kirkland* v. *New York State Department of Correctional Services* (2d Cir., 44 L.W. 2089, 1975), and said that in the absence of any evidence or proof of past discrimination, the imposition of permanent quotas to eradicate the effects of past discriminatory practices was unwarranted. The District Court order required the Department to promote at least one black or Hispanic employee for each three white employees promoted until the combined percentage of minority correction sergeants was equal to the combined percentage of minority correction officers. The opinion for the Court of Appeals stated:

> One of the most controversial areas in our continuing search for equal employment opportunity is the use of judicially imposed employment quotas. The replacement of individual rights and opportunities by a system of statistical classifications based on race is repugnant to the basic concepts of a democratic society....
>
> So long as civil service remains the constiutionally mandated route to public employment in the State of New York, no one should be "bumped" from a preferred position on the eligibility list solely because of his race. Unless the Fourteenth Amendment is applicable only to blacks, this is constitutionally forbidden reverse discrimination.

These cases are, of course, cases involving issues of governmental discrimination rather than private, but it would appear that the same constitutional questions are raised when a governmental decree—whether issued by a court or by a federal agency under an "affirmative action" guideline—directs the adoption of a quota system of employment. The Supreme Court had an opportunity to rule on the question in *DeFunis* v. *Odegaard,* 416 U.S. 312 (1974), involving a racial quota system for the admission of students to the University of Washington Law School. DeFunis' application was rejected, although based on his record his Predicted First Year Average score was higher than 36 of the 37 minority students who were admitted. He filed suit in state court contending that the admission procedures invidiously discriminated against him as a white applicant and therefore violated the Fourteenth Amendment. The trial court agreed and issued a mandatory injunction ordering his admission. The Washington Supreme Court reversed, but by this time DeFunis was in his second year of Law School. DeFunis petitioned the United States Supreme Court for certiorari, and the case was set for argument. By the time the decision was rendered, in April 1974, DeFunis was only a few weeks away from graduation, and the Law School stipulated that irrespective of the decision in the case, he would be allowed to graduate upon satisfactory completion of his work. The majority of the Court held that in view of this stipulation, the question had become moot, and thus it refused to reach the constitutional question presented. Four Justices dissented, arguing that the question was still extant, since DeFunis had not yet graduated, and that the issues "concern vast numbers of people, organizations and colleges and universities, as evidenced by the filing of twenty-six *amici curiae* briefs. Few constiutional questions in recent history have stirred as much debate, and they will not disappear."

Other Aspects of Race Discrimination

There is one area of state legislation classifying by race into which the Court did not venture until 1967. This is the statutory bar to marriages between whites and nonwhites, commonly known as antimiscegenation laws. Since miscegenous marriages represent one of the great fears of those who support race discriminations, it is understandable that neither the Court nor the nonwhite racial pressure groups were anxious to press the issue of the validity of such laws, at least until nondiscrimination in the more important areas of social and economic activity had been achieved. The line of decisions respecting classification by race in regulatory legislation, however, clearly presaged a holding that the miscegenation laws were unconstitutional.

At one period in the nineteenth century some thirty-eight states had statutes barring whites from marrying members of defined categories of nonwhites. During the Civil War period nine states repealed such statutes, and as of 1951 twenty-nine states retained them. [See Harvey H. Applebaum, "Miscegenation Statutes: A Constitutional and Social Problem," 53 *Geo. L. J.* 49 (1964).] Since that time a number of those states had repealed their statutes, and as of 1967 sixteen states remained with statutes outlawing interracial marriage. The statutes differed widely, both in the persons to whom they applied and in the definitions of categories. In general they prohibited whites from marrying nonwhites but did not bar intermarriage among the nonwhite categories, as, for example, between Indians and Negroes. The definition of Negro (or Indian or Oriental) varied, however, and a person of mixed white and Negro ancestry could be a white under the law of one state and a Negro under the law of another.

Shortly after the end of World War II, the California Supreme Court held the California antimiscegenation law unconstitutional, as a denial of equal protection of the law, in *Perez* v. *Lippold* [*Sharp*], 32 Cal. 2d 711, 198 P.2d 17 (1948). The United States Supreme Court had an opportunity to rule on the question in a case involving the Virginia law as applied to an attempted marriage between a white and an Oriental, but avoided a decision on the merits. The case was first remanded to the Virginia court on the ground of deficiencies in the record, and an appeal from the later decision was dismissed. [*Naim* v. *Naim*, 350 U.S. 985 (1956).]

More recently the Court took an appeal and rendered a decision in a case which bore closely on the miscegenation question. Defendants were convicted in a Florida state court of having violated a statute which made it a criminal offense for a white person and a Negro of opposite sexes, not married to each other, to habitually live in and occupy in the nighttime the same room. The Florida Supreme Court sustained the statute against a claim of denial of equal protection under the Fourteenth Amendment. On appeal the Court unanimously reversed in *McLaughlin* v. *Florida,* 379 U.S. 184 (1964). In his opinion for the Court, Justice White discussed the legislative power to classify and then stated: "Our inquiry, therefore, is whether there clearly appears in the relevant materials some overriding statutory purpose requiring the proscription of the specified conduct when engaged in by the white person and a Negro, but not otherwise. Without such justification the racial classification ... is reduced to an invidious discrimination forbidden by the Equal Protection Clause." He concluded that promiscuity by the interracial couple presented no particular problems which required separate or different treatment. Florida argued, however, that the interracial cohabitation law was valid because it was ancillary to and served the same purpose as the miscegenation law itself. Justice White responded, "We reject this argument without reaching the question of the validity of the State's prohibition against interracial marriage. ..."

The Court did reach the question in 1967, however, in an appeal involving the antimiscegenation policy of the state of Virginia. The case testing Virginia's statutes began, ironically, as *Virginia* v. *Loving,* a criminal prosecution for violation of the state's ban on interracial marriages. In *Loving* v. *Virginia,* 388 U.S. 1 (1967), the Court held the prohibition unconstitutional.

LOVING *v.* VIRGINIA
388 U.S. 1 (1967)

Mr. Chief Justice Warren delivered the opinion of the Court.

This case presents a constitutional question never addressed by this Court: whether a statutory scheme adopted by the State of Virginia to prevent marriages between persons solely on the basis of racial classifications violates the Equal Protection and Due Process Clauses of the Fourteenth Amendment. For reasons which seem to us to reflect the central meaning of those constitutional commands, we conclude that these statutes cannot stand consistently with the Fourteenth Amendment.

In June 1958, two residents of Virginia, Mildred Jeter, a Negro woman, and Richard Loving, a white man, were married in the District of Columbia pursuant to its laws. Shortly after their marriage, the Lovings returned to Virginia and established their marital abode in Caroline County. At the October Term, 1958, of the Circuit Court of Caroline County, a grand jury issued an indictment charging the Lovings with violating Virginia's ban on interracial marriages. On January 6, 1959, the Lovings pleaded guilty to the charge and were sentenced to one year in jail; however, the trial judge suspended the sentence for a period of 25 years on the condition that the Lovings leave the State and not return to Virginia together for 25 years, stating that:

"Almighty God created the races white, black, yellow, malay, and red, and he placed them on separate continents. And but for the interference with his arrangement there would be no cause for such marriages. The fact that he separated the races shows that he did not intend for the races to mix."

[The opinion then describes the various procedural attacks made by the Lovings on the judgment and sentence, culminating in an appeal to the Virginia Supreme Court.]

The Supreme Court of Appeals upheld the constitutionality of the antimiscegenation statutes and, after modifying the sentence, affirmed the convictions. The Lovings appealed this decision. . . .

The two statutes under which appellants were convicted and sentenced are part of a comprehensive statutory scheme aimed at prohibiting and punishing interracial marriages. The Lovings were convicted of violating §20–58 of the Virginia Code:

"*Leaving State to evade law.* If any white person and colored person shall go out of this State for the purpose of being married, and with the intention of returning, and be married out of it, and afterwards return to and reside in it, cohabiting as man and wife, they shall be punished as provided in §20–59, and the marriage shall be governed by the same law as if it had been solemnized in this State. The fact of their cohabitation here as man and wife shall be evidence of their marriage."

Section 20–59, which defines the penalty for miscegenation, provides:

"*Punishment for marriage.* If any white person intermarry with a colored person, or any colored person intermarry with a white person, he shall be guilty of a felony and shall be punished by confinement in the penitentiary for not less than one nor more than five years."

Other central provisions in the Virginia statutory scheme are §20–57, which automatically voids all marriages between "a white person and a colored person" without any judicial proceedings, and §§20–54 and 1–14 which, respectively, define "white persons" and "colored persons and Indians" for purposes of the statutory prohibitions. The Lovings have never disputed in the course of this litigation that Mrs. Loving is a "colored person" or that Mr. Loving is a "white person" within the meanings given those terms by the Virginia statutes. . . .

I

In upholding the constitutionality of these provisions in the decision below, the Supreme Court of Appeals of Virginia referred to its 1955 decision in *Naim* v. *Naim,* 87 S.E.2d 749, as stating the reasons supporting the validity of these laws. In *Naim,* the state court concluded that the State's legitimate purposes were "to preserve the racial integrity of its citizens," and to prevent "the corruption of blood," "a mongrel breed of citizens," and "the obliteration of racial pride," obviously an endorsement of the doctrine of White Supremacy. . . . The court also reasoned that marriage has traditionally been subject to state regulation without federal intervention, and, consequently, the regulation of marriage should be left to exclusive state control by the Tenth Amendment.

While the state court is no doubt correct in asserting that marriage is a social relation subject to the State's police power, . . . the State does not contend in its argument before this Court that its powers to regulate marriage are unlimited notwithstanding the commands of the Fourteenth Amendment. . . . [T]he State contends that, because its miscegenation statutes punish equally both the white and the Negro participants in an interracial marriage, these statutes, despite their reliance on racial classifications, do not constitute an invidious discrimination based upon race. . . . In the case at bar . . . we deal with statutes containing racial classifications, and the fact of equal application does not immunize the statute from the very heavy burden of justification which the Fourteenth Amendment has traditionally required of state statutes drawn according to race. . . .

There is patently no legitimate overriding purpose independent of invidious racial discrimination which justifies this classification. The fact that Virginia only prohibits interracial marriages involving white persons demonstrates that the racial classifications must stand on their own justification, as measures designed to maintain White Supremacy. We have consistently denied the constitutionality of measures which restrict the rights of citizens on account of race. There can be no doubt that restricting the freedom to marry solely because of racial classifications violates the central meaning of the Equal Protection Clause.

II

These statutes also deprive the Lovings of liberty without due process of law in violation of the Due Process Clause of the Fourteenth Amendment. The freedom to marry has long been recognized as one of the vital personal rights essential to the orderly pursuit of happiness by free men.

Marriage is one of the "basic civil rights of man," fundamental to our very existence and survival.... To deny this fundamental freedom on so unsupportable a basis as the racial classifications embodied in these statutes, classifications so directly subversive of the principle of equality at the heart of the Fourteenth Amendment, is surely to deprive all the State's citizens of liberty without due process of law. The Fourteenth Amendment requires that freedom of choice to marry not be restricted by invidious racial discriminations. Under our Constitution, the freedom to marry, or not marry, a person of another race resides with the individual and cannot be infringed by the State.

These convictions must be reversed.

It is so ordered.

Mr. Justice Stewart, concurring.

I have previously expressed the belief that "it is simply not possible for a state law to be valid under our Constitution which make the criminality of an act depend upon the race of the actor." *McLaughlin* v. *Florida* ... (concurring opinion). Because I adhere to that belief, I concur in the judgment of the Court.

Despite the long list of cases denying governments the power to classify by race in regulatory legislation, it should not be assumed that they are barred from taking any cognizance whatever of race or color. There are valid uses for such notations, and as long as data concerning race or color are maintained for legitimate statistical or other valid public purposes, such record-keeping does not violate the constitution. Drivers' licenses presumably may properly require an entry showing race or color as an aid to identification, and certainly birth records and census reports would seem justifiably to contain the same information. In *Tancil* v. *Woolls,* 379 U.S. 19 (1964), the Court, in a Per Curiam opinion, affirmed a three-judge district court's judgment [230 F. Supp. 156 (E.D. Va., 1964)] upholding a Virginia statute which required that the race of the parties be identified in divorce decrees. It is clear, however, that record-keeping by race which may be maintained must not in any way suggest differential treatment, such as occurred in the jury selection cases, for example, or the procedure will not pass muster under the equal protection clause.

In 1971 the Court examined the question of whether a city's closing of a public swimming pool, following a court order to integrate the facility, was a violation of the equal protection clause. There was disagreement among the justices as to whether the primary motivation behind the decision to close the pool was to avoid financial loss or to evade the integration order, but the majority held that the action was not unconstitutional.

PALMER v. THOMPSON
403 U.S. 217 (1971)

[After federal litigation had resulted in a judgment declaring unconstitutional a Mississippi city's operation of public swimming pools on a racially segregated basis—four for whites only and one for Negroes only—the city council decided not to operate public swimming pools at all, and the pools were closed. Some Negro residents brought suit in federal court seeking to require the city to reopen the pools and to operate them on a desegregated basis. The District Court declined to issue an injunction, and the Court of Appeals affirmed.]

Mr. Justice Black delivered the opinion of the Court.

Petitioners rely chiefly on the first section of the Fourteenth Amendment which forbids and State to "deny to any person within its jurisdiction the equal protection of the laws." There can be no doubt that a major pupose of this Amendment was to safeguard Negroes against discriminatory state laws—state laws that fail to give Negroes protection equal to that afforded white people. . . . Here there has unquestionably been "state action" because the official local government legislature, the city council, has closed the public swimming pools of Jackson. The question, however, is whether this closing of the pools is state action that denies "the equal protection of the laws" to Negroes. It should be noted first that neither the Fourteenth Amendment nor any act of Congress purports to impose an affirmative duty on a State to begin to operate or to continue to operate swimming pools. Furthermore, this is not a case where whites are permitted to use public facilities while blacks are denied access. It is not a case where a city is maintaining different sets of facilities for blacks and whites and forcing the races to remain separate in recreational or educational activities. . . .

Unless, therefore, as petitioners urge, certain past cases require us to hold that closing the pools to all denied equal protection to Negroes, we must agree with the courts below and affirm.

Although petitioners cite a number of our previous cases, the only two which even plausibly support their argument are *Griffin* v. *County School Board of Prince Edward County,* 377 U.S. 218 (1964), and *Reitman* v. *Mulkey,* 387 U.S. 369 (1967). For the reasons that follow, however, neither case leads to reverse the judgment here.

A. In *Griffin* the public schools of Prince Edward County, Virginia, were closed under authority of state and county law, and so-called "private schools" were set up in their place to avoid a court desegregation order. . . . In Prince Edward County the "private schools" were open to whites only and these schools were in fact run by a practical partnership between state and county, designed to preserve segregated education. We pointed out in *Griffin* the many facets of state involvement in the running of the "private schools.". . . That case can give no comfort to petitioners here. This record supports no intimation that Jackson has not completely and finally ceased running swimming pools for all time. . . .

B. Petitioners also claim that Jackson's closing of the public pools authorizes or encourages private pool owners to discriminate on account of race and that such "encouragement" is prohibited by *Reitman* v. *Mulkey, supra.*

In *Reitman,* California had repealed two laws relating to racial discrimination in the sale of housing by passing a constitutional amendment establishing the right of private persons to discriminate on racial grounds in real estate transactions. This Court [held] that the constitutional amendment was an official authorization of racial discrimination which significantly involved the State in the discriminatory acts of private parties.... *Reitman* v. *Mulkey* was based on a theory that the evidence was sufficient to show the State was abetting a refusal to rent an apartment on racial grounds. On this record, *Reitman* offers no more support to petitioners than does *Griffin*.

Petitioners have also argued that respondents' action violates the Equal Protection Clause because the decision to close the pools was motivated by a desire to avoid integration of the races. But no case in this Court has held that a legislative act may violate equal protection solely because of the motivations of the men who voted for it....

It is true there is language in some of our cases interpreting the Fourteenth and Fifteenth Amendments which may suggest that the motive or purpose behind a law is relevant to its constitutionality. *Griffin* v. *Prince Edward County, supra; Gomillion* v. *Lightfoot*, 364 U.S. 339 (1960). But the focus in those cases was on the actual effect of the enactments, not upon the motivation which led the States to behave as they did.... Here the record indicates only that Jackson once ran segregated public swimming pools and that no public pools are now maintained by the city.... It shows no state action affecting blacks differently from whites.... The judgment is

Affirmed.

Mr. Chief Justice Burger, concurring. . . .

Mr. Justice Blackmun, concurring. . . .

Mr. Justice Douglas, dissenting. . . .

I conclude that though a State may discontinue any of its municipal services—such as schools, parks, pools, athletic fields, and the like—it may not do so for the purpose of perpetuating or installing apartheid or because it finds life in a multiracial community difficult or unpleasant. If that is its reason, then abolition of a designated public service becomes a device for perpetuating a segregated way of life. That a State may not do....

Mr. Justice White, with whom Mr. Justice Brennan and Mr. Justice Marshall join, dissenting....

Let us assume a city has been maintaining segregated swimming pools and is ordered to desegregate them. Its express response is an official resolution declaring desegregation to be contrary to the city's policy and ordering the facilities closed rather than continued in service on a desegregated basis. To me it is beyond cavil that on such facts the city is adhering to an unconstitutional policy and is implementing it by abandoning the facilities. It will not do in such circumstances to say that whites and Negroes are being treated alike because both are denied use of public services. The fact is that closing the pools is an expression of official policy that Negroes are unfit to associate with whites.... The Equal Protection Clause is a hollow promise if it does not forbid such official denigrations of the race the Fourteenth Amendment was designed to protect....

Mr. Justice Marshall, with whom Mr. Justice Brennan and Mr. Justice White join, dissenting....

... [W]hen the officials of Jackson, Mississippi, in the circumstances of this case, detailed by Mr. Justice White, denied a single Negro child the opportunity to go swimming simply because he is a Negro, rights guaranteed to that child by the Fourteenth Amendment were lost. The fact that the color of his skin is used to prevent others from swimming in public pools is irrelevant....

SEX DISCRIMINATION

A variety of earlier cases held that the state does not violate the equal protection clause by singling out women for special treatment in the exercise of the state's protective power. Classification has been upheld based on differences either in their physical characteristics or in the social conditions surrounding their employment. One of the earliest pieces of social legislation to be held valid by the Court was a law limiting hours of work for women in laundries to a ten-hour workday. [*Muller* v. *Oregon,* 208 U.S. 412 (1908).] In *Radice* v. *New York,* 264 U.S. 292 (1924), a law prohibiting women from working in restaurants at night was upheld. More recently, in *Goesaert* v. *Cleary,* 335 U.S. 464 (1948), the Court sustained a state statute forbidding women to act as bartenders, but making an exception in favor of wives and daughters of the male owners of liquor establishments, although three justices dissented. Justice Frankfurter, for the majority, stated:

We are, to be sure, dealing with a historic calling. We meet the alewife, sprightly and ribald, in Shakespeare, but centuries before him she played a role in the social life of England. . . . The Fourteenth Amendment did not tear history up by the roots, and the regulation of the liquor traffic is one of the oldest and most untrammeled of legislative powers. Michigan could, beyond question, forbid all women from working behind a bar. This is so despite the vast changes in the social and legal position of women. The fact that women may now have achieved the virtues that men have long claimed as their prerogatives and now indulge in vices that men have long practiced, does not preclude the States from drawing a sharp line between the sexes, certainly in such matters as the regulation of the liquor traffic. . . . The Constitution does not require legislatures to reflect sociological insight, or shifting social standards, any more than it requires them to keep abreast of the latest scientific standards.

The experiences of World War II, however, had shown to many people clear proof that women could perform just as competently and safeguard their morals at least as well as men in occupations which formerly had been denied them. Women drove taxis, welded, riveted, flew airplanes, and even did heavy construction work. And they did these jobs at all hours of the day and night. Understandably, many such women chafed under the resumption after the war of the so-called "protective" laws limiting the types of of employment for women or the hours in which they could work. Their criticisms began to reach legislative bodies and political party platform committees, and they charged that the only thing "protective" about such restrictions was the protection of men from female competition for their jobs. The dissenting opinion of Justice Rutledge, joined by Justices Douglas and Murphy, in the *Goesaert* case indicated a willingness to look more closely into the reasonableness of classifications based on sex. He stated, in part:

The statute arbitrarily discriminates between male and female owners of liquor establishments. A male owner, although he himself is always absent from his bar, may employ his wife and daughter as barmaids. A female owner may neither work as a barmaid herself nor employ her daughter in that position, even if a man is always present in the establishment to keep order. The inevitable result of the classification belies the assumption that the statute was motivated by a legislative solicitude for the moral and physical well-being of women who, but for the law, would be employed as barmaids. Since there could be no other conceivable justification for such discrimination against women owners of liquor establishments, the statute should be held invalid as a denial of equal protection.

In 1967 the United States Supreme Court denied a petition for certiorari to review a Tennessee rule of tort liability involving an unusual aspect of discrimination on the basis of sex. The case was *Krohn* v. *Richardson-Merrell, Inc.,* 406 S.W.2d 166 (Tennessee, 1966), a tort action against a drug company following the rendering of a man impotent as a consequence of using the company's drug. As one assignment of injury, the wife claimed damages for loss of consortium. Following the common-law rule, the Tennessee Supreme Court held that the wife could not maintain such an action and rejected her contention that permitting a husband but not a wife to recover for loss of consortium is an impermissible discrimination under the equal protection clause.

The Civil Rights Act of 1964, while primarily designed to prevent racial discrimination, includes in the Title VII provisions on Equal Employment Opportunity a provision that it shall be an unlawful employment practice for an employer, as defined by the Act, "to fail to refuse to hire or to discharge any individual, or otherwise to discriminate against any individual with respect to his compensation, terms, conditions, or privileges of employment, because of such individual's . . . sex. . . ." Employment agencies and labor unions are also barred from making classifications or otherwise discriminating on the basis of sex. The Title permits an exception, however, "in those certain instances where . . . sex . . . is a bona fide occupational qualification reasonably necessary to the normal operation of that particular business or enterprise." In order to implement these and other provisions of Title VII, the Equal Opportunity Commission is created by the Act and is given authority "to issue, amend, or rescind suitable procedural regulations to carry out the provisions of this title."

On November 22, 1965, Franklin D. Roosevelt, Jr., Chairman of the Commission, published the first guidelines (30 Federal Register 14926) on how the Commission construed its statutory duties under the provisions barring discrimination based on sex. The statement is made that "The commission does not believe that Congress intended to disturb such laws and regulations which are intended to, and have the effect of, protecting women against exploitation and hazard." It goes on to point out, however, that many laws originally enacted to protect women have ceased to be relevant to the nation's technology or to the expanding role of the woman worker in the economy. And in cases where the clear effect of a law in current circumstances is not to protect women but to subject them to discrimination, the law will not be considered a justification for discrimination. As an example, the Commission said it would honor state restrictions on lifting weights except where the limit is set at an unreasonably low level that could not endanger women.

In *Phillips* v. *Marietta Corp.,* 400 U.S. 542 (1971), the Court held that §703 (a) of the Civil Rights Act of 1964, which prohibits discriminatory hiring practices because of sex, was violated by an employer who refused to accept applications from women with preschool-age children, although it did employ men with preschool-age children. In the Per Curiam opinion, however, the case was remanded with the suggestion that the existence of such conflicting family obligations, "if demonstrably more relevant to job performance for a woman than for a man, could arguably be a basis for distinction under §703 (e) of the Act."

In 1971 the Supreme Court for the first time in history held a law unconstitutional on the ground that it discriminated against women in violation of the equal protection clause. The case grew out of the appointment of an administrator for the estate of a minor child under a construction of the relevant Idaho law which accorded preference for the appointment of the father rather than the mother to such positions.

REED v. REED
404 U.S. 71 (1971)

[After the death of an adopted, minor son, the mother, who had separated from the father, filed a petition in the Probate Court of Ada County, Idaho, seeking appointment as administratrix of her son's estate. Prior to a hearing on the mother's petition, the father filed a competing petition seeking to have himself appointed administrator. Under the Idaho Probate Code, the parents of a decedent are in the same entitlement class for appointment as administrator. The Probate Court, apparently without attempting to determine the relative capability of the competing applicants, ordered that letters of administration be issued to the father, on the basis of a provision of the Probate Code that males must be preferred to females where persons of equal entitlement seek to administer an estate. On appeal by the mother, the District Court of Idaho reversed, holding that the statute violated the Fourteenth Amendment equal protection clause. The Supreme Court of Idaho reversed.]

Mr. Chief Justice Burger delivered the opinion of the Court....

... The court treated ... the Idaho Code as the controlling statutes and read those sections as compelling a preference for Cecil Reed because he was a male....

... Having examined the record and considered the briefs and oral arguments of the parties, we have concluded that the arbitrary preference established in favor of males by ... the Idaho Code cannot stand in the face of the Fourteenth Amendment's command that no State deny the equal protection of the laws to any person within its jurisdiction.

Idaho does not, of course, deny letters of administration to women altogether. Indeed, under §15–312, a woman whose spouse dies intestate has a preference over a son, father, brother, or any other male relative of the decedent. Moreover, we can judicially notice that in this country, presumably due to the greater longevity of women, a large proportion of estates, both intestate and under wills of decedents, are administered by surviving widows.

Section 15–314 is restricted in its operation to those situations where competing applications for letters of administration have been filed by both male and female members of the same entitlement class.... In such situations, §15–314 provides that different treatment be accorded to the applicants on the basis of their sex; it thus establishes a classification subject to scrutiny under the Equal Protection Clause.

In applying that clause, this Court has consistently recognized that the Fourteenth Amendment does not deny to States the power to treat different classes of persons in different ways.... The Equal Protection Clause of that Amendment does, however, deny to States the power to legislate that different treatment be accorded to persons placed by a statute into different classes on the basis of criteria wholly unrelated to the objective of that statute. . . . The question presented by this case, then, is whether a difference in the sex of competing applicants for letters of administration bears a rational relationship to a state objective that is sought to be advanced by the operation of [the statutes].

In upholding the latter section, the Idaho Supreme Court concluded that its objective was to eliminate one area of controversy when two or more persons, equally entitled, . . . seek letters of administration and thereby present the probate court "with the issue of which one should be named." The court also concluded that where such persons are not of the same sex, the elimination of females from consideration "is neither an illogical nor arbitrary method devised by the legislature to resolve an issue that would otherwise require a hearing as to the relative merits . . . of the two or more petitioning relatives. . . ." . . .

Clearly the objective of reducing the workload on probate courts by eliminating one class of contests is not without some legitimacy. The crucial question, however, is whether §15–314 advances that objective in a manner consistent with the command of the Equal Protection Clause. We hold that it does not. To give a mandatory preference to members of either sex over members of the other, merely to accomplish the elimination of hearings on the merits, is to make the very kind of arbitrary legislative choice forbidden by the Equal Protection Clause of the Fourteenth Amendment; and whatever may be said as to the positive values of avoiding intrafamily controversy, the choice in this context may not lawfully be mandated solely on the basis of sex. . . .

The judgment of the Idaho Supreme Court is reversed and the case remanded for further proceedings not inconsistent with this opinion.

Reversed and remanded.

In *Stanley* v. *Illinois*, 405 U.S. 645 (1972), Illinois statutes were challenged which permitted custody of illegitimate children by the unwed mother but did not even allow the unwed father a hearing to determine fitness for custody, presuming him to be unfit. A majority of the Court held that such discrimination violated the equal protection clause, and that both the father and the mother should be accorded equal rights to hearing on the issue of fitness before removing children from custody.

In 1972 a major victory was won by opponents of sex discrimination—the adoption by Congress of the Equal Rights Amendment. Section 1 of the proposed Amendment, the substantive section, states:

Equality of rights under the law shall not be denied or abridged by the United States or by any State on account of sex.

The second section gives Congress the power to pass appropriate legislation to enforce this provision. The amendment was proposed on March 22, 1972, and by December 1 twenty-two states had ratified. As of this writing, thirty-four of the required thirty-eight ratifications have been obtained. In many of the state legislatures the fight over ratification has been long and often bitter. The proponents of ratification have included a large number of men and the opponents have included a substantial female population. Debate over the impact of the proposed amendment has ranged from the question of whether women would be required to have combat assignments in the military to whether women might have to pay alimony in some divorce cases to whether separate restroom facilities would be unconstitutional. Some of the arguments which have appeared are to be found in the Court's opinion in a sex discrimination case involving military policy, *Frontiero* v. *Richardson.*

FRONTIERO *v.* RICHARDSON
411 U.S. 677 (1973)

[A servicewoman's application for increased quarters allowances and medical and dental benefits for her husband as a dependent was denied because she failed to demonstrate that her husband was dependent on her for more than one-half of his support, as required by various sections of the United States Code. Thereupon the servicewoman sued in the United States District Court in Alabama, contending that the statutes—which allow a serviceman to claim his wife as a dependent for such benefits without regard to whether she is in fact dependent upon him for any part of her support—unreasonably discriminated on the basis of sex in violation of the due process clause of the Fifth Amendment. The three-judge District Court upheld the constitutionality of the statutes.]

Mr. Justice Brennan announced the judgment of the Court and an opinion in which Mr. Justice Douglas, Mr. Justice White, and Mr. Justice Marshall join.

The question before us concerns the right of a female member of the uniformed services to claim her spouse as a "dependent" for the purposes of obtaining increased quarters allowances and medical and dental benefits ... on an equal footing with male members. Under these statutes, a serviceman may claim his wife as a "dependent" without regard to whether she is in fact dependent upon him for any part of her support.... A servicewoman, on the other hand, may not claim her husband as a "dependent" under these programs unless he is in fact dependent upon her for over one-half of his support.... Thus, the question for decision is whether this difference in treatment constitutes an unconstitutional discrimination against servicewomen in violation of the Due Process Clause of the Fifth Amendment....

At the outset, appellants contend that classifications based upon sex, like classifications based upon race, alienage, and national origin, are inherently suspect and must therefore be subjected to close judicial scrutiny. We agree and, indeed, find at least implicit support for such an approach in our unanimous decision only last Term in *Reed* v. *Reed* ... (1971)....

There can be no doubt that our Nation has had a long and unfortunate history of sex discrimination. Traditionally, such discrimination was rationalized by an attitude of "romantic paternalism" which, in practical effect, put women, not on a pedestal, but in a cage. Indeed, this paternalistic attitude became so firmly rooted in our national consciousness that, 100 years ago, a distinguished Member of this Court was able to proclaim:

"Man is, or should be, woman's protector and defender. The natural and proper timidity and delicacy which belongs to the female sex evidently unfits it for many of the occupations of civil life. The constitution of the family organization, which is founded in the divine ordinance, as well as in the nature of things, indicates the domestic sphere as that which properly belongs to the domain and functions of womanhood. The harmony, not to say identity, of interests and views which belong, or should belong, to the family institution is repugnant to the idea of a woman adopting a distinct and independent career from that of her husband....

"... The paramount destiny and mission of woman are to fulfill the noble and benign offices of wife and mother. This is the law of the Creator." *Bradwell* v. *Illinois,* 16 Wall. 141 (1873) (Bradley, J., concurring).

As a result of notions such as these, our statute books gradually became laden with gross, stereotyped distinctions between the sexes and, indeed, throughout much of the 19th century the position of women in our society was, in many respects, comparable to that of blacks under the pre-Civil War slave codes. Neither slaves nor women could hold office, serve on juries, or bring suit in their own names, and married women traditionally were denied the legal capacity to hold or convey property or to serve as legal guardians of their own children.... And although blacks were guaranteed the right to vote in 1870, women were denied even that right—which is itself "preservative of other basic civil and political rights" until adoption of the Nineteenth Amendment half a century later.

It is true, of course, that the position of women in America has improved markedly in recent decades. Nevertheless, it can hardly be doubted that, in part because of the high visibility of the sex characteristic, women still face pervasive, although at times more subtle, discrimination in our educational institutions, in the job market and, perhaps most conspicuously, in the political arena....

... [W]hat differentiates sex from such nonsuspect statutes as intelligence or physical disability, and aligns it with the recognized suspect criteria, is that the sex characteristic frequently bears no relation to ability to perform or contribute to society. As a result, statutory distinctions between the sexes often have the effect of invidiously relegating the entire class of females to inferior legal status without regard to the actual capabilities of its individual members.

We might also note that, over the past decade, Congress has itself manifested an increasing sensitivity to sex-based classifications. [The opinion here cites Title VII of the Civil Rights Act of 1964, the Equal Pay Act of 1963, and the Equal Rights Amendment, passed by Congress in 1972 and submitted to the States for ratification.] Thus, Congress itself has concluded that classifications based upon sex are inherently invidious, and this conclusion of a coequal branch of Government is not without significance to the question presently under consideration....

With these considerations in mind, we can only conclude that classifications based upon sex, like classifications based upon race, alienage, or national origin, are inherently suspect, and must therefore be subjected to strict judicial scrutiny. Applying the analysis mandated by that stricter standard of review, it is clear that the statutory scheme now before us is constitutionally invalid....

... [T]he Government concedes that the differential treatment accorded men and women under these statutes serves no purpose other than mere "administrative convenience." In essence, the Government maintains that, as an empirical matter, wives in our society frequently are dependent upon their husbands, while husbands rarely are dependent upon their wives. Thus, the Government argues that Congress might reasonably have concluded that it would be both cheaper and easier simply conclusively to presume that wives of male members are financially dependent upon their husbands, while burdening female members with the task of establishing dependency in fact....

... [O]ur prior decisions make clear that, although efficacious administration of governmental programs is not without some importance, "the Constitution recognizes higher values than speed and efficiency." *Stanley* v. *Illinois,* ... (1972). And when we enter the realm of "strict judicial scrutiny," there can be no doubt that "administrative convenience" is not a shibboleth, the mere recitation of which dictates constitutionality.... On the contrary, any statutory scheme which draws a sharp line between the sexes, *solely* for the purpose of achieving administrative convenience, necessarily commands "dissimilar treatment for men and women who are ... similarly situated," and therefore involves the "very kind of arbitrary legislative choice forbidden by the [Constitution]. ..." *Reed* v. *Reed*. ... We therefore conclude that, by according differential treatment to male and female members of the uniformed services for the sole purpose of achieving administrative convenience, the challenged statutes violate the Due Process Clause of the Fifth Amendment insofar as they require a female member to prove the dependency of her husband.

Reversed.

Mr. Justice Stewart concurs in the judgment, agreeing that the statutes before us work an invidious discrimination in violation of the Constitution. *Reed* v. *Reed*.

Mr. Justice Rehnquist dissents. ...

Mr. Justice Powell, with whom The Chief Justice and Mr. Justice Blackmun join, concurring in the judgment.

I agree that the challenged statutes constitute an unconstitutional discrimination against servicewomen in violation of the Due Process Clause of the Fifth Amendment, but I cannot join the opinion of Mr. Justice Brennan, which would hold that all classifications based upon sex, "like classifications based upon race, alienage, and national origin," are "inherently suspect and must therefore be subjected to close judicial scrutiny."... It is unnecessary for the Court in this case to characterize sex as a suspect classification, with all of the far-reaching implications of such a holding. *Reed* v. *Reed* ..., which abundantly supports our decision today, did not add sex to the narrowly limited group of classifications which are inherently suspect. In my view, we can and should decide this case on the authority of *Reed* and reserve for the future any expansion of its rationale.

There is another, and I find compelling, reason for deferring a general categorizing of sex classifications as invoking the strictest test of judicial scrutiny. The Equal Rights Amendment, which if adopted will resolve the substance of this precise question, has been approved by the Congress and submitted for ratification by the States. If this Amendment is duly adopted, it will represent the will of the people accomplished in the manner prescribed by the Constitution. By acting prematurely and unnecessarily, as I view it, the Court has assumed a decisional responsibility at the very time when state legislatures, functioning within the traditional democratic process, are debating the proposed Amendment. It seems to me that this reaching out to preempt by judicial action a major political decision which is currently in process of resolution does not reflect appropriate respect for duly prescribed legislative processes. ...

In *Cleveland Board of Education* v. *La Fleur*, 414 U.S. 632 (1974), certain pregnant teachers had challenged the constitutionality of the Board's maternity leave policy which provided that a pregnant teacher must take maternity leave beginning five months before the expected birth of the child, that the teacher give notice of her pregnancy at least two weeks prior to the time when she must begin her maternity leave, and that she could become eligible for reemployment no sooner than the beginning of the next school semester after her child was three months old, provided that a doctor issued a certificate attesting to the teacher's health. The Court held the policy unconstitutional, but the decision came on due process grounds rather than equal protection. The majority found the notice provision reasonable, but held that the mandatory employment termination provisions and the waiting period rule violative of the due process clause as not being necessary for continuity of instruction or for keeping physically unfit teachers out of the classroom since they established a conclusive presumption of the physical incapacity of the teacher during these periods and such presumptions were neither necessarily nor universally true. Justice Stewart, for the majority, stated, "While the medical experts in these cases differed on many points, they unanimously agreed on one—the ability of any particular pregnant woman to continue at work past any fixed time in her pregnancy is very much an individual matter." As to the three-months-of-age provision for eligibility to return, the opinion stated, "To the extent that the three-month provision reflects the school board's thinking that no mother is fit to return until that point in time, it suffers from the same constitutional deficiencies that plague the irrebuttable presumption in the termination rules." It was also considered unnecessary, since the requirement of a physician's certificate fully protected the school's interest in this regard.

In *Stanton* v. *Stanton,* 421 U.S. 7 (1975), Utah statutes were challenged which provided that males attained majority at age twenty-one and females at age eighteen, and thus a father's responsibility for child support payments following a divorce decree ceased at age eighteen for females but continued to age twenty-one for males. The Court held that *Reed* v. *Reed* was controlling, and that "in the context of child support the classification effectuated ... denies the equal protection of the laws, as guaranteed by the Fourteenth Amendment." The Court was unimpressed with the Utah court's "old notions" that females tend to marry earlier than males, and that since it is the man's primary responsibility to provide a home, it is salutary for him to have education and training before he assumes that responsibility. Justice Blackmun, for the Court, stated, "To distinguish between the two on educational grounds is to be self-serving: if the female is not to be supported so long as the male, she hardly can be expected to attend school as long as he does, and bringing her education to an end earlier coincides with the role-typing society has long imposed."

One of the most controversial developments in the movement toward abolition of sex discrimination has been the establishment of new guidelines by HEW for "Nondiscrimination on the Basis of Sex in Education Programs and Activities Receiving or Benefitting from Federal Financial Assistance." The regulations were issued to effectuate Title IX of the Education Amendments of 1972 and became operative as of July 21, 1975 (40 *Federal Register* 24128, 1975). While a variety of topics are covered, the application of the regulations to the athletic programs of colleges and universities seemed to stir the greatest opposition. Equal athletic opportunities must be provided for members of both sexes, including provision of equipment and supplies, travel and per diem allowance, provision of housing and dining facilities and services, and others. And if the school awards athletic scholarships or grants-in-aid, §86.37 requires that "it must provide reasonable opportunities for such awards for members of each sex in proportion to the number of students of each participating in interscholastic or intercollegiate athletics." In other areas, neither students nor employees may be discriminated against on the basis of pregnancy, and the schools are directed to treat pregnancy under the same policies as any other temporary disability. Admission and hiring policies must be absolutely nondiscriminatory, except to the extent that "sex is a bonafide occupational qualification." Schools may provide separate housing facilities by sex, but such facilities must be comparable in quality and cost to the student and must be proportionate in quantity to the number of students of each sex applying for housing. In general, the guidelines represent a full-scale effort to accomplish the purposes of Title IX, which provides that "No person in the United States shall on the basis of sex, be excluded from participation in, be denied the benefits of, or be subjected to discrimination under any education program or activity receiving Federal financial assistance." The only exceptions are for certain religious institutions, military and merchant marine educational institutions, and certain voluntary organizations such as social fraternities and sororities, the YMCA, the YWCA, and the Boy Scouts and Girl Scouts.

[The literature on sex discrimination and women's rights is now voluminous. A few useful items are: J. D. Johnston, Jr., "Sex Discrimination and the Supreme Court—1971–1974," 49 *N.Y.U. L. Rev.* 617 (1974); Panel, "Men, Women, and the Constitution: the Equal Rights Amendment," 10 *Colum. J. L. & Soc. Prob.* 77 (1973); Karen DeCrow, *Sexist Justice* (New York: Random House, 1974); "Equal Rights for Women: A Symposium on the Proposed Constitutional Amendment," 6 *Harvard Civil Rights-Civil Liberties L. Rev.* 2 (1971); Roxanne B. Conlin, "Equal Protection Versus Equal Rights Amendment—Where Are We Now?" 24 *Drake L. Rev.* 259 (1975); and E. Boyd Steele, "The Legal Status of Women," *Book of the States, 1972–1973* (Lexington: Council of State Governments, 1972).]

CHAPTER 8

Voting and Apportionment

The framers of the United States Constitution clearly contemplated that the basic power to regulate elections and fix voter qualifications would rest with the states. Except for the "dead letter" provisions of Section 2 of the Fourteenth Amendment, the only affirmative statements of qualifications of voters are found in Article I, Section 2, and the Seventeenth Amendment, and these provisions only go so far as to require that persons voting for members of the Congress "shall have the Qualifications requisite for Electors of the most numerous Branch of the State Legislature." Thus the states were left with broad leeway in determining the manner in which elections would be conducted and the persons who could participate in them. From 1964 to the present a number of changes have occurred, brought about by constitutional amendments, enactments by Congress, and judicial revision of some of the older provisions of the Constitution, which have resulted in greater uniformity in voter requirements. Before that time, while the general outlines were similar, there was considerable variation in the requirements for voting and candidacy and in the situations which would disqualify persons from continuing to exercise the franchise. For example, the age requirement was usually twenty-one years, but Georgia and Kentucky set the voting age at eighteen, Alaska at nineteen, and Hawaii at twenty. And while the usual residence requirement was one year, some states required only six months and others two years. Approximately one-third of the states employed literacy tests of one kind or another, and eleven southern states made prior payment of a poll tax a condition of voting. Although all states now require citizenship, there have been some twenty states which at one time or other have allowed aliens to vote before their naturalization was complete. [See Constance E. Smith, *Voting and Election Laws* (New York: Oceana Publications, 1960).]

If this were the whole of the picture of regulations concerning voting and elections, then any problems would be resolved simply by reference to the respective state laws. Complications are introduced, however, by the fact that the Constitution both gives to Congress certain powers to regulate elections and sets certain limits on the states in the exercise of their regulatory powers over certain voting and elections. It is in the treatment accorded these two areas by the Congress and the courts in the past hundred years, rather than in positive state laws, that the major developments have occurred in safeguarding and expanding the basic right to vote.

CONSTITUTIONAL LIMITATIONS ON STATE VOTING REGULATIONS

The provisions of the United States Constitution which serve to limit the states in the area of voting and elections are the Fourteenth Amendment's equal protection clause, the Fifteenth Amendment, the Nineteenth Amendment, the Twenty-fourth Amendment, and the Twenty-sixth Amendment. In brief, the equal protection clause denies the state the power to make unreasonable classifications in the matter of voting, the Fifteenth Amendment prohibits both the states and the United States from abridging the right to vote because of race or color, and the Nineteenth Amendment prohibits both the states and the United States from abridging the right to vote because of sex. The Twenty-fourth Amendment bars the states and the United States from requiring the payment of a poll tax as a condition of voting for federal officials, and the Twenty-sixth Amendment forbids the states and the United States from denying persons eighteen years of age or older the right to vote because of age. It should be noted that in each of the Amendments the prohibitions lie against action carried through by *governments,* and none of the restrictions runs against purely *private* action to interfere with voting. In a case alleging a violation of the equal protection clause, the court must make affirmative findings in response to two questions before it can offer a remedy: (1) Was the alleged interference accomplished by means of state action? and (2) Was the interference a result of improper classification either in a statute or in its administration? In a case alleging a violation of the other Amendments, the court must also make affirmative findings in response to certain questions, but they are slightly different from those which would be raised in an equal protection claim. In a Fifteenth Amendment case, for example, the issues would be: (1) Was the alleged interference accomplished by means of either state or federal action? (2) Was the attempted electoral participation of the kind guaranteed in the phrase "right to vote"? and (3) Was the alleged denial of electoral participation based on race or color? Only if the answer to all three questions is in the affirmative can the court offer a remedy.

Race Discrimination: The White Primary Cases

In the latter part of the nineteenth century the southern states adopted a variety of provisions directed largely toward disfranchisement of the Negro. These included such voter requirements as long residence, payment of a poll tax, literacy tests (often discriminatorily administered), and the production of a receipt proving payment of the previous year's taxes. But as the selection of candidates by primary elections instead of party conventions became general, the main thrust of the southern effort was directed toward preventing the Negro from participating in the Democratic primaries. In the "solid South" until fairly recently, winning the Democratic pimary was tantamount to election, and thus, even if participation in the general elections was permitted, it was largely futile. The first of the white primary cases to reach the Court was *Nixon* v. *Herndon,* 273 U.S. 536 (1927). The Texas election law of 1923 provided that "in no event shall a negro be eligible to participate in a Democratic Party primary election held in the State of Texas." This provision might appear at first glance to have been a clear-cut violation of the Fifteenth Amendment. But until 1941 the Court did not take a clear stand that the Fifteenth Amendment "right to vote" included the right to vote in a primary. With this uncertainty the Court in *Nixon* v. *Herndon* chose the safer course of ruling the provision unconstitutional as a denial of equal protection of the laws under the Fourteenth Amendment. A substitute statute was then passed authorizing the state executive committee of every political party to fix qualifications for participating in their respective primaries. The state executive committee of the Democratic Party then adopted a rule barring Negroes from participation in its primaries. In *Nixon* v. *Condon,* 286 U.S. 73 (1932), the Court held that this was a delegation of state power to the state executive committee and made its determination conclusive irrespective of any expression of the partys' will by its convention, and therefore the committee's action barring Negroes from the party primaries was "state action" prohibited by the Fourteenth Amendment. Undaunted, the Texas legislature then repealed its statutes regarding party membership and left the matter solely to the parties. In 1932 the state Democratic convention of Texas adopted a resolution limiting membership in the Democratic Party, and thereby participation in the primaries, to white persons. When this resolution as well was challenged, in *Grovey* v. *Townsend,* 294 U.S. 699 (1935), the Court's uncertainties regarding the right to participate in a primary election as well as the status of a state party convention's determinations under the "state action" definition combined to produce a decision that the petitioner was not denied "any right guaranteed by the Fourteenth and Fifteenth Amendments." The Court held that arguments directed toward the right to membership in a party and participation in its primaries were confused with the right to vote for one who is to hold a public office. "With the former the state need have no concern, with the latter it is bound to concern itself...." With regard to the status of the Democratic convention, the opinion stated, "We are not prepared to hold that in Texas the state convention of a party has become a mere instrumentality or agency for expressing the voice or will of the state."

In 1941, however, the Court held in *United States* v. *Classic* that a citizen's right to vote in a congressional primary and to have his vote properly counted is a federal right protected by the Constitution.

UNITED STATES *v.* CLASSIC
313 U.S. 299 (1941)

[Classic and others, election commissioners, were charged with willfully altering and falsely counting and certifying the ballots in a Democratic primary in Louisiana at which a candidate for representative in Congress was being nominated. The indictment was brought in a federal district court under Sections 19 and 20 of the United States Criminal Code. Section 19 makes criminal any conspiracy to injure a citizen in the exercise "of any right or privilege secured to him by the Constitution or laws of the United States." Section 20 makes it a crime for anyone "acting under color of any law" willfully to subject any person to the deprivation of any rights protected by the Constitution and laws of the United States. The constitutional question turned on the issue of whether Congress' power to regulate "elections" for Senators and Representatives under Article I, Section 4, extended to the regulation of primaries in which candidates for such positions were nominated. Convictions were obtained in the trial court, but the Court of Appeals reversed.]

Mr. Justice Stone delivered the opinion of the Court. . . .

. . . [T]he practical operation of the primary in Louisiana, is and has been since the primary election was established in 1900 to secure the election of the Democratic primary nominee for the Second Congressional District of Louisiana.

Interference with the right to vote in the congressional primary in the Second Congressional District for the choice of Democratic candidate for Congress is thus as a matter of law and in fact an interference with the effective choice of the voters at the only stage of the election procedure when their choice is of significance, since it is at the only stage when such interference could have any practical effect on the ultimate result, the choice of the Congressman to represent the district. The primary in Louisiana is an integral part of the procedure for the popular choice of Congressman. The right of qualified voters to vote at the congressional primary in Louisiana and to have their ballots counted is thus the right to participate in that choice.

We come then to the question whether that right is one secured by the Constitution. Section 2 of Article I commands that Congressmen shall be chosen by the people of the several states by electors, the qualifications of which it prescribes. The right of the people to choose, whatever its appropriate constitutional limitations, where in other respects it is defined, and the mode of its exercise is prescribed by state action in conformity to the Constitution, is a right established and guaranteed by the Constitution and hence is one secured by it to those citizens and inhabitants of the state entitled to exercise the right. *Ex parte Yarbrough,* 110 U.S. 651. . . . While, in a loose sense, the right to vote for representatives in Congress is sometimes spoken of as a right derived from the states, see *Minor v. Happersett,* 21 Wall. 162, . . . this statement is true only in the sense that the states are authorized by the Constitution, to legislate on the subject as provided by Section 2 of Article I, to the extent that Congress has not restricted state action by the exercise of its powers to regulate elections under Section 4 and its more general power under Article I, Section 8, clause 18 of the Constitution "to make all laws which shall be necessary and proper for carrying into execution the foregoing powers.". . .

Obviously included within the right to choose, secured by the Constitution, is the right of qualified voters within a state to cast their ballots and have them counted at congressional elections. This Court has consistently held that this is a right secured by the Constituiton. . . . And since the constitutional command is without restriction or limitation, the right, unlike those guaranteed by the Fourteenth and Fifteenth Amendments, is secured against the action of individuals as well as of states. *Ex parte Yarbrough.* . . .

. . . The right to participate in the choice of representatives for Congress includes, as we have said, the right to cast a ballot and to have it counted at the general election whether for the successful candidate or not. Where the state law has made the primary an integral part of the procedure of choice, or where in fact the primary effectively controls the choice, the right of the elector to have his ballot counted at the primary, is likewise included in the right protected by Article I, Section 2. And this right of participation is protected just as is the right to vote at the election, where the primary is by law made an integral part of the election machinery, whether the voter exercises his right in a party primary which invariably, sometimes or never determines the ultimate choice of the representatives. . . .

. . . The words of Sections 2 and 4 of Article I, read in the sense which is plainly permissible and in the light of the constitutional purpose, requires us to hold that a primary election which involves a necessary step in the choice of candidates for election as representatives in Congress, and which in the circumstances of this case controls that choice, is an election within the meaning of the constitutional provision and is subject to congressional regulation as to the manner of holding it. . . .

Reversed.

[Mr. Justice Douglas wrote a dissenting opinion, in which Justices Black and Murphy joined, arguing that as a matter of statutory construction, Congress did not intend to reach congressional primaries when it enacted the sections applied in this case.]

While the *Classic* case did not deal directly with the question of the validity of white primaries, the relevance of the decision to the problem in *Grovey* v. *Townsend* was obvious. If "elections" in Article I, Section 4, included primaries, then the "right to vote" protected by the Fifteenth Amendment should also extend to the right to participate in primaries. In short order, another case was brought up from Texas for a reexamination of the *Grovey* rule, and in *Smith* v. *Allwright* in 1944 *Grovey* was overruled.

SMITH *v.* ALLWRIGHT
321 U.S. 649 (1944)

Mr. Justice Reed delivered the opinion of the Court. . . .

. . . When *Grovey* v. *Townsend* was written, the Court looked upon the denial of a vote in a primary as a mere refusal by a party of party membership. As the Louisiana statutes for holding primaries are similar to those of Texas, our ruling in *Classic* as to the unitary character of the electoral process calls for a reexamination as to whether or not the exclusion of Negroes from a Texas party primary was state action. . . .

It may now be taken as a postulate that the right to vote in such a primary for the nomination of candidates without discrimination by the State, like the right to vote in a general election, is a right secured by the Constitution. . . .

Primary elections are conducted by the party under state statutory authority. The county executive committee selects precinct election officials and the county, district or state executive committees, respectively, canvass the returns. These party committees or the state convention certify the party's candidates to the appropriate officers for inclusion on the official ballot for the general election. No name which has not been so certified may appear upon the ballot for the general election as a candidate of a political party. No other name may be printed on the ballot which has not been placed in nomination by qualified voters who must take oath that they did not participate in a primary for the selection of a candidate for the office for which the nomination is made.

The state courts are given exclusive original jurisdiction of contested elections and of mandamus proceedings to compel party officers to perform their statutory duties.

We think that this statutory system for the selection of party nominees for inclusion on the general election ballot makes the party which is required to follow these legislative directions an agency for the state in so far as it determines the participants in a primary election. . . . If the state requires a certain electoral procedure, prescribes a general election ballot made up of party nominees so chosen and limits the choice of the electorate in general elections for state offices, practically speaking, to those whose names appear on such a ballot, it endorses, adopts and enforces the discrimination against Negroes, practiced by a party entrusted by Texas law with the determination of the qualifications of participants in the primary. This is state action within the meaning of the Fifteenth Amendment. . . .

The privilege of membership in a party may be, as this Court said in *Grovey* v. *Townsend,* no concern of a state. But when, as here, that privilege is also the essential qualification for voting in a primary to select nominees for a general election, the state makes the action of the party the action of the state. . . . *Grovey* v. *Townsend is overruled.*

Judgment reversed.

Mr. Justice Frankfurter concurs in the result.

Mr. Justice Roberts, dissenting. . . .

The reason for my concern is that the instant decision, overruling that announced about nine years ago, tends to bring adjudications of this tribunal into the same class as a restricted railroad ticket, good for this day and train only. I have no assurance, in view of current decisions, that the opinion announced today may not shortly be repudiated and overruled by justices who deem they have new light on the subject. In the present Term the Court has overruled three cases. . . .

Smith v. *Allwright* would seem to have settled the matter of the white primary once and for all, but this was not the case. The South Carolina legislature was called into special session and, taking its cue from the way Justice Reed found "state action" in the Texas case, repealed all statutes (nearly 150 in all) relating in any way to primaries and proposed amendments to the state constitution to remove any similar provisions in the constitution. The theory was that such action would leave the political party in the same position as any other private club, and its acts would in no way be construed as state action. This done, a Democratic state convention adopted a rule barring Negroes from membership in the Democratic Club and, therefore, from participation in its primaries.

A federal district court issued an injunction against an official of the Democratic Party to prevent his denying Negroes the right to vote in the primaries. [*Elmore* v. *Rice,* 72 F. Supp. 516 (E.D.S.C., 1947).] In *Rice* v. *Elmore,* 165 F.2d 387 (4th Cir., 1947), this ruling was affirmed by the Court of Appeals. [*Cert. denied,* 333 U.S. 875 (1948).] Judge Parker, speaking for the court of appeals, stated:

The fundamental error in defendant's position consists in the premise that a political party is a mere private aggregation of individuals, like a country club, and that the primary is a mere piece of party machinery. . . . [W]ith the passage of the years, poltical parties have become in effect state institutions, governmental agencies through which sovereign power is exercised by the people. . . .

The closing chapter in the white primary story saw a return to Texas and a challenge to the racially exclusionary practices of the Jaybird Democratic Association of Fort Bend County, Texas. The Jaybird Association was organized in 1889 and limited its membership to white registered voters. Candidates for county offices submitted their names to the Jaybird Committee and ran in a primary held by the Association prior to the regular Democratic primary. The winners normally ran subsequently in the regular Democratic primary without opposition and won both that and the general election folliwing. In *Terry* v. *Adams,* 345 U.S. 461 (1953), the Court held such a procedure violatlve of the Fifteenth Amendment. Justice Black, for three of the majority, stated:

> For a state to permit such a duplication of its election processes is to permit a flagrant abuse of those processes to defeat the purposes of the Fifteenth Amendment. The use of the county-operated primary to ratify the results of the prohibited election merely compounds the offense. It violates the Fifteenth Amendment for a state, by such circumvention, to permit within its borders the use of any device that produces an equivalent of the prohibited election. . . .

> . . . It is immaterial that the state does not control that part of this elective process which it leaves for the Jaybirds to manage. The Jaybird primary has become an integral, indeed the only effective part, of the elective process that determines who shall rule and govern in the county. The effect of the whole procedure, Jaybird primary plus Democratic primary plus general election, is to do precisely that which the Fifteenth Amendment forbids—strip Negroes of every vestige of influence in selecting the officials who control the local county matters that intimately touch the daily lives of citizens. . . .

Five other members of the Court concurred in the result, but for slightly different reasons. Justice Minton was the lone dissenter, arguing that the actions of the Jaybird Association could not properly be held to be state action. [On the white primary, see Douglas Weeks, "The White Primary: 1944–1948," 42 *Am. Pol. Sci. Rev.* 500 (1948); V. O. Key, *Southern Politics* (New York: Knopf, 1949), pp. 625–643; and Thurgood Marshall, "The Rise and Collapse of the 'White Primary,' " 26 *J. of Negro Ed.* 249 (1957).]

The Grandfather Clauses

Among other devices employed to impede voting by Negroes was the "grandfather clause," used by several states beginning in 1895. Without expressly disfranchising the Negro, it facilitated the permanent placement of white residents on the lists of registered voters while continuing to impose serious obstacles upon Negro registration. The typical provision required all prospective electors to be able to read and write any section of the state constitution, but no person who voted prior to January 1, 1866, or who was a lineal descendant of such person, could be denied the right to register and vote because of his inability to meet this literacy requirement. The clause did not, therefore, bar Negroes from being registered, but because of the operative date, all Negroes had to pass the literacy test while most white persons were exempt. In *Guinn* v. *United States,* 238 U.S. 347 (1915), the Court held that the employment by the state of Oklahoma of a standard based purely upon a period of time before the enactment of the Fifteenth Amendment and which so clearly set up a classification following racial lines was in violation of the protection accorded by that Amendment. Oklahoma promptly adopted a new statute in 1916 which provided that all persons, except those who voted in 1914, who were qualified to vote in 1916 but who failed to register between April 30 and May 11, 1916 (a twelve-day registration period) should be perpetually disfranchised. The Court was not impressed with this obvious subterfuge, and in *Lane* v. *Wilson,* 307 U.S. 268 (1939), held this statute also violative of the Fifteenth Amendment. In a sharply worded opinion, Justice Frankfurter stated that that Amendment "nullifies sophisticated as well as simple-minded modes of discrimination. It hits onerous procedural requirements which effectively handicap exercise of the franchise by the colored race although the abstract right to vote may remain unrestricted as to race."

Poll Taxes

There were at one time in the period following Reconstruction some eleven southern states which imposed a poll tax as a prerequisite to voting. The amount of the tax ranged from one to two dollars, and some statutes exempted women and older persons. Whether the tax had greater impact on Negroes than on white persons has been a matter of some dispute. Certainly in the manner of administration, and in the fact that it was cumulative in some states, it was a factor in discouraging voter registration whether there was special racial impact or not. Payment was normally voluntary and, since tax bills were not usually sent out, the voter had to keep track of annual deadlines and take the initiative in seeking out the proper officials to whom the poll tax was to be paid. Until a 1953 amendment was adopted, the Alabama tax was cumulative starting with age twenty-one and going through age forty-five. After 1953 the cumulative period was reduced to two years. V. O. Key, in his book *Southern Politics* (New York: Knopf, 1949), pp. 617–618, concluded that the poll tax had little or no bearing on the paucity of Negro voters because of the much greater effect of other methods of disfranchisement. He did feel, however, that removal of the poll tax would increase voting in most southern states by five to ten percent of the potential number of white voters.

The Court in *Breedlove* v. *Suttles,* 302 U.S. 277 (1937), upheld the Georgia poll tax law against the claims of a white male citizen that the law violated the equal protection clause, that it abridged the privileges and immunities of United States citizens, and that it violated the Nineteenth Amendment. The law exempted blind persons and women who did not register for voting.

Proposals in Congress for abolishing the poll tax as a prerequisite to voting were advanced for many years, beginning in 1939, but many members expressed reservations concerning the constitutionality of the proposals. Finally, in 1962, a constitutional amendment passed the Congress prohibiting the exacting of any tax as a requirement for voting in federal elections. It was ratified in 1964 as the Twenty-fourth Amendment. At the time, five states still required payment of the poll tax (Alabama, Arkansas, Mississippi, Texas, and Virginia), and they indicated plans to continue the requirement with respect to voting in state and local elections.

In 1963, in anticipation of the promulgation of the Twenty-fourth Amendment, a special session of the Virginia General Assembly was convened. It adopted a requirement that in order to qualify to vote in federal elections one must either pay a poll tax or file a witnessed or notarized certificate of residence. In *Harman* v. *Forssenius,* 380 U.S. 528 (1965), the Court unanimously held the requirement repugnant to the Twenty-fourth Amendment. Chief Justice Warren, for the Court, stated that the requirement of a poll tax clearly violated that Amendment, and "no equivalent or milder substitute may be imposed." He said further, "Any material requirement imposed upon the federal voter solely because of his refusal to waive the constitutional immunity subverts the effectiveness of the Twenty-fourth Amendment and must fall under its ban."

The closing chapter in the long history of the poll tax as a prerequisite to voting was presumably written in 1966. In *Harper* v. *Virginia State Bd. of Elections*, 383 U.S. 663 (1966), the Court by a six-to-three vote held the requirement of payment of a poll tax as a prerequisite to participation in *state* elections unconstitutional under the equal protection clause of the Fourteenth Amendment. Justice Douglas, for the majority, stated:

We conclude that a State violates the Equal Protection Clause of the Fourteenth Amendment whenever it makes the affluence of the voter or payment of any fee an electoral standard. Voter qualifications have no relation to wealth nor to paying or not paying this or any other tax.... The principle that denies the State the right to dilute a citizen's vote on account of his economic status or other such factors by analogy bars a system which excludes those unable to pay a fee to vote or who fail to pay.... To introduce wealth or payment of a fee as a measure of a voter's qualifications is to introduce a capricious or irrelevant factor. The degree of the discrimination is irrelevant. In this context—that is, as a condition of obtaining a ballot—the requirement of fee paying causes an "invidious" discrimination (*Skinner* v. *Oklahoma* ...) that runs afoul of the Equal Protection Clause. Levy "by the poll," as stated in *Breedlove* v. *Suttles,* ... is an old familiar form of taxation; and we say nothing to impair its validity so long as it is not made a condition to the exercise of the franchise. *Breedlove* v. *Suttles* sanctioned its uses as "a prerequisite of voting." ... To that extent the *Breedlove* case is overruled.

Literacy Tests

Literary tests for voting have been used by a number of states for many years. While there is a fairly obvious relationship between literacy and voting (although even here the case may be overstated), the literacy test at the same time lends itself more readily than most other requirements to discriminatory administration. The constitutionality of a Mississippi literacy requirement was attacked in *Williams* v. *Mississippi,* 170 U.S. 213 (1898) on the ground that unfettered discretion was vested in the registrars and that the provisions were administered in a racially discriminatory manner. The Court found the claim of discriminatory administration inadequately pleaded and held that literacy tests which are drafted so as to apply alike to all applicants for the voting franchise would be deemed to be fair on their face, and in the absence of proof of discriminatory enforcement could not be viewed as denying the equal protection of the laws guaranteed by the Fourteenth Amendment.

As recently as 1959, in *Lassiter* v. *Northampton Election Board,* 360 U.S. 45, the Court refused to hold invalid on its face a North Carolina requirement that all voters be able "to read and write any section of the Constitution of North Carolina in the English language." Justice Douglas, speaking for a unanimous Court, stated:

The states have long been held to have broad powers to determine the conditions under which the right of suffrage may be exercised....

We do not suggest that any standards which a State desires to adopt may be required of voters. But there is wide scope for exercise of its jurisdiction. Residence requirements, age, previous criminal record ... are obvious examples indicating factors which a State may take into consideration in determining the qualifications of voters. The ability to read and write likewise has some relation to standards designed to promote intelligent use of the ballot. Literacy and illiteracy are neutral on race, creed, color, and sex, as reports around the world show. Literacy and intelligence are obviously not synonymous. Illiterate people may be intelligent voters. Yet in our society where newspapers, periodicals, books, and other printed matter canvass and debate campaign issues, a State might conclude that only those who are literate should exercise the franchise. ... It was said last century in Massachusetts that a literacy test was designed to insure an "independent and intelligent" exercise of the right of suffrage. ... North Carolina agrees. We do not sit in judgment on the wisdom of that policy. We cannot say, however, that it is not an allowable one measured by constitutional standards. ...

In *Louisiana* v. *United States,* 380 U.S. 145 (1965), the Court held invalid a Louisiana requirement that applicants for registration be able to give a "reasonable interpretation" of any section of the Louisiana Constitution or the United States Constitution when read to them by the registrar. In his opinion for the Court, Justice Black stated:

... The applicant facing a registrar in Louisiana thus has been compelled to leave his voting fate to that official's uncontrolled power to determine whether the applicant's understanding of the Federal or State Constitution is satisfactory. As the evidence showed, colored people, even some with the most advanced education and scholarship, were declared by voting registrars with less education to have an unsatisfactory understanding of the constitution of Louisiana or of the United States. This is not a test but a trap, sufficient to stop even the most brilliant man on his way to the voting booth. The cherished right of people in a country like ours to vote cannot be obliterated by the use of laws like this, which leave the voting fate of a citizen to the passing whim or impulse of an individual registrar. ...

Other practices designed to hinder Negro registration in Louisiana are described in the chapter "The Louisiana Story" in the 1961 United States Commission on Civil Rights Report, *Voting* (Washington, D.C.: U.S. Government Printing Office, 1961). One feature of the registration requirements which appears to be unique is the requirement that the applicant state his exact age in years, months, and days. The report states that a registrar of voters of Plaquemines Parish, who was called on to give a step-by-step demonstration of the proper way to complete the application form, erred in her age computation by almost a month. And there appeared to be some confusion as to whether to include or exclude the day on which the application was filed. Nor was there agreement on whether an error of one day would be fatal to registration.

A group of provisions added to the Mississippi Constitution in 1954 and 1960 resulted in requirements that applicants for registration had to: (1) be able to read and copy in writing any section of the Mississippi Constitution, and (2) give a reasonable interpretation of that section to the county registrar, and (3) demonstrate to the registrar "a reasonable understanding of the duties and obligations of citizenship under a constitutional form of government," and (4) be "of good moral character."

The repeated use of literacy tests in a racially discriminatory manner led to the adoption of, first, the Voting Rights Act of 1965, which prohibited the use of any "test or device" for voter qualification in defined areas (predominantly the South), and, second, the 1970 Voting Rights Amendments, which operated nationwide to bar the use of literacy tests in all elections, state and national. (See *Oregon* v. *Mitchell,* below, for the decision upholding the validity of the latter prohibition.)

Residence Requirements

All states have established durational residence requirements as a condition of registering to vote. These have customarily included a period of residence in the state (from six months to two years), a period of residence in the county, and frequently a period of residence in the precinct. In earlier cases, the Court had indicated that such requirements did not violate the Constitution. [See *Pope* v. *Williams*, 193 U.S. 621 (1904), for example.] But in the 1970 Federal Voting Rights Act, Congress outlawed state durational residence requirements for presidential and vice-presidential elections and prohibited the States from closing registration more than thirty days before such elections. This provision was upheld in *Oregon* v. *Mitchell* in 1970. (See the case cutting below.) This still left the states free to impose such requirements for persons wishing to vote in state and congressional elections, however. In *Dunn* v. *Blumstein* these provisions were challenged as violative of the equal protection clause.

DUNN *v.* BLUMSTEIN
405 U.S. 330 (1972)

Mr. Justice Marshall delivered the opinion of the Court.

Various Tennessee public officials . . . appeal from a decision by a three-judge federal court holding that Tennessee's durational residence requirements for voting violate the Equal Protection Clause of the United States Constitution. The issue arises in a class action for declaratory and injunctive relief brought by appellee James Blumstein. Blumstein moved to Tennessee on June 12, 1970, to begin employment as an assistant professor of law at Vanderbilt University in Nashville. With an eye toward voting in the upcoming elections, he attempted to register to vote on July 1, 1970. The county registrar refused to register him, on the ground that Tennessee law authorizes the registration of only those persons who, at the time of the next election, will have been residents of the State for a year and residents of the county for three months. . . .

Durational residence laws penalize those persons who have traveled from one place to another to establish a new residence during the qualifying period. Such laws divide residents into two classes, old residents and new residents, and discriminate against the latter to the extent of totally denying them the opportunity to vote. The constitutional question presented is whether the Equal Protection Clause of the Fourteenth Amendment permits a State to discriminate in this way among its citizens.

To decide whether a law violates the Equal Protection Clause, we look, in essence, to three things: the character of the classification in question; the individual interests affected by the classification; and the governmental interests asserted in support of the classification. . . . First, then, we must determine what standard of review is appropriate. In the present case, whether we look to the benefit withheld by the classification (the opportunity to vote) or the basis for the classification (recent interstate travel) we conclude that the State must show a substantial and compelling reason for imposing durational residence requirements. . . .

We turn, then, to the question of whether the State has shown that durational residence requirements are needed to further a sufficiently substantial state interest. We emphasize again the difference between bona fide residence requirements and durational residence requirements. We have in the past noted approvingly that the States have the power to require that voters be bona fide residents of the relevant political subdivision. . . . But *durational* residence requirements, representing a separate voting qualification imposed on bona fide residents, must be separately tested by the stringent standard. . . .

It is worth noting at the outset that Congress has, in a somewhat different context, addressed the question whether durational residence laws further compelling state interests. In §202 of the Voting Rights Act of 1965, added by the Voting Rights Act amendments of 1970, Congress outlawed state durational residence requirements for presidential and vice-presidential elections, and prohibited the States from closing registration more than 30 days before such elections. . . . In our present case, of course, we deal with congressional, state, and local elections, in which the State's interests are arguably somewhat different; and, in addition, our function is not merely to determine whether there was a reasonable basis for Congress' findings. However, the congressional finding which forms the basis for the Federal Act is a useful background for the discussion that follows.

Tennessee tenders "two basic purposes" served by its durational residence requirements:

"(1) INSURE PURITY OF BALLOT BOX—Protection against fraud through colonization and inability to identify persons offered to vote, and

"(2) KNOWLEDGEABLE VOTER—Afford some surety that the voter has, in fact, become a member of the community and that as such, he has a common interest in all matters pertaining to its government and is, therefore, more likely to exercise his right more intelligently." Brief for Appellants. . . .

We consider each in turn.

A

Preservation of the "purity of the ballot box" is a formidable-sounding state interest. The impurities feared, variously called "dual voting" and "colonization," all involve voting by nonresidents, either singly or in groups. The main concern is that nonresidents will temporarily invade the State or county, falsely swear that they are residents to become eligible to vote, and, by voting, allow a candidate to win by fraud. Surely the prevention of such fraud is a legitimate and compelling government goal. But it is impossible to view durational residence requirements as necessary to achieve that state interest. . . . This contention is particularly unconvincing in light of Tennessee's total statutory scheme for regulating the franchise.

Durational residence laws may once have been necessary to prevent a fraudulent evasion of state voter standards, but today in Tennessee, as in most other States, this purpose is served by a system of voter registration. . . . There is no indication in the record that Tennessee routinely goes behind the would-be voter's oath to determine his qualifications. Since false swearing is no obstacle to one intent on fraud, the existence of burdensome voting qualifications like durational residence requirements cannot prevent corrupt nonresidents from fraudulently registering and voting. . . . Indeed, the durational residence requirement becomes an effective voting obstacle only to residents who tell the truth and have no fraudulent purposes. . . .

. . . If the State itself has determined that a three-month period is enough time in which to confirm bona fide residence in the State and county, obviously a one-year period cannot also be justified as "necessary" to achieve the same purpose. Beyond that, the job of detecting nonresidents from among persons who have registered is a relatively simple one. It hardly justifies prohibiting all newcomers from voting for even three months. . . . Objective information tendered as relevant to the question of bona fide residence under Tennessee law—places of dwelling, occupation, car registration, driver' slicense, property owned, etc.—is easy to double-check, especially in light of modern communications. . . . It is sufficient to note here that 30 days appears to be an ample period of time for the State to complete whatever tasks are necessary to prevent fraud—and a year, or three months, too much. . . .

Our conclusion that the waiting period is not the least restrictive means necessary for preventing fraud is bolstered by the recognition that Tennessee has at its disposal a variety of criminal laws that are more than adequate to detect and deter whatever fraud may be feared. . . .

B

The argument that durational residence requirements further the goal of having "knowledgeable voters" appears to involve three separate claims. . . .

Finally, the State urges that a longtime resident is "more likely to exercise his right [to vote] more intelligently." To the extent that this is different from the previous argument, the State is apparently asserting an interest in limiting the franchise to voters who are knowledgeable about the issues. . . .

. . . [T]he durational residence requirements in this case founder because of their crudeness as a device for achieving the articulated state goal of assuring the knowledgeable exercise of the franchise. The classifications created by durational residence requirements obviously permit any longtime resident to vote regardless of his knowledge of the issues—and obviously many longtime residents do not have any. On the other hand, the classifications bar from the franchise many other, admittedly new, residents who have become at least minimally, and often fully, informed about the issues. Indeed, recent migrants who take the time to register and vote shortly after moving are likely to be those citizens, such as appellee, who make it a point to be informed and knowledgeable about the issues. Given modern communications, and given the clear indication that campaign spending and voter education occur largely during the month before an election, the State cannot seriously maintain that it is "necessary" to reside for a year in the State and three months in the county in order to be knowledgeable about congressional, state, or even purely local elections. There is simply nothing in the record to support the conclusive presumption that residents who have lived in the State for less than a year and their county for less than three months are uninformed about elections. . . .

It is pertinent to note that Tennessee has never made an attempt to further its alleged interest in an informed electorate in a universally applicable way. Knowledge or competence has never been a criterion for participation in Tennessee's electoral process for longtime residents. . . . If the State seeks to assure intelligent use of the ballot, it may not try to serve this interest only with respect to new arrivals. . . .

Affirmed.

Mr. Justice Powell and Mr. Justice Rehnquist took no part in the consideration or decision of this case.

Mr. Justice Blackmun, concurring in the result.

Mr. Chief Justice Burger, dissenting. . . .

In the following year, in *Rosario* v. *Rockefeller,* 410 U.S. 752 (1973), the Court in a five-to-four decision upheld provisions of the New York election laws which required a person wishing to vote in a party primary to register his party affiliation eight months before a presidential primary and eleven months before primaries for other offices. The majority held that the requirement was not so severe as to constitute "a constitutionally onerous burden on petitioners' exercise of the franchise." It concluded that the goal of preventing "raiding" by members of the opposition party was a legitimate purpose and was neither invidious nor arbitrary.

Although *Dunn* held that a state could not constitutionally impose a one-year residence requirement for voting, in *Kanapaux* v. *Ellisor,* 419 U.S. 891 (1974), the Court in a summary action, without opinion, affirmed the judgment of a three-judge court which held that South Carolina's five-year durational residence requirement for candidates for Governor was not violative of the Fourteenth Amendment equal protection clause.

Filing Fees for Candidates

It has long been the practice for political parties to charge filing fees for persons who wished to enter party primaries as candidates for public office. While in some states these fees were fairly nominal, there were other states in which the filing fees amounted to very substantial sums of money. In support of such charges it was argued that since the parties usually had to bear the expenses for administering the primaries, such levies against the candidates were a reasonable method of financing the elections. In *Bullock* v. *Carter,* in 1972, the Court addressed the question of whether such fees, which had the effect of denying the poor entry into political contests, were violative of the equal protection clause.

BULLOCK *v.* CARTER
405 U.S. 134 (1972)

Mr. Chief Justice Burger delivered the opinion of the Court.

Under Texas law, a candidate must pay a filing fee as a condition to having his name placed on the ballot in a primary election. The constitutionality of the Texas filing-fee-system is the subject of this appeal from the judgment of a three-judge District Court.

Appellee Pate met all qualifications to be a candidate in the ... Democratic primary for the office of County Commissioner ... except that he was unable to pay the $1,424.60 assessment required of candidates in that primary. Appellee Wischkaemper sought to be placed on the Democratic primary ballot as a candidate for County Judge ... but he was unable to pay the $6,300 assessment for candidacy for that office. Appellee Carter wished to be a Democratic candidate for Commissioner of the General Land Office; his application was not accompanied by the required $1,000 filing fee.

After being denied places on the Democratic primary ballots in their respective counties, these appellees instituted ... actions in the District Court challenging the validity of the Texas filing-fee system. ... Following a hearing on the merits, the three-judge court declared the Texas filing-fee scheme unconstitutional and enjoined its enforcement. ...

Under the Texas statute, payment of the filing fee is an absolute prerequisite to a candidate's participation in a primary election. There is no alternative procedure by which a potential candidate who is unable to pay the fee can get on the primary ballot by way of petitioning voters, and write-in votes are not permitted in primary elections for public office. ...

Unlike a filing-fee requirement that most candidates could be expected to fulfill from their own resources or at least through modest contributions, the very size of the fees imposed under the Texas system gives it a patently exclusionary character. . . . To the extent that the system requires candidates to rely on contributions from voters in order to pay the assessments, a phenomenon that can hardly be rare in light of the size of the fees, it tends to deny some voters the opportunity to vote for a candidate of their choosing; at the same time it gives the affluent the power to place on the ballot their own names or the names of persons they favor. . . .

Because the Texas filing-fee scheme has a real and appreciable impact on the exercise of the franchise, and because this impact is related to the resources of the voters supporting a particular candidate, we conclude . . . that the laws must be "closely scrutinized" and found reasonably necessary to the accomplishment of legitimate state objectives in order to pass constitutional muster.

Appellants contend that the filing fees required by the challenged statutes are necessary both to regulate the ballot in primary elections and to provide a means for financing such elections. . . .

. . . There may well be some rational relationship between a candidate's willingness to pay a filing fee and the seriousness with which he takes his candidacy. But the candidates in this case affirmatively alleged that they were *unable,* not simply *unwilling,* to pay the assessed fees, and there was no contrary evidence. It is uncontested that the filing fees exclude legitimate as well as frivolous candidates. And even assuming that every person paying the large fees required by Texas law takes his own candidacy seriously, that does not make him a "serious candidate" in the popular sense. If the Texas fee requirement is intended to regulate the ballot by weeding out spurious candidates, it is extraordinarily ill-fitted to that goal; other means to protect those valid interests are available. . . .

. . . Appellants strenuously urge that apportioning the cost among the candidates is the only feasible means for financing the primaries. They argue that if the State must finance the primaries, it will have to determine which political bodies are "parties" so as to be entitled to state sponsorship for their nominating process, and that this will result in new claims of discrimination. . . . [T]he Court has recently upheld the validity of a state law distinguishing between political parties on the basis of success in prior elections. *Jenness* v. *Fortson* [1971]. We are not persuaded that Texas would be faced with an impossible task in distinguishing between political parties for the purpose of financing primaries.

We also reject the theory that since the candidates are availing themselves of the primary machine, it is appropriate that they pay that share of the cost that they have occasioned. . . .

Appellants seem to place reliance on the self-evident fact that if the State must assume the cost, the voters, as taxpayers, will ultimately be burdened with the expense of the primaries. But it is far too late to make out a case that the party primary is such a lesser part of the democratic process that its cost must be shifted away from the taxpayers generally. . . . Viewing the myriad governmental functions supported from general revenues, it is difficult to single out any of a higher order than the conduct of elections at all levels to bring forth those persons desired by their fellow citizens to govern. Without making light of the State's interest in husbanding its revenues, we fail to see such an element of necessity in the State's present means of financing primaries as to justify the resulting incursion on the prerogatives of voters.

Since the State has failed to establish the requisite justification for this filing-fee system, we hold that it results in a denial of equal protection of the laws. It must be emphasized that nothing herein is intended to cast doubt on the validity of reasonable candidate filing fees or licensing fees in other contexts. By requiring candidates to shoulder the costs of conducting primary elections through filing fees and by providing no reasonable alternative means of access to the ballot, the State of Texas has erected a system that utilizes the criterion of ability to pay as a condition to being on the ballot, thus excluding some candidates otherwise qualified and denying an undetermined number of voters the opportunity to vote for candidates of their choice. These salient features of the Texas system are critical to our determination of constitutional invalidity.

Affirmed.

Mr. Justice Powell and Mr. Justice Rehnquist took no part in the consideration or decision of this case.

In *Lubin* v. *Panish,* 415 U.S. 709 (1974), the Court followed the *Bullock* rule in holding invalid the California filing-fee requirement which, like that of Texas, provided no alternative access to the ballot. The State argued that the requirement was a useful device for minimizing the possibility of lengthy "laundry list" ballots cluttered with frivolous or otherwise nonserious candidates. The Court, as in *Bullock,* held that the State would have to use devices to accomplish this purpose other than mere distinctions based on wealth.

Property Requirements for Voting

While the States no longer make ownership of property a condition for eligibility for general voter participation, it has not been uncommon for them to require some specified ownership of taxable property as a prerequisite to voting in elections on the issuance of governmental bonds or other special categories of elections. In *Kramer* v. *Union Free School District,* 393 U.S. 818 (1969), the Court examined the validity of the New York election law provisions which regulated the selection of members of certain school boards in the state. The statutes limited the electorate for such positions to persons who were otherwise eligible to vote in state and federal elections and who, in addition, either owned or leased taxable real property within the school district or who were parents of children enrolled in the local public schools. The appellees argued that it was necessary to limit the franchise to those "primarily interested" in school affairs because "the very increasing complexity of the many interacting phases of the school system and structure make it extremely difficult for the electorate fully to understand the whys and wherefores of the detailed operations of the school system." Since the issue involved limitations on the right to vote, the majority of the Court adopted the "strict scrutiny" approach and could not find the degree of necessity for adopting this device which would justify denying the franchise to the excluded persons. In holding the exclusions invalid, the Court stated that the statutes "are not sufficiently tailored to limiting the franchise to those 'primarily interested' in school affairs," and, in fact, obviously would exclude many persons who might be both interested and informed on school matters.

Hill v. *Stone,* 421 U.S. 289 (1975), involved a challenge by residents of Fort Worth, Texas, to the state and city laws limiting the franchise in city bond elections to persons who had made available for taxation some real, mixed, or personal property in the election district in the year of the election. On authority of *Kramer* and subsequent cases, the Court held the limitation invalid. The bond issue was for the purpose of building a library, and although a general obligation issue, it was to have been paid for entirely out of property taxes. Appellant claimed that in view of this fact, the election was one of special interest and thus outside the rule of *Kramer.* The majority opinion cited *City of Phoenix* v. *Kolodziejski,* 339 U.S. 204 (1970), which had also held invalid a statute restricting the franchise in a general obligation bond election to real property owners, in which it was stated:

Property taxes may be paid initially by property owners, but a significant part of the ultimate burden of each year's tax on rental property will very likely be borne by the tenant rather than the landlord since . . . the landlord will treat the property tax as a business expense and normally will be able to pass all or a large part of this cost on to the tenants in the form of higher rent.

In addition, it was noted that property taxes on commercial property would normally be treated as a cost of doing business and would "be reflected in the prices of goods and services purchased by nonproperty owners and property owners alike." Appellant argued further that any resident could become eligible merely by listing personal property of even negligible value, and therefore it could not be considered a serious impediment to participation. The Court's answer was that if this were true, the requirement "can hardly be said to select voters according to the magnitude of their prospective liability for the city's indebtedness."

FEDERAL LEGISLATION TO PROTECT VOTING RIGHTS

Shortly after the Fifteenth Amendment was ratified in 1870, Congress passed a law to enforce its provisions [Act of May 31, 1870, 42 U.S.C. 1971(a) (1958)]. The relevant section provided:

All citizens of the United States who are otherwise qualified by law to vote at any election by the people in any State, Territory, ditsrict, county, city, parish, township, school district, municipality, or other territorial subdivision, shall be entitled and allowed to vote at all such elections, without distinction of race, color, or previous condition of servitude; any constitution, law, custom, usage, or regulation of any State or Territory, or by or under its authority, to the contrary notwithstanding.

[The discussion of this section and other legislation through the Civil Rights Act of 1960 is largely in the words of the 1961 Civil Rights Commission Report, *Voting,* pp. 73–78. See also, Note, "Voting Rights," 3 *Race Rel. L. Rep.* 371 (1958).]

While the Supreme Court has long since struck down much Reconstruction legislation as unconstitutional, this provision, Section 1971(a) of Title 42, survives as a cornerstone of Federal legislation to protect the right to vote.

But this section merely declared a right; it provided no legal remedy. And other relevant Reconstruction legislation has proved difficult to apply or depends on private initiative. Until the passage of the Civil Rights Act of 1957, therefore, the federal government could do little to combat discriminatory denials of the right to vote. The 1957 Act, and its successor Act in 1960, opened the way to more direct and effective federal action to protect the fundamental right of electoral participation.

For seventy years the federal government relied almost solely on two sections of the Criminal Code to prevent discrimination in voting. Both were Reconstruction measures, now Sections 241 and 242 of Title 18 of the United

States Code. Section 241 penalizes *conspiracies* of two or more persons to "injure, oppress, threaten, or intimidate any citizen in the free exercise or enjoyment of any right . . . secured . . . by the Constitution or laws of the United States. . . ." This provision applies to actions by either state officials or private persons that interfere with voting in federal elections, and also to state officials in state and local elections. (For a detailed analysis of Sections 241 and 242 and for discussion of the general distinction between the federal right to vote and the state right, see Chapter 3.) The other criminal provision, now Section 242, prohibits action "under color of law" which interferes with "rights . . . secured or protected by the Constitution or laws of the United States," including the right not to be discriminated against on grounds of race or color.

Section 241 was involved in the case of *Ex parte Yarbrough,* 110 U.S. 651 (1884), where the Court declared that the right to vote in federal elections arose from the federal Constitution and was, therefore, subject to protection by federal legislation. This was true, said the Court, despite the fact that state laws prescribe the qualifications of electors. Both sections were involved in *United States* v. *Classic,* 313 U.S. 299 (1941), where the Court held for the first time that the guarantees of the Constitution cover primary as well as general elections.

In 1939 Congress enacted, as part of the Hatch Act, another criminal provision to protect the right to vote. It is Section 594 of Title 18 of the Code and assesses criminal penalties as a misdemeanor for persons who intimidate, threaten, or coerce any other person for the purpose of interfering with his right to vote in federal elections. It does not appear to have been used to date.

Before 1957, in addition to these criminal remedies, three other provisions of the Code laid a basis for *civil* remedies for improper denials of the right to vote. Section 1971(a), quoted above, while it did not provide for specific remedies, did set up the federal right to vote without distinctions as to race or color. And two other sections set up the civil remedies. Section 1983 (the civil counterpart of Section 242) of Title 42 of the Code permits suits to be brought against persons acting "under color of any statute, ordinance, regulation, custom or usage" to deprive citizens of rights secured by the Constitution and laws of the United States. The injured party may bring "an action at law, suit in equity, or other proper proceeding for redress." The suit for injunctive relief or for damages is the usual type of action under this section. It was the basis for action, along with Section 1971(a), in a number of landmark cases, including *Nixon* v. *Herndon, Smith* v. *Allwright,* and *Rice* v. *Elmore.* The other section, Section 1985 (3) of Title 42, provides for a suit for damages (but not equitable action) in the case of a conspiracy to deprive persons of the equal protection of the laws or to prevent by force, intimidation, or threat, any qualified voter from voting as he chooses in a federal election. This section has been little used. (See Chapter 3 for the text of these sections and some of their applications.)

In summing up the effect of these provisions, the 1961 Civil Rights Commission *Voting* Report states (p. 75):

These provisions set the framework for a series of important cases expanding and defining the Federal right to vote—but they were weak. Most of these cases were civil, not criminal. The Federal Government was empowered only to bring criminal cases, and the criminal statutes were unwieldly and difficult to apply. Civil cases, with their flexible remedies and relative ease of proof, could be brought only by private persons, who are not always able to bear the expense and difficulty involved in long and complicated litigation.

Congress made a substantial change in adopting the Civil Rights Act of 1957 (71 Stat. 635). Basically, the Act is an amendment to the old Section 1971. It retains that section as subsection (a) and adds several other subsections. Subsection (b) is also a declaration of rights, adopting substantially the same language as 18 U.S.C. Section 594, the Hatch Act provision to punish for intimidation of voters in federal elections, except that it explicitly mentions primaries as well as general elections and provides for civil suits to be brought by either private parties or the Attorney General. Other provisions of the Act give the federal district courts jurisdiction of such civil proceedings without a requirement that state administrative or other remedies first be exhausted; provide for contempt proceedings in the event of disobedience of court orders under the section; and, by authorizing the appointment of an additional Assistant Attorney General, led to raising the Department of Justice's Civil Rights Section to the status of a full division. The Act also created the Civil Rights Commission.

Experience under the 1957 Act indicated that it was still insufficient to stop discriminatory denials of the right to vote. When the Commission issued its first report late in 1959, the Civil Rights Division had instituted only three actions under the section permitting the Attorney General to institute suits, and none had been successful. In one case, because the registrars against whom the suit was brought had previously resigned from office, a federal district court had held that there was no one the federal government could sue. [*United States* v. *Alabama,* 171 F. Supp. 720 (M.D. Ala., 1959), *aff'd,* 267 F.2d 808 (5th Cir., 1960), *vacated,* 362 U.S. 602 (1960).]

As a result of the experience under the 1957 Act, the Commission strongly urged the passage of another act to close up several loopholes. The Civil Rights Act of 1960 (74 Stat. 86) reflected the Commission's recommendations. It took care of the problem of resigning registrars by amending the 1957 law to provide that in actions brought under Section 1971(a) and (c), "the act or practice shall also be deemed that of the State and the State may be joined as a party defendant and if, prior to the institution of such proceeding, such official has resigned or has been relieved of his office and no successor assumed such office, the proceeding may be instituted against the State."

Another provision of the 1960 Act—Title III—declared voting records public and required their preservation for a period of twenty-two months following any general or special election. The provision opened the way for inspection and copying by the Attorney General both to help him to decide which cases might warrant prosecution and also to help him in gathering evidence for suits ultimately filed.

Title VI of the 1960 Act made provision for the substitution of federal voting referees for local registration officials when various judicial findings of discriminatory practices were made. The procedural requirements which had to be met preparatory to an actual registration order were quite formidable, however. First, the government had to file suit under Section 1971(a) and (c) and obtain a court finding that "a person has been deprived on account of race or color" of the right to vote. Second, the court was required to find that "such deprivation was or is pursuant to a pattern or practice." Third, any person found to be discriminated against because of race could apply for an order declaring him qualified to vote. To get such an order he had to prove: "(1) he is qualified under State law to vote, and (2) he has since such finding by the court been (a) deprived of or denied under color of law the opportunity to register to vote or otherwise to qualify to vote, or (b) found not qualified to vote by any person acting under color of law." Finally, the court (or an appointed referee) had to hold a hearing on the application and permit the state to appear to challenge the applicant's qualifications. Only then could a specific person be ordered to be registered and allowed to vote. Thus the machinery was provided to combat discrimination against voters, but it was cumbersome machinery indeed.

In the 1963 Report of the United States Commission on Civil Rights this statement is made (p. 27):

Abridgment of the right to vote on the grounds of race persists in the United States in direct violation of the Constitution. In fulfillment of its statutory obligation, the Commission has previously recommended to the President and the Congress a variety of corrective measures. In 1963 the continuing discriminatory denial of the right to vote has led this Commission to reexamine and reconsider each of its prior voting recommendations. The Commission now believes that the only effective method of guaranteeing the vote for all Americans is the enactment by Congress of some form of uniform voter qualification standards. The Commission further believes that the right to vote must, in many instances, be safeguarded and assured by the Federal Government. Adequate legislation must include both standards and implementation. . . .

In partial response to this and other recommendations, Title I of the Civil Rights Act of 1964 (78 Stat. 241) adds further amendments to Section 1971 of Title 42. It prohibits the employment of differential standards of qualification for applicants for registration, prohibits denial of right to vote in federal elections because of trivial errors or omissions on the part of applicants which are not material to the determination of qualification, and requires that literacy tests be administered wholly in writing and, further, that a certified copy of the tests and his answers be furnished to the applicant upon his request. In addition, the provision set up a rebuttable presumption that completion of the sixth grade in school is sufficient to meet the requirement of literacy which any state might impose.

Political pressures mounted, however, for even stronger federal legislation guaranteeing the right to vote. The answer came with the signing into law of the Voting Rights Act of 1965 (79 Stat. 437) on August 6 of that year. The Act was clearly aimed at the South, where most of the racially discriminatory denials of the franchise occurred, and was designed to sweep away all procedures which in the past had been used to deny the right to vote on racial grounds, whatever rational justification might be presented for the procedures. The key provision of the Act, in this respect, is Section 4, which prohibits the use of "any test or device" in certain defined states or political subdivisions thereof. The section states, in part:

Sec. 4. (a) To assure that the right of citizens of the United States to vote is not denied or abridged on account of race or color, no citizen shall be denied the right to vote in any Federal, State, or local election because of his failure to comply with any test or device in any State with respect to which the determinations have been made under subsection (b) or in any political subdivision with respect to which such determinations have been made as a separate unit, unless the United States District Court for the District of Columbia in an action for a declaratory judgment brought by such State or subdivision against the United States has determined that no such test or device has been used during the five years preceding the filing of the action for the purpose or with the effect of denying or abridging the right to vote on account of race or color....

(b) The provisions of subsection (a) shall apply in any State or in any political subdivision of a state which (1) the Attorney General determines maintained on November 1, 1964, any test or device, and with respect to which (2) the Director of the Census determines that less than 50 per centum of the persons of voting age residing therein were registered on November 1, 1964, or that less than 50 per centum of such persons voted in the presidential election of November 1964....

(c) The phrase "test or device" shall mean any requirement that a person as a prerequisite for voting or registration for voting (1) demonstrate the ability to read, write, understand, or interpret any matter, (2) demonstrate any educational achievement or his knowledge of any particular subject, (3) possess good moral character, or (4) prove his qualifications by the voucher of registered voters or members of any other class.

The Act authorizes the appointment of examiners with authority to examine the qualifications of applicants for registration and, if they are found qualified under state laws not in conflict with the Constitution or federal laws, to place their names on a list of eligible voters. The appointment of such examiners may be authorized by a federal court in appropriate proceedings begun by the Attorney General under Section 3 of the Act, or the Civil Service Commission will appoint such examiners if the Attorney General certifies that in specified areas as defined by Section 4(b) residents are being denied registration on account of race or color and that the appointment of examiners is necessary to enforce the guarantees of the Fifteenth Amendment.

Section 5 of the Act demands that, if states or political subdivisions falling within the category defined by Section 4 "enact or seek to administer any voting qualification or prerequisite to voting, or standard, practice, or procedure with respect to voting different from that in force or effect on November 1, 1964," they must either seek a declaratory judgment from the United States District Court for the District of Columbia that such provision will not abridge the right to vote on account of race or color, or submit such provision to the Attorney General, in which case if he does not interpose an objection within sixty days thereafter, the provision may be put into operation. In the latter case, however, the Attorney General's failure to object does not act as a bar to subsequent action to enjoin the enforcement of the new provision.

The Attorney General moved swiftly after the adoption of the Act, and several southern states were brought within the prohibitions of the Act in the late summer of 1965. South Carolina brought an action in the original jurisdiction of the United States Supreme Court challenging the constitutionality of the "triggering" provision, Section 4(b) of the Act (the characterization was by counsel for South Carolina, and referred to the coverage formula and the provisions for findings by the Attorney General and the Director of the Census which would "trigger" application of the coverage formula), as well as the Section 5 provision "freezing" the election procedures as they were on November 1, 1964, and the Section 6 provisions for registration by federal examiners. Five other southern states were permitted to file supporting briefs and participate in oral argument in the case—Alabama, Georgia, Louisiana, Mississippi, and Virginia. Twenty northern and western states filed briefs in support of the government's position that the Act was constitutional, and argument was heard beginning on January 17, 1966.

In less than two months, an exceptionally rapid disposition of the case, the Court handed down its decision upholding the constitutionality of the Act in *South Carolina* v. *Katzenbach.*

SOUTH CAROLINA *v.* KATZENBACH
383 U.S. 301 (1966)

[By leave of the Court, South Carolina filed on original bill a bill of complaint seeking a declaration that the Voting Rights Act of 1965 was unconstitutional and asking for an injunction against enforcement of its provisions. The attack centered on the provisions for suspension of literacy and other voting tests in the applicable geographic areas, the provisions suspending all new voting regulations in such areas pending review by federal authorities, the provisions for assignment of federal examiners to list qualified applicants for voting, and the designation of the United States District Court for the District of Columbia over litigation as to termination of the statutory coverage. It was contended that the coverage formula violated the principle of the equality of states, denied due process by employing an invalid presumption, constituted a forbidden bill of attainder, and impaired the separation of powers by adjudicating guilt through legislative action rather than through the courts.]

Mr. Chief Justice Warren delivered the opinion of the Court. . . .

Two points emerge vividly from the voluminous legislative history of the Act contained in the committee hearings and floor debates. First: Congress felt itself confronted by an insidious and pervasive evil which had been perpetuated in certain parts of our country through unremitting and ingenious defiance of the Constitution. Second: Congress concluded that the unsuccessful remedies which it had prescribed in the past would have to be replaced by sterner and more elaborate measures in order to satisfy the clear commands of the Fifteenth Amendment. . . .

In recent years, Congress has repeatedly tried to cope with the problem by facilitating case-by-case litigation against voting discrimination. . . .

Despite the earnest efforts of the Justice Department and of many federal judges, these new laws have done little to cure the problem of voting discrimination. . . .

. . . [T]he basic question presented by the case [is]: Has Congress exercised its powers under the Fifteenth Amendment in an appropriate manner with relation ot the States?

The ground rules for resolving this question are clear. The language and purpose of the Fifteenth Amendment, the prior decisions construing its several provisions, and the general doctrines of constitutional interpretation, all point to one fundamental principle. As against the reserved powers of the States, Congress may use any rational means to effectuate the constitutional prohibition of racial discrimination in voting. . . .

Congress exercised its authority under the Fifteenth Amendment in an inventive manner when it enacted the Voting Rights Act of 1965. First: The measure prescribes remedies for voting discrimination which go into effect without any need for prior adjudication. This was clearly a legitimate response to the problem, for which there is ample precedent under other constitutional provisions.... After enduring nearly a century of systematic resistance to the Fifteenth Amendment, Congress might well decide to shift the advantage of time and inertia from the perpetrators of the evil to its victims....

Second: The Act intentionally confines these remedies to a small number of States and political subdivisions which in most instances were familiar to Congress by name. This, too, was a permissible method of dealing with the problem. Congress has learned that substantial voting discrimination presently occurs in certain sections of the country, and it knew no way of accurately forecasting whether the evil might spread elsewhere in the future. In acceptable legislative fashion, Congress chose to limit its attention to the geographic areas where immediate action seemed necessary.... The doctrine of the equality of States, invoked by South Carolina, does not bar this approach, for that doctrine applies only to the terms upon which States are admitted to the Union, and not to the remedies for local evils which have subsequently appeared....

Mr. Justice Black, concurring and dissenting.

I agree with substantially all of the Court's opinion sustaining the power of Congress ... to suspend state literacy tests and similar voting qualifications and to authorize the Attorney General to secure the appointment of federal examiners to register qualified voters in various sections of the country.... I dissent from its holding that every part of §5 of the Act is constitutional. Section 4(a), to which §5 is linked, suspends for five years all literacy tests and similar devices in those States coming within the formula of §4(b). Section 5 goes on to provide that a State covered by §4(b) can in no way amend its constitution or laws relating to voting without first trying to persuade the Attorney General of the United States or the Federal District Court for the District of Columbia that the new proposed laws do not have the purpose and will not have the effect of denying the right to vote to citizens on account of their race or color. I think this section is unconstitutional on at least two grounds.

(a) The Constitution gives federal courts jurisdiction over cases and controversies only.... [I]t is hard for me to believe that a justiciable controversy can arise in the constitutional sense from a desire by the United States Government or some of its officials to determine in advance what legislative provisions a State may enact or what consitutional amendments it may adopt....

(b) My second and more basic objection to §5 is that Congress has here exercised its power under §2 of the Fifteenth Amendment through the adoption of means that conflict with the most basic principles of the Constitution.... Section 5, by providing that some of the States cannot pass state laws or adopt state constitutional amendments without first being compelled to beg federal authorities to approve their policies, so distorts our constitutional structure of government as to render any distinction drawn in the Constitution between state and federal power almost meaningless....

In 1971 the Court decided *Perkins* v. *Matthews*, which illustrates the "prior approval" provisions of the 1965 Act as applied to the decision of a Mississippi city to change the location of its polling places.

PERKINS v. MATTHEWS
400 U.S. 379 (1971)

[Section 5 of the Voting Rights Act of 1965 requires that changes in voting standards or procedures in those States covered by the Act receive prior approval from the District Court for the District of Columbia or be submitted to the Attorney General and receive no objection from him before becoming operative. The city of Canton, Mississippi, (1) changed the locations of certain polling places, (2) annexed adjacent areas, thereby enlarging the number of eligible voters, and (3) changed from ward to at-large election of aldermen, all without following the prior submission procedures outlined in the Voting Rights Act. Certain voters and candidates for election to city offices filed an action in federal court to enjoin the city elections, on the ground that the Act had been violated by instituting the electoral changes without a judgment that such changes did not have a discriminatory purpose or effect. Pending the convening of a three-judge court, a single judge issued a temporary restraining order. The three-judge court, after hearing, dissolved the injunction and dismissed the complaint. The elections were then held in October, 1969, with the challenged changes in effect. The case was heard on direct appeal by the Supreme Court.]

Mr. Justice Brennan delivered the opinion of the Court. . . .

The three-judge court misconceived the permissible scope of its inquiry into appellant's allegations. . . . The inquiry should have been limited to the determination whether "a state requirement is covered by Sec. 5, but has not been subjected to the required federal scrutiny." . . . What is foreclosed to such district court is what Congress expressly reserved for consideration by the District Court of the District of Columbia or the Attorney General—the determination whether a covered change does or does not have the purpose or effect "of denying or abridging the right to vote on account of race or color." . . .

[The opinion then gives an examination of each of the three changes in electoral procedure and concludes that since there is a potential for racial discrimination in the purpose or effect of each change, they should have followed the approval procedures outlined in Section 5 of the Voting Rights Act.]

The appellants have urged that, in addition to reversing the District Court judgment, the Court should set aside the elections held in October, 1969, and order new elections held forthwith in which the changes challenged in this case may not be enforced. . . . Since the District Court is more familiar with the nuances of the local situation than are we, and has heard the evidence in this case, we think the question of the appropriate remedy is for that court to determine, in the first instance, after hearing the views of both parties.

The judgment of the District Court is reversed, and the case is remanded to that court with instructions to issue injunctions restraining the further enforcement of the changes until such time as the appellees adequately demonstrate compliance with Sec. 5, and for further proceedings consistent with this opinion.

It is so ordered.

Mr. Justice Blackmun with whom the Chief Justice joins, concurring. . . .

Mr. Justice Harlan, concurring in part and dissenting in part.

Our role in this case, as the Court correctly recognizes, is limited to determination whether Sec. 5 of the Voting Rights Act of 1965 . . . required the city of Canton to obtain federal approval of the way it proposed to run its 1969 elections. For this reason, I am unable to join the dissenting opinion of Mr. Justice Black,

...although like him I see little likelihood that the changes here involved had a discriminatory purpose or effect.

I agree with the Court, and for substantially the reasons it gives, that the city should have submitted the relocation of polling places for federal approval. But I cannot agree that it was obliged to follow that course with respect to the other two matters here at issue.

... Section 5 requires submission of changes "with respect to voting" only.

The Court seems to interpret this restriction as including any change in state law which has an effect on voting, if changes of that type have "a potential for racial discrimination in voting." ... At least in the absence of a contrary administrative interpretation, I would not go beyond *Allen* [v. *State Board of Elections*] to hold that annexations are within the scope of Sec. 5. The Court's assertion that the Attorney General does in fact interpret the Act differently seems to me to give too much weight to the passing remark of an Assistant Attorney General. [The opinion here points out that there were over forty municipal annexations in South Carolina in 1967–1968 and over one hundred boundary changes in Georgia cities in 1965–1969, only one of which was submitted to the Attorney General.]

I must confess that I am somewhat mystified by the Court's discussion of the appropriate remedy in this case.... I would direct the holding of new elections if and only if the city fails to obtain approval from the appropriate federal officials within a reasonable time.... In any event, the District Court is entitled to more guidance on this score than the Court provides.

Mr. Justice Black dissenting.

In *South Carolina* v. *Katzenbach* ... I dissented vigorously from the majority's conclusion that every part of Sec. 5 of the Voting Rights Act was constitutional. The fears which precipitated my dissent in *Katzenbach* have been fully realized in this case. The majority, relying on *Katzenbach,* now actually holds that the City of Canton, Mississippi, a little town of 10,000 persons, cannot change four polling places for its election of aldermen without obtaining federal approval....

The city altered four of the local polling places. Two were moved because the old polling places had been located on private property and the owners would no longer consent to the use of their property for voting. I find it incredible to believe that Congress intended that the people of Canton would have to travel to Washington to get the Attorney General's consent to rent new polling places. Another polling place was moved because the old one did not have sufficient space to accommodate voting machines. Finally, the fourth place was moved from a courthouse to a public school to eliminate interference with courtroom proceedings. It is difficult for me to imagine a matter more peculiarly and exclusively fit for local determination than the location of polling places for the election of town aldermen. Nor is there the slightest indicaiton that any of these changes were motivated by or resulted in racial discrimination... Presumably, the majority is ready to hold, if necessary, that the City of Canton could not change from ballots to voting machines without obtaining similar federal approval. I dissent from any such utter degradation of the power of the States to govern their own affairs....

... It is beyond my comprehension how the change from wards to an at-large election can discriminate against Negroes on account of their race in a city that has an absolute majority of Negro voters....

This Act attempts to reverse the proper order of things. Now the Congress presumes—a presumption which the Court upholds—that statutes regulating voting are discriminatory and enjoins their enforcement until the State can convince distant federal judges or politically appointed officials that the statute is not discriminatory. This permits the Federal Government to suspend the effectiveness or enforcement of a state act *before* discrimination is proved. But I think the Federal Government is without power to suspend a state statute before discrimination is proved. The inevitable effect of such a reversal of roles is what has happened in this case—a nondiscriminatory state practice or statute is voided wholly without constitutional authority.

Except as applied to a few southern States in a renewed spirit of Reconstruction, the people of this country would never stand for such a perversion of the separation of authority between state and federal governments. Never would New York or California be required to come begging to the City of Washington before they could enforce the valid enactments of their own legislatures. Never would this law have emerged from congressional committees had it applied to the entire United States. Our people are more jealous of their own local governments than to permit such a bold seizure of their authority.

Finally, I dissent from the remedy adopted by the Court. . . . I am convinced that if the majority were to confront the issue of an appropriate remedy now, the Court would not void the election or compel the city to hold a new election. To the contrary, the 1969 election would be upheld because the alleged violations of the Act are so very minor and so clearly technical. We should not forget that while it is easy for judges to order new elections, it will be neither easy nor inexpensive for the little city of Canton to comply with such an order. . . .

The provisions of the Voting Rights Act of 1965 were, by the terms of the Act, to extend for a period of ten years. In 1975, prior to the expiration of the Act, Congress enacted amendments to expand the coverage slightly and to extend the operation of the Act ten more years to 1985.

In 1970 Congress adopted a major law of national application to lower the voting age, abolish literacy tests, and reduce the residence period for voters in the election of presidential electors. The Court considered a challenge to these provisions in *Oregon* v. *Mitchell* in 1970.

OREGON *v.* MITCHELL
400 U.S. 112 (1970)

Mr. Justice Black, announcing the judgments of the Court in an opinion expressing his own view of the cases.

In these suits the States resist compliance with the Voting Rights Act Amendments of 1970, . . . 84 Stat. 314, because they believe that the Act takes away from them powers reserved to the States by the Constitution to control their own elections. By its terms the Act does three things. First: It lowers the minimum age of voters in both state and federal elections from 21 to 18. Second: Based upon a finding by Congress that literacy tests have been used to discriminate against voters on account of their color, the Act enforces the Fourteenth and Fifteenth Amendments by barring the use of such tests in all elections, state and national. Third: The Act forbids States from disqualifying voters in national elections for presidential and vice presidential electors because they have not met state residency requirements.

For the reasons set out in Part I of this opinion, I believe Congress can fix the age of voters in national elections . . . but cannot set the voting age in state and local elections. For reasons expressed in separate opinions, my Brothers Douglas, Brennan, White, and Marshall join me in concluding that Congress can enfranchise 18-year-old citizens in national elections, but dissent from the judgment that Congress cannot extend the franchise to 18-year-old citizens in state and local elections. For reasons expressed in separate opinions, my Brothers The Chief Justice, Harlan, Stewart, and Blackmun join me in concluding that Congress cannot interfere with the age for voters set by the States for state and local elections. They, however, dissent from the judgment that Congress can control voter qualifications in federal elections. In summary, it is the judgment of the Court that the 18-year-old vote provisions . . . are constitutional and enforceable insofar as they pertain to federal elections and unconstitutional and unenforceable insofar as they pertain to state and local elections.

For the reasons set out in Part II of this opinion, I believe that Congress, in the exercise of its power to enforce the Fourteenth and Fifteenth Amendments, can prohibit the use of literacy tests or other devices used to discriminate against voters on account of their race in both state and federal elections. For reasons expressed in separate opinions, all of my Brethren join me in the judgment. Therefore the literacy test provisions of the Act are upheld.

. . . I believe Congress can set residency requirements and provide for absentee balloting in elections for presidential and vice presidential electors. [Seven justices concur in this judgment.] My Brother Harlan . . . considers that the residency provisions of the statute are unconstitutional. Therefore the residency and absentee balloting provisions of the Act are upheld. . . .

. . . In the very beginning the responsibility of the States for setting the qualifications of voters in congressional elections was made subject to the power of Congress to make or alter such regulations if it deemed available. This was done in Art. I, Sec. 4, of the Constitution, which provides:

"The Times, Places and Manner of holding Elections for Senators and Representatives, shall be prescribed in each state by the legislature thereof; *but the Congress may at any time by Law make or alter such Regulations,* except as to the Place of Chusing Senators." (Emphasis supplied.). . .

Any doubt about the powers of Congress to regulate congressional elections, including the age and other qualifications of the voters should be dispelled by the opinion of this Court in *Smiley* v. *Holm* . . . (1932). There, Chief Justice Hughes writing for a unanimous Court discussed the scope of congressional power under Sec. 4 at some length. He said:

"The subject matter is the 'times, places and manner of holding elections for Senators and Representatives.' It cannot be doubted that these comprehensive words embrace authority to provide a complete code for congressional elections. . . . The phrase 'such regulations' plainly refers to regulations of the same general character that the legislature of the State is authorized to prescribe with respect to congressional elections. In exercising this power, the Congress may supplement these state regulations or may substitute its own. . . . It 'has a general supervisory power over the whole subject.' ". . .

Similarly, it is the prerogative of Congress to oversee the conduct of presidential and vice presidential elections and to set the qualifications for voters for electors for those offices. It cannot be seriously contended that Congress has less power over the conduct of presidential elections than it has over congressional elections.

On the other hand, the Constitution was also intended to preserve to the States the power . . . to establish and maintain their own separate and independent governments. . . . It is obvious that the whole Constitution reserves to the States the power to set voter qualifications in state and local elections, except to the limited extent that the people through constitutional amendments have specifically narrowed the powers of the States. . . .

. . . I would hold that the literacy test ban of the 1970 Amendments is constitutional under the Enforcement Clause of the Fifteenth Amendment. . . . In this legislation Congress has recognized that discrimination on account of color and racial origin is not confined to the South, but exists in various parts of the country. Congress has decided that the way to solve the problems of racial discrimination is to deal with nationwide discrimination with nationwide legislation. Compare *South Carolina* v. *Katzenbach, supra*. . . .

In Title II of the Voting Rights Act Amendments Congress also provided that in presidential and vice presidential elections, no voter could be denied his right to cast a ballot because he had not lived in the jurisdiction long enough to meet its residency requirements. Furthermore, Congress provided uniform national rules for absentee voting in presidential and vice presidential elections. In enacting these regulations for national elections Congress was attempting to insure a fully effective voice to all citizens in national elections. What I said in Part I of this opinion applies with equal force here. Acting under its broad authority to create and maintain a national government, Congress unquestionably has power under the Constitution to regulate federal elections. . . .

Mr. Justice Douglas.

I dissent from the judgment of the Court insofar as it declares Sec. 302 unconstitutional as applied to state elections and concur in the judgment as it affects federal elections but for different reasons. I rely on the Equal Protection Clause and on the Privileges and Immunities Clause of the Fourteenth Amendment. . . .

Congress might well conclude that a reduction in the voting age from 21 to 18 was needed in the interests of equal protection. . . . Equality of voting by all who are deemed mature enough to vote is certainly consistent "with the letter and spirit of the constitution.". . . I would sustain the choice which Congress has made. . . .

Mr. Justice Harlan, concurring in part and dissenting in part. . . .

. . . I am of the opinion that the Fourteenth Amendment was never intended to restrict the authority of the States to allocate their political power as they see fit and therefore that it does not authorize Congress to set voter qualifications, in either state or federal elections. I find no other source of congressional power to lower the voting age as fixed by state laws, or to alter state laws on residency, registration, and absentee voting, with respect to either state or federal elections. The suspension of Arizona's literacy requirement, however, can be deemed an appropriate means of enforcing the Fifteenth Amendment, and I would sustain it on that basis. . . .

Mr. Justice Brennan, Mr. Justice White, and Mr. Justice Marshall dissent from the judgment insofar as it declares Sec. 302 unconstitutional as applied to state and local elections, and concur in the judgment in all other respects. . . .

. . . [T]here is no question but that Congress could legitimately have concluded that the use of literacy tests anywhere within the United States has the inevitable effect of denying the vote to members of racial minorities whose inability to pass such tests is the direct consequence of previous governmental discrimination in education. . . . Five years of experience with the 1965 Act persuaded Congress that a nationwide ban on literacy and other potentially discriminatory tests was necessary to prevent racial discrimination in voting throughout the country. . . .

Section 202 of the 1970 Amendments abolishes all durational state residence requirements restricting the right to vote in presidential elections. . . . For more than a century, this Court has recognized the constitutional right of all citizens to unhindered interstate travel and settlement. . . .

By definition, the imposition of a durational residence requirement operates to penalize those persons, and only those persons, who have exercised their constitutional right of interstate migration. . . . Congress has explicitly found both that the imposition of durational residence requirements abridges the right of free interstate migration and that such requirements are not reasonably related to any compelling state interests. . . . Accordingly, we find ample justification for the congressional conclusion that Sec. 202 is a reasonable means for eliminating an unnecessary burden on the right of interstate migration. *United States* v. *Guest, supra.* . . .

We believe there is serious question whether a statute granting the franchise to citizens over 21 while denying it to those between the ages of 18 and 21 could, in any event, withstand present scrutiny under the Equal Protection Clause. Regardless of the answer to this question, however, it is clear to us that proper regard for the special function of Congress in making determinations of legislative fact compels this Court to respect those determinations unless they are contradicted by evidence far stronger than anything that has been adduced in these cases. We would uphold Sec. 302 as a valid exercise of congressional power under Sec. 5 of the Fourteenth Amendment. . . .

Mr. Justice Stewart, with whom the Chief Justice and Mr Justice Blackmun join, concurring in part and dissenting in part. . . .

I agree with the Court in sustaining the congressional ban on state literacy tests, for substantially the same reasons relied upon by Mr. Justice Black. I also agree that the action of Congress in removing the restrictions of state residency requirements in presidential elections is constitutionally valid. . . . And finally, I disagree with the Court's conclusion that Congress could constitutionally reduce the voting age to 18 for federal elections, since I am convinced that Congress was wholly without constitutional power to alter—for the purpose of *any* elections—the voting age qualifications now determined by the several States. . . .

Congress, in my view, has the power under the Constitution to eradicate political and civil disabilities which arise by operation of state law following a change in residence from one State to another. Freedom to travel from State to State—freedom to enter and abide in any State in the Union—is a privilege of United States citizenship. . . . In the light of these considerations, Sec. 202 presents no difficulty. . . .

Contrary to the submission of my Brother Black, Article I, Sec. 4, does not create in the federal legislature the power to alter the constitutionally established qualifications to vote in congressional elections. . . . The "manner" of holding elections can hardly be read to mean the *qualifications* for voters, when it is remembered that Sec. 2 of the same Article I explicitly speaks of the "qualifications" for voters in elections to choose Representatives. It is plain, in short, that when the Framers meant qualifications they said "qualifications." That word does not appear in Article I, Sec. 4. . . .

To be sure, recent decisions have established that state action regulating suffrage is not immune from the impact of the Equal Protection Clause. But we have been careful in those decisions to note the undoubted power of a State to establish a qualification for voting based on age. . . . I cannot but conclude that Sec. 302 was beyond the constitutional power of Congress to enact.

The Twenty-sixth Amendment to the Constitution was ratified on June 10, 1971, in the record time of three months, seven days. It reinstates the eighteen-year-old vote provision held unconstitutional in *Oregon v. Mitchell* by providing:

The right of citizens of the United States, who are 18 years of age or older, to vote shall not be denied or abridged by the United States or by any State on account of age.

APPORTIONMENT OF LEGISLATIVE SEATS AND THE EQUAL PROTECTION CLAUSE

Prior to 1962, attacks on patterns of apportioning seats for legislative bodies based on the claim that such patterns violated the Article IV guarantee of "a republican form of government" or that population inequalities between districts had the effect of producing inequalities in the effective voting power of persons residing in different districts were unsuccessful in the federal courts. *Colegrove* v. *Green,* 328 U.S. 549 (1946), presented a challenge to the arrangement of Illinois' congressional districts, essentially unchanged since 1901. Petitioners asked that the Court restrain the state from holding a general election on the ground that the districts lacked compactness of territory and approximate equality of population, and that the inequality of voting power resulting was in violation of the Fourteenth Amendment and the provisions of Article I respecting the election of members of the House of Representatives. Three justices held that the matter was nonjusticiable. Justice Frankfurter, speaking for these, stated:

We are of opinion that the petitioners ask of this Court what is beyond its competence to grant. This is one of those demands on judicial power which cannot be met by verbal fencing about "jurisdiction." It must be resolved by considerations on the basis of which this Court, from time to time, has refused to intervene in controversies. It has refused to do so because due regard for the effective working of our Government revealed this issue to be of a peculiarly political nature and therefore not meet for judicial determination. . . .

. . . Nothing is clearer than that this controversy concerns matters that bring courts into immediate and active relations with party contests. From the determination of such issues this Court has traditionally held aloof. It is hostile to a democratic system to involve the judiciary in the politics of the people. And it is not less pernicious if such judicial intervention in an essentially political contest be dressed up in the abstract phrases of the law. . . .

The one stark fact that emerges from a study of the history of Congressional apportionment is its embroilment in politics, in the sense of party contests and party interests. . . .

Justice Rutledge concurred in the result, holding that the question *was* justiciable but that the bill should be dismissed because the Court could not provide a proper equitable remedy for the problem.

Justices Black, Douglas, and Murphy dissented, asserting that the question was justiciable, that appellants had made out a case for their allegations of injury, and that they were entitled to equitable relief. Justice Black suggested that if the state did not properly redistrict, the courts could order elections at large for members of the House, thereby equalizing voting power within the state.

Only seven members of the Court participated in the *Colegrove* decision. On the question of the Court's power to offer assistance in such a case the vote was four-to-three in the negative. With Justice Rutledge's split vote, however, the Court was divided four-to-three in *favor* of holding that the question presented a justiciable controversy. Thus the bill was dismissed, but the case was hardly a conclusive disposition of the whole question of judicial remedies for malapportionment.

In *South* v. *Peters*, 339 U.S. 276 (1950), an injunction was sought in a federal court to restrain the enforcement of the Georgia county-unit statute. The county-unit system provided that in primary elections the candidate receiving the largest vote in a county received its entire "electoral vote," which ranged from two for the small county to six for the most populous county. The complaint charged that gross inequality of voting power resulted from the system. The Court, citing *Colegrove* v. *Green,* affirmed a dismissal of the petition, with Justices Black and Douglas dissenting.

In *Baker* v. *Carr*, 369 U.S. 186 (1962), the Court for the first time held that allegations that malapportionment of legislative seats denied equal protection presented a justiciable cause of action and one for which the federal courts could fashion appropriate equitable relief upon finding that such apportionment was a denial of equal protection under the Fourteenth Amendment. The case presented a challenge to the apportionment of seats in the Tennessee House of Representatives. It was alleged that Tennessee continued to allocate representation on the basis of a 1901 statute and that subsequent population changes without reapportionment resulted in a denial to the plaintiffs of the equal protection of the laws by virtue of "the debasement of their votes." The trial court had dismissed the petition on grounds of nonjusticiability. By a six-to-two vote the Court reversed and remanded.

BAKER *v.* CARR

369 U.S. 186 (1962)

Mr. Justice Brennan delivered the opinion of the Court....

... [Petitioners] seek a declaration that the 1901 statute is unconstitutional and an injunction restraining the appellees from acting to conduct any further elections under it. They also pray that unless and until the General Assembly enacts a valid reapportionment, the District Court should either decree a reapportionment by mathematical application of the Tennessee constitutional formulae to the most recent Federal Census figures, or direct the appellees to conduct legislative elections, primary and general, at large....

I

... In light of the District Court's treatment of the case, we hold today only (a) that the court possessed jurisdiction of the subject matter; (b) that a justiciable cause of action is stated upon which appellants would be entitled to appropriate relief; and (c) because appellees raise the issue before this Court, that the appellants have standing to challenge the Tennessee apportionment statutes. Beyond noting that we have no cause at this stage to doubt the District Court will be able to fashion relief if violations of constitutional rights are found, it is improper now to consider what remedy would be most appropriate if appellants prevail at the trial.

II

Jurisdiction of the Subject Matter

The District Court was uncertain whether our cases withholding federal judicial relief rested upon a lack of federal jurisdiction or upon the inappropriateness of the subject matter for judicial consideration—what we have designated "nonjusticiability." The distinction between the two grounds is significant. In the instance of nonjusticiability, consideration of the cause is not wholly and immediately foreclosed; rather, the Court's inquiry necessarily proceeds to the point of deciding whether the duty asserted can be judicially identified and its breach judicially determined, and whether protection for the right asserted can be judicially molded. In the instance of lack of jurisdiction the cause either does not "arise under" the Federal Constitution, law or treaties (or fall within one of the other enumerated categories of Art. III, Section 2), or is not a "case or controversy" within the meaning of that section; or the cause is not one described by any jurisdictional statute. . . .

An unbroken line of our precedents sustains the federal courts' jurisdiction of the subject matter of federal constitutional claims of this nature. The first case involved the redistricting of States for the purpose of electing Representatives to the Federal Congress. . . . When the Minnesota Supreme Court affirmed the dismissal of a suit to enjoin the Secretary of State of Minnesota from acting under Minnesota redistricting legislation, we reviewed the constitutional merits of the legislation and reversed the State Supreme Court. *Smiley* v. *Holm,* 285 U.S. 355. . . . When a three-judge District Court . . . permanently enjoined officers of the State of Mississippi from conducting an election of Representatives under a Mississippi redistricting act, we reviewed the federal questions on the merits and reversed the District Court. *Wood* v. *Broom,* 287 U.S. 1. . . .

The appellees refer to *Colegrove* v. *Green,* 328 U.S. 549, as authority that the District Court lacked jurisdiction of the subject matter. Appellees misconceive the holding of that case. The holding was precisely contrary to their reading of it. Seven members of the Court participated in the decision. Unlike many other cases in this field which have assumed without discussion that there was jurisdiction, all three opinions filed in *Colegrove* discussed the question. Two of the opinions expressing the views of four of the Justices, a majority, flatly held that there was jurisdiction of the subject matter. . . .

Several subsequent cases similar to *Colegrove* have been decided by the Court in summary *per curiam* statements. None was dismissed for want of jurisdiction of the subject matter. . . .

. . . In *South* v. *Peters,* 339 U.S. 276, we affirmed the dismissal of an attack on the Georgia "county unit" system but founded our action on a ground that plainly would not have been reached if the lower court lacked jurisdiction of the subject matter. . . .

We hold that the District Court has jurisdiction of the subject matter of the federal constitutional claim asserted in the complaint. . . .

IV

Justiciability

. . . We understand the District Court to have read the cited cases as compelling the conclusion that since the appellants sought to have a legislative apportionment held unconstitutional, their suit presented a "political question" and was therefore nonjusticiable. We hold that this challenge to an apportionment presents no non-justiciable "political question." The cited cases do not hold the contrary.

Of course the mere fact that the suit seeks protection of a political right does not mean it presents a political question. Such an objection "is little more than a play upon words.". . . Rather, it is argued that apportionment cases, whatever the actual wording of the complaint, can involve no federal constitutional right except one resting on the guaranty of a republican form of government, and that complaints based on that clause have been held to present political questions which are nonjusticiable.

We hold that the claim pleaded here neither rests upon nor implicates the Guaranty Clause and that its justiciability is therefore not foreclosed by our decisions of cases involving that clause. . . .

Our discussion . . . requires review of a number of political question cases, in order to expose the attributes of the doctrine. . . . That review reveals that in the Guaranty Clause cases and in the other "political question" cases, it is the relationship between the judiciary and the coordinate branches of the Federal Government, and not the federal judiciary's relationship to the States, which gives rise to the "political question.". . .

. . . The nonjusticiability of a political question is primarily a function of the separation of powers. . . .

. . . Prominent on the surface of any case held to involve a political question is found a textually demonstrable constitutional commitment of the issue to a coordinate political department; or a lack of judicially discoverable and manageable standards for resolving it; or the impossibility of deciding without an initial policy determination of a kind clearly for nonjudicial discretion; or the impossibility of a court's undertaking independent resolution without expressing lack of the respect due coordinate branches of government; or an unusual need for unquestioning adherence to a political decision already made; or the potentiality of embarrassment from multifarious pronouncements by various departments on one question. . . .

We conclude that the nonjusticiability of claims resting on the Guaranty Clause which arises from their embodiment of questions that were thought "political," can have no bearing upon the justiciability of the equal protection claim presented in this case. . . . Only last Term, in *Gomillion* v. *Lightfoot,* 364 U.S. 339 (1960), we applied the Fifteenth Amendment to strike down a redrafting of municipal boundaries which effected a discriminatory impairment of voting rights, in the face of what a majority of the Court of Appeals thought to be a sweeping commitment to state legislatures of the power to draw and redraw such boundaries. . . .

. . . We conclude that the complaint's allegations of a denial of equal protection present a justiciable constitutional cause of action upon which appellants are entitled to a trial and a decision. The right asserted is within the reach of judicial protection under the Fourteenth Amendment.

The judgment of the District Court is reversed and the cause is remanded for further proceedings consistent with this opinion.

Reversed and remanded.

Mr. Justice Whittaker did not participate in the decision of this case.

Mr. Justice Douglas, concurring. . . .

The traditional test under the Equal Protection Clause has been whether a State has made "an invidious discrimination," as it does when it selects "a particular race or nationality for oppressive treatment.". . .

I agree with my Brother Clark that if the allegations in the complaint can be sustained a case for relief is established. We are told that a single vote in Moore County, Tennessee, is worth 19 votes in Hamilton County, that one vote in Stewart or in Chester County is worth nearly eight times a single vote in Shelby or Knox County. The opportunity to prove that an "invidious discrimination" exists should therefore be given the appellants. . . .

Mr. Justice Clark, concurring. . . .

The controlling facts cannot be disputed. It appears from the record that 37 per cent of the voters of Tennessee elect 20 of the 33 Senators while 40 per cent of the voters elect 63 of the 99 members of the House. But this might not on its face be "invidious discrimination,". . . for a "statutory discrimination will not be set aside if any state of facts reasonably may be conceived to justify it." *McGowan* v. *Maryland,* 366 U.S. 420, 426 (1961).

It is true that the apportionment policy incorporated in Tennessee's Constitution, *i.e.,* state-wide numerical equality of representation with certain minor qualifications, is a rational one. . . . Try as one may, Tennessee's apportionment just cannot be made to fit the pattern cut by its Constitution. . . . We must examine what the Assembly has done. The frequency and magnitude of the inequalities in the present districting admit of no policy whatever. . . . [T]he apportionment picture in Tennessee is a topsy-turvical of gigantic proportions. This is not to say that some of the disparity cannot be explained, but when the entire Table is examined . . . it leaves but one conclusion, namely that Tennessee's apportionment is a crazy quilt without rational basis. . . .

Although I find the Tennessee apportionment statute offends the Equal Protection Clause, I would not consider intervention by this Court into so delicate a field if there were any other relief available to the people of Tennessee. But the majority of the people of Tennessee have no "practical opportunities for exerting their political weight at the polls" to correct the existing "invidious discrimination." Tennessee has no initiative and referendum. I have searched diligently for other "practical opportunities" present under the law. I find none other than through the federal courts. The majority of the voters have been caught up in a legislative strait jacket. Tennessee has an "informed, civically militant electorate" and "an aroused popular conscience," but it does not sear "the conscience of the people's representatives." This is because the legislative policy has riveted the present seats in the Assembly to their respective constituencies, and by the votes of their incumbents a reapportionment of any kind is prevented. The people have been rebuffed at the hands of the Assembly; they have tried the constitutional convention route, but since the call must originate in the Assembly it, too, has been fruitless. They have tried Tennessee courts with the same result, and Governors have fought the tide only to flounder. It is said that there is recourse in Congress and perhaps that may be, but from a practical standpoint this is without substance. To date Congress has never undertaken such a task in any State. We therefore must conclude that the people of Tennessee are stymied and without judicial intervention will be saddled with the present discrimination in the affairs of their state government. . . .

. . . If judicial competence were lacking to fashion an effective decree, I would dismiss this appeal. However . . . I see no such difficulty in the position of this case. One plan might be to start with the existing assembly districts, consolidate some of them, and award the seats thus released to those counties suffering the most egregious discrimination. Other possibilities are present and might be more effective. But the plan here suggested would at least release the strangle hold now on the Assembly and permit it to redistrict itself. . . .

Mr. Justice Stewart, concurring. . . .

The complaint in this case asserts that Tennessee's system of apportionment is utterly arbitrary—without any possible justification in rationality. The District Court did not reach the merits of that claim, and this Court quite properly expresses no view on the subject. Contrary to the suggestion of my Brother Harlan, the Court does not say or imply that "state legislatures must be so structured as to reflect with approximate equality the voice of every voter.". . . The Court does not say or imply that there is anything in the Federal Constitution "to prevent a State, acting not irrationally, from choosing any electoral legislative structure it thinks best suited to the interests, temper, and customs of its people.". . .

Mr. Justice Frankfurter, whom Mr. Justice Harlan joins, dissenting.

The Court today reverses a uniform course of decision established by a dozen cases, including one by which the very claim now sustained was unanimously rejected only five years ago. The impressive body of rulings thus cast aside reflected the equally uniform course of our political history regarding the relationship between population and legislative representation—a wholly different matter from denial of the franchise to individuals because of race, color, religion or sex. Such a massive repudiation of the experience of our whole past in asserting destructively novel judicial power demands a detailed analysis of the role of this Court in our constitutional scheme. Disregard of inherent limits in the effective exercise of the Court's "judicial Power" not only presages the futility of judicial intervention in the essentially political conflict of forces by which the relation between population and representation has time out of mind been and now is determined. It may well impair the Court's position as the ultimate organ of "the supreme Law of the Land" in that vast range of legal problems, often strongly entangled in popular feeling, on which this Court must pronounce. The Court's authority—possessed neither of the purse nor the sword—ultimately rests on sustained public confidence in its moral sanction. Such feeling must be nourished by the Court's complete detachment, in fact and in appearance, from political entanglements and by abstention from injecting itself into the clash of political forces in political settlements.

A hypothetical claim resting on abstract assumptions is now for the first time made the basis for affording illusory relief for a particular evil even though it foreshadows deeper and more pervasive difficulties in consequence. The claim is hypothetical and the assumptions are abstract because the Court does not vouchsafe the lower courts—state and federal—guide-lines for formulating specific, definite, wholly unprecedented remedies for the inevitable litigations that today's umbrageous disposition is bound to stimulate in connection with politically motivated reapportionments in so many States. . . . For this Court to direct the District Court to enforce a claim to which the Court has over the years consistently found itself required to deny legal enforcement and at the same time to find it necessary to withhold any guidance to the lower court how to enforce this turnabout, new legal claim, manifests an odd—indeed an esoteric—conception of judicial propriety. One of the Court's supporting opinions, as elucidated by commentary, unwittingly affords a disheartening preview of the mathematical quagmire (apart from divers judicially inappropriate and elusive determinants), into which this Court today catapults the lower courts of the country without so much as adumbrating the basis for a legal calculus as a means of extrication. Even assuming the indispensable intellectual disinterestedness on the part of judges in such matters, they do not have accepted legal standards or criteria or even reliable analogies to draw upon for making judicial judgments. To charge courts with the task of accommodating the incommensurable factors of policy that underlie these mathematical puzzles is to attribute, however flatteringly, omnicompetence to judges. The framers of the Constitution persistently rejected a proposal that embodied this assumption and Thomas Jefferson never entertained it. . . .

In sustaining appellants' claim, based on the Fourteenth Amendment, that the District Court may entertain this suit, this Court's uniform course of decision over the years is overruled or disregarded. Explicitly it begins with *Colegrove* v. *Green, supra,* decided in 1946, but its roots run deep in the Court's historic adjudicatory process. . . .

The *Colegrove* doctrine, in the form in which repeated decisions have settled it, was not an innovation. It represents long judicial thought and experience. From its earliest opinions this Court has consistently recognized a class of controversies which do not lend themselves to judicial standards and judicial remedies. . . .

[The opinion then takes up various categories of cases falling under the "political question" doctrine.]

The influence of these converging considerations—the caution not to undertake decision where standards meet for judicial judgment are lacking, the reluctance to interfere with matters of state government in the absence of an unquestionable and effectively enforceable mandate, the unwillingness to make courts arbiters of the broad issues of political organization historically committed to other institutions and for whose adjustment the judicial process is ill-adapted—has been decisive of the settled line of cases, reaching back more than a century, which holds that Art. IV, Section 4, of the Constitution, guaranteeing to the States "a Republican Form of Government," is not enforceable through the courts. . . .

The present case involves all of the elements that have made the Guarantee Clause cases non-justiciable. It is, in effect, a Guarantee Clause claim masquerading under a different label. But it cannot make the case more fit for judicial action that appellants invoke the Fourteenth Amendment rather than Art. IV, Section 4, where, in fact, the gist of their complaint is the same. . . .

The notion that representation proportioned to the geographic spread of population is so universally accepted as a necessary element of equality between man and man that it must be taken to be the standard of a political equality preserved by the Fourteenth Amendment—that it is, in appellants' words "the basic principle of representative government"—is, to put it bluntly, not true. However desirable and however desired by some among the great political thinkers and framers of our government, it has never been generally practiced, today or in the past. . . .

Manifestly, the Equal Protection Clause supplies no clearer guide for judicial examination of apportionment methods than would the Guarantee Clause itself. Apportionment, by its character, is a subject of extraordinary complexity, involving —even after the fundamental theoretical issues concerning what is to be represented in a representative legislature have been fought out or compromised—considerations of geography, demography, electoral convenience, economic and social cohesions or divergencies among particular local groups, communications, the practical effects of political institutions like the lobby and the city machine, ancient traditions and ties of settled usage, respect for proven incumbents of long experience and senior status, mathematical mechanics, censuses compiling relevant data, and a host of others. Legislative responses throughout the country to the reapportionment demands of the 1960 Census have glaringly confirmed that these are not factors that lend themselves to evaluations of a nature that are the staple of judicial determinations or for which judges are equipped to adjudicate by legal training or experience or native wit. And this is the more so true because in every strand of this complicated, intricate web of values meet the contending forces of partisan politics. The practical significance of apportionment is that the next election results may differ because of it. Apportionment battles are overwhelmingly party or intra-party contests. It will add a virulent source of friction and tension in federal-state relations to embroil the federal judiciary in them. . . .

Dissenting opinion of Mr. Justice Harlan, whom Mr. Justice Frankfurter joins. . . .

In the last analysis, what lies at the core of this controversy is a difference of opinion as to the function of representative government. It is surely beyond argument that those who have the responsibility for devising a system of representation may permissibly consider that factors other than bare numbers should be taken into account. . . .

In short, there is nothing in the Federal Constitution to prevent a State, acting not irrationally, from choosing any electoral legislative structure it thinks best suited to the interests, temper, and customs of its people. I would have thought this proposition settled by *MacDougall* v. *Green*, . . . in which the Court observed that to "assume that political power is a function exclusively of numbers is to disregard the practicalities of government.". . .

Indeed, I would hardly think it unconstitutional if a state legislature's expressed reason for establishing or maintaining an electoral imbalance between its rural and urban population were to protect the State's agricultural interests from the sheer weight of numbers of those residing in its cities. . . .

In conclusion, it is appropriate to say that one need not agree, as a citizen, with what Tennessee has done or failed to do, in order to deprecate, as a judge, what the majority is doing today. Those observers of the Court who see it primarily as the last refuge for the correction of all inequality or injustice, no matter what its nature or source, will no doubt applaud this decision and its break with the past. Those who consider that continuing national respect for the Court's authority depends in large measure upon its wise exercise of self-restraint and discipline in constitutional adjudication, will view the decision with deep concern. . . .

[Mr. Justice Harlan attached an Appendix entitled "The Inadequacy of Arithmetical Formulas as Measures of the Rationality of Tennessee's Apportionment."]

The potential impact of *Baker* v. *Carr* on state and local government and politics was readily apparent. The decision was rendered on March 26, 1962, and a spate of articles, editorials, studies, and speeches in legislative bodies soon followed. Reaction ranged from anger or dismay at the Court's entry into the "political thicket" to warm expressions of enthusiasm for the cutting of the Gordian knot of malapportionment. Many observers, however, raised questions about the application of the *Baker* decision to such problems as the county unit system of Georgia, malapportionment of congressional districts, and the "little federal system" of according equal representation by counties in one house of the state legislature. Answers to these questions were not long in coming. In *Gray* v. *Sanders*, 372 U.S. 368 (1963), the Court held invalid the Georgia county unit system of weighting smaller county votes disproportionately in the Democratic primary where United States Senators and statewide officers were nominated. And while some of the opinions in *Baker* indicated that factors other than population might be relevant in setting up electoral districts, the majority in *Gray* v. *Sanders* held that the only acceptable test in statewide elections was equality of population. Justice Douglas, speaking for eight members of the Court, stated:

... If a State in a statewide election weighted the male vote more heavily than the female vote or the white vote more heavily than the Negro vote, none could successfully contend that that discrimination was allowable.... How then can one person be given twice or 10 times the voting power of another person in a statewide election merely because he lives in a rural area or because he lives in the smallest rural county? Once the geographical unit for which a representative is to be chosen is designated, all who participate in the election are to have an equal vote—whatever their race, whatever their sex, whatever their occupation, whatever their income, and wherever their home may be in that geographical unit. This is required by the Equal Protection Clause of the Fourteenth Amendment. The concept of "we the people" under the Constitution visualizes no preferred class of voters but equality among those who meet the basic qualifications. The idea that every voter is equal to every other voter in his State, when he casts his ballot in favor of one of several competing candidates, underlies many of our decisions....

The conception of political equality from the Declaration of Independence, to Lincoln's Gettysburg Address, to the Fifteenth, Seventeenth, and Nineteenth Amendments can mean only one thing—one person, one vote....

[Justice Harlan was the only dissenter in the case. In an "I-told-you-so" opinion he pointed to the rash of litigation spawned by the *Baker* decision:]

When *Baker* v. *Carr* ... was argued at the last Term we were assured that if this Court would only remove the roadblocks of *Colegrove* v. *Green* ... and its predecessors to judicial review in "electoral" cases, this Court in all likelihood would never have to get deeper into such matters. State legislatures, it was predicted, would be prodded into taking satisfactory action by the mere prospect of legal proceedings.

These predictions have not proved true. As of November 1, 1962, [only eight months after *Baker*] the apportionment of seats in at least 30 state legislatures had been challenged in state and federal courts, and, besides this one, 10 electoral cases of one kind or another are already on this Court's docket. The present case is the first of these to reach plenary consideration....

In the following year, in another Georgia case, *Wesberry* v. *Sanders*, 376 U.S. 1 (1964), the Court applied the "one man, one vote" rule to the matter of equalizing of population among congressional districts within a state. Petitioners lived in Georgia's Fifth Congressional District, in which Atlanta is located, which had a population of 823,680—as contrasted with a population of 394,312 for the average Georgia congressional district. They brought suit in a federal district court to enjoin defendants from conducting an election under the existing congressional districting statute on the ground that it was violative of the Constitution. The district court dismissed for nonjusticiability and want of equity, and on appeal the Supreme Court reversed. In an opinion by Justice Black, for six members of the Court, it was held that the statute was invalid as abridging the requirement of Article I, Section 2, that congressmen be chosen "by the People of the several States." In construing this section, Justice Black stated:

We hold that, construed in its historical context, the command of Art. I, Section 2, that Representatives be chosen "by the People of the several States" means that as nearly as is practicable one man's vote in a congressional election is to be worth as much as another's. This rule is followed automatically, of course, when Representatives are chosen as a group on a statewide basis, as was a widespread practice in the first 50 years of our Nation's history. . . . We do not believe that the Framers of the Constitution intended to permit . . . vote-diluting discrimination to be accomplished through the device of districts containing widely varied numbers of inhabitants. To say that a vote is worth more in one district than in another would not only run counter to our fundamental ideas of democratic government, it would cast aside the principle of a House of Representatives elected "by the People," a principle tenaciously fought for and established at the Constitutional Convention. The history of the Constitution, particularly that part of it relating to the adoption of Art. I, Section 2, reveals that those who framed the Constitution meant that, no matter what the mechanics of an election, whether statewide or by districts, it was population which was to be the basis of the House of Representatives.

[The opinion then treats the debates in the Philadelphia Convention on the structure of the Congress and gives some contemporaneous construction of the sections dealing with the House of Representatives indicating that equality of voting power was intended.]

While it may not be possible to draw congressional districts with mathematical precision, that is no excuse for ignoring our Constitution's plain objective of making equal representation for equal numbers of people the fundamental goal for the House of Representatives. That is the high standard of justice and common sense which the Founders set for us.

Apparently there was fairly general acceptance of the idea that fairness demanded that one house of the legislature and congressional districts be apportioned on the "one man, one vote" formula. But criticism erupted when in June 1964, in a group of Alabama cases cited as *Reynolds* v. *Sims*, the Court held that both houses of a bicameral state legislature were required by the equal protection clause to be apportioned strictly on the basis of population.

REYNOLDS *v.* SIMS
377 U.S. 533 (1964)

[Taxpayers and registered voters of two urban Alabama counties brought suit in the United States District Court challenging the validity of (1) the existing apportionment provisions for the Alabama legislature, which created a 35-member state senate elected from 35 districts varying in population from 15,417 to 634,864, and a 106-member state house of representatives with population-per-representative variances from 6,731 to 104,767; (2) a proposed state constitutional amendment creating a 67-member state senate with one senator per county, the counties varying in population from 10,726 to 634,864, and a 106-member state house of representatives with population-per-representative variances from 10,726 to 42,303; and (3) a "standby" statutory measure creating a 35-member state senate elected from 35 districts varying in population from 31,175 to 634,864, and a 106-member house of representatives with population-per-representative variances from under 20,000 to over 52,000. The three-judge court held that all three schemes were unconstitutional, but in order to "break the strangle hold" of the rural counties on the legislature so that it could reapportion itself, the court ordered a temporary reapportionment following the proposed amendment's provisions with respect to the house of representatives and the "standby" statute's provisions with respect to the state senate. Direct appeal to the Supreme Court.]

Mr. Chief Justice Warren delivered the opinion of the Court. . . .

Gray and *Wesberry* are of course not dispositive of or directly controlling on our decision in these cases involving state legislative apportionment controversies. Admittedly, those decisions, in which we held that, in statewide and in congressional elections, one person's vote must be counted equally with those of all other voters in a State, were based on different constitutional considerations and were addressed to rather distinct problems. But neither are they wholly inapposite. . . . *Wesberry* clearly established that the fundamental principle of representative government in this country is one of equal representation for equal numbers of people, without regard to race, sex, economic status, or place of residence within a State. Our problem, then, is to ascertain, in the instant cases, whether there are any constitutionally cognizable principles which would justify departures from the basic standard of equality among voters in the apportionment of seats in state legislatures. . . .

Legislators represent people, not trees or acres. Legislators are elected by voters, not farms or cities or economic interests. As long as ours is a representative form of government, and our legislatures are those instruments of government elected directly by and directly representative of the people, the right to elect legislators in a free and unimpaired fashion is a bedrock of our political system. . . . [I]f a State should provide that the votes of citizens in one part of the State should be given two times, or five times, or 10 times the weight of votes of citizens in another part of the State, it could hardly be contended that the right to vote of those residing in the disfavored areas had not been effectively diluted.

[In response to the claim that a state senate based on one member per county was reasonable because analogous to the Federal Senate, Chief Justice Warren stated:]

Much has been written since our decision in *Baker* v. *Carr* about the applicability of the so-called federal analogy to state legislative apportionment arrangements.* After considering the matter, the court below concluded that no conceivable analogy could be drawn between the federal scheme and the apportionment of seats in the Alabama Legislature under the proposed constitutional amendment. We agree with the District Court, and find the federal analogy inapposite and irrelevant to state legislative districting schemes. Attempted reliance on the federal analogy appears often to be little more than an after-the-fact rationalization offered in defense of maladjusted state apportionment arrangements. The original constitutions of 36 of our States provided that representation in both houses of the state legislatures would be based completely, or predominantly, on population. And the Founding Fathers clearly had no intention of establishing a pattern or model for the apportionment of seats in state legislatures when the system of representation

---

* For a thorough statement of the arguments against holding the so-called federal analogy applicable to state legislative apportionment matters, see, e.g., McKay, Reapportionment and the Federal Analogy (National Municipal League pamphlet 1962); McKay, The Federal Analogy and State Apportionment standards, 38 Notre Dame Law. 487 (1963). See also Merrill, Blazes for a Trail through the Thicket of Reapportionment, 16 Okla. L. Rev. 59, 67–70 (1963).

in the Federal Congress was adopted. Demonstrative of this is the fact that the Northwest Ordinance, adopted in the same year, 1787, as the Federal Constitution, provided for the apportionment of seats in territorial legislatures solely on the basis of population.

The system of representation in the two Houses of the Federal Congress is one ingrained in our Constitution, as part of the law of the land. It is one conceived out of compromise and concession indispensable to the establishment of our federal republic. Arising from unique historical circumstances, it is based on the consideration that in establishing our type of federalism a group of formerly independent States bound themselves together under one national government....

Political subdivisions of States—counties, cities, or whatever—never were and never have been considered as sovereign entities. Rather, they have been traditionally regarded as subordinate governmental instrumentalities created by the State to assist in the carrying out of state governmental functions.... The relationship of the States to the Federal Government could hardly be less analogous....

Since we find the so-called federal analogy inapposite to a consideration of the constitutional validity of state legislative apportionment schemes, we necessarily hold that the Equal Protection Clause requires both houses of a state legislature to be apportioned on a population basis. The right of a citizen to equal representation and to have his vote weighted equally with those of all other citizens in the election of members of one house of a bicameral state legislature would amount to little if States could effectively submerge the equal-population principle in the apportionment of seats in the other house. If such a scheme were permissible, an individual citizen's ability to exercise an effective voice in the only instrument of state government directly representative of the people might be almost as effectively thwarted as if neither house were apportioned on a population basis. Deadlock between the two bodies might result in compromise and concession on some issues. But in all too many cases the more probable result would be frustration of the majority will through minority veto in the house not apportioned on a population basis....

We do not believe that the concept of bicameralism is rendered anachronistic and meaningless when the predominant basis of representation in the two state legislative bodies is required to be the same—population. A prime reason for bicameralism, modernly considered, is to insure mature and deliberate consideration of, and to prevent precipitate action on, proposed legislative measures. Simply because the controlling criterion for apportioning representation is required to be the same in both houses does not mean that there will be no differences in the composition and complexion of the two bodies. Different constituencies can be represented in the two houses. One body could be composed of single-member districts while the other could have at least some multimember districts. The length of terms of the legislators in the separate bodies could differ. The numerical size of the two bodies could be made to differ, even significantly, and the geographical size of districts from which legislators are elected could also be made to differ. And apportionment in one house could be arranged so as to balance off minor inequities in the representation of certain areas in the other house. In summary, these and other factors could be, and are presently in many States, utilized to engender differing complexions and collective attitudes in the two bodies of a state legislature, although both are apportioned substantially on a population basis.

By holding that as a federal constitutional requisite both houses of a state legislature must be apportioned on a population basis, we mean that the Equal Protection Clause requires that a State make an honest and good faith effort to construct districts, in both houses of its legislature, as nearly of equal population as is practicable. We realize that it is a practical impossibility to arrange legislative districts so that each one has an identical number of residents, or citizens, or voters. Mathematical exactness or precision is hardly a workable constitutional requirement. . . .

[Justices Clark and Stewart concurred in the result, but on the ground that the Alabama legislature as constituted and the proposals for reapportionment offered by the state were not rationally based. Justice Clark stated, in part:]

It seems to me that all that the Court need say in this case is that each plan considered by the trial court is "a crazy quilt," clearly revealing invidious discrimination in each house of the Legislature and therefore violative of the Equal Protection Clause. . . .

I, therefore, do not reach the question of the so-called "federal analogy." But in my view, if one house of the State Legislature meets the population standard, representation in the other house might include some departure from it so as to take into account, on a rational basis, other factors in order to afford some representation to the various elements of the State. . . .

Mr. Justice Harlan, dissenting. . . .

Had the Court paused to probe more deeply into the matter, it would have found that the Equal Protection Clause was never intended to inhibit the States in choosing any democratic method they pleased for the apportionment of their legislatures. This is shown by the language of the Fourteenth Amendment taken as a whole, by the understanding of those who proposed and ratified it, and by the political practices of the States at the time the Amendment was adopted. It is confirmed by numerous state and congressional actions since the adoption of the Fourteenth Amendment, and by the common understanding of the Amendment as evidenced by subsequent constitutional amendments and decisions of this Court before *Baker* v. *Carr* made an abrupt break with the past in 1962. . . .

The Court's elaboration of its new "constitutional" doctrine indicates how far—and how unwisely—it has strayed from the appropriate bounds of its authority. The consequence of today's decision is that in all but the handful of States which may already satisfy the new requirements the local District Court or, it may be, the state courts, are given blanket authority and the constitutional duty to supervise apportionment of the State Legislatures. It is difficult to imagine a more intolerable and inappropriate interference by the judiciary with the independent legislatures of the States. . . .

Finally, these decisions give support to a current mistaken view of the Constitution and the constitutional function of this Court. This view, in a nutshell, is that every major social ill in this country can find its cure in some constitutional "principle," and that this Court should "take the lead" in promoting reform when other branches of government fail to act. The Constitution is not a panacea for every blot upon the public welfare, nor should this Court, ordained as a judicial body, be thought of as a general haven for reform movements. . . . This Court . . . does not serve its high purpose when it exceeds its authority, even to satisfy justified impatience with the slow workings of the political process. For when, in the name of constitutional interpretation, the Court *adds* something to the Constitution that was deliberately excluded from it, the Court in reality substitutes its view of what should be so for the amending process. . . .

The apportionment decisions are, by any test, landmark cases in the history of the Court's work. And they will inevitably have enormous impact on the organization, structure, and operation of state and local government in the United States. The Court has been both praised for its statesmanlike courage and condemned for its heavy-handed entry into matters deemed within the sole prerogative of the states. Illustrative of the former position, Dean Robert B. McKay, in the summary of his book *Reapportionment: The Law and Politics of Equal Representation* (New York: Twentieth Century Fund, 1965), stated: "It has been the theme of this volume that the *Reapportionment Cases* have opened the way for revitalization of representative democracy in the United States at the national, state, and even local levels." Other writers, while accepting the general line of the apportionment decisions, expressed doubt whether the Court had given adequate thought to some of the ramifications of its statements. In a thoughtful article by Professor Robert G. Dixon, Jr. ["Reapportionment Perspectives: What Is Fair Representation?" 51 *A. B. A. J.* 319 (1965)] for example, the point was made that the Court was actually dealing with representation, not voting, and thus was involved in "the most interesting, the most complex, the most baffling aspect of any democratic political system."

[For an exceptionally careful and thorough analysis of the cases and the views of the critics, through the *Reynolds* decision, see Carl Auerbach, "The Reapportionment Cases: One Person, One Vote—One Vote, One Value," 1964 *Supreme Court Review* 1 (Chicago: University of Chicago Press, 1964.)]

Permissible Population Variations

The "one man, one vote" rule of the Court in the *Apportionment Cases* raised the obvious question of just what degree of mathematical precision would be demanded to satisfy the constitutional test of equality. If, for example, only a one- or two-percent population deviation among districts was allowable, then it might be impossible to construct a valid system without splitting political subdivision lines. And once this approach is permitted, or even required, the potential for gerrymandered districts increases enormously.

In decisions subsequent to *Reynolds* the Court has adopted two different standards of permissible variance. In cases involving state legislative districts, substantial population variances have been upheld. But in the drawing of congressional district lines a much more restrictive rule of equality has been imposed. The cases to follow illustrate the differential standards employed by the Court.

MAHAN *v.* HOWELL

410 U.S. 315 (1973)

[In 1971, the Virginia legislature enacted statutes establishing districts for the election of members to the House of Delegates and Senate. The statute apportioning the House provided for a combination of fifty-two single-member, multimember, and floater delegate districts from which one hundred delegates would be elected. The maximum percentage population variation was 16.4 percent. The minimum population percentage necessary to elect a majority of the House was 49.29 percent. With the exception of one densely populated county which was allotted ten delegates and was subdivided into five-member districts, the delegate districts followed political subdivision lines of counties and cities. Suits were filed challenging the apportionment on the ground of excessive population variance. The statute apportioning the Senate establishtd forty single-member districts, but all naval personnel "homeported" at the Norfolk Naval Station were assigned to a single district. (A separate suit was filed attacking this grouping of naval personnel; the portion of the opinion holding this provision unconstitutional will be omitted.) The suits were consolidated in the District Court. The court held the variance in House districts excessive and substituted its own plan which had a variance of approximately 10 percent, but which did not follow subdivision lines in many instances.]

Mr. Justice Rehnquist delivered the opinion of the Court. . . .

In *Kirkpatrick* v. *Preisler* and *Wells* v. *Rockefeller,* this Court invalidated state reapportionment statutes for federal congressional districts having maximum percentage deviations of 5.97 percent and 13.1 percent respectively. The express purpose of these cases was to elucidate the standard first announcd in the holding of *Wesberry* v. *Sanders* . . . that "the command of Art. I, §2, that Representatives be chosen 'by the People of the several States' means that as nearly as is practicable one man's vote in a congressional election is to be worth as much as another's." . . . And it was concluded that that command "permits only the limited population variances which are unavoidable despite a good-faith effort to achieve absolute equality, or for which justification is shown." . . . The principal question thus presented for review is whether or not the Equal Protection Clause of the Fourteenth Amendment likewise permits only "the limited population variances which are unavoidable despite a good-faith effort to achieve absolute equality" in the context of state legislative reapportionment. . . .

Application of the "absolute equality" test of *Kirkpatrick* and *Wells* to state legislative redistricting may impair the normal functioning of state and local governments. Such an effect is readily apparent from an analysis of the District Court's plan in this case. Under . . . Virginia's Constitution, the General Assembly is given extensive power to enact special legislation regarding the organization of, and the exercise of governmental powers by, counties, cities, towns, and other political subdivisions. The statute redistricting the House of Delegates consistently sought to avoid the fragmentation of such subdivisions, assertedly to afford them a voice in Richmond to seek such local legislation.

[The opinion here shows that the result of the District Court's plan is to so fractionate the voter influence in several cities and counties as to make their representation "all but nonexistent" as a result of having split political subdivisions in twelve instances.]

We conclude, therefore, that the constitutionality of Virginia's legislative redistricting plan was not to be judged by the more stringent standards that *Kirkpatrick* and *Wells* make applicable to congressional reapportionment, but instead by the equal protection test enunciated in *Reynolds* v. *Sims, supra.* We reaffirm its holding that "the Equal Protection Clause requires that a State make an honest and good faith effort to construct districts, in both houses of its legislature, as nearly of equal population as is practicable." . . . We likewise reaffirm its conclusion that "[s]o long as the divergences from a strict population standard are based on legitimate considerations incident to the effectuation of a rational state policy, some deviations from the equal-population principle are constitutionally permissible with respect to the apportionment of seats in either or both of the two houses of a bicameral state legislature." . . .

We are not prepared to say that the decision of the people of Virginia to grant the General Assembly the power to enact local legislation dealing with the political subdivisions is irrational. And if that be so, the decision of the General Assembly to provide representation to subdivisions qua subdivisions in order to implement that constitutional power is likewise valid when measured against the Equal Protection Clause of the Fourteenth Amendment.... We hold that the legislature's plan for apportionment of the House of Delegates may reasonably be said to advance the rational state policy of respecting the boundaries of political subdivisions. The remaining inquiry is whether the population disparities among the districts that have resulted from the pursuit of this plan exceed constitutional limits. We conclude that they do not.

The most stringent mathematical standard that has heretofore been imposed upon an apportionment plan for a state legislature by this Court was enunciated in *Swann* v. *Adams*, ... where a scheme having a maximum deviation of 26 percent was disapproved. In that case, the State of Florida offered no evidence at the trial level to support the challenged variations with respect to either the House or Senate.... The relatively minor variations present in the Virginia plan contrast sharply with the larger variations in state legislative reapportionment plans that have been struck down by previous decisions of this Court....

Neither courts nor legislatures are furnished any specialized calipers that enable them to extract from the general language of the Equal Protection Clause of the Fourteenth Amendment the mathematical formula that establishes what range of percentage deviations is permissible, and what is not. The 16-odd percent maximum deviation that the District Court found to exist in the legislative plan for the reapportionment of the House is substantially less than the percentage deviations that have been found invalid in the previous decisions of this Court. While this percentage may well approach tolerable limits, we do not believe it exceeds them. Virginia has not sacrificed substantial equality to justifiable deviations....

Affirmed in part, reversed in part.

Mr. Justice Powell took no part in the consideration or decision of these cases.

Mr. Justice Brennan, with whom Mr. Justice Douglas and Mr. Justice Marshall join, concurring in part and dissenting in part....

In *Gaffney* v. *Cummings*, 412 U.S. 735 (1973), a Connecticut reapportionment plan was challenged which established a Senate with thirty-six districts, with a maximum population variance of 1.81 percent, and a House of Representatives with 151 districts, with a maximum population variance of 7.83 percent. The plan was based on a "political fairness" principle which was designed to reflect the relative strength of the major political parties by creating a certain number of "safe" districts for each party and a certain number of "swing" districts. A three-judge District Court held that the population variations were not shown to be justified by any sufficient state interest and were thus unconstitutional, and the policy of partisan political structuring was not a legitimate reason for violating the principle of numerical equality.

On appeal, the Supreme Court reversed by a six-to-three vote. The majority found that since the population variations constituted such minor deviations, the State was not required to justify them, and, further, the "political fairness" principle used in locating and defining the legislative districts was not invidiously discriminatory. In response to the contention that the State was required to establish substantial equality of population among districts, Justice White, for the Court, stated:

This is a vital and worthy goal, but surely its attainment does not in any commonsense way depend upon eliminating the insignificant population variations involved in this case. Fair and effective representation may be destroyed by gross population variations among districts, but it is apparent that such representation does not depend solely on mathematical equality among district populations. There are other relevant factors to be taken into account and other important interests that States may legitimately be mindful of. . . . An unrealistic overemphasis on raw population figures, a mere nose count in the districts, may submerge these other considerations and itself furnish a ready tool for ignoring factors that in day-to-day operation are important to an acceptable representation and apportionment arrangement. . . .

On the matter of the "political fairness" principle, Justice White's remarks indicate a rather more substantial understanding of political reality than may be found in some of the earlier apportionment opinions:

Politics and political considerations are inseparable from districting and apportionment. . . . It is not only obvious, but absolutely unavoidable, that the location and shape of districts may well determine the political complexion of the area. District lines are rarely neutral phenomena. . . .

It may be suggested that those who redistrict and reapportion should work with the census, not political, data and achieve population equality without regard for political impact. But this politically mindless approach may produce, whether intended or not, the most grossly gerrymandered results; and, in any event, it is most unlikely that the political impact of such a plan would remain undiscovered by the time it was proposed or adopted, in which event the results would be both known and, if not changed, intended. It is much more plausible to assume that those who redistrict and reapportion work with both political and census data. . . .

In *White* v. *Regester*, 412 U.S. 755 (1973), decided on the same day as *Gaffney*, the Court upheld a Texas plan for reapportionment of the House of Representatives in which the maximum population variance reached 9.9 percent, concluding that this variance was not sufficient to establish a prima facie case of invidious discrimination under the equal protection clause. At the same time, however, it found that in two of the counties in which multi-member districts had been established there was sufficient evidence to support a finding that the votes of Negroes, in one county, and Mexican-Americans, in the other, had been unconstitutionally diluted by the use of the multimember district device.

The cases treated above indicate that the majority of the Court is fairly tolerant of what might be considered to be rather substantial population variations between legislative districts, at least in the absence of any showing of invidious discrimination in the establishment of such districts. A quite different attitude is evident, however, when the Court scrutinizes the variance between congressional districts within a state, as shown in the case to follow.

WHITE *v.* WEISER
412 U.S. 783 (1973)

[In 1971 the Governor of Texas signed into law Senate Bill One (S.B.1), which established twenty-four congressional districts. The populations of districts created by S.B.1 varied from a high of 477,856 in one district to a low of 458,581 in another.

The former exceeded the ideal district by 2.43 percent and the latter was smaller by 1.7 percent, giving a total percentage deviation of 4.13 percent. The average deviation was .745 percent. Appellees filed suit in a District Court alleging that the reapportionment plan was unconstitutional and asked for an order requiring either a new apportionment or the use of a substitute plan (called Plan B) which they appended to their complaint. Plan B created districts varying in population from 466,930 to 466,234. The largest district exceeded the ideal by .086 percent and the smallest was under the ideal by .063 percent, for a total percentage deviation of .159 percent. Although the plan followed the district lines of S.B.1 where possible, in order to achieve maximum population equality, Plan B cut across eighteen more county lines than did S.B.1. After the three-judge court was convened, appellees suggested an alternative plan, Plan C, which substantially disregarded the configuration of districts in S.B.1. Instead, the authors admitted that Plan C represented an attempt to attain lower deviations without regard to any consideration other than population. The largest district was overpopulated by .139 percent and the smallest underpopulated by .145 percent, the total percentage deviation being .284 percent. The District Court found S.B.1 unconstitutional and enjoined the State from conducting elections under this plan. It further ordered the adoption of Plan C, even though the deviations were higher than in Plan B, because Plan C "is based solely on population and is significantly more compact and contiguous than either S.B.1 or Plan B." Direct Appeal to the Supreme Court.]

Mr. Justice White delivered the opinion of the Court. . . .

I

The command of Art. I, §2, that representatives be chosen "by the People of the several States" was elucidated in *Westbury* v. *Sanders* . . . (1964), and in *Kirkpatrick* v. *Preisler* . . . , to permit only those population variances among congressional districts that "are unavoidable despite a good-faith effort to achieve absolute equality, or for which justification is shown." . . . See also *Wells* v. *Rockefeller* . . . (1969). *Kirkpatrick* and *Wells* invalidated state reapportionment statutes providing for federal congressional districts having total percentage deviations of 5.97 percent and 13.1 percent, respectively. In both cases, we concluded that the deviations did not demonstrate a good-faith effort to achieve absolute equality and were not sufficiently justified.

The percentage deviations now before us in S.B.1 are smaller than those invalidated in *Kirkpatrick* and *Wells*, but we agree with the District Court that, under the standards of those cases, they were not "unavoidable," and the districts were not as mathematically equal as reasonably possible. Both Plans B and C demonstrate this much, and the State does not really dispute it. Also, as in *Kirkpatrick* and *Wells*, "we do not find legally acceptable the argument that variances are justified if they necessarily result from a State's attempt to avoid fragmenting political subdivisions by drawing congressional district lines along existing county, municipal, or other political subdivision boundaries." . . .

The State asserts that the variances present in S.B.1 nevertheless represent good-faith efforts by the State to promote "constituency-representative relations," a policy frankly aimed at maintaining existing relationships between incumbent congressmen and their constituents and preserving the seniority the members of the State's delegation have achieved in the United States House of Representatives. We do not disparage this interest. We have, in the context of state reapportionment, said that the fact that "district boundaries may have been drawn in a way that minimizes the number of contests between present incumbents does not in and of itself establish invidiousness." . . . But we need not decide whether this state interest is sufficient to justify the deviations at issue here, for Plan B admittedly serves this purpose as well as S.B.1 while adhering more closely to population equality. S.B.1 and its population variations, therefore, were not necessary to achieve the asserted state goal, and the District Court was correct in rejecting it.

Appellant also straightforwardly argues that *Kirkpatrick* and *Wells* should be modified so as not to require the "small" population variances among congressional districts involved in this case to be justified by the State. . . . It is clear, however, that at some point or level in size, population variances *do* import invidious devaluation of the individual's vote and represent a failure to accord him fair and effective representation. . . . Keeping in mind that congressional districts are not so intertwined and freighted with strictly local interests as are state legislative districts and that, as compared with the latter, they are relatively enormous, with each percentage point of variation representing almost 5,000 people, we are not inclined to disturb *Kirkpatrick* and *Wells*. This is particularly so in light of *Mahan* v. *Howell* . . . (1973), decided earlier this Term, where we reiterated that the *Wesberry, Kirkpatrick,* and *Wells,* line of cases would continue to govern congressional reapportionments, although holding that the rigor of the rule of those cases was inappropriate for state reapportionments challenged under the Equal Protection Clause of the Fourteenth Amendment.

II

The District Court properly rejected S.B.1, but it had before it both Plan B and Plan C, and there remains the question whether the court correctly chose to implement the latter. . . .

From the beginning, we have recognized that "reapportionment is primarily a matter for legislative consideration and determination, and that judicial relief becomes appropriate only when a legislature fails to reapportion according to federal constitutional requisites in a timely fashion after having had an adequate opportunity to do so." . . . Just as a federal district court, in the context of legislative reapportionment, should follow the policies and preferences of the State, as expressed in statutory and constitutional provisions or in the reapportionment plans proposed by the state legislature, whenever adherence to state policy does not detract from the requirements of the Federal Constitution, we hold that a district court should similarly honor state policies in the context of congressional reapportionment. In fashioning a reapportionment plan or in choosing among plans, a district court should not pre-empt the legislative task nor "intrude upon state policy any more than necessary." . . .

Here it is clear that Plan B, to a greater extent than did Plan C, adhered to the desires of the state legislature while attempting to achieve population equality among districts. . . .

. . . Despite the existence of Plan B, the District Court ordered implementation of Plan C, which, as conceded by all parties, ignored legislative districting policy and constructed districts solely on the basis of population considerations. The District Court erred in this choice. Given the alternatives, the court . . . should have implemented Plan B, which most clearly approximated the reapportionment plan of the state legislature, while satisfying the constitutional requirements. . . .

The judgment of the District Court invalidating S.B.1 is affirmed. The adoption of Plan C is, however, reversed, and the case is remanded for further proceedings consistent with this opinion.

It is so ordered.

Mr. Justice Powell, with whom the Chief Justice and Mr. Justice Rehnquist join, concurring. . . .

Mr. Justice Marshall, concurring in part. . . .

Whatever the merits of the view that a legislature's reapportionment plan will not be struck down merely because "district boundaries may have been drawn in a way that minimizes the number of contests between present incumbents," . . . it is entirely another matter to suggest that a federal district court which has determined that a particular reapportionment plan fails to comport with the constitutional requirement of "one man, one vote" must, in drafting and adopting its own remedial plan, give consideration to the apparent desires of the controlling state political powers. In my opinion the judicial remedial process in the reapportionment area—as in any area—should be a fastidiously neutral and objective one, free of all political considerations and guided only by the controlling constitutional principle of strict accuracy in representative apportionment. . . .

Multimember Districts

WHITCOMB v. CHAVIS
403 U.S. 124 (1971)

[Suit was filed in a three-judge federal court in Indiana attacking Indiana's state legislative apportionment insofar as it created a single district of Marion County for the at-large election of eight state senators and fifteen state assemblymen. The District Court redistricted Marion County into single-member districts on the ground that the multimember district minimized the voting power of the cognizable racial minority in the county's ghetto and, further, redistricted the entire state on the ground that the state was malapportioned. The Court affirmed the latter judgment to the extent that redistricting would be required, but portions of the opinions dealing with this latter issue are omitted from the extracts following.]

Mr. Justice White delivered the opinion of the Court with respect to the validity of the multi-member election district in Marion County. . . .

The question of the constitutional validity of multi-member districts has been pressed in this Court since the first of the modern reapportionment cases. These questions have focused not on population-based apportionment but on the quality of representation afforded by the multi-member district as compared with single-member districts. . . . That voters in multi-member districts vote for and are represented by more legislators than voters in single-member districts has so far not demonstrated an invidious discrimination against the latter. But we have deemed the validity of multi-member district systems justiciable, recognizing also that they may be subject to challenge where the circumstances of a particular case may "operate to minimize or cancel out the voting strength of racial or political elements of the voting population." . . . We have not yet sustained such an attack. . . .

On the record before us plaintiffs' position comes to this: that although they have equal opportunity to participate in and influence the selection of candidates and legislators, and although the ghetto votes predominantly Democratic and that party slates candidates satisfactory to the ghetto, invidious discrimination nevertheless results when the ghetto, along with all other Democrats, suffers the disaster of losing too many elections. But typical American legislative elections are district-oriented, head-on races between candidates of two or more parties. As our system has it, one candidate wins, the others lose. Arguably the losing candidates' supporters are without representation since the men they voted for have been defeated; arguably they have been denied equal protection of the laws since they have no legislative voice of their own. This is true of both single-member *and* multi-member districts. But we have not yet deemed it a denial of equal protection to deny legislative seats to losing candidates, even in those so-called "safe" districts where the same party wins year after year. . . .

The District Court's holding, although on the facts of this case limited to guaranteeing one racial group representation, is not easily contained. It is expressive of the more general proposition that any group with distinctive interests must be represented in legislative halls if it is numerous enough to command at least one seat and represents a majority living in an area sufficiently compact to constitute a single-member district. This approach would make it difficult to reject claims of Democrats, Republicans, or members of any political organization . . . who in one year or another, or year after year, are submerged in a one-sided multi-member district vote. There are also union oriented workers, the university community, religious or ethnic groups occupying identifiable areas of our heterogeneous cities and urban areas. Indeed, it would be difficult for a great many, if not most, multi-member districts to survive analysis under the District Court's view unless combined with some voting arrangement such as proportional representation or cumulative voting aimed at providing representation for minority parties or interests. At the very least, affirmance of the District Court would spawn endless litigation concerning the multi-member district systems now widely employed in this country. . . .

Reversed and remanded.

Mr. Justice Harlan. . . .

This case is nothing short of complete vindication of Mr. Justice Frankfurter's warning 10 years ago "of the mathematical quagmire (apart from divers judicially inappropriate and elusive determinants) into which this Court today catapults the lower courts of the country." . . . Hopefully, the day will come when the Court will frankly recognize the error of its ways in ever having undertaken to restructure state electoral processes.

I would reverse the judgment below and remand the case to the District Court with directions to dismiss the complaint.

Mr. Justice Douglas, with whom Mr. Justice Brennan and Mr. Justice Marshall concur, dissenting. . . .

It is said that if we prevent racial gerrymandering today, we must prevent gerrymandering of any special interest group tomorrow, whether it be social, economic, or ideological. I do not agree. Our Constitution has a special thrust when it comes to voting; the Fifteenth Amendment says the right of citizens to vote shall not be "abridged" on account of "race, color, or previous condition of servitude."

Our cases since *Baker* v. *Carr* have never intimated that "one man, one vote" meant "one white man, one vote." Since "race" may not be gerrymandered, I think the Court emphasizes the irrelevant when it says that the effect on "the actual voting power" of the blacks should first be known. They may be all Democratic or all Republican; but once their identity is purposefully washed out of the system, the system, as I see it, has a constitutional defect. It is asking the impossible for us to demand that the blacks first show that the effect of the scheme was to discourage or prevent poor blacks from voting or joining such party as they chose. On this record, the voting rights of the blacks have been "abridged," as I read the Constitution. . . .

I would affirm the judgment.

CHAPMAN v. MEIER
420 U.S. 1 (1975)

[Following protracted state and federal litigation challenging various apportionment plans for the North Dakota Legislative Assembly, a three-judge District Court in 1965 approved a plan which included a provision for five multimember senatorial districts. Appellants brought the present action alleging that substantial population shifts had occurred since 1965 and requested the court to order apportionment based on the 1970 census, to require single-member districts throughout, and to declare the 1965 order invalid. The three-judge District Court held the 1965 plan invalid and approved another plan which provided for five multimember senatorial districts and which contained a 20 percent population variance between the largest and smallest senatorial district. On direct appeal, the Supreme Court held that the population deviation "of that magnitude in a court-ordered plan is constitutionally impermissible in the absence of significant state policies or other acceptable considerations that require adoption of a plan with so great a variance." Finding no such justification, the Court reversed on this point. The Court's response to the multimember district aspect of the plan is extracted below.]

Mr. Justice Blackmun delivered the opinion of the Court. . . .

V

The Multimember Districts . . .

This Court has refrained from holding that multimember districts in apportionment plans adopted by States for their legislatures are *per se* unconstitutional. *White* v. *Regester* . . . (1973), and cases cited therein. On the contrary, the Court has upheld numerous state-initiated apportionment schemes utilizing multimember districts. . . . And, beginning with *Reynolds* v. *Sims* . . . , the Court has indicated that a State might devise an apportionment plan for a bicameral legislature with one body composed of at least some multimember districts, as long as substantial equality of population per representative is maintained.

Notwithstanding this past acceptance of multimember districting plans, we recognize that there are practical weaknesses inherent in such schemes. First, as the number of legislative seats within the district increases, the difficulty for the voter in making intelligent choices among candidates also increases. . . . Ballots tend to become unwieldy, confusing, and too lengthy to allow thoughtful consideration. Second, when candidates are elected at-large, residents of particular areas within the district may feel that they have no representative specially responsible to them. . . . Third, it is possible that bloc voting by delegates from a multimember district may result in undue representation of residents of these districts relative to voters in single-member districts. This possibility, however, was rejected, absent concrete proof, in *Whitcomb* v. *Chavis* . . . (1971). Criticism of multimember districts has been frequent and widespread. . . . See generally Carpeneti, "Legislative Apportionment: Multimember Districts and Fair Representation," 120 *U. Pa. L. Rev.* 666 (1972); Banzhaf, "Multi-Member Electoral Districts—Do They Violate the 'One Man, One Vote' Principle," 75 *Yale L. J.* 1309 (1966).

In *Fortson* v. *Dorsey* . . . we held that the mere assertion of such possible weaknesses in a legislature's multimember districting plan was insufficient to establish a denial of equal protection. Rather, it must be shown that

"designedly or otherwise, a multi-member constituency apportionment scheme, under the circumstances of a particular case, would operate to minimize or cancel out the voting strength of racial or political elements of the voting population." . . . Further, there must be more evidence than a simple disproportionality between the voting potential and the legislative seats won by a racial or political group. There must be evidence that the group has been denied access to the political process equal to the access of other groups. . . .

This requirement that one challenging a multimember districting plan must prove that the plan minimizes or cancels out the voting power of a racial or political group has been applied in cases involving apportionment schemes adopted by state legislatures. In *Connor* v. *Johnson,* 402 U.S. 690 (1971), however, which came to us on an application for a stay, we were presented with a *court-ordered* reapportionment scheme having some multimember districts in both bodies of the state legislature. We stated explicitly that "when district courts are forced to fashion apportionment plans, single-member districts are preferable to large multi-member districts as a general matter." . . . Exercising our supervisory power, we directed the District Court to devise a single-member districting plan, "absent insurmountable difficulties." . . . This preference for and emphasis upon single-member districts in court-ordered plans was reaffirmed in *Connor* v. *Williams* . . . and again in *Mahan* v. *Howell* . . . (1973). In the latter case a district court was held to have acted within its discretion in forming a multimember district as an interim remedy in order to alleviate substantial underrepresentation of military personnel in an impending election.

The standards for evaluating the use of multimember districts thus clearly differ depending on whether a federal court or a state legislature has initiated the use. The practical simultaneity of decision in *Connor* v. *Johnson* and in *Whitcomb* v. *Chavis* . . . so demonstrates. When the plan is court-ordered, there often is no state policy of mulitmember districting which might deserve respect or deference. Indeed, if the court is imposing multimember districts upon a State which always has employed single-member districts, there is special reason to follow the *Connor* rule favoring the latter type of districting.

Appellants do not contend that any racial or political group has been discriminated against by the multimember districting ordered by the District Court. They only suggest that the District Court has not followed our mandate in *Connor* v. *Johnson,* and that the court has failed to articulate any reasons for this departure. We agree. Absent particularly pressing features calling for multimember districts, a United States district court should refrain from imposing them upon a State. . . .

. . . Unless the District Court can articulate such a "singular combination of unique factors" as was found to exist in *Mahan* v. *Howell* . . . or unless the 1975 Legislative Assembly appropriately acts, the court should proceed expeditiously to reinstate single-member senate districts in North Dakota. . . .

The reapportionment decisions have led to probably the most widespread popular reexamination of representation theory since the famous debates on legislative composition in the state constitutional conventions in Massachusetts, New York, and Virginia in the decade 1820–1830. Basic "truths" are being scrutinized and tested, to be reconfirmed by some and discarded by others. Even the ancient belief that rural-dominated legislatures block urban demands has been challenged as not borne out by the voting patterns. [See Noel Perrin, "In Defense of County Votes," *The Yale Review* (Autumn, 1962), pp. 16–24, reprinted in Howard D. Hamilton, ed., *Legislative Apportionment* (New York: Harper & Row, 1964), which presents the background, litigation, and some divergent views on apportionment and representation.] It is doubtful that the more sophisticated nuances of representational theory will find their way into the judicial opinions or the legislative debates, but assuredly the simple phrase "one man, one vote" is insufficient to resolve the variety of problems presented by the commands to reapportion on a basis of equality.

Constitution of the United States

WE THE PEOPLE of the United States, in order to form a more perfect union, establish justice, insure domestic tranquility, provide for the common defense, promote the general welfare, and secure the blessings of liberty to ourselves and our posterity, do ordain and establish this Constitution for the United States of America.

ARTICLE I

SECTION 1. All legislative powers herein granted shall be vested in a Congress of the United States, which shall consist of a Senate and House of Representatives.

SECTION 2. (1) The House of Representatives shall be composed of members chosen every second year by the people of the several States, and the electors in each State shall have the qualifications requisite for electors of the most numerous branch of the State legislature.

(2) No person shall be a Representative who shall not have attained to the age of twenty-five years, and been seven years a citizen of the United States, and who shall not, when elected, be an inhabitant of that State in which he shall be chosen.

(3) Representatives and direct taxes[1] shall be apportioned among the several States which may be included within this Union, according to their respective numbers, which shall be determined by adding to the whole number of free persons, including those bound to service for a term of years, and excluding Indians not taxed, three fifths of all other persons.[2] The actual enumeration shall be made within three years after the first meeting of the Congress of the United States, and within every subsequent term of ten years, in such manner as they shall by law direct. The number of Representatives shall not exceed one for every thirty thousand, but each State shall have at least one Representative; and until such enumeration shall be made, the State of New Hampshire shall be entitled to choose three, Massachusetts eight, Rhode Island and Providence Plantations one, Connecticut five, New York, six, New Jersey four, Pennsylvania eight, Delaware one, Maryland six, Virginia ten, North Carolina five, South Carolina five, and Georgia three.

(4) When vacancies happen in the representation from any State, the executive authority thereof shall issue writs of election to fill such vacancies.

(5) The House of Representatives shall choose their Speaker and other officers; and shall have the sole power of impeachment.

SECTION 3. (1) The Senate of the United States shall be composed of two Sena-

---

[1] Modified as to income taxes by the 16th Amendment.
[2] Replaced by the 14th Amendment.

tors from each State, chosen by the Legislature thereof,[3] for six years; and each Senator shall have one vote.

(2) Immediately after they shall be assembled in consequence of the first election, they shall be divided as equally as may be into three classes. The seats of the Senators of the first class shall be vacated at the expiration of the second year, of the second class at the expiration of the fourth year, and of the third class at the sixth year, so that one third may be chosen every second year; and if vacancies happen by resignation, or otherwise, during the recess of the legislature of any State, the executive thereof may make temporary appointments until the next meeting of the legislature, which shall then fill such vacancies.

(3) No person shall be a Senator who shall not have attained to the age of thirty years, and been nine years a citizen of the United States, and who shall not, when elected, be an inhabitant of that State for which he shall be chosen.

(4) The Vice President of the United States shall be president of the Senate, but shall have no vote, unless they be equally divided.

(5) The Senate shall choose their other officers, and also a president pro tempore, in the absence of the Vice President, or when he shall exercise the office of President of the United States.

(6) The Senate shall have the sole power to try all impeachments. When sitting for that purpose, they shall be on oath or affirmation. When the President of the United States is tried, the Chief Justice shall preside: and no person shall be convicted without the concurrence of two thirds of the members present.

(7) Judgment in cases of impeachment shall not extend further than to removal from office, and disqualification to hold and enjoy any office of honor, trust or profit under the United States: but the party convicted shall nevertheless be liable and subject to indictment, trial, judgment and punishment, according to law.

SECTION 4. (1) The times, places and manner of holding elections for Senators and Representatives, shall be prescribed in each State by the legislature thereof; but the Congress may at any time by law make or alter such regulations, except as to the places of choosing Senators.

(2) The Congress shall assemble at least once in every year, and such meeting shall be on the first Monday in December, unless they shall by law appoint a different day.

SECTION 5. (1) Each House shall be the judge of the elections, returns and qualifications of its own members, and a majority of each shall constitute a quorum to do business; but a smaller number may adjourn from day to day, and may be authorized to compel the attendance of absent members, in such manner, and under such penalties as each House may provide.

(2) Each House may determine the rules of its proceedings, punish its members for disorderly behavior, and, with the concurrence of two thirds, expel a member.

(3) Each House shall keep a journal of its proceedings, and from time to time publish the same, excepting such parts as may in their judgment require secrecy; and the yeas and nays of the members of either House on any question shall, at the desire of one fifth of those present, be entered on the journal.

(4) Neither House, during the session of Congress, shall, without the consent of the other, adjourn for more than three days, nor to any other place than that in which the two Houses shall be sitting.

SECTION 6. (1) The Senators and Representatives shall receive a compensation

---

[3] Modified by the 17th Amendment.

for their services, to be ascertained by law, and paid out of the Treasury of the United States. They shall in all cases, except treason, felony and breach of the peace, be privileged from arrest during their attendance at the session of their respective Houses, and in going to and returning from the same; and for any speech or debate in either House, they shall not be questioned in any other place.

(2) No Senator or Representative shall, during the time for which he was elected, be appointed to any civil office under the authority of the United States, which shall have been created, or the emoluments whereof shall have been increased during such time; and no person holding any office under the United States, shall be a member of either House during his continuance in office.

SECTION 7. (1) All bills for raising revenue shall originate in the House of Representatives; but the Senate may propose or concur with amendments as on other bills.

(2) Every bill which shall have passed the House of Representatives and the Senate, shall, before it become a law, be presented to the President of the United States; if he approve he shall sign it, but if not he shall return it, with his objections to that House in which it shall have originated, who shall enter the objections at large on their journal, and proceed to reconsider it. If after such reconsideration two thirds of that House shall agree to pass the bill, it shall be sent, together with the objections, to the other House, by which it shall likewise be reconsidered, and if approved by two thirds of that House, it shall become a law. But in all such cases the votes of both Houses shall be determined by yeas and nays, and the names of the persons voting for and against the bill shall be entered on the journal of each House respectively. If any bill shall not be returned by the President within ten days (Sundays excepted) after it shall have been presented to him, the same shall be a law, in like manner as if he had signed it, unless the Congress by their adjournment prevent its return, in which case it shall not be a law.

(3) Every order, resolution, or vote to which the concurrence of the Senate and House of Representatives may be necessary (except on a question of adjournment) shall be presented to the President of the United States; and before the same shall take effect, shall be approved by him, or being disapproved by him, shall be repassed by two thirds of the Senate and House of Representatives, according to the rules and limitations prescribed in the case of a bill.

SECTION 8. (1) The Congress shall have power to lay and collect taxes, duties, imposts and excises, to pay the debts and provide for the common defense and general welfare of the United States; but all duties, imposts and excises shall be uniform throughout the United States;

(2) To borrow money on the credit of the United States.

(3) To regulate commerce with foreign nations, and among the several States, and with the Indian tribes;

(4) To establish an uniform rule of naturalization, and uniform laws on the subject of bankruptcies throughout the United States;

(5) To coin money, regulate the value thereof, and of foreign coin, and fix the standard of weights and measures;

(6) To provide for the punishment of counterfeiting the securities and current coin of the United States;

(7) To establish post offices and post roads;

(8) To promote the progress of science and useful arts, by securing for limited times to authors and inventors the exclusive right to their respective writings and discoveries;

(9) To constitute tribunals inferior to the Supreme Court;

(10) To define and punish piracies and felonies committed on the high seas, and offenses against the law of nations;

(11) To declare war, grant letters of marque and reprisal, and make rules concerning captures on land and water;

(12) To raise and support armies, but no appropriation of money to that use shall be for a longer term than two years;

(13) To provide and maintain a navy;

(14) To make rules for the government and regulation of the land and naval forces;

(15) To provide for calling forth the militia to execute the laws of the Union, suppress insurrections and repel invasions;

(16) To provide for organizing, arming, and disciplining the militia, and for governing such part of them as may be employed in the service of the United States, reserving to the States respectively, the appointment of the officers, and the authority of training the militia according to the discipline prescribed by Congress;

(17) To exercise exclusive legislation in all cases whatsoever, over such district (not exceeding ten miles square) as may, by cession of particular States, and the acceptance of Congress, become the seat of the government of the United States,[4] and to exercise like authority over all places purchased by the consent of the legislature of the State in which the same shall be, for the erection of forts, magazines, arsenals, dockyards, and other needful buildings; and

(18) To make all laws which shall be necessary and proper for carrying into execution the foregoing powers, and all other powers vested by this Contitution in the government of the United States, or in any department or officer thereof.

SECTION 9. (1) The migration or importation of such persons as any of the States now existing shall think proper to admit, shall not be prohibited by the Congress prior to the year one thousand eight hundred and eight, but a tax or duty may be imposed on such importation, not exceeding ten dollars for each person.

(2) The privilege of the writ of habeas corpus shall not be suspended, unless when in cases of rebellion or invasion the public safety may require it.

(3) No bill of attainder or ex post facto law shall be passed.

(4) No capitation, or other direct, tax shall be laid, unless in proportion to the census or enumeration herein before directed to be taken.[5]

(5) No tax or duty shall be laid on articles exported from any State.

(6) No preference shall be given by any regulation of commerce or revenue to the ports of one State over those of another: nor shall vessels bound to, or from, one State, be obliged to enter, clear, or pay duties in another.

(7) No money shall be drawn from the Treasury, but in consequence of appropriations made by law; and a regular statement and account of the receipts and expenditures of all public money shall be published from time to time.

(8) No title of nobility shall be granted by the United States: and no person holding any office of profit or trust under them, shall, without the consent of the Congress, accept of any present, emolument, office, or title, of any kind whatever, from any king, prince, or foreign State.

SECTION 10. (1) No State shall enter into any treaty, alliance, or confederation; grant letters of marque and reprisal; coin money; emit bills of credit; make anything but gold and silver coin a tender in payment of debts; pass any bill of attainder, ex post facto law, or law impairing the obligation of contracts, or grant any title of nobility.

---

[4] Modified by the 23rd Amendment.
[5] Modified by the 16th Amendment.

(2) No State shall, without the consent of the Congress, lay any imposts or duties on imports or exports, except what may be absolutely necessary for executing its inspection laws; and the net produce of all duties and imposts, laid by any State on imports or exports, shall be for the use of the Treasury of the United States; and all such laws shall be subject to the revision and control of the Congress.

(3) No State shall, without the consent of Congress, lay any duty of tonnage, keep troops, or ships of war in time of peace, enter into any agreement or compact with another State, or with a foreign power, or engage in war, unless actually invaded, or in such imminent danger as will not admit of delay.

ARTICLE II

SECTION 1. (1) The executive power shall be vested in a President of the United States of America. He shall hold his office during the term of four years,[6] and, together with the Vice President, chosen for the same term, be elected, as follows:

(2) Each State shall appoint, in such manner as the legislature thereof may direct, a number of electors, equal to the whole number of Senators and Representatives to which the State may be entitled in the Congress: but no Senator or Representative, or person holding an office of trust or profit under the United States, shall be appointed an elector.

The electors[7] shall meet in their respective States, and vote by ballot for two persons, of whom one at least shall not be an inhabitant of the same State with themselves. And they shall make a list of all the persons voted for, and of the number of votes for each; which list they shall sign and certify, and transmit sealed to the seat of the government of the United States, directed to the president of the Senate. The president of the Senate shall, in the presence of Senate and House of Representatives, open all the certificates, and the votes shall then be counted. The person having the greatest number of votes shall be the President, if such number be a majority of the whole number of electors appointed; and if there be more than one who have such majority, and have an equal number of votes, then the House of Representatives shall immediately choose by ballot one of them for President; and if no person have a majority, then from the five highest on the list the said House shall in like manner choose the President. But in choosing the President, the votes shall be taken by States, the representation from each State having one vote; a quorum for this purpose shall consist of a member or members from two thirds of the States, and a majority of all the States shall be necessary to a choice. In every case, after the choice of the President, the person having the greatest number of votes of the electors shall be the Vice President. But if there should remain two or more who have equal votes, the Senate shall choose from them by ballot the Vice President.

(3) The Congress may determine the time of choosing the electors, and the day on which they shall give their votes; which day shall be the same throughout the United States.

(4) No person except a natural born citizen, or a citizen of the United States, at the time of the adoption of this Constitution, shall be eligible to the office of President; neither shall any person be eligible to that office who shall not have attained to the age of thirty five years, and been fourteen years a resident within the United States.

[6] Modified by the 22nd Amendment.
[7] This paragraph was replaced in 1804 by the 12th Amendment.

(5) In the case of the removal of the President from office, or of his death, resignation, or inability to discharge the powers and duties of the said office, the same shall devolve on the Vice President, and the Congress may by law provide for the case of removal, death, resignation, or inability, both of the President and Vice President, declaring what officer shall then act as President, and such officer shall act accordingly, until the disability be removed, or a President shall be elected.[8]

(6) The President shall, at stated times, receive for his services, a compensation, which shall neither be increased nor diminished during the period for which he shall have been elected, and he shall not receive within that period any other emolument from the United States, or any of them.

(7) Before he enter on the execution of his office, he shall take the following oath or affirmation:—"I do solemnly swear (or affirm) that I will faithfully execute the office of President of the United States, and will to the best of my ability, preserve, protect and defend the Constitution of the United States."

SECTION 2. (1) The President shall be commander in chief of the army and navy of the United States, and of the militia of the several States, when called into the actual service of the United States; he may require the opinion, in writing, of the principal officer in each of the executive departments, upon any subject relating to the duties of their respective offices, and he shall have power to grant reprieves and pardons for offenses against the United States, except in cases of impeachment.

(2) He shall have power, by and with the advice and consent of the Senate, to make treaties, provided two thirds of the Senators present concur; and he shall nominate, and by and with the advice and consent of the Senate, shall appoint ambassadors, other public ministers and consuls, judges of the Supreme Court, and all other officers of the United States, whose appointments are not herein otherwise provided for, and which shall be established by law: but the Congress may by law vest the appointment of such inferior officers, as they think proper, in the President alone, in the courts of law, or in the heads of departments.

(3) The President shall have the power to fill up all vacancies that may happen during the recess of the Senate, by granting commissions which shall expire at the end of their next session.

SECTION 3. He shall from time to time give to the Congress information of the state of the Union, and recommend to their consideration such measures as he shall judge necessary and expedient; he may, on extraordinary occasions, convene both Houses, or either of them, and in case of disagreement between them, with respect to the time of adjournment, he may adjourn them to such time as he shall think proper; he shall receive ambassadors and other public ministers; he shall take care that the laws be faithfully executed, and shall commission all the officers of the United States.

SECTION 4. The President, Vice President and all civil officers of the United States, shall be removed from office on impeachment for, and conviction of, treason, bribery, or other high crimes and misdemeanors.

ARTICLE III

SECTION 1. The judicial power of the United States, shall be vested in one Supreme Court, and in such inferior courts as the Congress may from time to time ordain and establish. The judges, both of the Supreme and inferior courts, shall

---

[8] Replaced by the 25th Amendment.

hold their offices during good behavior, and shall, at stated times, receive for their services, a compensation, which shall not be diminished during their continuance in office.

SECTION 2. (1) The judicial power shall extend to all cases, in law and equity, arising under this Constitution, the laws of the United States, and treaties made, or which shall be made, under their authority;—to all cases affecting ambassadors, other public ministers and consuls;—to all cases of admiralty and maritime jurisdiction;—to controversies to which the United States shall be a party;—to controversies between two or more States;—between a State and citizens of another State;[9]—between citizens of different States;—between citizens of the same State claiming lands under grants of different States, and between a State, or the citizens thereof, and foreign States, citizens or subjects.

(2) In all cases affecting ambassadors, other public ministers and consuls, and those in which a State shall be party, the Supreme Court shall have original jurisdiction. In all the other cases before mentioned, the Supreme Court shall have appellate jurisdiction, both as to law and fact, with such exceptions, and under such regulations as Congress shall make.

(3) The trial of all crimes, except in cases of impeachment, shall be by jury; and such trial shall be held in the State where the said crimes shall have been committed; but when not commited within any State, the trial shall be at such place or places as the Congress may by law have directed.

SECTION 3. (1) Treason against the United States, shall consist only in levying war against them, or in adhering to their enemies, giving them aid and comfort. No person shall be convicted of treason unless on the testimony of two witnesses to the same overt act, or on confession in open court.

(2) The Congress shall have power to declare the punishment of treason, but no attainder of treason shall work corruption of blood, or forfeiture except during the life of the person attained.

ARTICLE IV

SECTION 1. Full faith and credit shall be given in each State to the public acts, records, and judicial proceedings of every other State. And the Congress may by general laws prescribe the manner in which such acts, records and proceedings shall be proved, and the effect thereof.

SECTION 2. (1) The citizens of each State shall be entitled to all privileges and immunities of citizens in the several States.

(2) A person charged in any State with treason, felony, or other crime, who shall flee from justice, and be found in another State, shall on demand of the executive authority of the State from which he fled, be delivered up, to be removed to the State having jurisdiction of the crime.

(3) No person held to service or labor in one State, under the laws thereof, escaping into another, shall, in consequence of any law or regulation therein, be discharged from such service or labor, but shall be delivered up on claim of the party to whom such service or labor may be due.

SECTION 3. (1) New States may be admitted by the Congress into this Union; but no new State shall be formed or erected within the jurisdiction of any other State; nor any State be formed by the junction of two or more States, or parts of

---

[9] Restricted by the 11th Amendment.

States, without the consent of the legislatures of the States concerned as well as of the Congress.

(2) The Congress shall have power to dispose of and make all needful rules and regulations respecting the territory or other property belonging to the United States; and nothing in this Constitution shall be so construed as to prejudice any claims of the United States, or of any particular State.

SECTION 4. The United States shall guarantee to every State in this Union a republican form of government, and shall protect each of them against invasion; and on application of the legislature, or of the executive (when the legislature cannot be convened) against domestic violence.

ARTICLE V

The Congress, whenever two thirds of both Houses shall deem it necessary, shall propose amendments to this Constitution, or, on the application of the legislatures of two thirds of the several States, shall call a convention for proposing amendments, which, in either case, shall be valid to all intents and purposes, as part of this Constitution, when ratified by the legislatures of three fourths of the several States, or by conventions in three fourths thereof, as the one or the other mode of ratification may be proposed by the Congress; Provided that no amendment which may be made prior to the year one thousand eight hundred and eight shall in any manner affect the first and fourth clauses in the ninth section of the first article; and that no State, without its consent, shall be deprived of its equal suffrage in the Senate.

ARTICLE VI

SECTION 1. All debts contracted and engagements entered into, before the adoption of this Constitution, shall be as valid against the United States under this Constitution, as under the Confederation.

SECTION 2. This Constitution, and the laws of the United States which shall be made in pursuance thereof; and all treaties made, or which shall be made, under the authority of the United States, shall be the supreme law of the land; and the judges in every State shall be bound thereby, anything in the constitution or laws of any State to the contrary notwithstanding.

SECTION 3. The Senators and Representatives before mentioned, and the members of the several State legislatures, and all executive and judicial officers, both of the United States and of the several States, shall be bound by oath or affirmation to support this Constitution; but no religious test shall ever be required as a qualification to any office or public trust under the United States.

ARTICLE VII

The ratification of the conventions of nine States, shall be sufficient for the establishment of this Constitution between the States so ratifying the same.

done in Convention by the unanimous consent of the States present the seventeenth day of September in the year of our Lord one thousand seven hundred and eighty-seven, and of the independence of the United States of America the twelfth. In witness whereof we have hereunto subscribed our names.

Go Washington—
Presidt. and Deputy from Virginia

AMENDMENTS

ARTICLE I[10]

Congress shall make no law respecting an establishment of religion, or prohibiting the free exercise thereof; or abridging the freedom of speech, or of the press; or the right of the people peaceably to assemble, and to petition the government for a redress of grievances.

ARTICLE II

A well regulated militia, being necessary to the security of a free State, the right of the people to keep and bear arms, shall not be infringed.

ARTICLE III

No soldier shall, in time of peace be quartered in any house, without the consent of the owner, nor in time of war, but in a manner to be prescribed by law.

ARTICLE IV

The right of the people to be secure in their persons, houses, papers, and effects, against unreasonable searches and seizures, shall not be violated, and no warrants shall issue, but upon probable cause, supported by oath or affirmation, and particularly describing the place to be searched, and the persons or things to be seized.

ARTICLE V

No person shall be held to answer for a capital, or otherwise infamous crime, unless on a presentment or indictment of a grand jury, except in cases arising in the land or naval forces, or in the militia, when in actual service in time of war or public danger; nor shall any person be subject for the same offense to be twice put in jeopardy of life or limb; nor shall be compelled in any criminal case to be a witness against himself, nor be deprived of life, liberty, or property, without due process of law; nor shall private property be taken for public use, without just compensation.

ARTICLE VI

In all criminal prosecutions the accused shall enjoy the right to a speedy and public trial, by an impartial jury of the State and district wherein the crime shall have been committed, which district shall have been previously ascertained by law, and to be informed of the nature and cause of the accusation; to be confronted with the witnesses against him; to have compulsory process for obtaining witnesses in his favor, and to have the assistance of counsel for his defense.

ARTICLE VII

In suits at common law, where the value in controversy shall exceed twenty dollars, the right of trial by jury shall be preserved, and no fact tried by a jury

10 The first ten Amendments were adopted in 1791.

shall be otherwise reexamined in any court of the United States, than according to the rules of the common law.

ARTICLE VIII

Excessive bail shall not be required, nor excessive fines imposed, nor cruel and unusual punishments inflicted.

ARTICLE IX

The enumeration in the Constitution, of certain rights, shall not be construed to deny or disparage others retained by the people.

ARTICLE X

The powers not delegated to the United States by the Constitution, nor prohibited by it to the States, are reserved to the States respectively, or to the people.

ARTICLE XI[11]

The judicial power of the United States shall not be construed to extend to any suit in law or equity, commenced or prosecuted against one of the United States by citizens of another State, or by citizens or subjects of any foreign State.

ARTICLE XII[12]

The electors shall meet in their respective States and vote by ballot for President and Vice-President, one of whom, at least, shall not be an inhabitant of the same State with themselves; they shall name in their ballots the person voted for as President, and in distinct ballots the person voted for as Vice-President, and they shall make distinct lists of all persons voted for as President, and of all persons voted for as Vice-President, and of the number of votes for each, which lists they shall sign and certify, and transmit sealed to the seat of the government of the United States, directed to the president of the Senate;—The president of the Senate shall, in the presence of the Senate and House of Representatives, open all the certificates and the votes shall then be counted;—The person having the greatest number of votes for President, shall be the President, if such number be a majority of the whole number of electors appointed; and if no person have such majority, then from the persons having the highest numbers not exceeding three on the list of those voted for as President, the House of Representatives shall choose immediately, by ballot, the President. But in choosing the President, the votes shall be taken by States, the representation from each State having one vote; a quorum for this purpose shall consist of a member or members from two thirds of the States, and a majority of all the States shall be necessary to a choice. And if the House of Representatives shall not choose a President whenever the right of choice shall devolve upon them, before the fourth day of March next following, then the Vice-President shall act as President, as in the case of the death or other constitutional disability of the President.—The person having the greatest number of votes as Vice-President, shall be the Vice-President, if such number be a majority of the

11 Ratified in 1795; proclaimed in 1798.
12 Adopted in 1804.

whole number of electors appointed, and if no person have a majority, then from the two highest numbers on the list, the Senate shall choose the Vice-President; a quorum for the purpose shall consist of two thirds of the whole number of Senators, and a majority of the whole number shall be necessary to a choice. But no person constitutionally ineligible to the office of President shall be eligible to that of Vice-President of the United States.

ARTICLE XIII[13]

SECTION 1. Neither slavery nor involuntary servitude, except as a punishment for crime whereof the party shall have been duly convicted, shall exist within the United States, or any place subject to their jurisdiction.

SECTION 2. Congress shall have power to enforce this article by appropriate legislation.

ARTICLE XIV[14]

SECTION 1. All persons born or naturalized in the United States, and subject to the jurisdiction thereof, are citizens of the United States and of the State wherein they reside. No State shall make or enforce any law which shall abridge the privileges or immunities of citizens of the United States; nor shall any State deprive any person of life, liberty, or property, without due process of law; nor deny to any person within its jurisdiction the equal protection of the laws.

SECTION 2. Representatives shall be apportioned among the several States according to their respective numbers, counting the whole number of persons in each State, excluding Indians not taxed. But when the right to vote at any election for the choice of electors for President and Vice President of the United States, Representatives in Congress, the executive and judicial officers of a State, or the members of the legislature thereof, is denied to any of the male inhabitants of such State, being twenty-one years of age, and citizens of the United States, or in any way abridged, except for participation in rebellion, or other crime, the basis of representation therein shall be reduced in the proportion which the number of such male citizens shall bear to the whole number of male citizens twenty-one years of age in such State.

SECTION 3. No person shall be a Senator or Representative in Congress, or elector of President and Vice President, or hold any office, civil or military, under the United States, or under any State, who, having previously taken an oath, as a member of Congress, or as an officer of the United States, or as a member of any State legislature, or as an executive or judicial officer of any State, to support the Constitution of the United States, shall have engaged in insurrection or rebellion against the same, or given aid or comfort to the enemies thereof. But Congress may by a vote of two thirds of each House, remove such disability.

SECTION 4. The validity of the public debt of the United States, authorized by law, including debts incurred for payment of pensions and bounties for services in suppressing insurrection or rebellion, shall not be questioned. But neither the United States nor any State shall assume or pay any debt or obligation incurred in aid of insurrection or rebellion against the United States, or any claim for the

[13] Adopted in 1865.
[14] Adopted in 1868.

loss or emancipation of any slave; but all such debts, obligations and claims shall be held illegal and void.

Section 5. The Congress shall have power to enforce, by appropriate legislation, the provisions of this article.

ARTICLE XV[15]

Section 1. The right of citizens of the United States to vote shall not be denied or abridged by the United States or by any State on account of race, color, or previous condition of servitude.

Section 2. The Congress shall have power to enforce this article by appropriate legislation.

ARTICLE XVI[16]

The Congress shall have power to lay and collect taxes on incomes, from whatever source derived, without apportionment among the several States, and without regard to any census or enumeration.

ARTICLE XVII[16]

The Senate of the United States shall be composed of two Senators from each State, elected by the people thereof, for six years; and each Senator shall have one vote. The electors in each State shall have the qualifications requisite for electors of the most numerous branch of the State legislatures.

When vacancies happen in the representation of any State in the Senate, the executive authority of such State shall issue writs of election to fill such vacancies: *Provided,* That the legislature of any State may empower the executive thereof to make temporary appointments until the people fill the vacancies by election as the legislature may direct.

This amendment shall not be so construed as to affect the election or term of any Senator chosen before it becomes valid as part of the Constitution.

ARTICLE XVIII[17]

Section 1. After one year from the ratification of this article the manufacture, sale, or transportation of intoxicating liquors within, the importation thereof into, or the exportation thereof from the United States and all territory subject to the jurisdiction thereof for beverage purposes is hereby prohibited.

Section 2. The Congress and the several States shall have concurrent power to enforce this article by appropriate legislation.

Section 3. This article shall be inoperative unless it shall have been ratified as an amendment to the Constitution by the legislatures of the several States, as provided in the Constitution, within seven years from the date of the submission hereof to the States by the Congress.

[15] Adopted in 1870.
[16] Adopted in 1913.
[17] Adopted in 1919. Repealed by Article XXI.

ARTICLE XIX[18]

The right of citizens of the United States to vote shall not be denied or abridged by the United States or by any State on account of sex.

The Congress shall have power to enforce this article by appropriate legislation.

ARTICLE XX[19]

SECTION 1. The terms of the President and Vice President shall end at noon on the 20th day of January, and the terms of Senators and Representatives at noon on the 3rd day of January, of the years in which such terms would have ended if this article had not been ratified; and the terms of their successors shall then begin.

SECTION 2. The Congress shall assemble at least once in every year, and such meeting shall begin at noon on the 3rd day of January, unless they shall by law appoint a different day.

SECTION 3. If, at the time fixed for the beginning of the term of the President, the President elect shall have died, the Vice President elect shall become President. If a President shall not have been chosen before the time fixed for the beginning of his term, or if the President elect shall have failed to qualify, then the Vice President elect shall act as President until a President shall have qualified; and the Congress may by law provide for the case wherein neither a President elect nor a Vice President elect shall have qualified, declaring who shall then act as President, or the manner in which one who is to act shall be selected, and such person shall act accordingly until a President or Vice President shall have qualified.

SECTION 4. The Congress may by law provide for the case of the death of any of the persons from whom the House of Representatives may choose a President whenever the right of choice shall have devolved upon them, and for the case of the death of any of the persons from whom the Senate may choose a Vice President whenever the right of choice shall have devolved upon them.

SECTION 5. Sections 1 and 2 shall take effect on the 15th day of October following the ratification of this article.

SECTION 6. This article shall be inoperative unless it shall have been ratified as an amendment to the Constitution by the legislatures of three-fourths of the several States within seven years from the date of its submission.

ARTICLE XXI[20]

SECTION 1. The eighteenth article of amendment to the Constitution of the United States is hereby repealed.

SECTION 2. The transportation or importation into any State, Territory or Possession of the United States for delivery or use therein of intoxicating liquors in violation of the laws thereof is hereby prohibited.

SECTION 3. This article shall be inoperative unless it shall have been ratified as an amendment to the Constitution by conventions in the several States, as provided in the Constitution, within seven years from the date of submission hereof to the States by the Congress.

[18] Adopted in 1920.
[19] Adopted in 1933.
[20] Adopted in 1933.

ARTICLE XXII[21]

Section 1. No person shall be elected to the office of the President more than twice, and no person who has held the office of President, or acted as President for more than two years of a term to which some other person was elected President shall be elected to the office of the President more than once. But this Article shall not apply to any person holding the office of President when this Article was proposed by the Congress, and shall not prevent any person who may be holding the office of President, or acting as President, during the term within which this Article becomes operative from holding the office of President or acting as President during the remainder of such term.

Section 2. This Article shall be inoperative unless it shall have been ratified as an amendment to the Constitution by the legislatures of three-fourths of the several States within seven years from the date of its submission to the States by the Congress.

ARTICLE XXIII[22]

Section 1. The District constituting the seat of Government of the United States shall appoint in such manner as the Congress may direct:

A number of electors of President and Vice-President equal to the whole number of Senators and Representatives in Congress to which the District would be entitled if it were a State, but in no event more than the least populous state; they shall be in addition to those appointed by the states, but they shall be considered, for the purposes of the election of President and Vice-President, to be electors appointed by a state; and they shall meet in the District and perform such duties as provided by the twelfth article of amendment.

Section 2. The Congress shall have power to enforce this article by appropriate legislation.

ARTICLE XXIV[23]

Section 1. The right of citizens of the United States to vote in any primary or other election for President or Vice-President, for electors for President or Vice-President, or for Senator or Representative in Congress, shall not be denied or abridged by the United States or any state by reason of failure to pay any poll tax or other tax.

Section 2. The Congress shall have power to enforce this article by appropriate legislation.

ARTICLE XXV[24]

Section 1. In case of the removal of the President from office or his death or resignation, the Vice President shall become President.

Section 2. Whenever there is a vacancy in the office of the Vice President, the President shall nominate a Vice President who shall take the office upon confirmation by a majority vote of both houses of Congress.

[21] Adopted in 1951.
[22] Adopted in 1961.
[23] Adopted in 1964.
[24] Adopted in 1967.

SECTION 3. Whenever the President transmits to the President pro tempore of the Senate and the Speaker of the House of Representatives his written declaration that he is unable to discharge the powers and duties of his office, and until he transmits to them a written declaration to the contrary, such powers and duties shall be discharged by the Vice President as Acting President.

SECTION 4. Whenever the Vice President and a majority of either the principal officers of the executive departments, or of such other body as Congress may by law provide, transmit to the President pro tempore of the Senate and the Speaker of the House of Representatives their written declaration that the President is unable to discharge the powers and duties of his office, the Vice President shall immediately assume the powers and duties of the office as Acting President.

Thereafter, when the President transmits to the President pro tempore of the Senate and the Speaker of the House of Representatives his written declaration that no inability exists, he shall resume the powers and duties of his office unless the Vice President and a majority of either the principal officers of the executive department, or of such other body as Congress may by law provide, transmit within four days to the President pro tempore of the Senate and the Speaker of the House of Representatives their written declaration that the President is unable to discharge the powers and duties of his office. Thereupon Congress shall decide the issue, assembling within 48 hours for that purpose if not in session. If the Congress, within 21 days after receipt of the latter written declaration, or, if Congress is not in session, within 21 days after Congress is required to assemble, determines by two-thirds vote of both houses that the President is unable to discharge the powers and duties of his office, the Vice President shall continue to discharge the same as Acting President; otherwise, the President shall resume the powers and duties of his office.

ARTICLE XXVI[25]

SECTION 1. The right of citizens of the United States, who are eighteen years of age, or older, to vote shall not be denied or abridged by the United States or by any state on account of age.

SECTION 2. The Congress shall have the power to enforce this article by appropriate legislation.

ARTICLE XXVII[26]

SECTION 1. Equality of rights under the law shall not be denied or abridged by the United States or by any State on account of sex.

SECTION 2. The Congress shall have the power to enforce, by appropriate legislation, the provisions of this article.

SECTION 3. This amendment shall take effect two years after the date of ratification.

[25] Adopted in 1971.
[26] Proposed to states for ratification March 22, 1972.

Selected References

Chapter 1

GENERAL

Henry J. Abraham, *The Judicial Process,* 3rd ed. (New York: Oxford University Press, 1975), Chapters 5, 7, 8.

Harold J. Berman and William R. Greiner, *The Nature and Function of Law,* 2nd ed. (Brooklyn: Foundation Press, 1966), Chapters 1–4.

Alexander M. Bickel, *The Least Dangerous Branch: The Supreme Court at the Bar of Politics* (Indianapolis: Bobbs-Merrill, 1963).

Edmond Cahn, *Can the Supreme Court Defend Civil Liberties?* (New York: Sidney Hillman Foundation, 1956).

Thomas E. Barth, "Perception and Acceptance of Supreme Court Decisions at the State and Local Level," 17 *J. of Pub. L.* 308 (1968).

Richard C. Cortner, "Strategies and Tactics of Litigants in Constitutional Cases," 17 *J. of Pub. L.* 287 (1968).

Jerome Frank, *Courts on Trial: Myth and Reality in American Justice* (Princeton: Princeton University Press, 1959).

Paul Freund, "Civil Rights and the Limits of Law," 14 *Buffalo L. Rev.* 199 (1964).

Paul Freund, "The Supreme Court and Civil Liberties," 4 *Vand. L. Rev.* 553 (1951).

Sheldon Goldman and Thomas P. Jahnige, *The Federal Courts as a Political System* (New York: Harper & Row, 1971).

Arthur Garfield Hays Conference, "The Proper Role of the United States Supreme Court in Civil Liberties Cases," 10 *Wayne L. Rev.* 457 (1964).

Robert H. Jackson, *The Supreme Court in the American System of Government* (Cambridge: Harvard University Press, 1955).

Herbert Jacob, *Justice in America: Courts, Lawyers, and the Judicial Process,* 2nd ed. (Boston: Little, Brown, 1972).

Samuel Krislov, *The Supreme Court in the Political Process* (New York: Macmillan, 1965), Chapters 2, 6.

Richard J. Richardson and Kenneth N. Vines, *The Politics of Federal Courts* (Boston: Little, Brown, 1970).

C. Herman Pritchett, *The American Constitutional System,* 4th ed. (New York: McGraw-Hill, 1976).

John P. Roche, *Courts and Rights,* 2nd ed. (New York: Random House, 1966).

Stephen L. Wasby, *The Impact of the United States Supreme Court: Some Perspectives* (Homewood: Dorsey, 1970).

ACTIVISM AND SELF-RESTRAINT

Charles L. Black, Jr., *The People and the Court: Judicial Review in a Democracy* (New York: Macmillan, 1960).

Howard Dean, *Judicial Review and Democracy* (New York: Random House, 1966).

D. F. Forte, ed., *The Supreme Court in American Politics: Judicial Activism v. Judicial Restraint* (Lexington, Mass.: Heath, 1972).

Martin Shapiro, "Judicial Modesty: Down with the Old!—Up with the New?" 10 *U.C.L.A. L. Rev.* 533 (1963).

Edward McWhinney, "The Great Debate: Activism and Self-Restraint and Current Dilemmas in Judicial Policy-Making," 33 *N.Y.U. L. Rev.* 775 (1958).

Robert J. Steamer, *The Supreme Court: Constitutional Revision and the New "Strict Constructionism"* (Minneapolis: Burgess, 1973).

Wallace Mendelson, "The Politics of Judicial Activism," 24 *Emory L. J.* 43 (1975).

Herbert Wechsler, "Toward Neutral Principles of Constitutional Law," 73 *Harv. L. Rev.* 1 (1959).

STANDING AND JUSTICIABILITY

Roaul Berger, "Standing to Sue in Public Actions: Is It a Constitutional Requirement?" 78 *Yale L. J.* 816 (1969).

Louis L. Jaffee, "The Citizen as Litigant in Public Actions: The Non-Hohfeldian or Ideological Plaintiff," 16 *U. Pa. L. Rev.* 1033 (1968).

T. P. Lewis, "Constitutional Rights and the Misuse of 'Standing'," 14 *Stan. L. Rev.* 433 (1962).

Note, "Advisory Opinions on the Constitutionality of Statutes," 69 *Harv. L. Rev.* 1302 (1956).

Note, "Non-Justiciable Controversy," 48 *Va. L. Rev.* 922 (1962).

C. G. Post, Jr., *The Supreme Court and Political Questions* (New York: Da Capo, 1969).

Victor G. Rosenblum, "Justiciability and Justice: Elements of Restraint and Indifference," 15 *Catholic U. L. Rev.* 141 (1966).

Fritz Scharpf, "Judicial Review and the Political Question: A Functional Analysis," 75 *Yale L. J.* 517 (1966).

Christopher L. Stone, "Should Trees Have Standing?—Toward Legal Rights for Natural Objects," 45 *So. Cal. L. Rev.* 450 (1972).

DELAY

Hans Zeisel, Harry Kalven, Jr., and Bernard Buchholz, *Delay in the Court* (Boston: Little, Brown, 1959).

APPEALS

Jerome Frank, *Courts on Trial: Myth and Reality in American Justice* (Princeton: Princeton University Press, 1950), Chapter 3–9, 15.

Paul Freund, "Why We Need the National Court of Appeals," 59 *Am. Bar Assn. J.* 247 (1973).

William J. Brennan, "The National Court of Appeals: Another Dissent," 40 *Univ. of Chi. L. Rev.* 473 (1973).

J. Woodford Howard, Jr., "Litigation Flow in Three United States Courts of Appeals," 8 *Law and Society Rev.* 49 (1973).

Samuel Krislov, "The Amicus Curiae Brief: From Friendship to Advocacy," 72 *Yale L. J.* 694 (1963).

Karl Llewellyn, *The Common Law Tradition: Deciding Appeals* (Boston: Little, Brown, 1960).

S. Sidney Ulmer, William Hintze, and Louise Kirklosky, "The Decision to Grant or Deny Certiorari: Further Consideration of Cue Theory," 6 *Law and Society Rev.* 640 (1972).

Kenneth Vines, "The Role of Circuit Courts of Appeal in the Federal Judicial Process," 7 *Midwest J. of Pol. Sci.* 305 (1963).

POVERTY AND JUSTICE

Norman Dorsen, ed., "Poverty, Civil Liberties, and Civil Rights: A Symposium," 41 *N.Y.U. L. Rev.* 328 (1966).

Robert Lefcourt, ed., *Law Against the People* (New York: Random House, 1971).

Report of the Attorney General's Committee on Poverty and the Administration of Criminal Justice, *Poverty and the Administration of Federal Criminal Justice* (Submitted to U.S. Attorney General, February 25, 1963).

Leonard Downie, Jr., *Justice Denied: The Case for Reform of the Courts* (New York: Praeger, 1971), Chapter 4.

Harry P. Stumpf and Robert J. Janowitz, "Judges and the Poor: Bench Responses to Federally Financed Legal Services," 21 *Stan. L. Rev.* 1058 (1969).

Arnold S. Trebach, *The Rationing of Justice: Constitutional Rights and the Criminal Process* (New Brunswick: Rutgers University Press, 1964).

Patricia M. Wald, *Law and Poverty: 1965* (Report to the National Conference on Law and Poverty, Washington, D.C., June, 1965).

JUDICIAL REVIEW OF ADMINISTRATIVE ACTION

Roaul Berger, "Administrative Arbitrariness and Judicial Review," 65 *Colum. L. Rev.* 55 (1965).

Walter Gellhorn and Clark Byse, *Administrative Law: Cases and Comments,* 6th ed. (Mineola, N.Y.: Foundation Press, 1974), Chapter 3.

Louis L. Jaffee, *Judicial Control of Administrative Action* (Boston: Little, Brown, 1965).

Symposium, "Judicial Review of Police Methods in Law Enforcement," 44 *Tex. L. Rev.* 939 (1966).

Chapter 2

Henry J. Abraham, *Freedom and the Court,* rev. ed. (New York: Oxford University Press, 1972), Chapter 3.

William J. Brennan, Jr., *The Bill of Rights and the States* (Santa Barbara: Center for Study of Democratic Institutions, 1961).

Robert F. Cushman, "Incorporation: Due Process and the Bill of Rights," 51 *Cornell L. Q.* 467 (1966).

Horace Flack, *The Adoption of the Fourteenth Amendment* (Baltimore: Johns Hopkins Press, 1908).

Charles Fairman, "Does the Fourteenth Amendment Incorporate the Bill of Rights? The Original Understanding," 2 *Stan. L. Rev.* 5 (1949).

Felix Frankfurter, "Memorandum on 'Incorporation' of the Bill of Rights into the Due Process Clause of the Fourteenth Amendment," 78 *Harv. L. Rev.* 746 (1965).

Louis Henkin, "Selective Incorporation in the Fourteenth Amendment," 73 *Yale L. J.* 74 (1963).

Roger Howell, "The Privileges and Immunities of State Citizenship," *The Johns Hopkins University Studies in History and Political Science,* Vol. 36, No. 3 (Baltimore: Johns Hopkins Press, 1918).

Alex B. Lacy, Jr., "The Bill of Rights and the Fourteenth Amendment: The Evolution of the Absorption Doctrine," 23 *Wash. and Lee L. Rev.* 37 (1966).

Chapter 3

GENERAL

Annotation, "Relief, under Federal Civil Rights Acts, to State Prisoners," 18 ALR Fed. 7 (1974).

Theodore L. Becker and Vernon G. Murray, eds., *Government Lawlessness in America* (New York: Oxford University Press, 1971).

Sydney Brodie, "The Federally-Secured Right to be Free from Bondage," 40 *Geo. L. J.* 367 (1952).

Ian Brownlie, ed., *Basic Documents on Human Rights* (London: Oxford, 1971).

A. B. Caldwell and Sydney Brodie, "Enforcement of the Criminal Civil Rights Statute, 18 U.S.C. 242, in Prison Brutality Cases," 52 *Geo. L. J.* 706 (1964).

Robert K. Carr, *Federal Protection of Civil Rights* (Ithaca: Cornell University Press, 1947).

W. E. Dellinger, "Of Rights and Remedies: The Constitution as a Sword," 85 *Harv. L. Rev.* 1532 (1972).

D. E. Engdahl, "Immunity and Accountability for Positive Governmental Wrongs," 44 *U. Colo. L. Rev.* 1 (1972).

Eugene Gressman, "The Unhappy History of Civil Rights Legislation," 50 *Mich. L. Rev.* 1323 (1952).

Alfred Hill, "Constitutional Remedies," 69 *Colum. L. Rev.* 1109 (1969).

N. D. Levy, "Personal Liability of Welfare Officials Under 42 U.S.C. 1983," 3 *Clearinghouse Rev.* 285 (1970).

Richard P. Longaker, *The Presidency and Individual Liberties* (Ithaca: Cornell University Press, 1961).

Will Maslow and Joseph B. Robinson, "Civil Rights Legislation and the Fight for Equality, 1862–1952," 20 *U. Chi. L. Rev.* 363 (1953).

Ruth P. Morgan, *The President and Civil Rights* (New York: St. Martin's Press, 1970).

Note, "Discretion to Prosecute Federal Civil Rights Crimes," 74 *Yale L. J.* 1297 (1965).

Note, "Federal Civil Action against Private Individuals for Crimes Involving Civil Rights," 74 *Yale L. J.* 1462 (1965).

Note, "The Fourth Amendment: Is a Lawsuit the Answer?" 23 *Syr. L. Rev.* 1227 (1972).

Note, "Tort Liability of Law Enforcement Officers Under Section 1983 of the Civil Rights Act," 30 *La. L. Rev.* 100 (1969).

Report of the President's Commission on Civil Rights, *To Secure These Rights* (Washington, D.C.: Government Printing Office, 1947).

1961 Report of the U.S. Commission on Civil Rights, 5 vols.: *Voting,* vol. 1; *Education,* vol. 2; *Employment,* vol. 3; *Housing,* vol. 4; *Justice,* vol. 5 (Washington, D.C.: Government Printing Office, 1961).

Report of the U.S. Commission on Civil Rights, *Civil Rights '63* (Washington, D.C.: Government Printing Office, 1963).

Jay A. Sigler, *American Rights Policies* (Homewood: Dorsey, 1975), esp. Chapter 17.

Joseph P. Witherspoon, "Civil Rights Policy in the Federal System: Proposals for a Better Use of Administrative Process," 74 *Yale L. J.* 1171 (1965).

Allan Wolk, *The Presidency and Black Civil Rights* (Cranbury, N.J.: Fairleigh Dickinson University Press, 1971).

THE "STATE ACTION" PROBLEM

Glenn Abernathy, "Expansion of the State Action Concept Under the Fourteenth Amendment," 43 *Cornell L. Q.* 375 (1958).

Michael J. Horan, "Law and Social Change: The Dynamics of the 'State Action' Doctrine," 17 *J. of Pub. L.* 258 (1968).

Richard A. Lang, Jr., "State Action Under the Equal Protection Clause of the Fourteenth Amendment and the Remaining Scope of Private Choice," 50 *Cornell L. Q.* 473 (1965).

Thomas P. Lewis, "The Meaning of State Action," 60 *Colum. L. Rev.* 1083 (1960).

Jerre S. Williams, "The Twilight of State Action," 41 *Tex. L. Rev.* 347 (1963).

Chapter 4

GENERAL

Abraham Blumberg, *Criminal Justice* (Chicago: Quadrangle Books, 1967).

George F. Cole, *Criminal Justice: Law and Politics* (North Scituate Mass.: Duxbury, 1972).

David Fellman, *The Defendant's Rights* (New York: Rinehart, 1958).

David Fellman, *The Defendant's Rights Under English Law* (Madison: University of Wisconsin Press, 1966).

Marvin E. Frankel, *Criminal Sentences: Law Without Order* (New York: Hill and Wang, 1972).

J. A. C. Grant, *Our Common Law Constitution* (Boston: Boston University Press, 1956).

Howard James, *Crisis in the Courts,* rev. ed. (New York: David McKay, 1971).

Yale Kamisar, ed., *Criminal Justice in Our Time* (Charlottesville: University Press of Virginia, 1965).

Leon Radzinowicz and Marvin E. Wolfgang, eds., *Crime and Justice,* 3 vols. (New York: Basic Books, 1971).

John A. Robertson, ed., *Rough Justice: Perspectives on Lower Criminal Courts* (Boston: Little, Brown, 1974).

Jerome H. Skolnick, *Justice Without Trial* (New York: Wiley, 1966).

Claude R. Sowle, ed., *Police Power and Individual Freedom* (Chicago: Aldine, 1962).

NOTICE

Oliver P. Field, "Ex post Facto in the Constitution," 20 *Mich. L. Rev.* 315 (1922).

Note, "Statutory Criminal Presumptions: Judicial Sleight of Hand," 53 *Va. L. Rev.* 702 (1967).

Note, "The Void-for-Vagueness Doctrine in the Supreme Court," 109 *U. Pa. L. Rev.* 67 (1960).

SEARCHES AND SEIZURES

William G. Buss, "The Fourth Amendment and Searches of Students in Schools," 59 *Iowa L. Rev.* 739 (1974).

Erwin N. Griswold, *Search and Seizure: A Dilemma of the Supreme Court* (Lincoln: University of Nebraska Press, 1975).

Melvin Gutterman, " 'Person Aggrieved': Standing to Suppress Illegally Seized Evidence in Transition," 23 *Emory L. J.* 111 (1974).

Jerold H. Israel, "Legislative Regulation of Searches and Seizures: the Michigan Proposals," 73 *Mich. L. Rev.* 222 (1974).

John Kaplan, "Limits of the Exclusionary Rule," 26 *Stan. L. Rev.* 1027 (1974).

Wayne R. LaFave, *Arrest* (Boston: Little, Brown, 1965).

Jacob W. Landynski, *Search and Seizure and the Supreme Court* (Baltimore: Johns Hopkins Press, 1966).

Nelson B. Lasson, *The History and Development of the Fourth Amendment to the United States Constitution* (Baltimore: Johns Hopkins Press, 1937).

Note, "Border Searches Revisited: the Constitutional Propriety of Fixed and Temporary Checkpoint Searches," 2 *Hastings Con. L. Q.* 251 (1975).

Note, "Police Power to Stop, Frisk, and Question Suspicious Persons," 65 *Colum. L. Rev.* 848 (1965).

Mark Rothstein and Laura F. Rothstein, "Administrative Searches and Seizures: What Happened to *Camara* and *See?*" 50 *Wash. L. Rev.* 341 (1975).

John B. Wefing, "Consent Searches and the Fourth Amendment: Voluntariness and Third Party Problems," 5 *Seton Hall L. Rev.* 211 (1974).

Welsh S. White, "Effective Consent to Search and Seizure," 113 *U. Pa. L. Rev.* 260 (1964).

Alan F. Westin, *Privacy and Freedom* (New York: Atheneum, 1967).

SELF-INCRIMINATION AND CONFESSIONS

Erwin N. Griswold, *The Fifth Amendment Today* (Cambridge: Harvard University Press, 1955).

Fred E. Inbau and John E. Reid, *Criminal Interrogation and Confessions* (Baltimore: Williams & Wilkins, 1962).

Leonard W. Levy, *Origins of the Fifth Amendment* (New York: Oxford, 1968).

R. C. Pittman, "The Colonial and Constitutional History of the Privilege Against Self-Incrimination in America," 21 *Va. L. Rev.* 763 (1935).

R. H. Seeburger and R. Stanton Wettick, Jr., "*Miranda* in Pittsburgh—A Statistical Study," 29 *U. Pitts. L. Rev.* 1 (1967).

Otis H. Stephens, Jr., *The Supreme Court and Confessions of Guilt* (Knoxville: University of Tennessee Press, 1973).

Arthur E. Sutherland, "Crime and Confession," 79 *Harv. L. Rev.* 21 (1965).

RIGHT TO COUNSEL

William M. Beaney, *The Right to Counsel in American Courts* (Ann Arbor: University of Michigan Press, 1955).

Fred P. Graham, *The Self-Inflicted Wound* (New York: Macmillan, 1970).

Anthony Lewis, *Gideon's Trumpet* (New York: Random House, 1964).

Lee Silverstein, *Defense of the Poor in Criminal Cases in American State Courts* (Chicago: American Bar Foundation, 1965).

S. Sidney Ulmer, *Military Justice and the Right to Counsel* (Lexington: University of Kentucky Press, 1970).

DOUBLE JEOPARDY

Walter T. Fisher, "Double Jeopardy, Two Sovereignties and the Intruding Constitution," 28 *U. Chi. L. Rev.* 591 (1961).

M. L. Friedland, *Double Jeopardy* (New York: Oxford, 1969).

J. A. C. Grant, "Successive Prosecutions by State and Nation," 4 *U.C.L.A. L. Rev.* 1 (1956).

Note, "Double Jeopardy: Its History, Rationale and Future," 70 *Dick. L. Rev.* 377 (1966).

Jay A. Sigler, *Double Jeopardy: The Development of a Legal and Social Policy* (Ithaca: Cornell University Press, 1969).

L. G. Miller, *Double Jeopardy and the Federal System* (Chicago: University of Chicago Press, 1968).

TRIAL BY JURY

M. J. Bloomstein, *Verdict: The Jury System* (New York: Dodd, Mead, 1968).

Sir Patrick Devlin, *Trial by Jury* (London: Stevens, 1956).

Francis H. Heller, *The Sixth Amendment to the Constitution of the United States:* A Study in Constitutional Development (Lawrence: University of Kansas Press, 1951).

Harry Kalven, Jr., and Hans Zeisel, *The American Jury* (Boston: Little, Brown, 1966).

Comment, "Should Jury Verdicts be Unanimous in Criminal Cases?" 47 *Ore. L. Rev.* 417 (1968).

CRUEL AND UNUSUAL PUNISHMENT

Larry C. Berkson, *The Concept of Cruel and Unusual Punishment* (Lexington, Mass.: D. C. Heath, 1975).

James S. Campbell, "Revival of the Eighth Amendment: Development of Cruel Punishment Doctrine by the Supreme Court," 16 *Stan. L. Rev.* 996 (1964).

Michael Meltsner, *Cruel and Unusual: The Supreme Court and Capital Punishment* (New York: Morrow, 1974).

Arthur E. Sutherland, Jr., "Due Process and Cruel Punishment," 64 *Harv. L. Rev.* 271 (1950).

HABEAS CORPUS

Paul M. Bator, "Finality in Criminal Law and Federal Habeas Corpus for State Prisoners," 76 *Harv. L. Rev.* 441 (1963).

Zechariah Chafee, Jr., "The Most Important Human Right in the Constitution," 32 *B. U. L. Rev.* 144 (1952).

H. J. Friendly, "Is Innocence Irrelevant? Collateral Attack on Criminal Judgments," 38 *U. of Chi. L. Rev.* 142 (1970).

Daniel J. Meador, *Habeas Corpus and Magna Carta* (Charlottesville: University Press of Virginia, 1966).

Note, "Habeas Corpus and the Military: The Crippled Attack on Courts Martial," 61 *Ky. L. J.* 333 (1972–73).

Chapter 5

Chester J. Antieau, Arthur T. Downey, and Edward C. Roberts, *Freedom from Federal Establishment* (Milwaukee: Bruce, 1964).

Donald E. Boles, *The Bible, Religion, and the Public Schools,* 3rd ed. (Ames: Iowa State University Press, 1965).

Kenneth M. Dolbeare and P. E. Hammond, *The School Prayer Decisions: From Court Policy to Local Practice* (Chicago: University of Chicago Press, 1971).

Thomas I. Emerson, David Haber, and Norman Dorsen, *Political and Civil Rights in the United States,* 3rd ed., 2 vols. (Boston: Little, Brown, 1967), Chapter 8.

David Fellman, *Religion in American Public Law* (Boston: Boston University Press, 1965).

Sidney Hook, *Religion in a Free Society* (Lincoln: University of Nebraska Press, 1967).

Mark DeWolfe Howe, *The Garden and the Wilderness* (Chicago: University of Chicago Press, 1964).

Paul G. Kauper, *Religion and the Constitution* (Baton Rouge: Louisiana State University Press, 1964).

Paul G. Kauper, "The Supreme Court and the Establishment Clause: Back to Everson?" 25 *Case West. Res. L. Rev.* 107 (1974).

Philip B. Kurland, *Religion and the Law* (Chicago: Aldine, 1962).

David R. Manwaring, *Render unto Caesar: The Flag Salute Controversy* (Chicago: University of Chicago Press, 1962).

Richardson E. Morgan, "The Establishment Clause and Sectarian Schools: A Final Installment?" 1973 *Supreme Court Review* 57.

Richard E. Morgan, *The Supreme Court and Religion* (New York: Free Press, 1972).

Note, "The Establishment Clause: Analysis of Legislative and Administrative Aid to Religion," 74 *Colum. L. Rev.* 1175 (1974).

Note, "Released Time Cases Revisited: A Study of Group Decisionmaking by the Supreme Court," 83 *Yale L. J.* 1202 (1974).

Note, "Private Colleges, State Aid, and the Establishment Clause," 1975 *Duke L. J.* 976.

Dallin H. Oaks, ed., *The Wall Between Church and State* (Chicago: University of Chicago Press, 1963).

Leo Pfeffer, *Church, State and Freedom* (Boston: Beacon Press, 1962).

Anson P. Stokes, *Church and State in the United States,* 3 vols. (New York: Harper & Row, 1950). See also the one-volume condensation by Leo Pfeffer, *Church and State in the United States* (New York: Harper & Row, 1964).

Hearings before the Subcommittee on Constitutional Amendments of the Committee on the Judiciary, United States Senate, 89th Congress, 2d Session, August 1966, on Senate Joint Resolution 148 relating to Prayers in Public Schools.

Chapter 6

GENERAL

Edmond Cahn, ed., *The Great Rights* (New York: Macmillan, 1963).

Zechariah Chafee, Jr., *Free Speech in the United States* (Cambridge: Harvard University Press, 1948).

Thomas I. Emerson, David Haber, and Norman Dorsen, *Political and Civil Rights in the United States,* 3rd ed. (Boston: Little, Brown, 1967), Vol. 1.

David Fellman, *The Limits of Freedom* (New Brunswick: Rutgers University Press, 1959).

Osmond Fraenkel, *The Supreme Court and Civil Liberties,* 2nd ed. (New York: Oceana, 1963).

Milton Konvitz, *Fundamental Liberties of a Free People: Religion, Speech, Press, Assembly* (Ithaca: Cornell University Press, 1957).

Paul L. Murphy, *The Meaning of Freedom of Speech: First Amendment Freedoms from Wilson to FDR* (Westport, Conn.: Greenwood, 1972).

DOCTRINES OF INTERPRETATION

Zechariah Chafee, Jr., *Free Speech in the United States* (Cambridge: Harvard University Press, 1948), Chapter 1.

Thomas I. Emerson, *Toward a General Theory of the First Amendment* (New York: Random House, 1967).

Laurent B. Frantz, "The First Amendment in the Balance," 71 *Yale L. J.* 1424 (1962).

Alexander Meiklejohn, *Free Speech and Its Relation to Self-Government* (New York: Harper & Row, 1948).

Wallace Mendelson, "On the Meaning of the First Amendment: Absolutes in the Balance," 50 *Calif. L. Rev.* 821 (1962).

Martin Shapiro, *Freedom of Speech: The Supreme Court and Judicial Review* (Englewood Cliffs: Prentice-Hall, 1966).

INTERNAL SECURITY

Association of the Bar of the City of New York, Report of the Special Committee on *The Federal Loyalty-Security Program* (New York: Dodd, Mead, 1956).

Ralph S. Brown, Jr., *Loyalty and Security* (New Haven: Yale University Press, 1958).

Digest of the Public Record of Communism in the United States (New York: Fund for the Republic, 1955).

Sidney Hook, *Political Power and Personal Freedom: Critical Studies in Democracy, Communism, and Civil Rights* (New York: Criterion, 1959).

Harold D. Laswell, *National Security and Individual Freedom* (New York: McGraw-Hill, 1950).

John O. Rogge, *The First and the Fifth* (New York: Nelson & Sons, 1960).

Telford Taylor, *Grand Inquest* (New York: Simon & Schuster, 1955).

PRESS

Arthur L. Berney, "Libel and the First Amendment—A New Constitutional Privilege," 51 *Va. L. Rev.* 1 (1965).

Francis X. Beytagh, "Privacy and a Free Press: A Contemporary Conflict in Values," 20 *N.Y. L. Forum* 453 (1975).

Zechariah Chafee, Jr., *Government and Mass Communication* (Chicago: University of Chicago Press, 1947).

Jerome Barron, "An Emerging First Amendment Right of Access to the Media?" 37 *Geo. Wash. L. Rev.* 487 (1969).

Council of State Governments, *Shield Laws* (Lexington, Ky.: Council of State Governments, 1973).

Sam J. Ervin, Jr., "In Pursuit of a Press Privilege," 11 *Harv. J. on Leg.* 278 (1974).

Edward G. Hudon, *Freedom of Speech and Press in America* (Washington, D.C.: Public Affairs Press, 1963).

Hearings on Freedom of the Press before the Subcommittee on Constitutional

Rights, Senate Committee on the Judiciary, 92d Congress, 1st and 2nd Sessions (1972).

Leonard W. Levy, ed., *Freedom of the Press from Zenger to Jefferson* (New York: Bobbs-Merrill, 1966).

Note, "Privacy and the Freedom of Information Act.,, 27 *Admin. L. Rev.* 275 (1975).

Note, "The Speech and Press Clause of the First Amendment as Ordinary Language," 87 *Harv. L. Rev.* 374 (1973).

Glenn Robinson, "The FCC and the First Amendment: Observations on 40 Years of Radio and Television Regulation,"," 52 *Minn. L. Rev.* 67 (1967).

Jerome A. Barron, *Freedom of the Press for Whom: The Right of Access to Mass Media* (Bloomington: Indiana University Press, 1973).

FREE PRESS AND FAIR TRIAL

American Bar Association Committee on Fair Trial and Free Press, *Standards Relating to Fair Trial and Free Press, Tentative Draft* (New York: Institute of Judicial Administration, 1966).

Association of the Bar of the City of New York, Special Committee on Radio, Television, and the Administration of Justice, *Freedom of the Press and Fair Trial: Final Report with Recommendations* (New York: Columbia University Press, 1967).

C. R. Bush, ed., *Free Press and Fair Trial* (Athens: University of Georgia Press, 1970).

Hearings on S. 290 before the Subcommittee on Constitutional Rights and the Subcommittee on Improvements in Judicial Machinery, United States Senate Committee on the Judiciary, 89th Congress, 1st Session (1965), *Free Press and Fair Trial.*

Edward G. Hudon, "Freedom of the Press Versus Fair Trial: The Remedy Lies with the Courts," 1 *Valparaiso U. L. Rev.* 8 (1966).

ASSEMBLY AND ASSOCIATION

Glenn Abernathy, *The Right of Assembly and Association* (Columbia: University of South Carolina Press, 1961).

Zechariah Chafee, Jr., "The Internal Affairs of Associations Not for Profit," 43 *Harv. L. Rev.* 993 (1930).

David Fellman, *The Constitutional Right of Association* (Chicago: University of Chicago Press, 1963).

Robert A. Horn, *Groups and the Constitution* (Stanford: Stanford University Press, 1956).

Charles E. Rice, *Freedom of Association* (New York: New York University Press, 1962).

CENSORSHIP OF BOOKS; OBSCENITY

John Chandos, ed., *To Deprave and Corrupt* (New York: Association Press, 1962).

Harry M. Clor, ed., *Censorship and Freedom of Expression* (Chicago: Rand McNally, 1971).

Robert B. Downs, ed., *The First Freedom* (Chicago: American Library Association, 1960).

Morris L. Ernst and Alan U. Schwartz, *Censorship: The Search for the Obscene* (New York: Macmillan, 1964).

David Fellman, *The Censorship of Books* (Madison: University of Wisconsin Press, 1957).

Walter Gellhorn, *Individual Freedom and Governmental Restraints* (Baton Rouge: Louisiana State University Press, 1958), Chapter 2.

Robert W. Haney, *Comstockery in America* (Boston: Beacon Press, 1960).

Richard P. McKeon, Robert K. Merton, and Walter Gellhorn, *The Freedom to Read* (New York: Bowker, 1957).

James C. N. Paul and Murray L. Schwartz, *Federal Censorship: Obscenity in the Mail* (New York: Free Press of Glencoe, 1961).

The Report of the Commission on Obscenity and Pornography (Washington, D.C.: U.S. Government Printing Office, 1970).

Norman St. John-Stevas, *Obscenity and the Law* (London: Secker & Warburg, 1956).

Martin Shapiro, "Obscenity Law: A Public Policy Analysis," 20 *J. of Pub. L.* 503 (1971).

Jay A. Sigler, "Freedom of the Mails: A Developing Right," 54 *Georgetown L. J.* 30 (1965).

Chapter 7

Morris Berger, *Equality by Statute: The Revolution in Civil Rights,* rev. ed. (Garden City: Doubleday, 1967).

Albert P. Blaustein and Clarence C. Ferguson, Jr., *Desegregation and the Law* (New Brunswick: Rutgers University Press, 1957).

Congressional Quarterly Service, *Revolution in Civil Rights,* 4th ed. (Washington, D.C.: Congressional Quarterly, Inc., 1968).

L. B. Barker, *The Black in the American Political System* (New York: Winthrop, 1974).

Thomas R. Dye, *The Politics of Equality* (Indianapolis: Bobbs-Merrill, 1971).

Thomas I. Emerson, David Haber, and Norman Dorsen, *Political and Civil Rights in the United States,* 3rd ed., Vol. 2 (Boston: Little, Brown, 1967.

John Frank and Robert F. Munro, "The Equal Protection of the Laws," 50 *Colum. L. Rev.* 131 (1950).

Jack A. Greenberg, *Race Relations and American Law* (New York: Columbia University Press, 1959).

Jack A. Greenberg, ed., "Blacks and the Law," *The Annals,* Vol. 407 (May 1973).

Karen DeCrow, *Sexist Justice* (New York: Random House, 1974).

"Equal Rights for Women: A Symposium on the Proposed Constitutional Amendment," 6 *Harv. Civil Rights-Civil Liberties L. Rev.* 2 (1971).

Roxanne B. Conlin, "Equal Protection Versus Equal Rights Amendment—Where Are We Now?" 24 *Drake L. Rev.* 259 (1975).

Oscar Handlin, *Fire-Bell in the Night: The Crisis in Civil Rights* (Boston: Little, Brown, 1964).

Robert J. Harris, *The Quest for Equality: The Constitution, Congress, and the Supreme Court* (Baton Rouge: Louisiana State University Press, 1960).

J. D. Johnston, Jr., "Sex Discrimination and the Supreme Court—1971–1974," 49 *N.Y.U. L. Rev.* 617 (1974).

Panel, "Men, Women, and the Constitution: The Equal Rights Amendment," 10 *Colum. J. L. & Soc. Prob.* 77 (1973).

Joseph Tussman and Jacobs ten Broek, "The Original Understanding of 'Equal Protection of the Laws'," 37 *Calif. L. Rev.* 341 (1949).

Clement E. Vose, *Caucasians Only: The Supreme Court, the NAACP, and the Restrictive Covenant Cases* (Berkeley: University of California Press, 1959).

Arthur I. Waskow, *From Race Riot to Sit-in: 1919 and the 1960's* (Garden City: Doubleday, 1966).

C. Vann Woodward, *The Strange Career of Jim Crow,* 3rd rev. ed. (New York: Oxford University Press, 1974).

Chapter 8

VOTING

William Gillette, *The Right to Vote: Politics and the Passage of the Fifteenth Amendment* (Baltimore: Johns Hopkins Press, 1965).

Alan P. Grimes, *The Puritan Ethic and Woman Suffrage* (New York: Oxford University Press, 1967).

R. Claude, *The Supreme Court and the Electoral Process* (Baltimore: Johns Hopkins Press, 1970).

C. V. Hamilton, *The Bench and the Ballot: Southern Federal Judges and Black Voters* (New York: Oxford University Press, 1973).

Paul Lewinson, *Race, Class, and Party: A History of Negro Suffrage and White Politics in the South* (New York: Russell and Russell, 1963).

V. O. Key, Jr., *Southern Politics in State and Nation* (New York: Knopf, 1949).

Thurgood Marshall, "The Rise and Collapse of the 'White Primary'," 26 *J. of Negro Ed.* 249 (1957).

Donald R. Matthews and James W. Prothro, *Negroes and the New Southern Politics* (New York: Harcourt Brace Jovanovich, 1966).

Note, "Private Economic Coercion and the Civil Rights Act of 1957," 71 *Yale L. J.* 537 (1962).

William W. Van Alstyne, "The Fourteenth Amendment, the 'Right' to Vote, and the Understanding of the Thirty-Ninth Congress," 1965 *Sup. Ct. Rev.* 33.

1961 U.S. Commission on Civil Rights Report No. 1, *Voting* (Washington, D.C.: U.S. Government Printing Office, 1961).

Hearings before the United States Commission on Civil Rights, held in 1965 in Jackson, Mississippi, Vol. 1, *Voting* (Washington, D.C.: U.S. Government Printing Office, 1965).

APPORTIONMENT

Richard C. Cortner, *The Apportionment Cases* (New York: Norton, 1970).

Gerhard Casper, "Apportionment and the Right to Vote: Standards of Judicial Scrutiny," 1973 *Sup. Ct. Rev.* 1.

Robert N. Clinton, "Further Explorations in the Political Thicket: The Gerrymander and the Constitution," 59 *Iowa L. Rev.* 1 (1974).

Robert G. Dixon, Jr., *Democratic Representation* (New York: Oxford University Press, 1968).

Alfred de Grazia, *Essay on Apportionment and Representative Government* (Washington, D.C.: Institute for Social Science Research, 1963).

Stanley A. Halpin and Richard L. Engstrom, "Racial Gerrymandering and Southern State Legislative Redistricting: Attorney General Determinations under the Voting Rights Act," 22 *J. of Pub. L.* 37 (1973).

Howard D. Hamilton, ed., *Legislative Apportionment* (New York: Harper & Row, 1964).

Roger A. Hanson and Robert E. Crew, "Policy Impact of Reapportionment," 8 *Law & Soc. Rev.* 69 (1973).

Calvin B. T. Lee, *One Man, One Vote: WMCA and the Struggle for Equal Representation* (New York: Scribner, 1967).

Robert B. McKay, *Reapportionment: The Law and Politics of Equal Representation* (New York: Twentieth Century Fund, 1965).

C. Herman Pritchett, "Equal Protection and the Urban Majority," 58 *Amer. Pol. Sci. Rev.* 869 (1964).

Glendon Schubert, ed., *Reapportionment* (New York: Scribner, 1964).

Index